MASTER THESE ADVANCED TOPICS	SEE
Understand Network Protocols	Chapter 16
Set Up and Configure a Simple Peer to Peer Network	Chapter 17
Create Shared Network Resources	Chapter 17
Create Hardware and User Profiles	Chapter 17
Connect a Windows 2000 Professional Workstation To an NT 4 Domain	Chapter 17
Create User and Group Accounts	Chapter 18
Set Permissions	Chapter 18
Keep Track of Who's Allowed to Use the Network and Who Isn't	Chapter 19
Implement Secure Telecommuting	Chapter 21
Protect Data with the Encrypting File System	Chapter 21
Create Basic Web Pages Using HTML	Chapter 22
Use VBScript to automate simple, repetitive tasks	Chapter 24
Use the Windows Scripting Host Engine to Execute Scripts	Chapter 25
Manipulate the Registry Using Scripts	Chapter 25
Support New Hardware and Install Drivers	Chapter 26
Avoid Windows 2000 Professional Crashes	Chapter 27
Maintain a Healthy System Using Disk Defragmenter, Disk Cleanup, and Check Disk	Chapter 27
Restore a Configuration	Chapter 27
Start and stop services, format drives, and repair your system using Recovery Console	Chapter 27
Use the Driver Verifier to keep an eye on how drivers utilize and access memory	Chapter 27
Back Up And Restore Valuable Data	Chapter 27
Use Disk Management to manage disk partitions and handle formatting chores	Chapter 28
Use Event Viewer to troubleshoot a problematic PC	Chapter 28
Use the Microsoft Management Console to Administer a Network	Chapter 29
Troubleshoot Your Windows 2000 Professional Setup	Chapter 30
Troubleshoot Your Windows 2000 Professional Network	Chapter 30

WINDOWS 2000 PROFESSIONAL

MASTERING™ WINDOWS® 2000 PROFESSIONAL

Mark Minasi

SYBEX®

San Francisco • Paris • Düsseldorf • Soest • London

Associate Publisher: Jordan Gold
Contracts and Licensing Manager: Kristine O'Callaghan
Acquisitions and Developmental Editor: Ellen L. Dendy
Editor: Sally Engelfried
Production Editor: Elizabeth Campbell
Technical Editors: Art Brieva, Steve Wisniewski
Book Designer: Franz Baumhackl
Graphic Illustrators: Tony Jonick, Elizabeth Creegan, Cuong Le, Inbar Berman
Electronic Publishing Specialist: Adrian Woolhouse
Proofreaders: Nanette Duffy, Laurie O'Connell, Erika Donald, Nancy Riddiough, Sarah Tannehill
Indexer: Ted Laux
Cover Designer: Design Site
Cover Illustrator/Photographer: Sergie Loobkoff

Library of Congress Card Number: 00-106458
ISBN: 0-7821-2853-X

Manufactured in the United States of America
10 9 8 7 6 5 4 3 2 1

This book is dedicated to everyone who has ever taken a seminar from TechTeach International, my firm. It's probably true that I've learned more over the years from my students than from anyone else.

--Mark Minasi

ACKNOWLEDGMENTS

As you can tell by lifting this tome, a lot of work went into creating all these pages about the workings of Windows 2000 Professional.

First, I'd like to thank Pat Coleman, who worked tirelessly to rework material and add valuable information when needed. Without her dedication and expertise, this book would not be possible.

Don Murdoch and Doug Toombs also deserve honorable mentions for their significant contributions.

I would be remiss if I didn't thank those at Sybex who helped get this book out on time. Thanks go to Jordan Gold, Publisher, and Ellen Dendy, Acquisitions and Developmental Editor, for helping get the book on the road, and providing guidance throughout the process. Thanks to our Editor, Sally Engelfried, for making sure the manuscript was beautiful and for being patient with a strict schedule. Thanks also to Art Brieva and Steve Wisniewski, Technical Editors, for keeping a technical eye on the book at all times. Thanks to Elizabeth Campbell, Production Editor, for keeping the book on schedule and making sure everything was in order, and to Adrian Woolhouse, Electronic Publishing Specialist, for making the pages look so good! Lastly, thanks go to the graphic artists: Elizabeth Creegan, Cuong Le, Inbar Berman, and Tony Jonick, who contributed to the wonderful illustrations enhancing this book, the proofreaders: Nanette Duffy, Laurie O'Connell, Erika Donald, Nancy Riddiough, and Sarah Tannehill, and also Ted Laux the indexer.

CONTENTS AT A GLANCE

CONTENTS

PART III • NETWORKING WINDOWS 2000 PROFESSIONAL 435

INTRODUCTION

What you have in your hands is a soup-to-nuts, beginner-to-expert, end-user-to-administrator handbook—the all-in-one guide to using and supporting Windows 2000 Professional, Microsoft's successor to Windows NT 4 Workstation.

This book is for you if you are upgrading from a previous version of Windows, including Windows 3.1, Windows 95/98, or Windows NT 4 Workstation, or if you're coming to the Windows world from another operating system. This book is also for you if you are new to networking or if you're thinking about setting up a network at home or in your business. In addition, this book is for you if you use a corporate client-server Windows 2000 network at the office. In other words, if you use Windows 2000 Professional in any environment, including a stand-alone system at home, you'll find here information you can use—all the way from installing Windows 2000 Professional to troubleshooting a large network.

What I Cover in This Book

This book is divided into four parts, building in a logical order from setting up your system to configuring advanced features.

Part I: Windows 2000 Professional Basics

Part I consists of nine chapters.

Chapter 1 is an overview of Windows 2000 Professional—what's new since the last incarnation (plenty!), what makes it different from other operating systems and other versions of Windows (including what makes it different from Windows 95/98), and what its main features are. Don't be misled if it seems there's a lot of jargon in this first chapter: I figured that power users who are already familiar with other operating systems will be looking to this chapter just to get an idea of what's different in Windows 2000 Professional; if you're not a power user on another system, you won't miss anything if you simply skim these comparisons.

In this Chapter 2, I take up the topic of *installing* Windows 2000 Professional, on your own as well as for other users. Like all advanced operating systems, Windows 2000 Professional has a somewhat complex, time-consuming installation process. *Unlike* Windows 3.*x*, you can't just install the operating system on one computer and then copy it to other, similar computers; you have to start Setup on every workstation that will be running Windows 2000 Professional. However, I'll show you how you can reduce the amount of work needed to install the system—by means of an automatic, "unattended" installation.

Chapter 3 contains information about programs you no longer need under this advanced type of operating system and also gives you some advice about how to run the programs you *will* be using. In other words, this is the chapter that gives you your first real introduction to *using* Windows 2000 Professional.

Nominally about organizing your programs and files in a useful and accessible hierarchy on your hard drive, Chapter 4 introduces the tools you'll be using to accomplish those goals: the Start menu (which you can organize as *you* see fit, to afford instant access to anything and everything on your system) and Explorer.

Chapter 5 unveils one of the key features of Windows 2000, shortcut menus, in very few pages. Shortcut menus pop up when you click your right mouse button on various objects found throughout the interface. In a single place, they provide only the commands that are most likely to be relevant to the operation you're currently performing! Shortcut menus also provide a highly convenient route to your *Properties dialog boxes*, which provide configuration options and settings specific to the object at hand, whether it be a file, a folder, a printer, a modem, or even another user's profile!

Chapter 6 will help you customize the look of your Desktop, including the way your programs' windows behave on screen, which fonts and colors your programs use, and settings for screen savers. I also discuss making changes to your default mouse properties, such as adjusting the double-click speed and using special mouse pointers for fun or for added visibility.

Chapter 7 is a must for virtually all users because everyone wants to print things, and printers are, for one reason or another, still a pain to set up and keep in working order. Add to that the number of options Windows 2000 Professional offers for controlling print jobs—such as prioritizing users on a network, changing the default fonts and graphics, adding and subtracting different types of printers, and so on—and the topic can quickly become bewildering unless you have a manual. This chapter functions as this manual.

If you have any intention of using audio or video with your system, you'll be happy to know that you can turn to Chapter 8 for an all-in-one guide to using multimedia on your Windows 2000 Professional workstation. Covering audio and video capabilities in depth, I discuss not only installing the hardware and software you'll be using, but I also discuss general instructions on *how* to use them. Discussions of the various standards in the field of audio and video recording/playback will help you ensure that your projects work for every member of your team, if not for widespread distribution as well.

No matter what kind of work you plan to do with your system, make plans now to set aside time for Chapter 9, because it covers the fundamental topic of putting your data where it will do the most good. In this chapter, I teach you how to move and share information of all types between different projects—such as inserting a spreadsheet or even an audio clip into a word processing report, adding a video sequence to a slide show, and moving a paragraph from the middle of a document to the beginning of the same document. If you're already familiar with simple cut, copy, and paste techniques, you'll be surprised at how much more you can do once you take advantage of the OLE methods available through Windows 2000 Professional applications.

Part II: Communications

The chapters in Part II start by introducing you to the communications tools that are included with Windows 2000 Professional. Chapter 10 also includes instructions for installing and configuring a modem. Chapter 11 explains the communications programs—Fax, HyperTerminal, and NetMeeting. Chapter 12 explains how to use the Internet Explorer Web browser, and Chapter 13 is an overview of Outlook Express—the news and mail client that's included with Windows 2000 Professional.

Part III: Networking Windows 2000 Professional

After you're past the "getting comfortable" stages of Parts I and II, you might feel like taking on the mantle of expert user—the user who is there to help other users get their work done most efficiently. That's the goal of the second half of the book (Parts III and IV).

Chapter 14 examines the architecture of Windows 2000 Professional—the pieces and parts of the operating system—which will, at the very least, equip you with an understanding of error messages. Chapter 15 is an introduction to overall networking concerns, delving just a bit into many fundamental topics.

Chapter 16 elaborates the down-and-dirty of those same topics; it describes everything from logical topologies to physical cabling and connectors. If you're fuzzy on the difference between an Internet router and Roto-Rooter, it will pay for you to take a hard look at this chapter.

In Chapter 17, I show you how to set up and configure a Windows 2000 Professional peer-to-peer network and how to connect Windows 2000 Professional machines to a Windows NT 4 domain. I think this latter situation is probably really common today as corporations and even small businesses migrate gradually to a total Windows 2000 environment.

One of the ways that Windows 2000 Professional is radically different from every other operating system is that it is *secure*; in fact, Windows 2000 Professional has been certified by the U.S. government as meeting the requirements for C2 level security. Security is a great thing to have, for obvious reasons, but it can also cause problems—the first time you can't access a file on your own computer, you'll want to know why! Chapter 18 takes you through the details of security so that you can address problems quickly and directly.

If you were lending half an ear to the prepublicity for Windows 2000, you most likely heard about Active Directory. Chapter 19 explains what it is and why it's important.

Chapter 20 deals with the very likely scenario of your planning to use your Windows 2000 Professional workstations over a Novell NetWare network. More than half the file servers in the world now run some version of Novell's popular NetWare operating system, and Microsoft, recognizing the reality of this situation, has worked with Novell to provide Windows 2000 Professional users with tools to make it easy to operate over such systems. In this chapter, you'll learn the idiosyncrasies of those tools, known collectively as Client Service for Novell NetWare.

Chapter 21 is about VPNs. A Virtual Private Network (VPN) is a tunnel through the Internet that connects your computer to a network. When you're on the road, you can dial up almost any ISP and set up a VPN session to your network over the Internet. If you're a road warrior, you shouldn't skip this chapter.

Part IV: Advanced Techniques and Troubleshooting

The chapters in this part of the book are primarily for system administrators. In other words, you probably shouldn't try some of this when you're home alone unless you have some programming skills and are really familiar with what's involved in setting up and administering a network.

I begin with four chapters that show you how to use scripts with Windows 2000 Professional. Chapter 22 covers HTML and VBScript, Chapter 23 covers DHTML and VBScript, Chapter 24 covers VBScript and Windows 2000 Professional, and Chapter 25 covers the Windows Scripting Host.

Windows 95/98 fans will find that most of what they like about Windows 95/98 is also present in Windows 2000 Professional. For example, try to install a new driver, say for a mouse or for many other necessary and/or popular devices, and you'll quickly see that one of the most significant changes from NT 4 is the inclusion of Plug and Play.

Chapter 26 simply and clearly explains what types of hardware Windows 2000 Professional does support and how to find, install, configure, and update drivers for that hardware. You won't realize how valuable this chapter is until the first time you spend 20 minutes on a "driver treasure hunt" trying to figure out how to install a new sound board driver!

In Chapter 27, I'll let you in on a little secret: Although Windows 2000 Professional is probably one of the most stable, crash-proof operating systems that's ever been available for the PC, it *can* still crash. When it does, anyone claiming to be an expert should expect to be asked to explain it, and the first thing you'll be asked is, "What's the deal with this blue screen?" Blue screens needn't make you blue, but they will give you food for thought. In this chapter, I'll show you how to interpret such screens and explain what you can do with the information. Chapter 28 follows up on this topic, with a look at how to use administrative and diagnostic tools to keep your system up to speed.

In Chapter 29, I've collected all the customization and optimization options that don't fit neatly into the other chapters. If you're a systems administrator, computer jock, or power user, and you haven't found the options you need discussed elsewhere in the book, be sure to check out this chapter.

In Chapter 30, I look at some advanced troubleshooting techniques. This chapter focuses on the methodology of troubleshooting Windows 2000 Professional, including using the Microsoft Knowledge Base to find answers, applying Service Packs, and learning to troubleshoot using the architecture of Windows 2000 Professional.

Typesetting Conventions Followed in This Book

As much as I could, I attempted to be consistent throughout the book with the capitalization of menu commands and dialog-box options. And all program-level filenames and command names appear in a `special font` to help distinguish them from the natural grammar of the sentence.

I've *italicized* terms for emphasis or as needed to avoid confusion. For example, key terms being defined for the first time are in italics. Furthermore, when I'm presenting the syntax of a command (yes, system administrators will still occasionally be dealing with command-line entry), placeholders and variables will be represented in italics.

Finally, anything I instruct you to type into an entry field or command line will be shown in **boldface** type.

Stay in Touch!

I hope you find the answers to all of your Windows 2000 Professional questions here. But if you have questions I didn't cover, or if you have a comment on the book, or if I made a mistake, I'd love to hear from you. Just e-mail `help@minasi.com` with questions, comments, or suggestions for future editions. I try to answer all of the e-mail that I get, but you can help me with that by doing a couple of things. First, please don't send me receipted mail. For various reasons that I won't go into here, I've set up my mail handler to automatically delete receipted mail; sorry. Second, if you're asking for advice, please try to keep the problem statement to a few paragraphs—if it gets any more involved than that, then, well, we're sort of moving into the field of network consulting, which is partially how I make my living…so I'm afraid your request will be slotted to be dealt with *after* those of my contracted clients. As you've probably guessed by now, I *do* receive a lot of mail. Much of it is highly complimentary, and I am very thankful to all of you who have corresponded! I *will* try to reply to all mail that I get—and thanks again for reading!

PART I

Windows 2000 Professional Basics

Learn To:

- ***Install Windows 2000 Professional***
- ***Install and organize remove programs***
- ***Add a local and a network printer***

CHAPTER 1

Introducing Windows 2000 Professional

FEATURING:

Since the advent of the personal computer, users have wanted three things in an operating system: power, stability, and usability. Windows 2000 Professional has all these and more in abundance. Since its inception in 1993, Windows NT has featured an indefatigable 32-bit architecture, complete with built-in networking and the capability to run almost every piece of Windows software on the market. Windows 2000 Professional now includes an interface, which has evolved from the NT 4 Explorer shell and is even easier to use.

NOTE Windows 2000 Professional is actually version 5 of Windows NT Workstation. Throughout the book, I make many references to NT in describing Windows 2000. The name change was a sign of the convergence of the Windows product lines.

What does all this mean to the consumer, the person sitting at a desk 52 weeks a year who just wants to be a productive computer user? It means a lot. It means a fast, up-to-date operating system with a slew of advanced features that ensure the computer will almost never crash. It means an operating system that can host the emerging multitude of 32-bit software applications, some of which offer amazing facilities for professional audio and video recording, editing, and broadcasting. It means a new interface, which gives users tremendous control over how the system performs its tasks and how it maintains its connections to peripherals and to other computers.

In this chapter, I'll give you an overview of Windows 2000 Professional: what's new, what's different, and what's under the hood. I'll compare Windows 2000 Professional to other operating systems you may be familiar with and emphasize comparisons between Windows 2000 Professional and previous versions of Windows. In later chapters, I'll expand on most of the topics I'll introduce in this chapter, but you'll find a lot here to whet your appetite.

Windows 2000 Professional, Windows 2000 Server: Which Is Which?

The two basic "flavors" of Windows 2000 are *Professional* and *Server*. It might be easier to think of Windows 2000 Server as the big brother of Windows 2000 Professional; they're from the same family but a little different in size and purpose. Both versions of Windows 2000 are solid, 32-bit operating systems, with C2 Level security and built-in networking. Both feature the Windows 2000 interface. Windows 2000 Professional is an operating system designed for corporate and high-end users who want a robust and powerful operating environment. Windows 2000 Server does everything that Windows 2000 Professional does and adds a comprehensive set of tools for managing and administering a network. It is designed to run on a network file server or application server. There are also additional versions of Windows 2000 Server intended for more specialized environments, such as cluster servers and data warehousing. For more information on these versions, see my book *Mastering Windows 2000 Server* (Sybex).

Everything that I discuss in this book is relevant for both flavors of Windows 2000, but I don't discuss the advanced networking administration features found in Windows 2000 *Server*. (Not to worry, though, networkers: in Part III of this book I *do* cover the administration features that let you manage the built-in networking capabilities of Windows 2000 *Professional*.)

The Road to Windows 2000 Professional

For many years people believed that microcomputer operating systems and mainframe operating systems were totally different entities, as different as bicycles and airliners. In the case of bikes and airliners, most of us would say, "Sure, they're both forms of transportation, but the similarity ends there." It's true. Microcomputer operating systems mainly ended up being launching pads for personal productivity tools such as word processors, drawing packages, e-mail, spreadsheets, and simple databases, as well as games. Mainframes, which make truly awful platforms for word processing (ask anyone who's ever tried to run the Unix version of WordPerfect or IBM's DisplayWrite/370), mainly ended up being the "data warehouses" of large corporations.

Because mainframe systems generally operate in well-managed, centrally administered, and very fault-tolerant environments, huge mission-critical database programs have found a home on them. The IRS keeps its "master file" on every U.S. citizen in a building full of huge mainframes in Martinsburg, West Virginia. The IRS must run a program to examine the master file every day—all 300+ million records of it—and that file is so valuable that parts of it are backed up *continuously*. Running that application on a few dozen Pentium Pros under Windows is hard to imagine, isn't it? (Try explaining to the president that we weren't able to issue refunds this year because the master file GPFed.)

But think about it: Why *doesn't* the IRS do its work on PCs? PCs are slower than mainframes, certainly, but by a smaller and smaller margin with every machine generation. No, the main reason is that corporate information technology (IT) managers don't trust PC software, and with good reason. PC users assume and take for granted the existence of bugs in the software we buy. It's just a fact of computer life. Our acceptance is somewhat odd, though, when you think about it. Consistent low quality is almost unheard of in the rest of the manufacturing world. If one in a thousand Big Macs gave you food poisoning, would you still frequent McDonald's? Probably not. If automobiles have manufacturing defects, do you meekly accept the answer, "Well, yes, it *is* a problem, but it's not a big one. We'll fix it in the next model." Nope. In fact, in most areas of commerce you usually don't need to worry about the issue of quality because laws protect consumers from shoddy products in most fields.

Why don't PC vendors work harder to produce high-quality, never-failing software? Well, some have; IBM's Personal Editor was one example of an essentially flawless piece of software. Operating systems haven't been quite as lucky, though; you'd pretty much need a CD-ROM to hold the list of known Windows 3.*x* bugs.

The Beginnings

The top people at Microsoft knew that they were vulnerable on a very key point: all their products ran on Intel *x*86 hardware, meaning the 8088, 80286, 80386, 80486, and eventually Pentium and Pentium Pro processors and beyond. Microsoft's fortunes, then, rode on the Intel horse, and at that time the Intel horse seemed the right one to back. But what about the future? Who could know what processor would be dominant in 10 years? Microsoft wanted to know that it would be on top no matter what processor the marketplace chose, so it needed an *architecture-independent* operating system.

Building an Architecture-Independent Operating System

Architecture-independent doesn't mean that the product works as well in a Victorian house as it does in a Bauhaus office. Architecture-independent means that it's built so that it can be modified fairly easily to work on a different processor. All of Microsoft's operating systems up to 1989 were firmly Intel entrenched, and porting any of them to another processor would have been difficult. (For example, IBM was forced to agree that portability was a problem when it announced that it had stopped work on a version of OS/2 for its PowerPC processor, a CPU of non-Intel architecture.)

A piece of software can easily become dependent on a particular processor because the writers of the operating system must become intimately familiar with the processor's strengths and weaknesses. Consequently, those strengths and weaknesses inevitably color a developer's sense of what's necessary and unnecessary for an operating system. For example, if you build an operating system on top of a 16-bit processor, you're probably going to make the operating system a 16-bit operating system. If the processor handles memory in chunks (*pages* is the exact word) of 4KB, as the Intel processors do, the operating system's pages will probably turn out to be 4KB as well. So converting the operating system to a machine with 1MB pages involves massive code rewriting unless the operating system is designed with flexible page sizes in mind.

Building an architecture-independent operating system might have been too difficult a task for Microsoft's development staff, but as luck would have it, a team of top-flight mainframe operating system designers became available in 1989. A group of former Digital Equipment Corporation programmers, led by a man named Dave Cutler, set up shop at Microsoft, promising to build the operating system of Microsoft's future. Influenced partly by an operating system called MACH, a Unix implementation created at Carnegie Mellon University, Cutler's team used a design approach that attempted to isolate all the processor-specific parts of the operating system into a single area called the *microkernel*. Most of the machine-specific parts of the operating system would live in a file called `hal.dll`, or the *Hardware Abstraction Layer*. The operating system would be stable, *carefully* debugged, and *scalable*—that is, able to grow to meet the requirements of the largest PCs imaginable (or, at least, imaginable in 1989).

To produce a stable and scalable operating system, the NT team would require a PC with at least 16MB of RAM and at least a 33MHz processor, quite an expensive machine for the time. Microsoft risked spending millions of dollars on an operating system that would be seen as a sluggish memory hog if in the long run memory prices didn't come down and CPU speeds didn't go up. Memory prices *have* come down, and processors *have* become faster; 400MHz is about the minimum speed you will find on a new computer nowadays.

The Early Releases

The first version of NT (which stands for New Technology) wasn't named NT version 1, probably out of some marketing notion that people are scared of any software labeled version 1. (Actually, going immediately to 3.1 was to coordinate with Windows 3.1.) The first release, called NT 3.1, was supposed to ship in late 1991 but was delayed—first until early 1992 and then until late 1992; it finally shipped in July 1993. This version of NT was dubbed NT Workstation 3.1 to distinguish it from its server sibling NT Advanced Server. NT Workstation 3.1 didn't sell all that well—mainly because it required a fairly expensive PC to run it and it lacked software. Despite the weak sales, NT got high marks from its users. I don't think I *ever* remember any of its detractors pointing to its bugs—because there were hardly any. I recall skeptically loading NT onto a few of my workstations and being pleasantly surprised at its stability—very few bugs and very stable multitasking.

About 14 months later, NT version 3.5 appeared in server and workstation configurations. NT Advanced Server had been renamed NT Server without the *Advanced* because people looked at its $1,500 price tag and said, "Hey, that's a lot of money, and I don't need that much power; where do I find the *basic* Server?" Again in version 3.5, the NT team showed its commitment to high-quality, bug-free software. Very few features had been added—just some improvements in the TCP/IP software and in NetWare connectivity tools. The NT development team had worked for a little more than a year, and what had it done? Simple: Instead of adding pointless features, the programmers focused on fixing bugs and tightening up the operating system. It got a little leaner, a little faster, and a bit more stable.

In the early summer of 1995, yet another version of NT appeared—version 3.51. Version 3.51 again produced very few new features. PCMCIA (Personal Computer Memory Card International Association) support, a client license management system, and file compression were the main new items. NT version 3.51 seemed a bit less stable, as evidenced by Microsoft's release of *three* Service Packs (that is, groups of files that patch up the operating system and repair bugs—in other words, bug fixes) for it by the end of 1995.

After 3.51's introduction, another Microsoft operating system appeared, Windows 95. Like NT, it claimed to be a 32-bit OS and sported a shiny new user interface and some new network management tools. Users soon wanted to know when NT would reach parity with Windows 95's features.

The answer to that question was, of course, "Soon," and NT 4 was the down payment on that promise. Windows 2000 Professional has carried on with that promise to provide many of the features formerly the exclusive domain of Windows 95/98.

What's New in Windows 2000 Professional?

Windows 2000 Professional is a mix of old and new. It carries on the legacy of Windows NT including most of NT's strengths and architecture, but it adds many new features. Windows 2000 Professional is much more than just Windows NT 5. It represents the convergence of technologies from Windows 95/98 and Windows NT Workstation. Once again, Microsoft has developed an operating system designed for ease of use, fantastic hardware support, and technology that sets new standards.

Nearly all the functionality of NT 4 Workstation has been preserved, though many of the tools have new locations and new looks in Windows 2000 Professional. The most obvious changes lie in the consolidation of the administration tools into the Microsoft Management Console (MMC), a one-stop shopping place for your management needs. The MMC lets you manage your entire computer from one toolbar. You will also notice changes in the appearance of Control Panel and Explorer. Even the Desktop has changed. Don't worry if the new interface and its new tools seem unfamiliar now; I'll be covering them in detail throughout this book.

Plug-and-Play Support

If you've ever installed a board in a PC, you know what a pain it can be. If you've ever installed a *complex* board, such as a sound card, you know that making it work can be a weekend project. That's why Microsoft and Compaq developed Plug and Play.

Plug and Play is an ambitious project, but here's a brief description of how it works. Every device inside your PC uses a combination of some or all of these components, known generically as *hardware resources*:

- Memory addresses
- Input/output (I/O) addresses
- Interrupt request (IRQ) levels
- Direct memory access (DMA) channels

If you've never come across any of these items, don't be intimidated by the terms; they only *sound* technical. All you have to know is this: Your computer has a limited number of memory addresses, I/O addresses, IRQ levels, and DMA channels. In general, you cannot assign two devices to use the same hardware resource. For example, if you try to put both your sound card and your local area network on IRQ5, neither the sound card nor the local area network card works, or one will work, but not the other.

NOTE The essence of PC expansion board configuration is to first find out what hardware resources a board needs. Some need just an I/O address, and others need an I/O address and an IRQ level; a few demand an I/O address, an IRQ level, and a DMA channel. The design of a board determines its requirements. The next step is to reconfigure the board so that it doesn't conflict with any other board's resources.

If I wanted to install a sound card into a system, I'd start by finding out that it required three I/O address ranges, an IRQ level, and two DMA channels. (I'm not making this up; your basic 16-bit sound card is a nightmare to configure.) Then I'd determine which resources (memory, I/O, IRQ, and DMA) were free and available on my computer before installing the sound card. After I know what resources my computer currently *uses*, I can then figure out what resources are *available*, and I'd tell the sound board to use those unused resources.

Telling the sound board to use those resources sometimes means physically taking the board in hand and moving small electronic contacts called *jumpers* or tiny switches called *dual in-line package (DIP) switches*. Or it may mean running a program that comes with the sound board, or a combination of the two. And I'm still not done. Next, I'll have to load drivers for the sound board, and the drivers will not work until they know which I/O addresses, IRQ level, and DMA channels I selected for the sound board. Reboot, and *then* I'm done, assuming that I did each step correctly.

In contrast, all Plug-and-Play devices contain *smart* boards, boards that can be interrogated by the system about their resource needs. At startup, a program in the BIOS called the Configuration Manager asks all Plug-and-Play hardware—Plug-and-Play hardware resides on the PC's motherboard as well as on expansion boards—to announce its existence. The Configuration Manager then asks each of the boards,

"What resources do you need?" They respond, and the Configuration Manager figures out what configuration will make all the boards happy. It then sets the memory addresses, I/O addresses, IRQ levels, and DMA channels on all the Plug-and-Play hardware and commences the boot process. This procedure sounds time-consuming but requires only a second.

Notice that so far, the operating system is irrelevant; a Plug-and-Play–compliant PC has a Configuration Manager in its BIOS ROM, which runs before the operating system even gets started. But recall that every Plug-and-Play computer completely reconfigures itself whenever you turn it on; this means, in theory, that if you insert a new sound card into your computer, it could set off a chain reaction that would cause the Configuration Manager to reassign all the resources to all the boards.

Reassigning resources would be a problem because all the driver programs that are such an important part of Windows 2000 Professional (and, for that matter, *any* operating system) must figure out what resources each board uses. Also, any Plug-and-Play–compliant operating system must be able to take the self-identification information provided by each Plug-and-Play expansion board and use it to choose drivers automatically. For example, suppose you install a 3Com 3C590 Ethernet card, which is a Plug-and-Play card, into your PC. The Configuration Manager sets its resources automatically, but then how do you tell the operating system to load the driver for a 3Com 3C590? Well, in a perfect world, you don't want to have to tell the operating system *anything*; it should figure it out for itself—and a Plug-and-Play–compliant operating system does just that.

Windows 2000 Professional includes Plug-and-Play support. For longtime users of Windows NT Workstation, that statement bears repeating: Windows 2000 Professional has Plug-and-Play! No more suffering through the mysteries of manual configuration when installing a new piece of hardware in your computer. After installing the hardware, all you have to do is boot the computer, and Plug-and-Play should take care of the rest.

Partial Plug-and-Play Systems

So, to review: If you have a non-Plug-and-Play system, you configure all the boards by hand, make notes on which memory addresses, I/O addresses, IRQ levels, and DMA channels each board uses, and relay that information to each of the drivers that you must load. If you have a Plug-and-Play system, the system configures itself. Each Plug-and-Play board can communicate its configuration to the corresponding driver.

But what about this fairly common configuration: a Plug-and-Play system with a number of non-Plug-and-Play boards? If your computer has both PCI (Peripheral Component Interconnect) and ISA (Industry Standard Architecture) slots—which is the case for most PCs nowadays—virtually all your PCI boards are Plug and Play, and virtually all your ISA boards are *not* Plug and Play. Thus, you must configure the ISA boards by hand. In other words, the PCI boards configure themselves without even asking for your opinion, and the ISA boards sit mutely waiting for your instructions.

NOTE Not all ISA boards are Plug-and-Play unaware. In fact, a number of ISA boards provide Plug-and-Play configuration. Examples include the Intel and 3Com ISA Ethernet cards and the Creative Laboratories Plug-and-Play 16-bit sound card. But the vast majority of ISA boards have no Plug-and-Play capability and must be configured by hand.

Suppose you configure one of your ISA boards to use IRQ10. The Configuration Manager, which knows nothing of the ISA boards, happens to assign one of the PCI boards to IRQ10. Result: instant, automatic conflict. What to do?

Some well-designed computers (Compaq is the premier example) have a user-configurable Configuration Manager that you can just plain tell to "stay away from IRQ10." Unfortunately, most computers aren't that well built, so here's my advice.

First, remove the ISA boards. Leave in the PCI boards, and boot the system under DOS or Windows 95/98. Let the Configuration Manager configure the PCI cards. You can then find out which resources the PCI cards used by examining the Windows 95/98 Device Manager. (On the Windows 95/98 Desktop, right-click My Computer to open the System Properties dialog box, and click the Device Manager tab.)

You can also run a DOS-based Plug-and-Play manager, which you can get from Intel or from the manufacturer of your PC. After you know where the PCI boards have settled, configure the ISA boards in the remaining resources. In effect, you let the PCI boards do whatever they want and then make the ISA boards tiptoe around them.

As you can see, configuring a Plug-and-Play system without a Plug-and-Play operating system makes the task more like "plug and pray" than Plug and Play.

Hot Plug-and-Play Support

Another neat feature of Windows 95/98 is *Hot* Plug and Play, which is useful in laptops with PCMCIA/PC Card slots.

If I turn on my laptop computer without a network card in it, Windows 95/98 does not load any network software. But if I insert a PCMCIA/PC network card into my system after it's booted up, the Configuration Manager recognizes that the network card needs network drivers. Then all the network software loads without the need for a reboot.

Hot Plug and Play is a neat feature for Windows 95/98 and is a feature that is shared by Windows 2000 Professional. When I insert a PCMCIA adapter into my laptop, Windows 2000 Professional recognizes the device, installs the driver (if needed), and starts using the device. Be careful, though. Some devices really don't like hot swapping. For that reason, there is an icon in your status area to prepare your PCMCIA cards for ejection.

NOTE Although Windows 2000 Professional doesn't require you to reboot or even ask if you want to do so, in many cases you'll need to reboot for a device to work properly.

Offline Files

Using Offline Files, you can work with network files and folders even when you aren't connected to your network. For example, if you lose your network connection or you undock your portable computer, anything that you've made available offline continues to be available to you, with the same access and permissions you'd have if you were connected to the network. To use Offline Files, use the options in My Computer.

Windows Management Instrumentation

Almost all hardware functions are now built around Windows Management Instrumentation (WMI), a software interface that lets an administrator view and modify any hardware settings on the computer you're sitting at as well as on any machine that you can see on the network. In addition you can format and partition disks locally or over the network.

Advanced Power Management Support

If you ran NT 4 on a notebook computer, you'll be glad to know that using Windows 2000 Professional on a notebook computer will double the life of a battery. Advanced Configuration and Power Interface (ACPI) is an industry standard, implemented in Windows 2000 Professional Advanced Power Management, that allows the operating system to conserve power by routing power away from unused hardware components.

Encrypting File System

Using encrypting file system (EFS), you can secure your documents and folders so that only you—or the people to whom you give the key—can view the documents, if you are using the NTFS file system. Encryption is a handy way to keep even shared documents private or to protect files on a machine that could easily be stolen, such as a laptop.

Support for Windows 2000 Server Deployment Tools

Windows 2000 Professional includes support for features of Windows 2000 Server that simplify getting an operating system on a new computer and then simplify installing applications on that computer. If your computer is part of a Windows 2000 Server/Professional network, the administrator can use Remote Installations Services (RIS) to configure a workstation and then install the operating system, necessary drivers, and so on. An administrator can then use the Software Installation (SI) tool to automatically install an application company-wide.

Microsoft Management Console

Microsoft Management Console (MMC) is a framework for management applications, providing a unified interface for Microsoft and third-party management tools. MMC doesn't replace management applications; it integrates them into one single interface. There are no inherent management functions in MMC at all. It uses component tools called snap-ins, which do all the work. MMC provides a user interface; it doesn't change how the snap-ins function.

Our old familiar administrative tools—such as the User Manager and User Manager for Domains, Server Manager, Event Viewer, and even Disk Administrator—have been assimilated into things called Microsoft Management Console (MMC) tools.

USB Support

Universal Serial Bus (USB) is an electronic pathway that supports Plug and Play and that allows you to connect and disconnect devices without shutting down or restarting your computer. The Windows 2000 Professional USB supports everything from game controllers to digital cameras.

Digital Camera Support

Setting up a digital camera in Windows 2000 Professional is a cinch using the Scanners And Camera applet in Control Panel. If your camera is Plug and Play, Windows 2000 Professional will detect it and install it automatically.

Multiple Monitor Support

Unlike NT 4 and like Windows 98, Windows 2000 Professional supports the use of multiple monitors with a single CPU. All you need is an additional PCI video card that supports multimonitor. If you're thinking of getting a bigger monitor, you might want to consider getting an additional monitor instead (if you have space on your physical desktop). For example, two 17-inch monitors have more display area than a single 21-inch monitor.

DirectX 7

DirectX is Microsoft's architecture for running multimedia applications using any hardware platform, and it is a tool that developers use to create multimedia content.

Windows 2000 Professional supports the entire suite of DirectX 7 components. DirectX 7 is composed of the following components:

DirectDraw Controls the graphics and video functions on your computer (the way that images are drawn on your screen).

DirectSound Controls the way that sound is played on your computer.

DirectInput Controls joystick commands on your computer.

Direct3D Controls the manipulation of 3-D images on your screen.

DirectPlay Provides network access for programs written to take advantage of DirectX 7.

For starters, all this means that your favorite Windows 95/98 games will work in Windows 2000 Professional exactly as they did in Windows 95/98.

Advanced VPN Security

A Virtual Private Network (VPN) is a tunnel through the Internet that connects your computer to a network. When you're on the road, you can dial up almost any ISP and set up a VPN session to your network over the Internet. VPN supports the following protocols:

Point-to-Point Tunneling Protocol (PPTP) Part of the TCP/IP family of protocols used to transmit data over serial lines and point-to-point dial-up telephone connection.

Layer-2 Tunneling Protocol (L-2TP) Based on a Cisco protocol, allows you to establish a tunnel from an ISP to a corporate site and transmit data through it.

IP Security (IP-Sec) A suite of communications protocols that add security to the Internet Protocol (IP).

NOTE For all the details about VPN and Windows 2000 Professional, see Chapter 21.

Recovery Console

Recovery Console is a program that you run from a command prompt to make changes to a Windows 2000 Professional system that refuses to start—if you are a knowledgeable system administrator. You can also use the Recovery Console to start or stop system services and to format disks.

Hibernation

Hibernation is a feature of power management in Windows 2000 Professional that saves everything in memory to the hard drive, turns off your monitor and hard disk, and then turns off your computer. You typically use hibernation when you are going to be away from your computer for an extended period or overnight. When you restart your computer, the Desktop is restored exactly as it was when the computer shut down. Hibernation is primarily for use on portable computers, but the computer's hardware must be set up by the manufacturer to support this feature.

Remote Desktop Sharing

Remote desktop sharing allows the user of a remote computer to take over another computer just as though they were in front of it. This is a new feature of NetMeeting that you cannot replicate using VPN or any other remote access service. For all the details, see Chapter 11.

Internet Connection Sharing

Internet Connection Sharing (ICS) is a feature that allows multiple computers to share a connection to the Internet whether that connection is a modem, ISDN, cable modem, DSL, or whatever. You run ICS on the computer that's dialed in (or cable-modemed or DSLed) to the Internet. When you enable Shared Access, the ICS machine acts as a DHCP server and as a router. For details about sharing an Internet connection, see Chapter 10.

Fax Services

Windows 2000 Professional includes a fax service, which sends and receives faxes through a separate fax queue (just like a printer) or through various fax-aware applications such as your favorite e-mail client software.

Internet Explorer 5

Internet Explorer (IE) is Microsoft's all-purpose Web browser. Much as in Windows 98, IE is integrated into the Desktop environment. IE functions are integrated into the entire operating system to make it easier to reach documents either on your local network or anywhere on the Internet.

Internet Information Services

Windows 2000 Professional includes the same Internet Information Services (IIS) as its big brother, Windows 2000 Server. IIS provides the ability to act as a Web server, File Transfer Protocol (FTP) server, Simple Mail Transfer Protocol (SMTP), and Post Office Protocol version 3 (POP3) server for e-mail.

Accessibility Options

Accessibility options are features that you can enable to help people with physical challenges use the computer easier. Features include Narrator, which reads items that are displayed on the screen, Magnifier, which displays magnified portions of your screen in a separate window, and an onscreen keyboard that you type on with the mouse.

Telnet Server

The Telnet Server service enables remote computers to connect to a Telnet server via the Telnet protocol. Telnet Server service in Windows 2000 Professional supports two simultaneous connections.

Personalized Menus

In Windows 2000 Professional, menus contain only the items you most frequently use. Those items that you don't use don't appear until you click the More button. Opinions vary as to whether this is a bug or a feature. But if you find this "feature" annoying, you can always to revert to the standard menu, using the options in the Taskbar And Start Menu Properties dialog box.

What's Not in Windows 2000 Professional?

The following is a very short list of features not available in Windows 2000 Professional.

MSN Support

The much-talked-about Microsoft Network (MSN) software that was a key part of Windows 95/98 is not available in Windows 2000 Professional. However, you can still use MSN as an Internet service provider (ISP), for use with Microsoft IE or the Web browser of your choice. Look for an MSN client to be released for Windows 2000 Professional in the near future.

Support for MIPS or PowerPC Chips

Windows 2000 Professional does not support the MIPS (millions of instructions per second) and PowerPC processors. These platforms haven't been very well represented in the marketplace, and the development effort put into the approximately 36 million lines of code for Windows 2000 Professional demands that only the most prevalent systems be supported.

Why Choose Windows 2000 Professional over Windows 98?

Given that their interfaces are so similar, it would be a fair question to ask why you should choose one over the other. The answer is straightforward. Windows 2000 Professional may look like Windows 98, but it does many things that Windows 98 can't. For starters, Windows 2000 Professional is a secure operating system. Just try to log on to a Windows 2000 Professional computer without the correct password. You can't do it. In Windows 98? Just press the Esc key and you're in! The lesson here is, if you have data that absolutely, positively needs to be kept secret, Windows 2000 Professional is the operating system for you.

Windows 2000 Professional is also the most complete 32-bit environment you can buy. If you need an operating system that won't crash and won't shut down on you, Windows 2000 Professional is the one for you.

How different is Windows 2000 Professional from Windows 98? Both use the same style interface; both are 32-bit operating systems. But after that, the similarity ends. Although they are both 32-bit operating systems, they implement their 32-bitness in much different ways. Table 1.1 lists the differences, which are explained below in greater detail.

TABLE 1.1: COMPARISON OF WINDOWS 2000 PROFESSIONAL AND WINDOWS 98

Windows 2000 Professional	Windows 98
Hardware Abstraction Layer (HAL) with Plug and Play	Plug and Play
Multiprocessor support (with either *x*86 or Alpha)	*x*86 support only
Runs entirely in protected mode	Runs in protected mode with some real-mode support
Separate 16-bit memory spaces	Shared 16-bit memory spaces
Multithreaded operating system	Single-threaded operating system
NT File System (NTFS), File Allocation Table (FAT), File Allocation Table 32 (FAT32)	File Allocation Table (FAT), File Allocation Table 32 (FAT32)
File and resource rights assignments	No rights
Complete user-level security	Limited password security

More Solid, Crashless

Ever since his days at DEC and before that at DuPont, Dave Cutler had a simple formula for making sure that a piece of code was as bug-free as possible: He forced the people who wrote the code to *use* the code. His phrase was that programmers should "have to eat their own dog food." From as early as possible, it was Alpo for breakfast, Ken-l-Ration for lunch, and Mighty Dog for dinner with the NT team. Putting a bug into the latest "build" of NT brought tons of peer disapproval and, worse, a *communication* from Dave.

Additionally, Cutler wrote some of the toughest pieces of the operating system himself. No one on the team just talked about what the system should do; everyone participated in building it. And Cutler carried all of NT in his head. Maybe this centralization was a *disadvantage*—after all, what would happen when Cutler left the project? But at that time, having at least one person with the grand overview—something that's rumored not to have existed for Windows 95/98—was a great strength.

NOTE Looking at some of the bug lists that accompany the Service Pack updates for NT 4 is a worthwhile exercise. A Service Pack may fix hundreds of bugs, but those bugs could be so minor that not a single one applies to your installation. And consider that Service Packs were never released for DOS or Windows 3.1. One appeared for Windows 95, but it fixed only two bugs, leaving the dozens of shell bugs untouched. We can expect to see Service Packs for Windows 2000 Professional too, so keep an eye on Microsoft's Web site from time to time.

When Windows 2000 Professional *does* die, it does a pretty good job of telling you who killed it. If you ever see Windows 2000 Professional crash, you'll see a distinctive sight. The screen clears and goes to a 50-line text screen with a blue background and bright white letters. When Windows 2000 Professional crashes, it fills up this blue screen—Windows 2000 Professional experts call this event *bluescreening*—with memory dump information and an error message or two. In my experience, what kills Windows 2000 Professional is a bad video driver, a bad disk driver, or a bad RAM chip, and the blue screen helps you identify which one is the culprit.

Furthermore, when Windows 2000 Professional crashes, it writes an entire image of the physical memory to disk in what is called a *crash dump*. You can use the crash dump analysis program `dumpexam.exe` (included on the Windows 2000 Professional installation CD) to look through the crash and narrow down the causes. You can also send the crash dumps to software and driver vendors, meaning that you have some leverage when you ask them to fix their software.

Complete Protected Mode over Protected Mode with Real-Mode Support

One of the selling points for Windows 95 was its emphasis on backward compatibility, which meant that it wasn't *completely* a 32-bit operating system. If you're running Windows 95 and you still have some old, real-mode, 16-bit drivers for your favorite peripheral, you can still use them with Windows 95. You can't use them with Windows 2000 Professional, though. That's because everything about Windows 2000 Professional must be able to run in protected mode.

What are these modes, and what difference do they make? Simply put, *real-mode* drivers can talk directly to your PC hardware. Although this is a direct and efficient way for things to work, it also causes crashes and other errors that often beset computer users. *Protected-mode* drivers, on the other hand, cannot talk directly to computer hardware; they must go through the operating system. In Windows 2000 Professional, all protected-mode drivers must talk to the HAL (Hardware Abstraction Layer) to get to the hardware, which makes for a more stable operating environment.

Faster

One thing that can't be denied about NT is that it runs slower on a given system than Windows 95/98. At first glance, that would suggest that NT and speed aren't subjects you'd often put in the same sentence. And if you're talking about the standard Pentium workstation with 16MB of RAM and a 100MHz processor, it's true that you'd be better off running most applications under Windows 95/98 than under NT 4.

But now consider the more powerful systems. The top end of the *x*86 world for a long time was the Pentium Pro processor. And believe it or not, the Pro runs NT faster than it runs 95/98.

Why? Well, when Intel started designing the Pentium Pro in the late '80s, it predicted that by 1995 most people would have converted from 16-bit to 32-bit operating systems. Consequently, Intel designed a CPU that ran fastest in 32-bit mode and not very fast in 16-bit mode; in fact, the Pentium Pro is usually slower than a Pentium in executing 16-bit code. Unfortunately, as we now know, Intel was a little optimistic in its beliefs about people's willingness to upgrade their operating systems. (The fact that memory prices didn't fall significantly until early 1996 certainly didn't help their willingness.) Hence, 16-bit operating systems, such as DOS or Windows 3.1, won't run very well on a Pentium Pro.

But what about Windows 95/98? Well, even though Windows 95/98 is advertised as being a 32-bit operating system, it's not, really. It combines a lot of the old 16-bit code with some new 32-bit code. In fact, a lot of the 32-bit code in Windows 95/98 is just 16-bit code with some programming fixes built in, a process called *thunking*. You won't find any such thunks in Windows 2000 Professional, because it's an actual 32-bit operating system. The upshot is, because Windows 95/98 is partially 16-bit, it takes a performance hit when running on a Pentium Pro.

Windows 2000 Professional, in contrast, gets *faster* on a Pentium Pro, because both use true 32-bit architecture. But the Windows 2000 Professional speed boost doesn't end with the Pentium Pro. The new Pentium IIIs have that 32-bit architecture as well, and at the time of this writing they're running at 800MHz and faster!

NOTE Although Windows 2000 Professional can support as many as 32 processors, the Hardware Abstraction Layer (HAL) that ships with Windows 2000 Professional supports only two processors. To use more, you'll need a custom HAL from your computer manufacturer. The HAL that ships with Windows 2000 Server supports four processors, and the higher versions of Windows 2000 Server support as many as 32 processors.

The first desktop PC to run at 1000MHz won't be running Windows 95/98—it'll most likely be running Windows 2000 Professional. So, while the lower-end workstations run fastest with one of the old 16-bit or hybrid 16/32-bit operating systems, the more powerful machines will find Windows 2000 Professional a better fit.

Home Directories

A home directory is the location where a user stores their files. The user can then access these files from any computer that they can log on to. Home directories supply another level of data protection that is not available in Windows 95/98.

Error Recording

Ever had a message appear on the screen while you booted a DOS or Windows 95/98 workstation, only to have the message scroll off the screen before you could read it? You won't have to endure this particular frustration under Windows 2000 Professional, because all important system messages are written to one of three logs: the System Log, the Security Log, or the Applications Log. You view all three with an application called the Event Viewer, which is in the Administrative Tools applet.

Event Viewer messages are not always the most useful things in the whole world, but you'll sometimes be able to get a lot of information out of them. Well-written applications (you *did* catch the weasel words *well-written,* didn't you?) write useful information into the Applications Log, so put "uses the Applications Log" on your list of things to look for when buying 32-bit applications for Windows 2000 Professional. One of the new features that Microsoft touted for Windows 2000 Professional is new, clearly written error messages. So far, the messages I've seen have been remarkably easy to work with.

Multiprocessor Support over *x*86-Only Support

Windows 2000 Professional is built to run on the Intel *x*86 and IA64 families of computer processors. It can also run on computers running more than one processor. As I mentioned earlier, Windows 2000 Professional can support up to two processors. What's the advantage to all this? Well, it means you can use Windows 2000 Professional on some very fast machines; you're not limited to the *x*86 series. On the other hand, Windows 95/98 can run only on an *x*86 processor and on only one of them at a time.

Separate 16-Bit Memory Spaces over Shared 16-Bit Memory Spaces

Despite all the advances brought about by 32-bit software, sooner or later you'll probably find yourself in a situation where you need to run 16-bit applications. Both Windows 2000 Professional and Windows 95/98 run 16-bit programs just fine, but they run them differently, and this affects performance and system reliability.

In the world of Windows 95/98, 16-bit Windows programs share the same memory space, or, if you prefer, the same room. If one 16-bit Windows application goes down, it will also crash any other 16-bit applications you may be running. Windows 95/98 runs 32-bit programs much the same way that Windows 2000 Professional does—it runs them in separate memory spaces. Windows 95/98 also runs MS-DOS programs in separate memory spaces because the operating system first must create the illusion of a computer running MS-DOS. This simulation is called the Virtual DOS Machine (VDM).

Windows 2000 Professional also uses a VDM to run MS-DOS applications, giving the appearance of a 486 computer with all the memory the program needs. Each VDM exists in its own memory space and runs as a 32-bit program. Windows 2000 Professional uses the VDM to create the Win16 on Win32 (WOW) environment too. The WOW is a simulation of Windows 3.1 on top of the simulation of MS-DOS. It runs just like Windows 3.1 with all the good points and the bad. By default, Windows 2000 Professional shares the same WOW environment for all 16-bit Windows applications, which means that if one crashes, they all crash. But Windows 2000 Professional differs from 95/98 in that you can start your 16-bit applications in separate memory spaces so they run just like 32-bit programs. That means you have the choice of using the default model of running the 16-bit applications in a shared memory space where they can crash one another or running them in a separate 32-bit memory space where you can take advantage of preemptive multitasking and multiprocessing.

Running 16-bit programs in a separate memory space may not always work. Some applications require a shared memory environment in order to exchange information or draw upon services provided by another program. Unfortunately, you may need to experiment some to find out if your 16-bit applications will run correctly on Windows 2000 Professional.

NT File System over FAT File System

DOS, Windows 3.*x*, and Windows 95/98 use the same type of file system, called FAT, for File Allocation Table. Here, when I mention a file system, I'm not just talking about the order in which your files are stored on your hard drive. Rather, I'm talking about the entire set of organizing principles that allow your operating system to communicate with your hard drive. The FAT approach to organizing this activity is to create a database (the FAT) at the boot sector of your hard drive. The boot sector is an area at the "beginning" of your hard drive. It's the place where the hard drive keeps the files that your operating system needs to talk to the drive, and the FAT is the most crucial of these.

NOTE The disk error messages you may have seen when running a disk utility under other operating systems are informing you of problems in the FAT!

NTFS (New Technology File System) is a high-performance file system used by Windows NT and Windows 2000 Professional. It incorporates more powerful features than the FAT system. For example, not only can NTFS understand long filenames, up to 255 characters (actually, Windows 95/98 can also do this), NTFS also creates backup records of its Master File Table (MFT), which is the NTFS version of the FAT. If the boot sector of your hard drive (the place where file table information is stored) happens to be damaged through some unfortunate incident, the information can be replaced from one of the MFT backup records. As a result, it's much less likely that you'll lose data because of disk problems under NTFS than under FAT.

NOTE Windows 2000 Professional includes the newer version of NTFS that was first released with Service Pack 4 on NT 4. If you want to multiboot Windows 2000 Professional and NT 4, be sure to install the latest Service Pack.

Moreover, it is much more difficult for viruses to infect NTFS volumes than it is for them to infect FAT volumes. This is because the data on the NTFS volume is written differently than it is under FAT. Most viruses are looking for FAT file types, and they don't know what to do when they encounter NTFS.

NTFS also allows security controls for individual files, programs, and folders—controllable by the Windows 2000 Professional Administrator or anyone with administrator privileges. FAT has no security features at all.

Neither DOS, nor Windows 3.*x*, nor Windows 95/98 understands NTFS. If you have two hard drives in your computer, and one of them is formatted as NTFS and the other as FAT, DOS, Windows 3.*x*, and Windows 95/98 systems will see only the FAT drive.

Similarly, if you make multiple partitions of a single hard drive and format each of them with a different file system, the non-NT/Windows 2000 Professional operating systems won't see the NTFS-formatted partitions. Table 1.2 lists the main differences between NTFS and FAT.

WARNING Earlier versions of Windows NT supported the High Performance File System (HPFS) from OS/2. NT 4 and Windows 2000 Professional do not support HPFS at all. If you have any partitions formatted with HPFS, you must convert them to NTFS before installing Windows 2000 Professional if you want the data on those partitions to be accessible.

NOTE Windows 2000 Professional does support the FAT32 file system, so multibooting with Windows 98 is now possible.

TABLE 1.2: A COMPARISON OF NTFS AND FAT

NTFS	FAT
Backup records	No backup records
Long filenames	Long filenames with Windows 95/98
	8.3 filenames with earlier Windows and MS-DOS
Full user security support	No security
Limit of 16EB	2GB under Windows 95/98
	(1EB = 1,073,741,824GB)
	4GBs under Windows NT
Windows NT only	MS-DOS, Windows 3.*x*,
	Windows 95/98, Windows NT

Security in Windows 2000 Professional

Security is an A-number-1 raison d'être for Windows 2000 Professional. NT was designed to fulfill the needs of people requiring high levels of security, and NT is one of the only microcomputer operating systems that has been reviewed for the U.S. government's C2 security standard. Windows 2000 Professional also incorporates this deep-seated need for security.

Here are some of the ways in which Windows 2000 Professional implements security:

- Requires users to log on to a workstation.
- Defines user rights that control a user's actions.
- Uses file and printer permissions to control access.
- Encrypts security information over networks.

Windows 2000 Professional Requires Users to Log On to a Workstation

Windows 95/98 (for comparison with Windows 2000 Professional) has a login screen that appears when you turn it on, but the login procedure is not really secure, for a couple of reasons. First, you can bypass it by pressing Esc. Second, you can always boot a Windows 95/98 computer with a floppy and run the `regedit.exe` program to export the Registry, a set of files that controls the configuration of Windows 95/98.

Windows 2000 Professional, in contrast, doesn't let you do anything on your computer until you log on, identifying yourself by name, password, and whether you want to be acknowledged by a local Windows 2000 Professional domain. (Windows 2000 Professional domains are methods of centrally storing user account information.)

Windows 2000 Professional Defines User Rights That Control a User's Actions

Have you ever loaned your machine to someone, only to get it back with all your settings changed? Or, worse yet, to find it loaded with a new piece of software that messed up your DLL files or program groups?

The good news is that Windows 2000 Professional divides the range of things that you can do with a computer into *user rights*. Local Users And Groups enables you to restrict what someone can do on your system. Giving someone else an account on your system doesn't necessarily mean giving them the keys to your system; it may mean giving them access to only a subset of your computer's capabilities.

The bad news is that you don't have the same fine control of user rights in Windows 2000 Professional that you do in Windows 2000 Server. The good news is that Windows 2000 Professional lets you define a local user account that can use the computer and run common programs but cannot install new programs. Members of the Users group can run programs and save data to their own folders, but they can't install programs or modify system files.

Windows 2000 Professional Uses File and Printer Permissions to Control Access

Like its bigger brother Windows 2000 Server, Windows 2000 Professional lets you point to any given folder and remove a user's access to that folder. Believe it or not, you can create a local account on a Windows 2000 Professional machine that, at the same time that it lets someone get on your computer and run a particular program, also prevents that user from doing anything else.

When you examine a file or a folder with Explorer, you can right-click a folder or file, choose Properties from the shortcut menu, select the Security tab, and see the permissions attached to that file or folder.

Printers, as well as folders and files, have permissions associated with them. You can prevent specific people from using your locally attached printers, and of course, domain network administrators can control which network printers those people can access.

Windows 2000 Professional Will Optionally Log All Security Events

Want to keep track of *everything* that happens on your computer? It's possible. Windows 2000 Professional includes a Security Log that will, at your option, log many events, including the following:

- Who logged on to your machine, when the person logged on, and when they logged off
- What files were used
- When others attempted and failed to log on to your system
- Whether the person who logged on to your system changed any user rights or permissions (if they had administrative privileges)

All that information goes in the Security Log, one of the three logs you can find in the Event Viewer.

How Is Windows 2000 Professional Different from Other Operating Systems?

I've discussed the differences and advantages of Windows 2000 Professional compared with Windows 95/98, but how does it stack up against other popular operating systems?

Windows 2000 Professional Compared with Windows 3.*x*

Windows NT, Windows 3.1, and Windows for Workgroups (Windows 3.11) all once had the same interface, and all were made by the same company, but that's where the similarities end. The Windows 3.*x* family of operating systems are 16-bit, completely real-mode operating systems and are also completely beholden to the DOS 640KB memory model. Although Windows for Workgroups has built-in networking capabilities and can coexist quite nicely with Windows 2000 Professional on a network, it offers no security features of its own, relying instead on the network for things like password validation and rights authorization. Whereas Windows 2000 Professional can run any program that the others can run, neither 3.1 nor 3.11 can take advantage of the 32-bit Windows programs that have become available in the wake of Windows 95/98.

Windows 2000 Professional Compared with OS/2

Both Windows 2000 Professional and OS/2 are 32-bit operating systems that also run 16-bit Windows applications and DOS applications in separate memory addresses. In terms of robustness, Windows 2000 Professional and OS/2 are on about even footing. Past that, OS/2 gets left in the dust. OS/2 is not a secure environment, and it lacks native networking capability—you must buy additional software so OS/2 can talk to its network brethren. Furthermore, it won't run 32-bit Windows applications. Because only about three native OS/2 applications are available, this is a serious shortcoming.

Windows 2000 Professional Compared with Unix

Of all the operating systems under discussion here, Unix is probably the most similar to Windows 2000 Professional in terms of architecture. There are many different flavors of Unix, however. Each flavor has a different user interface, and not all of them are graphical. As a group, Unix operating systems are 32-bit, secure, and capable of running on Intel, RISC, and DEC Alpha processors.

In the past, artists and designers have used high-end Unix-based workstations to create special effects for films. Windows 2000 Professional, however, supports high-end 3-D protocols such as Raydream. Running Windows 2000 Professional on a high-powered *x*86 processor such as the Pentium Pro or Pentium II or III will give you equal processing power to those Unix workstations, with the added punch of Windows 2000 Professional, for a fraction of the price.

Windows 2000 Professional Compared to Macintosh OS

Like Windows 2000 Professional, the Macintosh operating system (OS) is a 32-bit environment with built-in networking capabilities. Despite its well-known and intuitive interface, the Macintosh OS lacks many of the powerful features found in Windows 2000 Professional. Object linking and embedding (OLE), MAPI, and TAPI are all unfamiliar to Apple users. The Mac OS supports only a limited sort of cooperative multitasking, and you can switch between programs only with the mouse; there's no equivalent to the mighty Alt+Tab key combination in Windows. There is also a relatively limited amount of software available to the Macintosh market as compared with the Windows market.

What Are the Features of Windows 2000 Professional Architecture?

I've already discussed some of the Windows 2000 Professional architecture. In this section, I'll analyze it a little more closely to see what makes Windows 2000 Professional tick and why it is different from other operating systems. I'll go into the Windows 2000 Professional architecture in much greater detail later in the book (see Chapter 14), but this will serve as a primer for those of you who can't wait.

From a programmer's perspective, Windows 2000 Professional is divided into two layers. These are actually two separate operating modes. The *kernel mode* is where Windows 2000 Professional performs its internal tasks and controls interaction between programs and the operating system, and between programs themselves. It is generally protected from end users fiddling with it. The *user mode*, which is usually described as sitting above the kernel mode because it is closer to the end user, is where your applications run. The area is considered nonprotected, because you have access to it through your applications.

Kernel Mode

Nothing happens in the Windows 2000 Professional universe without the operating system knowing about it and giving its blessing. The *kernel* is the core of Windows 2000 Professional. It acts as a "gofer" between the operating system and the computer's processor. As such, it is responsible for scheduling all the operating system's interactions with your computer. The kernel also manages all the interrelationships between the different kernel mode operations. It does this by means of *threads*. A thread is a series of instructions that are attached to a command that is executed by a program. Threads include memory addresses, scheduling for the amount of time the process will take, and anything else that describes the process.

The kernel mode is divided into three subsections: the HAL, the kernel, and Executive Services. Executive Services is subdivided further into its own component parts; more on those parts a little later in the chapter.

The HAL and the Kernel

The HAL controls the interaction between the kernel and the system hardware. One of the design goals of Windows 2000 Professional was the capability to be easily ported from one type of computer to another. To this end, the HAL *abstracts* the hardware from the kernel so that the kernel does not need to know what type of hardware is installed in the computer. This extends to running multiple processors in your computer. Windows 2000 Professional is one of the only PC-based operating systems that can take advantage of symmetric multiprocessing. The abstraction provided by the HAL gives Windows 2000 Professional greater stability.

Because of the abstraction provided by the HAL, software that attempts to directly access the hardware is not permitted to run. The HAL, working with the kernel, stops those programs dead in their tracks. For performance reasons, many DOS programs—particularly games—use direct hardware access. Programs written for Windows 2000 Professional don't need to worry about how to access the hardware; they just ask the operating system for support, and Windows 2000 Professional takes care of the rest.

Windows 2000 Professional does have some communication that bypasses the HAL and goes directly to the hardware. In each of these cases, the communication is between the Executive Services and the individual drivers for hardware devices such as the video card and network card. But the concept of hardware abstraction is still maintained.

Executive Services

Executive Services is a set of separate components that complete the underpinnings of the Windows 2000 Professional kernel mode. Each of the Executive Services controls a specific function. The following is a brief overview of each of those functions.

I/O Manager

I/O Manager handles all communication between your applications and your hard disk. Additionally, it manages drivers for different file formats (FAT, NTFS) and keeps the Windows 2000 Professional kernel informed of the hard drive's status. I/O Manager also manages network cards and modems. In short, this manager controls any device that delivers data to or from the computer. Its components are illustrated in Figure 1.1.

FIGURE 1.1
I/O Manager is built to simultaneously control multiple devices and drivers.

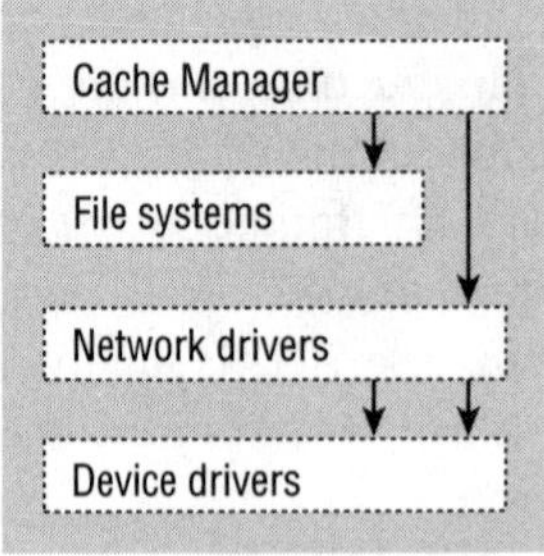

I/O Manager is divided into the following sections:

Cache Manager Monitors your use of disk cache and disk pages.

File systems Manages the file systems you have installed on your computer.

Network drivers Controls your network cards and network protocols.

Device drivers Manages the hardware you have in your computer. This includes everything from your hard drive(s) and modem to your keyboard and mouse.

Object Manager

Object Manager manages all the system objects that are used by Windows 2000 Professional. An *object* is a piece of data used by the operating system to create system events. Objects are acted upon by processes. Every object has a handle (yes, that's the technical term) that a process connects to in order to complete its job. The Object Manager is extensible, meaning that it can be expanded and added to as new object types are developed.

Security Reference Monitor

Security Reference Monitor is the "watchdog" for Windows 2000 Professional. Security Reference Monitor assigns security tokens and authenticates users each time they execute a task.

Process Manager

Process Manager is the complement to Object Manager. Process Manager manages the creation and deletion of processes. A *process* is a set of threads combined with a memory address and the necessary objects needed to complete a system task. The Process Manager works in conjunction with the Security Reference Monitor to ensure that every process is assigned a security token.

Local Procedure Call Facility

Local Procedure Call facility acts as a negotiator between user mode and kernel mode. From an internal standpoint, Windows 2000 Professional uses a client-server model to administer itself. Just as Windows 2000 Professional connects to Windows 2000 Server and requests services from it, the Windows 2000 Professional user mode requests services from the Windows 2000 Professional kernel mode. Those requests are handled by local procedure calls. Local procedure calls are also used in standard client-server networks.

Virtual Memory Manager

Virtual Memory Manager oversees how Windows 2000 Professional uses virtual memory. To increase the amount of usable memory space, Windows 2000 Professional uses hard-disk space as memory when it runs out of memory (which can happen fairly quickly with some high-powered programs). The disk memory is known as *virtual* memory.

Win32K and GDI

The Win32K and Graphics Device Interface (GDI) are the graphics subsystem of Windows 2000 Professional. The graphics functions in earlier versions of Windows NT were provided by the Win32 subsystem in user mode. Microsoft moved the graphics subsystem into the Executive Services for version 4 to give the graphics functions a performance boost. In fact, this resulted in the single greatest increase in the apparent speed of Windows NT 4.

User Mode

In the Windows 2000 Professional user mode, each of your programs runs in a separate memory space, an arrangement that protects each program from the others in case one should crash. This is true for 32-bit and 16-bit programs, both Windows and DOS.

The user mode is divided into subsystems. Each subsystem handles a different type of application and can report directly to the kernel mode. The subsystems are described briefly in Table 1.3.

TABLE 1.3: USER MODE SUBSYSTEMS

Subsystem	Description
Win32	Administers 32-bit and 16-bit Windows programs.
OS/2	Administers character-based OS/2 programs.
POSIX	Administers POSIX programs, which are Unix hybrids that can be run on any POSIX-compliant system, including Windows 2000 Professional. They are written to a series of application programming interfaces (APIs) that are platform independent. They control interaction with system components such as hard drives and memory.
Security	Administers system security and manages security tokens, monitors, and passwords. The user mode portion of the Security subsystem runs only during a user logon. For more information on security, see Chapter 18.

In addition to the subsystems noted in Table 1.3, user mode may also contain VDMs. A *VDM* simulates a computer running MS-DOS 5, with 16MB of RAM and conventional, expanded, and extended memory. As stated earlier in this chapter, this simulation makes it possible to run MS-DOS programs on Windows 2000 Professional. It also enables you to run 16-bit Windows applications by simulating Windows 3.1 running on that MS-DOS computer with 16MB of memory. By default, Windows 2000 Professional starts all 16-bit Windows applications in the same WOW environment. This simulates exactly the environment the programs were written to operate in under Windows 3.1. However, Windows 2000 Professional gives you the ability to start the application in a separate memory space, which creates another WOW for each 16-bit Windows application.

Remember that the WOW environment imitates Windows 3.1 so well that it even hangs just like the old Windows did! That means that if one of your 16-bit Windows applications crashes, it will take all the other 16-bit applications with it—unless you have chosen to start them in their own memory spaces, in which case the other 16-bit programs will keep running without a problem.

NOTE If a 16-bit application crashes, it will also crash any other program running in the same memory space. If this happens, you can stop the WOW by using Task Manager and restart the 16-bit program. All 32-bit applications will be unaffected by the crash and continue to run normally.

Windows 2000 Professional Weaknesses

Ah, but Windows 2000 Professional is not all wine and roses. Windows 2000 Professional isn't right for everybody, at least not yet. The problems tend to fall into the following categories:

Problems related to scale Some problems stem from the fact that a lot fewer people are using Windows 2000 Professional than are using Windows 95/98 or Windows NT. As a result, fewer people are writing applications and drivers for Windows 2000 Professional.

Problems related to expectations Other problems come from people's prior knowledge of Windows. People expect Windows 2000 Professional to have all the features of whatever operating system they already know, and Windows 2000 Professional doesn't always comply with that expectation.

Problems related to Windows 2000 Professional security The middle name of Windows 2000 Professional, security, gets it into trouble. Deciding to secure an operating system means that you can lock yourself out of your own computer. Believe it or not, it's actually possible to lock Windows 2000 Professional out of itself!

Problems related to the legacy of Windows 2000 Professional and problems that aren't really problems It inherits some unpleasant characteristics from earlier operating systems. Also, some "problems" are really shortcomings, things that it *should* be doing, but hasn't gotten to yet.

Problems Related to Scale

In more than 20 years of experience with microcomputer operating systems, I've seen a number of really good products go down in flames through no fault of their own, save for one thing: They never saw enough acceptance. Although it's true that most Windows 95/98 applications run under Windows 2000 Professional, a system requires more than applications. For example, drivers must be available to run for every piece of hardware that the application needs.

Fewer Drivers Are Available

Running your video board, network card, mouse, SCSI host adapter, or scanner requires a piece of software called a *driver*. Someone must sit down and write a driver program for each piece of hardware in your system. Of course, Windows 2000 Professional includes drivers right in the box for major pieces of hardware. But what about not-so-major pieces of hardware? For example, although obtaining a driver for the 3Com Ethernet board is easy enough, can you get one for the SMC Ethernet cards? And if a major vendor, such as 3Com, comes out with a new card, will anyone write a Windows 2000 Professional driver for that board?

The relatively small number of available drivers is definitely one of NT's main weaknesses. Windows 2000 Professional uses the same drivers as Windows 98 for *most* of its hardware, but not all. It includes a new version of the Network Device Interface Specification (NDIS) drivers for network cards. Now this isn't as bad as it may sound. In this case, the driver for Windows 98 works fine, but the information (INF) file that tells Windows 2000 Professional how to install the driver is in a different format.

The things to check out before you commit to Windows 2000 Professional are usually the drivers for your video card and sound card. SCSI and network card drivers are more plentiful, but you can't be positive that the generic Sound Blaster 16 driver will work on your Sound Blaster clone. Unless you're using a Microsoft or Logitech mouse, check for Windows 2000 Professional mouse drivers as well. Or restrict your purchases to devices on the Microsoft Hardware Compatibility List.

Now, after all the gloom, it has to be said that driver support for Windows 2000 Professional is getting better all the time. If in doubt, check the Web site for the company that made your hardware. There were many cases in which the support staff for a company told me that a driver for NT wasn't available, and then I found one right on their Web site! The moral here is that everyone, including Microsoft, has been surprised by the rapid acceptance of NT as the operating system of choice by savvy users, and we can expect that to continue with Windows 2000 Professional.

Not All Windows 95/98 Apps Run

Windows NT 4 did not include much support for Microsoft's game API DirectX, so there were many games and other applications that would not run correctly or not run at all under NT. Windows 2000 Professional includes the full DirectX 7 API set, so this should no longer be a major issue for users of Windows 2000 Professional. But there will still be issues if applications are written to look for a specific version of Windows. For instance, if a program is written to only run on Windows 95 by name, it won't run on Windows 2000 Professional. It probably won't even run on Windows 98, for that matter.

Additionally, many application programmers just plain haven't figured out the correct way to write a 32-bit application, so they cobble together some of the 16-bit things that they've already written and understand and wrap a bit of 32-bit code around it, calling the result a Windows 95 application. Before you know it, Windows 95 is out of memory and you end up with a Windows 95 application that doesn't run under Windows 2000 Professional.

Problems Caused by the Secure Nature of Windows 2000 Professional

Windows 2000 Professional can meet the U.S. government C2 security standards, as you read earlier. Security means more than requiring password encryption and forcing you to log on to your own computer. It also means that Windows 2000 Professional is engineered not to crash—after all, stability is a kind of security. Years ago, Bob Muglia, one of NT's product managers and a very influential force in the design of the first version of NT, said to me, "Our goal is for you to set up your NT machine and *never reboot it.* If it crashes, if an application brings it down, we haven't done our job." I have to admit that I smiled inwardly when Bob made that seemingly hubristic claim. But, as you've already read, NT has achieved much of that goal; it's very stable.

(And when Bob says something, he's serious. When I called him for the interview we had scheduled, he told me, "I'm a little distracted; my wife's in the hospital getting ready to have our baby." I told him that it wasn't *exactly* necessary to do the interview at that moment, but he told me he was just waiting around for the birth anyway. Now, *there's* dedication to a job....)

But the point I'm getting to is this: the stability of Windows 2000 Professional comes with a price. Think of it this way. You have a choice between Windows 95/98 and Windows 2000 Professional for your desktop operating system. Both are, as I've already observed, pretty good, particularly when stacked up against their predecessors.

The defining criterion boils down to this: You can buy Windows 95/98 and get speed and massive compatibility; virtually all your DOS and Windows 3.1 applications will run with little or no tweaking on your part. But when Windows 95/98 crashes, you're out of luck. Or you can buy Windows 2000 Professional, which almost never crashes. It examines everything that an application wants to do before it allows the application to do it. When Windows 2000 Professional *does* crash, it provides you with full disclosure of why the crash happened via the crash dump and the `dumpexam.exe` program. But the price of vigilance is performance; a computer running Excel under Windows 2000 Professional will not run as quickly as that same computer running the same application under Windows 95/98.

You make the choice: speed and compatibility versus stability. Personally, I choose stability, but that's probably because I've lost too many important files to unstable operating systems.

Some DOS and Windows 3.*x* Apps Run Slowly

Because DOS and Windows 3.1 programs require watching (they're likely to do something that violates Windows 2000 Professional security), Windows 2000 Professional runs them at a noticeable speed disadvantage. If they're written "clean" (that is, if they attempt to use only the operating system to access the drive, video, mouse, and other devices), Windows 2000 Professional won't demonstrate much of a slowdown at all when compared to Windows 3.1 or DOS. But you'll have to test each program in turn.

Some DOS and Windows Apps Will Not Run

Virtually all DOS and many Windows 3.1 applications bypass the operating system and directly manipulate the PC hardware. Windows 2000 Professional can't allow this behavior, of course.

Rather than terminate those applications, Windows 2000 Professional has a sneaky way of making them *think* they're directly accessing hardware. Windows 2000 Professional uses a set of programs called VxDs, or *virtual device drivers*. Basically, a VxD exists for each device—the keyboard, the mouse, the video board, and so on—and it detects attempts by an application to access its companion hardware. The VxDs then swoop in and impersonate the hardware, leading the DOS or Windows 3.1 application to think that it actually *has* directly twiddled the hardware, making the application happy.

You do, of course, pay a price—performance. As I said earlier, this can significantly slow down execution for a DOS or Windows 3.1 application. But, even worse, it may keep the application from running in the first place.

Here's why: The designers of Windows 2000 Professional had to know what kinds of devices to build VxDs for in the first place. Most devices are easy; everybody has a keyboard, a mouse, and a video board. But what about the marginal stuff, such as a proprietary scanner interface board, fax board, or possible factory control interface card? Microsoft figured that those were small markets and didn't try to write VxDs for those boards.

Now consider what happens when you run a DOS or Windows 3.1 program that was built to work with one of these "unusual" boards. Windows 2000 Professional sees the program attempt to directly access some hardware for which Windows 2000 Professional has no VxD. What should Windows 2000 Professional do? The Windows 2000 Professional design says, "When in doubt, leave it out," and so Windows must terminate the DOS program. Is this design feature good or bad? Well, remember your choice: fast and compatible versus stable.

Problems Related to Legacy

Some of the things that Windows 2000 Professional does are just plain dumb because it's missing relatively simple and eminently possible features that Microsoft hasn't taken the time to implement. Don't misunderstand this statement—most of the items in this section are not things that Microsoft has promised at any time. But I think they would make Windows 2000 Professional much more useful.

File Associations Rely on File Extensions

When you open a folder, you may see files with the PowerPoint, Excel, or Word icons attached to them. If you double-click the icon, Windows 2000 Professional automatically starts up the application and feeds the file to the application. But how does Windows 2000 Professional know that the file `household.xls` is an Excel spreadsheet? By its XLS file extension. This is a dumb idea for a number of reasons.

First, now that both Windows 95/98 and Windows 2000 Professional support long filenames—names that have as many as 255 characters with spaces and uppercase and lowercase letters—saving files with names such as `portfolio analysis done on 3 March 2000` makes sense; having to add .`xls` to the end of the filename is cumbersome.

Second, some file extensions could be in doubt. Whoever said that Microsoft Word should own the extension DOC? Lots of people that I know use the DOC extension for their WordPerfect documents. What, then, do they do if they want to load both Microsoft Word and WordPerfect on the same computer?

Windows 2000 Professional supports the notion of *file forking,* whereby a file contains two pieces: the data file and a small program, what Macintosh users call a *resource fork*. The resource fork is a little program that says, "To use me, run program *XYZ*." Thus, all Microsoft Word documents would get a resource fork that says, "To use me, run Microsoft Word." This convention would free us from file extensions and make the user interface considerably more user-intelligible. The PC world is one wherein we always seem be to hearing, "What's that? The tool we built for you doesn't fit your hand? Hmmm...have you considered surgery?"

Perhaps most embarrassing for Microsoft is (or *should* be) the fact that IBM included file forking with OS/2 way back in 1992.

Operating System Components Are Largely Static

Run Windows 2000 Professional for a while, and you'll be pleasantly surprised at how stable it is. So stable, in fact, that the only reason that I ever reboot my Windows 2000 Server machines is to add or remove a module. Some of the slightest modifications to your configuration cause Windows 2000 Professional to demand that you reboot the system.

There's no real reason to require rebooting, either. Today's mainframe and minicomputer operating systems go for months at a time without being rebooted. You can load new system software and keep on going. The big-iron folks abandoned the notion of a heavily static operating system more than a decade ago. Nevertheless, it persists in the microcomputer world as just another thing that seems to be acceptable.

Boot Windows 2000 Professional, and you can see why I feel that it's imperative for Microsoft to do something about how slowly their computers boot up. You can wait for 10 minutes for NT 4 to start a workstation with a whole bunch of drivers and services, and of course, demonstrating a slow startup on an NT Server machine is even easier. Now, Windows 2000 Professional *is* faster than NT 4 at booting, but some of us are never really satisfied when it comes to boot speed. All that is really required to reset Windows 2000 Professional during the installation of software is to stop and restart the devices and services involved in what you installed, so why doesn't someone write their program to stop and restart the services instead of requiring a reboot?

Shortcuts Don't Link Two Ways

One of the features of the Windows 2000 Professional graphical user interface is the *shortcut*. Shortcuts are small files with the extension LNK; they are usually smaller than 200 bytes. The value of a shortcut is that it provides a quick way to access some file or program.

For example, suppose you want to start up Microsoft Word. The path to the program is probably `C:\Program Files\Microsoft Office\Office\WINWORD.exe`. So to start it up, you might open My Computer, then the C drive, then the Program Files folder, then the Microsoft Office folder, then the Office folder, and then finally double-click the WINWORD icon, which represents `WINWORD.EXE`. But that's a lot of folder-diving. Instead, you could create a shortcut by putting an icon for Microsoft Word on the Desktop. Double-click the shortcut, and Word starts; so far, so good.

But this process falls down when you want to examine or change the properties of the `WINWORD` file. Right-click the Microsoft Word icon, and you'll get the option to examine the properties of that file; the tabs in the WINWORD Properties dialog box display information such as the file's version, size, and trademarks. But try right-clicking the shortcut, and all you'll get is an offer to find the original item. So, to modify the properties of Microsoft Word from a shortcut, you've got to open the Properties dialog box for the shortcut, which then offers you the opportunity to find the target of the original file. Right-click the original file, and choose Properties from the shortcut menu to open the Properties dialog for WINWORD an extra and annoying couple of steps.

In contrast, a truly object-oriented operating system would support shortcuts that act exactly like their original objects (objects such as Microsoft Word). Again, this feature *isn't* rocket science; OS/2 included it back in 1992.

No Bookmark Support Exists for Applications

Ever since Macintosh and Windows appeared, they—and subsequent graphical operating systems—have used the paradigm of a desktop. The basic idea has probably been to get across the notion that you get real work done with one of today's operating system, hence the desktop metaphor.

The problem is, computer desktops don't resemble my physical desktop at all. For one thing, when I leave for the day, my desktop pretty much stays the way it is. If I leave my stapler in the middle of the desktop, it doesn't spirit itself off to the upper-left corner automatically.

For another thing, my "data files" and "applications" return each day to the place where I left them. Books open to page 45 are still at page 45 the next day; folders are open to the same sheet of paper. Half-finished drawings and my drawing tool (a pen) are waiting for my return.

Compare this real-life scenario to how Windows 2000 Professional starts up in the morning. It remembers which folders you had open when you shut it down, and it reopens them, but that's it. You must restart all the applications by hand, tell them what files they were working on (or, of course, you can double-click the files themselves), and, after the files and apps are loaded, you still have to tell the application to go back to where you were yesterday.

Why not build a bookmark programming interface that application vendors could put into their applications, an interface that could remember where you left off when last running the application or, perhaps, the file? Then every data file could contain a bookmark pointing to where it was last edited. (After all, virtually every application keeps track of where you are *while* you're running it; why not just save that information?) The Desktop would then only have to remember which data files you had open when you shut down. When the Desktop started up again, it would open the files, and their file associations would enable them to tell the Desktop which applications to start. Then the bookmark pointer would restore the application to exactly the state that existed when the computer powered down. One of these days, I guess...

Summary

By now, you should have a good idea of what Windows 2000 Professional is and isn't. This may sound complicated (and it is), but it's also easy to learn. The new Explorer interface offers huge leaps in usability that make it a simple task to harness the power and complexity of this state-of-the-art operating system.

You may be saying to yourself at this point, however, "Who cares about C2 level security and flat memory models? I just want to get my work done and increase my productivity so I can get a raise." Well said, and rightly so. That's just what the rest of this book is about. Consider this, though: Now that you've begun to understand what the operating system does and how it differs from others that you may be more accustomed to, you're in a much better position to make the best use of the information you'll find in the following chapters.

So sit back, press Control+Alt+Delete to log on to your Windows 2000 Professional system, and let's go!

CHAPTER 2

Installing Windows 2000 Professional (and Automating Installation)

FEATURING:

Installing Windows 2000 Professional is a fairly straightforward procedure. It is even easier if you know your machine and think about the logistics for a moment before you begin. Although the installation procedure is more time consuming than it is for some applications, you do have an alternative to standing over the computer and responding to dozens of installation questions. You can write a setup batch script that will automatically answer all those questions. But first, this chapter provides a step-by-step guide to installing Windows 2000 Professional on its own and also as a link to the server. Then I explain how Windows 2000 Professional interacts with the server and other operating systems, and how to install it efficiently to several machines using the batch routine.

Before you do any of this, however, you need to make sure that your hardware can handle Windows 2000 Professional.

Knowing Your Computer Needs

First and foremost, make sure your computer has the CPU, disk space, and RAM necessary for the operating system. And just as important, be sure you have all the hardware you need to install and operate Windows 2000 Professional smoothly. Next, ascertain whether the computer will be a stand-alone workstation or part of a domain. Determine also if Windows 2000 Professional will be the only operating system on the machine or if another OS, such as Windows 95/98, will be present as well.

Reviewing Your Hardware Requirements

The first step is to make sure you have all the hardware necessary to install and operate Windows 2000 Professional effectively.

Processor

If you're definitely committed to Windows 2000 Professional, consider buying Pentium II– or Pentium III–based systems rather than Pentium systems. Recall that the Pentium Pro through Pentium III chips are especially tuned to run 32-bit programs particularly well, and they offer that performance without the great cost of RISC-based systems. (RISC is an abbreviation for reduced instruction set computing.)

No matter what processor you buy, get the most speed you can afford. I'm *not* going to tell you not to run Windows 2000 Professional on anything below 300MHz, but if all other things are equal, more megahertz means better performance.

NOTE Early versions of Windows NT ran on a 386 processor, but Microsoft stopped supporting NT on a 386 as of version 4. Windows 2000 Professional supports the Pentium as the minimum processor requirement.

Memory

I've run Windows 2000 Professional on a 333MHz computer and been disappointed by its sluggish performance. I've also run it on a 133MHz server and been satisfied with its performance.

The difference? The 333MHz computer had 32MB of RAM. The server had 64MB of RAM.

I haven't actually *found* the point at which Windows 2000 Professional stops thirsting for memory. For example, the computer on my desktop contains 128MB of RAM, and even *it* shuffles things from memory onto disk now and then.

Thankfully, memory prices have dropped (and risen, then dropped again), and today there aren't many reasons not to have enough memory. And while I still can't say what enough memory *is* for Windows 2000 Professional, I can say that today most Windows 2000 Professional users are running on computers with at least 128MB of RAM. Just check out the catalog from your favorite supplier, and you will notice that most of the current systems are equipped with 128MB of RAM.

NOTE You can't just put any arbitrary amount of RAM into a computer; the memory sockets in most Pentiums allow only a few memory configurations: 8MB, 16MB, 24MB, 32MB, 40MB, 48MB, 64MB, 72MB, 80MB, 96MB, or 128MB. Newer motherboards support much higher amounts of RAM but still have specific configurations.

As the price falls, people will say, "What the heck, as long as I'm upgrading, I'll go for more memory." Many folks will jump from 16MB all the way up to 64MB or 96MB, skipping 32MB altogether. Many will try to increase their system's RAM all the way up to 128MB or even 256MB—and then they may get an unpleasant surprise.

Part of a computer's configuration is contained in a chip commonly known as the complementary metal oxide semiconductor (CMOS) chip. Calling this specific chip *the* CMOS is quite misleading—*many* other chips in a PC could also be called CMOS chips—but that's the common term. Anyway, the standard CMOS configuration first appeared in 1984 with the IBM AT. The CMOS sets aside 2 bytes, which are defined as the amount of kilobytes of RAM above the first megabyte. The largest value that a 2-byte integer can hold is 64KB-1, or 65,535. So the greatest amount of kilobytes above the first megabyte on a system with a standard CMOS is 65,535KB, or 64MB.

What this bit of mathematics means is that no matter how many memory sockets are on your computer's motherboard, no matter how much memory you put on your computer, it will recognize only the first 65MB (the 64MB above the first megabyte and then the first megabyte). What's the answer? Make very certain when you buy the computer that it isn't afflicted with an ancient CMOS—fortunately, this isn't very common any more. Talk to the firm's technical support people, and be sure that (1) they understand the CMOS problem, and (2) their computer doesn't have the problem.

TIP The bottom line on memory is this: On a Windows 2000 Professional machine, the more memory, the merrier.

Video Card

Video cards are one of the most difficult types of hardware to choose for Windows 2000 Professional. First of all, what are you looking for? Games? Productivity? OK, admit it, you want a little of both. Today's games often use high-end 3-D technologies that make them very exciting. Unfortunately, finding the drivers for the 3-D video cards can be hard with NT. Again, thanks to the unified driver model, Windows 2000 Professional will use the same drivers as Windows 98. This means that the new video cards will very likely have driver support for Windows 2000 Professional right out of the box.

Your best bet is to find out which chipsets are providing the type of performance you want, which cards have that chipset, and finally which manufacturers are providing Windows 2000 Professional drivers.

Consult Microsoft's Hardware Compatibility List (HCL)

Microsoft is in something of a tough spot when it comes to support. As a Microsoft VP once explained, "There *is* no such thing as *PC-compatible*," meaning that every model has its own quirks. Because no two PCs are identical, building an operating system that will run on any PC is difficult for Microsoft (or anyone).

What Microsoft has done in response is to compile a list of machines that it has successfully tested and verified that Windows 2000 Professional will run on. That list is called the Hardware Compatibility List, or HCL.

The HCL is a good idea, but it has one problem: Getting on the list is expensive for a hardware vendor. A hardware vendor can't just give a computer to Microsoft to be tested for Windows 2000 Professional compatibility; Microsoft charges thousands of dollars to test a computer. The result is that you can find many perfectly good computers made by small firms that can't afford to pay Microsoft to test their computers and so they never make it onto the HCL. If the computers don't make it onto the HCL, choosing one of them is basically a crap shoot. The only way you'll know if Windows 2000 Professional will run on the computer is to try to install it. At least with the HCL you can know ahead of time whether the computer will work.

Nevertheless, if you receive any kind of Microsoft product support for Windows 2000 Professional (or if you *intend* to receive any kind of support), you pretty much *have* to buy computers on the HCL. If you don't, Microsoft technical support people "get stupid" all of a sudden. You can ask a perfectly valid question of a Microsoft technical support person, something like, "What's the difference between a workgroup and a domain in Windows 2000 Professional?" If the tech support person doesn't know the answer, he'll say, "Well, that depends. What kind of computer are you running this on?" If you answer, "I've got an Acme Thunderchip 586," he'll cluck his tongue and say, "Well, that's not on the Hardware Compatibility List." Ah, yes, the HCL—the last refuge of scoundrels.

NOTE If you work for a large company that has Microsoft Premier Support, you've pretty much got to buy machines on the HCL. If you're part of a smaller company, you *may* choose to save some money by buying cheaper machines whose firms opted not to give Microsoft money to test their machines–but you're removing yourself from a source of later support. Last time I checked, Microsoft Technical Support policy states that if your *system* isn't on the HCL they can give you one hour and their best effort or refund your money for the call and wish you luck.

By the way, you can find the most up-to-date copy of the HCL (I think Microsoft updates it at least twice a month) on Microsoft's Web site, `www.microsoft.com`.

Make Sure the Drivers You Want to Use Appear on the HCL

The *good* part of the HCL is that it includes a list of tested and approved video boards, SCSI host adapters, and LAN boards, among other things. Therefore, even if your machines aren't on the HCL, you can still use the HCL to choose add-in cards for those machines.

Additionally, it's not a bad idea to get onto the peripheral vendor's Web site and check out its Windows 2000 Professional driver support. The truth of the matter is that writing NT drivers is often a third- or fourth-order issue for hardware vendors—writing Windows drivers is the highest priority. Some sites seem to keep releasing newer and newer beta drivers for NT, promising the final version soon. The unified driver model in Windows 2000 Professional should help to relieve some of this, as the drivers for Windows 2000 Professional are usually the same as the drivers for Windows 98.

WARNING As someone who's spent far too much of my life waiting around for OS/2 drivers to appear, take my advice: Do not buy a piece of peripheral hardware for Windows 2000 Professional until you can get final drivers for Windows 2000 Professional and the hardware is on the HCL.

But be sure that the peripheral drivers are supported for your computer architecture. I met a fellow in class who'd been trying for weeks to get a particular network card to work in his NT 4 MIPS-based server. Because the card was a PCI board, it could be used in an Intel-based system, a MIPS system, an Alpha system, or a PowerPC system. The board, similarly, was on the HCL.

After calling the board vendor and Microsoft for weeks, he finally got an answer: The board's on the HCL, yes, but only for the Intel platform. The manufacturer had not yet written drivers for the MIPS machine.

TIP So my second piece of advice is this: If you're buying a RISC-based machine, buy the entire machine as a package from the vendor, and get a guarantee of Windows 2000 Professional compatibility.

If you've been using PC-compatible computers for years, you've been sheltered from the reality that users of Macintoshes, Amigas, Atari 1040s, and RISC machines are reminded of every day: Non-PC markets are so small that you cannot and should not assume *anything* about support and compatibility. If you're buying RISC machines, check everything once, twice, and three times, and *get it all in writing*. RISC machines are amazingly fast and wonderful when they work, but they can be so frustrating when they don't. And another thing to keep in mind: A small market doesn't sell enough software to support the kind of development effort that Microsoft puts into Windows 2000 Professional. The platform support in Windows 2000 Professional may be very different from the platform support in the future.

Reviewing Software Requirements

Windows 2000 Professional is very compatible with older operating systems. Yes, but running a DOS program under Windows 2000 Professional still isn't running a DOS program under DOS—it's running a DOS program under a DOS emulator. You are being unfair and unreasonable if you say to a vendor of some DOS program, "I'm running your application that I bought from you last year under Windows 2000 Professional , and it's not running right. It ran fine under DOS. What do I do?" The vendor never promised that the application would run under the DOS emulator in Windows 2000 Professional. And, truthfully, if it runs under DOS (or Windows 3.1) and doesn't run under the Windows 2000 Professional emulators of those two operating systems, the problem is in the DOS or Windows 3.1 emulators in Windows 2000 Professional, not in the DOS application.

For an occasionally used DOS or Windows 3.1 program, using Windows 2000 Professional is fine. But I wouldn't think about switching over to a Windows 2000 Professional machine full time (and didn't) until my most important applications supported Windows 2000 Professional directly; otherwise, as I've indicated, you're running without support.

TIP Minasi's law of operating systems: Do not move to a new desktop operating system until your top three applications have released stable versions that are native to the new operating system.

Now, what *are* your top three applications? For most of us, the top one is word processing. People reflexively say that spreadsheets are their second most-used application, but I wonder about that. Personally, I spend *lots* more time in my e-mail application than I do my spreadsheet; I use the Web all the time for researching computer topics, and so I'd have to say that my third most-used application is probably my Web browser.

Now that I've written that, I notice that Windows 2000 Professional goes a long way toward making a place for itself in my heart (and my PC) because it contains both an Internet-enabled e-mail client and a Web browser. The Outlook Express e-mail client that ships with Windows 2000 Professional can access Internet e-mail even if your company doesn't use Exchange Server. For those who speak the language, the Outlook Express client can act as a POP3 client, like the popular Eudora and Pegasus e-mail programs. The Web browser has shaped up to be a fine tool, and it's free. As for 32-bit word processing, well, I haven't found any *great* packages yet, but both Lotus's WordPro and Microsoft Word are available in 32-bit versions.

Make Sure the Apps Work

Painful experience reminds us that just because an application *claims* to work under a particular operating system doesn't mean that it actually *runs* under that operating system. Before you buy a thousand copies of Windows 2000 Professional and install them on your employees' PCs, get a few machines, build a small network, and run the applications for a while. When you've found the particular quirks caused by running Windows 2000 Professional (assuming that there *are* any; it's not a foregone conclusion), you can make an informed decision about whether to move everyone in your organization to Windows 2000 Professional.

Installing Windows 2000 Professional as a Stand-Alone Workstation or Domain Member

Determine whether this computer will be a stand-alone workstation or part of a domain. If it is to be part of a domain, the installation program will ask you several questions. The domain installation process is faster and easier if you know the following:

- The type of network card installed in the computer. Some network cards require the user to adjust the manufacturer's default settings. Before installing, run a diagnostic tool such as WinMSD to determine what these settings should be, and then write them down so that you can refer to them later.
- The protocol(s) the machine uses to connect to the domain controller (server).
- Your computer's set Internet Protocol (IP) address, unless you have a Dynamic Host Configuration Protocol (DHCP) server to determine your computer's IP address. If you do have a DHCP server on your network, a static IP address isn't required. Ask your system administrator if you don't know whether your network has a DHCP server.

As you can see, making the machine part of a domain necessitates the addition of a network card. If you do not have a network card set up when you install Windows 2000 Professional, you can still continue the installation process. Just set up the computer as a stand-alone machine and make it part of a domain after you install the network card.

Yes, you read that correctly. Changing your mind about having the workstation as part of a domain does not mean completely reinstalling Windows 2000 Professional. One great feature of Windows 2000 Professional is that you can work through those kinds of administrative details quite simply by running a program. The option of quickly adding a workstation to a domain at any time can be rather handy.

Deciding Whether to Keep Other Operating Systems

You need to decide whether you want the current operating system(s) to remain in place or if you want Windows 2000 Professional to be your only operating system. As you've probably just surmised, the good news is that you can have more than one operating system on your computer.

Simply copying the files from one folder to another does not work because the applications still look for the files in the other operating system folder that it can't open. Hence, you'll need to install the applications on both operating systems. Reinstalling software takes time and can use a lot of space on the hard drive. Therefore, you must think carefully about how you will use that space before opting to have applications run on more than one operating system. See the "Using Dual Operating Systems" section toward the end of this chapter for more help with this option.

Understanding Windows 2000 Professional Terminology

The bad news is that some applications installed on your old operating system will not run on Windows 2000 Professional without being reinstalled.

NOTE Some applications install files in the system folder. When you try to run these applications on Windows 2000 Professional, it looks for those files in the Windows 2000 Professional folder when they are really in the Windows folder.

Windows 2000 Professional is in some ways a server and workstation built into one. It has some of the same diagnostic tools that Windows 2000 Server has. Windows 2000 Professional can accommodate different users on the workstation by providing each user with Desktop settings and file security. It also requires an administrator to oversee all activity on the workstation, just as a server has an administrator to oversee the domain. This similarity of function and terminology can get confusing, especially when a connection exists between the workstation and a domain. Let's take a moment to avoid some confusion by defining a few frequently used terms:

Domain A logical group of interconnected computers on a network controlled by a domain controller.

Domain controller A computer that controls the domain. This computer functions as a "gatekeeper" for all of a domain's shared items. The domain controller keeps a database of security information and uses that information to validate requests from workstations for network resources.

Administrator Traditionally, a person who has administrator privileges on a server—that is, abilities (which users do not have) to control the server and domain. Now it gets trickier. A workstation requires an administrator just as a domain does. A workstation administrator has nothing to do with a domain administrator, however. A workstation administrator has control over the workstation settings (for example, network card or display settings) and its users. A domain administrator controls aspects of the domain such as controlling user access or backup operations. The two are separate entities. Anyone who logs on as a workstation administrator cannot automatically make changes to the domain, and vice versa.

User Again, users are users regardless of whether they are working on a standalone workstation or have access to the server files.

Installing a Stand-Alone Windows 2000 Professional Computer

Find a form of installation—from a CD-ROM or network location—that works for your setup needs. If you are upgrading from NT, installing from a network might be your best bet because it is faster and you can copy files from multiple locations at the same time. More on that later.

If you have the room, I recommend putting a copy of the installation folder for your machine and its contents on the hard drive where you are installing Windows 2000 Professional. Why? First, you may need to reinstall Windows 2000 Professional on your computer when you do not have a Windows 2000 Professional CD available. Second, when installing on some machines, the CD-ROM becomes inaccessible halfway through the installation. Installing Windows 2000 Professional from your hard disk can save you a lot of aggravation and wasted time. Third, putting a copy of the Windows 2000 Professional CD on the server is a good backup measure in case the CD is missing. However, do remember that you can't install a workstation using this folder because you will not be able to access the network from the workstation until the installation has finished.

Installing Windows 2000 Professional from a CD-ROM

If you're installing Windows 2000 Professional from a CD, you may want to note the drive letter that your CD-ROM uses. Even though your CD-ROM may use a drive letter, say, Z, when installing Windows 2000 Professional, that won't be the drive letter Windows 2000 Professional uses during the installation process. Windows 2000 Professional automatically chooses the next available drive letter for the CD-ROM instead of the one that you previously assigned to it. For example, if you have a hard drive using drive C, and D is not being used, Windows 2000 Professional would pick D for the CD-ROM drive. However, the Setup program still thinks that the drive letter for your CD-ROM is drive Z. To install Windows 2000 Professional, you have to change the drive letter of your CD-ROM drive to the next unused letter. Your other option is to install from your hard disk.

You can install from a CD-ROM in two ways. The first (and easiest) way is to install Windows 2000 Professional directly from the CD. The other way is to use floppy disks to start the installation and to use the CD to finish the setup process. The first method works well if you have the CD-ROM driver installed on your system already. If you don't, you need to either boot from floppies first or install the driver to DOS before you can install Windows 2000 Professional. Here is the process for installing on an Intel or compatible platform:

1. Go to the command prompt and change to the I386 directory on your CD-ROM.

2. Type **WINNT32** (or **WINNT** when running from MS-DOS or Windows 3.*x*) at the command line.

NOTE If an operating system is already installed on the computer that you want to upgrade to Windows 2000 Professional, simply insert the installation CD-ROM, and follow the onscreen instructions.

Using the Installation Command

The initial command used to start the installation process depends on what kind of operating system you are using. If you are using a 32-bit operating system such as Windows 95/98 or Windows NT, you need to use WINNT32. Otherwise, on systems such as Windows 3.*x* or DOS, you'll have to use the WINNT command. Table 2.1 lists the parameters for these commands.

NOTE The WINNT and WINNT32 commands both use the same switches listed in the table below.

TABLE 2.1: PARAMETERS FOR WINNT32 COMMANDS

Parameter	Description
/s:*sourcepath*	Specifies the source location of Windows NT files. *Sourcepath* must be a full path in the form of x:\[path] or \\server\share[\path].
/tempdrive:*drive_letter*	Specifies a drive to contain temporary setup files. If not specified, Setup attempts to locate a drive for you. This is usually the C drive. If your C drive doesn't have enough space (about 300MB), you'll have to choose another drive or start the install with boot floppies.
/checkupgradeonly	Checks your computer to see if it complies with the minimum setup requirements for Windows 2000 Professional.
/cmd:*command_line*	Tells Setup to open a command prompt and execute the command listed before Setup completes the final phase.
/cmdcons	Adds the Recovery Console option to the Setup options screen to help recover a failed installation.

TABLE 2.1: PARAMETERS FOR WINNT32 COMMANDS (CONTINUED)

Parameter	Description
`/copydir:`*folder_name* or `/copysource:`*folder_name*	Both these switches allow you to copy an additional folder to the Winnt folder during Setup and use the drivers contained in that folder during Setup. The difference is that `/copydir` keeps the subfolder permanently, while `/copysource` deletes the subfolder after Setup completes.
`/m`	Tells Setup to copy files from an alternative location. This is useful if you need to provide newer drivers for a specific device. Setup will look for files first in the folder you specify with the `/m` switch, then in the distribution folder.
`/makelocalsource`	Instructs Setup to make a local source folder for all of the installation files. This switch replaces the old `/b` switch to perform a floppyless install.
`/noreboot`	Tells Setup not to reboot after the file copy phase is complete so that you can execute another command first.
`/syspart:`*drive_letter*	Tells Setup that you want to copy the startup files for installation to a specific hard drive, mark the partition as active, and then move the drive to a different computer. This enables you to create disks for new computers, which will then complete Setup once they are booted in the new machine.
`/unattend`	Tells Setup that you want to upgrade your previous installation of Windows 2000 Professional in unattended mode. In this case, Setup will take all its settings from the existing version and won't prompt the user for any settings.
`/unattend[`*num*`]:[`*answer file name*`]`	This switch has replaced the old `/u` unattended setup switch. This unattended mode setup requires an answer file to provide all of the necessary parameters to successfully complete Windows 2000 Professional setup. The *num* parameter specifies the number of seconds to wait after copying files and before rebooting. This is only available on Windows 2000 Professional computers.
`/udf:`*id*`,`*UDF_file*	Specifies the station *id* for an unattended setup and the name of the Uniqueness Database File (*UDF*) that will provide the variables for this particular computer.

For example, if you are running Windows 95 and want to install Windows 2000 Professional using the installation files on your hard disk, type the following command from the command prompt:

```
WINNT32 /makelocalsource /s:c:\i386
```

If you wanted to accomplish the same thing from a DOS workstation, simply replace the WINNT32 with WINNT.

The first thing that Setup will prompt you to do is to decide whether you are upgrading or installing a fresh copy to a new folder. Though upgrading works fine, you really do get the very best install when you use a new folder. Setup will prompt you with the License Agreement. You must accept this agreement in order to continue with Setup. Figure 2.1 shows the next dialog box, where you can select any special option you need for the installation.

FIGURE 2.1
The Select Special Options dialog box lets you set Language or Accessibility options.

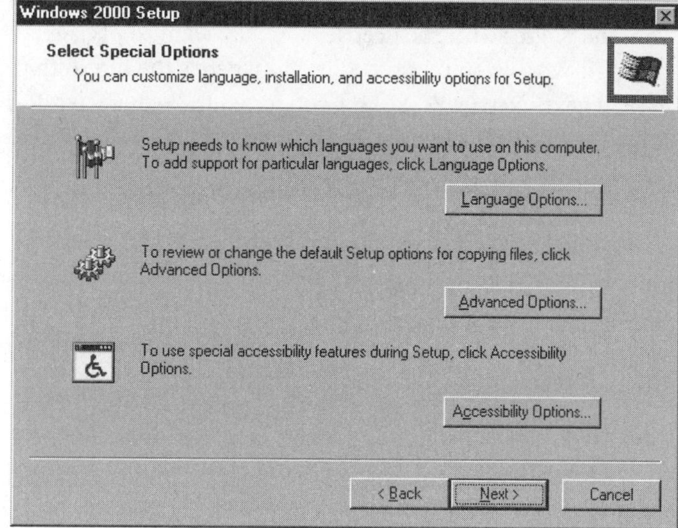

Setup will want to know if you want to upgrade your drive to use NTFS. This is actually a good way to describe it since this is a newer version of the NT File System than you may be currently using if you are running NT 4. Definitely do not upgrade, though, if you are planning to multiboot with Windows 95/98 on FAT or FAT32.

Setup copies the Windows 2000 Professional files to a temporary folder on your hard drive and then asks you to restart your computer to continue Windows 2000 Professional Setup. If you are in DOS mode, just press Enter to restart Setup automatically. If you are in Windows 95/98 or NT, close the command prompt window, and restart the computer.

When the computer restarts, the screen displays the current NT Workstation version (if any) and the available memory and welcomes you to Setup. You have several options at this point. You can

- Set up Windows 2000 Professional
- Repair a damaged Windows 2000 Professional installation
- Quit Setup without installing Windows 2000 Professional

For now, you'll want to set up Windows 2000 Professional. Setup continues with the installation and asks you a variety of questions.

End User License Agreement

It is a good idea to read through the license at least once, though you won't want to read it every time. Basically, it tells you not to pirate the software and how many computers you can install it on. When you feel that you've read enough to make a decision, select an option button to accept the license or to quit the installation process. If you don't agree with the license, you may want to pack everything up and return it to the store where you purchased it. But where's the fun in that?

The next screen will prompt you for your 25-character license key. This code can be found on the back of your CD-ROM case for Windows 2000 Professional.

Where to Put Windows 2000 Professional

Now you can choose where to put Windows 2000 Professional on your hard disk. You can choose to put it in a partition already created on your disk, or Setup will partition an unpartitioned space for you. You must have at least 650MB of unused space on either a partitioned or unpartitioned area. If you have another operating system, it is more convenient and efficient to install Windows 2000 Professional and its applications onto a separate partition or another hard drive if you have one.

TIP Locating and maintaining Windows 2000 Professional and its applications is easier if you keep them separate from other operating systems. Of course, you are not obligated to do so if space doesn't permit.

Formatting an Unpartitioned Space

If you choose to install Windows 2000 Professional onto an unpartitioned space, just select the space and Setup partitions and assign a drive letter to it. Highlight that new space, and continue with the installation. You can also choose to delete a partition at this screen, which enables you to reorganize your disk if necessary.

File System Type and the Formatting of Space

If you are partitioning free space, you must select either an NTFS or File Allocation Table (FAT) system for that space. NTFS was designed specifically for use with Windows NT and Windows 2000 Professional. The main differences between NTFS and the FAT system are

- NTFS supports filenames of up to 255 characters (including spaces and periods), with multiple extensions; FAT on Windows 2000 Professional supports filenames of up to 255 characters including the full path.
- NTFS is designed with system security in mind, providing features such as auditing and built-in file-level permissions; FAT has no file system security.
- NTFS supports larger volumes up to a practical limit of 2 terabytes and a theoretical limit of 16 exabytes (EB). FAT supports only 2GB partitions on MS-DOS and Windows 95/98 and 4GB on Windows 2000 Professional.
- NTFS supports file auditing; FAT does not.
- NTFS is more efficient on larger disks than FAT and supports a larger partition size (16EB per partition).
- NTFS keeps a log of activities in order to be able to restore the disk after a power failure or other interruptions in service; FAT is not able to do this.

If you choose to install Windows 2000 Professional on a FAT file system, you can convert the partition to NTFS before installing to that virtual drive. Be aware, though, that conversion to NTFS is a one-way street. There is no going back to FAT without repartitioning and formatting. You also need to decide if you want to install to the Winnt folder. If you don't, type in the name of the folder you want.

NOTE This point in Setup is one of the few places that you can delete an NTFS partition. If you ever need to remove an NTFS partition, you can run Setup to this point and choose to delete the partition and create a new partition. You can also delete an NTFS partition by using either Disk Management in Windows 2000 Professional or Fdisk from MS-DOS 6.2 or higher. In Fdisk, you choose to delete a non-DOS partition.

Installation Continues

As the installation continues, Setup prompts you to restart the computer. You advance through the license agreement and then a series of informational screens before getting to the Setup Preferences window.

The Plug-and-Play device detection occurs at this point. During the detection, your screen may flicker for a few seconds. Windows 2000 Professional will detect and load drivers for all your supported hardware. It's possible that it won't have drivers for something in your computer, but you can always install the drivers after Setup has completed.

Regional Settings

You use the Regional Settings dialog box to configure things such as the keyboard layout, date, time, and currency formats.

Name and Organization

In this dialog box, you need to enter your full name and the name of your organization. If you are uncertain what to enter here, check with your network administrator. If this Windows 2000 Professional computer is to be used at home, you can enter anything you want in these spaces.

Computer Name and Administrator Password

The name that you choose for your computer is arbitrary but necessary for identification. You can name it anything you like as long as that name isn't being used by another computer connected to the same domain. My advice, however, is to avoid using the name of the person currently using the workstation. Two years from now, the computer may still be in use, but it would be confusing for Joe, Martin, and Laura to all have been using Bobscomputer, while Bob himself has long since moved to another office—and now uses Lynnscomputer.

NOTE Keep in mind that computer names are limited to 15 characters on network protocols other than TCP/IP. If you have TCP/IP installed, you can have names up to 63 characters in length, but they won't be visible from other operating systems. You can use spaces in the names, but this may cause problems with older network operating systems such as Windows for Workgroups.

In this same dialog box, there is a prompt to set the password for the local Administrator account. You will need to type it into the space provided and then type it again to confirm it. The passwords in Windows 2000 Professional can be up to 256 characters in length, allowing for some *very* secure user accounts. (For much more detail about passwords and users, see Chapter 18.)

Remember that the administrator administers this machine only, not the domain (that is, if you're a domain member). As the local administrator, you can choose any password—it doesn't have to be the same as your domain administrator account, and for security purposes it shouldn't be the same. You can add user accounts and users with administrator permissions to the workgroup after Setup is complete.

Date and Time

You use the Date And Time Settings dialog box to select the correct time and date, obviously, but it also has settings for the correct time zone for your location. Setup will read the time and date settings from the computer's BIOS and will display those settings as the suggested configuration. If they aren't right, use the up and down arrows to adjust them.

Networking Settings

Windows 2000 Professional will detect the network card and install default components. The default components include the Client for Microsoft Networks, File and Print Sharing for Microsoft Networks, and the TCP/IP protocol with automatic addressing. You can select to install the network with Custom Settings, and then choose the proper settings for the default components; you'll also have the opportunity to install additional services.

You will next be prompted to decide whether this computer will be part of a domain or a workgroup environment. If you decide to add this computer to a domain, you will be prompted for an account and password for an account with the privileges to add computers to the domain.

NOTE Windows 2000 Professional Setup will install only the first network adapter it finds. If your computer is multihomed (that is, it has more than one network adapter), you will need to install the other adapter after Setup has completed.

Final Phase

Next, Setup will begin copying the files necessary to install the selected components. Once the file copy is complete, Setup enters its final phase, which includes the following tasks:

Install Start menu items Setup installs and configures the utilities on the Start menu.

Register components Builds the OLE Registration database information in the Registry for the standard components.

Save settings Builds the final copy of the Registry and initializes it.

Remove temporary files Setup cleans up after itself by deleting any temporary files used during the installation.

Reboot This is the final step in Setup. Once the computer is restarted, Windows 2000 Professional has been installed.

Installing to a Network

If you chose Do Not Connect This Computer To A Network At This Time during installation, you can still add your computer to a domain any time after the installation. Before you can do so, an administrator must create the machine object within the domain. You then need to have the following information at hand, which you can get from your network administrator:

- User name
- Password
- Domain name
- Computer name
- Computer domain

To add your workstation to a domain or to change the domain for your workstation, follow these steps:

1. On the Desktop, right-click My Computer to open the System Properties dialog box.
2. Click the Network Identification tab, and then click Network ID to start the Network Identification Wizard:

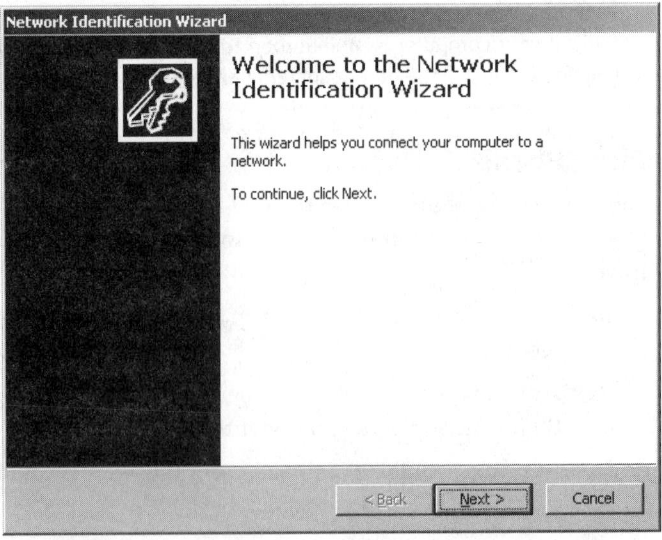

3. Click Next to open the Connecting To The Network screen.
4. Click the option to connect to other computers at work, and then click Next to open the second Connecting To The Network screen.
5. Click the My Company Uses A Network With A Domain option, and then click Next to open the Network Information screen.
6. If you followed my suggestion earlier in this section, you've already collected this information. If not, gather it now, and then click Next to open the User Account And Domain Information screen.
7. Now you are asked to supply your user name, password, and the name of the domain you want to join. Windows 2000 Professional will attempt to contact a domain controller to verify your computer account. If it cannot find your computer account (as is the case when your administrator has not made the account yet), the Wizard will prompt you to enter your computer name and domain name.
8. You will very likely be prompted for a name and password for an account with the rights to make a new computer account. If you have that information, enter it in the dialog box, and click Next. If not, this would be a great time to talk to your administrator.
9. Next, the Wizard wants to help you add a user account to your local computer. This will grant the domain user account local access to your computer. It does not prevent you from using this computer with a domain user account, but it will make it easier for that domain account to access local resources on your computer. You can also choose not to add a new user at this time.
10. Click Next to display the summary screen for the Wizard. Click Finish to restart your computer automatically, or click Close to exit to Windows 2000 Professional without rebooting.

DHCP Service

The installation program asks you if you have a DHCP (Dynamic Host Configuration Protocol) server on your network. If so, it should provide the IP address for your workstation. If you don't have a DHCP server, or if you don't want to use it, enter a static IP address. If you're not sure what the static address should be, ask your system administrator. You're probably thinking, "Are you kidding?" but this time I mean it. Make sure that this address isn't already in use by another computer; if you use an address that another computer is using, either your workstation or the one that is using the same IP address will not have full access to the network. If that happens, you'll definitely have to see your system administrator, who won't be happy.

The ability to automatically configure your computer to use a reserved IP address if your computer is unable to locate a DHCP server on the network is new to

Windows 2000 Professional. In this case, Windows 2000 Professional will attempt to use a Class C reserved address to at least get on the network. Chances are, if you're using static addressing, this won't be the correct address for your network. Consult your network administrator for help in getting the correct address.

Network Card

Windows 2000 Professional will automatically detect your network card during Setup. If your card can be recognized by Plug and Play or if it's on the PCI bus, Setup will find it. Setup will then ask if you want to install network support with Typical Settings or Custom Settings. If your card isn't detected, choose Custom Settings so that you can install the Microsoft Loopback adapter, which is an imitation network adapter. The benefit is that you can install all your network services here during Setup and install the correct drivers later.

Network Protocol

Windows 2000 Professional will automatically install TCP/IP as your network protocol. You can easily add another protocol or remove TCP/IP if your network uses a different protocol. Your choices are as follows:

- TCP/IP (default)
- AppleTalk Protocol
- DLC Protocol
- NetBEUI Protocol
- NWLink IPX/SPX/NetBIOS Compatible Transport Protocol
- Network Monitor Driver

For information and the steps to set up network protocols, see Chapter 17.

TIP Because network protocols use resources such as memory, it's a good idea to install only the protocol(s) you need. Excess protocols also contribute to network congestion. Try to resist the temptation to install all of them just because you can.

Using Setup Manager to Automate Installation for Multiple Machines

Installing Windows 2000 Professional is time consuming. With an installation time of 20 to 30 minutes per machine, installing Windows 2000 Professional on 20 machines can take a full day. Fortunately, you can use the Windows 2000 Professional Setup

Manager to create a batch file called `unattend.txt` that will do a lot of the dirty work for you by automating the process. You'll find Setup Manager on the Windows 2000 Professional Resource Kit.

When you install Windows 2000 Professional on the machines you've selected, you run an automatic installation from this batch file rather than from a typical setup boot floppy or CD-ROM by simply adding the `/unattend` switch to the `WINNT32` command. The installation program then looks for the `unattend` file in a distribution server folder, copies it to a temporary folder called `\$win_nt$.~ls`, and runs from there.

To automate user input, you must of course provide Setup Manager with all the answers that would normally be required from users during a regular setup. (Otherwise, the installation program pauses for user input, even when the program is running in unattended mode, and just sits there waiting for someone to notice and deal with the situation.) Fortunately, Setup Manager provides all the options you'd run into during almost any type of installation; moreover, using information already available to it via your network server, Setup Manager performs some of the browsing necessary for suggesting likely defaults.

Setup Manager is easy to run; just find `setupmgr.exe` in the Windows 2000 Professional Resource Kit, run the program, and check all the options appropriate for each machine on which you'd like to install Windows 2000 Professional. The options are available through Setup Manager's three main sets of dialog boxes: General Setup, Networking Setup, and Advanced Setup. Be sure to look through all the tabs in these dialog boxes to ensure that you don't miss some important settings, and remember to save the `unattend.txt` answer file that is created as a result of your input.

Running the Unattended Installation

When using the `WINNT32/unattend` command or the `WINNT/unattend` command, by default, files are installed on the same drive as the temporary folder that your computer created. However, you can override the default location by specifying a `/t` parameter in the unattended Setup mode command.

To override the default location of a new installation on a computer running Windows 2000 Professional, type the following command at the command prompt:

```
WINNT32 /unattend:<answerfile> /t:<destination> /s:<source>
```

<destination> Indicates the path where Windows 2000 Professional temporary files should be stored.

<source> Indicates the path where the Windows 2000 Professional files are located. Usually, these files are found the I386 folder.

If you are starting Setup from a 16-bit operating system such as MS-DOS or Windows 3.*x*, you can use the `WINNT` command in place of `WINNT32`.

Using Dual Operating Systems

What if you have Windows 95/98 (or any other operating system) already installed on your machine and you want to add Windows 2000 Professional (or vice versa)? Having more than one operating system on a machine can be a tricky business. Problems can arise when you install an application that has already been installed on one operating system on another. Separate operating systems and their applications need to stay separate. Having two operating systems generally means installing your applications twice. There is no easy way out, although individual software specs can vary.

TIP What do you do if you use the same application on multiple operating systems? The only answer that I can see is to install your applications on each operating system, because applications can't be shared. The applications can usually be installed in their original folders because they will place their operating system-specific files in the proper locations within the operating system folders.

Making a Dual Boot Work

A dual boot refers to the `boot.ini` file that creates a Startup menu, from which you can choose an operating system for a session. Windows 2000 Professional creates the `boot.ini` during the installation process when it locates one or more preexisting operating systems.

The `boot.ini` file is created and stored in the root of the drive on which the preexisting operating system is installed. For example, I have partitioned my hard drive so that I have drives C and D. Before I installed Windows 2000 Professional, I had Windows 98 Second Edition installed on drive C. I then installed Windows 2000 Professional on drive D. My `boot.ini` file is in the root of drive C and looks like this when open in Notepad:

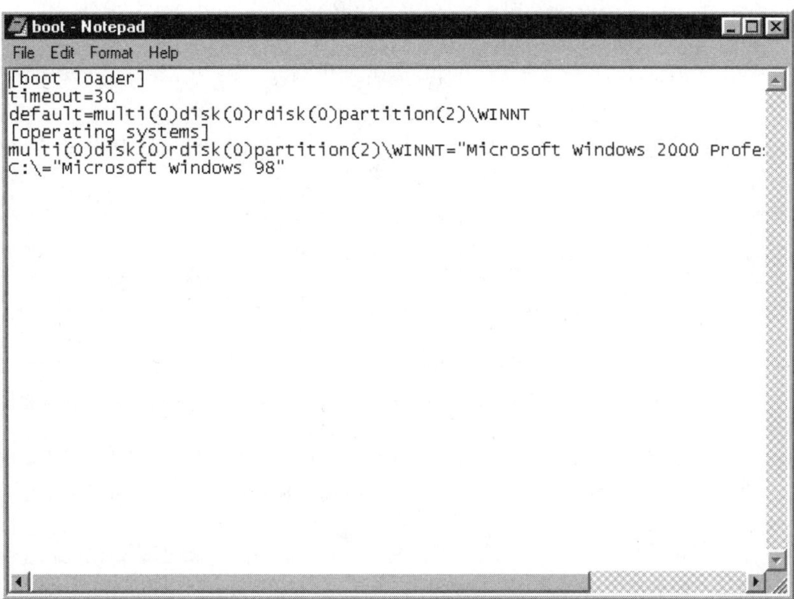

Before you can open `boot.ini`, you need to tell Windows 2000 Professional to display some hidden files. Follow these steps:

1. In Explorer, choose Tools ➢ Folder Options to open the Folder Options dialog box.
2. Click the View tab.
3. In the Advanced Settings list, be sure that the Show Hidden File And Folders option is selected, and then clear the Hide Protected Operating System Files (Recommended) check box.
4. Click OK.

Every time you install Windows 2000 Professional on your system, a new menu entry is created. If you have installed Windows 2000 Professional into more than one folder on your machine, you will encounter identical menu entries for Windows 2000 Professional. For example, one user created two Windows 2000 Professional installations on one workstation: One version was installed with a FAT file system; the other uses NTFS. Even though the entries may look alike, they point to different directory trees on the hard drive. To distinguish the difference between entries, you'll probably want to edit the `boot.ini` file.

Editing the file is simple. Using any text editor, you can make the changes necessary to distinguish between the menu entries. Why edit the file? Well, as I mentioned, there may be more than one entry in the menu. Also, you may have deleted or renamed a Windows 2000 Professional installation. If so, you need to either change the folder name in the `boot.ini` file or delete the entry entirely. As long as `boot.ini` has at least one valid entry, you can load an operating system.

As you can see in the earlier graphic that shows my `boot.ini` file, the `boot.ini` file has two sections: boot loader and operating systems. The first item in the boot loader section is the timeout, which specifies the amount of time you are given to select an operating system. Windows 2000 Professional creates a timeout of 30 seconds by default, but you can change this to any length of time that you like.

NOTE You can also change the timeout in the System Properties dialog box. On the Desktop, right-click My Computer, and choose Properties from the shortcut menu. In the System Properties dialog box, click the Advanced tab, and then click the Startup And Recovery button to open the Startup And Recovery dialog box. In the System Startup section, click the arrow in the spin box to reset the time that the list of operating systems is displayed.

The other item in this section is the default operating system, which is automatically chosen if the user doesn't select one during the timeout period.

NOTE If Windows 2000 Professional is the only operating system present on the computer, the boot menu usually displays less than five seconds. In this case, the delay is only there to enable you to get to the troubleshooting boot options by pressing the F8 key.

In the Operating Systems section, you need to provide information in order for the system to locate where Windows 2000 Professional and other operating system files reside. Knowing on which hard disk and partition the Windows 2000 Professional files are located is very important here. Without this information, Windows 2000 Professional can't locate the rest of the files it needs in order to boot.

Each menu entry for Windows 2000 Professional has four parts:

`multi`*(#)* With # starting at 0; designates the hard disk controller for the disk on which Windows 2000 Professional is located.

`disk`*(#)* With # starting at 0; designates the hard disk on which Windows 2000 Professional is located.

`rdisk`*(#)* With # starting at 0; designates the hard disk on which Windows 2000 Professional is located.

`partition`*(#)* With # starting at 1; designates the hard disk partition on which Windows 2000 Professional is located.

For example, you might have two hard disks and two partitions on the second hard disk. Let's say that you installed Windows 2000 Professional three times (once on the first hard disk and once in each partition). The entries in the `boot.ini` file would look like this:

```
multi(0)disk(0)rdisk(0)partition(1)\WINNT="Microsoft Windows 2000
Professional"
```

```
multi(0)disk(0)rdisk(1)partition(1)\WINNT="Microsoft Windows 2000
Professional"
multi(0)disk(0)rdisk(1)partition(2)\WINNT="Microsoft Windows 2000
Professional"
```

You can also designate any other systems that may exist. For example, if you have Windows 98 residing on your system, you'll want to create an entry like this:

```
C:\="Microsoft Windows 98"
```

When `boot.ini` is finished, it should look like this:

```
[boot loader]
timeout=30
default=multi(0)disk(0)rdisk(0)partition(1)\WINNT[operating systems]
multi(0)disk(0)rdisk(0)partition(1)\WINNT="Microsoft Windows 2000
Professional"
multi(0)disk(0)rdisk(1)partition(1)\WINNT="Microsoft Windows 2000
Professional"
multi(0)disk(0)rdisk(1)partition(2)\WINNT="Microsoft Windows 2000
Professional"
C:\="Microsoft Windows 98"
```

Save the file, reboot your machine, and you should be able to load Windows 2000 Professional or any other operating system by clicking one of the options you just created. The path to the operating system files is called an Advanced RISC Computing (ARC) path. It came originally from the RISC platforms and was chosen to facilitate the porting of Windows NT to those platforms. Table 2.2 has more information about the sections of an ARC path.

TABLE 2.2: SECTIONS OF AN ARC PATH

Keyword	Description
`multi(#)`	Identifies the hard disk controller and is used for either IDE or SCSI with an active BIOS. Numbers start from 0.
`scsi(#)`	Identifies the hard disk controller and is used only when Windows 2000 Professional is installed on a SCSI disk without an active BIOS. Numbers start at 0.
`signature(#)`	Indicates a disk controller by an internal serial number. The number portion is represented by an eight-digit hexadecimal value. It only appears when Windows 2000 Professional is installed on a FAT32 partition.
`disk(#)`	Identifies the hard disk and is used only with the scsi(#) keyword. It will be ignored otherwise. Numbers from 0.
`rdisk(#)`	Identifies the hard disk when the path begins with the multi(#) keyword. It will be ignored otherwise. Numbers start at 0.

TABLE 2.2: SECTIONS OF AN ARC PATH (CONTINUED)

Keyword	Description
`partition(#)`	Identifies the partition number where Windows 2000 Professional is installed. Numbers start at 1.
`\<folder>`	The name of the root of the folder structure in which the Windows 2000 Professional system files are located.

Here are some examples of valid ARC paths:

```
Multi(0)disk(0)rdisk(3)partition(2)\winnt
Scsi(2)disk(2)rdisk(0)partition(1)\winnt4
Signature(ea9b9c97)disk(0)rdisk(0)partition(1)\winnt
```

Obtaining Debugging Information

If you have started the boot process but are unable to load Windows 2000 Professional after choosing your operating system, the problem may be with one or more of the drivers that Windows 2000 Professional needs to run properly. If this is the case, you can find out which drivers failed during the boot by adding an `/SOS` parameter to the end of your Windows 2000 Professional version line in the `boot.ini` file. Adding this parameter lets you view the drivers that Windows 2000 Professional attempts to load during the boot.

TIP The `/SOS` parameter may be annoying if you use it all the time, but it's helpful when trying to diagnose problems.

Another parameter you might want to use is `/MAXMEM=`*n*, which enables you to fool Windows 2000 Professional into thinking that it has less memory when you want to test your system's memory. The values for *n* can be anywhere in the range of 8 through 16 (the default). Reducing the value of *n* reduces the amount of physical memory and the total space for page files. The main result of changing this parameter is that applications run slower because of the increased amount of disk access by the Virtual Memory Manager, depending on the amount of memory available.

You can also add several other switches to your `boot.ini` file:

/NODEBUG Does not collect or transmit debugging information collected during startup. This setting is the default.

/DEBUG Enables debugging with a debugger such as I386KD. The last standard COM port found will be used unless a different port is specified using the /DEBUG-PORT=COM*x* parameter.

/DEBUGPORT=COM*x* Sends output to a specific COM port.

/BAUDRATE=*nnnnn* Specifies the baud rate at which data is sent through the COM port; used for remote debugging purposes. The default for *nnnnn* is 19200.

/CRASHDEBUG Enables a certain amount of stackable pages to be accessible via the debugger. For remote debugging, the default number of stackable pages is 9600. The pages are accessible only after the system encounters a fatal error and begins checking for bugs.

/NoSerialMice Disables the serial mouse detection on certain COM ports. This switch excludes ports that are used by an Uninterruptible Power Supply (UPS) system because the detection signal causes some UPS units to power down, thereby turning off the computer. You can use multiple /NoSerialMice parameters. The format is /NoSerialMice- [COM*x* | COM*x*,COM*y*,COM*z*,…]. If /NoSerialMice is specified without parameters, serial mouse detection will be disabled on all the serial ports.

Booting Windows 2000 Professional in Safe Mode

If you've spent any time working with Windows 95/98, you're no doubt familiar with Safe Mode. Any time the system won't boot due to a newly installed driver or minor hardware problems, you could choose to boot in Safe Mode, which loads only the drivers necessary to start the operating system. Most of the time, this allows you to boot the computer and begin making repairs.

To use Safe Mode, simply press the F8 key when you see the boot menu. You'll see a screen with the following options:

Safe Mode Boots Windows 2000 Professional with only the basic drivers needed to load the operating system. Uses basic drivers for mouse, keyboard, display (VGA), mass storage, default system services and drivers, and absolutely no network components. Creates a log file to track the progress of the system boot.

Safe Mode With Networking Loads the Safe Mode configuration, but also enables the network devices and services. Creates a log file to track the system boot.

Safe Mode With Command Prompt Loads Safe Mode, displaying a list of the files that are loading, and then displays the graphical interface in 640 by 480. Rather than loading the Desktop, Windows 2000 Professional uses the command prompt for its shell. Creates a log file to track the progress of the system boot.

Enable Boot Logging Boots Windows 2000 Professional with all the normal files and drivers but writes their status to a log file at each step. This log file, like the log files in the Safe Mode options, is located in the Windows 2000 Professional folder and is named ntbtlog.txt.

Enable VGA Mode Boots Windows 2000 Professional using a plain vanilla VGA 16-color 640 by 480 display driver for the highest level of compatibility with video cards. This option is an old favorite with NT users.

Last Known Good Configuration Boots Windows 2000 Professional using the last Registry configuration that is known to actually work. Last Known Good is a way of undoing problems created by installing incorrect drivers or possibly by Registry corruption. It will not, however, fix problems caused by corrupted or missing files.

Directory Services Restore Mode Displays the main boot menu, showing in blue text at the bottom of the screen that you're in Directory Services Restore Mode. The system then boots in Safe Mode With Networking, runs CHKDSK on all volumes, and displays the logon screen for you to log on as the Administrator of the local domain. This option is for those times when you want to be doubly sure that Active Directory is back and reindexed.

Debugging Mode Boots Windows 2000 Professional while sending debug information through a serial port to another computer. It's useful in the case of a persistent Blue Screen or Stop error.

Installing Fonts on Windows 2000 Professional

Windows 2000 Professional contains a number of excellent fonts, but you can also install other fonts. For information about fonts and printing in Windows 2000 Professional and for the steps to follow to install a new font, see Chapter 7.

Special Topic: Using Batch Routines for Multiple Installations

In an ideal world, loading desktop operating systems would be simple and painless. You'd just have to wave a magic wand (Microsoft Wand 2000?) that would automatically get any Windows operating system installed on a computer. After a few minutes, you'd come back to find a pristine new operating system installed on your computer (optionally, with all your previous applications migrated successfully).

Unfortunately, we don't live in an ideal world. We live in a world where desktop operating systems have become so complex that the difficulties involved with installing them are beyond the realm of most nontechnical people. However, Microsoft has added a number of features to the Windows 2000 Professional suite in order to make

Windows 2000 Professional easier to install. Microsoft supports three primary methods for unattended installations of Windows 2000 Professional:

- Via an unattended "script" file, which automatically answers the questions normally asked by the Windows 2000 Professional installation routines
- Via the Remote Installation Service included with Windows 2000 Server
- Via imaging the hard drive and copying it to a new computer (with the assistance of the SYSPREP utility)

Each of these methods has advantages and disadvantages. In this chapter, I'll briefly discuss the merits of each method of installation and when you might want to use it. Then, I'll take a more in-depth look at each installation method and how you can use it to your advantage.

Unattended Script Files

Just as a writer produces scripts for actors so that they know what to do and say, you can provide a "script" to the Windows 2000 Professional installation routine. In this script, you'll tell Windows 2000 Professional all the things it will want to know—the correct time zone, where to install the operating system, what your license key is, and so on. You place this information in a specially formatted text file, and the installation routine looks at this file whenever it has a question instead of displaying a prompt on the screen. Assuming that you have prescripted all the questions that the installation routine needs to ask, your installation can proceed from start to finish without any intervention whatsoever.

In my opinion, unattended script files are the most versatile means of installing the Windows 2000 Professional operating system. Period. But pay close attention to my phrasing there—unattended script files are the best for installing *the Windows 2000 Professional operating system.*

There's the catch. Unattended script files are excellent for installing Windows 2000 Professional, but they do very little to help you install any additional applications you might need. For example, a properly configured unattended script file can completely automate the installation of Windows 2000 Professional from start to finish. But let's say you also have a core set of applications you'd like to install at the same time—Adobe Acrobat Reader, WinZip, Office 2000, pcAnywhere, an antivirus program, a few service packs or patches. The unattended installation script will not do anything about installing these programs other than give you the ability to launch a few executables at the end of the Windows 2000 Professional installation. In order to automate the installation of third-party applications or patches, you will need to look elsewhere.

Remote Installation Service

OK, I've got to admit it. The Remote Installation Service (RIS) included with Windows 2000 Server falls within my category of "cool new things" in Microsoft's flagship network operating system. Using RIS, you can quite literally turn on a brand-new computer—with nothing more than a network connection and a blank hard drive—and see a menu of Windows 2000 Professional installation options on your screen. Simply choose a configuration to completely install Windows 2000 Professional from your network. No boot floppy is required as long as your network interface card supports a PXE (preexecution environment) boot, which allows the system to download the code necessary to begin the installation routine. If your network has the bandwidth to support it, RIS is a great way to deploy Windows 2000 Professional.

You can completely customize builds of Windows 2000 Professional deployed via RIS, much in the same manner that you would customize a build via an unattended installation routine. You can configure additional applications to be installed after the operating system has completed, define custom hardware and networking settings, and so on. Because RIS is included with Windows 2000 Server, it is covered at length in *Mastering Windows 2000 Server* (Sybex, 2000) and won't be discussed here.

SYSPREP

The deployment tools included with Windows 2000 Professional are the most comprehensive Microsoft has ever offered. However, you may find that there are occasions when they just simply won't get the job done. On those occasions, you'll need to embark on the road less traveled: disk imaging.

Disk imaging is, basically, making a complete copy of a hard drive and then loading that image on another hard drive. Much like copying a floppy diskette, but on a much larger scale. When it comes to deploying large numbers of Windows computers, this approach seems to make sense at first. After all, installing Windows, a host of productivity applications, and making all the other necessary fine-tuning adjustments to get a system "just right" takes a lot of time. So why not just do it once and then copy it over and over again, right?

Unfortunately, it's not quite that simple. For a number of reasons—too technical to discuss here—simply making a copy of a Windows 2000 Professional system won't work well if you ever intend to network those systems. Each Windows 2000 Professional system has a unique identifier on it called a SID (security ID) that computers use to keep track of one another. Duplicate SIDs on a network cause the Windows operating system to behave erratically in the areas of networking. Therefore, it is necessary to have a unique SID on every single system.

For many years, this has been a problem for enterprises that needed to do large-scale rollouts of the Windows operating system. Microsoft has responded by providing a tool called SYSPREP, which is used to prepare a system for drive imaging (sometimes referred to as cloning). Basically, SYSPREP removes all the SIDs from your system, at which point you can make a complete image of the hard drive (via Ghost or another third-party tool) and load it onto another system. You can then boot up both systems and use them on the same network without any problems.

However, this ease of deployment is not without its drawbacks. Due to the nature of disk imaging and SYSPREP, you will face some hardware limitations onto what you will be able to install your disk image. For organizations with thousands of similar desktops to rollout, this is often one of the most economical solutions.

Using Unattended Installation Scripts

OK, so let's assume that you've decided to use unattended installation files to automate the installation of Windows 2000 Professional. You'll need to determine the following:

- Where will the Windows 2000 Professional source code come from? Common choices are a CD-ROM (either the original or your own custom CD), a network share point, or from the hard drive of the machine that's being installed.
- Where will the unattended script file come from? Common choices are a floppy disk, a CD-ROM, a network share point, or the hard drive of the machine being installed.
- Will any additional third-party hardware drivers (not included with Windows 2000 Professional) be required for any of your systems?

Depending on your situation, any combination of source location and script location might make sense. For example, let's say that you are planning to deploy Windows 2000 Professional throughout a large centralized organization. If you will have plenty of bandwidth available internally, sending installers out with a bootable floppy disk and an unattended script file on it might make sense. The floppy disk could boot a set of network drivers that would then attach to a share containing the \I386 directory from the Windows 2000 Professional source CD.

Or, let's suppose that your organization has no more than a handful of computers at each location but has multiple locations. In that case, it might make more sense to use a CD-based installation, either with an unattended script file contained on a floppy or (my personal preference) on the CD itself.

In any case, you can approach your deployment in a number of ways, but the one thing that will remain the same throughout all the possible scenarios is the script file itself. So let's start taking a look at how you can build an unattended script file, the things you can do with it, and where to put it.

UNATTEND.TXT

Although you might see references to two types of unattended installation files—`unattend.txt` and `winnt.sif`—these files are actually the same. To be honest, you could name your unattended installation file whatever you wanted. The name of the file doesn't matter; it's the content inside the file that does.

In essence, a Windows 2000 Professional installation file looks similar to a Windows INI file—for those of you who have been around long enough to remember what those files look like. For those of you who are unfamiliar, INI files were the files that Microsoft used in earlier versions of Windows to store system settings. The same type of formatting—with sections and data items—is used in an unattended installation file.

The lines in an unattended installation file are one of three types: blank, a section header, or a data item (referred to in Microsoft parlance as a key). Blank lines—well, they're obvious. Section headers are enclosed in square brackets [ ] and are used to consolidate groups of related settings. For example, language type, keyboard layout, and time zone are settings that are usually determined by the same characteristic—where the computer is located. Therefore, these settings are grouped together within the unattended installation file.

The third type of line in an unattended installation file is the actual data item itself. This might be something as simple as telling the installation routine where to install Windows 2000 Professional or something more complicated such as launching a post-installation executable with a number of command-line switches. Data items can be single or multivalued, depending on the type of information that is needed.

So, how do you go about building an unattended installation file? Well, you can take two primary approaches. The first is to use some of the tools that Microsoft has included to automatically build one for yourself. The second is to "roll your own" and build the file by hand. Personally, I'm an advocate of using the Microsoft tool to get a start and then adding any additional information I need by hand. So let's start by taking a look at the tool Microsoft has included to make this job easier, the Setup Manager.

Setup Manager

You won't find the Setup Manager on any of the Windows 2000 Professional menus—it's a separate program that you must add to your system. You'll find it in a file called `DEPLOY.CAB`, located in the \Support\Tools folder of your Windows 2000 Professional CD-ROM. Open `DEPLOY.CAB`, and copy all the files in `DEPLOY.CAB` to a folder on your computer. Run the application called `SETUPMGR.EXE` to begin creating an unattended installation file for your system.

Setup Manager will walk you through a series of Wizard panels (from 10 to over 30, depending), asking you the necessary questions to build an appropriate unattended installation file. The first panel of the Wizard is shown in Figure 2.2.

FIGURE 2.2
Using Setup Manager

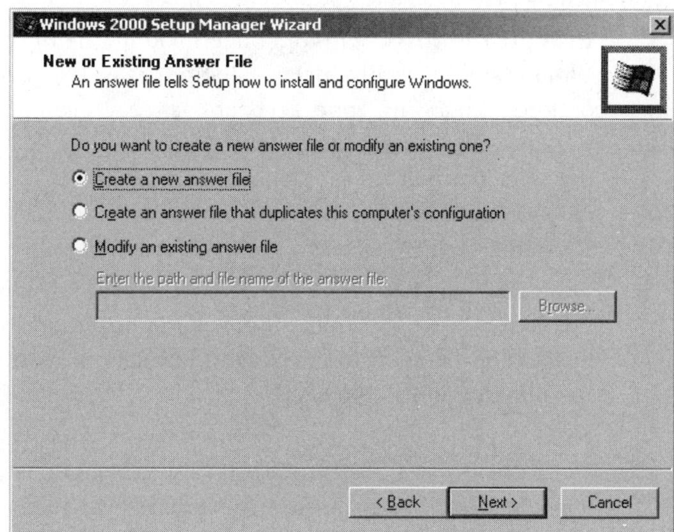

At this first step of the Wizard, Setup Manager wants to know whether you are going to work on a new file or an existing file or if it should create a file based on the settings used on your current system. For our purposes here, let's assume that you want to create a new unattended installation file. Select the first option, and then click Next to continue with the Wizard.

Now, instead of showing each of the 10 to 20 Wizard screens (which would take up a lot of space without adding much content), I'll walk through each screen and tell you which settings are required and how they will impact your unattended installation file.

Product To Install At this screen, Setup Manager wants to know what you want to build your answer file for—a Windows 2000 Unattended Installation, SYSPREP (discussed later in this chapter), or Remote Installation Service (discussed previously in this chapter). For the purposes of what we'll be discussing in this section, choose the Windows 2000 Unattended Installation, and then click Next to continue.

Platform You can use unattended installation files to install Windows 2000 Server or Windows 2000 Professional. Since we're dealing with Windows 2000 Professional in this book, select that option, and then click Next to continue.

User Interaction Level This stage of the Wizard lets you define how the unattended installation will actually execute. Specifically, this Wizard screen lets you select how much user interaction is involved in the setup process, from no involvement to requiring that the user click through each step of the installation. This option will set the UnattendMode= key in the [Unattended] section of your unattended file. The available options are as follows:

Provide Defaults This option lets you specify the default values for the Windows 2000 Professional installation instead of having the user select options such as time zone, keyboard, language, computer name, and so on. Windows 2000 Professional installation will proceed as it normally would—asking users for input at each step along the way—but for each item that the installation routine asks for, the value provided in the unattended file will be the selected default.

Fully Automated For a 100 percent start-to-finish unattended installation, this is the option to use. The user will not be prompted for anything in the installation—no decision making will be necessary on the part of whoever is installing Windows 2000 Professional.

Hide Pages Similar to the provide defaults value, this option will allow for an unattended file that has default values for all the information that the Windows 2000 Professional installation routine will need to know. However, this value functions differently. If all the values in an installation screen are supplied, that screen will not be presented to the user during the installation routine. In the case of screens that have some or all of the information missing from the unattended file, the entire screen will be displayed for the user to enter the correct information. This value is an ideal choice for people who need to roll out an installation that is less than 100 percent fully automated but is still very automated. This would be most useful for an installation that had defaults supplied for almost everything except the computer-specific items such as computer name, IP address, and so on. The user or installer can install those items when prompted for them, and then the rest of the installation routine will proceed uninterrupted (assuming values are provided for all other parts of the installation).

Read-Only Similar to the hide pages value, this option will display only installation screens that need information, but this value lets you narrow down things even further to the specific field value. Therefore, if you need information from a user during the installation routine but only need one value on one of the installation screens (instead of all the values on an installation screen) choose this option.

GUI Attended This option automates the non-GUI (Graphical User Interface) portion of the Windows 2000 Professional installation routine. The GUI portion of the installation routine will be fully attended, meaning that the user will have to answer all the installation screens that are presented.

License Agreement This option is rather self-explanatory. Just as with any other Microsoft product, you must indicate somewhere that you have accepted the

End User License Agreement (EULA). Check this option, and then click Next to proceed to the next step of the Wizard.

Customize The Software Again, as is typical with most Microsoft product installations, you must provide a user name and an organization name. This may be one area where the read-only unattended value (discussed above) might be of use to you. For example, you may want your installation routine to prompt users for their user name, but you may want to provide the organization name. Since these values are both presented on the same screen of the Windows 2000 Professional installation, leaving the name blank while entering an organization here (in conjunction with the read-only value specified above) will let users enter a name but force the same organization name on all systems.

Computer Names If you've been networking with Windows NT or 2000 for any length of time, you are no doubt aware that every computer must have a unique name. In this screen of the Setup Manager, you have four options for providing names: leaving the entire screen blank (not an option if you selected the fully unattended installation mode), entering a single name (which will be used for every computer that you install), providing a list of computer names to use, or letting the installation routine come up with a name based on your organization name. If you are going to use an unattended installation routine to deploy multiple Windows 2000 Professional systems, I recommend either leaving the name blank and allowing the end-user to define a name or providing a list of names in a plain old text file with one computer name on each line of the file. This file will be converted into a UDF (Uniqueness Database File) which you will use along with your unattended installation file. The Windows 2000 Professional installation routine will use this file to come up with unique names for each of your computers that are installed.

Administrator Password The first and foremost user on any computer, the Administrator account, should always have a password. You can either provide a password for your Windows 2000 Professional installation, or you can let the user provide a password during the installation routine by choosing the appropriate radio button. In either case, if you would like Windows 2000 Professional to automatically log in as Administrator once installation is complete, check the When The Computer Starts, Automatically Log On As Administrator check box. This is useful if you have an installation team that doesn't need to know the Administrator password you intend to assign but needs to be logged in to complete an installation. You can even specify how many times the Administrator should automatically be logged in by increasing the Number Of Times To Auto Logon value.

Display Settings In this day and age of high-resolution computers, it's helpful to be able to specify the starting resolution for Windows 2000 Professional. Personally, I don't see why any systems nowadays should be working with less than 800 by 600 resolution and at least 256 colors, but maybe some still do. In any case, choose the acceptable resolutions for your Windows 2000 Professional systems in this screen of the Wizard.

Network Settings If your installations of Windows 2000 Professional will consist solely of the TCP/IP protocol (with a DHCP-assigned address) and the Microsoft Networking client, you can select the Typical Settings radio button on this screen of the Wizard. However, if you need to add additional protocols (NWLink IPX/SPX, NetBEUI) or other options, you will need to specify custom parameters by selecting the Custom Settings radio button. Selecting custom settings will run you through two additional Wizard screens (not discussed here) covering how many network adapters you will be adding and which networking components you want to add.

Workgroup Or Domain All Windows 2000 Professional computers that have networking installed on them are either part of a workgroup or a domain. If your installation routines call for adding computers to a domain during the installation process, you will need a way to define your machines in your domain. This will require either adding the names of the computers into your domain before the Windows 2000 Professional installation begins or selecting the Create A Computer Account In The Domain option. If you choose the second option, you will need to provide your users and/or installers with an account name to use that has the rights to add a machine to your domain, or pre-enter the account information in this screen of the Wizard. It is not necessary to provide the domain's Administrator account for this purpose (although that will work), just an account with enough rights to successfully add a machine to a domain.

Time Zone This setting is rather obvious—if you know what time zone your Windows 2000 Professional system(s) will be in, you can enter this value in advance.

At this point, you have a bare-bones unattended installation file that can be used to install Windows 2000 Professional. You can quit here and have the Setup Manager create your file for you, or you can continue and specify some additional settings. Let's walk through the additional settings screens as well, as there are a number of useful features in them.

Telephony If your Windows 2000 Professional computers will be doing any dial-up networking, you can predefine any country codes, local area codes, or dialing prefixes necessary.

Regional Settings Each version of Windows 2000 Professional has a set of pre-assigned regional settings associated with it. For example, the English (United States) version of Windows 2000 Professional uses the default time, date, and currency displays for the United States. If you need to override these values, or if you want to allow your user and/or installer to override these values, choose the correct option at this Wizard screen.

Languages If you want to install support for additional languages, choose them at this screen of the Wizard.

Browser And Shell Settings This is one of the best options in the additional settings you can define in Setup Manager. You can automatically predefine proxy, home page, and favorites for your automated Windows 2000 Professional installations. For example, you might want your user's default start page to be your company's home page, or you might want to add Favorites to supplier and vendor's Web sites in your custom configuration. You can customize all these settings by choosing the radio button for Individually Specify Proxy And Default Home Page Settings, and then clicking the Proxy Settings and Browser Settings buttons to define proxies and home pages/favorites, respectively.

Installation Folder One thing that Windows 2000 Professional has inherited from its predecessor, Windows NT Workstation, is the installation path. By default, Windows 2000 Professional will try to install itself in a folder on your system called Winnt. I've found that more often than not, this is acceptable to me, but if your requirements call for something different, you can specify a custom folder name here, or you can allow Setup to create a unique folder name for you.

Install Printers Printers have typically been one of the most annoying parts of any Windows installation—especially in large corporate roll-outs. No routines existed for easy, automatic installation of printers—until now. Now, if you want to define a set of printers for every user who installs Windows 2000 Professional, you can simply specify the server names and printer share names to install by using the format `\\`*<servername>*`\`*<printername>*. During your installation routine, Windows 2000 Professional will install these printers (along with their appropriate drivers) into your system.

Run Once If you would like to execute anything once a user first logs on to their Windows 2000 Professional system, you can specify this in the Run Once Wizard screen. This is the best method to use for installing additional software packages onto your Windows 2000 Professional installation. If you can run the installation routines for your additional applications in a silent or unprompted mode, you can completely automate the installation of those applications as well. For example, using an InstallShield silent installation script, I have been able to automatically add Adobe Acrobat Reader to my Windows 2000 Professional installations by placing the command line `c:\acroread\setup.exe -s` in Run Once. Of course, this assumes that the installation routine for Adobe Acrobat Reader is stored in C:\acroread (see additional files or folders covered later in this section).

TIP Newer versions of InstallShield (I'm not exactly certain how new) can create a recording of a typical installation by appending the -r switch to the installation routine when you run it. If you do this and step through what a typical installation should look like, you should find an ISS file on your system after you've completed the normal setup. These are commonly referred to as InstallShield Silent install files (hence, the ISS). After you have the necessary ISS file for the application you want to install, all you need to do is execute the setup routine with an -s option, and InstallShield will "play back" the answers you provided to the setup routine, without prompting the user for any additional information. This is a quick and easy (and reliable!) way to automate the installation of third-party applications that use InstallShield as their primary mechanism of installation.

Distribution Folder In order to make your deployment of Windows 2000 Professional easier, the Setup Manager will gladly build a "distribution folder" for you. I'll discuss this in detail a bit later, but a distribution folder is basically the \I386 folder from your Windows 2000 Professional installation media, slightly customized to meet your installation needs. You can place this distribution folder on a network share, or you can burn it on to a custom CD-ROM if you like (my favorite option).

Distribution Folder Name If you elected to have Setup Manager build a distribution folder for you, you can create a new folder or modify an existing folder at this Wizard screen. Setup Manager will copy the entire Windows 2000 Professional \I386 subfolder into the folder you specify here, along with some additional supporting files (if necessary). Setup Manager will then share the folder on your system.

Additional Mass Storage Drivers This Wizard screen is one of the main reasons it is beneficial to have Setup Manager create a distribution folder for you—it will automatically add in support for additional hardware devices, such as mass storage drivers. If you will be deploying Windows 2000 Professional to any devices that have mass storage drivers that aren't recognized by default by Windows 2000 Professional, you can add the drivers to the Windows 2000 Professional distribution so that the installation routine will be able to find the necessary driver. Having this capability available in a GUI interface is a welcome addition, because the behind-the-scenes changes that are necessary to support additional hardware are a bit of a pain. If you have additional mass storage drivers that you need to support, click Browse here, and then find your drivers (probably on a floppy) to add to your distribution folder.

Hardware Abstraction Layer The same as the mass storage drivers above. If you have a custom Hardware Abstraction Layer (HAL) that you need to support on a Windows 2000 Professional system that you deploy, this is the area to define those files.

Additional Commands Any commands that you enter into this dialog box will be put into a special file called `CMDLINES.TXT`, which needs to go wherever your `UNATTEND.TXT` file goes. All commands found in `CMDLINES.TXT` will be executed after Windows 2000 Professional setup has completed but before the final reboot. This is a perfect time to install additional Microsoft service packs, hot fixes, and so on.

OEM Branding Although this is more of an aesthetic option, you can customize the background bitmap displayed during the installation routine and optionally put a logo in the upper-right corner. Although this is commonly used by computer manufacturers (OEM is an abbreviation for original equipment manufacturer), it is simple enough to configure for anyone and adds a nice touch to the installation process. It also serves as a visual cue for whoever is installing Windows 2000 Professional to know that they are installing the correct version—your custom version—and not using the Microsoft defaults. Background bitmaps must be no more than 640 by 480 in resolution, with a maximum of 16 colors. Logos should be no larger than 175 by 175. Setup Manager will copy your files into the distribution folder.

Additional Files Or Folders Having this option available via the GUI interface of Setup Manager is also a welcome addition to unattended installations. Previously, installing any additional files into a user's system required creating some special folders under the \I386 folder of the distribution folder. Now, the Setup Manager can handle this for you. So, if you have any files that need to be installed to your Windows 2000 Professional system(s) in addition to the base operating system, this is the place to do it. Want to put your company's complete set of operating manuals into a folder called Manuals on each user's C drive? Simply navigate to the Other Drives > C folder in this Wizard screen and then click Add Files. Select the files you want to include, and Setup Manager will automatically build them into your distribution point. I've found this particularly useful for including all the source code to additional applications I build on systems. I typically build a folder called Source and place all the third-party installation routines I want in there—such as Acrobat PDF Reader, WinZip, pcAnywhere, and so on. That way, I always know that the source code is there if I need it.

Answer File Name If you skipped the option to create a distribution folder, this will be the last step of the Wizard for you. Setup Manager simply needs to know where to put your unattended installation file. Give it the appropriate folder, and then click Finish. Your unattended installation file will be written out with a default name of `unattend.txt`, unless you provide it with another name to use. If you told Setup Manager to create a distribution folder, click Next to continue to the final step of the Wizard.

Location Of Setup Files The final step of the Wizard is to tell Setup Manager where it can find the Windows 2000 Professional \I386 folder, either from a CD or from another location. Choose the appropriate location, and Setup Manager will begin building your distribution folder. Your distribution folder will contain all the mass storage drivers, custom HALs, background bitmaps and logos, and additional files that you've defined.

Custom UNATTEND.TXT Modifications

Although Setup Manager will do most of the work for you when it comes to building an unattended installation file, there are some commands that Setup Manager won't put into your file. Let's look at a few of the more useful commands and the sections that they fall under.

Useful Additional Commands—[Unattended] Section

ExtendOEMPartition= This option lets you extend the partition onto which you are installing Windows 2000 Professional. The valid values for this key are 0, 1, or a size in megabytes. If you choose 0, setup will not extend the partition into which you are installing Windows 2000 Professional. If you choose 1, setup will extend the partition as far as it can. If you specify a size in megabytes, the setup routine will increase the size of the target partition by a specified amount. Therefore, if you begin installing in a 2GB partition on your system, and you specify an `ExtendOEMPartition=` value of 4GB, you will end up with a final partition size of 6GB.

FileSystem= If you plan to use the `ExtendOEMPartition` option, you must specify this key in your unattended installation file, as only NTFS partitions can be extended. Valid values for this field are `ConvertNTFS` and `LeaveAlone`. If you want to extend your installation partition, you must set this value to `ConvertNTFS`.

Useful Additional Commands—[SetupParams] Section

This section of the unattended file is not well documented and in some cases, not documented at all. However, I have had some success in getting this section to function properly, but I am providing it with no guarantees.

The SetupParams section is a way to execute commands on your Windows 2000 Professional installation right at the very end of the GUI setup but before the system reboots for the first time and is ready for a login. Microsoft's documented way to achieve the same functionality is to create a file called `CMDLINES.TXT`, which is executed at the end of setup, but I like using this approach as it centralizes everything into one file—the unattended installation file.

Although you can use the SetupParams file to install third-party applications onto your system, I have found that it is best used for installing Microsoft patches into the operating system. By specifying multiple `Userexecute=` lines within the SetupParams section, you can specify multiple commands that should be executed at the end of Windows 2000 Professional setup. Therefore, if you are reading this and you want to deploy Windows 2000 Professional with Service Pack 1, you might include a line such as `Userexecute="c:\patches\servpak1 -z"` within the SetupParams section of your unattended installation file. Of course, this would require that you actually have an executable program called servpak1 in the C:\patches folder of your user's system (Hint, hint: remember the "Additional Files" option I mentioned earlier?). I've also found that "-z" is a commonly used option for a silent-mode installation of Microsoft service packs and updates.

Useful Additional Commands–[Components] Section

Setup Manager will automatically assume that you'd like to install all the typical components of the Windows 2000 Professional operating system, including things like FreeCell, MineSweeper, Pinball, and Solitaire. Through this section of the unattended file, you can select or deselect any and all of the applications that Windows 2000 Professional installs. The list of optional components is rather exhaustive and can be found in the `UNATTEND.DOC` file inside the `DEPLOY.CAB` file mentioned earlier in this section.

Useful Additional Commands–[UserData] Section

Although the Setup Manager will not prompt you for a product ID, you can enter one in advance by manually editing the `SYSPREP.INF` file and adding the string `ProductID=` to the [UserData] section. Include a valid Windows 2000 Professional product ID in this key value. An example entry would look like the following:

```
ProductID="XXXXX-YYYYY-ZZZZZ-AAAAA-BBBBB"
```

What to Do with Your UNATTEND.TXT File

OK, so now that Setup Manager has helped you build an `UNATTEND.TXT` file (and optionally, a `CMDLINES.TXT` file and an `UNATTEND.UDF` file), and you've tweaked it with your own commands, what do you want to do with it? At this point, your options depend entirely on what will work best for your environment.

As I stated earlier in the chapter, you can put the file on a network share and simply connect a workstation to that share (via a DOS boot disk or other means) for your installation purposes. Or, you could put it on a floppy diskette and use it in conjunction with your Windows 2000 Professional CD. Or, you could put it on a custom CD along with the Windows 2000 Professional source files and other files you want to install. Go with whatever works best for your environment. Here are a few common uses for the `UNATTEND.TXT` file.

Floppy Boot Disk You can use a floppy boot disk to install Windows 2000 Professional in one of two ways. First, you can use a floppy boot disk to boot a set of network drivers, attach to your Windows 2000 Professional distribution folder on a server, and then execute the Windows 2000 Professional installation routine with an unattended installation file that is either stored on your network or the floppy itself. In this case, all that would be on your floppy disk is a set of drivers necessary to boot up your system and attach to a network. Having said that, let me also say that building a bootable DOS network disk can often be quite a complicated task, one that we won't be tackling here.

The second way that you can use a floppy boot disk is during a CD-ROM based installation of Windows 2000 Professional. If the Windows 2000 Professional setup routine is executed from a booted CD-ROM, it will look for a file called `Winnt.sif` in your floppy drive. The `Winnt.sif` file is exactly the same as the `unattend.txt` file created earlier. Therefore, all you need to do is copy your `unattend.txt` file to a floppy, rename it to `Winnt.sif`, and then boot your Windows 2000 Professional CD-ROM. As soon as your computer starts booting from the CD-ROM, insert the floppy disk into the drive. The installation routine will start building your Windows 2000 Professional system using the unattended installation file you built.

Custom CD-ROM (the Author's Preferred Choice) As a writer and a consultant, there are so many times that I end up installing, reinstalling, and re-reinstalling Windows 2000 Professional that it's enough to make my head spin. After doing this enough, I finally decided to break down and build my own sort of customized installation routine. Personally, I think it's the best choice around, but hey—I might be a bit biased.

What I've done, more or less, is to make my own bootable CD-ROM with the Windows 2000 Professional source files on it (the \I386 folder), several `UNATTEND.TXT` files for varying purposes, and installation files for other applications that I typically need. This makes it very easy to get everything I need onto any system at any time—as long as the system can boot from a CD. This type of setup CD is actually quite easy to make.

Believe it or not, the most challenging part of creating my own custom Windows 2000 Professional installation CD-ROM was making it a bootable CD. Without going into lengthy technical details, let me just say that there are a couple of ways to make a bootable CD-ROM. One of the *easiest* ways is to make a CD-ROM that has its own sort of "virtual A drive floppy" embedded into the media.

TIP I can't even begin to count how many CD-Rs I went through trying to figure out how to make a bootable CD-ROM. It's a bit of a quirky process and not very well documented, but once you do it successfully for the first time it will start to make sense. I found the Australian Bootable CD FAQ was extremely helpful. You can find that site at `www.ozemail.com.au/~rossstew/drs/bootcd.html`.

How this actually works was confusing at first, but after enough trial and error it was actually quite easy. What you do is make a bootable DOS floppy, which has all the device drivers, CD-ROM drivers, MSCDEX (the Microsoft CD Extensions), and the startup files you need on it. Test your floppy on as many machines as possible, making sure that all the machines will boot from that floppy. Make sure that once the machine has booted, you can connect to the CD-ROM drive and access it from DOS. Getting to this point is actually quite challenging (hint: I've got a shortcut I'll tell you about in just a bit), but once you get there, you're all set.

Once you're sure that you have a "universal" boot floppy—one that will work on any machine—all you need to do is "burn" that bootable floppy image into a special area of a CD-ROM. Personally, I do it with Adapted EZ-CD Creator. You will need to create an ISO-9660 CD-ROM (not a Joliet) in order to support booting from CD-ROM (these steps are specifically covered in the Australian Bootable CD FAQ).

When your system boots up with a CD-ROM in the drive that has this virtual A drive floppy on it, it will actually boot from that area, just as if it was a floppy drive. As a matter of fact, once it's done booting you should have at least two drive letters available on your system—A, which won't access your floppy but instead will access the special area of the CD-ROM, and then whatever letter you mapped to your CD-ROM drive via MSCDEX. If you have a working C drive on your system, you should have a drive letter for that as well.

So, there's no more need to carry around a bootable floppy! You can burn that floppy image into a CD-ROM and use that to boot from—and once you've booted you can then access your CD-ROM to begin your installations.

TIP If you're having trouble making a boot disk that will work on most any machine and successfully mount the CD-ROM drive, try booting a Windows 98 CD-ROM and then exiting to DOS. Change the drive letter to A (*without* a floppy in the drive), and take a look at the directory. Lots of stuff there, right? Good stuff, like drivers and startup files that Microsoft has already tested and debugged for you. From that "virtual" A drive, copy all the contents to another location–such as the C drive on the system. Then, all you will need to do is format a floppy so that it is bootable and copy all those files from your hard drive onto your floppy. You've now "borrowed" a copy of the bootable code on Microsoft's Windows 98 CD-ROM to use for your own purposes (keeping within the restrictions of your software licensing, of course). You will probably want to change around your `AUTOEXEC.BAT` and `CONFIG.SYS` files a bit so that they don't try to launch a Windows 98 install, but now all you need to do is use your software to burn a CD-ROM with this diskette as your virtual A floppy and whatever other files you want. Voila! Instant bootable, custom Windows 2000 Professional CD-ROM!

Now, for the CD-ROM portion of the content, I'm prone to put as much as I can on a single CD. Therefore, I'll often put a copy of the Windows 2000 Professional \I386 folder on the CD-ROM and then create individual folders for each of the additional applications I want to install on my system. For me, that includes putting the source files for Adobe Acrobat Reader, WinZip, pcAnywhere, and a host of other applications on the same CD-ROM and installing everything I need all at once, from one single location. It makes my life a lot easier when it comes time to rebuild a system!

Sample UNATTEND.TXT file

Once you've got it all together, your `UNATTEND.TXT` file should look similar to the example provided here. As you can see, a number of options are defined in a complete `UNATTEND.TXT` file, and you can modify them as you see fit. You should also take a few minutes to review the Word document `UNATTEND.DOC`, which is included in the

\SUPPORT\TOOLS\DEPLOY.CAB file on your Windows 2000 Professional installation CD. That document contains complete information about every possible option available in a Windows 2000 Professional unattended installation file.

```
[Data]
    AutoPartition=1
    MsDosInitiated="0"
    UnattendedInstall="Yes"
[Unattended]
    UnattendMode=FullUnattended
    OemSkipEula=Yes
    OemPreinstall=No
    TargetPath=\WINNT
[GuiUnattended]
    AdminPassword=*
    OEMSkipRegional=1
    TimeZone=35
    OemSkipWelcome=1
[UserData]
    FullName="Douglas Toombs"
    OrgName="NetArchitect Consulting"
    ComputerName=COMPNAME
[Display]
    BitsPerPel=8
    Xresolution=800
    YResolution=600
[TapiLocation]
    CountryCode=1
    Dialing=Tone
    AreaCode=703
    LongDistanceAccess="9,"
[FavoritesEx]
    Title1="Minasi Research & Development.url"
    URL1="http://www.minasi.com"
[Branding]
    BrandIEUsingUnattended=Yes
[URL]
    Home_Page=http://www.netarchitect.com
[Proxy]
    Proxy_Enable=1
    Use_Same_Proxy=1
    HTTP_Proxy_Server=10.0.0.1:80
```

```
    Proxy_Override=<local>
[GuiRunOnce]
    Command0=c:\runonce.exe
[Identification]
    JoinWorkgroup=WORKGROUP
[Networking]
    InstallDefaultComponents=Yes
```

Tying It All Together: Launching a Windows 2000 Professional Installation

OK, so you've got it all together now. You've got a distribution folder, you've got an unattended installation file. So, what do you do with them?

Unless you're using the first floppy-based installation method I discussed (letting the standard setup routine read your `winnt.sif` file), you will need to launch one of the two Windows 2000 Professional installation routines. They are `winnt.exe` (for starting DOS-based installations) and `winnt32.exe`. Both can be found in the \I386 folder of your distribution folder, and both provide for similar command-line options that you will use in an unattended installation. There are two primary things that you will need to tell the installation routine: where your distribution folder is and where your unattended file is.

The `/U` command-line switch will instruct the Windows 2000 Professional installation routine to use an unattended file and where it should look for it. The `/S` command-line switch will tell the Windows 2000 Professional installation routine where your distribution folder is located. If you are using `WINNT` to install Windows 2000 Professional, you can provide the additional /T command-line switch to define the target drive for your Windows 2000 Professional installation. Therefore, a properly formatted Windows 2000 Professional installation command-line might read as follows:

```
WINNT /U:A:\UNATTEND.TXT /S:G:\WIN2000DIST /T:C:\
```

This would launch the Windows 2000 Professional setup from DOS, using an `unattend.txt` file stored on A, and a distribution folder located at `G:\WIN2000DIST`. Windows 2000 Professional would be installed to the C drive, in whatever folder the unattended installation file specified. Of course, you would need to have your network drive mapped to access a G drive for this to work.

My personal preference is to build a batch routine that copies the entire \I386 folder down to the C drive of the machine that I am installing and then execute the Windows 2000 Professional installation routines from there, using the local \I386 folder as the distribution folder. I find that eventually, I always need to refer to my \I386 folder when I'm trying to install something, and it's nice to not have to track down a CD-ROM and know that the files are already on my hard drive.

Using SYSPREP

Let's assume that, for whatever reason, your configuration is simply too complicated for an unattended installation routine. Running SYSPREP on a system and then copying the drive image might be the only solution. But there are some hardware limitations on what you can do with drive imaging. For drive imaging to work, your source and target systems must have the following characteristics:

- They must have the same number of CPUs.
- They must be running identical Hardware Abstraction Layers (HALs).
- They must be running identical mass storage controllers (IDE or SCSI).

If your systems do not match in all three of these areas, you will have a hard time using an image of your Windows 2000 Professional system to deploy other systems. That's why most organizations use drive imaging as a solution when they are deploying multiple systems that are all the same (for example, rolling out 100 new desktops that are all the same type). If drive imaging will suit your needs, the following procedures should get you started with SYSPREP and preparing a system to be cloned.

Preparing a System To Be Cloned

Now, before you get ready to clone a system, you've got to tidy it up a bit. You want things such as applications, drive mappings, and shortcuts to be propagated to all the target systems that you deploy. However, you don't necessarily want your default settings, preferences, histories, and so on deployed to thousands of desktops throughout your organization. Here's a list of things you should do to prepare your system for cloning.

Install Windows 2000 Professional. This should be rather straightforward if you've gotten to this chapter in the book. Although you can clone existing systems, it is *strongly* recommended that you clone a brand new system with a fresh copy of Windows 2000 Professional on it. Trust me, your deployments will go much smoother if you do.

Install SYSPREP. SYSPREP v1.1 (the latest version at the time of this writing) can be downloaded from `www.microsoft.com/windows2000/downloads/deployment/sysprep/default.asp`. Unpack the files to a folder on your computer (such as C:\sysprep).

Configure Desktop wallpapers, color schemes, shortcuts, and so on. If you've got a custom background you want to use for your users, a special screen saver, shortcuts, or other such items, set all these options before preparing your system for copying.

Install all necessary service packs. Check to see if there are any updates or service packs available for Windows 2000 Professional. If there are, you might as well install them once on your source computer instead of multiple times on all your deployed systems. Be sure to reboot after all updates in order to initialize the changes that have been made.

Make any persistent drive connections. Although the preferred method for mapping drive letters is to use login scripts, if you prefer to do so through client-based persistent drive mappings, map all the appropriate drives before creating an image of your system. Remember that all the drives that you are mapping will need to be accessible by anyone who will be logging in on a cloned system—otherwise their system will try to map the drive (as it should) and they will receive an error message.

Install and connect all necessary printers. Just as with making drive connections, make sure that all *network* printers are installed with appropriate drivers. If you plan on having a local printer attached to each and every cloned workstation (highly unlikely in most cases), install the appropriate driver for that printer as well and connect it to the appropriate local printer port.

Install and configure all third-party applications. After you've installed all your Windows 2000 Professional settings, install any and all third-party applications that your users will need. Office 2000, Internet Explorer, WinZip, whatever your users need—remember to install each application and make all of the necessary settings to the program (such as IE favorites or start pages). If you forget to install an application or make a necessary setting on your source system, you'll end up fixing it later, one desktop at a time.

Remove the computer from the domain. If your source computer is in a domain, remove it from the domain and make it a member of a workgroup instead. Once you have deployed your system image on a target system, re-add the target system to the domain.

Remove any IP configurations. In case you will be installing multiple computers on the same network, you should remove any TCP/IP configuration from your source system and set it to use DHCP instead. TCP/IP configurations can be installed on each target computer once the system is built.

Set the Administrator's password to blank. Another safety precaution, just in case something goes wrong with the installation process.

Reboot one last time. After you've done all these steps, you're almost ready to take the snapshot image of your source system. Just to be safe, reboot your computer one last time to make sure that any pending changes are implemented on the system.

Copy the Administrator's profile to the default profile. During the final boot-up for your source system, there's only one task that you will need to complete: copying the Administrator's profile to the default user's profile. This is a bit trickier than it sounds, however.

First, you've got to enable your system to show hidden files and folders, because the default user profile is stored in a hidden folder. Set this option by opening My Computer and then choosing Tools ➢ Folder Options. Click the View tab, and then select the Show Hidden Files And Folders radio button.

Next, you need to copy the Administrator's profile to the default profile. Open Control Panel, click System to open the System Properties dialog box, and then select the User Profiles tab. You should see all the profiles that are currently on your system. Select the Administrator's profile, and then click the Copy To button. You will see a screen similar to the one shown in Figure 2.3.

FIGURE 2.3
Copying the Administrator's profile

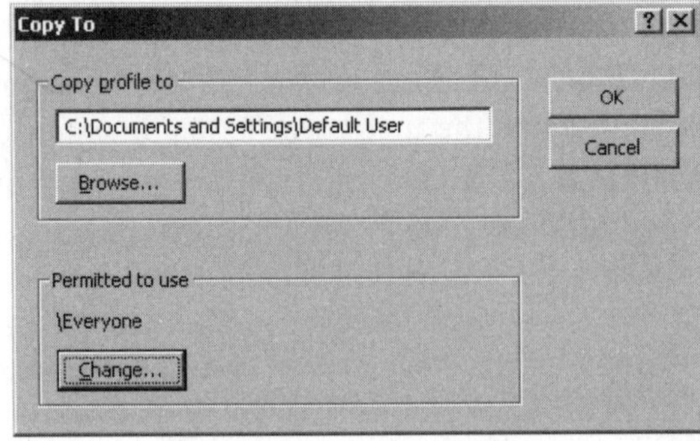

At this point, you want to copy the profile into the path C:\Documents and Settings\Default User (assuming you have your copy of Windows 2000 Professional installed on C). You can get there by browsing to the path (this is recommended to make sure that you can actually see the hidden folder) or typing in the path directly.

In addition to copying the Administrator's profile to the default user, you also need to make sure that everyone can access the profile. Click the Change button in the Permitted To Use check box, and change the permission to the Everyone group. This will ensure that any new user logging in will be able to access the default user's profile and make it their own.

Create a SYSPREP answer file. Although SYSPREP helps you make an exact copy of an existing machine's hard drive onto a new machine, it also needs to have an answer file to guide it along. Use the Setup Manager (SETUPMGR.EXE) discussed earlier in this chapter to make an answer file for a SYSPREP install (selected at the second screen of the Wizard). The file that Setup Manager will create will be called SYSPREP.INF—store this in the same folder that SYSPREP.EXE is in.

Optionally, add a product ID to SYSPREP.INF. The SYSPREP.INF file created by Setup Manager will not contain a product ID—something that Windows 2000 Professional typically wants to see during an installation. Manually edit the SYSPREP.INF file and add the string ProductID= to the [UserData] section. Include a valid Windows 2000 Professional product ID in this key value. An example entry would look like the following:

```
ProductID="XXXXX-YYYYY-ZZZZZ-AAAAA-BBBBB"
```

Cover your tracks—clear document and IE histories. No one wants to get a new computer that looks like someone else lived on it before they did. So, cover your tracks, if you've made any, by removing document and program histories from your system. Right-click the Taskbar, and choose Properties from the shortcut menu to open the Taskbar And Start Menu Properties dialog box. Click the Advanced tab, and then click the Clear button to remove all document histories, Internet Explorer history, and so on.

Run SYSPREP. After you've gone through all the steps above, you're ready to run SYSPREP. The actual tool, SYSPREP.EXE, can be found in the Tools folder of wherever you unpacked the SYSPREP files. Once you've run SYSPREP, your system will shut itself down. Your system is now ready to be imaged and deployed.

Imaging a System and Deploying It

Once you've reached this step, you can begin imaging your drive and deploying it throughout your organization. Obviously, this step will vary from one organization to the next, but ideally at this point you should have some sort of drive-imaging software available (Norton Ghost, ImageCast, and so on.)

Start your imaging software, and take an image of your hard drive. Obviously, you will need to store that image somewhere other than on your source system (and you can expect your image file to be rather large), so you will probably need some sort of network connectivity as well. Once you've taken the image of your hard drive, you can begin deploying copies of that hard drive into target systems and then booting the target systems up.

Once you boot up your target systems, you will need to correct the primary items that were removed from your source system—namely the IP configuration (assuming you weren't using DHCP)—and adding the computer into the domain. Once you've accomplished all this, you should be able to sit a user down at the computer and have them log in. All the applications that they need will be available, along with all the necessary printer mappings, drive mappings, shortcuts, and so on.

Summary

In this chapter, we discussed the various methods of Windows 2000 Professional installation. You learned about installing Windows 2000 Professional both at a standalone computer and on a network. We talked about installing hardware at setup time and finished by looking at techniques to automate the install procedure.

CHAPTER 3

Running Your Applications

FEATURING:

Without software, your computer is nothing but an expensive hunk of plastic and metal. It takes software to make your computer come alive and do something useful. An operating system, such as Windows 2000 Professional, serves as the platform for running your application software. Although it is most helpful to learn how to use your favorite applications so that you can be productive with them, it is also important to learn how your software interacts with your operating system. This knowledge will not only help make you a happier and more informed computer user, it will also help you diagnose and solve problems—and perhaps become the envy of your office.

Eliminating Programs You Won't Need Anymore

When you make the move to Windows 2000 Professional, you won't need to take all your old DOS and Windows programs with you. Some just won't work, and others have been replaced by utilities that are built into Windows 2000 Professional. In fact, you can leave behind many of your Windows 95/98 utilities since they have been replaced by new built-in utilities. In this section, I'll discuss which programs you won't need anymore, why you don't need them, and with what Windows 2000 Professional has replaced them, if anything.

TSRs

Terminate and Stay Resident programs (TSRs) are small programs that DOS would run at boot-up and then leave in memory for as long as DOS was in operation. They were a mainstay in the days of DOS. As a rule, TSRs provided functionality not found in DOS. The most common TSRs were those that enabled DOS to use memory more effectively, to load support for your sound card, to use CD-ROM drives or other Small Computer System Interface (SCSI) devices, or to connect to a network.

The functionality of TSRs is replaced by the Windows 2000 Professional services such as the Microsoft Client Service for NetWare and the File Replication Service. If you need to support a program or hardware device with a TSR under DOS or even Windows 95/98, there is likely a Windows 2000 Professional counterpart that runs as a service.

Disk Utilities

Hard disks need ongoing care to keep them running smoothly and happily. This is still true under Windows 2000 Professional, but because of the way Windows 2000 Professional interacts with your computer's hardware, including hard disks, you can't use your old disk utilities from DOS, Windows 3.1, or Windows NT4. Windows 2000 Professional provides its own set of tools for such purposes, and third-party, 32-bit utility programs provide even more features than the ones that come with Windows 2000 Professional. Just be sure that the utility you choose is compatible with the file system you are using.

Desktop Replacements

In earlier versions of Windows, you could easily replace the default shell with a third-party add-on. A shell is the user interface of the operating system, the part you actually interact with. In Windows 3.*x* and Windows NT 3.*x*, the shell was called Program Manager (`progman.exe`), and you could easily replace it with another program. The shell for Windows 95 and NT 4 was Explorer (`explorer.exe`). It introduced features that made the operating system more intuitive and easier to use, for example, the Start menu and the Taskbar. You will still find those features in Windows 2000 Professional, but many of the others have either been replaced or updated with new functionality.

With the advent of Internet Explorer 4 (IE4) from Microsoft, there has been at least one modified shell available for Windows 95 or NT 4. When you installed this Web browser, you could choose to replace the Explorer shell with Internet Explorer's Active Desktop. In Windows 2000 Professional, as in Windows 98/98 SE, Internet Explorer is integrated into the operating system. There aren't any shell replacements for Windows 2000 Professional at this time, but have no doubt that some will be available in the future.

Discovering Programs You Can't Run Anymore

You probably didn't buy Windows 2000 Professional just to play with its features. You bought this operating system to run your applications, right? With the possible exception of older DOS and some 16-bit Windows applications, you won't have many problems running your programs in Windows 2000 Professional. Keep in mind that some of these applications will suffer a slight performance hit when they are run in Windows 2000 Professional, and many DOS games won't run at all. Just as with earlier versions of Windows NT, Windows 2000 Professional will need to do some extra work when it runs older programs. These older applications often try to talk directly to the hardware, and Windows 2000 Professional can't permit this and still maintain its security and stability.

Windows 2000 Professional will run all your 32-bit Windows programs and most of your older DOS and Windows applications. If the program runs in protected mode and lets Windows 2000 Professional handle the hardware access, everyone will be happy, and the program will run correctly. If a program tries to go past the operating system to the hardware and Windows 2000 Professional can't handle the access with a Virtual Device Driver (VxD), Windows 2000 Professional will shut down the application.

To be blunt, every program and every file you run under Windows 2000 Professional must operate in protected mode. All 32-bit programs run in this mode; not all 16-bit programs do. I'll discuss the difference between these two modes later in this section in a sidebar titled "What Are the Differences between 16-Bit and 32-Bit Programs?"

A brief additional word about games: You can run most Windows games under Windows 2000 Professional, but some will run noticeably slower, as discussed in the next section. Any DOS game that creates its own *virtual environment* will also probably run, albeit slowly, and those that don't, won't. However, new 32-bit, protected-mode games are appearing almost faster than your local computer store can keep track, so you're sure to find plenty of titles that will run on Windows 2000 Professional. Many of the most popular games today will run fine on Windows 2000 Professional; in fact, some will actually run better than they did on Windows 98. The best bet is to check the manufacturer's recommendations to see if they support Windows NT or Windows 2000 Professional. You'll likely notice better support for these applications in Windows 2000 Professional than in previous versions of Windows NT since Windows 2000 Professional has added Plug-and-Play support and uses the common driver model (meaning it uses the same drivers as Windows 98).

What Are the Differences between 16-Bit and 32-Bit Programs?

At present in the world of Windows computing, there are two types of programs: *16-bit* and *32-bit*. Technically, the difference between them is that 16-bit programs are written in accordance with the Win16 API, and 32-bit programs are written in accordance with the Win32 API. API stands for application programming interface, which is a set of guidelines that programmers use when they are writing programs for specific operating systems.

More to the point, an API functions as a programmer's rule book. The rules concern how the program should go about its tasks: how it should write instructions into memory, how it should create windows, how it should send e-mail, and how it should handle every other function that a program needs an operating system for. Practically, there are two significant differences between 16-bit and 32-bit programs:

- 32-bit programs will run only on Windows 95/98 or Windows 2000 Professional, and they'll sport far more sophisticated features than a 16-bit version of the program ever could. Thirty-two–bit programs will not run on Windows 3*x*.

Continued

- 16-bit programs will run on any Windows platform (including NT and Windows 2000 Professional). In fact, they'll run better (fewer crashes) on Windows 2000 Professional than they will on Windows 3*x* because of Windows 2000 Professional protected-mode support for 16-bit programs.

The real strength of 32-bit programs is that they take advantage of the strengths of Windows 2000 Professional: preemptive multitasking, a flat memory model, and the aforementioned protected-mode support. When looking for new programs, choose the 32-bit program if you are presented with a choice between a 32-bit program and a 16-bit program performing essentially the same function. You will get better performance, experience fewer crashes, and obtain better integration with your Windows 2000 Professional operating environment.

Some Windows 95/98 Apps Won't Run

Yes, it's true. The sad fact is that not *all* 32-bit Windows applications will run under Windows 2000 Professional. When Microsoft originally designed the requirements for creating Windows 95 programs, one of the specifications was that 32-bit applications that were designed for Windows 95 had to run under Windows NT as well. Microsoft later changed that requirement to state that programs don't *have* to run on Windows NT—but *if* they don't, they're required to "degrade gracefully." This means they aren't allowed to freeze the operating system when they fail.

You can find out if an application is compatible with Windows 2000 Professional Professional in at least three ways:

- If you're buying new software, be sure that the packaging copy says the product is for Windows 2000 Professional.
- Run the Windows 2000 Professional Readiness Analyzer tool, which compares devices and applications on a system against a list of known issues and reports any potential incompatibilities. You'll find the Readiness Analyzer on your installation CD. At a command prompt, type **`WINNT32.exe /checkupgradeonly`** to start it.
- Do your own compatibility testing by following these steps:
  1. Install and open the application in Windows 2000 Professional.
  2. Verify that the following functions work:
     - Printing
     - Saving files
     - Customizing menus
     - Exporting data
     - Cutting and pasting through the Clipboard
  3. Run routine tasks to verify that their stability has not been affected.

Running Programs

In Windows 2000 Professional, you can run an application in a number of ways, but before I get into that, I need to show you around the Desktop. If you've used Windows 98, you'll be familiar with many of the Desktop elements, but you'll find that some are new, some are in new locations, and some have different functionality.

But First...The User's View of the Desktop

In Windows 2000 Professional, the Desktop is a fully integrated and essential part of the operating system. You can drag programs, files, and system objects onto it in order to organize them or launch them. (And you can also customize the look of the Desktop.)

Figure 3.1 shows my current Desktop, which is almost in its virgin state. One thing that's missing is the Connect To The Internet icon. Clicking that icon starts the Internet Connection Wizard, which lets you set up your connection to the Internet. When you finish with the Wizard, this icon disappears from the Desktop. I also have an icon for FullShot99, which is the program I'm using to create the illustrations for this book.

FIGURE 3.1
The Windows 2000 Professional Desktop

The Taskbar

Located at the bottom of your screen (you can move it any time you want to), the Taskbar is the Windows 2000 Professional information system. It constantly tells you which applications and files you have open and whether you are printing, have e-mail, or have sound. Most important, the Taskbar (see the following illustration) is the permanent home of the Start button. Click this button to pop open the Start menu, which I'll discuss in the next section.

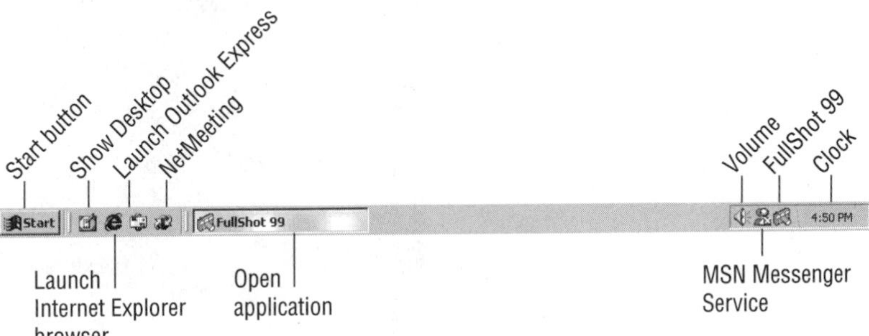

The Taskbar you see here includes a couple of items that you probably don't have on your Taskbar. When you configure NetMeeting, which I'll discuss in Chapter 11, Windows 2000 Professional places a NetMeeting icon on the Taskbar. In order to use the directory services in NetMeeting, you have to install MSN Messenger Service. When you do so, Windows 2000 Professional also places an icon for that program in the status area of the Taskbar.

Here's how to use the icons on the Taskbar:

Show Desktop If you have multiple windows open and you need to access something on your Desktop, click Show Desktop to minimize all the open windows. For this to work, you need to be able to see the Taskbar. I'll discuss hiding and displaying the Taskbar in the next chapter.

Launch Internet Explorer Click to open Internet Explorer.

Launch Outlook Express Click to open Outlook Express.

Volume Click once to display the volume control slider bar and the Mute check box.

Clock Place the mouse cursor over the time to display the current date. To change the time or the date, double-click the time to open the Date/Time Properties dialog box.

The Start Menu

As the name implies, everything on your computer can be initiated from the Start menu. Click the Start button to open the Start menu, and you can launch any program, configure your computer, and access your most recently used documents, all with a click of your mouse—and all without ever stopping the program you are using. You can also customize the Start menu: You can drag icons for your most frequently used applications or files to the Start button, which turns them into menu items that you can click. The following Start menu includes items for Microsoft Office, which I've already installed on my Windows 2000 Professional system.

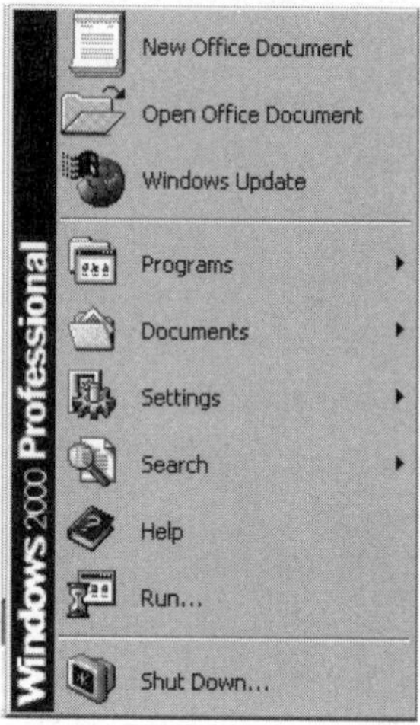

Shortcut Menus

Throughout the work you've done with Windows, you may have noticed that you have two mouse buttons and that most of the time the right one (well, the one that isn't set up as your primary button) is useless. The new Windows 2000 Professional interface rectifies that situation by assigning the right-click action to pop up some kind of context-sensitive menu, called a shortcut menu, for almost every file, folder, drive, or any other object you'll encounter. The items that a shortcut menu includes depend on what you right-click. Common commands include the ability to cut, copy, and paste, as well as the ability to send a document (using the Send To choice) directly to the printer or attach it to an e-mail message. In addition, almost every shortcut menu provides a Properties choice, which is usually your fastest route to discovering the location of a program file in the path and folder hierarchy and for adjusting the way the program or file behaves. An example of a shortcut menu is shown in Figure 3.2. (I'll discuss the Properties item in detail in Chapter 5).

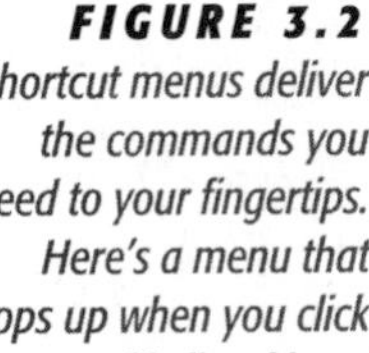

FIGURE 3.2
Shortcut menus deliver the commands you need to your fingertips. Here's a menu that pops up when you click a file listed in an Explorer window.

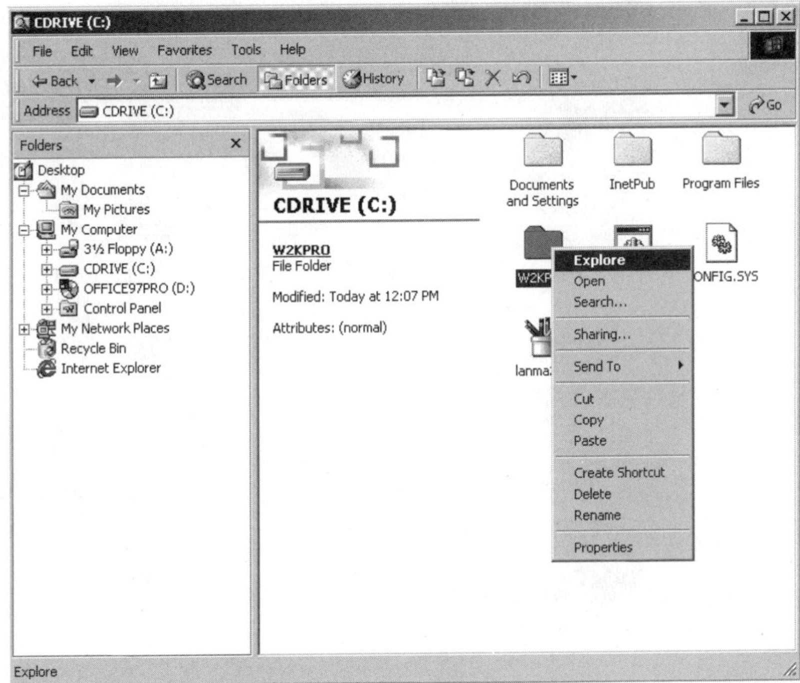

NOTE Some people refer to shortcut menus as right-click menus. Others call them context-sensitive menus. In this book, I'll use the term *shortcut menu,* since that is what Microsoft uses.

TIP You can right-click in Windows 2000 Professional and almost always display something useful. So when in doubt, right-click. At the very least you'll get nothing, and right-clicking can never do any harm.

Folders

The concept of folders is not new to Windows 2000 Professional, but the ways that you can configure and view them is. Figure 3.3 shows the contents of the Winnt folder in Large Icon view, and Figure 3.4 shows the contents of the same folder in List view. You can also move or copy folders anywhere you want, including to the Start menu and the Desktop.

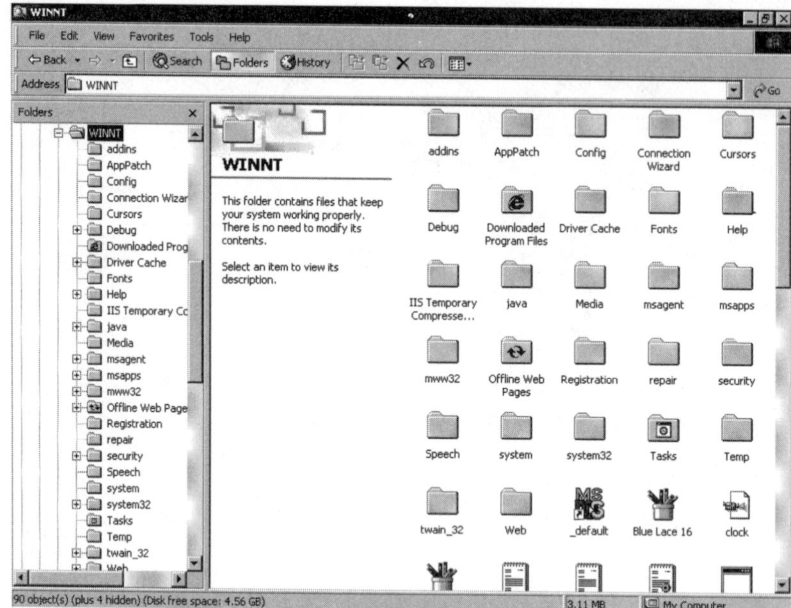

FIGURE 3.3
The Winnt folder in Large Icon view

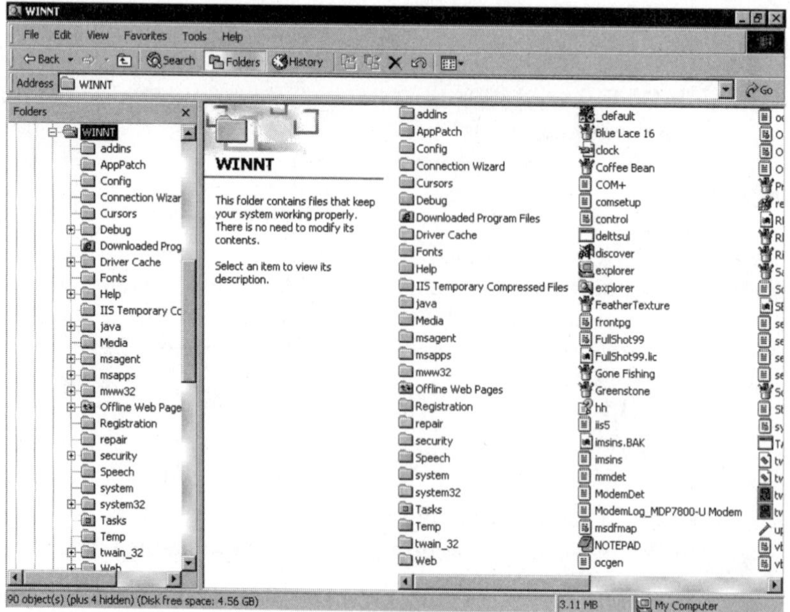

FIGURE 3.4
The Winnt folder in List view

Explorer

In Windows 2000 Professional, Explorer creates the views of everything you interact with, defines how things are displayed, and provides the basic functionality of the Desktop. In a way, Explorer is a part of every Windows 2000 Professional component. Explorer opens a window that lists, hierarchically, the contents of *everything* connected to your computer: whether it be a hard drive or a printer, a device driver or the operating system's Registry, or the hard drives or peripherals connected to another computer on your network. You can move and copy the items in Explorer to initiate connections and to open or run files and applications.

My Computer

My Computer is really just Explorer with a special default presentation: it displays a certain *set* of folders—the top-level folders for your computer's operating system and peripherals. Double-click the My Computer icon to gain instant access to the folders for Control Panel and any storage devices (hard drives, floppy drives, tape drives, CD-ROM drives, and so on) attached to your computer. The default view you see when you double-click My Computer uses a simple one-pane version of Explorer (see Figure 3.5). If you'd rather see the typical two-pane Explorer approach to the same information, simply right-click the My Computer icon (rather than double-click), and choose Explore.

FIGURE 3.5
Double-click My Computer to display a one-pane view.

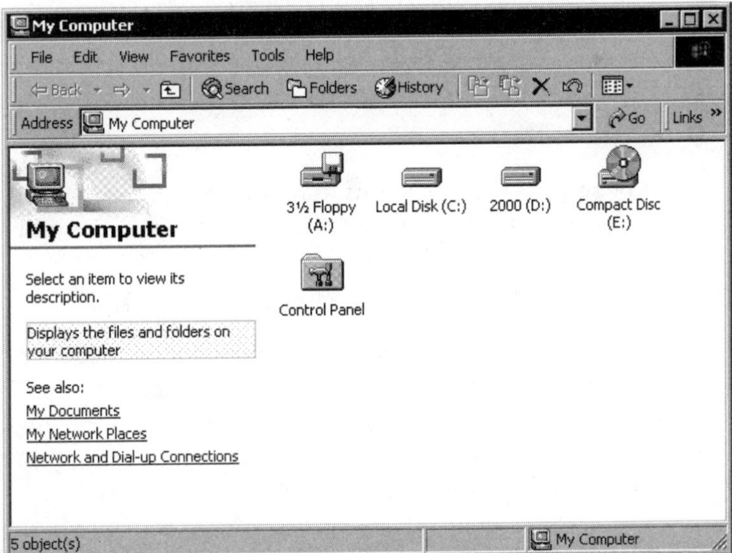

My Network Places

In Windows 2000 Professional, My Network Places replaces Network Neighborhood (found in Windows NT 4 and Windows 95/98). My Network Places is a window to your local network, but it also lets you add persistent network connections, add network printers, and browse the network. My Network Places uses the same Explorer view as My Computer; it supplies Web content on the left side to provide help and guidance (see Figure 3.6).

FIGURE 3.6
My Network Places is a new doorway to all the computers on your network.

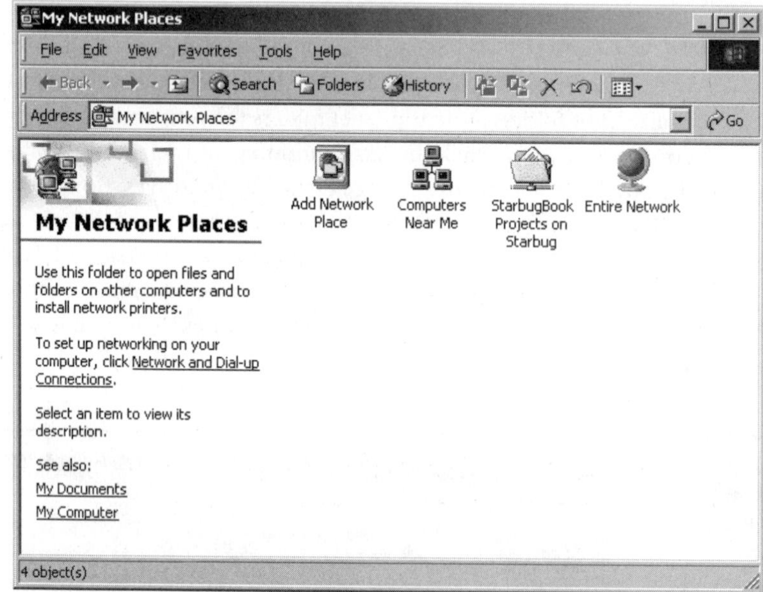

Browsing the network means using an intuitive approach to clicking icons representing servers, hard drives, and files to find the resources you want to use.

Running Programs from the Start Menu

The Start menu is just what its name implies, the place to start working with Windows 2000 Professional. From the submenus, you can access all the various functions of your system. In addition, you can select individual options to show or hide on the Start menu (such as the Administrative Tools group). You can still add your favorite programs to the Start menu too.

To access a program that is installed on your computer system, follow these steps:

1. Click the Start button to open the Start menu.
2. Click Programs.

3. Click the program group that includes the program you want to launch.
4. From the program group's submenu, click the program you want to launch.

NOTE When you install programs on your computer, you can install them into any folder or program group you like, but as a rule, programs create their own program group by default and then place that group on the Start menu's Programs submenu.

The Keyboard Approach to the Start Menu

You can also use the keyboard to access the Start menu:

- To open the Start menu at any time, press Ctrl+Esc, or press the Windows key if it is present on your keyboard.
- To navigate the Start menu and submenus, use the arrow keys as you would in any other graphical user interface, and press Enter to launch the highlighted item.

Running Programs from Explorer and Explorer-Type Windows

From Explorer or any Explorer-type window, you can access any device, program, or file you are authorized to use. What do I mean by "an Explorer-type window"? Well, I mentioned previously that My Computer and My Network Places are simply special sets of folders and devices presented in an Explorer window. You will find in your work with Windows 2000 Professional and with applications in Windows 2000 Professional that other sets of folders and files also appear in windows that behave similarly to Explorer. For example, the window that displays the results of a Find or a Browse action has many of the Explorer menu options built in; similarly, when you choose File ➢ Open in an application, the Open dialog box that lists the available files also shares many characteristics of Explorer.

You can open Explorer in the following ways:

- Right-click the Start button, and choose Explore. Explorer opens with the Start Menu folder selected.
- Choose Start ➢ Programs ➢ Accessories ➢ Windows Explorer.

As you navigate the hierarchical structure of drives and folders presented by Explorer, you will see the icons for each installed program. After you find the program you are looking for in Explorer or in an Explorer-type window, you can launch it in one of two ways:

- Double-click the program's icon.
- Select the program you want to run, and then either press Enter or choose File ➢ Open.

Running Programs from Search

Been looking for the Find command? Think Search instead. In Windows 2000 Professional, the Find command has been replaced with the Search utility. Not only can you use Search to locate files, folders, and people and to look for information on the Internet, you can also use Search to launch any programs that appear in the Search Results window. Simply double-click the program name, or select the program, and choose File ➢ Open.

To find programs and run them from the Search Results window, use the following steps:

1. Choose Start ➢ Search ➢ For Files or Folders to open the Search Results window.

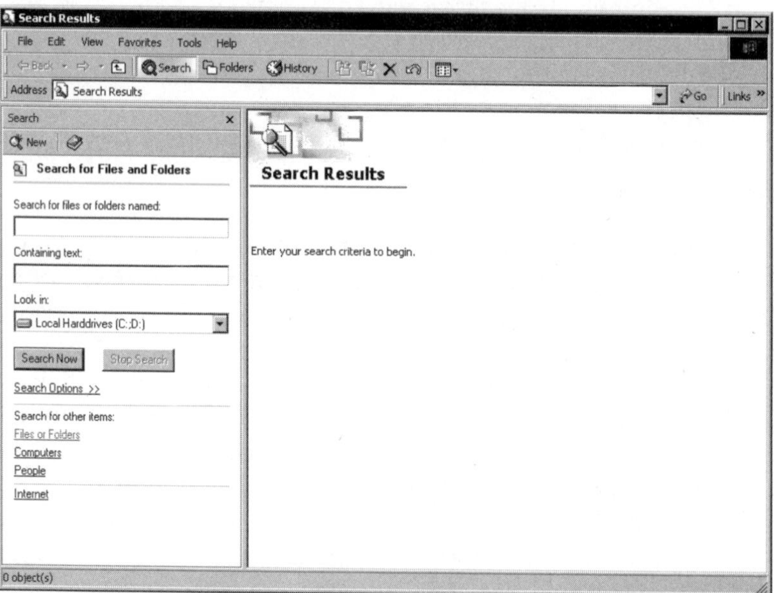

2. Enter the name of the file you want to locate in the Search For Files Or Folders Named text box. You can use wildcards to search for files that have similar spellings, or if you don't know the name of a program you are looking for, enter ***.exe**. You can also search for names containing a particular string of text using the Containing Text field.

3. In the Look In field, use the drop-down list to specify the drive you want to search. You can search any drive connected to your computer, including floppy drives, CD-ROM drives, and mapped network drives. A mapped network drive is any shared folder on the network to which you have assigned a drive letter. You can also search other network locations by browsing for the network folder that you want to search. Use the Look In drop-down list box, and choose Browse from the list to select a local folder or a network folder.
4. Click the Search Now button to start the search. Figure 3.7 shows the results of my search on `*.exe`.

FIGURE 3.7
The results of searching on `*.exe`

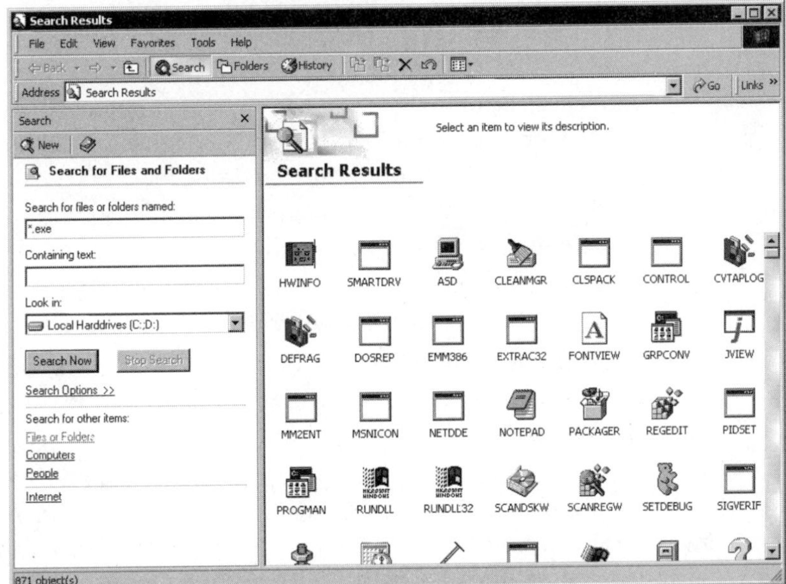

Running Programs by Accessing the Files They Create

You don't necessarily need to *find* a program to launch it. You can also start a program by opening a file or document that has been *associated* with that program. For example, you can double-click a Microsoft Word document in Explorer or in the Search Results window to open Word and also load the file.

You can also start a program by choosing a document from the My Documents list. Choose Start ➢ Documents to open My Documents, and then click a document to open it in its associated program.

Running Programs from Shortcuts

The history of humanity has been spent searching for faster, easier ways to do things. That's why we have microwave ovens, drive-through windows, and *shortcuts*. In Windows 2000 Professional, you can make a shortcut to any object that exists in the operating system—files, folders, programs, hard drives, and other computers on the network. Anything. You can even make shortcuts to other shortcuts!

The shortcut appears as an icon that you can click to open the associated file or resource. Because you can put a shortcut anywhere on the Desktop or anywhere in an Explorer or Explorer-type window, the shortcut can save you a lot of browsing to find your favorite items. Taking a mere 1KB of drive space on average, a shortcut is an economical way to set up quick access to your programs.

To create a shortcut from within an Explorer or Explorer-type window, do one of the following:

- Right-click the object you want to create a shortcut to, and drag the object to the Desktop or to the folder or drive of your choice. Release the mouse button, and choose Create Shortcut(s) Here from the shortcut menu. The item (file, folder, resource, whatever) remains in its original location; the shortcut appears where you dragged it.
- Copy the item you want to create a shortcut to, select the folder in which you want the shortcut to appear, and choose Edit ➢ Paste Shortcut.
- Select an object, choose File ➢ Create Shortcut, and then drag or copy the shortcut thus created to the Desktop or to the folder or drive of your choice.

Anything you can do to a file you can do to a shortcut. If you send a shortcut via e-mail to another MS Exchange Mail user, the recipient can double-click the shortcut to access the original file, or the recipient can copy the shortcut to their Desktop or anywhere else in their computer. This is a great way to distribute information across a network!

Running Programs by Using Run

You can also use the Start menu's Run command to launch applications. When you choose Start ➢ Run, you'll see the following dialog box:

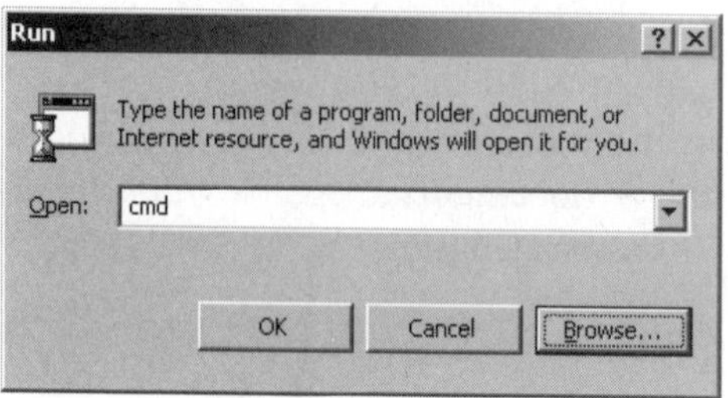

If you're like most users, you don't know or care where your application files are living on your hard drive, and you might not notice how their names are spelled. For you, the Browse button was invented. Click the Browse button in the Run dialog box to open the Browse dialog box:

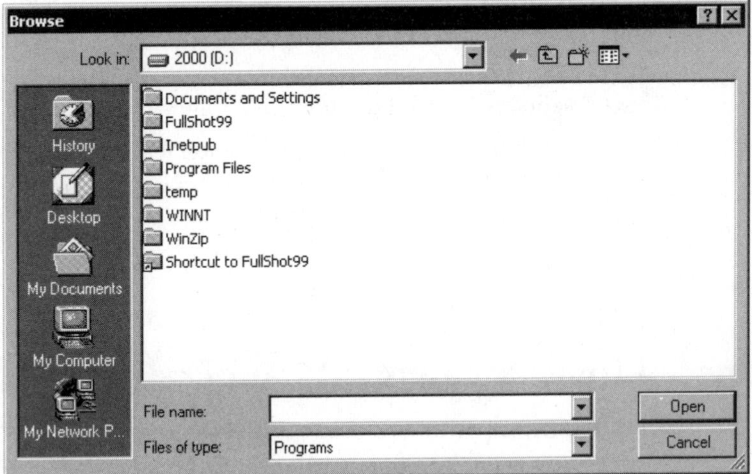

After you find the file, launch it as you would in Explorer.

NOTE If you are one of those people who remember precisely where your files are and how their names are spelled, you could type the path and the name of the application you want to run in the Run dialog box. But you have to know the full path, meaning you have to know what drive and folder the file is in. For most people, it's a lot easier to click the Browse button.

Here are some added benefits of the Run dialog box:

- You can use it to open and explore the contents of any disk device attached to your computer. For example, if you have two floppy drives and you want to see the contents of your B drive, open the Run dialog box, type **B:**, and press Enter. An Explorer window opens and displays the contents of the disk or drive.
- The Run command remembers what it has done for you in the past. Each time you use Run, it adds every file, folder, or drive that you launch or open to its drop-down list. Let's say you just ran a program, either by typing the application's path and filename or by using the Run dialog box's Browse feature. You would never again need to type that program's path or browse for it; you can just choose it from the drop-down list.

Running Programs Minimized

You can set every program on your hard drive to run minimized. When you minimize a program, you shrink the size of the program window so that it appears as a button on your Taskbar. Running a program minimized can be helpful if you want to start a program that you know you will need to use, but not immediately. Or, if you start certain programs automatically, you can have them run minimized and not clutter your Desktop right away.

To set an application to run minimized, follow these steps:

1. Right-click the shortcut to the application (either on the Desktop or in Explorer), and choose Properties from the shortcut menu to open the Properties dialog box for the application.
2. In the Run drop-down list box, select Minimized.
3. Click OK.

Special Topic: Running DOS Applications

You can run DOS applications under Windows 2000 Professional in two ways. You may ask, "Why would I want to bother with DOS, anyway?" Well, it's not always a question of wanting to; sometimes it's a question of needing to run DOS. There is a tremendous installed base of DOS software, and you never know when you might have to run some of it in order to finish a project started by someone else or to look at something historical in its original application. (Or maybe you just can't get enough of your favorite DOS games. That's a necessity, right?)

NOTE You don't need to have DOS installed on your system to run a DOS application under Windows 2000 Professional.

The easiest way to run a DOS program is to run it the same way you would run a Windows program: locate the DOS program by using Explorer, and then double-click its icon to launch it. No problem.

Many computer users are also comfortable using the command prompt (sometimes called the DOS prompt, even though in Windows 2000 Professional it isn't DOS) to give instructions to their computer, including instructions to run programs. In some cases, using the command prompt is faster because you avoid the overhead used by the Windows GUI (graphical user interface).

To use the command prompt to run a DOS program, follow these steps:

1. Choose Start ➢ Programs ➢ Accessories ➢ Command Prompt to open a window that looks remarkably like DOS but that is actually the 32-bit command line interface of Windows 2000 Professional:

2. At the prompt, type the path and name of the DOS program you want to run, for example, type **C:\wp5\wp51**, to run WordPerfect version 5.1.

When you use the command prompt, most of the old DOS commands you may remember will work. The exceptions, as I mentioned earlier, are any commands that try to access hardware directly:

- You can't use `SCANDISK` (formerly used to check hard disk errors). Instead, in Explorer, right-click a drive to open that drive's Properties dialog box. Select the Tools tab, and in the Error-Checking section, click Check Now to open the CHKDSK dialog box. Select the appropriate options, and click Start to check the disk for errors. Or, at the command prompt type **CHKDSK/F** to run Check Disk.
- You can't use `DEFRAG` (formerly used to defragment your hard disk). Instead, use Disk Defragmenter. Choose Start ➢ Programs ➢ Accessories ➢ System Tools ➢ Disk Defragmenter to open the Disk Defragmenter dialog box. Select the disk, and click Defragment.
- You can't use `LOCK` (formerly used to reserve direct access to the hard drive). Instead, you can use the Windows 2000 Professional administration features to grant and verify rights to specific users and objects.
- You can't use any DOS commands that compromise security.

Switching from One Window to Another

Windows 2000 Professional provides some easy ways to go back and forth between your open windows and applications.

Using Alt+Tab to Switch

The keyboard approach to switching from one task to another is the Alt+Tab key combination. When you press these two keys together, a dialog box opens, showing icons and names for each of the items you have open. (Actually, this was available in earlier versions of Windows as well, but from many reports the technique wasn't well known.) Hold down the Alt key while repeatedly pressing the Tab key to highlight each icon in a cycle. When the item you want to go to is highlighted, release the Alt+Tab keys to go to that item's window.

Using the Taskbar to Switch

Everything you have open, including windows for folders and drives, is listed on the Taskbar. The Taskbar isn't just for display, however. Each smaller bar you see on the Taskbar (shown in the following graphic) acts as a button. You can click the button to move the Desktop's focus to the item it represents, thus bringing its window to the front if it has been obscured or maximizing it if it has been minimized.

Configuring the Taskbar

You can customize the Taskbar in many ways to make switching between applications even easier.

- The simplest thing you can do is to *reposition* the Taskbar to whichever side of your monitor screen you prefer: bottom (the default), top, left, or right. To reposition the Taskbar, just click it and drag it where you want it to go.
- Almost as easy as repositioning the Taskbar is *resizing* it, to allow more or less of each Taskbar button to appear. Coincidentally, beyond a certain point, resizing also causes more or fewer of the buttons to appear, because a much greater height creates space for an extra row of buttons. To resize the Taskbar, move the mouse pointer to the boundary line between the Taskbar and the Desktop, at which point the pointer should change to a drag pointer, and then click and drag to increase or decrease the height or width of the bar.

NOTE One edge of the Taskbar always extends across the full width or height of the screen, depending on which edge it is positioned along. You can resize only its smaller dimension.

You can further customize the Taskbar, and we'll look at how to do so in Chapter 4.

Making File Associations

Not all your files and documents will hang out with just any program that will buy them a drink. Many types of documents need to be properly introduced to specific programs, and a real relationship must be defined, before they'll go out together. The way to do this is by *file association*. Essentially, this means that when you open files with certain filename extensions (such as DOC, WP, and XLS, for example, among many, many others), Windows 2000 Professional always identifies those files as ones to be opened in certain applications (such as Word, WordPerfect, and Excel, respectively, to continue the example).

For the most part, you don't need to worry about file associations—the associations are set up automatically when you first install an application. Occasionally, however, associations are lost after a program crashes. Also, you might occasionally receive a file of an indiscernible file type from a business associate or a friend. In these cases, you may have to force the file into an association with the most likely application. If this happens, Windows 2000 Professional prompts you to associate the file.

You can associate a program with a file in a couple of ways. Here's a really safe and easy way:

1. In Explorer, hold down Shift and right-click a file.
2. From the shortcut menu, choose Open With to open the Open With dialog box:

3. Select the program, click the Always Use This Program To Open These Files check box if that's what you want to do, and click OK.

NOTE You can also use the My Computer folder to associate files, and I'll discuss that procedure in the next chapter.

NOTE Windows 2000 Professional uses file associations to keep track of which programs you use to open different types of applications. Each time you install a new application, it registers itself and the types of files it can open in the Windows 2000 Professional *Registry*. The Registry is a database that keeps track of how your computer is configured, down to the tiniest detail. An in-depth description of the Registry is beyond the scope of this book. For a thorough discussion, see *Mastering Windows 2000 Professional Registry,* by Peter D. Hipson (Sybex, 2000).

WARNING Unless you are absolutely sure that you know exactly what you're doing, don't fiddle with the Registry. Most users never have a need to do so, and if you are on a corporate network, you probably don't have permission anyway. Messing up the Registry can turn your computer into an enormous doorstop, that is, render it completely useless. And if this warning seems overly severe, I've gotten my point across.

Finding Programs

Finding the programs that are installed on your system should be easy, right? But it's not, especially if you have lots of programs and different versions of the same programs. Some programs install themselves in their own folders, and others install themselves a level deeper than that. They install inside their own folders, to be sure, but those folders are in turn installed in a folder called Program Files (see Figure 3.8). The idea behind this is that finding all your programs is easier if they are installed in the same place.

TIP Keep in mind that with most programs, you are given the option to install your program into any folder you like. Install your programs where they make the most sense to you, but remember that if you ever need to refer to the program's manual for troubleshooting help, it will refer to files as though they are in the default setup location—so for your own sake write your changes in the manual.

FIGURE 3.8
The Program Files folder is the keeper of many programs.

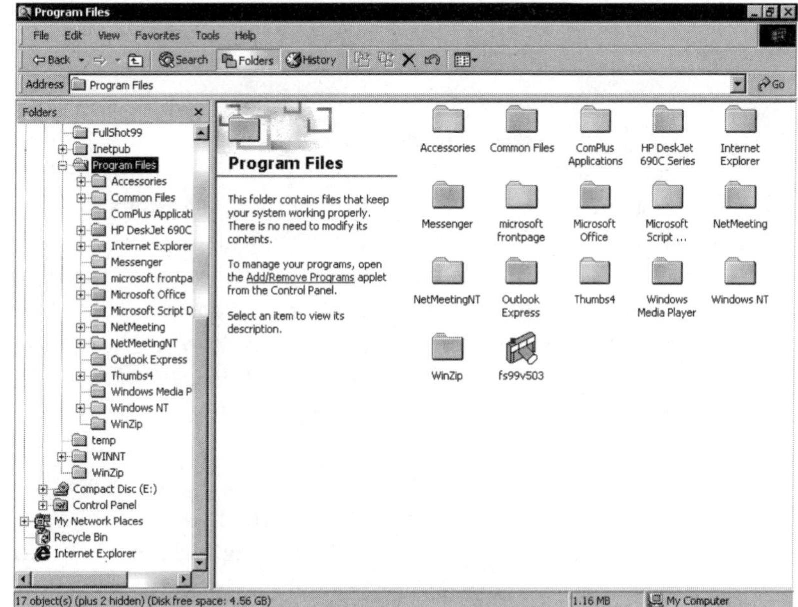

Installing and Removing Programs

Installing and removing programs under Windows 2000 Professional is easy. Almost without exception, programs include their own installation utility that not only copies all their files to the necessary folders but also takes care of creating program groups and placing them on the Program submenu. Removing programs, which has become more and more difficult as programs have become more and more sophisticated and powerful, is also easy, provided you installed them using the better of the three installation procedures outlined below.

Installing Programs

You can install programs under Windows 2000 Professional in three ways. Here's the way you'd probably expect:

1. Insert the CD-ROM or floppy disk that contains the program you want to install.
2. Open Explorer, and navigate to the floppy or CD-ROM drive.
3. Double-click the program's Setup or Install program. Follow the directions that the installation routine gives you for installing the program. Many programs

have numerous installation options, including Custom, which usually lets you select how many utilities and features you want to install and where you want to install them. Install these programs according to your needs and available disk space. If a program offers you a feature you don't need, don't install it. You can always go back later and install the program's extra features if you change your mind.

Another easy way to install an application in Windows 2000 Professional is to use the program's Auto Run feature. Most of the applications written for Windows can automatically run the Setup program when you insert the CD-ROM into the computer. This is often the easiest method to use, and you can usually remove the program using the Add/Remove Programs applet in Control Panel.

The best way to install programs, however, is to take advantage of the Add/Remove Programs applet, which launches a program's installation routine for you while offering the added protection of monitoring the software that is being installed. This monitoring process is useful for two reasons:

- When a program is installed, it places files in several locations on your hard drive. These files are difficult to locate if you want to completely remove a program from your hard drive. By keeping track of what it installs onto your system, Windows 2000 Professional makes it easier for you if you ever want to uninstall the program at some later time.
- Windows 2000 Professional can enforce a higher measure of security, preventing deleterious programs from causing damage while being installed.

To use the Windows 2000 Professional Add/Remove Programs applet, follow these steps:

1. Choose Start ➢ Settings ➢ Control Panel to open Control Panel.
2. Double-click Add/Remove Programs to open the Add/Remove Programs dialog box.
3. Click the Add New Programs icon to open the dialog box shown in Figure 3.9.

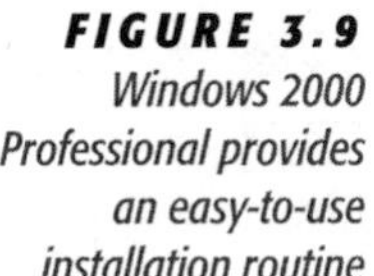

FIGURE 3.9
Windows 2000 Professional provides an easy-to-use installation routine

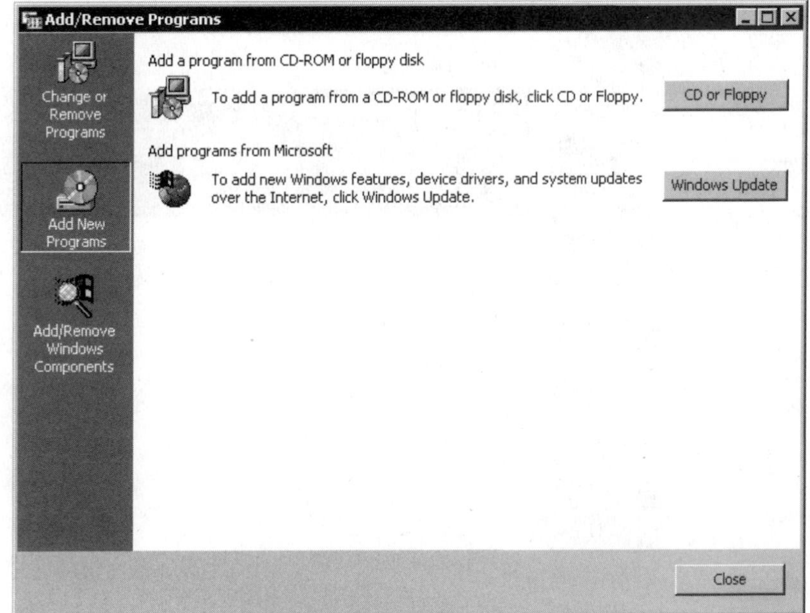

4. If the program is on a CD or floppy, click the CD Or Floppy button to open the Install Program From Floppy Disk Or CD-ROM dialog box.
5. Insert the CD or floppy, and then click Next.
6. Click Finish, and then follow the on-screen instructions.

Removing Programs

As I mentioned earlier, Windows 2000 Professional can remove programs for you as well as install them.

To remove programs, do the following:

1. Choose Start ➢ Setting ➢ Control Panel to open Control Panel.
2. Double-click Add/Remove Programs to open the Add/Remove Programs dialog box. You'll see a list of currently installed programs (see Figure 3.10).

FIGURE 3.10
Windows 2000 Professional provides a list of installed programs you can remove.

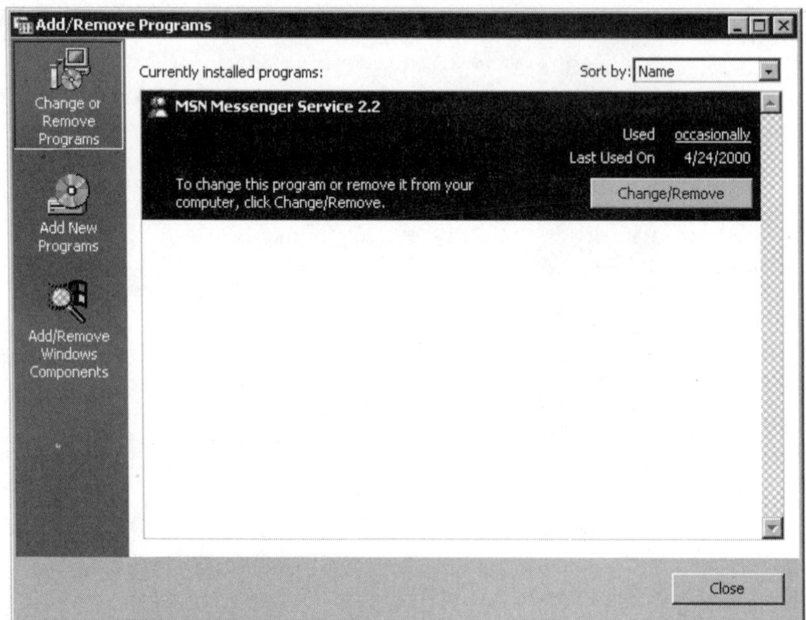

3. Select the program on the list that you want to remove.
4. Click the Change/Remove button to begin the removal process. Follow the on-screen instructions.

Special Topic: Running Programs in Dual-Boot Mode with Windows 95/98

If hard-drive space is not an issue, you might do well to consider running your system in dual-boot mode, with both Windows 2000 Professional and Windows 95/98, because doing so lets you take advantage of the strengths of both operating systems. For example, you could switch to Windows 95/98 to play the games that Windows 2000 Professional won't permit and then switch to Windows 2000 Professional to use your word processing program to write about the games in your award-winning hint book. Another use for this arrangement is to check out how well your favorite applications run under two different systems: You could run them first under 95/98 and then switch to Windows 2000 Professional to see if it really makes any difference in the way they work.

Unfortunately, it takes a little work to get the programs you installed under Windows 98 operating and running smoothly under Windows 2000 Professional. The main obstacle to being immediately able to run all your preinstalled programs is that you now have two system folders. In general, Windows system folders contain all the DLLs and other essential program files that enable your programs to run in the first place. Windows 2000 Professional and Windows 95/98 (and Windows 3.1, for that matter) each have separate system folders. They are set in the path statements for each operating system. The problem is, if you've installed Windows 2000 Professional on a system that was already running Windows 95/98, all your previously installed applications have their DLLs in your Windows 95/98 system folder. When you try to run those same programs under Windows 2000 Professional, Windows 2000 Professional looks for them in its own system folder and of course can't find them there.

The quick solution to the system folder discrepancy problem is to add your Windows 95/98 system folder to your Windows 2000 Professional path. By doing that, Windows 2000 Professional looks in both its own and the Windows 95/98 system folders. (I discussed this procedure in Chapter 2.)

But the best way to have programs available to you in both Windows 95/98 and Windows 2000 Professional is to reinstall the programs in Windows 2000 Professional. This isn't as bad as it sounds. You should choose to install the program in the same folder where it is already installed. Setup programs won't overwrite any data; they just copy the files that are missing. In the case of the application files, none are missing in the Programs folder, but all are missing from the Windows 2000 Professional system folder. By reinstalling the application, you are installing the system files Windows 2000 Professional needs to run the application and making the correct Registry entries so the program will run properly.

If you're jumping ahead of the discussion here, be careful: Don't copy the contents of one system folder into another. Despite the similar natures of Windows 2000 Professional and Windows 95/98, they often use different versions of the same files. Replacing even one file with the wrong version can prevent either operating system from running with full functionality or perhaps even booting at all!

Summary

Running all your favorite applications (and even the programs you don't like) is easier under Windows 2000 Professional than in previous versions of Windows. More than being easier, it's more convenient. You now have a variety of ways to run and open files, and with shortcuts, you can put the buttons that you click right where you want them.

Even though Windows 2000 Professional is a 32-bit operating system, it still runs 16-bit Windows and DOS programs as well or even better than Windows 3.1 or DOS. As you'll recall, this is because Windows 2000 Professional uses a separate memory space for 16-bit Windows and DOS programs, protecting them from one another and keeping your operating system safe from crashing programs. Remember, if a program does go errant on you, you can put it out of its misery with a swift Ctrl+Alt+Delete key combination.

In short, Windows 2000 Professional enables you to run your programs—almost all of them—better, faster, and more easily.

CHAPTER 4

Organizing Programs and Documents

FEATURING:

An operating system is like your desk. Or more accurately, it's like your whole office. If your office is cluttered, you will find it harder to find things and to be as productive as you like. The same goes for your operating system. Like other operating systems, Windows 2000 Professional not only offers its own filing system, it pretty much forces you to use it. However, just as you may be in the habit of keeping stacks of mail in a drawer of your office filing cabinet because you never get around to buying those special hanging folders, you can misuse (or under-use) the Windows 2000 Professional file system and not capitalize on its strengths. Fortunately, Windows 2000 Professional has numerous tools, tricks, and enhanced usability features to keep you organized.

Using the Start Menu

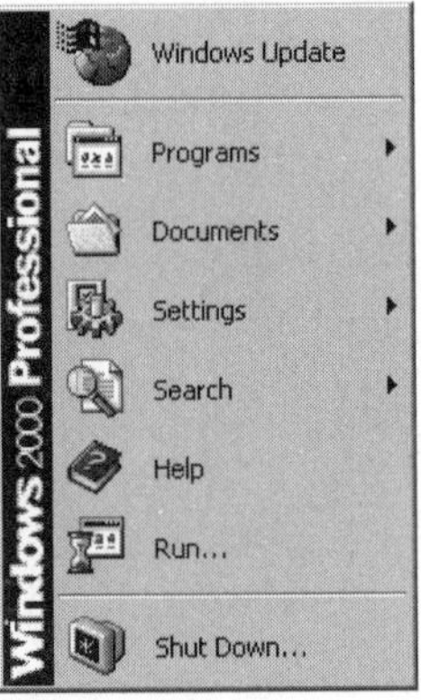

Clicking the Start button displays the Start menu, which, as the name implies, is the place to go first. From the Start menu, you can find anything you need or want on your system—and that includes anything on any machines to which you have permissions to through a shared or network arrangement. You can easily modify the Start menu to display shortcuts to any program, file, or resource (such as a printer or an external tape drive). By default, it provides a fast way to access the Help system, a command for opening Control Panel (to change your computer's settings), commands for launching tools such as Search, and the command for shutting down the system. Because you can access the Start menu no matter which application you're using, you always have instant access to the "controls" for your computer. If you have a Windows keyboard, you can quickly access the Start menu by pressing the special Windows key; you can also press the Ctrl and Esc keys simultaneously to display the Start menu.

Adding Your Favorite Programs to the Start Menu

If you copy any file, program, or system object (printers, hard drives) to the Start menu, Windows 2000 Professional automatically creates a shortcut to that item—and because it's on the Start menu, you can access those shortcuts any time, no matter what other programs you are running.

To create a shortcut on the Start menu, drag the file you want onto the Start button. The next time you click the Start button, the shortcut to that file will appear at the top of the Start menu.

TIP A damaged or accidentally deleted shortcut won't affect the file to which it points. If the shortcut is damaged, Windows 2000 Professional will automatically search for the object the shortcut points to when you try to open it.

Arranging Open Windows with the Taskbar

Like most objects you can click in the Windows 2000 Professional environment, the Start menu and Taskbar provide shortcut menus that you can use to set options for controlling their behavior and appearance. (I'll get into details about shortcut menus in Chapter 5. In this chapter, you get to see some of the most immediate advantages of using them.)

You can quickly change the size and position of all open applications on the Desktop by making choices from the Taskbar's shortcut menu. Simply right-click any empty area on the Taskbar to display a menu with the following choices:

Toolbars Lets you add or customize the toolbars that appear on the Taskbar. The default toolbar is the Quick Launch toolbar with icons for Show Desktop, Launch Internet Explorer Browser, and Launch Outlook Express.

Adjust Date/Time Lets you adjust the date, time, and time zone. Click Adjust Date/Time to open the Date/Time Properties dialog box.

Cascade Windows Places each of your open applications across your Desktop, one almost on top of another. Your windows look somewhat like a deck of cards spread across a dealer's table.

Tile Windows Horizontally Arranges your current applications in equal-sized horizontal windows so that you can see some contents of every window at once.

Tile Windows Vertically Arranges your current applications in equal-sized vertical windows so that you can see some contents of every window at once.

Minimize All Windows Minimizes all your open applications to the Taskbar. This is probably the fastest way to clear the Desktop when it is cluttered, although the Show Desktop icon on the Quick Launch toolbar performs the same function.

TIP When you click a program that has been minimized (shows up as a button on the Taskbar), it returns to its former size and position on the Desktop.

Undo Tile and Undo Minimize All Undoes whatever Taskbar action you last performed. The first time you right-click the Taskbar, these commands do not appear.

Task Manager Opens Task Manager, which is useful for terminating an unresponsive application or getting a quick view of the system's performance.

Properties Displays the Taskbar and Start Menu Properties dialog box. The options in this dialog box not only let you arrange items on the Start menu and the Taskbar, but also let you specify the opening and closing behaviors of those items. You can control which options are displayed in the Start menu by selecting the Advanced tab in the Taskbar And Start Menu Properties dialog box. For example, you can choose to display the Administrative Tools group, Favorites, and Logoff.

Customizing the Start Menu and Taskbar

To customize the Start menu and the Taskbar, you use the Taskbar And Start Menu Properties dialog box:

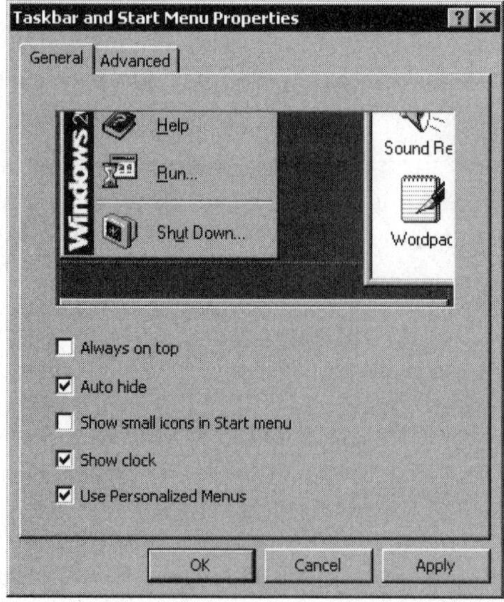

Let's look at the options on both the General and the Advanced tabs.

The General Tab

You use the options on the General tab to specify some basic settings:

Always On Top Keeps the Taskbar visible at all times. This is the default setting. (Screen saver programs ignore this setting, however, as they blank the entire screen.)

Auto Hide Hides the Taskbar until you move your mouse pointer to where the Taskbar is hidden. Auto Hiding the Taskbar is useful if you have limited screen space or if you just don't like the look of the Taskbar.

Show Small Icons Un Start Menu Shrinks the size of the icons on the Start menu and removes the Windows 2000 Professional label that appears on the left side of the Start menu. If you have limited screen space or just want to reduce the size of the Start menu, select this option.

Show Clock Adds or removes the clock that by default is displayed at the far end of the Taskbar.

Use Personalized Menus Tells Windows 2000 Professional to remember the items you most often use and display only them on menus. Clear this check box if you don't want to use personalized menus.

TIP Remember, you don't need to set any options to reposition the Taskbar. At any time, you can simply click the Taskbar and drag it to whichever edge of the screen you like.

The Advanced Tab

Although I wouldn't suggest using the Advanced tab to add or remove programs to your Start menu (it is no match for the ease of the drag-and-drop approach outlined at the beginning of this chapter), using the options on the Advanced tab gives you more control over the appearance of the items on your Start menu, allowing you to change such items as the following:

- The icon that appears next to an item on the Start menu
- The order of the items on the Start menu
- The size of an item's window after it is opened
- Other options, depending on your system configuration

Of Wizards and Mini-Explorers

The route you'll follow to change settings in Windows 2000 Professional will often take you to one of the following types of assistant programs:

- A Wizard, which is a series of dialog boxes and folders programmed specifically to prompt you for additional information relating to the option you initially chose
- An Explorer-like window (or sometimes Explorer itself) that knows from the context of what you're doing to open folders and menus from which you can make appropriate selections

You'll see a couple of minor examples of these assistants in the following discussions. If you haven't yet mastered Explorer, don't worry; you'll just get a taste of what it can do in these next few paragraphs. I'll discuss Explorer in detail in the rest of this chapter.

Removing Programs from the Start Menu

To remove programs from the Start menu, follow these steps:

1. Right-click the Taskbar and choose Properties from the shortcut menu to open the Taskbar And Start Menu Properties dialog box.
2. Click the Advanced tab.

3. Click the Remove button to open the Remove Shortcuts/Folders dialog box.
4. Select the item you want to remove, and then click Remove.
5. A dialog box asks if you are sure you want to delete the program. (Are you? Click OK if you are sure.)
6. Click the Close button to finish the process.

The Advanced Button and Explorer

If you go to Explorer, you can use its View menu to rearrange the items in the Start Menu folder (or any of its subfolders). You can go to Explorer any way you like, but if you don't remember where your Start Menu folder lies in the hierarchy of your hard drive, you may need to hunt for it. (In fact, your computer may have a confusing multitude of Start Menu folders. Remember that because Windows 2000 Professional is a multiuser environment, you can have different Start menus for the different types of work you do. Also, all other users who log on to your system have their own profile, and that profile includes their individual folder of Start menu items.)

Windows 2000 Professional can help you make short work of this confusion by taking you directly to your own current Start Menu folder. Clicking the Advanced button on the Advanced tab opens an Explorer window with your Start Menu folder open, the Start menu's items listed, and the commands and buttons for rearranging, renaming, and copying those items right at hand. While you're there, you can continue to use Explorer to do just about anything else you might normally want to do with Explorer, just as you would if you had run Explorer by itself.

NOTE When you right-click the Start button and choose Explorer in Windows 2000 Professional, the default view is your own Start Menu folder. To access the common groups of the Start menu, browse to the All Users folder, and edit the Start menu there. This enables you to modify the Start menu programs that everyone using the computer will see.

Using Explorer

Explorer could almost *be* your Desktop, really, because anything you might want to do to a file or program, and any configuration changes you want to make to your operating environment, can be done right from Explorer.

NOTE Actually, Explorer is the shell for Windows 2000 Professional as well as a separate utility for browsing local resources on your computer.

In Windows 98, Explorer added some active content that uses HyperText Markup Language (HTML) files to describe the contents of individual folders. This helped to decrease the separation of your computer from the Internet. Windows 2000 Professional has carried on that idea, but Microsoft changed the emphasis in the GUI away from the Internet and more toward ease of use. You can enable the same functionality that Windows 98 includes, but the default configuration of Windows 2000 Professional has more separation between your computer and the Internet.

Opening vs. Exploring

One thing you'll notice right away when you use Explorer is a difference between *opening* a Desktop object and *exploring* a Desktop object. Figure 4.1a and b shows the difference. Opening a Desktop object opens a window that shows only the contents of the object or the folder. When you open the program called My Computer, for example, you'll see its contents, but nothing else: no toolbar, no double panes. However, if you explore the same program (that is, if you right-click the My Computer icon, either on the Desktop or in a file list where it appears) and choose Explore from the shortcut menu, the window that opens proudly displays a toolbar full of useful buttons and a right pane for displaying the contents of whatever you select in the left pane. These are the telltale features of Explorer. If you already know where you want to go, that is, the location of the file or object you want to access, Open is the way to go. But, as the name suggests, Explorer functions best when you want to "explore" the computer for the file or application you want to use.

FIGURE 4.1a
Opening My Computer produces a single window.

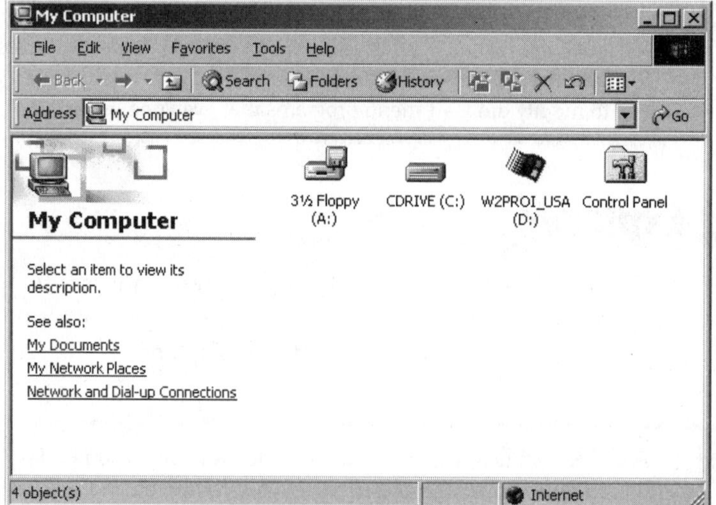

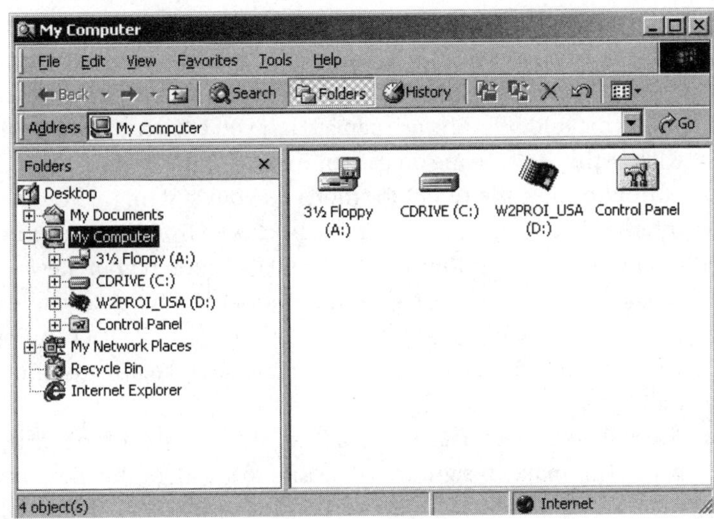

FIGURE 4.1b
Exploring My Computer opens the entire Explorer window for the same set of objects.

Branches

It's easy to think of Windows Explorer as the filing system of Windows 2000 Professional. It may be more accurate, though, to describe it as a window to the filing system of Windows 2000 Professional. The views in Windows Explorer depict an upside down tree with its root being My Computer. It branches down from there showing the various connected drives and other resources. The simplest way to access this view is to right-click My Computer on the Desktop and select Explore from the shortcut menu. When you open Explorer, you'll notice two panes: on the left is a view of the tree structure of your system; on the right is a group of icons and names representing all the main branches or resources of your computer.

TIP Each item that appears in Explorer is considered an object. Every object has its own properties, many of which you can modify to suit your needs, regardless of whether you're working with a file, a folder, a program, or a network computer. Although Explorer is often thought of as a method to view or locate objects, you could just as easily think of it as the glue that holds this diverse environment together.

Views

You can arrange objects in Explorer in many ways, all of which are called *views*. The View menu not only controls how objects in the right Explorer pane appear, but also how Explorer itself can be configured to work best for you.

The view that you choose affects only the right Explorer pane. The left pane, the Folders pane, always looks the same—an expandable list of the folders and files—but you can eliminate it in Windows 2000 Professional by clicking its Close button. (To restore the Folders pane, click the Folders button on the toolbar.) The default view shows the folders in the left pane, but if you click the Search button in the toolbar, you will see the Search pane on the left instead of the folders. You can also click the History button to show the recent locations on your system (or your network, or even the Internet) that you've visited. You can choose from five views in Explorer, and you can arrange the icons in four ways after you've chosen your view.

Large Icons view (see Figure 4.2) is probably the view you're most familiar with. In this view, the icons are large and easily recognizable. Depending on how many files you have in a particular folder, the icons can take up most if not all the space in the right Explorer pane.

Small Icons view (see Figure 4.3) shrinks the size of the icons on the right Explorer pane. This makes it significantly easier to see all of the files in a folder—particularly if there are a lot of them, as in the Windows folder.

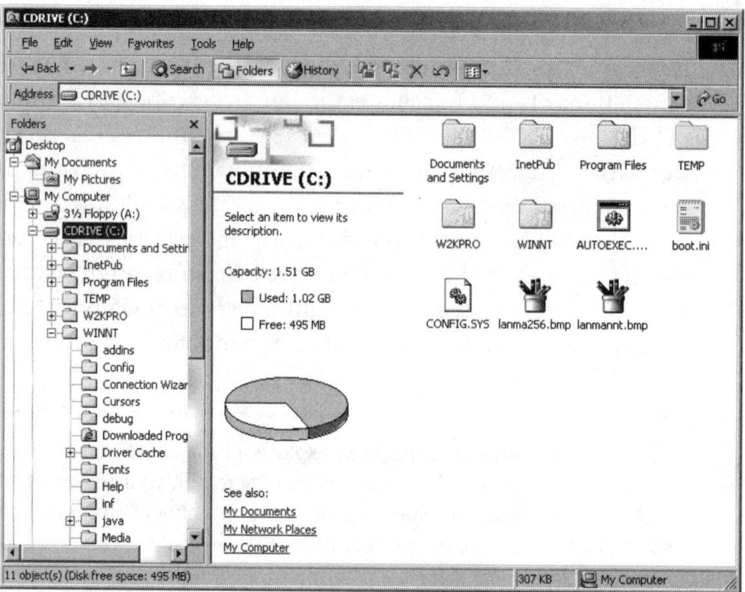

FIGURE 4.2
This is Large Icons view, which is Explorer's default view.

List view (see Figure 4.4) looks much like Small Icons view except that the objects are displayed in columns. Folders appear first, arranged alphabetically along the left side of the pane, and then the rest of the files appear, also arranged alphabetically.

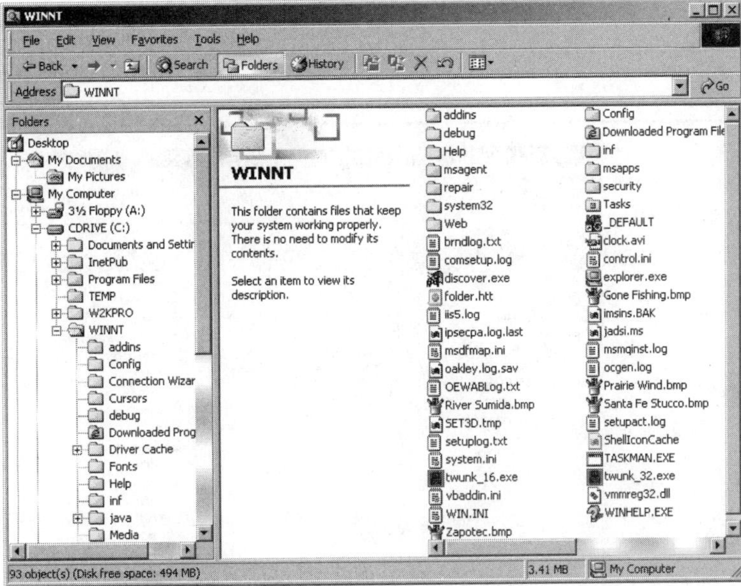

FIGURE 4.3
This is Small Icons view.

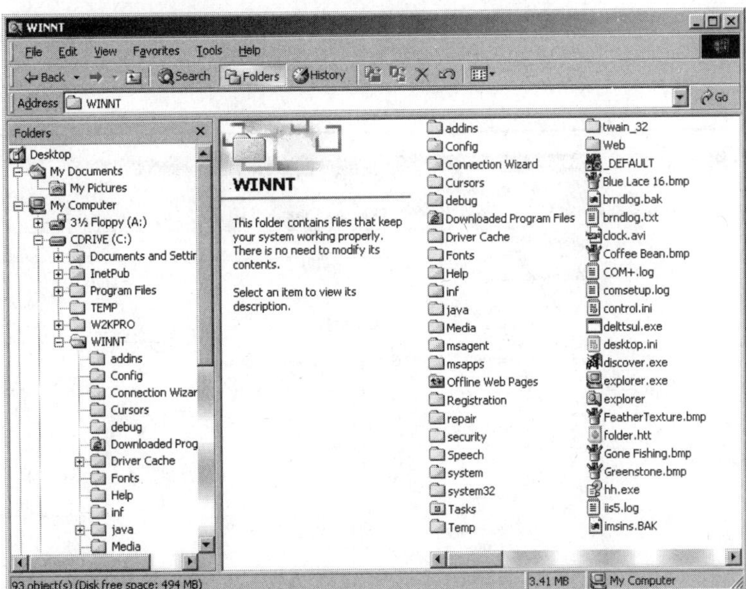

FIGURE 4.4
This is List view.

Details view (see Figure 4.5) moves all the icons to the left-most column and uses the other columns for file/object information. This information includes the file type (which is determined by how the file is associated), the size of the file, and the date the file was last modified or saved.

Thumbnails view (see Figure 4.6) is particularly useful for sorting through graphic files. With this view, the graphic files are displayed as miniatures that you can sort through quickly to find just the picture you need.

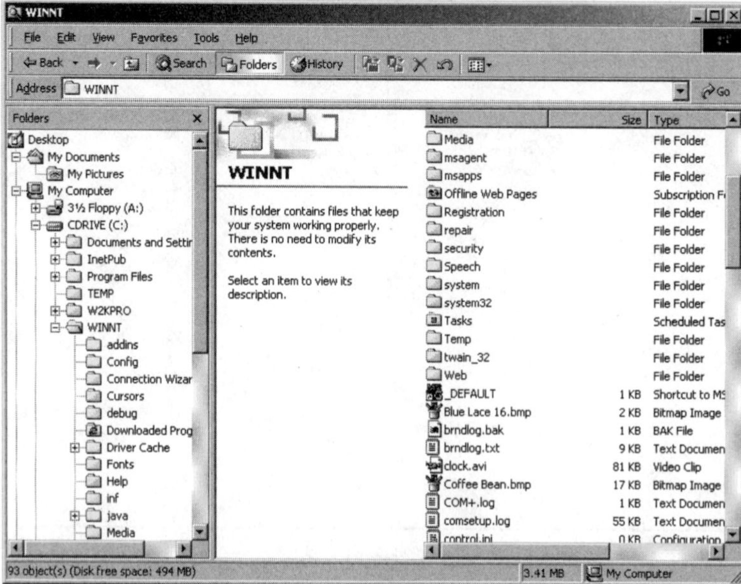

FIGURE 4.5
This is Details view.

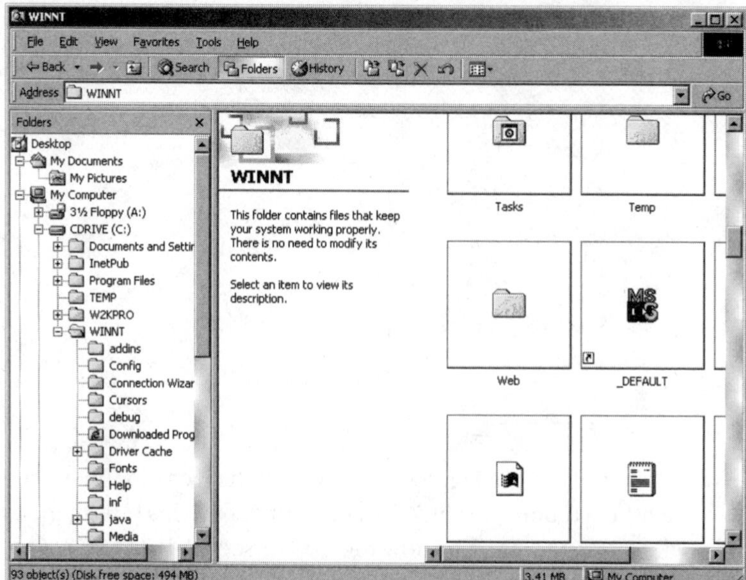

FIGURE 4.6
This is Thumbnails view.

So why do you care about all this organizing? What if you can't remember the name of a file you need, but you do remember the date it was created? Or what if you know which application created the file and what the file extension is? With Explorer, you can arrange the items in the right pane so that they are sorted or organized by name, size, date, or file type. You can then see at a glance what is and isn't inside the folder.

To rearrange the order of your files in Explorer's right pane, choose View ➢ Arrange Icons, and then select an option from the submenu. Name and date are self-explanatory; type refers to the three-character extension at the end of the filename (for example, this book was written as a DOC file); and size refers to the size of the file in bytes, kilobytes, or megabytes, whichever is appropriate.

You can also set the View using the Views button on the toolbar, and you can arrange the icons by right-clicking anywhere in the right pane, clicking Arrange Icons, and selecting an order from the submenu.

TIP Select Auto Arrange if you want the folders to always arrange automatically.

Toolbar

Toolbars are one of the great inventions in personal computing. They place the most common functions in a program where you can easily get to them when you want. Figure 4.7 shows the toolbar in Explorer.

FIGURE 4.7 *The Explorer toolbar brings common commands to your fingertips.*

From left to right, here's what each of the Explorer toolbar buttons do for you:

Back Returns you to the previous folder location. This works just like the Back button in your favorite Web browser.

Forward This button also works just like the Forward button in your Web browser in that it moves you forward one step in your browsing (assuming that you have already been there and moved back with the Back button).

Up This button moves you up one folder in the hierarchy.

Search This button opens the Search pane on the left side of Explorer. You can use this Search pane just like the Search utility on the Start menu—to find files, folders, people, and computers.

Folders This button is on by default when you open Explorer. Its purpose is to display and hide the Folders pane.

History Click the History button to display the History pane, which shows you a list of where you've been lately both locally (on your own computer) and remotely (on the local network or the Internet).

Move To Select a file or folder and click the Move To button to open the Browse For Folder dialog box. Select the folder to which you want to move the file, and click OK.

Copy To Select a file or folder and click the Copy To button to open the Browse For Folder dialog box. Select the folder to which you want to copy the file, and click OK.

Delete This button sends the selected object to the Recycle Bin.

Undo This button reverses the last action. If you just copied or moved a file, the Undo button will...*undo* that action.

Views This button enables you to select the view you want to use in Explorer, as I discussed earlier in this chapter.

To customize the Explorer toolbar, follow these steps:

1. Choose View ➢ Toolbars ➢ Customize to open the Customize Toolbar dialog box:

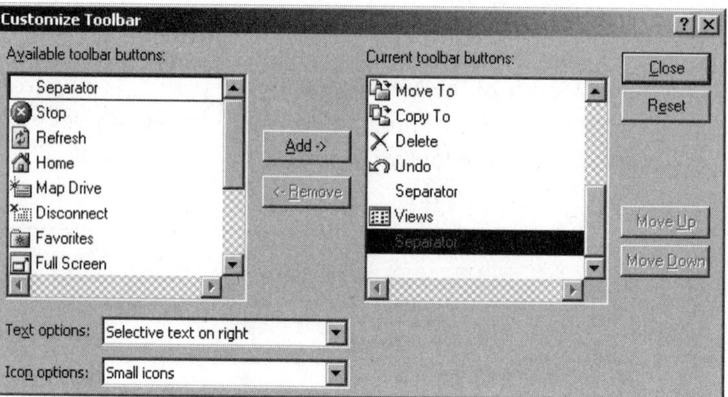

2. To add a button, select it from the list on the left, and click Add.
3. To remove a button, select it from the list on the right, and click Remove.
4. To change the order of the buttons on the toolbar, click the Move Up or Move Down button until the arrangement is to your liking.
5. Click the drop-down lists to take a look at text and icon options.
6. When you're finished, click Close.

Using Explorer's Main Menus and Shortcut Menus

With Explorer, you get a lot more menu for your money. The menus are context sensitive, meaning that the commands you see depend on what you are doing at the time. For example, when you select a file, the commands on the File menu reflect the activities that are appropriate for working with files.

In this section, I'll briefly describe all the main menu options and then provide an overview of shortcut menu options in Explorer.

NOTE By default, the menus in Windows 2000 Professional are personalized, as I mentioned earlier. Therefore, unless you've chosen not to use personalized menus, the commands you see will depend on which commands you've used most recently, as well as on which commands are appropriate for the task at hand.

Using the File Menu

The File menu contains commands for opening files and creating and administering folders. You can also access the Properties dialog box from the File menu. Here are some commands commonly found on the File menu.

Open Opens your selected file using its associated application. If the file you selected does not have an associated application, you are prompted to select the application to use when opening the file.

NOTE Not all files can be opened. Many of the files you see in Explorer are system files that the operating system or applications use. As a rule, files that can be opened have the extension EXE or are represented by easily recognizable icons. Also, if you select a file and then click the File menu, you won't see an Open command if the file can't be opened.

Print Sends a file directly to your default printer. You'll see this command when a file is selected.

Open With This option appears if you do not have a program associated with a particular file type and you have a file selected. Choosing File ➢ Open With opens the Open With dialog box, in which you can select a program to associate with the file.

Explore Displays an Explorer view of the selected folder, which seems a bit redundant given that you're already *in* Explorer (appears when you have selected a folder).

Search Opens the Search utility in the left pane of Explorer and sets the default location to search as the folder you have selected (appears when you have selected a folder).

New Creates a new folder or shortcut in your current folder and names the folder New Folder and the shortcut New Shortcut. You can also choose File ➢ New to create a new document in most of your installed applications.

Send To Sends your selected file or folder to any of the locations you have placed in your Send To folder. The Default choices are 3½ Floppy, Desktop (create shortcut), Mail Recipient, and My Documents.

Create Shortcut Creates a shortcut to the selected file in the current folder.

Delete Sends selected files and folders to the Recycle Bin.

Rename Highlights the name of the selected file or folder and enters edit mode. Type your new name for the file or folder, and then press Enter or click outside the name area to accept it.

WARNING Do not rename program or system files. For example, leave `excel.exe` and `system32.dll` alone. As a rule, only rename files and folders that you have created.

Properties Displays the Properties dialog box for the selected file or folder. For more information on Properties, see Chapter 5.

Close Closes the active Explorer window.

Using the Edit Menu

The Edit menu contains the commands you would expect to find in the Edit menu of an average Windows application. Here are some of the commands commonly found on the Edit menu:

Undo Reverses or undoes the last action you completed. Even if you send a file to the Recycle Bin, Undo restores it to the folder from which you deleted it. In Windows 2000 Professional, this command usually indicates the last action. For example, when you have deleted a file, this command becomes Undo Delete.

Cut Removes files and folders from their present location. You can paste them into a new folder or use Cut as a means of deleting them.

Copy Copies selected files and folders so that you can paste them elsewhere.

Paste Inserts files and folders you have cut or copied from other folders into the selected folder.

NOTE Cut, Copy, and Paste work just like they do in a word processor or spreadsheet. Whatever you cut or copy is placed on the Clipboard until you choose Paste or shut down Windows 2000 Professional.

Paste Shortcut Inserts a shortcut that you've cut or copied in another file or folder.

Copy To Folder Opens the Browse For Folder dialog box, which you can use to select a folder in which to copy selected files or folders.

Move To Folder Opens the Browse For Folder dialog box, which you can use to select a folder in which to insert a selected file or folder. When you move a file or a folder, it is deleted from its original location.

Select All Selects (highlights) the entire contents of a folder.

Invert Selection Reverses the item selection in the current folder. For example, if you have two items selected, Invert Selection selects all but the two files you originally selected.

Using the View Menu

You use the commands on the View menu to change the display of items in Explorer. The View menu includes all the functionality of the Views button on the toolbar and much more. The commands are as follows:

Toolbars Displays a submenu from which you can choose to display or hide the standard buttons, the Address bar, links, and the Radio toolbar. Choose Toolbars ➢ Customize to open the Customize Toolbar dialog box, as I discussed earlier.

Status Bar Displays or hides the Status bar at the bottom of the Explorer window.

Explorer Bar Opens a submenu from which you can choose to display or hide the Search, Favorites, History, and Folders panes as well as the Tip Of The Day.

Large Icons Displays the contents of the right pane in Large Icons view.

Small Icons Displays the contents of the right pane in the Small Icons view.

List Displays the contents of the right pane in List view.

Details Displays the contents of the right pane in Details view.

Thumbnails Displays the contents of the selected folder as a miniature view of each file. As I mentioned previously, the Thumbnails view is useful for sorting through multiple graphics files.

Arrange Icons Displays a submenu from which you can choose to arrange file and folder icons by name, type, size, or date.

Line Up Icons Maintains the current order of the icons but aligns them with an unseen grid so that they appear neater.

Choose Columns Available when Explorer is in Details view, this command opens the Column Settings dialog box, which you can use to display and hide columns and rearrange the order of columns.

Customize This Folder Starts the Customize This Folder Wizard, which you can use to change the appearance of the selected folder.

Go To Opens a submenu of commands that you can choose to easily return to any recent locations on your computer, your local network, or the Internet.

Refresh Renews the video display.

Using the Favorites Menu

The Favorites menu has the same functionality in Explorer and in Internet Explorer. (I'll discuss Internet Explorer in Chapter 12.) You use the Favorites menu to mark locations on your local hard drive, your local network, or the Internet so that you can access them quickly. The Favorites menu contains only two commands:

Add To Favorites Opens the Add Favorite dialog box, which you can use to add the current location to the Favorites list.

Organize Favorites Opens the Organize Favorites dialog box (see Figure 4.8), which you can use to create a new Favorites folder, rename or delete an item on the Favorites list, and move items to other folders.

FIGURE 4.8
You use the Organize Favorites dialog box to organize your favorite locations.

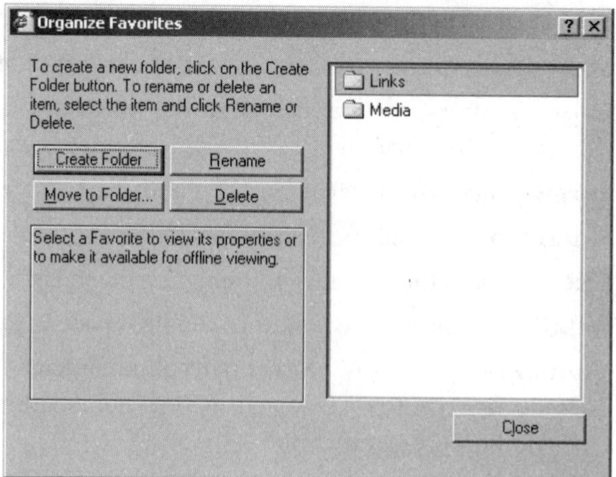

Using the Tools Menu

You use the commands on the Tools menu to configure network drives, to configure files for offline viewing, and to specify folder options.

Map Network Drive Opens the Map Network Drive dialog box, which you can use to make a new network connection, connect using another name, or connect to an Internet server.

Disconnect Network Drive Opens the Disconnect Network Drive dialog box, which you can use to disconnect from a selected network drive.

Synchronize Opens the Items To Synchronize dialog box, which you can use to set the properties of various folders on your network for offline viewing.

Folder Options Opens the Folder Options dialog box, which has four tabs. Use the General tab to define how the Desktop and folders will work. Use the View tab to specify folder views and to specify advanced settings for files and folders. Use the File Types tab to make file associations. Use the Offline Files tab to specify which network files will be cached locally on your computer.

Using the Help Menu

Choose Help ➢ Help Topics to open the Windows 2000 Professional Help file. Choose Help ➢ About Windows to display version information. Press F1 at any time to get context-sensitive help.

Using Shortcut Menus

Thanks to the Windows 2000 Professional shortcut menus, you probably won't need to use the main Explorer menus often. In fact, the shortcut menus give you just as many or more options than the main menus do. As you may recall from Chapter 3, you open a shortcut menu by right-clicking an object. Which commands appear on a shortcut menu depends on such factors as the current folder's location, the current file or folder type, user privileges, and which programs are installed on your computer.

Here are some of the commands that most commonly appear on shortcut menus:

- New
- Cut, Copy, and Paste
- Map Network Drive
- Send To
- Rename
- Delete
- Create Shortcut

- Properties

Of these commands, most are equivalent to what you'd find on the application's File or Edit menu. Choosing Properties, which usually appears at the bottom of a shortcut menu, generally takes you to the object's Properties dialog box, a topic I'll discuss in detail in Chapter 5.

Organizing Your Files and Folders

Managing your files in Explorer is easy and logical. After you learn a few commands, you can use them over and over for a variety of tasks. After a short time using Explorer, you'll wonder how you ever did it any other way.

Creating New Folders

To create a new folder in Explorer, follow these steps:

1. Choose where you want to create a new folder. You can create a folder on the Desktop, at the root of a hard drive or a floppy drive, or inside another folder.
2. In Explorer, choose New ➢ Folder, or right-click the item in which you want to create the folder, and choose New ➢ Folder from the shortcut menu. To create a folder on the Desktop, right-click an empty area, and choose New ➢ Folder from the shortcut menu.
3. The folder is created with the default name New Folder. By default the name is highlighted. To give a new name to the folder, type it now. You can always rename a folder by selecting it and choosing File ➢ Rename or by right-clicking the folder and choosing Rename from the shortcut menu. (I'll discuss renaming in detail later in this chapter.)

Moving Items

You can move files and folders anywhere on your computer or over the network as long as you have permission to do so. To move a file or folder, follow these steps:

1. Select the file or folder you want to move. To select more than one object, hold down Ctrl while you click each one. If the objects constitute an uninterrupted group, hold down Shift while you click the first object and the last.)
2. Choose Edit ➢ Cut (or press Ctrl+X).
3. Select the destination, and choose Edit ➢ Paste (or press Ctrl+V).

You can also drag items from one place to another:

- Drag from the right Explorer pane to the left.
- Drag from either Explorer pane to another Explorer or Explorer-type window.

- Drag from either Explorer pane to the Start button. (Actually, this doesn't *move* the item; instead, it creates a shortcut on the Start menu.)
- Drag from either Explorer pane to the Desktop. (Optionally, if you hold down the right mouse button while you drag, you can create a shortcut or shortcuts on the Desktop for the object or objects you are dragging.)
- Drag from the Desktop to an Explorer folder.

TIP If you drag a folder from the right Explorer pane to the left on a *different* drive, Windows 2000 Professional defaults to *copying* the file instead of *moving* it. (As long as you are dragging the object to the *same* drive, Windows 2000 Professional moves the file or folder by default.) If you don't want Windows 2000 Professional to copy the file, hold down the Shift key while you drag the object to another drive. That way it will be moved rather than copied.

Copying Items

You can also copy files and folders anywhere on your computer or the network as long as you have permission to do so. To copy a file or folder, follow these steps:

1. Select the file or folder you are going to copy. To select more than one object, hold down Ctrl while you click each object. To select objects that constitute an uninterrupted group, hold down Shift, click the first object, and then click the last object.
2. Choose Edit ➢ Copy (or press Ctrl+C).
3. Select the destination, and choose Edit ➢ Paste (or press Ctrl+V).

   You can also drag the items from one place to another, as described in the previous section, with one difference: to ensure that the objects you are dragging are copied and not moved, hold down the Ctrl key while you are dragging.

TIP If you drag a folder from the right Explorer pane to the left on the *same* drive, Windows 2000 Professional defaults to *moving* the file instead of *copying* it. (As long as you are dragging the object to a *different* drive, Windows 2000 Professional copies the file or folder by default.) If you don't want Windows 2000 Professional to move the file, hold down the Ctrl key while you drag the object to another drive. It will be copied, not moved.

Saving Files and Folders to the Desktop

You can keep files on your Desktop for quick and easy access. To store files and folders on the Desktop, do one of the following:

- Drag a file from Explorer to the Desktop.

- If you are saving the file from within an application, select Desktop (it's at the very top of your local drive hierarchy) in the application's Save As dialog box.

Dragging with the Right Mouse Button

When you right-click a file, drag it, and then release the button, you'll see a shortcut menu with the following options:

Copy Here Copies the file to the new location.

Move Here Moves the file to the new location.

Create Shortcut(s) Here Creates a shortcut to the file at the new location. As I've discussed, a shortcut is a pointer to the real file or folder and can be stored anywhere on your computer.

Cancel Cancels the operation.

TIP If you are new to Windows 2000 Professional or are confused about when to use Ctrl or Shift when moving or copying files, the safest thing to do is to drag the file with the right mouse button. This way, you are always presented with a choice of whether to move or copy the file.

Renaming Documents and Folders

You can quickly and easily rename files and folders. Because Windows 2000 Professional keeps track of file associations, you don't have to worry about including the three-character file extensions. To rename a file or folder, follow these steps:

1. In Explorer, select the file or folder you want to rename.
2. Choose File ➢ Rename, or right-click the file and choose Rename from the shortcut menu.
3. When only the name of the file (the text associated with the icon) becomes highlighted, do one of the following:
   - If you want to simply replace the entire name, start typing the new name; the old name disappears the moment you start typing.
   - If you want to make only a correction or two to the existing name, use the arrow keys to move to specific characters within the existing name. The highlight disappears the moment you start moving within the name, enabling you to insert or delete specific characters without deleting the entire name.
4. To accept the name, press Enter or click outside the name area. If you make a mistake, press Escape.

TIP You can also rename files and folders with two single-clicks (but not so fast that Windows 2000 Professional interprets it as a double-click) on the name of the object so that it is highlighted. Then follow steps 3 and 4.

Deleting Files and Folders

If you decide that you don't want a file or a folder, you can easily delete it. By default, the file is not actually deleted when you tell Windows 2000 Professional to delete it: instead, it is compressed and sent to the Recycle Bin folder. A file in the Recycle Bin hasn't been removed from your hard drive, only placed on inactive duty, so to speak. (You can periodically delete items within the Recycle Bin to *actually* remove them entirely, or you can empty the Recycle Bin to delete everything in it.)

The Recycle Bin is a good intermediate place to keep files you're pretty sure you want to delete, because if you change your mind after "deleting" them to the Recycle Bin, you can always open the Recycle Bin and resurrect the object. Mutter your apologies for treating the item so shabbily, and it's ready for use once more.

TIP If you're the kind of person who hates being pestered by second thoughts, and you'd prefer to avoid the nice little safeguard of the Recycle Bin, you can *really* delete an item by selecting it and pressing Shift+Delete.

Sending Items to the Recycle Bin

You can send a file or a folder to the Recycle Bin in several ways:

- Select the item, and then press the Delete key.
- Select the item, and then choose File ➢ Delete.
- Right-click the file or folder, and then choose Delete from the shortcut menu.
- Select the item, and then drag and drop it on the Recycle Bin icon.

Emptying the Recycle Bin

By default, the size of the Recycle Bin folder is set at 10 percent of your hard drive. If you have more than one hard drive or if you have a dual-partitioned drive, you will have a Recycle Bin folder for each drive, and the size of the folder is set at 10 percent for each drive. For example, if drive C is 3.44GB, the Recycle Bin folder is 353MB; and if drive D is 6.09MB, its Recycle Bin folder is 624MB.

When the Recycle Bin folder is full, Windows 2000 Professional automatically deletes enough items, starting with the oldest, to accommodate whatever you are currently sending to it. When an item is removed from the Recycle Bin, it is gone forever.

To better control the Recycle Bin and maintain its intended functionality (which is to provide second chances), you can periodically empty it manually. You can delete all the items it contains or only selected items.

- To delete selected items, double-click the Recycle Bin to open the Recycle Bin folder. Now delete items as you would in Explorer.
- To totally empty the Recycle Bin, right-click its icon, and choose Empty Recycle Bin from the shortcut menu.

WARNING When a file is deleted in Windows 2000 Professional, it is really deleted. Other operating systems such as MS-DOS or Windows 95/98 delete only the first byte from a file and mark the space as available. Windows 2000 Professional is much more thorough because of its secure nature. When you delete a file in Windows 2000 Professional, all the bytes in the file are set to a zero value. This is like formatting the space where the file was so it can be reclaimed.

Restoring Items from the Recycle Bin

To restore items from the Recycle Bin you can do one of the following:

- Open the Recycle Bin folder, select an item, and drag it to the folder of your choice.
- Open the Recycle Bin, select the item you want to restore, and click the Restore button. The item is restored to its original location.

Understanding Windows 2000 Professional as a Multiuser Environment

From the ground up, Windows 2000 Professional is designed as a multiuser networking environment. Because security is so integral to the way that Windows 2000 Professional operates, it is possible for two or more users to use the same workstation without stepping on each other's toes. That is, one user can log in and do the work they want to do without necessarily knowing who else has access to the computer or without having access to another user's files.

For multiuser access to work the way it should, the system Administrator needs to set up the appropriate accounts in the Users And Passwords applet. For more information on system administration and the Users And Passwords applet, see Chapter 28.

User Profile Folders

When a user logs on to a Windows 2000 Professional workstation, the operating system assigns that user a security token. The Windows 2000 Security Manager portion of the Executive Services manages security tokens. Each time that user attempts to do something in Windows 2000 Professional, be it open a file, send e-mail, or change the way the Desktop looks, the Security Manager checks that person's token to see if they have the rights and permissions to perform the task they've requested.

As a result of the token-based security system, Windows 2000 Professional administers multiuser environments logically. User profile information is stored in the user's folder in the Documents And Settings folder on the drive where Windows 2000 Professional is installed. Inside the Documents And Settings folder is a folder for each user that logs in to a workstation (see Figure 4.9), and inside each user's folder is a set of folders that customize the Windows 2000 Professional environment for that user.

Following is a list and a description of some of the folders commonly found inside each user's folder. Some of these folders are hidden folders. To display hidden folders, choose Tools ➢ Folder Options to open the Folder Options dialog box. Select the View tab, and then in the Advanced Settings list, click Show Hidden Files And Folders.

FIGURE 4.9
Inside the Documents and Settings folder is a separate folder for each user that logs on to a specific Windows 2000 Professional workstation.

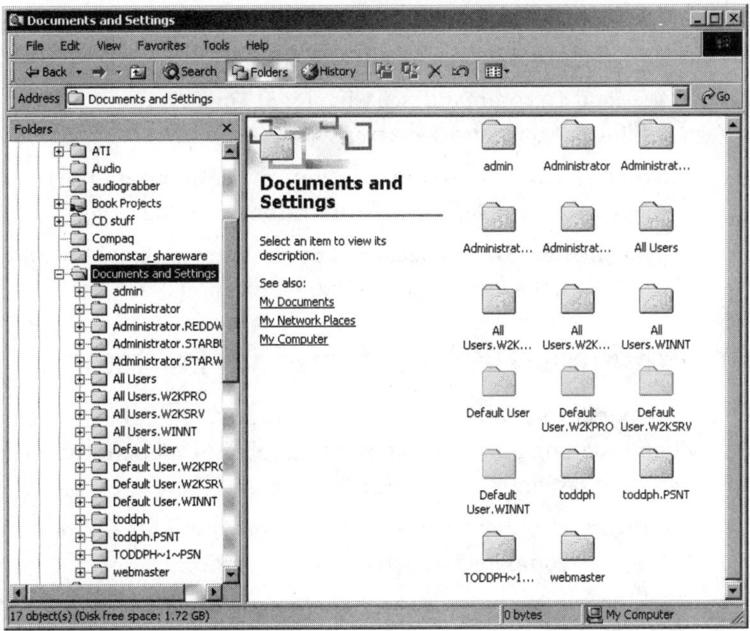

Cookies Contains any cookies that you may have stored from Web sites. Cookies are a small bit of text information that enables a Web site to customize its appearance just for you.

Desktop Contains any files that a user stores on the Desktop. This does not include My Computer, My Network Places, or the Recycle Bin.

Favorites Stores your favorite programs, files, and Web sites. You can add files to this folder and delete files from it as you would with any other folder.

Local Settings Contains a portion of the user-specific information of the Registry, as well as some personal settings for your History, Temporary Internet Files, and a system Temp folder.

My Documents Keeps files that you don't want any other users to access, even though the users may share other aspects of your workstation. The My Documents folder is empty by default, except for a subfolder called My Pictures. My Pictures is the default location for storing your picture files.

NetHood This folder contains some cached information that normally appears in My Network Places. This is where you will store the browse list for your local network and any persistent network connections.

PrintHood Stores the mappings for any network printers you have installed. Network printers are actually part of the user profile and are not part of the overall system configuration.

Recent Stores files and folders you have accessed recently.

Send To Stores customizations to your Send To menu. For more information on the Send To command, see Chapter 5. The Favorites folder is a good candidate for adding to your Send To menu.

Start Menu Stores configurations and customizations you have made to your Start menu. For example, it shows all the shortcuts you have added to your Start menu.

Templates This folder stores the system templates for various applications that can be installed on Windows 2000 Professional.

The Windows 2000 Professional Folder

Your Windows 2000 Professional folder (or Winnt folder, if you use the default name when installing it) contains several subfolders that perform specific functions for the operating system, including the following:

Addins Contains configuration information for additional Windows 2000 Professional components such as the Fax service.

Cursors Stores Windows 2000 Professional mouse cursors. This folder may be empty if you did not choose to install all the cursors during Windows 2000 Professional Setup.

Debug Stores some information useful in recovering from a system failure. The files in this folder track the installation of the network during setup and back up the user's environment settings.

Downloaded Program Files Contains the programs needed to display different types of active content on the Web. When you download a program that lets you view an animation on a Web page, the program is stored here.

Driver Cache Contains a subfolder that holds all the drivers that Windows 2000 Professional might use at some point. This may save you from needing the CD-ROM when installing some new hardware.

Fonts Contains all your installed fonts. For more information on installing or removing fonts, see Chapter 7.

Help Contains all the Windows 2000 Professional Help files. You can open Help from individual applications or from Explorer. Help files for nonoperating system programs—Word, Excel, and so on—are not stored here.

Inf Contains the information files (`.inf`) needed to install new hardware drivers.

Java Contains any Java applets and class libraries you may have downloaded when browsing the Internet or an intranet.

Media Stores system sound files. When you assign system sounds to operating system events (for example, Start Windows, New Mail, and so on), you call files from this folder. You can store any WAV file in this folder and make it available to Windows 2000 Professional. For more information on assigning system sounds, see Chapter 6. For more information on WAV files, see Chapter 8.

MSAgent Contains the Microsoft Agent, an animated character that can be scripted into a document or a Web page to provide interactive help for users.

Msapps Provides an install point for various Microsoft applications. By default, it contains the MSInfo subfolder.

Offline Web Pages Holds any Web pages and their contents that you may have selected for offline caching.

Registration Contains the encrypted product registration information for your installation of Windows 2000 Professional.

Repair Contains backup copies of some essential system files so that you can restore them in the case of a system crash. The Setup file provides a map to all Windows 2000 Professional essential system files that were installed during installation. Use this file as a guide if you need to make Windows 2000 Professional repairs.

TIP In Windows 2000 Professional, the files in the Repair folder are not compressed. If you need to access these files directly (other than during an emergency repair), you should be able to use them without having to uncompress them first.

Security Contains some Windows 2000 Professional security policy information. It would be wise to leave this information alone.

Speech Contains the files that support the speech capabilities of Windows 2000 Professional. They are normally called upon when you use the Narrator to read selected text from the screen. For information about the Narrator, see Chapter 6.

System Stores 16-bit system files that may be required to support Windows 3.1 applications. It also provides some backward compatibility for 16-bit Windows applications that really want to see a System folder.

System32 Contains most of the files and program code that make Windows 2000 Professional operate. This is the most important folder in Windows 2000 Professional. In addition to essential system files, System32 contains many Windows 2000 Professional applets and utilities.

WARNING As a rule, you should not manually move or change files in the System32 folder except as instructed by your Management Information Service (MIS) department or a technical support representative.

Tasks Contains tasks that are scheduled for Windows 2000 Professional, for example, defragmenting a hard drive.

Temp Contains any temporary files you may be creating through your interaction with different applications.

Twain32 Contains files that support scanning images.

Web Contains Web documents that provide the Tips shown at logon, templates for basic Web pages used in Windows 2000 Professional, and subfolders that contain the wallpapers that can be displayed with the Active Desktop.

Summary

In this chapter, I've covered a lot of information that is essential if you want to use Windows 2000 Professional effectively—in particular, if you want to know how to use and customize the Start menu and how to use Explorer.

If you've used previous versions of Windows, you should know how to use Explorer, but I'm always surprised at the number of people who use their computer a lot and don't even know that Explorer exists. Understanding how to use Explore to organize your files and folders is key to using Windows 2000 Professional.

In the next chapter, I'll give you details about right-clicking in Windows 2000 Professional and show you how to use Properties dialog boxes.

CHAPTER 5

Setting Object Properties

FEATURING:

In this chapter, I discuss Properties dialog boxes in detail. Also, because one of the easiest ways to display an object's properties is to right-click it with your mouse, I'll present a comprehensive description of the other things you can do with a right-click to get your work done faster. You've already had the opportunity to use these features in earlier chapters. This time around, though, we get into the essentials. Let's start with a brief recap of right-clicking.

Right-Clicking around Windows 2000 Professional

Right-clicking objects throughout the Windows 2000 Professional interface displays a shortcut menu that contains options pertaining to the objects at hand. The same options are typically available from the main menus but are more conveniently reached with the right-click.

The "rightness" and "leftness" of these clicks will, of course, be reversed if you have reversed the mouse buttons (because you're left-handed, for example, or for some other reason). If you have a trackball, a GlidePoint, or another nonmouse pointing device, your right-click button may be somewhere unexpected. You may need to refer to your pointing device's Help files to find out how to trigger the right-click event. In addition, if you have a special Windows keyboard, you have a "right menu" key (next to the Windows key) that you can press to display the shortcut menu for whatever screen object has the current focus.

Right-clicking doesn't belong only to the Windows 95/98 and Windows 2000 Professional interface—it has been incorporated into recently written Windows programs too. For example, Microsoft Office programs such as Word and Excel have had shortcut menus for some time. Most of the Accessory programs supplied with Windows 2000 Professional also have shortcut menus. In general, the contents of shortcut menus in Windows programs depend on the type of object. For example, if you right-click a table in Word, the shortcut menu contains items that are different from the shortcut menu items you'll see when you right-click a worksheet in Excel or frames, text, graphics, and so on.

As a rule, I suggest you start using the right-click button whenever you can. You'll learn through experimentation which of your programs do something with the right-click and which don't. Many NT 3.51 (and 16-bit Windows) programs won't respond to the click; others may do something unexpected, but in almost every case, right-clicking results in a shortcut menu. Incidentally, as with any menu in Windows, you can close the shortcut menu by clicking elsewhere or by pressing Esc; so don't worry about doing anything dangerous or irreversible.

A good example is right-clicking the Taskbar. Right-click an empty place on the Taskbar, and you'll see this menu:

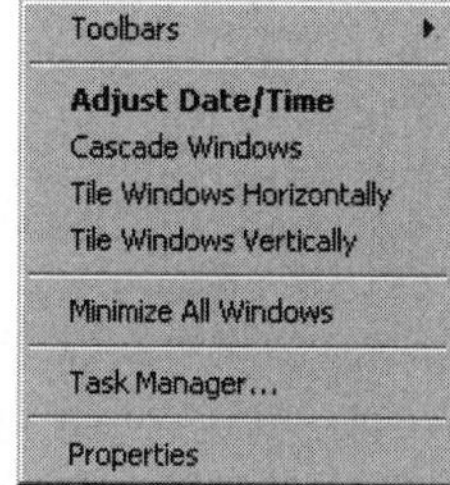

Now right-click the Start button, and you'll see the following menu:

Other shortcut menus often have Cut, Copy, Paste, Open, Print, and Rename commands on them. Here are a few other right-clicking experiments to give you a feel for the usefulness of this facility:

- Right-click My Computer, and notice the menu options. You'll see different shortcut menus depending on whether you right-click the My Computer icon on the Desktop or right-click the My Computer window after it's open. In fact, you'll get different shortcut menus within the open window depending on which part of the window you click. For example, right-clicking the title bar, the list area of the window, and an object highlighted within the list will each display a different shortcut menu.
- When you right-click a printer in the Printers folder, you can quickly set the printer to be the default printer or to work offline. Printing offline is handy when the printer you want to use is not connected (or is turned off), because the result of offline printing is that your print jobs are queued up, ready, and waiting until your printer is reconnected and ready to print. To begin printing again, simply right-click the printer, and select Work Online, and all the print jobs in your queue are sent to the printer. (Work Offline and Work Online appear on a printer's shortcut menu only if the printer is located on a network.)
- Right-click the Desktop to display the options for setting the screen colors, wallpaper, screen saver, and so forth. This also lets you set the Active Desktop options for displaying Web content on your Desktop.
- Right-click any program's title bar, and notice the options for resizing the window or closing the application. This menu is the same as the program's System menu.

- Right-clicking a minimized program's button in the Taskbar also displays the System menu.

Many objects such as folders, printers, and My Network Places have a shortcut menu item called Explore that displays the object in Explorer's format (two vertical panes). You'll see the object in the left pane and its contents listed in the right pane. In some cases, the contents are print jobs; in other cases, they are fonts, files, folders, disk drives, or computers on the network.

Sharable items, such as printers, hard disks, and folders, have a Sharing option on their shortcut menu. Selecting Sharing opens a Properties dialog box for the object. Click the Sharing tab to specify sharing options and permissions. I'll discuss sharing in Part III.

Using Properties Dialog Boxes

Just as most objects have shortcut menus, many also have Properties dialog boxes, which provide a simple and direct means for making settings to everything from how the screen looks to whether a file is hidden or what a shared printer is named.

Virtually every object in Windows 2000 Professional—whether a printer, modem, shortcut, hard disk, folder, networked computer, or hardware driver—has a *Properties dialog box* that contains such settings. These settings affect how the object works and, sometimes, how it looks. And Properties dialog boxes not only *display* the settings for the object but also usually enable you to easily *alter* the settings.

You've probably noticed that many shortcut menus have a Properties choice at the bottom. This choice is often the quickest path to an object's Properties dialog box—not that there aren't other ways. Many dialog boxes, for example, have a Properties button that displays the object's Properties dialog box when clicked. And you can use Control Panel to set numerous properties throughout Windows 2000 Professional. Still, as you become more and more comfortable with Windows 2000 Professional, you'll find the right-click approach the most expedient.

Deciding When to Use Properties Dialog Boxes

Most Windows 2000 Professional users will rarely bother viewing or changing Properties settings because Windows 2000 Professional is well-behaved enough to govern itself (for example, repairing shortcuts when the target file or folder has been moved) and to prompt you when necessary for details about objects. As a case in point, when you install Windows 2000 Professional for the first time, or when you add new hardware or create a new printer, Wizards conscientiously assume the responsibility of setting up properties appropriately. The upshot is that tweaking the Windows 2000 Professional internals and objects isn't as necessary as it was in earlier versions of Windows. In those rare instances when it is necessary to make adjustments, unearthing the required dialog box for the job isn't an exercise reminiscent of dismantling a Chinese box puzzle.

Any self-respecting power user will want to know all about properties for performing such tasks as sharing a folder on the network, changing the name of a hard disk volume, checking the status of the computer's ports, displaying a font or other file's technical details, or checking the amount of free disk space on a hard disk.

TIP To display an object's Properties dialog box even more quickly, highlight the object and press Alt+Enter. Or simply press the Alt key at the same time you double-click the object.

Trying Out a Few Properties Dialog Boxes

The Properties option is always the last command on a shortcut menu. For example, if you right-click the My Computer icon on the Desktop, you'll see this menu:

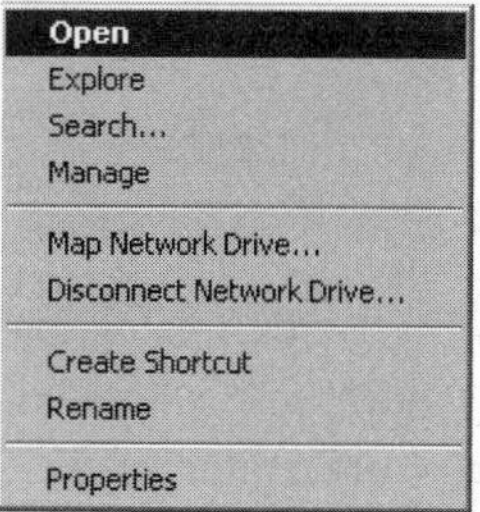

Here's another example. Suppose you're browsing through some folders using Explorer, and you come across an item identified as a Word document. Wondering what it is, when it was created, and who created it, you right-click and choose Properties to open the Properties dialog box for that file, as shown in Figure 5.1. Notice that there are several tabs. That's because Word stores its property information in several locations. Other applications might display only a single-tabbed Properties dialog box.

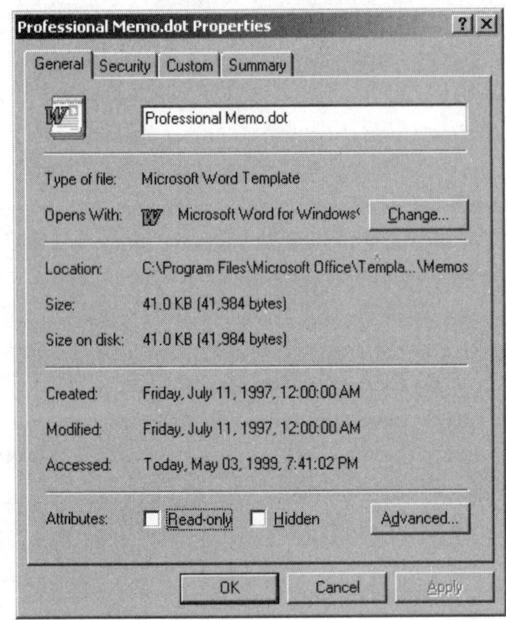

FIGURE 5.1
A typical Properties dialog box for a document file. This one is for a Word 97 file, so it has several tabs listing its editing history, who created it, keywords, title, and so forth.

As you might guess, Properties dialog boxes for other kinds of files may have more or less information than the one shown in Figure 5.1. In fact, most document Properties dialog boxes are truly useful only if you want to examine the history of the file or set its attributes, such as whether it should be read-only (to prevent others from using it) or hidden from view in folders, or whether its archive bit should be set. (A check mark in the Archive box means the file hasn't been backed up since it was last altered or since it was created.) The point is that you can usually only view the status of the document, not alter it.

Properties dialog boxes for objects *other* than documents, however, often let you make more substantive changes to them. A shortcut's Properties dialog box, for example, lets you adjust some goodies about how the shortcut works, the file it points to, and so on, as shown in Figure 5.2.

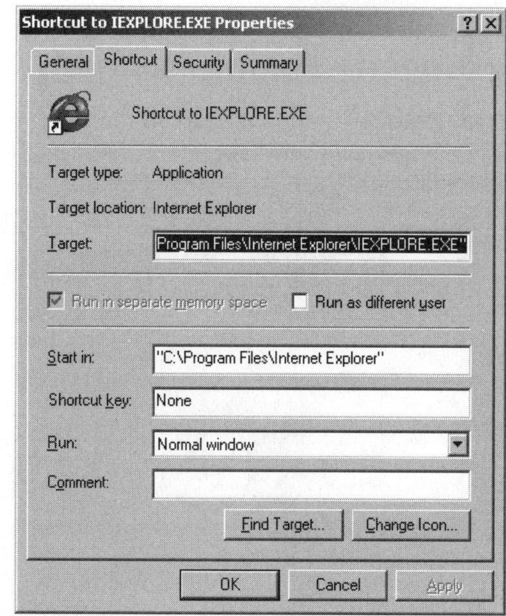

FIGURE 5.2
Shortcuts have Properties dialog boxes that list the particulars of the shortcut and which you can modify. Here you can change settings that control how the document or program runs when you double-click the shortcut.

You can click the question mark (?) button (found in the upper-right of most Properties dialog boxes as well as other dialog boxes) for help on any of the options. Click the question mark, and then click the item for which you want help. The two handiest items in this dialog box are Shortcut Key and Run.

You use the Shortcut Key field you to assign a key combination that will run the shortcut from anywhere. For example, to jump to My Computer without minimizing all your other windows first (you *do* need to minimize the other windows to complete this procedure, though), follow these steps:

1. From the Desktop, right-click My Computer, and choose Create Shortcut from the shortcut menu. You'll immediately see a new shortcut on the Desktop called Shortcut To My Computer.
2. Right-click the new shortcut, and choose Properties to open the Shortcut To My Computer Properties dialog box.
3. If necessary, click the Shortcut tab, and then click in the Shortcut Key field.
4. Press Ctrl+Alt+C to assign the shortcut key to Ctrl+Alt+C.
5. Click OK to finish.

Now whenever you want to open My Computer, simply press Ctrl+Alt+C, which does take a little manual dexterity, but is quick. Use this same trick for any object you use regularly and often need to fish around to open.

The Run field in a shortcut's Properties dialog box determines whether the object opens in a maximized, minimized, or normal (floating) window.

Changing Property Settings from My Computer

Right-clicking the My Computer icon on the Desktop and choosing Properties from the shortcut menu opens the System Properties dialog box, as shown in Figure 5.3.

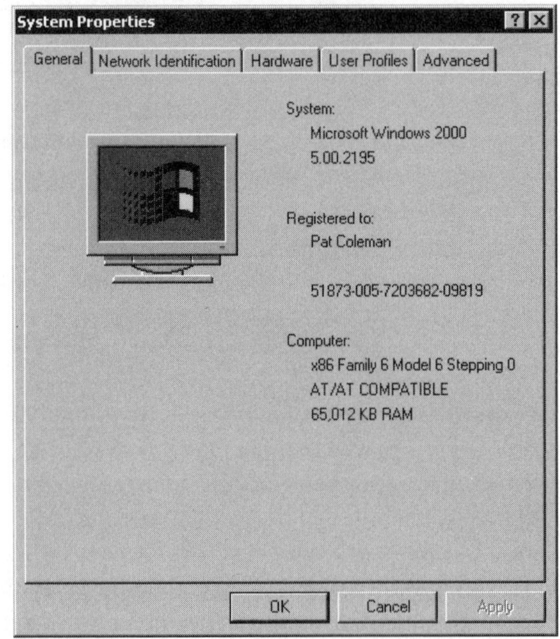

FIGURE 5.3 *A grand overview of your computer's attributes is available by right-clicking My Computer and choosing Properties. Use some caution with these settings. You can also open this dialog box by clicking the System icon in Control Panel.*

The General tab gives you some useful information about the version of Windows you are running, how much memory your computer has, and what type of CPU chip is in your machine. This information will come in handy the next time someone asks you what's in the computer you're running. Instead of drumming your fingers on the desk and feeling like a doofus, you can open this dialog box and read what it says.

NOTE The General tab of the System Properties dialog box is one of the only places where you can see which Service Packs, if any, have been installed on the system.

The Network Identification tab, which is shown in Figure 5.4, displays the full name of your computer as it appears in the table of your local Domain Name System (DNS) and WINS (Windows Internet Naming Service) servers, if you are using either of these.

It also displays the name of the domain to which your computer belongs. Clicking the Network ID button starts the Network Identification Wizard. Clicking the Properties button opens the Identification Changes dialog box, which you can use to change the name and membership of the computer.

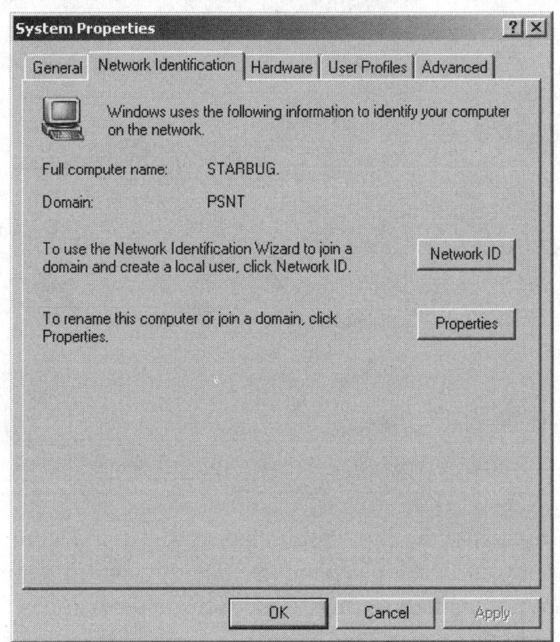

FIGURE 5.4
The Network Identification tab contains information on your computer name and domain.

The Hardware tab, which is shown in Figure 5.5, provides access to a number of hardware management tools in Windows 2000 Professional. You can use the Hardware Wizard to add, remove, or troubleshoot hardware. Device Manager is a snap-in for the Microsoft Management Console, so when you start Device Manager, it opens in a separate window with the same basic interface as the other administrative tools. Clicking the Hardware Profiles button opens the System Properties dialog box at the Hardware tab, which you can use to specify different configurations for your computer.

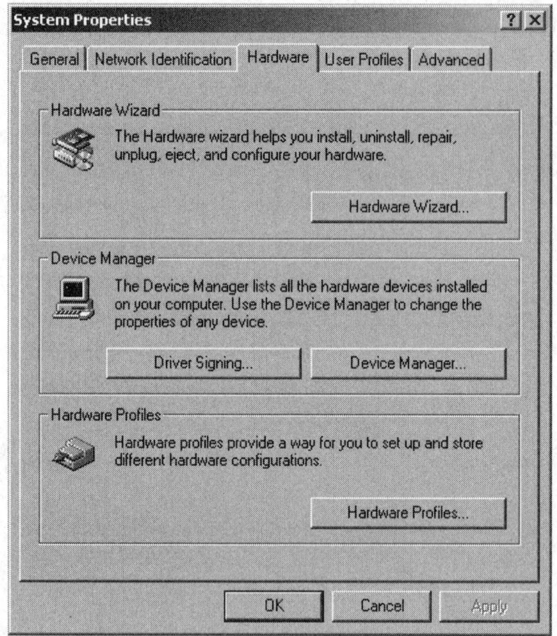

FIGURE 5.5 *The Hardware tab gives you access to the main hardware configuration tools in Windows 2000 Professional.*

You can use the User Profiles tab, as shown in Figure 5.6, to save different configurations of your Desktop *appearance*, including which items appear on your Start menu and other interface settings, and associate these appearances with different users logging into the system. You can also specify a "roaming" configuration, which makes your Desktop appearance available to every machine on your network when your profile is stored on a network file server. This way you can work at other machines using your own familiar interface.

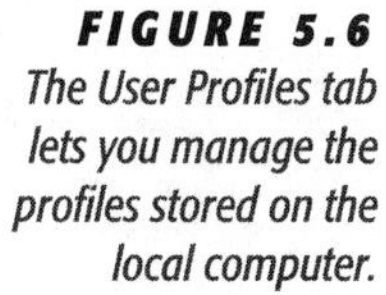

FIGURE 5.6
The User Profiles tab lets you manage the profiles stored on the local computer.

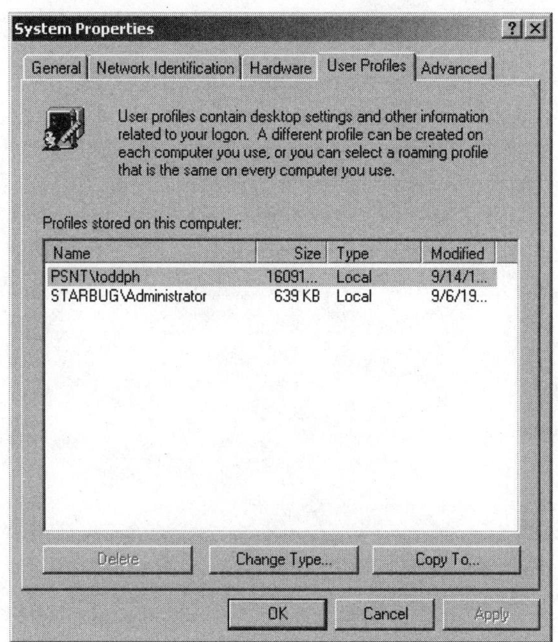

You use the Advanced tab, which is shown in Figure 5.7, to change some of the performance and recovery options for Windows 2000 Professional. Clicking the Performance Options button opens the Performance Options dialog box, which you can use to set the size of the page file and to optimize performance for either desktop applications or background services. Clicking the Environment Variables button opens the Environment Variables dialog box, in which you can set the various system or user level variables, such as the location and name of the temporary folder or the system path statement. Clicking the Startup And Recovery button opens the Startup And Recovery dialog box, which you can use to determine how the computer starts up and what to do if a critical error occurs.

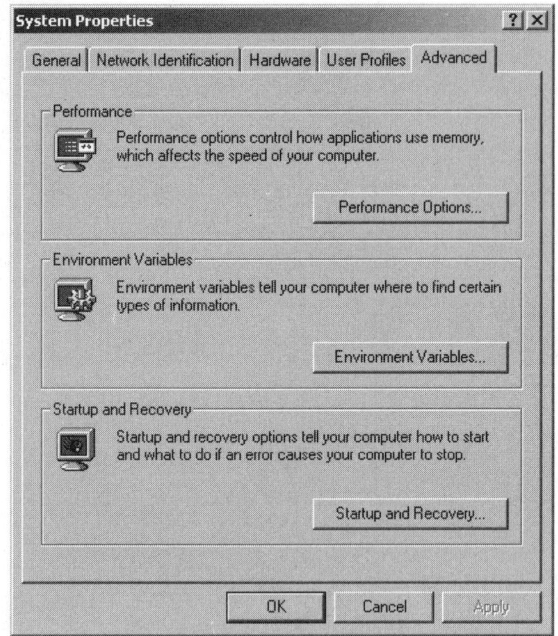

FIGURE 5.7
You use the options on the Advanced tab to change performance and recovery options for Windows 2000 Professional.

WARNING As a rule, don't mess with the settings in the System Properties dialog box unless you know what you're doing. Adjusting the virtual memory settings, for example, will more likely negatively impact your system's performance than accelerate it. Examining all the tabs is fine if you click Cancel after viewing the information.

Summary

In this chapter, you learned how to adjust properties for many of the objects in Windows 2000 Professional. Whether you prefer to use the shortcut menu by right-clicking an object or by highlighting an object and pressing the special shortcut menu key on your Windows keyboard, you can easily access Properties settings in Windows 2000 Professional.

Properties dialog boxes are available for many parts of Windows 2000 Professional right from the Desktop. Right-clicking My Computer and selecting Properties gets you to the most important of these settings, the System Properties dialog box.

CHAPTER 6

Customizing Your Desktop via Control Panel

FEATURING:

You can make numerous alterations to customize Windows 2000 Professional to your liking—adjustments to screen colors, modems, mouse speed, passwords, key repeat rate, fonts, and networking options, to name just a few. Most of these adjustments are not necessities as much as they are niceties that make using Windows 2000 Professional a little easier. Others are more imperative, such as setting up Windows 2000 Professional to work with your brand and model of printer or getting your mouse pointer to slow down a bit so you can reasonably control it.

You set preferences of this sort through Control Panel. After you change a setting with Control Panel, alterations are stored in the Windows Registry. The settings are reloaded each time you run Windows 2000 Professional and stay in effect until you change them again with Control Panel.

You can alter a few Control Panel settings from other locations. For example, you can set up printers by choosing Start ➢ Settings ➢ Printers and opening the Printers folder, and you can change your screen's settings by right-clicking the Desktop and choosing Properties from the shortcut menu, which opens the Display Properties dialog box. However, such approaches essentially run the Control Panel option responsible for the relevant settings, so Control Panel is still doing the work. Running Control Panel to make system changes is often easier because it displays all the options for controlling your system in one place.

NOTE I won't discuss all the Control Panel settings in this chapter. Those that pertain to larger topics, such as networking, printing, multimedia, and communications, are covered in greater depth in their respective chapters later in the book. Those that don't fall into a single chapter are gathered into Chapter 29.

Opening Control Panel

You can open Control Panel, which is shown in Figure 6.1, in the following ways:

- Chose Start ➢ Settings ➢ Control Panel.
- Double-click the My Computer icon on the Desktop, and then click Control Panel.
- Open Explorer, and double-click Control Panel.

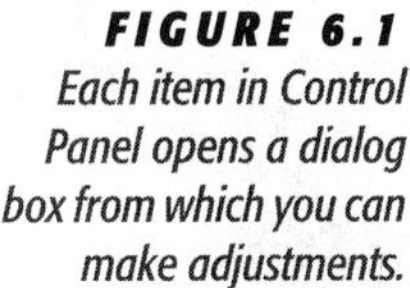

FIGURE 6.1
Each item in Control Panel opens a dialog box from which you can make adjustments.

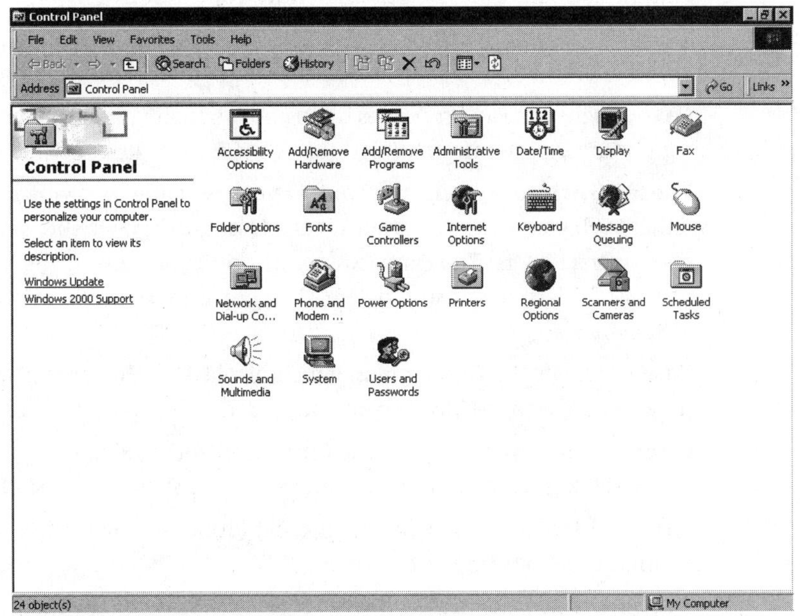

The items you see depend on your computer's hardware, and software and on which items you opted for during installation of Windows 2000 Professional. As you add new software or hardware to your system, you'll occasionally see new options in Control Panel as well, or your mouse icon might look different from the one you see in Figure 6.1. Computers that use a Microsoft Ballpoint mouse, for example, may have an icon that looks like a trackball rather than a tabletop mouse.

Each icon in Control Panel represents a little program (called an *applet*) that runs when you double-click it, typically displaying one or more dialog boxes in which you can specify settings. The following list describes all the standard Control Panel applets.

Accessibility Options Opens the Accessibility Options dialog box, which you can use to set keyboard, mouse, sound, display, and other options that make a Windows 2000 Professional computer easier to use by those who are visually, hearing, or motor impaired.

Add/Remove Hardware Starts the Add/Remove Hardware Wizard, with which you can add, remove, unplug, and troubleshoot hardware.

Add/Remove Programs Opens the Add/Remove Programs dialog box, which you can use to add, change, and remove programs as well as Windows components.

Administrative Tools Opens the Administrative Tools folder, which you use to configure administrative settings for your computer.

Date/Time Opens the Date/Time Properties dialog box, in which you can set the current date and time, as well as identify your time zone.

Display Opens the Display Properties dialog box, in which you can set a background color, a screen saver, resolution, and other aspects of your screen display.

Fax Opens the Fax Properties dialog box, which you use to design cover pages, supply cover page information, and set Status Monitor and other options.

Folder Options Opens the Folder Options dialog box, which you use to specify either Web view or Classic view for the Desktop and whether single-click or double-click opens folders. You can also use the options in this dialog box to specify the view for folders, to add and delete file types, and to enable or disable the use of offline files.

Fonts Opens the Fonts folder, which displays all the fonts installed on your computer. You use this dialog box to add or delete fonts from your system.

Game Controllers Opens the Game Controllers dialog box, which you can use to install, configure, and test a game controller such as a joystick or gamepad.

Internet Options Opens the Internet Properties dialog box, which you use to configure all your Internet settings.

Keyboard Opens the Keyboard Properties dialog box, which you can use to set the rate at which keys repeat when you hold them down, set the cursor blink rate, determine the language your keyboard will be able to enter into documents, and troubleshoot your keyboard.

Message Queuing Opens the Message Queuing Properties dialog box, which you can use to perform certain administrative tasks for Message Queuing. This applet is not installed by default, and you must have Administrator privileges to install and use it.

Mouse Opens the Mouse Properties dialog box, in which you can set the speed of the mouse pointer's motion relative to your hand motion and set the double-click speed. You can also reverse the function of the right and left buttons, set the shape of the various Windows 2000 Professional pointers, and tell Windows 2000 Professional that you've changed your type of mouse.

Network And Dial-Up Connections Opens the Network And Dial-Up Connections folder, which you can use to create a new connection and access settings and components of a connection.

Phone And Modem Options Opens the Phone And Modem Options dialog box, which you use to establish dialing rules and to add, remove, and set the properties of the modem(s) connected to your system.

Power Options Opens the Power Options Properties dialog box, which you use to set the power conservation scheme and to set options for how long your computer will sit idle before turning off the monitor and hard drives or even to enter hibernation.

Printers Opens the Printers folder, which displays the printers installed on your system, lets you modify the property settings for those printers, and lets you display and manage the print queue for each of those printers. Use this applet to install printer drivers.

Regional Options Opens the Regional Options dialog box, which you use to specify how Windows 2000 Professional displays languages, times, dates, numbers, and currency.

Scanners And Cameras Opens the Scanners And Cameras dialog box, which you use to install, configure, and troubleshoot digital cameras or scanners.

Scheduled Tasks Opens the Scheduled Tasks folder, which you use to specify when Windows 2000 Professional performs system maintenance tasks, such as cleaning up a hard disk.

Sounds And Multimedia Opens the Sounds And Multimedia Properties dialog box, with which you can add and configure sounds to specific system events if your computer has built-in sound capability or an installed sound card. You can also set up sound *schemes*—preset collections of sounds that your system uses to alert you to specific events—and configure and troubleshoot multimedia equipment on your computer.

System Opens the System Properties dialog box, which displays information about your system—devices, amount of random access memory (RAM), type of processor, environment settings, user profiles, hardware profiles, and start-up configuration.

Users And Passwords Opens the Users And Passwords dialog box, which you use to create and manage user and group accounts for your computer.

NOTE To display context-sensitive help for any option in an applet dialog box or folder, click the question mark (?) button in the upper-right corner, and then click the option.

Understanding the Active Desktop

Before I get into the details about some of the applets in Control Panel, I need to talk briefly about how you customize the general appearance and behavior of the overall user interface. In Windows 2000 Professional, you can choose the classic Windows interface or a Web view of the interface, or you can mix and match.

In the classic Windows interface, you double-click to open an item whether it's on the Desktop or elsewhere, and folders and folder contents do not look or work like

Web pages. In the Web view, icons on the Desktop are underlined and behave like links in a Web document; that is, pointing to an item displays a hand as on a Web page, and you single-click to open an item.

By default, the Windows 2000 Professional interface is a hybrid: the Desktop displays in classic form, but Web content is enabled in folders. Thus, you double-click to open an item from the Desktop, and the contents of folders are displayed as Web pages. In this book, the illustrations show this default interface.

To specify Web view, classic view, or some combination, you use the Folder Options dialog box, as shown in Figure 6.2, which you can open in the following ways:

- Open Control Panel, and double-click Folder Options.
- On the Desktop, double-click My Computer to open the My Computer folder, and choose Tools ➢ Folder Options.
- Right-click the Start button, and choose Explore to open Explorer. Choose Tools ➢ Folder Options.

FIGURE 6.2
The Folder Options dialog box

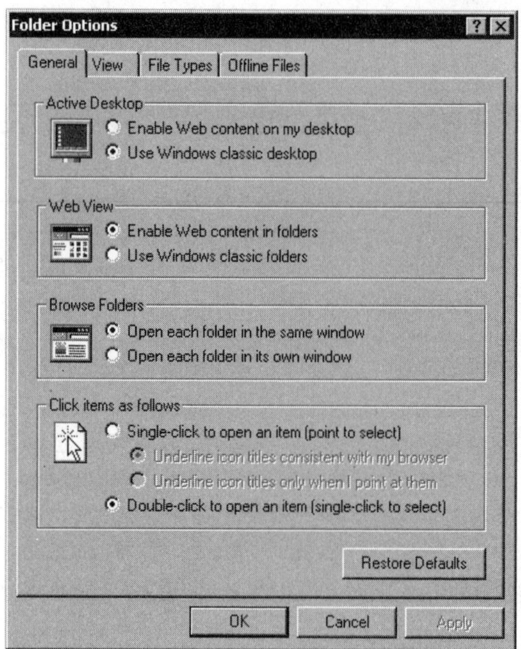

In the Active Desktop section, specify whether you want the classic or Web view of the Desktop. In the Web View section, specify how you want folders to look and work. In the Browse Folders section, specify whether to open each folder in the same window or in its own window. In the Click Items As Follows section, select single- or double-clicking.

Opinions seem to vary about which view is best. I've heard some so-called experts say that Web view is the wave of the future and that we should just use it and get used to it. Others really dislike it. I personally don't think it's a matter of consequence. Use whichever appeals to you. You do, however, need to know how each option works so that if you ever sit down at someone else's computer and see the icons underlined on the Desktop, you'll know how to navigate it.

Using Accessibility Options

Accessibility technology makes a computer easier to use for those with physical challenges, and in recent years we have seen many advances in these tools and utilities. Speech recognition systems, alternative keyboards, and adaptive devices for people with spinal cord injuries are but a few.

Enhancing the accessibility options was key in the development of Windows 2000 Professional. Nevertheless, the current tools provide only a minimal level of functionality for users with special needs. Most physically impaired users will need special programs and devices. For a list of these and some very helpful information, check out Microsoft's Accessibility Web site at `www.microsoft.com/enable/`.

In Windows 2000 Professional, you set up some accessibility options using the Accessibility Options applet in Control Panel, and you set up others through the Accessibility accessory, including the Accessibility Wizard. In this section, I'll start with a look at the applet, and then I'll look at the accessory.

NOTE To customize some of these features you'll need Administrator privileges on your Windows 2000 Professional computer.

Using the Accessibility Options Applet

You can set keyboard, sound, display, mouse, and administrative options using the Accessibility Options applet. To open it, click its icon in Control Panel. Figure 6.3 shows this applet open at the Keyboard tab.

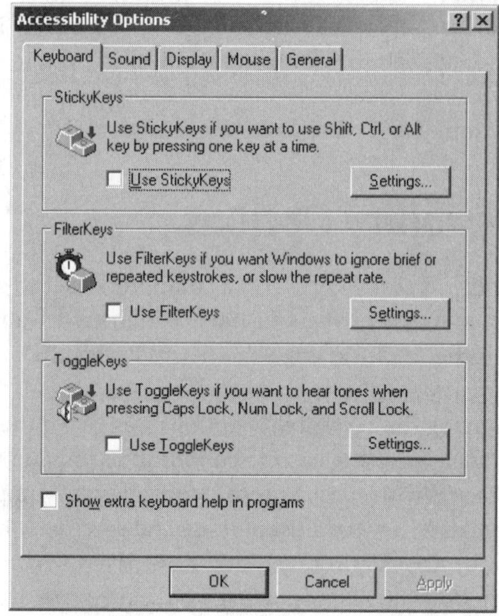

FIGURE 6.3 *To set keyboard options, you can use this tab, the Keyboard applet, and the Accessibility Wizard.*

- Click Use StickyKeys if you have trouble pressing two keys simultaneously, such as Ctrl+Alt.
- Click Use FilterKeys if you want brief or repeated keystrokes to be ignored.
- Click Use ToggleKeys if you want to hear a high-pitched sound when you press Caps Lock, Scroll Lock, or Num Lock and to hear a low-pitched sound when you turn off these keys.

To further modify any option, select it, and then click Settings to open the Settings dialog box for that option.

Here are the features available on the other tabs:

Sound Click Use SoundSentry if you want a visual clue when your system generates a sound. Click Use ShowSounds if you want to display captions for speech and sounds.

NOTE Not all programs work cooperatively with these sound options. As more programs are written to take advantage of these settings, you'll see more use of *closed captioning*, in which sound messages are translated into useful captions on the screen.

Display Click Use High Contrast and then click Settings to specify a black-and-white or a custom color scheme instead of a standard color scheme. You might consider enabling this feature if you are color-blind.

Mouse Click Use MouseKeys to control the mouse pointer with the keys on the numeric keypad.

General Use this tab to set a time after which accessibility features are turned off, to tell Windows 2000 Professional that you want a message or sound when turning a feature on or off, to enable an alternative mouse or keyboard device, and to select administrative options.

NOTE If you are an administrator, you can choose to apply the settings in the Accessibility Options dialog box to all users or to new users only.

Using the Accessibility Accessories

The Accessibility accessories include the Accessibility Wizard, the Magnifier, the Narrator, the On-Screen Keyboard, and the Utility Manager. Let's start with the Accessibility Wizard.

Using the Accessibility Wizard

This Wizard helps you customize Windows 2000 Professional for your vision, hearing, and mobility needs. To open it, choose Start ➢ Programs ➢ Accessories ➢ Accessibility ➢ Accessibility Wizard. At the Welcome screen, click Next, and then follow the on-screen instructions to configure such features as text size, display size, options for vision, hearing, and mobility, and the size and color of the mouse pointer. Figure 6.4 shows the Display Settings screen, which you use to specify font size, increase the size of items on the screen, use Magnifier, and disable personalized menus.

FIGURE 6.4
The Display Settings screen in the Accessibility Wizard

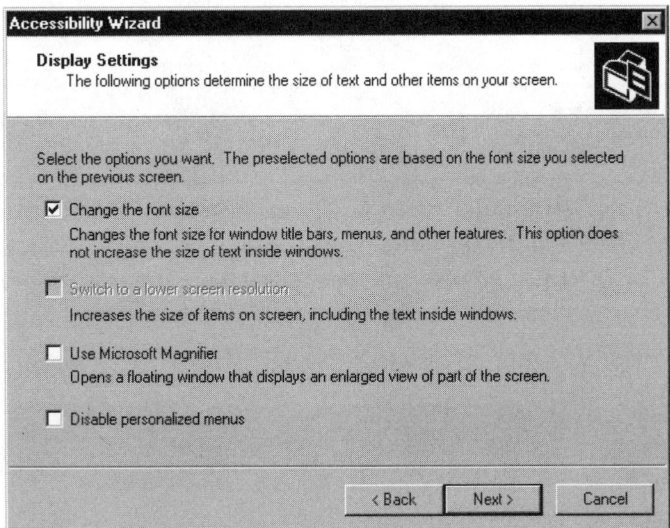

Using Magnifier

Magnifier is a utility that displays a magnified portion of your screen in a separate window. To start Magnifier, choose Start ➢ Programs ➢ Accessories ➢ Accessibility ➢ Magnifier. To configure Magnifier, follow these steps:

1. Open the Accessibility Wizard, and on the Text Size screen, choose Use Microsoft Magnifier And Large Titles And Menus, and then click Next.
2. Set the options you want in the Magnifier dialog box, which is shown in Figure 6.5. You can set Magnifier to follow the mouse, the keyboard focus, or text editing.

FIGURE 6.5 *The Magnifier dialog box*

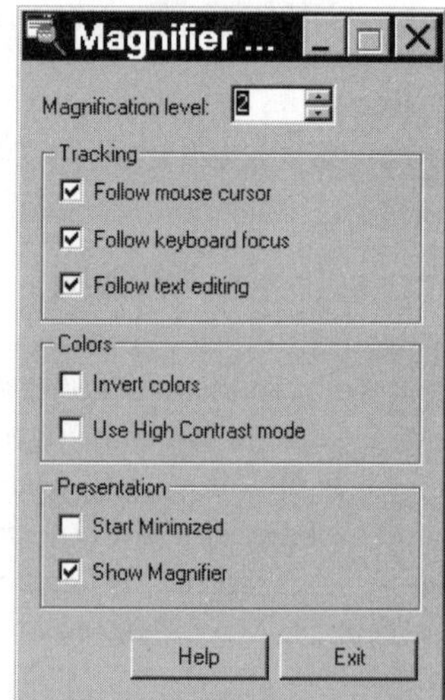

3. Click the Close button to return to normal view.

NOTE When Magnifier is running, you must make selections in the magnified portion of the screen.

Running Narrator

If you have a sound board, speakers, and a text-to-speech program, you can run Narrator. His name is Sam, and as you can see in Figure 6.6, he will tell you what's happening on the screen.

FIGURE 6.6
The Narrator can read items that are displayed on the screen.

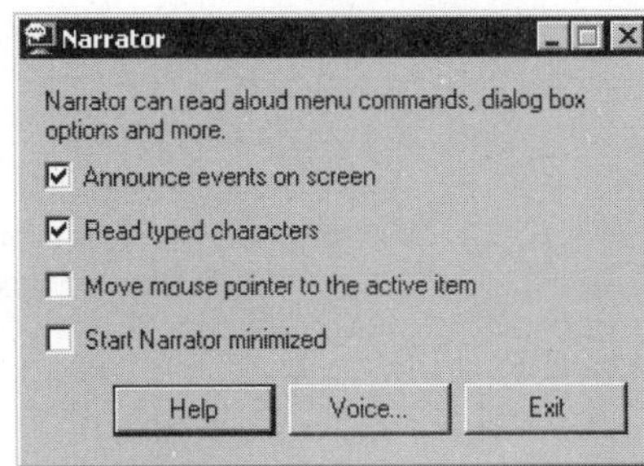

NOTE Narrator will read to you if you are working with Notepad, WordPad, Control Panel applets, Internet Explorer, the Desktop, and Windows 2000 Professional Setup. He may not read words correctly in other programs and is not available in all languages.

To adjust the speed at which Sam reads, his volume, and his pitch, click the Voice button to open the Voice Settings dialog box. To silence Sam, click the Exit button in the Narrator dialog box.

Using the On-Screen Keyboard

If you aren't a good typist or if you have a physical disability that makes typing difficult, you can display the keyboard on the screen and use the mouse to type. To see how this works, follow these steps:

1. Choose Start ➢ Programs ➢ Accessories ➢ Notepad to open Notepad.
2. Maximize Notepad.
3. Choose Start ➢ Programs ➢ Accessories ➢ On-Screen Keyboard.
4. Click the keys with your mouse to enter text in Notepad. You can alternate between "typing" on the keyboard and choosing commands from the menu in Notepad. Figure 6.7 shows the on-screen keyboard and my typing in Notepad.

FIGURE 6.7
To enter an uppercase character, click Shift, and then click the character. Did you notice that this is a Windows keyboard?

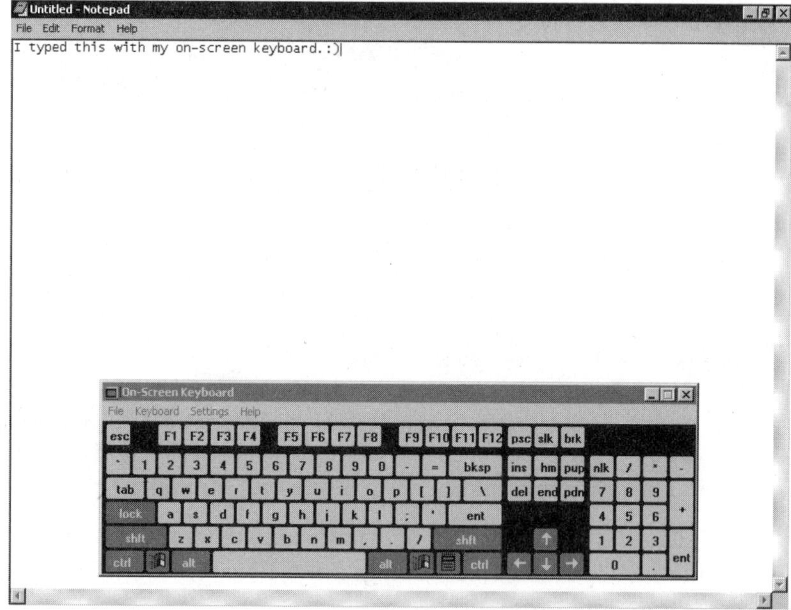

5. When you're finished, click Close to close both Notepad and the keyboard.

Using Utility Manager

You use Utility Manager, which is shown in Figure 6.8, to start and stop Magnifier, Narrator, and On-Screen Keyboard. You can specify that any one of the three start when Windows 2000 Professional starts or when you start Utility Manager. To start Utility Manager, choose Start ➢ Programs ➢ Accessories ➢ Accessibility ➢ Utility Manager, or press the Windows key+U.

FIGURE 6.8
Use the Utility Manager to establish accessibility settings.

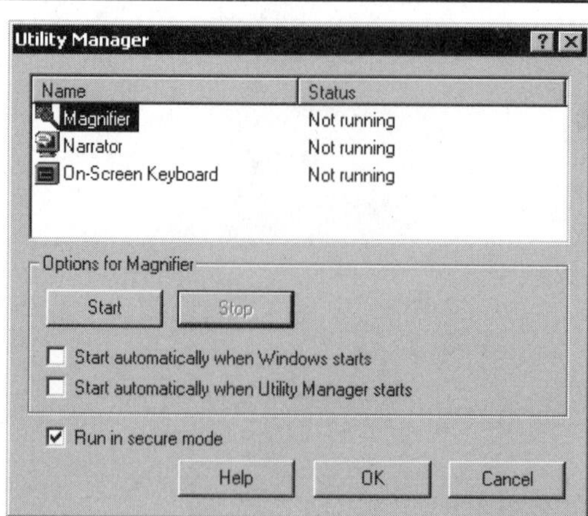

Setting the Date and Time

To adjust the system's date and time, you use the Date/Time applet in Control Panel. The system date and time are used for a number of purposes, including date- and time-stamping the files you create and modify as well as e-mail messages and scheduling fax transmissions. All programs use these settings, regardless of whether they are Windows or non-Windows programs. (You can't change the format of the date and time using this applet—just the actual date and time. To change the *format*, you use the Regional Options applet.) To set the date and time and change the time zone, follow these steps:

1. Open Control Panel, and double-click the Date/Time icon to open the Date/Time Properties dialog box, which is shown in Figure 6.9.

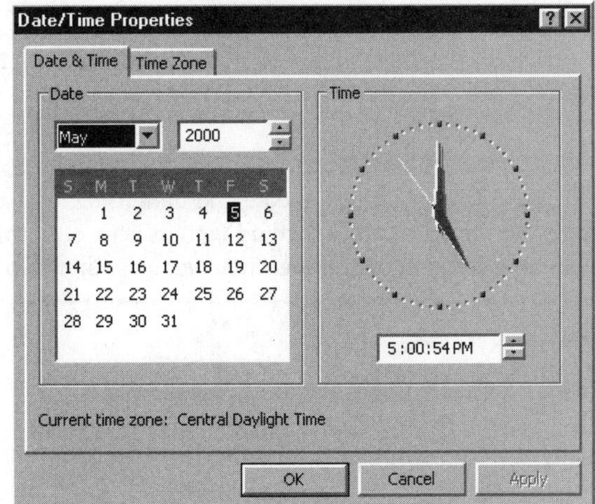

FIGURE 6.9
Adjust the date, time, and local time zone from this dialog box. A shortcut to this box is to double-click the time in the Taskbar.

2. Adjust the date and time by typing the corrections or clicking the arrows.

NOTE You have to click the hours, minutes, seconds, or AM/PM area before the little arrows to the right of them will modify the correct value.

3. Next, you can change the time zone. Who cares about the time zone, you ask? Good question. For many users it doesn't matter. But because people fax to other time zones, and some programs help you manage your transcontinental and transoceanic phone calling, time zone functionality is built in to Windows 2000 Professional. Some programs need to know where in the world you and Carmen Sandiego are. So, click the Time Zone tab to see a world map (see Figure 6.10).

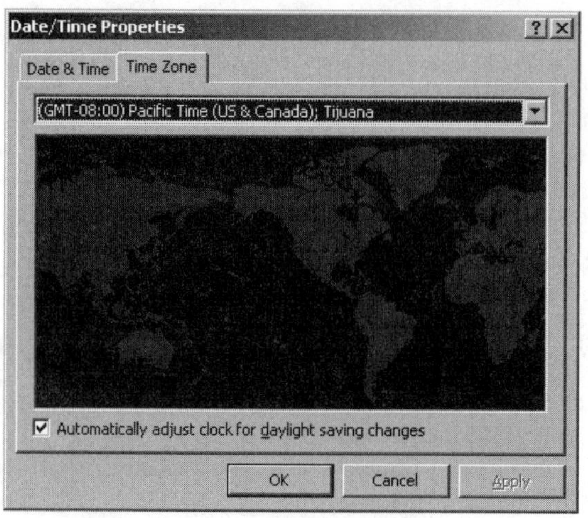

FIGURE 6.10
Check and set your time zone if necessary. Some programs use this information to help you schedule mail or fax transmissions to other time zones. For laptop users who travel, this can be a great boon. Just point to your new location and click. The computer's time is automatically adjusted.

TIP You can also adjust the date and time using the `date` and `time` commands from the command prompt. Another method is to use the `net time` command to synchronize your system time and date with a specific server on your network.

Customizing Your Screen Display

To alter the screen display, you use the Display applet. You can open it in a couple of ways:

- Choose Start ➢ Settings ➢ Control Panel, and double-click Display.
- Right-click an empty area of the Desktop, and choose Properties from the shortcut menu.

In either case, you'll see the Display Properties dialog box, as shown in Figure 6.11.

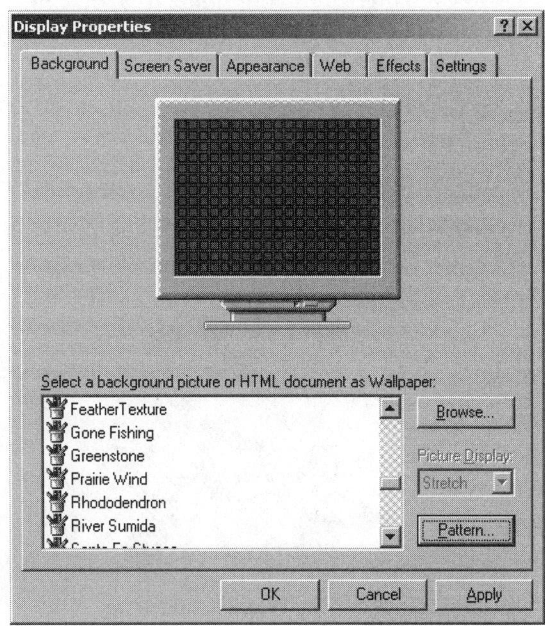

FIGURE 6.11
Use the Display Properties dialog box to alter the appearance of your screen.

Here are the functional and cosmetic adjustments you can make to your Windows 2000 Professional display from this applet:

- Set the background and wallpaper for the Desktop.
- Set the screen saver and energy conservation.
- Set the color scheme and fonts for Windows elements.
- Set the display device driver and adjust resolution, color depth, and font size.
- Adjust the display properties of multiple monitors if you have them.

Setting the Background and Wallpaper

If you want to decorate the Desktop with something a little more festive than the default screen, you can play around with the pattern and wallpaper setting. Patterns are repetitious designs, such as the woven look of fabric. Wallpaper uses larger pictures that were created by artists with a drawing program. You can create your own patterns and wallpaper, use the ones supplied, or even download art from the Web to use as wallpaper. You can wallpaper using a single copy of a picture placed in the center of the screen, or you can tile the picture, which gives you multiple identical images covering the whole screen.

If you are using the Active Desktop, you can use JPEG (JPG) files as wallpaper just as you would use them for backgrounds on your Web pages. These files are great because they occupy significantly less space on the hard drive than bitmap files. Of course, with the Active Desktop you can display entire Web pages as your background if you choose. This can range from your home page or some favorite Web site to custom-defined pages that you specify—something that really shows what's unique about you.

Loading a Pattern

To load a new pattern:

1. In the Display Properties dialog box, click the Background tab.
2. Set the Wallpaper to None, and click the Pattern button to open the Pattern dialog box:

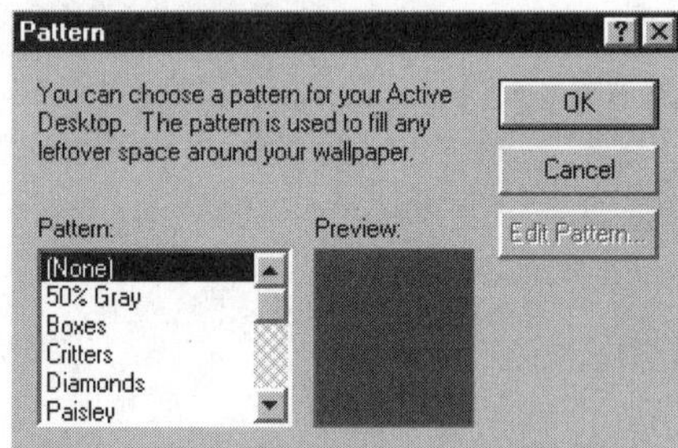

   Or, if you want to use wallpaper *and* a pattern, make sure the Picture Display setting is Center. This setting allows the pattern to show around the borders of the wallpaper.

3. From the Pattern list, select a pattern. The Preview box displays the design.
4. When you're satisfied with the pattern you've chosen, or if you just want to try it out, click OK to close the Pattern dialog box, and then click OK in the Display Properties dialog box.

NOTE For a pattern to show up, wallpaper must be set to None or the Picture Display option must be set to Center because wallpaper always sits on top of the Desktop's pattern.

Editing a Pattern

If the supplied patterns don't thrill you, make up your own with the built-in bitmap editor. You can either change an existing pattern or design your own. If you want to design your own, choose None from the drop-down list before you begin. Otherwise, choose a pattern you want to play with, and then follow these steps:

1. On the Background tab of the Display Properties dialog box, click the Pattern button to open the Pattern dialog box.
2. Select a pattern, and then click the Edit Pattern button to open the Pattern Editor dialog box:

3. In the Name text box, type a name for the new pattern.
4. To create the pattern, click in the Pattern box. What you are doing is defining the smallest element of the repeated pattern (a cell). The cell is enlarged to make editing easier. Each click reverses the color of one pixel. The effect when the pattern is applied across a larger area and in normal size is shown in the Sample section to the right.
5. When you like the pattern, click Add to add the pattern to your list of patterns.
6. Click the Done button when you're finished creating new patterns.

If you later want to remove a pattern, select it in the Pattern dialog box, click Edit Pattern to open the Pattern Editor, and click Remove. If you want to edit an existing pattern, open the Pattern Editor, select an existing pattern, make changes to it, and click Change.

TIP If you want to abandon changes you've made to a pattern, click the Close button (X) in the upper-right corner, and answer No to the question about saving the changes.

Loading a New Slice of Wallpaper

The images used in wallpaper are usually bitmap (BMP) files created by programs such as Paintbrush. Other programs create bitmap files too, so the sky's the limit as far as what you can use as wallpaper. For example, you could use a scanned color photograph of your favorite movie star, a pastoral setting, some computer art, a scanned Matisse painting, or a photo of your pet lemur.

To load a new BMP file and display it as wallpaper, follow these steps:

1. Create or otherwise obtain the image with whatever program you want, as long as the program saves the image as a BMP file.
2. In the Display Properties dialog box, click the Browse button to open the Browse dialog box.

3. Switch to the folder containing your BMP file, select the file, and click OK.
4. Click OK to apply the new wallpaper and close the dialog box.

To use an image you find on the Internet as wallpaper, simply right-click it, and choose Set As Wallpaper from the shortcut menu.

Setting the Screen Saver

A screen saver blanks your screen or displays a moving image or pattern if you don't use the mouse or keyboard for a predetermined amount of time. Screen savers were originally developed to prevent a static image from burning the delicate phosphors on the inside surface of the monitor, which could leave a ghost of the image on the screen for all time regardless of what was displayed. Although today's monitors are not susceptible to this problem, many people continue to use screen savers for their decorative and entertainment value.

The screen saver options enable you to choose or create an entertaining video ditty that will greet you when you return to work. You also can set how much time you have after your last keystroke or mouse skitter before the show begins.

Loading a Screen Saver

Here's how it's done:

1. In the Display Properties dialog box, click the Screen Saver tab:

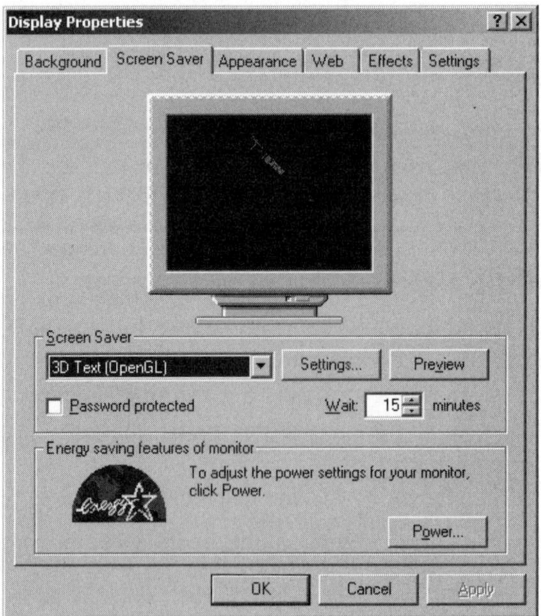

2. Choose a name from the drop-down list. You'll see a preview in the little screen.

3. Want to see how it will look on your whole screen? Click the Preview button. Your screen goes black and then begins its antics. The show continues until you press any key or move your mouse.
4. If you want to change anything about the selected screen saver, click Settings to open the Setup dialog box for that screen saver. Here's the Setup dialog box for the 3D Text (OpenGL) screen saver:

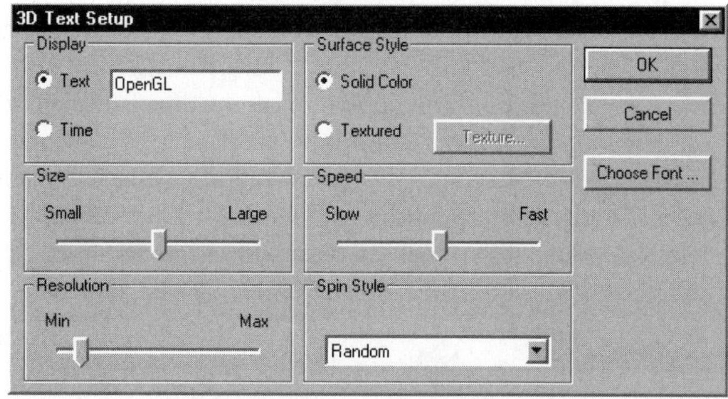

5. Most of the option boxes have fun sliders and stuff you can play with to get an effect you like. Depending on the screen saver you chose, you may need to make a few adjustments, such as speed, placement, and details pertinent to the graphic. Play with the settings until you're happy with the results, and then click OK.
6. Back at the Screen Saver tab, the next choice you might want to consider is Password Protected. If you set password protection on, every time your screen saver is activated you must type your password into a box to return to work. This is good if you don't want anyone else tampering with your files or seeing what you're doing. It can be a pain, though, if there's no particular need for privacy at your computer. To cancel the screen saver, you must press Ctrl+Alt+Del and enter the same password you use to log on to Windows 2000 Professional. If you cannot get back in, don't worry. An administrator can unlock the machine by entering their password. If they do this, it will log off your session, so the Administrator can't see your work. Click the Password Protected check box if you want protection, and proceed to the next two steps.
7. Set the number of minutes you want your computer to be idle before the screen saver springs into action. Next to Wait, either type a number or use the up and down arrows to change the time incrementally.
8. When all the settings are correct, click Apply or OK.

NOTE Have you ever wondered about the difference between the OK and Apply buttons? Clicking Apply makes the change but leaves the window or dialog box open; clicking OK makes the change and closes the window or dialog box. You can use either one. You do not have to click Apply and then OK in order to save your changes.

Adjusting the Power Settings

Many of today's monitors have an EPA Energy Star, Video Electronics Standards Association (VESA), or other kind of energy-saving strategy built into them. Because far too many people leave their computers on all the time (although it's not really true that they will last longer that way), efforts have been made by power regulators and electronics manufacturers to devise energy-conservation schemes for computers. If your monitor has an Energy Star rating and your video board supports this feature, the screen saver in Windows 2000 Professional can power down the monitor after it senses you went out to lunch or got caught up at the water cooler for a longer-than-expected break.

TIP For an energy-saving screen saver to work properly, the monitor must adhere to the VESA Display Power Management Signaling (DPMS) specification or to another method of lowering power consumption. Some LCD screens on portable computers can do this. You can assume that if your monitor has an Energy Star emblem, it probably supports DPMS. Energy Star is a program administered by the U.S. Environmental Protection Agency (EPA) to reduce the amount of power used by personal computers and peripherals. The Energy Star emblem does not represent EPA endorsement of any product or service. If you notice that your screen freaks out or the display is garbled after your power-management screen saver turns on, you should turn off these settings.

To enable the energy-saving features, follow these steps:

1. In the Display Properties dialog box, click the Screen Saver tab, and then click Power to open the Power Options Properties dialog box:

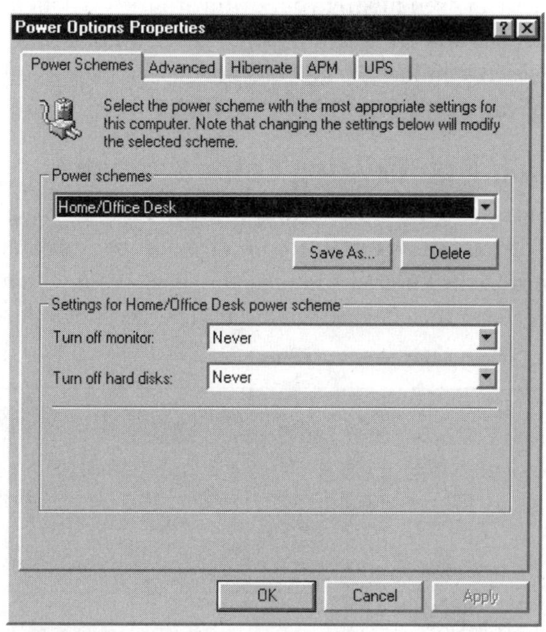

2. Click the Power Schemes tab, if necessary.
3. In the Power Schemes drop-down list, select the power scheme that is appropriate for your system.
4. In the Settings For Home/Office Desk Power Scheme section, select the amount of time after which you want your monitor and hard disks to turn off.
5. Use the options on the other tabs to show a power management icon on the Taskbar, set hibernation options, enable Advanced Power Management support, and configure an Uninterruptible Power Supply (UPS).
6. Click OK when you have set all your options.

Adjusting the Appearance

You use the Appearance tab in the Display Properties dialog box to change the way Windows 2000 Professional assigns colors and fonts to various parts of the screen. If you're using a monochrome monitor (no color), altering the colors may still have some effect (how much effect depends on how you installed Windows 2000 Professional).

Windows 2000 Professional sets itself up using a default color scheme that's fine for most screens—and if you're happy with your colors as they are, you might not want to futz around with them.

However, the color settings options for Windows 2000 Professional are flexible, and you can modify the color setting of just about any part of a screen. For those of you who are particular about color choices, you can do this manually, choosing colors from a palette or even mixing your own with the Custom Colors feature. Once created, custom colors and color setups can be saved on disk for later use or automatically loaded with each Windows 2000 Professional session. A number of color scheme options are supplied.

Loading an Existing Color Scheme

The various parts of the Windows 2000 Professional graphical environment that you can alter are shown in the top portion of the Appearance tab (see Figure 6.12) and are named in the lower portion. As you select color schemes, these samples change so that you can see the effect without having to go into Windows 2000 Professional proper.

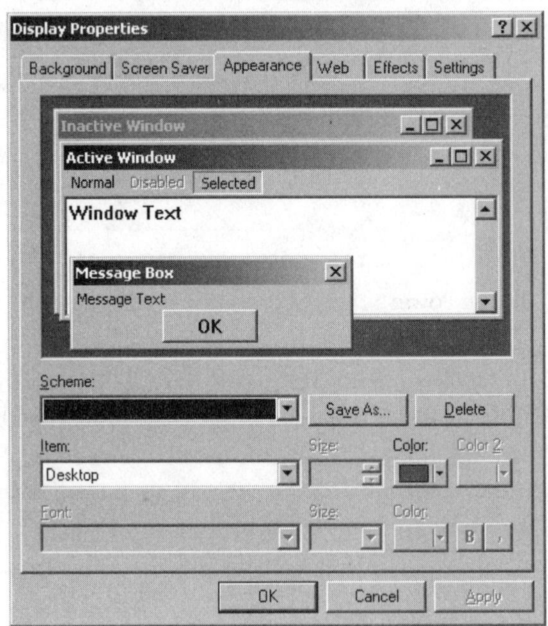

FIGURE 6.12
The dialog box for setting the colors, fonts, and metrics of the Windows 2000 Professional environment

Before playing with the custom color palette, first try loading the supplied ones; you may find one you like. Follow these steps:

1. Click the Scheme drop-down list box.

TIP You can always toggle a drop-down list box open and closed from the keyboard by pressing Alt+down arrow or Alt+up arrow.

2. You can cycle through the color schemes without selecting them from the drop-down list: with the Scheme space highlighted, press the up arrow and down

arrow keys. The sample screen elements change to reflect each color scheme as its name appears in the Scheme box.

3. Click the Apply button or click OK to apply the settings to all Windows 2000 Professional activities.

Microsoft has incorporated a few color schemes that may enhance the operation of your computer:

- On LCD screens that you'll be using in bright light, you might try the setting called High-Contrast White.
- If your eyes are weary, you might want to try one of the settings with the words Large or Extra Large in the name. These settings display menus, items in dialog boxes, and the names on title bars in large letters.

Choosing Your Own Colors and Changing Fonts

If you don't like the supplied color schemes, you can create your own. The easiest way to do this is to start with a scheme that's close to what you want and then modify it. Once you adjust the scheme to your liking, you can save it under a new name for later use. To create your own color scheme, follow these steps:

1. In the Appearance tab of the Display Properties dialog box, select a scheme from the Scheme list, select a Windows element from the Item list, and then click the Color button to display the Color palette:

2. To assign a color to the item, click the color. Repeat the process for each color you want to change. Want more colors? Click the Other button to open the Color dialog box.
3. Once the color scheme suits your fancy, click the Save As button to open the Save Scheme dialog box.
4. Give your new scheme a name, and then click OK.

TIP If you want to remove a scheme (for instance, there may be schemes that you know you'll never use), select it from the Scheme drop-down list, and click the Delete button.

You can make two other major adjustments to your display—the fonts used for various screen elements and Windows *metrics* that affect the size of some screen elements.

To change the font of elements, follow these steps:

1. On the Appearance tab, simply click the element whose font you want to change. In the Size spin box next to the Item drop-down list, you'll see the current font size.
2. To change the font, the font size, the color, or the style (boldface or italic), click the appropriate box at the bottom of the dialog box.
3. To save your scheme, click Save As, give the scheme a name, and click OK.

Many screen elements—such as the borders of windows—have a constant predetermined size; however, you might want to change these settings. If you have trouble grabbing the borders of windows, for example, you might want to make them larger. If you want icons on your Desktop and in folders to line up closer or farther apart, you can do that too. To change the size of screen elements, follow these steps:

1. Select an element from the Item list, and then click the up or down arrow in the Size box

   You'll see the effect of your choice in the Window Elements display.
2. Click the Apply button to check out the effects of the changes. You might want to switch to another application via the Taskbar to see how things look.
3. If you don't like the effects of the changes you've made, you can either return to the Appearance tab and click Cancel, or, because the screen metrics are recorded on each color scheme, you can select another color scheme.

Changing the Web Settings

You can use the Web tab (see Figure 6.13) in the Display Properties dialog box to customize the Desktop with animations, graphics, and even live content from the Internet.

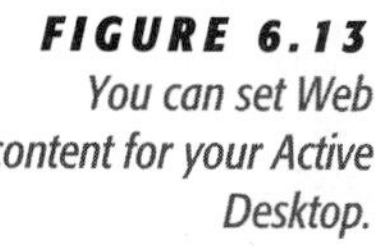

FIGURE 6.13
You can set Web content for your Active Desktop.

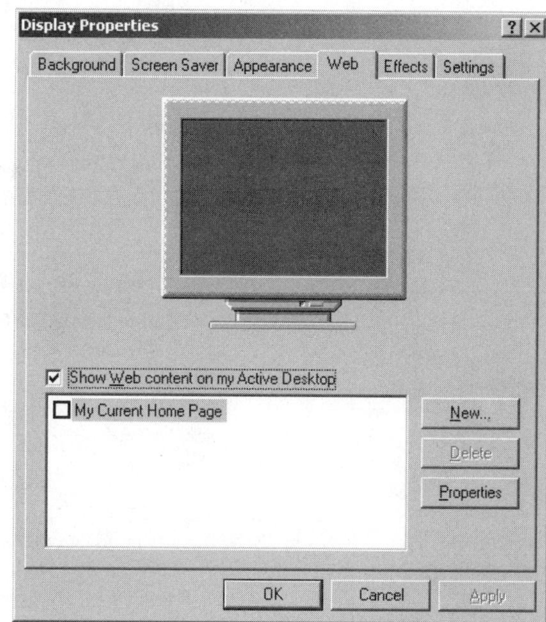

To set up Web content for your Active Desktop, follow these steps:

1. In the Web tab, click the Show Web Content On My Active Desktop check box.
2. To use your current home page, simply click OK. Figure 6.14 shows my Active Desktop with a page from `minasi.com`.

FIGURE 6.14
My Active Desktop, using a page from my Web site

3. To add other live content or pictures to your Active Desktop, click the New button to open the New Active Desktop Item dialog box:

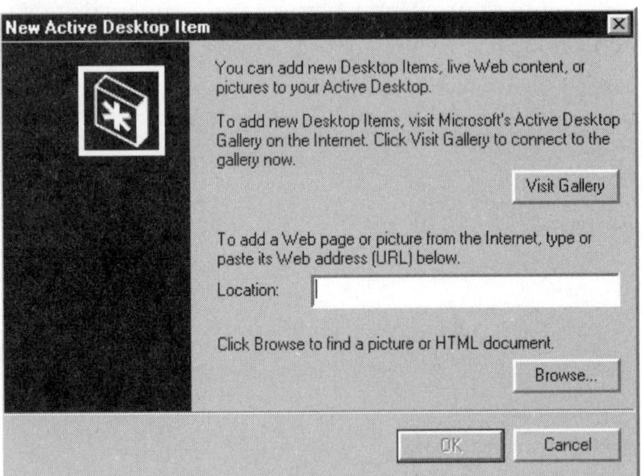

4. To select an item from Microsoft's Internet gallery, click the Visit Gallery button.
5. To add a Web page or a picture from the Internet, enter its URL in the Location box.

6. To find a picture or an HTML document, click the Browse button to open the Browse dialog box.
7. Click OK when you have selected an item to add the content to your Desktop.

In the Web tab, click the Properties button to open the Properties dialog box for the item you select to display on your Active Desktop. Click the Schedule tab to specify that the page be cached locally for display when you aren't connected to the Internet. When you do connect, you can update the offline page by choosing Tools ➢ Synchronize In Internet Explorer.

NOTE See Chapter 12 for information about Internet Explorer.

Changing the Visual Effects

You use the Effects tab (see Figure 6.15) of the Display Properties dialog box to change the appearance of icons and other visual effects.

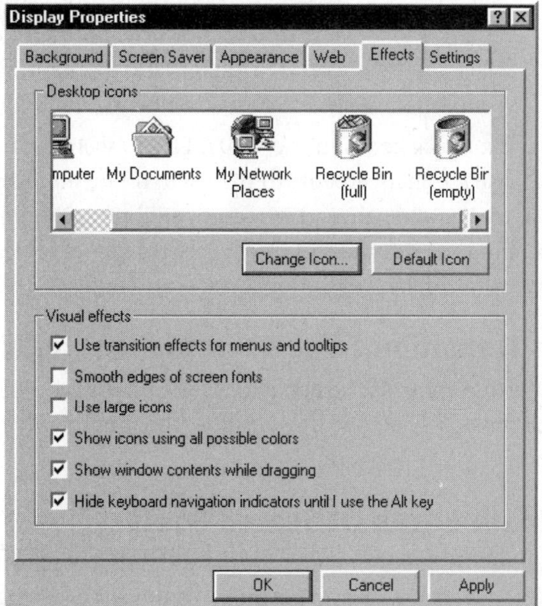

FIGURE 6.15
The Effects tab

Yes, this means that you aren't stuck with using the wastebasket for the Recycle Bin or any of the other Desktop icons. If you don't like some of them, select another. To do so, follow these steps:

1. In the Effects tab, select an icon from the Desktop Icons section, and then click the Change Icon button to open the Change Icon dialog box:

2. Select the new icon you prefer, and click OK. If you have other icon graphics stored on your system or your network, click the Browse button to locate one.

The six check boxes in the Visual Effects section of the Effects tab provide additional visual enhancements to the shell. If you are running in greater than 256-color mode, try enabling all of them, and you'll notice quite a difference. These options exemplify the usefulness of multiple settings—at lower resolutions, you won't want them, but at higher resolutions, they can make your system look great.

Use Transition Effects For Menus And ToolTips

This setting controls the behavior of your menus in Windows 2000 Professional. If you check the box to enable these effects, the menus will appear to be animated as they unfold.

Smooth Edges Of Screen Fonts

Enabling this option requires video modes that support more than 256 colors. This option uses shades of gray to smooth out the jagged edges of certain letters in large font sizes. You will especially notice the jagged edges (or "jaggies" as some folks refer to them) if you look at letters that have rounded edges—*o*, *p*, *q*, *s*, and so on. Although font smoothing does takes care of the jaggies problem, it might make your characters appear slightly blurry or fuzzy around the edges. Try it in any case; you'll probably like it.

Use Large Icons

If you've played around with different screen resolutions, you've probably noticed how, as the screen resolution is increased, the relative size of everything on your Desktop decreases. At 1024 or 1280 resolution, especially on a 17-inch or larger display, your icons start to look like Shrinky Dinks, and this is where Use Large Icons becomes helpful. Some applications (and the shell) supply a set of larger-sized icons, and the system makes use of these. Otherwise, the larger-sized icons are created on the fly by expanding the standard-sized ones.

Show Icons Using All Possible Colors

This option has a pleasing effect—particularly with icons that were designed using more than 16 colors. The shell contains a set of high-color icons for the folder icons, My Computer, My Network Places, Recycle Bin, and so on. As time goes on, more applications will likely ship with a set of high-color (and larger) icons built-in. As with the Smooth Edges Of Screen Fonts option, you must be running in greater than 256-color mode to use this option.

Show Window Contents While Dragging

This is a fun option, provided your video controller is up to speed. In addition to letting you see the full window contents while dragging, it also gives instant feedback when resizing a window—no need to let go of the window to see how it will look when resized. This option works better (that is, the windows slide more smoothly) if your Desktop isn't covered by wallpaper.

Hide Keyboard Navigation Indicators Until I Use The Alt Key

Selecting this option turns off keyboard shortcuts (the underlined characters in menus and controls) so that you see cleaner menus throughout the interface. In addition, selecting this option turns off the focus indicators (that little dashed line that indicates the default button in dialog boxes). With this option checked, these items are not displayed until you use the Alt key to display a menu. After you start using the keyboard to navigate, the keyboard shortcuts and focus indicators are turned on again.

Adjusting the Driver Settings

You use the options on the Settings tab (see Figure 6.16) to manipulate the video driver responsible for your video card's capability to display Windows. These settings are more substantial than those that adjust whether dialog boxes are mauve or chartreuse because they load a different driver or bump your video card up or down into a completely different resolution and color depth. This changes the amount of information you can see on the screen at once.

FIGURE 6.16
The Settings tab of the Display Properties dialog box controls the video card's device driver. With most video systems, the slider lets you adjust the screen resolution on the fly. Changing color depth may require a restart, however.

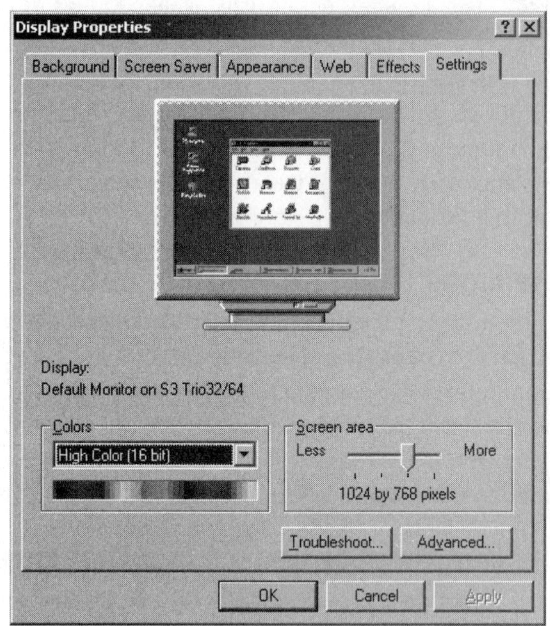

Next, let's take a look at the individual settings on the Settings tab.

Colors

Assuming your video card was properly identified when you installed Windows 2000 Professional, the Colors drop-down list box includes all the legitimate options available for your card. As you may know, the number of colors that your monitor can display depends on the video card. Your monitor is not the limiting factor (with the exception of color LCD screens such as those on laptops, which do have limitations); the limitations have to do with how much RAM is on your video card. All of today's analog color monitors for PCs can display 16 million colors, which is dubbed True Color.

It's possible that the drop-down list will include color amounts (called *depths*) that exceed your video card's capabilities, in which case such a choice won't have any effect. On the other hand, if your setting is 16 colors and your screen can support 256 or more, Windows 2000 Professional will look a lot prettier if you choose 256 and then choose one of the 256-color schemes from the Appearance tab.

TIP There is a trade-off between higher color depth and system resources: the more colors you choose to have available at any one time, the slower your video system performs. The price may be only marginal on systems with today's fast video cards, and you probably won't notice any slowdown, but keep it in mind.

Windows 2000 Professional doesn't require you to reboot after adding a new display driver. You can choose the new settings and click either Apply or OK to make the change. Windows 2000 Professional will tell you that it will apply the change for 15 seconds, at the end of which time it will revert to the old setting if you don't decide to keep the new setting. If you click OK to this warning and you can see the new setting correctly, click OK to keep the new setting.

Screen Area

Some jobs—such as working with large spreadsheets, databases, Computer Aided Design (CAD), or typesetting—are much more efficient with more data displayed on the screen. To display more data, you need to change the screen resolution, and you do so using the Settings tab in the Display Properties dialog box.

Because higher resolutions require a trade-off in clarity and make on-screen objects smaller, eyestrain can be minimized by going to a lower resolution, such as 640 by 480 pixels (a pixel equals one dot on the screen). A relationship exists between the color depth and the resolution that's available because your video card can have only so much RAM on it. That RAM can be used to display extra colors *or* extra resolution, but not both. So, if you bump up the number of colors, you won't have as many resolution options. If the dialog box won't let you choose the resolution you want, try dropping the color palette setting to a lower color depth.

To change the resolution, you move the slider in the Screen Area section of the Settings tab. The little screen in the dialog box indicates how you screen will look once you apply the setting.

NOTE As of this writing, many laptops still have screens that can display only one resolution, often 800 by 600. This has been changing with the advent of the newer Thin Film Technology (TFT) LCD screens. Laptops now have much the same capabilities as desktop computers.

After you adjust the slider, click OK to apply the changes to your settings. Windows 2000 Professional will apply the changes and ask you if you want to keep the new settings. If you can't see the new settings, don't panic. Windows 2000 Professional will automatically resume the previous settings in 15 seconds if you don't confirm the new configuration.

TIP Even if you change the Colors setting, you should be able to change the Screen Area setting without restarting Windows 2000 Professional.

Troubleshoot

Clicking the Troubleshoot button opens Windows 2000 Help directly to the Display Troubleshooter. This troubleshooting tool can help you find the cause of and resolution to most of the common video display problems you encounter. I highly recommend that you take a look at this feature at least once, even if you don't need it. Just knowing that it's there can be a help in itself.

Advanced

Clicking the Advanced button displays a dialog box that is specific to your display adapter and monitor. Figure 6.17 shows this dialog box, for my monitor.

FIGURE 6.17
Use this dialog box to control advanced settings for your display.

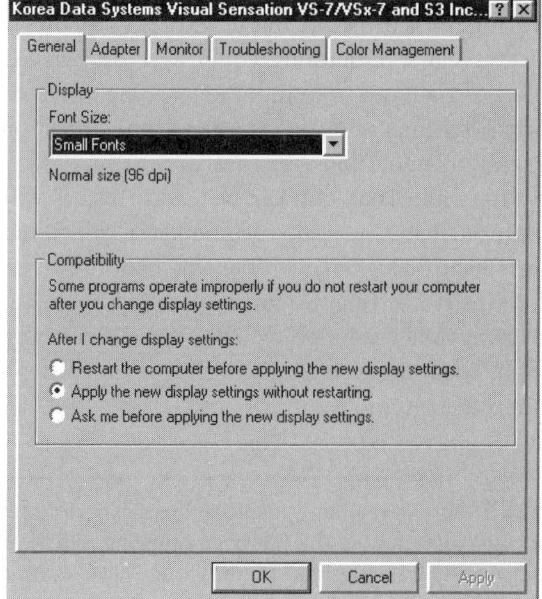

The General Tab

As you may know, some screen drivers use different font sizes for screen elements such as dialog boxes and menus. When you switch to a high Desktop area resolution, such as 1280 by 1024, these screen elements can get quite small, blurry, and difficult to read. For this reason, you can adjust the font size. Of course, you can do this via the

Fonts settings on the Appearance tab as discussed earlier, but doing it here is a little simpler. If you select a Desktop area greater than 640 by 480, you have the choice of Small Fonts or Large Fonts. Especially for resolutions of 1024 by 768 or above, you might want to check out the Large Fonts selection from this drop-down list. If you want, you can also choose a custom-size font. Select the Font Size drop-down list to open the Custom Font Size dialog box, which lets you declare the amount that you want the fonts scaled. The range is from 75 to 200 percent.

The Adapter Tab

You use the Adapter tab to view and change the properties for the display adapter. Click the Properties button to open the Properties dialog box for your adapter. If you want to change the driver or add another display adapter, you will need to visit the Add/Remove Hardware applet in Control Panel.

The Adapter Information section shows the information about the currently installed display adapter such as memory installed, BIOS, and manufacturer. Click the List All Modes button to open the List All Modes dialog box, which displays a list of all of the possible modes that this driver and adapter can produce.

The Monitor Tab

This tab gives you access to the driver properties and settings that deal with the monitor itself. The Monitor Type section shows the currently installed monitor type. Use the Refresh Frequency drop-down list box in the Monitor Settings section to change the refresh rate for the monitor.

NOTE If you specify a refresh rating that is too high for your monitor, trying to expand the Desktop area to a larger size may not work. You'll just get a mess on the screen. If this happens, try using a setting with a lower refresh rate, such as 60Hz or interlaced. The image may flicker a bit more, but at least it will be clearly visible.

A check box below the Refresh Frequency list box tells Windows 2000 Professional to hide any video mode that is inappropriate for your current configuration. This is a great idea, because setting your monitor to a refresh frequency that is too high can permanently damage your monitor.

The Troubleshooting Tab

The Troubleshooting tab includes a slider control that adjusts the amount of hardware acceleration that Windows 2000 Professional will use. Hardware acceleration settings control how Windows uses your graphics hardware. Some hardware configurations don't like the highest acceleration setting. If you are experiencing some display anomalies such as flickering, corrupted images, and mouse cursor problems, experiment with the hardware acceleration settings that disable portions of the acceleration. As you move the slider from Full to None, you'll see a description of each setting:

Full (All Accelerations Are Enabled) This is the default setting, with all performance enhancements enabled.

Disable Cursor And Bitmap Accelerations This setting can help resolve problems with the mouse cursor or issues with displaying bitmap images.

Disable All Cursor And Advanced Drawing Accelerations This setting disables the optimizations for drawing images on the screen.

Disable All DirectDraw And Direct3D Accelerations This setting is helpful in determining if DirectX is causing the problem with your display.

Disable All But Basic Accelerations This turns off all but the most basic accelerations in your graphics display.

None (Disable All Accelerations) This setting disables all graphics accelerations. If this setting solves the issues you're having with the display, it may be time to think seriously about a new video card.

The Color Management Tab

The settings on this tab have to do with the overall colors that you see displayed on your monitor. Anyone remember being yelled at by Dad to leave the hue, color, and tint settings alone on the TV? These settings are basically the same as those on a TV, but they're packed into management schemes that are appropriate for your monitor. Using one of these Color Profiles may give you a much more pleasing view on your monitor.

Adjusting the Mouse

You can adjust the following six aspects of your mouse's operation:

- Left/right button reversal
- Double-click speed
- Appearance of the pointers
- Tracking speed
- Mouse trails
- Mouse type and driver

NOTE The Mouse Trails option appears only if your mouse driver provides support for this feature.

Switching the Buttons and Setting Double-Click Speed

If you're left-handed, you may want to switch the mouse around to use it on the left side of the computer and reverse the buttons. The main button then becomes the right button instead of the left one. If you use other programs outside Windows that don't allow this, however, switching the buttons might just add to the confusion. If you use the mouse only in Windows programs and you're left-handed, it's worth a try. Follow these steps to reverse your mouse buttons:

1. In Control Panel, double-click Mouse to open the Mouse Properties dialog box:

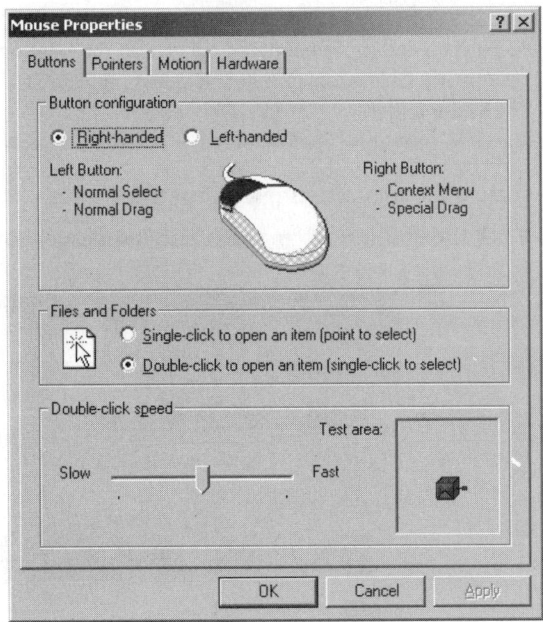

2. Click the Left-Handed option button, and then click Apply to check it out. Don't like it? Revert to the original setting, and click Apply again.

In the Files And Folders section, choose whether you want to single-click or double-click to open files and folders.

In the Double-Click Speed section, move the slider to specify a slower or faster double-click speed. Double-click the Jack-in-the-Box to try out the new double-click speed. Jack jumps out or back into the box if the double-click registered. If you're not faring well, adjust the slider, and try again.

NOTE You don't need to click Apply to test the slider settings. Just moving the slider instantly affects the mouse's double-click speed.

Setting Your Pointers

Your mouse pointer's shape depends on what you are pointing at and what Windows 2000 Professional is doing. If you are pointing to a window border, the pointer becomes a two-headed arrow. If Windows 2000 Professional is busy, the pointer becomes an hourglass. When you are editing text, the pointer becomes an I-beam, and so on.

You can customize your pointers for the fun of it or to increase visibility. You can even install animated cursors that look really cute and keep you amused while you wait for some process to complete.

TIP You can find more animated cursors on the Internet and through information services such as America Online and CompuServe. Just copy the ANI files into your Cursors folder, which is in the Winnt folder.

To change the cursor settings, follow these steps:

1. Click the Pointers tab in the Mouse Properties dialog box:

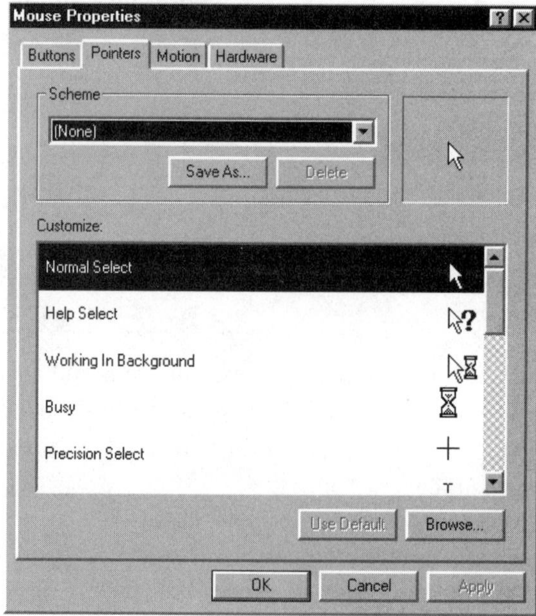

2. The list shows the pointers currently assigned to each activity. To change an assignment, click an item in the list.
3. Next, if you've changed the shape and want to revert, click Use Default to go back to the standard pointer shape that Windows 2000 Professional came with. Other-

wise, choose Browse, and use the Browse dialog box to load the cursor you want. When you click a cursor in the Browse box, it is displayed in the Preview box.

4. Click the Open button. The cursor is now applied to the activity in question.

You can save pointer schemes just as you can colors. If you want to set up several schemes (one for each person in the house, for example), assign the settings the way you like, click Save As to open the Save Scheme dialog box, enter a name, and click OK. To select a scheme later, open the drop-down list, select the scheme's name, and click Apply or OK.

Setting the Pointer Motion

You can make two useful adjustments to the way the mouse responds to the motion of your hand—speed and trails—and you do so using the Motion tab, which is shown in Figure 6.18.

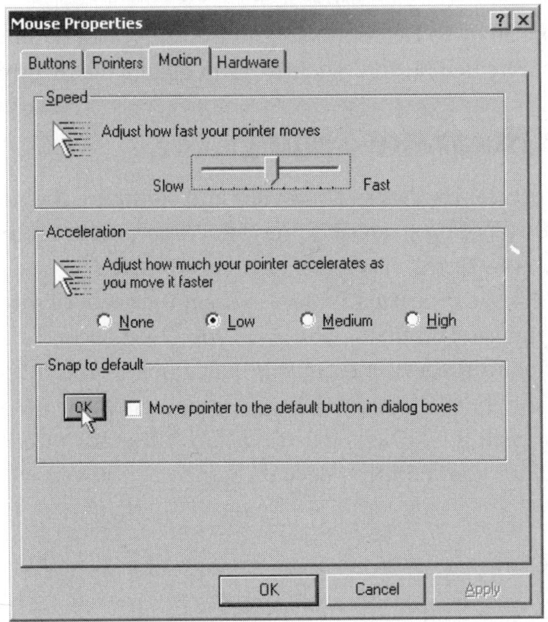

FIGURE 6.18
You can adjust the speed at which the mouse pointer moves and whether the cursor snaps to the default button in dialog boxes.

Pointer speed is the speed at which the mouse pointer moves relative to the movement of the mouse. Believe it or not, mouse motion is measured in *Mickeys*! (Somebody out there has a sense of humor.) A Mickey equals 1/100 of an inch of mouse movement. You use the Speed setting to adjust the relationship of Mickeys to pixels. If you want to be exact in your cursor movement, you'll want to slow the tracking speed, requiring more Mickeys per pixel. However, this requires more hand motion for the same corresponding cursor motion. If your desk is crammed and your coordination is good, you can increase the speed (fewer Mickeys per pixel).

If your mouse driver supports the option, mouse trails create a shadow of the mouse's path whenever you move it. Some people find it annoying, but for those who have trouble finding the pointer on the screen, it's a blessing. Mouse trails are particularly helpful when using Windows on passive-matrix or dual-scan laptop computers, where the pointer often disappears when you move it.

Here are the steps for changing these items:

1. Drag the speed slider one way or another to increase or decrease the motion of the pointer relative to your hand (or thumb in the case of a trackball) motion. Nothing may happen until you click Apply. Adjust as necessary. Try aiming for an item on the screen, and see how well you succeed. Setting the motion too fast can result in muscle strain and in holding the mouse too tight. It's ergonomically more sound to use a little slower setting that requires more hand motion.
2. Click OK or Apply to make it all official.

The Snap To Default setting causes the cursor to automatically move to the default or highlighted button whenever you open a dialog box.

Mouse Hardware Settings

You use the Hardware tab to view and configure the hardware settings for your installed pointing device. Click the Troubleshoot button to start the Mouse Troubleshooter in Help.

Click the Properties button to open the Mouse Properties dialog box for your specific mouse. This dialog box gives you direct access to the driver settings that control your pointing device. From this dialog box, you can update the driver to a newer version using the Driver tab, change resources on the Resource tab, and make advanced settings on the Advanced Settings tab. These advanced settings are specific to the driver for your pointing device.

Summary

As you have seen, most of the adjustments you can make through Control Panel are not necessities as much as they are niceties. You can change settings to match the way your equipment behaves, but you can also change settings to match the way *you* like to behave. Remember, after you change a setting with Control Panel, your alterations are stored in the Windows Registry. Your settings are reloaded each time you run Windows 2000 Professional and stay in effect until you change them with Control Panel.

CHAPTER 7

Printers and Printing

FEATURING:

With the advent of computers came the notion of the "paperless office." In fact, the goal of the paperless office was heralded as practically the eighth wonder of the world, and computers were to be the key to this promised miracle. My, how times change.

Doing without paper is a wild fantasy in most businesses today. Working completely without a printer to produce most of that paper is totally unthinkable. Go into any office, and you'll hear printers churning out reports, receipts, payroll checks, and even the boss's daughter's eighth-grade term paper. No, the paperless office is a miracle that is far too good to be true. The speed of the printer, color of the page, and clarity of the graphics are products much more important these days than a lack of file drawers.

As necessary as they are, however, printers are still big and expensive, and printers aren't used every minute that a computer is used. Sharing a printer between 2 workstations or even among 20 workstations can be a practical solution to money and space constraints. Windows 2000 Professional provides easy, efficient, and helpful tools for sharing a printer among workstations.

At times, however, not sharing a printer is important as well. For example, when the weekly newsletter is printed, all other printing tasks must take a back seat. Windows 2000 Professional comes with security measures that can be easily arranged to give one person or a group of people particular access rights and to give people access at different times of the day. If your printer seems overused, the auditing feature can provide detailed accounts of who used the printer when so that you can allocate resources more efficiently.

Printing in Windows 2000 Professional

The first thing to get out of the way is some basic terminology. In the language of Windows 2000 Professional printing, a *printer* is the software that controls a *print device*, which is the hardware. This can be confusing, but knowing this terminology can be valuable when trying to describe printing issues. The printer is the combination of the printer driver, support files, and the print queue. The print device is the part that we can't seem to live without and that costs all the money.

When you choose to print something in Windows 2000 Professional, unless you indicate otherwise, Windows programs hand off data to the operating system, which in turn *spools* the data to a specified printer. Spooling means temporarily putting information that's headed for the printer on the hard disk. Your document is then sent to the printer at the slow speed that the printer can handle. This lets you get back to work with your program(s) sooner. You can even print additional documents, stacking up a load of jobs for the printer to print. This stack is called a *queue*.

In Windows 2000 Professional, each printer you've installed appears in the Printers folder, along with an additional icon called Add Printer that lets you set up new printers. Printer icons in the folder appear and behave like any other objects. You can delete them, create new ones, and set their properties. Double-clicking a printer displays its print queue and lets you manipulate the queue. Commands on the menus let you install, configure, connect, disconnect, and remove printers and drivers.

You can open the Printers folder in the following ways:

- Choose Start ➢ Settings ➢ Printers.
- In Control Panel, click the Printers icon.

The Windows 2000 Professional print feature mix is quite rich. Here are the highlights:

- You can add, modify, and remove printers right from the Printers folder.
- You can set up multiple printers for one physical print device, or vice versa, and set different schedules, priorities, and permissions for the device.
- You don't need to think about the relationship of printer drivers, connections, and physical printers because an object-oriented interface using printer icons eliminates that abstraction. You can simply add a printer and set its properties. Once added, it appears as a named printer in the Printers folder.
- After you set up a printer, you can easily share a printer on the network so that others can print to it. You can give the device a useful name, such as LaserJet in Fred's Office, so that people on the network know what it is.
- When sharing a printer on the network, you can choose to also install one or more Windows 2000 Professional printer drivers for other Windows 2000 Professional platforms, for versions of NT, and/or for Windows 95/98 stations. These drivers are then provided "automagically" to other printer users, sparing them the task of loading their own printer driver manually (and ensuring that the correct printer driver will always be used by the others accessing this printer). If you're on a network, you can manage network-printer connections by displaying available printers, sharing your local printer, and connecting to and disconnecting from network printers.
- When sharing a printer on the network, you can conduct printer-access auditing, set ownership, set which time periods the printer is available for use on the network, and restrict who has access to the printer.
- You can start printing and immediately go back to work; you don't need to wait until spooling is done. While one document is printing, other programs can start print jobs. Additional documents are simply added to the queue and print in turn.
- You don't need to manually set options such as number of copies, paper tray, page orientation, and so forth. Defaults are automatically used during print jobs.

- To quell your curiosity, you can open a window displaying jobs being printed or jobs in the queue waiting to be printed, along with an indication of the current print job's progress.
- You can easily rearrange the order of the print queue and delete print jobs.
- You can choose whether printing begins as soon as the first page is spooled to the hard disk or after the last page of a document is spooled.
- You can temporarily pause or resume printing without causing printer time-out problems.

Adding a New Printer

If your printer is already installed and seems to be working fine, you can probably skip this section. In fact, if you're interested in nothing more than printing from one of your programs without viewing the queue, printing to a network printer, or adjusting your current printer's settings, skip to the "Printing from a Program" section. However, if you need to install a new printer, modify or customize your current installation, or add printers to your setup, read on to learn how to do the following:

- Add a new printer
- Select the printer port and make other connection settings
- Set preferences for a printer
- Install a printer driver that's not listed
- Set the default printer
- Select a printer when more than one is installed
- Delete a printer from your system

About Printer Installation

Before installing hardware, including printers, you should read any last-minute printed or on-screen material that comes with Windows 2000 Professional. Often, such material is full of useful information about specific types of hardware, including printers. Because these are last-minute details, I can't include them in this book. Look for a `readme` file (or something similar) on your Desktop that you can open by double-clicking. Then look through the file for information about your printer.

With that said, here is the overall game plan for adding a new printer. It's an easy process thanks to the Add Printer Wizard that walks you through it.

1. In the Printers folder, click Add Printer to start the Add Printer Wizard.
2. Specify whether the printer is local (directly connected to your computer) or on the network.

3. Specify what kind of printer it is.
4. Give the printer a name.
5. Print a test page.
6. Check and possibly alter the default printer settings, such as the dots per inch (dpi) and memory settings.

After these steps are complete, your printer should work as expected. After a printer is installed, you can customize its setup by modifying its properties. In the Printers folder, right-click your printer, and choose Properties from the shortcut menu to open the Properties dialog box for that printer. Figure 7.1 shows the Properties dialog box for my printer, open at the Device Settings tab. The tabs that are present in this Properties box depend on the features and capabilities of the printer. In the Properties dialog box for my printer, I can do the following:

- Specify the amount of time I want Windows to keep trying to print a document before alerting me to a printer problem.
- Specify the share name for the printer so that other network users can find it when they search the network for printers.
- Set job defaults pertaining to paper tray, two-sided printing, and paper orientation.
- Stipulate a *separator file* (a file, usually one page long, that prints between each print job).
- Select the default printer if more than one printer is installed.
- Choose whether my printer should substitute its own fonts for certain Windows TrueType fonts.
- Select printer settings relevant to page orientation, color matching, grayscaling, size scaling, type of paper feed, halftone imaging, and when file header information (such as a PostScript preamble) is sent to the printer.
- Set whether to share the printer for use by others on the network.
- Set whether documents will go directly to the printer or will go through the spooler.

FIGURE 7.1
You use the Device Settings tab to fine-tune the options for your printer.

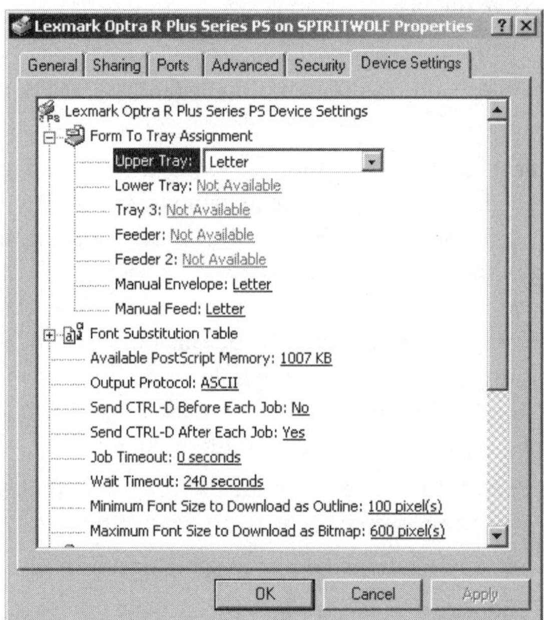

The good news is that normally you won't need to fuss with any of these settings.

About Adding Printers

Before running the Add Printer Wizard, let's consider when you would need to add a new printer to your Windows 2000 Professional configuration:

- You're connecting a new printer directly to your computer.
- Someone has connected a new printer elsewhere on the network, and you would like to use it from your computer.
- You want to print to disk files that can later be sent to a particular type of printer.
- You want to set up multiple printer configurations (preferences) for a single physical printer so you can easily switch between them without changing your printer setup between print jobs.

Notice that a great deal of flexibility exists here, especially in the case of the last item. Because of the modularity of the Windows 2000 Professional internal design, even though you might have only one physical printer, you can create any number of printer definitions for it, each with different characteristics (and different descriptive names).

NOTE These printer definitions are actually called *printers*, but you can think of them as printer names, printer aliases, or named virtual devices.

For example, you might want to set up one definition to print on legal-sized paper in landscape orientation and another to print with standard-sized paper in portrait orientation. Each of these two "printers" would use the same physical printer to print. The word *printer* often doesn't refer to a physical printer. It usually means a printer setup that you've created with the Wizard. It's a collection of settings that typically point to a physical printer, but they could just as well create a print file instead of a paper printout.

About Printer Drivers

A printer can't just connect to your computer and mysteriously print a fancy page of graphics or even a boring page of text. You need a printer *driver*. The printer driver (a file on your hard disk) translates your text file to commands that tell your printer how to print your file. Because different brands and models of printers use different commands for such actions as "move up a line, print a circle in the middle of the page, print the letter *A*," and so on, a specialized printer driver is needed for each type of printer.

NOTE Because some printers are functionally equivalent, a driver for a popular brand and model of printer (for example, an Epson or a Hewlett-Packard) often masquerades under different names for other printers.

When you add a printer, you may be asked to choose the brand and model of printer. Windows 2000 Professional has the benefit of Plug-and-Play technology and can usually detect your printer correctly. If you own a printer that cannot be detected by Windows 2000 Professional, you will need to tell the system what kind of printer you have so that the correct driver can be installed.

A good printer driver takes advantage of all your printer's capabilities, such as its built-in fonts and graphics features. A poor printer driver might succeed in printing only draft-quality text, even from a sophisticated printer.

If you're the proud owner of some offbeat brand of printer, you may be alarmed when you can't find your printer listed in the box when you run the Wizard. But don't worry, the printer's manufacturer might be able to supply a driver. I'll cover the procedure for installing manufacturer-supplied drivers later in this chapter.

About the Add Printer Wizard

Microsoft has made the previously arduous chore of adding a printer somewhat simpler, though it is still a multistep process. You may be adding a network print server or a local computer, which is one that is attached to your computer. Let's start with the procedure for adding a network printer.

Adding a Network Printer

Assuming your Windows 2000 Professional network system is successfully cabled and running, network printing should be possible. Before a network user can access a network printer, the following must be true:

- The printer must be cabled to the sharing computer. If the printer has a direct network interface, the sharing computer must be on the same network as the printer.
- The printer must be created; that is, you need to complete all the steps in the Add Printer Wizard to create the printer, and it must be working properly for local use.
- The printer must be shared.
- The security settings for the printer and network users wanting access must match.

By default, new printer shares are given a security setting that gives all users (the Everyone group) access for printing. Only the creator, power users, and administrators can *manage* the printer, however. Managing the printer means rearranging the print-job queue: starting, stopping, and deleting print jobs.

Connecting to a shared printer using Windows 2000 Professional is so easy that it's tempting to believe that you didn't do it right until you print successfully. To connect to a printer on the network, all you do, in essence, is point to the printer you want to use and say: "Print here." Of course, the print server Administrator has control over who can use the printer you just pointed to, but apart from giving the print server Administrator flowers and candy, you have no control over the printer settings. This makes connecting to a networked printer easy, and it also makes Windows 2000 Professional flexible and controllable (for the printer administrators).

Because Windows 2000 Professional workstations use the printer drivers stored on the print server, Windows 2000 Professional workstations will use them automatically even if you install a newer version of a driver on the print server. You don't need to tweak the workstation connection.

Here are the steps for connecting to a network print server:

1. Choose Start ➢ Settings ➢ Printers to open the Printers folder:

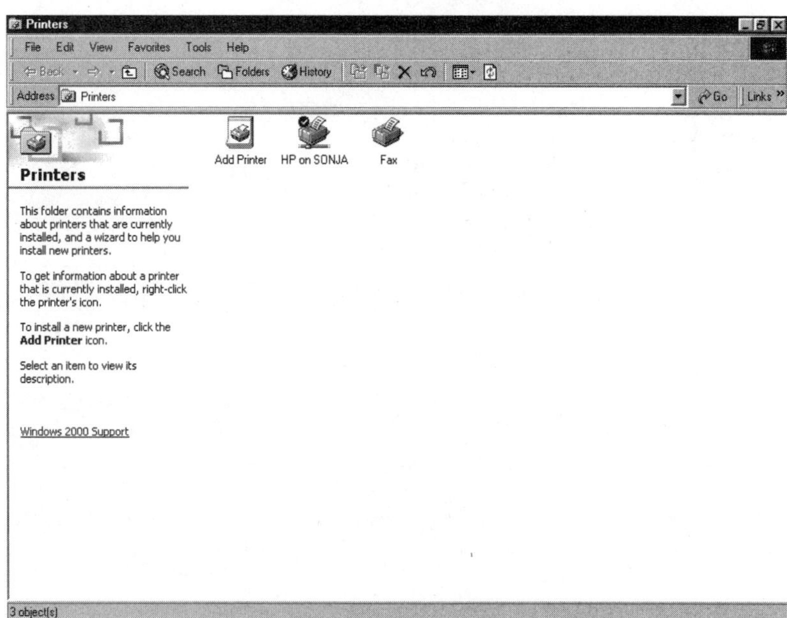

2. Double-click Add Printer to start the Add Printer Wizard:

3. Click Next.

4. In the Local or Network Printer screen, select Network Printer, and click Next.

5. Next you'll be given a choice of how you want to find the shared printer. If you don't know the name or URL of the printer you want to connect to, click Next to open the Browse For Printer screen:

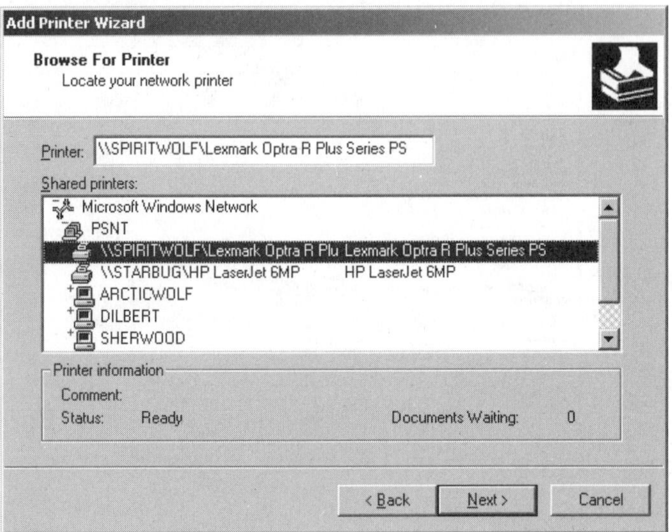

If the printer you want to connect to isn't listed in the Shared Printers list, don't despair. You can easily type the path to the printer in the Printer box. Simply type two backslashes (\\) followed by the name of the server, another backslash (\), and the name of the printer. Browse lists are often incomplete, and you can't change that. Of course, this method requires that you know the name of the server and the printer, but you really should try this before calling your Administrator for help. This path is referred to as a Universal Naming Convention (UNC) path and can be entered directly from the Run command if you really want a shortcut.

NOTE For a printer to appear in the Shared Printers list, it must have been added to the host computer's setup (the computer the printer is directly attached to) using the steps for adding a local printer. It must also be set as Shared for use on the network.

6. If the network printer is currently offline, you are told that you need to wait until it comes back online before you can use it but that you can go ahead and install it if you want. In this case, you may be asked to specify the brand and model of the printer, because the Wizard can't figure out the type of printer when it is unavailable for your computer to question. If you can alert the owner of the printer to put it online (that user can right-click the printer's icon at their

computer and turn off the Work Offline setting), you may not need to specify these settings. If this isn't possible, just select the brand name and model from the list, and click Next.

7. The Default Printer screen asks whether you want the printer to be the *default* printer:

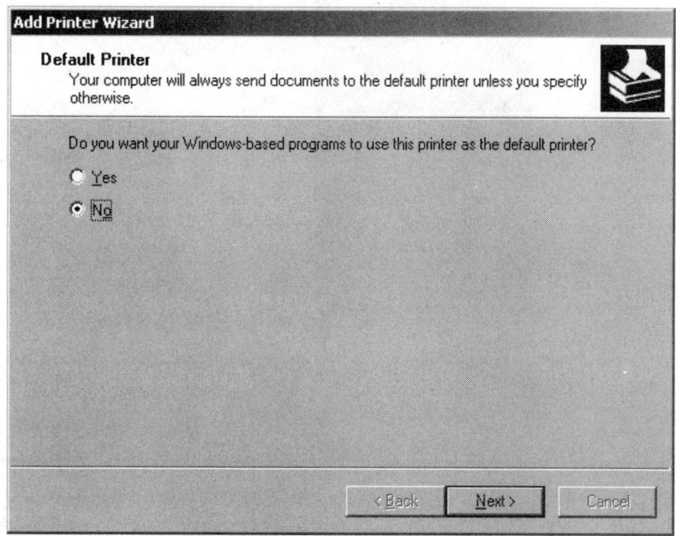

The default printer is the one that programs will assume you want to print to. Some programs don't let you choose which printer a document will print to, so setting the default printer can be important. If you want this network printer to be the default printer, remember that the computer the printer is directly connected to must be up and running for the printer to work. So, if you have a local printer on your machine as well, it might be better to make that the default printer. After you select an option, click Next.

8. The last thing the Wizard will do for you is display a list of the options you've chosen to install for the printer, as shown in Figure 7.2.

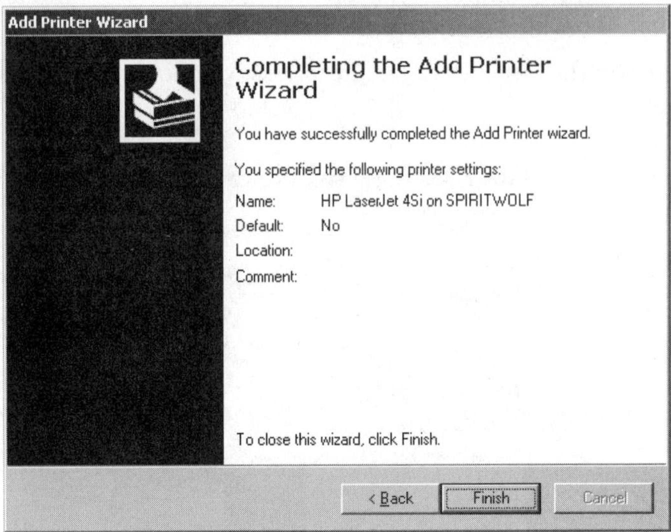

FIGURE 7.2
Windows 2000 Professional displays a summary of the options you selected for your printer.

NOTE If the print server recognizes the printer and has a driver already installed for your Windows 2000 Professional computer, then steps 5 through 8 will be skipped and the printer will be created automatically. These last steps will only be necessary if your Windows 2000 Professional computer cannot detect what kind of printer is being installed.

If all went well, you now have a network printer set up and ready to go. The new printer appears in your Printers folder.

Adding a Network Printer Using the Directory

If your computer is in a native Windows 2000 Professional network, you'll see a third option on the Locate Your Printer screen: Find A Printer In The Directory. This indicates that all the Domain Controllers maintaining the security are Windows 2000 Professional Servers using Active Directory.

Using the capabilities of Active Directory, you don't need to know the name of the printer, its location, or anything else. Of course, the more you know, the easier it will be to find the right printer.

To install a network printer using the Directory, follow these steps:

1. Open the Printers folder, and double-click Add Printer to start the Add Printer Wizard. Click Next.
2. Select Network Printer, and then click Next.

3. In the Locate Your Printer screen, specify the path. If you don't know the path, click Next.
4. In the Browse For Printer screen, you can search the Directory for any printer that meets your criteria. Click the Printers tab to search for a shared printer by name, location, or model. Click the Features tab to find a shared printer based on its installed features. Click the Advanced tab to search based on any criteria that have been published in the Directory for shared printers. Enter the criteria you want to search for, and click Find Now to begin the search.
5. When you locate a suitable printer in the list, double-click it to close the Find Printers screen and return to the Add Printer Wizard.
6. If this printer is not the first printer installed, you will be asked whether your Windows applications should use this printer as the default printer. Answer Yes or No, and then click Next.
7. The Add Printer Wizard will display a summary of the options you have chosen:

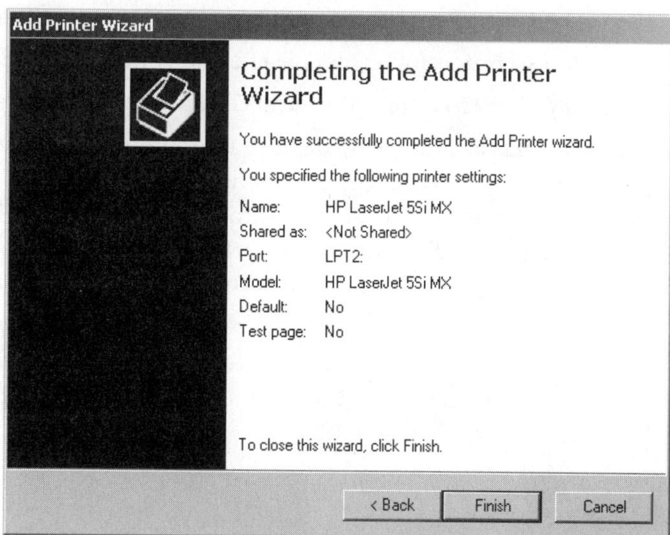

8. If you are satisfied with the options, click Finish.

Printing a Test Page

In some cases, you are asked if you want to print a test page after you add a printer. Test pages are useful troubleshooting tools. Even though they appear simple, they prove that you can print graphics *and* text. The text they print is also useful because it contains the list of files supporting the printer and their versions. It's a good idea to print a test page after installing a new printer and then to keep the page on file in case of problems later.

You are not asked to print a test page if you are installing a network printer. The assumption is that the printer has already been tested when it was installed locally on the print server. If you do want to print a test page for this printer, you can easily do so from the printer's Properties dialog box after it is installed. To print a test page, follow these steps:

1. In the Printers folder, right-click the printer you want to test, and choose Properties from the shortcut menu to open the Properties dialog box for this printer.
2. On the General tab, click the Print Test Page button.
3. If the test page prints correctly, click OK when you are prompted. If it doesn't print at all or doesn't print correctly, click the Troubleshoot button to open the Print Troubleshooter in Help.

Adding a Local Printer

Adding a local printer is easy. Thanks to Plug and Play, Windows 2000 Professional can detect your printer if it is physically connected to your computer and turned on. If you want to add a local printer rather than a networked printer, follow these steps:

1. In the Printers folder, double-click Add Printer to start the Add Printer Wizard.
2. Click Next to display the Local Or Network Printer screen.
3. Click Local Printer. By default, the Automatically Detect And Install My Plug And Play Printer check box is checked. This allows Windows 2000 Professional to automatically detect any locally attached printer. If Windows 2000 Professional can detect the printer, this is the last step. If the printer cannot be detected, you will need to run the Wizard again with the option for automatic detection disabled. Click the Next button.
4. If you need to run the Add Printer Wizard again because your printer could not be detected, first be certain that it is connected and turned on, and then proceed with the following steps.

5. Click the Next button to open the Select The Printer Port screen:

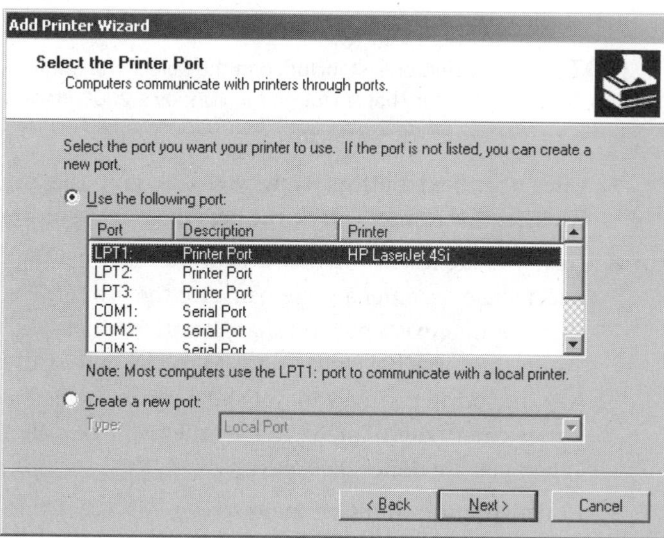

Select the printer port to use. (A port usually refers to the connector on the computer.) Most often the port will be the parallel printer port called LPT1 (Line Printer 1). Unless you know your printer is connected to another port, such as LPT2 or a serial port (such as COM1 or COM2), select LPT1. Here are some additional guidelines for choosing port settings:

- The most common setting is LPT1 because most PC-type printers hook up to the LPT1 parallel port.
- If you know your printer is of the serial variety, it's probably connected to the COM1 port. If COM1 is tied up for use with some other device, such as a modem, use COM2.

TIP You can select more than one port if you like. This means you can configure a "printer" to actually be more than one printer. Any jobs sent to this printer name are printed on the first available printer. A single printer controlling multiple print devices is called a "printer pool" and is used to provide fast printing in high-volume printing environments.

NOTE If your printer is attached through the Universal Serial Bus (USB), it should be detected immediately. USB devices depend upon Plug and Play for their detection and installation. If your printer is not automatically detected when you start Windows 2000 Professional, use the Add/Remove Hardware applet in Control Panel to detect it.

6. Select the manufacturer and model of your printer, and click Next.

NOTE If your printer isn't included in the Select The Printer Port screen, see the next section, "Adding a Printer That Is Not on the Windows 2000 Professional List."

7. Click the Next button. Now you can give the printer a name and specify whether this printer will be the default. When you are done, click Next.
8. Next you are asked whether this printer is to be shared on the network. If you select Share As, enter a share name for the printer. You can even conceal the fact that a printer exists but still share it with the network for a chosen few to access. To do this, attach a dollar sign ($) to the end of the printer share name. This way, the printer name will not show up on the list of networked printers, but if a user enters the name by hand, they will be able to connect to the printer. When you are done, click Next.
9. In the Location And Comment screen, fill in any information you want to publish about this printer. It's helpful to provide a location for the printer and possibly a comment that describes the printer. When you are satisfied, click Next.
10. Now you are prompted to print a test page. It is a good idea to print and save the test page at this point, since it displays your printer's ability to print graphics and text and gives you a list of the necessary files for this printer's configuration. Click Next.
11. Windows 2000 Professional displays a summary of the configurations you have chosen. Read through the list before clicking Finish just to be sure you have everything you need. When you click Finish, Windows 2000 Professional copies the necessary files to create the printer configuration on your computer. Notice that Windows 2000 Professional already has the drivers on the hard disk. This is because the driver and information files are preloaded when you install Windows 2000 Professional.

Adding a Printer That Is Not on the Windows 2000 Professional List

When you're adding a local printer, you need to supply the brand name and model of the printer because Windows 2000 Professional needs to know which driver to load into your setup to use the printer correctly. When you are adding a network printer and the correct printer driver is installed on the print server, you will get the driver automatically. If the print server doesn't have a driver for your printer, you need to follow the steps later in this section to install a copy of the driver locally on your computer.

What if your printer isn't on the list of recognized printers? Many off-brand printers are designed to be compatible with one of the popular printer types, such as the Apple

LaserWriters, Hewlett-Packard LaserJets, or the Epson line of printers. Refer to the manual that came with your printer to see whether it's compatible with one of the printers that *is* listed. Some printers require that you set the printer in compatibility mode using switches or software. Again, check the printer's manual for instructions.

Finally, if it looks as if there's no mention of compatibility anywhere, contact the manufacturer of the driver. If you're lucky, the manufacturer will have one. It's also possible that Microsoft has a new driver for your printer that wasn't available when your copy of Windows 2000 Professional was shipped. Contact Microsoft at (206) 882-8080 and ask for the Windows 2000 Professional Driver Library Disk, which contains all the latest drivers. Another option is to look for the latest drivers on the Internet, either at Microsoft's site (`www.microsoft.com`) or at your printer manufacturer's Web site.

Assuming you do obtain a printer driver, follow these steps to install it:

1. Follow the instructions in the earlier section for adding a local printer.
2. Instead of selecting one of the printers in the Manufacturers or the Printers list (it isn't in either list, of course), click the Have Disk button to open the Install From Disk dialog box:

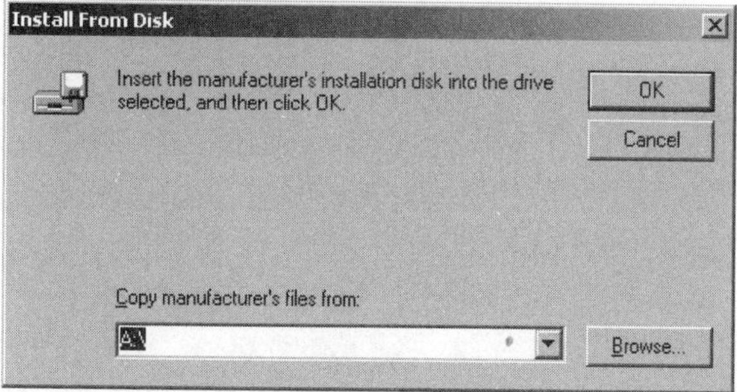

3. Enter the drive letter, insert the disk (or make sure the files are available somewhere and enter the path), and click OK. You might need to choose a driver from a list if multiple options exist.

NOTE The Add Printer Wizard is looking for a file with an INF extension. This is the standard file extension for manufacturer-supplied driver-information files.

4. Continue with the Wizard, as explained in the earlier section.

If none of the drivers you can lay your hands on will work with your printer, try choosing Generic from the Manufacturers list and then select the Generic/Text Only driver from the Printers list. This driver prints only text—no fancy formatting and no graphics—but it works in a pinch with many printers. Make sure the printer is capable of or is set to an ASCII or ANSI text-only mode; otherwise, your printout may be a mess.

PostScript printers don't have such a text-only mode. For a PostScript laser printer, you can try the Apple LaserWriter, which most PostScript printers can emulate.

Sharing a Printer for Network Use

You need to *share* a printer before it becomes available to other network users. After you add a local printer, follow these steps:

1. In the Printers folder, right-click the printer's icon, and choose Properties or Sharing from the shortcut menu.
2. Either command opens the Properties dialog box for that printer. Click the Sharing tab if it's not selected. The tabs in this dialog box depend on the printer.

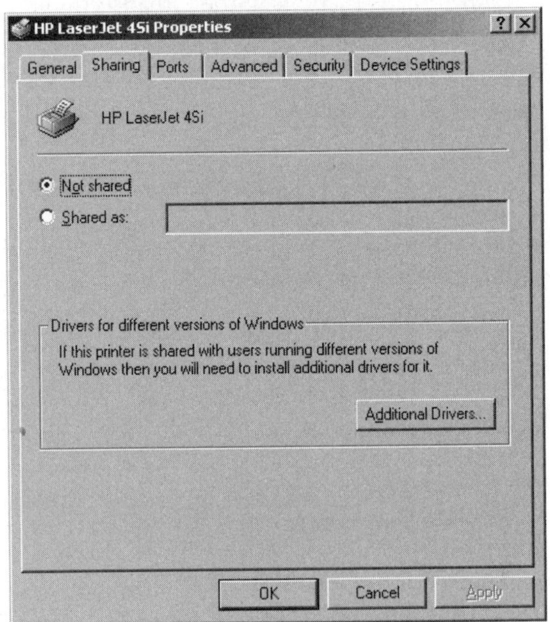

3. Click Shared As. A *share name* based on the printer name is automatically generated. You can leave the share name as is or change it.
4. Click the General tab, and fill in Location and Comment information. Any text that you add here will be seen by other users who browse the network for a printer.

TIP You can preinstall printer drivers for other Microsoft operating systems (Windows 95/98 and all flavors of NT). This can be a great time-saver for the other printer users because they will not need to supply the driver files from their computer. It also eliminates one more thing that could go wrong for users on the network.

5. Click the OK button, and your printer is shared! Its icon now has a hand under it, as shown here. Pretty soon you'll start to see unexpected print jobs rolling out of your printer.

HP LaserJet 4Si

To prevent the sharing of your printer, open the Properties dialog box for your printer, click the Sharing tab, and click Not Shared.

Another approach to preventing overuse of a printer (at least temporarily) is to right-click its icon and choose Pause Printing from the shortcut menu. This method may not be a very elegant way to deter people from printing to your printer, but it *will* stop print jobs. Of course, anyone viewing the print queue will be able to resume printing, so this technique may not buy you much time. Clicking the Not Shared option is a much better practice.

Creating a Second Printer for the Same Print Device

It's often desirable to have two (or more) names for the same print device you are sharing with others. Having different people access the same device from different names lets you assign different printing priorities to different users, specify different hours that the printer is available for printing, make one printer for network use and another for local use, and so forth. Having two or more names lets you fine-tune the network's access to the printer.

The process of creating a second printer for the same print device is identical to that of creating the first one, but make sure that you select a new name for the additional printer. Windows 2000 Professional will remember the last printer you installed and automatically select the same manufacturer and model when you install the second printer. If you don't give the new printer a different name, Windows 2000 Professional won't actually create the printer.

Choose the same printer driver for the printer that the other printer on this print device uses, and make sure that all other settings are as they should be. You don't need to share all printers you create, even if they're attached to the same printing device. If you do choose to share the new printer, it will be available to other workstations on the network.

Creating a Printer Pool

Just because you send a print job to a particular printer name doesn't mean that that print job must print to one particular printer. To save time for print jobs, you can use the Details dialog box to pool several *identical* printers into one logical one. If you do this, when you send a print job to that printer name, the first available printer will do the job. This is called *printer pooling*.

Printer pooling will not work unless the pooled printers are physically identical—the same make and model and the same amount of memory.

To set up printer pooling, follow these steps:

1. In the Printers folder, right-click the printer's icon and choose Properties from the shortcut menu to open the Properties dialog box for that printer.
2. Select the Ports tab, and click the Enable Printer Pooling check box.
3. Select the ports that correspond to the ports where you've plugged in the other printers. If the ports you need aren't on the list, you can add them by clicking the Add Port button (discussed in the next section).
4. When you have added all of the ports, click OK to apply the changes. Any job sent to this printer will now go to the first available port.

TIP You can actually create a printer pool with dissimilar print devices if they emulate a common printer. Install the driver for the emulation, and adjust the physical printers to use the emulation. If they aren't identical physically, this may work with varying degrees of success.

Customizing Your Printer

The settings pertaining to a printer are called *properties*. As I discussed earlier, properties abound in Windows 2000 Professional. Almost every object has properties that you can examine and change. When you add a printer, the Wizard makes life easy for you by giving the printer default properties that usually work fine and don't need to be tampered with. You can change them later, but only if you need to. However, it may be worth looking at the properties for your printer, especially if the printer's acting up in some way when you try to print. Here are the steps:

1. Open the Printers folder.
2. Right-click the printer's icon, and choose Properties from the shortcut menu to open the Properties dialog box for that printer.

TIP You can also press Alt+Enter to open the Properties dialog box. This is true with many Windows 2000 Professional objects.

3. Click the various tab pages of the Printer Properties dialog box to view or alter the great variety of settings. It may not be clear to you what some of these settings do, but you can usually get help by clicking the ? button in the upper-right corner and then clicking the setting or button whose function you don't understand.

The following sections describe some of the options in the tabs of the Printer Properties dialog box. As I've mentioned several times now, the tabs you see depend on the features and configuration of your printer.

Using the General Tab

The General tab contains basic information as well as buttons to set the printing preferences and to print a test page. The General tab for an HP LaserJet 4Si printer is shown in Figure 7.3.

FIGURE 7.3
The General tab contains basic identification of installed features and other information.

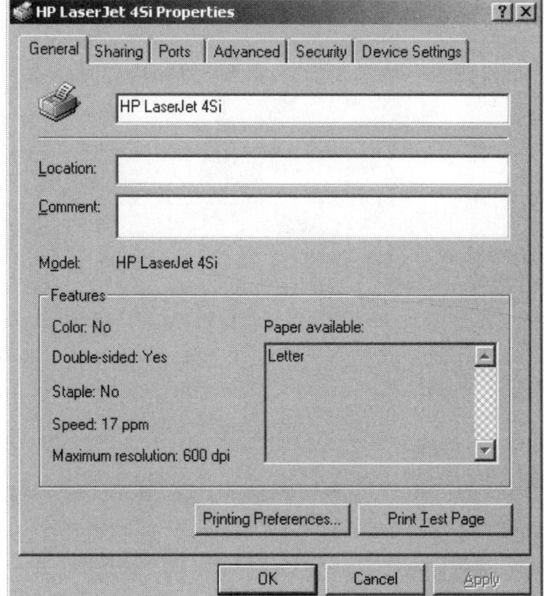

Working with Port Settings

The Ports tab of the printer Properties dialog box, shown in Figure 7.4, shows you which port the printer is using. You can add a port by simply double-clicking the box of the additional port you want. Using multiple ports enables several print jobs to be queued at once.

FIGURE 7.4
The Ports tab of the printer Properties dialog box

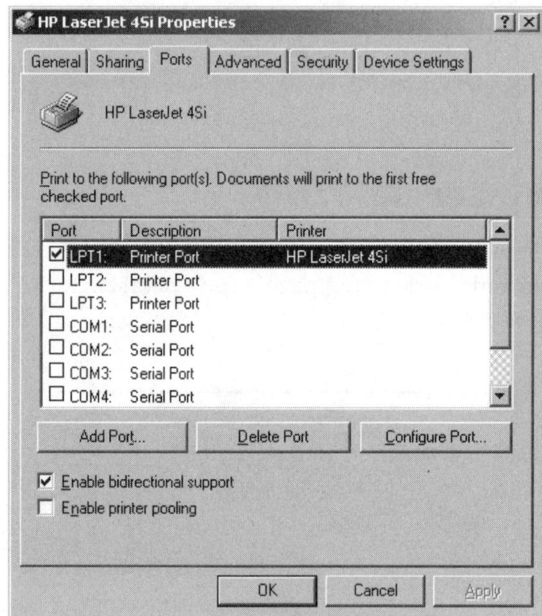

Adding a Port

Adding a port is relatively straightforward. Follow these steps:

1. Click the Add Port button to open the Printer Ports dialog box:

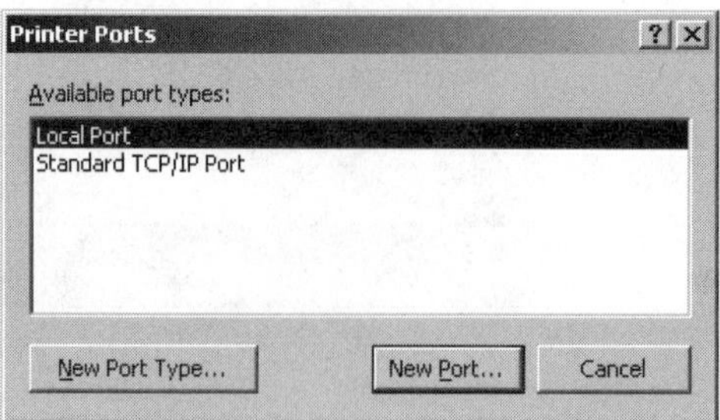

2. Double-click either Local Port or Standard TCP/IP Port to open the Port Name dialog box.
3. Enter a port name, and click OK.
4. Click Close in the Printer Ports dialog box. You'll now see the port you added in the list of ports in the Ports tab.

To add a different type of port, follow these steps:

1. In the Ports tab, click Add Port to open the Printer Ports dialog box.
2. Click New Port Type to open the Installing Print Monitor dialog box.
3. In the Copy Files From box, enter the path to the driver file (or click Browse to find it), and click OK.

Deleting a Port

To delete a port, select it in the Ports tab, and click the Delete Port button. Windows 2000 Professional will ask if you are sure you want to delete the port. If you are, click Yes.

Windows 2000 Professional won't allow you to delete a system port such as the physical parallel port LPT1. If you do manage to delete a port that you need, you should be able to add it again by using the procedure to add a new port I outlined earlier. If that doesn't work, you will need to edit the Registry directly to recover the port.

Retrieving a Port

To retrieve a printer port (perhaps after accidentally deleting it), you must edit the Registry. Contact your network administrator. This is not a task for 99.9 percent of end users.

Configuring a Port

If the printer you are setting up is connected to a parallel port, you can specify the time lapse before Windows 2000 Professional decides that the printer is not responding and notifies you (as the user) of an error. Setting the Transmission Retry number higher or lower adjusts the amount of time that the system will wait for a printer to prepare itself to accept data.

This setting affects not only the printer that you've selected, but also any other local printers that use the same printer driver. To set the timeout value, follow these steps:

1. In the Ports tab, select the port you want to configure, and click the Configure Port button to open the Configure Port dialog box:

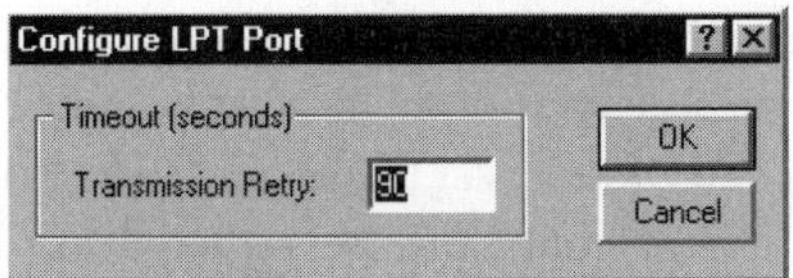

2. Enter the time for the Transmission Retry in seconds, and click OK.

Scheduling Print Jobs

Another way to control access is to schedule print jobs, which you do using the Advanced tab in the printer Properties dialog box, as shown in Figure 7.5.

FIGURE 7.5
The Advanced tab in the printer Properties dialog box

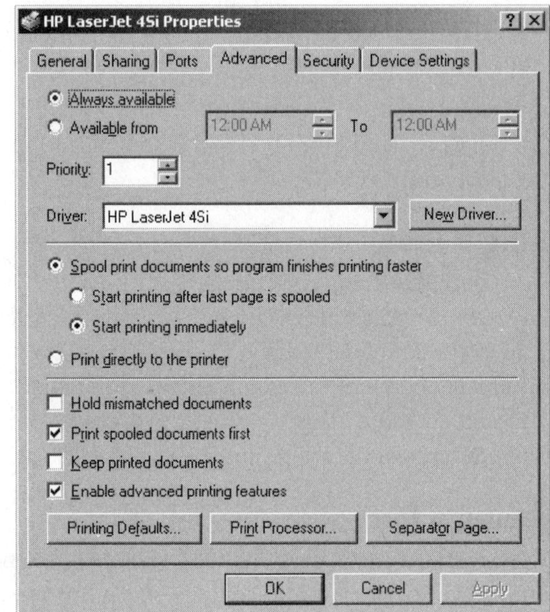

Setting Availability Times

By default, the printer is always available. If you'd rather it be available only at certain times, follow these steps:

1. In the Advanced tab, click the Available From option.
2. In the first spin box, click the up or down arrows to select a starting time or enter a time.
3. In the To spin box, click the up or down arrow to select an ending time or enter a time.
4. If you are not setting other options in this tab, click OK.

If a print job is sent to a printer during its "off" hours, that job won't disappear, but it will sit in the queue until the printer is authorized to print again.

Although you can set user logon hours and printer hours, you must set the same printer hours for all groups and users who have access to a particular printer. For example, you can't restrict a group of users to accessing a printer only between 9 AM and 5 PM if the Administrators can access it at any time. There are exceptions to this rule, however:

- You can adjust users' logon times so that they are forcibly disconnected when their logon hours expire.
- You can set up two printer names: one name for the window of time when the printer is open for use and the other name with a different time window. Those who connect to the printer name with the limited hours will be able to use the printer only during those hours.

Using Scheduling

Let's look at some of the ways you can use scheduling. Suppose that Jose and Fred need different access rights to different printers. You, as the printer Administrator, want Jose to be able to use the inkjet printer all the time, but to use the laser printer only on Fridays when the graphics department goes home early. You want Fred, who is in the graphics department, to go home early instead of racking up overtime pay and therefore you don't want him to use the laser printer at all on Fridays. Fred still needs access to the inkjet printer on Friday mornings and the rest of the week.

Because both Jose and Fred can have access to the inkjet printer all week, no special restrictions need to be made. The laser printer is another matter. Here, you need to set up two printers with different access times for the laser printer. You call one *Week Use Laser Printer*, share it with the network, restrict access times to Monday through Thursday, and connect Fred's workstation to that printer. You then set up another printer with the same specifications, except it's called *Friday Use Laser Printer*, restrict the hours of use to Fridays, and connect Jose's workstation to that printer (which is physically the same printer as Fred's laser printer).

Setting Printer Priorities

If you want to share your printer with the network but don't want everyone else's print jobs crowding out your own, you can give the printer two names: one name for you to use that has a high priority and a name for everyone else to use that has a lower priority. To further hone print priorities for different user groups, you can give the printer three or more names, each with its own priority attached, and then assign each group access to a printer name according to their priority.

Another way to set priorities is by document. Priorities affect where the document goes in the print queue. When a high-priority document enters the queue, it jumps over the lower-priority jobs that are waiting in line. As soon as the print device is available, the high-priority job is printed. When you're setting the printer priorities, don't forget that higher numbers (up to 99) have priority over lower ones. The default value is 1.

For purposes of example, let's assume that you have composed a WordPad document and want to set its priority in the print queue. Follow these steps:

1. Choose Start ➢ Programs ➢ Accessories ➢ WordPad to open WordPad.
2. Create a document, or open an existing one.
3. Choose File ➢ Print to open the Print dialog box.
4. Right-click the printer you want to use, and choose Properties from the shortcut menu to open the Properties dialog box for that printer.
5. Select the Advanced tab, and give the document a high priority.
6. Click OK.
7. Back in the Print dialog box, click Print.

If you like, you can send print jobs directly to the port connected to the printer. If you do this, however, you won't be able to use your application until the print job is done. To send a WordPad document, for example, directly to the printer port, follow steps 1 through 4 above, select the Advanced tab, and click the Print Directly To The Printer option.

Spooling

By default, documents for printing are spooled to the printer before they are printed. (The Spool Print Documents So Program Finishes Printing Faster option on the Advanced tab is selected.) When a document is spooled, it is sent first to your hard drive, then across the network to the print server's hard disk, and then to the printer. This allows users to get back to what they were doing as soon as possible and is called *printing in the background.* You can choose whether printing starts during or after spooling and turn spooling off entirely (Print Directly To The Printer), through the Advanced tab.

Windows 2000 Professional always wants to spool the documents so that you can get control of your application faster. In other words, the hourglass goes away sooner. If you find that your printer has trouble processing print jobs with this spooling enabled, you can select the option to Print Directly To The Printer. This will turn off the spooling for the printer and send the job directly to the print device. This could solve your printing problem, but it will result in slower printing.

Setting Up Separator Pages

Another organizational tool is a separator page. Separator pages are extra pages printed before the main document. These extra pages can be used to identify the owner of the print job, record the print time and date, print a message to users of the printer, or record the job number. They're useful for keeping documents sent to the printer separate from one another. If a number of people are using the same networked printer, separator pages help them keep their documents sorted. Several separator page files are included with Windows 2000 Professional. They are stored in the Winnt\system32 folder and have a SEP extension. You can also create your own using Notepad.

WARNING The separator files included with Windows 2000 Professional may not work with all printers.

Choosing a Separator Page

To specify a particular separator page, follow these steps:

1. In the printer Properties dialog box, select the Advanced tab, and click Separator Page to open the Separator Page dialog box:

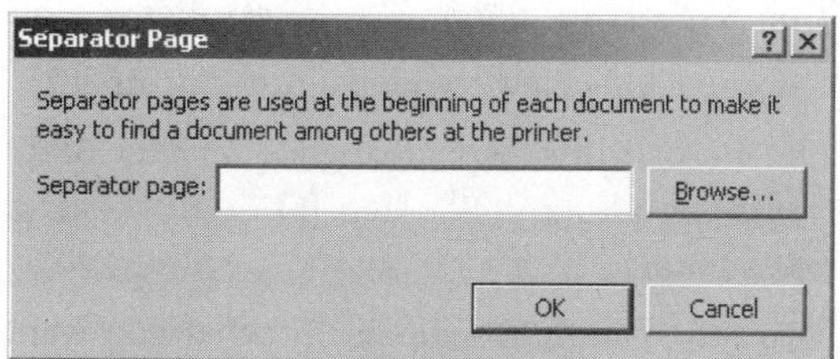

2. Click Browse to open another Separator Page dialog box, select one of the files with the SEP extension, click Open, and then click OK. Table 7.1 describes the four separator pages that come with Windows 200 Professional.
3. Click OK again, and the page you selected will print before every print job.

TABLE 7.1: DEFAULT SEPARATOR PAGES

File Name	Description	Compatibility
SYSPRINT.SEP	Prints a blank page before print jobs	PostScript
PCL.SEP	Switches a dual-language printer to PCL (Printer Control Language) mode	PCL
PSCRIPT.SEP	Switches a dual-language printer to PostScript mode	PostScript
SYSPRTJ.SEP	Prints a blank page before print jobs sent to a PostScript Printer	PostScript

If you no longer want to use the separator page you selected, click Separator Page on the Advanced tab to open the Separator Page dialog box, delete the document part of the path name, and click OK.

When specifying a separator page, you can type a filename (if you're already in the proper path to find the file) or the filename and path (if you're in another path). You must, however, use a file that is *physically* located on the computer that controls the printer for which you're specifying the separator page. Why can't you use just any file that's accessible from the network? The computer that controls the printer stores separator page information in its Registry, and so it needs that information available locally. If you tell the printer to use a separator file that is not located on its hard disk or one that is not in the path that you've indicated, you may see an error message that says, "Could not set printer: The specified separator file is invalid."

Creating a Separator Page

To make your own separator page file, follow these steps:

1. Choose Start ➢ Programs ➢ Accessories ➢ Notepad to open Notepad.
2. Choose File ➢ New to open a new document.
3. On the first line, type a single character that you don't anticipate needing for anything else (a dollar sign [$] or a pound sign [#] are good candidates), and press Enter.
4. Enter the variables that specify what you want printed on your separator page. Table 7.2 lists the possibilities. Enter each variable on a separate line, and press Enter.
5. Choose Files ➢ Save As to open the Save As dialog box.
6. In the Save As Type box, choose All Files, and save the file with a SEP extension. If you save it as a text file, you won't be able to load it as a separator page.

The character you enter on the first line becomes the *escape character*. It tells the system that you're performing a function, not entering text.

TABLE 7.2: PRINTER SEPARATOR PAGE VARIABLES

Variable	Effect
BS	Prints text in block characters with pound signs (#) until you insert a $U. You probably don't want to use this option because printing text like this takes a lot of room.
$D	Prints the date the job was printed, using the format defined on the Date tab of the Regional Options dialog box. (In Control Panel, click Regional Options to open this dialog box.)

TABLE 7.2: PRINTER SEPARATOR PAGE VARIABLES (CONTINUED)

Variable	Effect
$E	Ejects a page from the printer. Use this code to start a new separator page or to end the separator page file. If an extra blank separator page prints, remove this code from your separator page file.
$F*pathname\filename*	Prints the contents of the file specified by path, starting on a blank line. Only the text is printed, without any formatting.
$H*nn*	Sets a printer-specific control sequence, where *nn* is a hexadecimal ASCII code sent directly to the printer. To determine the specific numbers, see your printer manual.
$I	Prints the job number.
$L*xxxx*	Prints all the characters (*xxxx*) following it until another escape code is encountered. You can use this code to enter text exhorting people not to waste paper on unnecessary print jobs, to have a nice day, to save the planet, or anything else that you like.
$N	Prints the login name of the person who submitted the print job.
$*n*	Skips *n* number of lines (from 0 through 9). Skipping 0 lines moves printing to the next line.
$T	Prints the time the job was printed, using the format defined in the Time tab of the Regional Options dialog box. (In Control Panel, click Regional Options to open this dialog box.)
$U	Turns off block character printing.
$W*nn*	Sets the line width of the separator page. The default width is 80; the maximum width is 256. Any printable characters beyond this width are truncated.

For example, the following Notepad separator page file:

```
$
$N
$D
$L This is a test separator file.
```

```
$T
$E
```

results in this output:

```
Mark 11/11/2000 This is a test separator file. 9:21:22 AM
```

Even though I pressed Enter after each entry, the output is all on one line because I didn't use the $*n* character to tell the separator page to skip lines between entries.

Setting User Permissions to the Printer

Just because you share a printer doesn't necessarily mean that you want everyone on its domain to be able to access it. Maybe it's the color printer with the expensive ink that only the graphics people need to use, or you want to reduce the risk of security breaches by limiting the people who can print copies of company secrets. Either way, you'll want to control access to the printer just as you would to any other network device.

By default, only administrators have full access to the printer. Only those with Manage Printers permission can pause or resume a printer or change its permissions. Those who have only print access can administer only their own documents.

NOTE The default print permissions in Windows 2000 Professional are as follows: Administrators and Power Users have Manage Printers permission; the Everyone group has Print permission; Creator Owner (the person who submits a job) has Manage Documents permission for the job they have submitted.

Users on a workstation are automatically given the right to use the printer connected to the workstation. They are, therefore, automatically given the ability to connect to another printer on the domain for which they also have user permissions. These default limitations and permissions can be modified by the Administrator. Just as you can control devices on a network, you are able to control printer use by setting the permissions on it.

To set printer permissions, follow these steps:

1. Choose Start ➢ Settings ➢ Printers to open the Printers folder.
2. Right-click the printer for which you want to set permissions, and choose Properties from the shortcut menu to open the Properties dialog box for that printer.

3. Click the Security tab:

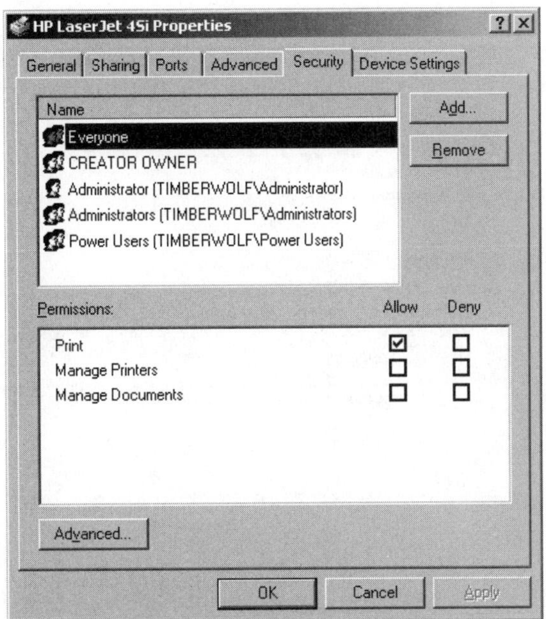

The Security tab lists the accounts that have set up some kind of printer access. From here, you can change each user group's level of access. Printing permissions are granted to groups, not individual users. Therefore, granting user permission means making a user a member of a group with the printing permission you want that user to have.

The default permission levels are as follows:

Print Members of that user group can print documents and manage their own documents.

Manage Printers Members can do anything with the printer—print; control document settings; pause, resume, and delete documents and printers; change the printing order of documents; and change printer properties and permissions.

Manage Documents Members can control document settings and pause, resume, restart, and delete documents lined up for printing, including documents submitted by others.

4. To change a printer permission, select the group, and then clear or check the Allow check box or the Deny check box. To implicitly deny access, select the group, and clear all the check boxes.

5. To add a user group or user to the printer permissions list, click the Add button to open the Select Users, Computers, Or Groups dialog box:

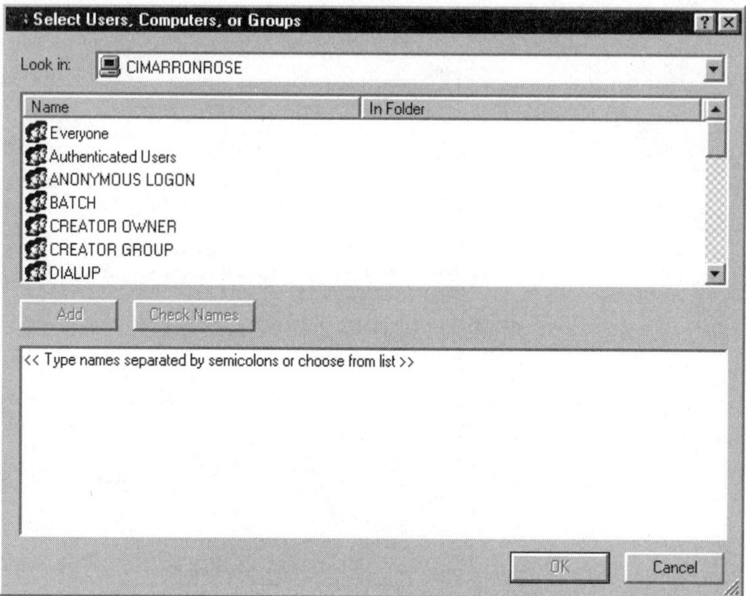

By default, the Name list displays only the accounts in the context you've logged on to. For example, if you've logged onto the domain, the list will display all the accounts for the domain. If you logged on to the local computer instead, you will see the accounts on your local computer. You can still drop down the Look In list box to see the other accounts.

6. To add a group or a user, select the name in the Name list, click Add, and then click OK.

7. To remove a group or user from the printer permissions list, back on the Security tab, highlight the name of the user or group, click Remove, and then click OK.

TIP If a user is a member of more than one group with different printer permissions, the system grants the highest-level permission. So, if Jane is a member of one group with Print permission and a member of another group with Full Control permission, she'll always have Full Control permission. The only time that print permissions are *not* cumulative is when one of the groups that a user belongs to has No Access to the printer. In that case, that permission level overrides all higher levels, and the user has no access to the printer, regardless of a user's access level or membership in other user groups.

Changing Ownership

The user with administrative privileges who created the printer is considered the owner of it, just as files are owned by their creators.

Only an administrator or someone with Manage Printers permission can change ownership of a printer, and that event can be traced through the Auditing feature if it is turned on. To change ownership of a selected printer, follow these steps:

1. Log on to Windows 2000 Professional as the user who will be the new owner.
2. Choose Start ➢ Settings ➢ Printers to open the Printers folder.
3. Right-click the printer of which you want to take ownership, and choose Properties from the shortcut menu to open the Properties dialog box for that printer.
4. Click the Advanced button to open the Access Control Settings dialog box for the printer:
5. Click the Owner tab:

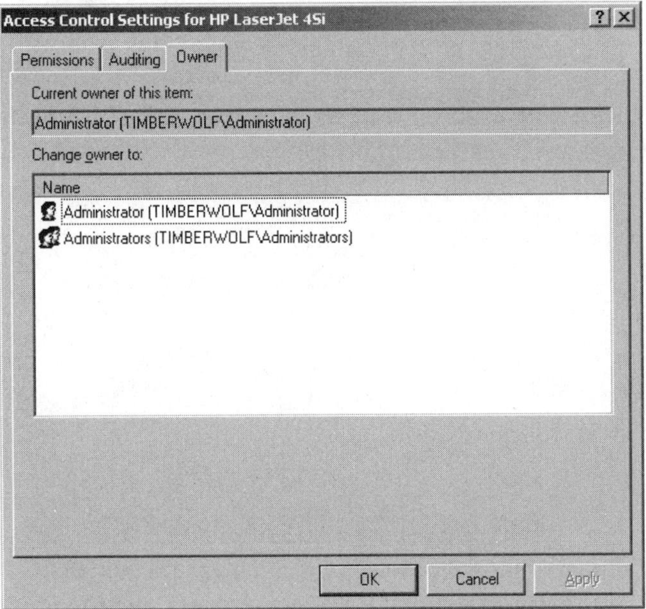

6. In the Change Owner To section, select your account name from the list, and click Apply or OK.

Auditing Printer Usage

To get a good idea of what is happening with your printer, you can audit its use. Perhaps the printer is overused, or perhaps you want to know who is using the printer after regular work hours. Auditing these events gives you the answer.

TIP To set up auditing, you must be logged in as an administrator.

Before you can set up auditing, you must enable it. To do this, you use the Group Policy add-in. Follow these steps:

1. Choose Start ➢ Run to open the Run dialog box.
2. In the Open box, type **gpedit.msc**, and press Enter to open the Group Policy window:

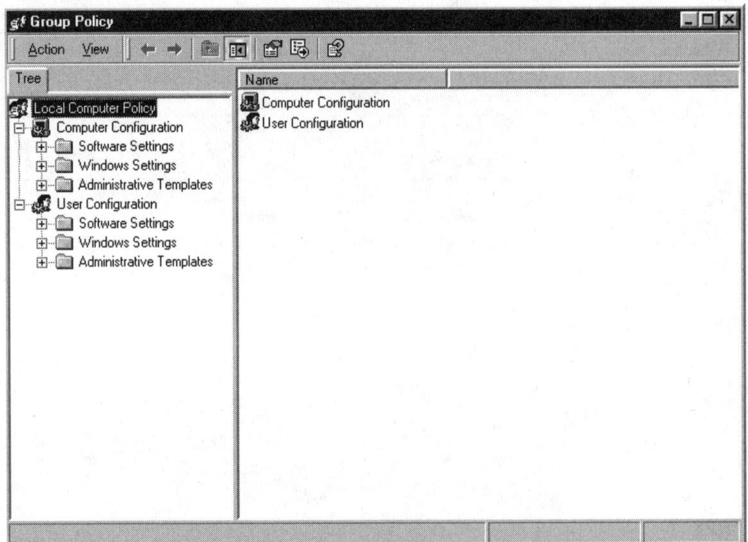

3. In the Tree pane, click Computer Configuration, click Windows Settings, click Security Settings, click Local Policies, and then click the Audit Policy folder to display the audit policies in the pane on the right.

4. Select Audit Policy Change, and then choose Action ➢ Security to open the Local Security Policy Setting dialog box:

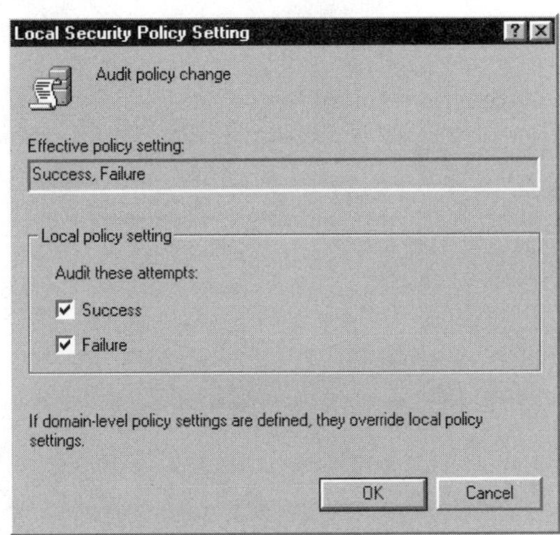

5. Check the Success and the Failure check boxes, and click OK. Back in the Group Policy window, you'll see that auditing has been enabled for Success and Failure.
6. Close the Group Policy window.

NOTE The Group Policy snap-in is part of Computer Management, an administrative tool that I'll discuss in Chapter 30.

After you've turned on auditing, you can choose what to audit. Follow these steps:

1. Choose Start ➢ Settings ➢ Printers to open the Printers folder.
2. Right-click the printer you want to audit, and choose Properties from the shortcut menu to open the printer Properties dialog box.

3. Click the Advanced button top open the Access Control Settings dialog box for the printer, and select the Auditing tab:

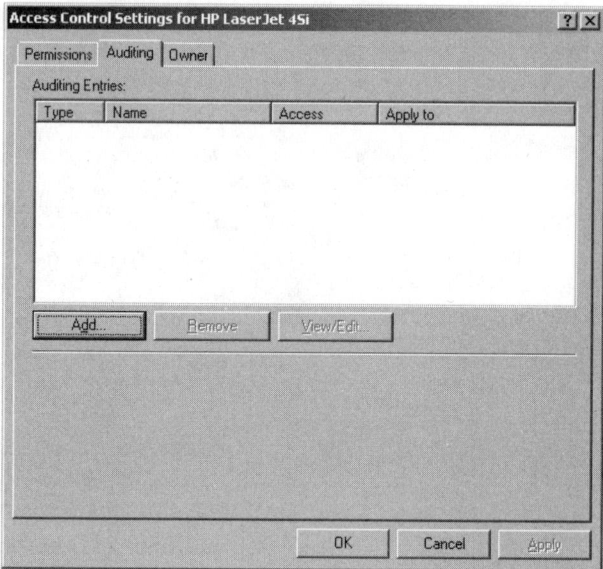

4. Click Add to open the Select User, Computer, Or Group dialog box.
5. Select a user or a group, and click OK to open the Auditing Entry For *Printer* dialog box:

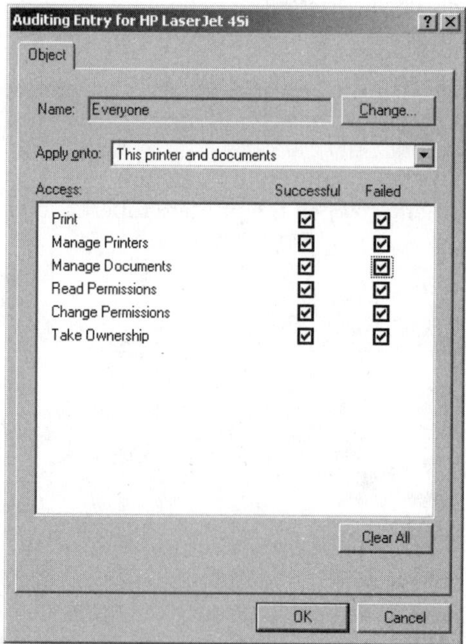

6. Click the Successful or the Failed check box for each item that you want to audit, and then click OK. The Auditing Entries list in the Access Control Settings dialog box will now look similar to the following:

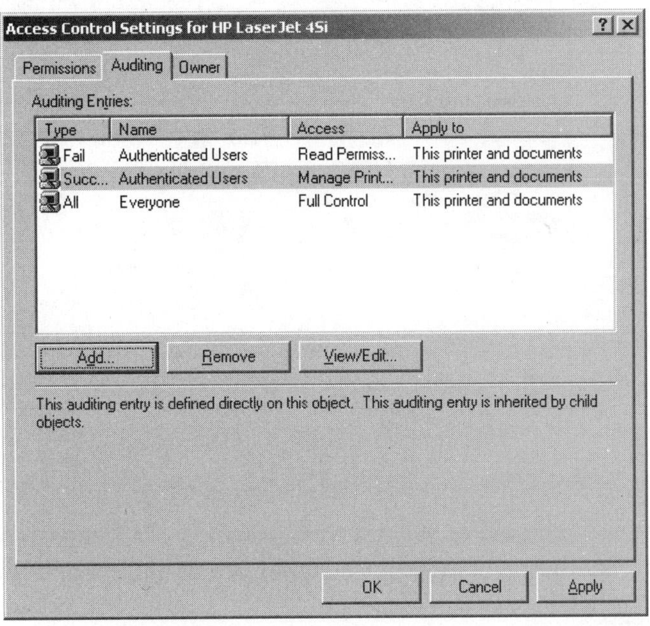

7. Highlight an account in the Auditing Entries list to display some basic information for the type of audit. To see the actual settings, highlight the account, and click the View/Edit button to open the Auditing Entry dialog box.
8. Click OK to close all open dialog boxes.

To view the auditing information, use the Event Viewer in the Administrative Tools applet. In Chapter 30, I'll discuss Event Viewer in detail. For now, just so you know how, follow these steps to open Event Viewer:

1. Choose Start ➢ Settings ➢ Control Panel to open Control Panel.

2. Click Administrative Tools to open the Administrative Tools folder:

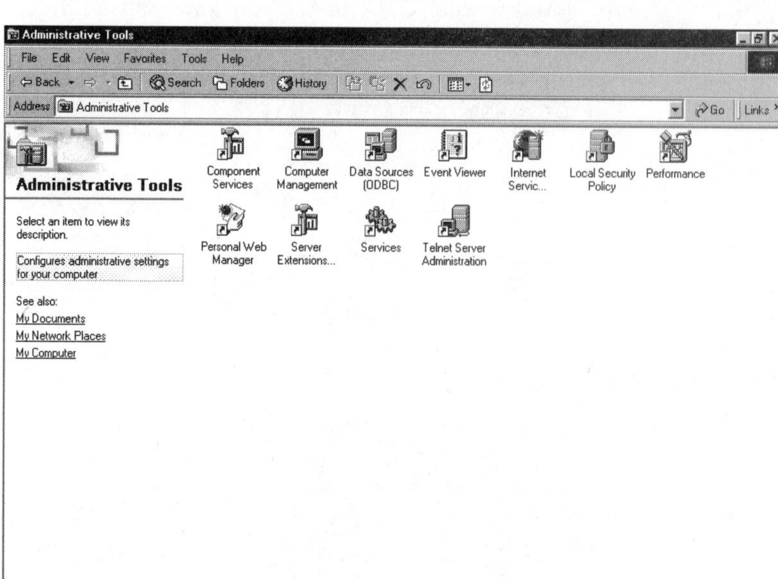

3. Click Event Viewer to open the Event Viewer window.

Deleting a Printer from Your Printers Folder

After you've added it, you might want to decommission a printer for several reasons, including the following:

- You've connected a new type of printer to your computer, and you want to delete the old setup and create a new one with the correct driver for the new printer.
- You want to disconnect from a network printer that you've finished using.
- You've created several slightly different setups for the same physical printer, and you want to delete the ones that you don't use.

In any of these cases, the steps are the same:

1. Choose Start ➢ Settings ➢ Printers to open the Printers folder.
2. Right-click the icon for the printer setup you want to delete, and choose Delete from the shortcut menu (or select the printer and press the Delete key).
3. You will see at least one confirmation box before the printer is deleted. You may see another warning if print jobs are in the queue for the printer. Verify that you want to remove this printer.

NOTE Deleting a network printer or a local printer removes that printer from every user profile on the system.

When you delete a printer by following the preceding steps, the related driver file and font files are not deleted from the disk. Therefore, if you want to recreate the printer, you don't need to insert disks, and you won't be prompted for the location of driver files.

Printing Documents from Your Programs

By now your printer(s) are added to your system and ready to go. To print documents from your programs, simply open the document, choose File ➢ Print, and set a few options, such as which pages to print. You might also need to set the print area first or make some other settings, depending on the program.

If you're already happy with the ways in which you print, you might want to skim over this section. However, there *are* a couple of conveniences you might not know about, such as using drag-and-drop techniques to print or right-clicking a document to print it without opening the program that created it.

Printing from a Program

The appearance of your printed documents varies somewhat from program to program because not all programs can take full advantage of the capabilities of your printer and printer driver. For example, simple word processing programs such as Notepad don't let you change the font; a full-blown word processing program such as Microsoft Word can print all kinds of fancy graphics, fonts, columns of text, and so forth.

When you print from any program, the file is printed to a disk file instead of directly to the printer. Windows 2000 Professional then spools the file to the assigned printer(s), coordinating the flow of data and keeping you informed of the progress. Jobs are queued up and listed in the Printers folder, and you can view their status, rearrange them, delete them, and so on.

To print from any program, follow these steps:

1. Check to see that the printer and page settings are correct. Some program's File menus provide a Printer Setup, Page Setup, or other option for this. Settings you make from such a dialog box temporarily (sometimes permanently, depending on the program) override settings made from the Print dialog box.

2. Open the document, and choose File ➢ Print to open the Print dialog box. The following is the Print dialog box in WordPad:

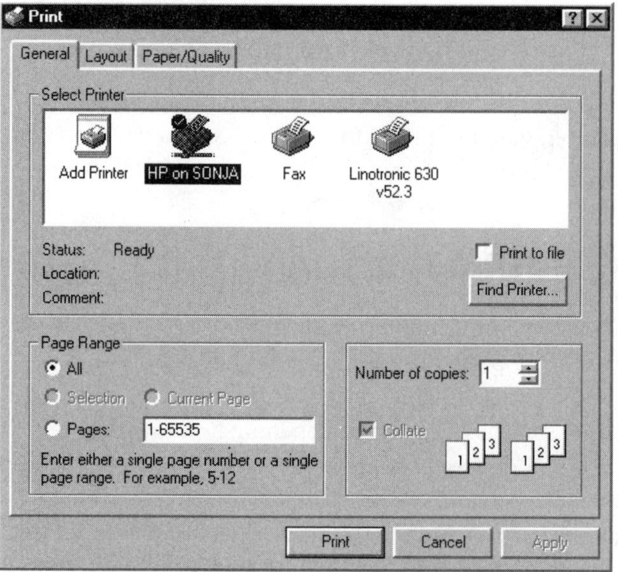

NOTE The options you see in a Print dialog box depend on the printer or printers you have installed on your system.

3. Select the printer you want to use, and specify any other appropriate options, such as the number of copies, whether you want to print the whole file or a portion of it, whether you want to print horizontally or vertically (click the Layout tab to do this), and so on, and then click OK (or otherwise confirm printing). Windows 2000 Professional intercepts the print data and writes it in a file and begins printing it. If an error occurs (a port conflict, the printer is out of paper, or another problem), you'll see a message such as the following:

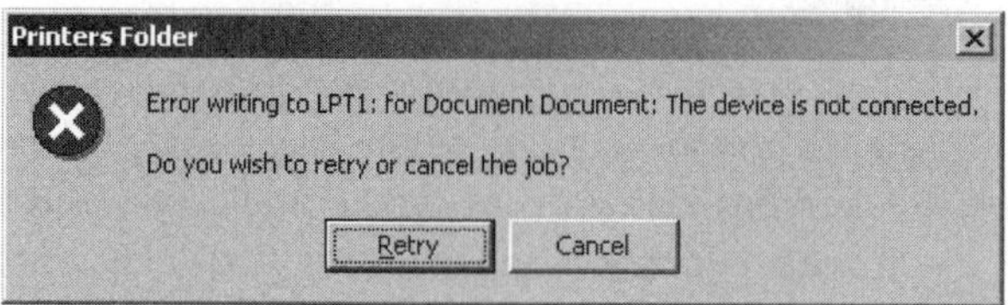

4. If you see this message, check the paper supply, check that the printer is turned on, and check that the printer is online (there may be a switch on the printer for this). If it's a network printer, make sure it's shared and that the computer it's connected to is booted up and has shared the printer for use.

TIP When printing commences, a little printer icon appears in the Taskbar next to the clock. You can double-click this icon to see details of your pending print jobs.

Printing by Dragging Files

You can quickly print Windows program document files by dragging them onto a printer's icon or window. This works only with documents that have an association with a particular program. To check whether a document has an association, right-click it. If the shortcut menu includes an Open command (not Open With), the file has an association.

To use this technique, follow these steps:

1. Arrange your screen so that you can see the file(s) you want to print as well as either the printer's icon or its window. (You open a printer's window by double-clicking its icon in the Printers folder.)
2. Drag the document file(s) onto the printer's icon or window. The file is loaded into the source program, the Print command is automatically executed, and the file is spooled. The document isn't moved out of its home folder; it's just printed.

A benefit of using this approach is that you can drag multiple files onto a printer's icon or open window at once. All the documents will be queued up for printing, one after another, via their source programs. You'll see the following message asking for confirmation before printing commences:

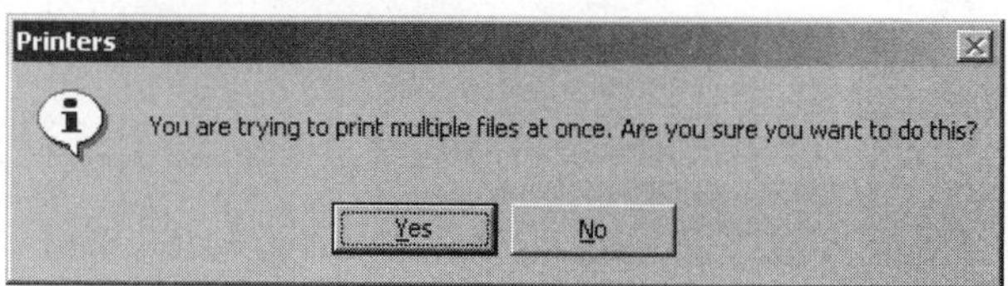

One caveat about this technique: As you know, some programs don't have a built-in facility for printing to a printer other than the default one. Try to drag a document that requires the default printer to a different printer, and you may see this message:

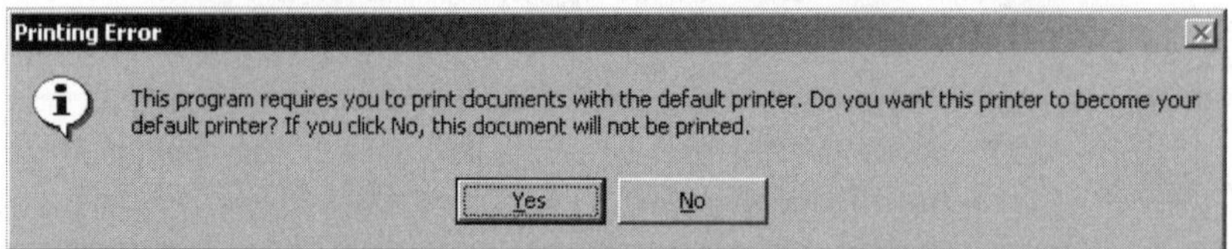

TIP You can use the drag-and-drop method with shortcuts too. You can drag shortcuts of documents to a printer or even to a shortcut of a printer, and the process will still work. If you like this way of printing, keep a shortcut of your printer on the Desktop so that you can drag documents to it without needing to open the Printers folder. Double-clicking a shortcut provides an easy means of checking that it's a printer's print queue too. The only downside is that you are stuck with the default print options, such as orientation, number of copies, and so on.

Printing by Right-Clicking a Document

Another printing shortcut you can use with some documents doesn't even require you to have a printer icon in view. Right-click the icon of any document you want to print, and choose Print from the shortcut menu. The file opens in its source program and starts printing right away. Once spooled, the document closes automatically. If the shortcut menu does not list a Print command, press Escape to cancel the menu; you can't print the document using this technique.

Working with the Print Queue

If you print more than a few files at a time, or if you share your printer for network use, you'll sometimes want to check the status of a printer's print jobs. You also might want to see how many jobs need to print before you turn off your local computer and printer if others are using it. Or you might want to know how many other jobs are ahead of yours.

You can check on these items by double-clicking the printer's icon to open a printer's window. You'll see something like this:

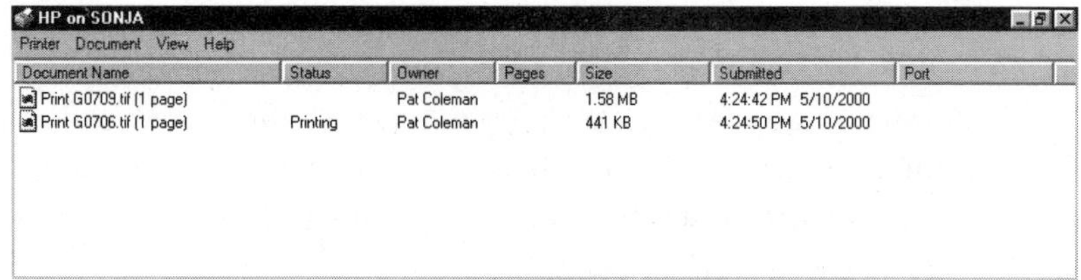

The printer's windows supplies the following information:

Document Name Name of the file being printed and possibly the source program

Status Whether the job is printing, being deleted, or paused

Owner Who sent each print job to the printer

Pages The number of pages to be printed

Size The size of the document in megabytes

Submitted The time and date the job was sent to the printer

Port The port to which the printer is attached

If necessary, adjust the size of the printer window so that you can see all the columns. You can resize the columns to see more data in a small window. Move the pointer to the dividing line in the header display, and drag the line left or right.

If the printer in question is a network printer, and the printer is offline for some reason, such as that its computer isn't turned on, you'll be forced to work *offline*. An error message will alert you to this, and until the issue is resolved, you won't be able to view the queue for that printer. You can still print to it, however.

When an error occurs during a print job, Windows 2000 Professional tries to determine the cause. For example, the printer might be out of paper, or the printer might be offline or unplugged from the AC outlet. You may be forced to work offline until the problem is resolved. Opening the printer's queue should display an error message approximating the nature of the problem. Check the printer's File menu to see if the Work Offline setting has been activated. When you think the problem has been solved, turn off this setting to begin printing again.

Refreshing the Network Queue Information

The network cabling that connects workstations and servers is often busy, so Windows 2000 Professional usually doesn't bother to add more traffic to the network by polling each workstation for printer-queue information. This is done when necessary, such as when a document is deleted from a queue.

If you want to refresh the window for a printer to get the absolute latest information, press F5. This immediately updates the queue information.

Deleting a File from the Queue

After sending a file to the queue, you might change your mind about printing it. For example, you might discover that you need to make some changes before printing the document. If so, you can simply remove the file from the queue. Here's the procedure:

1. Open the printer's window.
2. Select the file.
3. Choose Document ➢ Cancel, or press Delete. Or you can right-click the printer icon and choose Cancel from the shortcut menu. The document item is removed from the printer's window. If you're trying to delete the job that's printing, you might have some trouble. At the very least, the system might take some time to respond.

You can delete other people's print jobs if the printer in question is connected to *your* computer. However, normally, you can't delete someone else's print jobs on a remote printer. If you try to, you are told that this is beyond your privileges and that you should contact your system administrator. If you want to be able to delete jobs on a remote computer, someone must alter the security settings on the remote computer to enable remote administration of the printer.

You may find, especially with PostScript laser-type printers, that after deleting a file while printing, you need to reset the printer to clear its buffer or at least eject the current page (if you have a page-eject button). To reset, you typically need to push a button on the printer's front panel or turn off the printer for a few seconds, and then turn it on again.

NOTE Because print jobs in Windows 2000 Professional are stored on the hard drive of the print server as files, pending print jobs are not lost when computers are powered down. Any documents in the queue when the system goes down reappear in the queue when you power up. When you turn on a computer that is the host for a shared printer that has an unfinished print queue, you are alerted to the number of jobs in the queue and asked whether to delete or print them.

Canceling All Pending Print Jobs on a Printer

Sometimes, because of a megalithic meltdown or some other catastrophe, you'll decide to bail out of all the print jobs that are stacked up for a printer. Normally, you don't need to do this, even if the printer has gone wacky. You can just pause the queue (as described in the next section) and continue printing after the problem is solved. But sometimes you'll want to resend everything to another printer and remove the queue on the current one. It's easy:

1. Open the printer's window.
2. Choose Printer ➢ Cancel All Documents. Or you can right-click the printer's icon in the Printers folder, and choose Cancel All Documents from the shortcut menu.

WARNING Make sure you really want to cancel the jobs before you choose Cancel All Documents. This is a good way to make enemies if people on the network were counting on their print jobs being finished any time soon.

Pausing (and Resuming) the Printing Process

If you're the administrator of a printer with a stack of jobs in the print queue, you can temporarily pause a single job or all jobs on a particular printer at any time. This can be useful for taking a minute to add paper, answer a phone call, or have a conversation in your office without the noise of the printer in the background.

Pausing or Resuming a Specific Print Job

You can pause documents anywhere in the queue. Paused documents are skipped, and subsequent documents in the list print ahead of them. When you feel the need to pause or resume a specific print job, follow these steps:

1. Open the printer's window.
2. Right-click the document you want to pause, and choose Pause from the shortcut menu.

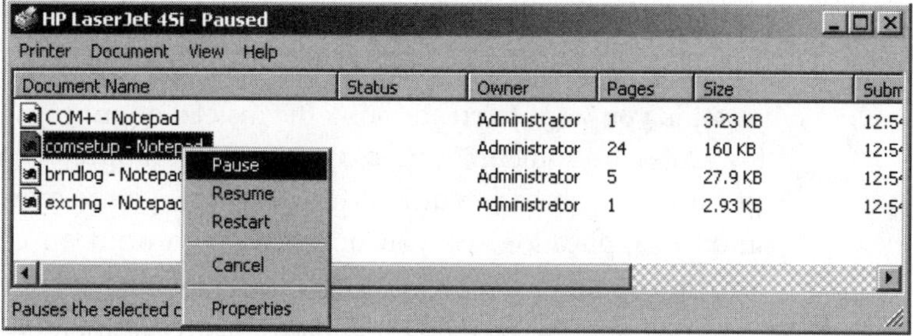

The current print job is temporarily suspended, and the word *Paused* appears in the status area.

NOTE The printing might not stop immediately when you choose Pause, because your printer might have a buffer that holds data in preparation for printing. The printing stops when the buffer is empty.

To resume printing the document, right-click the document, and choose Resume from the shortcut menu.

Pausing or Resuming All Jobs on a Printer

In a similar fashion, you can temporarily pause all jobs on a printer. You might want to do this to load paper or otherwise adjust the physical printer or to alter printer settings from the printer's Properties dialog box.

To pause or resume all jobs for a printer, in the Printers folder, right-click the printer you want to pause, and choose Pause Printing from the shortcut menu.

Printing to a Disk File

In some cases, you may want to print to a disk file rather than to the printer. What does this mean? When you print to a disk file, the codes and data that would normally be sent to the printer are shunted off to a disk file—either locally or on the network. The resulting file typically isn't just a copy of the file you were printing; it contains all the special formatting codes that control your printer: codes that change fonts, print graphics, set margins, break pages, and add attributes such as underline, bold, and so on. Print files destined for PostScript printers typically include their PostScript preamble too.

NOTE A PostScript preamble is a special file that prepares the printer to receive the instructions that are about to come and the fonts that are included in the document.

Why would you want to create a disk file instead of printing directly to the printer?

- Print files are sometimes used by programs for specific purposes. For example, printing a database to a disk file might enable you to more easily work with it in another application. Or you might want to print an encapsulated PostScript graphics file to be imported into a desktop publishing document.
- You can send the file to another person who can then print the file directly to a printer. The person doesn't need the program that created the file and doesn't need to worry about any of the printing details, such as formatting, setting up margins, and so forth. All that's in the file.

To print to a file, follow these steps:

1. In your application, choose File ➢ Print to open the Print dialog box.
2. Select the printer, and then click Print To File.
3. Click Print.
4. Enter a name for the file in the Print To File dialog box, and click OK.

By default, these files have a PRN extension and are stored in your My Documents folder.

Troubleshooting

If your print job isn't coming out quite like you expected (or at all), check the simple things first:

- Is the printer plugged in? Check the cable from the computer to the printer *and* the power cord.
- Is the printer turned on? The power switch for some printers is in a hard-to-find location.

Answering these questions can often fix the problem. If it doesn't, your second line of defense is the Print Troubleshooter that's included with Windows 2000 Professional. To use the troubleshooter, follow these steps:

1. Choose Start ➢ Help to open the Windows 2000 Professional Help system.
2. Click the Contents tab, click Troubleshooting And Maintenance, and then double-click Windows 2000 Professional Troubleshooters to open a list and description of the troubleshooters in the pane on the right.

3. Scroll down until you see the Print link:

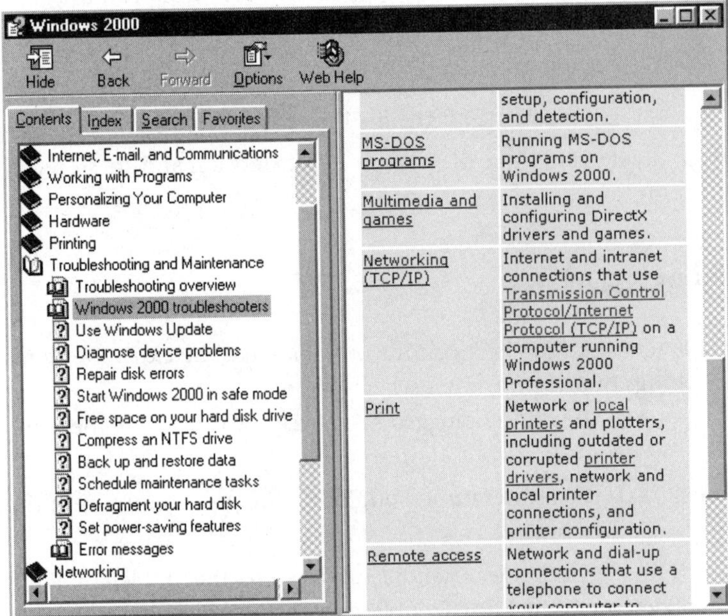

4. Click the Print link to open the Print Troubleshooter:

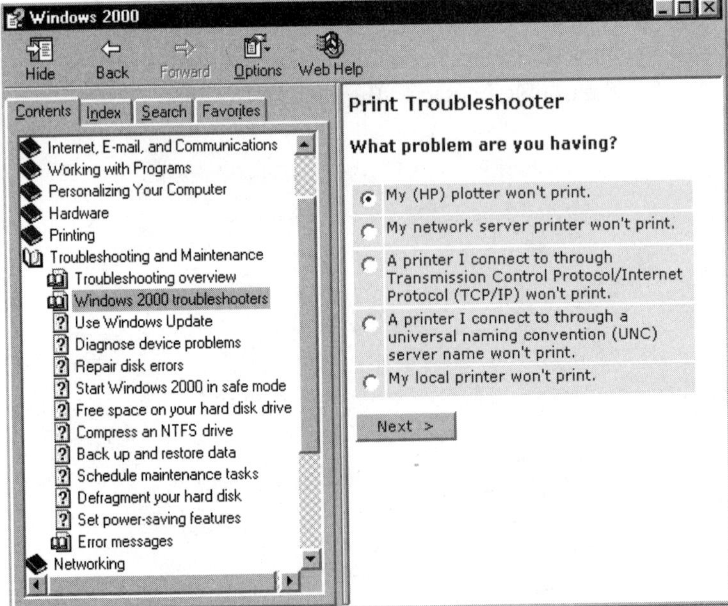

5. Click a problem that corresponds to your situation, click Next, and then follow the on-screen instructions.

A Word about Fonts

In Windows 2000 Professional, a font is the name of a typeface, and a font can have size, which is usually described in points (a point is 1/72-inch), and a style, such as bold or italic. To see the fonts installed on your system, click the Fonts icon in Control Panel to open the Fonts folder:

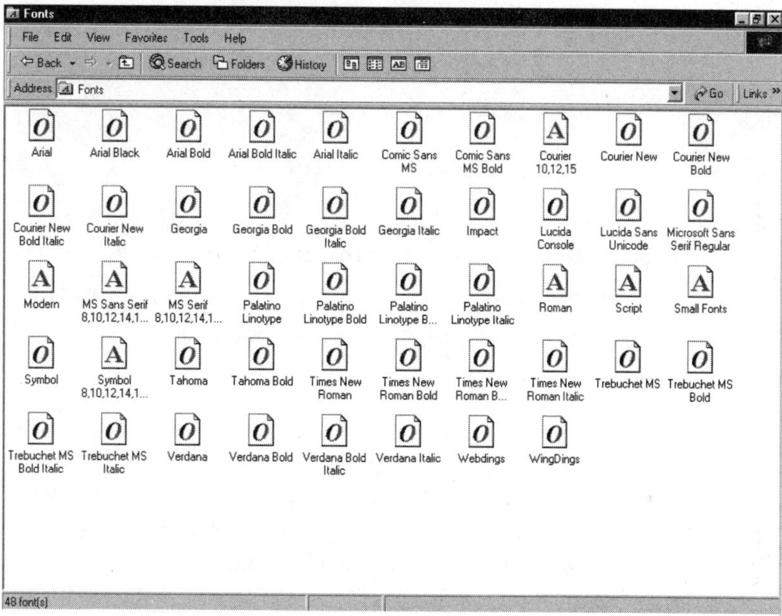

To see what an individual font looks like in several sizes, double-click a font.

Windows 2000 Professional provides three types of fonts:

- OpenType fonts are indicated by the letter *O* and are an extension of TrueType fonts that came with previous versions of Windows. OpenType fonts look the same on the screen and when printed, and you can rotate and scale them.
- Vector fonts are indicated by the letter *A* and are used primarily with plotters. The three vector fonts are Modern, Roman, and Script.
- Raster fonts are also indicated by the letter *A* and are stored in files as bitmap images. The five raster fonts are Courier, MS Sans Serif, MS Serif, Small, and Symbol. Raster fonts cannot be scaled or rotated, and if your printer does not support them, they won't print.

To install a new font on your system, follow these steps:

1. In the Fonts folder, choose File ➢ Install New Font to open the Add Fonts dialog box:

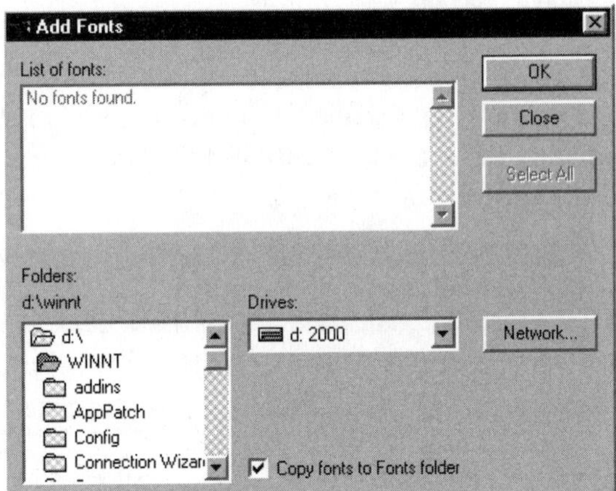

2. Select the drive and folder that contain the files for the new font.
3. Click OK.

By default, fonts are installed into the Fonts folder.

Summary

Printing is an everyday task we often take for granted. Windows 2000 Professional makes this task easy once you learn some of the techniques covered in this chapter.

Windows 2000 Professional provides an easy-to-use Wizard that helps you add printers to your computer and to share them for use on the network. It also provides the printer drivers to other users automatically. After you share a printer for network use, a person with the correct permissions can adjust the queue, manage documents, and even manage the printer itself.

CHAPTER 8

Running Multimedia Applications

FEATURING:

Multimedia—few terms have been used so much that confuse so many. Just what is multimedia, anyway?

Multimedia applications integrate different types of media—graphics (two-dimensional and three-dimensional), digital video, wave audio, and synthesized music—to more dramatically present information on just about any subject. A picture is worth a thousand words. For instance, it may be interesting to read about a cheetah running at 70mph, but it's far more compelling to see a digital video clip of this majestic animal sprinting across a field. Reading text about how music sounds doesn't tell us much, but hearing it, maybe with an annotated narration, can convey far more information than just text on a screen. Computer games are a kind of multimedia; they use all these capabilities to create a compelling environment for you to enter.

You can also create your own multimedia shows. For example, by peppering a computer-based slide presentation with digital video and audio clips, you can add panache to what might be an otherwise dreary business presentation.

The Windows 2000 Professional multimedia capabilities include being able to use the full range of DirectX 7's application programming interfaces (APIs). In this chapter, we'll take a look at these APIs and how they process multimedia data. Next, I'll step you through the instructions for installing multimedia hardware to run with Windows 2000 Professional. Then we'll explore the Windows 2000 Professional multimedia tools for viewing or listening to multimedia content.

Understanding How Multimedia Works in Windows 2000 Professional

DirectX is a group of technologies for running multimedia applications and is built directly into Windows 2000 Professional. You don't really need to know anything about DirectX to use it, but if you are a multimedia enthusiast, understanding how it works will be important.

From a user's point of view, the main thing you want to know is that DirectX lets you run multimedia applications that require hardware that is not installed on your system. For example, a DirectX game that uses 3-D imagery can run on your Windows 2000 Professional computer even if you don't have a 3-D accelerator card. DirectX simulates the features that an accelerator card would provide.

In the past, game developers were notorious for writing their programs straight to the hardware (especially true of graphics code), often bypassing many operating system components that normally handle graphics drawing routines. This programming style works fine provided you know exactly what hardware users will have. But because that wasn't the case, some programs would crash running on certain kinds of hardware, which was a real nightmare for users.

DirectX provides developers with a set of APIs that give improved access to the advanced features of hardware such as accelerator chips and sound cards. An API is a piece of *middleware*, to which developers write their programs, rather than writing directly to hardware. The key concept with DirectX is hardware abstraction, whereby software developers don't need to worry about their programs being able to "talk" to specific hardware. Hardware vendors, in turn, write their drivers to the API. In addition to eliminating many compatibility nightmares, these APIs are much faster at handling their respective duties than their predecessors, a requirement for great multimedia. Figure 8.1 shows how applications get at the DirectX APIs, which in turn communicate with your multimedia hardware.

FIGURE 8.1
Applications communicate with multimedia hardware through DirectX.

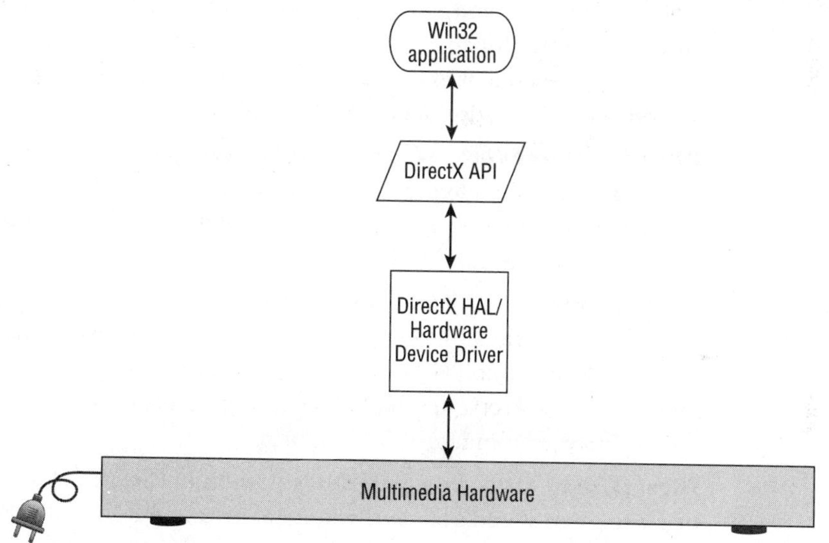

Windows 2000 Professional has implemented the entire DirectX 7 API set. In Windows 2000 Professional, there are essentially two layers of DirectX support:

- The DirectX Foundation layer provides the low-level hardware services for things such as video accelerators and joysticks.
- The DirectX Media layer provides high-level support for media streaming (digital audio and video), animation, and interactivity.

Understanding the Foundation Layer of DirectX

The Foundation layer of DirectX 7's APIs is designed to handle the interaction of applications with today's high-performance multimedia hardware such as video accelerators, sound cards, and video capture cards. This layer of services automatically detects your computer's hardware capabilities and sets the application's configuration to match, giving you the best performance possible.

The Foundation layer provides support for 3-D graphics and sound, 2-D graphics acceleration, and input devices such as joysticks and keyboards. The following components make up the Foundation layer:

DirectDraw This API provides many of the same graphics functions as the Graphics Device Interface (GDI) in the Executive Services of Windows 2000 Professional, but actually it can process most of them much faster than GDI. DirectDraw provides extremely fast direct access to the accelerated abilities of the video adapter. It also provides vendors with a great opportunity to develop hardware for Windows 2000 Professional, as all they need to do is take advantage of DirectDraw's hardware-independent graphics functions. DirectDraw supports 2-D graphics acceleration and video codecs (compression and decompression services).

Direct3D Immediate Mode This API gives applications a way to directly access the advanced 3-D rendering ability of most new video cards without requiring extra configuration from the user. Direct3D can use all of the features of Intel's MMX and Pentium III architecture, as well as AMD's 3DNow! processors.

DirectSound Many of us remember multimedia programs or games that didn't quite match up the sounds with the pictures on the screen. One of DirectSound's best features is the ability to sequence sound and video so that this problem no longer occurs. DirectSound provides hardware-independent access to a sound card's mixing, playback, and recording features.

DirectMusic This is the pure music portion of DirectX. DirectMusic handles message-based sound such as the Musical Instrument Digital Interface (MIDI) format. It also gives application developers the ability to design completely immersive soundtracks that can respond to the user's activities. Immersive soundtracks contain audio tracks to create the full surround-sound experience when played back over theater-style speakers.

NOTE MIDI enables synthesizers made by different manufacturers to "talk" to one another with a common set of commands. A specification called General MIDI is commonly implemented on PC sound cards. General MIDI commands can be recorded and saved as a MIDI sequence, which is basically a batch file of commands to turn specific notes on and off at exact times, using instruments from different synthesizers if more than one is present. The important distinction between a MIDI sequence and an audio wave file is that a MIDI sequence doesn't contain audio data, only instructions to be passed to a synthesizer that will produce the sounds. The main numbers you'll probably want to know are that the General MIDI patch set consists of 128 patches (a patch is a specific instrument sound, such as that made by a clarinet), and MIDI data can be transmitted and received on 16 MIDI channels.

DirectInput This API handles the user input from a variety of hardware such as force-feedback controllers, gamepads, joysticks, mice, and more. It includes support for the new Universal Serial Bus (USB) game controllers. It gives the application developer the ability to work with these devices in a completely hardware-independent manner.

Understanding the Media Layer of DirectX

The Media layer is responsible for high-level functions and works with the Foundation layer to provide a full-featured multimedia experience.

Among the responsibilities of the Media layer are handling animation, media streaming, and interactivity. The media streaming is one part that you probably already use. It's the download and display of media from Internet sites that feature streaming media such as movie clips, audio programs such as radio, or broadcasts. The Media layer is composed of the following API sets:

Direct3D Retained Mode This API provides high-level support for 3-D graphics and animation. This is the Media layer counterpart of the Direct3D Immediate mode that is part of the Foundation layer. It provides access to real-time 3-D graphics and animation capabilities for Internet applications, multimedia, and games.

DirectAnimation The DirectAnimation API provides the integration and timing support for 2-D and 3-D images, sound, movies, text, and vector graphics. This is the piece of code that ensures that the individual components of your 3-D action game all work at the same time.

DirectPlay This API's job is to provide that thrilling, head-to-head competition across modem, LAN, or other Internet connections. DirectPlay allows game designers to concentrate on building the game rather than dealing with the network hardware.

DirectShow Spend any time watching movies on your computer? This API enables Windows 2000 Professional to display MPEG and AVI format videos and even to play WAV audio files. DirectShow is also useful when using video capture hardware to record and edit digital video in Windows 2000 Professional.

DirectX Transform This API set has an odd name, but it's very useful. DirectX Transform enables developers to build tools for editing and manipulating digital 2-D or 3-D images. It aids in animation and in the development of graphics for Internet applications.

Installing Multimedia Hardware

These days you'll have to search diligently to find a computer on the market that is not replete with rather sophisticated multimedia hardware. But in the event that you are upgrading an older model or that you want to increase the horsepower that comes with a new so-called multimedia computer, I'm providing the information in this section.

Not everybody is just aching to get under the hood, however, and if you are one of those who approach such a task with fear and trembling, you can always take your machine to the local guru's shop and have it done. Regardless of whether you do it yourself or outsource, you'll need some guidelines for selecting your multimedia hardware. Following the guidelines, I'll go into the specifics of how to install a sound card and a graphics card.

Choosing Multimedia Hardware

Adding multimedia hardware to your Windows 2000 Professional system livens things up, but hardware costs can add up too, so shop around. Because new products are coming out at such a rapid rate, any specific product recommendations made here would be old news by the time you read this book. But a few simple guidelines can help you through the process.

Graphics Boards

A wide variety of graphics boards are currently on the market. Before you shop for a board, consider how you'll be using it:

Is the board mostly for business applications?

- Will you be running digital video-intensive multimedia applications that use Moving Pictures Experts Group (MPEG) standards?
- Will you be watching DVD movies or using the television output to display movies or games on your TV?

After you decide what kind of applications you want to run, you can buy exactly the horsepower you need.

Most cards support some digital video acceleration, but better boards support x-y interpolation (also called bilinear interpolation) and color space conversion. You'll want a minimum of 4MB of RAM on any graphics board you buy so that you can run programs at higher resolutions. In fact, the minimum RAM for all but the cheapest cards is now 8 or 16MB. For less than $200, you can buy a graphics accelerator that should be more than adequate for your multimedia adventures.

Sound Cards

Here again, you have many options. Sound Blaster is always a good bet because of its market dominance. As when you shop for graphics boards, it's good to have an idea how you'll be using the sound board. In some cases, it's better to skimp a little here and spend the saved money on higher quality speakers. On the other hand, many of the better (and more expensive) sound cards support 3-D surround-sound suitable for a home theater experience. If this is your dream, do some research to find the card that supports all the features you want, but be prepared to spend some money.

NOTE In PCs today, there are two types of MIDI synthesizers: FM and wavetable. FM synthesis was brought to the market by Yamaha in the 1980s and became popular with professional musicians. FM synthesis uses several sine waves (called operators) to produce its sounds. Although some of the sounds are convincing, many lack authenticity. Less-expensive sound cards usually have only FM synthesizers. But a synthesis technique called wavetable lookup gained favor in the late 1980s for its superior instrument quality. Wavetable lookup stores short recordings (called samples) of the instrument being synthesized. Many mid- and high-end sound cards have wavetable lookup synthesizers on them. But not all that glitters is gold. If you're going to be getting into MIDI, try to listen to a demo of a sound card's wavetable lookup synthesizer before you buy. All performance numbers aside, your ears are the best judge.

Speakers

As with a home stereo, your overall audio quality depends heavily on the quality of your speakers. If you spend the money to get a good sound card with lots of bells and whistles but play it through squawk-box speakers, the overall effect will be disappointing.

You'll want good computer speakers and a subwoofer for extra bass response. You can also run your PC's audio into your home stereo, though if your sound card is given to popping and crackling, these types of noises can damage speaker drivers. Be sure to either turn your amplifier volume down when powering your PC up or down or switch the amplifier to another input channel.

Installing a Sound Card

Sound cards are infamous for their cruel and unusual installation procedures, making you learn far more than you probably wanted to about the inner workings of your PC. Most installation woes stem from a sound card's need for many I/O resources. Some sound cards need at least two base I/O addresses, two IRQs, and two direct memory access (DMA) channels. If you're installing a sound card into an already-crowded system, it's easy to wind up with I/O resource conflicts—the sound card and another hardware device fight to use the same resources. The result is often that neither device will work correctly.

This is one of the areas where the Plug-and-Play capabilities of Windows 2000 Professional really shine. Installing a sound card in Windows 2000 Professional is a much less painful experience than it was in NT 4. Of course, you still must have available hardware resources in your computer, or you *will* have conflicts.

Tracking Hardware Device I/O Resources

It's a good idea to keep a table of I/O resources that each of your installed hardware devices uses. When you add a new device, you can check this information and avoid the headaches of I/O resource conflicts. Table 8.1 shows typical hardware you might find in a garden-variety PC and the I/O resources used.

TABLE 8.1: TYPICAL PC HARDWARE AND I/O RESOURCES

Device	Base I/O Address	IRQ	DMA Channel
SCSI controller	140	11	3
Network card	330	2	None
Modem on COM2	2F8	3	None
Mouse on COM1	3F8	4	None
Printer port	378	7	None
Floppy disk	3F7	6	2
System clock	None	1	None

Installing a Sound Board in Your PC

Windows 2000 Professional ships with drivers on its installation CD-ROM for the most popular sound cards out there. For our example, let's install a Sound Blaster 16 sound card with a Roland SCD-10 General MIDI daughterboard to make it interesting (this will help show off the Windows 2000 Professional MIDI functionality later).

The first step is to check which I/O resources the Sound Blaster needs. It turns out that the Sound Blaster requires two base I/O addresses, one IRQ, and two DMA channels. Its default settings are as follows:

Base I/O addresses 220 and 330

IRQ 5

DMA channels 1 and 5

Checking the table of I/O resources, you see that the second base I/O address will conflict with your network card, so you need to use another address. Sound Blaster can use either 330 or 300 for its MPU-401/General MIDI, and because no devices are using 300, you select that address. Looking at the rest of the requirements, you see no other I/O conflicts, so you're ready to install the board into the PC. Be sure to add the I/O resources you're using to your table of installed devices, because you'll need to tell Windows 2000 Professional what they are.

WARNING Make sure that your PC is turned off and that you first touch your PC's metal chassis to discharge any static electricity before adding or removing any expansion boards!

Installing the Sound Card Driver

After you insert the sound board in your PC and replace the PC's cover, restart the system, and follow these steps to install the sound card driver:

1. Choose Start ➢ Settings ➢ Control Panel ➢ Add/Remove Hardware to start the Add/Remove Hardware Wizard, and then click Next to open the Choose A Hardware Task screen:.

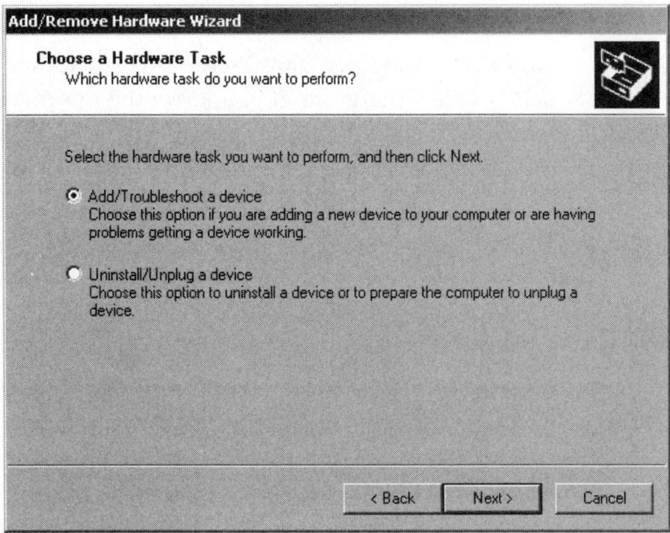

2. Select Add/Troubleshoot A Device, and then click Next to open the New Hardware Detection screen.

3. Windows 2000 Professional begins searching for the newly installed sound card. At this point, Windows 2000 Professional will only be looking for Plug-and-Play devices that can be installed and configured without user intervention. If the

device is detected correctly, Windows 2000 Professional installs the driver. If nothing was detected, you will be presented with the Choose A Hardware Device screen:

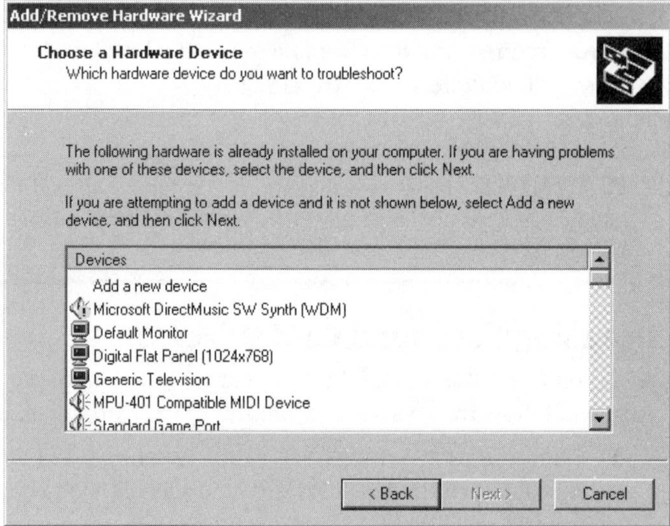

4. Select Add A New Device, and then click Next to open the Find New Hardware screen.
5. If you want Windows 2000 Professional to search for the device, click Yes, Search For New Hardware. If you know the information for the device and do not want to search, or if you have drivers from the manufacturer, select No, I Want To Select The Hardware From A List.
6. Select Next, and Windows 2000 Professional searches for any non-Plug-and-Play hardware installed in the computer and, if possible, installs a driver for it. If the hardware is not detected, click Next to open the Hardware Type screen.
7. Select the type of hardware you are installing. For a sound card, select Sound, Video, And Game Controllers, and then click Next to open the Select A Device Driver screen:

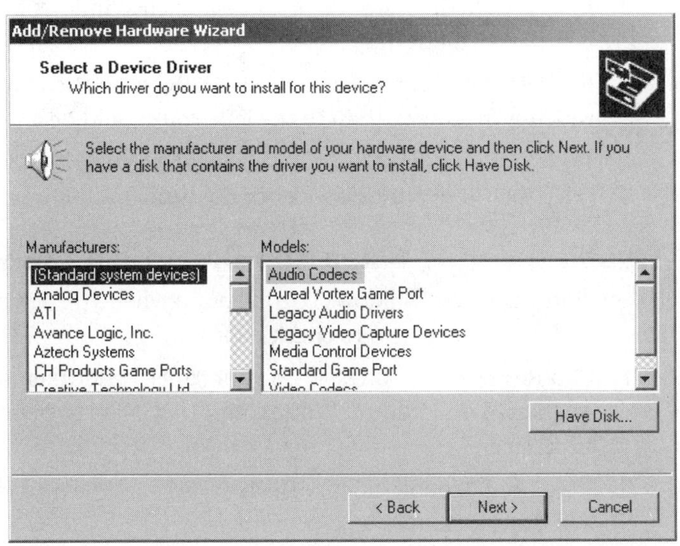

8. Select the manufacturer and model of the device you are installing. If it isn't listed, you can click the Have Disk button to specify the location of the updated driver. Click Next to open the Start Hardware Installation screen.
9. Click Next to start the installation. Windows 2000 Professional will copy the files for your device and then display a summary of the installation. If you need to make settings for the card, a dialog box will ask for the correct settings. The default options will often be correct, but it's a good idea to check them anyway. Click OK to accept the settings. Click Finish to complete the installation process and close the Wizard.

You may or may not need to reboot the computer before the sound card will work. Either way, plug in some speakers or headphones to hear some sound.

WARNING Be careful using headphones with a sound card. When first testing your sound card after driver installation, hold the headphones near your ear, but don't cover your ears with them. The Windows 2000 Professional start-up sound can be painfully loud, so adjust your mixer settings before wearing headphones.

After you reboot and log on to Windows 2000 Professional, you should hear the Windows Logon Sound, which is the Windows default start-up sound. If you don't hear this sound, follow the instructions in the next section. If you heard the Windows Logon Sound, the wave audio portion of your sound card is working fine. To test the General MIDI portion of the sound card, follow these steps:

1. In Explorer, go to the Winnt\media subfolder, and find a file called `canyon.mid`.

2. Double-click the `canyon.mid` file to launch Windows Media Player. (Media Player is covered later in this chapter.)
3. If the music doesn't start automatically, click the Play button in Media Player, which is the one farthest to the left. You should hear a tune—in this case a MIDI sequence.
4. Click the Close button to silence the tune.

Troubleshooting When You Don't Hear the Start-Up Sound

If you didn't hear the Windows Logon Sound when you restarted Windows 2000 Professional, follow these steps to check your settings:

1. Choose Start ➢ Settings ➢ Control Panel ➢ Add/Remove Hardware to start the Add/Remove Hardware Wizard, and click Next to open the Choose A Hardware Task screen.
2. Select Add/Troubleshoot A Device, and click Next to open the Choose A Hardware Device screen.
3. Select the sound card, and click Next. A sample list is shown in Figure 8.2.

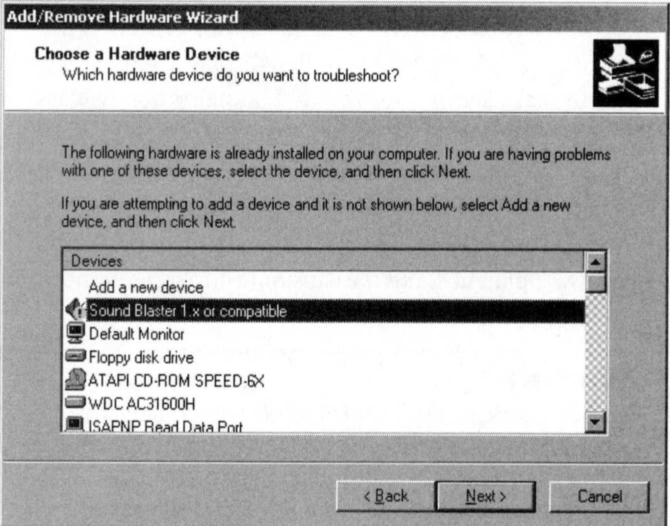

FIGURE 8.2
You can troubleshoot an installed device using the Add/Remove Hardware Wizard.

4. The Wizard displays a summary of the device status, indicating what it thinks the problem is. When you click Finish, the Add/Remove Hardware Wizard closes and the Troubleshooter opens.
5. Windows 2000 Professional Help opens with the entry for the specific error code displayed.

If the resource settings match the ones you selected on the hardware, either your hardware settings are incorrect or the sound card may be defective. Power the computer down, and open it up, being careful to ground yourself to the PC's metal chassis by touching the metal frame of the computer. Remove the card and verify its settings. If the settings are correct, they match the ones you selected in Control Panel, and you're sure there are no I/O conflicts with other devices, the sound card may be defective. You will need to replace the sound card itself.

Installing a Graphics Card

Fortunately, installing a graphics board is a somewhat less involved endeavor than installing a sound card, but there are still a few pitfalls to avoid. Suppose that you've got a sluggish graphics board, and you've decided to replace it with a faster one with more features. First, you need to make sure that any new graphics accelerator you purchase has Windows 2000 Professional drivers. Many new boards do have them, but check with the vendor to be sure. After you have your Windows 2000 Professional–ready graphics accelerator, you can begin.

The drivers for Windows 2000 Professional are compliant with the Windows Driver Model (WDM), which unifies the drivers for Windows 95/98 and 2000 into one library. This means that if you don't have a driver specific to Windows 2000 Professional you can try a driver for Windows 95/98.

TIP If you're running your old graphics adapter at 800 by 600 or 1024 by 768, move all your icons toward the center of the display, so that when you reboot at 640 by 480 to install your new drivers you'll be able to see your Start button and all your icons.

Follow these steps to install the graphics board and driver:

1. Open your PC, being sure to touch its metal chassis to discharge any static electricity (it can fry a computer circuit) before touching any of the boards. Remove your old graphics adapter, and replace it with the new one. Replace the cover on your PC, and power up the unit.
2. When you first boot the computer with the new video card in place, let it boot normally. With its Plug-and-Play capability, Windows 2000 Professional should be able to detect the new card and automatically use the default settings to boot. If it does, you can stop here. If not, proceed to step 3.
3. Boot the computer again, and this time use the VGA Mode. The boot menu displays the options for booting the computer, if you have more than one copy of Windows 2000 Professional installed. If not, you'll see the option to boot Microsoft Windows 2000 Professional. You can press F8 to get to the advanced boot menu. On this menu, if you have any problems booting with the new video card, select Enable VGA Mode and press Enter.

NOTE VGA (Video Graphics Adapter), first developed in 1987, has become the most standard display mode that graphics boards support and is usually a 640 by 480 pixel display with 16 colors.

4. After the machine boots up, open Control Panel and start the Add/Remove Hardware Wizard.
5. Click Next to open the Choose A Hardware Task, select Add/Troubleshoot A Device, and then click Next to open the New Hardware Detection screen.
6. The Wizard will search for any Plug-and-Play devices and very likely will find the new video card at this point. If it doesn't, select Add A New Device, and click Next.
7. Tell the Wizard to search for new hardware, and then click Next.
8. The Add/Remove Hardware Wizard should locate your new video card during the first portion of the search. If it doesn't, you may need to verify that there aren't any hardware conflicts. The Wizard should display a list of detected hardware and allow you to choose which device you want to install drivers for. Click Next to proceed.
9. Windows 2000 Professional will copy the drivers or prompt you for the location of the driver from the manufacturer. When you click Next, the Wizard will display a list of the options you installed.
10. On the Summary page, click Finish to complete the installation. You may be prompted to shut down and restart the computer.

After you reboot, you can change your screen resolution. Follow these steps:

1. Right-click the Desktop, and choose Properties from the shortcut menu to open the Display Properties dialog box.
2. Click the Settings tab.
3. In the Screen Area section, move the slider bar to increase or decrease the screen resolution.
4. In the Colors area, click the down arrow to select a setting that increases the color depth.
5. To change the refresh rate, click the Advanced button to open the Properties dialog box for your graphics card.
6. Click the Monitor tab, and in the Refresh Frequency box, click the down arrow to select a new rate. Click OK.
7. Click OK again.

You'll see a dialog box telling you that the display will be reset for 15 seconds and then automatically revert if you don't decide to keep the new setting. You need not reboot for the changes to take effect.

NOTE As a rule, you want to run your monitor at a minimum vertical refresh rate of 72Hz. This faster rate cuts down on perceptible flicker, decreasing eye fatigue during long periods of uninterrupted viewing. Windows 2000 Professional can use Plug and Play to detect the settings for your monitor, if you have a Plug-and-Play monitor. Before increasing your monitor's refresh rate, consult its documentation to find out its maximum refresh rate at the screen resolution and color depth at which you're running. Although you can run most monitors at a setting beyond their specified maximum refresh rate, you will more than likely damage the monitor's display circuitry by pushing it faster than it is intended to run.

Assigning Sounds to System Events

When a sound card is installed in your system, you will hear occasional sounds when certain system events occur. You can assign different sounds for different events, ranging from the default system beep to the sound that is played when a window is minimized. The Windows 2000 Professional default sounds give aural cues to system events, but they're not particularly exciting. The good news is you can easily change the default system event sounds. If you've downloaded WAV files you like from the Internet or some online service, you can swap these sounds for the default sounds. Here's how:

1. Choose Start ➢ Settings ➢ Control Panel ➢ Sounds And Multimedia to open the Sounds And Multimedia Properties dialog box:

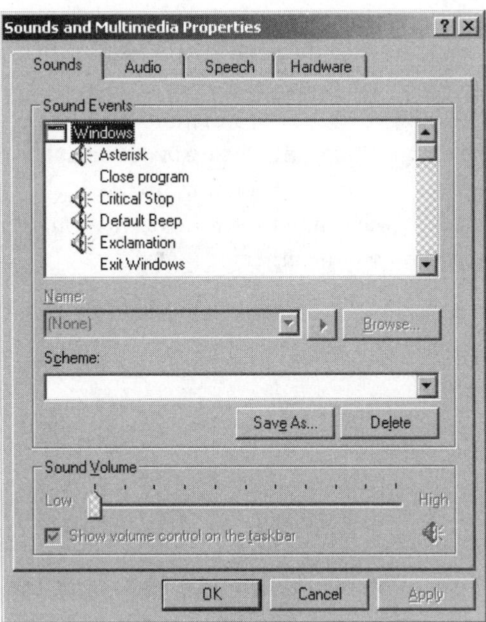

2. You can click any event and assign a WAV file sound to it. If you're not sure what a certain WAV file sounds like, you can preview it by clicking the Play button.
3. If you've assigned certain WAV files to events and like that configuration, you can save it as a sound scheme by clicking Save As and giving the scheme a name. If you change sound event assignments and then decide that you want to return to your original scheme, you can select it from the Scheme list, and those WAV files will be reassigned to the system events you previously chose.
4. Click OK when you've made your selections.

NOTE If you (or your neighbors) find system events a bit annoying, you can select (None), and no sound will play when that event occurs.

Using Multimedia Tools

So now you've installed your sound card and that burnin' new graphics accelerator, and you're ready to rock and roll. Let's check out some of the multimedia software components and controls that make the cool stuff happen. Open Control Panel and double-click the Sounds And Multimedia icon. The Sounds And Multimedia Properties dialog box contains a variety of tools for working with sounds and graphics.

Audio Tools

Click the Audio tab in the Sounds And Multimedia Properties dialog box (see Figure 8.3) to see your selected audio device, which is the ESS Maestro in my example. If you're one of those brave souls who has more than one sound card in their system, you can select which one you want to use as your default audio device. Some wave editors let you select the audio device you want to use. If you click the Use Only Preferred Devices check box, any wave audio software will use only the device that you select, and it won't be able to see the others.

FIGURE 8.3
The Audio tab in the Sounds And Multimedia Properties dialog box shows your selected audio device.

NOTE A *wave editor* is a program that lets you perform complex audio editing functions on WAV files and audio files in other formats such as Apple's AIFF or Sun's AU. These functions include adding effects such as reverb, chorus, fade-ins, and fade-outs; flanging/phase shifting; applying new equalizer (EQ) parameters; and mixing several WAV files. Wave editors are used by professional audio engineers and enthusiasts alike, and several excellent wave editors such as CoolEdit are available for download from the Internet.

Adjusting Audio Levels

In the Audio dialog box, you can also adjust the audio level for both playback and recording by clicking the Volume button next to the option you want to adjust. This opens the Volume Control dialog box for either recording or playback devices.

In the Volume Control dialog box, you can adjust the volume for one specific device or the overall volume for all devices by moving the slider controls. This dialog box mimics the actions of a mixer board and is in fact the interface to your sound card's mixer capabilities.

Enabling or Disabling the Speaker Icon

You can also enable or disable the display of a speaker icon on the Taskbar. In the Sounds And Multimedia Properties dialog box, click the Sounds tab, and then click the Show Volume Control On The Taskbar check box.

Specifying Recording Quality

You can also specify the default recording quality that the Sound Recorder applet uses. To adjust these settings in the Sounds And Multimedia Properties dialog box, select the Audio tab, and then click the Advanced button in the Sound Recording section to open the Advanced Audio Properties dialog box. You can now select the quality versus the processor usage using a pair of slider controls.

MIDI Tools

You use the Preferred Device drop-down list in the MIDI Music Playback section on the Audio tab of the Sounds And Multimedia Properties dialog box to specify which MIDI device you want to use. If you don't have any external MIDI devices connected to your PC (via your sound card's joystick port), you'll want to use your sound card's default device, which in the example is the Sound Blaster FM Synthesis device. But remember, in the installation example, you have a Roland SCD-10 General MIDI daughterboard attached to your Sound Blaster. To make it the default MIDI device, select the Creative Labs Sound Blaster 1.5 device. MIDI instructions are then redirected to the Sound Blaster's MIDI Out and the Roland daughterboard, which delivers markedly better instrument sound quality.

To change the settings of your MIDI device, follow these steps:

1. In the Sounds And Multimedia Properties dialog box, select the Hardware tab:

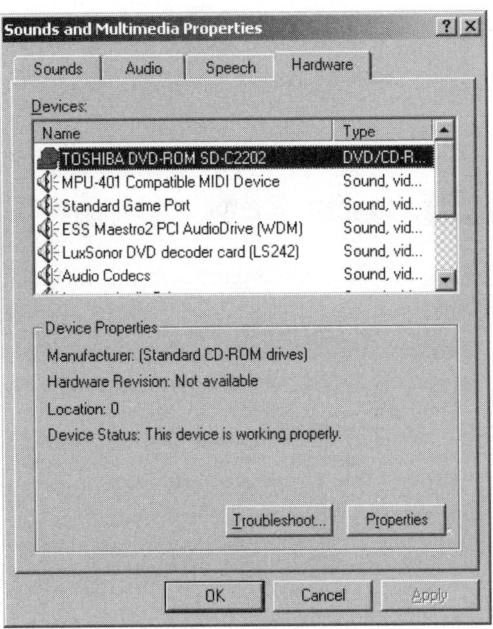

2. Scroll down and double-click Media Control Devices in the Devices list to open the Media Control Devices Properties dialog box.
3. Click the Properties tab, select your sound card, and click Properties to open the Properties dialog box for that sound card.
4. On the General tab of the Properties dialog box, click the Settings button to display the resources for the sound card.
5. Click OK as many times as necessary to close all the open dialog boxes.

Multimedia Device Information

Of the four tabs in the Sounds And Multimedia Properties dialog box, the Hardware tab conveys about as much information as the other four combined. This dialog box lists your installed multimedia hardware, software controls, audio and video decompression types, as well as video capture devices.

In addition to being able to change settings for multimedia hardware, you can also access the Windows 2000 Professional Troubleshooters for each of the devices through this interface if you are having trouble with them. To display the installed devices, click a category in the Name list, click Properties to open the Properties dialog box for that category, and then click the Properties tab to see a list of installed devices.

Multimedia File Information

A cool new feature in Windows 2000 Professional provides a quick way to get lots of information about multimedia files. In Explorer, right-click any multimedia filename, and select Properties from the shortcut menu to open a Properties dialog box for that file. You will see specific information about each of the media types. This information ranges from total playing time to sample rates and the codec the file uses for playback.

Running Multimedia Applications

Windows 2000 Professional includes four multimedia applications:

- CD Player
- Sound Recorder
- Volume Control
- Windows Media Player

To open any of them, choose Start ➢ Programs ➢ Accessories ➢ Entertainment, and then select the application from the submenu.

All these applications are easy to use, and, in fact, you may use them at times and not even realize it. For example, if you open a video clip in Internet Explorer, it runs in Windows Media Player automatically. In this section, we're going to look at each of these accessories briefly.

Running Media Player

You can open Windows Media Player from the Accessories menu, or you can enter **mplayer2** at a command prompt. In either case, you'll see the window shown in Figure 8.4.

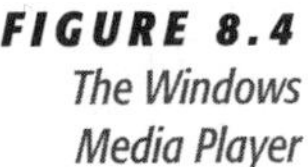

FIGURE 8.4
The Windows Media Player

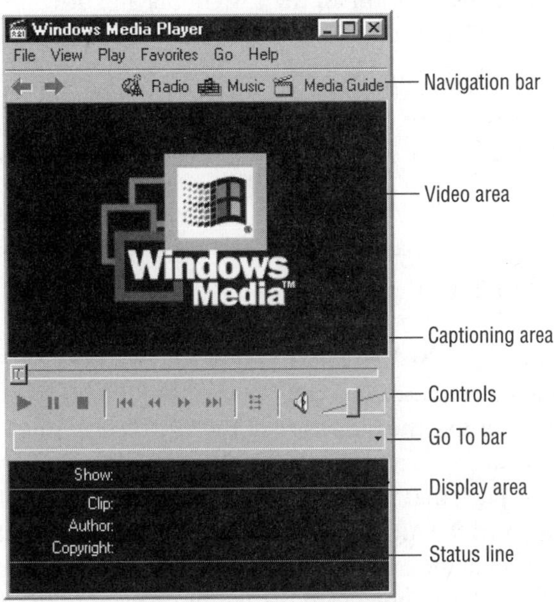

Using Media Player Controls

Depending on the type of media file you are playing, you'll see the following components in the Windows Media Player:

Navigation bar Click the Forward and Back buttons to open a file you played earlier in the current session; click Web Events to go to WindowsMedia.com, which contains a number of links to media files that you can play and download.

Video area The video you are viewing displays in this area.

Captioning area If the file you are viewing provides it, this area displays closed-captioning. (Choose View ➢ Captions.)

Seek bar If the content of the file you are playing makes the Seek bar available, you can drag the slider bar to play a specific section of the clip.

Controls The controls in Media Player correspond to those on your audio CD player, and you use them in exactly the same way.

Go To bar Click the down arrow to display a list of markers in the file, if the file provides them. Click a marker to play the section of the file associated with the marker.

Display area If the file provides it, this area displays the shot title, clip title, author, and copyright notice.

Status line This area displays icons for sound and closed captioning and the following information for the current playing file:

- Connecting
- Buffering
- Playing
- Paused
- Reception quality
- Time elapsed
- Total time

Using Media Player Features for AVI Files

A lesser-known trick you can use with AVI files in Media Player is to double, triple, or even quadruple the frame size of the Video area. An AVI file may have an original (or *native*) frame size of only 320 by 240 pixels. If you play this back on an 800 by 600 pixel display, that frame will be small. Before clicking the Play button, press Alt+2 (hold down the Alt key and press the 2 key) to double the frame size. Press Alt+3 to triple the frame size, and press Alt+4 to quadruple the frame size. This trick is especially handy if your graphics card has hardware features to smooth video playback image quality at larger frame sizes.

WARNING Watch out though—if your graphics card lacks these features, and the frame size is too big, the video playback will seriously suffer and will look blocky. To return the frame to its original size, press Alt+1.

Running CD Player

When you insert a data CD-ROM or audio CD in your CD-ROM drive, Windows 2000 Professional checks its format information. If it's a data CD, Windows 2000 Professional looks for a file called `autorun.bat`, which is a batch file telling Windows 2000 Professional which program on the CD to execute. If the CD is an audio CD, Windows 2000 launches CD Player.

To manually launch CD Player, choose Start ➢ Programs ➢ Accessories ➢ Entertainment ➢ CD Player. Figure 8.5 shows the CD Player window. The first things you see are the transport controls like those found on a home CD player: Play, Pause, Stop, Previous Track, Scan Back, Scan Forward, Next Track, and Eject.

FIGURE 8.5
The CD Player window

You will also notice that there are no drop-down menus in CD Player. You configure CD Player using the items on the Options item, which include the following:

Preferences Opens the Preferences dialog box, which you can use to configure CD Player and the CD volume control. In this dialog box, you can also set your preferences for Album Information, such as how to connect over the Internet to download track information, and you can specify how to view your playlist.

Playlist Opens the Preferences dialog box at the Playlists tab.

Tiny View Displays CD Player in compact view, showing only the Options, Play, Stop, Eject, and Track buttons. It also shows a small timer display. If you are already in Tiny View, this command is replaced with Normal, which you can choose to resume the default view of CD Player.

CD Player Help Opens the online help utility for CD Player.

About CD Player Displays the version information for CD Player. This is a traditional Windows About dialog. It contains information on the registered owner of the operating system and the amount of physical memory available to Windows.

Exit Closes the CD Player utility.

Using CD Player, you can download album information from the Internet. This is a great timesaver for those of us who like to have the track names entered for each audio CD. The Internet button in the main interface gives you access to these features. When you start CD Player, it will automatically try to download the information for the album from one of two Internet sites, either Music Boulevard or Tunes.com. If your Internet connection is not currently available, CD Player will queue the request and wait until the next time you connect to the Internet to retrieve the information. You can customize this behavior in the Preferences dialog box on the Album Options tab.

Editing CD Player Information

You can enter album and track title information for discs that aren't located on the Internet. This way, the album information is displayed the next time you run CD Player just as the album information that is automatically downloaded from the Internet is. It's also useful if your favorite album isn't in the databases on either of the Internet sites. You can enter the correct information and upload it to the sites so that they can add it to their database. Follow these steps:

1. Insert an audio CD into your CD-ROM drive.
2. Click the Options button, and select Playlist. Highlight the disc that's currently in the drive, and click Edit Playlist to display the dialog box shown in Figure 8.6.

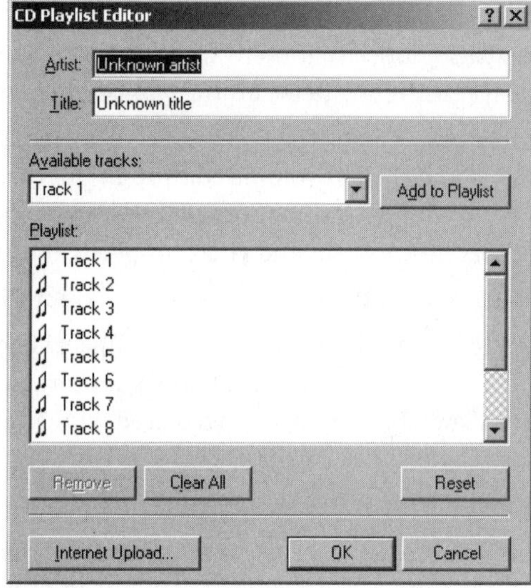

FIGURE 8.6
Using the CD Playlist Editor, you can edit disc and track names, as well as specify play orders.

3. To change the Artist name, highlight the text in that field, and begin typing.
4. Press the Tab key and enter the CD title.
5. For each of the tracks, you can highlight a given track either in the Playlist box or in the Available Tracks box, and enter a name in the field in the middle of the dialog box, which displays the track number.
6. When you've finished, click the Add To Playlist button. You'll see that the name is updated in both the Available Tracks and Playlist boxes.
7. After you enter all the track names, click OK.
8. As a test, remove the CD from the drive, and then put it back in. CD Player reads and recognizes the disc and shows you the information you've just input.

Changing Time Display Options

The four CD Player time display options are straightforward. To specify the display you want, choose Options ➢ Preferences to open the Preferences dialog box. On the Player Options tab, choose from the following options in the Time Display Options section:

Track Time Elapsed Shows how far you are in playing a track

Track Time Remaining Displays the amount of time left for a given track

CD Time Elapsed Shows the total time that the disc has been playing

CD Time Remaining Shows the total amount of play time left for the entire disc

Specifying CD Player Preferences

In the Player Options tab in the Preferences dialog box, you can also specify the following:

- Whether CD Player begins playing when you open it
- Whether CD playback stops when you exit CD Player
- Whether you want CD Player to always be the top window
- Whether you want to display the control on the Taskbar

You can also adjust the Preview Time interval, which defaults to five seconds.

Running Sound Recorder

If you have the appropriate equipment, you can make your own voice recordings or record from another sound source. To make voice recordings, you need a microphone and a sound card. To record sounds from another device such as an audio CD or a stereo receiver, you'll need a Line In connector to your sound card.

To open Sound Recorder, which is shown below, choose Start ➢ Programs ➢ Accessories ➢ Entertainment ➢ Sound Recorder.

Use the buttons at the bottom of the Sound Record window to control recording and playback.

To make a voice recording, follow these steps:

1. Choose File ➢ New.
2. Turn on your microphone.
3. Choose File ➢ Properties to open the Properties For Sound dialog box.
4. In the Choose From drop-down list, select Recording Formats, and click Convert Now to open the Sound Selection dialog box.
5. In the Name drop-down list, select a recording quality—CD, radio, or telephone.
6. Click OK twice.
7. Click the Record button, and speak into the microphone.
8. When you're finished, click Stop.
9. Choose File ➢ Save As to save your recording as a file.

Running Volume Control

The Volume Control accessory lets you set both playback and recording levels for all your sound card's devices (WAV, MIDI, Audio CD, Microphone, and Line In). Choose Start ➢ Programs ➢ Accessories ➢ Entertainment ➢ Volume Control to open the Volume Control window, as shown in Figure 8.7.

FIGURE 8.7
The Volume Control window

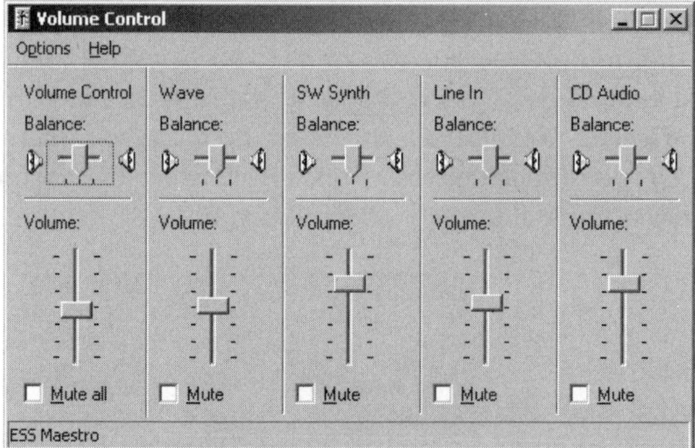

TIP Another way to launch the Volume Control accessory is to double-click the speaker icon on the Taskbar. Right-click the speaker icon and choose Adjust Audio Properties from the shortcut menu to open the Sounds And Multimedia Properties dialog box, in which you can adjust your audio settings.

In the Volume Control window, two types of slide controllers set the levels—one set moves vertically and the other horizontally. You control the volume using the vertical sliders, and you control the balance using the horizontal sliders.

Recording Levels

To view recording levels, choose Options ➢ Properties to open the Properties dialog box, as shown in Figure 8.8.

FIGURE 8.8
The Volume Control Properties dialog box

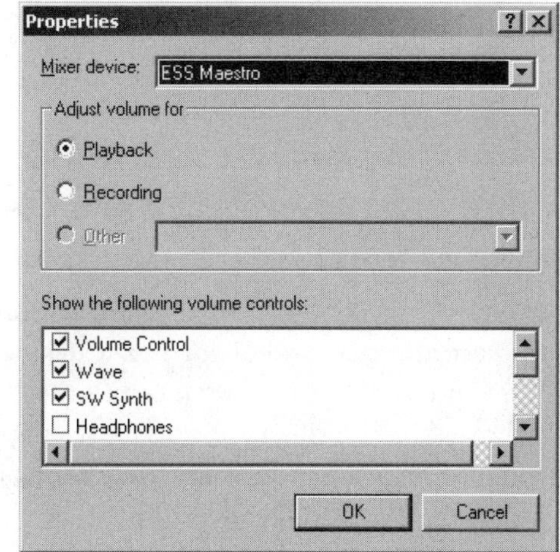

In the Properties dialog box, you can select which items will be visible and whether you want to look at Playback, Recording, or Other level settings. Select Recording for now and click OK.

You'll notice that the mixer window's title changes to Recording Control, as shown in Figure 8.9, and that some of the level settings are different. From here, you can adjust each setting's recording level, including the Line In and Microphone settings. After you've played with these settings a while, reset Volume Control to display playback levels.

FIGURE 8.9
The Recording Control window

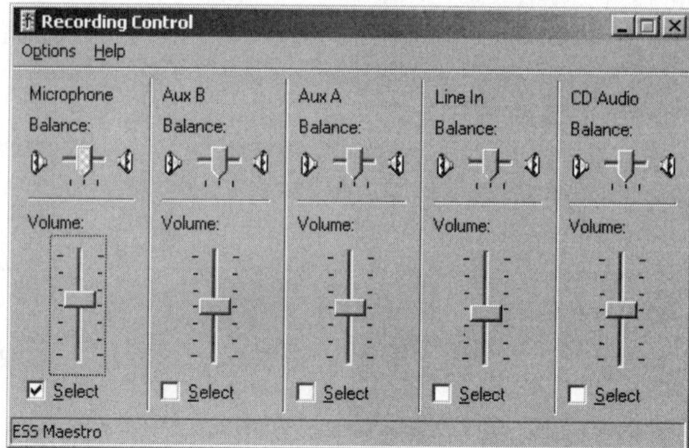

Advanced Controls

Clicking the Advanced button in the Recording Control window opens the Advanced Controls for Recording Control dialog box. Clicking the Advanced button in the Volume Control window opens the Advanced Control for Volume Control dialog box. Both dialog boxes contain slider controls for setting the bass and treble volume. Unless you have exceptionally good speakers, these controls won't change the overall sound quality very much.

Summary

I've covered a lot of technical information about numerous media data types and multimedia tools that you'll encounter in Windows 2000 Professional. The main thing to know is that multimedia can make using Windows 2000 Professional much more compelling, not to mention fun. Because Windows 2000 Professional incorporates the DirectX APIs, you'll be able to play most games written for Windows 95/98 on Windows 2000 Professional.

Although the Windows 2000 Professional multimedia tools provide only basic functionality, you can still have some fun with them. You can also customize your CD Player to recognize and display information about your favorite CDs. As the Windows 2000 Professional interface suggests, explore!

CHAPTER 9

Sharing Data Between Applications

FEATURING:

As you know, you can run several applications at one time and switch between them with a click of the mouse or a press of Alt+Tab. You may also know that you can cut, copy, and paste information between programs and documents, embedding bits and pieces of information, graphics, sound, and video from multiple sources into a single destination source to create complex documents.

As a result of the standardization of the Windows interface and API, users have become accustomed to being able to cut, copy, and paste not only within a given program, but also between Windows programs. Nowadays, thousands of applications can easily share data with one another through these commands that use the Windows Clipboard.

In this chapter, we look at data sharing on the Windows 2000 Professional platform, paying particular attention to the techniques you can use to create complex documents, including OLE.

Exchanging Data

Actually, much more interesting than simply being able to use one program's document in another program is the ability to mix and match a great variety of document types, such as text, sound, graphics, worksheets, databases, and so forth. This mixing and matching lets you construct complex documents previously requiring physical cutting and pasting and possibly the aid of an art department. Such operations are dependent on the operating system's capacity to exchange data between dissimilar applications: worksheets and word processors, for example.

Windows 2000 Professional provides three internal vehicles for exchanging data between programs:

- The Windows Clipboard (and ClipBook, which is an extension of Clipboard)
- Dynamic Data Exchange (DDE)
- Object linking and embedding (OLE)

In this chapter, I'll explain each of these and then describe some special considerations for data sharing across the network.

If you're new to Windows applications, you may want to read only the portion about the Clipboard and the Cut, Copy, and Paste commands. You'll use these commands much more often than the other techniques covered here. If you're using a network and want to share little bits of information with other people, read about ClipBook too. If you want to take full advantage of what OLE has to offer under Windows, read the entire chapter. Using OLE, you can construct complex documents by putting, say, a portion of a worksheet or a fancy chart into a word processing document.

NOTE Many of the examples in this chapter refer to Microsoft products. This isn't necessarily an endorsement of Microsoft products over other competing products! I'm just using the most common examples to reach the widest audience, and the most commonly used products just happen to be Microsoft products.

Using the Clipboard

Although the Clipboard is not capable of converting data files between various formats (such as XLS to WK3 or RTF to DOC), it is great for many everyday data-exchange tasks. Just about all Windows programs support the use of the ubiquitous Cut, Copy, and Paste commands, and it's the Clipboard that provides this functionality for you.

The Clipboard makes it possible to move any kind of material—whether it's text, data cells, graphics, video, or audio clips—and OLE objects between documents and, with Windows 2000 Professional, between folders, the Desktop, Explorer, and other portions of the interface. The form of the source data doesn't matter that much, because the Clipboard and Windows together take care of figuring out what's being copied and where it's being pasted, making adjustments when necessary or providing just a few manual options for you to adjust.

Understanding How the Clipboard Works

The Clipboard is built into Windows 2000 Professional and uses a portion of the system's internal resources (RAM and virtual memory) as a temporary holding tank for material you're working with. For example, suppose you cut some text from one part of a document in preparation for pasting it into another location. Windows 2000 Professional stores the text on the Clipboard and waits for you to paste it into its new home.

The last item you copied or cut is stored in this no man's land somewhere in the computer until you cut or copy something else, exit Windows 2000 Professional, or intentionally clear the Clipboard. As a result, you can paste the Clipboard's contents any number of times.

You can examine the Clipboard's contents using the ClipBook utility supplied with Windows 2000 Professional. If you've used previous versions of Windows NT, you're familiar with this application. You can also use this application to save the Clipboard's contents to disk for later use or to share specific bits of data for use by others on your network.

Selecting, Copying, and Cutting in Windows Applications

In Windows 2000 Professional, the earlier Windows standards and procedures for copying, cutting, and pasting apply, because Windows 2000 Professional supports all the

Windows calls for these services. Even if you're mixing and matching 16- and 32-bit applications, the Clipboard works just fine, because in the internals of Windows 2000 Professional, the 16-bit subsystem shares the same Clipboard as the 32-bit section.

In a Windows 2000 Professional application, you can cut, copy, and paste in three ways:

- By using the commands on the Edit menu or their shortcut keys
- By dragging and dropping
- By right-clicking an item and using the shortcut menu

To cut, copy, and paste using the Edit menu, follow these steps:

1. Open the source document, and select what you want to cut or copy.
2. Choose Edit ➢ Cut (or press Ctrl+X) or Edit ➢ Copy (or press Ctrl+C). The item is now stored on the Clipboard.
3. Open the destination document, and place the insertion point where you want the item (although you can always move it later).
4. Choose Edit ➢ Paste (or press Ctrl+V).

That's all there is to it. Figure 9.1 shows a selection that's being copied from the Sybex Web site, and Figure 9.2 shows that selection copied into WordPad.

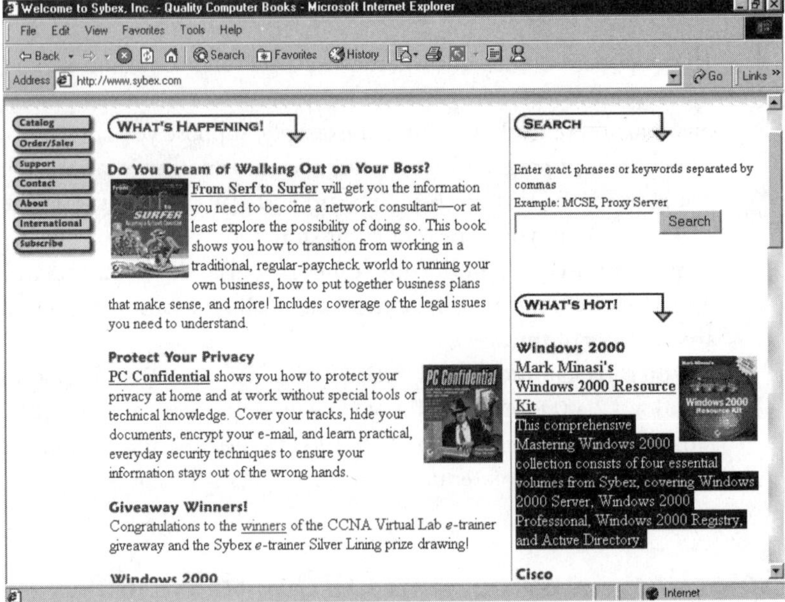

FIGURE 9.1
Copying a selection from the Sybex Web site

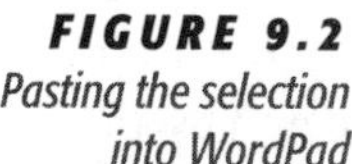

FIGURE 9.2
Pasting the selection into WordPad

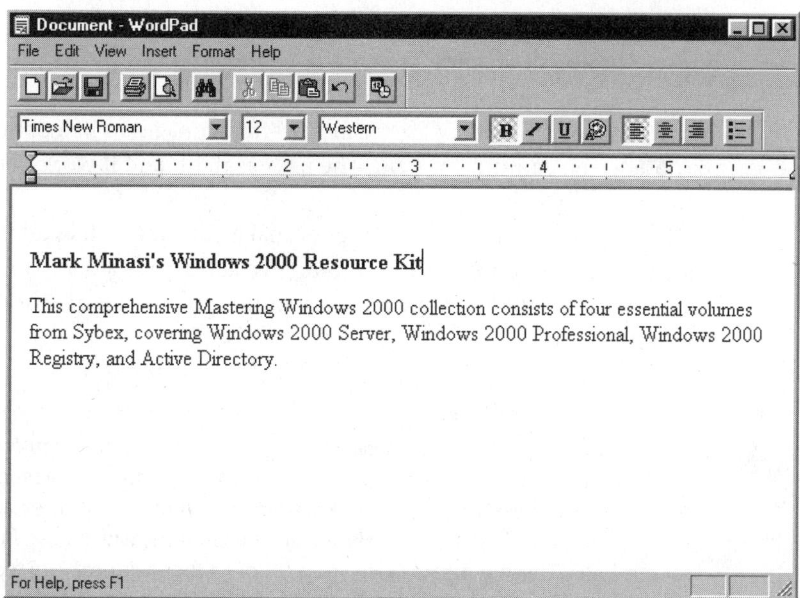

To cut, copy, and paste using drag and drop, follow these steps:

1. Open both the source document and the destination document so that both are visible on the Desktop.
2. Select what you want to cut or copy, right-click the selection, drag it to the destination document, and release the mouse button.
3. From the shortcut menu that appears, choose Move Here, or choose Copy Here.

To cut, copy, and paste using the shortcut menu, follow these steps:

1. Right-click the source item (for example, a filename in Explorer) to open the shortcut menu.
2. Choose Cut or Copy.
3. Right-click the destination item (for example, a folder in Explorer), and choose Paste from the shortcut menu.

NOTE If you're using the shortcut menu to copy an item to a document, open the destination document, right-click where you want the item inserted, and choose Paste from the shortcut menu.

Capturing Screens with the Clipboard

You can capture all or part of a screen image while running an application. Screen captures are useful for creating program documentation, software education materials, or promotional material about software.

The Clipboard is handy for capturing screen images in lieu of purchasing a special-purpose screen-capture program. The price is right, and it works, albeit with some limitations.

Although you can't edit your files or make changes such as adding borders when using this economy approach to captures, you can save a file to disk for later use. The Clipboard and ClipBook both let you save files to disk. I'll discuss this in more detail later in this chapter.

TIP Professional programs designed for screen capture help you organize, crop, and edit your screen captures, among other things. If you regularly use screen captures, you might want to check these programs out. Programs you might want to explore are Collage Complete, Tiffany, PixelPop, Hotshot, Hijaak, and FullShot 99, which I used to capture the screens for this book. These programs give you a lot of latitude with capture techniques, file formats, color settings, grayscaling, and so forth, which the Clipboard doesn't allow.

With the Clipboard, you can capture the entire screen or only the active window. The capture is converted to a bitmapped format for pasting into graphics programs, such as PageMaker and Paint.

NOTE The active window is the window that contains the display or document that will be affected by any cursor movement, command, or text entry.

To copy the active window's image onto the Clipboard, follow these steps:

1. With the application whose screen you want to capture open and running in a window, adjust and size the window as desired.
2. Press Alt+Print Screen. The image of the active window is copied to the Clipboard.

To capture the entire screen, press only Print Screen. To paste the screen into a document, open the document, and choose Edit ➢ Paste or press Ctrl+V. Figure 9.3 shows a Windows 2000 Professional screen pasted into a Word document.

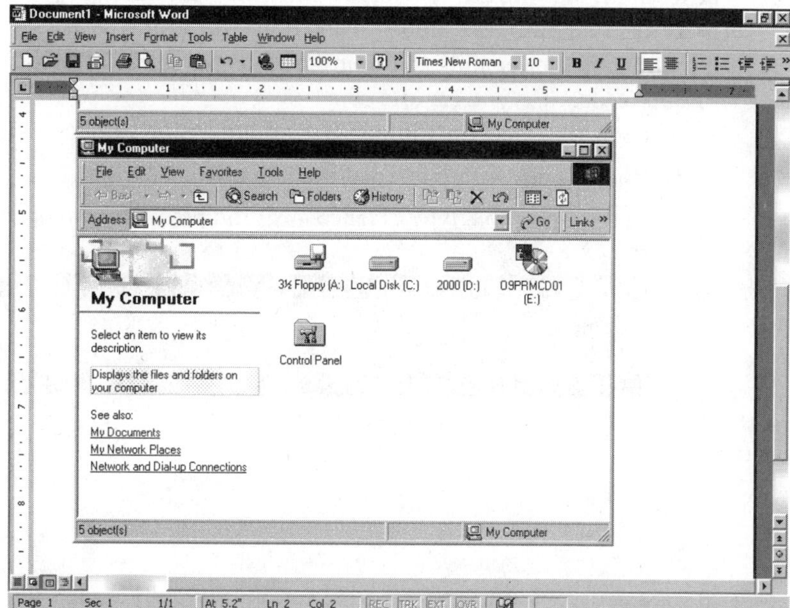

FIGURE 9.3
A screen capture of My Computer window pasted into a Word document

Working with ClipBook Viewer

In Windows NT 4, two programs handled viewing objects that had been placed on the Clipboard: Clipboard Viewer and ClipBook Viewer. In Windows 2000 Professional, these two programs have been combined into one program, ClipBook Viewer (`clipbrd.exe`). This program lets you do some useful Clipboard-related tasks, such as the following:

- View the Clipboard's contents
- Save and retrieve the Clipboard's contents to or from a file
- Clear the Clipboard's contents
- Set up pages of the Clipboard, with each page storing information you plan to use later or want to make available to networked colleagues

Let's look at each of these simple tasks in order.

Viewing the Clipboard's Contents

You may simply forget what information is on the Clipboard; you don't remember what you cut or copied last. Before you paste it into an application (especially if that application doesn't have an Undo command) you might want to check out what will be inserted. Viewing the Clipboard's contents is also useful when you've tried to get a particular item into the Clipboard and don't know how successful you've been. Opening ClipBook Viewer and positioning it off in the corner of the screen can give you instant feedback as you cut and copy.

Here's how to view the Clipboard's contents using ClipBook Viewer:

1. Choose Start ➢ Run to open the Run dialog box.
2. In the Open box, type **`clipbrd.exe`**, and press Enter to open ClipBook Viewer:

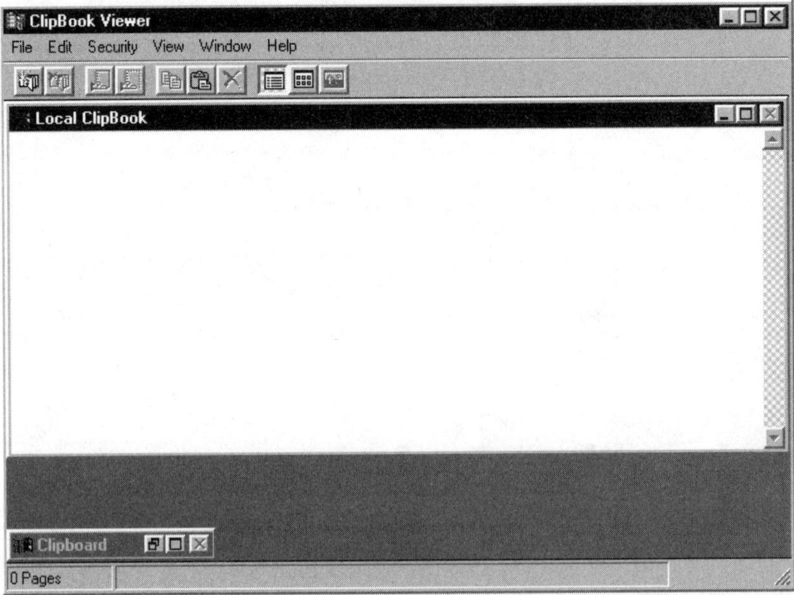

3. Double-click Clipboard in the bottom left corner to display the contents of the Clipboard. As Figure 9.4 shows, my Clipboard contains the screen I copied using Alt+Print Screen earlier in this chapter.

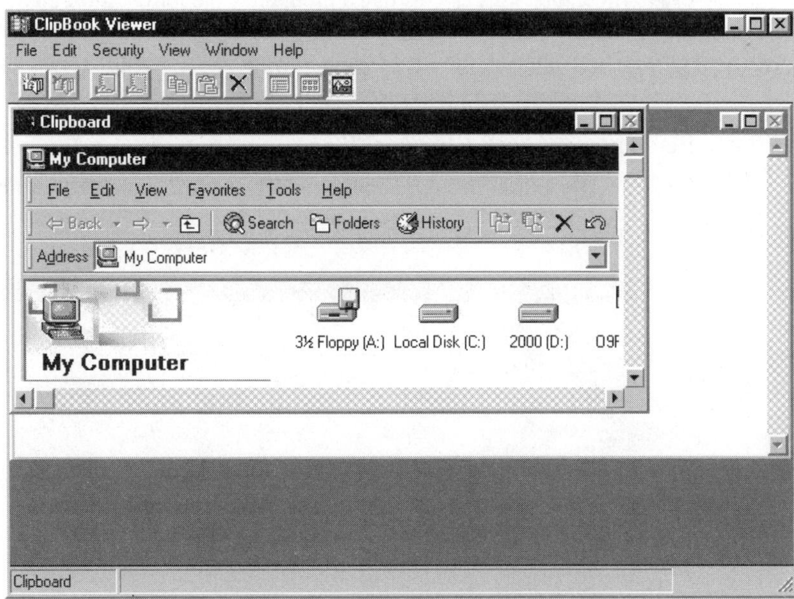

FIGURE 9.4 *The contents of my Clipboard*

NOTE If you use ClipBook Viewer frequently, you'll find it helpful to create a shortcut on your Desktop or even to add a shortcut to your Start menu.

Storing the Clipboard's Contents in a File

When you place new material onto the Clipboard, reboot, or shut down the computer, the Clipboard contents are lost. Also, because the Clipboard itself is not *network-aware* (meaning it can't interact with other workstations on the network), you can't share the Clipboard's contents with other network users. You'll want to take advantage of ClipBook pages for that, as described later in this chapter.

You can, however, save the Clipboard's contents to a disk file. Clipboard files have the extension CLP. After the Clipboard's contents are stored in a disk file, it's like any other disk file—you can later reload the file from disk. If you do a lot of work with clip-art and bits and pieces of sound, video, text, and the like, this technique can come in handy. Also, if you give network users access to your CLP file directory, they can, in effect, use your Clipboard.

TIP The Clipboard CLP files use a proprietary file format; no other popular programs can use these files. So, to use a CLP file, you *must* open it in Clipboard before pasting it where you want it to appear. If this is a hassle for you, you're a prime candidate for using ClipBook.

Here's how to save a Clipboard file:

1. With the Clipboard contents open in ClipBook Viewer, choose File ➢ Save As to open the Save As dialog box:

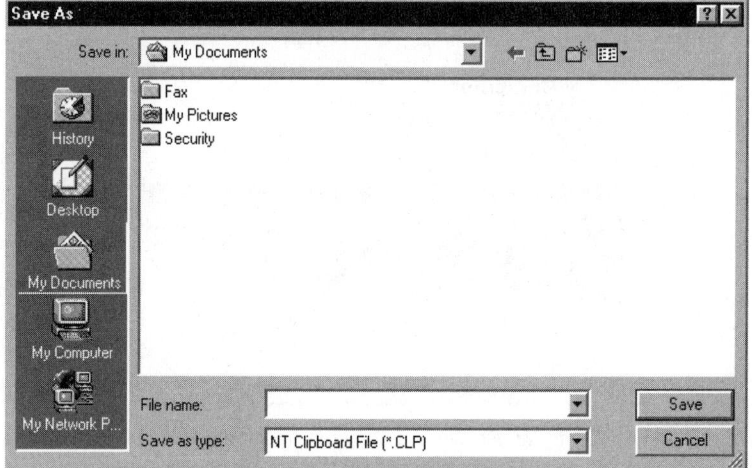

2. Enter a name. As usual, you can change the folder, name, and extension. Leave the extension as CLP, because Clipboard uses this as a default when you later want to reload the file.
3. Click the Save button.

Retrieving the Contents of a Stored Clipboard File

After the CLP file is on disk, you can reload it. However, you should be aware that when you reload a CLP file, anything currently on the Clipboard is lost.

Follow these steps to open your saved Clipboard file:

1. Run ClipBook Viewer.
2. Choose Window ➢ Clipboard to open the Clipboard.
3. Choose File ➢ Open to display the Open dialog box.
4. Select the file you want to pull onto the Clipboard. (Only legitimate CLP files can be opened.)

5. If there's something already on the Clipboard, you are asked if you want to erase it. Click Yes.
6. Change the display format via the View menu if you want to (assuming there are options available on the menu).
7. Paste the contents into the desired destination.

Clearing the Clipboard to Save Resources

While you're using the Clipboard, keep in mind that the information you store there, even temporarily, can affect the amount of memory available for use by the system and other applications. If you're cutting and pasting small bits of text and graphics as most people do during the course of a workday, this shouldn't be a concern, especially because Windows 2000 Professional's new memory management is more efficient than its predecessor's.

But some items you might place on the Clipboard can be large. For example, graphics, video, sound samples, or large amounts of formatted text take up considerable space on the Clipboard. Some items are stored in a number of formats for pasting into different kinds of destinations and thus may be more memory-hogging than you might expect.

The moral of the story is that if you're running into memory shortages, you may occasionally want to clear the contents of the Clipboard using the technique described here.

To clear the Clipboard, follow these steps:

1. From ClipBook Viewer, double-click Clipboard.
2. Click the X in ClipBook Viewer toolbar, or choose Edit ➢ Delete.
3. Click Yes when you are asked if you want to clear the Clipboard contents.

Using ClipBook Instead of the Clipboard

Although it's very handy, the Clipboard does have several drawbacks:

- You can't easily share information on the Clipboard with network users.
- Copying or cutting a new item erases the previous one, so you're limited to one item on the Clipboard at a time.
- Saving and retrieving Clipboard files is a hassle. Accessing, say, several small sound clips or clip-art pictures requires giving each one a CLP filename and later remembering their names so you can reload them.

So, what to do? Use ClipBook, which has the following advantages over Clipboard:

- You can store Clipboard memory on *pages* within ClipBook. There can be as many as 127 of these pages, each one acting like a separate Clipboard.

- You can give each ClipBook page a description to help you remember what it contains. The description can be a maximum of 47 characters. This means you can give a page a name such as "Joe's logo version 10."
- You can share all or selected pages of your ClipBook for use by colleagues at other network workstations.
- You can display thumbnail representations of each page so that you can visually scan many pages of your ClipBook at once to find the one you want.

Running ClipBook

If you've been following the steps in this chapter, you already know how to run ClipBook Viewer. This program is your connection to ClipBook, just as it is to the Clipboard. To open ClipBook, in ClipBook Viewer choose Window ➢ Local ClipBook.

Figure 9.5 identifies the buttons on ClipBook Viewer's toolbar, and the following list describes their use.

FIGURE 9.5 *The buttons on ClipBook Viewer's toolbar*

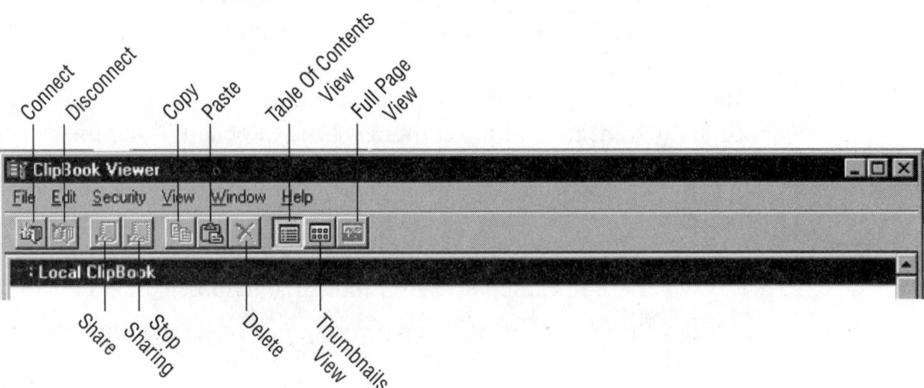

Connect Connects to a ClipBook on a remote (networked) computer.

Disconnect Disconnects from a ClipBook on a remote (networked) computer.

Share Shares a page of your ClipBook for network users to access.

Stop Sharing Stops sharing a page.

Copy Pastes a selected ClipBook page to the Clipboard.

Paste Pastes the contents of the Clipboard to ClipBook.

Delete Deletes the contents of a selected page (or of Clipboard if showing).

Table Of Contents Lists the named pages in ClipBook.

Thumbnails Displays thumbnails of ClipBook's pages.

Full Page Displays a selected ClipBook page.

Pasting Items into ClipBook

ClipBook doesn't replace the Clipboard; it simply works in concert with it. In Windows 2000 Professional, cutting, copying, and pasting within and between your various applications is still orchestrated by the Clipboard. ClipBook supplies a convenient repository for Clipboard items—items that would normally be wiped out of the Clipboard when you shut down Windows or when you copy something new onto the Clipboard. Figure 9.6 illustrates the relationship of the Clipboard to ClipBook.

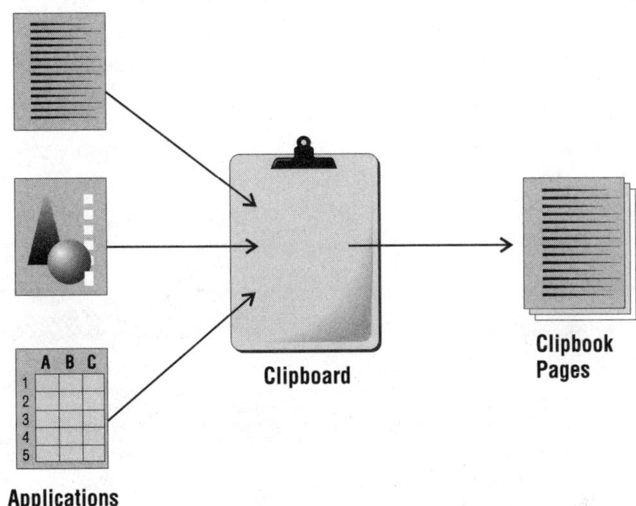

FIGURE 9.6 *Items are added to ClipBook by pasting them from the Clipboard.*

To use ClipBook, paste an item onto one of the 127 pages in your ClipBook. Then give the page a name and description for later reference. Here are the steps:

1. Cut or copy the desired information onto the Clipboard.
2. Run or switch to ClipBook Viewer.
3. At this point, it doesn't matter whether the Clipboard or Local ClipBook window is the active window. Choose Edit ➢ Paste from within ClipBook Viewer to open the Paste dialog box, which asks for a name for the new page, as shown here. Each time you paste into ClipBook, you need to name the page.

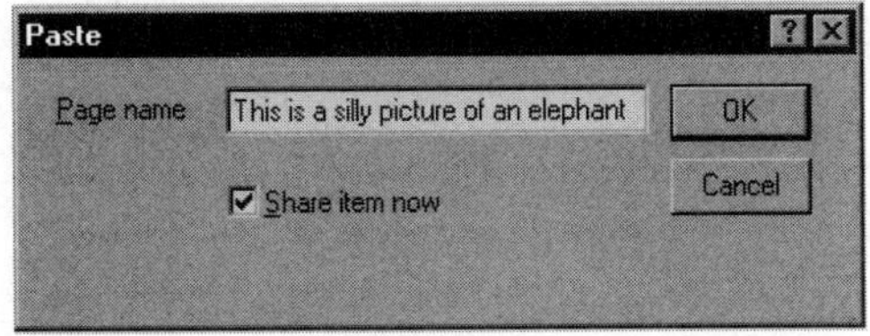

4. If you want to make the new ClipBook page immediately available to other users on the network (if you're on a network), click the Share Item Now check box. When you click OK, you'll see the Share ClipBook Page dialog box, which asks how you want to share the item. See the next section for details.

After you've stowed your items on ClipBook pages, how do you use them again? No problem. You can easily paste them into documents or share them for use by others on your network. Let's take these two situations separately.

Pasting Items from ClipBook

Here's how to paste something from ClipBook into a document you're working on. Suppose you've saved a piece of clip-art on a page and now you want to paste it:

1. Run ClipBook Viewer (or switch to it, if it's already running).
2. Display the Local ClipBook window by double-clicking it or by choosing Window ➢ Local ClipBook. You can change the display from the View menu or from the toolbar. Figure 9.7 shows a typical view of pages.

FIGURE 9.7
To paste a ClipBook page, start by selecting it. You can then copy and paste it into the destination application. The Clipboard is used as an intermediary.

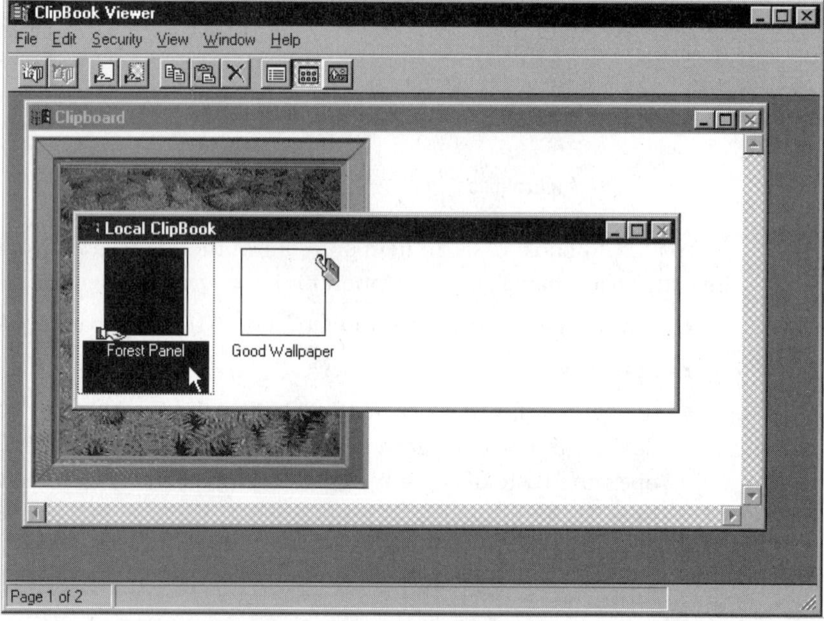

3. Select the page containing the information you want by clicking its thumbnail or name.

4. Within ClipBook Viewer, click the Copy button, or choose Edit ➢ Copy to copy the page onto the Clipboard.
5. Switch to the destination application. Position the cursor or do any setup in that application that might be necessary, and then choose Edit ➢ Paste from that application.

Sharing Your ClipBook Pages with Network Users

When you want to share a ClipBook page so others on the network can link or copy it into their documents, do the following:

1. Run or switch to ClipBook Viewer.
2. Choose Window ➢ Local ClipBook.
3. Select the item you want to share. If you want to examine the item before sharing it, click the Full Page button.

TIP You can quickly toggle between Full Page and Thumbnail or Table of Contents view by double-clicking an item.

4. Choose File ➢ Share to open the Share ClipBook Page dialog box:

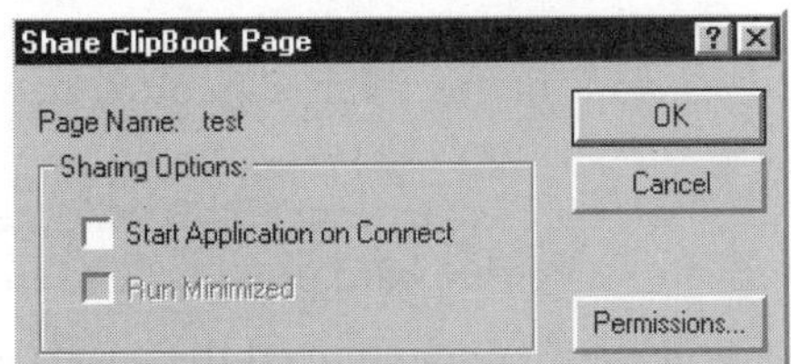

5. Check the Start Application On Connect check box if the data on the ClipBook page is anything more complex than a bitmap or unformatted text. If you don't, network users won't be able to access the data. When the option is selected, the source application runs when a remote user accesses the page. If you don't want the running of the application to interrupt your work by opening a window on the serving workstation, check the Run Minimized check box.

TIP If you're in doubt about whether to turn on the Start Application On Connect option, share the page with the setting turned off, and let others try to use it. If this doesn't work, turn the setting on.

6. Unless you specify otherwise, pages are shared with a type of Full Control permission. This means other people can erase or edit the page as well as copy it. If you want to prevent others from editing or erasing the page, click the Permissions button to open the ClipBook Page Permissions dialog box:

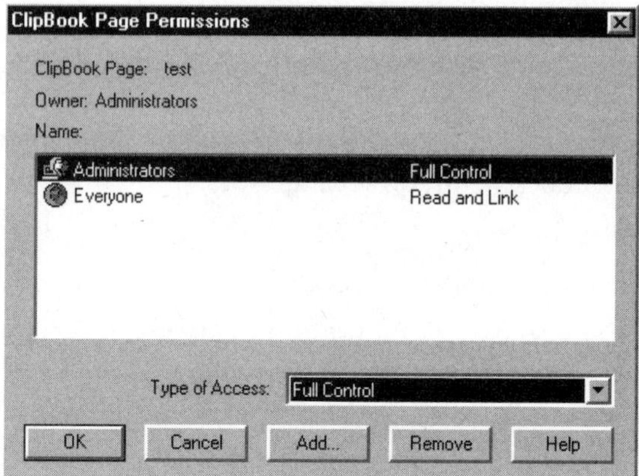

You can specify users and user groups who will have access, and set their permissions.

Connecting to a Shared ClipBook Page

So much for creating your own ClipBook pages, using them locally (that means on your computer), and sharing them with other network users. What about connecting to another network station's ClipBook to use those pages? And, by the same token, how do other users connect to your ClipBook pages after you've shared them?

It's a relatively straightforward process. Here are the steps:

1. Run ClipBook Viewer and open the Local ClipBook window.
2. Choose File ➢ Connect to open the Select Computer dialog box:

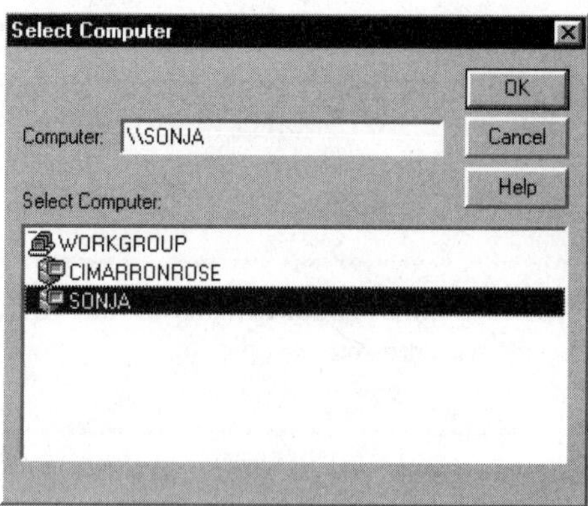

3. Browse to select the computer whose ClipBook has the information you want, or type in its name.
4. Click the OK button. If a password is required for the remote ClipBook, you are prompted to enter it. The newly available pages now appear in a new window within your ClipBook Viewer. When you attempt to access one of its pages, you may be prompted for a password.
5. When you're finished using another person's ClipBook, you may want to disconnect from it. Simply activate the particular remote ClipBook's icon or window within your ClipBook Viewer, and choose File ➢ Disconnect.

Using OLE

When you use the Clipboard to insert an item from a document in one application into a document in another application, you are inserting a static element. For example, if you insert an Excel worksheet or a portion of a worksheet into a Word document, it is what it is. Even though you might update the worksheet in Excel, the inserted portion will not change; nor can you edit the worksheet in Word.

Most of the time, this is probably what you want. However, in some cases it is really helpful to insert a document that changes whenever it's edited in the originating application; it can also be useful to be able to edit the source document right inside the destination document. For example, you are working on a report that contains the next quarter's budget, which is in a state of flux. The report is created in Word, and the budget worksheet is being created in Excel. You have a couple of choices here:

- Insert a new copy of the worksheet every time it is updated.
- Insert a link to the worksheet so that changes to it are reflected in the Word document.

Obviously, the most efficient choice is to link to the worksheet. The technology that makes this possible is OLE (object linking and embedding), which has been available in the Windows family of operating systems since Windows 3.1. OLE allows you to create *compound* documents that contain linked or embedded *objects*.

A compound document is simply one that consists of portions created in different applications. For example, your report might contain text created in Word, the budget worksheet created in Excel, and a company logo created in Paint. An object is the portion of the document that you either link or embed, and it can be text, graphics, sound, or video.

To use OLE, all the programs involved must support it. How can you tell if this is the case? If the Paste Special item is not present on the Edit menu, the program does not support linking and embedding. You'll see why this is important in the next section.

Before I get down to the nuts and bolts of linking and embedding, though, I need to define both these terms and explain the differences between them. When you *link* an object to a document, the document contains only a link to the object. To change the object, you edit the original file. Any such changes are reflected in the linked object.

When you *embed* an object in a document, the document contains a copy of the object. Any changes made to the original object are not reflected in the document unless the embedded object is updated. Embedding an object is rather similar to inserting a static element via the Clipboard; the difference is that you can click an embedded object to edit it in the application in which it was created.

Whether you link or embed an object depends on the situation. If it's important for the document to be current at all times, link the object. Otherwise, you can embed the object. Now, let's walk through the steps for doing both and take a look at how you edit an object.

Embedding Objects

To embed an object, follow these steps:

1. Open the application that contains the information you want to embed, and select the information.
2. Choose Edit ➢ Copy.
3. Open the document that will contain the embedded object.
4. Choose Edit ➢ Paste Special to open the Paste Special dialog box:

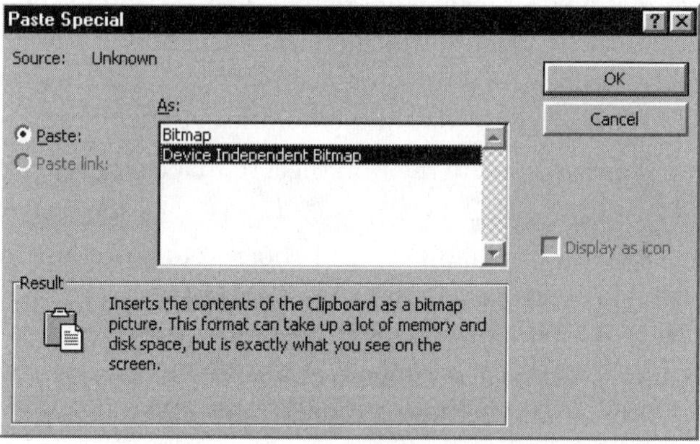

5. Click Paste, and select the format you want to use.
6. Click OK.

To edit an embedded object, follow these steps:

1. Open the document that contains the object.
2. Double-click the object to open it in an editing window that displays the tools and menus of the application in which the object was created.
3. Edit the object, and then click outside it.

Figure 9.8 shows an embedded object ready for editing.

TIP To view an embedded object in Word, you need to be in Page Layout view.

FIGURE 9.8
This Excel chart is ready for editing in a Word document.

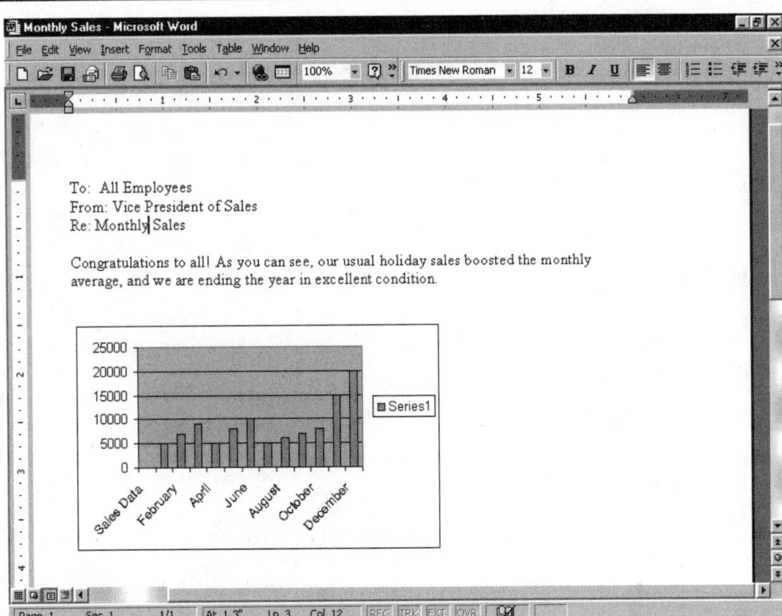

Linking Objects

To link an object, follow these steps:

1. Open the application that contains the information you want to link, and select the information.
2. Choose Edit ➢ Copy.
3. Open the document that will contain the embedded object.
4. Choose Edit ➢ Paste Special to open the Paste Special dialog box.
5. Click Paste Link, and select a format for the object.
6. To display an icon of the object, click Display As Icon.
7. Click OK.

Figure 9.9 shows a Word document with an icon that indicates an Excel worksheet is linked to the document.

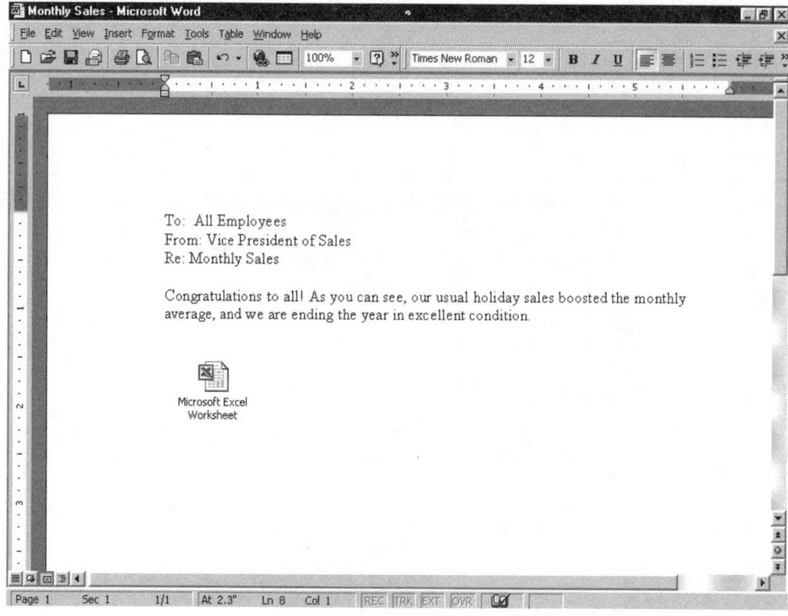

FIGURE 9.9
A Word document with a linked Excel worksheet

To edit a linked object, follow these steps:

1. Open the document that contains the link.
2. Double-click the link to open the originating application and the document that contains the information that was linked.
3. Save the file, and then close the application. The change is reflected in the linked object.

What Is DDE?

An older and less ambitious means for intercommunication between applications is called Dynamic Data Exchange (DDE), and it is also included in Windows 2000 Professional. Some older applications used DDE to achieve some of the same results you get nowadays with OLE. Windows NT Workstation 4, Windows for Workgroups, and Windows 95/98 have included an updated network version of DDE called NetDDE that enables applications to talk to one another over the network as well as on the same machine, and in Windows 2000 Professional, the Clipboard uses NetDDE. And actually, OLE uses DDE as its communications link between programs.

Continued

The downside of DDE is that although it provides a way for applications to share information in a *live* way as OLE does (meaning that altering one document updates any linked documents too), how you, the user, set up the link varies considerably from program to program. Another problem inherent in DDE is that the links it sets up between documents are too easy to sever. Simply moving a file to a new location or upgrading one of the source applications could result in a document losing one of its objects.

Since OLE's debut (with Windows 3.1), the bulk of serious Windows applications support OLE rather than DDE for user-created data sharing. Few programs used DDE internally to communicate between modules of a program or between multiple documents running under the same program. DDE has essentially been left to the domain of hackers working with such tools as Excel macros—one of the few DDE-enabled tools.

Maintaining Your OLE Links

Although Windows 2000 Professional can usually maintain a link between the source and destination documents, at times a link may be broken for some reason. A traditional example is an application crashing before its links can be recorded properly. And although OLE is intelligent about keeping your links in working order, it's not impossible to mislead it by copying source and destination files from folders, erasing folders, and so forth. A broken link typically manifests itself as a hole where data was to appear in a document or as data that isn't up-to-date. In the next few sections, I'll explain how to manually make changes to a link to modify its properties.

Manually Updating a Linked Object

Under normal circumstances, when you make changes to a source document, your changes appear immediately in any other documents that contain copies of that object. Actually, *immediate* updating requires that the other destination documents be open. If they aren't open, destination documents are updated the next time you open them.

In any case, there are times when you might want to delay the updating of objects linked to other documents. You can stipulate that a given link will update destination documents only when you manually execute an update command. This might be useful when your source document is undergoing repeated revision that would cause the destination document to read inaccurately or appear unfinished, or if the source document is linked to many destination documents and the automatic updating process slows your computer too much, ties up the network (in the case of links to documents across the network), or is otherwise annoying.

To deal with this, just set up your link for manual updating. Here's how:

1. Open the destination document.
2. Click the object to select it.
3. Choose Edit ➢ Links to open a Links dialog box similar to the one in Figure 9.10. (The box may vary depending on the application you're running.)

FIGURE 9.10
Use the Links dialog box to change the details of a link.

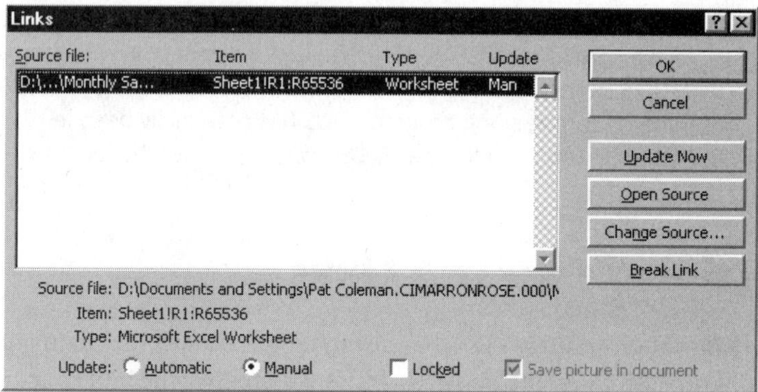

NOTE If the Links dialog box lists two or more links, you can select multiple consecutive links by holding down the Shift key while you click with the mouse. You can also select multiple links that don't appear consecutively by pressing Ctrl while you click.

4. Select the link, click the Manual option button, and click OK.

If you want to reset the updating to the automatic mode later, open the Links dialog box again and click Automatic.

After you've set a linked object to manual updating, no changes you make to the source document will be reflected in the destination document until you manually update the source. To do that, you'll need to open the Links dialog box, highlight the link in question, and choose Update Now.

Taking Care of Other Link-Management Tasks

You probably noticed some other buttons in the Links dialog box that suggest other possible link-related tasks. For example, you might want to break, delete, reestablish, or alter existing links to refer to different source documents. Here's the rundown on each of these activities.

Breaking a Link

In certain circumstances, you'll want to break a link between two documents. When you break a link, the data continues to appear in the destination document; it just can no longer be edited from within that document. If the destination application is capable of displaying the data, you will still see it. If it's not capable of displaying it, you will see an icon representing the material.

TIP In most cases, double-clicking an object whose link has been broken doesn't have any effect; that is, it doesn't open the source application or enable you to edit the object. But here's another method: Select the object, copy it to the Clipboard, and paste it back into the originating program. Then edit it as you need to, copy it onto the Clipboard again, and paste it back into the destination.

But now for the obvious question. Why would you want to break a link? You would break a link if having the link is more hassle than it's worth, such as when you separate the source and destination documents. For example, suppose you want to copy the destination document onto a floppy disk to send to someone. When the recipient opens the document, they would see empty sections in the document and a dialog box saying that parts of the document are missing. So, breaking the link keeps the data in the document, with the only downside being that it can no longer be edited.

To break a link, follow these steps:

1. Open the document containing the object with the link you want to break.
2. Select the object, and choose Edit ➢ Links to open the Links dialog box. (In some applications, such as Word, you don't need to select the object, because all linked objects appear in the Links dialog box.)
3. In the list of links, highlight the one whose connection you want to break.
4. Click the Break Link button, and then click OK.

What about deleting a link? Deleting a link wipes out the linked material in the destination document. The source document is left intact, of course, but the previously linked object is purged from the destination document. To delete a link, select it in the destination document, and press Delete.

Fixing Broken Links

As I mentioned earlier, links can be broken inadvertently, especially on a network. Links made from within Windows 2000 Professional are robust and can survive even when you move source and destination documents between folders or rename files. However, links are still sometimes broken, especially if a document is composed of information on different workstations across the network. When a destination document can't find the filename and path name to locate a linked object, the application gets confused and breaks the link. The data may still appear in the destination document, but you won't be able to edit it, and the connection will no longer be live.

Here's how to reestablish a link so that the source and destination documents are once again connected:

1. Open the document containing the object whose link is broken.
2. Select the object, and choose Edit ➢ Links to open the Links dialog box.
3. Click the Change Source button to open the Change Source dialog box, as shown in Figure 9.11.

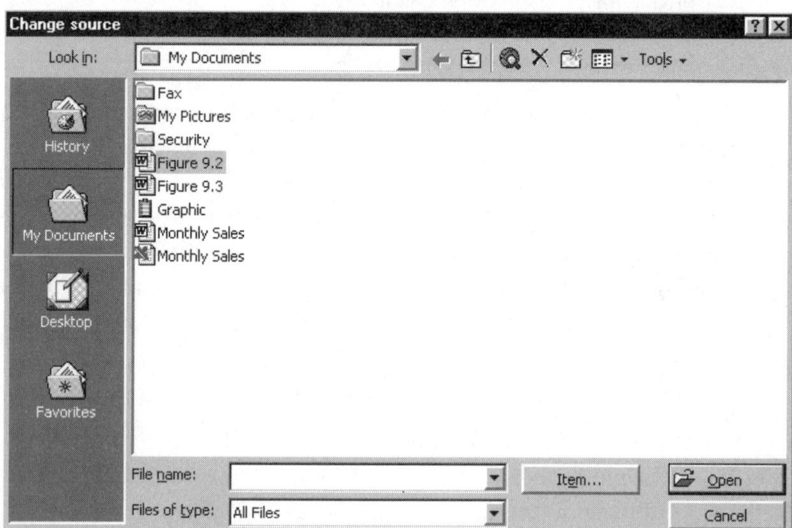

FIGURE 9.11
The Change Source dialog box

NOTE In some applications, you may see a Change Link button instead of a Change Source button.

4. Select the computer, drive, folder, and file as necessary to select the filename of the source document that contains the source material. Click the Open button. The Links dialog box then reappears, listing the updated location and name of the source document. If the source is on a workstation across the network, look for a Network button to click.

5. Click the OK button to finalize the new link information. When the box closes—and assuming the link is set for automatic updating—the current version of the linked object appears in the destination document.

Summary

This chapter introduced the concepts of object linking and embedding (OLE) and discussed how OLE enables many of the features found in Windows 2000 Professional. From the basics of cutting and pasting to inserting one type of document into another, OLE enhances your ability to easily create complex documents.

We also looked at how OLE creates the special capabilities of the Clipboard and ClipBook for cutting and pasting many types of data.

PART II

Communications and the Internet

Learn To:

- *Connect to the Internet*
- *Use the communications programs*
- *Use Internet Explorer and other Internet services*
- *Use Outlook Express*

CHAPTER 10

Introduction to Communications

FEATURING:

Will Rogers once explained that the telephone is like a very big dog; when you pulled on its tail in New York, the dog would bark in Los Angeles. Radio, he said, works exactly the same way, but without the dog. In Windows 2000 Professional, communications functions—including data transfer, electronic mail, and control of voice telephone calls—are integrated into the operating system. Maybe Will Rogers would have said that the dog is now using a keyboard and a modem.

When you first got your computer, you probably planned to use it for word processing, financial record keeping and analysis, and maybe playing some games. You would tap information into the keyboard, the computer would do its thing, and after a while, it would print the result on a piece of paper or display the result on your screen. At that point, your computer was probably a stand-alone device, not connected to any other computers. If you needed to exchange data with somebody else, you could use a floppy disk to move files from one machine to the other (this technique is sometimes called sneakernet).

But when you start connecting stand-alone computers together, they become extremely flexible tools for communication. Relatively early in the development of computer technology, people figured out that it wasn't particularly difficult to transfer information through a wire from one computer to another. As long as the computers on both ends use the same technical standards, you can move messages, programs, text, and data files back and forth. And when you connect a *lot* of computers together through a network, you can communicate with any other computer on the same network, just as you can reach any other telephone connected to the global telecommunications system from the one on your desk.

Under the broad category of communications, your PC can send and receive text, program files, sounds, and images. It can also exchange images of fax pages with a distant fax machine. This data can enter and leave your PC through a modem, a network interface card, or a direct cable connection to another computer.

Communications capability has been part of DOS and Windows since the earliest IBM PCs. Windows 2000 Professional includes an extensive set of communications tools that enable you to exchange electronic mail with other computers, browse the Internet, and use your computer to control telephone calls. This chapter starts with an overview of the communications features of Windows 2000 Professional, shows how to configure Windows 2000 Professional to work with your modem, discusses how to use the Internet Connection Wizard to connect to the Internet, and concludes with information about how to share an Internet connection and how to connect via cable modem, DSL (Digital Subscriber Line), and ISDN (Integrated Services Digital Network).

You can find more specific information about communications applications in the remaining chapters of this part of the book:

- Chapter 11 covers Fax, HyperTerminal, NetMeeting, and Phone Dialer.

- Chapter 12 covers the Internet Explorer Web browser.
- Chapter 13 covers Outlook Express, the Windows 2000 Professional control center for messaging components and news.

Discovering What's New in Windows 2000 Professional Communications

Windows 2000 Professional includes some major improvements over the way earlier versions of Windows handled communications:

- It's a lot happier about sending and receiving data at high speeds.
- It can transfer data in the background without interfering with other applications.
- It doesn't require you to shut down a program that waits for incoming messages or faxes before you try to use the same modem to place an outgoing call.

In addition, Microsoft has replaced the old Terminal program in previous versions of Windows with a completely new set of applications for connecting to distant computers through a modem and for sending, receiving, and managing messages, data files, and faxes. Windows 2000 Professional also has a Telephony Application Program Interface (TAPI) that integrates your PC with a telephone system. You may notice, in Control Panel, the Phone And Modem Options applet. This provides an interface for installing future telephony drivers, once they become more widely available. Two Microsoft-supplied drivers are installed with Windows 2000 Professional, namely, the Unimodem driver and TAPI. Overall, Windows 2000 Professional goes a long way toward turning your stand-alone computer into a tool that can be linked to other computers and other communications devices anywhere in the world.

Using the Windows Telephony Interface

Windows NT 4 and Windows 95/98 included TAPI—a set of software hooks to applications that control the way your computer interacts with the telephone network. Windows 2000 Professional implements a newer version of TAPI that gives you some additional capabilities. TAPI is an internal part of Windows 2000 Professional rather than a specific application program—it provides a standard way for software developers to access communications ports and devices, such as modems and telephone sets, to control data, fax, and voice calls. Using TAPI, an application can place a call, answer an incoming call, and hang up when the call is complete. TAPI also supports features such as hold, call transfer, voicemail, and conference calls. TAPI-compliant applications work with conventional telephone lines, Private Branch Exchange (PBX), and Centrex systems; these applications also work with specialized services such as cellular and ISDN.

By moving these functions to a common program interface, Windows 2000 Professional prevents conflicting demands for access to your modem and telephone line from multiple application programs. Therefore, you no longer need to shut down a program that's waiting for incoming calls before you use a different program to send a fax.

Unless you're planning to write your own communications applications, you won't ever have to deal directly with TAPI, but you will see its benefits when you use the communications programs included in Windows 2000 Professional—HyperTerminal, Outlook Express, Phone Dialer, and Fax—and when you use Windows NT or Windows 95/98–compatible versions of third-party communications programs such as ProComm and WinFax.

Windows 2000 Professional includes a fairly simple telephony application called Phone Dialer (which I'll talk about in Chapter 11), but this application only begins to show what TAPI can do. Windows NT 4 also included Phone Dialer, but the version in Windows 2000 Professional is a whole new animal. Phone Dialer now delivers on some of the promise that TAPI showed us in Windows NT. This application can not only dial the phone, it can connect to videoconference sessions over your local area network (LAN) or place a voice call to an Internet address by modem or network connection.

Eventually, you can expect to see a lot of new Windows telephony products that will move control of your telephone to the Windows 2000 Professional Desktop. For example, you might be able to use the telephone company's caller-ID service to match incoming calls to a database that displays detailed information about the caller before you answer, or you may be able to use an on-screen menu to set up advanced call features such as conference calling and call forwarding, which now require obscure strings of digits from the telephone keypad.

Installing a Modem

Every time you installed a new communications application in earlier versions of Windows, you had to go through another configuration routine—you had to specify the port connected to your modem, the highest speed the modem could handle, and so forth. Because there was no central modem control, each program required its own setup.

This changed in Windows NT 4 (and Windows 95/98), which uses a *universal modem* driver called *Unimodem*. Unimodem is the software interface between all your computer's 32-bit Windows-compatible communications applications (including the ones that use TAPI) and your modem or other communications hardware. It includes integrated control for port selection, modem initialization, speed, file transfer protocols, and terminal emulation. Because Unimodem handles the modem configuration, you only have to specify setup parameters once.

If you're using third-party communications applications left over from earlier versions of Windows, they'll usually work with Windows 2000 Professional, but you'll still have to configure them separately. When you replace them with newer, Windows 2000 Professional–compatible updates, they'll use the settings already configured in Control Panel.

In most cases, you need a modem to use the communications features of Windows 2000 Professional. Your modem might be an internal expansion board, an external modem plugged into a serial port, or a credit-card–sized PCMCIA (Personal Computer Memory Card International Association) modem. If your modem is Plug and Play (and it probably is if you acquired your computer recently), Windows 2000 Professional will recognize and install it automatically during the installation of the operating system.

If your modem is not Plug and Play or if for some other reason you want to install it manually, you can use the Phone And Modem Options applet in Control Panel, or you can configure the modem from a communications application such as Phone Dialer or HyperTerminal.

Follow these steps to install a modem from Control Panel:

1. If you're using an external modem, turn it on, and make sure it's connected to both the telephone line and a serial port on your computer.
2. Choose Start ➢ Settings ➢ Control Panel to open Control Panel.
3. Double-click the Phone And Modem Options icon to open the Phone And Modem Options dialog box, which is shown in Figure 10.1.

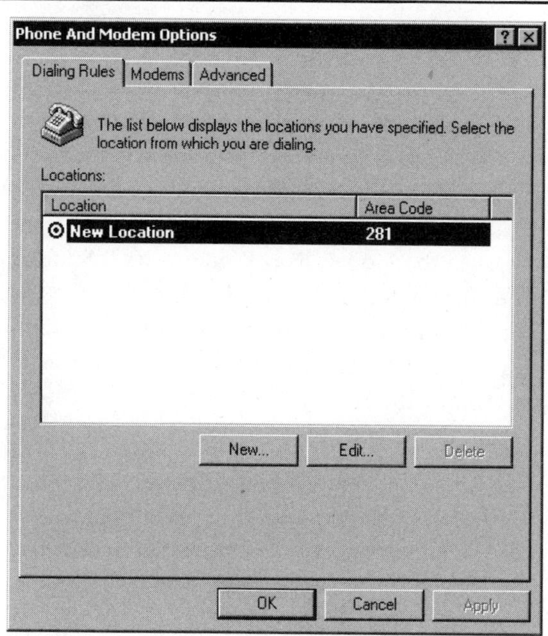

FIGURE 10.1
This is the Phone And Modem Options dialog box. Click the Add button on the Modems tab to install a new modem.

4. Click the Modems tab, and then click the Add button to start the Add/Remove Hardware Wizard.
5. Because you turned on the modem in step 1, you can let the Wizard try to identify your modem type. Click the Next button.
6. If you have an external modem, you will see the lights flash on the front panel while the Wizard tests it. When the tests are complete, the Wizard displays the final dialog box, which is shown in Figure 10.2.

FIGURE 10.2
The Add/Remove Hardware Wizard tells you that it has finished installing a new modem.

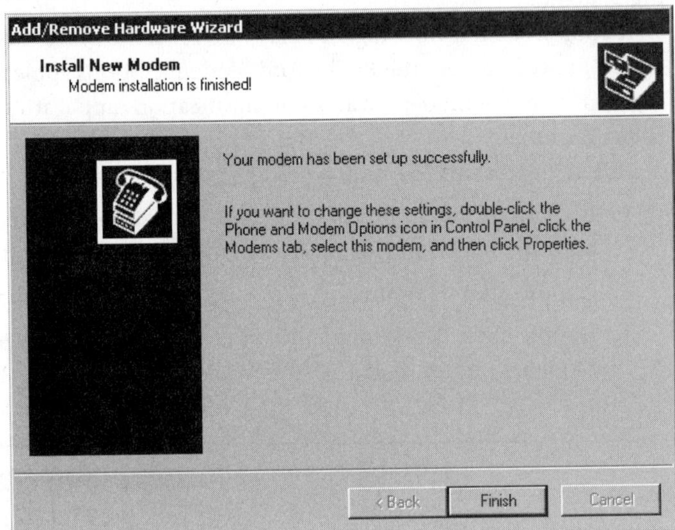

7. If the Wizard is not able to identify your modem, you will be prompted to choose its make and model from a list. If your modem is not listed, look in the modem manual for an equivalent type or select one of the standard modem types in the Models list. Windows 2000 Professional supports most modems on the market today, but it also allows for new models that will inevitably be released in the future. If you own a modem that is not listed, contact the vendor for updated drivers, or check the disk that was provided with the modem. In this case, click the Have Disk button to open the Install From Disk dialog box, and install the driver.
8. Click the Next and Finish buttons to complete the modem installation.

Changing Modem Properties

After you install your modem, all your TAPI-aware communications programs will use the same configuration settings. When you change them in one application, those changes carry across to all the others. In general, you won't want to change the default modem properties, which specify settings such as the loudness of the modem's speaker and the maximum data-transfer speed. If you replace your modem, or if you use different modem types in different locations, you can install an additional modem from Control Panel.

To change the modem properties after installation is complete, open Control Panel, and double-click the Phone And Modem Options icon to open the Phone And Modem Options dialog box. Click the Modems tab, select the modem you want to modify, and then click the Properties button to display the Properties dialog box for that modem. Figure 10.3 displays the Properties dialog box for a U.S. Robotics modem.

NOTE Other applications that work with modems, such as HyperTerminal, also provide access to the Modem Properties dialog box. The tabs visible in this dialog box depend on whether you are working from Control Panel or from another application.

FIGURE 10.3 *Use this Properties dialog box to change your modem configuration.*

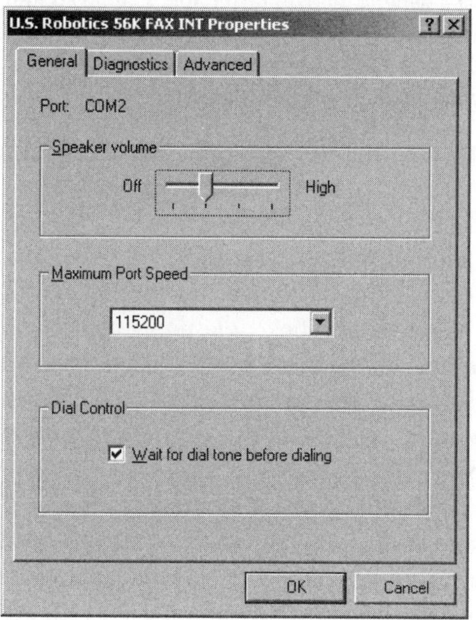

General Properties

The General tab of the Modem Properties dialog box has four settings:

- Port
- Speaker Volume
- Maximum Port Speed
- Dial Control

Port

The port that your modem is using is displayed in this area. Unlike in Windows NT 4, you can't change the port setting here. Instead, use the Advanced tab to alter the port usage for the modem. (We'll look at the settings on the Advanced tab later in this section.) Internal modems are usually installed on COM port 3 or 4. External modems are normally installed on COM2.

Speaker Volume

The Speaker Volume control is a slider bar that you can use to specify the loudness of the speaker inside your modem.

NOTE Some modems support only one volume level besides Off, and if you happen to be using a generic modem driver, this volume control may be disabled. In this case, you can still control the speaker. In the Modem Properties dialog box, click the Advanced tab, and in the Extra Initialization Commands box, enter **ATM1** (for sound) or **ATM0** (for no sound). For more information on the AT commands for your modem, consult the manual that came with your modem.

Maximum Port Speed

When your modem makes a connection, it will try to use the maximum speed to exchange data with the modem at the other end of the link. As a rule, if you have a 33,600 bits per second (bps) or faster modem, the maximum speed should be three or four times the rated modem speed (for example, set your modem speed to 115,200) to take advantage of the modem's built-in data compression.

Dial Control

This setting is a simple check box that enables or disables the option to Wait For Dial Tone Before Dialing. If your modem doesn't recognize the dial tone used by your current location, or if you need to manually dial your modem connection, clear this check box.

Not all modems support this setting. If your modem does not, the check box will be grayed out.

Diagnostics

The Diagnostics tab is new to many Windows NT users, but should be familiar to users of Windows 95/98. The Diagnostics tab is extremely useful for troubleshooting communications issues. Clicking the Diagnostics tab displays the dialog box shown in Figure 10.4.

FIGURE 10.4
The Diagnostics tab of the modem Properties dialog box lets you test your modem configuration and set logging options.

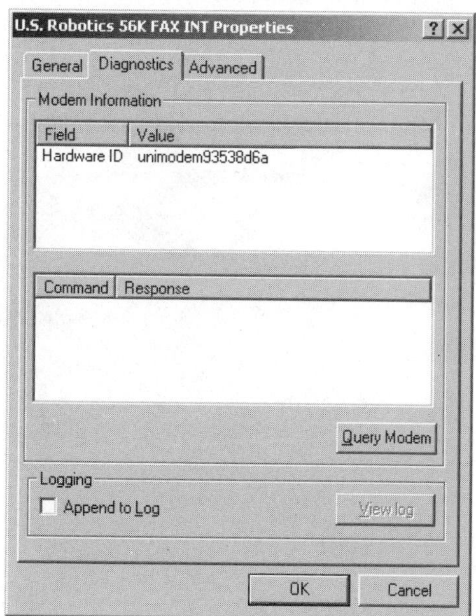

Query Modem

Clicking the Query Modem button sends a series of commands to your modem, testing its response. The first thing this tells you, hopefully, is that you actually *have* a modem and that it is working correctly. The next thing it reveals is which attention commands (AT commands) are supported by your hardware.

The responses to your test, if any, will be displayed in the two text boxes of the Modem Information area of the Diagnostics tab.

Logging

The Logging section is at the bottom of the Diagnostics tab. The first option that you can control here is whether to create a new modem log for each session or to append the new information to the existing file. To add new information to the end of an existing file, check the Append To Log check box.

Clicking the View Log button opens the log file in Notepad. These log files contain information gathered while the modem was being queried for diagnostics and information gathered while the modem was in normal use.

Advanced Settings

Many of the, pardon the term, *advanced* settings have been moved out of the way and consigned to the Advanced tab (see Figure10.5). This is partly an effort to shield the average user from the possible complexities of configuring a modem in Windows 2000 Professional and partly because you just won't have to use these settings often.

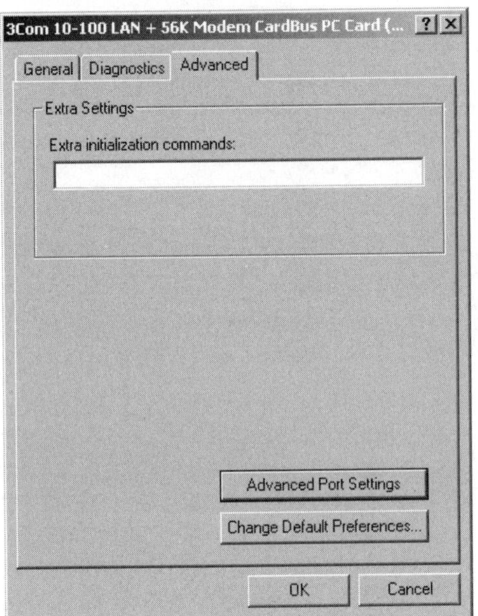

FIGURE 10.5
The Advanced tab of the Modem Properties dialog box

Extra Settings

The Extra Settings section contains the Extra Initialization Commands text box for entering any additional AT commands you want to use while initializing the modem. I've found this area useful when working with several modems, such as the U.S. Robotics Sportster. This modem and several others by various manufacturers don't seem to like the initialization string that Microsoft wrote for them. Symptoms of this may be anything from dropped sessions to failed file transfers. You can use the Extra Settings section to correct this problem. Simply type **&F1** in the Extra Initialization Commands box, and click OK. This command tells the modem to ignore the initialization string it just received and to use its built-in factory settings instead. Perfect!

WARNING You should exercise some caution here, though, and consult the documentation for your modem to verify the actions of the command before using it. If the command isn't right for your modem, using it could cause some real damage to your modem.

The Extra Initialization Commands option enables you to control all the functions of your modem, such as the speaker volume or whether it waits for a dial tone before dialing.

Change Default Preferences

Clicking the Change Default Preferences button opens the Default Preferences dialog box for your modem. Using the General and the Advanced tabs, you can alter the configuration for your modem, including port speeds, compression, and advanced port settings.

The General tab contains settings for Call Preferences and Data Connection Preferences. The Call Preferences section has a couple of settings that govern how the call session will be handled. The first is whether the modem should hang up automatically after it has been idle for a set number of minutes. Check the box next to Disconnect A Call If Idle For More Than *x* Minutes, and enter the number of minutes that you want the modem to sit idle before being disconnected. The default is 30 minutes.

The second option under Call Preferences is Cancel The Call If Not Connected Within *x* Seconds. The default is 60 seconds. This option tells your modem to continue trying to connect for up to the number of seconds you specify.

The Data Preferences section contains the following settings that affect the transfer of data across this modem session:

Port Speed Sets the data transfer rate for the communications port. As a rule, set this to at least twice the rated speed of your modem to allow for modem data compression.

Data Protocol Controls the error-correction scheme that your modem will use for sessions. The default setting of StandardEC enables your modem to negotiate the highest level of error correction that both modems in a session will support. This is usually the best setting since it allows for some flexibility. The ForcedEC setting causes the modem to use only V.42 error correction. If this fails, the call will be terminated. The Disabled setting turns off error correction entirely. Click the down arrow to display the ForcedEC and Disabled settings.

Compression Tells the modem to use hardware-based data compression. This usually results in faster communications, except when you are transferring large files that are already compressed. In this case, enabling hardware compression can actually slow down your session because you are trying to compress something that is already compressed.

Flow Control This setting controls the method used to signal transmission of data. Many programs require some kind of indication that the data sent was received on the other end. Typically, this can be done through hardware or software methods. The hardware method uses a scheme called Ready to Send/Clear to Send (RTS/CTS), which depends on the modem hardware to handle the signaling. The software method is called XON/XOFF, which relies on the operating system to send a signal when the modem is through transmitting. The Disabled option disables flow control altogether. Use this option mostly for troubleshooting.

The Advanced tab has the following settings, some of which you may recognize if you've been using your modem for a while under older operating systems:

Data Bits Sets the number of bits that will be used for transmitting a single character of text. Typically, most online services and bulletin board systems use 8 bits per character, though some systems use 7. If you don't you use the same setting that the modem you are calling is using, you won't be able to communicate correctly.

Parity Determines whether the session will use parity bits for error checking. If you are using this method of error checking, the modem will append a single bit that indicates whether the number of bits set to the value of 1 in a character is even or odd. This is a fairly primitive method of checking for errors and has been replaced with much more sophisticated routines. Typically, this option is set to None. This setting must match that of the other modem with which you are communicating.

Stop Bits Tells the system that a byte of data has been sent. Stop bits are almost always set to a value of 1.

Modulation This setting determines the protocol used to translate the data signals from the digital form used by computers to the sounds that can be transmitted across the phone line. Normally, you use the Standard modulation protocol, but if you are having problems connecting, try changing to the Nonstandard (Bell, HST) modulation.

Dialing Rules

This is one of the new areas in Windows 2000 Professional. In Windows NT 4, you used the Dialing Properties dialog box to dictate the configuration of your TAPI location. Windows 2000 Professional uses the Dialing Rules tab of the Phone And Modem Options dialog box. You can access this information in a couple of ways: you can use Control Panel, or you can use any TAPI-aware application.

When TAPI was first released (with Windows 95), it was a great boon to people who traveled with their computers. Establishing the communications settings just once and having them apply equally to all communications programs was really nice. But you probably live in a place where the phone companies have been splitting areas into smaller geographic segments and assigning these segments new area codes. If you use an ISP in an area code different from your own but access that ISP as a local call, that can be enough to drive you crazy.

Windows 2000 Professional can help end *that* suffering by enabling you to set up rules for your 10-digit dialing pleasure. The Dialing Rules tab of the Phone And Modem Options dialog box enables you to create, modify, or delete TAPI locations. Put simply, a TAPI *location* is a collection of the dialing properties for the place from which you are calling.

To create a new location or to edit a location, follow these steps:

1. Open Control Panel, and double-click the Phone And Modem Options icon to open the Phone And Modem Options dialog box.
2. On the Dialing Rules tab, click New to open the New Location dialog box, or click Edit to open the Edit Location dialog box, which is shown in Figure 10.6.

FIGURE 10.6
The Edit Location dialog box gives you access to all the important settings to control dialing from one place.

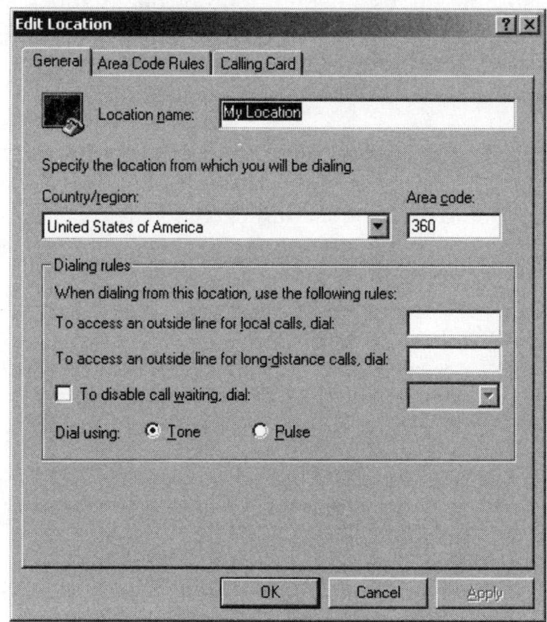

NOTE Both the New Location and the Edit Location dialog boxes contain the same options, and you can also open them from any TAPI-aware communications program in Windows 2000 Professional.

3. Type a name that you will use to identify this location in the Location Name text box.
4. Under Country/Region, select the appropriate country. This will determine the correct country code for dialing long distance. In the United States, the country code is 1.
5. In the Area Code text box, type the area code for the location you are creating or editing.
6. In the Dialing Rules section, you need to tell Windows 2000 Professional how to dial from this location. If you dial a special number to access an outside line (such as 9 on a PBX system at work), enter that in the first text box. In the second text box, you can enter the number you use to dial an outside line for long distance, if it's different from the first number.
7. If you have call waiting, you can disable it by checking the To Disable Call Waiting, Dial check box and then selecting the correct numeric code.

NOTE To find out the correct code for disabling call waiting in your area, look in the front of your local telephone directory or call your telephone business office.

8. Finally, select the correct radio button for the type of modulation your phone system uses to dial. This will most likely be Tone dialing, but if your phone system uses pulse dialing you will need to select Pulse in order to dial correctly.
9. Click OK.

If you want to change the area code settings to outsmart the new 10-digit dialing for local calls, you will need to complete a few more steps. On the Area Code Rules tab, you can establish the rules for dialing within your area code and for calling other area codes. Basically, you need to separate long distance from local calling whether it's in your own area code or another. To create a new area code rule, follow these steps:

1. On the Area Code Rules tab of the New Location dialog box or the Edit Location dialog box, click the New button to open the New Area Code Rule dialog box, which is shown in Figure 10.7.

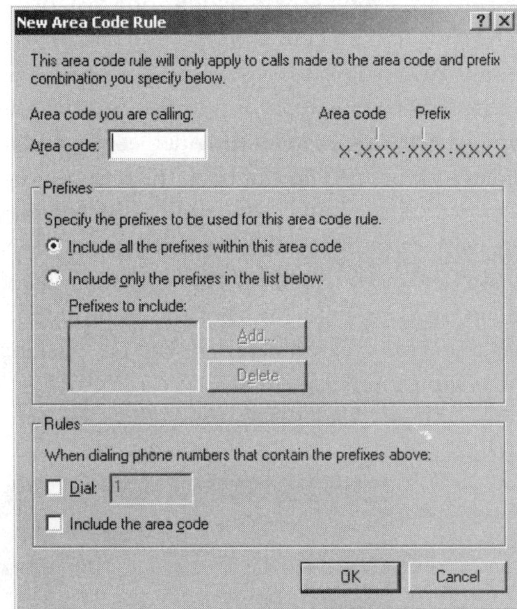

FIGURE 10.7 *The New Area Code Rule dialog box enables you to define combinations of area code and prefix that are to be dialed as local calls.*

2. Type the area code for which you want to create the rule in the Area Code text box.
3. In the Prefixes section, click either Include All The Prefixes Within This Area Code to dial all the prefixes as local, or click Include Only The Prefixes In The List Below if you want to customize the list. To add new prefixes to the list, click the Add button to open the Add Prefix dialog box, as shown here, and type the prefixes in the Prefixes box. Separate multiple prefixes with either a space or a comma.

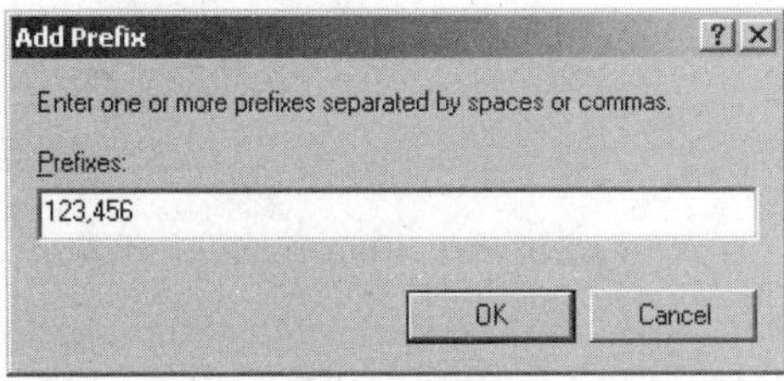

4. Finally, check the check boxes in the Rules section that describe how this rule should be applied. The first box tells Windows 2000 Professional to dial your country code before the area code and number. The second check box tell the system to include the area code when dialing any area code and prefix in the list.
5. Click OK.

Calling Card

Calling cards are a good way to handle long distance charges, especially if you will be expensing costs back to your employer. To pay for a call with a calling card (a telephone company credit card), you must dial a special string of numbers that includes a carrier access code, your account number, and the number you're calling. In some cases, you have to call a service provider, enter your account number, and wait for a second dial tone before you can enter the number you want to call.

To use your calling card automatically when dialing, you need to specify the card to use along with the account number and Personal ID Number (PIN). To do this, click the Calling Card tab of either the New Location dialog box or the Edit Location dialog box, and in the Card Types list, click the name of the calling card you use. If your card isn't listed, you can create a new definition by clicking the New button. The Calling Card tab is shown in Figure 10.8.

FIGURE 10.8
Use the Calling Card tab in either the New Location dialog box or the Edit Location dialog box to specify your telephone credit card type and number.

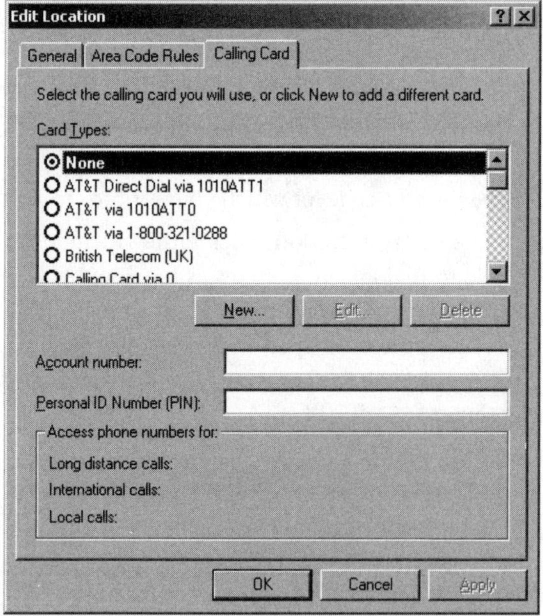

The Card Types list includes the most commonly used telephone credit cards in the United States—those issued by AT&T, MCI, and Sprint, as well as some of the more common international cards such as British Telecom. If you choose a calling card from the list, the program automatically uses the correct calling sequence for that long-distance carrier. But if you need a special calling sequence, click the New button, and type the sequences for local, long distance, and international calls in the New Calling Card dialog box.

To create a new calling card definition for a card that's not on the list, follow these steps:

1. In Control Panel, open the Phone And Modem Options applet.
2. Click the Dialing Rules tab, and select the TAPI location you want to edit. If you are creating a new location, use the steps from earlier in this chapter, and then use the following steps to modify the calling card.
3. Click Edit to open the Edit Location dialog box, and then click the Calling Card tab to display the list of predefined calling cards available.
4. Click the New button to open the New Calling Card dialog box, as shown in Figure 10.9.

FIGURE 10.9
The New Calling Card dialog box lets you create your own calling card definitions.

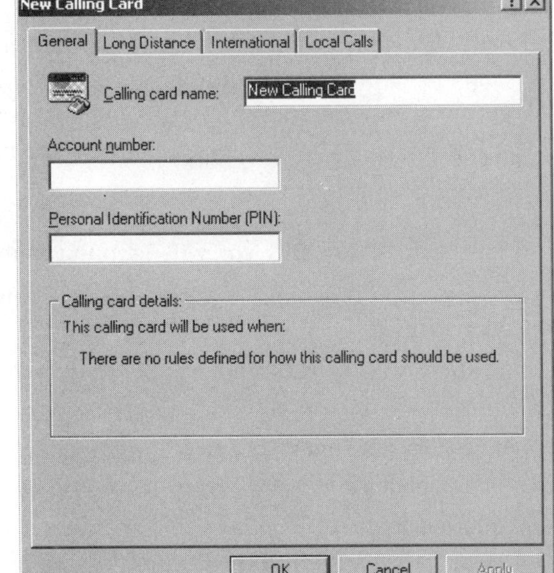

Communications and the Internet

5. On the General tab, fill in the name you want to use to describe this card. This is a name to help you identify this card definition; it is not *your* name. Fill in the account number of your calling card, if it has one, and then fill in the PIN.
6. On the Long Distance tab, enter the phone number you call to place your long distance calls with this card.
7. Select the steps you need to perform to place a call. This sets the exact order in which the information needs to be provided so the computer can use the calling card. For instance, if your card requires you to enter your PIN and then the destination number, click the PIN button, and then click the Destination Number

button. The steps will be displayed in the Calling Card Dialing Steps text box. You can easily move them up or down by highlighting them and pressing the Move Up or Move Down buttons until the order is correct.

8. Repeat steps 6 and 7 for the International and Local Calls tabs until you have provided the information for every type of call you will be making with this card.
9. Click Apply or OK to save your card definition.

In Windows 95/98 and Windows NT 4, you needed some complicated scripting to create the procedure you just completed. Windows 2000 Professional has made calling cards much easier to deal with by shielding you from the need to understand script variables and formatting.

Using the Internet Connection Wizard

In times past, setting up a connection to the Internet was quite a complex operation, but that is no longer the case. The Internet Connection Wizard walks you through the steps of setting up your Internet connection. All you need is an account with an Internet Service Provider and your credit card number. You can start the Internet Connection Wizard in several ways:

- Click the Connect To The Internet icon on the Desktop. Once you set up your Internet connection, this icon will disappear from the Desktop.
- Choose Start ➢ Programs ➢ Accessories ➢ Communications ➢ Internet Connection Wizard.
- From the Windows 2000 Professional Help system, choose Using the Internet Connection Wizard topic.
- Choose Start ➢ Settings ➢ Control Panel ➢ Internet Options to open the Internet Properties dialog box, select the Connections tab, and click the Setup button.
- In Internet Explorer, choose Tools ➢ Internet Options to open the Internet Options dialog box, select the Connection tab, and click the Setup button.

No matter which method you use, the Welcome screen shown in Figure 10.10 gives you three choices:

I Want To Sign Up For A New Internet Account. (My Telephone Line Is Connected To My Modem.) Select this option if you do not already have an account. The Wizard takes you through the steps of finding an ISP and starting an account and sets up the dial-up link for you.

I Want To Transfer My Existing Internet Account To This Computer. (My Telephone Line Is Connected To My Modem.) Establishes a connection to an existing Internet account. Select this option to set up a connection to your existing Internet account or to revise the settings for your current account.

I Want To Set Up My Internet Connection Manually, Or I Want To Connect Through A Local Area Network (LAN). Allows you to set up your account configuration manually.

Click Tutorial to learn more about the Internet, or click Cancel if you want to close the Internet Connection Wizard without setting up your account.

FIGURE 10.10 *The Internet Connection Wizard Welcome screen*

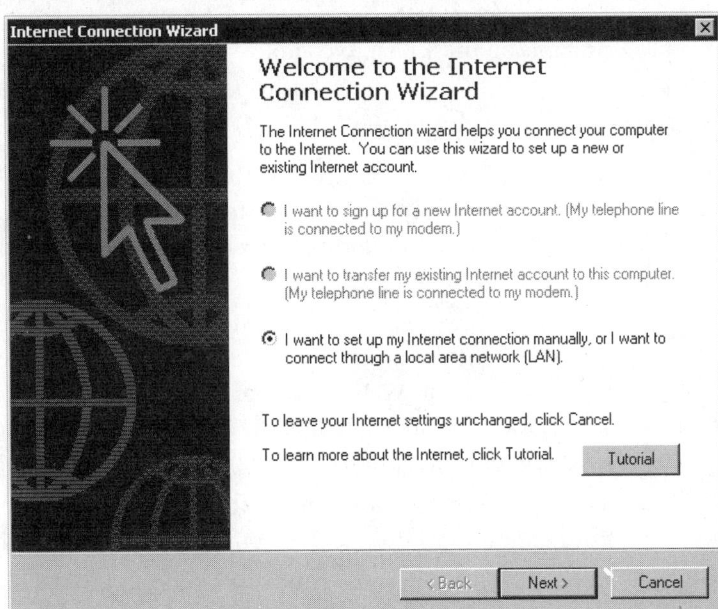

Creating a New Connection to the Internet

To create a new dial-up connection to the Internet, start the Internet Connection Wizard, and then follow these steps:

1. In the opening dialog box, choose the first option to select an ISP and set up a new Internet account, and then click Next.
2. The Wizard dials out on your modem, connects to the Microsoft Internet Referral Service, and downloads information on ISPs. Not all the ISPs available in your area will be listed here; most of those listed are actually nationwide services. (If you want to set one up that's not listed, you'll have to do it manually, as detailed in the next section.)
3. Select one of the ISPs, and click Next. The information shown in the next two dialog boxes depends on which of the ISPs you chose in the last step.

4. Enter your name, address, and phone number in the next dialog box. This information is used for billing purposes only and is only sent to the ISP you selected. Click Next.
5. Choose a billing option from those shown on the screen, and click Next.
6. Choose a method of payment, enter the details of your credit card, and click Next.
7. The Internet Connection Wizard connects to the ISP, selects a user ID and password, and completes the configuration of your Internet connection. Follow the prompts on the screen to complete your setup.

Setting Up Your Connection to the Internet Manually

You don't have to use the ISPs listed by the Microsoft Internet Referral Service. If you want to use an ISP whose name is not listed by the Internet Connection Wizard—perhaps a local ISP known for offering a particularly good service or an ISP recommended by a friend—follow these steps:

1. Phone the ISP you have chosen, and ask for a dial-up account that will give you e-mail and Internet access; some ISPs also assign space on their systems so you can create a small Web site of your own. The ISP will send you details of the servers they operate, including the names of the mail and news servers; you will need that information to complete the steps outlined below.
2. Start the Internet Connection Wizard, and in the opening dialog box, select the third option to set up a connection manually, and click Next.
3. Choose the method you want to use to connect to the Internet. Most people will check the I Connect Through A Phone Line And A Modem option. Click Next.
4. In the next dialog box, enter the phone number to dial to make the connection to your ISP.
5. In the next dialog box, enter your user name and password information. These will be provided by your ISP, and remember to enter them in the same case, either uppercase or lowercase, as specified by your ISP. Click Next.
6. Enter the name you want to use for this connection; choose something easy to remember. Click Next.
7. You'll then be asked if you want to set up an Internet e-mail account; click Yes and then Next to specify whether you want to use an existing account or create a new one. If you opt to continue using an existing account, you will be asked to confirm your e-mail account settings; if you establish a new account, you will have to enter this information from scratch. Click Next.
8. Finally, click the Finish button to complete the configuration, close the Wizard, and connect to the Internet.

Connecting to the Internet with a Cable Modem

It's amazing how much times have changed. Less than five years ago, everyone wanted the latest and greatest in computer hardware——the fastest processors, the best video, the biggest hard drives. Nowadays, if you offer someone a choice between a computer with all the best hardware on the market or an average computer with a really fast Internet connection, 9 out of 10 people would choose the computer with the Internet connection.

Internet bandwidth is king, and there is no sign that things will change in the near future. So, what can you do when you decide it's time to upgrade from your 56K modem to something a bit faster? One option is to sign up for Internet access over the same cable that brings TV into your home.

That might sound a bit strange at first, but it actually makes good sense. Millions of homes across the country (roughly 100 million) are already wired for cable access. Cable service can bring hundreds of channels of full audio and video content into your home over a single wire. If a cable signal can carry that much content, adding a bit of data into the mix isn't much of a problem.

Cable Internet Access—How Does It Work?

A cable modem has at least two (and maybe more) interfaces on it. The first is a standard F port connector, a coaxial cable connector that is similar to the one on the back of a television or a VCR. Your cable service is connected to that port. The second interface is a 10Base-T connector, which connects your cable modem to your computer. Your computer needs a 10Base-T port on the back of it in order to connect the two together. If your computer does not have a 10Base-T port, your cable service provider can probably install one for you.

Once your cable modem is up and running, data comes down to your system on a special channel on your cable signal and, unlike an analog modem, is always on.

How Fast Is It?

Being the techie that I am, I like absolutes. I like to know exactly how things work and exactly how fast something will run. So I did a bit of research to find out how fast cable modem service actually is. What I learned is that you can't find out.

When determining how fast a cable modem will actually run, you must consider a number of factors. Some factors (but not all) are out of the control of the cable Internet service providers, so their common answer—if you really press them on it—will be "it depends." Of course, this doesn't prevent them from bragging that their service is up to 1,000 times faster than a 33.6 modem. In theory, it is.

Let's take a look at that theory. On a typical cable modem installation, a 6MHz analog carrier channel is dedicated to carrying downstream data from the Internet to your computer. Now, the way all the bits and bytes are put together over a cable modem yields a throughput of 36Mb on a 6MHz carrier channel. So, in theory, 36,000,000bps is 1,000 times greater than 33,600bps.

Ah, but a few factors get in the way. First, let's start with your computer. Your computer interfaces with your cable modem over a 10Base-T connection. It's called a "10"Base-T connection because the maximum throughput it will support is 10,000,000 bps (10Mbps). That's a bit less than 36Mbps—about 73 percent less. So much for the claim of being 1,000 times faster.

But that's not the only possible bottleneck. The signal that is coming down the 6MHz carrier channel and into your computer is mixed in with other signals headed to other nearby computers. Your cable Internet traffic is traveling across the same cable that connects all the other homes and apartments in your neighborhood. Now, in theory, that cable can carry the entire 36Mbps of signal into your area. But how many users does it take to completely saturate that connection to your neighborhood? Four computers using 9Mbps each? What about 40 users running 900,000 kilobits per second (Kbps) each? What about 400 users running 90Kbps (less than two 56K modems) each? Each combination would saturate the cable signal for your neighborhood and—believe it or not—it is not uncommon for 500 to 2,000 cable TV subscribers to all be running on the same cable (that is, running into the same cable "head-end" or "node"). Hopefully, not all of them are subscribing to cable Internet access as well. If they were, and if everyone were using their cable modems, your connectivity might not be much better than that of two 56K modems, but I admit I'm stretching things a bit to make a point. Simply put, the best neighbor to have is one that doesn't even have a computer.

There is also the potential for a bottleneck from your cable company out to the Internet itself. Now, in all fairness, this is a bottleneck point for any ISP—whether you have dial-up, DSL, cable modem, or whatever. Just as airlines make their money by selling more seats on a plane than they actually have, ISPs make money by selling more bandwidth than they actually have. They wouldn't be able to survive if they didn't.

A close companion who has a cable modem was able to confirm my speed rating of "it depends." In his particular scenario, he was able to see average throughputs of 256Kbps to 512Kbps, with his best connection being about 1.3Mbps—roughly the speed of a T-1 connection. So, cable modems are definitely faster, but don't buy into the hype about their being 1,000 times faster than a regular modem.

Cable Internet Access—Advantages and Disadvantages

A number of advantages and disadvantages are associated with cable modem service (in comparison with typical analog modems). I've outlined a few of the positives and negatives for you.

Advantages of Cable Modem Internet Access

Always on Full-time dedicated Internet access—you'll definitely appreciate this once you have it.

High-speed Despite the possible bottlenecks I discussed earlier, 99 times out of 100, cable modems will give you far better speed and reliability than analog modems. Once you get connected, you'll never be willing to move somewhere that *doesn't* have high-speed access.

One less phone line required If you had a dedicated second phone line installed in your house for computer access, you can drop that phone line. This should save you $10–$20 per month, which can offset the cost of the cable modem service.

Affordable In comparison with other high-speed Internet access options, cable modems are one of the most affordable.

Disadvantages of Cable Modem Internet Access

Privacy Since all systems in a "neighborhood" of cable Internet subscribers use the same connection to send and receive data, someone may be able to intercept your traffic and analyze it—a security risk.

Few choices Unlike phone companies and Internet service providers, cable companies are more or less a monopoly here in the United States. You usually won't be able to choose from multiple cable Internet providers; you'll have to take whatever is available in your neighborhood.

Getting Hooked Up

OK, so let's assume you've decided to take the plunge and get hooked up to the Internet with a cable modem. Let's take a look at what you might go through, from start to finish.

Questions to Ask Your Provider

You should definitely ask your cable provider a number of questions before getting hooked up. You might not get answers to all of them, but I would want any provider to be able to answer at least some of the following questions to my satisfaction:

- How can you ensure that my neighbors won't be able to intercept my data and read it?
- Is yours a two-way service? (Avoid one-way services. One-way means that your computer can receive data quickly from a cable modem, but it must transmit data through an analog modem.)

- Will I receive a public IP address? If so, will it be fixed or dynamic? (Fixed IP addresses are better if you need to access your computer remotely; dynamic IP addresses are better from a security point of view.)
- How fast can I expect it to be? Can you guarantee a certain level of service? (By all means, e-mail me if you get any provider to actually guarantee a certain level of bandwidth—I'd like to hear about them!)
- Are there any speed restrictions on my uplink speed? (Uplink refers to data sent from your computer to the Internet. Uploading a large e-mail message, video-conferencing, or transferring a large file to someone are all affected by slow uplink speeds.)
- Are there any restrictions on the type of services I can run on my computer?

Service Delivery

Once you've talked with your provider and agreed to purchase the service, they will set up a time to send an installer out to your location. Now, I don't have cable modem Internet access, but I would expect the service to be just about as prompt as my regular cable service (meaning: not very prompt). Once they're at your location, they will work with the cables a bit and hook up their cable to a box—the cable modem.

Once the box is hooked up, it is time to hook the computer up. If your computer already has an Ethernet adapter in it, they will most likely connect the cable modem to the Ethernet adapter. If your system doesn't have an Ethernet adapter, they should add one to your computer for you (make sure that you have your original Windows 2000 Professional software handy, just in case they need it).

After your Ethernet adapter is installed and connected to the cable modem, the technician will probably change around your network settings a bit—maybe load some optional authentication software on your computer—and you'll be ready to surf the Internet in style. If the installer did not configure your network settings for you, you will need the minimum TCP/IP configuration necessary to access the Internet. Make sure you find out the following from your provider if they did not configure your computer:

- Should you use DHCP or a static IP address? (If you are supposed to use DHCP, you can probably ignore the rest of these items.)
- What is the subnet mask?
- What is the default gateway?
- What DNS servers should be used?

Once you have this information, you can configure the TCP/IP properties of your Ethernet connection accordingly and start accessing the Internet.

High-Speed Internet Utilities

For high-speed Internet access, I simply can't live without two utilities: Zone Alarm and ICB 2000. ZoneAlarm is a personal firewall package that resides on your computer and protects it from outside intrusions. It is by far the best firewall package I've seen for personal use. The real reason that I like it is that you must "authorize" each application on your computer before it is allowed to transfer information to the Internet, a feature that none of the other personal firewalls have as far as I know. Plus, you can't beat the price—it's free! You can find ZoneAlarm at `www.zonealarm.com`.

ICB (Internet Connection Benchmark) 2000 is a package that will sit and watch your Internet traffic and determine what your uplink and downlink throughput actually is. This was particularly helpful for me to determine the true speed of my 1.1Mb DSL connection. Running this utility and then starting a large download from `www.microsoft.com` revealed that I was indeed getting a 1.1Mb DSL connection. You can find ICB 2000 at `www.byzantine.nl/icb`.

Connecting to the Internet with DSL

Another popular high-speed Internet option is Digital Subscriber Line (DSL) service. DSL typically comes in two varieties: Asymmetric DSL (ADSL) and Symmetric DSL (SDSL). Since the two technologies move data in a similar manner, you may also see these commonly referred to as xDSL.

Asymmetric DSL is called asymmetric because the uplink and downlink speeds are different, with more of the speed usually being allocated to the downlink (what you use to download content from the Internet). With Symmetric DSL, the same amount of bandwidth is available in both directions—up and down.

DSL—How Does It Work?

DSL uses the existing copper phone lines already in your house to send a high-speed data signal. Your plain old telephone service (POTS) typically uses a low frequency range for all the types of signals you're accustomed to: voice, fax, and data. DSL operates on the same line—at the same time—by using a higher (inaudible) set of frequencies to transmit data. Since the DSL signal is operating in a different frequency range, you can still use your phone, fax machine, or even a modem at the same time you are using your DSL service to access the Internet.

When you have a DSL modem installed in your home, the device will have at least two or three interfaces on it. The first will be a standard RJ11 phone connector that you're probably very familiar with. Your phone line will be connected to that port. The second interface on your DSL modem will be a 10Base-T connector (also known as an RJ45), which will connect your DSL modem to your computer. Your computer will need a 10Base-T port on the back of it in order to connect the two together. If your computer does not have a 10Base-T port, your DSL provider will probably install one for you. The third port that you might have on the back of your DSL modem is another RJ11 jack—this is for connecting your phone to the DSL modem.

How Fast Is It?

Unlike cable modems, DSL service usually has very defined levels of service associated with it, from 1.5 all the way up to 9Mbps. A speed of 1.5Mbps is the same as a T1 Internet access line, the same type of line that many businesses use for their Internet access needs, and it's probably more than enough for the average individual user.

NOTE A T1 line is a long-distance circuit that provides 24 channels of 64Kbps each, giving you a total bandwidth of 1.544Mbps.

You will usually have at least a few providers to choose from. Compare the speed offerings from all the providers able to service your neighborhood and choose what is best for you.

Depending on how your provider's network is configured, the potential for a bottleneck exists from your DSL provider out to the Internet itself. Remember, this is a bottleneck point for any ISP, whether you have dial-up, DSL, a cable modem, or whatever. As I mentioned earlier, ISPs make their money by selling more bandwidth than they actually have, in the expectation that not everyone will use it at once.

Having DSL myself, I can tell you that—in my case—it has lived up to its service speed. I've been able to verify a full 1.1Mbps worth of connectivity on my service, which is exactly what I paid for. Being able to download Windows service packs in five minutes instead of four hours is a definite advantage in my line of business.

DSL—Advantages and Disadvantages

A number of advantages and disadvantages are associated with DSL service (in comparison with typical analog modems). I've outlined a few of the positives and negatives for you.

Advantages of DSL Service

Always on Full-time dedicated Internet access—once you've had it, you'll never want to go back. You'll definitely appreciate this once you have DSL.

High-speed Once you get connected, you'll never be willing to move somewhere that doesn't have high-speed access.

One less phone line needed If you had a dedicated second phone line installed in your house for computer access, you can drop that phone line because you can still use your DSL line as a voice line—even when you are on the Internet. This should save you $10–$20 per month, which can offset the cost of the DSL service.

Disadvantages of DSL Service

Limited service area Due to technical limitations, your location must be within three miles (some providers say anywhere from 12,000 to 20,000 feet) of the phone company's DSL-capable switching location. And that distance is based on the length of cabling between you and the phone company's office, not the "as the crow flies" distance. So, even if you live two miles from a DSL-capable switching location, you won't be able to get DSL if there are more than three miles of cable between you and the switch.

Getting Hooked Up

OK, so let's assume you've decided to take the plunge and get hooked up to the Internet through DSL service. Let's take a look at what you might go through, from start to finish.

Questions to Ask Your Provider

Before ordering service, you should probably ask any prospective provider a few questions. Although this isn't a complete list of items you may need to consider, it's a good start.

- Will I receive a public IP address? If so, will it be fixed or dynamic? (Fixed IP addresses are better if you need to access your computer remotely; dynamic IP addresses are better from a security point of view)
- Do you guarantee the level of service that I am purchasing?
- Are there any speed restrictions on my uplink speed? (Uplink refers to data sent from your computer to the Internet—uploading a large e-mail, videoconferencing, or transferring a large file to someone are all affected by slow uplink speeds)
- Are there any restrictions on the type of services I can run on my computer?

Service Delivery

Once you've decided on a provider and agreed to a level of service, your provider will set up a time to send an installer out to your location (or, in some areas, they can send you a kit to install the DSL modem yourself—although you should have more technical knowledge than the average casual Internet user does if you're going to do this). Once they're at your location, they may have to work with your phone lines a bit before hooking up your DSL modem, and then they'll hook up your phone line to the DSL modem.

Once the DSL modem is hooked up, it is time to hook up the computer. If your computer already has an Ethernet adapter in it, they will most likely connect the DSL modem to the Ethernet adapter. If your system doesn't have an Ethernet adapter, they should add one to your computer for you (make sure that you have your original Windows 2000 Professional software handy, just in case they need it).

After your Ethernet adapter is installed and connected to the cable modem, the technician will probably change your network settings a bit—maybe load some optional authentication software on your computer—and then you'll be ready to surf the Internet in style. If the installer did not configure your network settings for you, you will need to have the minimum TCP/IP configuration necessary to access the Internet. Make sure you find out the following from your provider if they did not configure your computer:

- Should you use DHCP or a static IP address? (If you are supposed to use DHCP you can probably ignore the rest of these items.)
- What is the subnet mask?
- What is the default gateway?
- What DNS servers should be used?

Once you have that information, you can configure the TCP/IP properties of your Ethernet connection accordingly and start accessing the Internet.

Connecting to the Internet with ISDN

ISDN is another option for providing high-speed Internet connectivity, but it has taken a back seat to other modern technologies due to two primary factors: cost and speed. Although ISDN can provide high-speed access to the Internet, it is typically slower than other commercial alternatives. In addition to its lack of speed, in some cases it is also more costly than other services, with some providers even charging by the minute. However, ISDN has one advantage over all other high-speed options: it is available almost anywhere. In addition, you aren't tied to an ISP as you usually are with DSL or cable modem. Depending on your situation, ISDN might be a good choice for you.

ISDN—How Does It Work?

ISDN (Integrated Services Digital Network) is an international standard for sending voice, video, and data over normal telephone lines. It works by sending a data signal over a pair of copper wires and then dividing the data signal into three separate channels. A separate function and bandwidth are allocated to each channel.

The first type of channel is a bearer channel, commonly referred to as a B channel. A B channel can support data, voice, or fax transmissions and is capable of moving data at 64Kbps. With the exception of commercial-grade circuits, most ISDN lines can support two B channels, yielding a maximum throughput of 128Kbps. As you can see, even a single B channel by itself is already faster than the fastest 56K modem.

The second type of channel is a data channel, commonly referred to as a D channel. A D channel typically carries data at16Kbps and is primarily used for transmitting connection maintenance data such as call signaling and setup information, requests for network services, tearing down a call when it's complete, and so on. Since a D channel is typically used to maintain the connection, it is not typically used for data transmission. Therefore, the most common configuration you will see for an ISDN connection is what's referred to as a 2B+D connection—two bearer channels, one data channel. The maximum data throughput (before compression) allowed through such a circuit is 128Kbps.

ISDN—Advantages and Disadvantages

A number of advantages and disadvantages are associated with ISDN (in comparison with typical analog modems).

Advantages of ISDN Service

Widely available ISDN is available almost everywhere. As a matter of fact, only the existing analog phone network has a wider reach. Depending on your location, ISDN might be the only option for high-speed Internet access.

High-speed With speeds more than 125 percent faster than the fastest 56K analog modems available, you will definitely appreciate the added bandwidth of an ISDN connection.

One less phone line needed If you had a dedicated second phone line installed in your house for computer access, you can drop that phone line and run your voice and data communications over the same ISDN line. This can help offset some of the cost of your ISDN service.

Multipurpose You can use the same ISDN line for voice calls, fax, data, and so on.

Disadvantages of ISDN Service

Cost ISDN, in some markets, is still a bit expensive in comparison with the additional bandwidth that it provides. Some providers are even charging per-minute fees for ISDN usage, which can add up to some hefty monthly bills if you are a heavy user.

Getting Hooked Up

If you've looked at your connectivity options and decided that ISDN is the best route for you, let's take a look at the process you'll need to go through to get access to the Internet.

ISDN Modem

The first thing that you will need to install into your system is an ISDN modem. Basically, an ISDN modem is no different from a regular analog modem, except for the fact that it works on an ISDN line instead of an analog line. We've already covered modems and modem installation earlier in this chapter, so I won't readdress that information here—you'll simply need to walk through the proper steps to install an ISDN modem into your system.

NOTE Although we typically refer to the little box that connects your computer to your DSL, ISDN, or cable line as a modem, it really isn't a modem in the true sense of the word. A modem converts digital signals to analog signals and vice versa. So-called DSL, ISDN, and cable modems transmit and receive all data as digital signals, and so they are really terminal adapters.

Once your ISDN modem is installed (and Windows 2000 Professional recognizes it correctly), some configuring may be involved.

After you've finished configuring your ISDN modem, the steps to connect to the Internet are amazingly similar to the steps used for connecting to the Internet with an analog modem. That brings us to the next part of the picture…

You Need an ISP Too

Unlike other high-speed Internet options, which typically include an ISP account, you will probably have to set up an account with an ISDN-capable ISP. ISPs don't actually run the ISDN line to your location, they just set up banks of ISDN modems at their location to receive calls—just as they do with analog modems. It's up to you to purchase your connection and then to use it to call into them.

This allows you to easily switch from one ISP to another while keeping your high-speed ISDN line. This is also a good option if your existing analog dial-up ISP supports

ISDN connections, as you can keep all of your existing e-mail address and other services. The only thing that will change as far as your ISP is concerned is which line you dial in on, the analog or the ISDN.

Service Delivery

When you're ready to get started with ISDN, you will need to purchase the service directly from your phone company or, optionally, from your ISP if they offer the service (they will most likely order the line from the phone company on your behalf). A technician from your phone company should arrive at your location to set up your ISDN circuit. Once their work is finished, you should have an ISDN jack installed in your home or office.

At this point, you should refer to your modem manufacturer's directions about how to connect your ISDN modem to your ISDN line. Although most ISDN modems will have a jack for the ISDN connection (and optionally one or two jacks to plug in regular phone equipment), you may need to manually configure some items—such as the ISDN switch type you are connected to, the service profile identifiers (SPIDs), and so on. Although most good ISDN modems autodetect most of these items for you, you may have to configure some of them manually. Results will vary with each modem manufacturer, so follow their directions carefully in conjunction with the paperwork from your ISDN provider.

Dialing In via ISDN

Once your modem is hooked up, it is time to dial into your ISP. By following the steps in the Internet Connection Wizard (covered earlier in this chapter), you should be able to create an ISDN dial-up networking entry for your system. Launching that entry and supplying your username and password for your ISP account should get you connected. Once you are connected, your ISP will most likely give you a dynamically assigned IP address, which should configure the following TCP/IP settings for your computer:

- Subnet mask
- Default gateway
- DNS servers

Sharing an Internet Connection

As you can see, you can end up spending some time and resources getting a high-powered computer, complete with a high-speed Internet connection, set up in your home or office. And after you spend all that time getting your master system set up, guess what will happen? You'll get a second computer. That will leave you with a high-speed Internet connection on one system and nothing on the other.

Well, if Windows 2000 Professional is able to share its other resources (such as files and printers), you should be able to share its Internet connection, right? Fortunately for you, the answer is yes. And I say fortunately, because in Windows NT Workstation this was not possible without adding third-party software to your system. Fortunately, Microsoft saw the demand for Internet connection sharing and decided to build the capability directly into Windows 2000 Professional.

TIP Although I'll talk about using Windows 2000 Professional to share a high-speed Internet connection, you may want to talk to your ISP to see if you can simply hook their connection into an Ethernet hub and then plug multiple computers directly into the hub. My DSL provider allows me to do this, giving each of my internal computers its own IP address and its own connection to the Internet. Since I am paying for a set amount of bandwidth, they don't care how many computers I use as long as I stay below my purchased bandwidth amount. Connecting all your computers directly to your high-speed Internet connection might be the quickest and easiest solution if your ISP allows it, and it only requires the purchase of a hub.

So, what do you need to get started? This list should cover all the basics that you will need in most situations:

- Your Windows 2000 Professional system, with a high-speed Internet connection such as one of the types covered in this chapter—xDSL, ISDN, cable modem, and so on.
- Your secondary computer—this could be any Windows-based system or even a Macintosh or Linux system. You must have the ability to change the IP address and configuration on your secondary computer (no other applications must be running that require another IP configuration or address).
- Two network cards installed in your computer—one to connect to your high-speed Internet connection, and a second to connect to your other computer. Or, one network card and a dial-up networking entry for an ISDN connection.

TIP Although I haven't had a chance to work with them yet, I have heard good reports about a set of wireless network adapters from WebGear, Inc., called the Aviator. If you would like to have Internet access from another location in your house without installing wiring, you might want to give these adapters a try. Personally, I plan to try them soon with my laptop, so that I can share my high-speed Internet access with it and use it anywhere in my home.

- A "crossover" cable—a special Ethernet cable—if you plan to connect both your computers directly. You should be able to find one at most computer supply stores. Optionally, you can also use an Ethernet hub to connect your computers (recommended if you plan to share your Internet connection with more than one system).

Configuring Windows 2000 Professional to Share an Internet Connection

Once you've got everything you need in place to share an Internet connection, start by working on your primary Windows 2000 Professional system (the one with the high-speed Internet connection). To begin, you should have two network adapters installed in your computer, and both should be working properly. You can check this by choosing Start ➢ Settings ➢ Network And Dial-Up Connections. In the Network And Dial-Up Connections folder, verify that you have two network adapter icons and that neither of them is grayed out.

To keep the adapters straight, I will refer to them as the *public adapter* and the *private adapter*. The public adapter is the network adapter that is connected to your high-speed Internet service. It is connected to the "public" Internet (hence, the name public adapter). The private adapter is the one that is connected to the computers within your home or office—your private systems.

TIP Since I typically use the same type of network cards in most of my computers, I like to name each of my connections by renaming the adapter icons in the Network And Dial-Up Connections folder. Now, instead of seeing icons with vague names such as Intel EtherExpress 1 and Intel EtherExpress 2, I see icons for Public Adapter and Private Adapter.

To start installing Internet Connection Sharing, follow these steps:

1. In the Network And Dial-Up Connections folder, right-click the icon for your public adapter, and choose Properties from the shortcut menu to open the Properties dialog box for that adapter.

2. If everything on your system is configured correctly, you should see a Sharing tab, similar to the following:

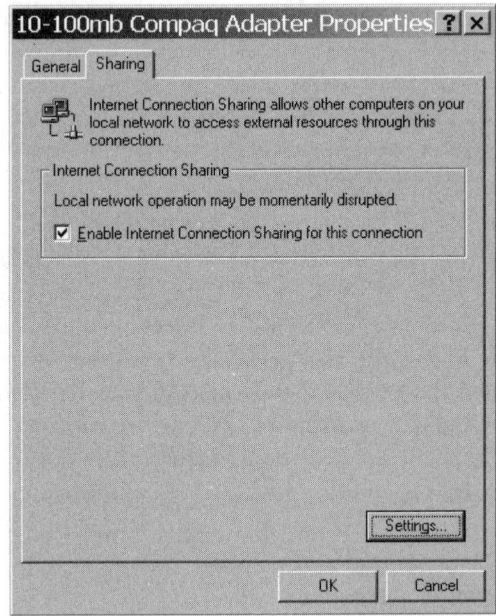

This dialog box is deceptively simple. It has one check box—Enable Internet Connection Sharing For This Connection. Go ahead and check that box, but don't expect miracles yet. Notice the simple little Settings button at the bottom of the dialog box? That's where most of the configuration occurs for sharing an Internet connection. Go ahead and click the Settings button to open the Internet Connection Sharing Settings dialog box:

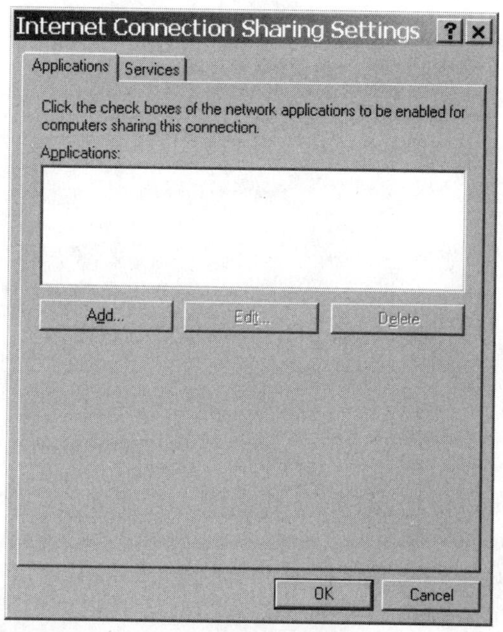

Now, to a novice user (and even some intermediate users) this dialog box can be a bit misleading. It would have been nice if Microsoft had made a Wizard for this configuration item or preinstalled some of the more common settings, but they didn't. So, you'll have to configure each application you want to share over the Internet.

So what's an "application"? As far as Internet Connection Sharing is concerned, an application is really just a TCP/IP protocol. Think of it as a function that comes from your internal computers (on the private adapter) and goes out to the Internet (through your public adapter). Web browsing would be considered an application. Secure Web browsing would also be considered an application—but a different one from Web browsing. Downloading e-mail would be considered an application, and sending e-mail would also be considered an application—but again, a different one from downloading e-mail. Each and every function that your computer performs on the Internet is most likely a separate application, which means you will have to define each and every application that you want to share. This can be useful if you want to control which types of Internet access you are sharing with your internal systems.

So let's start configuring an application. Click the Add button to open the Internet Connection Sharing Application dialog box:

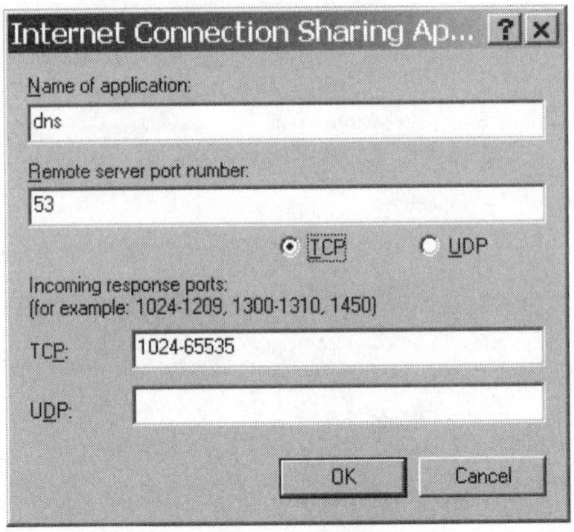

In order to allow shared access for a TCP/IP application, Windows 2000 Professional needs to know the "application" (that is, the protocol) functions. Now, all TCP and UDP protocols use certain source and destination "ports" in order to communicate from one computer to another. You will need to define those ports for Windows 2000 Professional.

The first application that you should probably define is DNS. As you're probably aware, DNS is the application that translates human-friendly names (such as `www.netarchitect.com`) into Internet IP addresses (such as 206.135.150.39) that your computer needs in order to connect to a remote system. Without DNS support, all the systems connected to your private adapter would have to connect to systems on the Internet by numbers instead of names. So let's walk through adding support for DNS.

First, you will need to create a friendly name for the application you are defining. I use simple names for these, usually based on the protocol I am working with. In this case, you'll use DNS as the name of your application—enter that in the Name Of Application field. Next, you'll need to know the correct port number for DNS communication. According to Internet standards, DNS communications should take place over port 53, either via TCP or UDP, depending on how your Internet service provider is running their DNS systems. For your purposes, assume that it's a TCP protocol, and go ahead and type 53 in the Remote Server Port Number field, and then click the TCP radio button.

Now, when the remote DNS server receives a request from one of your internal systems, it will reply to that computer on a different port. In the case of DNS (and many other Internet protocols), this can be on any port in the range of 1024–65535, so go ahead and enter that exact value (complete with the hyphens) in the Incoming Response Ports field for TCP. Click OK, and you will have configured your Windows 2000 Professional system to route DNS traffic from your private network out into the Internet.

Of course, in order to really test your connection, you will probably also want to enable Web browsing (the HTTP protocol). Using the information in Table 10.1 and repeating the steps above, you should be able to add an additional application to your system for HTTP.

TABLE 10.1: TCP/IP WELL KNOWN PORTS AND SERVICES

Protocol Type	Destination Port/Protocol	Response Port(s)/Protocol(s)
FTP	21/TCP	1024-65535/TCP
Telnet	23/TCP	1024-65535/TCP
SMTP	25/TCP	1024-65535/TCP
Gopher	70/TCP	1024-65535/TCP
HTTP	80/TCP	1024-65535/TCP
POP3	110/TCP	1024-65535/TCP
NNTP	119/TCP	1024-65535/TCP

Once you have added support for the HTTP protocol, it's probably a good time to test your work and make sure that everything is working properly. Click OK in the Internet Connection Sharing Settings dialog box to store your application definitions, and then click OK on the adapter Properties dialog box to enable Internet Connection Sharing on your system. You should see a warning dialog box like the following:

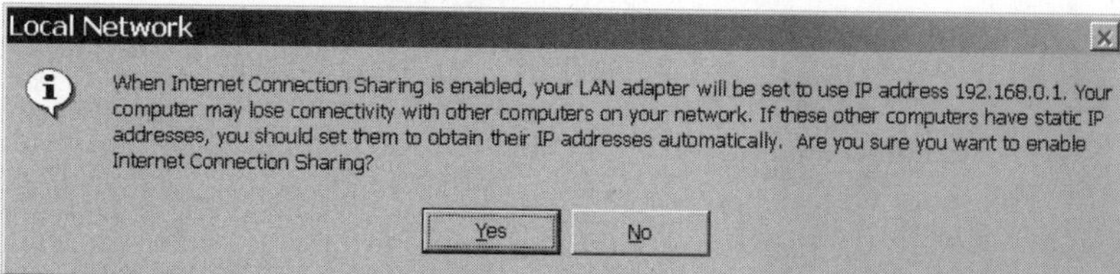

In order for Internet Connection Sharing to work, Windows 2000 Professional requires that you use a specific IP address, 192.168.0.1, for your private adapter. Windows 2000 Professional also requires a specific subnet mask as well—255.255.255.0. If you select Yes at this dialog box, Windows will make the necessary changes to the TCP/IP configuration of your private adapter.

Once you click Yes, Windows 2000 Professional will change your TCP/IP configuration, after which you should be sharing your Internet connection. In order to test this, you'll need to change the TCP/IP configuration of your other computer(s).

Configuring Clients

Three primary components usually make up a TCP/IP configuration: the IP address, the subnet mask, and the (optional) default gateway. For your clients to be able to share your Windows 2000 Professional Internet connection, they must be configured with the following parameters:

TCP/IP Address Any address from 192.168.0.2 through 192.168.0.254

Subnet mask 255.255.255.0

Default gateway 192.168.0.1

DNS You will need to configure the DNS settings of your second computer to use the DNS servers provided by your ISP. This will vary from one provider to the next. If you don't know the correct IP addresses for the DNS servers that your ISP uses, on your Windows 2000 Professional system, type `ipconfig /all | more` at a command prompt. You should see one or more IP addresses listed under DNS Servers for your public adapter. Or, call your ISP (or check their Web page) to find out the correct DNS server addresses. Enter those DNS addresses in the DNS configuration of your private computer(s) so that they can correctly resolve host names to IP addresses.

Once you have your workstation properly configured, start up the Web browser on your second computer, and see if you can connect to the Internet. If you can, you have successfully set up Internet Connection Sharing on your computer. You can add additional "applications" to your system as needed to support additional protocols within your network.

Troubleshooting Internet Connection Sharing

If, for some reason, you aren't able to browse the Internet successfully, it's time to troubleshoot your networking. Although this isn't a complete list of troubleshooting steps, these are the first tests that you should perform to make sure that everything is working properly.

Test your main computer. OK, even though it may sound as simple as checking the power switch, check to make sure that you can still browse the Internet from your main computer. If you can't, odds are you won't be able to browse it from your second computer.

Ping yourself. From your main computer and from your second computer, "ping" yourself via the `PING` command at a command prompt. On your main Windows 2000 Professional computer, do this by typing `PING 192.168.0.1` at the command prompt. You should see a successful response from your pings (not a response timeout). Do the same from your second computer—ping its IP address to see if you get a response. If you fail either of these tests, you have a general TCP/IP networking problem or connectivity issue that needs troubleshooting.

Ping the other guy. From your main Windows 2000 Professional system, try to ping your second computer. And from your second computer, ping your Windows 2000 Professional system. Again, if you fail either of these tests (that is, you get a response timeout), you have a basic TCP/IP networking problem or connectivity issue that needs troubleshooting.

Do a DNS lookup. If all your pings worked successfully, go to your second workstation and try to ping a host out on the Internet. Try typing in something like **`PING www.microsoft.com`**. In this case, if you get a request timeout you're actually in good shape—your DNS definition is working correctly. If you receive a `Bad IP Address` response from the ping command, your DNS query is not making it to your ISP's DNS server, or the response isn't making it back. Check your definitions of the DNS application again in the Internet Connection Sharing Settings dialog box.

Check your HTTP definition. If all the above steps worked correctly, the problem is most likely in your definition of the HTTP application (or else it is beyond the scope of what I can cover in the book). Recheck your HTTP application configuration to make sure everything is set correctly. You could also try building another application such as POP3 (for downloading e-mail) to see if that works correctly.

Summary

This chapter covered the basics of installing and configuring a modem for use in Windows 2000 Professional. I discussed configuring the dial-up connection and how TAPI makes our lives easier when dialing from multiple locations. I ended the chapter with information about how to set up various kinds of Internet connections.

In the next chapter, you'll find specific information about the communications programs that are included with Windows 2000 Professional.

CHAPTER 11

Using the Communications Programs

FEATURING:

You may never have an occasion to use the programs I'm going to discuss in this chapter, but I'm including information about them so that you'll know they exist, what each is best suited for, and how to access them when the need arises. I'm guessing that the one you might use the most, especially if you run a small business and have a small network of computers, is Fax.

In Windows 2000 Professional, all these programs have been improved over their earlier versions in NT and Windows.

Using the Windows 2000 Professional Fax Service

If you're in business today, a fax machine is as essential as an office copier or a coffeepot. The most common tool for facsimile communication is still the stand-alone fax machine, but there are some real advantages to using your PC as a personal fax machine instead.

To send a fax through a fax machine you need to: create the document, print a copy on paper, write up a cover sheet, carry the document and cover sheet to the fax machine, wait for your turn to use the machine, dial the recipient's fax number, feed the document and cover sheet through the fax machine, and, finally, walk back to your office. When somebody sends you a fax, it spills out of the machine and waits for you to come get it—meanwhile, everybody who walks past the fax machine has a chance to read your messages before you do.

On the other hand, you can send and receive faxes through your PC and a fax modem without leaving your chair. If you have a home office or a *really* small business with a tight budget, you can do PC-based faxing without spending a couple of hundred dollars or more for a separate machine. And when you're traveling with a portable computer, you can use it to exchange faxes with your office and your customers.

In this section, you will learn how to use Fax to send and receive faxes from your PC just as if you were printing the document or sending e-mail. You'll also learn how to create personalized, custom cover pages for your faxes.

Installing Fax

You don't really have to install Fax; Windows 2000 Professional does that for you when you install the operating system. These days, most modems have fax and data capabilities. If you don't know whether your modem has fax capabilities, choose Start ➢ Settings ➢ Printers to open the Printers folder. If you have an icon for a fax printer, your modem has fax capabilities.

Configuring Windows 2000 Professional Fax

To configure Fax, you use the Fax applet in Control Panel. This applet contains the basic information that Windows 2000 Professional uses to fill in your cover page, as well as your list of personal cover pages and other service settings.

Choose Start ➢ Settings ➢ Control Panel ➢ Fax to open the Fax Properties dialog box, which is shown in Figure 11.1.

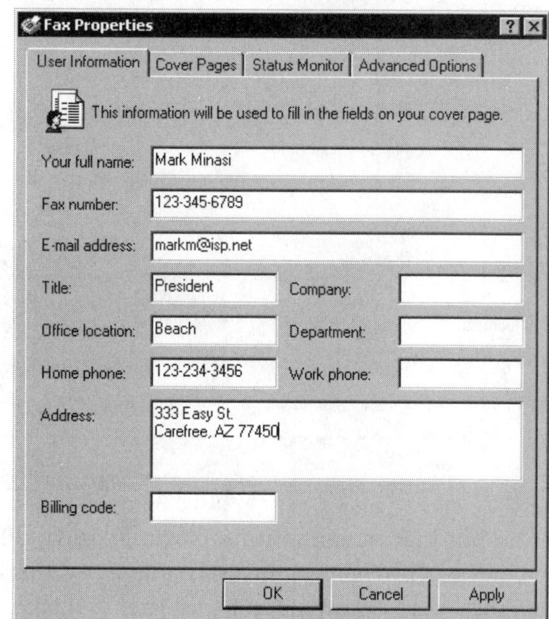

FIGURE 11.1 *The User Information tab of the Fax Properties dialog box contains your personal fax information.*

User Information

The User Information tab contains the basic information that will populate your cover page when you send a fax. It has fields for your name, fax number, address, company name, and so on.

You don't have to fill in every single field on the tab, but the more you fill out, the more complete your cover page will be. At least, the more complete it will be without your having to fill it in every time.

Most businesses consider the minimum information to be the person's name, company name, and fax number. You can decide how much information is enough.

Cover Pages

If you're like most people, you have several cover pages. Probably, you have one for formal business communications, one for personal business communications, and one just for fun. Maybe you have more than this, maybe less. Whatever your personal needs, you can use the Cover Pages tab, which is shown in Figure 11.2, to organize cover pages.

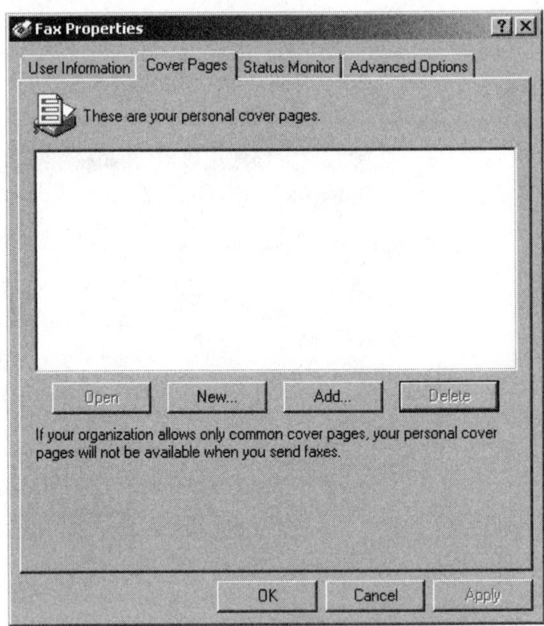

FIGURE 11.2
The Cover Pages tab of the Fax Properties dialog box

The list box that contains the list of cover pages available for use occupies the main portion of the tab. When you first start to use Fax, this list will be empty. We will go through the steps to create a cover page later in this chapter.

The Cover Pages tab has four buttons that you'll be using:

Open Highlight a cover page and click Open to open the page in the Cover Page Editor. You can then make changes to the page.

New Click New to open the Cover Page Editor with a blank cover page loaded, ready for you to create your own page.

Add Click Add to open the Browse For New Cover Page File dialog box, from which you can add a new cover page from a previously created file.

Delete Highlight a cover page and click Delete to remove a currently installed cover page from the list.

Status Monitor

The Status Monitor tab, which is shown in Figure 11.3, controls the behavior of the Fax Status Monitor, a tool that will help you track the activity of Fax.

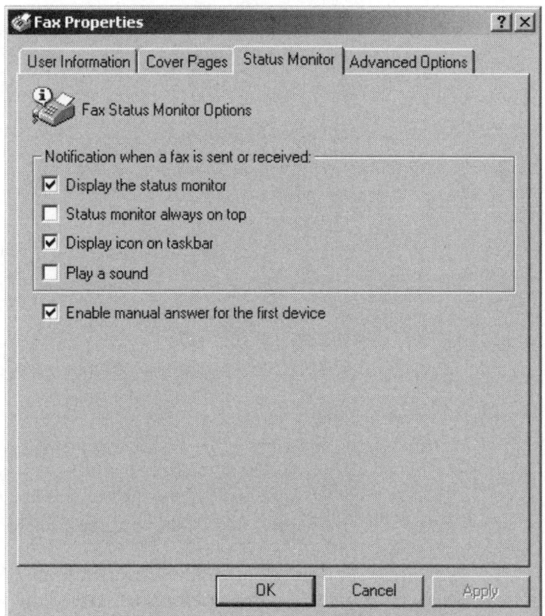

FIGURE 11.3
The Status Monitor tab contains settings that control the Fax Status Monitor.

The Status Monitor tab displays the status of faxes being sent or received and records fax-related events in the log files. It contains the following options:

Display The Status Monitor Determines whether the Fax Monitor dialog box is displayed when you send or receive faxes.

Status Monitor Always On Top Tells Windows 2000 Professional to always display the Fax Monitor dialog box on top of other windows when it is in use.

Display Icon On Taskbar Tells Windows 2000 Professional to display the Fax Printer icon in the status area of the Taskbar. Whenever you want to view the status of Fax, simply click this icon.

Play A Sound Tells Windows 2000 Professional to play a sound when you receive a fax. The default sound associated with receiving a fax is a ringing telephone. To select another sound, use the Sounds And Multimedia applet in Control Panel.

Enable Manual Answer For The First Device This setting is useful if a fax modem and a telephone share the same phone line. With this option selected, you are prompted to answer with the fax modem when an incoming fax is detected.

Advanced Options

The Advanced Options tab, which is shown in Figure 11.4, provides access to some of the management tools for Fax.

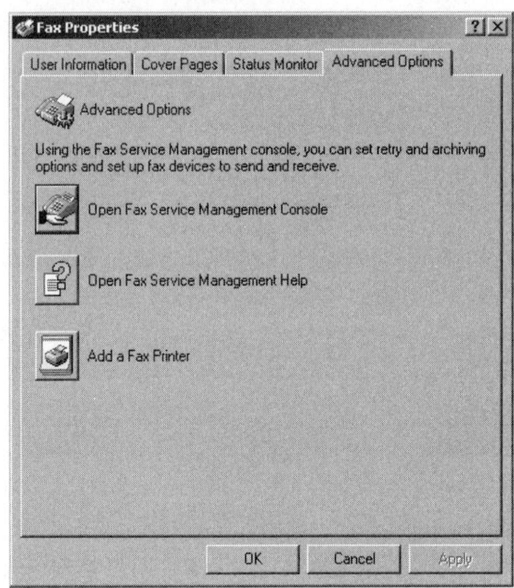

FIGURE 11.4
The Advanced Options tab of the Fax Properties dialog box

Let's take a look at each of the options on this tab.

Open Fax Service Management Console

Clicking the Open Fax Service Management Console button opens the Fax Service Management dialog box, which is shown in Figure 11.5. You use this dialog box to manage the settings for your installed fax devices and for the logging of sent and received faxes.

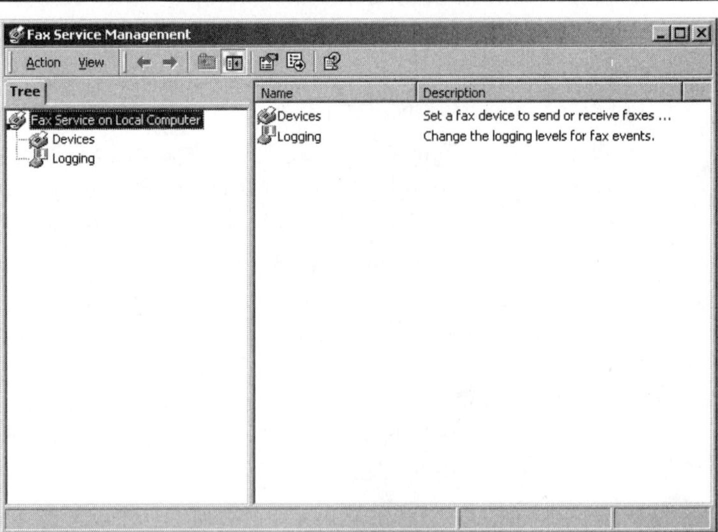

FIGURE 11.5
The Fax Service Management dialog box

The Tree pane on the left contains entries for Devices and Logging. Click Devices to display the fax devices installed on your Windows 2000 Professional system in the pane on the right. Click Logging in the left pane to display the log options in the right pane.

To display the properties of a fax device, double-click its name in the right pane, or right-click its name and choose Properties from the shortcut menu. The Properties dialog box has two tabs, General and Received Faxes.

On the General tab (see Figure 11.6), you can select whether the fax device will send, receive, or both. For greater efficiency, you might want one fax device to receive incoming faxes and another to send your outgoing faxes. You can configure that arrangement using the options in the General tab.

FIGURE 11.6
The General tab of the fax modem Properties dialog box lets you choose whether to send or receive.

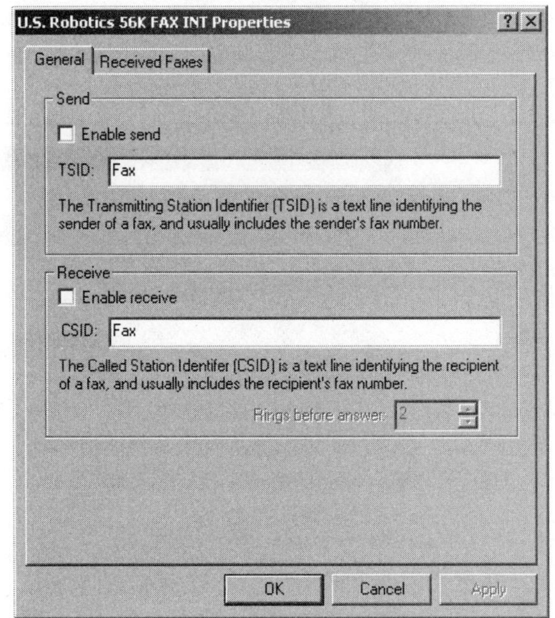

In the Send section, click the Enable Send check box to specify that the device will send faxes, and specify the Transmission Station Identifier (TSID) of the fax device in the TSID text box.

NOTE The TSID is usually the fax number of the device, and it will be displayed on the cover sheet automatically. The TSID may also be displayed in the Fax Queue when you are receiving a fax.

In the Receive section, click the Enable Receive check box to specify that this device will receive faxes. The Called Station Identifier (CSID) is the recipient of a fax and normally includes the recipient's fax number. Enter this information in the CSID box. When you receive a fax, the CSID is displayed in the Event Viewer in Computer Management. (See Chapter 29 for information about Computer Management.)

Specify the number of rings to wait before answering an incoming fax call in the Rings Before Answer spin box.

You use the Received Faxes tab, which is shown in Figure 11.7, to specify what Fax will do with incoming faxes. Select the Print On check box to direct all incoming faxes on this device to a printer. Click the Save In Folder check box to specify where incoming faxes will be saved. The default is the Fax folder in the My Documents folder in your user profile. To specify a different folder, enter the pathname, or click the Browse button (the button with ellipses) to open the Browse For Folder dialog box and select a folder.

FIGURE 11.7
The Received Faxes tab of the fax modem Properties dialog box

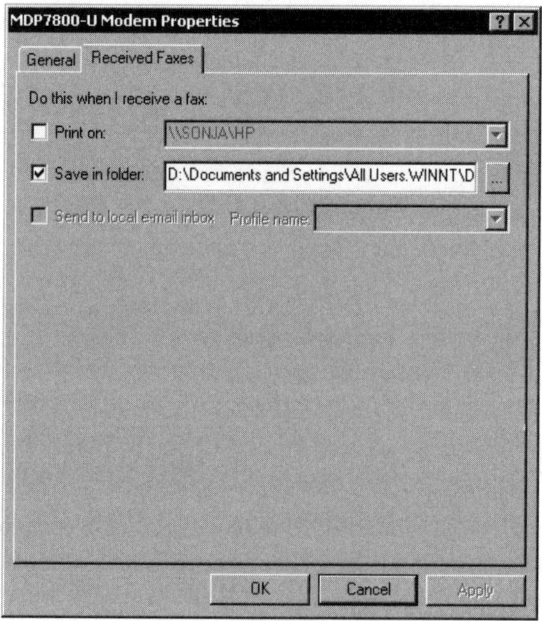

To specify that a device forward faxes to a Microsoft Exchange inbox, click the Send To Local E-mail Inbox check box, and enter a name in the Profile Name box. This profile will receive the faxes as e-mail attachments. You can set this option to different inboxes for each installed fax device.

Open Fax Service Management Help

Click the Open Fax Service Management Help button to open the Help files for Fax Service Management. The online Help in Windows 2000 Professional is really outstanding when compared with that in earlier versions of the operating system. If you have questions about Fax Service Management, this is the place to go.

Add A Fax Printer

It is sometimes helpful to have more than one configuration for a fax printer. The easiest way to create and manage multiple configurations for a printer is to create several icons for that printer. You then give each icon its own group of settings, and you're ready to go.

When you click the Add A Fax Printer button, the Fax Service Management places a new Fax Printer icon in your Printers folder and displays a message telling you that the new Fax Printer was created successfully. By default, the new fax printer is named Fax (Copy *x*).

TIP To delete a fax printer from the Printers folder, select it, and press Delete.

Sending Faxes in Windows 2000 Professional

OK, you've read through the entire configuration section, and you're ready to start faxing, so let's get to it. You can fax a document from within any Windows program that contains a Print command. For purposes of example, let's fax a document from WordPad and assume that this is your first time to fax a document in Windows 2000 Professional. Follow these steps:

1. Choose Start ➢ Programs ➢ Accessories ➢ WordPad to open WordPad.
2. Open an existing document, or create a new one.
3. Choose File ➢ Print to open the Print dialog box.
4. Select the Fax icon, and then click the Fax Options tab, which is shown in Figure 11.8.

FIGURE 11.8
The Fax Options tab of the Print dialog box

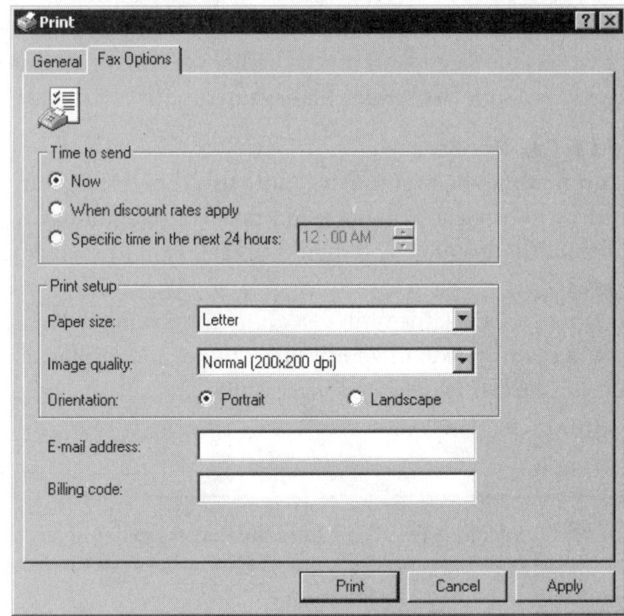

5. Click Print to start the Send Fax Wizard, as shown in Figure 11.9.

FIGURE 11.9
Sending a fax with the Send Fax Wizard

6. Click Next to open the Recipient And Dialing Information screen, shown in Figure 11.10.

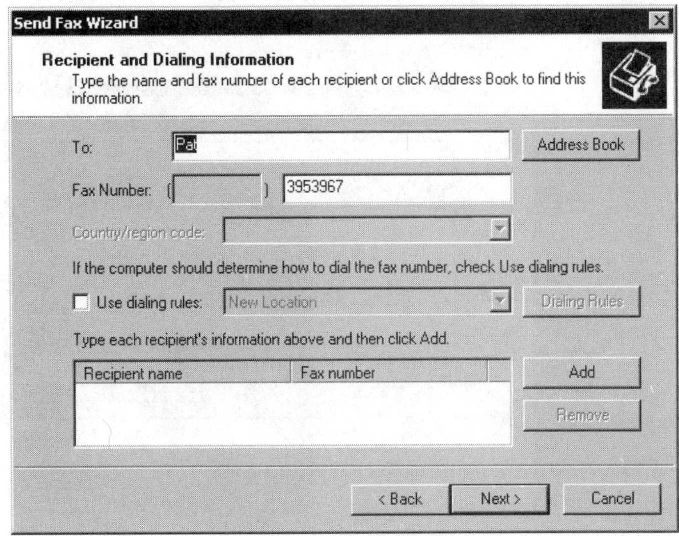

FIGURE 11.10
The Recipient And Dialing Information screen of the Send Fax Wizard

7. Enter the recipient's name and fax number. If the number is in an area code that is different from yours or is long distance, check the Use Dialing Rules check box. If you want to send this fax to multiple recipients, click the Add button, and then enter the information for the other recipients. Click Next when you are done.

8. In the Adding A Cover Page screen (shown in Figure 11.11), you specify a cover page to use for this fax. Four cover page templates are provided with Windows 2000 Professional: confidential, FYI, generic, and urgent templates. If you have created your own cover pages, they will also appear in the Cover Page Template drop-down list. You will also need to enter a subject line on this page before you can send the fax. Optionally, you can type a message in the Note field that will be sent on the cover page. Often, you just need to send a small bit of text information in a fax; using the Note field lets you do this without adding another page. Click Next when you're ready to proceed.

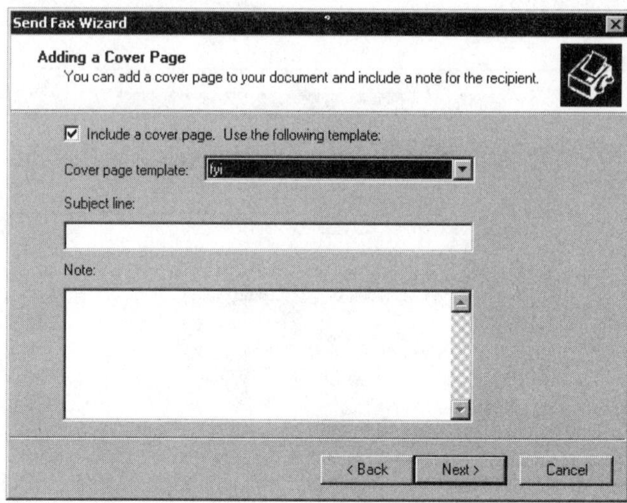

FIGURE 11.11 *Selecting a template for a cover page*

9. Next, you need to decide when to send the fax. On the Scheduling Transmission screen (see Figure 11.12), you have three options:
   - Now
   - When Discount Rates Apply
   - Specific Time In The Next 24 Hours

   If you need to enter a billing code to keep track of the faxes for accounting purposes, enter it in the appropriate field. When you are ready to proceed, click Next.

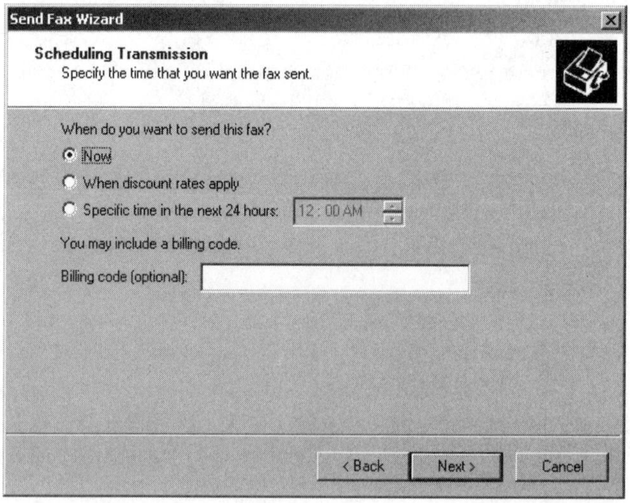

FIGURE 11.12 *The Scheduling Transmission screen lets you control when the fax is sent.*

10. The Completing The Send Fax Wizard screen summarizes your selected options. This gives you one more chance to correct any mistakes you may have made. Click Finish to add your fax to the Fax Queue and to have it be sent at the time you specified.

To make faxing a little easier, you can add a shortcut to your fax printer in the Send To menu. Follow these steps:

1. Choose Start ➢ Settings ➢ Printers to open your Printers folder.
2. Open Explorer and size both windows so that you can see Explorer and your Printers folder simultaneously.
3. In Explorer, browse to your Send To folder, and select it.
4. In the Printers folder, right-click and drag the icon for your fax printer to the Send To folder in the right pane of Explorer. Release the icon in Explorer, and choose Create Shortcut Here from the shortcut menu. You might want to rename the shortcut something other than Shortcut To Fax Printer. It's up to you.
5. Close both the Printers folder and Explorer, and you're all done.

Now when you right-click a document, you will have an option to send a fax on the shortcut menu. When you use this method, Windows 2000 Professional opens the Send Fax Wizard to gather the information about your recipient and the cover page you want to use, and then it will send the fax.

Creating a Cover Page

Are you finding the cover pages provided by Windows 2000 Professional a little dull? They just don't seem to reflect your sense of taste and style? Maybe you want something a little flashier? In this section, you will learn how to create a new custom cover page.

The process starts in Control Panel with the Fax applet. On the Cover Pages tab of the Fax Properties dialog box, you will see a New button that will open the Cover Page Editor. (Remember this from earlier in this chapter?) That's where we're going now. Follow these steps to open the Cover Page Editor:

1. Open the Fax Properties dialog box by double-clicking the Fax icon in Control Panel.
2. Select the Cover Pages tab, and then click the New button to open the Fax Cover Page Editor, as shown in Figure 11.13.

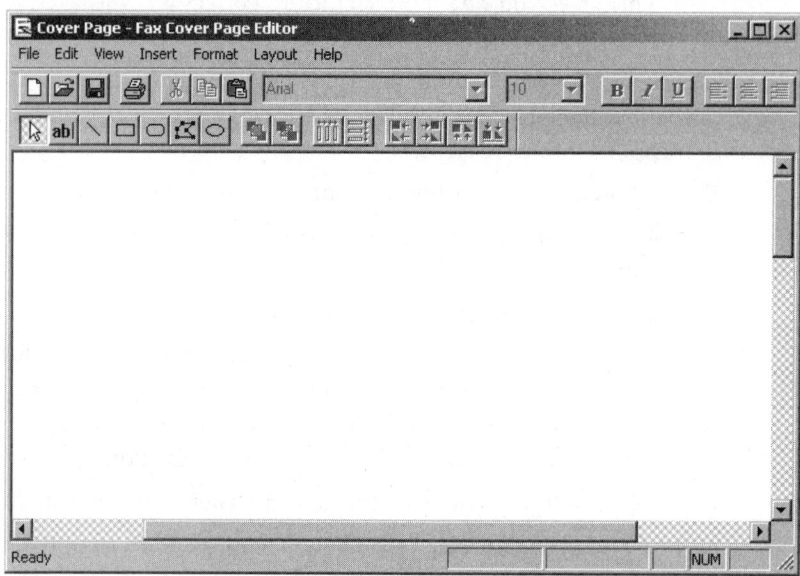

FIGURE 11.13
You can use the Fax Cover Page Editor to create your own custom cover pages.

3. Click OK to close the Tips dialog box. The Tips are worth reading through if you are new to Fax and editing cover pages, but we'll pass on them for now.

The Cover Page Editor is now ready to work with a blank document already loaded for use. The Cover Page Editor looks like a simple word processor, such as WordPad, at first glance. But if you browse through the menus and toolbars a little, you'll soon discover that the editor is more akin to a desktop publishing program. The Cover Page Editor is more concerned with placement of fields on the page and the overall layout and appearance of the page than with entering text. Let's take a closer look at some of the capabilities of this editor.

The Basics of Cover Pages

Every cover page needs certain bits of information: the name of the recipient, the fax number of the recipient, the name and phone number of the sender, and so on. Let's start our exploration of the Cover Page Editor with a look at adding these basic fields, and then we'll move on to some of the more advanced features.

First, let's make it easier to place the fields evenly on the page by turning on grid view: choose View ➢ Grid Lines.

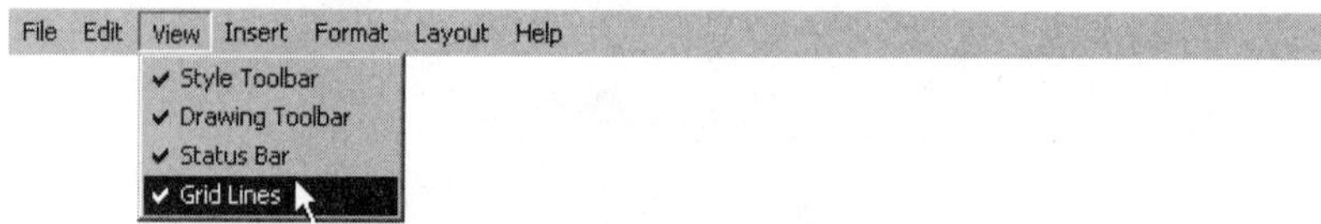

The Insert menu contains commands that place the common fields on your cover page. The fields are dropped into the center of the page, and you will need to drag them to their final destination. The fields are divided into three groups:

- Recipient
- Sender
- Message

The Recipient menu contains fields for the person's name and fax number. You will most likely want to include these in your cover page unless you're certain that the recipient is the only person at that number.

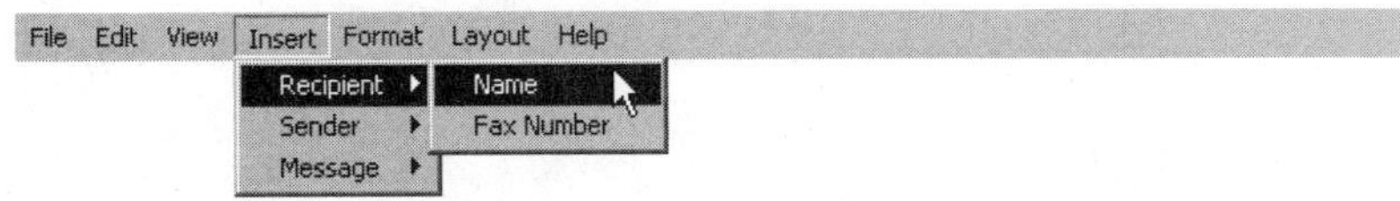

The Sender menu has a few more options. You can mix and match until you find the balance that's right for you. A good minimum might be to include your name and number, though your company name, office location, and department also might be useful.

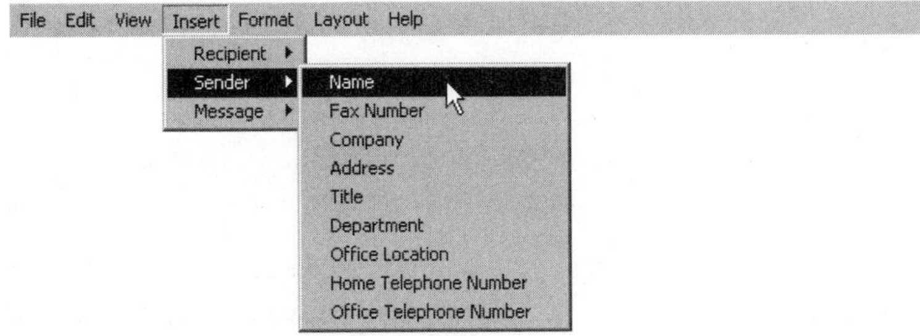

The Message menu has only four options:

- Note
- Subject
- Date/Time Sent
- Number Of Pages

At a minimum, include a Subject field and a Date/Time Sent field. Most cover pages include all four of these options as standard practice. Again, you'll have to decide what works best for you.

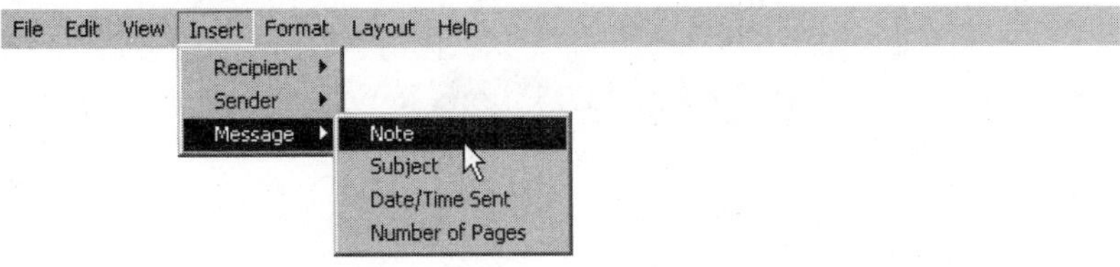

After you insert the fields that you want to include, you can drag them anywhere you want. In Figure 11.14, you can see that the Subject fields are highlighted with drag handles at the corners. These handles signify that you can move the fields by clicking anywhere in them and dragging them to a new position. You can also use the handles to resize the fields.

FIGURE 11.14
You can easily move any of the fields on your cover page.

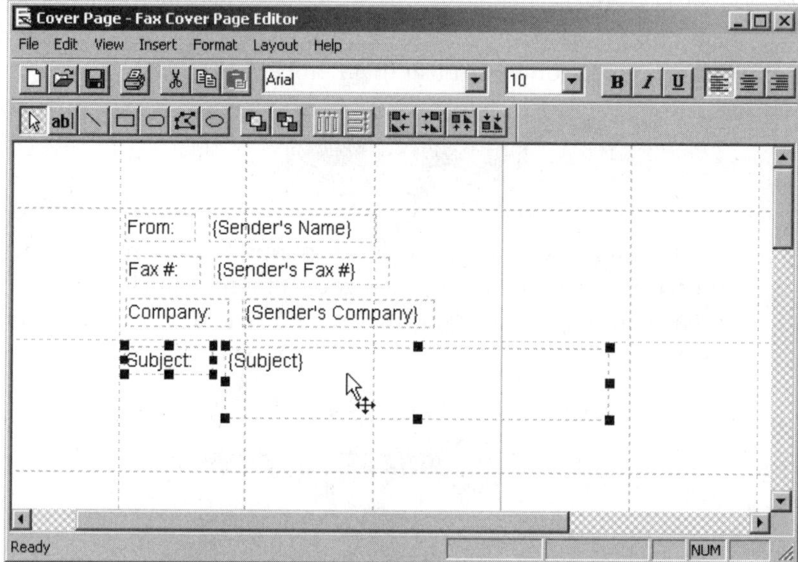

To select multiple fields, click somewhere near the outermost field in the group, and then, holding the mouse button down, drag the cursor until you've selected all the fields in the group. When you let go of the mouse button, all those fields will be selected, and you can move them as a unit.

Advanced Cover Page Editing

Well, now you can create a simple cover page that contains all the necessary information. But just having the basic information is, yawn, so dull. You need to spice it up a bit with some graphics.

You can use the tools on the Drawing toolbar to add some visual interest to your cover page. The shapes and text buttons are much like those in the Paint program included with Windows 2000 Professional, but the Fax Cover Page Editor also includes some tools such as Send To Back and Send To Front that make it simple to create some great layered looks. Figure 11.15 shows some basic shapes and fill styles you can add to your cover page.

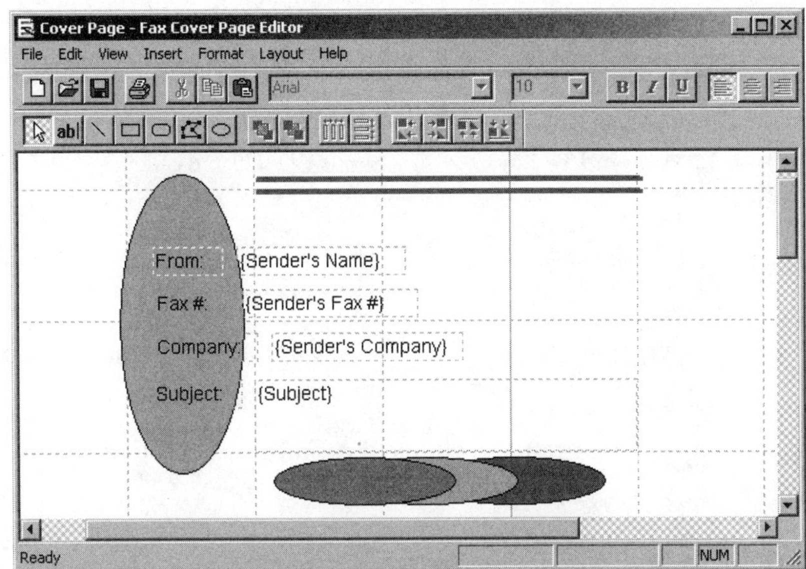

FIGURE 11.15 *You can add simple graphics to your cover page to add interest.*

Here are the buttons you'll be using in the Cover Page Editor:

Select	The standard arrow cursor that you can use to select and move items on the page.
Text	Changes the cursor to a crosshair style and lets you draw a box in which to place text.
Line	Draws lines of different types based on the Format settings.
Rectangle	Draws a simple rectangular shape. If you configure the fill settings before drawing, the rectangle can be filled or colored.
Rounded Rectangle	Draws a rectangle that has rounded corners.
Polygon	Draws, well, *polygons*. That may not be too clear, but each time you click your mouse button you will define a vertex of a polygon. When you are satisfied with the shape, double-click the last "corner" to stop drawing.

	Ellipse	Draws circles or ovals.
	Bring To Front	Moves the selected field or object to the front of the picture or to the top of the stack of images.
	Send To Back	Sends the selected object to the back of the picture.
	Space Across	Evenly spaces the selected objects across the page horizontally.
	Space Down	Evenly distributes the selected objects vertically on the page.
	Align Left	Aligns the selected objects with the left of the page.
	Align Right	Aligns the selected objects with the right side of the page.
	Align Top	Aligns the selected objects with the top of the page.
	Align Bottom	Aligns the selected objects with the bottom of the page.

Using these tools, you can create very complex or very simple cover pages. When you have finished your work of art, be sure to save it so that it will be available in the future.

You should take note of the message on the Cover Pages tab of the Fax Properties dialog box. If your network administrator has decided that only the official company cover pages are going to be allowed, you won't be able to use your personal cover pages.

If you are the one sharing the fax device and want to be certain that people are using the right cover pages, follow these steps:

1. Choose Start ➢ Programs ➢ Accessories ➢ Communications ➢ Fax ➢ Fax Service Management to open the Fax Service Management dialog box.
2. Right-click the Fax Service On Local Computer entry in the Tree pane, and select Properties from the shortcut menu to open the Fax Service On Local Computer Properties dialog box, which is show in Figure 11.16.

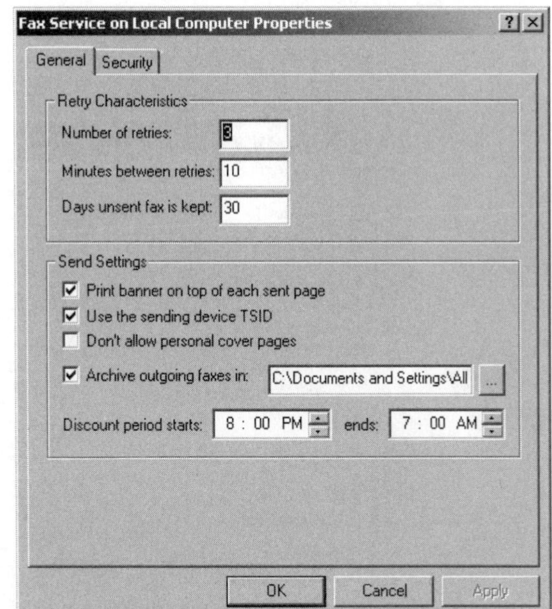

FIGURE 11.16
The Fax Service On Local Computer Properties dialog box

3. Click the Don't Allow Personal Cover Pages check box, and then click OK.

You use the Retry Characteristics section in the General tab to specify the number of times the service will attempt to send a fax if it doesn't succeed the first time. You can set the number of minutes between each retry and the number of days that the unsent fax will be kept in the Fax Queue.

The Send Settings section contains several settings that determine how a fax is sent. In addition to the Don't Allow Personal Cover Pages option, the settings are as follows:

Print Banner On Top Of Each Sent Page Prints a banner containing the sender's information at the top of each page.

Use The Sending Device TSID Tells Windows 2000 Professional to include the specific TSID for the fax device that was used to send the fax.

Archive Outgoing Faxes In Defines the path where all outgoing faxes will be copied. This is particularly useful if your organization needs to maintain copies of all documents.

Discount Period Starts/Ends Defines the period of time when the lowest prices exist for using the phone lines for the fax service.

The Security tab, which is shown in Figure 11.17, contains the permissions settings for Fax. You can fine-tune the permissions for users or for groups defined either on the local computer or in your domain.

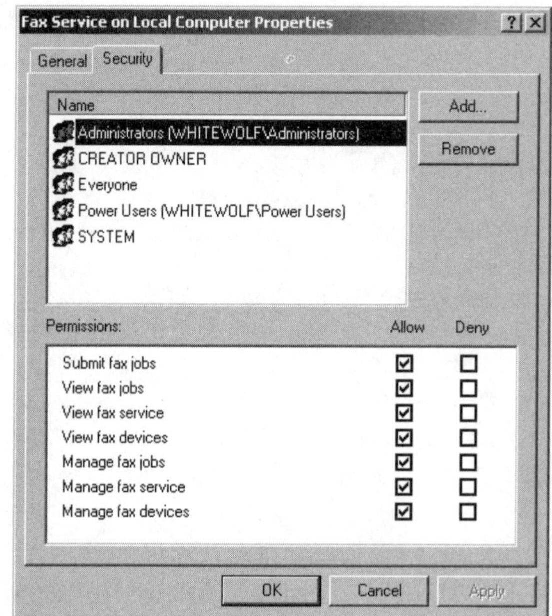

FIGURE 11.17
The Security tab lets you define permissions for Fax.

Using Phone Dialer

In previous versions of Windows, Phone Dialer was a simple application that you could use to place outgoing telephone calls through your modem—if you used the same phone line for voice and data. Whether this was easier than picking up the phone and dialing the number is an issue I won't get into here, but you could use your computer as a telephone if you had a modem, a microphone, a sound card, and speakers.

In Windows 2000 Professional, Phone Dialer has been enhanced. In addition to using it to make voice calls, you can now use it to make video calls and conference calls and to connect to an Internet directory. To open Phone Dialer, choose Start ➢ Programs ➢ Accessories ➢ Communications ➢ Phone Dialer. You'll see the dialog box shown in Figure 11.18.

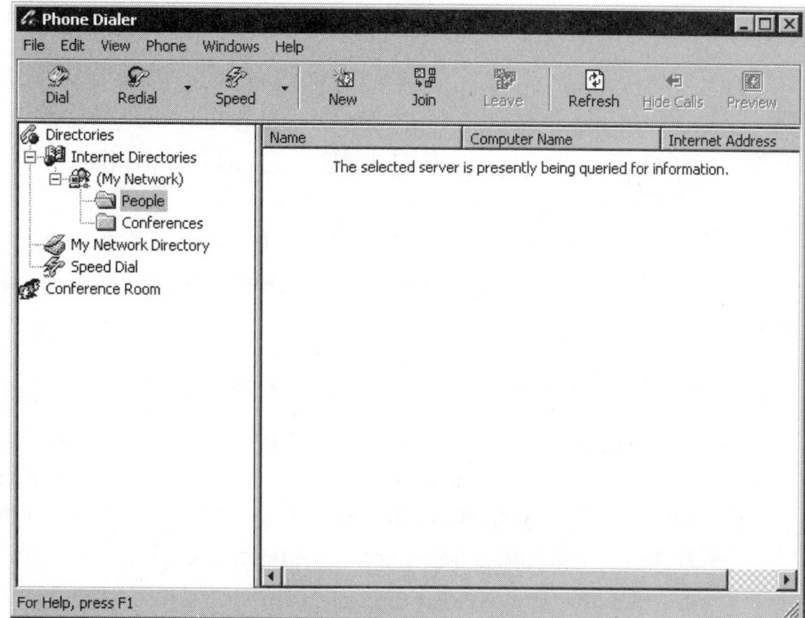

FIGURE 11.18
The Phone Dialer

Placing a Call

To place a simple phone call, follow these steps:

1. Open Phone Dialer, and click Dial to open the Dial dialog box.
2. Click the Phone Call option button, and enter the phone number in the text box.
3. Click Place Call.

That's really all there is to it. If you want to add the number to your speed-dial list, click Add Number To Speed Dial List. To add a number to the list manually, choose Edit ➢ Add To Speed Dial List.

NOTE To receive a call, Phone Dialer must be running.

Connecting to an Internet directory or placing a video call involves a few more steps, and I'll go through those in the next sections.

Configuring Phone Dialer to Link to a Directory

An Internet directory is a listing of people and conferences that can receive Internet calls. The directory can be on your local server or on the Internet. Before you can connect to an Internet directory, you need to add the name of the server to the list on your system. To add a directory and connect to it, follow these steps:

1. In Phone Dialer, choose Edit ➢ Add Directory to open the Add Directory Server dialog box.
2. Enter the server name in the Directory Name box, and click Add.
3. The name now appears in the directories list, and you can click it to access the server.

Configuring Phone Dialer for Video Calls

To fully participate in a video call, you need speakers and a camera installed on your PC. If you do not have a camera, you can view and hear the other participant, but that person cannot see you. For each video call you want to make, follow these steps:

1. In Phone Dialer, choose Edit ➢ Options to open the Options dialog box.
2. Click the Audio/Video tab, select the line to use, and click the Video Playback check box.
3. Click OK.

NOTE You can also make conference calls using Phone Dialer, but conferencing is much more convenient with NetMeeting, which I'll describe later in this chapter.

Connecting with HyperTerminal

HyperTerminal is a utility program you can use to connect to another computer (perhaps one that uses a different operating system such as Unix), to an information service such as the book catalog at your local library, or to a bulletin board. You can use this type of connection to download or transfer files.

TIP HyperTerminal is a class of program known as *terminal emulation software.* In other words, it pretends to be a terminal attached to the remote computer. HyperTerminal is not a Web browser and cannot access Web sites on the Internet. For that particular task, see the description of how to use Internet Explorer in Chapter 12.

Creating a New HyperTerminal Connection

To create the phone numbers and specifics for initiating a HyperTerminal connection, follow these steps:

1. Choose Start ➢ Programs ➢ Accessories ➢ Communications ➢ HyperTerminal to open the Connection Description dialog box in the foreground and the HyperTerminal window in the background.
2. In the Name box, enter the descriptive name you want to assign to this connection, and then choose one of the icons from the selection displayed at the bottom of the dialog box. Click OK to open the Connect To dialog box.
3. Verify the country and area code, type the telephone number you want to use with this connection, and confirm your modem type. Click OK to open the Connect dialog box.
4. Check the phone number for this connection, and if it is incorrect, click Modify to change it. To look at or change any of the settings associated with the phone line or with dialing, click Dialing Properties to open the Phone And Modem Options dialog box. (See Chapter 9 for information about this dialog box.)
5. When you are ready to make the connection, click Dial. You will be connected to the other computer, and a named window for the connection will open. If you do not want to dial now, click Cancel, and the named window for the connection will be displayed, as shown in Figure 11.19.

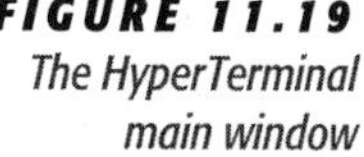

FIGURE 11.19 *The HyperTerminal main window*

The next thing that you see in the window will depend on the service or computer you have connected to; you may be asked to select a terminal type, to enter a password, or to make a selection from a menu. When you are finished, use the appropriate command to log off the remote computer before you close the HyperTerminal window.

Sending and Receiving Files

While using HyperTerminal, you can send and receive files and capture what you see on your screen to your printer. To send a file, follow these steps:

1. Choose Transfer ➢ Send File to open the Send File dialog box.
2. Enter the name of the file in the Filename box, or click Browse to locate it.
3. In the Protocol box, accept the protocol that HyperTerminal suggests, or click the down arrow to select another protocol from the list.

NOTE If you know the specific protocol for the system to which you are connected, select that protocol. If you don't know the protocol, stick with Zmodem, which is a generic, commonly used protocol.

4. Click Send.

To receive a file, follow these steps:

1. Choose Transfer ➢ Receive File to open the Receive File dialog box.
2. Indicate where the received file should be stored, and specify the protocol if necessary.
3. Click Receive.

To capture what you see on your screen to the printer, choose Transfer ➢ Capture To Printer.

Communicating and Sharing with NetMeeting

NetMeeting is an application that you can use to do the following:

- Chat with someone over the Internet, via a telephone or by typing on the screen
- Audio conference
- Videoconference
- Share applications
- Collaborate on documents
- Transfer files

- Draw on the Whiteboard
- Control a remote PC

Obviously, you need the proper equipment to do some of these, and, as we look at the individual features of NetMeeting, I'll point that out.

Starting NetMeeting

Before you can use NetMeeting for the first time, you need to configure it a bit and give it some information about yourself. You do this with a Wizard that starts up the first time you open NetMeeting (choose Start ➢ Programs ➢ Accessories ➢ Communications ➢ NetMeeting). After you complete the setup, NetMeeting places a shortcut to itself on your Desktop so that you need only to click the shortcut to start the program.

Let's go quickly through the steps you need to take before you can work (and have fun) with NetMeeting. The first screen presents an overview of NetMeeting. Take a look at it, click Next, and then follow these steps:

1. In the boxes provided, enter at least your first name, your last name, and your e-mail address, and then click Next.
2. If you want to log on to a directory server whenever you start NetMeeting, click Log On To A Directory Server When NetMeeting Starts. If you don't want your name to appear in the directory listing for that server, click Do Not List My Name In The Directory. Click Next.

NOTE Directory servers are maintained by organizations or companies and provide a list of people who are logged on to the server and have chosen to display their names. If you are connected to the Internet and log on to a directory server, you can click a name in the list to connect to that person. We'll look at exactly how this works later in this chapter and also talk about why you might or might not want to display your name.

3. In the next screen, specify your modem speed or connection mode, and then click Next.
4. If you want quick access to NetMeeting, leave the options selected in this screen so that you display a shortcut to NetMeeting on your Desktop and an icon on the Quick Launch toolbar. Click Next to start the Audio Tuning Wizard, and then click Next again.
5. If you have sound equipment (speakers and a sound card), click the Test button to sample the volume, and then change it as necessary.
6. If you have a microphone, speak into it to ensure that the record volume is correct. Click Next.

7. Click Finish.

You're now ready to start using NetMeeting, which is shown in Figure 11.20.

FIGURE 11.20
The opening NetMeeting window

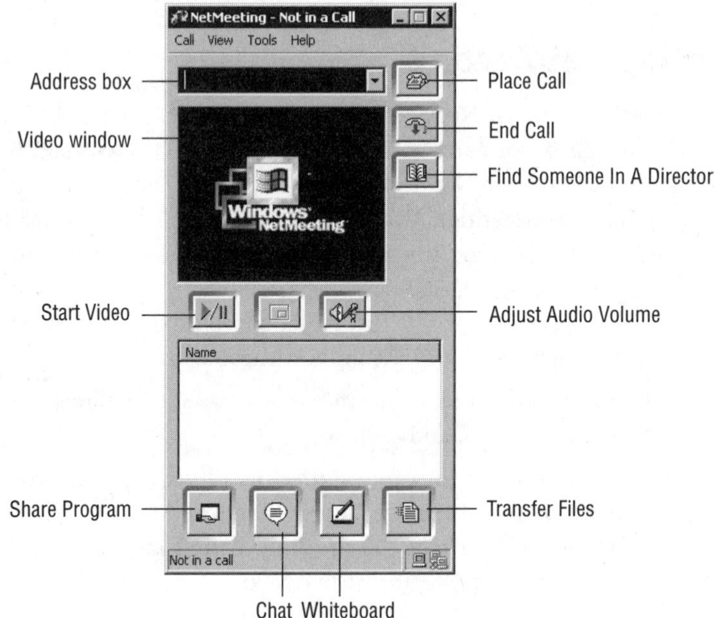

Making a Call

When you make a call in NetMeeting, you can use an e-mail address, a computer IP address, a computer name, or a modem phone number for the person you are calling. The only requirement is that both people must be running NetMeeting.

When you make the connection, you can communicate in several ways, depending on your equipment:

- If both people have microphones, sound cards, and speakers, you can talk just as you would over the telephone.
- If both people have microphones, sound cards, speakers, video cards, and video cameras, you can talk and be seen on the screen.
- If you don't have any of this equipment or just prefer it, you can communicate via the Chat application.

NOTE You can see video even if you don't have a camera, and you can hear another person who is using a microphone if you have speakers. Video runs in the Video window.

To make a call, follow these steps:

1. Click the Place Call button to open the Place A Call dialog box:

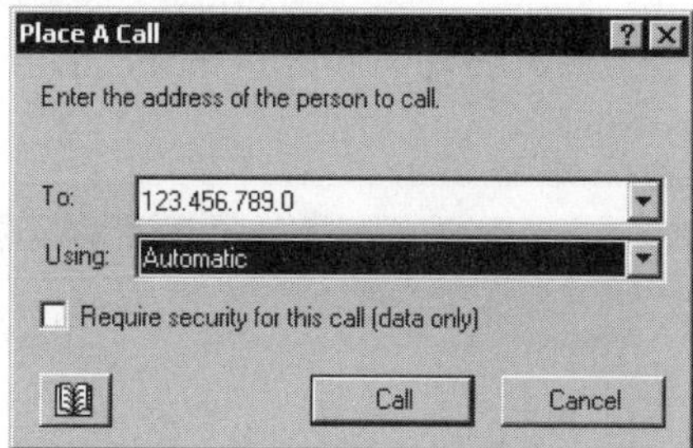

2. In the To box, enter the address (an IP address, an e-mail address, a modem phone number, or the name of the computer).
3. Click Call.

Finding an IP Address

An IP (Internet Protocol) address is a unique number that identifies your computer on the Internet; for example, `209.254.117.155`. The first three parts of this number refer to your ISP (Internet Service Provider), and the last three digits refer to your computer. Unless you have a permanent connection to the Internet such as your ISP has, each time you log on you are assigned a different IP address. As I've mentioned, using an IP address is one way to connect through NetMeeting with others who are on the Internet.

To find out what your current IP address is, follow these steps:

1. Choose Start ➢ Programs ➢ Accessories ➢ Command Prompt to open the Command Prompt window.
2. At the prompt, type **`ipconfig`** and press Enter to open the IP Configuration dialog box.

Now you can share your IP address with someone who wants to call you. We've done this via e-mail before, and it works great. If the person you want to call is not running Windows 2000 Professional but Windows 95/98 instead, they can type **`winipcfg`** to find out their IP address. Remember, though, every time you disconnect from the Internet or lose your connection, you lose that IP address. You'll get another one when you connect again.

Using the Chat Application

If you've visited chat rooms on the Web, you know how to use chat. What you type appears on the screen for you and others to see. Figure 11.21 shows the Chat window. To open Chat, click the Chat button in the main NetMeeting window.

FIGURE 11.21
Chatting in NetMeeting

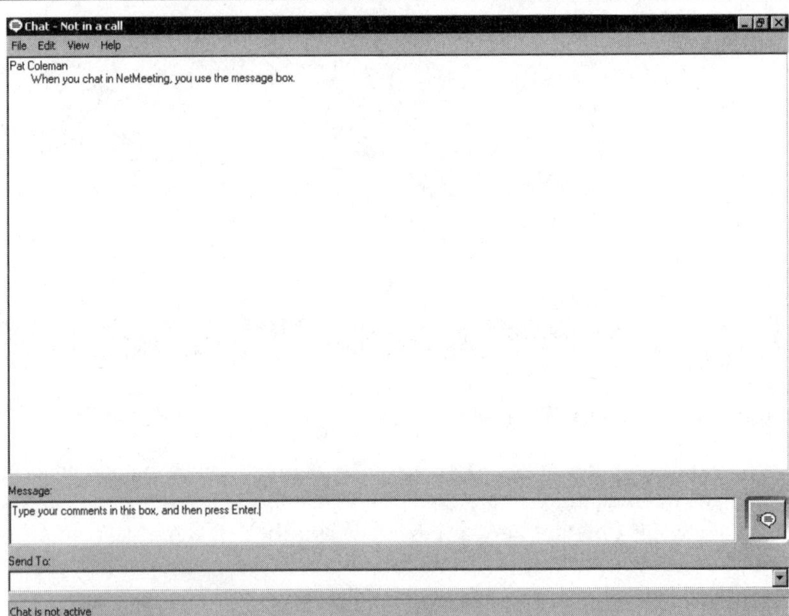

To use Chat, you need to know only the following:

- Click in the Message box, type, and press Enter to send your words of wisdom.
- If the session involves more than one person, click the down arrow in the Send To box to specify whether to send your chat lines to an individual or to the whole group.
- To save the contents of a Chat session, choose File ➢ Save As.
- To end a session, close the Chat window.

TIP To customize the format of the Chat window, such as the fonts used and the display of information, choose View ➢ Options.

Using Directory Servers

As I mentioned earlier, a directory server is a service maintained by an organization or a company, and when you connect to it, you can see the names, e-mail addresses, and so on of all the others who are logged on and have chosen to display their names. You can also see whether they are available for video and audio transmission.

By default, NetMeeting points you to the Microsoft Internet Directory service. To log on to it, choose Call ➢ Directory, which opens the Find Someone dialog box, as shown in Figure 11.22. Before you can use the new Microsoft Internet Directory, you must download and install MSN Messenger. Follow the on-screen instructions.

FIGURE 11.22
The Find Someone dialog box

Hosting a Meeting

You can also use NetMeeting to hold a meeting. To set this up, choose Call ➢ Host Meeting to open the Host A Meeting dialog box, as shown in Figure 11.23. Specify the parameters for the meeting, such as whether only you can place or accept calls, share applications, and so on, and then click OK. Now others can call you or you can call others. The meeting lasts until you end it (or until you or the others lose their connections).

FIGURE 11.23
Setting the guidelines for a meeting

Using Video

When you are receiving or sending video, images are displayed in the video window. To set up video transmissions, choose Tools ➢ Options to open the Options dialog box, and click the Video tab, which is shown in Figure 11.24. You can specify when to send and receive video, the size of the image, its quality (do you want speed or clarity?), and the properties of your camera.

FIGURE 11.24
Setting up video transmission

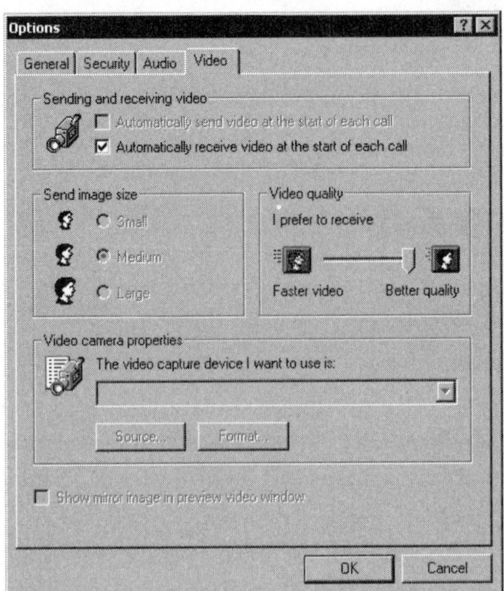

Sharing Applications

While you are in a call or in a meeting, you can share documents and applications. To do so, open the program you want to share, and then click the Share Program button to open the Sharing dialog box, as shown in Figure 11.25. Specify the program to share and who will control it, and then click Close. Others will now be able to see and interact with you and your application.

FIGURE 11.25
Getting ready to share an application

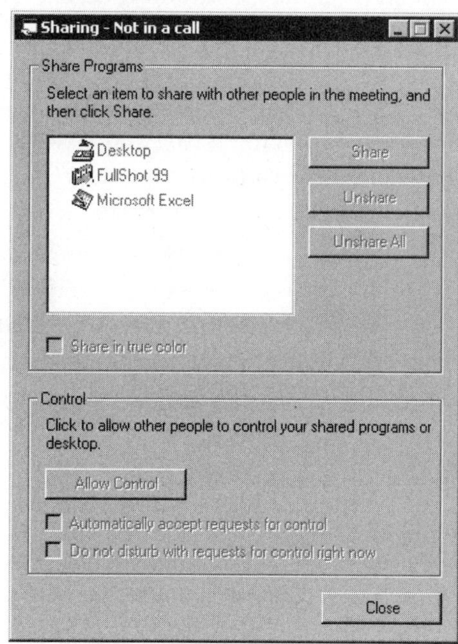

NOTE To share the Whiteboard, click the Whiteboard button.

Transferring Files

Whenever you are in a call, you can transfer files. Simply click the Transfer Files button to open the File Transfer dialog box, and follow these steps:

1. Click Add File to select the file to send.
2. Click the name of the person to whom you want to send the file.
3. Click Send All.

To receive a file, click Accept. Received files are stored in the Received File folder in the NetMeeting folder, unless you specify otherwise.

PC Remote Control with NetMeeting

NetMeeting includes a feature called Remote Desktop Sharing (RDS). Suppose you want to control a computer named Slave from a computer named Master, using RDS. Here's an overview of what you need to do that:

1. Set up Slave to accept incoming RDS connections. I'll talk more specifically about how to do that below. (You must have an administrator-level account on Slave.)
2. Master and Slave must be connected somehow. The easiest way to do a remote connection is for both Master and Slave to be on the Internet or on the same corporate network. Alternatively, RDS can work over a temporary connection: you can set up Slave with Dial-Up Networking to accept incoming calls and then have Master call Slave before seizing control with RDS.
3. Once Master and Slave are connected, you sit at Master and "call" Slave using NetMeeting. Slave answers, but only because you've told it in Step 1 to be ready to receive incoming NetMeeting calls.
4. Slave prompts you for a password. You type the account name and password of the Administrator account.
5. You then see a window on your screen that contains Slave's Desktop.

You can now watch what the person sitting at Slave is doing. But your connection isn't passive—you can move your mouse or press keys on the keyboard and override whatever Slave's local operator is doing. Here are the specifics.

NOTE Before you can use NetMeeting on either Master or Slave, you've got to set up NetMeeting, as discussed earlier in this chapter.

Setting Up Slave to Allow a Remote Computer to Control It

Slave now has NetMeeting running but won't allow other machines to take control of it. To set that up, follow these steps:

1. In NetMeeting, choose Tools ➢ Remote Desktop Sharing to start the Remote Desktop Sharing Wizard.
2. Click Next to display a screen that tells you that anyone wanting to connect to this machine and control the machine remotely must be an administrator; click Next once you've read the message.

3. The next screen lets you set up NetMeeting with a password-protected screen saver. The idea is that if some is sitting at a distant computer and you use RDS to control this computer (Slave), forget that you're controlling Slave from your distant computer (Master), and walk away, then someone could sit down at Master and have free rein of Slave. Using a password-protected screen saver prevents anyone sitting down at Master after some inactivity from doing anything with Slave without reentering the password of your Administrator account. Choose the options you prefer, and click Next.
4. Click Finish.

Listening for Incoming Calls

Look in the status area on the Taskbar, and you'll see a small icon that looks like a globe; this globe indicates that NetMeeting is ready to receive an incoming call. But that's only a NetMeeting call—that is, a voice-and-perhaps-video connection. Slave is still not ready to accept remote control. Here are the next steps:

1. Close NetMeeting.
2. Right-click the NetMeeting icon in the status area, and choose Activate Remote Desktop Sharing from the shortcut menu.

Setting Up Master to Control Slave

Now let's set up another computer called Master that will remotely control Slave. Follow these steps:

1. Set up NetMeeting on Master, running through NetMeeting's setup Wizard. You needn't run through the Remote Desktop Sharing Wizard.
2. Ensure that Master has connectivity with Slave. Pinging Slave is a nice simple way to check connectivity.
3. With NetMeeting open on Master, choose Call ➢ New Call to open the Place A Call dialog box.
4. In the To field, enter the IP address or DNS name of the Slave machine. Check the Require Security For This Call (Data Only) check box, and then click Call.
5. When Master finds Slave, you'll be prompted for an account name and password. Enter the name and password of any account that Slave recognizes as an administrator, and you'll see a window on your screen that is Slave's Desktop. You now remotely control Slave from Master.

Summary

In this chapter, we've taken a quick look at four communications programs included with Windows 2000 Professional: Phone Dialer, HyperTerminal, Fax, and NetMeeting. As I said at the outset, you may never have occasion to use any of these applications, or you may need only one of them from time to time. All are easy to learn and use, and if you frequently use any of them, you'll be up to speed with it in no time.

Now let's turn our attention to something you'll probably use every day—Internet Explorer.

CHAPTER 12

Web Browsing with Internet Explorer

FEATURING:

Obviously, the most important thing about Internet Explorer is not the program itself but all the resources you can access using it. And, to be completely honest about it, Internet Explorer is so easy to use that you hardly need a how-to book, a manual, or even this chapter. If you know how to open any Windows 2000 Professional program, you know how to open Internet Explorer, and you can start browsing immediately by simply clicking links.

Thus, in this chapter I'm going to move briskly through the tasks you most commonly perform with Internet Explorer. As I proceed, I'll point out some new features of version 5 and show you how to expand on what comes naturally. For example, you probably know that you can access an Internet resource by typing its URL in the Address bar. That's rather easy in the case of something such as `www.microsoft.com`, but what about `http://finance.yahoo.com/q?s=msft+brka+csco+ald+mmm+sci+lhsp+yhoo&d-v1`? In this chapter, you'll see that in Internet Explorer you have at least a half-dozen ways to access a lengthy URL such as this without ever typing it.

The good news is that as the cost of personal computers continues to drop, browsers such as Internet Explorer become easier to use and more powerful. The only bad news is that most of us usually don't have enough hours in the day even to skim the surface of the abundance of the Internet. You can, however, use the skills you acquire here to streamline your activities and make more efficient use of your time.

Starting Internet Explorer

Unless you've been hiding in a cave and forgot to take along your cell phone, TV, or laptop, you've heard about the integration of Windows and Internet Explorer. Nowhere is this more apparent than in the myriad ways in which you can start Internet Explorer.

When you first start Internet Explorer after installing Windows 2000 Professional, you'll see the start page shown in Figure 12.1. Later in this chapter, you'll see how to specify any page you want as your start page. In the next section, I'll identify and discuss the components of the Internet Explorer interface.

FIGURE 12.1
You can retain the page at www.msn.com as your start page or select any other page that suits your fancy or interests.

From the Desktop

From the Desktop, you can start Internet Explorer in three ways:

- Click the Launch Internet Explorer Browser button on the Quick Launch toolbar.
- Double-click the Internet Explorer shortcut.
- Choose Start ➢ Programs ➢ Internet Explorer.

From a Hyperlink

You can also start Internet Explorer from any document in any Windows application that includes a hyperlink if Internet Explorer is your default browser. For example, if you receive an e-mail that includes a URL in the body of the message, simply click the URL to open Internet Explorer at that page. A hyperlink can be text or an image, and it is usually underlined and in a color that is different from normal text.

NOTE If you have only one browser, Internet Explorer, installed, it is your default browser. If you have more than one browser installed, you'll need to specify one as the default. I'll show you how to do this later in this chapter.

From Windows Explorer

In Windows Explorer, HTML files are indicated by the Internet Explorer icon, and when you double-click such a file, it opens in Internet Explorer.

You can also open any file on your hard drive, a floppy, or your network by choosing File ➢ Open. If it is not an HTML file, it will open in its associated program.

A Look Behind the Scenes: Viewing HTML Pages

HTML is the abbreviation for HyperText Markup Language, the programming language that is used to create Web pages. HTML uses tags to tell the browser how to display the page on the screen. Tags are enclosed in angle brackets, and most come in pairs. For example, the <H1> tag defines a first-level heading, like this:

<H1>This is a level 1 heading.</H1>

An HTML file is really just a plain text file that can be created with a text editor such as Notepad or with a program such as Microsoft FrontPage. To view the HTML behind any page you open in Internet Explorer, choose View ➢ Source. The file is displayed in Notepad and looks similar to the following:

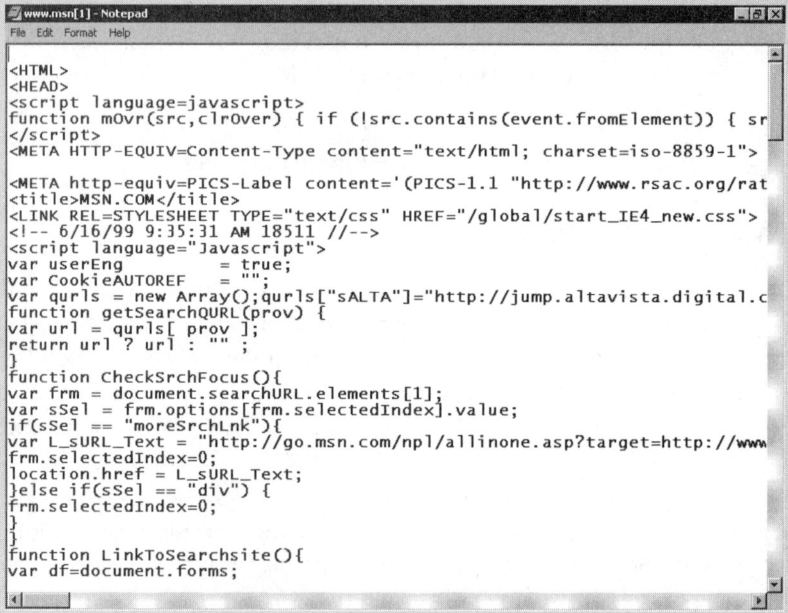

www.msn[1] - Notepad

File Edit Format Help

```
<HTML>
<HEAD>
<script language=javascript>
function mOvr(src,clrOver) { if (!src.contains(event.fromElement)) { sr
</script>
<META HTTP-EQUIV=Content-Type content="text/html; charset=iso-8859-1">

<META http-equiv=PICS-Label content='(PICS-1.1 "http://www.rsac.org/rat
<title>MSN.COM</title>
<LINK REL=STYLESHEET TYPE="text/css" HREF="/global/start_IE4_new.css">
<!-- 6/16/99 9:35:31 AM 18511 //-->
<script language="Javascript">
var userEng          = true;
var CookieAUTOREF    = "";
var qurls = new Array();qurls["sALTA"]="http://jump.altavista.digital.c
function getSearchQURL(prov) {
var url = qurls[ prov ];
return url ? url : "" ;
}
function CheckSrchFocus(){
var frm = document.searchURL.elements[1];
var sSel = frm.options[frm.selectedIndex].value;
if(sSel == "moreSrchLnk"){
var L_sURL_Text = "http://go.msn.com/npl/allinone.asp?target=http://www
frm.selectedIndex=0;
location.href = L_sURL_Text;
}else if(sSel == "div") {
frm.selectedIndex=0;
}
}
function LinkToSearchsite(){
var df=document.forms;
```

Continued

To return to Internet Explorer and the page displayed in the browser, click the Close button in Notepad.

If you're interested in learning more about HTML and creating Web pages, check out the following Sybex titles: *Mastering FrontPage 2000* (or *Mastering FrontPage 98*) and *Mastering HTML 4, Second Edition.*

Getting Help

You have at your fingertips several ways to get help with Internet Explorer. For starters, choose Help ➢ Contents And Index. As in Windows Help, enter a word or phrase to search for a topic. If you want to search the Web for help, choose Help ➢ Online Support. If you're connected to the Internet, you'll go to the Microsoft Product Support Services page at `http://support.microsoft.com/directory/`.

If you're new to Internet Explorer, choose Help ➢ Tour. Click any hyperlink to get information about that topic. If you're new to Internet Explorer but have used Netscape Navigator, choose Help ➢ For Netscape Users to access a list of tips and corresponding terminology.

A Quick Tour of Internet Explorer

The Internet Explorer window has much in common with other Windows application windows: vertical and horizontal scroll bars display as necessary, you can size various portions of the window by clicking and dragging, and you can display a ToolTip by placing the mouse cursor over an item. In the upper-right corner are the Minimize, Restore, and Close buttons.

In this section, we'll look briefly at the components of the Internet Explorer window, and in later sections we'll look at some specific components that you can use to enrich and supplement your browsing experience. Figure 12.2 is your components roadmap.

FIGURE 12.2
Many Internet Explorer window components are similar to those in other Windows applications.

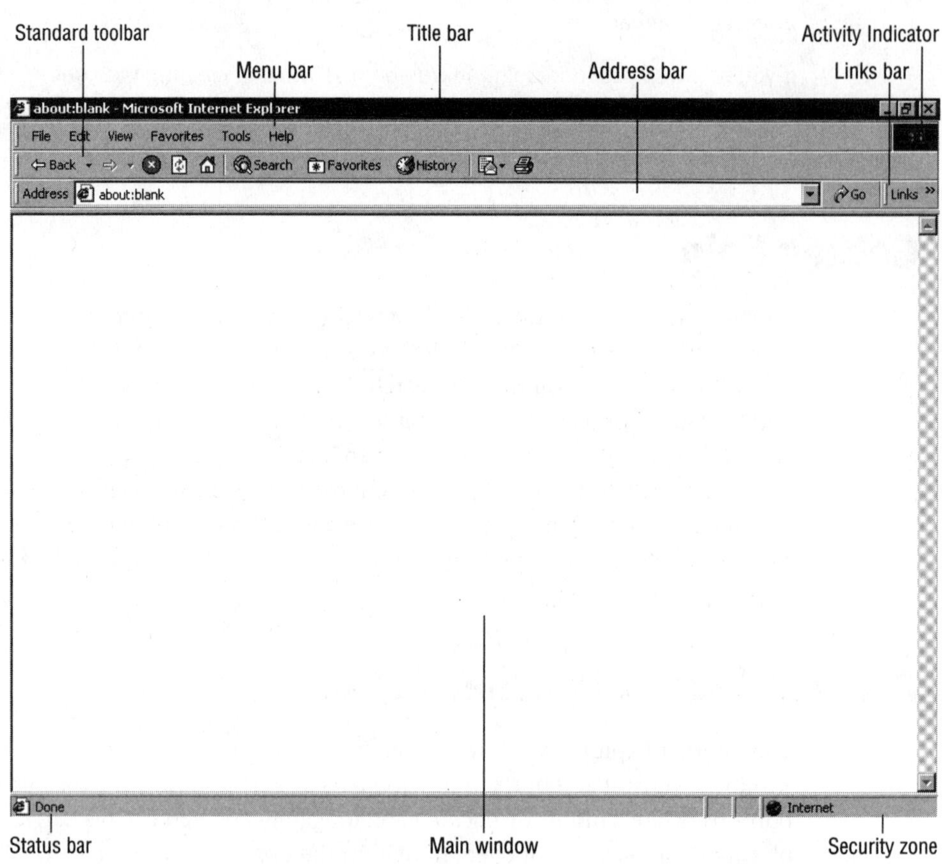

Here is a general description of each component:

Title bar Displays the name of the current Web page or other file that is displayed in the Internet Explorer window.

Menu bar Contains a set of menus, some of which contain the same items that appear on that menu in other Windows programs.

Standard toolbar Contains several buttons that correspond to items on the Menu bar, as well as navigation buttons such as Back, Forward, and Home.

Address bar Contains a drop-down box in which you can enter or select the resource you want to access.

Links bar Contains a short list of preselected hyperlinks. You can add to this list.

Activity Indicator Is animated when Internet Explorer is sending or receiving data.

Main window Displays the resource—Web page, document file, image, and so on—that you most recently accessed.

Status bar Displays information about the current state of Internet Explorer.

- When you choose a menu command, the status bar displays a description of what it does.
- When you point to a hyperlink, the status bar displays its URL.
- When you click a hyperlink to open another page, the status bar displays a series of messages related to the progress of that process.

Security zone Displays the security zone currently active. I'll show you how to select security zones later in this chapter.

Moving around the Web

To even begin to describe what you'll find on the Web these days is an exercise in futility. What was suspect a year ago is commonplace today, and what appears today to be well in the future may be up and running tomorrow. You can buy and sell almost any commodity, search the world's vast storehouse of information, play blackjack, chat with somebody on another continent, witness the birth of a baby, locate a lost relative, book a cruise, scout new business opportunities—the list is indeed endless. And, as the saying goes, one thing leads to another.

The items on the Internet Explorer toolbars are your best friends in this quest, and in this section we'll take a look at their typical and not-necessarily-so-typical uses.

Going to Specific Sites

You know, of course, that you can enter a URL in the Address bar and press Enter to go to that site. You are probably also aware that you can click the down arrow at the right of the Address bar, select a URL from the list, and press Enter. (You can click Go instead of pressing Enter if you want.) And you may have noticed that on occasion when you start to type an address, it sort of finishes itself for you. That's the AutoComplete feature at work. If the address is the one you want, simply press Enter, and you're on your way to that page. If you wanted another site, just continue typing.

TIP AutoComplete also comes to your aid in just about any other field you fill in on a Web page—stock quotes, search queries, passwords, and so on. You can often click a drop-down list and make a selection. This information is encrypted and stored on your computer and is not accessible to Web sites, so you needn't be concerned about security when you use AutoComplete. AutoComplete is enabled by default. To disable it, choose Tools ➢ Internet Options to open the Internet Options dialog box, and select the Content tab. Click AutoComplete to open the AutoComplete Settings dialog box, and clear specific items.

Internet Explorer assumes that when you enter a URL in the Address bar you want to go to a Web page or some other HTML document. Therefore, whether you enter `http://www.sybex.com` or `www.sybex.com`, you'll reach the Sybex Web site. If you want to access another type of resource, such as an FTP archive, a Telnet host, or a Gopher server, you'll need to enter the full URL, for example, `ftp://ftp.archive.edu`.

TIP If you want to edit only part of an address that's already displayed in the Address bar, place the cursor in the Address bar, hold down Ctrl, and press the right or left arrow to jump forward or backward to the next separator character (\\ \ . , ? or +).

You can also run a program from the Address bar. Simply type its path (for example, **`C:\Program Files\FrontPage.exe`**), and press Enter. To find a file using the Address bar, enter the drive letter (for example, **`D:`**), and press Enter. Internet Explorer opens a window similar to that shown in Figure 12.3.

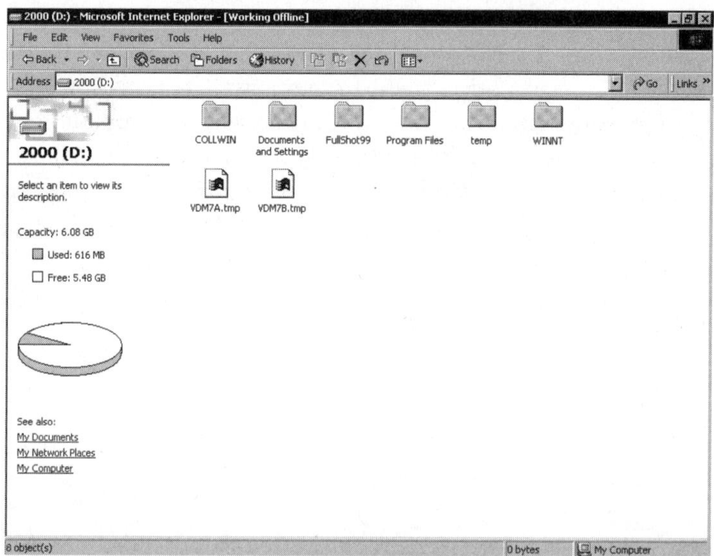

FIGURE 12.3
Finding a file with Internet Explorer

In addition, you can search from the Address bar. Enter the word or phrase you want to find and click the Search button. We'll look at searching in detail later in this chapter.

Using and Managing Links

The term *link* is short for hyperlink, which is a term, a phrase, an image, or a symbol that forms a connection with another resource that can reside on your local computer, your local network, or the Internet. You may also hear these connections referred to as hot links, hypertext links, or hypermedia. They all mean the same thing, and clicking one takes you to that resource. Links are the heart and soul of the Internet, and in the incipient days of browser development, they gave rise to ponderous discussions about the linear structure of books, film, and speech versus the nonlinear format of the World Wide Web.

Today, we seldom discuss links; we just take them for granted and click. In Internet Explorer, textual links are underlined and are usually in a different color from normal text. After you click such a link to jump to that resource and then return to the page on which the link resides, the link will be in yet another color, indicating that you've "visited" it.

To find out if an image or a symbol is a link, place the mouse pointer over it. If it's a link, the pointer becomes a hand with a pointing finger.

Moving Backward and Forward

In the past, you could easily get lost following links. You still can lose your way when you're just mindlessly surfing the Net, but Internet Explorer provides several tools that can help you retrace your steps, starting with the drop-down list in the Address bar, as I discussed in the previous section. Perhaps even handier are the Back and Forward buttons.

Click the Back button to return to the page you just visited. Click the down arrow next to the Back button to select from the last four pages you visited.

Click the Forward button to return to the page you visited before you clicked the Back button. Click the down arrow next to the Forward button to select from the last few pages you visited.

Adding Your Own Links to the Links Bar

Another way to keep track of links that you follow and want to revisit is to add them to the Links bar. When you first install Windows 2000 Professional, the Links bar contains the following:

- Customize Links, which takes you to a Microsoft page that gives you information on how to add, remove, and rearrange items on the Links bar

- Free Hotmail, which takes you to a page where you can sign up for a Hotmail e-mail account
- Windows, which takes you to the Microsoft Windows site

To add a link, simply drag it from the Web page to the Links bar. To remove a link, right-click it and choose Delete from the shortcut menu. To rearrange items on the Links bar, click the item and then drag it to a new location.

Another quick and easy way to keep track of pages you want to revisit is to add them to your Favorites list, and we'll look at how to do that in the following section.

Keeping Track of Your Favorite Sites

As I've mentioned, Internet Explorer provides several devices you can use to prevent getting lost in cyberspace, and a particularly handy one is the Favorites bar. To open it, click the Favorites button on the Standard toolbar, or choose Favorites from the menu bar. Figure 12.4 shows the screen you'll see if you click the Favorites button, and Figure 12.5 shows the Favorites menu.

FIGURE 12.4
Click the Favorites button to open the Favorites bar.

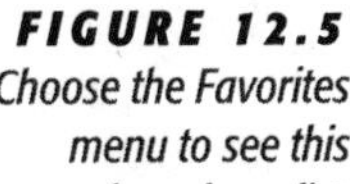

FIGURE 12.5
Choose the Favorites menu to see this drop-down list.

Adding a Site to Your Favorites List

Clicking a Favorites item takes you to that resource. Initially you'll see the following items on the Favorites menu or in the Favorites bar:

- Links, which opens the same list that you see on the Links bar
- Media, which contains links that take you to a variety of sites such as Disney, ESPN Sports, MSNBC, and the Windows Media Showcase, a page where you can search for online audio and video
- MSN, which takes you to the msn.com home page
- Radio Station Guide, which takes you to a page where you can click a button to hear a radio Webcast from stations such as the BBC and CNN
- Web Events, which takes you to the WindowsMedia.com page, where you can access audio and video headlines, check the weather forecast and your horoscope, get stock quotes, and so on

NOTE On some Web pages, you will see a suggestion that you "bookmark" this page. Netscape and some other Web browsers refer to a list of sites that you want to revisit as a bookmark list rather than as a Favorites list.

To add a site to your Favorites list, follow these steps:

1. Go to the site you want to add.
2. Click Favorites to open the Favorites bar.

3. Click Add to open the Add Favorite dialog box:

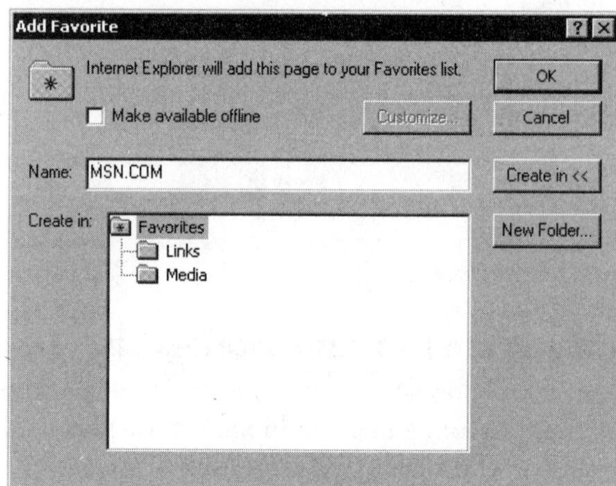

4. If you want to place this page in your top-level Favorites menu, click OK. If you want to add it to an existing folder, click Create In, select a folder, and click OK. If you want to create a new folder for this item, click New Folder, enter a name for the folder, and click OK.
5. In the Add Favorites dialog box, Internet Explorer provides a name for this Favorite site. To give the site another name in your Favorites list, replace the default name with the name you want.
6. Click OK.

You can also add items to your Favorites list in some other ways:

- Right-click a link, and choose Add To Favorites from the shortcut menu.
- Right-click on the current page outside a link, and choose Add To Favorites from the shortcut menu to add that page.
- Drag and drop a link on a Web page to the Favorites button on the Standard toolbar.

Maintaining Your Favorites List

You'll find out soon enough that your Favorites list will grow quickly, and before too long the titles that seemed patently clear when you added the site to the list will, unfortunately, be meaningless. In addition, you may no longer really care what's happening on the Learn2.com site. To keep your list manageable, you need to do some periodic housekeeping, weeding out what you don't want and rearranging or retitling what you do keep so that it is meaningful.

Deleting a site from your Favorites list is simple: right-click it in the list, and choose Delete from the shortcut menu. You might, however, want to get in the habit of following the link before you right-click—just in case the site is more important than you remembered and you want to keep it in the list.

To move an item to another place in the list or to another folder, simply click and drag it. To create a new folder, click Organize to open the Organize Favorites dialog box, and click Create Folder.

To rename an item, right-click it and choose Rename from the shortcut menu. Type the new name, and press Enter.

Returning to Where You Were

Yet another way to keep track of where you've been and to quickly revisit sites of interest is the History list. To display it, click the History button on the Standard toolbar. You'll open the History bar, which will look similar to that in Figure 12.6. Simply click a link to go to that page. Click a folder to see pages in that site that have links in the History list. To specify how many days you want to keep links in the History list, choose Tools ➢ Internet Options, and on the General tab change the number in the Days To Keep Pages In History box.

FIGURE 12.6
You can use the History bar to see where you went today and in previous days and weeks.

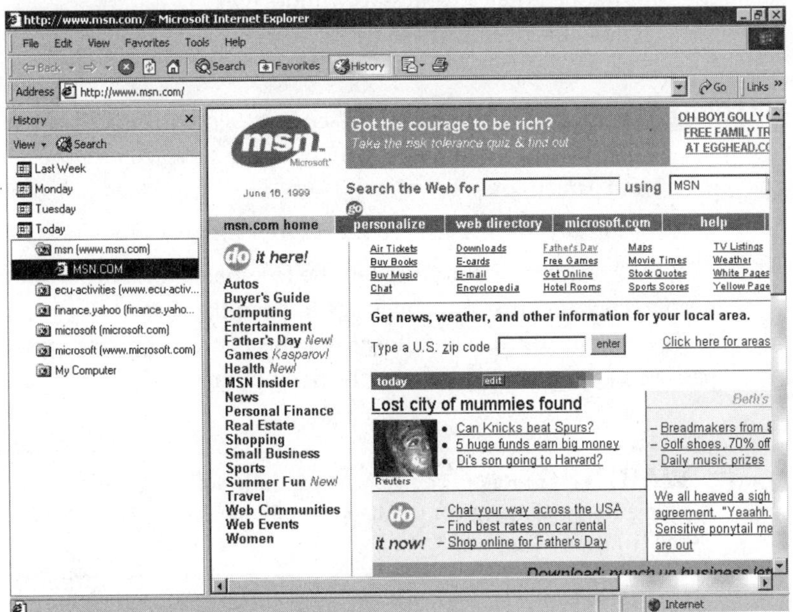

You can display the items in the History list by date, by site, by most visited, and by the order in which you visited sites today. Click the View down arrow to choose an order. If you want to search for something on the History list, click Search, enter a word or a phrase, and click Search Now.

To delete an item from the History list, right-click it, and choose Delete from the shortcut menu. To clear the History list completely, click the Clear History button on the General tab of the Internet Options dialog box.

TIP If you want really quick access to a Web site, create a shortcut to it on the Desktop. Right-click in an empty area of the page, and choose Create Shortcut. You'll see a message that the shortcut will be placed on your Desktop. Now all you need to do to open Internet Explorer and connect to that page is to double-click the shortcut.

Reading Mail and News and Sharing Pages

If you hear the You've Got Mail beep as you're exploring the Internet, you can quickly open your Inbox in Outlook Express by clicking the Mail button on the Standard toolbar and choosing Read Mail. To check a newsgroup, click the Mail button, and choose Read News. To compose an e-mail message, click the Mail button, and choose New Message to open the New Message window.

To send a link, follow these steps:

1. Open the page.
2. Click the Mail button, and choose Send A Link. The New Message window opens with the link in the body of the message and the site title in the Subject and Attach lines.
3. Address your message, compose your message, and click Send.

If your recipient is connected to the Internet and has a Web browser, they merely need to click the link in the message to open that page.

To send the page itself, follow the same steps but choose Send Page. The current page you are viewing appears in the body of the message.

WARNING Before you willy-nilly include Web pages in your e-mail, be sure that your recipient's e-mail program can handle HTML messages. For more information about e-mail and HTML, see Chapter 13.

Listening to the Radio over the Internet

If you've used previous versions of Internet Explorer, you'll find something new on the menu when you choose View ➢ Toolbars—the Radio toolbar, which is shown in Figure 12.7. Windows Radio is a feature that gives you direct access to radio stations throughout the United States and around the world through the Internet.

FIGURE 12.7 *To tune in to music or news of your choice, use the Radio toolbar.*

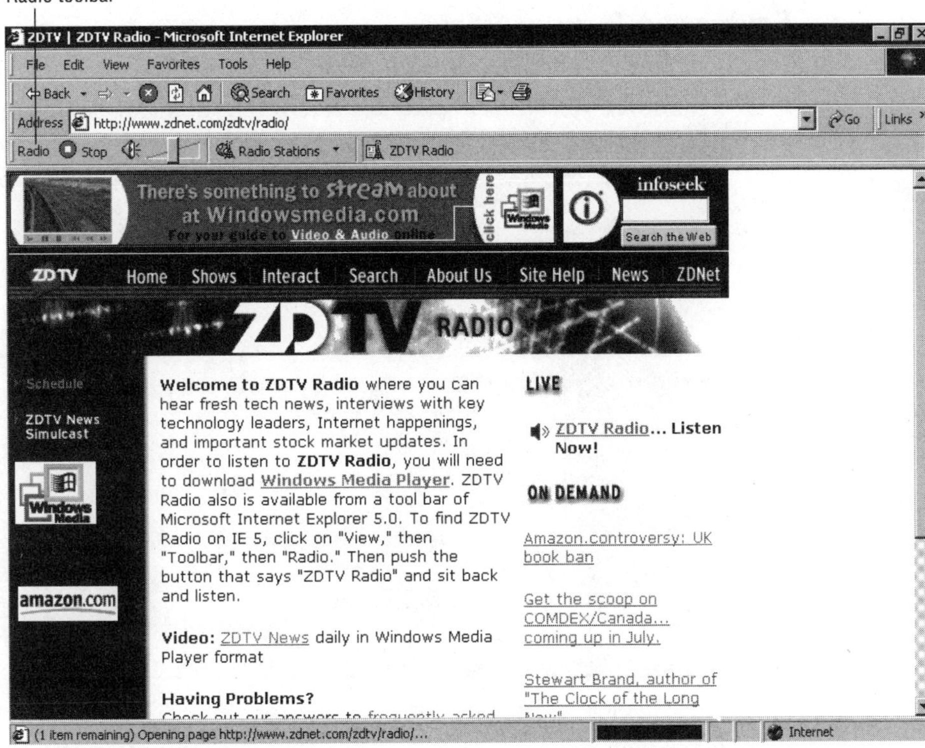

To select a station, click the Radio Stations button, and choose Radio Station Guide to open the WindowsMedia.com site. Click a button to listen to a Webcast. The station's home page loads while the station is being found. To adjust the volume, move the slider on the Volume Control. To turn the radio off, click the Stop button on the Radio toolbar.

The quality of your listening experience will depend on your speakers, your system, and the speed at which you are connected. An Internet access speed of at least 56Kbps is recommended.

Saving and Printing Web Pages

If you always want to see the most current version of a Web page, you probably want to place a link to it on the Links bar or the Favorites bar. However, in some cases, you'll want to save it to your local hard drive or to a drive on your network. For example, I recently wanted easy access to a rather long U.S. government document. In this case, the document had been written and distributed over the Internet and was not going to change. It was what it was, so I saved it to my local network so that I could get to it quickly without being connected to the Internet.

Saving the Current Page

To save the current page, follow these steps:

1. Choose File ➢ Save As to open the Save Web Page dialog box:

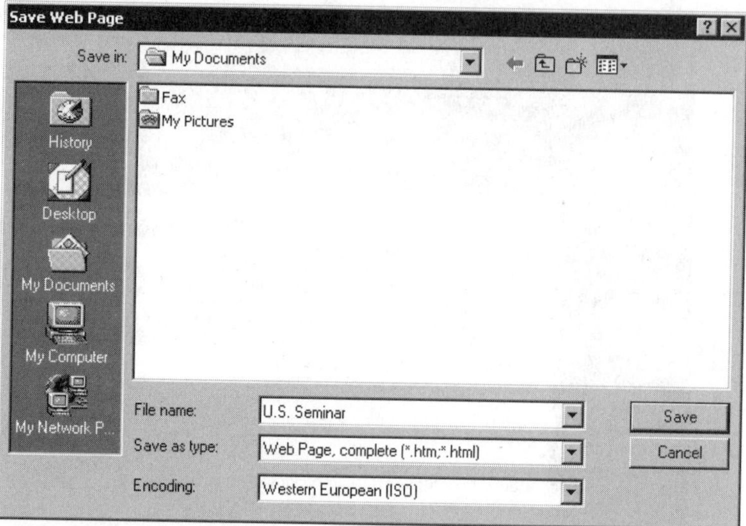

2. Select a folder in which to save the page, and in the File Name box enter a name if you want something different from that which Internet Explorer proposes.
3. In the Save As Type drop-down box, select the format in which you want the page saved.
4. Click Save.

You can also save a Web page without opening it if its link is displayed. Follow these steps:

1. Right-click the link, and choose Save Target As from the shortcut menu. You'll see a dialog box that shows you that the page is being downloaded.
2. In the Save As dialog box, select a folder, and specify a filename.
3. Click Save.

Saving Portions of a Page

You can also save only a portion of text from a Web page or an image. To save a portion of text to use in another document, select the text, and then press Ctrl+C. Open the other document, place the insertion point where you want the text, and press Ctrl+V.

To save an image, follow these steps:

1. Right-click the image, and choose Save Picture As from the shortcut menu to open the Save Picture dialog box.
2. Select a folder, a filename, and a type, and click Save.

To save an image as wallpaper, right-click the image and choose Set As Wallpaper from the shortcut menu. To specify how you want the wallpaper displayed, right-click the image on the Desktop, choose Properties to open the Display Properties dialog box, and select an option in the Picture Display drop-down box.

Printing the Current Page

If you want to quickly print the current page, simply click the Print button on the Standard toolbar. If, however, you want more control over what's printed and how, choose File ➢ Print to open the Print dialog box, as shown in Figure 12.8.

FIGURE 12.8
The Print dialog box, open at the Options tab

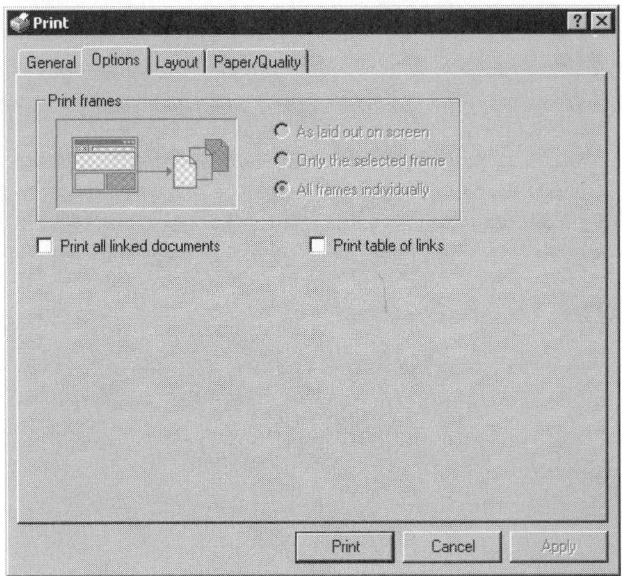

For the most part, this is your standard Windows Print dialog box. (For details about printers and printing in Windows 2000 Professional, see Chapter 7.) The difference is the Options tab, which you can use to specify how frames and links are printed; it is shown in Figure 12.8. Here are the specifics:

- Select the As Laid Out On Screen option in the Print Frames section to print the Web page exactly as it is displayed on your screen.

- Select the Only The Selected Frame option to print only a frame you have previously selected. (To select a frame, click inside it in an empty space—in other words, not on a link.)
- Select the All Frames Individually option if you want to print each frame on a separate sheet of paper.
- Select the Print All Linked Documents option if you want to print the pages that are linked to the current page as well. (Be sure you really want to do this; you could need lots of paper.)
- Select the Print Table Of Links option if you want to print a table that lists the links for the page at the end of the document.

When you have all your options selected, click the Print button on any tab to print the document.

To print the target of any link, right-click the link, and choose Print Target from the shortcut menu to open the Print dialog box.

TIP By default, Windows does not print the background colors and background images of Web pages. First, the printed output could be illegible, and, second, unless you have a rather powerful printer, spooling and printing could be really slow. If, for whatever reason, you want or need to print the background, choose Tools ➢ Internet Options to open the Internet Options dialog box. Click the Advanced tab, scroll down to the Printing section, check the Print Background Colors And Images check box, and click OK.

Working Offline

As I mentioned earlier in this chapter, if you want to view Web pages when you aren't connected to the Internet, and their currentness is not important, you can simply save them to your local hard drive. If their currentness is important, you can choose to "work offline."

To make the current page available for offline viewing, follow these steps:

1. Right-click in an empty spot on the page, and choose Add To Favorites to open the Add Favorite dialog box.
2. Click the Make Available Offline check box.
3. If you want to view only certain content offline, click the Customize button to start the Offline Favorite Wizard. Follow the onscreen instructions. You can also establish a schedule for updating the page using this Wizard. Click Finish when you're done.

4. Before you close your connection to the Internet, choose Tools ➢ Synchronize to ensure that you have the most up-to-date content for the page you want to view offline.

To view pages offline, choose File ➢ Work Offline, and in the Favorites bar, select the page you want.

TIP In the previous version of Internet Explorer, offline viewing was called "subscribing."

Finding Exactly What You Want on the Internet

The serendipitous experience of clicking and following hyperlinks may suffice while you're polishing off your lunch of tuna sandwich and chips or filling the occasional lazy, rainy afternoon, but most of the time when you connect to the Internet, you have something specific in mind that you want to do or find. Regardless of what you're looking for—information about a topic, an e-mail or a mailing address, a business, a Web page, and so on—the way to find it is to use a search service. *Search service* is a relatively new term for what we referred to in the past as a search engine, a program that can search a file, a database, or the Internet for keywords and retrieve documents in which those keywords are found.

Examples of search services that you may have used include Yahoo!, Excite, InfoSeek, AltaVista, and Lycos. To search with one of these services, you go to the site (for example, `www.yahoo.com`); optionally, select a category, enter a keyword or phrase, and click Search (or some similar button). Although these search services are very efficient, you are accessing only one of them at a time.

In Internet Explorer 5, you can use the Search Assistant to search several services simultaneously. Let's do a simple search to see how this works.

Performing a Simple Search

Follow these steps to perform a simple search:

1. In Internet Explorer, click the Search button on the Standard toolbar to open the Search bar:

TIP If you don't see all the categories shown here, click More.

2. In the Find A Web Page Containing box, type a word or a phrase on which you want to search.
3. Click Search.
4. Scroll down the Search bar until you see something that answers your query, and click it. You'll see the page displayed in the pane on the right.

TIP If you want to find Web pages similar to the current page, choose Tools ➢ Show Related Links. A list of links is displayed in the Search bar.

Power Searching

In the Search bar, you can specify to search for any of the following by selecting that option:

- A Web page
- A person's address
- A business
- Previous searches
- A map
- A word
- A picture
- A word or phrase in a newsgroup

You can further refine your searches in the Customize Search Settings dialog box (click the Customize button in the Search bar). Scroll down this dialog box to survey all your options. At the bottom of this dialog box, click Autosearch Settings to specify which search service is used when you search from the Address bar. If you want to return to the default set of search options, click the Reset button.

Customizing Internet Explorer

In Windows 2000 Professional, you can view or change the configuration options relating to Internet Explorer in two ways:

- Use Internet Options in Control Panel
- Choose Tools ➢ Internet Options from within Internet Explorer

Regardless of which you choose, you open the same dialog box. However, if you open it from Control Panel, it is called Internet Properties, and if you open it from within Internet Explorer, it is called Internet Options. In both cases, the contents of the dialog boxes are identical. In this section, we'll use Control Panel.

Choose Start ➢ Settings ➢ Control Panel ➢ Internet Options, and you'll see the Internet Properties dialog box open on your screen. This dialog box has six tabs, and in the next few sections, I'll review the most important configuration choices you can make on each of these tabs. I'll start with the General tab.

Configuring the General Tab

The General tab, which is shown in Figure 12.9, contains these groups of settings:

Home Page Lets you choose which Web page opens each time you connect to the Internet. A home page is the first Web page you see when you start Internet Explorer. Click Use Current to make the current page your home page (if you are online to the Internet), click Use Default to return to the default setting, and click Use Blank to start each Internet session with a blank screen. To use a different Web page as your home page, type the URL in the Address box.

Temporary Internet Files Lets you manage those Web pages that are stored on your hard disk for fast offline access. If these files are occupying too much hard disk space, click the Delete Files button to remove them. To control how these files are stored on your hard disk, click Settings to open the Settings dialog box. Click the option that applies to when you want Internet Explorer to check for newer versions of these stored Web pages. You can use the slider to specify how much hard disk space is given over to these temporary Internet files. Click Move Folder if you want to use a different folder to hold your temporary Internet files; you must remember to restart your computer after making this change so that the new folder is used in place of the default. Click View Files to open an Explorer window listing all the Web and graphics files in the folder, or click View Objects to open an Explorer window listing all the other Web-related files such as ActiveX controls and Java-related files.

History Contains a list of the links you have visited so that you can return to them quickly and easily using the History button on the Internet Explorer toolbar. You can specify the number of days you want to keep pages in the History folder; if you are running low on hard disk space, consider reducing this number. To delete all the information currently in the History folder, click the Clear History button.

Colors Lets you choose which colors are used as background, links, and text on those Web pages for which the original author did not specify colors. By default, the Use Windows Colors option is selected.

TIP You can always change the Windows colors. In Control Panel, click Display, and then select the Appearance tab.

Fonts Lets you specify the font style and text size to use on those Web pages for which the original author did not make a specification.

Languages Lets you choose the character set to use on those Web pages that offer content in more than one language. English is rapidly becoming the most common language in use on the Internet, so you may not use this option often.

Accessibility Lets you choose how certain information is displayed in Internet Explorer, including font styles, colors, and text size. You can also specify that your own style sheet is used.

FIGURE 12.9
The General tab in the Internet Properties dialog box

Looking at the Security Tab

The Security tab, which is shown in Figure 12.10, lets you specify the overall security level for each of four zones. Each zone has its own default security restrictions that tell Internet Explorer how to manage dynamic Web page content such as ActiveX controls and Java applets. The zones are:

Internet Sites you visit that are not in one of the other categories; default security is set to Medium.

Local Intranet Sites you can access on your corporate intranet; default security is set to Medium-Low.

Trusted Sites Web sites in which you have a high degree of confidence will not send you potentially damaging content; default security is set to Low.

Restricted Sites Sites that you visit but do not trust; default security is set to High.

FIGURE 12.10
The Security tab in the Internet Properties dialog box

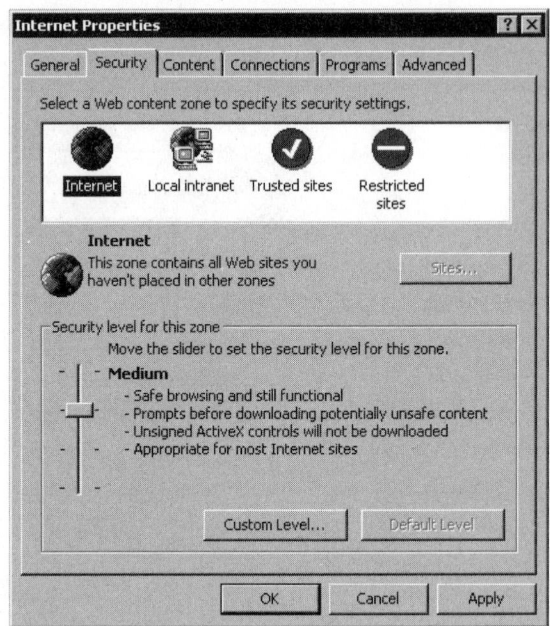

To change the current security level of a zone, just move the slider to the new security level you want to use:

High Excludes any content capable of damaging your system. Cookies are disabled, and so some Web sites will not work as you might expect. This is the most secure setting.

Medium Opens a warning dialog box in Internet Explorer before running ActiveX or Java applets on your system. This is a moderately secure setting that is good for everyday use and is selected by default.

Medium-Low Same as Medium but without the prompts.

Low Does not issue any warning but runs the ActiveX or Java applet automatically. This is the least secure setting.

Click the Custom Level button to create your own settings in the Security Settings dialog box, which is shown in Figure 12.11. You can individually configure how you want to manage certain categories, such as ActiveX controls and plug-ins, Java applets, scripting, file and font downloads, and user authentication.

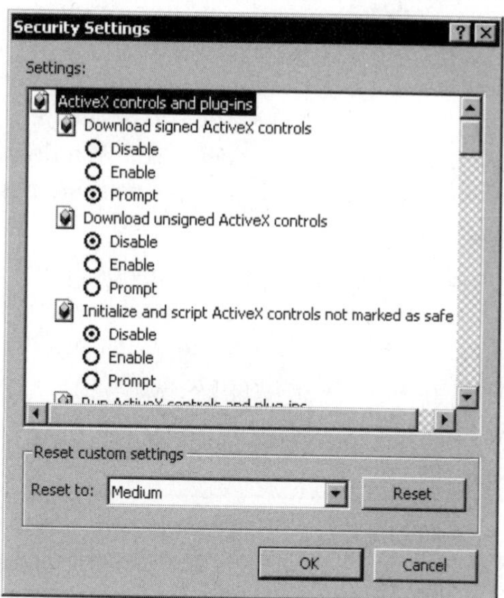

FIGURE 12.11
The Security Settings dialog box

Using the Content Tab

The Content tab, which is shown in Figure 12.12, contains settings you can use to restrict access to sites and specify how you want to manage digital certificates:

Content Adviser Lets you control access to certain sites on the Internet and is particularly useful if children have access to the computer. Click Enable to establish a password, and then click OK to open the Content Advisor dialog box. Use the tabs in this dialog box to establish the level of content you will allow users to view:

Ratings Lets you use a set of ratings developed by the Recreational Software Advisory Council (RSAC) for language, nudity, sex, and violence. Select one of these categories, and then adjust the slider to specify the level of content you will allow.

Approved Sites Lets you create lists of sites that are always viewable or always restricted regardless of how they are rated.

General Specifies whether people using this computer can view material that has not been rated; users may see some objectionable material if the Web site has not used the RSAC rating system. You can also opt to have the Supervisor enter a password so that users can view Web pages that may contain objectionable material. You can click the Change Password button to change the Supervisor password; remember that you have to know the current Supervisor password before you can change it.

Advanced Lets you look at or modify the list of organizations providing ratings services.

Certificates Lets you manage digital certificates used with certain client authentication servers. Click Certificates to view the personal digital certificates installed on this system, or click Publishers to designate a particular software publisher as a trustworthy publisher. This means that Windows 2000 Professional applications can download, install, and use software from these agencies without asking for your permission first.

Personal Information Lets you look at or change the settings for Windows AutoComplete and your own personal profile. Click AutoComplete to change the way that this feature works within Windows 2000 Professional, or click My Profile to review the information sent to any Web sites that request information about you when you visit their site.

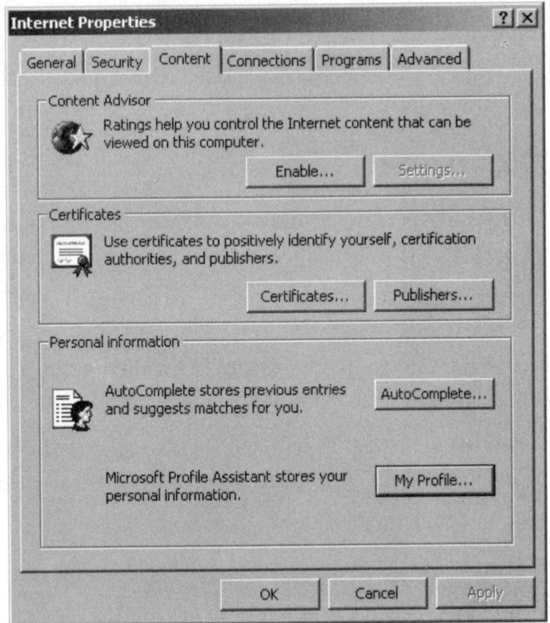

FIGURE 12.12
The Content tab in the Internet Properties dialog box

Setting up the Connections Tab

The Connections tab, which is shown in Figure 12.13, allows you to specify how your system connects to the Internet. Click the Setup button to run the Internet Connection Wizard and set up a connection to an Internet Service Provider. (See Chapter 10 for complete details on this.) If you use a modem, click the Settings button to open the

My Connection Settings dialog box, where you can specify all aspects of the phone connection to your ISP.

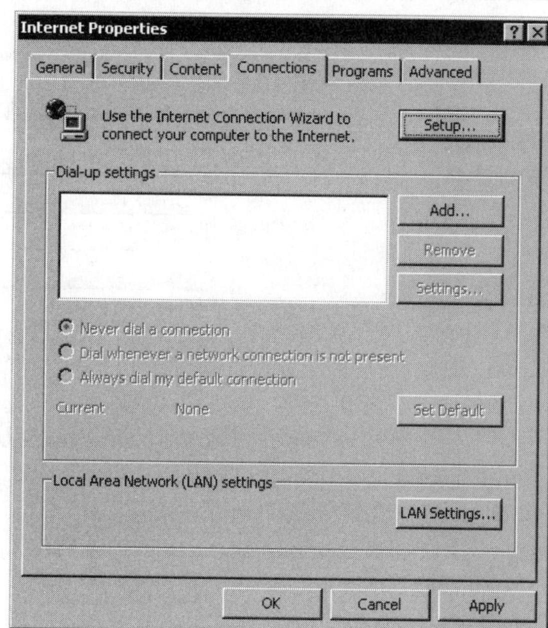

FIGURE 12.13
The Connections tab in the Internet Properties dialog box

Looking at the Programs Tab

The Programs tab, which is shown in Figure 12.14, lets you set your default program choices for HTML editor, e-mail, newsgroup reader, Internet call, calendar, and contact list. Finally, you can specify that Internet Explorer check to see if it is configured as the default browser on your system each time it starts running.

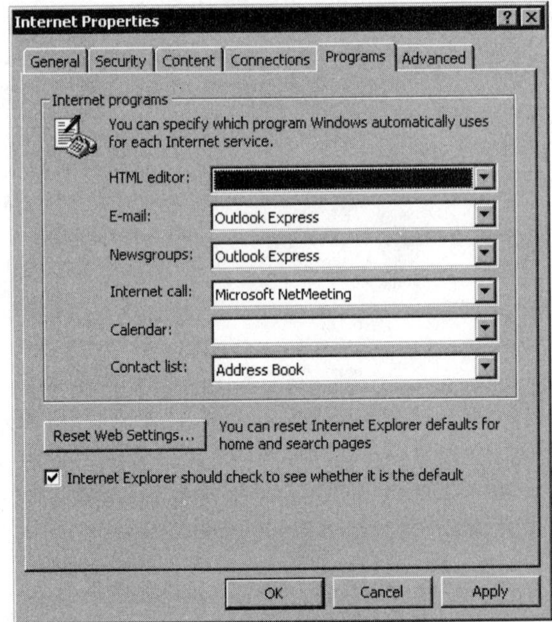

FIGURE 12.14
The Programs tab in the Internet Properties dialog box

Configuring the Advanced Tab

The Advanced tab, which is shown in Figure 12.15, lets you look at or change a number of settings that control much of Internet Explorer's behavior, including accessibility, browsing, multimedia, security, the Java environment, printing and searching, the Internet Explorer toolbar, and how HTTP 1.1 settings are interpreted. Click a check box to turn an option on; clear the check box to turn the option off.

Changes you make here stay in effect until you change them again, until you download an automatic configuration file, or until you click the Restore Defaults button, which returns the settings on the Advanced tab to their original values.

FIGURE 12.15
The Advanced tab in the Internet Properties dialog box

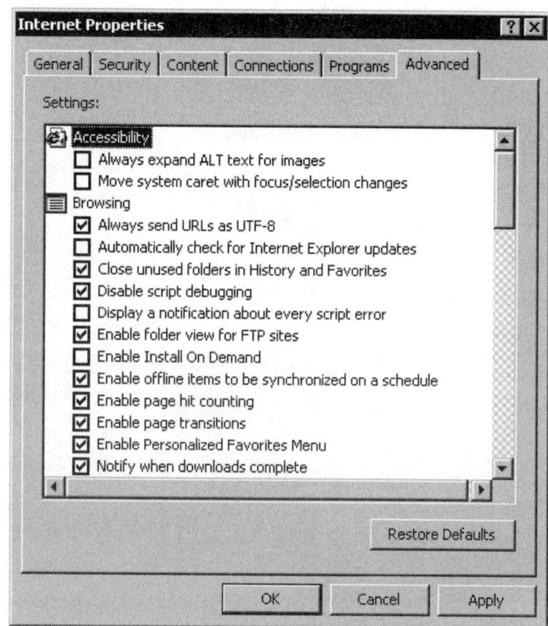

Using Built-In Internet Utilities

Windows 2000 Professional includes several standard Internet utilities. These programs are in most cases functionally identical to the same programs or commands found on pretty much every flavor of Unix. Although most people are not going to use these nearly as often as they will their Web browsers, I describe each in the following sections so you at least know what they are. It is useful to acquaint yourself, for example, with FTP—if you are ever on a Windows 2000 Professional system that for some reason does not have a Web browser, knowing how to use FTP to transfer files enables you to connect to Spry, Netscape, or Microsoft and download a browser.

Following this brief rundown of each of the tools, we will look at other Internet applications you can download via the Internet. Note that with each of the following programs, you can get help by typing the program name at the command prompt followed by **-?** (dash, question mark).

To open any of the following utilities, you type a command at a command prompt. To open a command prompt window, do one of the following:

- Choose Start ➢ Run, and in the Open text box, type the command (the name of the utility).
- Choose Start ➢ Programs ➢ Accessories ➢ Command Prompt.

Address Resolution Display and Control (ARP)

The ARP program is used to display and/or modify entries in the Internet-to-Ethernet (or Token Ring) address translation tables that are used by the Address Resolution Protocol (ARP). Various command-line switches are documented in the -? option. To use ARP, type **arp** at the command prompt.

File Transfer Protocol (FTP)

FTP is the standard TCP/IP file transfer protocol used for moving text and binary files between computers on the Internet. If you have an account on a distant computer on the Internet, you can use FTP to download files from the other computer to your PC and to upload files from your PC to the host. In addition, there are tens of thousands of *anonymous* FTP archives all over the Internet that accept logins from anybody who wants copies of their files.

The Windows 2000 Professional FTP program (and the others mentioned here) can be found in the `Winnt\System32` folder, which is included in your search path. Therefore, you don't have to specify the path when you enter an FTP command. To connect to an FTP server, follow these steps:

1. At a command prompt, type the following, and then press Enter:

   FTP <host name>

2. Windows 2000 Professional displays the `ftp>` prompt:

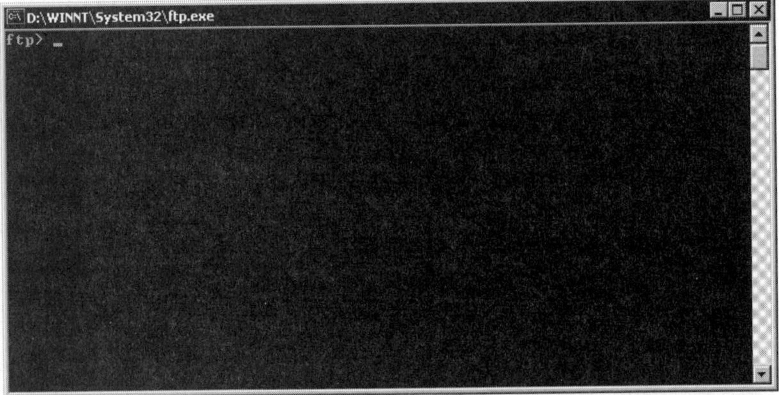

3. After FTP connects to the server, the server asks for your username and password. If you're connecting to an anonymous FTP server, type **anonymous** as your username, and type your e-mail address as your password or leave the password field blank and press Enter. Use the standard *`name@address.domain`* format.

Most FTP servers use the same system of directories and subdirectories that you may be familiar with from DOS and Windows. To see the contents of the current directory, type **dir** or **ls** at the ftp> prompt.

A *d* as the first letter in a listing indicates that the item in that line is a directory. If a dash is the first character, the item is a file. The name of the file or directory is at the extreme right.

Use the command cd *name* (typing the name of the subdirectory in place of *name*) to move to a subdirectory.

Use the command cd .. to move to the next higher level. (Press the spacebar after you enter the "d" and before you type the first period.)

When you download a file from an FTP server, you must specify that it is either an ASCII text file or a binary file. As a general rule, binary files that you can read on a PC have a DOS file extension (rather than TXT for a text file or PS for a Postscript print file), but you really can't be certain. ASCII text files may or may not have a file extension.

When you initially connect to an FTP server, you're in ASCII mode. Before you try to transfer a binary file, you have to change modes. To switch to binary mode, use the command binary. To switch back to ASCII mode, use the command ascii. The host acknowledges your mode-change command.

To download a file from the server, use the command get *filename* (typing the name of the file in place of *filename*). If you want to store the file on your PC with a different name, use the command get *filename newname* (typing the file you want to get in place of *filename* and the name you want to store the file under in place of *newname*). When the file transfer is complete, the host sends you another message, shown here:

```
ftp> get Yellball.gif
200 PORT command successful.
150 Opening BINARY mode data connection for Yellball.gif(582 bytes).
226 Transfer complete.
ftp: 582 bytes received in 0.01Seconds 58.20Kbytes/sec.
ftp>
```

When you are finished with your FTP session, type **disconnect** to break the connection to the server. You can connect to another host by typing the new server's address.

To close the FTP utility, type the command **quit**.

TIP One handy use for the command-line FTP client is automating file transfers. Because FTP accepts scripts (via the -s:filename switch), you can easily create a script (which is just a text file of FTP commands) to log on to an FTP server, switch to a particular directory, transfer a long listing of files in one or both directions, and then log off. You can even set this to occur at a given time of day, by using the Windows 2000 Professional at command. (For details on using the at command, type **help at** from any command prompt.)

Finger

The finger program can be used to retrieve user-supplied information about a user (or host computer). Unfortunately, many users do not have a finger file for others to retrieve and view (or even know about creating one), and some host computers do not provide finger services, so your mileage will vary. On the other hand, some universities and institutions do use finger services, and on these you can find some useful (or at least interesting) information. To use finger, type **`finger`** ***`auser@someplace.com`*.** Enter a valid username or at least a host name, and press Enter, and you may get a listing of information.

Ping

Ping is a useful diagnostic utility that tests your ability to connect your computer to another device through the Internet by sending an echo request and displaying the number of milliseconds required to receive a reply. Whenever you need to diagnose your Internet connection problems, pinging a known host computer is a good first test.

To set up a ping test, follow these steps:

1. At a command prompt, type **`ping`** ***`destination`***. Use the domain name or the IP address of the host you want to test in place of *`destination`*. If you do not get a response when using the domain name of the destination, try the IP address of the destination instead.
2. Ping sends four sets of Internet Control Message Protocol (ICMP) echo packets to the host you specify and displays the amount of time it took to receive each reply, as shown here:

```
C:\W2KPRO\System32\cmd.exe

C:\>ping spiritwolf

Pinging spiritwolf [10.1.0.1] with 32 bytes of data:

Reply from 10.1.0.1: bytes=32 time<10ms TTL=128
Reply from 10.1.0.1: bytes=32 time<10ms TTL=128
Reply from 10.1.0.1: bytes=32 time<10ms TTL=128
Reply from 10.1.0.1: bytes=32 time<10ms TTL=128

Ping statistics for 10.1.0.1:
    Packets: Sent = 4, Received = 4, Lost = 0 (0% loss),
Approximate round trip times in milli-seconds:
    Minimum = 0ms, Maximum =  0ms, Average =  0ms

C:\>_
```

The important part of the ping display is the time</>*nnn*ms section of the Reply lines. Ping's capability to connect to the distant host tells you that your connection to the Internet is working properly; the number of milliseconds can tell you if you have an efficient connection to this particular host (anything less than about 500ms is usually acceptable).

Protocol Statistics (Netstat)

Use the `netstat` command to display a list of currently active Internet connections. At the command prompt, type **`netstat`**. A list of connections similar to the ones in the following illustration appears:

```
C:\W2KPRO\System32\cmd.exe

C:\>netstat

Active Connections

  Proto  Local Address          Foreign Address        State
  TCP    STARBUG:1274           SPIRITWOLF:nbsession   ESTABLISHED
  TCP    STARBUG:1352           STARBUG.psnettech.com:nbsession  TIME_WAIT

C:\>
```

A `netstat` report includes the following information:

Proto Shows the networking protocol in use for each active connection. For PPP or SLIP connections to the Internet, the Proto column always reads TCP, which specifies a TCP/IP connection.

Local Address Indicates the identity of your PC on the network.

Foreign Address Shows the address of each distant computer to which a connection is currently active.

State Shows the condition of each connection.

Remote File Copy (RCP)

If you've ever wanted to copy a file from one directory or drive to another on a remote computer, without having the file go through your modem twice (as a normal copy or xcopy would), you understand the purpose of the RCP program. You can also use RCP to copy files from one remote computer to another remote computer without being copied to your computer first. Not all systems permit you to use this command, and if they do, of course you are limited to the directory areas for which you have access rights. Type **`-?`** for specific usage and option information. To use RCP, open a command prompt, and type **`rcp`**.

Remote Program Execution (REXEC)

The REXEC program is just as powerful as Remote Shell/Script (RSH; discussed in the next section), if not more so, and likewise is quite restricted by most system administrators. It functions just like RSH, except that it starts binary programs rather than scripts on the remote host. Windows 2000 Professional stations *do* permit remote execution of programs, provided the system administrator has enabled this and given you the necessary access rights. To run REXEC, type **rexec** at a command prompt.

Remote Shell/Script (RSH)

Another potentially powerful utility, RSH is used to start a script program on a remote host. Again, some host computers do not support this, and of those that do, your access rights may preclude or severely limit what you can do. To use RSH, type **rsh** at a command prompt.

Remote Terminal (Telnet)

Telnet is one of the utilities you are somewhat more likely to use, particularly in university settings or when data you need to access without using HTML is stored on a remote host (a less and less common scenario, thankfully). When you connect through a Telnet connection, your PC becomes a terminal on the distant system. In most cases, a Telnet login requires an account on the host (remote) machine, but many systems accept logins from anybody who wants to connect. Among the most common public Telnet sites are online library catalogs. Other public Telnet sites let you use certain character-based Internet services that may not be available on your computer.

To set up a Telnet connect, type **Telnet *hostname*** at a command prompt (using the domain name or IP address of the computer to which you want to connect in place of *hostname*). Telnet connects your computer to the host whose name you supplied and displays messages from that host in the Telnet window.

Most Telnet hosts display a series of login prompts as soon as you connect. If you're connecting to a public Telnet host, it will probably tell you how to log in.

NOTE Telnet is also used to configure most routers. If you are interested in network design and management, you might want to focus some attention on Telnet.

Route

You can use `route` to view, add to, or modify a routing table on a Windows 2000 Professional computer with more than one network interface. If you have a *multihomed* computer (one with multiple network cards) and have enabled IP forwarding in the TCP/IP Properties dialog box, you can use the `route` command to view and modify the table of information that tells Windows 2000 Professional where to direct TCP/IP data from one interface to another. Using this command on a computer with one network interface will also display basic routing information. To use `route`, type **`route`** at a command prompt.

Trace Route (tracert)

In most cases, when you set up a connection to a distant computer through the Internet, your signal path passes through several routers along the way. Because this is all happening in a fraction of a second, these intermediate routers are usually invisible. But when you're having trouble making a connection, the trace route command can help isolate the source of the problem.

To run a trace route test, type **`tracert`** ***`target`*** at a command prompt. In place of *`target`*, type the address of the distant system. A trace route report appears in the prompt window.

In many cases, your connection will pass through one or more backbone networks between your connection to the Internet and your ultimate destination. For example, the `tracert` report in Figure 12.16 shows a route from a PC in Seattle to The WELL, near San Francisco. In this case, the connection passes through backbone networks operated by Sprintlink and AlterNet.

FIGURE 12.16 *The `tracert` command produces a list of intermediate routers between your PC and an Internet host.*

```
C:\WINNT\System32\cmd.exe

C:\>tracert well.com

Tracing route to well.com [206.15.64.10]
over a maximum of 30 hops:

  1    47 ms    47 ms    47 ms  gateway.gte2.rb1.bel.nwlink.com [209.20.176.1]
  2    15 ms    31 ms    16 ms  gte1-rb1-bel-cr1.nwlink.com [209.20.128.14]
  3    16 ms    31 ms    31 ms  902.Hssi4-0.GW2.SEA1.ALTER.NET [137.39.136.129]
  4    16 ms    31 ms    31 ms  104.ATM3-0.XR2.SEA1.ALTER.NET [146.188.200.54]
  5    15 ms    32 ms    31 ms  194.ATM3-0.TR2.SEA1.ALTER.NET [146.188.200.118]
  6    32 ms    46 ms    63 ms  110.ATM5-0.TR2.SCL1.ALTER.NET [146.188.137.189]
  7    31 ms    31 ms    47 ms  198.ATM6-0.XR2.SJC1.ALTER.NET [146.188.146.49]
  8    46 ms    47 ms    47 ms  192.ATM3-0-0.SAN-JOSE9-GW.ALTER.NET [146.188.144
.133]
  9    47 ms    47 ms    47 ms  198.32.184.34
 10   141 ms    46 ms    63 ms  sf-cust1-fe0-0.core.hooked.net [206.80.17.13]
 11    47 ms    63 ms    47 ms  well.com [206.15.64.10]

Trace complete.

C:\>_
```

`Tracert` steps through the connection route, one step at a time. For each step, it shows the amount of time needed to reach that router, in milliseconds. If an intermediate router or a connection between two intermediate routers fails, `tracert` will not display any steps beyond that point in the route. If that happens, you can assume that the failed site is the reason that you are unable to connect to your intended destination.

Trivial File Transfer Protocol (TFTP)

This program is similar in usage and functionality to the more well-known FTP utility but is used to transfer files to or from a remote computer that is running Trivial File Transfer Protocol (TFTP).

FTP uses the TCP protocol, which guarantees safe delivery of the data. TFTP uses User Datagram Protocol (UDP), which does not provide reliable delivery and hence is somewhat faster. Windows 2000 Professional does not provide a TFTP server, but some are available for download on the Internet.

Summary

Within the space of a very few years, many of us have come to consider access to the Internet an essential component of daily life. It is now the first place I turn when I want information about almost anything, and it's rare that I don't find what I'm looking for. An equally essential component is e-mail, which is the topic of the next chapter.

CHAPTER 13

Using Outlook Express for E-mail and News

FEATURING:

Of all the features of the Internet, intranets, and local area networks, e-mail is, without question, the most used. Instead of playing phone tag with colleagues at work, you send them e-mail. Millions of extended families stay in touch via e-mail, and an e-mail address has become an expected component of a business card.

Outlook Express is an Internet standards e-mail reader you can use to access an Internet e-mail account. An Internet e-mail account is not the same thing as an account with an online information service. The difference is that an Internet account provides services such as Point-to-Point protocol Internet access and e-mail but does not include services such as chat rooms, access to databases, conferences, and so on. Consequently, you cannot use Outlook Express to access an e-mail account with MS Mail, cc:Mail, CompuServe, America Online, or versions of Microsoft Exchange Server prior to version 5.

TIP You can use Outlook Express to set up and access a free Hotmail account. To set up a Hotmail account, choose Tools ➢ New Account Signup ➢ Hotmail, and follow the onscreen instructions.

In addition to being an e-mail reader, Outlook Express is also a news reader. In the first part of this chapter, I'll look at e-mail features, and in the second part I'll look at how to access newsgroups and post to them.

Using Outlook Express As Your Mail Reader

The quickest way to start Outlook Express is to click the Launch Outlook Express icon on the Quick Launch toolbar. You can also start it by choosing Start ➢ Programs ➢ Outlook Express or, from within Internet Explorer, by choosing Tools ➢ Mail and News and then selecting an item from the submenu.

NOTE Before you can open and use Outlook Express to send and receive e-mail, you need to configure your Internet connection. You'll find information on how to do this in Chapter 10.

A Quick Tour

When you first open Outlook Express, you'll see a screen similar to that shown in Figure 13.1.

FIGURE 13.1
The opening screen in Outlook Express

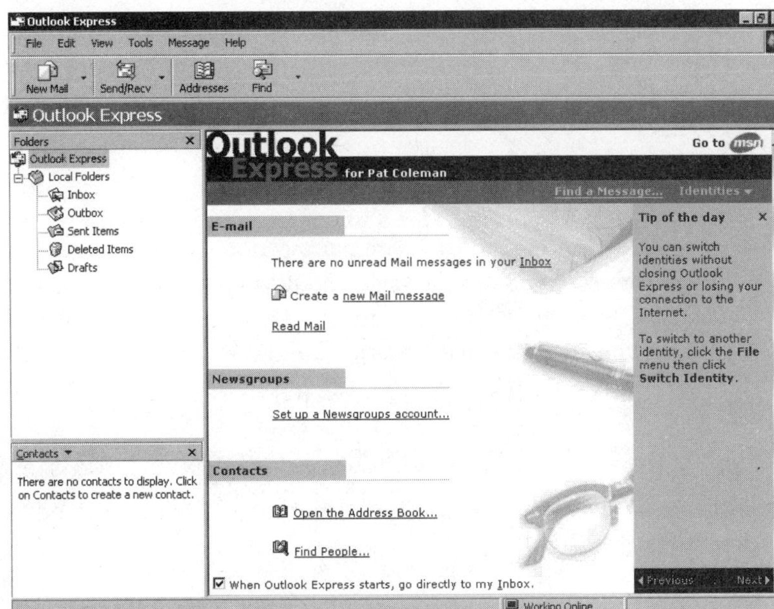

To read your mail, click Read Mail, or click Inbox in the Folders list. Initially the Preview pane is split horizontally; header information is displayed in the upper pane, and the message is displayed in the lower pane.

TIP To change the arrangement of the Preview pane, choose View ➢ Layout to open the Window Layout Properties dialog box, and select options to show or hide certain parts.

The Folders List

The Folders List is a tool for organizing messages. Initially, it contains the following folders, although you can create additional folders, as you'll see shortly:

Inbox Contains newly received messages and messages that you have not yet disposed of in some way.

Outbox Contains messages that are ready to be sent.

Sent Items Contains copies of messages that you have sent (a handy device if you send lots of e-mail).

Deleted Items Contains copies of messages that you have deleted.

Draft Contains messages that you are working on but which are not yet ready to be sent.

The Contacts Pane

The Contacts pane contains the names of people in your Address Book. To compose a message to anyone on this list, simply double-click the name.

Retrieving Your Mail

If you are connected to your Internet account, Outlook Express will automatically check the server for new messages and download them when you open Outlook Express. By default, Outlook Express will also check for new mail every 30 minutes, as long as you are connected. To adjust this time interval, follow these steps:

1. Choose Tools ➢ Options to open the Options dialog box:

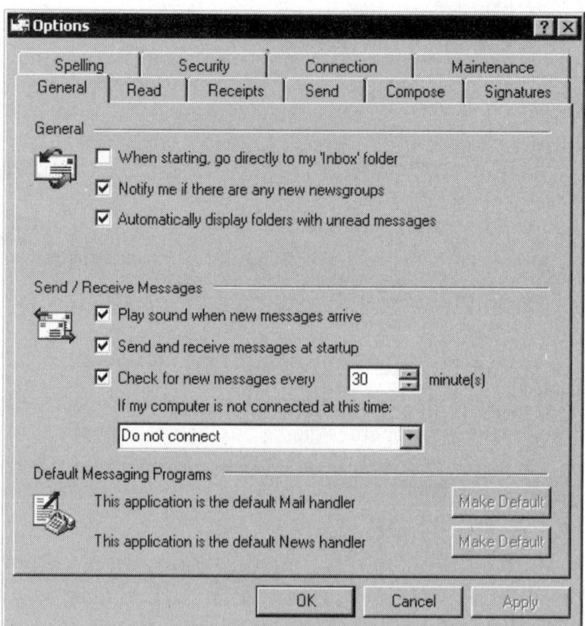

2. In the General tab, click the up or down arrow to change the Check For New Message Every *x* Minutes option.
3. Click OK.

You can also check for new mail by choosing Tools ➢ Send and Receive ➢ Receive All or by clicking the Send/Recv button on the toolbar in the main window.

Reading and Processing Messages

If you are working in the split Preview pane view, simply click a message header to display the message in a separate window. Otherwise, simply double-click a header to view the message.

Printing Messages

For various reasons, it's often handy to have a paper copy of e-mail messages. You can print in a couple of ways:

- To print a message without opening it, select its header and click the Print icon on the toolbar in the main window.
- To print an open message, click the Print icon on the toolbar in the message window.

Marking Messages

If you're like me, you don't always handle each message as you receive it or immediately after you read it, and it's easy to forget that you need to take some action or follow up on a message unless it stands out from the others in the header list. One trick that I use is to mark a message as unread even though I have read it (select the header and choose Edit ➢ Mark As Unread). You can also select the header and choose Message ➢ Flag Message to display a red flag to the left of the message header.

In addition, you can mark a message as read, and you can mark all messages as read.

Moving Messages

You can easily move a message from one folder to another by dragging and dropping it. For example, if you receive a message that you want to modify and send to some else, select the message header and then drag it to the Drafts folder. Open it, revise it, and then send it on its way.

Saving Messages

You can save messages in folders you created in Windows Explorer, and you can save messages in Outlook Express folders. You can also save attachments as files.

Saving Messages in Windows Explorer Folders

To save messages in a folder in Windows Explorer, follow these steps:

1. Open the message or select its header.

2. Choose File ➢ Save As to open the Save Message As dialog box:

3. Select a folder in which to save the message. Outlook Express places the subject line in the File Name box. You can use this name or type another name.
4. Select a file type in which to save the message, and then click Save.

Saving Messages in Outlook Express Mail Folders

As I've mentioned, you can create your own Outlook Express folders. For example, you might want to create folders for people with whom you regularly correspond, or you might want to create folders for current projects. To create a new folder, follow these steps:

1. Choose File ➢ New ➢ Folder to open the Create Folder dialog box:

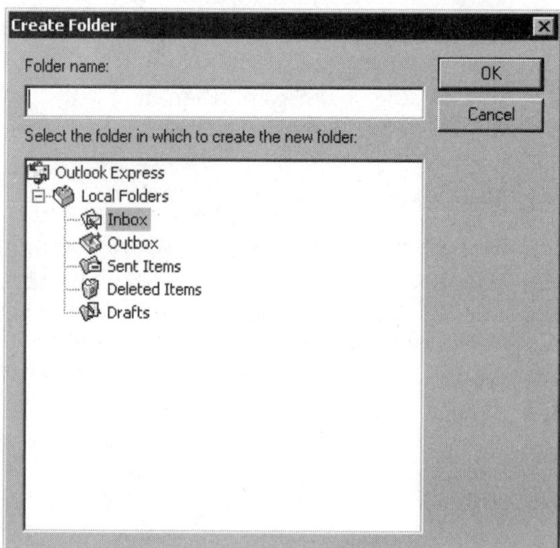

2. In the Folder Name box, type a name for your folder.
3. Select a folder in which to place the new folder, and click OK.

You now have a new folder in your folders list, and you can drag any message to it. You have, however, an even easier and more efficient way to save messages in Outlook Express folders, and I'll look at that in the Apply Message Rules section, later in this chapter.

Saving Attachments

An attachment is a file that is appended to an e-mail message. You'll know that a message has an attachment if the header is preceded by the paper clip icon. When you open the message, you'll see the filename of the attachment in the Attach line in the header. To open an attachment, double-click its filename.

To save an attachment, follow these steps:

1. Open the message, and choose File ➢ Save Attachments to open the Save Attachments dialog box:

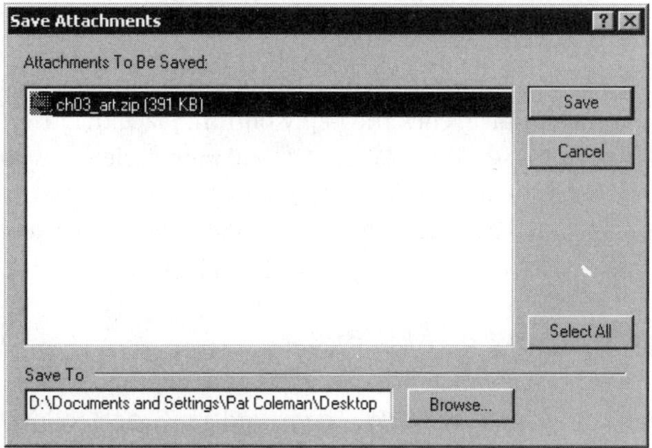

2. Select a folder in which to save the file, and click Save.

I'll discuss how to attach a file to a message later in this chapter.

Replying to a Message

To reply to a message, click the Reply button on the toolbar in the message window. If the message is addressed to multiple recipients and you want to reply to all of them, click the Reply All button.

TIP This is a quick and easy way to note the person's e-mail address. By default, Outlook Express automatically places the names of the people you reply to in your Address Book.

By default, Outlook Express includes the text of the original message in your reply. According to Internet tradition, this squanders bandwidth, and it's better not to include the original message unless it's really necessary. When is it necessary?

- When you want to be sure that the recipient understands the nature of your reply and the topic to which it is related
- When your message is part of a series of messages that involve some sort of question-and-answer sequence
- When it's important to keep track of who said what when

An alternative is to include only the relevant portions of the original message in your reply. To do so, follow these steps:

1. Open the message and click the Reply button.
2. The message is now addressed to the original sender, and the original subject line is preceded by Re:.
3. In the body of the message, edit the contents so that the portions you want are retained, and then enter your response.
4. Click the Send button.

If you don't want to include the original message in your reply, you can simply open the message, click the Reply button, place the insertion point in the body of the message, choose Edit ➢ Select All, and press Delete. If you're sure that you don't want to include the original message, choose Tools ➢ Options, and in the Options dialog box, click the Send tab. Clear the Include Message In Reply check box. If once in a while you need the message included, simply recheck the option.

Forwarding a Message

Forwarding an e-mail message is much easier than forwarding a letter through the U.S. mail, and it actually works. To forward a message, follow these steps:

1. Open the message.
2. Click the Forward button on the toolbar in the message window.
3. Enter an address in the To field.
4. Add your own comments if you want.
5. Click Send.

Deleting Messages

To delete a message, you can select its header and click Delete, or you can open it and then click Delete. The message is not yet really deleted, however; Outlook Express has placed it in the Deleted Items folder. By default, the Deleted Items folder is emptied when you close Outlook Express.

If you want to delete items from the Deleted Items folder yourself, follow these steps:

1. Select the Deleted Items folder.
2. Choose Edit ➢ Empty 'Deleted Items' Folder.
3. When Outlook Express asks if you are sure you want to delete these items, click Yes.

Creating and Sending Messages

In this section, I'll walk through the steps to create a simple message and send it. You can, however, create messages in HTML (HyperText Markup Language) and include hyperlinks, pictures, colorful formatting, sounds, and so on. We'll look at that in the next section.

To begin a new message, you can click the New Mail button in the main window to open the New Message window, as shown in Figure 13.2. Or, if the intended recipient is in your Address Book, you can double-click that person's name in the Contacts pane to open the New Message window; the To line will display the recipient's name.

FIGURE 13.2
You create a new message in the New Message window.

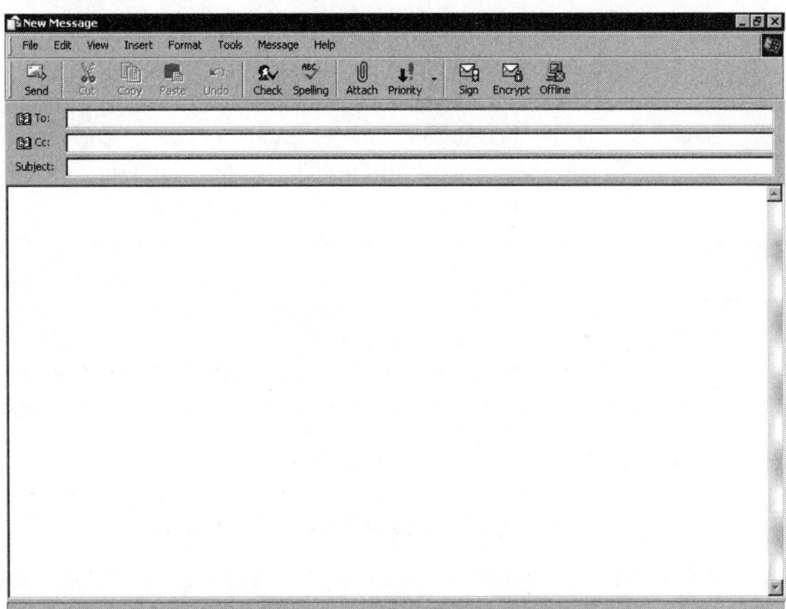

If your New Message window includes a Formatting toolbar, the message you compose will be formatted as HTML. For my purposes here, I want only plain text. So, if necessary, choose Format ➢ Plain Text before you begin composing your message. Now, follow these steps:

1. If necessary, enter the address of the primary recipient in the To field. If you are sending a message to multiple primary recipients, separate their addresses with semicolons.
2. Optionally, enter e-mail addresses in the Cc (carbon copy) and Bcc (blind carbon copy) fields. To enter a Bcc recipient, click the Cc icon, enter the name in the Select Recipients dialog box, and click Bcc.
3. Enter a subject line for your message.

NOTE If you don't enter a subject line, Outlook Express will ask if you're sure you don't want a subject line. Unless you have a good reason not to do so, enter some text in the subject line. Your recipient will see this text in the header information for the message and will then have a clue as to the nature of your message.

4. Enter the text of your message.
5. If appropriate, establish a priority for your message. Choose Message ➢ Set Priority, and then choose High, Normal, or Low. The default is Normal.
6. Click Send to start your message on its way.

You can send your message immediately by clicking the Send button, or you can save it in your Outbox to send later by choosing File ➢ Send Later. The message will be sent when you choose Send And Receive All or when you choose Send All.

TIP You can use Copy and Paste in Outlook Express just as you use those commands in other Windows programs. For example, to include a portion of a Word document in a message, open the document, select the text, and copy it to the Clipboard. In Outlook Express, open the New Message window, place the insertion point where you want to copy the text, and press Ctrl+V. Use this same process to copy portions of e-mail messages to other messages or to documents in other applications.

Creating E-mail Messages with HTML

In the previous section, I created a plain text message, but as I mentioned, you can also compose messages in HTML and include all sorts of neat effects. Before you send a formatted message, be sure that your recipient's e-mail program can display it effectively. When you open the New Message window and choose Format ➢ Rich Text (HTML), the message you compose is essentially a Web page. Newer e-mail programs such as Netscape Messenger and the commercial version of Eudora, Eudora Pro, can read, compose, and send HTML messages, but many others cannot, including America Online and the freeware version of Eudora. An easy way to find out if your recipient's e-mail program can handle HTML is to send a simple plain text message and ask.

That said, let's look at some bells and whistles you can include in Outlook Express e-mail messages. Click the New Mail icon to open the New Message window, and be sure that the Rich Text (HTML) option is selected. You'll see the screen shown in Figure 13.3. Notice the Formatting toolbar, which contains many of the same tools you see and use in your Windows word processor. You'll also see the Font and Font Size drop-down list boxes that are present in your word processor.

FIGURE 13.3
You can use the Formatting toolbar when creating a message in HTML.

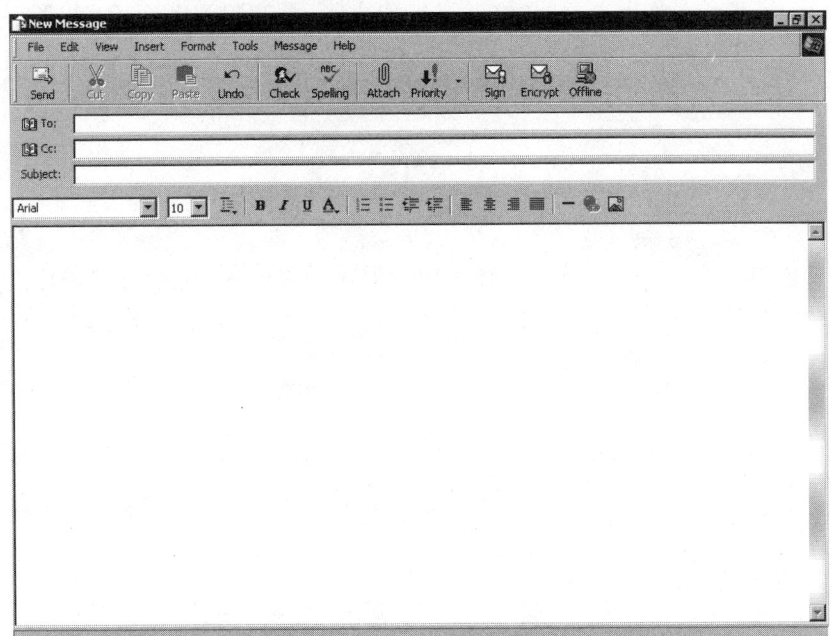

As you create your message, just pretend that you're using a word processor, and use the Formatting tools to apply emphasis to your message. All the usual design rules apply, including the following:

- Don't use a lot of different fonts.
- Remember, typing in all capital letters in e-mail is tantamount to shouting.
- Don't place a lot of text in italics. It's hard to read on the screen.
- Save boldface for what's really important.

To insert a horizontal line that spans the message window, choose Insert ➢ Horizontal Line.

To apply HTML styles such as Definition Term or Definition, click the Paragraph Style button on the Formatting toolbar.

Using Stationery

In addition to formatting, there is another way to add some class or some comedy to your e-mail messages: stationery. In the New Message window, choose Message ➢ New Using, and then choose a predesigned format from the list in the submenu or click Select Stationery to open the Select Stationery dialog box and select from a larger list. Here's one example of what you'll find:

To customize stationary, click Create New in the Select Stationery dialog box to start the Stationery Setup Wizard. Follow the onscreen instructions.

Adding a Picture to Your Messages

You can insert a picture in a message in two ways:

- As a piece of art
- As a background over which you can type text

To insert a picture as a piece of art that you can size and move, follow these steps:

1. In the New Message window, choose Insert ➢ Picture to open the Picture dialog box.
2. Enter the filename of the picture in the Picture Source text box, or click the Browse button to locate it.
3. Optionally, in the Alternate Text box, enter some text that will display if the recipient's e-mail program cannot display the picture, and specify layout and spacing options if you want. (You can also size and move the picture with the mouse once you place it in the message.)
4. Click OK.

To insert a picture as background, follow these steps:

1. In the New Message window, choose Format ➢ Background ➢ Picture to open the Background Picture dialog box.
2. Enter the filename of the picture, or click Browse to select a predesigned stationery background or locate another file.
3. Click Open, and then click OK to insert the background.

Adding a Background Color or Sound to Your Message

To apply a color to the background of your message, choose Format ➢ Background ➢ Color, and select a color from the drop-down list. Now type something. Can you see it on the screen? If not, you have probably chosen a dark background and your font is also a dark color—most likely black if you haven't changed it from the default.

To make your text visible, click the Font Color button, and select a lighter color from the drop-down list.

To add a background sound, follow these steps:

1. In the New Message window, choose Format ➢ Background ➢ Sound to open the Background Sound dialog box.
2. Enter the filename of the sound, or click Browse to locate a sound file.
3. Specify the number of times you want the sound to play or whether you want it to play continuously. (In my opinion, a sound that plays continuously while the recipient is reading the message is far more likely to annoy than to entertain.)
4. Click OK.

Including Hyperlinks in Your Message

When you insert a hyperlink in a message, the recipient can go directly to the resource simply by clicking the hyperlink. You can insert a hyperlink in three ways:

- Simply type it in the message body. Be sure to include the entire URL.

- In the New Message window, choose Insert ➢ Hyperlink to open the Hyperlink dialog box, and then enter the URL in the text box.
- In Internet Explorer, choose Tools ➢ Mail and News ➢ Send A Link to open the New Message window. The URL of the current page is automatically inserted in the message body.

Adding a Signature to Your Messages

I know people who never sign their e-mail messages. After all, their name is in the From line in the message header. I also know people who append elaborate signatures, touting their accomplishments or advertising their businesses. I usually just sign my first name at the bottom of messages, but what you do depends on your personal style or whether you're sending business or personal correspondence.

To create a signature that's automatically added to all your outgoing messages, follow these steps:

1. Choose Tools ➢ Options to open the Options dialog box.
2. Click the Signatures tab.
3. Click New.

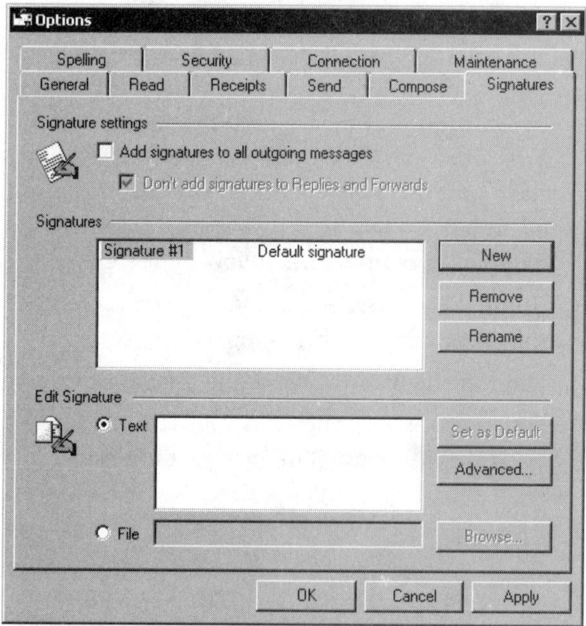

4. To create a text signature, in the Edit Signature section, enter the content in the box next to the Text option button.

5. If you want to use a file you've already created as your signature, click the File option button, and enter the filename or click Browse to locate it.
6. If you have multiple e-mail accounts, click the Advanced button to open the Advanced Signature Settings dialog box, and specify which accounts should use this signature.
7. Click the Add Signature To All Outgoing Messages check box, and click OK.

If you don't want the signature automatically appended to all outgoing messages, leave the Add Signature To All Outgoing Message check box unselected. Then, to add this signature to a message, choose Insert ➢ Signature in the New Message window.

Attaching Files to Your Messages

In Outlook Express, sending a file or multiple files along with your message is painless and simple. Follow these steps:

1. In the New Message window, choose Insert ➢ File Attachment to open the Insert Attachment dialog box:

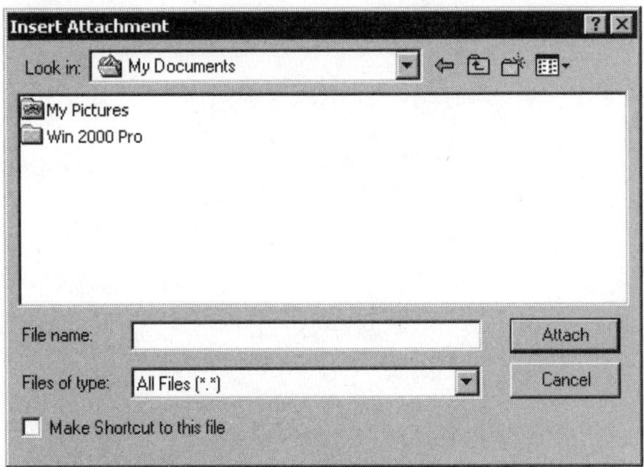

2. Select a file and click Attach.

Your message now contains the name of the file in the Attach line.

TIP If the file is large or if you know that the recipient has a slow connection, you'll want to compress it using a program such as WinZip. For a list of Web pages from which you can download or purchase such a program, in Internet Explorer search on *compression utilities.* See Chapter 12 for information on searching in Internet Explorer.

Applying Message Rules

Using the Rules Editor, you can specify where messages go after they are downloaded, block unwanted messages, and, in general, manage incoming messages more efficiently—especially if you deal with a lot of e-mail. In this section, I'll give you a couple of examples that illustrate the possibilities, but, as you will see, there are lots of possibilities, and you'll need to apply the options that make the most sense for your situation.

Let's start by establishing a rule that sends all mail from a particular person to that person's Outlook Express folder. Follow these steps:

1. In the main Outlook Express window, choose Tools ➢ Message Rules ➢ Mail to open the New Mail Rule dialog box:

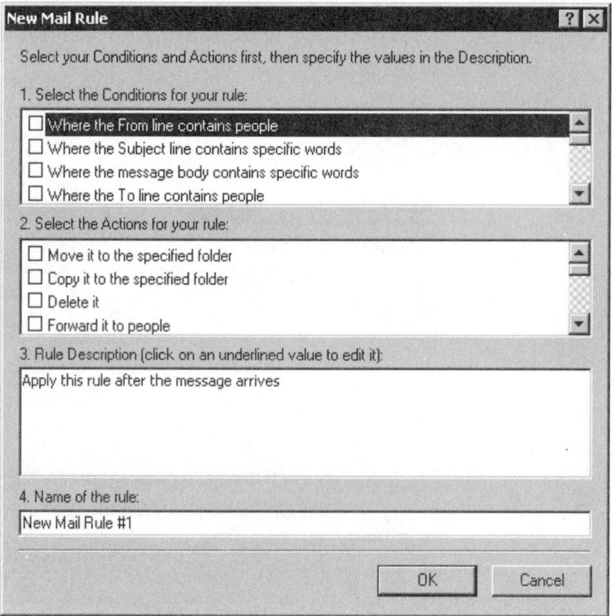

2. In the Select The Conditions For Your Rule section, click the Where The From Line Contains People check box.
3. In the Select The Actions For Your Rule section, click the Move It To The Specified Folder check box.

4. In the Rule Description section, click Contains People to open the Select People dialog box:

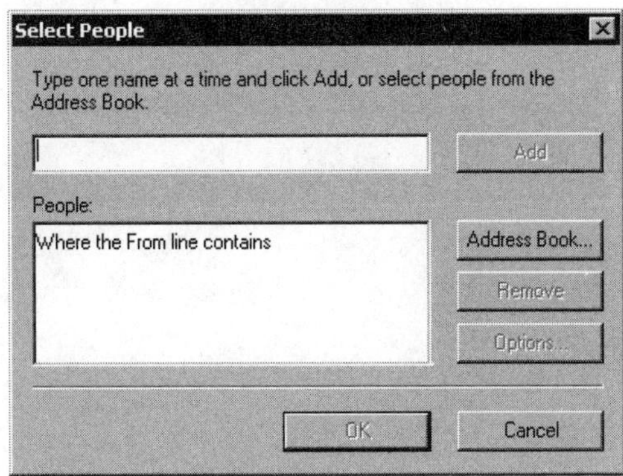

5. Enter a name and click Add, or select a name from your Address Book, and click OK.
6. Click Specified to open the Move dialog box.
7. Select the folder where you want this person's messages to go, and click OK. If you need to create a folder, click New Folder.
8. Accept the name of the rule that Outlook Express proposes, or type a new name.
9. Click OK.

Now, when messages arrive from that person, you'll find them in their folder rather than in your Inbox.

TIP To delete a rule, select it and click Remove in the Message Rules dialog box. To modify a rule, select it and click Modify.

To establish a rule that blocks unwanted messages, follow these steps:

1. In the main Outlook Express window, choose Tools ➢ Message Rules ➢ Blocked Senders List to open the Message Rules dialog box at the Blocked Senders tab.

2. Click Add to open the Add Sender dialog box:

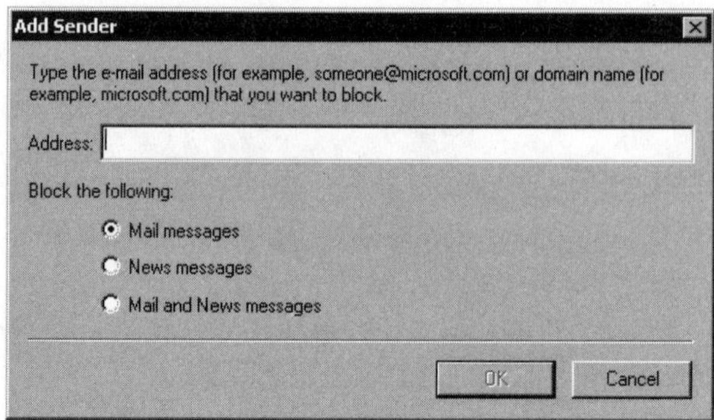

3. Enter the e-mail address that you want to block, specify whether you want to block mail, news, or both from this person, and click OK.
4. Click OK again in the Message Rules dialog box.

Now, mail from that address will go immediately to the Deleted Items folder. News from that person will simply not be displayed. (More on news in the last part of this chapter.) To change or delete this rule, open the Message Rules box, select the address, and click Modify or click Remove.

Adding and Managing Identities

If several people use the same computer either at home, at the office, or elsewhere, and thus also use Outlook Express, you'll probably want to take advantage of the Identities feature, which lets each person view their own mail and have individualized settings and contacts. Once you set up Identities, you can switch between them without shutting down the computer or disconnecting from and reconnecting to the Internet.

TIP You can also set up Identities in Address Book if you open it by choosing Start ➢ Programs ➢ Accessories ➢ Address Book.

When you install Windows 2000 Professional, you are set up in Outlook Express as the Main Identity. To set up other identities in Outlook Express, follow these steps:

1. In the main Outlook Express window, choose File ➢ Identities ➢ Add New Identity to open the New Identity dialog box:

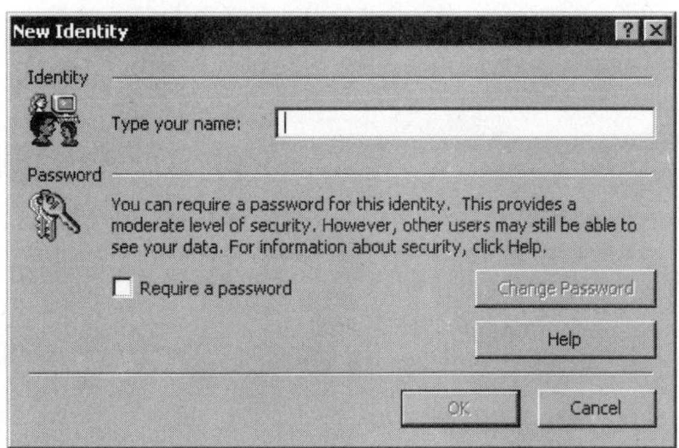

2. Enter the name of the identity you want to establish.
3. If you want to password protect this identity, click the Require A Password check box. Enter the password twice—once in the New Password box, and again in the Confirm New Password box. Click OK twice.
4. Outlook Express asks if you want to switch to this new identify now. If you do, click Yes; otherwise, click No.
5. In the Manage Identities dialog box, click New if you want to set up another identity; otherwise, click Close.

The first time you log on as a new identity, you will be asked for some information about your Internet connection. To switch from one identity to another, choose File ➢ Switch Identity to open the Switch Identities dialog box. Select the identity, and click OK. To log off from an identity, choose File ➢ Identities ➢ Logoff Identity.

To delete an identity, select the identity in the Manage Identities dialog box, and click Remove.

Using Outlook Express As Your Newsreader

A *newsgroup* is a collection of articles about a particular subject. A newsgroup is similar to e-mail in that you can reply to what someone else has written (the newsgroup term for this is *posted*), and you can send a question or a response either to the whole group or to individuals.

The primary (but not sole) source of newsgroups is Usenet, which is a worldwide distributed discussion system consisting of newsgroups that have names which are classified hierarchically by subject. In a newsgroup name, each component is separated from the next by a period. For example, `rec.crafts.metalworking` is a recreational group devoted to the craft of metalworking. The leftmost portion represents the largest hierarchical category, and the name gets more specific from left to right. Table 13.1 lists the major top-level newsgroup categories and explains what topics each discusses. Currently, there are thousands and thousands of newsgroups on every conceivable topic. For an extensive listing of them, go to `sunsite.unc.edu/usenet-i/hier-s/master.html`.

TABLE 13.1: THE MAJOR NEWSGROUPS

Newsgroup	What It Discusses
alt	Newsgroups outside the main structure outlined in this table
comp	Computer science and related topics, including operating systems, hardware, artificial intelligence, and graphics
misc	Anything that does not fit into one of the other categories
news	Information on Usenet and newsgroups
rec	Recreational activities such as hobbies, the arts, movies, and books
sci	Scientific topics such as math, physics, and biology
soc	Social issues and cultures
talk	Controversial subjects such as gun control, abortion, religion, and politics

You access newsgroups by accessing the server on which they are stored. Not all servers store the same newsgroups. The network administrator or the owner of the site determines what to store. Almost all news servers "expire" articles after a few days or, at most, a few weeks because of the tremendous volume. Although they might be archived at the site, these articles are no longer available to be viewed by users.

NOTE Newsgroups are uncensored. You can find just about anything at any time anywhere. Nobody has authority over newsgroups as a whole. If you find certain groups, certain articles, or certain people offensive, don't go there, or use the Rules Editor that I talked about earlier to prevent certain articles from even being displayed. But, remember, anarchy reigns in newsgroups, and you never know what you might stumble upon in the least likely places.

Setting Up a Newsgroup Account

Before you can read newsgroups, you must set up a newsgroups account. Before you start, get the name of your news server from your ISP, and then follow these steps:

1. In the main Outlook Express window, select the Outlook Express folder, and in the pane on the right click Set Up A Newsgroups Account to start the Internet Connection Wizard.
2. Supply the information that the Wizard requests, and click Finish when you are done.

You'll now see a folder in the Folders list for your news server.

Connecting to Newsgroups

The next task is to download the list of newsgroups from your server. When Outlook Express asks if you want to do this, click Yes. This may take a while if you have a slow connection, but notice the incrementing number of newsgroups in the Downloading Newsgroups dialog box. In the process of writing this section, I downloaded a list of more than 25,000 newsgroups.

TIP Only the names of the newsgroups are downloaded to your computer; their contents remain on the news server. Periodically, you can update this list by clicking Reset List.

When the list has finished downloading, you'll see the Newsgroup Subscriptions dialog box, as shown in Figure 13.4.

FIGURE 13.4
Use this dialog box to search for and subscribe to newsgroups.

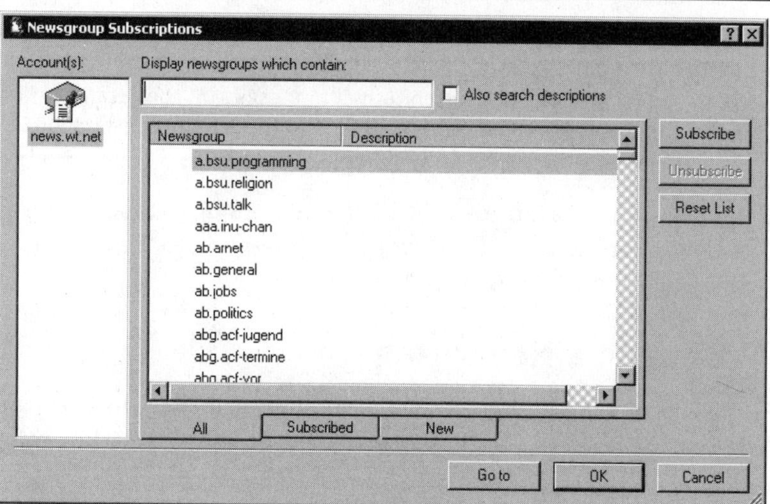

Finding a Newsgroup of Interest

You can select a newsgroup to read in two ways:

- You can scroll through the list (this will take a lot of time).
- You can search on a term.

Just for the sake of doing it, scroll the list a bit. As you can see, it's in alphabetic order by hierarchical categories. If you don't see anything right away that strikes your fancy, you can perform a search. Enter a term in the Display Newsgroups Which Contain text box, and then don't do anything! In a second, you'll see a list of newsgroups that contain articles about your topic.

Subscribing to a Newsgroup

Subscribing to a newsgroup doesn't involve a fee or any other transaction. Subscribing means simply creating a subfolder for a particular newsgroup in your news folder. Then, instead of selecting it from the Newsgroup Subscriptions dialog box, you can simply click the newsgroup's folder to see the list of articles in it.

Once you've located a newsgroup you want to read, you can select it, click Subscribe, and then click Go To to open it, or you can simply click Go To. To unsubscribe to a newsgroup, right-click its folder, and choose Unsubscribe.

Reading a Newsgroup

To read an article, simply click its header to display the message in the lower pane.

Outlook Express is a threaded newsreader in that it groups messages that respond to a subject line. If you see a plus sign to the left of a newsgroup header, you can click the plus sign to display a list of related messages. The more up-to-date term for threads is *conversation*. Newsgroup articles are grouped by conversations by default.

TIP You can also organize mail messages by conversations. With your Inbox selected, choose View ➢ Current View ➢ Group Messages by Conversation.

To read the articles from another newsgroup or to search for another newsgroup, double-click your main news folder, and then click Newsgroups to open the Newsgroup Subscriptions dialog box.

Posting to a Newsgroup

Replying to a newsgroup article or sending a message to a newsgroup is known as posting. You post to a newsgroup in much the same way that you compose and send e-mail.

To send an original message to a newsgroup, open the newsgroup and click the New Post button. The New Message window will open with the group's name in the To line.

To reply to an individual article, click the Reply button, and to reply to the entire newsgroup, click the Reply Group button.

Customizing Outlook Express

Throughout this chapter, I've mentioned from time to time ways that you can specify how Outlook Express handles certain features, such as signatures. In most cases, you do this through the Options dialog box (shown in Figure 13.5), which you open by choosing Tools ➢ Options. Here's a quick rundown of what to use each tab for in the Options dialog box:

General Use this tab to specify settings for how Outlook Express starts and for sending and receiving messages.

Read Use this tab to set options for reading news and mail. For example, you can specify a maximum number of news article headers to download at one time.

Receipts Use this tab if you want to verify that your message has been read by the recipient.

Send Use this tab to set, among other things, the format (HTML or Plain Text) in which you will send all messages and the format you'll use to reply to messages. You can also specify whether copies of sent messages will be stored and whether you want Outlook Express to put the names and addresses of people you reply to in your Address Book.

Compose Use this tab to specify the font and font size for mail messages and news articles that you create and to select stationery fonts for HTML messages.

Signatures Use to create a signature, as discussed earlier in this chapter.

Security Use this tab to specify your desired Internet Security zone and to get a digital ID.

Connection Use this tab to specify how Outlook Express handles your dial-up connection.

Maintenance Use this tab to specify what Outlook Express does with deleted items and to clean up downloaded messages, as well as to specify that all server commands are stored for troubleshooting purposes.

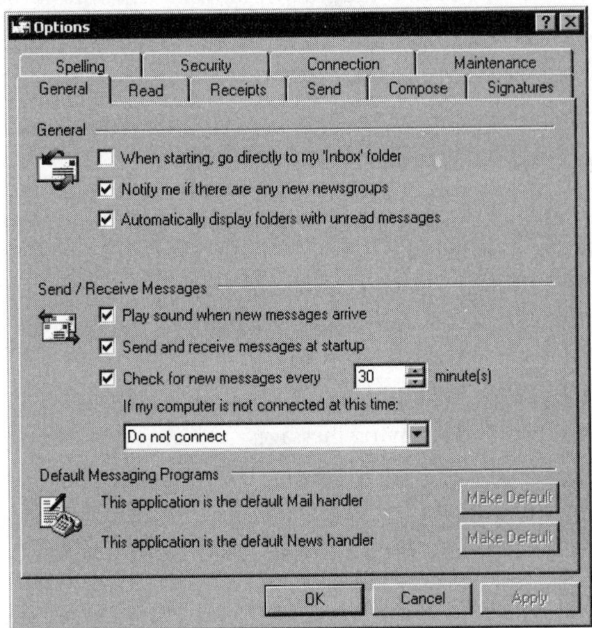

FIGURE 13.5
You use the Options dialog box to customize Outlook Express for the way you work.

NOTE If you have installed any of the Microsoft Office applications that include a spell checker, you will also see a Spelling tab in the Options dialog box.

Summary

The information in this chapter completes our look at how to use Windows 2000 Professional to communicate with the outside world and to connect to the Internet. In the next chapter, I'll lay the foundation for the rest of this book by describing the architecture—the operating system internals—of Windows 2000 Professional.

PART III

Networking Windows 2000 Professional

Learn To:

- ***Work with the Windows 2000 Professional and network architecture***
- ***Connect to Windows 2000 Professional networks***
- ***Use Active Directory***
- ***Telecommute securely***

CHAPTER 14

Understanding the Architecture

FEATURING:

Building an operating system is all about choices and trade-offs. Consequently, no single operating system is the best for every user and every need, although I'd argue that Windows 2000 Professional is in the running. Understanding those choices and trade-offs makes understanding Windows 2000 Professional easier.

Judging by most books on operating systems, publishers and writers seem to believe that operating system internals are of interest only to programmers. I don't think that point of view is defensible. Support people, power users, and troubleshooters will have a better understanding of the problems and strengths in Windows 2000 Professional if they are comfortable with terms such as *GDI, user,* and *WOWEXEC.*

In this chapter, I'll take you on a tour of the main components in Windows 2000 Professional, its client-server structure, and its environment subsystems. We also look at a controversial change in architecture—the decision to move the graphical user interface (GUI) from ring 3 into ring 0—that happened back in the NT 4 days but still affects the robustness of Windows 2000 Professional. Now, if you're not a hardware type and are saying to yourself, "Hmm...I try to answer the phone by the third ring. What's ring 0?" stay tuned; it'll all be clear soon.

Understanding Rings and Things: CPU Privilege Levels

Despite the intention that Windows 2000 Professional would be an architecture-independent operating system, Windows 2000 Professional does include a few elements that are common to most processors. (*Architecture-independent* really means processor-independent.) One of the most important concepts related to architecture independence is the notion of *memory protection and privilege.*

A Major Software Problem: Clobbering Memory

Put two programs into a computer, and you'll soon experience the problem of keeping those programs from damaging each other. Even if your computer is running a *multitasking operating system*—that is, an operating system that supports more than one program running at a time—a potential problem lurks. Applications can grow and shrink dynamically, as required by their owners. You start up Microsoft Word, and it may initially ask the operating system for only a couple of megabytes of RAM. But insert a few big graphics, and before you know it, Word is grabbing megabytes by the fistful.

What happens if Word needs four more megabytes, but the operating system has only two more to give it? A well-behaved application would accept the bad news and deal with it. But a buggy application (and unfortunately every application is at least a *little* buggy) might start writing to the memory that it owns and then keep going and going and going, right on past its allotted memory region. In the process, the errant application would overwrite another application's memory, damaging that application. This problem is probably the most common and most troublesome of programming errors, and it's known by many names. Back when I wrote mainframe Fortran for a living, I called it an 0C1 or an 0C4, for the error messages that it generated. Some programmers would say the bad application was "scribbling" all over another application's memory; still others would refer to the application "clobbering" the other application's memory.

Windows 3.1 programs caused this problem all the time. When the Windows 3.1 operating system noticed the problem, it would report a *general protection fault*, or GPF.

Anti-Clobber Features

Now, GPFs aren't necessarily a bad thing. When a GPF occurs, it means that the CPU and the operating system are working together to detect and stop berserk applications before they start destroying other applications. GPFs were a problem in Windows 3.1 because Windows 3.1 didn't use the built-in protection of the CPU chip effectively. As a result, Windows 3.1 was good at sounding the alarm, but not so good at mustering the troops to keep the infidels from the gate; although this isn't a book about Windows 3.1, I explain a bit more about GPFs later.

Applications strayed out of their assigned memory areas so often in Windows 3.1 programs that a company named Numega has made a fair amount of money selling a product called Bounds-Checker that helps you catch a program in the act of stepping out of its allowed memory space. Although Bounds-Checker is one of the truly great debugging applications of our time, Numega should never have *needed* to write it—checking for memory clobbering is the operating system's job, not the job of some third-party utility.

A large portion of the instability in Windows 3.1 can be traced to the system's laissez-faire attitude about how its applications use memory. An example is a word processor scribbling all over a spreadsheet—what's to keep the word processor from scribbling all over the *operating system*?

In the case of Windows 3.1, *nothing* stopped the word processor from scribbling all over the operating system, and that's why Windows 3.1 was so easy to crash. From NT's very beginning, its designers wanted to offer better crashproofing.

As it turns out, most of today's processors include a built-in feature called the *memory protection model* that makes building an operating system with zero tolerance for memory clobbers fairly simple.

Process Privilege Levels: Kernel and User Mode

Most of today's processors enable you to designate any program running in the processor as either a kernel mode application or a user mode application. A *kernel mode application* is allowed to, among other things, allocate memory to all other applications.

Kernel mode programs are the only programs allowed to modify a very important piece of data in the computer's memory: a table of memory boundaries that defines each application currently running and exactly what memory each application is allowed to access. You'll see that this table of memory boundaries is vitally important.

Here's the sequence of events for allocating memory boundaries:

1. An application asks the operating system (which is a kernel mode program) to load it.
2. The operating system asks the application how much memory it needs.
3. The application tells the operating system its required amount of memory.
4. The operating system loads the application into memory, securing the memory boundaries around the application.

From that point on, whenever the application tries to access memory, the CPU consults a table of application memory boundaries that indicates which RAM goes with which application. Using that information, the CPU can either allow the memory access or declare a *memory access fault.* (I *would* use the term general protection fault, as a memory access fault *is* a GPF, but that term is applied only to Intel processors, and recall that NT was originally designed to run on non-Intel processors, so NT architects tend to use terms that aren't Intel-specific, even though at this point NT *is* Intel-specific, as Microsoft killed Alpha support in Windows 2000 Professional. In any case, "memory access fault" is the more generic term applying to all processors, so think of it as architecture-independent jargon.)

Only a kernel mode application can modify the table that the CPU consults. The major difference between kernel mode programs and user mode programs is that kernel mode programs define the memory boundaries and user mode programs live in them.

The dichotomy between programs that can define memory boundaries and those that can't is built into the processors that Windows 2000 Professional currently runs on (the Intel *x86* chips) and into the processors it will soon run on (the IA64 chips). Although RISC (reduced instruction set computing) chips support only two levels of privilege (kernel mode and user mode), the Intel chips support *four* levels of privilege, which are called *rings*. You'll never see the terms *kernel mode* and *user mode* in an Intel programming manual. Ring 0 applications (Intel-speak for *kernel mode*) can control anything about memory but can also leave some memory control to ring 1 applications. Ring 1 applications, in turn, cannot modify memory protections set by a ring 0 application but can set memory protection on memory that *they* own; ring 1 restrictions must be followed by ring 2 applications. Ring 2 applications get to bully around the last kind, ring 3 applications, and ring 3 applications can't modify any memory and therefore have no one to boss around.

NOTE Windows 2000 Professional on Intel computers uses only ring 0 (for kernel mode) and ring 3 (for user mode). Windows 2000 Professional does not use rings 1 or 2, because many RISC CPUs support only two levels of privilege, and Windows 2000 Professional must be able to run on many kinds of CPUs.

Even though the concept of rings took a few pages to describe, it's a basic and fundamentally important thing to understand about Windows 2000 Professional—how it protects the memory of one application from all other applications.

You've also got the tools now to understand why Windows 3.1 was so unstable: *All applications lived in ring 0.* Every single device driver, screen saver, application—you name it—had the capability to reallocate the table of memory boundaries anytime one felt like it.

Now you can easily understand an important Windows 2000 Professional design goal: *Don't let the applications get within 10 miles of the kernel mode* (ring 0 on Intel, recall). If an application tries to exceed its allotted memory space, the processor will detect a memory access fault and remove the offending application from memory.

NOTE An operating system will not protect an application from itself. If an application uses several memory areas and one area overflows into another, Windows 2000 Professional will probably not detect the overflow unless the application tries to read or write outside of its allotted memory space. That's not an immutable truth, however; a programmer can design a program to take advantage the built-in memory protection capabilities of Windows 2000 Professional, but doing so is not a requirement for building an application.

This distinction of kernel mode programs versus user mode programs turned out to be crucial in the design of Windows 2000 Professional, as you'll see in the rest of this chapter.

Designing Architecture Independence

I've already peppered this discussion with references to PCs with processors other than the standard Intel *x*86 chips. But to the average user, architecture independence may seem like a fairly unimportant concept—after all, doesn't everybody use Intel Pentiums, Pentium Pros, and Pentium IIs and IIIs? Well, no, not exactly.

Architecture Independence in Windows 2000 Professional: The Big Picture

You don't get massive power from Intel *x*86 systems; you get it from a four-processor Alpha with 512MB of RAM running at 500MHz. Windows 2000 Professional is positioned to capture the high end of the desktop workstation market; if it happens to end up in the midrange, pushing out Windows 95/98 machines in business and in the home, well, then, so be it. You can be sure that Microsoft won't complain—but taking market share from Windows 95/98 wasn't the initial goal.

NOTE Late in the beta process of Windows 2000 Professional, Compaq announced that they would no longer pursue development efforts with Microsoft on the Alpha processor. Microsoft then announced that they were dropping their support for the Alpha as well. Microsoft does, however, plan to support Intel's new 64-bit RISC platform, IA64, so Windows 2000 Professional will continue to carry on NT's cross-platform development.

Computer manufacturers will always be making a chip that's bigger, faster, and, most important, *newer*. But the days are gone when consumers would wait five years for an operating system for that chip. The vital and central importance of architecture independence for Windows 2000 Professional is that its easily portable structure usually enables Windows 2000 Professional to be the first operating system implemented on a new CPU, and in this business, being first often means being the only one in the game.

Minimum CPU Requirements to Be Windows 2000 Professional–Possible

Well, how architecture-independent *is* Windows 2000 Professional?

Not every CPU *can* host Windows 2000 Professional. Obviously, the 80286 lacks the 32-bit strength that Windows 2000 Professional needs. But Windows 2000 Professional doesn't demand much. Before Microsoft can implement Windows 2000 Professional on a CPU, it must have the following:

- Data registers that are 32 bits or larger
- Memory address registers that are 32 bits or larger

NOTE Windows 2000 Professional needs to be able to allocate a space up to 2^{32} bits, or 4GB. (No, Windows 2000 Professional doesn't need that much RAM; it's just that the underlying architecture is laid out on a 4GB memory map, as you'll learn later in this chapter.)

- A memory protection model
- At least two levels of privilege for processes so that Windows 2000 Professional can implement kernel mode and user mode privilege
- The capability to control how any arbitrary process accesses any given block of memory in the following ways:
  - A given process can or cannot read the block of memory.
  - A given process can or cannot write the block of memory.
  - A given process can or cannot execute the block of memory.
- A memory *paging* ability, or CPU support for virtual memory

That looks like a fair number of requirements, but it isn't really. These requirements describe most advanced microprocessors on the market today, as well as larger computers. A Microsoft source once said that they were looking into building NT/370, NT for an IBM mainframe. In theory, that would be possible due to NT's fairly liberal requirements; of course, whether it's *advisable* is a different matter. (Where do you plug in the mouse?)

The Windows 2000 Professional Baseline: the HAL, the Kernel, and the Drivers

The HAL, the kernel, and the drivers—sounds like a rock band, doesn't it? To keep Windows 2000 Professional as architecture-independent as possible, Microsoft minimized the amount of the operating system that is hardware-specific. Just three parts of the operating system must change with different computers:

- The Hardware Abstraction Layer, `hal.dll`
- The kernel, `ntoskrnl.exe`
- The device drivers for the computer's specific hardware, such as video drivers, network card drivers, and mouse drivers

Next, we take a brief look at each of these components.

"Open the Drive Bay Door, HAL"

Well, you never have to tell it that, really. The HAL (Hardware Abstraction Layer) exists to smooth out differences *within* the many implementations of a particular microprocessor. For example, the Motorola 68000 was the processor upon which the Apple Macintosh, the Amiga, and the Atari 520 ST were built. They were all desktop microcomputers with GUIs, but any other similarity ends there. Some of the computers made heavy use of interrupts; others used more programmed input-output and direct memory access (DMA). Additionally, a *huge* difference exists between the structure of a PC with one processor and a PC with two or more processors.

The HAL's job is to smooth out those differences, presenting to the operating system a standard-looking set of computer hardware. The HAL is implemented as a file called `hal.dll`. In the 68000 example, the Macintosh, Atari ST520, and Amiga versions would all have the same kernel because they all use the same processor, but they'd need different HALs.

The basic HAL that ships with Windows 2000 Professional supports two processors, and the HAL that ships with Windows 2000 Server supports as many as four processors. NT can support as many as 32 processors in theory, but you'd need a new HAL to support them. Similarly, if a new peripheral bus were to appear, such as a 128-bit version of PCI, Windows 2000 Professional would need only a new HAL and then it would run with no problems.

We Have a Kernel, but Not a General

Unix systems were built in pieces, somewhat similar to the way Windows 2000 Professional is built today, and the central manager or heart of the operating system was called the *kernel*. That name is used to describe the heart of virtually every operating system, and Windows 2000 Professional is no exception.

The kernel is mainly a piece of software that schedules tasks on your computer. If several programs all want to run at the same time, the kernel locates the one that has the highest priority and runs that task. The kernel also makes sure that all the processors in a multiprocessor system keep busy.

The kernel also manages all the Windows 2000 Professional subsystems, which are the subject of most of the remainder of this chapter. Managing subsystems turns out to be a key concept in understanding the notion of Windows 2000 Professional borrowing from the microkernel and client-server models of operating systems, as you'll later in this chapter.

They're Called Drivers Because They Can Drive You Crazy

Support for particular pieces of hardware could be built into an operating system—for example, Microsoft could have built support for a Microsoft mouse right into the kernel—but that isn't a particularly good idea. For one thing, if you had a computer that didn't include a Microsoft mouse, the memory required to hold the Microsoft mouse support would be wasted.

Instead, Windows 2000 Professional, like other operating systems, segregates support for hardware devices into separate software modules called *device drivers*. Although most descriptions of Windows 2000 Professional do not include device drivers in the hardware-specific part of Windows 2000 Professional (most just show the HAL and the kernel), these drivers are quite hardware-specific. That fact is worth knowing; support for a particular network card on an Intel system doesn't necessarily mean that it's supported on an Alpha system. (*That's* the part that can drive you crazy.)

Perhaps the other reason that drivers can drive you crazy (and why you care about what they are in the first place) is that they're usually not written by the people who write the operating system. Instead, they're written by somebody at a company that makes a peripheral such as a video board, a mouse, a LAN board, or a SCSI host adapter. These people often don't understand Windows 2000 Professional all that well, with the result that drivers are often not written very well.

Now, the scary part is that drivers pretty much *must* be kernel mode programs, so a badly written driver can crash your system.

WARNING In my experience, a bad driver is usually the cause of a Windows 2000 Professional crash.

More than 90 percent of the Windows 2000 Professional crashes I've seen were caused either by bad SCSI (Small Computer System Interface) drivers or bad Enhanced Integrated Drive Electronics (EIDE) drivers. Of course, the great strength of Windows 2000 Professional is that when it dies, it points the finger at who killed it, so at least you can go back to the vendor who wrote the driver and ask the company to fix it. The vendor may not fix the driver, but at least they won't be able to do any finger-pointing at other vendors. The culprit's name is printed in black and white for anyone to see when you run the `dumpexam.exe` program.

"But wait a minute," you cry, "I thought Windows 2000 Professional was stable." Well, yes, it's stable, but there's no such thing as a bulletproof operating system; as I've already said, designing an operating system involves trade-offs—which is the topic of the next section.

Designing Robustness

I've made much of how the structure of Windows 2000 Professional lends it a stability that most of us haven't seen in desktop operating systems, but I haven't really gone too much into the details. I'll do that now.

A Basic Layered Operating System

Most PC operating systems are *layered* operating systems, meaning that they consist of a bunch of pieces of software stacked one atop the other. The pieces tied most closely to the hardware are always represented at the bottom and application software is always at the top. Sandwiched between the applications that users want to run and the hardware on which they want to run, the applications are the intermediary programs that communicate between the two. Figure 14.1 depicts a basic representation of a layered operating system.

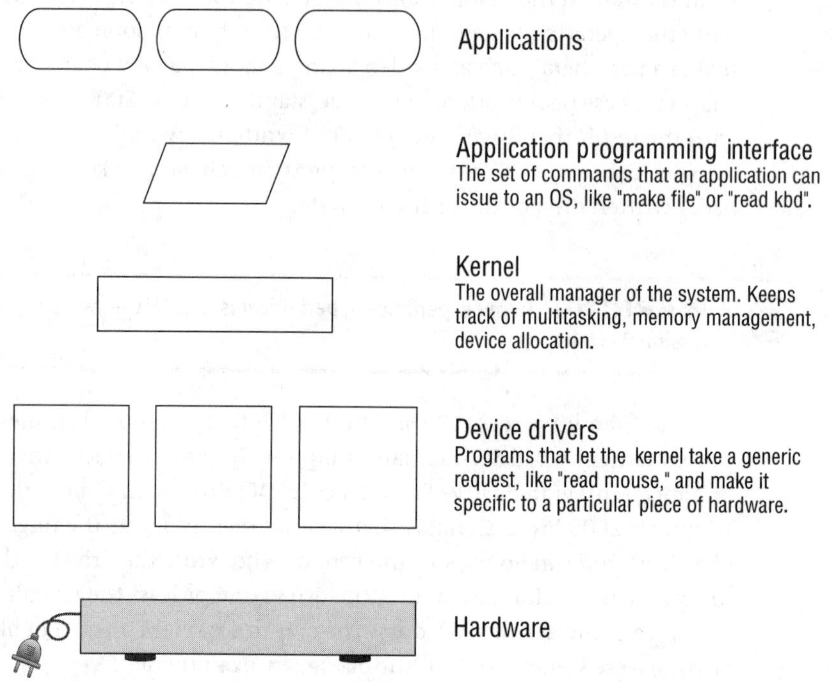

FIGURE 14.1
The structure of a typical layered operating system, the very basis of more advanced architectures

To a certain extent, the layered structure in Figure 14.1 also represents the design of DOS, OS/2, Windows 3.1, and Windows 95/98.

At the lowest level of software are the device drivers, which manipulate the system hardware. The APIs, or *application programming interfaces*, are the doorway to the operating system as far as the applications are concerned. If an application wants to create a file, read a keystroke, or paint the screen blue, it must go through the operating system, and it must access the operating system through the APIs. DOS has an API of its own, as do Windows 3.1 and Windows 95/98, so today's layered operating systems often support multiple APIs to allow backward compatibility.

An API is the published set of legal tasks that an operating system can do for an application—examples include opening a file, reading a keystroke, or ending a program. Of course, since we are dealing with computers, there are *i*'s to be dotted and *t*'s to be crossed. For example, one operating system might open a file with the command `DOSOPENFILE`, and another might open a file with the `makefile` command. Those two commands do the same thing, but they do it in different operating systems in much the same way that you express the idea *hello* differently in different languages.

Windows NT, OS/2, and Windows 3.*x* all used different APIs, and so developers have always had to decide which API to focus their efforts on. Because of the large size of the Windows market, most vendors work first in Windows and then port their applications from Windows to some other operating system. An application trying to access one of today's operating systems from anything other than the APIs will crash. (I say *today's* operating systems because it was possible under DOS to jump into the operating system at any old place, leading to a host of compatibility nightmares for people trying to build "compatible" PC computers.)

In between the APIs and the device drivers is the kernel, which manages the whole thing.

A Client-Server, Microkernel Operating System

The only thing wrong with the previous model is that virtually all the applications themselves must live in kernel mode. That *does* make securing the operating system a bit harder, at least when compared with a *client-server* or *microkernel* architecture, which is depicted in Figure 14.2. (It's called client-server because parts of the operating system treat each other as clients or servers.)

FIGURE 14.2

The microkernel or client-server operating system model moves more of the software into the user mode.

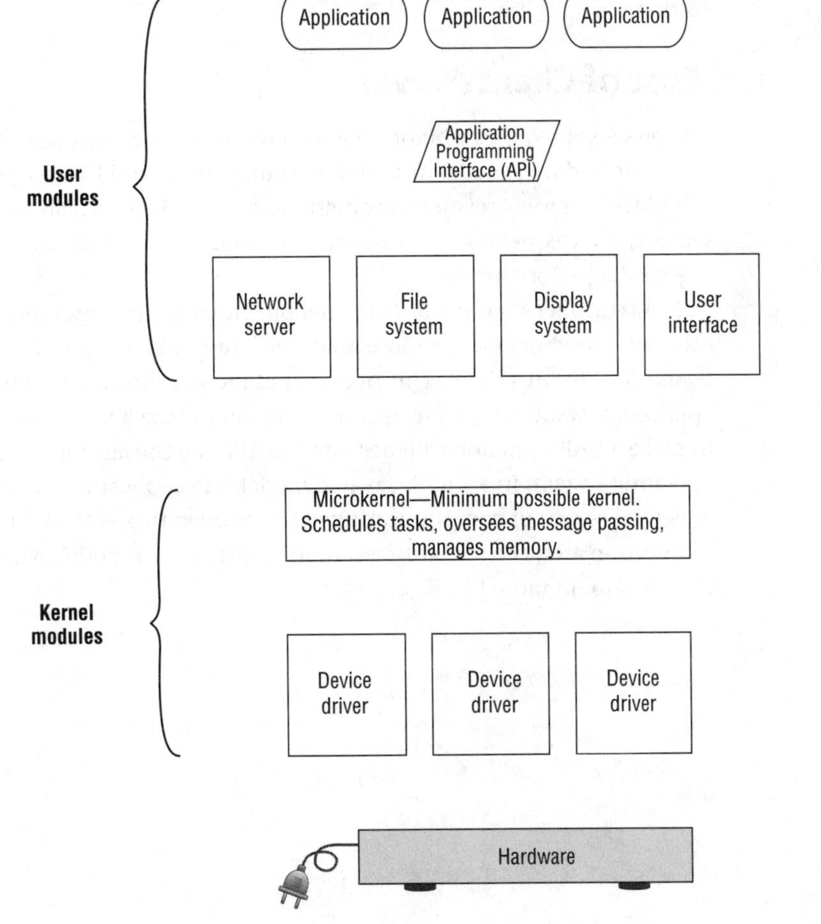

Notice that Figure 14.2 distinguishes between kernel mode and user mode. The basic layered operating system presented in the preceding section puts everything but the applications in the kernel mode. The client-server or microkernel model puts only the bare minimum (hence the *micro* part of microkernel) in kernel mode. One reason that the client-server model seems worth the effort is that operating system designers want their systems to be robust and stable.

One way to accomplish those goals is to simply write operating systems without bugs in them. (Now that we've had a little laugh, let's look at another way.) Another way is to exploit the memory protection functions built right into today's processor chips. Kernel mode programs are scary in that they can scribble all over *any* part of the system's memory. Also, user mode programs can be imprisoned in memory areas, and if they try to escape by exceeding their bounds, the CPU hardware automatically sounds the alarm.

One of the major goals of the client-server model is, then, to minimize the number of parts that run in kernel mode. There is, of course, a downside to the client-server model, one that can significantly affect performance and that I'll consider in the next section.

The Cost of Client-Server

The processor requires a bit of time—a few tens of microseconds—to shift between kernel mode and user mode. Although that may not sound like very much, consider that a 100MHz microprocessor can sometimes get *1,000 instructions* to execute in 10 microseconds. Consequently, every user/kernel mode shift is expensive in terms of operating system performance.

Now consider that in a microkernel operating system, user modules cannot see other user modules (applications that don't run in kernel mode) and cannot directly communicate with them. This necessitates mode shifts. For example, imagine that an application wants to tell the operating system to read a keystroke. To do this, it needs to make an API function call, because the APIs are the authorized doorways into the operating system. In a simple layered model, the application simply calls the API, which takes care of communicating with the operating system. But the lines of communication aren't so straightforward in a microkernel model, where the communication flow looks more like Figure 14.3.

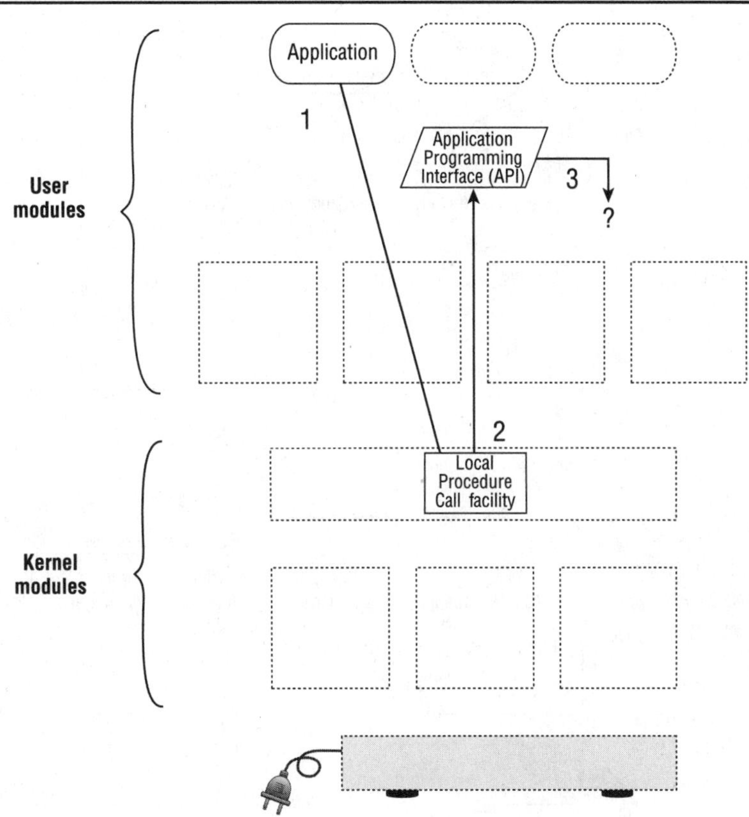

FIGURE 14.3
User module communication in a microkernel model

In the microkernel model, the application, instead of calling the API, calls a piece of the microkernel whose only job is to pass messages (in Windows 2000 Professional, it's called the *Local Procedure Call* facility or *LPC*). The LPC forwards the message to the API.

Here's the path of the message: The message goes from the application across the user/kernel boundary to the LPC, and from the LPC back to the API across the user/kernel boundary again. That's the point at which the API knows to ask the operating system to do something, and this of course generates another user/kernel mode shift. Further, accessing the network, the file system, the display, or the user interface involves piles of mode shifts. The latter are all user modules as well, so messages passed between them must go through the user/kernel boundary.

The Windows 2000 Professional Compromise

A pure microkernel model, then, would be tremendously inefficient because of the massive number of context shifts it requires. So Windows 2000 Professional settles on a kind of modified microkernel structure, as you see in Figure 14.4.

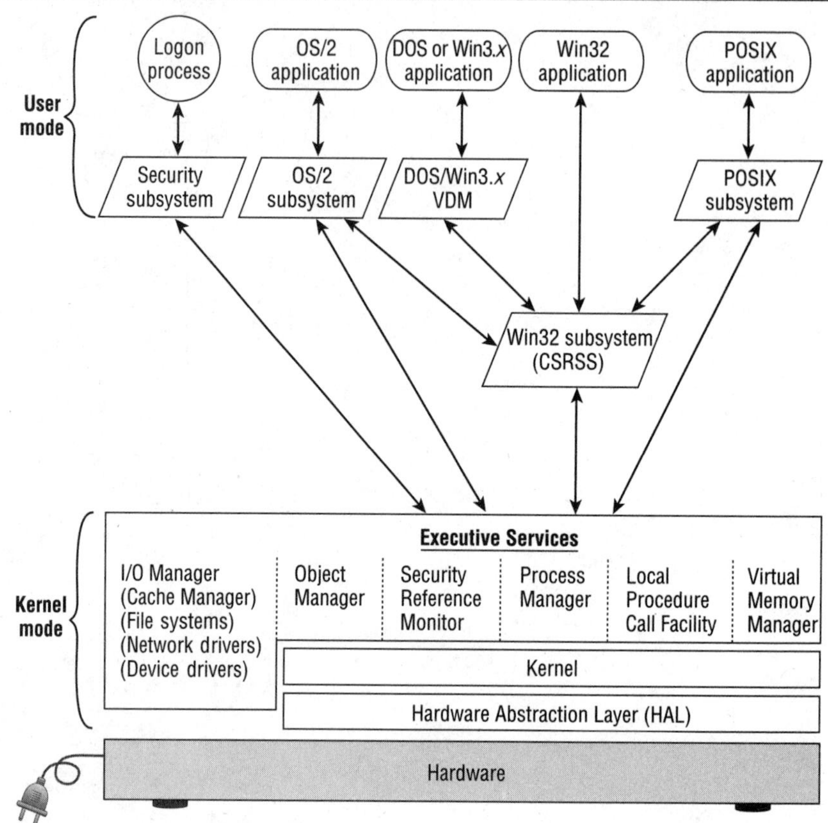

FIGURE 14.4 *The Windows 2000 Professional modified client-server structure (simplified)*

Now, whenever we see a figure like this, our eyes tend to glaze over; lest *yours* do the same, let's break it down. You need to understand this diagram if you want to stay with this chapter. Also, I couldn't fit an important flow of information on the figure, so read on to see what's *not* in this picture.

The Hardware box represents only the hardware on which you're running Windows 2000 Professional. You've already met the HAL and the kernel. Although this picture shows the kernel as sitting atop the HAL, that representation is not 100 percent accurate. Some small parts of the kernel interact directly with the hardware rather than through the HAL.

The I/O Manager is vitally important because:

- It contains all the device drivers that keep the hardware working.
- It contains most of the networking part of Windows 2000 Professional.
- It contains the file systems—FAT, FAT32, and NTFS.

Windows 2000 Executive Services (which were first mentioned way back in Chapter 1) is just a catch-all phrase for a few modules that are important to Windows 2000 Professional and that live in kernel mode. They are also called Windows 2000 Executive functions. I'll get to all of them a bit later.

In user mode, you see the OS/2, POSIX, DOS/Windows 3.*x*, and client-server (Win32) subsystems (usually abbreviated CSRSS) of Windows 2000 Professional. Although they're an important part of the operating system, they live out in user mode—and for a very good reason.

Operating system designers have always struggled with the dilemma that I described a bit earlier. They want to segregate the operating system from the applications, because the applications can't be trusted. But allowing the applications to be more closely knit to the underlying operating system makes for smaller applications and faster operating systems. Running OS/2 or Windows 3.*x* applications, then, *requires* that Windows 2000 Professional allow these applications to peek and poke into the OS/2 and Windows 3.*x* subsystems. That kind of intimacy is necessary for Windows 2000 Professional to fool those applications into thinking that they are running on their native operating systems rather than on simple Windows 2000 Professional subsystems that are mimicking the native systems.

In fact, any program running on a Windows 2000 Professional machine ends up using the native Windows 2000 Professional programming interface; the environment subsystems resemble translators that convert an OS/2, DOS, Windows 3.*x*, or POSIX operating system request to an equivalent Windows 2000 Professional request and then pass that request to Windows 2000 Professional. The front end for requests to Windows 2000 Professional is the CSRSS. The word for the native Windows 2000 Professional programming interface, by the way, is *Win32*—something I'll have more to say about a bit later.

But first, let me clear up something *very important* that underscores yet again the cost of using even a hybrid client-server approach as Windows 2000 Professional does. Look at the lines running between the subsystems, the CSRSS, and the Windows 2000 Professional Executive. They're not actually correct because I've depicted each environment subsystem communicating directly with CSRSS—do you remember why? Take a look at Figure 14.5, and you'll see what I'm talking about.

FIGURE 14.5
A more accurate view of subsystem communication in the Windows 2000 Professional modified client-server structure

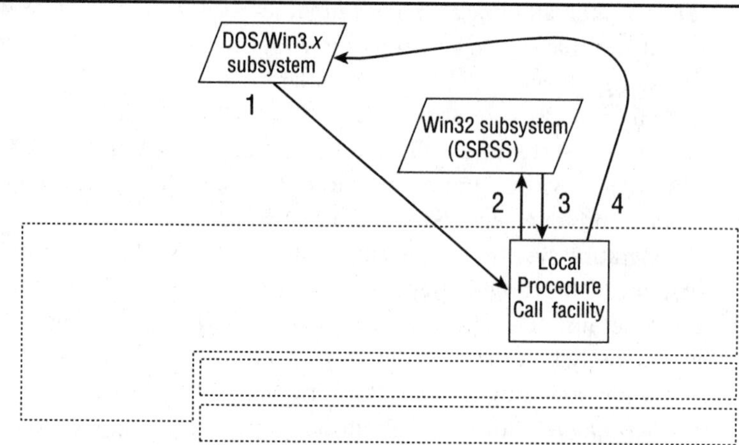

Figure 14.5 illustrates how just one user mode subsystem, the DOS/Windows 3.*x* subsystem, communicates with another user mode subsystem, the CSRSS. Figure 14.4 shows a double-sided arrow between the DOS/Windows 3.*x* subsystem and the CSRSS. But two user modules can't directly communicate—*pass messages* is the more accepted Windows 2000 Professional term—under Windows 2000 Professional. Instead, the DOS/Windows 3.*x* subsystem must pass a message to the Windows 2000 Professional Executive, which lives in kernel mode, which then passes the message to CSRSS.

Similarly, CSRSS can respond only to a request from the DOS/ Windows 3.*x* subsystem by first sending a message to the Windows 2000 Professional Executive, which then forwards the note to the DOS/Windows 3.*x* subsystem. Here you see that I'm 'fessing up for having oversimplified things a bit. Go back to Figure 14.4, and visualize all of the user mode communications that are represented as double-headed arrows as really being four single-headed arrows. I didn't want that oversimplification to cause you to miss exactly *how* expensive the client-server model is in terms of user/kernel shifts.

Is the Microkernel a Bad Compromise?

The whole idea of a microkernel or client-server operating system is that it is a stable approach, which puts drivers and subsystems all at arm's length, so to speak—out in user mode (ring 3 on Intel systems). And if they crash, they crash only themselves.

Well, yes, that of course sounds good, but to a certain extent, it's a moot point. If the keyboard driver is in user mode and it crashes, then certainly it has crashed only itself and the kernel continues to run. But what can you do with an operating system without a functioning keyboard?

On yet another hand, some of the things that you want to do might be possible even without a working keyboard. On a Windows 2000 Server machine, your server processes would continue to run as long as they didn't need keyboard input. You could then *choose* when to take down the server and bring it back up, rather than potentially have the entire system crash on the errant driver's schedule.

TIP The best approach for stability is probably to keep applications in user mode and put the operating system in kernel mode—but to debug the operating system extremely well.

NOTE You can tell whether an error occurred in user mode or kernel mode. Kernel mode errors lead to blue screens. User mode errors lead to Dr. Watson messages.

NT 4's Additional Architectural Change

All this discussion of where different operating system pieces should go is particularly relevant to NT Workstation 4. Prior to this release, Microsoft put the Windows NT native programming subsystem, the Win32 API, out in user mode—but with NT 4, Win32 moved to kernel mode.

Microsoft says it made the change to improve NT's performance as a workstation operating system, and the switch did, indeed, improve NT's performance. Animation-based Windows 3.1 programs that ran painfully slow under Windows NT 3.51 and earlier versions run at about the same speed under NT Workstation 4 as they do under Windows 95.

Mainly, there were three pieces of NT that moved from user mode to kernel mode:

- USER, the user interface manager
- GDI, the graphics manager
- The video display drivers

USER is a set of routines that responds every time a user clicks or drags a user control. (*Control* is the generic phrase for a window, button, slider bar, radio button, check box, list box, combo box, or toolbar.) The GDI (Graphics Device Interface) is a set of routines that handles much of the low-level work required to keep a graphical user interface going. GDI routines manipulate bitmaps, colors, cursor shapes, icons, and fonts. Every time your word processor wants to show you a line of text in Times Roman, GDI puts those characters on the screen.

NOTE Whenever you load a bitmap as wallpaper, you see another example of GDI at work.

Both GDI and USER are central, integral parts of Windows NT and they're pretty well debugged. Putting them into kernel mode, then, is probably a good idea. But the display drivers, well, that's another story…

I've already said that the only times I have ever seen Windows 2000 Professional crash were when I loaded a badly written SCSI or EIDE driver. Because those drivers are part of the I/O Manager, they live in kernel mode, which is why they can bluescreen the system when they fail.

Display drivers, in contrast, weren't able to kill a Windows NT machine in versions 3.51 and earlier. That changed in NT 4 (and continues in Windows 2000 Professional) because the display drivers now live in kernel mode. Again, a reasonable person could say, "Hey, wait a minute, *who cares*? After all, what can you get done on a computer that doesn't have a display driver?" And again, I answer that a server has very little use for a display driver. Windows 2000/NT Server works just fine no matter how strange the screen looks; after all, the file and application server part comes up automatically, and you needn't even log into an NT Server machine for it to act as a file server.

My worry is that display drivers are, like disk drivers, often not written by people inside Microsoft, and so they don't get tested as well. Not, mind you, that Microsoft is any paragon of virtue when it comes to bug-free code—although NT's pretty darn good that way—but because a Microsoft tester has access to thousands of different machines, a huge network, and the ear of people with intimate knowledge of the innards of NT. A Microsoft tester is in a good position to beat the stuffing out of a display driver. In contrast, a display driver programmer at a video board company wouldn't have access to nearly that number of resources. When working at a company whose focus is hardware, testers often see software drivers as a kind of necessary evil—and the result is a display driver that hasn't been properly tested.

So, in the end analysis, what's the best course of action for *you*? Well, ultimately, Microsoft's decision to put the Win32 subsystem into kernel mode has meant that we get a snappier response out of our desktop applications on NT 4 and now Windows 2000 Professional. Yes, it probably means some small reduction in stability in NT/2000, but that problem probably comes from the drivers. I suggest, therefore, confining video board purchases to the boards on the Hardware Compatibility List (HCL)—they've been beaten around and are presumably fairly trustworthy.

In the end analysis, moving graphic and printing drivers into kernel mode was probably a bad idea. But Microsoft built some entirely new tools while creating Windows 2000 Professional that allowed them to really run drivers through the wringer. The result is that Windows 2000 Professional's kernel mode components are pretty reliable, and so you won't see too many blue screens under 2000. The new *user* mode modules, however, may bedevil us, so I've found in general that Windows 2000 Professional means fewer blue screens but more frequent visits from the good Dr. Watson.

By the way, those driver testing tools shipped *with* Windows 2000 Professional in the form of `verify.exe`. It's a cool tool that lets you put a particular driver under intense scrutiny and prove pretty reliably whether it's buggy or not.

Working with the Major Modules in Windows 2000 Professional

By now, you've met some of the major components in Windows 2000 Professional. But I haven't been able to work *all* of them into the discussion yet, so let me make amends for that now.

The HAL, Kernel, and I/O Manager

The HAL, kernel, and I/O Manager are some of the pieces of Windows 2000 Professional you've already met. The HAL enables many dissimilarly designed computers to look like Windows 2000 Professional. The HAL also smooths out any differences created by running Windows 2000 Professional with a single processor on some machines and as many as 64 processors on other machines.

The kernel is the central manager, the part that knows at any moment which processes are running in the system, what memory they take up, what their priority is, and what (if anything) they're waiting for. Part of the system's memory management takes place in the kernel as well, and you'll read about how Windows 2000 Professional manages memory in a few pages.

The I/O Manager contains the network system, including the *redirector* (which makes it possible for a workstation to use resources on the network) and the server. The network board drivers are part of the I/O Manager as well, as are the file systems, the Cache Manager, disk interface drivers, and other device drivers.

The Windows 2000 Professional Executive

Remember back a few pages when I showed you an overview of the structure of Windows 2000 Professional? I included a piece of Windows 2000 Professional that is a kernel mode piece but didn't say much about it. That piece is called the Windows 2000 Professional Executive, and I'll describe it here.

The Executive consists of Windows 2000 Professional modules that were deemed important enough to live in kernel mode, ring 0 on an Intel processor. They are

- Local Procedure Call (LPC) facility
- Process Manager

- Object Manager
- Security Reference Monitor
- Virtual Memory Manager

The LPC facility is the part of the Windows 2000 Professional Executive that manages the messages passed between one user mode module and another—recall that two user mode modules can't communicate directly with each other.

The Process Manager has the job of handling the nitty-gritty detail of starting and shutting down processes (programs or parts of programs). Whenever you start a program, the Process Manager does much of the hard work. After the Process Manager starts a process, the process is usually handled by the kernel until the process terminates, at which time the process is, again, handled by the Process Manager—think of it as both obstetrician and undertaker for processes. The Process Manager oversees the creation and destruction of processes and a kind of subprocess called a *thread*.

The Object Manager, well, manages objects. Hmmm, let's try that another way. Windows 2000 Professional is built atop the whole notion of *objects*. Everything—and I mean *everything*—is implemented as an object. A file is viewed by Windows 2000 Professional as an object, as is a serial port, a process, and many of the programming constructs in Windows 2000 Professional.

Defining these elements as objects serves two purposes. First, making something into an object gives it properties in common with other objects, so Windows 2000 Professional offers a uniform way of accessing all of them. You see, in most operating systems, grabbing a serial port and communicating with it involves massively different code than grabbing a file and reading it. By putting an object interface on everything in Windows 2000 Professional, Microsoft made it a bit easier for programmers to use different parts of the operating system. So simplifying programmers' lives is the first benefit of an object-oriented operating system; the second is security.

By creating a single point of contact between an application program and a peripheral (another program, a file, an input/output device, and so on), Windows 2000 Professional makes the tasks of tracking which program uses which object and checking whether that program has the *right* to use that object much easier for itself. Keeping track of what objects are in the system and who's using them and deciding whether programs can access objects are the jobs of the Object Manager.

The Security Reference Monitor is the part of the Windows 2000 Professional Executive that oversees the security modules in Windows 2000 Professional.

The Virtual Memory Manager is the parking lot attendant for all the processes running in Windows 2000 Professional. It's the program that makes sure that every process has all the memory that it needs—even if the system doesn't *have* enough memory! You'll see how the Virtual Memory Manager accomplishes this feat a little later in this chapter.

Having exhausted all the modules in kernel mode under Windows 2000 Professional, we can now move on to the pieces that live in user mode. They're called the environment subsystems and the security subsystems.

Environment Subsystems

The pieces that enable you to run programs reside within user mode modules in Windows 2000 Professional; they are called *environment subsystems*. Here's a quick look at them.

Win32

Although Windows 2000 Professional is built to run programs from several other, competing, operating systems, it also has a programming interface of its own. Even before Windows 2000 Professional existed, Microsoft sought to get the programming industry as a whole to agree on which programming interface would serve the needs of programmers in building most programs.

The result was the Win32 API. Win32 is the closest thing that Windows 2000 Professional has to a native programming interface, but it's not totally owned by Windows 2000 Professional.

NOTE Microsoft knew that Windows 95/98 and Windows NT would have separate lives in the marketplace, but the company didn't want to have to write both NT and Windows 95/98 versions of the applications. (Microsoft knew also that third-party programmers wouldn't want that either.) So it set out to create a programming interface that could sit atop either Windows 95/98 or Windows NT. Win32 is the result.

The different structures of the two Windows—Windows 95/98 and Windows 2000 Professional—mean in practice that Windows 2000 Professional can do some things that 95/98 can't, and vice versa. As a result, writing a program that runs under Windows 95/98 but not under Windows 2000 Professional is possible—and those programs are out there; watch for them.

Another way in which the 95/98 and Windows 2000 Professional implementations of Win32 differ significantly is in how Windows 95/98 applications run on non-Intel platforms—they *don't*. What I mean is this: If you're running Windows 2000 Professional on an IA64 processor, you can also run DOS and Windows 3.1 programs, even though you don't have a Pentium or like processor. They work simply because Windows 2000 Professional on an IA64 system includes software to emulate the Intel processor command set on a RISC chip. When running a DOS program on an IA64, you'll see that it runs, but it runs very slowly.

NOTE The *x*86 emulator runs the DOS or Windows 3.1 program by loading the first pieces of code and then examining the next few statements in the DOS or Windows 3.1 program. It then converts those statements to the native processor language of the RISC system and gives those statements to the RISC chip to execute. When the RISC chip is done, it goes back to the emulator program for more. This simultaneous translation of *x*86 opcodes (short for operation codes) to RISC opcodes is impressive, but slow.

If you want to run a Win32 program on your IA64, you've got to find out if the software vendor has written it for the IA64 in the first place. Although virtually every Win32 application has been built to run on the *x*86 line, most Windows 2000 Professional applications never get translated to IA64. Windows 2000 Professional's much-vaunted portability is of value only if software vendors take the short extra time needed to recompile their programs for both platforms—and, sadly, most have not.

As Windows 95/98 programs are usually also Windows 2000 Professional programs, RISC users are in the odd position of being pretty much guaranteed compatibility with Windows 3.1, but not with Windows 95/98. Too bad we don't have an *x*86 emulator for Win32 code, isn't it?

NOTE Buggy and *x*86-only programs aside, a number of types of programs will not run under both NT and 95/98. But the Win32 API supports enough NT and 95/98 programs to be called a common programming interface.

The Win32 programming interface is a bit different in NT Workstation 4 and Windows 2000 Professional than it was in previous versions; as mentioned earlier, Microsoft moved the Win32 programming interface from user mode to kernel mode in version 4.

WOWEXEC

Windows 2000 Professional doesn't run Windows 3.1 programs natively; rather, it runs a large program that supports old Windows 3.1 programs called the "Win16 on Win32," or WOW. A program called WOWEXEC creates the WOW environment. You already know that Windows 2000 Professional can run Windows 3.1 programs, and I don't intend to belabor the point here. But there are some useful side effects caused by the way that Windows 2000 Professional runs Windows 3.1 programs that make 2000 *superior* to 3.1 for running its 3.1 programs. Specifically:

- Windows 2000 Professional optionally provides separate memory spaces for each Windows program.
- Windows 2000 Professional separates the Windows modules far enough from the system that a Windows 3.1 application basically *cannot* crash the system.

- Windows 2000 Professional multitasks Windows 3.1 applications far better than does Windows 3.1 or Windows 95/98.

Separate WOWEXECs

By default, all Windows 3.1 programs run in the same WOWEXEC module. To make WOWEXEC as backward-compatible as possible, Windows 2000 Professional enables Windows 3.1 applications to do a certain amount of fiddling around in their "operating system"—that is, in WOWEXEC, not in Windows 2000 Professional. As a result, a Windows 3.1 application *could* trash WOWEXEC. For example, you might find that a Windows 3.1 application just stops responding. It doesn't change the screen, you can't choose menu items, and you can't close it down. You *can*, of course, always press Ctrl+Alt+Del and tell the Task Manager to shut down any application, whether it's a Windows 2000 Professional or a Windows 3.1 application.

When you tell Windows 2000 Professional to shut down an application, it often returns a dialog box that says "This application is not responding" and advises you to either wait a bit and try again (a fruitless endeavor in my experience) or tell it to force the application to shut down. The second choice often does the trick.

Sometimes, however, it doesn't, and Windows 2000 Professional offers to go a step further, shutting down the whole of WOWEXEC. Be aware that this step shuts down not only the errant Windows 3.1 application, but also any other Windows 3.1 applications.

You have an option when running a Windows 3.1 application under Windows 2000 Professional to run the application in a separate memory space. *Separate memory space* means that Windows 2000 Professional creates a completely separate WOWEXEC for that one application. That's potentially good because no matter how crazy that application gets, it cannot damage anything except itself. That extra protection isn't without a cost, however. Each WOWEXEC takes up some memory, so running many Windows 3.1 applications, each in its own memory space, places a greater strain on your system's available RAM than if you run all of them in a single WOWEXEC.

Sturdier Multitasking

Those separate WOWEXECs obviously improve the crash-proof nature of Windows 2000 Professional. But they offer something else as well: better multitasking.

Under Windows 3.1, all applications multitask using a method called *cooperative multitasking*. Explaining cooperative multitasking works best when using an unlikely analogy—a vaudeville show.

Windows 3.1 applications multitask in much the same way as vaudeville performers. The kernel—the stage manager in Windows 3.1—shoves an application out onto the Desktop, hoping that it won't stay there for long. A cooperative application runs only for a few tenths of a second at most, yielding to the kernel. The kernel can then select the next application to get some CPU time, and so on. Some Windows 3.1 applications, however, aren't very cooperative. They just slap the hourglass up on the screen and continue to work away, oblivious to the other applications that are waiting to run.

In vaudeville, the stage manager had a course of action: *the hook*. With the hook, a stage manager could yank a performer off stage. Sadly, Windows 3.1 lacks a hook.

To maintain compatibility with Windows 3.1, Windows 2000 Professional also lacks a hook in WOWEXEC. Consequently, a Windows 3.1 application can monopolize all the CPU power allocated to WOWEXEC. However, a Windows 3.1 application cannot take all the CPU time under Windows 2000 Professional because Windows 2000 Professional gives only a percentage of its CPU power to WOWEXEC—and that restriction is very important.

A Short Detour into Vaudeville

Back before TV and movies were popular, but after Americans started getting more leisure time and more income, more and more road shows started popping up around the country. Around the turn of the century, the most common format for these road shows was the variety show, with a dozen or so acts, each running for three to six minutes. These became known as vaudeville shows.

Now, the trick to managing a variety show is to understand that while *some* people will be spellbound by the guy who's balancing plates on poles, *others* came to see the woman whose dog can do square roots. As a result, each act can't go on for very long, or there won't be enough time for the other acts. The job of making sure that the schedule is rigidly adhered to falls to the stage manager. Standing just in the wings, he directs each act out onto the stage and, when time is up, he signals the performer to exit.

Now, here's where the cooperative part comes in.

The performer really *shouldn't* have to be reminded that his time is up, but sometimes it happens. Some performers feel that they're making the crowd happy and should be allowed to overstay their time on stage. A cooperative performer puts those thoughts aside for the good of the show, however, and takes her bows. Less cooperative performers don't.

For one thing, no matter how poorly behaved your Windows 3.1 application is, no matter how much of a CPU thief it is, it still can't affect your 32-bit applications. A rude application *can* keep your other Windows 3.1 applications from getting CPU time—but there's even a way to work around that. Think about it for a minute, and you'll see what it is: running separate WOWEXECs.

Separate WOWEXECs cost you in memory, yes, but they also get separate CPU time allocations from Windows 2000 Professional, which means that you can use

Windows 2000 Professional to get around Windows 3.1's uncooperative multitasking nature. Put each one of your Windows 3.1 applications in its own separate memory space, and they'll multitask like a charm. Oh, by the way, that cooperative multitasking problem doesn't pop up with Win32 applications; you might say that they're all built with a preinstalled hook.

OS/2 and POSIX

Windows 2000 Professional is a platform for client-server applications, and many client-server applications were built to run atop LAN Manager or Unix. LAN Manager ran on OS/2 version 1.3, so backward compatibility with Microsoft's previous network product required that Windows 2000 Professional be able to run LAN Manager applications. The OS/2 subsystem makes sure that happens.

Similarly, Unix is a platform for many client-server applications. Windows 2000 Professional would like to be able to support those applications, but, sadly, Unix isn't one operating system; it's an umbrella name for many different companies' implementations of the whole idea of Unix. The closest we come to a "standard" Unix is a government implementation called POSIX, and so Windows 2000 Professional supports POSIX applications.

Virtual DOS Machines (VDMs)

No operating system could call itself Windows compatible if it didn't support DOS programs; Windows 2000 Professional does that through a system called Virtual DOS Machine, or VDM. *How* Windows 2000 Professional achieves compatibility is an interesting story.

DOS programs have two basic needs: unrestricted access to 1MB of memory and unrestricted access to 64K of I/O addresses.

I'm sure you know what a memory address is, so I'll lay aside for the moment discussion of how Windows 2000 Professional solves that problem for DOS. But many people don't understand I/O addresses, so let me take a minute to explain them. All hardware devices, both chips on the motherboard and add-in cards, have hardware or I/O addresses. It's not unusual for us to say something like, "The communications program uses COM1," when we mean that the communications program sometimes needs to send data out of a serial port. It finds that serial port somewhere. From the CPU's point of view, nothing is actually called COM1. Instead, the CPU recognizes a piece of hardware at a particular address—hexadecimal address 3F8, in the case of COM1.

Windows 2000 Professional programs don't control a communications port by directly sending data to I/O address 3F8. Instead, they let the operating system do the controlling. Rather than sending the commands to COM1 to tell the modem to dial, for example, Windows 2000 Professional programs instruct the operating system to tell the modem to dial a particular number. Windows 2000 Professional applications, therefore, don't have to control hardware directly. DOS programs see the matter differently.

Virtually all DOS programs choose not to leave hardware control to the operating system and instead twiddle the hardware directly via that hardware's I/O addresses. Now, that could be a problem for Windows 2000 Professional because Windows 2000 Professional doesn't want any software addressing hardware directly except for the operating system itself. Disallowing DOS programs from communicating directly with I/O addresses, however, would make about 99 percent of the DOS programs crash, which would damage somewhat Windows 2000 Professional's claim to be DOS compatible. What, then, to do? The answer: Make use of *virtual device drivers*, or VxDs.

A VxD is a piece of operating system software that essentially shields the hardware from the program. When an application program, such as a DOS program, tries to access I/O address 3F8 directly, the action triggers a VxD for that address. As the VxD was attached by Windows 2000 Professional's designers to I/O address 3F8, that particular VxD is designed to handle serial port I/O. VxDs exist for the keyboard, the display screen, the hardware timer circuitry, the parallel port, you name it—just about all the standard PC hardware.

But what about the *not*-so-standard hardware? What kind of VxD support does Windows 2000 Professional have for it? Well, that's sort of a problem. Keyboards, mice, parallel ports, and the like are all pretty standard, so writing VxDs for them was possible. But no real market leader or standard in fax boards exists, so Windows 2000 Professional can't include a VxD for fax boards. Result: A number of DOS-based or Windows 3.1–based fax programs don't run under Windows 2000 Professional. (Actually, Windows 2000 Professional has a VxD that handles many fax boards, but not all of them.) Other examples of devices that lack VxD support: factory automation interfaces and proprietary boards. If Windows 2000 Professional runs across a DOS program that tries to access an address that Windows 2000 Professional doesn't have a VxD for, Windows 2000 Professional terminates the DOS program. This inability to run some DOS apps costs Windows 2000 Professional in terms of compatibility, but it's the price to pay for stability.

Managing Memory in Windows 2000 Professional

Let's wrap up this chapter with a quick look at how Windows 2000 Professional allocates memory to applications in its quest to be the most stable operating system around.

All Windows 2000 Professional applications start life being told that they have access to 2GB of RAM. Not only is that not true (I've seen Windows 2000 Professional machines with more than 2GB of RAM, but not many), but NT keeps on telling this little lie to *all* the applications running under NT!

The Virtual Memory Manager As Producer

Have you ever seen Mel Brooks's movie *The Producers*? It's a farce about a crooked producer who comes up with a surefire way to make a pile of money. He finds a number of rich people who'd like to back a Broadway play and, talking to each person privately, sells 90 percent of the interest in the play over and over again. By the time he's done, he's probably sold 1,000 percent of the play to unsuspecting investors. Then he sets off to create a play that will definitely flop, allowing him to tell the unwitting investors that oh, well, that's how it goes, as the play closes on its first night—and the crooked producer walks away with all the investment money. Of course, the plan backfires; the play is a big hit, and the producer encounters an endless string of problems.

Windows 2000 Professional's Virtual Memory Manager is kind of like that producer.

NOTE To be precise, Windows 2000 Professional applications (or, rather, Win32 applications, as there's really no such thing as a Windows 2000 Professional application) can work within a memory space equal to 2048MB, *minus* 128K. You'll see in a moment why that 128K is reserved.

The Numbers behind Windows 2000 Professional's Memory Requirements

Windows 2000 Professional requires that any machine it uses support a 32-bit memory structure, and 2^{32} bits is 4096MB, or 4GB. The first chip on which Microsoft implemented NT, however, was the MIPS chip, which supports 4GB but with a requirement—applications can't have more than 2GB of that 4GB total, and the operating system must get the other 2GB. It's dumb, but it's not the dumbest thing I've ever seen built into an operating system. Microsoft decided to follow suit and designed Windows 2000 Professional to require the same thing.

NOTE Just as an aside here, in my opinion the decision to restrict apps to 2GB max was a severely dumb move. No other 32-bit CPU that I know of imposes this limitation, and there's no *a priori* good reason to impose the limitation. Incorporating it into the architecture of Windows 2000 Professional makes about as much sense as saying that my Honda Civic is a hatchback and gets good mileage, so you should buy only hatchback cars for good mileage.

Remember I mentioned in a previous note that, to be precise, 128K of that 2GB is not available? That's because Microsoft defines the memory space of each Win32 program as 2GB but restricts the bottom 64KB and top 64KB of that memory; no program can address it. *Why* Microsoft restricts that space reflects a small stroke of genius, and the story is told in the following section.

Memory Mistakes That Programmers Make

Every programmer makes mistakes. Some mistakes are, however, more likely and more prevalent than others. Here are two of them: accidentally filling a memory address pointer to all zeros and then trying to write data, and accidentally filling a memory address pointer to all ones and then trying to write data.

The first error would lead a program to damage data in the bottom 64KB of its memory space. The second error would lead a program to damage data in the top 64KB of its memory space. By including those two memory address areas but marking them off-limits to a program, Microsoft guarantees that any accidental attempts at writing in the bottom or top 64KB—a symptom of a common programming error—*must* trigger an error message. A very clever feature.

Virtual Memory

And what if a Windows 2000 Professional application tries to *use* all 2GB of its memory space? Well, obviously most of us don't have computers with that much RAM. So, Windows 2000 Professional relies on an old dodge that operating systems have been using for years—*virtual memory*. All processors that run Windows 2000 Professional support virtual memory via *paging*. Here's how the dodge works.

First, CPUs divide their memory spaces into areas called *pages*. The 386, 486, Pentium, and Pentium Pro use 4KB pages, as do the MIPS and PowerPC chips. The Alpha uses 8KB pages. The Pentium and Pentium Pro have an option that enables them to use 4096KB pages, but probably no one uses that feature.

Second, CPUs enable their operating systems to readdress any given page. If a page is physically addressed as (for example) address 2000KB–2004KB, there's nothing saying that a program *using* that page must think that its address is 2000KB–2004KB. The CPU can just say to the program, "Oh, you needed address 124KB through 128KB? Well, here it is," and hand it that memory that is actually addressed from 2000KB–2004KB. In that case, we'd say that the *physical address* of the block is from 2000KB–2004KB but the *logical address* is 124KB–128KB. *Physical* and *logical* are the common words, but if they're not too clear, just substitute *actual* and *apparent,* as I do: The memory that is actually at address range 2000KB–2004KB appears to be in the range 124KB–128KB.

TIP The value of virtual memory can't be overstated.

Suppose you have a computer that's running 15 programs of various sizes and you exit from a random 7 of those programs. Unless all the programs were sitting right next to one another, your computer's RAM is probably *fragmented*—you have a block of used space, then a block of unused space, a block of used space, a block of unused space, and so on. So you load another program, and it wants *all* that space. Your operating system wants to give that RAM to the application all in one piece, so what does it do?

Well, on earlier operating systems, your system would defragment its memory, in a process somewhat like the `DEFRAG` command in MS-DOS 6.*x* or the SpeedDisk application in Norton Utilities. That's a tricky operation, because it means that you have to move an application *while* the application is working; it's like tuning a car while it's running down the road at 65mph. The ability to just readdress a block of memory with some bogus address and then tie that bogus address to a piece of software (and, best of all, to have that piece of software *believe* you) enables you to avoid defragging in the Norton Utilities way. Instead, all an operating system has to do is to grab all the free RAM, assign it contiguous memory addresses, and voilà! Instant block of contiguous memory.

Now let's put those two facts together and see how CPUs help with virtual memory. First, I kind of indicated that the CPU lies about a memory block's address only when necessary; not so. An inveterate liar from way back, the CPU insists on *always* supplying logical, not physical addresses to Win32 programs. Ignoring Mark Twain's advice that if you always tell the truth, you never have to remember anything, the CPU maintains *page tables,* which remember the physical and logical addresses of all the system's memory. In the page table is a bit that says whether a page is located in memory.

In effect, the CPU can hand out a bogus 2GB to each and every application regardless of how much or how little RAM exists on the system. Also, at any given moment, a lot more pages than the computer could *ever* supply have been handed out to applications. And if an application tries to access a page that's not in RAM at the moment, the Virtual Memory Manager swings into action. It has a large file called the *paging file* (stored on the hard disk as `pagefile.sys`), which acts as a holding tank for RAM pages. You see, if you're loading a 10MB application and you already have a 15MB application loaded but only 15MB of RAM available, the Virtual Memory Manager takes the pages for the now-dormant 10MB application and writes them to the paging file. That leaves space to put the entire 15MB application into RAM, at least for a moment or two. And if only some of the pages in both applications are being used or if the sum of the used pages for both applications is less than 15MB, you can load 25MB of applications into 15MB of RAM!

Summary

In this chapter, I've given you an overview of the pieces of Windows 2000 Professional and how they fit together. I have reviewed some of Windows 2000 Professional's history and how it compares with other operating systems available today. I've also delved into the hidden mysteries of Windows 2000 Professional's architecture that separate it from those other systems.

CHAPTER 15

An In-Depth Introduction to Networks

FEATURING:

By now, you're fully aware that the operating system on your computer is Windows 2000 Professional and that it was designed as a *network* operating system. You've patiently read through the earlier chapters, learning all there is to know about using Windows 2000 Professional on your own, but you're intensely interested in learning the best way to set up your network. And by "set up," you mean you want the nitty-gritty: You want to know what's *physically* involved. You want advice about cabling and connectors, protocols and topologies, and a heads-up about any additional software you might need to connect to or install your own network.

Well, you asked for it. In this part of the book, you'll get detailed information on networks—probably more than you need to get started with your installation, but, as with so many complicated topics, the more you know, the better off you'll be in the long run.

This chapter is designed to take you through the theories and preliminaries of planning a network. I'll begin with a look at various ways to use a network successfully and then present the types of cables that can be used for networking.

Early Networking: Sneakernet

The oldest form of the computer network is commonly referred to as the *sneakernet*, an official-sounding name for a very unofficial way of doing business. In this popular networking arrangement, a user copied information to a floppy disk, put on a good pair of Reeboks, and ran the file over to another machine or user. Not a very efficient method of sharing information by today's standards, but it got the job done. For some purposes, it may still be the best way to get information from one place to another.

Though wonderful for encouraging interoffice interaction, sneakernet poses a few serious disadvantages. Losing data is a big risk with this system because if you misplace or accidentally reformat the data disk, you lose the information. Making sure that everyone who's working on a document or worksheet has the same information is also cumbersome:

- What happens if you have a copy of the original disk and someone makes changes to the original without telling you?
- What happens if more than one person is working on a document and you need to incorporate everyone's changes into one copy?
- How do you keep people from leaving the building with disks full of sensitive information?

Obviously, if you want data integrity, security, and the best use of the creativity of all the people working on a document (and who doesn't?), sneakernet is not the way to go. What you need instead is some way of tying your network together other than having to rely on the trustworthiness and good will of your coworkers. What you need is a LAN.

LAN: The Alternative

Strictly speaking, a *local area network* (LAN) is a group of computers that is connected within a certain area. LANs vary greatly in size—you can make a LAN out of two computers sitting across from each other in the same room or out of several thousand computers in the same building. The key part to the definition of a LAN is that all the computers on the network are *grouped together in some fashion and are connected.*

NOTE A network that extends over a larger area, such as a city block or a country, is known as a *wide area network* or WAN. I've also run across the abbreviations MAN (Metropolitan Area Network) and CAN (Citywide Area Network), but most of the time citywide networks are referred to as WANs.

On most LANs, cables connect the LAN by linking the network cards that reside within each computer or printer on the network. I'll talk about situations in which cable is *not* the means of connection later in this chapter.

The preceding definition is the strict, textbook definition. However, in the real world, LANs are generally defined less by their physical characteristics and more by their function. In this sense, a LAN is a system in which linked computers and peripheral devices can share common information, software applications, printers, scanners, fax services, CD-ROMs, and/or the use of group scheduling programs and e-mail. The quick electronic dispersal of computer-generated information to people striving toward a common goal and existing in a single-user-per-computer environment truly defines a local area network.

With a LAN, you can do all the following:

- Perform file-management tasks:
    - Share files
    - Transfer files
- Share applications
- Share peripheral devices:
    - Printers
    - CD-ROMs
    - Scanners

- Fax modems
- Tape drives

- Interact with other users on the network:
  - Schedule group meetings
  - Send and receive e-mail
  - Hold electronic meetings
  - Play network games

File Management: Sharing and Transferring Files

One of the primary purposes of a LAN is to provide a common storage area so that several people can access the same files. File sharing can help ensure that only one version of a file is circulating at a time so that anyone who uses that file is always working with the most recent version. If you don't want to share a file with the network but you need someone else to do some work on it, you can transfer the file to someone else—just move it from your folder to theirs or send it as an e-mail message.

I'd like to point out that the act of sharing a file with the network does *not* automatically give everyone on the network access to it. In many network operating systems, you can attach a password to your files so that only people who have the password can access them. In most network operating systems, you can determine whether other users will have full access or read-only access to your files, folders, and hard drives. This capability can prevent others from seeing your work or making changes to your work when they're not supposed to.

Sharing, transferring, and securing information between computers on a network is generally known as *file management*. You can share entire drives and folders—you're not limited to sharing individual files.

NOTE As with individual files, you can restrict access to your shared resources (printers, CD-ROMs, scanners, tape drives, and so on) with passwords.

Concurrent Use of Applications

Many, but not all, software packages will work fine if you install them onto the *file server* and let people access them from their workstations. Here are a few of the advantages to locating software centrally (that is, on a file server):

- It frees disk space on individual computers. The bulk of the applications is stored on the file server and not at each user's computer.
- More than one user can use an application at one time (almost a necessity in many database applications).

- Upgrading software is easier because the application that needs to be updated is the copy of the software that is installed on the server. This feature is not true of all software packages. Some, such as Windows, have a certain number of files that need to be updated at each user's computer even though the major part of Windows is located on the file server. These files usually include configuration information that is specific to each computer system in your office.

WARNING If you store applications on a file server and let users access them from their workstations, *you are still required to buy more than one license*. You should have proper software licensing for every user, even if you load only one copy of the software onto the server. If you don't have proper licenses for all your users, you are committing software piracy—stealing from the developers of that software. Software piracy is a federal crime.

LAN-dependent applications, such as e-mail, are usually licensed for a specific number of users. When you access the program from the file server, a full-blown copy of the program is transported from the hard drive of the file server to the memory of your computer. As you interact with the program, you are interacting with the copy that is stored in the memory of your computer. If you activate a new feature of the program, such as invoking the spell-check feature of your favorite word processing program, the spell-check portion of the word processing program is transported from the hard drive of the file server to the memory of your computer. You need a license for every computer that will store part of the program in its memory.

Again, having more users than your LAN-dependent application allows is considered software piracy.

Peripheral Sharing

A lot of people get confused about the nature of peripherals these days, but basically a peripheral device is anything that is external to the CPU and memory.

NOTE The words *peripheral device* and *peripheral* are just tech-speak for "a device that attaches to your computer system." Printers, scanners, sound cards, CD-ROM players, fax modems, and joysticks are all peripheral devices.

A LAN enables its users to share high-cost peripheral devices and manage them so that two users do not attempt to use the devices simultaneously.

Peripheral sharing saves network users time and money. Of course, even without a network, you don't have to buy printers or other expensive peripheral devices for every workstation in the office. One or two devices will work just as well—if people don't mind standing in line to use them. However, if people must wait for a device to be free, you are spending the money you saved (by not buying the extra printer) on wasted time.

As with file management, a network administrator can restrict access to the peripheral devices on a network so that only those people authorized to use them can access them. For example, you may not want people to print out rough drafts or résumés on the $8,000 color printer.

Group Scheduling

Group scheduling could be one of your office manager's favorite network features. Organizing departmental meetings can be an administrator's nightmare, as they try to sort through everyone's schedules to find a time when everyone can meet. Group scheduling software can make this nightmarish task much more manageable.

Group scheduling software keeps track of all users' schedules, either separately or together as one large calendar. Each person on the network keeps track of their own appointments in the virtual day planner. This information is automatically stored in a central database.

Now, let's say that you want to call a meeting of all the MIS people in your company. All you have to do is list the names of the people who should attend this meeting and then choose a date. The computer can tell you of any scheduling conflicts and let you modify the meeting time accordingly. Some scheduling software packages let you tell the computer to choose the first time that everyone is available, to save you the trouble of having to guess. After you've settled on a time, you can use the scheduling program to send "invitations" and ask people to confirm their attendance.

Some group scheduling software enables users on the network to see or modify one another's schedules, but only if the owner of the schedule permits it.

Electronic Mail

Electronic mail, or e-mail, is one of the most popular features of a LAN. Using e-mail, you can do the following:

- Send messages to other users on the network—either individually or in a kind of mass mailing.
- Get receipts for messages that have been sent—never again will anyone be able to say, "I didn't get your memo," because your e-mail system has recorded the exact time and date of receipt. Whether people *remember* the memo's contents is another matter.
- Attach files—text, pictures, or worksheets—to messages.

E-mail works like the traditional postal service except that it is faster, more reliable, and doesn't require a fortune in postage. First, you write a message to someone on your network, address it, and send it. Second, the recipient of the message is notified by the mail system that they have new mail. (The method of notification depends on the mail software.) Third, your mail system notes the time that the message arrived at the other person's computer.

Most mail systems are flexible. You can send private messages to one person or distribute a departmental memo—you control who receives any messages by the way you address the message. To make sure that your intended recipients get their mail, you can ask for a return receipt; the computer will then automatically notify you of the date and time the message was read.

Another advantage to e-mail is that most systems let you attach text, graphics, or worksheet files to a message, just as you would put attachments on an interoffice memo. The recipient of your message can then pull up the attachment in an application and edit the information. This process is a lot like sharing files, but attaching files to messages has three advantages over just sharing files:

- You can attach a note to the file to explain anything that might be confusing to the recipient or to convey how important the information is.
- You ensure that the recipient is getting the correct file and hasn't confused it with another one.
- You don't have to muck around with passwords or define access rights to restrict access to the file—no one on the network gets the file except the people you send it to.

Network Games

Playing games probably isn't one of the loftier goals of your LAN, but you should be aware of it anyway. Most LANs come with a network game that lets multiple players participate from their own workstations, and hundreds of network games are available over the Internet and at your local software emporium.

Playing network games is a great way to spend the day, but if your boss catches you playing Blackjack during working hours, they are not likely to buy any excuses you might offer about getting more comfortable with the network. People often use the excuse that playing games helps them get used to the mouse. By now, everyone really should know how to use the mouse!

Networking Vocabulary

Like most other specialized fields, networking has its own jargon. This list is far from exhaustive—in the following chapters, I'll introduce more terms—but it gives you a good starting place. Remember these definitions. I try to keep the jargon to a minimum (I don't like jargon either), but to a certain extent it lets me explain things in fewer words than I could if I had to explain the concepts every time they came up. You'll also need to know these words if you do any more reading about networks:

Workstation Any machine that has the capability to provide input to the network environment is a *workstation,* the key element in this definition being *input.* This definition includes personal computers, handheld scanners, dumb terminals, and so on. Each workstation has its own Network Interface Card (NIC).

Packet A *packet* is the smallest unit of information that can be sent across a network. A packet contains the sending node's address, the receiving node's address, and the data being sent between the two nodes. The term *frame* is often used synonymously with packet, though it might be more precise to use packet for the data being sent, and frame to describe the format of that data as it travels the wire. In general, either term is correct.

Node Each workstation, fax, printer, file server, or anything else that has its own unique address is a *node.* How does a node get a unique address? Via the Network Interface Card. The manufacturer of your NIC placed a network address on your card that you cannot change. This permanent address is commonly referred to as the *hardware* or *Media Access Control* (MAC) address.

The purpose of placing addresses on the card is akin to addressing houses on a street. Just as your postal deliverer needs to be able to identify one house from another on a street, your network must be able to separate one network device from another network device. Your network will be transporting many network packets of information from one node to another, and it wants to make sure that the packet arrives at the proper location. The NIC address identifies the destination location.

Server The technical definition of a *server* is a centralized depository for a specific function.

All types of servers have one thing in common: They are all central locations where a specific function of the network is carried out. For example, a print server is a machine that queues and processes print jobs for a group of users. By creating a print server, you free up the processor of the individual workstation and give this specific task to only one machine. Likewise, a fax server collects fax requests, queues the fax jobs, and faxes these jobs.

The most common server is a file server. *A file server* is a machine that holds, manages, and secures access to files, applications, and data. It provides centralized control for and to your data and acts as a common location for your files for the purpose of centralized backup.

Topology This term relates to the physical and logical relationship of the nodes on the network. In a nutshell, it is the "look" of your network. You can look at your network in two ways—physically and logically.

Physical topology Describes where every node on the network lies physically in relation to all the other nodes and what the overall configuration looks like.

Logical topology Describes how information is passed along the network.

Basic Requirements: Hardware, Software, and Connections

Okay, you're convinced. Your office is never going to enter the twenty-first century unless you have a network up and running. What, then, do you need to make a network?

Network Interface Cards

The *Network Interface Card* (NIC), or the *adapter card*, is a card that you use to connect your workstation to the file servers or to other workstations. You need to be aware of various components of a NIC:

- Base I/O address
- Direct memory access (DMA) chips
- Interrupt request (IRQ) settings

How you connect your computers will depend on the type of topology you are using—specifically, peer-to-peer versus client-server. (I'll discuss these in the next chapter.) Also, the card will probably be cable-specific; that is, it may need to use coaxial cable or fiber-optic cable, depending on the card. You'll find details about adapter cards later in this chapter.

Cabling Systems

Copper wire or fiber-optic cable connects the nodes on a LAN. Planning is essential to implementing a successful LAN design, and one of the most important parts of your planning is your cabling. What kind of physical and logical topologies do you want to use in your network? What kind of cable fits into your budget and fulfills your transmission needs? What kinds of connectors will you need to put it all together?

Topologies

If you were to draw a blueprint of where all the computers are located in your network and how the cable is run throughout the building to attach all the computers, you would be looking at the *physical topology* of your network. Examples of physical topologies are bus, ring, and star.

If you have heard the terms *Ethernet* or *Token Ring*, you have been introduced to logical topologies. Each kind of logical topology is usually associated with a particular physical topology, but the physical topology may not necessarily look anything like the logical one. This distinction is important because it will help determine what type of Network Interface Card you will need to purchase and how much money you will spend on your network. I'll discuss both types of topologies in detail in Chapter 16.

Servers

Even with the growing popularity of peer-to-peer networks, client-server networks are more common by far. Therefore, you have to think about the computers that will run your network. How fast do they need to be? Which network operations can you run from a server and which need to be located at the individual workstations?

Network Operating Systems

After you choose your LAN's topology and setup, you need to start thinking about what kind of operating system best fits your needs and your cabling plan. Will you need one of the client-server network operating systems, such as Windows NT Server 4, Windows 2000, or NetWare, or does your LAN design require no more than Windows 2000 Professional built-in peer-to-peer networking?

Network-Based Applications

You've got a LAN and an operating system. Now you need something to do with it. You might say the network world is divided into four kinds of applications: LAN-dependent, LAN-aware, LAN-unaware, and LAN-hostile.

LAN-dependent Comprises the entire field of groupware. Groupware relies on the existence of networks in order to work. Here are a couple examples:

Lotus Notes A document organization system. Its rather steep price means that Lotus Notes isn't something you'll run into at every mom-and-pop shop, but it has a strong following among the Fortune 500. Most Lotus Notes–like systems require a LAN.

Any e-mail system E-mail systems enable you to send and receive messages from multiple users on a network. The e-mail system can be confined to your network or connected to the Internet. This can be helpful if there are many users on your network. Sending messages to yourself gets dull after a while.

LAN-aware Comprises applications that work fine without a LAN but have more features when connected to a network. For example, IBM's For Comment can interact with other PCs on a LAN, if the LAN exists, or it can communicate with Lotus Notes over a network.

LAN-unaware Comprises most word processors, worksheets, and games and is the status of most applications. To LAN-unaware applications, the network looks like no more than another physical hard drive. Rather than having only a C drive and perhaps a D drive, the network can have drives up to Z if you like. These applications don't care whether they run on a LAN or not.

LAN-hostile Comprises applications that directly address the disk's hardware. They are dangerous in combination with networks. They work fine on local drives—that is, on drives directly attached to the PC. If you use them on network drives, however, these programs either terminate (that's the good news) or trash the local drive (that's the bad news). Specifically, be careful with housekeeping programs if you're working on a network.

Wireless Networks

Now that I've talked about cables, I want to briefly discuss a kind of network that doesn't use them: the wireless network.

In recent years, several hardware companies have developed technology that enables computers to plug into a network without cables or connectors, as illustrated in Figure 15.1. This wireless connection requires a special network card in the network server, a receiving and broadcasting adapter for the computer to be connected, and an antenna that attaches to the server and thus broadcasts to and receives from the wireless workstation. Wireless nodes have a range of up to several hundred feet, but this range may be restricted by heavy steel or concrete floors or walls.

FIGURE 15.1
Wireless LAN

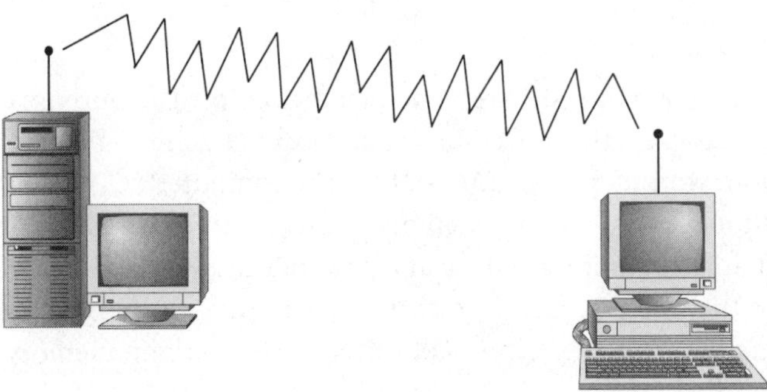

Another type of wireless connection is infrared line of sight. High-frequency light waves transmit data between nodes as much as 80 feet apart if the path is not obstructed. Infrared beams cannot pass through masonry walls.

Why would you want a wireless LAN? Depending on your situation, a wireless LAN could prove to be cost effective and convenient. The biggest chunk of your LAN's cost is the cabling, and the more difficult the cabling job, the more expensive that part of your LAN will be. A LAN that has no wires at all or one that is partially wired and partially wireless could save you money if your building is especially hard to wire. As for convenience, a wireless LAN could enable you to roam the building with a laptop or even go outside if you didn't go too far. For someone who needs to be mobile but also needs instant access to the network (such as a stock person at a grocery store), a wireless workstation is very handy.

You can have either an entirely wireless LAN or a mixed LAN with wired and wireless nodes. Wireless adapters and network cards are expensive, so you have to decide whether the more cost-effective option for you is to spend money on the wireless cards and adapters or on cables. Infrared connections, though limited in distance, have relatively high data transfer rates, in the tens of megabits per second range.

Specifics: The Network Interface Card

All cards have certain standard features—the settings that enable the cards to work correctly and to avoid hardware conflict with other cards that are sitting in the computer. So we will begin our adventure by taking a look at IRQs, base I/O addresses, and DMAs.

NOTE As you know, Windows 2000 Professional is Plug and Play. Most NICs that you buy today are also Plug and Play, which means that the operating system recognizes their settings. You normally don't have to do any further configuration. In this section, though, I'll explain how these settings work–information that every network professional should know.

IRQs

Sitting on your NIC are some memory chips. The purpose of these memory chips is to give packets that are addressed to your machine some place to go when they arrive at your workstation. Unfortunately, the computer's CPU, which is the brains of the operation, cannot see that memory sitting on the NIC. Therefore, something has to move that information from the memory of the NIC to the main memory of your system so that the CPU can process it. The component charged with the task of moving information from the memory of the NIC to your main memory is a chip set located on the network adapter.

NOTE The terms *NIC*, *network card*, and *network adapter* all refer to the same thing–the Network Interface Card.

If you open your computer, you will notice metal traces or wires sitting on the motherboard that act as pathways to connect various cards sitting in their bus slots to the CPU. Some of these pathways are known as *interrupt request* (IRQ) lines. You need to be concerned with 16 of them.

NOTE Because we are techie folk, we always start counting with the number zero. And so the IRQ numbers start from 0 and go all the way up to 15.

Each device that needs to use an IRQ must use a unique IRQ. Otherwise, you can expect your computer to crash! Using different IRQs for different cards in your system is not optional; it is imperative.

NOTE Windows 3.*x* sometimes lets you share IRQs with the assumption that only one of the devices will be in use at a time. Windows 95/98 doesn't like to share IRQs and often fails because of this. Windows NT and Windows 2000 Professional do not allow you to share IRQs at all. Each device must have a separate and unique IRQ to function with Windows 2000 Professional.

Now you are wondering how to find out which IRQs are in use and which ones are available. In Windows 95/98, follow these steps:

1. On the Desktop, right-click My Computer, and choose Properties from the shortcut menu to open the System Properties dialog box.
2. Click the Device Manager tab, and then double-click Computer (which is at the top of the list) to open the Computer Properties dialog box at the View Resources tab:

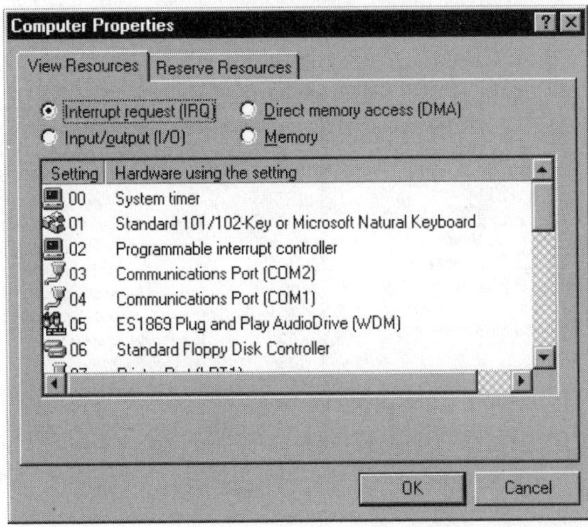

PART III

Networking Windows 2000 Professional

In Windows 2000 Professional, follow these steps:

1. At a command prompt, type **winmsd.exe** to open the System Information dialog box:

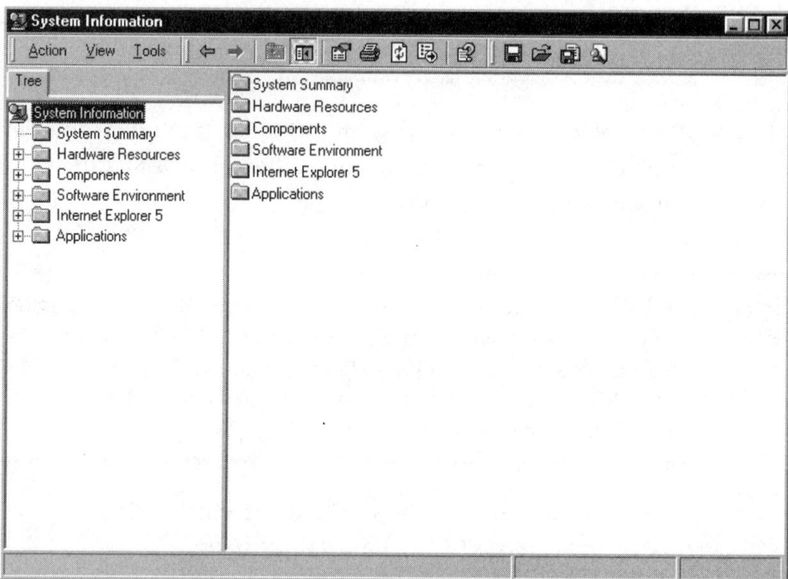

2. In the Tree pane, click the plus sign next to the Hardware Resources folder, and then click the IRQs folder to display the IRQ numbers and devices in the pane on the right:

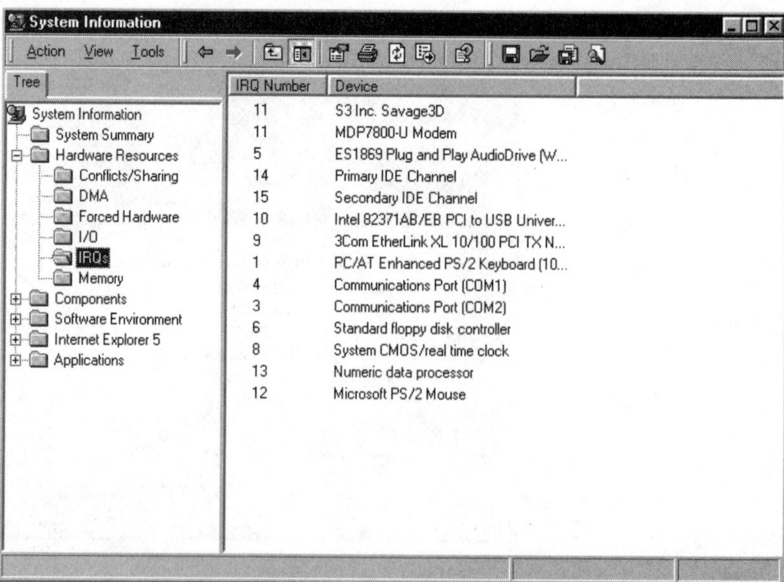

Base Memory Address

The location that an adapter card occupies in memory is referred to as its *base memory address* or *base I/O address*. This is the location that the CPU goes to when it needs to exchange information with the adapter card. The IRQ signals the CPU that information is waiting. The CPU then accesses these memory addresses to retrieve that information. This process works in reverse when the system is sending information to the network.

This is one of the hardware resources that Windows 2000 Professional needs to know about in order to access the adapter card's functions.

Direct Memory Access—Memory Movers

The next order of business is to find out how DMA (*direct memory access*) chips move the information from the NIC to main memory.

Your motherboard contains two DMA chips, and each chip supports four DMA channels, making a total of eight DMA channels on your motherboard. (Again, because we are techie folk, they're numbered DMA0 through DMA7.) Every device that needs to use DMA must use a unique DMA channel. I'll discuss this topic in detail in Chapter 17.

Cabling Considerations

Cables are the backbone of the network. All information runs through the cables, either in the form of electrical radio frequency (RF) transmissions, as in coaxial or twisted-pair cable, or in the form of light, as in fiber-optic cable. For your network to work well, information must pass through the cabling unaffected by RF noise. The noise generally won't corrupt the data, but it can slow down the network considerably.

Therefore, the biggest potential problem with any RF transmitting cables is that of unwanted RF transmissions getting into the cable. Here are some sources of unwanted RF transmissions:

- Fluorescent lights
- Large motors
- Local radio stations
- Other network cables

To avoid problems caused by RF interference, you need either to shield the signal going through the wires or to somehow make the signal indifferent to RF noise. Twisted-pair and coaxial cable take the first approach, whereas fiber-optic cable takes the second.

A cable design is one of the most important and most often neglected parts of network planning. Depending on your mindset and your budget, you may want to opt for unshielded twisted-pair, just because it's the cheapest cabling available. At the other extreme, you may read about fiber-optic's speed and security and decide to use it—to heck with the costs. (Given that you've probably got a business manager breathing down your neck and wanting you to account for every penny, the first scenario seems more likely.)

Ultimately, however, state-of-the-art technology and cost are not the only considerations. You should choose your cabling system based on your networking. This section is intended to help you figure out what you are trying to make your network do and then help you select the cable type (or types) that will let you reach your goals most effectively.

Understand that most people do not install the cabling system themselves. They hire contractors to perform this function. However, you need to ensure that you are cable literate so that the cable you choose will keep you in good stead over the long haul.

In thinking about which type of cabling will best meet your needs, you need to consider the following:

- Cost
- Ease of installation and maintenance
- Reliability
- Speed
- Distance

Cost

As you may be aware, the various types of cables have very different costs. Because your cabling expenses can be as much as half your total outlay on networking hardware, cost is not an insignificant consideration. You do not want to install a cable system today that will not meet your growing network needs tomorrow. Of course, the cost of cabling isn't entirely with the cables themselves. When comparing costs, don't forget to include installation and connection. For example, unshielded twisted-pair cabling is cheap, but it's used in a star physical topology (discussed in detail in Chapter 16) that requires expensive hubs.

Ease of Installation and Maintenance

The ease of installation and ease of maintenance are related to the cost consideration. The more difficult it is to install and maintain a network, the more it will cost. In the short term, you must pay your network professionals (in-house or contractors) for their time spent installing the cables. Let's consider what happens down the road.

Reliability

The more reliable your network is, the better you will like it in the long run. This is where the long-term costs come in. Although you may be able to save that short-term money and get something really easy to install, you could instead invest that money to prevent your network from slowing down or crashing altogether. Depending on your type of organization, network downtime can be either an expensive pain in the neck or a major disaster.

Speed

Transmission speed is measured in millions of bits per second. A *bit* is a negative or positive electrical pulse. If you string eight of them together, you get a byte. A *byte* is equivalent to one character. If the *b* in the abbreviation is capitalized—MBps—you are talking about millions of *bytes* per second.

Speed becomes a major consideration now and in the future. If your old cable can't keep up with the transfer rate of your new network, you'll need to replace it when you upgrade parts of the network, and that upgrade could be expensive. Clearly, the need for upgrades is yet another reason to plan your network ahead of time.

Distance

Distance can adversely affect cables if they aren't designed to deal with it. Here are the three ways distance most often affects cables:

- Signal strength and quality (attenuation)
- Possibility of packet collision
- Susceptibility to RF noise

Attenuation

Some kinds of cables just aren't capable of extending very far, due to their inability to maintain signal quality and strength over a certain distance. This capability varies according to the thickness and composition of its conducting wire and its type of insulating material. Twisted-pair, which consists of copper wires surrounded by an insulator, is one example of cable affected by attenuation. You can get around attenuation problems with devices such as repeaters.

Repeaters are devices that "repeat" a signal so that it can travel a distance that would otherwise be too long to maintain proper signal strength. These devices aren't exactly internetworking devices but rather devices to extend an existing network. Imagine that you and a friend are standing at a little distance from each other, calling back and forth. As long as you don't move too far apart, you can hear each other fine. If you move too far, though, you either won't hear what your friend said or it'll come out garbled. In that case, you'd need a repeater (perhaps a mutual friend) to stand in the middle and relay messages. In the same way, a repeater receives packets and either amplifies them or retransmits them as new so that the packet can go farther across your network.

Your best defense against the terrible threat of attenuation is to buy good cabling and to follow the IEEE standards.

Possibility of Packet Collision

Long cable runs can throw off the timing of packets moving through a network. On an Ethernet system, each node transmits for itself, sending a packet of information to wherever it needs to go on the network. If two nodes transmit at the same time, their packets collide, and they must retransmit, which takes time. Therefore, before a node sends out its packet, it "listens" to see if the network is clear.

Think of it like this: Suppose you are a stock clerk in a warehouse that stocks large boulders—rather like the one in *Raiders of the Lost Ark*. Each small stockroom in your warehouse opens onto a large corridor. If you need to move boulders from one stockroom to another, you certainly can't do it at the same time that someone else is moving another boulder because they won't fit past each other. So you must first listen out your door to make sure that the coast is clear before beginning the move. The rolling boulders make enough noise to alert you when other stock clerks are moving boulders.

What happens, however, if your warehouse expands and the corridor becomes longer (but no wider)? You might not be able to hear stock clerks moving boulders at the far end of the corridor, so you might hear nothing and head out with your boulder—and run into your colleague. Although you might expect that only one of you has to return to their stockroom until the other one has passed, the company rules are that both of you have to return to your respective stockrooms and wait a preset time before venturing out again.

Time wasting, isn't it? The above situation is analogous to what happens if you use cables that are too long for your Ethernet topologies. The nodes can't "hear" the other nodes at the far end of the cable and so transmit at the same time, causing the packets to collide and requiring the nodes to resend them. This kind of problem could seriously slow down a network because there's no guarantee that the packets wouldn't collide on the *next* try either.

This situation can be troublesome with only two people attempting to access the network cable, but imagine how monumental this problem can become if a thousand people are attempting to access the network.

Susceptibility to RF Noise

As I discussed earlier, wires are affected by RF noise and therefore act as antennas. The longer a wire is, the better antenna it makes—that's why, if you want to improve the signal on your car radio, you pull the antenna out farther. Also, the longer a cable is, the more likely it is to pick up RF noise that interferes with transmission. A poorly insulated cable is liable to pick up RF noise under the best of circumstances, and the longer it is, the more chances the noise has to interfere with it.

Types of Cables

The first solution to the interference problem led to the development of various kinds of protection against interference. Conductors can be protected from RF noise by insulating them with another conductor. This kind of protection is seen in twisted-pair and coaxial cables.

Twisted-Pair

Twisted-pair cable is made of several pairs of two wires intertwined along their entire length. Because each wire is a conductor, wrapping the wires over each other serves to insulate each wire from RF noise. The two kinds of twisted-pair cable are *shielded twisted-pair* (STP) and *unshielded twisted-pair* (UTP). The only difference between them is that in STP a conducting layer surrounds the twisted wires, providing an extra layer of protection from interference. STP costs a little more than UTP, but it is more immune to outside RF noise and therefore can run in places where UTP would not work well.

The Electronic Industries Association (EIA), Telecommunications Industry Association (TIA), and National Electrical Manufacturers Association (NEMA) established a standard and commissioned Underwriters Laboratories (UL) to certify cable as meeting the EIA/TIA-586 standards. The higher the grade number, the more twists per foot and the better attenuation—that is, the less interference will affect the conducting wire.

Category 1 For unshielded twisted-pair telephone cable; the old-style telephone cable with which telephone companies wire most residences and with which they wired business telephones until 1983. Category 1 cable is not suitable for high-speed data transmission because its only requirement is that it be twisted.

Category 2 UTP cable that is certified for data transmission up to 4Mbps. Its specifications match those of IBM's type 3 cable: four unshielded, solid (as opposed to stranded) twisted pairs of wire for voice or data.

NOTE The next three categories are more regulated and share the following characteristics: at least three twists per linear foot, and no two pairs have the same twist pattern. The purpose of ensuring that no two pairs have the same twist pattern is to reduce cable crosstalk.

Category 3 UTP cable that is the lowest-rated cable that you should use with any LAN. It can transmit up to 10Mbps and is better constructed than cable from Categories 1 and 2.

Category 4 For 16Mbps Token Ring networks, this cable is the lowest-grade cable you should use. In fact, to get the best use from your LAN, you should probably consider this your minimum rather than Category 3 cable.

Category 5 100-ohm, four-wire twisted-pair copper cable that runs at speeds up to 100Mbps with Ethernet or ATM (Asynchronous Transfer Mode). Crosstalk is minimal if Category 5 cable is installed correctly.

Category 5e This cabling was designed to further increase performance over Category 5 cabling and has better specifications for NEXT and attenuation that will support 1Gb Ethernet when you use all four pairs of cabling. At the time of this writing, Category 5e is comparable in price to Category 5 and should be the minimum rated cable for new installations.

Category 6 By the time you read this, the Category 6 specification will probably have been ratified by the IEEE. Category 6 is designed to exceed Category 5e specifications for bandwidth. Category 6 supports 250Mbps.

If you've heard all your life that UTP was unsuitable for networks, these data rates (and the possibility of using UTP as an alternative to fiber) probably surprise you. In recent years, however, twisted-pair's design has improved considerably. When Category 3 cable was specified to have at least three twists per foot, that requirement was far better quality than any existing twisted-pair. Today, high-quality twisted-pair has between 8 and 15 twists per foot and uses special plastics that improve its data rate.

NOTE The terms *coax* and *coaxial* are two forms of the same name. They can be used interchangeably. Coaxial cable is covered in more detail in the next section.

Twisted-pair is still inferior to coax in some ways. Whereas UTP and STP can extend only 300 feet before the signal fades (even Category 5 cable), thick coax (10Base-5) can stretch for 2,500 feet without a problem. However, if your network won't need high rates of data transfer (necessary for video, audio, and large graphics files) and you can keep the wires away from areas prone to electrical interference, UTP could suit you just fine. Twisted-pair is cheaper than coax and fiber-optic, and it requires less sophisticated installation techniques. Twisted-pair will work fine as long as you don't ask it to do more than it's capable of.

TIP If you're installing Category 5 twisted-pair cabling to speed up your network to 100Mbps, you need a Category 5 rating end-to-end. In other words, all your connectors along that wire must also be rated at Category 5.

Cable Crosstalk

Crosstalk occurs when electrical signals move across several wires that are close together. As I discussed earlier, cables are just long antennas. As the signals go across the cable, they create radio frequency noise. If the noise is too loud, a cable nearby can pick up the signal. If you have ever driven between states, you probably noticed that as your favorite radio station faded out, a new one started to fade in. For an interval, you could hear both radio stations simultaneously. That's crosstalk. (And you thought it was just annoying static noise.)

The more twists per foot you have in a cable, the greater protection you have against crosstalk. By varying their twist pattern (one pair has 3 twists per foot and another pair within the same case has 3-1/8 twists per foot), you are also providing greater protection against crosstalk.

Coaxial Cable

Coaxial cable, often referred to as *BNC* cable (the initials refer to the Bayonet-Naur Connector—a bayonet-shaped connector for thin coaxial cables), is made of a single copper wire encased in insulation and then covered with a layer of aluminum or copper braid that protects the wire from outside interference. If you need more bandwidth and noise protection than twisted-pair can provide but can't afford fiber-optic, coaxial cable is the way to go.

Coaxial cable has four parts:

Inner conductor A central wire

Dielectric A layer of insulation that surrounds the inner conductor

Shield A layer of foil or metal braid that covers the dielectric

Jacket A final layer of insulation

You can see a drawing of coaxial cable in Figure 15.2 and a coaxial cable with a connector in Figure 15.3.

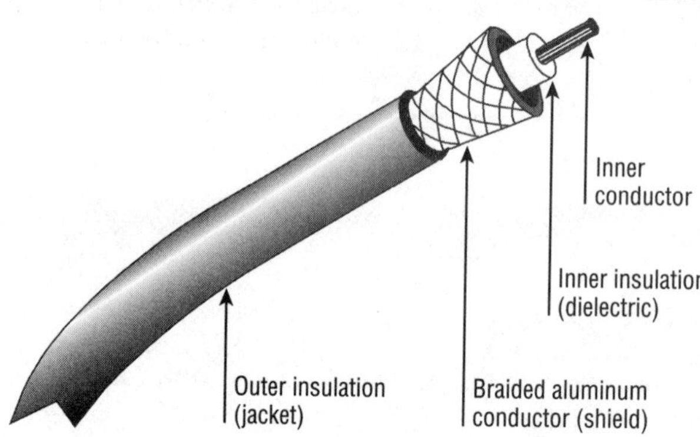

FIGURE 15.2
Coaxial cable

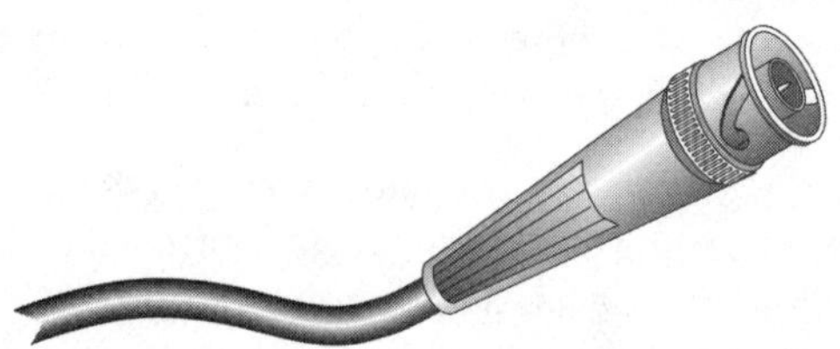

FIGURE 15.3
Coaxial cable with connector

Coaxial cable operates on the same theory that twisted-pair does: If you surround a conducting wire with another conductor, the second conductor protects the first from electrical interference. Whereas twisted-pair expects the wires to protect each other, coaxial cable dedicates a part of the cable to insulating the inner conductor so that it can neither pick up outside signals nor broadcast its own. Because the inner conductor that is doing the transmitting is encased by the shield, it can neither transmit nor receive RF signals and is thus prevented from either interfering with other network cables or being slowed down by rogue RF signals. All coaxial cable is shielded cable by design. Its better protection also enables it to extend farther than twisted-pair cable can, because signal deterioration is one of the key factors that determines how far a cable can extend.

Four varieties of coaxial cable are available. Each is used with a different type of LAN:

Ethernet Ethernet thick, also known as *thicknet,* was popular for backbones because it exceeded the distance limitations of Ethernet thin. It is uncommon to see thicknet in newer installations because the price of fiber-optic cable has dropped dramatically and because of the benefits of fiber-optic cable, which include faster data rates, lack of electromagnetic interference concerns, and longer distances.

RG-58A/U Used in coax Ethernet networks. Often referred to as 10Base-2 and also called *thinnet.*

RG-59/U Used on CATV (cable TV) and ARCnet (an older network topology).

RG-62/U Used on ARCnet and IBM terminals.

The Ethernet cable is the thickest, about 0.4 inches in diameter, whereas RG-58A/U is 0.18 inches, RG-59/U is 0.25 inches, and RG-62/U is 0.25 inches. Keep in mind that even though the latter three cables are roughly the same size, they are not interchangeable.

Of these four cables, only two are used in LAN settings—10Base-5 and 10Base-2. These names describe the specification of each cable. The information specified in these titles can be divided into *speed* of the cable, *bandwidth* of the cable, and *distance* a signal can be sent across the cable before attenuation sets in.

For example, in *10Base-5* the number 10 is the speed designation and refers to 10Mbps; 5 is the distance measure and indicates 500 meters (roughly 1640 feet); and then there is bandwidth.

Understanding Bandwidth

What is *bandwidth*? Well, it's just bandwidth! Sorry, but this response is the one I generally get from many of my techie friends when I ask them to describe bandwidth. It's a difficult concept to define in a few words, but it's intuitively easy when someone describes it by example. The one thing they all agree on is that you need a lot of it.

To understand the concept of bandwidth, think of a four-lane highway. If cars represent data and data can travel on any of the four lanes, you could say that the highway has a bandwidth of 4. During non–rush hours, you could move along at 55mph with no problem. But what happens during rush hour? A lot more cars are accessing the highway, and traffic slows down or comes to a screeching halt. In the same fashion, the more nodes that are accessing and communicating across your network cable, the slower the network traffic flows across the cable, or your network could come to a screeching halt.

Solutions?

- You could publish a procedure that says only a certain number of people can access the network, thus reducing the traffic. This idea does not sound very practical, though.
- You could install more pathways for data to travel across. In other words, you could increase your bandwidth.

Two terms define bandwidth. The first is *baseband,* which designates that the data has one pathway (or lane) available for travel. The second term is *broadband,* which designates that many pathways are available for the traveling data.

The *Base* in 10Base-5 signifies that this cable is a baseband cable with only one data pathway. Most LAN cable is baseband cable, whereas most WAN cable is usually broadband.

Now try your hand at deciphering 10Base-2.

The *10* refers to 10Mbps. The *Base* refers to baseband cable. And of course the *2* refers to 200 meters; well, not exactly. When the specification was first designed, signals were supposed to be able to travel 200 meters. It was a good theory, but in practice the signal gives out at 185 meters. So the *2* really stands for 185 meters. Nonetheless, the name is 10Base-2; 10Base1.85 just doesn't roll off the tongue as nicely.

Of course, being of better quality than twisted-pair, coax is more expensive on a per-foot basis. As you will soon discover, though, you generally use a lot less coax than twisted-pair wire in your physical network topology, so in practice it is cheaper.

Fiber-Optic Cable

Here are two new terms for your techie cocktail party (you know, the one where everybody tries to out-tech one another): *electronic medium* and *photonic medium*. The cables that I have discussed up to this point have been electronic; they conduct electronic signals. *Fiber-optic cable*, on the other hand, conducts photonic signals, or light.

Fiber-optic cable is indifferent to RF noise because of the difference in its conductive medium: Whereas twisted-pair and coaxial cable transmit with electronic signals, fiber-optic cable transmits using light. The light is conducted along a slender plastic or glass fiber that has a thin coating called *cladding*. The fiber is then surrounded by a plastic jacket intended to protect the delicate fiber.

NOTE You've probably seen fiber optics in action. Remember the feather lamps so popular in the late 1970s and early '80s? Each strand on those lamps is a fiber-optic strand.

Take a look at Figure 15.4 to see the structure of a fiber-optic cable.

FIGURE 15.4
Fiber-optic cable

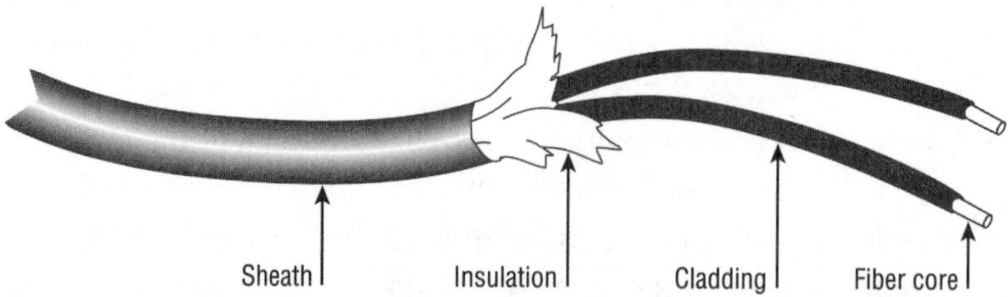

In Figure 15.4, the straight, darker wires running more or less horizontally from left to right are the fibers with cladding on them, and the feathery stuff is insulation.

How does fiber transmit data? Information travels along a fiber-optic cable by means of a high-powered light-emitting diode (LED) or by laser technology used in network equipment that sends signals through the core of the fiber-optic cable. These devices are generically called *codecs*—coder/decoders. When the signal reaches the receiving end of the transmission, it is reconstructed into its original form with a photo-diode. If the sending and receiving sources of the transmission are very far apart, a device called a fiber-optic repeater can be placed at strategic locations to amplify the signal so that it arrives at its destination at full strength.

Fiber-optic cabling doesn't limit you to one path for your data. As you saw in Figure 15.4, each cable can have more than one fiber in it, enabling data to move to its destination more quickly. The more fibers the cable has, the more data can pass through the cable at any given time, just as a four-lane highway can carry more traffic than a single-lane road. Also, fiber-optic cable comes in a variety of sizes, some intended for outside work and some for inside, as shown in Figure 15.5.

FIGURE 15.5 *Various sizes of fiber-optic cable*

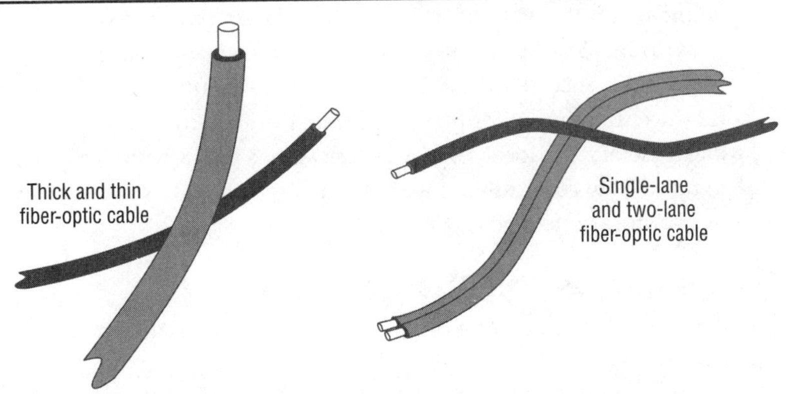

NOTE The thick gray cable in Figure 15.5 is about 1/2-inch thick and very stiff (it's outside cable), whereas the thinner black one is about 1/8-inch in diameter (and is commonly used indoors).

Some fiber-optic cables run information in both directions like the slender black cable does in Figure 15.5, but some cables are like two-lane streets. Traffic in each lane goes in only one direction, so each direction has its own lane: one to come, and one to go.

Types of Fiber-Optic Cable

The two types of fiber-optic cable are *single mode* (or monomode) and *multimode*.

Single mode Sends the light signal along a single path. This type of transmission is used for networks that need very high rates of data transfer, such as long-distance telephones.

Multimode Contains several light signals that move along inside the cable. The two kinds of multimode cable are *step index* and *graded index*.

Step index The light beams bounce around inside the cable in a zigzag pattern.

Graded index The light movement has a more rounded pattern like a sine wave.

Both kinds of multimode cable are prone to modal dispersion—spreading of the received light impulse—due to the number of light beams traveling through the cable. When the signal spreads, it moves more slowly, so single-mode cable transmits faster than multimode cable. To understand why, try imagining what happens if you throw a ball down a pipe. If you toss just one ball and it goes through without hitting the walls of the pipe, it would move faster and more accurately than if it bounced off the walls of the pipe. Just as bouncing off the walls of the pipe slows the ball's traveling speed, bouncing off the walls of the cable slows down the light signal.

With its 155Mbps throughput of multiple gigabits per second, fiber-optic cable has had notable success as a LAN backbone. Because it's still costly to run this type of cable for the entire system, only high-powered engineering or graphics applications seem to make use of it for local segments. Certainly a cost advantage can be realized by opting to run UTP to connect your workstations, which allows you the flexibility to upgrade to fiber-optic as prices go down.

Advantages and Disadvantages

Fiber-optic cable has a lot of advantages and two disadvantages. Here are some of the advantages:

- Its huge data transfer rates (up to 155Mbps), are especially useful for transferring video or audio images generally referred to as multimedia.
- Because fiber-optic transmits light, not electricity, fiber-optic is immune to electrical interference.
- Some kinds of fiber-optic can transmit up to three miles in LAN environments and across the country via a high-power laser device in WAN environments.
- Fiber-optic cable is useful in hazardous environments: First, it can't spark (as electric transfer cables could), and second, it doesn't have any metal in it, so it resists corrosion.
- Fiber-optic cabling is harder to tap into than coaxial or twisted-pair cable, so it's more secure. (Of course, no cable is totally immune from tapping.)

As you might have guessed, fiber's two disadvantages are cost related:

- Fiber-optic cable is far more expensive than either coax or twisted-pair.
- Fiber-optic cable is generally more difficult to install, so its installation costs are higher.

Fiber-optic is dropping in price as it becomes more common, however, so don't eliminate it from your list of possibilities just because of cost. If nothing else, you could follow the example of companies that run a fiber backbone and use high-grade UTP for taps to the nodes.

Types of Connectors

You can't just go out and get cables and expect to run your network. First, you need some way to hitch your computer to the network via those cables. In other words, you now need to investigate connector possibilities.

The kind of connectors you need depends a lot on the kind of cable that you use. If you buy sale-priced Ethernet T-connectors in preparation for your future network, you'd better be prepared to go with an Ethernet network because Ethernet connectors won't work with twisted-pair or fiber. Each kind of cable uses different connectors.

Connectors

You'll use three kinds of connectors on an Ethernet bus network:

T-connectors Link the cables to the cards (see Figure 15.6). The T-connector plugs into the card you've installed in your PC. The cables connect to the crossbar of the T, as shown in Figure 15.7.

FIGURE 15.6
T-connector

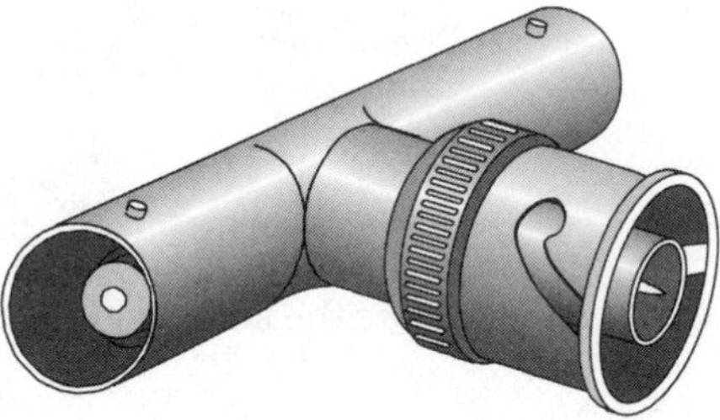

FIGURE 15.7
Network card with T-connector and cables attached

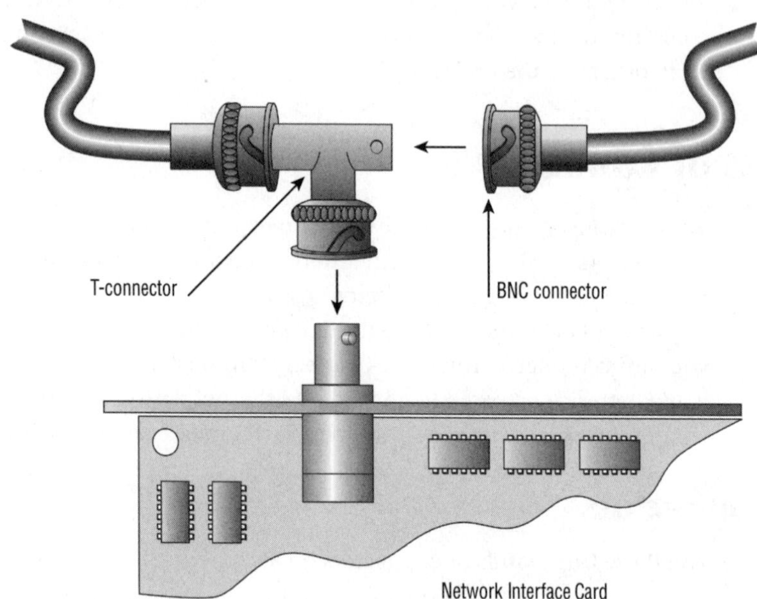

BNC connectors Link cables and connect them to T-connectors (see Figure 15.8).

FIGURE 15.8
BNC connector

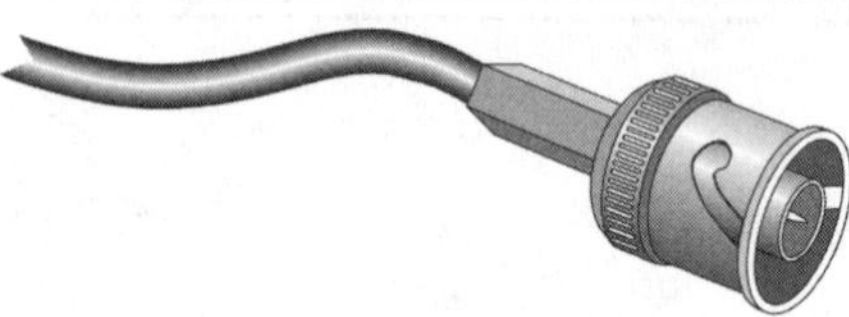

Terminators Terminate the LAN on either end (see Figure 15.9).

FIGURE 15.9
Terminator

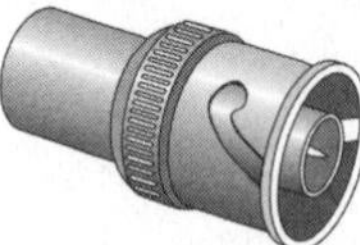

Terminators are made for either 50-ohm or 75-ohm cable; 50-ohm terminators are usually the standard. Pay attention when you're buying terminators because they won't work if you mix them up. Most coax network cable systems need 50-ohm terminators.

RJ45

Most unshielded twisted-pair cable terminates using connectors that look like chunkier versions of the connectors used to plug your telephone into the wall, as shown in Figure 15.10. These are called RJ45, whereas your telephone uses RJ11 connectors. One end plugs into your computer card, and the other plugs into a punch-down block in the wiring closet or a hub. I'll discuss network topologies in Chapter 16, but for the moment just understand that the way UTP terminates renders it unsuitable for any kind of wiring other than the star topology.

FIGURE 15.10
RJ45 connector

D-Shells and Data Connectors

STP is bulkier than UTP and, correspondingly, needs a different connector. In a Token Ring topology, a D-shell connector links STP cable to the machine's network card (see Figure 15.11), whereas an IBM Token Ring Connector attaches the other end of the cable to the *multistation access unit* (MAU) or *hub* (see Figure 15.12).

FIGURE 15.11
D-shell connector

FIGURE 15.12
IBM Token Ring Connector

Fiber-Optic Connectors

Fiber-optic connectors are an important part of the cabling process. Unlike twisted-pair, in which the medium itself is the biggest source of signal loss, fiber-optic is most susceptible to signal dispersion at its connectors. Fiber-optic cable use several different kinds of connectors; some of the most common are screw-mounted adapters (SMA), spring-loaded twist (ST), and subscriber connector (SC), which is a common latch connector. The ST connector, as shown in Figure 15.13, uses a spring-loaded twist to clamp to the cable; the SMA screws onto the end; and the SC latches into a connector and locks onto place.

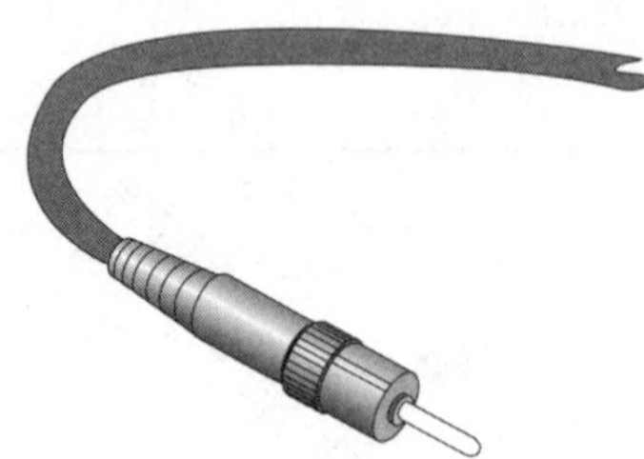

FIGURE 15.13
ST connector and connector cover

Wiring Systems

To help you get started, a number of companies have developed their own complete wiring systems. Here, I'll discuss IBM's and Ethernet's wiring plans.

IBM Cabling System

IBM has developed standards for a variety of cables, all of which are either fiber-optic or, more commonly, twisted-pair. IBM uses eight types of cable in its wiring plan.

Unlike the EIA/TIA (The Electronic Industries Association/Telecommunications Industry Association, remember?) categories of UTP, IBM cables are not rated in order of immunity to RF noise. (Yes, we've arrived in acronym hell [AH]. Get used to it; all LAN terminology looks like this.)

The following list is provided for your reference and does not have to be memorized. You don't have to know everything; you just have to know where to find it.

Type 1 Shielded cable with two twisted-pairs made from solid (as opposed to stranded) wire. It's used for data transmission, generally over Token Ring networks.

Type 2 Four unshielded pairs of solid wire for voice telephone communication and two more shielded data pairs in the same sheath. It's designed so that you can run your telephone and your Token Ring network from the same cable.

Type 3 Four unshielded, solid twisted-pairs of wire for voice or data. This is IBM's version of twisted-pair telephone wire.

Type 5 Two fiber-optic strands.

Type 6 Shielded cable with two twisted-pairs made from stranded wires. This is a lot like Type 1 but more flexible because it's made from stranded (rather than solid) wire. It's designed for data transmission, usually between a computer and a data jack in the wall.

Type 8 A special "under the carpet" shielded twisted-pair cable—it's designed to make a smaller lump when it's run under carpet.

Type 9 Plenum cable. Two shielded, twisted-pairs covered with a special flame-retardant coating, meant to be used between floors in a building. It's extra fireproof to help prevent fire on one floor from following the cable to the rest of the building.

Type Z Fiber-optic cable. This is the new fiber-optic standard, and it allows for distances of up to 130 nanometers (or microns).

Plenum cable, by the way, is a cable covered with plenum insulation. This particular kind of insulation is fire resistant, so it's safer to use than other materials, and no conduit is required for its installation in the office. Without plenum insulation, the cable itself could become the catalyst needed for a fire to spread very quickly.

WARNING Some fire ordinances require organizations to use only plenum-rated cable in certain situations—so before selecting cable, check your local fire codes to make sure the cable meets all fire codes in force.

To review, this is IBM's proprietary wiring system, based on the logical ring and physical star topologies. Its standard rate of transmission is 4Mbps, but in 1989 IBM introduced a version that transmits at 16Mbps. Token Ring generally uses UTP but can use fiber-optic cable if the network calls for it. One of the Token Ring architectures is

IBM's Systems Application Architecture (SAA), which supports peer-to-peer computing on a mainframe network.

What's special about this wiring system? Token Ring has the following special features that make it a good choice for many offices:

- It's easy to troubleshoot.
- It can use a smart hub (not an IBM standard, but it can work with Token Ring) to remove faulty nodes from the network without disrupting transmissions.
- It has a transmission design that ensures that one node can't tie up the network.

One of the potential problems with Token Ring is that although it's better equipped to deal with a broken cable connection than Ethernet is, if one adapter in a Token Ring network fails, so does the entire segment. This doesn't happen often, but it's a big enough pain if it does, so it might be worth the extra money to get a *smart hub.* A smart hub can tell if there's trouble and can remove the problem node from the network without disrupting traffic (IBM's standard MAUs aren't capable of this). Token Ring is also expensive to install. Because Token Ring is less popular than Ethernet, technology for Token Ring typically arrives on the market anywhere from three to six months after it arrives for Ethernet. This can be a disadvantage if your organization must always have the latest and greatest.

Ethernet Options

10Base-T and 10Base-2 have the same maximum transmission rate—about 10Mbps—but, as always, you should remember that a lot of factors affect network speed besides transmission rate over the cable. If your network seems slow, don't blame your wiring system first.

10Base-2

This wiring system uses both the logical and physical bus topologies. Using thin coaxial (RG-58A/U) cable, it connects the nodes of the network in a daisy chain.

Why use the 10Base-2 standard? It has two major advantages:

- It uses significantly less cable than a network using a star topology, such as 10Base-T.
- It doesn't require a hub to operate, so you don't need to allocate room, power, or money to connect all the network nodes—they connect directly to one another.

10Base-T

When discussing the bus physical and logical topologies, I will mention 10Base-T as an example of a network type that uses a bus logical topology and a connected-star physical topology. 10Base-T is more commonly used in physical star topologies. 10Base-T is a special type of Ethernet, as it runs on twisted-pair cable rather than coax; 10Base-2 is the more traditional bus-style Ethernet.

By way of review, the *10* stands for 10Mbps, the *Base* stands for baseband transmissions (one pathway for data to go across), and the *T* stands for twisted-pair. Keep in mind that the distance limitation for twisted-pair cable is 300 feet without a repeater.

Theoretically, the advantage of the 10Base-T standard is that it could enable you to use existing twisted-pair telephone wire and thus save on cabling costs. Practically, most LAN planners find that they have to pull any other type of wire you may have (wrongly) anticipated they might need. In any case, when installing 10Base-T, consider that more people are familiar with twisted-pair than with coax, so you could save money on hiring the technicians you need. A bigger potential advantage of 10Base-T is that troubleshooting is easier than it is in a physical-bus LAN. Like the spokes of a wheel, the LAN's cables extend from a wiring closet to the nodes of the network. If one cable breaks or shorts, that node is out of commission, but the rest of the LAN is unaffected.

Other Ethernet cabling options, such as 10Base-5 and 10Broad-36, appear from time to time but are much less common than the two options described above.

100Base-T

100Base-T is functionally just like 10Base-T in that it uses Category 5 UTP cable and works with the same topologies and similar hardware. What's the difference? Speed. 100Base-T functions at 100Mbps, 10 times faster than 10Base-T networks. It does require Category 5 UTP as a minimum and Network Interface Cards, hubs, and routers that are specially designed to work at these speeds.

1000Base-*X*

Gigabit Ethernet networks are becoming increasingly more common. These networks are being used to connect campus-wide networks and high-speed backbones. 1000Mb Ethernet has the ability to span miles over fiber media using high-powered lasers. Gigabit Ethernet has also been designed to reach workstations using Category 5 UTP cabling, although it's more likely to use Category 5e or Category 6. If you are laying down new cabling, consider that your network could be using this newer technology. You should always use the highest grade cabling that your budget can afford.

Summary

In this chapter, I've discussed various types of cable, wiring systems, and connector types. This chapter will not make you an expert cable installer, but it will give you some ideas about how you want to tackle the job. In the next chapter, I'll provide more specifics about network architecture, including details on topologies and protocols, and discuss how to choose between a client-server and a peer-to-peer network.

CHAPTER 16

Network Architectures

FEATURING:

If you've thoroughly digested your networking basics up to this point, you may have already decided which cabling system or systems to use for your network, which means now it's time to figure out how to put them and your computers together. The best way to approach this task is to delve more deeply into topologies, a topic that I mentioned in the preceding chapter and which I'll concentrate on in depth here. To refresh your memory, here's a quick overview of the two types of topologies:

Physical topologies Describes how the computers connect to each other. You can think of a physical topology as an actual map of how your computers and cables might look in an aerial photograph. The physical topology includes the cables, connectors, NICs (Network Interface Cards), and hubs. If it is a part of the network and you can tangibly touch it, it is part of the physical topology of your network.

Logical topologies Describes how signals pass between networked computers or how information passes from node A to node B. The same words (bus, ring) are used to describe specific physical and logical topologies, so be sure you understand the distinction.

After you've mastered the various specific topologies available in each of the above two categories, we'll move bravely to the *protocols* that can be used for networking your computers. I make no bones about it: protocols for sending information across your network are easily the most technically intensive part of this chapter. So make sure you block out an hour of your time to get through it and have a strong cup of coffee on hand. But I promise you, if you make it through this section of the chapter, the ride is all downhill from there.

Physical Topologies

If you wanted to, you could conceivably run cables from each network node to all other network nodes. Technically, assuming that you had enough places to plug in all those cables, this configuration could work fine. The only real problem is the amount of cable you would use.

If you draw a diagram for yourself, you can easily see how connecting all the computers in a network directly to one another could quickly get very complicated. For example, take a look at Figure 16.1. With 5 computers, you would need 10 cables, which doesn't seem too bad, really; but if you added just 3 more computers, you would have to connect 18 more cables! It gets worse: 10 computers require 45 cables; 25 computers require 300 cables.

FIGURE 16.1
Direct-cabling requirements for a five-node network and an eight-node network

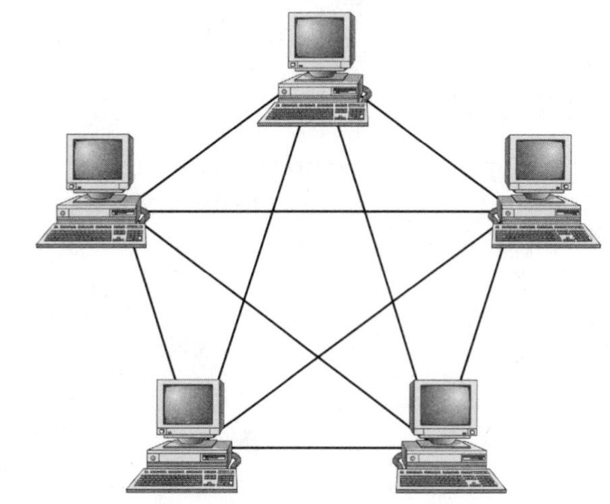

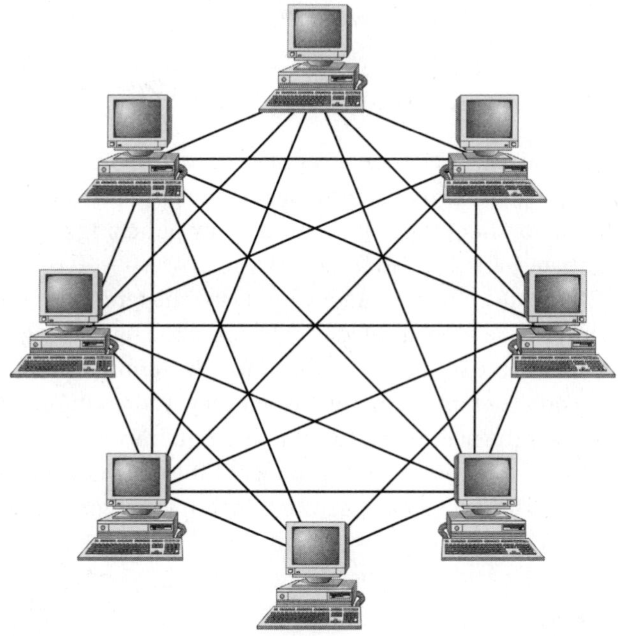

To figure out how many cables your organization would need to interconnect all your computers this way, take the number of computers (*n*), multiply it by (*n*–1), and then divide the result by 2. Hence:

Number of cables = $n\,(n-1) \div 2$

As you can see, the number of cables adds up quickly. If you don't want to spend your entire budget on cable, therefore, you need to devise a more efficient way of linking your network nodes. Most networks use a star topology or a bus topology.

The Star Topology

In the star topology, the network's server is the center of attention. Each workstation on the network connects directly to the server. Seen from above, a network with a star topology would look something like Figure 16.2.

FIGURE 16.2
Star physical topology

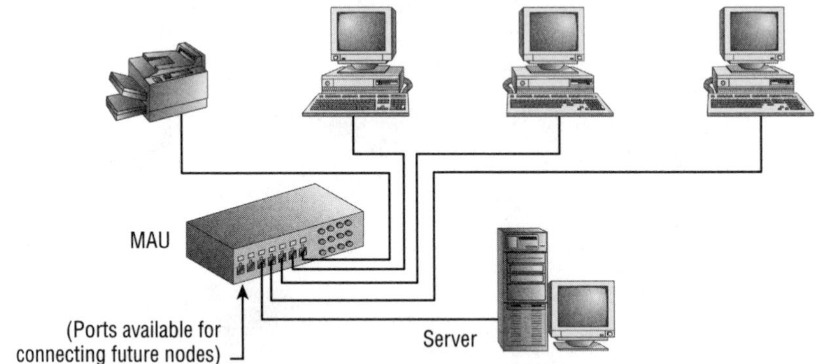

The star topology takes advantage of how computers worked in the early days of computing, when the mainframe was the primary way to network. People could get information from the mainframe only by punching cards, feeding them into the mainframe, and then waiting for their answer.

Eventually, new technology produced the terminal, which was a slightly (but only slightly) more sophisticated way of doing the same thing. Each terminal connected to the mainframe separately, and because the terminals possessed no computing power, they contacted the mainframe when they wanted information. They still had to wait in line for the mainframe to get to their question.

If the star topology is the product of the early days of computing, why is it still around today, when most new terminals have become smart workstations? The answer is threefold:

- Ease of transmission
- Ease of troubleshooting
- Ease of cabling

Getting to the Hub of the Problem

The centerpiece of the star topology is a hub, a multistation access unit (MAU), or a concentrator. All three of these devices provide a centralized location where all the cables in your physical star meet. Any node that is connected to these devices can talk to any other node that is connected. Thus, the similarity of these three devices, but how are they different?

Hub

A *hub* is a device that provides a meeting location for all your cables. Any device attached to the hub has physical access to any other device that is connected to the hub. Hubs generally fall into one of two categories: passive or active.

Passive hub Provides a central location where all your cables meet; it provides no additional functions.

Active hub Provides a central location where all your cables meet as well as at least one other function. The other function can be acting as a repeater (which is the most common) or acting as a bridge or router.

Multistation Access Units (MAUs)

IBM generally refers to its hubs as *multistation access units* (MAUs). MAUs serve the same functions as hubs and are used to accommodate the IBM connector. Most MAUs are active by design.

Concentrators

Concentrators are like build-it-yourself active hubs. A concentrator is a big box with expansion slots in it. An average concentrator could have up to 16 expansion slots. If you want the concentrator to be a straightforward hub, you can purchase a port card with 4, 8, or 16 ports to which you can attach computers. You can put your first port card in slot 0. Assuming that your port card had 8 ports on it, you would then be able to attach as many as 8 devices to the concentrator. This would be a good setup for a small network. The advantage of a concentrator is the capability to add more port cards as your network grows. If you want to add another small department of six people, add another 8-port card in slot 1.

And the fun is just beginning. As your network grows, you may have to provide a gateway service to your mainframe system in your office. No problem—just purchase a gateway card and put it into slot 2. Now all 16 of your current users (8 attached to slot 0 and 8 attached to slot 1) can go through the gateway card to get to the mainframe system. If distance between nodes is becoming a problem, add a repeater card so that all network packets are repeated as they flow through the hub. You can keep adding cards to the concentrator as your needs grow. If you are concerned that you might run out of slots, fear not. There is a slot specifically reserved for a backbone card that enables you to connect one concentrator to another so that they act as one large concentrator.

Of hub, MAU, and concentrator, the concentrator is the most expensive, but it does provide the greatest flexibility in terms of growth for your network.

NOTE In practice, the preceding terms are often used interchangeably. For instance, many folks use the term *hub* when they are referring to a concentrator. In the paragraphs above, I've given the true definitions of each term, but some of you may think those definitions are wrong because you've been hearing the industry use the terms loosely and often incorrectly. So don't be thrown when you are looking through articles or catalogs and you see mention of an 8-port stand-alone concentrator with no space to add additional cards. It is just the industry's way of keeping us on our toes. For the rest of this book, I bow to common usage and use the term *hub* to refer to all three options.

Star Topology Continued

On a network with a star topology, the server never has to wonder how to get information back to the terminal that asked the question. The server just finds the port to which the node in question connects and relays the information.

The star topology is nice for awkwardly arranged networks. As a simple example, imagine a network with four computers: three workstations and one server. If one workstation is upstairs and two are downstairs but in separate rooms, cabling the network is relatively easy if you don't have to worry about connecting all the nodes to each other and can concentrate on connecting the individual workstations to the hub.

Of course, the star topology has one major drawback—the large amount of cable it uses. Having a centralized hub isn't the most cable-efficient arrangement, so if you're concerned about cable costs and your nodes are close together, you might want to consider the bus topology.

Troubleshooting a Star Topology

Another big advantage to the star topology is that it's easy to troubleshoot. As you'll see in the discussion of the bus topology, if your bus network fails, you will have difficulty pinpointing exactly where the problem lies without a node-to-node search. On a star network, in contrast, finding the source of a problem is easy. If one node doesn't work, the problem probably lies somewhere between the port of the hub and the node. You should check to see if the problem lies with:

- The terminal itself
- The cable between the hub and the terminal
- The port on the hub that services the troubled terminal

Continued ›

First, check whether the NIC is configured correctly. Ensure that no hardware conflicts exist in terms of I/O addresses, IRQs (interrupt requests), or DMA (direct memory access) channels. You may also want to run a memory test on the workstation and run a hard drive testing utility.

If none of the network nodes work, the problem probably lies with the server, and it's time to hope that you planned for fault tolerance and that you did your backups.

The Bus Topology

The bus topology, known in the Mac world by the more descriptive term *daisy chaining*, is much more cable efficient than the star topology. In the bus topology, the cable runs from computer to computer, making each computer a link of a chain. You can run a bus topology in three ways. Ethernet is the best-known example of a logical bus topology; the others are called thicknet (10Base-5) and thinnet (10Base-2), based on the type of cable that you use to connect the network.

Thicknet, sometimes referred to as *frozen yellow garden hose* because of its stiffness and color, uses a thick, central cable as a sort of backbone for the network; then from the backbone it runs thinner cables known as *taps* or *drops* to the network's nodes, as depicted in Figure 16.3. What connects the thinner cable to the thicknet cable is a transceiver. In generic terms, a *transceiver* is a device that connects one cable type to a dissimilar cable type.

FIGURE 16.3
A thicknet configuration

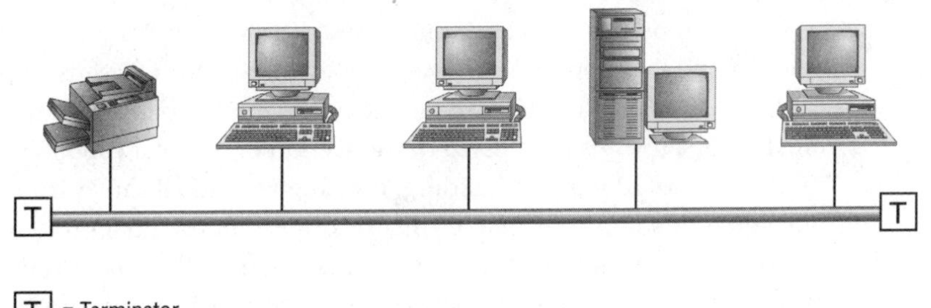

The *T*'s at either end of the network in Figure 16.3 indicate the terminators.

The thicknet configuration is typically used in mainframe and minicomputer networks, but its popularity is diminishing as PCs get smarter and mainframe-based networks less common.

Thinnet, on the other hand, eschews the backbone idea and connects all network devices directly. Rather than using thick cable, thinnet uses the more flexible coaxial cable, as depicted in Figure 16.4. Thinnet is becoming a more popular networking topology than its thick counterpart, if for no other reason than that the thick cable in thicknet is a pain to work with—it's very stiff and clumsy.

FIGURE 16.4
A thinnet configuration

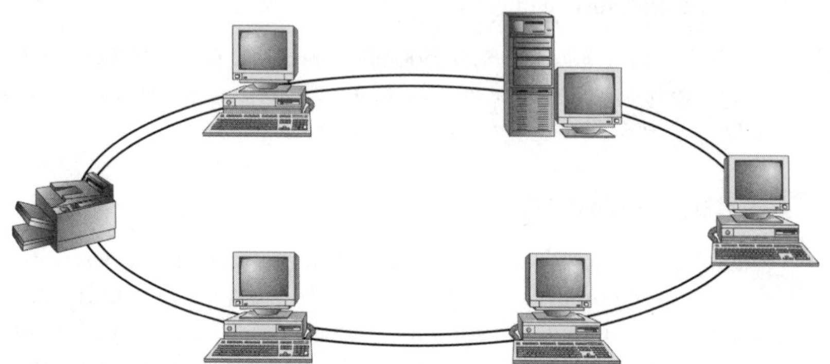

The biggest potential problem with a bus network is that you have to tell it when to quit. If you haven't terminated your network, your network can't transmit. Nor can it transmit if even one node on the network is malfunctioning, because the system depends on every node being in proper working order so that it can pass the data along.

There is an important distinction between a node malfunctioning and a node being off. If the node is off, data will pass through the T connector to the next active node. In this case, the network is unaware that an inactive node is present. However, if the node is on, or active—but malfunctioning—problems will occur. The active node will still attempt to process a packet, but will do it inaccurately, thus slowing down the whole network or bringing it to a screeching halt.

The bus topology does have one great advantage over the star topology: it's cable efficient and therefore can save you money on the most expensive part of your network. On the other hand, it can be difficult to implement if your network is not neatly lined up in a row. As I discussed in the section on the star topology, if the network is spread haphazardly over a building, running individual cables from each node to a hub could be a lot easier than trying to connect all the nodes to one another.

Another big minus to the bus is troubleshooting. If *one node* is down, the network can't relay messages, and the network stops dead. This factor not only makes your network vulnerable to failures (remember, the only way an entire star network dies is if the server or hub dies), but also makes it difficult to troubleshoot. To find a problem on a bus network, you might need to inspect every node on the segment to make sure that the cables are securely fastened, that no one tried to reboot or log off when a signal was being passed, or that any number of other things are in order.

Logical Topologies

Logical topologies (occasionally referred to as *electrical topologies*) describe the way in which a network transmits information from one node to the next node—as opposed to physical topologies, which merely represent what your network looks like. This topic is not all theory, however; the way you want your network to transmit information can directly affect your options when it comes to purchasing NICs and cabling.

As we head into logical topology, remember that the physical topology does not have a direct bearing on the logical topology. You can have a physical bus and a logical ring, a physical star and a logical bus, and so on.

The best way to visualize a logical topology is by way of an analogy. If you had a 400-page document that absolutely, positively had to be to sent across the country overnight, you would probably send it via Federal Express. In the process of sending this document, you would have to use a FedEx envelope and addressing slip. When addressing the FedEx package, you would have to provide a source address, a destination address, and the document.

Your network needs the same pieces of information: source address, destination address, and data. All this information taken together constitutes the *packet*. The logical topology has to handle how this packet is going to be sent across the network. It's a three-step process:

1. The logical topology determines the format of the packet, just as FedEx has predetermined the format of its address slip. You must have the addresses in a certain format.
2. The logical topology determines how much information the packet will carry, just as FedEx says that only 30 pages can be sent in its letter envelope.
3. The logical topology determines the method of tracking the packet across the network.

Actually, in regard to step 3 of the process, some logical topologies do not track the packet at all; they just hope for the best. Other topologies track the packet along each step of its path.

Bus Topology

As mentioned earlier, Ethernet is probably the best-known example of a logical bus network; it certainly is the most popular LAN type. Ethernet is an example of a *logical* bus topology, but—as you'll see in a minute—it is not always a *physical* bus topology. (Yes, I keep hammering that home, but the concept isn't easy to grasp.)

How does the bus topology work? Simply put, each time a node on the network has data for another node, it broadcasts the data to the entire network. The various nodes hear the broadcast and look to see if the data is for them. If it is, they keep it. If it's not, they pass it down again until it reaches the correct destination.

Whatever anyone on the bus says, everyone hears. It's something like the old telephone party lines, in which several neighbors shared a telephone number. A distinctive ring was assigned to each person on the line so that everyone could answer their own calls. If your code was, say, three quick rings, and you heard the telephone ring three quick rings, you could pick it up and know it was for you. On the other hand, if you heard two long rings and one short ring, you'd know that the call was for your neighbor Burt and ignore it. In all cases, everyone heard the rings but only one person responded—the person whom the call was for.

The bus topology works in a similar fashion. Every Ethernet card has a 48-bit address peculiar to itself, and each piece of data that travels the network is directed to the address of the card in the node that should receive the data. All nodes on the network can see the data, but if it's not addressed to them, they ignore it and pass it down until it reaches the correct destination. (Bus networks work better than the old party lines that way—your neighbor's machine can't eavesdrop on data not sent to it.)

So now you know how data finds its destination on the network, but how do networked computers send the data in the first place? On a bus network, every workstation can send out information in a package called a *packet*. Data transmitted on a network of *any* type must conform to a strict format called the *Data Link Layer Frame format,* which that network type uses for arranging data. Ethernet's format looks like Figure 16.5.

FIGURE 16.5
The composition of a Data Link Layer Ethernet frame

Preamble 8 bytes	Destination address 6 bytes	Source address 6 bytes	Message type 2 bytes	Data 46-1500 bytes	Frame check sequence 4 bytes

Each packet can be no more than 1,518 bytes, just to make sure that one workstation doesn't hog the network for too long. Before a workstation broadcasts to the network, it listens to see if anyone else is using the network. If the coast is clear, the workstation broadcasts.

What if the coast isn't clear? Ethernet is the topology that has to worry about that situation. When a node has a packet to send across the network, it "listens" to the cable to hear if any frequencies are going across the cable. If the sending node, I'll call it node A, detects a frequency on the cable, it will wait for the current packet to go by and then send its packet. If node A detects that the line is free, it will go ahead and send its packet.

The biggest problem with this broadcast method is distance, as I discussed in Chapter 15. If the distance between node A and node B is too great, the nodes might not "hear" each other on the line and might both send packets at the same time. What follows is known as a *packet collision.* If a collision occurs, it will cause a frequency "ripple" on the cable. The first node to detect this increased frequency ripple sends out a high-frequency signal, which cancels out all other signals. This signal tells all nodes that a collision has occurred and that all nodes on the network should stop sending packets. At this point each node waits a random amount of time and then tries broadcasting again. Nodes can repeat this wait-and-listen routine as many as 16 times before giving up.

The way that nodes decide when to resend their data is actually pretty neat. The system is known by the unfortunate name of *truncated binary exponential backoff.* (No, unlike almost everything else in the LAN world, it doesn't have a convenient and commonly used abbreviation.) In English, this name means that after two nodes collide, each node on the network randomly generates a whole number between 1 and 2, multiplies that number by 0.5, and then waits that number of milliseconds before retransmitting. Of course, the first time out the chances are 50-50 that nodes A and B will pick the same number, so they might have to retry again. The next time, A and B randomly pick a number between 1 and 4 and do the same thing. If they pick the same number again, they'll pick a number between 1 and 8. This goes on, doubling each time, either until A and B choose different numbers and send their information or the 16 tries are up and they stop trying. The chances are good that both A and B will get to send their data, however, by the time they get to the 16th try. The delay could be up to half a second, which for a network that transmits data at 10 million bits per second is an eternity. A bus network rarely needs that many retries.

How likely are collisions? Having cable no longer than it's supposed to be decreases your chance of a collision because the nodes can "hear" other nodes broadcasting more easily; but the way the bus logical topology works *increases* the likelihood of packet collisions. Consider: If a node can't broadcast until the network is clear and more than one node has information to send, what's going to happen as soon as the line is free? Both nodes will leap to get their information out first, and the result is a collision.

Keep in mind that all this processing takes place at the Ethernet NIC. Therefore, if you are going to use the Ethernet topology, all your nodes must have Ethernet cards. Ethernet can run on top of a physical bus, physical star, or physical ring.

Ethernet isn't the only example of a bus topology, but it is the most used. For a while, AT&T marketed a one-megabit-per-second (Mbps) version of Ethernet called StarLAN. StarLAN is now a 10Mbps network, but now and then you'll see installations using the old StarLAN. Another, perhaps better known example is the LocalTalk/AppleTalk network built into Macintosh computers. LocalTalk transmits at only 250,000bps but employs many of the basic design principles found in Ethernet.

Token Ring Topology

IBM originally bought the design for the Token Ring logical topology from Olaf Soderblom, a Dutch scientist. The original Token Ring used a 4Mbps signaling speed, but in 1989 IBM released a 16Mbps version. Other Token Ring networks are available but they are not as well known as IBM's, partially because they were late getting on the market. In addition, other companies developing their own Token Ring systems have to decide whether to fight or accommodate Soderblom's claim of proprietary rights. At this point, the battle is still in progress.

Although the Token Ring network has a ring logical topology, it uses a connected star system like that of 10Base-T Ethernet for its physical topology. Instead of hubs, Token Ring uses devices called either concentrators or, more commonly, multistation access units (MAUs), as discussed previously.

NOTE Don't confuse these MAUs with an Ethernet adapter's *media attachment unit*—a transceiver connecting to the Attachment Unit Interface (AUI) port.

A Token Ring board attaches to the MAU with a D-shell type connector on one side and an odd-looking IBM connector on the other. The Token Ring connector plugs into the MAU. Eight PCs can attach to a MAU, and then those MAUs attach to *other* MAUs. Token Ring networks do not have terminators; instead, one end of the cable plugs into the board, and the other end plugs into the MAU.

As with the hubs for 10Base-T, you can most easily arrange your Token Ring network so that cables extend from a central wiring closet (a place where all the cables can be gathered together) on each floor to workstations on that floor, and the MAUs go into the wiring closet. The cables between the MAU and the network device can be as long as 45 meters, providing enough space for most floor plans to be cabled with a wiring closet.

Remember that Ethernet is a broadcast system; that is, what one station says, all stations hear. But Token Ring doesn't work that way. In Token Ring, every station must repeat what it hears from the previous station, making a kind of "bucket brigade" of data.

The heart of the Token Ring topology is the token packet. To avoid packet collisions, the token topologies ensure that only one workstation can send information across the network at any given time. The method used to ensure that only a single transmission occurs is the token packet, or "talking stick." Only the node that has control of the token packet can send information across the network.

How does the token move around the network? When a workstation is done with the token, it releases it to whatever station is next in line. If nobody grabs the token, the workstation releases it a second time. If nobody responds to the token for a second time, the workstation sends out a general query, known as a *solicit successor frame*, over the network, asking, "Who's supposed to get the token next?" If a workstation responds, the sending workstation addresses the token to that workstation and passes the token. Because no single node can transmit for longer than it takes for a piece of data to make a complete circuit of the network, no one ever waits more than one circuit's worth of information before getting a chance to transmit. Unlike Ethernet, where collisions could conceivably keep other nodes from transmitting by tying up the network, Token Ring ensures that everyone gets a turn.

The fact that Ethernet *broadcasts* and that Token Ring *repeats* affects the kinds of cable that each network topology uses. Fiber-optic lines are not well suited to broadcasting but work well for point-to-point communications. Consequently, Token Ring is better suited to fiber usage than Ethernet is unless you use some kind of star configuration such as 10Base-T Ethernet. Token Ring is designed to support a variety of cable types, but most commonly uses IBM Type 1, IBM Type 2, and IBM Type 3 cables.

When a Bus Is Not a Bus: 10Base-T

To really understand how a network can use one physical topology and another logical topology, let's take a look at 10Base-T, a kind of Ethernet network that has a bus logical topology and a star physical topology. Figure 16.6 shows how a 10Base-T network is cabled.

FIGURE 16.6
A 10Base-T-distributed star configuration

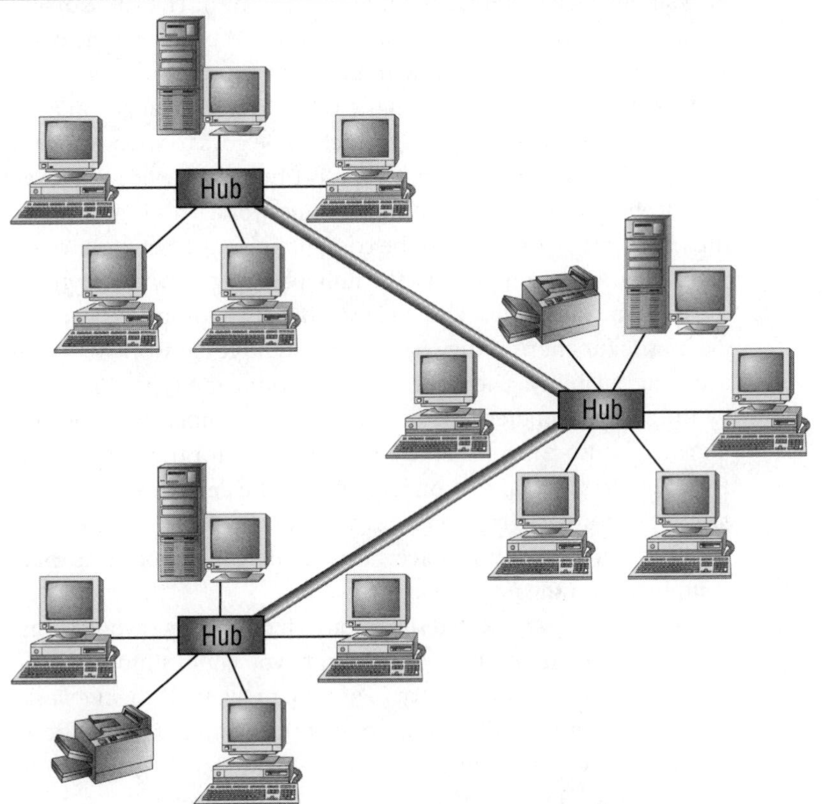

10Base-T looks like a set of stars connected by a bus. It still behaves as if it were a bus—it broadcasts to the network—but it's cabled like a star, using unshielded twisted-pair (UTP). Therefore, this network is a *logical* bus but a *physical* star. Why does 10Base-T use this connected-star approach? It might seem contrary to logic, because a star network involves more cable than a bus and so should not be a preferred cabling scheme from a cost-of-wiring point of view.

But this connected-star approach has a major benefit: it is easy to troubleshoot. Suppose you're setting up a network in a building with multiple floors. On each floor, you create a wiring closet. You then run cables (the 10Base-T specifications limit each cable's length to no more than 100 meters) from the wiring closet to each workstation on that floor. Next, connect each floor's wiring closet to the next floor's wiring closet with a cable. Now you've got a connected star—a star network on each floor and a bus connecting the floors.

The cable that is used to connect one hub to another hub is generally referred to as a *backbone*. You always want to make sure that the cable that you use for the backbone is rated for speeds that meet or exceed the speed of the cable that you are using throughout the network (from hub to the nodes). The value of all this extra cable lies in your test instruments in the wiring closet. When someone complains that their workstation no longer works with the network, you can go straight to the wiring closet and test the particular cable. All the cables will be arranged in a nice, neat order, with clearly marked labels indicating which cable goes to what workstation.

Inside each wiring closet is a 10Base-T hub, the device that enables all the computers on a floor to interact as an Ethernet network. This hub connects to the next hub, thus connecting each hub to the computers on the network. You can test the hub by taking a portable computer to the hub, plugging it in, and trying to make a network connection. Some hubs (known as *smart hubs*, appropriately enough) can even assume diagnostic functions if they have SNMP (Simple Network Management Protocol) management capability. They monitor the amount and type of information being supplied by the client computers and detect errors on computers in the network.

You can also pay for software that will monitor the hubs from a central location. For example, I've said that on a LAN only one device can "talk" at a time. One particular type of hardware failure makes a computer chatter away endlessly, locking up the network, but a smart hub detects this failure and disconnects that malfunctioning computer from the network.

Of course, the connected star approach of 10Base-T would simplify this debugging step even if you didn't have a smart hub; you could simply connect a portable computer to the hub—and then try to use the network. If the network is busy because of a chattering computer, disconnect one of the computers at the hub and try the portable again. Because all the connections are right at your fingertips, you need only a minute or two to test all the connections to find the chatterer.

IEEE's Topological Protocols

In 1980, the Institute of Electrical and Electronics Engineers (IEEE) attempted to make some sense out of all the conflicting standards, protocols, and manufacturing methods of cabling and logical topologies. The following sections, though not exhaustive, should give you a feel for some of the characteristics of these standards and how the IEEE committees work. Some of this information also appears elsewhere in the book, so don't worry if something looks familiar.

The 802.3 Standard

When the IEEE 802.3 committee met, Ethernet standards were already a powerhouse in the cabling configuration field, thanks to industry acceptance. However, the 802.3 committee was reluctant to force all new networks' topologies to follow the strict Ethernet as set out by Xerox and DEC, so it said, "Let's try to come up with an Ethernet-*like* standard," and the 802.3 standard was born. The 802.3 standard includes the older Ethernet protocol specifications in addition to changes in the basic structure of the data packets.

Although all Ethernet-type networks use the 802.3 standard, 10Base-2, which uses both a physical and a logical bus topology, is the most common. It uses 50-ohm coaxial baseband cable (refer to Chapter 15 if you need to) and can send data at 10Mbps. Information travels the network in packets consisting of the following parts (see Figure 16.7):

Preamble Eight bytes of information used to coordinate the rest of the information in the packet.

Start delimiter Indicates that the frame is about to begin.

Destination address The network address of the workstation or workstations that are to receive this information.

Source address The address that enables the receiving workstation or workstations to recognize the workstation that sent the information.

Type or length The type of information that is held within the data part of this packet, whether it is graphics information, ASCII text information, or any other type of data. If the type is not listed, this field will contain the length of the packet. This information is crucial to the sending process because the receiving station can't understand bitmaps if it's expecting text (or vice versa). Think of what happens when you drink orange juice when you're expecting milk. It doesn't taste like either one, and you probably can't identify it, at least not right away.

Actual data The data can be anywhere from 46 to 1,500 bytes long.

Frame-check sequence A "packing slip" to verify that the rest of the packet reached its destination intact.

FIGURE 16.7
The composition of an 802.3 frame

Preamble 8 bytes	Start delimiter 1 byte	Destination address 2-6 bytes	Source address 2-6 bytes	Length 2 bytes	Data 46-1500 bytes	Frame check sequence 4 bytes

Not only did the IEEE 802.3 committee have to determine how information would travel through the network and the kind of cable and topology that would best suit the method of data travel, it had to determine how far the cables could stretch before the data faded or corrupted. The committee found that length to be 185 meters (607 feet) per cable segment. This length clearly limits the distance between workstations and may affect the choice of network type in some situations.

TIP Remember, the length issue is important because it determines how far one workstation can be from another workstation or how closely the workstations have to be grouped together. If the workstations are too far apart, the information will fade away or become corrupted in transit. To avoid this problem, welcome to the wonderful world of repeaters. Recall that a repeater is simply a device that is placed periodically throughout the network to enhance or to strengthen the signal. As the signal reaches its length threshold, a repeater gives the signal a boost so that it can be sent another set distance before it hits the workstation that is to receive the information or before another repeater needs to enhance the signal again.

Carrier Sense Multiple Access/Collision Detection (CSMA/CD)

The 802.3 standard's most salient feature is the *Carrier Sense Multiple Access/Collision Detection* (CSMA/CD) designation. CSMA/CD gets to the heart of a basic Ethernet problem: how can you send vast amounts of information simultaneously across the network without causing collisions? After all, the network can handle only one packet at a time.

The best way to understand why Ethernet needs CSMA/CD is to visualize the boulder warehouse I talked about in Chapter 15. Recall how each clerk sat alone in a room with a boulder the size of the one in *Raiders of the Lost Ark*. The halls of this warehouse are pretty narrow, so the boulders only just fit—there's certainly no room for two to pass each other. Before the clerks can move the boulders, they have to listen outside their doors to make sure that no one else is moving a boulder in the corridor. Because the clerks have to move the boulders around fairly often, they spend a lot of time listening and then leaping out the door as soon as it's quiet—which, of course, leads to collisions because all the other clerks are doing the same thing. When the boulders collide, each clerk has to go back to their storeroom and wait for quiet before trying again.

Your Ethernet LAN works in much the same way. If you send one packet of information from one workstation to another workstation, the network has no trouble controlling the flow of this packet. If more than one workstation tries to broadcast at the same time, however, the packets will collide, the transmission will abort, and the workstations will have to try transmitting again.

CSMA/CD provides a means for reducing packet collision. Before transmitting, CSMA/CD broadcasts a signal known as the *carrier-sensing signal* to see if any other workstations are broadcasting. If not, it gives the workstation the "all clear," and the workstation transmits its packet. If, however, the carrier-sensing signal (as shown in Figure 16.8) detects another workstation's transmittal, CSMA/CD tells the workstation to wait before broadcasting.

FIGURE 16.8 *The carrier-sensing signal at work*

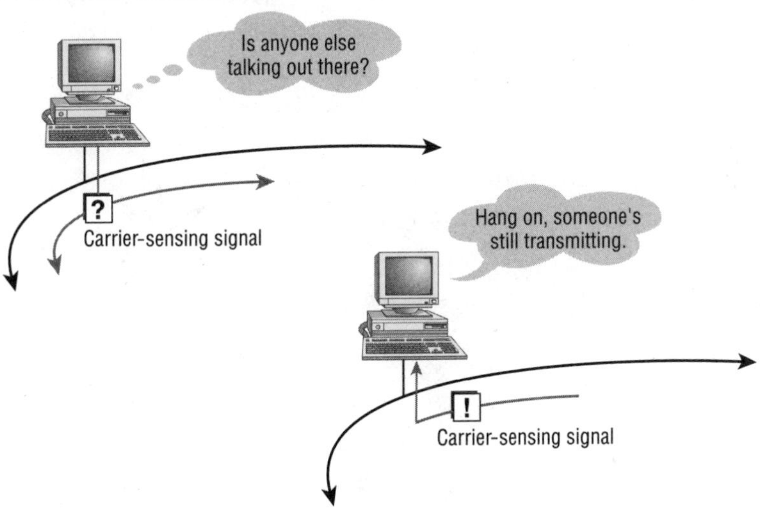

This process works fine as long as network traffic isn't heavy and the LAN's cables aren't any longer than they're rated for. If either of those conditions exist, collisions are likely to happen regardless of CSMA/CD. CSMA/CD isn't in charge of making sure that only one workstation transmits at a time; it's in charge of making sure that all workstations are quiet before one transmits. If two workstations happen to *begin* transmitting at the same time, there's nothing that CSMA/CD can do to prevent the collision.

If two packets collide, CSMA/CD tries to avoid a repeat collision, as shown in Figure 16.9. As I discussed earlier, each workstation chooses a random number between 1 and 2 before transmitting again. If the workstations choose the same number, they each choose a number between 1 and 4 and try again. This process goes on until either the workstations have both successfully completed their transmissions or they've tried 16 times without success. If they flunk out by the sixteenth try, both workstations have to pause and give the other workstations a chance to transmit.

FIGURE 16.9
How CSMA/CD prevents repeat collisions

How CSMA/CD Prevents Repeat Collisions

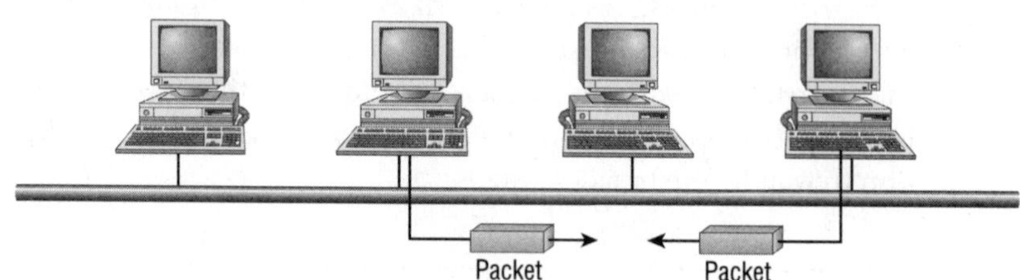

Two packets, not having heard each other, both start down the network.

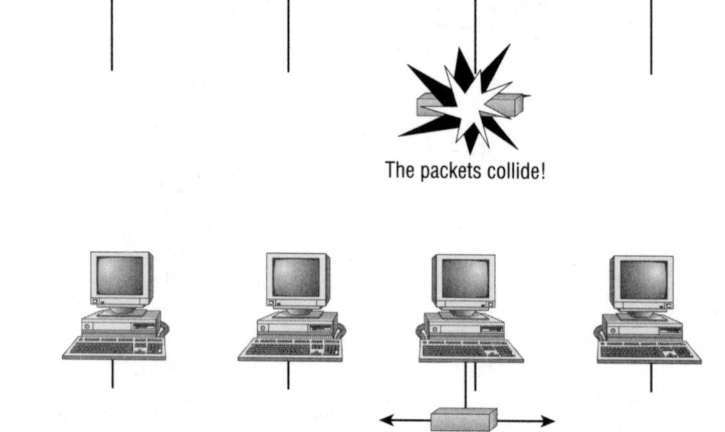

The packets collide!

The node closest to the collision detects it and sends out a jamming signal, notifying all nodes that a collision has taken place.

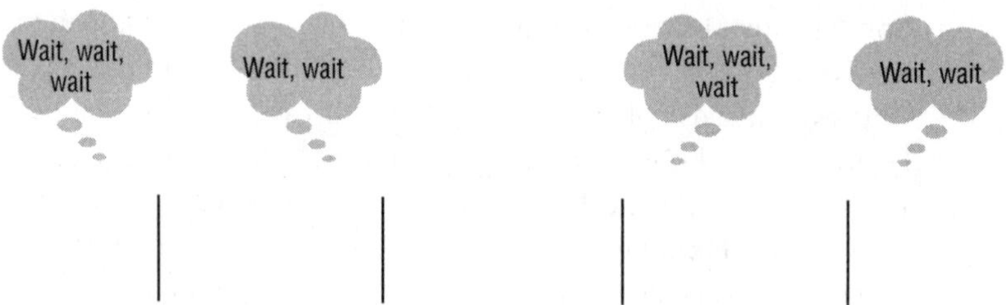

Each node on the network waits a random number of milliseconds before transmitting, in hopes that they won't coincidentally wait the same amount of time and send packets at the same time again.

In short, CSMA/CD can't prevent every collision, but it tries to minimize the time that collisions tie up the network.

Another Ethernet protocol called 802.2 is a variation on this theme. People use 802.3 primarily in a Novell environment because it is faster than 802.2. However, 802.3 is proprietary to the IPX (Internetwork Packet eXchange) protocol from Novell. In a heterogeneous environment with different types of servers and network operating systems, 802.2 is preferred because it is more universal in nature.

The 802.4 Standard

In an effort to design a standard that was less prone to collisions than the 802.3, the IEEE 802.4 subcommittee designed a combination bus/ring topology that transmitted information via a token. Using the bus physical topology and the ring logical topology, the 802.4 standard is designed on the principle that computers are prone to the same fallibility as humans: Give 'em half a chance, and they'll talk right on top of each other. To get around this problem, the 802.4 committee designed a token that the network could use in much the same way that discussion groups use "talking sticks"—whoever's got the stick has the floor (usually for a preset period of time) and no one else can talk until they've got the stick. So it is with the 802.4 standard.

Only the workstation that has the token can send information, and after that workstation has received acknowledgment of the receipt of that information, it must then pass the token to the next workstation in line. How does the network determine who's next in line? In the 802.4 standard, the network keeps track of who gets the token next. Just as the business manager could get the talking stick more often than the person in charge of office decorations, it's possible for some workstations to have priority over others to get the token.

The method of controlling collisions isn't the only way in which the 802.4 standard differs from the 802.3 standard. An 802.4 packet, also called a token bus, looks different from an 802.3 packet. The 802.4 contains a preamble, a start frame delimiter, frame control, destination address, source address, information, frame check sequence, and frame delimiter, as shown in Figure 16.10.

FIGURE 16.10
The composition of an 802.4 frame

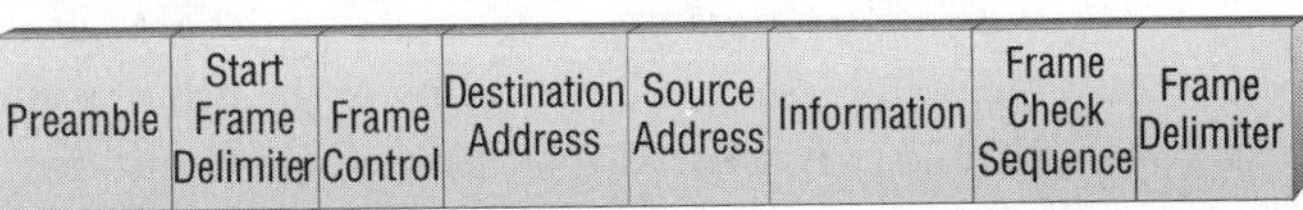

Although the token bus combination avoids collisions, the 802.4 standard still has some disadvantages that have kept it from common usage. Most shortfalls of the token bus format come from malfunctioning hardware, which can result in the token being lost, or from shadowed tokens that make it look as though the network has multiple tokens. Imagine a board meeting with more than one talking stick!

The 802.5 Standard

The IEEE 802.5 committee developed the 802.5 standard in conjunction with IBM. This standard is specifically designed for Token Ring networks that use the token specification to pass information from one workstation to another. As you'll remember from the earlier discussion of the Token Ring LAN, the 802.5 standard uses a star physical topology and a ring logical topology.

As in the 802.4 standard, the workstations on a Token Ring network use a token to determine which workstation gets to transmit. If a workstation doesn't need to transmit anything, it passes the free token to the next workstation, and so on until a workstation needs to transmit something.

Data travels from the originating workstation to every node on the network in succession. Each workstation examines the address on the data packet. If the data is for that station, the workstation keeps a copy of the data and sends the original on. If the data isn't for that station, it merely sends it to the next workstation on the network. When the sending workstation gets back the copy of its first data packet, it knows that it's time to stop transmitting and passes the free token to the next workstation.

The 802.5 standard has some qualities to recommend it. With a smart hub, the Token Ring protocol also allows for malfunctioning hardware—a nice feature that the token bus standard doesn't have. If a workstation malfunctions, either not releasing the token when its turn is up or jabbering over the network, the smart hub can recognize trouble and cut that workstation from the LAN, enabling the rest of the network to function normally. An 802.5 network can also extend for longer distances than either the 802.3 or the 802.4 because the packet travels from one workstation to another and is retransmitted at every step; therefore, it never has very far to go before being retransmitted.

Peer-to-Peer versus Client-Server

In the computing world, some issues are so divisive that debates about them have something of the quality of religious argument. If you don't believe us, have you ever eavesdropped on an argument between a diehard Mac user and a PC aficionado?

To date, the peer-to-peer versus client-server debate hasn't reached this point of passion, but some people *really* believe in one or the other, sometimes for no other reason than one technology is the first that they ever encountered. If you'd like to take a slightly more intellectual look at the debate, read on.

Neither type of network is perfect for all situations. Client-server networks have better security whereas peer-to-peer networks are more flexible and are often cheaper. Windows 2000 supports both platforms, with Windows 2000 Professional primarily providing peer-to-peer networking capabilities and Windows 2000 Server providing both.

Client-Server Networks

Client-server networks are similar in some ways to the old mainframe/terminal networks. In each, a central computer is in charge of the network and handles all requests. The main difference is that the client computers are able to compute on their own (assuming that they're PCs), unlike the dumb terminals. Figure 16.11 shows a client-server network configuration.

FIGURE 16.11
An example of a client-server network

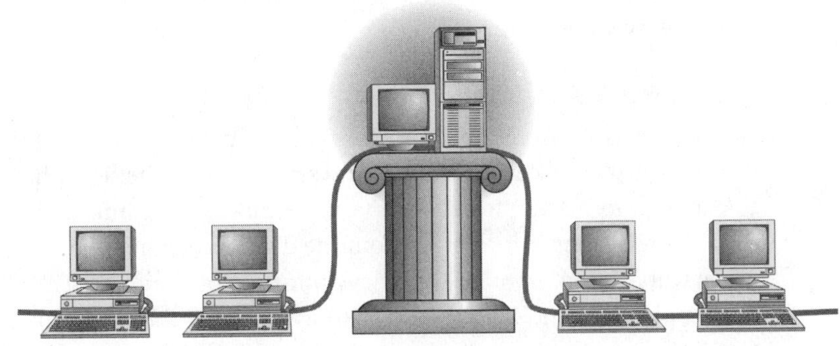

For large organizations, client-server networks have several advantages:

- They are often more upgradeable than peer-to-peer networks.

  Client-server networks are often more flexible than peer-to-peer networks. They have more options available to them and more software is written for client-server networks than for peer-to-peer. In addition, more industry information is available, which is helpful when you're trying to figure out a problem.

- They give their administrators better control of the network.

  In peer-to-peer networks, each user is, to an extent, their own administrator. Client-server networks are controlled by an administrator who decides which peripherals and files each user may attach to.

- They are infinitely expandable.

  Peer-to-peer networks can expand easily but don't work well with more than about 15 nodes. Client-server networks, on the other hand, can expand to hundreds of machines, even tens or hundreds of thousands in a wide area network (WAN).

- They are more secure from unauthorized access.

  Client-server networks use much tighter and more efficient security than peer-to-peer networks use. Most client-server networks require a user to provide a password and a logon ID before accessing the network from a client computer. That password and ID give that user access only to the files and devices that the user is authorized to access. In addition, the password and ID tell the file server exactly what kind of file access that user has (read-only or full) and how they can manipulate files, by moving them or marking them for other users to share.

Client-server networks have their liabilities, of course. They're generally much more expensive per node than peer-to-peer networks, and they are harder to set up. Even for an experienced administrator, setting up the server could entail hours of work. And adding new clients to the network can be time consuming.

Expense and administration aside, however, client-server networks are best suited for large companies. Let's take a look at some of the kinds of servers you might see on a client-server network.

Disk Servers

A *disk server* is a central repository for files and data, attached to the network like any other node and appearing to each workstation as another local hard disk.

Saving information to a disk server is just like saving information to a local hard disk, but retrieving information from the disk server is a bit more complex. On a stand-alone workstation, in order to retrieve information from the hard disk, the computer must look up the file's location in the *File Allocation Table* (FAT) or the *Master File Table* (MFT), depending on whether you are using the FAT file system or the NTFS (New Technology File System) file system. After the computer finds the file's location, it moves the read/write heads to that location on the hard disk and copies the file into memory.

NOTE As you will recall from either Chapter 2 of this book or from your own experience installing Windows 2000 Professional, you must decide which file system you want to use—NTFS, FAT, or FAT32. MFT is the NTFS version of the FAT.

It's not quite as easy to retrieve information from a disk server. You see, the disk server keeps its *own* FAT or MFT, and any time a workstation wants to retrieve information from the disk server, the disk server must send a copy of its FAT or MFT to the workstation. The workstation then stores a copy of the FAT or MFT in memory. To access information on the disk server, the workstation will first get a copy (to keep) of the disk server's FAT or MFT and then use that copy to see where the file is on the disk server's hard disk. Thus, when a workstation accesses a disk server, the following drama occurs.

The disk server can probably see the potential hazard. The whole point of a network is to give a number of people access to the network's capabilities, right? However, the first time someone accesses the disk server, the user will get a copy of the FAT or MFT as it looked *at that time*. Every time anyone adds or deletes a file from the server's hard disk, the FAT or the MFT changes. Therefore, if you get a copy of the disk server's FAT or MFT at 8:00 in the morning, by 2:30 that afternoon it's likely that your copy no longer matches the original. Because the disk server's CPU uses its outdated map to search for the data on the hard disk, your data retrieval could slow down or grind to a halt.

To get around this potential hazard, disk servers are usually divided or partitioned into several volumes, each volume reserved for a different workstation. In order to share information, it's saved on the "read-only" public volume, protecting the FAT's or the MFT's integrity on the disk server.

File Servers

Disk servers, as you can see, can be complicated and are potentially dangerous to work with. These days, *file servers* are much more common. File servers are a more complex animal than their predecessor. A file server usually has its own operating system, forming a shell around the disk operating system environment. This operating system filters out network commands and DOS commands, translating DOS commands to network commands, and vice versa.

File servers and disk servers are similar in function; that is, they provide a central place for workstations to store data. The main difference between a file server and a disk server is that a file server maintains its own FAT or MFT and does its own searching for files on its hard disk. When a workstation requests a file, the file server checks its FAT or MFT to see where the file is located on the hard disk and then moves the hard drive's rewrite heads to that location. After copying the data from the hard disk, the file server sends the copy of the file to the workstation that made the request.

The difference between a disk server and a file server could perhaps be expressed like this: When a workstation asks a disk server for a file for the first time that day, the disk server rummages in its drawer and finds a map of the storeroom where it keeps the files, telling the workstation, "Go ahead and get the file, kid, but keep the map; I've got better things to do than keep you supplied with maps." Every time a workstation gets something from the storeroom or returns something, the storeroom gets a little reorganized, but because it has an automatic update, the disk server always hands out accurate maps. When workstations come back to look for files using their old maps, however, it's quite possible that the storeroom will be rearranged and that they won't be able to find anything.

The file server, on the other hand, would rather find things itself than have a bunch of workstations rummaging through its hard disk. When a workstation asks for a file, the file server says, "I'll send it right out—no, really, I'd rather do it." It then finds the file, makes a copy of it for the workstation, and sends it through the network to the workstation that requested it.

File servers have a number of advantages over disk servers. First, because file servers don't need to copy the FAT or the MFT to the workstation, only one record of file locations exists, and the file server maintains it. Second, the server no longer has to divide its hard disk into volumes, so the server's entire disk can be shared with all workstations. This arrangement, as you recall, was *not* the case with the disk server.

NOTE The server's entire disk *can* be shared with all workstations but isn't necessarily. File servers generally have stringent security measures that restrict file access to users with the proper access rights. The files a user can access depend on his or her access rights.

Dedicated and Nondedicated File Servers

When you hear discussions of file servers, you'll sometimes hear people talking about dedicated file servers and nondedicated file servers. A *dedicated file server* has its own hard disk drive, and its only goal in life is to be a file server. By dedicating a computer as a file server, you restrict its memory to file server functions. A *nondedicated file server,* on the other hand, is a workstation that moonlights as a file server—its memory is divided between workstation functions and file server functions.

Why would you want a dedicated file server? A dedicated file server is faster, safer, and more efficient than one also being used as a workstation.

- It's faster because all the memory and all the processes that this computer does are file-server related.
- It's safer because no one's using the machine as a workstation and possibly crashing it (everyone crashes *sometimes*).
- It's more efficient because it does not have to divide its time between being a file server and being a workstation.

In short, dedicating your file server greatly improves your network's performance. Of course, the downside of a dedicated file server is that it can be expensive, because you must buy a computer just to hold and maintain the integrity and security of your information. Because your file server will have a lot of demands on it, you're going to want something fast with a big hard disk, and that type of machine isn't cheap.

The expense of a dedicated file server gives nondedicated file servers their place in life. A lower price tag is just about the only advantage you get from using your file server as a workstation. Nondedicated file servers tend to be slower than dedicated ones because any time the server needs CPU time to perform workstation tasks, the other workstations have to wait to access the server. This wait time can slow down your entire network.

Also, if your file server crashes—something far more likely to happen on a server that someone's using for a workstation than one used only for administration purposes—you can lose data all over your network. Having worked on networks with both dedicated and nondedicated file servers, I can honestly say that dedicated is a better bet if you can afford the extra machine. Nondedicated file servers may be a viable option for very small networks, but if you have 50 or 100 nodes on your network, the risk of data loss is more expensive than the extra machine. In the long run, the cost of buying an extra computer to be a dedicated file server will turn out to be less than that of losing your network's data.

If you *must* use a server as a workstation, it's best to make it a server that won't cause disaster if it crashes. Many nondedicated servers today are printer servers, fax servers, or e-mail servers. If one of those crashes, it's a pain in the neck but probably won't cause the annual report to go down in flames.

Peer-to-Peer Networks

Peer-to-peer networks represent an entirely different concept in networking. Rather than giving every computer on the network a central storage ground, peer-to-peer networking connects a group of totally independent computers, as depicted in Figure 16.12. Each computer generally keeps its applications on its own hard disk so that if something happens to the network, it simply breaks down into a group of individual yet functional computers. If one workstation goes down, life can go on for the rest of the network if all users keep their needed files at their own workstation. In other words, a peer-to-peer network enables every workstation to lead a double life: to be a workstation *and* a file server.

FIGURE 16.12
An example of a peer-to-peer network

NOTE In the next chapter, I'll get into the details of using Windows 2000 Professional to connect a peer-to-peer network.

Peer-to-peer networks give their users many of the same capabilities that client-server networks do. Each user decides what capabilities and peripheral devices they will share with the rest of the network and then shares them. You can share things selectively, saying, perhaps, "Accounting gets to use the C drive, and Personnel gets to use the printer," and you can attach passwords to your resources so that unauthorized people can't access them. On the subject of sharing resources, remember that because important information on a peer-to-peer LAN is distributed throughout the network, you'll have to leave networked machines on and logged on to the network as long as anyone is working who needs the information on those machines.

Judging Peer-to-Peer Packages

When shopping for a peer-to-peer network operating system, you should keep three things in mind:

- How good are its communications abilities?

  Most peer-to-peer packages include their own e-mail and chat capabilities, allowing both e-mail and real-time communications. A good package provides users with a list of other users available for chats and has both single-mode and multimode chat utilities.

- How capable is its resource sharing?

  Although peer-to-peer networks often expect each workstation to keep its own applications on file, you may prefer to locate some applications centrally and let people pick them up from another machine. You'll also be sharing devices such as drives, CD-ROMs, and printers. The best packages notify users when a workstation with shared resources leaves the network.

- How suitable is it for small-office use (since that's likely what you'll be using it for)?

  Because peer-to-peer networks rarely have network managers, you'll want a network that is as easy to control as possible. A good peer-to-peer should be easy to install and set up and have good print and file management tools to control shared resources. Although peer-to-peer networks are not famous for their security, you'll also want some way of controlling access to shared resources.

Understanding Peer-to-Peer Operations

We have explored how a client-server network operates, but how does a peer-to-peer network work? On a stand-alone machine, when you ask your operating system to access the drive, it can do it directly. The application talks directly to the operating system, which sends the information to the BIOS, which sends the information to the computer's disk. The operating system needs no go-between to help it access information and peripherals on its own computer.

If you're working on a network, however, the situation is a little different. The operating system needs help accessing information on other computers on the network. Its helper is called the *redirector* (or the *shell,* if you're a Novell user). I'll discuss the redirector in more detail in Chapter 17.

Weighing the Advantages of Using a Peer-to-Peer Network

At first glance, client-server networks seem to have all the advantages. When you look again, however, you discover that isn't necessarily the case. For small networks, peer-to-peer has a number of advantages:

- It doesn't require a dedicated workstation (although using one is still a good idea for the reasons I discussed earlier).
- It's an easy way to connect and share information on the workstations that you already have in your office.
- It's cheaper than duplicating your purchases of printers, CD-ROMs, and so on, for every person in the office, and probably more efficient for printer sharing than products such as print buffers and physical print spoolers.
- It costs less than a client-server LAN and doesn't require a degree in engineering to set up and administer.

In short, peer-to-peer networking does not offer the flexibility or the complete security of a file server workstation relationship, but for a small installation, it will probably more than fit the bill.

Summary

You should now have enough information under your belt to describe your needs to any network cabler you might run into. What more is there to know? Well, for starters, in the next chapter I'll discuss how to set up a Windows 2000 Professional peer-to-peer network, and in Chapter 20, I'll discuss one more specific type of network you may want to connect to: a Novell NetWare network.

CHAPTER 17

Connecting to Windows 2000 Peer-to-Peer Networks and NT4 Domains

FEATURING:

One of the most powerful features of Windows 2000 Professional is its capability to attach to and become part of a networking environment. In this chapter, we'll look at many of the decisions you will need to make in order to get the networking features to run reliably in that environment.

The whole idea of a network is to share things: space on a large disk drive, a particular file on that disk drive, a printer, and so on. As an example, let's consider a small office that needs to do some sharing.

In our office, Jennifer has more storage capacity on her machine than Joe does on his, but the office laser printer is attached to Joe's PC. Jennifer and Joe work on the office accounting system, so they need to share the accounting files—or they'll have to pass floppies back and forth. Because Jennifer has more disk space, they put the accounting files on her machine. So, the network problems that we need to solve are as follows:

1. Sharing Joe's printer with Jennifer
2. Sharing Jennifer's disk with Joe

Let's solve their problem with a basic Microsoft network. With this type of network, Jennifer puts her hard disk on the network, and Joe puts his printer on the network. Assuming that both computers are running Windows 2000 Professional, here's how to get Joe onto Jennifer's disk and Jennifer onto Joe's printer:

1. Jennifer tells the Windows 2000 Professional networking software, "Offer the Acctng subfolder on my C drive to anyone who wants it. Call it Acctng." In Microsoft enterprise networking terminology, Acctng becomes the *share name* of that drive on Jennifer's machine (GTW09), and it's the name that others will use to access the drive over the network. In a few pages, I'll show you exactly how to share such a resource on the network so others can access it, but for now, remember this: a machine (named GTW09) is sharing a resource called Acctng with anyone on that network who's able to use it.

NOTE Here's an important concept in Microsoft networking: You must name each machine in the network, whether it is a server or a workstation. You also must name each user (in our example, Joe and Jennifer). Because the PCs need names, we may as well name the PCs with their inventory numbers, which in this example are DELL05 and GTW09.

TIP Naming machines after their users is a bad idea, because PCs may be reassigned to other users.

2. Joe then tells the networking software on his PC, "Attach me to the Acctng resource on Jennifer's machine."
3. Joe, meanwhile, runs his network software and tells it to share the printer on his LPT1 port, giving it a name—again, a share name—of JOLASER. Joe's machine is called DELL05, so the UNC name of that printer will be `\\DELL05\JOLASER`.

NOTE UNC stands for Universal Naming Convention. In the printer's UNC name, `\\DELL05` is the *machine* name, and `\JOLASER` is the *share* name.

4. Jennifer then tells her networking software to attach JOLASER on Joe's machine to her LPT1 port.

From now on, whenever Jennifer tells an application program to print to a laser printer on LPT1, the network software will intercept the printed output and will direct it over the network to Joe's machine. The networking software on Joe's machine will then print the information on Joe's printer.

I know I left out some of the "how do we do this?" information; it's coming right up.

Connecting Your Network

In the first part of this chapter, I'm going to show you how to set up a simple peer-to-peer network that solves the problems of Joe and Jennifer that I just described. Using the information in the previous chapter, you first need to design your network, and then you probably need to go shopping—either on the Internet or at one of many computer centers that are springing up all over the place.

You need a network interface card (NIC) for each computer on the network, a hub, and some cables. You can even buy a starter kit that contains everything you need—probably for less than $100. With that and a couple of screwdrivers, you're ready to get started. Follow these steps:

1. Turn off and unplug each computer that will be part of your network.
2. At each computer, open the case, and insert a NIC in an empty slot, screwing the card in securely so that it won't come loose.
3. Replace the case.
4. Insert one end of the cable into the RJ45 socket on the card, and snap the other end of the cable into the hub, starting with port 1.
5. Plug the hub into the power supply.
6. Turn on the hub and all connected computers. You'll see some lights start blinking on the hub.

Now you're ready to configure your network.

Configuring Your Network

Because Windows 2000 Professional is Plug and Play, when you restart your computer after inserting the NICs and connecting the cables and hub, the system loads the device drivers you need for the NICs. If, for some reason, Windows 2000 Professional does not detect your NICs, you can run the Add/Remove Hard Wizard. In Control Panel, click Add/Remove Hardware, and follow the on-screen instructions.

NOTE If Windows 2000 Professional is still unable to detect your NIC, you may need to contact its manufacturer for a Windows 2000 Professional driver. In some cases, you may also be able to use an NT driver. If you have an older NIC that is not listed on the Hardware Compatibility list, my advice is to bid it a fond farewell. If you're a super techie, you may be able to use an older NIC if you jump through some complicated hoops that involve IRQs, the I/O port, memory addresses, and EPROM or the BOOT ROM. This can take a while, and you won't necessarily be successful. Give it up and shell out what could easily be fewer bucks than you'd spend to buy one of the latest computer games.

Specifying Protocols

Windows 2000 Professional doesn't know which networking protocols you want to use, so your first order of business is to take care of that. Follow these steps:

1. Log on to Windows 2000 Professional as an administrator.
2. Right-click My Network Places, and choose Properties from the shortcut menu to open the Network And Dial-Up Connections window.
3. Right-click Local Area Connection, and choose Properties from the shortcut menu to open the Local Area Connection Properties dialog box:

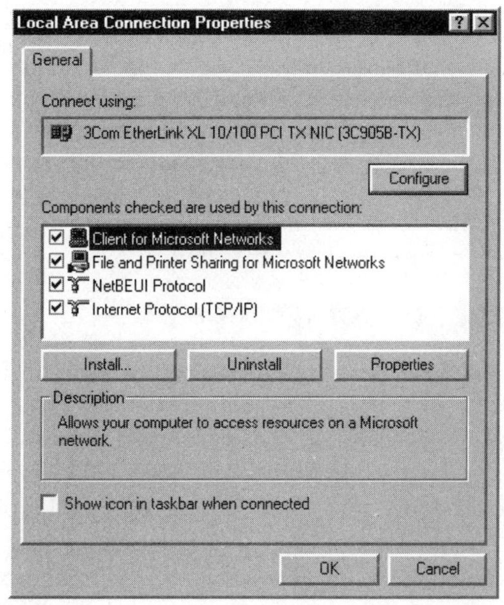

4. In the Components Checked Are Used By This Connection list in the middle of this box, you need to see at least the following protocols (you may see more, and that's OK):
   - Client for Microsoft Networks
   - File and Printer Sharing for Microsoft Networks
   - NetBEUI Protocol
5. If any of these components are not installed, click Install to open the Select Network Component dialog box.
6. Select Client to install Client for Microsoft Networks, select Service to install File and Printer Sharing for Microsoft Networks, or select Protocol to install NetBEUI Protocol, and then click Add.
7. Click OK, and then click OK again when you are asked to restart Windows 2000 Professional.

After you reboot your computer, you can follow these steps to see if everything is in working order:

1. In Control Panel, click Administrative Tools, and then click Computer Management to open the Computer Management window.
2. In the Tree pane, expand System Tools, and then click Device Manager to display the device installed on your computer in the right pane.
3. Expand Network Adapters. If you don't see a yellow exclamation point or a red arrow next to the icon for your adapter, all is working as it should.

NOTE Often, as you configure your system to support multiple protocols, you are concerned with the order in which your computer will search the protocol stacks to perform a specific network function. If the search order for the protocols is not efficient, you can spend a lot of time waiting for your computer to time out because it is searching the wrong protocol stack. Do not be concerned about the order of the protocols as they appear at this time. If you need to, you can change the search order of the protocols by using the Advanced menu in the Network And Dial-Up Connections window.

Connecting to Workgroups

In a Windows 2000 Professional peer-to-peer network, you join a workgroup, which is simply the group of users who are on the network. If you are on a client-server network, for example, workstations that are running Windows 2000 Professional and connect to a server running NT 4 Server or Windows 2000 Server, you can connect to a domain. In a special section at the end of this chapter, I'll explain how to connect to a domain.

By joining a workgroup, you have the ability to share your resources across the network with other Microsoft clients. Through this process you can provide limited security to these shared resources. To join a workgroup, follow these steps:

1. On the Desktop, right-click My Computer, and choose Properties from the shortcut menu to open the System Properties dialog box.
2. Click the Network Identification tab:

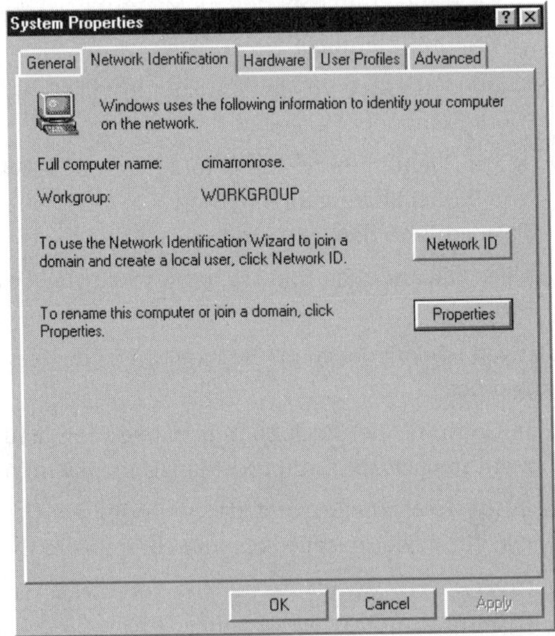

3. Click the Properties button to open the Identification Changes dialog box:

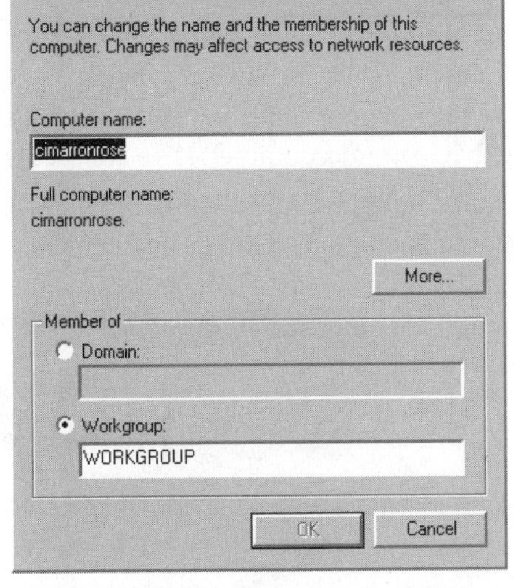

4. In the Computer Name box, you can name or change the name of your computer.
5. Click the Workgroup option button, and enter a name for the workgroup you will join. If you are the first one to log on to a workgroup with this workgroup name, you will create a workgroup. Otherwise, you will join one that already exists.

NOTE Capitalization of the workgroup name does not matter; *instructors* is identical to *Instructors*, which is identical to *INSTRUCTORS*. Capitalization may not count, but spelling does. Also, do not give a machine the same name as any other machine in your environment.

6. When you are done, click OK.

Creating Shares

Before users on your network can get to resources on your computer, you must share those resources. To do this, you must be logged on as an administrator. You can create shares using Explorer or Computer Management. Using Explorer is simple and direct, so in this section that's what I'll use.

NOTE To open Computer Management, in Control Panel click Administrative Tools and then click Computer Management.

A share can be a folder, a drive, a program, a file—any resource on your computer that you want to share over the network. For this example, I'm going to share the WinZip utility that's on my computer. Here are the steps:

1. In Explorer, right-click the WinZip folder, and choose Sharing from the shortcut menu to open the WinZip Properties dialog box at the Sharing tab:

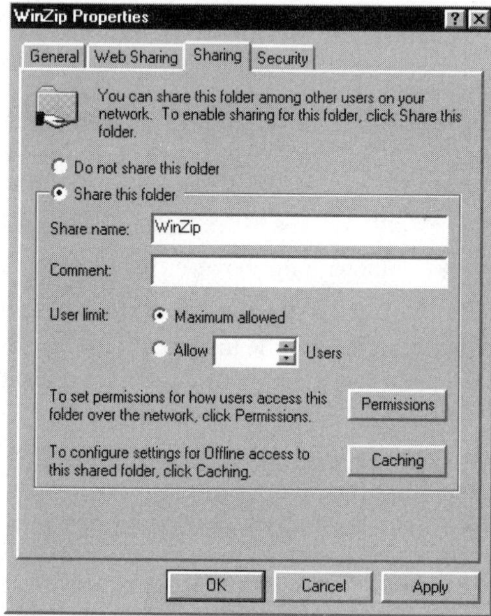

2. Click the Share This Folder option button.
3. In the Share Name box, you can accept the name that Windows 2000 Professional suggests or enter another name.
4. In the Comment box, you can briefly describe the share. This information will be visible to users when they browse for available shares.
5. In the User Limit section, click Maximum Allowed, or click Allow and then specify the number of users who can access this share simultaneously. The maximum that Windows 2000 Professional allows is 10 users.
6. The next step is securing your share, which I'll discuss in the next chapter. I'll also discuss what lies behind the Caching button later in this chapter. For now, click OK, and your resource is ready to be used by others on your network.

The options in the User Limit section can assist you with software licensing. For example, if you know that you have only five licenses for a program that you are sharing, and the licensing states that it is a five-user concurrent license, you can set the number of connections to this share to Allow 5 Users. Thus you can enforce the licensing of any program.

What If More Than the Maximum Number of Users Attempts to Connect to the Share?

If a client workstation tries to attach to a share that is already being used by the maximum number of allowable users, it will receive a warning message. The exact error message varies from operating system to operating system, but a DOS workstation would receive the following message:

```
Error 71: This request is not accepted by the network. The server may
have run out of resources necessary to process your request. Try the
request again. If the error persists, contact your network
administrator. For more information, type NET HELP 71 at the command
prompt.
```

Windows 95/98 workstations are more terse, saying:

```
An extended error has occurred.
```

Windows for Workgroups workstations also believe in keeping it brief, with the following rather uninformative warning:

```
This request is not accepted by the network.
```

NT or Windows 2000 Professional clients are a bit more chatty and descriptive:

```
No more connections can be made to this remote computer at this time
because there are already as many connections as the computer allows.
```

Now, before you start relying on this feature, let me tell you about a problem in NT Workstation 3.1 and 3.5 and Windows for Workgroups machines. The user-maximum feature seems not to work. You can create a share, give it a maximum number of users of 1, and then fire up 20 Windows for Workgroups machines—and they can all get onto the share. My experience with Windows 2000 Professional leads me to believe that Windows 2000 Professional *does* enforce the user maximum, but test it before you build a security system around this feature.

After you create shares, you may want to specify who can do what with them. For example, you may want to let some users only read a file, not change it or delete it. I'll discuss all the permission options in detail in the next chapter.

Attaching to Network Resources

After your network software is installed, one of the easiest ways to test your network connections is to attach to network resources. You can do so in the following ways:

- By browsing My Network Places
- By mapping a network drive
- By using UNCs to connect directly

Browsing My Network Places

Double-click My Network Places on the Desktop to open a window that displays the options on your network. Double-clicking Computers Near Me displays the computers that are sharing resources in your workgroup. Double-click a computer to view and connect to its shared resources.

Mapping a Network Drive

Mapping a network drive involves assigning a drive letter to a network location. For example, if you frequently connect to another user's shared folder, you might assign it an unused drive letter on your computer. It then appears in My Computer, and all you need to do to access it is to click it.

One of the benefits to networking is being able to back up your files and folders on another computer. You'll find that some applications won't recognize other network drives unless they are mapped—so that's another reason you need to know how to map network drives.

To map a drive, follow these steps:

1. On the Desktop, right-click My Network Places, and choose Map Network Drive to open the Map Network Drive dialog box:

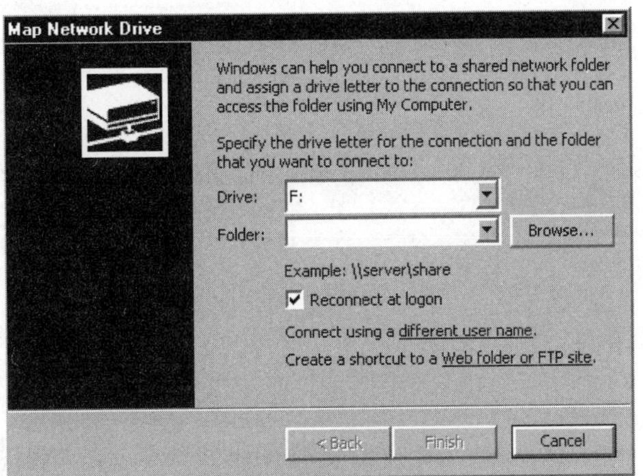

2. From the Drive drop-down list, select an unused drive letter.
3. From the Folder drop-down list, select the folder you want to map to, or click Browse to find the folder on your network.
4. If you want to use this mapping every time you log on, click the Reconnect At Logon check box.

NOTE Clicking the Connect Using A Different User Name link opens the Connect As dialog box, and I'll discuss that option in the last section in this chapter.

5. Click Finish. The drive now appears in My Computer along with your local drives.

To disconnect a mapped drive, follow these steps:

1. In Explorer, choose Tools ➢ Disconnect Network Drive to open the Disconnect Network Drive dialog box.
2. Select the drive, and click OK.

Making a Direct Connection via a UNC

At the beginning of this chapter, I mentioned UNC names. Using UNC names is yet another way to attach to network resources. You do this by executing `net use` statements at the command prompt. But before you can attach to resources with the `net use` statements, you need to know which resources are available on the network. I already showed you how to use My Computer to attach to network resources, but you can also do so at the command prompt using the `net view` command.

NOTE Up to now in this chapter, I've been primarily talking about how to set up and configure a Windows 2000 Professional peer-to-peer network, although some of the information, such as mapping network drives, applies equally to a client-server network and domains, which I'll discuss in the last part of this chapter. This section, however, contains information that sometimes applies to workgroups and sometimes applies to domains. You know which kind of network you have, so you'll know which instructions apply to your situation.

Here's how to use the `net view` command:

1. To display a list of the machines on your network, type **`net view`** at the command prompt. You'll see something similar to the following:

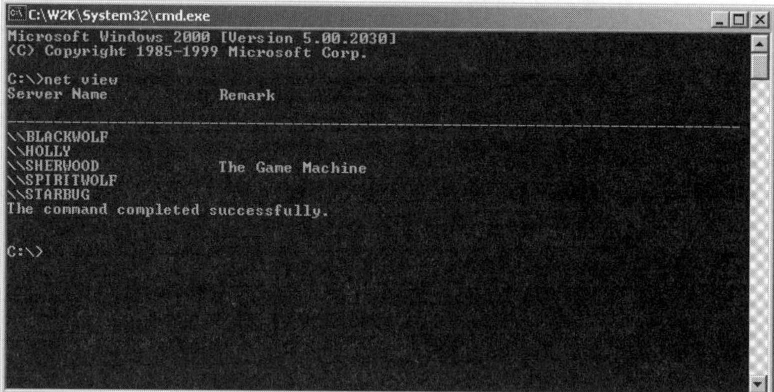

2. To display a list of the resources on a particular machine, append the name of the machine. For example, if the machine name was spiritwolf, you'd enter **`net view \\spiritwolf`**, and you'd see something similar to the following:

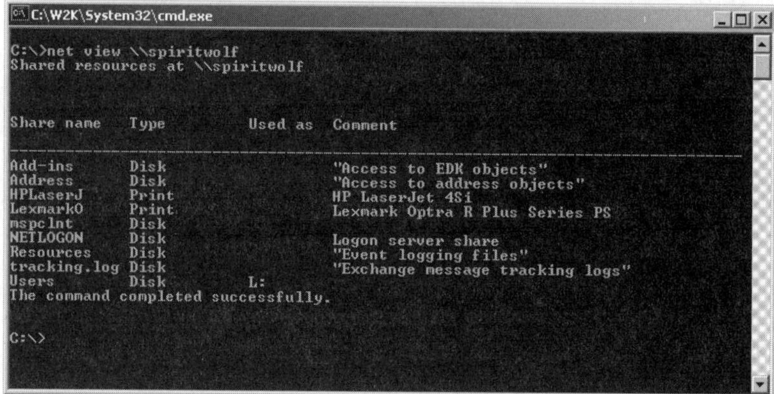

3. To view the resources of a machine in another domain, for example, the server spiritwolf in the domain hq, you'd enter the following:

   `net view \\spiritwolf /domain:hq`

   You'd then see something similar to the following:

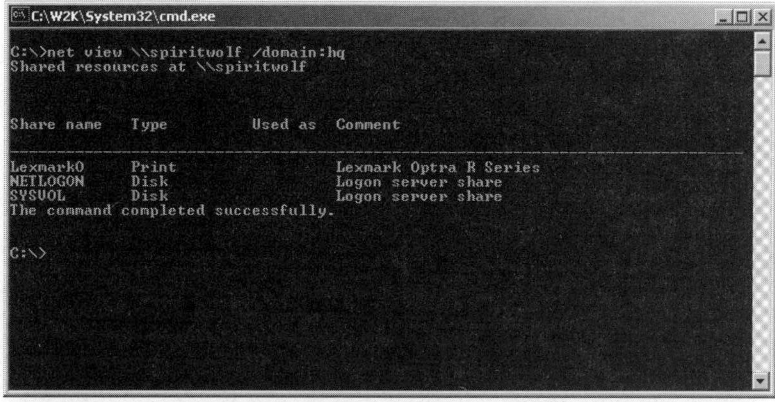

4. To display a list of all the domains on the network, simply enter **`net view /domain`**. You'll see something similar to the following:

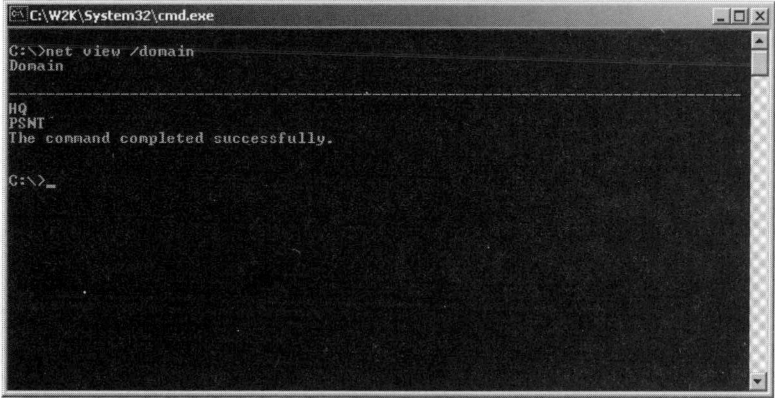

Using Net Use: Connecting to Other Drives and Printers

After you've browsed the network with the `net view` command, you can connect to all the available goodies (or disconnect from those you don't want) with the `net use` command. Use this command to connect to network resources as drives D through Z and printer ports LPT1 through LPT9.

NOTE The Help file on this command claims that you can use only printer ports LPT1 through LPT3. Technically, this statement isn't true, but the Help file probably puts it this way because some MS-DOS applications are not able to access printer ports with numbers higher than 3.

To display information about the workstation's current connections, type **`net use`** without options, and you'll see something like this:

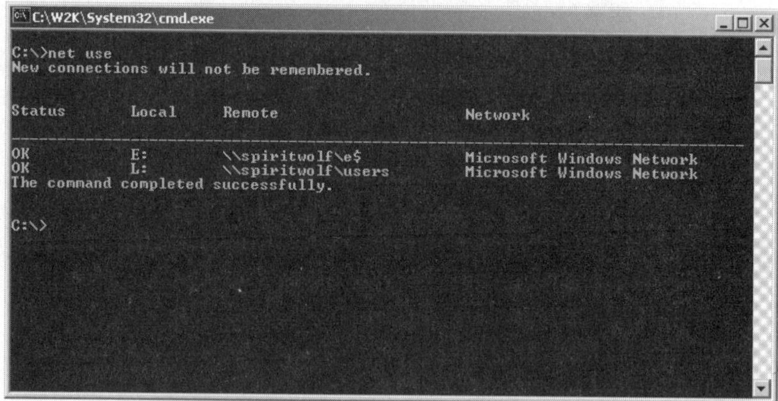

Connecting to a Resource in the Local Domain

To connect to a shared resource, such as a printer shared as lexmarko on server spiritwolf, type **`net use lptl: \\spiritwolf\lexmarko`**. You'll see something similar to the following:

Using Long Filenames in UNCs

If you wanted to connect to a folder called Wpfiles on a server and to make that your E drive, you'd substitute **`E:`** for **`lptl`**: and **`Wpfiles`** for **`lexmarko`** in the preceding example.

You get to specify the port name or drive letter that you want to connect a resource to, but, again, you're restricted to drive letters D through Z and ports LPT1 through LPT9. Also, if the computer that you're getting the resource from has a blank character in its name (that is, has two words in it), you must put the name in quotation marks, like this:

```
"\\eisa server"
```

If a password (let's say it's "artuser") is attached to the resource that you're trying to connect to, you need to include that in your connection command, like this:

```
net use lpt1: \\ted\hp4m artuser
```

Or, if you want the computer to prompt you for the password so that it isn't displayed on the screen, append an asterisk:

```
net use lpt1: \\ted\hp4m *
```

Creating a Drive Mapping for Your Home Folder

To connect to your home folder (the folder on the server that has been assigned to you, assuming that there is one), type:

```
net use /home
```

with the (optional) password on the end as explained above.

If you want to make the connection for another user, rather than for yourself, add the user's name (Frank) to the end of the line, like this:

```
net use lpt1: \\ted\hp4m user:frank
```

Passwords go before the user's name in the statement. If the user for whom you are making the connection is in another domain, the user part of the statement looks like this:

```
user:domainname/frank
```

where *domainname* is the name of that user's home domain.

Connecting to a Resource in Another Domain

If you want to connect to a resource in a domain that is not your usual one, you must first log on to that domain. If your domain and the other domain don't have a trust relationship with each other, you need to create a user account for yourself on the second domain. After you've logged on to the proper domain, the process is the same as described above.

Using Other Switches

No matter what kind of connection you make, you can make it persistent (that is, remake it every time you connect to the network), by adding the switch `/persistent:yes` to the end of the command. If you don't want it to be persistent, use `/persistent:no` instead.

If you don't specify one or the other, the default is whatever you chose last. If you want to make all future connections persistent, type:

```
net use /persistent:yes
```

(Or type `:no` if you want all future connections to be temporary.) Typing `/persistent` by itself at the end of the line won't do anything.

To disconnect from a resource, type:

```
net use devicename /delete
```

where *devicename* is the connection (such as D or LPT1). You don't have to provide a password or say anything about persistency to disconnect from a resource.

Using Profiles

Windows 2000 Professional uses two types of profiles: user and hardware. Each serves a specific purpose, and in this section we'll look at how to create them and manage them.

Creating Hardware Profiles

If you use a laptop for business, you likely have encountered the following problem. When you bring your laptop into the office, you would like your computer to recognize the NIC and maybe an external monitor and keyboard. But when you take your laptop on the road, you want it to know that you do not currently have any of the "office" devices attached. Most laptops get their information by timing out on each device, which adds five minutes to the boot process and wastes time, not to mention wasting valuable battery life.

A feature of Windows 2000 Professional that was designed to alleviate this problem is a hardware profile. You can create a profile of the hardware that is attached to your machine when you are in the office and specify a different hardware profile for when you are on the road. And the fun doesn't stop there. You can create profiles for all the places in which you use your computer.

To create a hardware profile, follow these steps:

1. On the Desktop, right-click My Computer, and choose System from the shortcut menu to open the System Properties dialog box.
2. Select the Hardware tab, and click Hardware Profiles to open the Hardware Profiles dialog box:

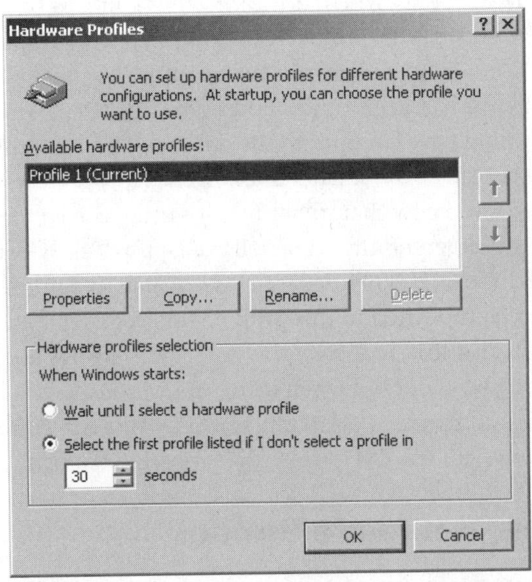

3. To create a new hardware profile, choose a configuration from the Available Hardware Profiles list, and then click Copy to open the Copy Profile dialog box.
4. Give the hardware profile a new name, and click OK. (I'll show you how to configure a profile a bit later in this section.)
5. To play with the docking properties of this profile, click Properties to open the Properties dialog box for the profile you are creating:

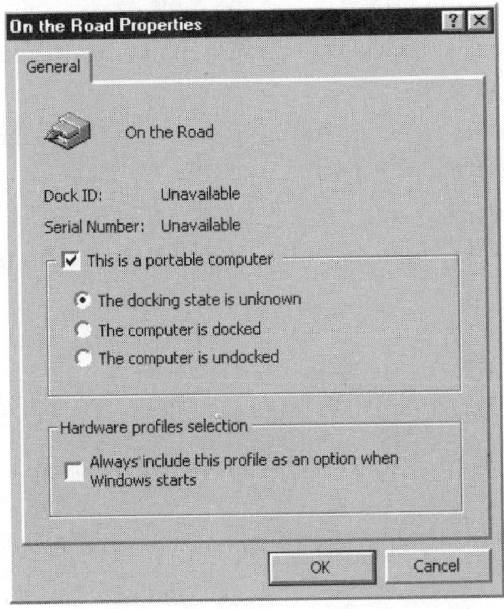

You can specify whether the system is going to be attached to a docking station when it is using this profile. A docking station is a box that sits on your desk (usually at the office) that you plug your laptop into. You use it because you can attach peripherals to it such as a larger monitor and keyboard. Then, when you come into the office, you simply plug your laptop into the dock, and you can use the larger monitor and keyboard instead of the smaller ones on the laptop. However, when you do this, your laptop needs to know that sometimes it's using the laptop screen, whereas other times it's using the larger monitor. You tell the laptop this by configuring the docking properties.

If Windows 2000 Professional is not able to automatically detect the docking status of your laptop when in this profile, The Docking State Is Unknown option is selected. You can also strictly specify the state if it is always docked when using this profile or if it is *not* always docked when using this profile.

If this computer is a desktop, uncheck This Is A Portable Computer. When you've set your options, click OK to close the Properties dialog box, and then click OK twice more.

Managing Hardware Profiles

Now that you have created your hardware profile, you can begin to enable the services and devices that will be available through it. When you reboot your computer, choose a hardware profile. To enable or disable devices or services in this profile, follow these steps:

1. In Control Panel, click Administrative Tools, and then click Computer Management to open the Computer Management window.
2. Expand System Tools, and then select Device Manager to display the list of devices in the pane on the right.
3. Double-click the device that you want to enable or disable to open its Properties dialog box.
4. In the General tab, use the Device Usage drop-down list to enable or disable a device in this profile, and then click OK.
5. To enable or disable services, expand Services And Applications, and then select Services to display the list of the services in the pane on the right:

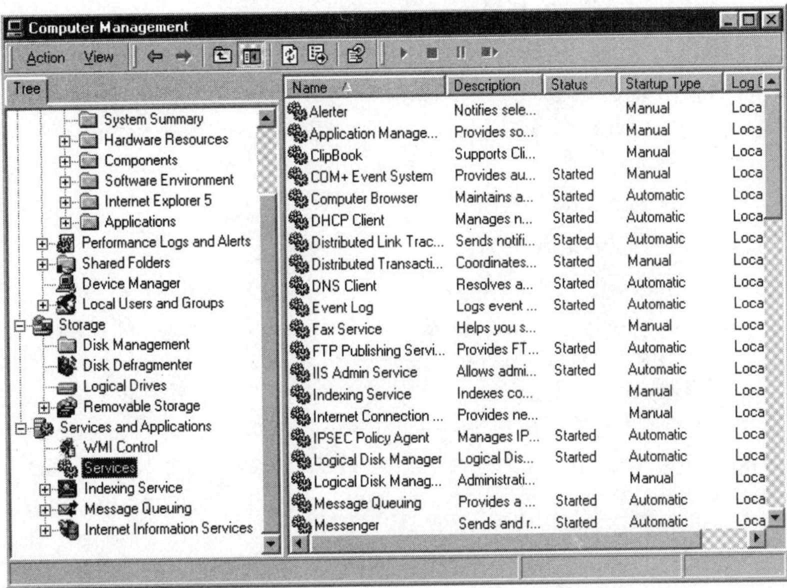

6. Double-click the service that you want to manage to open its Properties dialog box, and then click the Log On tab:

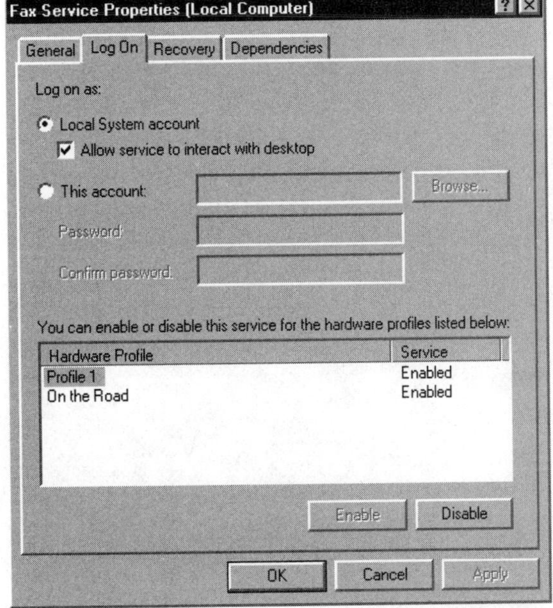

7. Enable or disable the service for this hardware profile, and then click OK.

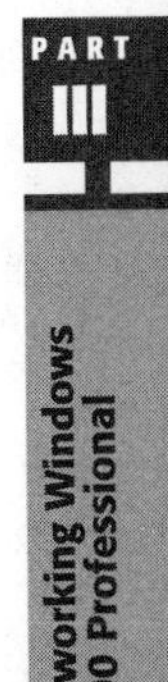

Surviving User Profiles

In Windows 2000 Professional, a *user profile* is a collection of environment settings that customize a user's interface. It can include display settings, network settings, printer settings, and so on. User profiles are of three types:

- Local
- Roaming
- Mandatory

The first time you log on to a computer, whether it's yours or that of someone else on your network, Windows 2000 Professional creates a *local user profile* for you that is specific to that machine; this is also called a *default user profile*. When you log off, any changes you've made to the environment during the sessions are saved in your local user profile. A *roaming user profile* can only be created by your system administrator, and it is stored on the server. A roaming user profile contains settings that are specific to you and is loaded whenever you log on to any computer on the network. A *mandatory user profile* specifies settings for an individual or a group of users and can only be created or modified by your system administrator.

To customize a default user profile so that each new user of the machine gets the same settings, follow these steps:

1. Log on to the computer as a new user.
2. Establish the settings, such as Start menu options, network connections, and so on, and then log off the computer.
3. Log back on to the computer as Administrator.
4. Right-click My Computer, and choose Properties from the shortcut menu to open the System Properties dialog box.
5. Click the User Profiles tab, highlight the profile that you want each new user to use, and then click Copy To to open the Copy To dialog box:

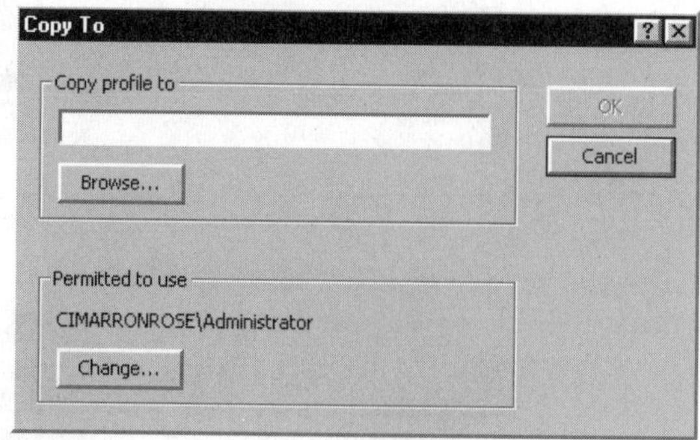

6. In the Copy Profile To box, enter the following path:

   `%SYSTEMROOT%\Documents and Settings\Default User`

7. Click OK, and then click OK again.

If you should happen to delete a profile folder in the Documents And Settings folder, Windows 2000 Professional will react as if the user has never logged on to the system before. When the user logs on again, Windows will create a new profile folder for the user. This feature can be useful if the user has placed icons and information all over the Desktop and is now complaining that it keeps coming up as a mess. You can simply delete the profile folder, and a new one will be created the next time that that user logs on. It will be the default environment as created in the Default User folder.

Understanding Windows 2000 Professional Profiles versus 95/98 Profiles

If you've used Windows 95/98, you know that it also has user profiles. Windows 95/98 stores a lot of its user environment information in a file called `user.dat` that is in the Windows folder. If you are in an NT Server or NetWare environment, you can easily network your user profiles so that your wallpaper, icons, start menu, and so on can follow you around the network, regardless of which Windows 95/98 machine you sit at.

Windows 2000 Professional profiles are stored in `ntuser.dat`. However, they work only if you are sitting at a Windows 2000 Professional machine, and Windows 95/98 profiles work only if you are sitting at a Windows 95/98 machine.

Special Topic: Connecting a Windows 2000 Professional Workstation to an NT4 Domain

When a new operating system appears on the horizon, those of us who are in the business of technical writing usually have to start using it long before it's a finished product and certainly long before the installed base of users is of any significance. Even after the product hits the streets, it's a matter of some time before an entire enterprise has upgraded or switched over. Normally the upgrade or switch occurs in stages, and I believe that currently a lot of you are in a mix-and-match stage: you are using Windows 2000 Professional as a workstation but are still connecting to an NT4 Server. The purpose of this section then is to talk about how you do that.

Before you can connect to an NT4 domain, you will need to get the following information from your system administrator:

- Your user name
- Your password
- The name of the domain that you will join
- Your computer name
- The name of your computer's domain

Once you are armed with this information, you can join a domain using the Identification Changes dialog box or the Network Identification Wizard. Since using the Wizard is more descriptive, I'll walk through the process using it. If you want to use the Identification Changes dialog box, follow these steps to open it:

1. Right-click My Computer, and choose Properties from the shortcut menu to open the System Properties dialog box.
2. Click the Network Identification tab, and then click Properties to open the Identification Changes dialog box.

Now, let's step briskly through the Wizard:

1. In the System Properties dialog box, click the Network Identification tab, and then click Network ID to start the Network Identification Wizard.
2. At the Welcome screen, click Next to open the Connecting To The Network screen.
3. Click the option that tells Windows 2000 Professional this is a business network, and then click Next to open the next Connecting To The Network screen.
4. Click the option that tells Windows 2000 Professional that your network has a domain, and then click Next.
5. Be sure that you have all the information listed on the Network Information screen, and then click Next.
6. On the User Account And Domain Information screen, enter your user name, your password, and your domain name.
7. On the Computer Domain screen, enter the name of your computer and your domain, and click Next.
8. You'll see the Domain User Name And Password dialog box. Enter a user name, password, and domain that has sufficient permissions to add this Windows 2000 Professional machine to the domain (usually Administrator), and then click OK. At this point, Windows 2000 Professional creates a machine name within the domain. Depending on your network, this could take a few minutes. When Windows 2000 Professional has created the machine name, it will return you to the User Account dialog box. Click Next.
9. On the Access Level Wizard, select the type of access that you want for the local computer. You can choose from three radio buttons: Standard Users, Restricted User, and Other. Standard users can modify the computer and install applications but have no rights to read files that do not belong to them. Restricted users can save documents but have no rights to modify the computer or add applications. The Other option allows you to insert the user into a different group, such as Administrators, which would grant complete rights to the entire Windows 2000 Professional computer. Select a radio button, and then click Next.

10. The final dialog box, Completing The Network Identification Wizard, will appear. Click Next and then select Yes to reboot.

After the computer reboots, follow these steps to log on to the domain:

1. At the Windows logon prompt, press Ctrl+Alt+Del as you normally would to log on to Windows 2000 Professional.
2. Enter a user name to log on to the domain (this is not always the same name as the local user name), a password, and select the appropriate domain. You can either type in the domain name or select it from the drop-down list that Windows 2000 Professional automatically builds for you.
3. Click the OK button to complete the domain authentication process.

Receiving the Error Message "No Domain Server Was Available…"

When logging on to the server, you may get an error message stating that no domain server is available to authorize you to log on to a domain. Often this error message will prevent you from seeing some resources in My Network Places and prevent you from accessing the network entirely.

This message appears when the system is unable to contact a domain controller for the domain that you are logging on to. The obvious problem could be that the server is down. Another common cause of this error is that a bridge, router, or gateway is malfunctioning in your environment; so check the hub and the bridges to make sure that they are operating normally.

Easily the most common occurrence of this problem is when TCP/IP is the primary transport protocol in your environment. If the workstation is on one physical segment of the network and the domain controller is on another segment of the network, often the client machine is unable to see the server via NetBIOS. To test this situation, see if you can ping the server's address. If you can ping the server but are unable to contact the server for domain logon authentication, you have determined the cause of your dilemma.

The most common solution is to install a Windows Internet Naming System Server (WINS Server) in your environment. It will handle the NetBIOS to IP address name resolution (in much the same way that a DNS server handles IP host name to IP address conversions). For more information on how to install the WINS Service on an NT Server, see my book *Mastering Windows NT Server 4, Seventh Edition* (Sybex Inc., 2000).

Configuration Testing

All the changes that you have made in the network configuration will require you to reboot your system. When the system restarts, you will know if Windows 2000 Professional can see the network during the logon procedure. You may see error messages, for example, if your TCP/IP address went awry or if the NT domain controller refuses to validate you into the domain. Even if no errors are immediately apparent, take a look in Event Viewer for potential conflicts. Follow these steps:

1. In Control Panel, click Administrative Tools, and then click Computer Management to open the Computer Management window.
2. In the Tree pane, expand System Tools, and then expand Event Viewer.
3. Click System to display events in the pane on the right.
4. Look for red stop signs or yellow exclamation points. If you see one of these symbols, double-click it to open the Event Properties dialog box for that event, which will look similar to the following:

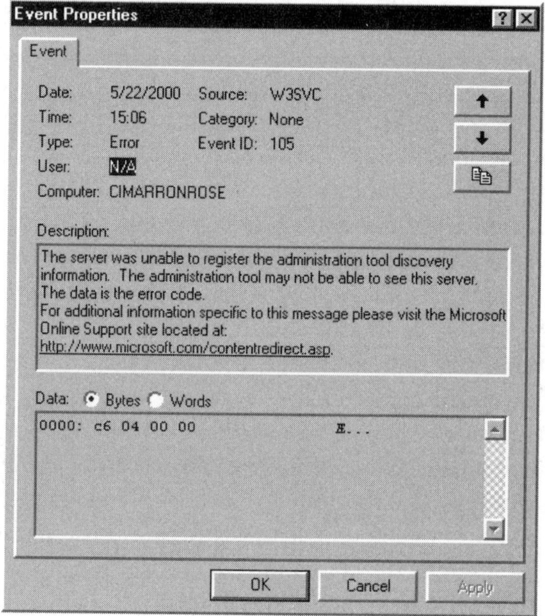

5. If the information in the Event Properties dialog box isn't sufficient to solve the problem, check the configuration of the component. In some cases, you may need to remove and reinstall it.
6. Click the Close button to close the Computer Management window.

TIP When using Event Viewer to troubleshoot network problems, start at the top of the list and work down until you find event ID number 6005 with a source of eventlog. This represents the last time you booted the computer. The most likely source of your problems will be the event immediately above or immediately below the 6005 event. You should focus most of your efforts resolving these before moving on to the others.

The ultimate test of your configuration is being able to attach to all the resources that you need. Taking a look in My Network Places and double-clicking Computers Near Me can give you insight into which parts of the networks you can and cannot communicate with.

To understand what is happening with your TCP/IP configuration, you will want to look at the IPCONFIG utility. Type `ipconfig /all` at the command prompt, and you will get a report that looks similar to the one in Figure 17.1.

FIGURE 17.1
An ipconfig /all report

```
Command Prompt
Microsoft Windows 2000 [Version 5.00.2030]
(C) Copyright 1985-1999 Microsoft Corp.

C:\>ipconfig /all

Windows NT IP Configuration

        Host Name . . . . . . . . . : STARBUG
        Node Type . . . . . . . . . : Hybrid
        IP Routing Enabled. . . . . : No
        WINS Proxy Enabled. . . . . : No

Ethernet adapter Local Area Connection:

        Adapter Domain Name . . . . :
        DNS Servers . . . . . . . . : 209.20.130.35
                                      209.20.130.33
        Description . . . . . . . . : 3Com (3C562D-3C563D) EtherLink III LAN+336
 Modem PC Card
        Physical Address. . . . . . : 00-60-97-85-83-27
        DHCP Enabled. . . . . . . . : Yes
        Autoconfiguration Enabled . : Yes
        IP Address. . . . . . . . . : 10.1.0.21
        Subnet Mask . . . . . . . . : 255.255.0.0
        Default Gateway . . . . . . : 10.1.0.1
        DHCP Server . . . . . . . . : 10.1.0.1
        Primary WINS Server . . . . : 10.1.0.1
        Lease Obtained. . . . . . . : Saturday, July 10, 1999 2:50:07 PM
        Lease Expires . . . . . . . : Tuesday, July 13, 1999 2:50:07 PM
```

`Ipconfig /all` reports all the vital information regarding your TCP/ IP connection, even down to lease duration of your IP address if you are using the Dynamic Host Configuration Protocol (DHCP) on your network. To test your TCP/IP configuration, follow this procedure:

NOTE Some of these tests assume that your LAN is connected to the Internet.

1. Test that you've installed the IP software by pinging the built-in IP loopback address. Type **`ping 127.0.0.1`**. If that fails, you know that you've done something wrong in the initial installation, so check that the software is installed on your system. This test does not put any messages out on the network; it just checks that the software is installed. By the way, the same thing happens if you ping your IP address, except that pinging your address also tests the network card.

   If that fails, your TCP/IP stack probably isn't installed correctly, or perhaps you mistyped the IP number (if it failed on your specific IP address but not on the loopback), or perhaps you gave the *same* IP number to another workstation.

2. Ping your gateway to see that you can get to the gateway, which should be on your subnet. For example, if your gateway were at 199.34.57.2, you would type **`ping 199.34.57.2`**, and all should be well.
3. If you can't get to the gateway, check that the gateway is up and that your network connection is all right. There's nothing more embarrassing than calling in outside network support, only to find that your LAN cable fell out of the back of your computer.
4. Ping something on the other side of your gateway, such as an external DNS server. (Ping me, Mark Minasi, if you like; 199.34.57.1. I ought to be up just about all the time.) If you can't get there, it's likely that your gateway isn't working properly.
5. Next, test the name resolution on your system. Ping yourself *by name*. Instead of typing something such as **`ping 199.34.57.35`**, you'd type **`ping nec.Mmco.Com`** (the machine you're on at the moment). That tests HOSTS and/or DNS.
6. Then, ping someone else on your subnet. Again, try using a DNS name, such as `mizar.Ursamajor.Edu`, rather than an IP address. If that doesn't work, use the IP address. If the IP address works, but the host name doesn't, double-check the HOSTS file or DNS.
7. Finally, ping someone outside your domain, such as `house.gov` (the U.S. House of Representatives) or `www.yahoo.com` or `orion01.Mmco.Com`. If that doesn't work but all the pings inside your network work, you've probably got a problem with your Internet provider.

If you're successful on all these tests, your TCP/IP connection should be set up properly.

Attaching to Network Resources Using Login Scripts

The most common way in which you will attach to network resources is through network rove mappings that the network Administrator created in a login script. Often drive letters such as H and M are pointing to files on a file server on the network. These drive icons appear in My Computer. In Figure 17.2, you can see that an L drive is mapped to a share called users on a server called spiritwolf.

FIGURE 17.2
My Computer contains drive icons.

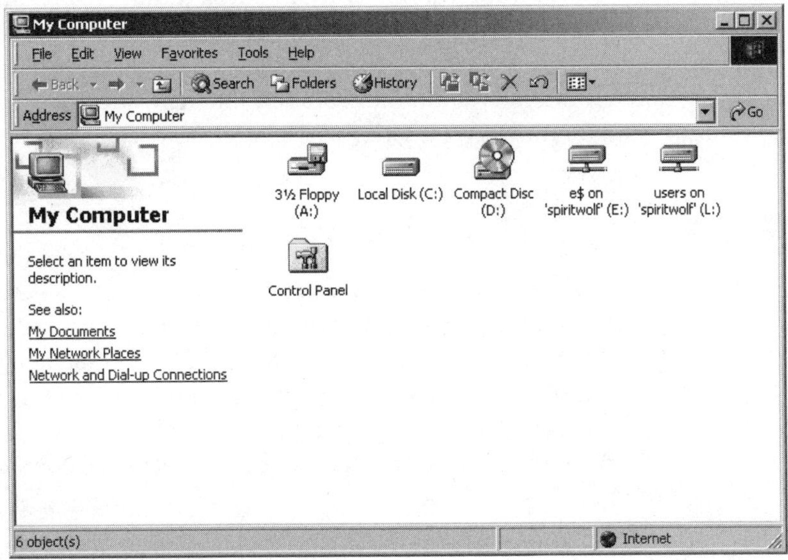

You will be able to distinguish between network drives and local hard drives by the icon associated with the drive. Network drives have the little T connector and cable beneath the icon. From time to time, you may see a drive with a red *X* across it. This symbol indicates that you formerly had a drive mapped to this drive letter, but the system cannot find the network location at this time. This situation happens most frequently if you are accessing the network remotely via a modem.

Using the Connect As Option

You can use the Connect As dialog box to attach to a resource with another user account. (Right-click My Network Places, choose Map Network Drive from the shortcut menu to open the My Network Drive dialog box, and then click the link Connect Using A Different User Name.) By default, when you map a network drive, you are attached to the resource using the same user account that you originally use to log on to the workstation. But what if you are attaching to another server and you do not have an account on that server? This happens a lot to administrators.

If you have an administrator called Sheila Sanders, Sheila will have an account on her primary server that she logs on to. In addition, Sheila may need to attach to other servers that have resources that she wants to use, even though she doesn't have an account on those servers. Another classic example would be that Sheila logs on to a Windows 2000 Server as Sheila but has an account named SSanders on a NetWare server.

To resolve this issue, Sheila could log on to the Windows 2000 Server as Sheila, but when she maps a drive to a Novell server, Sheila could use the Connect As dialog box to connect to the NetWare server as SSanders. If the Sheila password on Windows 2000 Server and the SSanders account on NetWare are the same, Sheila gets direct access to the NetWare directory. If the passwords are different, Sheila will be prompted to enter a password for the NetWare server when she clicks OK to map the network drive.

Summary

In this chapter, we've looked at how to set up and configure a network, create shares, attach to network resources, use user profiles and hardware profiles, and connect a Windows 2000 Professional workstation to an NT4 server. But an important aspect of networking is still missing: how to set up rights and permissions for shares and for files and folders. I'll discuss this in detail in the next chapter, because, as you well know by now, security is the main reason that people migrate to Windows 2000 Professional in the first place.

CHAPTER 18

Living with Windows 2000 Professional; Strict Security

FEATURING:

In the previous chapter, I walked you through the steps for creating and configuring a network, but one big piece of the networking pie is still missing: securing the resources on your network. From its inception, the NT family of operating systems was designed with security as a primary feature, and, of course, this architectural element is omnipresent in the Windows 2000 family.

Unlike some other operating systems, Windows 2000 Professional requires you to create a user account for yourself right on your PC before you can do anything on that PC. Yes, the idea that you must create your own user account on your personal PC before you can do anything with the PC is unusual—after all, most of us are accustomed to requiring *network* accounts, but not particular accounts on a workstation. But—as your father might say when you complain that something you don't like isn't fair—get used to it!

The user account is an integral part of Windows 2000 Professional and has some great benefits. For example, suppose you and Sue share a computer. You can set up the computer so that you own a folder on the hard disk and Sue owns another folder on the hard disk, and *it is completely impossible for Sue to access your data* (and vice versa) unless you give her permission.

In addition, you can restrict access to files and folders by setting permissions. As you may recall, in Windows 2000 Professional you can use the FAT, FAT32, or NTFS file system. If you use either FAT system, you can exercise only a limited amount of control over file and folder access, but if you use the NTFS system, you can exercise a great deal of control—whether the files are on your local computer or on your network.

In this chapter, we'll first look at how to set up user accounts, and then we'll look in detail at establishing permissions for shares, files, and folders.

Understanding User Accounts in Windows 2000 Professional

As you have just read, you must create separate user accounts on a Windows 2000 Professional machine before any user can log on to the workstation—and, unlike Windows 95/98, Windows 2000 Professional won't let you get anywhere until you log on. You can't avoid the logon screen.

If your computer is part of a Windows 2000 Professional client-server network, two types of user accounts are available: domain accounts and local accounts. A domain account gives you access to the network and to the network resources for which you have permission. The manager of the server normally sets up domain accounts, which are stored in Active Directory on the server.

A local user account is valid only on your local computer; local user accounts sit in a database called the *Security Accounts Manager*, or SAM. You create user accounts with the Users And Passwords applet, which you'll meet later in this chapter.

In this chapter, I'm going to talk about local user accounts only. If you happen to be the administrator of a domain on a network and you need help creating domain user accounts, take a look at Chapter 8 in *Mastering Windows 2000 Server* (Sybex Inc., 2000).

Before I get into how you change or create an account, we need to look at the types of accounts in Windows 2000 Professional. The two broad categories are users and groups. A user account identifies a user on the basis of their user name and password. A group account contains other accounts, and these accounts share common privileges.

User accounts are of three types:

Normal user account A regular old user has rights such as being able to log on locally, shut down the system, create files, delete files that the user owns (more about ownership later in this chapter), and any other rights that an administrator assigns the user.

Administrator account This account has full and complete rights to the computer and can do just about anything to the computer. The Administrator account was created during installation and setup of Windows 2000 Professional when you assigned a password to it. The Administrator account cannot be deleted. You'll need to log on as Administrator when you want to create new accounts, take ownership of files or other objects, install software that will be available to all users, and so on.

Guest account This is a built-in account that allows a user to log on to the computer even though the user does not have an account. It is disabled by default, and you should leave it that way. If you want to give a visitor or an occasional user access to the system, create an account for that person, and then delete the account when it is no longer needed.

As I said earlier, a group is an account that contains other accounts, and a group is defined by function. Using groups, an administrator can easily create collections of users who all have identical privileges. By default, every Windows 2000 Professional contains the following built-in groups:

Administrators Can do just about anything to the computer. The things that they can do that no other type of user can do include loading and unloading device drivers, managing security audit functions, and taking ownership of files and other objects.

Backup Operators Can log on to the computer and run backups or perform restores. You might put someone in this group if you wanted them to be able to get on your system and run backups, but not to have complete administrative control. Backup operators can also shut down the system but cannot change security settings.

Guests Have minimal access to network resources. As I mentioned earlier, creating user accounts for occasional users is a much safer bet than using Guest accounts.

Power Users Can create new printer and file shares, change the system time, force the system to shut down from another system, and change priorities of processes in the system. They can't run backups, load or unload device drivers, or take ownership.

Replicator Enables your computer to receive replicated files from a Windows 2000 Server machine. I won't discuss that process here since you can't do it without a Windows 2000 Server PC.

Users Can run programs and access data on a computer, shut it down, and access data on the computer from over the network. Users cannot share folders or create local printers.

Understanding User Rights

But what's this about shutting down the machine or loading and unloading drivers? Well, actually, the notion of a *user right* is an integral part of how Windows 2000 Professional security works. Basically, the difference between regular old users and administrators lies in the kinds of actions that they can perform; for example, administrators can create new user accounts but regular old users cannot. In Windows 2000 Professional terminology, the ability to perform a particular function is a user right. To take a look at the user rights in Windows 2000 Professional and the types of users to whom they are assigned, follow these steps:

1. In Control Panel, click Administrative Tools, and then click Local Security Policy to open the Local Security Settings window:

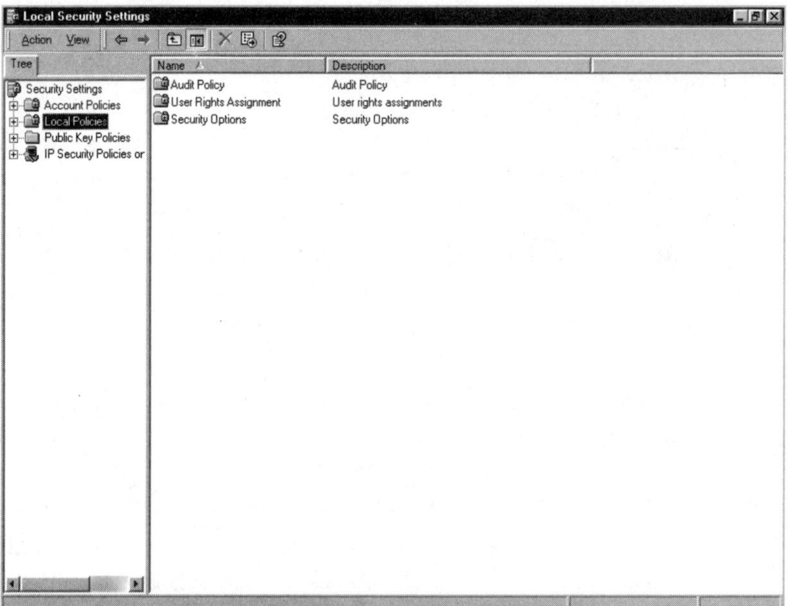

2. In the Tree pane, expand Local Policies, and then click User Rights Assignment to display a list of user rights in the pane on the right:

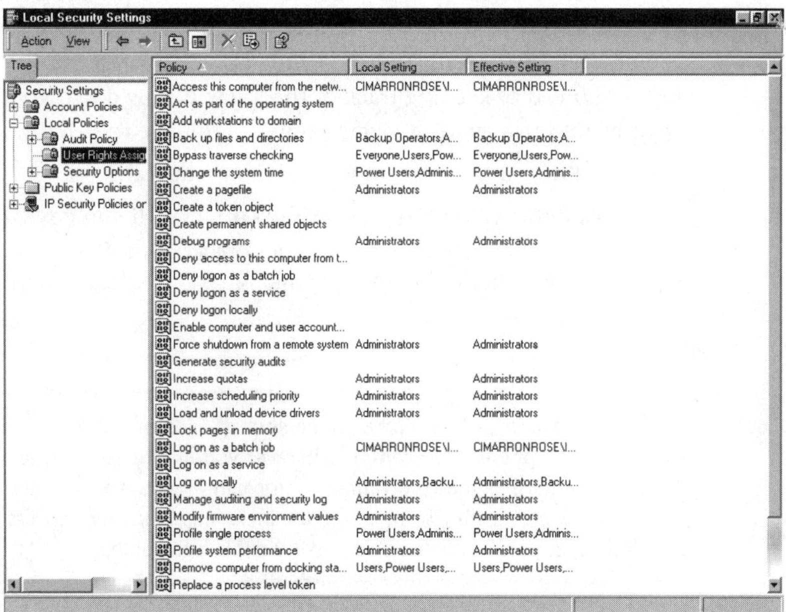

Most user rights are self-explanatory, but a few can use some clarification. Here's a list some of the rights and, where necessary, what they mean and what they're good for:

Back Up Files and Directories Run backup utilities.

Change the System Time Because the system time is important to the functioning of a network, not just anybody can change the system clock; it's a right. (Of course, you could always reboot the computer in DOS or go straight to the setup program in CMOS to reset the time, so it's not a very airtight security feature.)

Force Shutdown from a Remote System Some utilities let you select a Windows 2000 Professional machine and force it to shut down, even though you're not logged on to that machine. (One such utility comes with the Resource Kit.) Because you wouldn't want just anybody doing a forced shutdown, Microsoft made this a right.

Load and Unload Device Drivers A device driver is not only a video driver or SCSI driver; a device driver may be part of a software application or operating system subsystem. Without this right, you'll often be unable to install new software, and you'll usually be unable to change drivers or add and remove parts of the operating system.

Log on Locally Sit down at the computer and log on.

Manage Auditing and Security Log You can optionally turn on a Windows 2000 Security Log, which will report every single action that woke up any part of the security subsystems in Windows 2000 Professional. In general, I don't recommend using the Security Log because the output is quite cryptic and can be *huge*; logging all security events can fill up your hard disk quickly, and the CPU overhead of keeping track of the log will slow down your computer. You can't enable any security logging unless you have this right.

Restore Files and Directories As the name states.

Take Ownership of Files or Other Objects If you have this right, you can seize control of any file, folder, or other object even if you're not *supposed* to have access to it. This right is obviously quite powerful, which is why only administrators have it.

NOTE The user right to Take Ownership of Files or Other Objects is the secret to the administrator's power. You can do whatever you like to keep an administrator out of your data, but remember that the Administrator can always take ownership of the file, and as owner, do whatever they want to the file including changing permissions. You cannot keep an administrator out; you can only make it difficult to get in.

Creating a User Account

OK, now that you understand about the types of accounts and the concept of rights, let's create a new user account. You can do so in a couple of ways: using the Users And Passwords applet and using Computer Management. I'll start with the steps for creating a new user account with the Users And Passwords applet:

1. Log on as Administrator.
2. Choose Start ➢ Settings ➢ Control Panel to open Control Panel, and then click Users And Passwords to open the Users And Passwords dialog box:

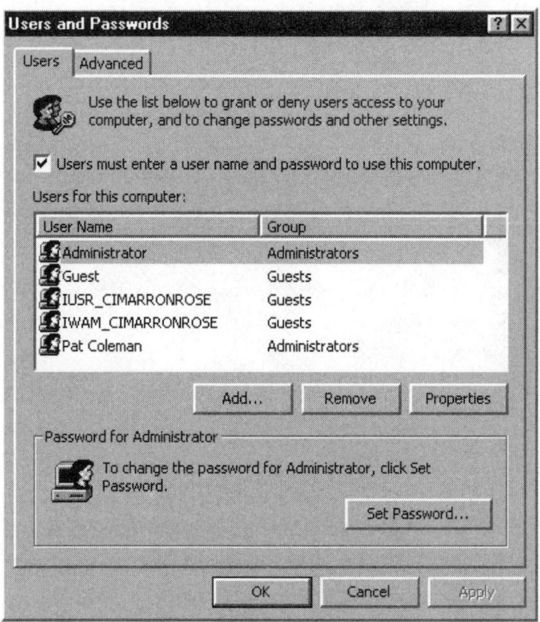

3. Click Add to open the Add New User dialog box:

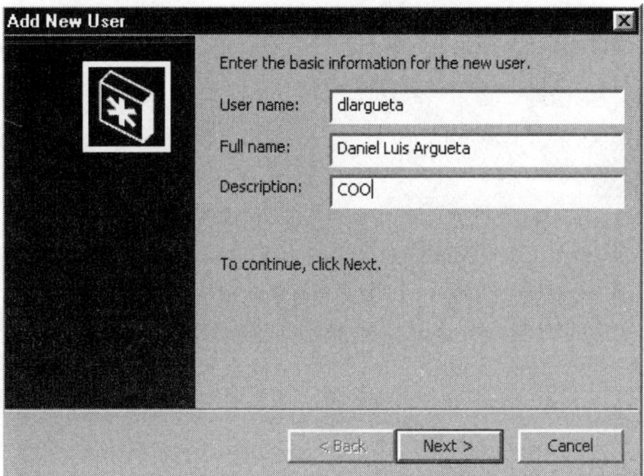

4. Enter a user name for the person, the person's full name, and a description, and then click Next.

NOTE In Windows 2000 Professional, a user name can be a maximum of 20 characters and is not case sensitive.

5. Enter a password for this user, retype it to confirm, and then click Next.

NOTE In Windows 2000 Professional, a password can be a maximum of 127 characters if you are in a pure Windows 2000 Professional environment. If you have Windows 95/98 machines on your network, keep the password to a maximum of 14 characters. Passwords are case sensitive.

6. Now you must indicate the level of access you want this user to have. In effect, you are specifying the group to which this user will belong. You have the following choices:

   Standard User This account will be a member of the Power Users group and will be able to modify the computer by installing new software and changing system settings.

   Restricted User This account will be a member of the Users group and will be able to run programs on the computer and save documents, but cannot install new software.

   Other This account will be a member of the Administrators, Backup Operators, Guests, Power Users, Replicator, or Users group. Click the drop-down arrow to make a selection.

7. Select a group, and then click Finish. Shortly, you'll see this account added to the list of users in the Users And Passwords dialog box.

To gain more control over the process of managing user accounts on Windows 2000 Professional, you will need to use the Local User Manager. You can access this tool in two ways.

- In Control Panel, click Administrative Tools, and then click Computer Management to open the Computer Management window. In the Tree pane, expand System Tools, expand Local Users And Groups, and then select Users to display a list of users in the right pane. Choose Action ➢ New User to open the New User dialog box.
- In Control Panel, click Users And Passwords to open the Users And Passwords dialog box, click the Advanced tab, and then click the Advanced tab to open the Local Users And Groups window. Select Users, and choose Action ➢ New User to open the New User dialog box.

As you can see, in either case you end up at the New User dialog box, as shown in Figure 18.1.

FIGURE 18.1
Use the New User dialog box to add a new user to your system.

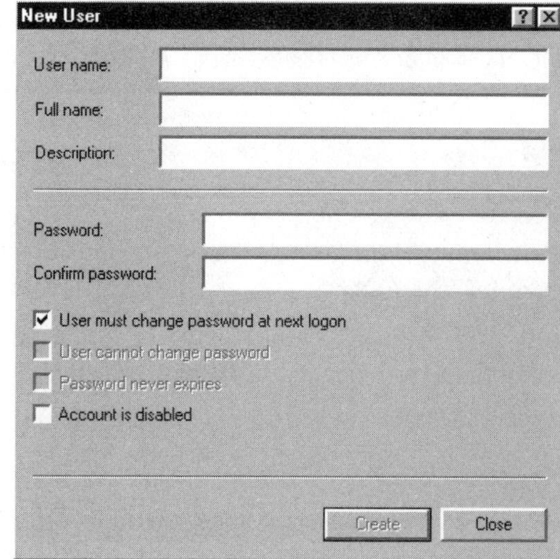

Now follow these steps:

1. Enter a user name for this new account.
2. Enter the person's full name.
3. Enter a description.
4. Enter and confirm a password.
5. Set the password options. The default option is User Must Change Password At Next Logon. This option means that only that user will know the password, which means better security. If you uncheck this option, the other two options become available. Select User Cannot Change Password if this account will be used for a service or for someone that you do not want to give the ability to change their own password. Select Password Never Expires if this password should be considered "permanent" and not have an automatic expiration.
6. The final option is to specify whether the account should be disabled. This is often a good idea if you want to change other properties of the account before it can be used, such as setting permissions on files and folders that this user will use. If this is the case, check the Account Is Disabled box.
7. When all options are selected, click Create to complete the process of making the new user account.

NOTE To enable a disabled account, in the Local Users And Groups window, right-click the account, and choose Properties from the shortcut menu to open the Properties dialog box for that account. Clear the Account Is Disabled check box.

Creating a Group Account

The process of creating a new group account is similar to creating a new user account. Local groups are useful for assigning permissions to resources. To create a new group account, follow these steps:

1. In Control Panel, click Administrative tools, and then click Computer Management to open the Computer Management window.
2. Expand System Tools, expand Local User And Groups, right-click Groups, and choose New Group from the shortcut menu to open the New Group dialog box:

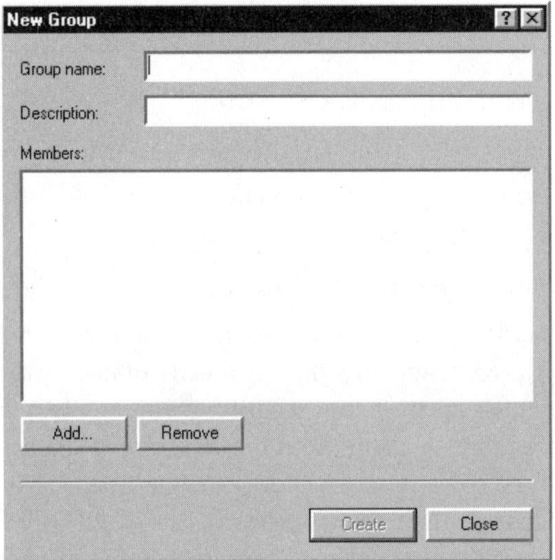

3. Type a name for the group in the space provided. The name can contain any numbers or letters and can be a maximum of 256 characters. The name must be unique in the local database.
4. Enter some text in the Description field that will describe the membership and purpose of this group.
5. Click the Add button to open the Select Users, Computers, Or Groups dialog box.
6. In the Look In drop-down list box, select the local computer.
7. To add users or groups to the group, select a name or a group, and click Add for each entity you want to add.

8. When you've added all the entities, click OK, and then click Create.
9. Click Close to close the New Group dialog box, and then close the Computer Management window.

Setting Permissions

The capability to restrict access to data is a really great feature of NT and Windows 2000 Professional. Prior to NT, my experience with operating systems of all kinds was that if you could gain physical access to a computer, you could get to its data; before NT, the only way to secure data with any confidence was to put the data on a server and put the server behind a locked door.

But network security is only as good as you make it. If a person can gain physical access to your machine, they can remove your hard disk and have all your data. Data security includes educating users to protect passwords and to apply permissions responsibly.

In this section, I'm going to show you how to set permissions at the share level and at the file and folder level. Remember, however, that you can establish file and folder security only if you are using the NTFS file system.

Setting Share-Level Permissions

In the previous chapter, I showed you how to share resources on your computer with others on your network. Now we need to look at what kind of access you want to give those who use your shared resources. To do this, you set the permissions.

To set share permissions, follow these steps:

1. In Explorer, right-click the shared resource, and choose Sharing from the shortcut menu to open the Properties dialog box for the share at the Sharing tab.

2. Click the Permissions tab to open the Permissions dialog box:

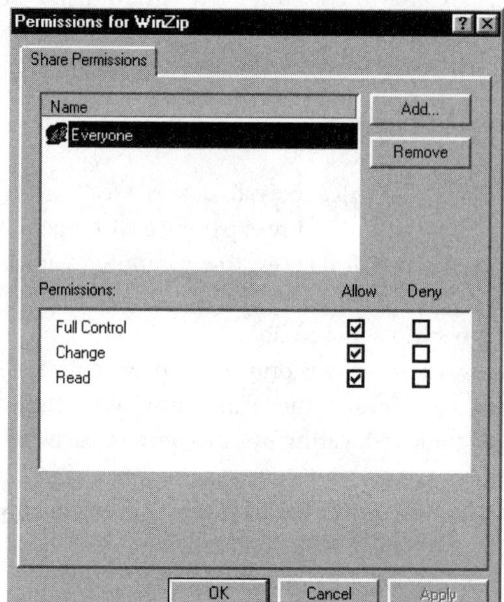

NOTE The default shared permission in Windows 2000 Professional is for the Everyone group to have Full Control. In a secure environment, be sure to remove this permission before assigning specific permissions to users and groups.

3. Click Add to open the Select Users, Computers, Or Groups dialog box, in which you can select which groups have access to a shared file or folder:

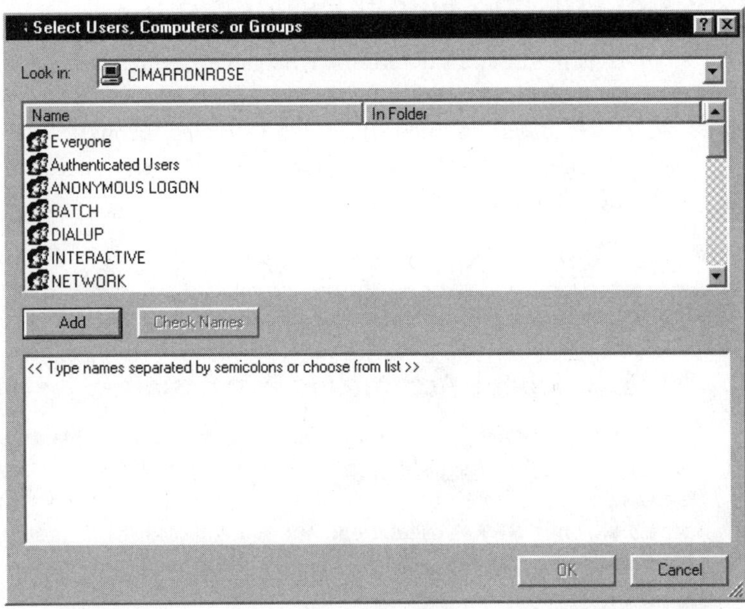

4. Select to whom you want to give access, click Add, and then click OK.
5. Back in the Permissions dialog box, you'll see that the user or group has been added to the Name list. In the Permissions section, click Allow or Deny to specify the type of permission you want to grant this user or group. Table 18.1 explains the choices.
6. When you've granted the permissions, click OK.

TABLE 18.1: FILE PERMISSIONS

Permission	Description
Full Control	The assigned group can perform any and all functions on all files and folders through the share.
Change	The assigned group can read and execute, as well as change and delete, files and folders through the share.
Read	The assigned group can read and execute files and folders but cannot modify or delete anything through the share.

Types of File and Folder Permissions

Share-level permissions determine who can access resources across the network and the type of access they will have. However, you can still assign more detailed permissions to the folders and files that can be accessed through the share. In addition, by using file- and folder-level permissions, you can restrict access to resources even if someone logs on to the system.

Multiple Groups Accumulate Permissions

You might have one group in your network called Accountants and another called Managers, and they might have different permission levels—for example, the Accountants might be able to only read the files, and the Managers might have Change access, which in NT was called Read and Write access. What about the manager of the Accounting department, who belongs to both the Managers and the Accountants groups—does he have Read access or does he have Change access?

In general, your permissions to a network resource *add up*—so if you have Read access from one group and Change from another group, you end up with Read *and* Change access. However, because Change access *includes* all the things that you can do with Read access, there's no practical difference between having Read and Change and having only Change access.

You've already seen that network shares have three types of permission levels: Read, Change, and Full Control. The permission types for files and folders are much more extensive, and each primary type includes still other types. Here are the primary types:

Read Allows you to view the contents, permissions, and attributes associated with a resource. If the resource is a file, you can view the file. If the resource is an executable file, you can run it. If the resource is a folder, you can view the contents of the folder.

Write Allows you to create a new file or subfolder within a folder if the resource is a folder. To change a file, you must also have Read permission, although you can append data to a file without opening the file if you have only Write permission.

Read & Execute Allows you the permissions associated with Read and with Write and also allows you to traverse a folder, which means you can pass through a folder for which you have no access to get to a file or folder for which you do have access.

Modify Allows you the permissions associated with Read & Execute and with Write, but also gives you Delete permission.

Full Control Allows you the permissions associated with all the other permissions I've listed so far and lets you change permissions and take ownership of resources. In addition, you can delete subfolders and files even if you don't specifically have permission to do so.

List Folder Contents Allows you to view the contents of folders.

If these levels of access are a bit coarse for your needs, you can fine-tune someone's access with what Microsoft calls *Special Access*. To modify the special access permissions for a file or folder, follow these steps:

1. In Explorer, right-click the resource whose permissions you want to modify, and choose Properties from the shortcut menu to open the Properties dialog box for that resource.
2. Click the Security tab, and then click Advanced to open the Access Control Settings dialog box:

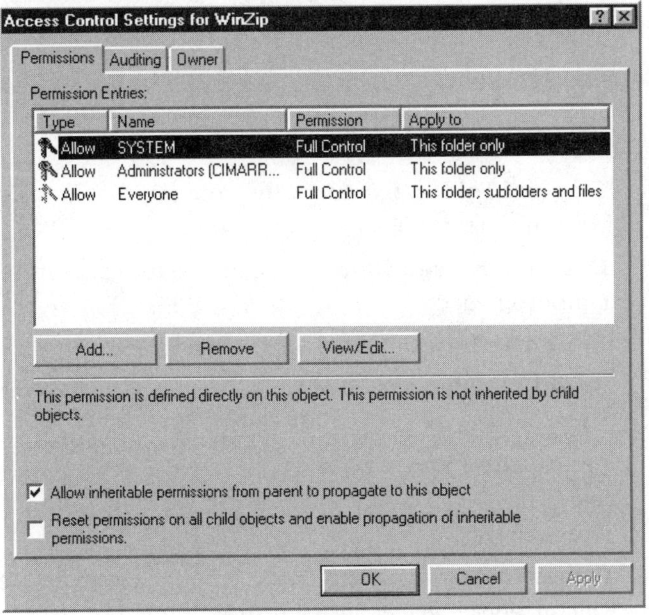

3. Click View/Edit to open the Permission Entry dialog box:

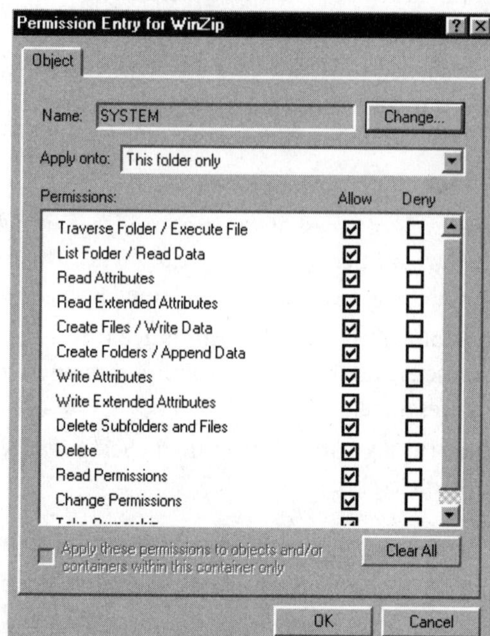

Here's a description of each of these permissions:

Traverse Folder/Execute File You can change folders through this folder, and you can run this file.

List Folder/Read Data You can read the contents of a file and display the contents of a folder.

Read Attributes You can display the current attributes of a file or folder.

Read Extended Attributes You can display the extended attributes of a file or folder, if there are any.

Create Files/Write Data You can write data to a new file. When applied to a folder, this permission means you can write files into the folder, but you can't view what's already in the folder.

Create Folders/Append Data You can create new folders in this location, and you can append data to existing files.

Write Attributes You can modify the attributes of a file or folder.

Write Extended Attributes You can create extended attributes for a file or folder.

Delete Subfolders and Files You can remove folders contained within the folder you're working in, and you can remove the files contained in them.

Delete You can delete files.

Read Permissions You can display the current permissions list for the file or folder.

Change Permissions You can modify the permissions for the file or folder. This permission is normally only included in Full Control.

Take Ownership You can claim ownership of a file or folder.

These permissions have changed quite a bit from NT, in which you had only six permissions to make up the standard permissions: Read, Write, Execute, Delete, Take Ownership, and Change Permissions. The new levels of granularity make security considerations more difficult to grasp initially, but they give a skilled administrator much finer control over how files and folders will be accessed.

One subtle change you may have already noticed is that there is no longer an explicit No Access permission. This is very likely a good thing, since No Access had several pitfalls. For example, if you assigned No Access for the Everyone group to the root of your C drive or to the System32 folder, you could actually prevent NT from booting. Other problems included not getting access to a resource you *should* have been able to access, because one of the groups you belong to had been given No Access.

To prevent someone from accessing a file or folder, you have two choices. The first, and usually the best, is to simply not grant the person access to the file or folder. That means, don't add their account to the list of permissions. Not having explicit permission is like having No Access; either way, you don't get in. The second method is to add the person's account to the permissions list, but check Deny for each permission. This creates an explicit No Access–type permission.

NOTE The special access items are all check boxes, not radio boxes, so you can mix and match as you like.

Assigning File and Folder Permissions

Now that you know something about the types of permissions you can place on files and folders, let's walk though the steps to assign them:

1. In Explorer, right-click the file or folder for which you want to establish permissions, and choose Properties from the shortcut menu to open the Properties dialog box for that file or folder.

2. Click the Security tab:

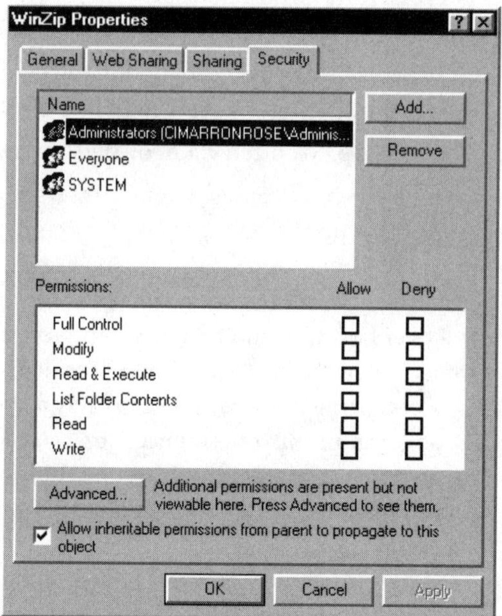

3. Click Add to open the Select Users, Computers, Or Groups dialog box.
4. Click a user or a group to whom you want to give permission, and then click Add. When you have added all the names of groups or users you want, click OK.
5. Back in the Properties dialog box, you'll see that those groups or users have been added to the Name list. Click OK.

Auditing Files and Folders

In addition to assigning file and folder permissions, Windows 2000 Professional lets you keep track of who accessed a file and when. You can audit everyone or only specific users or groups. To enable, set up, and view auditing, you need to be logged on as an administrator. Enabling auditing is a bit of a pain, but you have to do it before you can set up auditing. Bear with me, and follow these steps:

1. In Control Panel, click Administrative Tools, and then click Computer Management to open the Computer Management window:

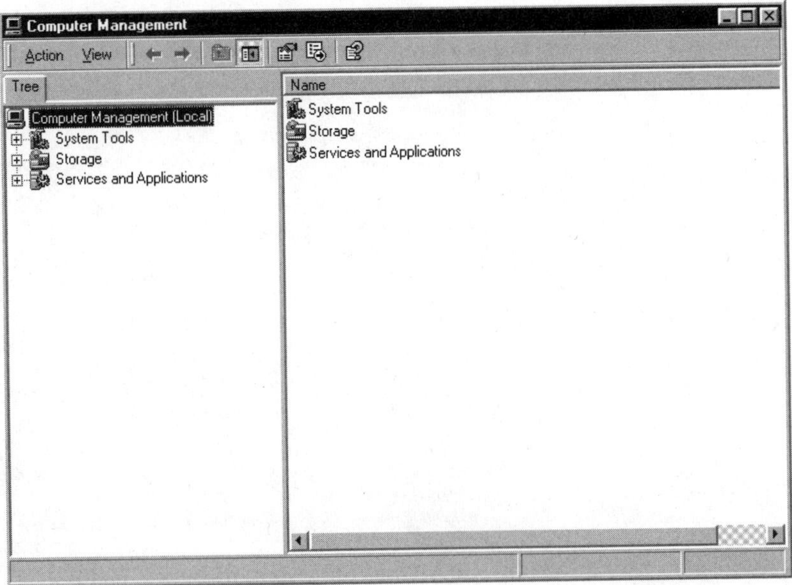

2. Choose Console ➢ Add/Remove Snap-in to open the Add/Remove Snap-in dialog box:

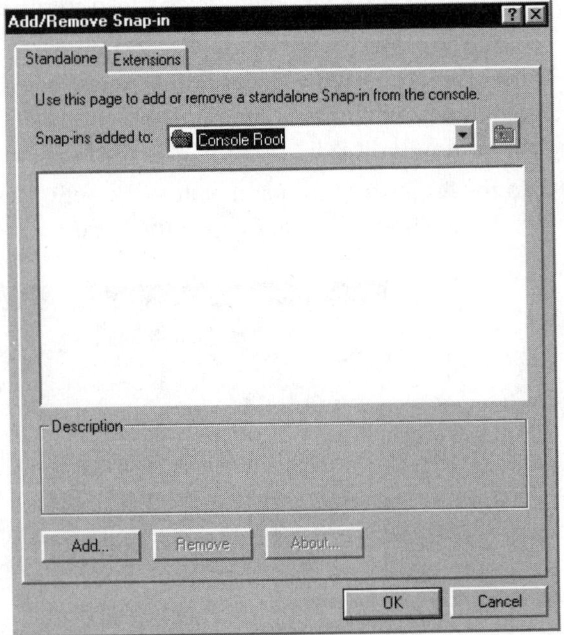

3. In the Standalone tab, click Add to open the Add Standalone Snap-in dialog box.

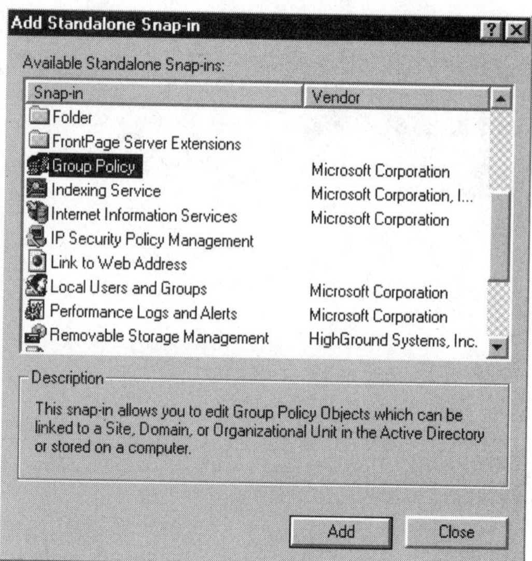

4. Scroll down to the Group Policy snap-in, select it, and click Add.
5. In the Select Group Policy Object dialog box, click Finish.
6. Close the Add Standalone Snap-in dialog box.
7. You'll see Local Computer Policy added to the list in the Add/Remove Snap-in dialog box. Click OK.
8. Back in the Console, click Local Computer Policy, click Computer Configuration, click Windows Settings, click Security Settings, click Local Policies, and then click Audit Policy to display a list of logging types you can audit.
9. In the list in the right pane, right-click Audit Privilege Use, and choose Security from the shortcut menu to open the Local Security Policy Setting dialog box:

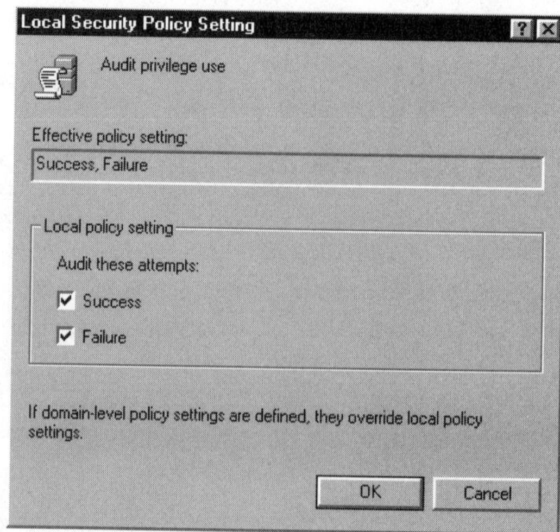

10. Select to audit for success and failure, and click OK.
11. Close the Computer Management window, and when you are asked if you want to save the settings, click Yes.

Whew…now you're ready to set up auditing. Follow these steps:

1. In Explorer, right-click the share you want to audit, and choose Properties from the shortcut menu to open the Properties dialog box for that share.
2. Click the Security tab, click the Advanced button to open the Access Control Settings dialog box, and click the Auditing tab:

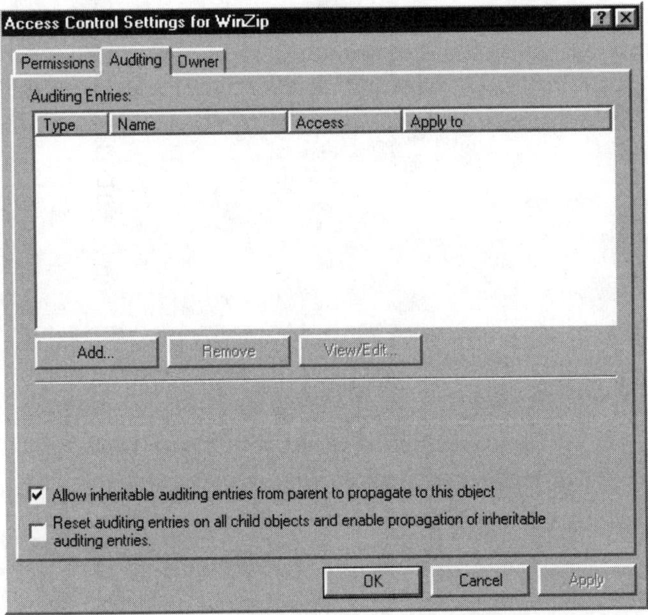

3. Click Add to open the Select Users, Computers, Or Groups dialog box.
4. Select a user or a group to audit, and then click OK to open the Auditing Entry dialog box, as seen next.

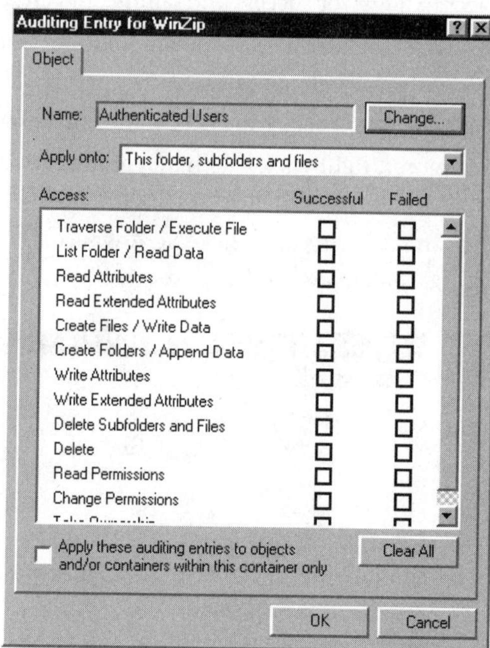

5. Select the entries that you want to audit, and then click OK three times.

To take a look at the events you've selected to audit, follow these steps:

1. In Control Panel, click Administrative Tools, and then click Event Viewer to open the Event Viewer window:

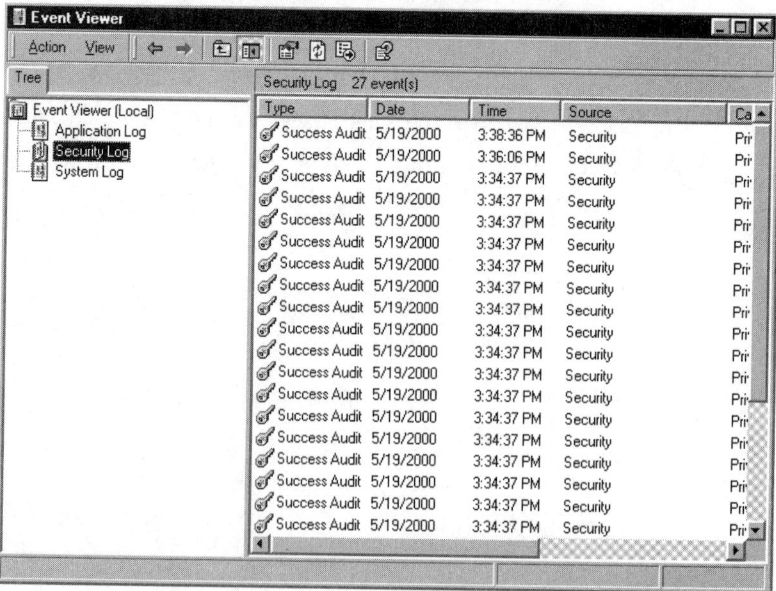

2. In the Tree pane, select Security Log to display a list of audited events in the right pane.

Understanding Ownership

Ownership—what a confusing concept. *Ownership* is a process by which you can take exclusive control over a file or a folder; and you can do all of this with a click of a button. But before you get power drunk with the possibilities, let's take a closer look at what being the owner of a file really means.

Defining Ownership

Now, having worked with NT since its inception, I don't mind telling you that the whole idea of a folder or file's "owner" seemed a bit confusing until I finally figured out the definition. Here's a definition—and from this point on, let me shorten the term *file* or *folder* to *object*:

Minasi's Definition of an Owner An object's owner is a user who can *always* modify that object's permissions.

Ordinarily, only an administrator can control settings such as an object's permissions. But you want your users to be able to control objects in their own area, their own home folder, without having to involve you at every turn. For example, suppose you want to give another user access to a folder in your home folder. Rather than having to seek out an administrator and ask the administrator to extend access permissions to another user, you as the owner can change the permissions directly. Ownership lets users become mini-administrators, rulers of their small fiefdoms.

To find out who owns an object, follow these steps:

1. In Explorer, right-click an object, and choose Properties from the shortcut menu to open the Properties dialog box for that object.
2. Select the Security tab, and then click Advanced to open the Access Control Settings dialog box.

3. Select the Owner tab:

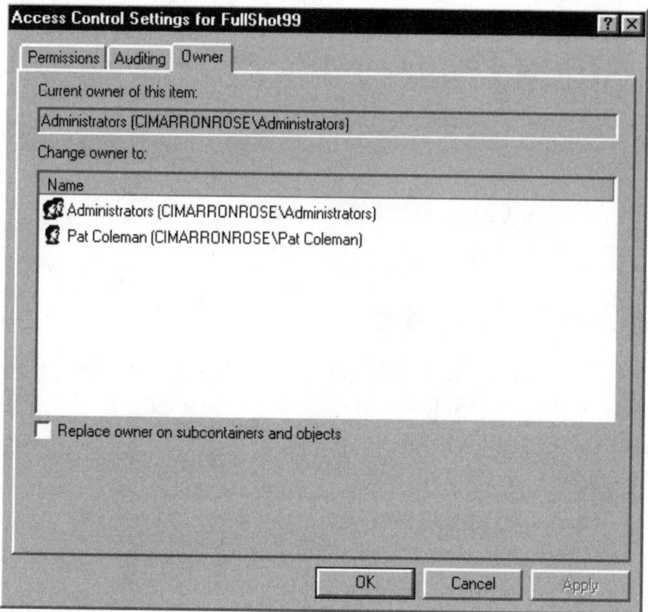

Taking Ownership

Users can't force themselves onto the permissions list for an object, but if they have the Take Ownership permission they *can* become the owner, and once they are the owner, *then* they can add themselves to the permissions list.

If you highlight your name in the Change Owner To list and click OK, you can become the owner of the object, but you can't see what's in the object because you are still not on the permissions list.

NOTE Owners of files can't necessarily access those files. All that the owners of files can do is change the permissions on those files.

Okay, then, how do you get to the object? Well, since you are an owner, you can change permissions. So you will add yourself to the permissions list and *then* gain access to the object.

Now, why were you able to do that? Because of a user right that all administrators have by default: Take Ownership. Perhaps if you were a more user-oriented than administrator-oriented company, you could remove the Administrators group from that right. By doing so, however, an administrator would be unable to poke around a user's area.

Further, users can always shore up their security just a bit by taking control of their home folder from the administrators. Recall that users have Full Control of their home folder, and Full Control includes the ability to take ownership of an object.

And if you're concerned about an administrator being able to take control at any time—where's the security in that?—consider that an administrator must *take* ownership in order to add themselves to the object's permissions list. In doing that, they leave fingerprints behind; if you log on one day and find that you're no longer the owner of something that you owned yesterday, you know that an administrator has been snooping—and if file auditing is in place, you can even find out who snooped.

NOTE You can't *give* ownership; you can only exercise the permission to take ownership. If an administrator were to take ownership of a file, they could not edit the file and then give ownership back to the original owner.

To summarize permissions and ownership:

- By default, new files and new subfolders inherit permissions from the folder in which they are created.
- A user who creates a file or a folder is the owner of that file or folder, and the owner can always control access to the file or folder by changing the permissions on it.
- When you change the permissions on an existing folder, you can choose whether those changes will apply to all files and subfolders within the folder.
- Users and groups can be denied access to a file or a folder simply by not granting the user or group any permissions for it. You don't have to assign No Access to every user or group that you want to keep out of a file or a folder.

It is possible to lock out everyone including the operating system itself if you do not apply permissions correctly.

Summary

In this chapter, we've looked at creating user and group accounts and at the rights that the various kinds of users and groups can have. I've also walked you through the steps involved in setting permissions for shares, files, and folders. Understanding and following these procedures is essential if you want the information on your Windows 2000 Professional system to be secure. And presumably that's one of the main reasons you're working with Windows 2000 Professional anyway, right?

CHAPTER 19

Active Directory Essentials

FEATURING:

The first thing that you probably ever heard about Microsoft's latest network operating system, Windows 2000, was that it can support larger networks than its predecessor, Windows NT Server 4, and that it accomplishes that with something called Active Directory (AD). To read the marketing literature, you'd think that Microsoft believes that AD is the single most important piece of Windows 2000.

Well, actually, they probably think that because AD probably *is* the single most important piece of Windows 2000. Unfortunately, it's also one of the most complex parts of Windows 2000 and one of the most pervasive—virtually every major feature of Windows 2000 requires Active Directory, with the possible exception of Plug and Play.

Veterans of NT 4 networks get a tired, resigned look on their faces when I talk to groups about AD. The new name and the new user interface for AD's management tools makes most NT 4 experts feel that all of their hard-won expertise is now useless, that "everything they know is wrong." A bunch of new terms are relevant to AD—*trees, forests, organizational units*, and so on.

If you're one of the despairing, cheer up! I've got good news. AD is really nothing more than NT 4 domain structures with a bunch of cool improvements. The problem is, of course, that Microsoft not only came up with a bunch of new things and gave them new names, they gave most of the old concepts new names as well. But if you're up-to-speed on NT 4 networks, you actually won't find AD terribly daunting, once someone gives you the NT-4-to-Windows-2000 decoder ring. Think of this chapter as that ring.

Not that long ago, networks were small (remember when the only "networks" you cared about were CBS, NBC, and ABC?), and so were their problems. But nowadays it's not unusual to see worldwide networks connecting hundreds of thousands of PCs and users. Managing that kind of complexity brings up big problems—oops, we're supposed to call them challenges; I always forget. One of the answers to the obvious question "Why bother with Windows 2000, anyway?" is that it was designed with some of those challenges in mind. That's important because NT 4 *didn't* address many of those problems.

You'll notice that for most of this chapter I'll be talking about Windows 2000 Server. And, yes, I realize that this book is about Windows 2000 Professional. If you're using Windows 2000 Professional on a standalone computer or a small peer-to-peer network that connects Windows 2000 Professional machines and Windows 95/98 machines, you don't need to know anything about Active Directory. But if you're part of a large client-server network, and your Windows 2000 Professional workstation is connected to a Windows 2000 Server machine, you do need to understand Active Directory, and the information in this chapter is important to you. After I explain what the hoopla is all about, I'll give you step-by-step instructions for connecting to an AD domain.

Security: Keeping Track of Who's Allowed to Use the Network and Who Isn't

A network's first job is to provide service:

- To provide central places to store simple things such as files or more complex things such as databases, shared printing, or fax services
- To make it possible for people to communicate by means of e-mail, videoconferencing, or whatever technology comes up in the future
- And, more recently, to make it easier for people to buy things

Fast on the heels of that first job, however, is the second job of every network: to provide security. Once, most computer networks were unsecured or lightly secured, but human nature has forced a change, and there's no going back. Just as businesses have locks on their doors, file cabinets, and cash registers to protect their physical assets, so also do most modern firms protect their information assets. And no matter which vendor's network software you're using, computer security typically boils down to two parts: authentication and authorization. To see why, consider the following example.

Acme Industries sells pest control devices. They've got a sales manager named Wilma Wolf; Wilma wants to see how the sales of a new product, Instant Hole, is doing. Acme's got it set up so that Wilma can review sales information through her Web browser—she just surfs over to a particular location on one of the company's internal Web servers, and the report appears on her screen.

Of course, Acme management wouldn't be happy about just *anybody* getting to these sales report pages, so the pages are secured. Between the time that Wilma asked for the pages and the time that she got them, two things happened:

Authentication The Web server containing the sales reports asked her workstation, "Who's asking for this data?" The workstation replied, "Wilma." The server then said, "Prove it." So the workstation popped up a dialog box on Wilma's screen asking for her username and password. She types in her name and password, and assuming that she types them in correctly, the server then checks that name and password against a list of known users and passwords and finds that she is indeed Wilma.

Authorization The mere fact that she's proven that she's Wilma may not be sufficient reason for the Web server to give her access to the sales pages. The Web server then looks at another list sometimes known as the Access Control List, a list of people and access levels—"Joe can look at this page but can't change it," "Sue can look at this page and can change it," "Larry can't look at this page at all." Presuming Wilma's on the "can look" list, the server sends the requested pages to her browser.

Now, the foregoing example may not seem to contain any deep insights—after all, everyone's logged into a system, tried to access something, and either been successful or rejected—but understanding how Windows 2000 Server and in particular AD is new requires examining these everyday things a bit. Here's a closer look at some of the administrative mechanics of logins.

Maintain a "Directory" of Users and Other Network Objects

Every secure system has a file or files that make up a database of known user accounts. NT 4 only used a single file named SAM, short for the less-than-illuminating Security Accounts Manager. It contained a user's username (the logon name), the user's full name, password, allowed logon hours, account expiration date, description, primary group name, and profile information. Of course, the file was encrypted; copy a SAM from an existing NT 4 system and pull it up in Notepad, and you'll see only garbage.

Windows 2000 Server stores most of its user information in a file called `ntds.dit`, but `ntds.dit` is different from SAM in a couple of ways:

- First, `ntds.dit` is a modified Access database, and Windows 2000 Server actually contains a variant of Access's database engine in its machinery. (Microsoft used to call the Access database engine JET, which stood for Joint Enterprise Technology—no, the meaning isn't obvious to me either, I think they just liked the acronym—but now it's called ESE, pronounced "easy," which stands for the equally useful name Extensible System Engine.)
- Second, as you'll see demonstrated over and over again, `ntds.dit` stores a much wider variety of information about users than SAM ever did.

The information in `ntds.dit` and the program that manages `ntds.dit` are together called the *directory service* (DS). (As a matter of fact, most folks will never say "`ntds.dit`"; they'll say "directory service.") Which leads to a question: What exactly is a "directory"?

It would seem (to me, anyway) that what we've got here is a database of users and user information. So why not call it a database? No compelling reasons; mostly convention, but there *is* one interesting insight. According to some, databases of users tend to get *read* far more often than they get *written*. That allows a certain amount of database engine tweaking for higher performance. This subset of the class of databases gets a name—*directories*. I guess it makes sense, as we're used to using lists of people called office directories or phone directories. I just wish the folks in power had come up with some other name; ask most PC users what a directory is, and they start thinking of hard disk structures: C:\Windows—isn't that a directory?

Centralizing the Directory and *Directories*: a "Logon Server"

"Please, can't we set things up so I only need to remember *one* password?"

Consider for a moment when Windows 2000 Server will use that user information located in AD. When you try to access a file share or print share, AD will validate you. But there's more at work here. When fully implemented, AD can save you a fair amount of administrative work in other network functions as well.

For example, suppose your network requires SQL database services. You'll then run a database product such as SQL Server or Oracle on the network. But adding another server-based program to your network can introduce more administrative headaches because, like the file and print servers, a database server needs authentication and authorization support. That's because you usually don't want to just plunk some valuable database on the network and then let the world in general at it—you want to control who gets access.

So the database program needs a method for authentication and authorization. And *here's* where it gets ugly: In the past, many database programs required their administrators to keep and maintain a list of users and passwords. The database programs required you to duplicate all that work of typing in names and passwords, to redo the work you'd already done to get your Novell, Banyan, NT, or whatever type LAN up and running. Yuk. But it gets worse. Consider what you'd have to do if you ran both NT as a network operating system *and* Novell NetWare as a network operating system: yup, you're typing in names and passwords yet again. Now add Lotus Notes for your e-mail and groupware stuff, another list of users, and hey, how about a mainframe or an AS/400? More accounts.

Let's see—with a network incorporating NT, Oracle, NetWare, and Notes, you got each user owning *four* user accounts. Which means each user has *four* passwords to remember. And, every few months, four passwords to remember to change.

This seems dumb; why can't you just type those names and passwords once into your Windows 2000 Server and then tell Oracle, NetWare, and Notes to just ask the local Windows 2000 Server machine to check that you are indeed who you say you are rather than making Oracle, NetWare, and Notes duplicate all that security stuff? Put another way, you have a centralized computer that acts as a database server, another that acts as a centralized e-mail server, another as a print server—why not have a centralized "logon" server, a centralized "authentication" server? Then your users would have to remember (and change) only one password and account name rather than four.

Centralized logons would be a great benefit, but there's a problem with it: how would Notes actually *ask* the Windows 2000 server to authenticate? What programming commands would an Oracle database server use to ask a Microsoft "logon server" (the actual term is *domain controller*, as you'll learn later) if a particular user should be able to access a particular piece of data?

Well, if that domain controller were running NT 4, the programming interface wouldn't have been a particularly well-documented one. And third parties such as Oracle, Lotus, and Novell would have been reluctant to write programs depending on that barely documented security interface because they'd be justifiably concerned that when the *next* version of NT appeared (Windows 2000 Server), Microsoft would have changed the programming interface, leaving Lotus, Novell, and Oracle scrambling to learn and implement this new interface. And some of the more cynical among us would even suggest that Lotus and Oracle might fear that Microsoft's Exchange and SQL Server would be able to come out in Windows 2000 Server–friendly versions nearly immediately after Windows 2000 Server's release...

Instead, Microsoft opted to put an industry standard interface on its AD, an interface called the Lightweight Directory Access Protocol (LDAP). Now, LDAP may initially sound like just another geeky acronym, but it's more than that—what Microsoft's done by putting an LDAP interface on Active Directory is to open a doorway for outside developers. And here's how important it is: Yes, LDAP will make Oracle's or Lotus's job easier should they decide to integrate their products' security with Windows 2000 Server's built-in security. But LDAP also means that it's (theoretically, at least) possible to build tools that create Active Directory structures—domains, trees, forests, organizational units, user accounts, all of the components. It means that if Windows 2000 Server gets popular but Microsoft's Active Directory control programs turn out to be hard to work with, some clever third party can just swoop in and offer a complete replacement, built atop LDAP commands.

Which, after you spend a bit of time with the Microsoft Management Console (MMC), may not seem like a bad idea—but I'll leave you to make your own judgment about that once you meet the MMC. (I'll explain the MMC in Chapter 29.)

Searching: Finding Things on the Network

Thus far, I've been talking about the directory service as if it only contains user accounts. But that's not true—the DS not only includes directory entries for people, it also contains directory entries describing servers and workstations. And that turns out to be essential, for a few reasons.

Finding Servers: "Client-Server Rendezvous"

Client-server computing is how work gets done nowadays. You check your e-mail with Outlook (the client), which gets that mail from the Exchange machine down the hall (the server). You're at your PC (the client) accessing files on a file server (the server). You buy a shirt at L.L. Bean's Web server (the server) from your PC using Internet Explorer (the client).

In those three cases, the copy of Outlook on your desktop had to somehow know where to find your local Exchange server, you couldn't get files from your file server until you knew which file server to look in, and you couldn't order that shirt until you'd found the address of the L.L. Bean Web server, `www.llbean.com`.

In every case, client-server doesn't work unless you can help the client find the server; hence, the phrase "client-server rendezvous." In the Outlook case, your mail client knows where your mail server is probably because someone (perhaps you) in your networking group set it up, feeding the name of the Exchange server into some setup screen in Outlook. You may have found the correct file server for the desired files by poking around in Network Neighborhood in Windows 95/98 or in My Network Places if your workstation is running Windows 2000 Professional, or perhaps someone told you where to find the files. You might have guessed L.L. Bean's address, saw it in a magazine ad, or used a search engine such as Yahoo! or AltaVista.

Those are three examples of client-server rendezvous; many more happen in the process of daily network use. When your workstation seeks to log you in, the workstation must find a domain controller, or to put it differently, your "logon client" seeks a "logon server." Want to print something in color and wonder which networked color printers are nearby? More client-server rendezvous.

In every case, AD can simplify the process. Your workstation will be able to ask AD for the names of nearby domain controllers. You can search the AD for keywords relevant to particular file shares and printers.

Name Resolution and DNS

But merely getting the name of a particular mail, Web, print, or file server (or domain controller) isn't the whole story. From the network software's point of view, `www.llbean.com` isn't much help. To get you connected to the Bean Web server, the network software needs to know the *IP address* of that server, a four-number combination looking something like 208.7.129.82. That's the second part of client-server rendezvous.

In the case of a public Web site such as Bean's, your computer can look up a Web server by querying a huge network of publicly available Internet servers called the *Domain Name System*, or *DNS*. The public DNS contains the names of many machines you'll need to access, but chances are good that your company's internal network doesn't advertise many of its machines' names on the Internet; rather, your internal network probably runs a set of private DNS servers.

After its inception in 1984, DNS didn't change much. But RFC 2052 (introduced in October 1996) and RFC 2136 (introduced in April 1997), transformed DNS into a naming system that's good not only for the worldwide Internet but also for internal intranets. Many of the pieces of DNS software out in the corporate world don't yet support 2052 and 2136, so it's a great convenience that Windows 2000 Server's DNS server supports those features.

NOTE RFC stands for *Request for Comment*, which is a document or a set of documents in which proposed Internet standards are described or defined.

Creating New Types of Subadministrators

The next network challenge becomes apparent after a network has grown a bit. When a network is small or new, a small group of people do everything, from running the cables and installing the LAN adapter boards to creating the user accounts and backing up the system. As time goes on and the network gets larger and more important to the organization, two things happen:

- First, the organization hires more people—*has* to hire more people, because there are more servers to tend and user accounts to look after—to handle all the different parts of keeping a network running.
- Second, networks get political: all of a sudden, some of the higher-ups get clued to the fact that *what those network geeks do affects our ability to retain our power in this organization.*

Both of those things mean that your firm will soon start hiring more network helpers. In some organizations, these newly created positions get to do much of the scut work of network administration, stuff that is (a) pretty simple to train people to do and (b) of no interest to the old-timer network types. Examples of the I-don't-want-it-you-can-have-it jobs in a network include:

Resetting passwords For security's sake, we network administrators usually require users to change their passwords every couple months or so. We also inveigh against the evils of writing those passwords down, so it's common for users to forget what they set their most recent passwords to. Resetting passwords to some innocuous value is something that really needs to be done quickly—the natives get restless when you take a week to let them back on the network—and it's a relatively simple task, so it's perfect for the newly hired, minimum-wage network assistant.

Tending the backups For tediousness, nothing matches the sheer irritation of backups. Most of us are forced to use tape drives for backups, and, well, some days it seems like tape drives were invented by someone who was abused by network administrators as a small child. They're balky and prone to taking vacations at random times, and you never can predict exactly how much data you can get on 'em—eight gigs one day, three the next, and as a result, *someone's* got to be around ready to feed in another blank tape. And somebody's got to label them and keep track of them; ask most network admin types what job they'd most like to give someone else to worry about, and backups are likely to be at the top of their wish list.

Hiring a few low-wage backup watchers and password fixers also gives a firm a sort of a "farm team," a place to try out folks to see if they're capable of learning to eventually become network analysts with more responsibilities (and, they hope, more salary).

But regular old users can't do things such as resetting passwords and running backups—you need at least some administrative powers to do those things. Recall that we'd like to hire this "network scut work" person or persons at a pretty low hourly rate, and that's troublesome from a security point of view. If they can leave this job and go off to one with the same pay level whose main challenge is in remembering to say, "Would you like fries with that, sir?" it might not be the brightest idea to give them full administrative control over the network. Is there a way to create a sort of partial administrator?

NT 4 gave us *some* of that, as there was a prebuilt group called Backup Operators, but there wasn't a Reset Password Operators group, and besides, all NT 4 offered was a small set of prebuilt groups of types of administrators—the groups were called Server Operators, Account Operators, and Backup Operators—with different levels. There wasn't a way to create a new type of group with a tailor-made set of powers. Windows 2000 Server changes that, offering a sometimes bewildering array of security options.

Delegation: Subdividing Control over a Domain

In the last section, I offered two examples of things that might motivate changing how the network works—a growing set of network duties that require some division of labor (which I covered in that section) and growing attention from upper management as it becomes increasingly aware of the importance of the network in the organization. That second force in network evolution is perhaps better known as "politics." Despite the fact that it's something of a bad word, we can't ignore politics—so how does Windows 2000 Server address an organization's political needs?

To see how, consider the following scenario. Some fictitious part of the U.S. Navy is spread across naval facilities across the world, but perhaps (to keep the example simple) its biggest offices are in Washington, DC; San Diego, CA; and Norfolk, VA. There are servers in DC, San Diego, and Norfolk, all tended by different groups. For all the usual reasons, the officers in charge of the Norfolk facility don't want administrators from DC or San Diego messing with the Norfolk servers; the DC folks and the San Diego folks have similar feelings, with the result that the Navy technology brass wants to be able to say, "Here's a group of servers we'll call Norfolk and a group of users we'll call Norfolk Admins. We want to be able to say that only the users in Norfolk Admins can control the servers in Norfolk." They want to do similar things for San Diego and DC. How to do this?

Well, under NT 4, they could do it only by creating three separate security entities called *domains*. Creating three different domains would solve the problem because separate domains are like separate *universes*—they're not aware of each other at all. With a DC domain, a Norfolk domain, and a San Diego domain, they could separate their admins into three groups that couldn't meddle with one another. It's a perfectly acceptable answer and indeed many organizations around the world use NT 4 in that manner—but it's a solution with a few problems.

For one thing, enterprises usually want *some* level of communication between domains, and to accomplish that, the enterprises must put in place connections between domains called *trust relationships*. Unfortunately, trust relationships are a quirky and unreliable necessity of any multidomain enterprise using NT 4. With Windows 2000 Server, in contrast, the Navy need only create *one* domain and then divide it using a new-to-NT notion called *organizational units*, usually abbreviated *OUs*.

More specifically, the Navy would solve their problem in this way:

- They'd create one domain named (for example) NAVY.
- Inside NAVY, they'd create an organizational unit named Norfolk, another called DC, and a third named San Diego. They would set up their servers and then place each server into the proper OU.
- Also inside NAVY, they'd create a user group named Norfolk Admins, and two others named San Diego Admins and DC Admins. They'd create accounts for their users and place any administrators into their proper group, depending on whether they were based in DC, San Diego, or Norfolk.

At this point, understand that the San Diego Admins (kinda sounds like a baseball team, doesn't it?) don't yet have any power: there's no magic in Windows 2000 Server that says, "Well, there's an OU named San Diego and a group named San Diego Admins, I guess that must mean I should let these Admin guys have total control over the servers in the San Diego OU." You have to create that link by *delegating control* of the San Diego OU to the user group San Diego Admins. (Windows 2000 Server has a Wizard that assists in doing this.) OUs are an excellent tool for building large and useful domains.

Satisfying Political Needs

"That's *my* data, so I want it on *my* servers!" As information has become the most important asset of many firms—for example, I once heard someone comment that the majority of Microsoft's assets resided in the crania of their employees—some firms have been reluctant to yield control of that information to a central IT group. Nor is that an irrational perspective: if you were the person in charge of maintaining a five-million-person mailing list, and if that list generated one half of your firm's sales leads, you might well want to see that data housed on a machine or machines run by people who report directly to you.

Of course, on the other side of the story there is the IT director who wants Total Control of all servers in the building, and her reasoning is just as valid. You see, if a badly run server goes down and that failure affects the rest of the network, it's *her* head on the chopping block.

So on the one hand, the department head or VP wants to control the iron and silicon that happen to be where his data lives, and on the other hand, the IT director who's concerned with making sure that all data is safe and that everything on the network plays well with others wants to control said data and network pieces. Who wins? It depends—and that's the "politics" part.

What does Windows 2000 do to ameliorate the political problems? Well, not as much as would be nice—there is no "make the vice presidents get along well" Wizard—but Windows 2000's variety of options for domain design gives the network designers the flexibility to build whatever kind of network structure they want.

Got a relatively small organization that would fit nicely into a single domain, but one VP with server ownership lust? No problem, give the VP an OU of their own within the domain. Got a firm with two moderately large offices separated by a few hundred miles? Under NT 4, two domains and a trust relationship would be the answer, and you could choose to do that under Windows 2000, but that's not the only answer. As Windows 2000 is extremely parsimonious with WAN bandwidth in comparison with NT 4, you might find that a single domain makes sense as it's easier to administer than two domains, but not impossible from a network bandwidth point of view. And bandwidth utilization is our next topic…

Connectivity and Replication Issues

More and more companies don't live in only one place. They've purchased another firm across the country, and what once were two separate *local* area networks are now one firm with a wide area network need. If that WAN link is fast, there's no network design headache at all: hook the two offices up with a T1 link, and you can essentially treat them as one office.

That's beneficial because each site will usually contain a domain controller—one of those servers that hosts the AD database and that acts as a machine to accomplish logins. But those domain controllers must communicate whenever something changes, as when a user's password changes or when an administrator creates a new user account. This is called *AD replication*. The same thing happened with NT 4, as NT 4 also allowed you to put multiple domain controllers in an enterprise.

In NT 4, suppose you've got two offices connected by a slow WAN link. Suppose further that you've got a domain controller in each of these offices. They need to replicate their SAM database between domain controllers (recall that NT 4 used a user database named SAM; Windows 2000's database is called AD). NT 4's domain controller updates happened every five minutes. That means that a domain controller might try to replicate changes to another domain controller every five minutes, even if they're only connected with a very slow link. All that chatter could well choke a WAN link and keep other, more important traffic from getting through.

Windows 2000 improves upon that by allowing you to tell Windows 2000 domain controllers about how well they're connected. The idea is that you describe your enterprise in terms of *sites*, which are basically just groups of servers with fast connections—groups of servers living on the same local area network, basically. You can then define how fast (or probably, slow) the connections *between* those sites are, and Windows 2000 will then be a bit smarter about using those connections.

In particular, Windows 2000 AD servers compress data before sending it over slow WAN links. Taking the time to compress data requires a certain amount of CPU power, but it's well worth it, as AD is capable of a 10:1 compression ratio!

Not only do you often face slow links, you often must live with *unreliable* links, ones that are up and down or perhaps only up for a short period of time every day. Windows 2000 lets you define not only a WAN link's speed but also the times that it is up.

NT 4's directory replications require a real-time connection called a *Remote Procedure Call (RPC)*. RPCs are like telephone calls—the domain controller programs on each side must be up and running and actively communicating simultaneously. Inasmuch as domain controllers can be more or less busy as the day wears on, requiring this kind of shared concentration in order to get a simple directory replication accomplished is a bit demanding. It might be nicer if replications could work less like a telephone call and more like a mailing—and to a certain extent, Windows 2000 allows this, or rather points to a day in the future when it'll be possible.

It's possible for one domain controller to simply *mail* part of its replication data to another domain controller. Then, even if the receiving domain controller is not currently online, the mail message is still waiting for it, ready to be read when the receiving domain controller is again awake. Sounds good, but unfortunately, not *all* of the directory replication can happen over mail. Microsoft says that'll change in a future release, but not in Windows 2000.

Site control will make life considerably easier for those managing multilocation networks.

Scalability: Building Big Networks

Large enterprise networks found NT 4 lacking in the number of users that its SAM database could accommodate. Although you could theoretically create millions of user accounts on an NT domain, it's not practical to create more than about 5,000 to perhaps

10,000 user accounts in a domain. (If you took the MCSE exam for NT Server and are looking at that number oddly, it's because they made you memorize 40,000 as the answer to the question "How many user accounts can you put on an NT domain?" In my experience, that's just not realistic, hence my 5,000 to 10,000 number.)

Five thousand user accounts are more than most companies would ever need. But some large firms need to incorporate more user accounts into their enterprise, forcing them to divide their company's network into multiple domains—and multiple domains were to be avoided at all costs under NT 4 because of the extra trouble in maintaining them.

AD can accommodate many more user accounts than NT's SAM. Microsoft claims that they have stress-tested Windows 2000 domains with 1.5 million users in them, and Compaq engineers in France have successfully created and worked with 16 million user accounts on a single domain using *beta 2* of Windows 2000. Although it'll be a while before we get enough real-world experience to know exactly how many users we can reasonably expect to add to Windows 2000 networks, it's clear that Windows 2000 systems will support far larger lists of users than did NT 4.

Furthermore, AD allows you to build larger networks by making the process of building and maintaining multidomain networks easier. Whereas once an administrator of a multidomain network had to build and maintain a complex system of interdomain security relationships—the *trust relationships* I've already referred to—now Windows 2000 will let you build a system of domains called a *forest*. A forest's main strength is that once a group of domains has been built into a forest, the trusts are automatically created and maintained. There are additionally smaller multidomain structures called *trees* that also feature automatic trusts.

Simplifying Computer Names or "Unifying the Namespace"

Devices on a network mainly identify themselves by some long and unique number. On an intranet or the Internet, it's a unique 32-bit number called an *IP address*. Networks also commonly exploit a 48-bit address burned into each network interface card called a *MAC* (Media Access Control) *address*. Any Ethernet, Token Ring, ATM (Asynchronous Transfer Mode), or other network interface has one of these addresses, and some conventions that network manufacturers have agreed upon have ensured that no matter whom you buy a NIC (Network Interface Card) from, the NIC will have a 48-bit address that no other NIC has. Some parts of NT identify PCs by their IP address (or addresses—a machine with multiple NICs will have an IP address and MAC address for each NIC), others by the PC's MAC address or addresses.

But people don't relate well to long strings of numbers—telling you that you can send me mail at `mark@11001110111101101111110111001000` is technically accurate (presuming that you can find a mail client that will accept network addresses in binary) but not very helpful. It's far more preferable to be able to instead tell your mail program to send mail to `help@minasi.com`, which you can do. Somehow, however, your mail client must be able to look up `minasi.com` and from there find out where to send mail for `minasi.com`. In the same way, pointing your Web browser to `www.microsoft.com` forces the browser to convert `www.microsoft.com` into the particular IP address or addresses that constitute Microsoft's Web site. This process of converting from human-friendly names such as `minasi.com` to computer-friendly addresses such as 11001110111101101111110111001000 is called *name resolution*. It's something every network must do.

So why is name resolution a problem with NT? Because most of the networking world uses *one* approach to name resolution, and up through version 4, NT used a different one.

Most every firm is on the Internet, has an internal intranet, or both. Intranets and the Internet use the DNS form of name resolution. DNS names are the familiar Internet names such as `www.microsoft.com`. PCs resolve DNS names by consulting a group of servers around the world called, not surprisingly, DNS servers. Your company or Internet Service Provider operates one or more DNS servers, and your Internet software uses these nearby DNS servers to resolve (for example) `www.minasi.com` to the Internet address 206.246.253.200.

NT-based networks using Internet software don't use DNS for much of their work. Instead, Microsoft invented its own name servers somewhat like DNS but using NetBIOS names; they called these name servers *Windows Internet Name Service*, or *WINS*, servers. The NetBIOS naming systems is incompatible with DNS; NetBIOS names are simpler—no more than 15 characters, no periods.

That leads to this problem: nearly every firm is on the Internet—*has* to be on the Internet—and so every firm must give DNS names to their computers. But if they're also using NT, they need to give their systems NetBIOS names. That in and of itself is not a great burden; what *is* a burden is that these names are important to the programs that use them, and programs can typically need one of the two names and can't use the other of the two.

Let's take an example. Suppose someone wants to log on to an NT 4 domain at Acme Technologies. To accomplish that, this person's workstation must find a domain controller for that domain. The workstation does that by searching for a machine with a particular NetBIOS name. Let's say that Acme does indeed have a domain controller around named LOGMEIN (its NetBIOS name) which *also* acts as a Web server with the DNS name `reptiles.pictures.animalworld.com`, as it hosts pages of pictures of local reptiles. Let's also suppose that for some reason ACME has no WINS servers but has a great network of DNS servers.

DNS names are of no value to the workstation looking for a logon. You could have the finest set of DNS servers in the world, but it would make no difference—without a functioning WINS server, that workstation would probably be unable to locate a domain controller to log you in. On the other hand, if someone sitting at that very same workstation sought to view the reptile pictures on `http://reptiles.pictures.animalworld.com`, they'd just fire up Internet Explorer and point it at that URL. Internet Explorer is, of course, uninterested in NetBIOS names, relying mainly on DNS names. The workstation would quickly locate the Web server and browse its pages, even as that same workstation was unable to detect that the very same server could perform logins.

Windows 2000 solves this problem by largely doing away with WINS, using DNS for all its name resolution needs. Unfortunately, however, Windows 2000 uses DNS for all *its* name resolution needs—older Windows 95/98 and Windows NT 4 systems still rely on WINS. So while WINS' role is diminished, it'll still be around until you've pulled the plug on the last Windows 95/98 and NT machines.

Satisfying the Lust for Power and Control

Well, okay, maybe it's not *lust*, but it's certainly *need*. Put simply, there just plain aren't enough support people around, and there is no shortage of users to support. In 1987, many firms retained one support person for every 100 users; in many companies nowadays, that ratio is more like one support person for every 2,000 users.

Although it was once possible for a support person to physically visit every user's PC to perform support tasks, it's just not reasonable to expect that any more. Support people need tools that allow them to get their work done from a central location as much as is possible. And, although not every user is all that happy about it, one way to simplify a support person's job is to standardize each PC's desktop. In some cases, support staffs need software tools to allow them to *enforce* that standard desktop. (As you can imagine, it's a very political issue for many firms.)

In NT 4, Microsoft started helping support staffs centralize their desktop control with something called *system policies*. But system policies were lacking in a few ways. AD improves upon system policies with a kind of "system policies version 2" called *group policies*.

Better security, more flexible administration options, wiser use of bandwidth, and providing godlike control to administrators: that's basically what AD is trying to accomplish.

Connecting a Windows 2000 Professional Machine to an AD Domain

So now that you know all about Active Directory and what it's for, let's take a look at how you can connect your Windows 2000 Professional workstation to an Active Directory domain. The steps are actually quite easy, and if you work along with the examples that follow, you should be connected to an Active Directory domain in no time.

Checklist

First, there are a number of things that you should make sure you know in advance before trying to connect to an Active Directory domain. Specifically, be sure you have the following information available before starting:

- The name of the AD domain you will be joining.
- Your username and password, as they are defined in the AD.
- Whether an account has already been added to the AD for your machine (each machine has an account, as does each a user).
- If an account has not been added for your machine, you will need a login and password in the Active Directory that has the rights to create an account for your machine.

Connecting to AD

Once you have verified all of the items on the checklist, you've got what it takes to add your machine to an Active Directory domain. The next step is to verify that the correct components are installed on your Windows 2000 Professional computer (and to install them if they're not) and then to add your machine to the Active Directory domain.

Verify Operating System Prerequisites

In order to connect to an Active Directory domain, two networking components must be in place on your system:

- Client for Microsoft Networks
- An appropriate communications protocol (NetBEUI, NWLink IPX/SPX, or TCP/IP).

Both components are necessary for any Microsoft operating systems to talk to each other, so it is important to make sure they are properly installed before trying to join an Active Directory domain.

To verify that both components are installed, follow these steps:

1. Choose Start ➢ Settings ➢ Network And Dial-Up Connections to open the Network And Dial-Up Connections folder.

2. Right-click the icon that represents your network, and choose Properties from the shortcut menu to open the Properties dialog box for your network.
3. In the list of configured components you should see the Client for Microsoft Networks and an appropriate protocol—TCP/IP, NWLink IPX/SPX, or NetBEUI. Make sure that both items are enabled (the check box next to the item is selected).

You now have everything you need to connect to a domain. You just need to tell Windows 2000 Professional to do it.

Change Computer Network Identification

To tell Windows 2000 Professional to join an Active Directory domain, you change the network identification information on your system. However, the configuration for doing so is a bit hidden. Instead of being with the other networking items, the Active Directory domain items are configuration parameters in My Computer. To change network identification, follow these steps:

1. On the Desktop, right-click My Computer, and choose Properties from the shortcut menu to open the System Properties dialog box.
2. Click the Network Identification tab, and you will see the current identification of your system consisting of a machine name and the current domain or workgroup your system is configured to use.
3. To change this configuration, click the Properties button to open the Identification Changes dialog box:

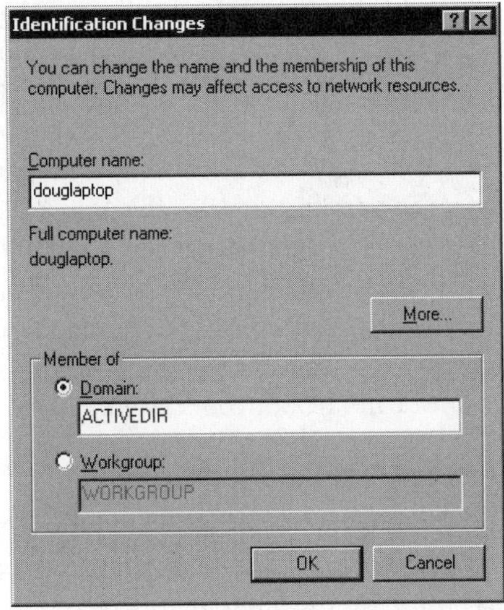

As you can see, the name of my machine is douglaptop, and it was originally a member of a workgroup called WORKGROUP. I've told Windows 2000 Professional to join an Active Directory domain called ACTIVEDIR by clicking the Domain radio button and entering the name of the domain that my system should join. After you make the necessary changes to your system, click OK. Either one of two things will happen.

First, you might see a dialog box welcoming you to the domain you specified. What that means is that someone—an administrator or someone else—has already set up an account for the name of your computer within the Active Directory. If this is the case, all you will need to do is reboot to complete your changes. You can now proceed to the Logging In to Active Directory section of this chapter.

However, more often than not there won't be an account for your computer within the Active Directory, so you'll need to add one. You'll know this is the case if you get prompted for a username and password, as shown in Figure 19.1.

FIGURE 19.1 *Your username and password are required to add a machine account in Active Directory.*

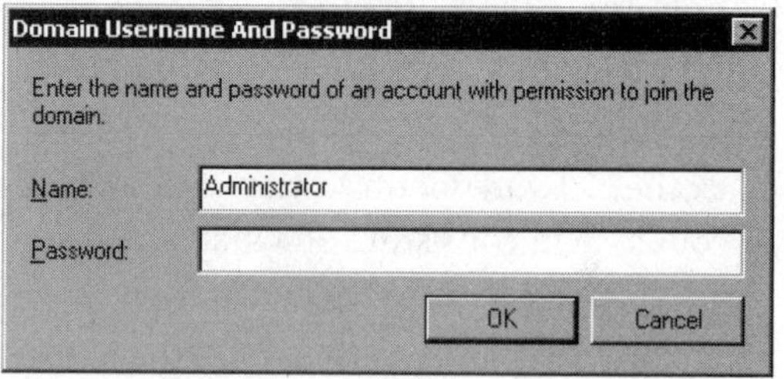

Active Directory doesn't let just anyone add machine accounts to its database; you need an Active Directory user account that has the right to do so. The Administrator account will work for these purposes, but depending on your circumstances, you may not have been provided with the administrative password to the Active Directory. There are also ways to create special accounts for one purpose—to add machines to domains—but ultimately if you don't know of an account to use at this point, you will need to contact an administrator for the Active Directory in order to complete this process (that's why this information was listed in the prerequisites).

Assuming you have the correct username and password to use (or that someone has entered it for you), the next thing you should see is a dialog box welcoming you to the domain you've joined. Your machine will need to be rebooted for the changes to take effect, so go ahead and reboot your system

Logging In to Active Directory

The next time your computer boots up, it probably won't look much different. You'll be presented with the same login box that you've always seen. However, if you click the Options button on the main login screen, you will see a drop-down list of domains to choose from. By default, your system will continue to use its own local accounts database for logging in, so you will need to click the drop-down list and choose the domain you just joined. Select the appropriate domain, and then enter your Active Directory username and password in the appropriate fields. If everything is configured correctly, you should end up logging in to the Active Directory domain. Congratulations!

Summary

The purpose of this chapter was to introduce you to AD. As you can tell from even these few pages, AD is a complicated topic. If you're interested in learning more, I recommend that you take a look at a couple of Sybex books: *Mastering Windows 2000 Server, Second Edition,* by Mark Minasi, Christa Anderson, Brian M. Smith, and Doug Toombs (Sybex Inc., 2000); and *Mastering Active Directory, Second Edition,* by Robert R. King (Sybex Inc., 2000).

CHAPTER 20

Connecting to Novell NetWare Networks

FEATURING:

If your business is like thousands of others around the world, there's a good chance you have a Novell NetWare network already in place. And if you've just made the move to using Windows 2000 Professional, you'll be pleased to know that it's not difficult to connect your Windows 2000 Professional computer to the Novell NetWare server. In other words, you've come to the right chapter.

Microsoft provides a special solution for this situation, which it calls the Client Service for NetWare. The benefits of the Client Service for NetWare include the following:

Novell script processing The Client Service for NetWare processes the system and individual logon scripts created by the network administrator of the Novell network. The Client Service for NetWare still has limited support for NetWare Directory Services (NDS) in this iteration of Windows 2000 Professional; therefore, the script processing takes place when logging onto a NetWare 4 or 5 server.

Long filename support If you enable OS/2 naming support on your Novell server, you can save files with names of as many as 255 characters. With the OS/2 naming support enabled, your NetWare server appears as a High Performance File System (HPFS) volume to the Windows 2000 Professional client.

Single peripheral systems Because you are using the 32-bit drivers for connectivity, you can use the dial-up services that are part of the Microsoft enterprise network. Historically, Microsoft products have referred to the dial-up services as Remote Access Service (RAS), but in Windows 2000 Professional, this function is known as Dial-Up Networking. If you use the Client Service for NetWare, Dial-Up Networking lets you attach directly to the Novell servers and process NetWare logon scripts remotely.

Before we look at the procedure for installing the Client Service for NetWare, let's look at the different versions of NetWare to which you may have to connect—NetWare 3, 4, or 5. We will also look at the printing resources that are available to you after you install the Client Service for NetWare. I'll conclude this discussion with some notes about utilizing logon scripts and mapping drives to NetWare servers.

Defining Novell's Point of View: Common Terms

A lot of the concepts that you are familiar with in Windows 2000 Professional are present in Novell NetWare. Let me take a moment to clarify the Novell terms.

Novell Security

NetWare security distinguishes four issues:

- The login procedure
- Trustee rights

- Directory rights
- File attributes

Each of these levels provides a different and more complete level of security.

The Login Procedure

Every time a user logs on to the network, they must provide their identification name and a password. This password is NetWare's guide to the access rights that the user has on the network. If the password has read-only rights attached to it, that user can't modify files on the server. Conversely, if that password has full rights to a file server and all file servers are treated as one on the network (as in NetWare 4 or 5), that user has full rights to all servers. When a user logs into NetWare, they are logging into a network. This means that the user can go anywhere around the world and, as long as their account has the appropriate trustee rights, they can log into their local server and have access to the same resources.

Trustee Rights

Each user or group of users on a Novell network is considered a trustee. Each user has a list of possible rights or permissions linked to their password (as you saw earlier), including but not limited to:

- Reading from open files
- Writing to open files
- Opening existing files
- Creating new files
- Deleting existing files
- Setting trustee rights for others at the directory/subdirectory level
- Modifying file attributes

Although these rights can apply evenly to entire disks, they don't necessarily have to. A network administrator can vary a user's rights according to a particular directory of a drive. (A user's rights are limited by the container—their individual trustee rights and their group memberships—to which they belong.) In other words, you could have full access to most of a drive, but read-only access to a particular directory on that drive. This concept leads to the next topic—directory rights.

Directory Rights

Directory rights are similar to folder permissions in Windows 2000 Professional. Although NetWare, by default, gives child directories (subdirectories) the same rights as their parent directories, each trustee can set the above rights for each directory and subdirectory on the network. Subdirectories do inherit the rights of their parent directories, just as subfolders inherit the rights of their parent folders in Windows 2000 Professional.

File Attributes

As a final level of security, the network administrator can mark individual files with certain attributes that limit how and when users can use them, similar to setting file-level permissions in Windows 2000 Professional. (NetWare just has fewer of them.) These attributes are:

- Sharable versus nonsharable. If one person is using a sharable file, others can access it as well. If a file is nonsharable, no more than one person at a time can use (even read) that file.
- Read/write versus read-only.

You're probably familiar with read/write and read-only file attributes. If a file is read-only, any user with those rights can read it and make changes but can't save those changes to the original document. They could save those changes if they saved the amended file under another name, however. This kind of restriction is handy for a group project in which one person is in charge and other people are contributing. If the helpers can't modify the original, the person in charge has to incorporate only the changes that they approve. This process saves the helpers from frantically looking for the original file's backup after modifying the file in a way in which the project leader rejected. (And unless the helpers made a backup copy, the old file would no longer exist.)

Any user with read/write capability (such as that project manager) could update a file and then save it under the same name as before, incorporating the new information. Again, unless a backup file is made, the old file will no longer exist.

Using the Novell Administration Utilities

To help you set up these myriad directories—users directory, trustee directory, and file attributes—NetWare comes with a complete set of network utilities. Of these, the main utility for administrative purposes is known as the *system configuration utility* (SYSCON for short) for NetWare 2 and 3 and NETADMIN for NetWare 4 (NWADMIN is the Windows version of this utility). NetWare 5 brings a new administration tool, ConsoleOne. With SYSCON and NETADMIN, you can set up accounting and metering features and set time restrictions for user logons. For example, let's say that Jane has rights to use the file server only from Monday through Friday, from 8:00 AM to 3:00 PM. If she tries to log on at 4:00 PM Friday, she will get an "access denied" or "invalid logon" error message.

ConsoleOne is a one-stop tool for administering both a NetWare 5 server and NDS. Accessed from a NetWare client, ConsoleOne gives you full access to the administration duties of your NetWare network with one tool. ConsoleOne is shown in Figure 20.1.

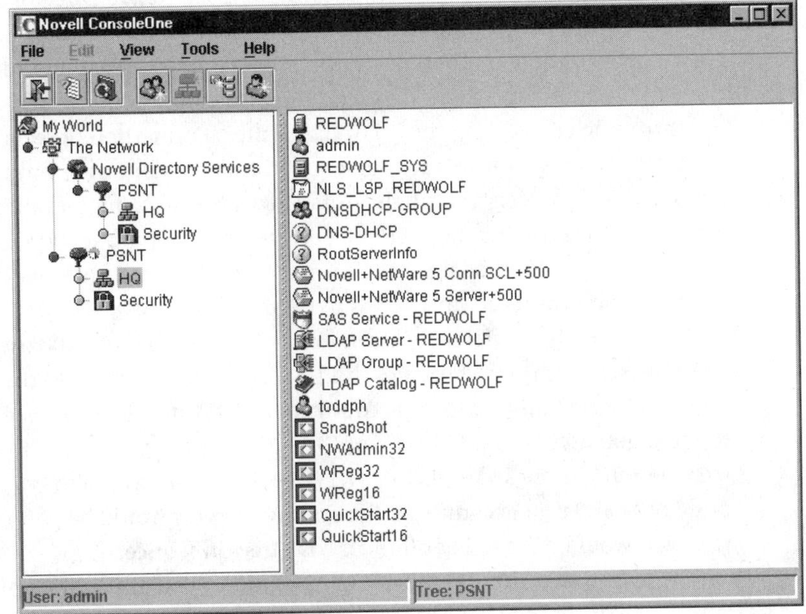

FIGURE 20.1
The ConsoleOne tool lets you manage your NetWare 5 network from Windows 2000 Professional.

With ConsoleOne, you can create users, groups, and organizational units (OUs). You can set trustee rights for the containers in your NDS tree, and you can set directory rights. Essentially, the functions of SYSCON and NETADMIN have been combined into a single tool that can be run either from the new GUI of NetWare 5 or from any Windows-based client. That's the good news.

The bad news for people who want to use Windows 2000 Professional to manage their NetWare 5 network is that the tool does not have full functionality with Microsoft's Client Services for NetWare. As with NT 4 and earlier, you must map a drive letter to access the Sys volume before you can run any NetWare administration tool. UNC (Universal Naming Convention) paths will not work at all with these tools. If you are serious about managing your NetWare environment from within Windows 2000 Professional, you should strongly consider downloading Novell's Client32 when it is available for Windows 2000 Professional.

Talking to NetWare 3 Servers versus Talking to an NDS Tree

Face it: you have to be aware of some facts of life regarding Novell and its three primary network operating systems—NetWare 3, 4, and 5. The heart of the difference lies in the way that NetWare versions view and handle security and validation of users.

NetWare 4 and 5 both use NetWare Directory Services (NDS), which is an X.500 directory structure that is much like the Windows 2000 Active Directory.

A NetWare 3 server holds its security information in a security database called the *bindery*. The bindery method of security views each server as an individual entity, and the security that you assign to various directories and print queues is kept independently on each server. On the other hand, the NDS method of security that NetWare 4 and 5 use no longer treats each server as an independent unit, but instead treats a conglomeration of servers as a single unit called a *tree*. As a matter of fact, we really don't care about the individual server in NetWare 4 and 5. Instead we look to the different resources, or *objects*, that are being offered on each server, and the NDS tree keeps track of these objects and controls access to them.

To illustrate the difference, assume that you had to build 100 user accounts on five NetWare servers and that each of the 100 users needed access to the five NetWare servers. If you were building these accounts in a NetWare 3 environment, you would have to build 500 user accounts—each of the 100 users on each of the five servers. If you were building these accounts in a NetWare 4 or 5 environment, you would have to build only 100 user accounts because all five servers would be part of the same NDS tree; you would have to log on to an NDS tree only once.

The reason that this difference is important to you at the Windows 2000 Professional level is that the levels of access and control that you have on a NetWare 3 server are different from those on a NetWare 4 or 5 server. Therefore, a Windows 2000 Professional machine interacts with NetWare 3 and 4 or 5 in different fashions.

Accessing a NetWare Server

After you install the Client Service for NetWare (discussed later in this chapter), you can access the resources of a NetWare 3 server as well as a NetWare 4 or 5 tree, as long as you have a valid login ID on the NetWare servers. The login scripts that reside on the Novell server will run even on your Windows 2000 Professional workstation, mapping your drives and capturing your printer ports.

NOTE You must configure and assign the user account to a print queue when mapping your network drives. The print queue is an object which contains the printer, and you must assign trustee rights to the user account to allow the user to use a particular printer.

Administering a NetWare Server from a Windows 2000 Professional Computer

After the Client Service for NetWare is installed, you can still go to the command line prompt and run SYSCON (the system console) on a NetWare 3 server to build users, manage groups, and assign trustee rights to the various resources on this NetWare server. Life proceeds normally as long as all you want to do is administer a NetWare 3 server.

However, if you turn your attention to a NetWare 4 server, life is much different. You cannot run the NETADMIN or NWADMIN utilities to manage a NetWare 4 NDS tree. At this time, the Client Service for NetWare does not support logging on to the NDS as Administrator to allow direct administrative access to the NDS. Look for this to change in subsequent patches for this service, especially in the Service Packs that Microsoft will release for this product.

WARNING Many administrators may have gotten around the NDS administration limitation in NT Workstation 4 with 32-bit Novell Administrator software provided by Novell. This utility does not work on Windows 2000 Professional. In most cases, it will bring your system to a screeching halt, generally making it difficult (if not impossible) to reboot Windows 2000 Professional. Look on Novell's Web site (`www.novell.com`) for the Windows 2000 Professional version of the utility.

NetWare 5 uses the ConsoleOne tool to manage the network resources from a client computer. Currently, this tool won't work correctly with Windows 2000 Professional. To really use this tool's functions, you will need to install the Client32 software from Novell. The key issue appears to be some proprietary functions supplied in some dynamic link libraries (DLLs) that are installed with the Client32 software.

Understanding How Windows 2000 Professional and NetWare Interact

A Novell NetWare network may incorporate Windows 2000 Professional machines solely as workstations. This task is fairly simple because it requires no work on the server side at all. All you need to do to access the Novell servers directly from Windows 2000 Professional is use the Client Service for NetWare, which is provided with Windows 2000 Professional.

Here are a few things you should know about this solution:

- It may require dual network client software, which can be hard to manage and require additional memory.
- It *does* provide access to both Novell NetWare and Windows 2000 Server resources, but security and programming interfaces are not integrated.
- It is difficult to share remote access and backup processes under this system.
- It involves no special software installation on the servers and so may be attractive to some network administrators.

Running NetWare and Windows 2000 Server Together

The idea here is simple: Your office contains both Windows 2000 servers and a NetWare server or servers. The Windows 2000 servers talk NetBIOS/NetBEUI and perhaps TCP/IP, and the Novell servers talk IPX/SPX or TCP/IP. Getting the two server families (NetWare and Windows 2000) to talk to one another is a mite tricky, goes the reasoning, *so don't bother*. Instead, load both IPX/SPX and NetBIOS/NetBEUI stacks on your Windows 2000 Server clients.

NOTE There is a very common belief in the networking world that the Microsoft operating systems use only NetBEUI and that NetWare uses only IPX/SPX. Today you will typically find that both are coexisting quite well using TCP/IP to communicate. You need to ensure that you have at least one protocol in common among all the computers that will communicate on your network.

WARNING Although both operating systems can use TCP/IP to communicate over the network, the Microsoft Client Services for NetWare will work *only* with NWLink installed. Here again, Microsoft is fostering the belief that NetWare only uses IPX/SPX for network communication.

The Older Solution: Windows for Workgroups and Windows 95

To better understand how Windows 2000 Professional is providing NetWare support, let's take a brief look at how Microsoft handled this problem in the past.

Windows for Workgroups ships with an IPX/SPX stack that runs in combination with NetBIOS/NetBEUI, making it possible to carry on conversations with both Windows 2000 Server and NetWare servers. Here are some features of the NetWare and Windows 2000 Server parallel solution:

Simplicity (kind of) You needn't install any software on the servers. You needn't put NWLink on your Windows 2000 Server machines or install some kind of odd NetWare Loadable Module (NLM) on your NetWare servers.

Lack of drivers 1 To date, Windows for Workgroups does not ship with a NetWare redirector. The IPX/SPX protocol is in place, but the redirector is not, requiring that you run the redirector that came with Windows for Workgroups version 3.1. Microsoft doesn't warn you about this deficiency until you're part way through the installation of Windows for Workgroups version 3.11. (Nice touch, boys and girls!) In addition, the combination of 3.11 and the old 3.1 driver is a bit wobbly.

Lack of drivers 2 If you're running NetWare 4 or 5 servers, then there's just no way that you can make the old Windows for Workgroups 3.1 NetWare drivers work reliably. You have to download a bunch of drivers from one of Novell's online resources or from one of their support CDs. They seem to work fairly well talking to the NetWare servers but tend to eliminate some of the benefits of Workgroups. Besides, they cut off your connections to Windows 2000 Server machines periodically.

Memory management Insufficient memory becomes a problem in that you're loading a *lot* of programs on the workstation.

Sharing Because you're still running two different server environments, they don't share anything. You've got to create separate user accounts on the Windows 2000 Server side of the house from the NetWare side. This is because two different server operating systems, Novell and Windows 2000 Server, are running simultaneously, and they don't share any resources from each other's respective environment. Remote access services aren't shared, requiring twice as many modems. Backup services aren't shared, so you've got to keep track of twice as many tapes.

TIP Windows 2000 Professional greatly simplifies matters because Microsoft has written complete protocol stacks and client software for both Windows 2000 Professional and Novell networks. Use all Microsoft client software, and you'll be dealing with only one vendor.

Configuring Windows 2000 Professional to Run in Parallel with NetWare

Running Windows 2000 Professional in parallel with NetWare requires that the Client Service for NetWare be installed on the Windows 2000 Professional machine. Installing the Client Service for NetWare is a straightforward procedure. Follow these steps:

1. Right-click My Network Places on the Desktop, and choose Properties from the shortcut menu to open the Network And Dial-Up Connections dialog box.
2. Right-click Local Area Connection, and choose Properties from the shortcut menu to open the Local Area Connection Properties dialog box.
3. Click the Install button to open the Select Network Component Type dialog box.

4. Select Client from the list, and click Add to open the Select Network Client dialog box:

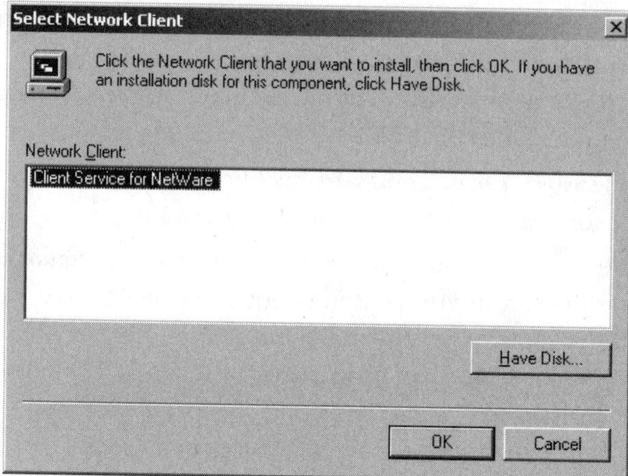

5. Double-click Client Service For NetWare to open the Local Area Connection Properties dialog box.
6. Click Install. Windows 2000 Professional copies the appropriate drivers to your system and makes changes to your Registry that enable the Client Service for NetWare to load the next time you start your system.

If you are loading the Client Service for NetWare and have not previously loaded the NWLink IPX/SPX–compatible transport protocol, this protocol will load automatically as you install the service. The NWLink IPS/SPX Properties screen (see Figure 20.2) prompts you for the frame type that your NetWare server is using. Contact the NetWare Administrator to ensure that you select the correct frame type, even though Auto Detect frame type works most of the time.

NOTE The Client Services for NetWare will not work at all without NWLink installed. If you disable NWLink, Windows 2000 Professional will automatically disable the Client Services for NetWare.

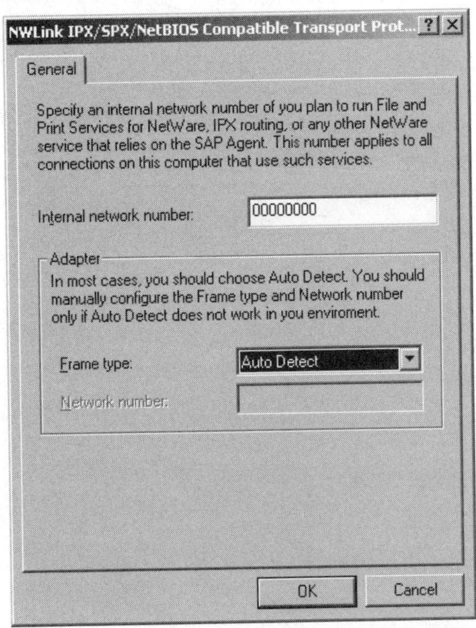

FIGURE 20.2
Setting the frame type during install

After you reboot the system, Windows 2000 Professional attempts to log on to Novell for the first time, as shown in Figure 20.3.

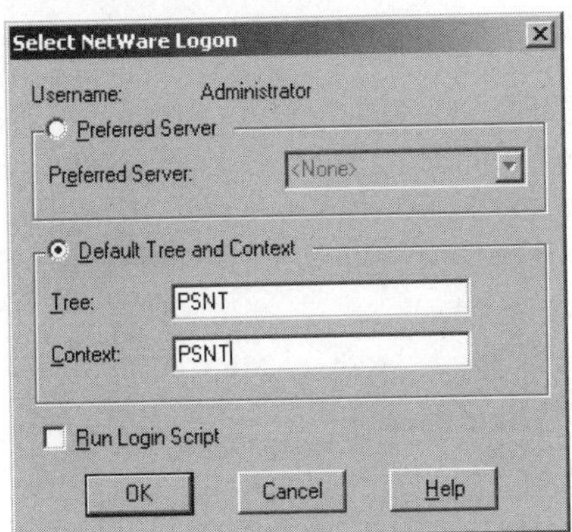

FIGURE 20.3
Logging on to Novell for the first time

With the client software provided by Microsoft, you can either log on to a Novell 3 bindery by clicking the Preferred Server radio button shown in Figure 20.3 or log on to a 4 NDS tree by clicking the Default Tree And Context radio button. If you are going to log on to an NDS tree, do not provide the parameter codes before each option (that is, omit the o= and the cn=). You can see an example of these selections in Figure 20.4.

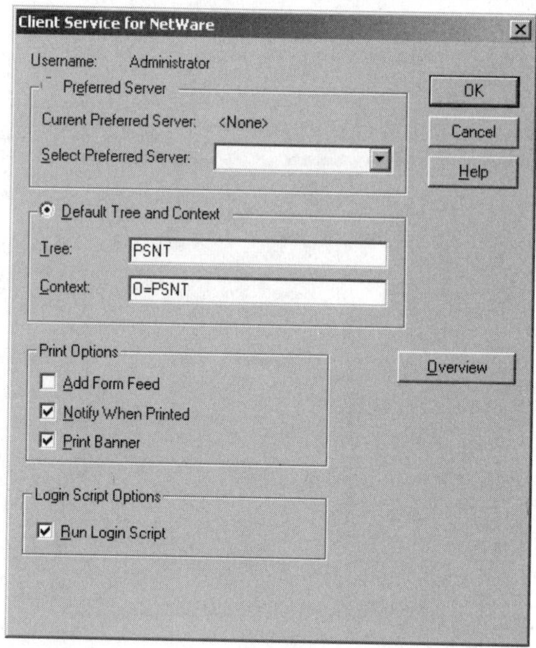

FIGURE 20.4
Configuring the Client Service for NetWare

It is the nature of being a client in a networked environment that you can log on to one server one day and log on to another server on another day. If you are an administrator, you can switch between servers more frequently. You can change the NetWare server that you log on to with great ease. In My Computer, click Control Panel. Now that you have installed the Client Service for NetWare, you will notice the CSNW icon in Control Panel. By clicking this icon, you can adjust your settings and the NetWare servers or tree that you log on to, as shown in Figure 20.4.

From this screen you can specify or change the server, or you can log on to a NetWare 4/5 NDS tree. In addition, you can set the print settings. The three options are as follows:

Add Form Feed Adds a form feed to the end of each print job

Notify When Printed Displays a screen message when your print job finishes printing

Print Banner Adds a cover page to the beginning of each print job, specifying who printed the job and the date and time

Any settings that you make here will apply to any Novell print queue that this Windows 2000 Professional computer accesses.

The final option in CSNW determines whether the system logon script that resides on the NetWare server will run. This feature will run either a 3 logon script or a 4/5 logon script.

Using Novell Commands Available from Windows 2000 Professional

At the Windows 2000 Professional computer, you can open a command line and run a number of Novell commands by changing the directory to the public directory of the NetWare server. Here are some of the commands, in simple alphabetic order:

chkvol	help	rconsole	settts
colorpal	listdir	remove	slist
dspace	map	revoke	syscon
fconsole	ncopy	rights	tlist
filer	ndir	security	userlist
flag	pconsole	send	volinfo
flagdir	psc	session	whoami
grant	pstat	setpass	

You can also run NetWare-aware applications (some of them, anyway) with some support programs. Windows-based, NetWare-aware applications may require files `netware.386`, `nwcalls.dll`, and `nwnetapi.dll`. They are in your System32 directory.

Novell supplies a file called `nwipxspx.dll` that some client-server applications depend on; Gupta SQLBase and Lotus Notes are two examples.

WARNING You must map a drive to the NetWare volume where these utilities are located in order to run them. Windows 2000 Professional will not run them correctly from a UNC path.

Printing to Novell Printers

Earlier in this chapter, I described the print options that are available after you install the Client Service for NetWare. To connect to a NetWare print queue, follow these steps:

1. Choose Start ➢ Settings ➢ Printers to open the Printers folder.
2. Click Add Printer to start the Add Printer Wizard.
3. At the Welcome screen, click Next to open the Local Or Network Printer screen.
4. Click Network Printer, and then click Next to open the Select The Printer Port Screen.
5. Select a printer port, and click Next.

6. At the Printer Selection dialog box, select the printer manufacturer and printer model.
7. Have the appropriate driver CD or disk ready, or know the location where the driver is stored. At the Printer Driver dialog box, insert the disk driver when prompted, and click OK.
8. Click Finish. This will complete the printer installation.

Enabling Long Filename Support on the Novell Server

To enable long filename support on the NetWare server, you need to load the OS/2 name space support. Here's how you do it:

1. At the NetWare server prompt, type the following:

   ```
   Load os2
   add name space os2 to volume sys
   ```
2. Add the following to the `startup.ncf` file:

   ```
   load os2
   ```
3. Down the server (that is, bring down the server by typing **Down** at the server prompt), and when you see the C: prompt, copy the `os2.nam` file from the NetWare disks or CD-ROM to the same directory as `server.exe`.
4. Type **SERVER** at the C: prompt to restart the NetWare server.

Choosing a 32-Bit Novell Solution

Some of you may be familiar with the 32-bit drivers for NT that Novell provides. You may choose to use the Novell solution if you need to ensure driver compatibility with NetWare. Choosing this option is also preferable if you attach to different types of servers that are using IPX as their primary protocol.

TIP Client Service for NetWare may talk directly to Novell servers with few problems, but if you need to talk to many types of servers using the IPX protocol, you really want to use the NetWare client.

NOTE Remember that this is one time when you cannot use the NT 4 version of this service. Go to Novell's Web site, `www.novell.com`, to download the latest and greatest version of this software for Windows 2000 Professional.

The Client32 solution provides another nice selling point. Novell has a package of network tools they call Zero Effort Networking or *Z.E.N.works*. Z.E.N.works lets you gain complete control over desktop and user management from the NetWare 4 and 5 environments. It's actually similar in many ways to Microsoft's Zero Administration Windows (ZAW) initiative in that it uses policies and login scripts to manage users and computers. But in the case of Z.E.N.works, the policies are being applied based on NDS objects across all client platforms, not just one version of Windows.

The full version of Z.E.N.works provides several useful help desk functions as well, including a ticketing system for reporting problems and remote control ability. The version that is supplied with NetWare 5 is the "light" version, which includes everything except the help desk tools and is supported by all the current Client32 platforms.

Client32 integrates very well with Windows 2000 Professional, offering a single login that can be configured between the NetWare and Windows 2000 Professional environments. Figure 20.5 shows the login screen offered by Novell's Client32 software.

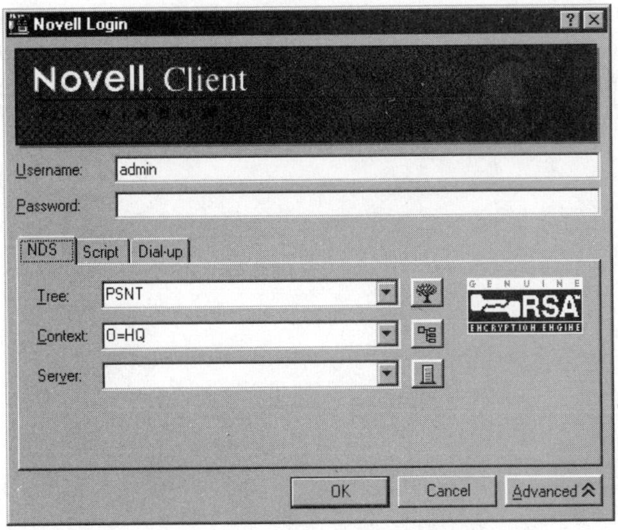

FIGURE 20.5
The Client32 login screen lets you log on to both NetWare and Windows 2000 Professional networks.

Accessing NetWare Servers from Windows 2000 Professional Clients

If you install the client software for NetWare that comes with Windows 2000 Professional, you will be given the option of processing the NetWare login script. The login scripts usually contain map statements such as the following:

```
map z:=den02\sys:public
```

This command will make the Z drive represent the public directory on a NetWare server known as DEN02. This result would occur on most DOS client machines. But Windows 2000 Professional clients map only to the root directory, regardless of the map statements. That is to say, if you processed this same statement from a Windows 2000 Professional client, the Z drive would be DEN02\SYS:, not the "public" directory. The fix for this is easy to implement; instead of using the `Map` command, use the `Map root` command, as follows:

```
Map root z:=den02\sys:public
```

Now the public directory becomes the root directory of Z. If you want to get something from the public directory, simply go to `Z:\` (the root directory of Z).

Summary

That's it for the relatively simple task of connecting to an existing NetWare network with Windows 2000 Professional. In this chapter, I've introduced you to NetWare terminology, showed you how to connect to a NetWare printer, and how to log on to a NetWare system.

CHAPTER 21

Secure Telecommuting

FEATURING:

In this chapter, we'll take a look at a common scenario—a corporate user who wants (or needs) to telecommute a portion of the time and needs to do so as securely as possible. We'll look at some of the common threats that a telecommuting user must face, along with what Windows 2000 Professional can do to protect against those threats.

Telecommuting Overview: Risks and Rewards

As telecommuting becomes more commonplace, the risks and rewards associated with it are becoming more apparent. The rewards are obvious: no dealing with traffic jams, being able to work in your bathrobe (if you want to), no office distractions, and so on. The risks, however, are a little less obvious. One of the biggest problems is the risk involved when corporate data is moved outside the corporation's walls.

The risks of telecommuting fall into three distinct areas: the interception of corporate data, the impersonation of an authorized user, and the potential abduction of confidential data. It's interesting to look at the irony of the situation. Corporations are increasing their efforts to secure their data within their walls, but at the same time they are allowing more and more employees to telecommute. I can imagine that people who want to steal corporate data will eventually start to focus their efforts on telecommuting workers instead of the corporation's main systems, because most telecommuters make much easier targets.

The interception of data is an obvious threat: as data passes from your Windows 2000 Professional computer into your corporation's main systems, someone eavesdrops on the data transmission and reads the data. If your transmission is crossing the Internet, it will travel through many systems outside your company's control before it reaches its final destination. The same is true with dial-up modems, although the risks are slightly less as your traffic is being carried over the telephone network (a bit more secure). Still, risks do exist, and the main way to deal with the risk of data interception is through data encryption between the source and destination computers. I'll talk about some of the ways you can protect against data interception by encrypting transmissions leaving your Windows 2000 Professional computer.

The impersonation of a user is also a threat. If someone obtains your username and password, and if your account has dial-in access, that person can log in to your company's systems under your account, effectively, impersonating you. Although the problem of account/password discovery happens within the corporation's walls as well (for example, users writing passwords down on yellow sticky notes and sticking them on their monitors), it becomes more of a problem when a user's account is granted dial-in access. The pitfalls of this type of security breach are many—corruption of data, deletion of data, abduction of data, and the introduction of malicious viruses, just to name a few. You can take steps to prevent user impersonation. Some of them are built into Windows 2000 Professional, and others are security measures that your corporation must implement, and we'll take a look at a number of possible solutions later in this chapter.

Finally, the risk of having data abducted is also a threat. Corporate espionage is a significant problem in many large organizations (although corporations usually keep silent about it since reporting it would have a negative impact on the company's stock price). Again, although corporations are taking significant steps to increase the security of their data within the company's walls, they are allowing users to keep copies of some data on their own home computers or laptops. Instead of targeting a corporate network, it will eventually be easier for someone to target a telecommuting user if they want to obtain a copy of sensitive corporate data. After all, which would be more difficult—breaking into a company and trying to steal a computer, or breaking into someone's home and stealing their computer or laptop? We'll take a look at some of the utilities provided in Windows 2000 Professional that will allow you to secure data on your system so that even in the worst-case scenario—your computer is completely stolen—your company's sensitive data won't fall into the wrong hands.

Protecting Against the Interception of Data

If you are telecommuting, odds are you are connected to your corporation's network in one of three ways: directly—through some sort of wide-area network connection, indirectly—through an analog dial-up networking connection, or through a high-speed digital connection or possibly a Virtual Private Network (VPN). No matter how you are connected, you can take steps to secure your communications.

Securing RAS Dial-in Sessions

The dial-in scenario is probably familiar if you've been using computers for any length of time. You install a modem, you define a dial-up networking entry to call into a remote network, and then your computer initiates a connection over your phone line. This is a relatively secure means of communicating with a remote network, but it still could be compromised: someone could tap into your phone line and record the data conversations traveling back and forth between your computer and the remote computer. Therefore, the primary means to protect RAS (remote access server) dial-in sessions is via encryption. Windows 2000 Professional makes it easy to implement (and require) encryption on any dial-up networking connection.

NOTE Encryption is the process of encoding information so that it is secure from unauthorized access. Decryption is the reverse of this process.

Assuming you have a working dial-up networking connection, setting up encryption is relatively easy. Follow these steps:

1. Choose Start ➢ Settings ➢ Network And Dial-Up Connections to open the Network And Dial-Up Connections folder.
2. Right-click the icon for your dial-up connection, and choose Properties from the shortcut menu to open the Properties dialog box for that connection.
3. Click the Security tab, click the Advanced (Custom Settings) option button, and then click the Settings button to open the Advanced Security Settings dialog box:

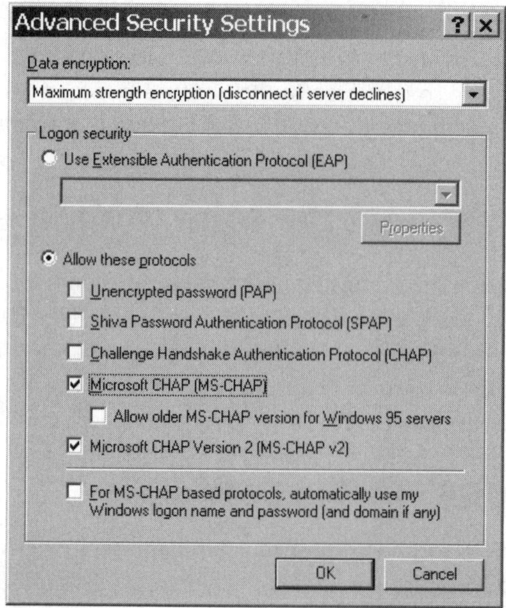

You'll notice that the very first item in the Advanced Security Settings dialog box is the Data Encryption drop-down list box. This option has four possible settings:

No Encryption Allowed This setting will attempt to force your computer into a nonencrypted communication session. If the remote system that you are dialing into will allow any type of connection (encrypted or not), you will be able to connect. However, if the remote system will accept only encrypted connections, you will not be able to connect.

Optional Encryption This setting will defer to whatever is required by the remote system you are calling into. If the remote system does not require encryption, this setting will let you connect. If the remote system does require encryption, this setting will also let you connect.

Require Encryption Enabling this setting will implement a 40-bit encryption channel between your Windows 2000 Professional computer and the remote system. If the remote system cannot support encryption, your session will immediately disconnect with an error message similar to the one in Figure 21.1.

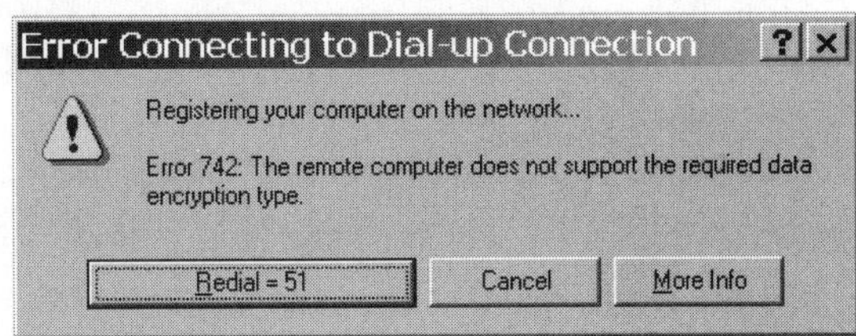

FIGURE 21.1 *You'll see this disconnection error message if the remote system doesn't support encryption.*

Maximum Strength Encryption Enabling this setting will require a strong (128-bit) encryption channel between your Windows 2000 Professional computer and the remote system. You will see this option only if you purchased Windows 2000 Professional in the United States. If the remote system cannot support strong encryption, your session will immediately disconnect with an error message (similar to the one in Figure 21.1).

Enabling a data encryption option ensures that all your communications are kept private, even if someone is able to intercept them.

To enable encryption on your dial-up connection, select one of the protocols in the Logon Security section of the Advanced Security Settings dialog box. Currently, only MS-CHAP, MS-CHAP v2, or EAP authentication will allow for successful encryption.

Virtual Private Networking Connections

Virtual Private Networking (VPN) connections are—by definition—meant to be private. VPNs were originally developed as a means to route confidential, private data across untrusted networks. As a result of the reach and popularity of the Internet, VPNs have enjoyed a considerable amount of success in the current market.

One of the better analogies I've found for explaining the concepts of a Virtual Private Network is to refer to them as "pipes." To conceptualize VPNs, think of two pipes, one large and one small. Now, imagine that the small pipe actually runs *inside* of the large one. It starts and ends at the same places the large pipe does, and it can carry materials on its own completely independent of whatever is happening in the large pipe. As a matter of fact, the only thing the small pipe is dependent on the large pipe for is the determination of the start and end points. Beyond that, the small pipe can operate independently of the large pipe in terms of direction of travel, materials it carries, and so on.

To add another layer to this analogy, let's assume that the large pipe is made of a transparent material and that the small pipe is made of metal. Anyone taking a look at the pipe-within-a-pipe would easily be able to see whatever is moving through the outside (large) pipe. However, whatever is traveling through the inside pipe would remain a mystery.

If this is starting to make sense, you should be thinking to yourself that the large pipe represents the unsecured network (that is the Internet) and that the small pipe represents the Virtual Private Network. VPN is a way of tunneling data packets through a connection that already exists but that can't be used on its own for privacy reasons. Obviously, the Internet is a perfect example of a network that often can't be used on its own for privacy reasons.

To establish a VPN connection to your corporate network, your company must have set up a VPN server, capable of receiving those connections. (More information on setting up a Virtual Private Networking server is available in *Mastering Windows 2000 Server*, available from Sybex.) If your company has set up a VPN server for you to dial in to, you will need to know the answers to the following questions:

- Which authentication type does it require?
- Which encryption strength does it require?
- What is the IP address or DNS (Domain Name Service) name to connect to?

Once you know the answer to these questions, you can set up a VPN connection on your Windows 2000 Professional computer.

Since a VPN (typically) runs over the Internet, the first thing you must have on your system is a functional Internet connection. Whether your connection is a dial-up modem or a dedicated cable/xDSL connection is mostly irrelevant. Assuming you have an Internet connection in place, you can easily create a VPN connection. Follow these steps:

1. Choose Start ➢ Settings ➢ Network And Dial-Up Connections to open the Network And Dial-Up Connections folder.
2. Double-click Make New Connection to start the Network Connection Wizard.

3. Click Next to open the Network Connection Type screen:

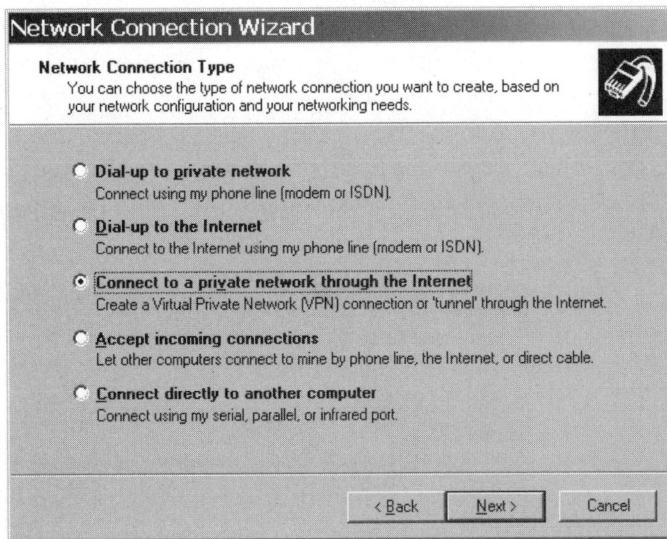

4. Select the Connect To A Private Network Through The Internet option, and then click Next to open the Public Network screen:

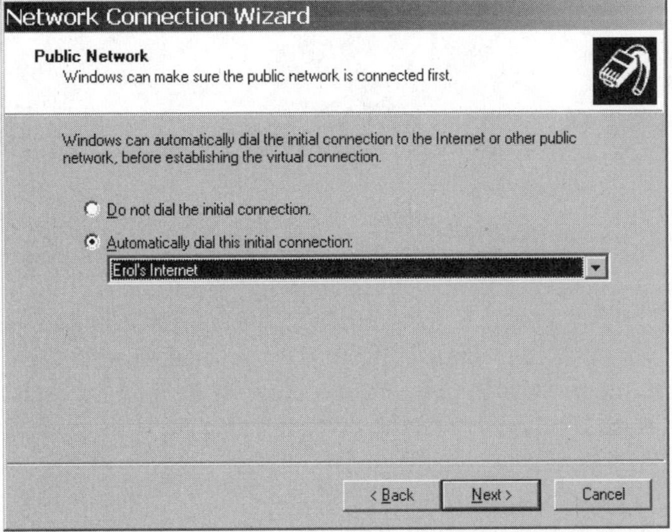

As I discussed earlier, connecting to a VPN (over the Internet) requires that a functional Internet connection be in place before establishing the VPN connection. Now, your connection to the Internet will most likely be one of two types—either a dial-up connection (such as a modem or an ISDN [Integrated Services Digital Network] line) or a dedicated connection that you do not need to dial (that is, it's always there, always

on). If you are using a dial-up connection to connect to the Internet, you can instruct Windows 2000 Professional to automatically establish that connection first before initiating your VPN connection by selecting the Automatically Dial This Initial Connection option. Select your Internet dial-up connection from the drop-down list, and then any time you launch your VPN connection, Windows 2000 Professional will automatically log you in to the Internet. If you have a direct connection to the Internet (cable, xDSL, other), simply skip this step by selecting the Do Not Dial The Initial Connection option. When you are finished with this step, click Next to open the Destination Address screen:

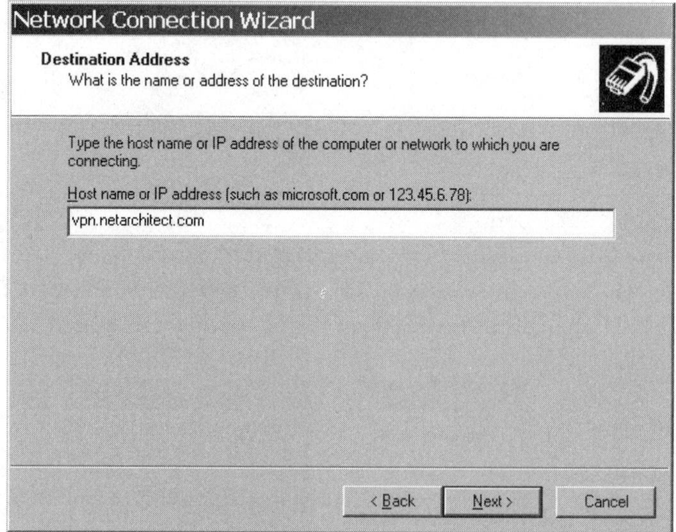

Since Virtual Private Networks function over the Internet, you will connect to a VPN either via an IP address or a DNS name (which resolves into an IP address). Enter the name of your target VPN server, or enter the IP address of the destination system, and then click Next to finish your VPN connection.

The final step of the Network Connection Wizard is to specify whether you want your VPN connection available only for yourself or for any user who logs in to your Windows 2000 Professional computer. Make the appropriate choice, and then click Next. You have now successfully created a VPN connection.

Now, if your corporation has implemented their VPN server correctly, it should be set up so that you can't connect unless your connection is encrypted. Assuming that is the case, you may need to set the appropriate encryption level for your VPN connection the same way you would set one for a RAS connection (as discussed earlier in the chapter).

NOTE You won't be able to connect securely to a Microsoft VPN unless you use an encrypted authentication such as: <<< >>>.

Once you've got everything correctly defined on your system, you should be able to double-click your VPN icon on your Windows 2000 Professional system and get connected—securely—to your corporate network. Once you're connected, you should be able to navigate throughout your company's corporate network just as if you were sitting in the office.

VPN Performance Considerations

Our look at Virtual Private Networking wouldn't be complete without taking a bit of time to discuss performance issues. Although Virtual Private Networking is a neat technology, some performance drawbacks are associated with it.

In the right set of circumstances, Virtual Private Networking can provide fast, reliable, and secure connections to your company's network from across the Internet (or another unsecured network). However, in the wrong set of circumstances, Virtual Private Networking can make an already slow dial-up connection seem even slower.

So what are the right circumstances? In my professional opinion, high-speed connectivity on the corporate side of your VPN, and preferably high-speed connectivity on both the corporate side and your personal connection. On occasions when I have been able to implement VPN circuits at locations with a T-1 or better available at both the company and client ends, performance has been wonderful and the connections reliable. However, due to the protocol overhead involved with PPTP (Point-to-Point Tunneling Protocol) and L2TP (Layer 2 Tunneling Protocol) and the inherent latency of the Internet, don't have high-performance expectations if you are planning to implement a VPN with a dial-up modem.

If you are using a dial-in modem, nothing will ever be faster than a direct dial-in connection. Period. Dial-in connections are simple. There's no encryption, and there's no VPN protocol overhead involved. Plus, your traffic does not have to cross through a countless number of routers before reaching its destination. Simply put, with a direct dial-in connection your packets go out of your computer, across the phone line, and directly into the corporate network.

If you are implementing a VPN connection over a dial-up modem, your packets must first be encrypted. They must then be bundled into a VPN protocol and then bundled again into another TCP/IP packet. After that, they are transmitted across the Internet, where they will probably pass through anywhere from 4 to 12 routers before reaching the VPN server at your corporation. Once the VPN server receives the packet, it must unpackage all the payload and then decrypt it. Although computers can do this quickly, it does add overhead to the process.

How much overhead? Well, there are no official numbers to go by, but I'd say you can expect a decrease in your performance ranging anywhere from 10 to 50 percent. Now, without getting into all the technical details, it is worthwhile to note that this isn't entirely Microsoft's fault; after all, they can't be blamed for the fact that the Internet can be inherently slow at times (or can they?). However, even with the worst-case scenario of a 50 percent reduction in performance, if there is 1Mb worth of bandwidth available on each side of the VPN, the effective speeds of the network are still roughly in the 500Kbps range—a very respectable amount. However, if you're using a 56K modem on your Windows 2000 Professional workstation (which probably won't connect much faster than 48Kbps), you can easily see how a 50 percent performance penalty can make a connection go from "slow" to "unusable."

Everything in life is a trade-off, and it will be up to you to decide if this will work adequately enough for your needs. After all, what is adequate to one person might be great to another and unacceptable to yet another. In either case, expect a performance penalty when implementing Virtual Private Networking and plan accordingly.

Protecting Against the Impersonation of a User

Compromising a valid user's account name and password is a network administrator's worst nightmare. An unauthorized user—posing as a valid one—can steal, compromise, or sabotage data from the company's network. If that user has remote dial-in access capabilities as well, the problem is even worse as someone can dial in from anywhere in the world and make trouble for the network. Therefore, it is important to prevent your user ID and password from falling into the wrong hands.

Common Sense Guidelines

It still amazes me how many times I run into users who have written down their usernames and passwords on a yellow sticky note and then stuck the note to their monitor. Talk about a security nightmare! Even if people don't stick their passwords on their monitors, users have a tendency to write them down on cards in their wallets or put them into an organizer such as a Palm. The first measure of good security is to never write your username and password down. If, for some reason, you must write them down, at least write them on separate sheets of paper and store them in different places. Don't store them with each other.

Another common security problem is users who choose passwords that are easily guessed. For example, it's common for many people to use simple things for passwords, such as what type of car they drive, their favorite sport they play or a favorite athlete, their mother's maiden name, their middle name, and so on. All those types of passwords can be easily guessed if someone is determined enough.

The best types of passwords are complex combinations that have nothing whatsoever to do with you. You can make your passwords a bit more complex—but still easily remembered—by substituting letters, numbers, or symbols in place of actual words. This is the same type of logic that people use to spell out phrases on custom license plates. For example, you could use the phrase "No soup for you today!" as a password (with all due respects to the *Seinfeld* "Soup Nazi" episode) by using "nosoup4u2day". Such a password is still easily remembered, but is much harder to guess. Other suggestions for substitutions are:

- Instead of the word "to" or "too", use the number 2.
- Instead of the word "for", use the number 4.
- Instead of the word "at", use the @ symbol.
- Instead of the word "and", use the & symbol.
- Instead of the word "you", use the letter U.
- Instead of the word "are", use the letter R.

I'm sure you get the point. The object is to keep the password something that you can remember while making it difficult to compromise. I've had good success using this formula.

Encrypted Authentication

If you are dialing into a remote network—either via a direct dial-in line or a VPN connection—Windows 2000 Professional must pass your user credentials (your username and password) to the remote system for authentication. The remote system will then check those credentials to determine if your account has been granted dial-in access. But how does Windows 2000 Professional send your credentials to the remote computer?

The answer can be found in the Advanced Security Settings dialog box. As you can see in that dialog box, Windows 2000 Professional can send your user credentials to the remote system in a number of ways, as long as the remote system is able to understand. Some of these authentication methods are encrypted, and some are not.

Extensible Authentication Protocol (EAP) Since security and authentication is a constantly changing field, embedding authentication schemes into an operating system is impractical at times. To solve this problem, Microsoft has included support for Extensible Authentication Protocol, which is simply a means of "plugging in" new authentication schemes as needed. Presumably, any type of extensible authentication would be encrypted, but that could vary from one case to the next.

Unencrypted Password (PAP) Password Authentication Protocol (PAP) is one of the first options and is also one of the least secure. It is no more secure than a simple conversation from your server saying "What is your name and password?" to the client, the client responding with "My name is Doug and my password is 'let-me-in'." There is no encryption of authentication credentials whatsoever.

Shiva Password Authentication Protocol (SPAP) SPAP is an encrypted password authentication method used by Shiva LAN Rover clients and servers. Windows 2000 Professional can provide SPAP authentication if needed.

Challenge Handshake Authentication Protocol (CHAP) Defined in RFC (Request for Comments) 1334, and later revised in RFC 1994, CHAP is a means of encrypting authentication sessions between a client and server. Since this protocol is defined by an RFC, it enjoys a broad base of support among many operating systems and other devices.

Microsoft CHAP (v1 and v2) (MS-CHAP) Microsoft's derivative of CHAP, or Challenge Handshake Authentication Protocol. An encrypted authentication method that also allows you to encrypt an entire dial-up session, not just the original authentication, which is important when it comes to setting up virtual private networking sessions.

Caller-ID/Callback Security

Although Caller-ID/Callback Security isn't an option for Windows 2000 Professional, it is worth discussing in terms of security. Simply put, let's assume that you have dial-in access to your corporate network, and the worst-case scenario comes true—someone obtains your user ID and password. Caller-ID and callback security can still provide your corporation with some level of protection. Both features work by verifying that you are actually calling from an authorized phone number—a phone number that has been predefined by the administrators of your corporate network.

Caller-ID Security If the dial-in systems on your corporate network can support it, your account can be set up with a Caller-ID–based security option. In this scenario, when the computers on your corporate network receive your incoming call, they take note of the phone number. Once you provide a username and password authentication, your username is checked for an associated Caller-ID number. If the two numbers match, your call is granted. If the two numbers don't match, your call is denied. Therefore, even if someone has your username and password, this type of security can protect your corporation's computers. The drawback is that whenever you want to connect to your company's network, you must be calling in from the approved number.

Callback Security This functions in a similar manner to Caller-ID security, but is a bit more secure (I've read that Caller-ID information can be spoofed with the correct equipment). With callback security enabled, your user account is associated with a call-back number. When you initiate a dial-in session to your company's network, you will provide your username and password. The system that verifies your dial-in credentials will see that you have a call-back number associated with your account and immediately disconnect you. After it disconnects you, it will then initiate a call to your system and establish the connection. This is a very secure method of verifying a dial-in user; however, it comes at the price of having to always log in from the same phone number.

If you are concerned that your account credentials might fall into the wrong hands, talk to your network administrators to see if either of these options are available for your dial-in system. Windows 2000 Server supports both of them.

Third-Party Products: SecurID, SafeWord

Although this is a book about Windows 2000 Professional, I want to mention two products that fall into the "extremely cool" category of security products: SecurID from RSA Security and SafeWord from Secure Computing.

The nature of these two products is similar—they are what's known as a "second factor" authentication method. What that means is that your "first factor" of authentication—your username and password—is not good enough to obtain access to a resource; you must authenticate yourself in another (second) manner before access is granted. You can think of a second factor authentication as being similar to having two different locks on a door—a regular one and a deadbolt. You won't be granted access until you can provide the correct authentication (a key) for both.

How they work—from a user perspective—is quite simple. When you start a dial-up networking session, you will are prompted for your username and password. That is your first authentication. After successfully negotiating a dial-in connection to your corporation's network, you are then prompted for a second authentication—a second "password," if you will. What's unique about this second password is that it's a different password every time.

SecurID works through a small key fob that has a digital readout on it. Every 60 seconds, a new number appears on the readout. The key fob is given to a user and must be used to gain access to the company's network. Let's take a look at a typical example.

Let's assume that a user named Wendy is trying to dial in to her company's network. Now, Wendy has a password for her account—let's assume that it's "arlington". Wendy also has a SecurID key fob that has been assigned to her. At the moment she is trying to sign in, her key fob is displaying the six-digit number 378265. As an added measure, Wendy also has a four-digit "pin" number assigned to her. Let's assume that she used 1234 for her pin number.

When Wendy dials in, she'll type in her username and password (wendy / arlington) just as in a normal dial-up connection. Her Windows 2000 Professional system will dial in to the company's network and negotiate a connection. Once the connection is negotiated, Wendy will be prompted for her SecurID passcode. At the moment she is logging in, the correct passcode for her will be "1234378265". Her passcode is validated by a SecurID server within the company's network, and if the passcode is correct, she is granted access to the network. The SafeWord system also functions on a similar, one-time password concept.

As you can see, this is an *extremely* secure means of authenticating a user. If someone manages to obtain Wendy's username and password, they are useless without her SecurID key fob. And even if someone were to obtain the key fob itself, it would still be useless without knowing Wendy's individual pin number.

Protecting Against the Abduction of Data

OK, I'll admit it, the word "abduction" sounds a bit too much like an *X-Files* episode, but the word just fits so well with the concept I am trying to get across. In any case, the abduction of data is simply someone without authorization copying corporate data off your system. You know, your typical corporate espionage stuff.

As I stated earlier in the chapter, I can imagine that this will become more and more of a problem as companies allow increasing amounts of data outside their corporate walls. After all, who is it more difficult to steal data from—the well-guarded and physically secured corporate network, or Joe the account executive walking out of the building late at night with his laptop? A quick bop on Joe's head and a grab of the laptop would compromise all the data stored on the laptop.

Or would it? Microsoft has added new encryption technologies into Windows 2000 Professional specifically to address this type of situation. The encrypting file system (EFS) can ensure that no one other than you will be able to read your encrypted files if your computer is ever stolen.

The encryption capabilities available in Windows 2000 Professional (right out of the box) are very good. And with a few additional precautions, you can make sure that they are absolutely secure—that no one will be able to ever read your encrypted files.

NOTE It goes without saying that if someone gets hold of your username and password, all bets are off. As far as Windows 2000 Professional is concerned, if someone logs in with your username and password, it must be you! Windows 2000 Professional will gladly decrypt all your files in that scenario. So, it's critical to make sure that your password is not discovered.

Encrypting Files with EFS

Although I'm not usually one to bestow outlandish praise on Microsoft for their products, I have to admit that they've really hit a home run with the encrypting file system (EFS) included with Windows 2000 Professional. Encrypting data is merely a matter of a few clicks of the mouse, and an entire folder or folder structure can be protected from prying eyes.

Having said that, you should try to follow a few "best practices" principles when working with EFS:

Don't encrypt the Windows 2000 Professional folders. This would have a significant impact on your system—most likely it wouldn't boot. Fortunately, EFS will always try to prevent you from encrypting system files, but you probably shouldn't even try to in the first place.

Don't encrypt your My Documents folder. This runs 100 percent contrary to Microsoft's suggested practices. The reason I recommend that you *don't* encrypt your My Documents folder is because there are almost no visual clues in the Windows interface that a file or folder has been encrypted. I've already read a few accounts of users who were "playing around" with EFS and followed Microsoft's suggestions to encrypt the My Documents folder, but months later they forgot that they had done it. Because of some sort of failure (in one instance, a simple HAL [Hardware Abstraction Layer] upgrade), the users reloaded Windows 2000 Professional. Guess what? Since they hadn't taken the additional step to back up their recovery keys, all their documents were irrecoverable. Gone. Personally, I like to make a folder called Encrypted Stuff, which gives me an obvious visual reminder that anything within that folder will be encrypted.

Encrypt your Temp folder. Your temporary folder (which can usually be found by typing **SET** at a command prompt and looking for the TEMP= and TMP= folders) is often a repository for fragments of your data, documents, and so on. Sometimes programs don't properly clean up after themselves, and they leave fragments of your files in this folder. If this folder is encrypted, no leftover fragments could be used by anyone else.

Encrypt entire folders, not just files. As I mentioned earlier, I like to make a special folder on my machine and call it Encrypted Stuff—then I just copy everything into it that I want protected.

Encrypting files and folders is really quite simple. Follow these steps:

1. Right-click the Start button, and choose Explore to open Windows Explorer.
2. Right-click the file or folder, and choose Properties from the shortcut menu to open the Properties dialog box for that item.

3. Click the Advanced button to open the Advanced Attributes dialog box:

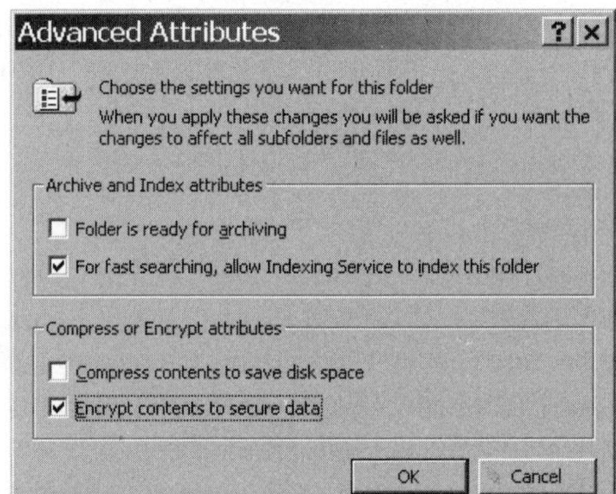

   Notice the two check boxes at the bottom of this dialog box: Compress Contents To Save Disk Space and Encrypt Contents To Secure Data. These two items are mutually exclusive, meaning that if you compress a file you can't encrypt it, and if you encrypt a file, you can't compress it.

4. If necessary, uncompress the file, and check the Encrypt Contents To Secure Data check box.
5. Click OK, and then click OK again to encrypt the file.

It almost seems too easy, doesn't it? Well, don't take my word for it—try logging in as someone else and see if you can read the file. You can't. Even if you have full access to the file under another user account, you won't be able to open the file, copy it, or do anything else with it. Only the user account that encrypted the file can decrypt it. Well, almost the only one...

The Recovery Agent

You're probably wondering the first thing that I wondered when it came to encrypting my files: OK, but what if something goes wrong? What if my account is accidentally deleted? What if my machine crashes? Will I lose my data?

Well, your data—once it is encrypted—will stay encrypted on your system and on any backups that you make. The only person that can decrypt the data is either you or your designated recovery agent.

Now, who is your designated recovery agent? Well, that depends on how your Windows 2000 Professional system is configured. If your system is a member of a Windows 2000 Professional domain, your recovery agent will most likely be the domain administrator or another administrative-type user. If your Windows 2000 Professional system is not a member of a domain or is a member of an NT 4 domain, your recovery agent is the local Administrator account on your machine.

The encrypting file system will not encrypt files unless a designated recovery agent is in place. So—what does that mean in your case? It means that by default, another account (either on your system or in your domain) will also be able to decrypt your files.

Now, if you are participating in a domain, this is probably a good thing, as your organization probably wouldn't appreciate it if you simply took their data and encrypted it so that no one else could ever use it. You could, inadvertently, hold your company's data hostage since no one else would be able to decrypt it but you. Of course, there's always the "What if you get hit by a bus..." analogy that goes along with that problem. So, there must be a designated recovery agent, and your domain administrators should (hopefully) take care of that in advance. You might want to check with them to make sure that they have the necessary capabilities in place to decrypt anything that you choose to encrypt, in a worst-case (that is, got-hit-by-the-bus) scenario.

But, what if you're on a stand-alone machine? Microsoft recommends exporting the recovery agent's private key to a (secure) floppy disk and then removing it from your system. In that case, if your computer is ever stolen, the recovery agent's private key is not stolen along with it, so no decryption can take place through the recovery agent.

Exporting the Recovery Agent Private Key

To export the private key from your recovery agent, follow these steps:

1. Log on to your computer as the local Administrator account (not just as an account with administrative access).
2. Choose Start ➢ Run to open the Run dialog box.
3. In the Open box, type **`secpol.msc`** to open the Local Security Settings window.
4. In the Tree pane, expand the Public Key Policies folder, and then select the Encrypted Data Recovery Agents folder.
5. In the pane on the right, right-click the name in the Issued To column, and choose All Tasks ➢ Export to start the Certificate Export Wizard.

The Certificate Export Wizard will walk you through the process to export a certificate from your system. As a part of the export process, you can export only the certificate or the certificate and the private key. Your system won't be adequately secured unless you remove both items from your computer, so select Yes, Export The Private Key in the second screen of the Wizard, and then click Next.

The next step of the Wizard allows you to select a file format for exporting your recovery agent certificate and private key. For most purposes, the default format (Personal Information Exchange) will be acceptable. I would also recommend selecting the Delete Private Key If The Export Is Successful option. Click Next to proceed to the next step of the Wizard.

One of the final steps is to choose a password to protect the keys you will be exporting. The password you choose here will be required by anyone who tries to import the certificate and private key from this file, so make sure that it is something you will be able to remember. Without this password, you won't be able to reimport your recovery agent key in the event of an emergency. Choose a password, and then click Next to continue.

The last screen of the Wizard will ask you for a path to use for storing the exported certificate and private key. You can store the file on a floppy disk or on another medium, but you must do everything possible to make sure that the file is never lost or destroyed.

Restoring the Recovery Agent Private Key

If ever the time comes that you must reinstall this key into your system, the installation is actually much easier. Again, you will want to make sure that you are logged into your computer as Administrator—as that is the key we previously removed.

To begin the import process, all you have to do is simply double-click the export file you created. That will launch the Certificate Import Wizard, which will walk you through the process to reimport your exported certificate and private key. After double-clicking a certificate file, you will be prompted to confirm the name of the file you are importing. Confirm that you are importing the correct file, and then click Next.

At the next step of the Wizard, you will have to re-enter the password you will need to enter the password you assigned to your export file. If you do not have the correct password, you will not be able to import the certificate file and the private key. Enter the correct password, and then click Next to continue.

By default, Windows 2000 Professional can automatically try to determine where your certificates should be placed on your system. However, some of Microsoft's online help documents indicate that you should not choose this default option—instead, you should select the Place All Certificates In The Following Store radio button, and then click Browse to select an appropriate store to use. In most circumstances, you will want to import the certificate into the Personal store.

Click Finish to finish the Certificate Import Wizard, and your Administrator's certificate and private key should now be restored onto your system.

Summary

In this chapter, I talked about the security of corporate data once it moves outside your corporation's walls. I covered how to encrypt the data as it is transferred to your computer and even how to encrypt the data once it is stored on your computer. I've talked about how to protect your account credentials and proposed solutions that you can provide to your corporate network administrators if an additional level of security is necessary.

PART IV

Advanced Techniques and Troubleshooting

Learn To:

- *Use VBScript*
- *Use the Windows scripting host*
- *Support new hardware and install drivers*
- *Fix Windows 2000 Professional when it breaks*
- *Customize advanced options and troubleshoot*

CHAPTER 22

HTML and VBScript

FEATURING:

As you know by now, on its surface, Windows 2000 Professional looks much like Windows 98. Of course, there's a lot beyond the new look. The inclusion of Internet Explorer 5 is probably the least important of the new features. The really new element is the integration of the browser and its function with the operating system. This integration isn't limited to Web-like folders and the single-click activation of the icons. As I'll discuss in this and the next three chapters, the technology that's made the Web such a popular place is now used by the operating system itself.

To exploit the integration of Web technologies into the Windows operating system, you need to understand Web pages: how to design them, how to activate them, and how scripting languages relate to the Web. One way to personalize your Desktop is to place custom-designed Web pages on it (which means you need to understand the structure of a Web page). To design Web pages that interact with the user, you need to be able to script them with VBScript and add ActiveX controls to them. To totally customize your environment, you'll need to know how to create scripts that control the operating system itself. Many of you remember the old DOS batch files. Windows never had a batch language of its own until Windows 98, which supports VBScript and exposes many of its objects, which you can program through VBScript (or JScript).

Windows 2000 Professional also supports VBScript, and in this chapter you'll learn how to:

- Develop simple Web pages with HTML
- Activate your Web pages with VBScript
- Build interactive Web pages
- Manipulate the contents of a Web page with VBScript

My goal in this chapter and the next three is to expose you to HTML, VBScript, and DHTML and ease your entry into the field of customizing and automating the administration of the Windows 2000 Professional environment.

As you may remember from Chapter 6, you can view Web content on your Active Desktop. To set this up, right-click an empty area of the Desktop, choose Display from the shortcut menu to open the Display Properties dialog box, click the Web tab, and check the Show Web Content On My Active Desktop check box. Before I get into the nitty-gritty of developing Web pages, though, I want to introduce you to a feature of Windows 2000 Professional that you can use to create your own personal Web server—Internet Information Services.

An Overview of Internet Information Services

If you used NT 4 Workstation, you might be familiar with something called Internet Information Server (IIS). IIS version 2, which was included with NT 4 Server and NT 4 Workstation, was a powerful, sophisticated Web server that included some very advanced tools such as JavaScript. With Windows 2000 Professional, Internet Information Server has evolved into Internet Information Services version 5 (also known as IIS), a collection of programs that you can use to do the following:

- Set up a personal Web server
- Share files and folders via the Web
- Access databases
- Create an intranet

IIS is not installed by default when you install Windows 2000 Professional, although if you do a custom installation, you can choose to install. You can also install later at any time. To do so, follow these steps:

1. Choose Start ➢ Settings ➢ Control Panel to open Control Panel.
2. Click Add/Remove Programs to open the Add/Remove Programs applet.
3. Click Add/Remove Windows Components to start the Windows Components Wizard.
4. In the Components list, click the Internet Information Services (IIS) check box, and then click Next to install all the IIS services, which include the following:
    - Common Files
    - Documentation
    - File Transfer Protocol (FTP) Server
    - Internet Information Services Snap-in
    - Personal Web Manager
    - SMTP Service
    - Visual InterDev RAD Remote Deployment Support
    - World Wide Web Server

    To install only certain services, click the Details button, select the services from the Subcomponents of Internet Information Services (IIS) list, click OK, and then click Next.
5. When the Wizard finishes installing the services, click Finish.

To take a quick tour of what you just installed, open Internet Explorer and type **//localhost.asp** in the Address bar. If you have not created a home page (which we'll do next), you'll see the following:

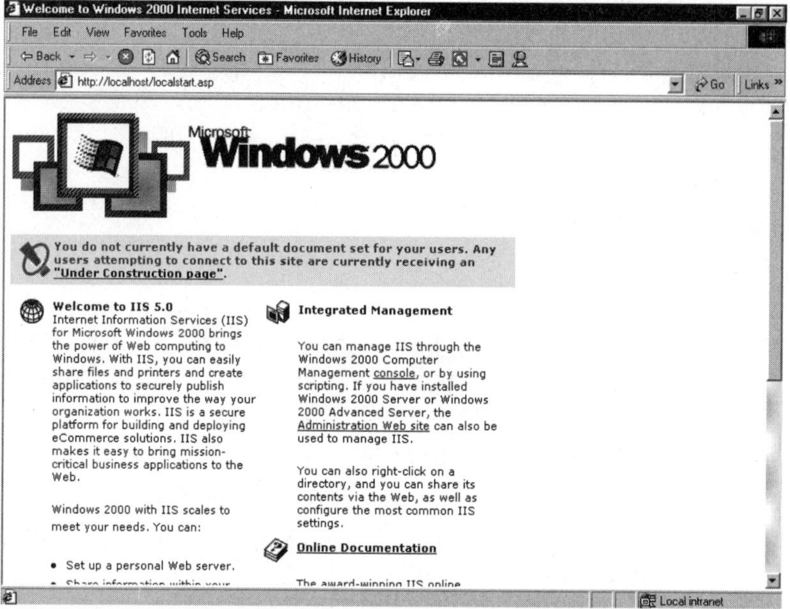

You'll also see the documentation for IIS open in a separate browser window.

When you installed Windows 2000 Professional, IIS created a default Web site and an FTP site, and you can publish information on both those sites. Follow these steps:

1. Create a home page using the techniques described in the rest of this chapter.
2. Save your home page as `Default.htm` or `Default.asp`.
3. Copy your home page into the default Web publishing folder that Setup created: \Inetput\Wwroot.
4. To view your home page, open Internet Explorer, and in the Address bar, enter **//localhost.asp**.

I need to mention one more thing before I leave this necessarily all-too-brief look at IIS. If you want to exercise super, geeky control over any IIS service, you can use the Computer Management console. Follow these steps to get to the services nodes:

1. Right-click My Computer, and choose Manage from the shortcut menu to open Computer Management.
2. Expand Services And Applications, expand Internet Information Services, and then drill down to the node you want to modify.

This breezy discussion of IIS probably leaves you dangling and maybe even a bit confused. For example, you may be asking yourself, "What in the world is an IIS snap-in, and why would I need to use it?" You'll find all the details about IIS in Chapter 19 of *Mastering Windows 2000 Server, Second Edition,* by Mark Minasi, et al. (Sybex Inc., 2000).

Now, let's get on with the business of developing Web pages.

Merging the Web and the Desktop

HTML (HyperText Markup Language) was originally the language of the Web. Every page you view with your browser is written in HTML. With the enormous success of the Web, which led to an explosion of Web-related technologies, new tools were introduced to offset the limitations of HTML. One of them was VBScript, a scripting language that allows developers to embed small programs into Web pages. VBScript started as a seriously limited subset of Visual Basic, but it's constantly evolving.

The next step was to couple HTML with VBScript. HTML was revised so that its elements could be programmed with VBScript (or other scripting languages, such as JScript). The result was Dynamic HTML (or DHTML). DHTML is not a programming language, either, but its elements can be programmed with VBScript. If you are not familiar with HTML or scripting, the example in Figure 22.1 will give you an idea of the structure of an HTML document and how VBScript is used to control its elements.

FIGURE 22.1
A simple HTML page

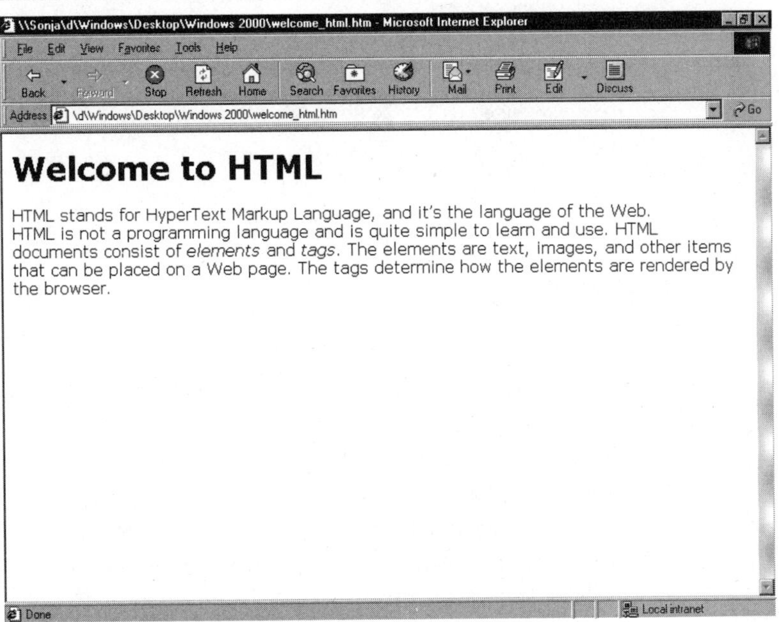

I created the page shown in Figure 22.1 with the following HTML code:

```
<HTML>
<FONT FACE="Verdana">
<H1>Welcome to HTML</H1>
HTML stands for HyperText Markup Language, and it's the language of the Web.
<BR>
HTML is not a programming language and is quite simple to learn and use.
HTML documents consist of <I>elements</I> and <I>tags</I>. The elements are
text, images, and other items that can be placed on a Web page. The tags
determine how the elements are rendered by the browser.
</HTML>
```

HTML is quite simple. The <H1> tag is a special command that tells the browser to render the following text (up to the </H1> tag) as a level-1 header. The <BR> tag inserts a line break and the pair of <HTML> and </HTML> tags delimit the document.

HTML is a language for specifying the appearance of the document. There's nothing programmable in HTML. With any other language, it would be really trivial to program an item (such as the header) to react to user actions such as the movement of the mouse. For example, let's say you want to change the color of the header when the user moves the mouse over it and reset the color when the pointer leaves the area. You can't do this with HTML, but you can do it with DHTML. Here's the same document implemented in DHTML:

```
<HTML>
<SCRIPT LANGUAGE=VBScript>
Sub Head_OnMouseOver()
    Head.Style.Color = "#FF0000"
End Sub
Sub Head_OnMouseOut()
    Head.Style.Color = "#000000"
End Sub
</SCRIPT>
<FONT FACE="Verdana">
<DIV ID="Head">
<H1>Welcome to HTML</H1>
</DIV>
HTML stands for HyperText Markup Language, and it's the language of the Web.
<BR>
HTML is not a programming language and is quite simple to learn and use.
HTML documents consist of <I>elements</I> and <I>tags</I>. The elements are
text, images, and other items that can be placed on a Web page. The tags
determine how the elements are rendered by the browser.
</HTML>
```

Notice that the header appears in a <DIV> tag, which makes it a distinct, addressable item of the document. The tag is

```
<DIV ID="Head">
```

which tells the browser that the header is named "Head." Then, in the SCRIPT section of the document, you can control the appearance of this element through VBScript code.

The `Head_OnMouseOver()` routine is activated when the mouse pointer enters the area of the header, and the `Head_OnMouseOut()` routine is activated when the mouse pointer leaves the area of the header. Both routines contain VBScript code, which is executed when each routine is activated. The routines are activated in response to external actions (such as the movement or the click of the mouse), which are called *events*. The document contains code that determines how it should react to various events. The code that causes the page to react to an event is called an *event handler*. It's a subroutine (a block of VBScript statements) that is activated automatically when an item on the page detects an event. When the user moves the mouse over the area of the item called Head, the event `OnMouseOver` is detected automatically, and the event handler `Head_OnMouseOver()` is called. You don't have to monitor the movement of the mouse. All you have to do is provide the code to be called when a specific event takes place. The event handler is called automatically in reaction to an event.

To test this example, you can enter the code shown here to a text file, save it with extension HTM on your disk, and then double-click its icon.

In the following pages, I'm going to discuss briefly HTML and VBScript. If you are going to customize your environment, you need to familiarize yourself with HTML and VBScript. Then, depending on the degree of customization you want to achieve, you can explore ActiveX controls, Java applets, channels, and more. In the next chapter, we'll look at DHTML and a few more advanced examples of VBScript. In Chapter 24, I'll discuss the mechanisms of VBScript that allow you to access the objects of the Windows 2000 Professional operating system and design highly customized Web pages for your Desktop. In Chapter 25, you'll see how you can use VBScript to manipulate the Windows 2000 Professional environment without HTML.

Designing with HTML

HTML is a document formatting language, like RTF (Rich Text Format). HTML is not a programming language and is quite simple to learn and use. Strictly speaking, you don't have to learn HTML. There are many WYSIWYG tools for designing Web pages, such as FrontPage, which is include in the Microsoft 2000 Office suite of applications. But even when you're using a visual environment such as FrontPage to design your Web pages with drag-and-drop operations, you should know what HTML looks like and understand its limitations—what it can and can't do for you.

An HTML document consists of *elements* and *tags*. The elements are text, images, hyperlinks, and, in general, the items that can be viewed on the page. The tags are commands that determine how the various elements are rendered on the page. The following line will produce a level-1 header:

```
<H1>Welcome to HTML!</H1>
```

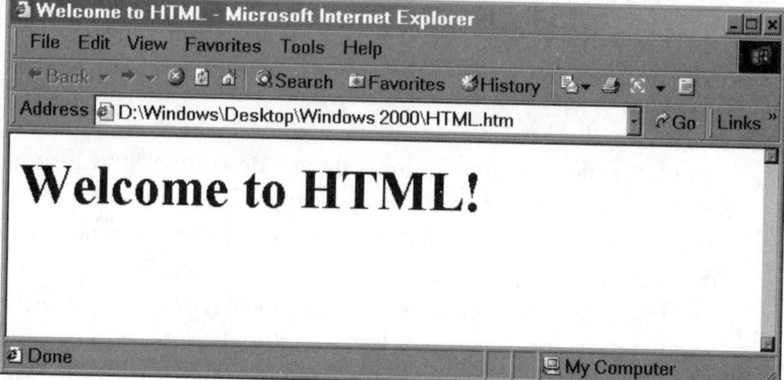

As you can guess, <H1> is the tag, and the string "Welcome to HTML!" is the element. HTML tags appear in pairs, as shown above. The first tag turns on a specific feature, and the matching, closing tag turns it off. As you will see in the following example, the tag <I> sets the text that follows it in italics up to the matching </I> tag (the forward slash indicates the closing tag). To stress one or more words in the text, use a line such as the following:

```
Welcome to <I>HTML!</I>
```

You can also nest tags. For example, you can italicize a few words within a level-1 header with a line like this:

```
<H1>Welcome to <I>HTML</I></H1>
```

Tags have attributes too. The <H1> tag recognizes the ALIGN tag, which centers the header on the page:

```
<H1 ALIGN="CENTER"> Welcome to HTML</H1>
```

Attributes are listed next to the opening tag, and they need not appear in the closing tag. The other possible values of the ALIGN attribute are LEFT and RIGHT (LEFT being the default value). Other tags accept multiple attributes. The <FONT> tag, which sets the font to be used for rendering the following text, recognizes the attributes COLOR (the text's color), FACE (the typeface), and SIZE (the size of the typeface). To render a sentence in Verdana typeface and red color, you can use a line like the following:

```
<FONT COLOR=#FF0000 FACE="Verdana">
This text is rendered in Verdana and red color
</FONT>
```

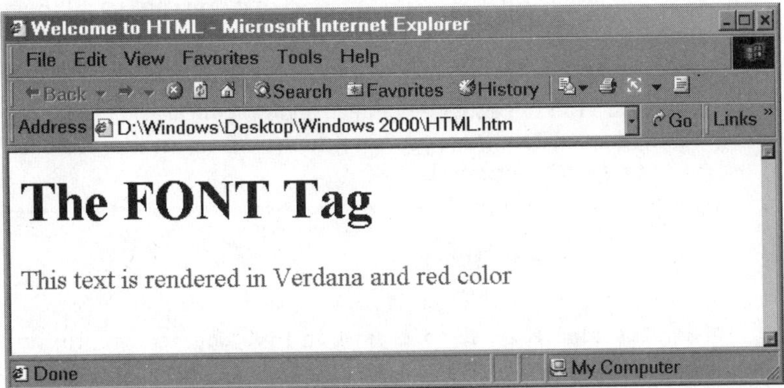

HTML tags and their attributes are described in many resources, and my goal isn't to cover every HTML tag or teach you how to write HTML pages. There are many good books on HTML. You might want to start with *Mastering HTML 4* by Deborah S. Ray and Eric J. Ray (Sybex Inc., 1999). Some excellent tutorials and reference material are available at the Microsoft Web site (www.microsoft.com).

In the following pages, I'll discuss the basic HTML tags you need to build simple Web pages. This information will be adequate to get you started. At the very least, you'll be able to understand other people's HTML code and see how they did it. (To see the HTML code that produced the page you're viewing in Internet Explorer, choose View ➢ Source.)

I'm including here the shortest introduction to HTML you'll probably ever find. This quick reference will give you the information you need to continue working through the following three chapters and customize your Desktop with Web pages. It's not my goal to cover exhaustively the topic of HTML, but to convince you that not knowing HTML shouldn't stop you from getting involved with the Web and starting to develop Web pages immediately.

The Absolute Essentials

Let's start our exploration of HTML with the simplest example. We will create a plain text document and then convert it to HTML format, suitable for viewing with Internet Explorer. We will create a very simple document to demonstrate the structure of an HTML document and a few simple HTML commands so that you'll get a feel for the language. We'll then move on to more complicated examples, one step at a time.

HTML documents are plain text files; therefore, you can use any text editor to create them. To simplify things even further, for this exercise we will use Notepad, the simplest text editor on your system. Follow these steps:

1. Choose Start ➢ Programs ➢ Accessories ➢ Notepad to open Notepad.
2. Choose Format ➢ Word Wrap so that you can see all the text on the line.

NOTE You can also use WordPad and save the files in text format, as long as you keep in mind that any formatting you apply to the document with WordPad's menus isn't going to affect the HTML document.

3. Enter the following text:

```
My First HTML Document
The simplest way to create an HTML document is to start with a regular
text document, format it with a few HTML tags (bold, italic, and so on),
and then save it as an HTML file.
This sample document contains a header, individually formatted words,
and a list of bulleted items. Later, we will add a table, images, and an
interesting background, and we will turn the HTML file into an
attractive Web page.
We will demonstrate how to create:
Lists
Tables
Couldn't be simpler!
```

4. Save the document as text with the extension HTM (name it `HTMLDOC1.HTM`). To save a file with an extension different from TXT with Notepad, choose All Files in the Save As Type list. If you don't, the file's extension will be TXT, even if you supply the HTM extension (you'll get a text file with a name like `HTMLDoc1.htm.txt`).
5. Locate the file's icon, and double-click it (or single-click, if you've chosen the single-click configuration of the Desktop). Internet Explorer will start and display the document, as shown in Figure 22.2.

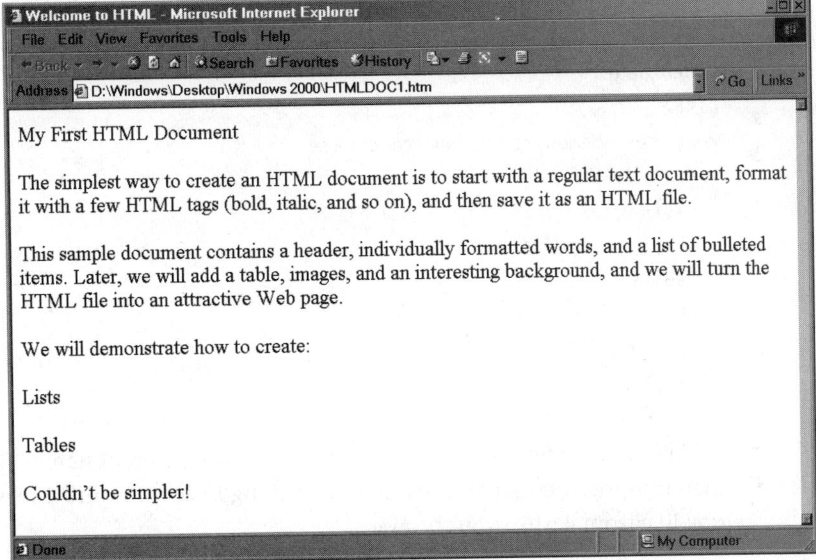

FIGURE 22.2
This is what the previous text segment looks like within Internet Explorer.

The first thing you'll notice about the way your document is displayed is that all information about paragraphs was lost. To insert a paragraph break, you must specify it explicitly with the <P> tag. The <BR> tag inserts a line break (which changes the line but doesn't insert any additional space between the current line and the next one).

Also notice that multiple spaces and tabs are rendered as single spaces. Normal text is left-justified, and line breaks are determined by the width of the window on which the document is viewed. Let's convert the previous document to a proper Web page.

First, enclose everything in a pair of <HTML> tags. HTML documents consist primarily of two segments, the *head* and the *body*, which are marked with the <HEAD> and <BODY> tags. The head contains information such as the document's title (which appears on the browser's title bar) and other information that doesn't usually appear in the browser's window.

The document's contents (in other words, what you see in the browser's window) are placed in the body segment. Here's the previous text in proper HTML format:

```
<HTML>
<HEAD>
```

```
<TITLE>Sample HTML document</TITLE>
</HEAD>
<BODY>
My First HTML Document
<P>
The simplest way to create an HTML document is to start with a regular text
document, format it with a few HTML tags (bold, italic, and so on), and then
save it as an HTML file.
<P>
This sample document contains a header, individually formatted words, and a
list of bulleted items. Later, we will add a table, images, and an
interesting background, and we will turn the HTML file into an attractive
Web page.
<P>
We will demonstrate how to create:
<P>
Lists
<P>
Tables
<P>
Couldn't be simpler!
</BODY>
</HTML>
```

Now save the file as an HTML document with a different name (`HTMLDoc2.htm`), and open it in Internet Explorer by double-clicking its icon. Figure 22.3 shows what it will look like from within your browser.

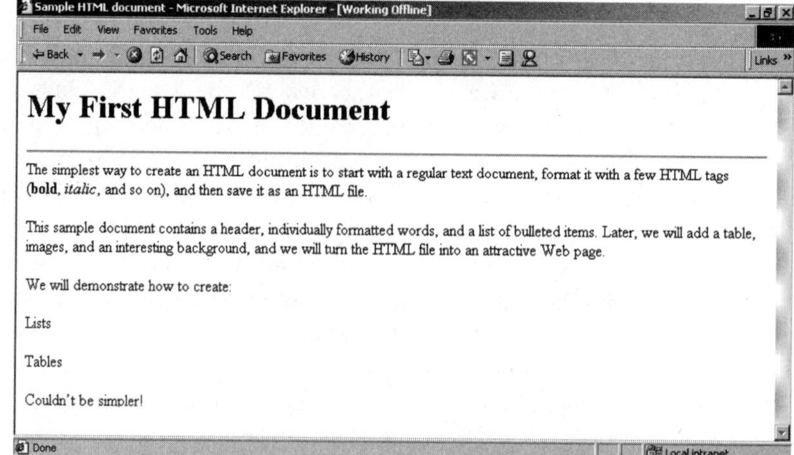

FIGURE 22.3 *A few tags were enough to create an HTML document any browser can understand.*

This time it looks better—at least it retains the paragraph structure of the original. Notice also that although the title of the document does not appear in the document itself, it does appear in the title bar of the browser. Change the width of the browser's window, and watch how the document is reformatted automatically to fit within the window. Recall that the source document contains no other formatting information, except for paragraph breaks. It is the browser's responsibility to display your document according to the embedded commands as best it can.

Now we're ready to format the document and make it look much more like a Web page. To begin with, let's make the first paragraph into a formatted header, by surrounding it with <H1> and </H1> tags. The <H1> tag specifies a level-1 header. There are similar tags for level 2 (<H2>), level 3 (<H3>), and headers up to level 6 (<H6>).

NOTE A header takes up an entire line, and there's no reason to insert a <P> tag to change lines.

To convert the first line of the body to a header, use tags as follows:

```
<H1>My First HTML Document</H1>
```

The matching </H1> is required; if you omit it, the entire document is rendered as a level-1 header.

Text Formatting Tags

The next step is to emphasize a few words in the text to make them stand out. To emphasize one or more words, use either italics or boldface characters. Italicized words are usually called *emphasized*, and bold words are called *strong*. Bold words are reserved for headers and should be avoided as much as possible in the text, because they disrupt the flow of the text. The tags for italics are <I> and </I>, and the tags for bold are <B> and </B>. There are two more equivalent tags, <EM> (for emphasis) and <STRONG> (for bold). The advantage of using the <EM> and <STRONG> tags is that the browser decides how to best display both styles. Using these tags will make your documents more portable.

Now open the HTML version of the example and make the following changes:

1. Enter the tag **<H1>** in front of the first line of the document's body and the tag **</H1>** after it.
2. Select the word *bold* in the text, and surround it with the tags **<B>** and **</B>**.
3. Select the word *italic,* and surround it with the tags **<I>** and **</I>**.

A third character formatting tag is the <U> tag, which underlines one or more characters or words. You should avoid underlining parts of your document, however, because underlining (along with a different color) is usually reserved for hyperlinks. If you want to underline an entire line to make it stand out, you can use a horizontal rule.

4. Add a horizontal rule under your document's header by inserting the tag **<HR>** under the header.

At this point, your HTML document should be

```
<HTML>
<HEAD>
<TITLE>Sample HTML document</TITLE>
</HEAD>
<BODY>
<H1>My First HTML Document</H1>
<P>
<HR>
The simplest way to create an HTML document is to start with a regular text
document, format it with a few HTML tags (<B>bold</B>, <I>italic</I>, and so
on), and then save it as an HTML file.
<P>
This sample document contains a header, individually formatted words, and a
list of bulleted items. Later, we will add a table, images, and an
interesting background, and we will turn the HTML file into an attractive
Web page.
<P>
We will demonstrate how to create:
<P>
Lists
<P>
Tables
<P>
Couldn't be simpler!
</BODY>
</HTML>
```

The equivalent Web page is shown in Figure 22.4.

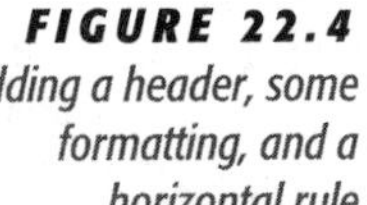

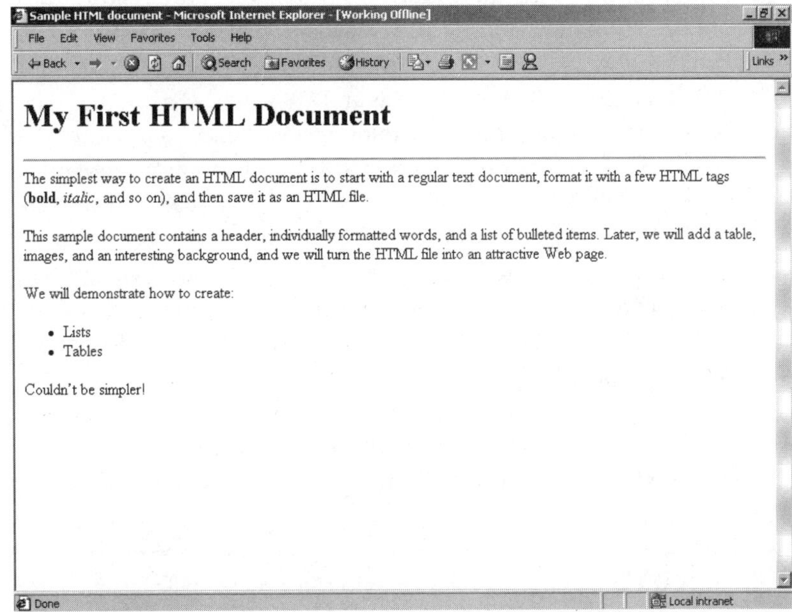

FIGURE 22.4
Adding a header, some formatting, and a horizontal rule

Specifying Fonts and Color

With the `FONT` tag, you can specify the typeface, size, and color of the text. The `COLOR` attribute accepts a color name (one of the names listed in Table 22.1) or an RGB value.

TABLE 22.1: COLORS SPECIFIED BY NAME

Aqua	Gray	Navy	Silver
Black	Green	Olive	Teal
Blue	Lime	Purple	White
Fuchsia	Maroon	Red	Yellow

The second way to define colors, by their *RGB value*, is a bit more complicated, but it lets you define any color possible. Each color is described in terms of three values, which correspond to the percentages of each of the three basic colors: red, green, and blue. Each value is expressed as a hexadecimal number. The smallest possible value (00) corresponds to absence of the corresponding color, and the largest possible value (FF, or 255 in decimal) corresponds to full intensity. For example, the value 00FF00 corresponds to a pure green tone, and the value 008000 corresponds to a mid-green tone (hex 80 is decimal 128, midway between 0 and 255).

You can combine percentages of the three basic colors to get nearly every color in the spectrum. The value FFFF00 corresponds to pure yellow, because it contains red and green in full intensity and no blue. A medium-yellow tone would be 808000. Color values such as 7A8100 and 808200 produce very similar tones.

To specify a COLOR attribute as an RGB value, you use the # symbol in front of the value; if you don't, Internet Explorer will attempt to interpret the value as a color name. Here are a few examples of valid color specifications with the RGB method:

```
<FONT COLOR = "#FF0000">This text should appear in red<P>
<FONT COLOR = "#800080">and this text should appear in a mid cyan tone
```

Black color corresponds to the RGB value #000000 (all basic colors are absent), and white corresponds to #FFFFFF (all basic colors in full intensity). Any RGB value with equal percentages of the three basic colors corresponds to a gray tone. Here are a few examples of gray tones:

```
<FONT COLOR = "#101010">This is a very dark gray tone,
<FONT COLOR = "#808080">this is a mid-gray tone
<FONT COLOR = "#B0B0B0">and this is a very light gray tone
```

NOTE Again, color values are given in hexadecimal notation. The # symbol in front of the number indicates that it's a hexadecimal number.

The same color specifications apply to other color-related attributes such as the BGCOLOR attribute of the BODY tag, which specifies the background color for the document's body.

The last attribute of the FONT tag, FACE, lets you specify the typeface to be used at each point in the document. You can use the FACE attribute to mix different typefaces in the same document. The FACE attribute is followed by the names of one or more typefaces. The browser will use the first font name if it's available on the system. If not, it will use the second font, and so on. The line

```
<FONT FACE="Arial,Times Roman">This text will most likely appear in Arial
```

instructs a browser that supports this modifier to display the text with the Arial typeface, available on almost any system. If the Arial typeface isn't available, the text will be rendered in Times Roman. However, there's no guarantee that any specified font will exist on the client.

Lists

Now we are going to create a more convincing list. The items of the list in Figure 22.4 look like a list, but they'd look much better if we indented each line and displayed a bullet (or sequence number) in front of each item. HTML supports two types of lists:

- Unordered lists, in which each item is marked with a bullet
- Ordered lists, in which each item is numbered

The two tags are <UL> for unordered lists and <OL> for ordered lists. The entire list must be contained within a pair of <UL> and </UL> (or <OL> and </OL>) tags. Each item in the list is distinguished with the <LI> tag.

Let's use these tags to create a true list with bullets in front of each item. Open your document in Notepad again, and enclose the entire list in a pair of <UL> </UL> tags. Then insert the tag <LI> in front of each item (or line) in the list. Here's what the revised document should look like:

```
<HTML>
<TITLE>Sample HTML document</TITLE>
<BODY>
<H1>My First HTML Document</H1><HR>
The simplest way to create an HTML document is to start with a regular text
document, format it with a few HTML tags (<B>bold</B>, <I>italic</I>, and so
on), and then save it as a HTML file.
<P>
This sample document contains a header, individually formatted words, and a
list of bulleted items. Later, we will add a table, images, and an
interesting background, and we will turn it into an attractive Web page.
<P>
We will demonstrate how to create:
<UL>
<LI>Lists
<LI>Tables
</UL>
Couldn't be simpler!
</BODY>
</HTML>
```

To change the unordered bulleted list to an ordered list, all you have to do is change the <UL> tag to <OL> and the closing </UL> tag to </OL>. It's also possible to create lists within lists—mixing both unordered and ordered lists. Let's see an example of a nested list with elements of both types.

Nested Lists

Nesting a list within another list is a straightforward process: insert an entire list in place of an item in the outer list. The inner list is usually called a *nested list* and must end before you move to the next element of the outer list. Of course, you can interrupt the inner list to start a new list nested within it. Here's the general structure of two nested lists:

```
<H1>Nested List Example</H1>
<OLO>
<LI> item description
<LI> item description
```

```
<UL>
    <LI> nested item description
    <LI> nested item description
        ...
    <LI> nested item description
</UL>
<LI> item description
<LI> item description
</OL>
```

The indention makes the structure easier to read—it does not affect the appearance of the list in any way. Figure 22.5 is an example of a nested list as displayed in Internet Explorer. Here's the source document that created the list shown in Figure 22.5:

```
<HTML>
<TITLE>Nested Lists Demonstration</TITLE>
<BODY>
<H1>Nested Lists<HR></H1>
<UL>
<LI>List 1, Item 1
<LI>List 1, Item 2
    <OL>
    <LI>List 1a, Item 1a.1
    <LI>List 1a, Item 1a.2
    <LI>List 1a, Item 1a.3
    </OL>
<LI>List 1, Item 3
<OL>
    <LI>List 1b, Item 1b.1
    <LI>List 1b, Item 1b.2
        <UL>
        <LI>List 1c, Item 1c.1
        <LI>List 1c, Item 1c.2
        <LI>List 1c, Item 1c.3 <STRONG>(some list items can span
          multiple lines, depending on the window's width)</STRONG>
        <LI>List 1c, Item 1c.4
        </UL>
    <LI>List 1b, Item 1b.3
    </OL>
<LI>List 1, Item 4
<LI>List 1, Item 5
</UL>

</BODY>
</HTML>
```

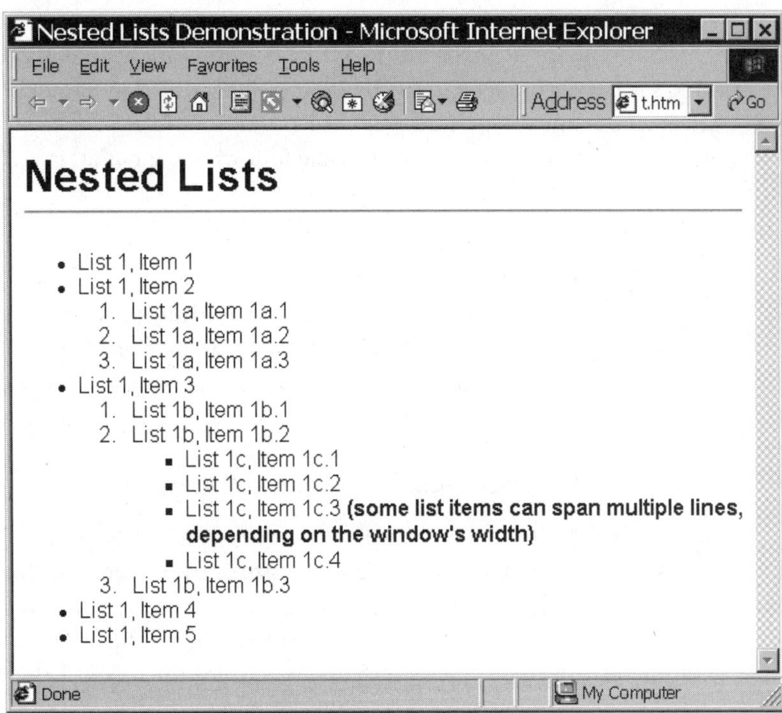

FIGURE 22.5
Three nested lists

Images

To insert an image into an HTML document, use the `IMG` tag, which can be followed by several attributes. In its simplest form, the `IMG` tag, with the `SRC` attribute, specifies the location of the image file

```
<IMG SRC = "image_file_location">
```

The *`image_file_location`* attribute is usually a relative path to the image file but can be an absolute reference (if there's a good reason for it). The common practice is to move all the images you are going to use in a Web page into the same folder as the document or into a subfolder under it. For example, if the image `MyFamily.gif` resides in the same folder as the document that contains it, use either of the following tags to insert it in the document:

```
<IMG SRC = "MyFamily.gif">
```

or

```
<IMG SRC = "./MyFamily.gif">
```

If the same image resides in the `WebImages` folder under the current folder, use the following tag:

```
<IMG SRC = "./WebImages/MyFamily.gif"
```

Here are the other attributes you can use with the IMG tag.

BORDER

This attribute specifies the size of a border around the image. If the image is a hyperlink, the border is drawn in the hyperlink color, which is determined by the browser. If the image is not a hyperlink, the border is an invisible space around the image. The image inserted in a document with the following tag has an invisible space of three pixels around it:

```
<IMG SRC=".\Images\Logo.jpg" BORDER = 3>
```

HSPACE, VSPACE

These attributes specify the horizontal and vertical space (in pixels) to be inserted around the image. They behave in a way similar to the BORDER tag, except that the margins are not colored when the image is a hyperlink. The IMG tag of the following example would have the same effect as the BORDER example (except if the image were a hyperlink):

```
<IMG SRC=".\Images\Logo.jpg" HSPACE = 3 VSPACE = 3>
```

WIDTH, HEIGHT

Together, these attributes determine the size of the image. You don't have to use these attributes; the browser will figure out the image's size. If you specify them, however, you're saving the browser the time spent to calculate the dimensions of the image. Another reason to specify a width and height for the image is that the browser will stretch the image to fit in the specified rectangle.

ALIGN

This attribute determines the alignment of the text around the image, as well as the alignment of the image on the page. To specify the alignment of the text, assign one of the following values to the ALIGN attribute: TOP, MIDDLE, or BOTTOM. The TOP value aligns the first line of the text with the top of the image. The MIDDLE value aligns the first line of text with the middle of the image, and the BOTTOM value aligns the first line of text with the bottom of the image. To specify the alignment of the image on the page, use one of the two values LEFT or RIGHT. Unfortunately, there's no option that will cause the text to flow around the image.

ALT

This attribute specifies the text that will be displayed in place of the picture, should the browser's ability to display images be turned off. If an image is inserted into a document with the following tag, users who have turned off the display of images, as well as users of text-only browsers, will see the string "Company Logo" in place of the image.

```
<IMG SRC=".\Images\Logo.jpg" BORDER = 3 ALT = "Company Logo">
```

The image's alternate description will also be displayed while the image is being downloaded.

Hyperlinks

The tag that makes the Web tick is the <A> tag, which inserts a *hyperlink* into a document. A hyperlink is a string, usually rendered in blue, that reacts to the mouse pointer. When the mouse pointer is over a hyperlink, the pointer assumes the shape of a hand pointing up. If you click the mouse button on a hyperlink, the browser reads the destination of the hyperlink, contacts the server, and displays the page. Here's how you would insert a hyperlink to Microsoft's home page into an HTML document:

```
For more information visit the <A HREF="http://home.microsoft.com">Microsoft
Web site</A>
```

The string `Microsoft Web site`, which is enclosed by <A> and </A> tags, is displayed as a hyperlink when the document is rendered on the client computer. When the visitor clicks this hyperlink, the browser displays Microsoft's home page.

The most common use of hyperlinks is to take the visitor to another document on the same Web site. The following hyperlinks create a table of contents when displayed:

```
<HTML>
<FONT FACE="Verdana">
<H1>Useful Resources</H1>
Click on the following hyperlink to view a document on the corresponding
topic:
<P>
<A HREF="HTMLDoc.htm">HyperText Markup Language</A>
<P>
<A HREF="VBSDoc.htm">Programming with VBScript</A>
<P>
<A HREF="JSDoc.htm">Programming with JScript</A>
<P>
```

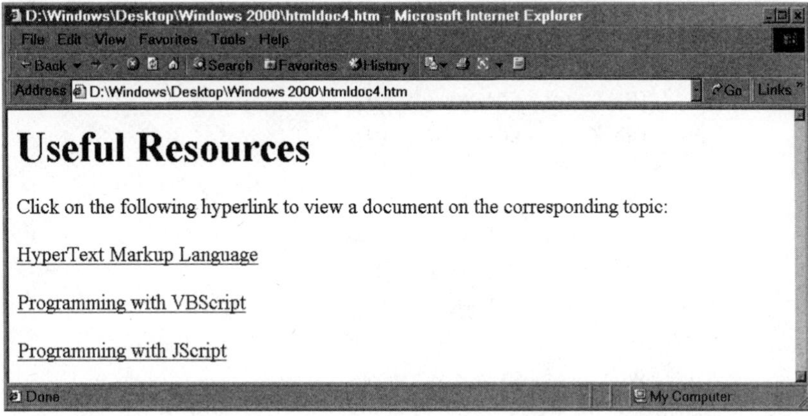

The HREF attribute determines the destination of the hyperlink, which is another HTML document. The destinations of the three hyperlinks of the previous example are stored on the same computer (and in the same folder) as the document that contains them. You can also specify destination documents that live on other computers. The following hyperlink, for example, will open a page on the Microsoft Web site (the VBScript documentation site):

```
For more information on VBScript, <A HREF="http://www.microsoft.com/
vbscript">click here.</A>
```

The words *click here* will be rendered as a hyperlink, which will take the visitor to the VBScript page on the Microsoft Web site.

Tables

One of the most advanced features of HTML is its support of tables. Designing a table with HTML tags is straightforward. First, you specify the section of the document that is to be treated as a table with the <TABLE> and </TABLE> tags. Each row of the table begins with the <TR> (Table Row) tag and ends with the </TR> tag. Finally, each row in the table contains cells, which are delimited by the <TD> and </TD> tags (Table Data). Here's the general structure of a table:

```
<HTML>
<H1>A Simple 3 X 3 Table</H1>
<FONT FACE="Verdana">
<TABLE>
<TR>
   <TD> Row 1, Column 1 </TD>
   <TD> Row 1, Column 2 </TD>
   <TD> Row 1, Column 3 </TD>
</TR>
<TR>
     <TD> Row 2, Column 1 </TD>
   <TD> Row 2, Column 2 </TD>
   <TD> Row 2, Column 3 </TD>
</TR>
<TR>
   <TD> Row 3, Column 1 </TD>
   <TD> Row 3, Column 2 </TD>
   <TD> Row 3, Column 3 </TD>
</TR>
</TABLE>
</HTML>
```

Each row of the table is delimited by the TR tag, and each cell is delimited with the <TD> tag. The closing tags </TR> and </TD> are not required, because the next <TD> or <TR> tag ends the scope of the previous one.

Figure 22.6 shows what the previous example looks like in Internet Explorer. The cells are arranged in a tabular form and are aligned properly, but there is no border or grid around them.

FIGURE 22.6
The table in Internet Explorer

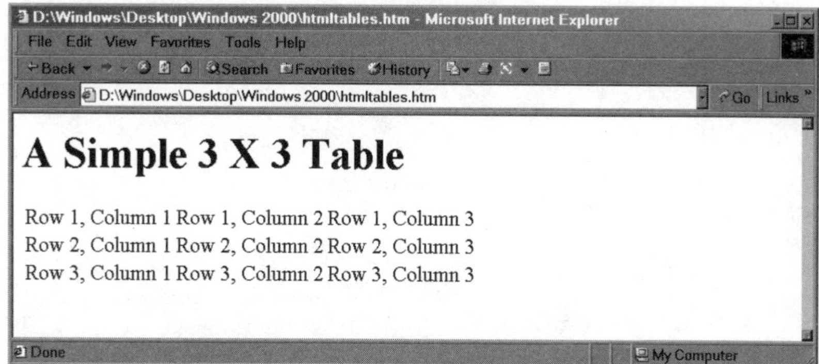

Let's add a border around the cells, to help us visualize the tabular structure of the data. To do so, insert the attribute BORDER into the TABLE tag. In other words, replace the string <TABLE> with the <TABLE BORDER> string. This attribute adds a border with the default thickness (one pixel) around each cell. The BORDER attribute can have a value, which is the width of the border in pixels.

Multiple Row and Multiple-Column Cells

Quite often, tables don't contain identically shaped rows and columns. Some rows may contain fewer and wider cells than the others, and some cells in a column may span multiple rows. The figures in this section contain tables with peculiar formatting.

Figure 22.7 shows a table with cells that span multiple columns and rows. These cells use the ROWSPAN and COLSPAN tags, which let you create really elaborate tables. Both COLSPAN and ROWSPAN, when placed between the <TD> and </TD> tags, act to merge the current cell with one or more of its adjacent cells, in the same row (in the case of the COLSPAN attribute) or column (in the case of the ROWSPAN attribute). The number of adjacent cells to be merged with the current one is the value specified for the COLSPAN and ROWSPAN attributes.

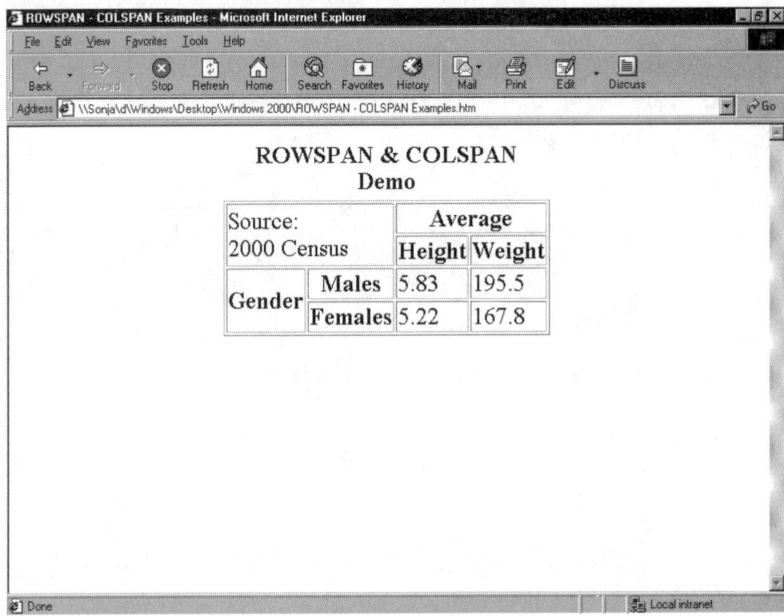

FIGURE 22.7
This table contains cells that span multiple rows and columns.

The table in Figure 22.7 was created with the following HTML lines. The only thing I've done differently here is to add the COLSPAN attribute (in the appropriate <TD> tags), to force some cells of the first row to span two columns, and the ROWSPAN attribute, to force some cells of the first column to span multiple rows. Other than that, the new table is as simple as the ones in the previous examples.

```
<HTML>
<HEAD>
<TITLE>ROWSPAN - COLSPAN Examples</TITLE>
</HEAD>
<BODY>
<CENTER>
<TABLE BORDER>
<CAPTION><FONT SIZE = 5><B>ROWSPAN & COLSPAN Demo</B></CAPTION>
<TR>
    <TD COLSPAN=2 ROWSPAN=2 ><FONT SIZE = 5>Source:<BR>2000 Census</TD>
    <TH COLSPAN=2><FONT SIZE = 5>Average</TH>
</TR>
<TR>
    <TH><FONT SIZE = 5>Height</TH>
    <TH><FONT SIZE = 5>Weight</TH>
</TR>
```

```
<TR>
    <TH ROWSPAN=2><FONT SIZE = 5>Gender</TH>
    <TH><FONT SIZE = 5>Males</TH>
    <TD><FONT SIZE = 5>5.83</TD>
    <TD><FONT SIZE = 5>195.5</TD>
</TR>
<TR>
    <TH><FONT SIZE = 5>Females</TH>
    <TD><FONT SIZE = 5>5.22</TD>
    <TD><FONT SIZE = 5>167.8</TD>
</TR>
</TABLE>
</CENTER>
</FONT>
</BODY>
</HTML>
```

Activating Web Pages with VBScript

Web pages are by definition interactive: each time visitors click a hyperlink, they are taken to another page. But this isn't the type of interaction Windows users are familiar with. In addition, this type of interaction requires a trip to the server at each step. The Web page can't respond to events, such as the click of a button, because HTML isn't a programming language. It can't display the date or do a simple calculation.

A few years ago Web pages started to change from being fairly static—pages with links and content—to being active and dynamic. An active page is one that behaves like an application, and a dynamic page is one that is generated "on the fly" by the server, usually based on information from the previous page or by parameters passed into the page.

The embedded application is called a *script*. Scripts are simple programs that are embedded into the HTML page as ASCII text. When the page is downloaded, the script is downloaded with it and is executed by the browser on the client computer. The idea behind active pages is to exploit the computing power of the client computer. With straight HTML, the client computer's task is to render the HTML documents on the screen. But most clients out there are powerful PCs, and they could do much more than simply display Web pages. Active pages can exploit available computing power by passing to the client much of the processing that would otherwise take place on the server.

Embedding Scripts in HTML Documents

The programs that you write in VBScript are called *scripts*. To embed a script in an HTML document, you must insert a pair of <SCRIPT> tags and place your script between them. In the opening <SCRIPT> tag, you must specify the language of the script.

NOTE For the examples in this book, the language is VBScript, but it's possible to develop scripts in JScript too.

The SCRIPT section of an HTML document looks like this:

```
<SCRIPT LANGUAGE = VBScript>
   your script goes here
</SCRIPT>
```

Any code you place in the script section of a document is executed as soon as the document is loaded onto the browser and before any element is rendered on the browser's window. For example, the script

```
<SCRIPT LANGUAGE = VBScript>
   MsgBox "The Date is " & Date()
</SCRIPT>
```

will display the current date as soon as it's loaded.

A typical application, however, isn't executed unconditionally. Normally, applications react to external events, such as a mouse click on a button. A typical script consists of subroutines, which are called when an event occurs. Let's say your page contains a button named DateButton (you'll see later in this chapter how you can place buttons and other common elements of the Windows interface on your pages). If you want to display the current date when this button is clicked, you must provide a subroutine called `DateButton_onClick`:

```
<SCRIPT LANGUAGE = VBScript>
Sub DateButton_onClick()
   MsgBox "The Date is " & Date()
End Sub
</SCRIPT>
```

The subroutine `DateButton_onClick()` is invoked every time the DateButton control receives the `onClick` event. You don't have to monitor the mouse from within your script. All you have to do is provide a subroutine made up of the name of the control and the event you want to react to. When the user clicks the DateButton, the subroutine `DateButton_onClick` is executed automatically.

There are more events that your page can react to, and you'll read about them later in this chapter and the following one.

VBScript Variables

To begin with, VBScript is not a strongly typed programming or scripting language. What this means is that you can use the same variable to hold different types of data. By types, I mean integer (numbers in the range 0 through 4 billion), float (numbers that have decimal places), and string data. To use VBScript (and Visual Basic, VBScript's big brother), variables are stored as a variant, and the VBScript engine coerces, or changes, the underlying data to the correct type before using the variable.

If you want to find out the type of a variable, use the `VarType()` function, which returns information about how your data is currently stored in a variable. The `VarType()` function returns an integer that represents the type of its argument. The `TypeName()` function returns the actual name of a variable's type (integer, double, date, string, and so on). You can also check for a specific data type by using the `Is` functions:

```
IsArray()   IsDate()   IsEmpty()
IsError()   IsNull()   IsNumeric()
IsObject()
```

For example, you can use the function `IsDate()` to find out whether the user has entered a valid date. If the `IsDate()` function returns `True`, the value entered is a valid date. If not, you can prompt the user to enter a new value:

```
If Not IsDate(Expires) Then
    Expires = InputBox("Please enter a valid expiration date")
End If
```

These lines of code examine the value stored in the variable `Expires`, and if the variable doesn't represent a valid date, they prompt the user to enter another value. You will soon see the control flow statements (`If...End If`) and the basic Input/Output functions (such as InputBox).

Traditionally, you had to declare variables and their types before they could be used. The declaration

```
Dim age As Integer
```

declares (in Visual Basic) a variable that will be used to store an integer value. The *age* variable can't be used to store a date, for example. With VBScript, variables can store all types of information.

VBScript Procedures

A *procedure* is a block of statements that can be called from anywhere in an application by name. Let's say you are going to write a script that formats and displays dates. If you must repeat this operation in many places of the script, you can implement a procedure and call it `MyDate()`. The procedure could be implemented as follows:

```
Sub MyDate(someDate)
    newDate = WeekdayName(someDate) & ", "
    newDate = MonthName(someDate) & " " & Year(someDate)
    MsgBox newDate
End Sub
```

You can then call this procedure from every other place of the script that needs to display the date in the format "Monday, January 12, 2001." (Actually, VBScript provides the `FormatDateTime()` function that can format dates and times in many ways, but let's say you need a format that's not available with the `FormatDateTime()` function.)

The `MyDate()` procedure is implemented as a subroutine. A subroutine performs its calculations and doesn't return a result. When you call a subroutine with a statement like

```
MyDate("1/12/01")
```

or

```
MyDate(Date())
```

the subroutine formats the date and displays it in a message box.

A different type of procedure returns a result. You could implement the same procedure as a function, as shown here:

```
Sub MyDate(someDate)
    newDate = WeekdayName(someDate) & ", "
    newDate = MonthName(someDate) & " " & Year(someDate)
    MyDate = newDate
End Sub
```

The `MyDate()` function returns the result (the formatted date). The value to be returned by the function must be assigned to the name of the function; this is done by the last line of the code. The `MyDate()` function can be called as follows:

```
MsgBox MyDate("1/12/01")
```

The function `MyDate()` will return a date like "Monday, January 12, 2001," which is displayed on a message box by the `MsgBox()` function.

Procedures—subroutines and functions—let you break your script into smaller, more manageable parts and implement them separately. Once the `MyDate()` function has been written and tested, you can use it as though it were another built-in function.

Controlling the Program Flow

Normally, a script is executed one line at a time, beginning to end. You can control the flow of your script with conditional and looping statements. With conditional statements, you can write VBScript code that makes decisions and repeats certain statements. In this section, we'll look at the statements that let you change the flow of the script.

Conditional Statements

VBScript supports the `If...Then...Else` and `Select Case` conditional statements, which we'll look at next.

The *If...Then...Else* Statement

The If...Then...Else statement examines a condition, and, depending on the result, a different set of statements is executed. The syntax of the If...Then...Else statement is

```
If <Expression> Then
    block1
Else
    block2
End If
```

<Expression> is a logical expression such as Age>18 or Country="USA". If the expression is True, the following block of statements is executed. If not, the block of statements following the Else keyword is executed. Here's an example that uses the If...Then...Else conditional statement:

```
If Hour(Time()) < 12 Then
    MsgBox "Good morning!"
Else
    MsgBox "Good evening!"
End If
```

If the current time is before noon, the first greeting is displayed. If it's past noon, the second greeting is displayed.

The Else clause is optional. If you want to execute one or more statements only under certain conditions, use the simpler version of the conditional statement:

```
NextDay = NextDay + 1
If NextDay = 8 Then
    NextDay = 1
    Weeks = Weeks + 1
End If
```

This code segment scans the days of the week, by increasing the value of the NextDay variable by one. If NextDay reaches 8, we move to the first day of the next week. You can also nest If statements, as shown in the next example:

```
NextDay = NextDay + 1
If NextDay = 8 Then
    NextDay = 1
    Weeks = Weeks + 1
    If Weeks = 5 Then
        Weeks = Weeks + 1
    End If
End If
```

Of course, most months have more than four weeks, but we'll ignore this for the sake of simplicity. We'll discuss how to handle days and months at the end of this chapter.

The *Select Case* Statement

A variation on the If...Then...Else statement is the ElseIf clause. To display a different message for each day of the week, you can use the following structure:

```
DayNum = WeekDay(Date())
If DayNum = 2 Then
    MsgBox "Have a nice week!"
ElseIf DayNum = 3 Then
    MsgBox "One down, four to go!"
ElseIf DayNum = 4 Then
    MsgBox "Two down, one to go!"
ElseIf DayNum = 5 Then
    MsgBox "Three down, two to go!"
ElseIf DayNum = 6 Then
    MsgBox "TGIF!"
Else
    MsgBox "Have a nice weekend!"
End If
```

The output produced by this code is shown in Figure 22.8.

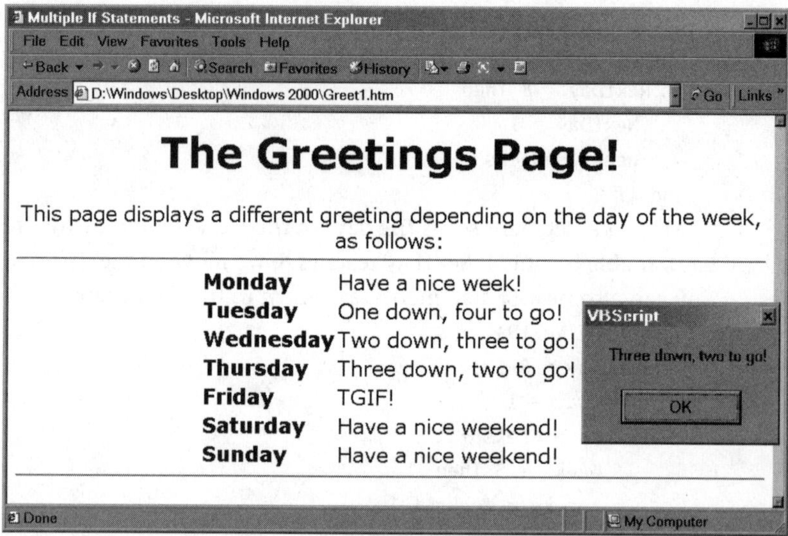

FIGURE 22.8 *The GREET1.HTM document displayed in Internet Explorer*

This VBScript code isn't very compact or easy to understand. An alternative conditional statement is the Select Case statement, whose syntax is:

```
Select Case var
    Case value1: block1
```

```
        Case value2: block2
        ...
        Case Else: blockn
    End Select
```

The `Select Case` statement examines the value of the variable *var* and executes one of the following blocks of statements depending on its value. If the value of *var* is `value1`, the first block of statements is executed; if it's `value2`, the second block of statements is executed, and so on. If *var* has a value different from the ones specified, the `Case Else` clause is executed. The code that displays a different message for each day can be implemented with a `Select Case` statement as follows:

```
DayNum = WeekDay(Date())
Select Case DayNum
    Case 2: MsgBox "Have a nice week!"
    Case 3: MsgBox "One down, four to go!"
    Case 4: MsgBox "Two down, three to go!"
    Case 5: MsgBox "Three down, two to go!"
    Case 6: MsgBox "TGIF!"
    Case Else: MsgBox "Have a nice weekend!"
End Select
```

Notice that the `Select Case` structure evaluates an expression once at the top of the structure. In contrast, the `If...Then...ElseIf` structure can evaluate a different expression for each `ElseIf` statement.

Looping Statements

You can use looping statements to execute a set of statements repeatedly. Some loops repeat statements until a condition is `False`; others repeat statements until a condition is `True`. There are also loops that repeat statements a specific number of times.

The following looping statements are available in VBScript:

- `For...Next`
- `While...Wend`
- `Do...Loop`

The *For...Next* Loop

The `For...Next` loop executes a block of statements a specific number of times. This loop uses a counter to keep track of how many times the loop has been executed so far. For example, the following procedure scans the days of the week with a `For...Next` loop:

```
For iDay = 1 To 7
    {process current day}
Next
```

The variable *iDay* is incremented by one automatically (you don't have to manipulate this variable from within the loop—and you shouldn't, either).

You can also use the Step keyword to go through the loop with a different step. The following loop scans the even months of the year (2, 4, 6, 8, 10, and 12):

```
For iMonth = 2 To 12 Step 2
    {process current month}
Next
```

The Step can be negative, so you can scan a range backward. The following loop processes each year, starting with the most recent one:

```
For iYear = 2001 To 1990 Step -1
    {process current year}
Next
```

You can exit any For...Next statement before the counter reaches its end value by using the Exit For statement. Because you usually want to exit only in certain situations, such as when an error occurs, you should use the Exit For statement in the True statement block of an If...Then...Else statement. If the condition is False, the loop runs as usual.

```
For i = 1 To 10
   If income(i) < 0 Then
       Exit For
   End If
   {more statements}
Next
```

The *While...Wend* Loop

The While...Wend statements execute a block of statements until a condition becomes False (or while it's True). To repeat some statements while a condition is True, use this structure:

```
While condition
    {statements}
Wend
```

The condition is evaluated at each iteration, and if it's True, the statements are executed. Somehow, the condition must be revised in the loop so that the While loop will eventually end. To scan the days of the week with a While...Wend loop, use this structure:

```
iDay=1
While iDay < 8
    {process current day}
    iDay = iDay + 1
Wend
```

The *Do...Loop* Loop

The Do loop is the most flexible one, as it repeats a block of statements while a condition is either True or False. To repeat a block of statements while a condition is True, use this structure:

```
Do While condition
    {statements}
Loop
```

The block of statements will be executed as long as *condition* is True. To repeat some statements until a condition becomes True (in other words, while it's False), use the following structure:

```
Do Until condition
    {statements}
Loop
```

Both forms of the Do loop examine the condition before the block of statements is executed even once. You can also test the condition after the execution of the statements, by moving the test to the end of the loop:

```
Do
    {statements}
Loop While condition
```

and

```
Do
    {statements}
Loop Until condition
```

To exit a Do loop prematurely, use the Exit Do statement.

A common use for the Do loop is to keep prompting the user for valid data. To make sure that the user has entered a valid age, use a loop such as the following:

```
Do
    Age = InputBox("Please enter your age")
Loop Until Age > 0
```

If the user enters a negative or zero age, the loop is executed, and it keeps prompting the user for a valid age.

Here's another loop that allows the user to enter a set of numeric data. When done, the user must enter the value -1 (which presumably is an invalid data value). The program keeps track of the sum of the data values and their count to calculate their average.

```
Do
    newVal = InputBox("New data value, or -1 to end")
    If NewVal <> -1 Then
        Sum = Sum + NewVal
        DataNum = DataNum + 1
    End If
Loop while NewVal <> -1
MsgBox "The average value is " & Sum / DataNum
```

Input/Output Functions

VBScript is limited when it comes to input and output functions. It supports the `InputBox()` and `MsgBox()` functions, which prompt the user to enter a value and display a message in a dialog box. To prompt the user for a data value, call the `InputBox()` function, passing the prompt you want to appear on the dialog box as an argument:

```
UserAge = InputBox("Please enter your age")
```

The dialog box provides the usual OK and Cancel buttons. If the user cancels the operation by clicking the Cancel button, the *UserAge* variable will be empty. To validate the data, use a structure such as the following:

```
UserAge = -1
While UserAge<1
   UserAge = InputBox("Please enter your age")
Wend
```

This is a loop that keeps executing while the variable's `UserAge` value is negative (you can apply any other constraint that suits your application).

The `MsgBox()` function displays a message in a dialog box. In its simplest form, this function accepts the message to display in a dialog box. The user can click the OK button to close the dialog box.

```
MsgBox "Can't Access Printer!"
```

Because the `MsgBox()` function can also display other buttons, you can use it in other situations. The complete syntax of the `MsgBox()` function is:

```
MsgBox(prompt, buttons, title)
```

Only the `prompt` argument is mandatory; the other two are optional. The `buttons` argument can have one of the values shown in Table 22.2, and it determines which buttons will appear in the message box. The `title` argument, finally, is the title that will appear on the title bar of the message box.

TABLE 22.2: THE CONSTANTS THAT DETERMINE WHICH BUTTONS WILL APPEAR

Constant Name	Value	Description
`vbOKOnly`	0	Display OK button only
`VbOKCancel`	1	Display OK and Cancel buttons
`VbAbortRetryIgnore`	2	Display Abort, Retry, and Ignore buttons
`VbYesNoCancel`	3	Display Yes, No, and Cancel buttons
`VbYesNo`	4	Display Yes and No buttons
`VbRetryCancel`	5	Display Retry and Cancel buttons

You can also add a constant that determines which icon will appear in the message box. These constants are listed in Table 22.3.

TABLE 22.3: THE CONSTANTS THAT DETERMINE WHICH ICON WILL APPEAR

Constant Name	Value	Description
`vbCritical`	16	Display Critical Message icon
`VbQuestion`	32	Display Warning Query icon
`VbExclamation`	48	Display Warning Message icon
`VbInformation`	64	Display Information Message icon

For example, to display the Yes and No buttons with the critical icon, use the value 20 (`vbYesNo + vbCritical`). To display this message box, use the following statement:

```
MsgBox "File not found. Do you want to locate it yourself?", vbYesNo +
vbCritical
```

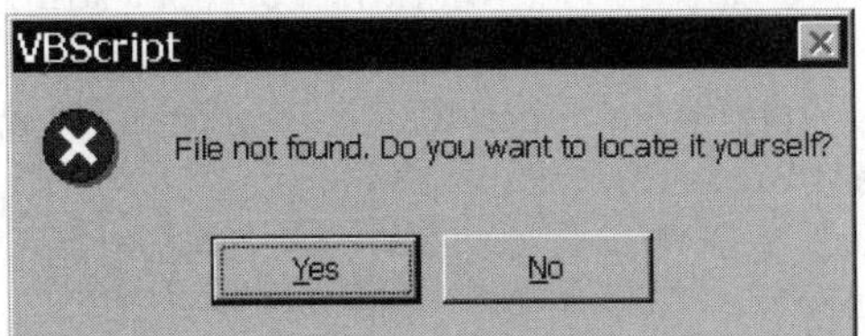

Finally, you can add another constant to the `buttons` argument, which determines which button is the default (in other words, which button will be activated when a user clicks the Enter button). Table 22.4 shows the values you can use to specify the default button.

TABLE 22.4: THE CONSTANTS THAT DETERMINE THE DEFAULT BUTTON

Constant Name	Value	Description
VbDefaultButton1	0	First button is default
VbDefaultButton2	256	Second button is default
VbDefaultButton3	512	Third button is default
VbDefaultButton4	768	Fourth button is default

String Manipulation Functions

Contrary to common belief, most programs don't crunch numbers; they crunch text instead. The proper term for text in computer programming is *string*. A string is a sequence of characters, such as a word, a sentence, or an entire document. VBScript provides the following functions for manipulating strings.

LCase(), UCase()

These two functions convert a string to lower- or uppercase. If the variable *message* contains the following string

```
message = "Welcome to VBScript"
```

the statement

```
MsgBox LCase(message)
```

will display "welcome to vbscript" and the statement

```
MsgBox UCase(message)
```

will display "WELCOME TO VBSCRIPT".

Left(), *Right()*, and *Mid()*

These three functions let you extract part of a string. The function `Left()` extracts a specified number of characters from the left of the string; the function `Right()` extracts a specified number of characters from the right side of the string. Let's say you assign a string to the variable *message*:

```
message = "Welcome to VBScript"
```

The statement

```
Left(message, 7)
```

will return the string "Welcome" (without the quotes), and the statement

```
Right(message, 8)
```

will return the string "VBScript".

The Mid() function can extract any part of the string and has the following syntax:

```
Mid(string, start, len)
```

The *start* argument is the location of the first character to be extracted, and *len* is the number of characters to be extracted. The statement

```
Mid(message, 9, 5)
```

will return the string "to VB".

Len()

The Len() function accepts a string as its argument and returns the length of the string.

InStr()

The Instr() function returns the location of a string within a longer string. Its syntax is

```
Instr(str1, str2)
```

The *str1* argument is the string being searched, and *str2* is the string searched for. To locate the word "VBScript" in the message string, use the statement

```
position = InStr(message, "VBScript")
```

The value of the position variable after the execution of the above statement will be 12.

Let's say you want to validate the variable *eMail*, which holds an e-mail address. A valid e-mail address contains the at character (@), and you must search for this character in the *eMail* variable. The following lines prompt the user for an e-mail address and then validate it:

```
eMail = InputBox("Please enter your e-mail address")
If InStr(eMail, "@") < 2 Then
    MsgBox "This is an invalid address"
Else
    MsgBox "Thank you!"
End If
```

If the eMail string doesn't contain an at character (in which case the InStr() function will return 0), or if it starts with this character (in which case InStr() will return 1), the e-mail address entered by the user is invalid, and the program displays the appropriate error message.

Other String Manipulation Functions

Other string manipulation functions include the StrReverse() function, which reverses the order of the characters in a string, and the StrComp() function, which compares two strings. Many other string manipulation functions are described in the VBScript documentation.

In addition to the string manipulation functions, there is a special string operator, the *concatenation operator*. Its symbol is &, and it concatenates the strings that appear before and after it. The statement

```
newString = "Welcome to " & "VBScript"
```

assigns the string "Welcome to VBScript" to the variable *newString*. The & operator concatenates strings only, even if they represent numeric values. The & operator, when applied to strings, is synonymous to the + operator. The previous statement could have also been written as

```
newString = "Welcome to " + "VBScript""
```

The statement

```
newString = "123" & "4.5"
```

will assign the value "1234.5" to the newString variable. However, the + operator will treat the two strings as numeric values and return a different result. The statement

```
newString = "123" + "4.5"
```

will assign the value 127.5 to the newString variable (which is now a numeric variable).

Date/Time Functions

VBScript provides a rich set of functions for handling dates and times, which are used quite frequently in programming. I'll discuss only the most basic and most commonly used ones in this section.

Date(), Time()

These two functions return the system's date and time. To display the date and time on a message box, use the statements

```
MsgBox Date()
MsgBox Time()
```

You can also combine these two functions on the same line with the & operator (which concatenates two strings):

```
MsgBox "The date is " & Date() & " and the time is " & Time()
```

DateAdd()

The DateAdd() function returns a date to which a specified time interval has been added and has the following syntax:

```
DateAdd(interval, number, date)
```

The *date* argument (the last argument) is the starting initial date, *interval* is the interval to be added to the string, and *number* is the number of intervals. The interval to be added to the initial date can be one of those shown in Table 22.5.

TABLE 22.5: THE VALUES OF THE DATEADD() FUNCTION'S INTERVAL ARGUMENT

yyyy	for year	q	for quarter	m	for month
d	for day	w	for week day	ww	for week of year
h	for hour	n	for minute	s	for second

To add three months to the date "30/11/2000" use the statement

```
MsgBox DateAdd("m", 3, "30/11/00")
```

The value displayed in the dialog box will be 02/28/01, which is the last day of February.

DateDiff()

The `DateDiff()` function returns the number of intervals between two dates. Its syntax is

```
DateDiff(interval, date1, date2)
```

The *`date1`* and *`date2`* arguments are the two days you want to use in the calculations, and *`interval`* determines the format of the result. To find out the difference between the dates "30/11/00" and "02/28/01" in months, use the statement

```
MsgBox DateDiff("m", "30/11/00", "02/28/01")
```

The result will be 3 months. If you reverse the order of the dates in the function, the result will be –3.

The same difference in days can be calculated with the statement

```
MsgBox DateDiff("d", "30/11/00", "02/28/01")
```

This time the result will be 90. Use the expression `"s"` as the first argument to calculate the same difference in seconds.

Day(), Month(), Year()

These three functions return the day of the month, month, and year of a date specifically. The `WeekDay()` function returns the day of the week (a value in the range 1 through 7). The statements

```
Day(Date())
```

and

```
Month(Date())
```

return the current day and month. The results are returned as numbers. If you need the name of the day or the month, use the following two functions.

Hour(), Minute(), Second()

These functions return the hour (a number from 0 to 23), the minute (0–59), and the second (0–59) of a specified date or time. If the current time is "6:14.48 PM," these functions will return the following values:

```
Hour(Time())        ' will return the value 18
Minute(Time())      ' will return the value 14
Second(Time())      ' will return the value 48
```

WeekdayName(), MonthName()

These two functions return the name of the day and the month of the specified date. The statements

```
WeekdayName(Date())
```

and

```
MonthName(Date())
```

return the name of the day and month of the current date.

Forms and Controls

VBScript looks and feels very much like a programming language. It provides numerous functions (you've seen just a few of them, and we'll discuss a few more in the following chapters), but it lacks the tools for designing user interfaces. Windows applications don't rely on `InputBox()` and `MsgBox()` functions to interact with the user. To design user interfaces, you must rely on HTML.

As you know already, HTML pages contain controls that let the user enter information, similar to the usual Windows controls: text boxes, option buttons, and so on. The areas on the HTML page where these controls appear are called *Forms*, and the controls themselves are called *intrinsic controls*. HTML provides special tags for placing intrinsic controls on a Form.

Before placing a control on the page, you must create a Form, with the `<FORM>` tag. Its syntax is

```
<FORM NAME=name>
</FORM>
```

All the controls must appear between these two tags. The *NAME* attribute (it's optional) is the name of the Form and is used when a page contains multiple Forms.

HTML provides support for the following intrinsic controls, which must appear within a pair of `<FORM>` tags. Figure 22.9 shows a Web page with a Form that contains most of HTML's intrinsic controls.

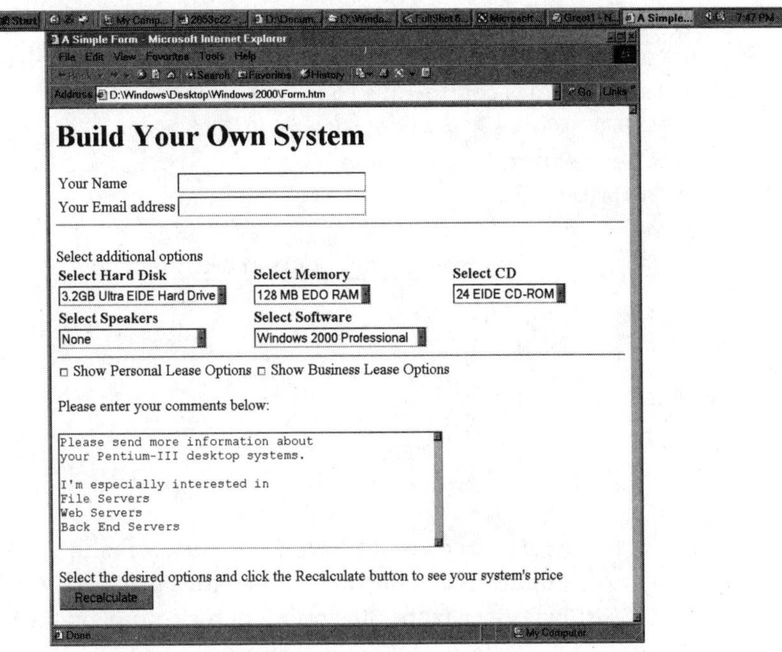

FIGURE 22.9
This Form contains all the intrinsic HTML controls.

The Text Control

The Text control is a box in which users can enter a single line of text (such as name, address, and so on). To insert a Text control on a Form, use the following tag:

```
<INPUT TYPE = TEXT NAME = "Publisher" VALUE = "Sybex">
```

The VALUE attribute specifies the initial value. After the user enters a new value, VALUE holds the new string. To edit the contents of a Text control, the visitor can use the common editing keys (Home, Delete, Insert, and so on), but the text can't be formatted.

To control the size and contents of the control, use the SIZE and MAXLENGTH attributes. The SIZE attribute specifies the size of the control on the Form, in number of characters, and the MAXLENGTH attribute specifies the maximum number of characters the user can type in the control. A variation of the Text control is the Password control, which is identical but doesn't display the characters as they are typed. Instead, it displays asterisks, and it is used to enter passwords.

The TextArea Control

The TextArea control is similar to the Text control, but it allows the entry of multiple lines of text. All the usual navigation and editing keys work with the TextArea control. To place a TextArea control on a Form, use the <TEXTAREA> tag:

```
<TEXTAREA NAME = "Comments" ROWS = 10 COLS = 30>
The best editor I've ever used!
</TEXTAREA>
```

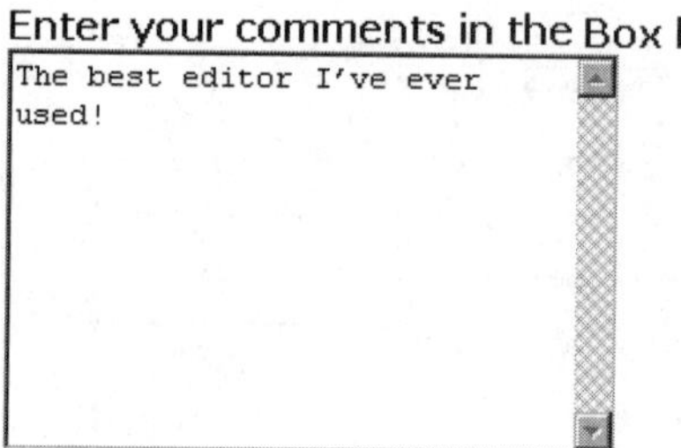

Because the TextArea control allows you to specify multiple lines of initial text, it's not inserted with the usual <INPUT> tag, but with a pair of <TEXTAREA> tags. The ROWS and COLS attributes specify the dimensions of the control on the page in number of characters. Any line breaks you insert between the two <TEXTAREA> tags are preserved when the text is displayed on the control. Even if you include HTML tags in the initial text, they will appear on the control.

The CheckBox Control

The CheckBox control is a little square with an optional check mark, which acts as a toggle. Every time the user clicks it, it changes state. It is used to present a list of options, from which the user can select one or more. To insert a CheckBox control on a Form, use the <INPUT> tag:

```
<INPUT TYPE = CHECKBOX NAME = "Check1">
```

To initially check a CheckBox control, specify the CHECKED attribute in the corresponding <INPUT> tag. The control's value can be 0 or 1, indicating whether it's checked (1) or cleared (0).

The following lines insert three CheckBox controls into the Form. The user can select one of them by clicking it; the previously selected one is cleared automatically.

```
<H4>Select an option by clicking a CheckBox</H4>
<INPUT TYPE = CHECKBOX NAME = "Images">Include images<BR>
<INPUT TYPE = CHECKBOX NAME = "Sound">Include sounds<BR>
```

```
<INPUT TYPE = CHECKBOX NAME = "Video">Include video <BR>
```

Select an option by clicking a CheckBox

☑ Include images
☑ Include sounds
☐ Include video

The RadioButton Control

The RadioButton control is round and contains a dot in the center when selected. RadioButton controls are used to present lists of options, similar to the CheckBox controls, but only one option can be selected at a time. Each time a new option is checked by the user, the previously selected one is cleared. To insert a RadioButton control on a Form use the following:

```
<INPUT TYPE = RADIO NAME = "Radio1">
```

Whereas each CheckBox control has a different name, a group of RadioButtons all have the same name. This is how the browser knows that a number of RadioButton controls belong to the same group and that only one of them can be checked at a time. To specify the control that will be initially checked in the group, use the CHECKED attribute. The following lines insert a group of four RadioButton controls on a Form:

```
<INPUT TYPE = RADIO NAME = "Level">Beginner <BR>
<INPUT TYPE = RADIO NAME = "Level">Intermediate <BR>
<INPUT TYPE = RADIO NAME = "Level" CHECKED>Advanced<BR>
<INPUT TYPE = RADIO NAME = "Level">Expert <BR>
```

Select your level by clicking one of the radio buttons below

○ Beginner
○ Intermediate
◉ Advanced
○ Expert

The Multiple Selection Control

The Multiple Selection control is basically a list that can contain a number of options. The visitor can select none, one, or multiple items in the list. The list is delimited with a pair of <SELECT> tags. Each item in the list is inserted with a separate <OPTION> tag. To place a Multiple Selection List on the Form, add the following lines:

```
<SELECT  NAME = "MemoryOptions" SIZE = 3 MULTIPLE = multiple>
<OPTION VALUE=16> 16 Mbytes</OPTION>
<OPTION VALUE=32> 32 Mbytes</OPTION>
```

```
<OPTION VALUE=64> 64 Mbytes</OPTION>
<OPTION VALUE=128> 128 Mbytes</OPTION>
<OPTION VALUE=256> 256 Mbytes</OPTION>
</SELECT>
```

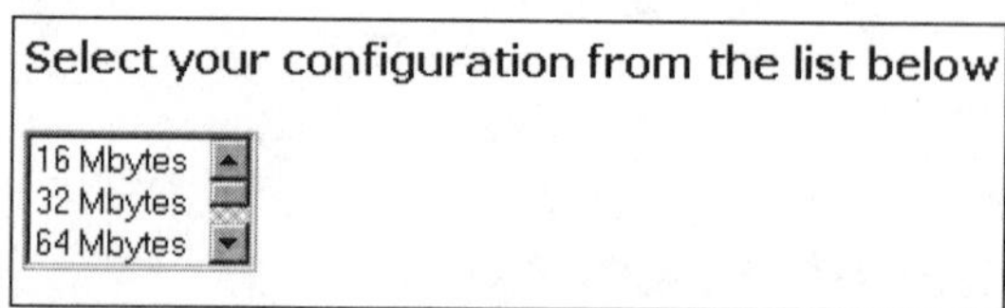

The SIZE attribute specifies how many lines will be visible. If you omit it, the list will be reduced to a single line and the user must use the up and down arrow keys to scroll through the available options. If the list contains more lines, a vertical scroll bar is automatically attached to help the user locate the desired item. The MULTIPLE attribute specifies that the user can select multiple items in the list by clicking their names while holding down the Shift or Ctrl key. If you omit the MULTIPLE attribute, each time an item is selected, the previously selected one is cleared.

The Command Button Control

Clicking a Command button triggers certain actions. To insert a Command button on a Form, use a tag such as the following:

```
<INPUT TYPE = BUTTON NAME = "ShowDate" VALUE="Date">
```

The *VALUE* attribute specifies the string that will appear on the Command Button. Every time this button is clicked, it triggers the ShowDate_Click event. Obviously, you must place the code that you want to execute every time this button is clicked in this event's handler:

```
Sub ShowDate_Click()
   MsgBox "The date is " & Date()
End Sub
```

The *FORM.HTM* Page

Now that you have seen the tags for placing controls on a Form, we can look at the HTML code that produced the Form shown in Figure 22.9. The FORM.HTM document is quite lengthy, but it's easy to read and understand. It contains the tags discussed in the previous sections for placing controls on a Form (the ORDER Form). The controls are all placed on a table to simplify their alignment. Tables are used by most Web pages as alignment tools, and the FORM.HTM page is a typical example.

The script at the beginning of the file handles the Click event of the Button at the bottom of the Form, whose name is RECALC. The button doesn't really recalculate the value of the selected configuration. Instead, it displays the values of all controls on the Form in a message box. Once you can read the value selected in each control, you can easily recalculate the value of the computer. Notice that the names of the controls in the script are prefixed by the name of the Form they belong to (the ORDER Form).

All controls have a Value property, which returns the value stored in the control or the value of the selected item for radio buttons. The CheckBox control has a Checked property, which is True or False, depending on whether it is checked. Take a look at the script to see how it accesses the values of the controls on the Form and displays their values. The expression vbCrLf is a built-in constant that inserts a line break. The script builds the string msg one step at a time and passes it as an argument to the MsgBox() function to display it.

Here's the listing of the FORM.HTM page:

```
<HTML>
<SCRIPT LANGUAGE=VBScript>
Sub RECALC_onClick()
   msg = "Customer Name " & ORDER.Name.Value & ORDER.EMail.Value & vbCrLf
   msg = msg & "Hard Disk " & ORDER.HardDisk.Value & vbCrLf
   msg = msg & "Memory " & ORDER.Memory.Value & vbCrLf
   msg = msg & "CD-ROM " & ORDER.CD.Value & vbCrLf
   If ORDER.PLease.Checked Then
      msg = msg & "Personal lease" & vbCrLf
   End If
   If ORDER.BLease.Checked Then
      msg = msg & "Business lease" & vbCrLf
   End If
   msg = msg & vbCrLf & "YOUR COMMENTS" & vbCrLf
   msg = msg & ORDER.Comments.Value
   MsgBox msg
End Sub
</SCRIPT>
<TITLE>A Simple Form</TITLE>
<H1>Build Your Own System</H1>
<FORM name=ORDER method="POST" action="http://127.0.0.1/aspages/param.asp">
<TABLE>
<TR>
<TD>Your Name</TD> <TD><INPUT TYPE=TEXT SIZE=30 MAXSIZE=30 NAME="Name"></TR>
<TR>
<TD>Your Email address</TD> <TD><INPUT TYPE=TEXT SIZE=30 MAXSIZE=30
NAME="EMail"></TR>
</TABLE>
<HR>
<P>
Select additional options
```

```
<TABLE>
<TR>
<TD><B>Select Hard Disk</B></TD>
<TD></TD>
<TD><B>Select Memory</B></TD>
<TD></TD>
<TD><B>Select CD</B></TD>
</TR>
<TR>
<TD><SELECT name="HardDisk" size="1">
<OPTION selected value="3.2G">3.2GB Ultra EIDE Hard Drive </OPTION>
<OPTION  value="4.3G">4.3GB Ultra EIDE Hard Drive </OPTION>
</SELECT>
</TD>
<TD>
      
</TD>
<TD>
<SELECT name="Memory" size="1">
<OPTION value="64 MB">64MB EDO RAM</OPTION>
<OPTION selected value="128">128 MB EDO RAM</OPTION>
<OPTION value="256">256 MB EDO RAM</OPTION>
</SELECT>
</TD>
<TD>
      
</TD>
<TD>
<SELECT name="CD" size="1">
<option value="CD12">12 EIDE CD-ROM</option>
<option selected value="CD24">24 EIDE CD-ROM</option>
</SELECT>
</TD>
</TR>
<TR>
<TD><B>Select Speakers</B></TD>
<TD></TD>
<TD><B>Select Software</B></TD>
<TD></TD>
</TR>
<TR>
```

```
<TD>
<SELECT name="Speaker" size="1">
<option selected value="">None</option>
<option value="S90">Altec ACS90 Speakers</option>
<option value="S290">Altec ACS290 Speakers</option>
</SELECT>
</TD>
<TD></TD>
<TD>
<SELECT name="Software" size="1">
<option selected value="WIN2K">Windows 2000 Professional</option>
<option value="WIN2K">Windows 2000 Professional</option>
<option value="WINNT">Windows NT Workstation 4.0 </option>
</SELECT>
</TD>
</TABLE>
<HR>
<INPUT NAME="Please" TYPE=CHECKBOX VALUE=1> Show Personal Lease Options
<INPUT NAME="Please" TYPE=CHECKBOX VALUE=2> Show Business Lease Options
<P>
Please enter your comments below:
<P>
<TEXTAREA NAME=Comments ROWS=8 COLS=50>
Please send more information about
your Pentium-III desktop systems.

I'm especially interested in
File Servers
Web Servers
Back End Servers
</TEXTAREA>
<P>
Select the desired options and click the Recalculate button to see your
system's price
<INPUT TYPE=BUTTON NAME="RECALC" VALUE="Recalculate">
</FORM>
</HTML>
```

VBScript and HTML

I mentioned already that VBScript and HTML are combined in DHTML. Since VBScript is embedded in HTML documents, you would expect to be able to access the container document from within the script. This is indeed possible, through the `Document` object. As you will see in the following three chapters, VBScript can access a number of objects (such as the folder of the hard disk, their files, and so on). One of the objects available to VBScript is the `Document` object, which represents the document that contains the script.

Through the methods and properties of the Document object you can manipulate the appearance, or even the contents, of the current document. If you are not familiar with objects, think of them as variables that represent programmable entities. The `Document` object, for instance, exposes the `bgColor` property, which is the document's background color. Likewise, the `Title` property is the document's object. To retrieve the current document's title from within the script, use the expression `Document.Title`. To change the document's background color, use a statement such as `Document.bgColor=red`. Objects have methods too, which are actions that each object can perform. The `Document` object, for example, has the Write method, which you call to write something to the document.

The Properties and Methods of the *Document* Object

Let's start by examining the most important properties of the `Document` object.

bgColor, fgColor

These two properties return or set the page's background color and the color of the text. You use the `Document` object's methods to manipulate the contents of the document.

Write

The `Write` method writes a string to the current document. The string is inserted at the current location in the document.

WriteLn

The `WriteLn` method is similar to the `Write` method, only it appends a new line character at the end of the string written to the document.

Open

This method opens the document for output. Its contents are cleared, and new strings can be placed in the document with the `Write` and `WriteLn` methods.

Close

This method closes the document and updates the browser's window (renders the text on the screen).

The `Document` object's properties and methods let you create HTML documents on the fly. Normally, HTML documents exist on some disk and are rendered on the browser. If you are using the browser to surf the Web, HTML documents live on a server. You can also open local HTML files by double-clicking their icons. Moreover, HTML documents are prefabricated. All users who open the same HTML document see the same window.

Using the *Document* Object

With the help of the Document object and VBScript, you can design pages that are rendered differently on each user's screen. Let's say you want to create an HTML document that displays the current date and/or time. Clearly, you can't keep changing the document constantly. As you may have guessed, we'll use VBScript's Date() and Time() functions to display the current date and time. Here's a document that uses these two functions to build a document whose contents change according to when it was opened. Notice that even the greeting is adjusted according to the time of the day:

```
<HTML>
<SCRIPT LANGUAGE=VBScript>
If Time < #12.00.00# Then
    Document.Write "<H1>Good morning</H1>"
Else
    Document.Write "<H1>Good afternoon</H1>"
End If
Document.Write "<H2>and welcome to VBScript</H2>"
Document.Write "<H3>The current date is " & Date() & "</H3>"
Document.Write "<H3>and the current time is " & Time() & "</H3>"
</SCRIPT>
<BODY>
<FONT FACE=Verdana SIZE=4>
<HR>
The first two lines of this page are generated the moment the document is
opened and they display the <I>actual date and time</I>.
The rest of the page is a regular HTML document, which remains the same,
regardless of when it's opened.
</BODY>
</HTML>
```

You can see the output generated by this document in Internet Explorer's window in Figure 22.10. The document is called DATE.HTM. The script in this document isn't contained in a subroutine or a function. Any lines of VBScript code inserted directly into the SCRIPT section of the document are executed as soon as the document is loaded. After the code is executed (and the initial headers are displayed), the rest of the document is rendered on the screen. The document's body is a regular HTML document made up of text and HTML tags.

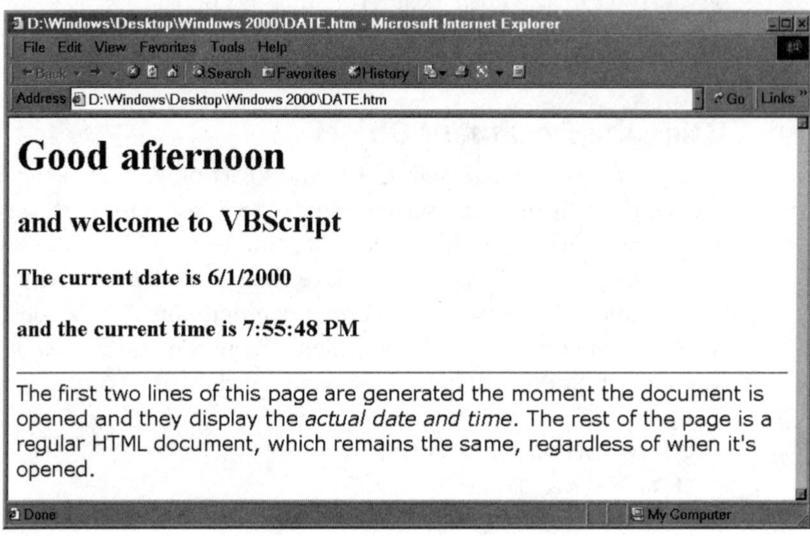

FIGURE 22.10
The DATE.HTM document uses a short script to display the current date and time, as well as a greeting according to the time.

In the next section, you will see a more advanced example that uses VBScript to generate a calendar on the fly.

The Calendar Page

The material in this chapter is rather dull, and I can't give you many practical examples. In the following three chapters you'll find interesting examples, but I must first discuss a few more topics that are really necessary for building nontrivial examples. However, I want to end this chapter with a useful document enhanced with VBScript commands, which you can use to experiment with. This example is shown in Figure 22.11. The `CALENDAR.HTM` page displays the current month's calendar. The document need not be changed every month; the calendar is generated automatically by VBScript code on the client computer.

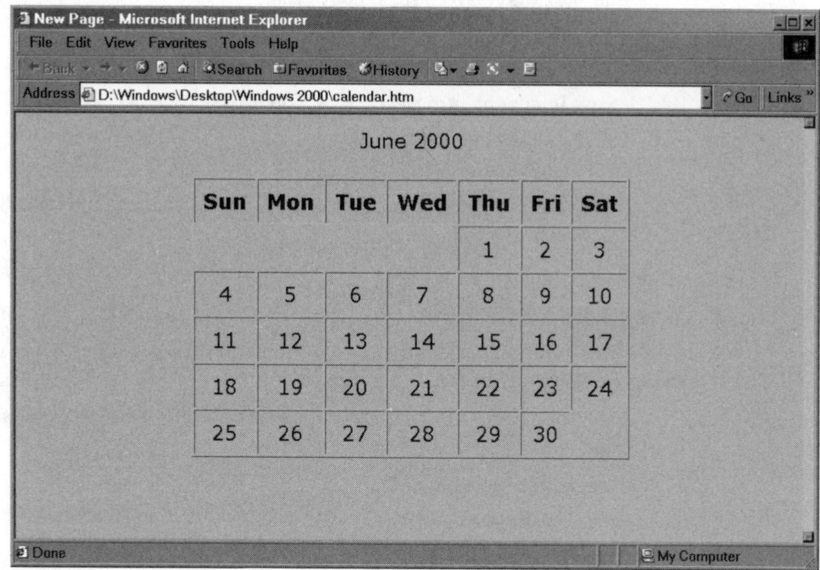

FIGURE 22.11
The CALENDAR.HTM page displays the current month's calendar.

The code for the CALENDAR.HTM file is shown here. You may find the listing complicated, but I'll go through it and explain how it works.

```
<HTML>
<HEAD>
<TITLE>New Page</TITLE>
<SCRIPT LANGUAGE="VBSCRIPT">
Dim imonth, thisdate, nextday, cday
imonth=Month(date)

    Document.bgColor="#C0C0C0"
    Document.Write "<CENTER>"
    Document.Write "<FONT FACE='Verdana' SIZE=5>"
    Document.Write MonthName(Month(date)) & " " & Year(date)
    Document.Write "<P>"
    Document.Write "<TABLE CELLPADDING=10 BORDER><TR>"
    Document.Write
"<TD><B>Sun<TD><B>Mon<TD><B>Tue<TD><B>Wed<TD><B>Thu<TD><B>Fri<TD><B>Sat"
    Document.Write "<TR>"
    thisdate=DateSerial(Year(date), Month(date), 1)
    nextday=1
```

```
    For cday=1 to 7
        If WeekDay(thisdate)>cday Then
            Document.Write "<TD></TD>"
        Else
            Document.Write "<TD ALIGN=CENTER><FONT SIZE=3>" & nextday &
            "</TD>"
            nextday=nextday+1
            thisdate=DateSerial(Year(Date), imonth, nextday)
        End If
    Next
    Document.Write "<TR>"
    weekDays=1
    while Month(thisdate)=imonth
        Document.Write "<TD ALIGN=CENTER><FONT SIZE=3>" & nextday & "</TD>"
        nextday=nextday+1
        weekDays=weekDays+1
        If weekDays>7 then
            WeekDays=1
            Document.write "<TR>"
        End If
        thisdate=DateSerial(Year(Date), imonth, nextday)
    Wend
    Document.Write "</TABLE>"
    Document.Write "</CENTER>"

</SCRIPT>
</HEAD>
<BODY>
</BODY>
</HTML>
```

Notice that the document doesn't contain a BODY section. Everything is generated on the fly with `Document.Write` statements. First, the script displays the current month as a header:

```
Document.Write "<CENTER>"
Document.Write "<FONT FACE='Verdana' SIZE=5>"
Document.Write MonthName(Month(date)) & " " & Year(date)
```

Then the scripts create a table, with the names of the days on the first row. The statement

```
thisdate=DateSerial(Year(date), Month(date), 1)
```

uses the `DateSerial()` function, which accepts as arguments the year, month, and date and returns a date variable, which is assigned to the `thisdate` variable. We select the current year (Year(Date()) and the current month (Month(Date()), but not the current date; instead, we select the first day of the month (the last argument).

The days of the first week of the month are displayed with a For...Next loop. The first week of the month is frequently incomplete, and the first few cells in the table are likely to be empty. This loop goes through the seven days in the week until it hits the first day in the month.

After it finds the first day in the month, the program creates cells in which it places the value of the variable nextday, which is increased with every iteration (it goes from 1 to 31). The following string produces a cell with a number:

```
"<TD ALIGN=CENTER><FONT SIZE=3>" & nextday & "</TD>"
```

This is HTML code, and any references to variables are replaced by the actual value of the nextday variable. For example, if the value of the variable is 24, the following line is actually written to the document:

```
<TD ALIGN=CENTER><FONT SIZE=3>24</TD>
```

After the first week of the month is displayed, the program continues with the subsequent weeks. These weeks are complete, except for the last one, of course.

A While...Wend loop handles the remaining days of the month. With each iteration, the nextday variable is increased by one day, and the loop continues to the end of the month.

You can easily turn each day of the month into a hyperlink that points to another file with information specific for that day. Instead of writing the number of the day to the output, you can insert the appropriate <A> tags to turn the day number into a hyperlink. For example, if the current value of the nextday variable is 24, the following VBScript line

```
"<A HREF=" & imonth & "-" & nextday & ".HTM>" & nextday & "</A>"
```

writes the following line to the document:

```
<A HREF=1-24.HTM>24</A>
```

which is a hyperlink to the document 24.HTM. This file must also exist on the same folder as the CALENDAR.HTM file.

Summary

In this chapter, I introduced you to Internet Information Services (IIS) and then got you started using HTML and VBScript to create Web pages. In the next chapter, I'll build on this information as we use DHTML and VBScript.

CHAPTER 23

DHTML and VBScript

FEATURING:

The trend in Web page design today is to create highly interactive and dynamic pages. An *interactive* page interacts with the user, as though it were an application. When the user clicks a button or issues a voice command, the page responds by carrying out an action. Web pages have always been interactive because they contain hyperlinks. Even so, they are hardly interactive when compared with Windows applications. VBScript, ActiveX controls, and Java applets can make Web pages even more interactive. A page that contains these elements can react to user actions in a way similar to a Windows application (as opposed to simply displaying another page).

A *dynamic* page is also interactive, but it can change its own content by hiding or displaying elements, sometimes not in response to user actions. You have certainly seen Web pages that contain rotating ads. These pages don't react to user actions, but their content is dynamic. Many pages on the Web use a navigational frame and adjust their contents depending on the item that the user selects in the navigational frame. These pages react to user actions, but they are also dynamic: their main feature is that they change their content right on your computer (without downloading another page from the server).

The distinction between interactive and dynamic pages has blurred along the way, and it's not really necessary to distinguish pages as either interactive or dynamic. Perhaps this is why Microsoft introduced the term *active pages* to describe Web pages that interact with the user and behave dynamically. Because interactivity is not new to the Web, in this chapter I'll use the term *dynamic.*

In the last chapter you learned the basics of VBScript and how to use VBScript to design interactive forms. You also saw an example of how to use VBScript to control the various elements of an HTML page. In this chapter you'll learn how to:

- Extend HTML with styles and classes
- Use VBScript to control the entire document and design Web pages with Dynamic HTML (DHTML)
- Use some of the new controls for creating dynamic contents, including the Structured Graphics Control and the Sequencer Control (which come with Internet Explorer—you need not install them separately)
- Include ActiveX controls, such as the Agent Control from Microsoft, which will allow you to design voice-enabled pages (pages that understand voice commands and reply in voice)

Extending HTML with Styles and Classes

DHTML originated with the so-called *styles*. As you recall from the previous chapter, many HTML tags recognize attributes, which allow the Web author to modify certain properties of the elements. For example, the COLOR attribute of the <FONT> tag lets you specify the color of the text, and the SRC attribute of the <IMG> tag lets you specify the image to be displayed. The basic look produced by most HTML tags, however, can't be changed. The <H1> tag, for instance, displays a level-1 header, and you can't change the look of the headers.

With styles, you can change the look of the elements and redefine just about any HTML tag. For example, the following tag definition will make all level-1 headers in a page blue and all level-2 headers red:

```
<STYLE>
H1 {color:blue}
H2 {color:red}
</STYLE>
```

If you insert this statement at the beginning of an HTML document, usually in the HEAD section of the document, it will take effect for all following <H1> and <H2> tags.

NOTE Styles are used in Web page design in the same way they are used in word processors: you define the style and then apply it to selected words or paragraphs. Because HTML is a language—not an environment with visual tools like a word processor—you must define the styles yourself with the <STYLE> tag.

In addition to the modified headers, you might also want to use the original, plain <H1> and <H2> tags. Or you might want two types of <H1> headers: a blue one and a red one. It is possible to define classes to differentiate custom tags. A *class* is a category of tag that lets you create a unique set of tags in addition to the existing ones.

Let's say you want to define two <H1> headers: one for title and another one for summaries. Here are the definitions of the two custom <H1> tags:

```
<STYLE>
H1.title {font-weight: bold; background:white; color:black}
H1.summary {font-weight: bold; color:blue}
</STYLE>
```

To use the <H1> tag in a title, you would insert the following:

```
<H1 CLASS=title>
This is a document section title
</H1>
```

To use the <H1> tag in a summary, you would insert the following:

```
<H1 CLASS=summary>
```

```
This is a summary section title
</H1>
```

Practically, a class is a new tag, but because it's derived from an existing tag instead of defining an entirely new tag, we define a class (a variation) of an existing tag. The tag `<H1 CLASS=title>` has all the attributes of the `<H1>` tag, except for the attributes specified in the definition of the class: the font's weight, the background color, and the foreground color.

You can use classes to customize existing HTML tags as needed in a document. Nevertheless, when you insert a tag into a document, it can't be changed later. The page is still a static one. As you will see, DHTML lets you redefine the styles after the page has been rendered on the screen. For example, you can specify that the color property of an `<H1>` header changes when the pointer is moved over it or when the user takes another action.

As you might guess, the attributes of custom tags are changed through a script, either in response to a user action or in a predefined program sequence. You provide the subroutines for the events the script should react to, and these subroutines are activated automatically. The same scripting model we used for programming forms is also used with DHTML.

Reacting to Mouse Events

In this section, we are going to look at a simple example of an HTML page containing a script that reacts to mouse events. Just as the intrinsic controls can have names, the various elements of HTML can also have names. For example, you can assign a name to a hyperlink and then use this name to react to the movement of the pointer while it's dragged over the hyperlink. The tag

```
<A HREF="http://www.sybex.com">SYBEX Home Page</A>
```

will insert a hyperlink on the page. To name this hyperlink, use the `NAME` attribute:

```
<A NAME=SYBEXLINK HREF="http://www.sybex.com">SYBEX Home Page</A>
```

Now you can write handlers for the various events that this element can recognize. One such event is the `Click` event, and the corresponding event handler would be a subroutine named

```
Sub SYBEXLINK_onClick()
    {your code comes here}
End Sub
```

Of course, there's very little reason to react to the `Click` event of a hyperlink; hyperlinks react to the mouse click on their own. But there's another mouse event you can react to, the `onMouseOver` event. Look at the following subroutine:

```
Sub SYBEXLINK_onMouseOver()
    {your code comes here}
End Sub
```

This subroutine will be called automatically as the user drags the pointer over the `SYBEXLINK` hyperlink. The `LINKS.HTM` page demonstrates how to program an HTML document to react to the movement of the mouse. The document, shown in Figure 23.1, contains two hyperlinks. Each time the pointer moves over them, a message is displayed on the browser's status bar. To access the status bar, use the `Status` property of the `Window` object, which represents the browser:

```
Window.Status = "your status message goes here"
```

FIGURE 23.1
The `LINKS.HTM` page reacts to the movement of the mouse over the two hyperlinks.

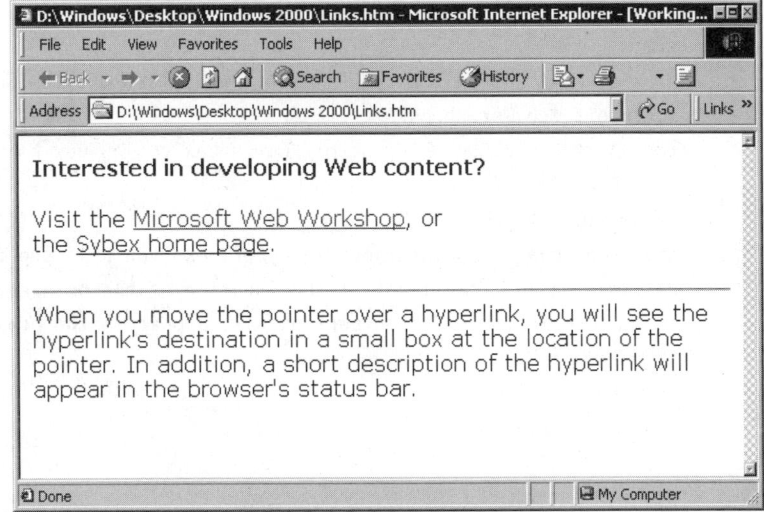

The two hyperlinks were inserted with the statements

```
<A NAME=MSLINK HREF="http:/www.microsoft.com/workshop">Microsoft Web
Workshop</A>
```

and

```
<A NAME=SYBEXLINK HREF="http://www.sybex.com">SYBEX Home Page</A>
```

The two event handlers for the `onMouseOver` event of the two hyperlinks appear at the beginning of the page, shown here:

```
<HTML>
<HEAD>
<TITLE>The Links Page</TITLE>
<SCRIPT LANGUAGE="VBScript">

Sub MSLink_onMouseOver()
    Window.status="The ultimate resource for Web authors and developers."
End Sub
```

```
Sub SBXLink_onMouseOver()
    Window.status="Books for all your computing needs."
End Sub

</SCRIPT>
</HEAD>

<BODY>
<FONT FACE="Verdana" SIZE=5>
<B>Interested in developing Web content?</B>
<P>
Visit the <A NAME=MSLINK HREF="http://www.microsoft.com/workshop/">
Microsoft Web Workshop</A>, or <BR>
the <A NAME=SBXLINK HREF="http://www.sybex.com">Sybex home page</A>.
<BR><BR><HR>
<FONT SIZE=2>
When you move the pointer over a hyperlink, you will see the hyperlink's
destination in a small box at the location of the pointer. In addition, a
short description of the hyperlink will appear in the browser's status bar.
</FONT>
</BODY>
</HTML>
```

The *<DIV>* Tag

HTML documents are rendered in one pass: the browser processes the page from the beginning to the end. As a result, there is no way to go back and place one element on top of another. For example, with plain HTML you can't place a caption over an image. You can place it above or below, but not on top of the image. Once the image has been rendered on the screen, you can't step back and overlay any elements on it.

This limitation can be overcome with the help of the <DIV> tag, which lets you break a document into separate entities that can be placed on the page with respect to one another. The <DIV> tag is at the core of DHTML, because it lets you break the page into entities that can be manipulated independently of each other. Let's look at a deceptively simple example. The STYLES.HTM page, shown in Figure 23.2, looks as though it has a background image, on top of which the text appears.

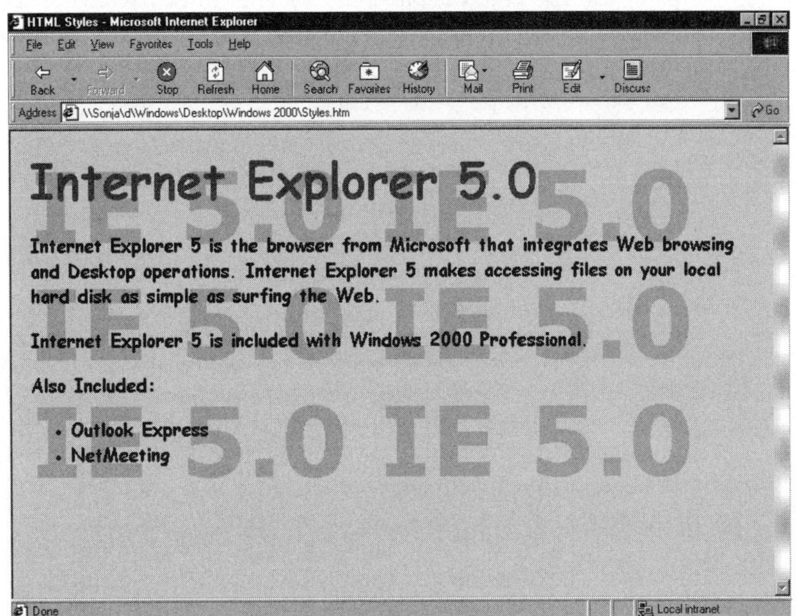

FIGURE 23.2 *The STYLES.HTM page uses the <DIV> tag to overlap HTML elements.*

The file STYLES.HTM contains two sections, each one delimited by the <DIV> tag. The first section contains a header (the string IE5.0) that is tiled in the document's background. The second section contains the text. The two sections overlap, so that the text appears on top of a background. Without the ability to overlap elements, the background would require that an image be downloaded.

The string IE5.0 that appears on the background is rendered with the custom <H1> tag, shown here:

```
<STYLE>
H1.LargeText {color:"#B0E080"; font-family:"Verdana"; font-size:600%}
</STYLE>
```

The definition of the first <DIV> tag, which creates the background, is shown next:

```
<DIV STYLE="position:absolute; left:20">
<H1 CLASS=LargeText>IE 5.0 IE 5.0 IE 5.0
IE 5.0 IE 5.0 IE 5.0</H1>
</DIV>
```

The position of the <DIV> section is defined as absolute and is 20 pixels from the left edge of the document.

The second section is displayed at the same location so that it will appear on top of the first one. Its origin is also 20 pixels from the left edge of the document.

```
<DIV STYLE="position:absolute; left:20">
</DIV>
```

In between the <DIV> and </DIV> tags, the text appears.

The position attribute may also have the value `relative`. Relative positions are defined with respect to the previous element on the page. The following statements will place an image on the document and then a title over the image:

```
<DIV>
<IMG SRC="c:\images\texture1.bmp">
</DIV>
<BR>
<DIV STYLE="position:relative; top:-10">
Image Caption
</DIV>
```

The second <DIV> section would normally appear below the image. Because its position is relative, it's raised by 10 pixels and is rendered on top of the image, near the image's bottom.

Besides the position of a <DIV> section, you can also specify its dimensions with the `Width` and `Height` attributes. The elements of the section are placed in the specified dimensions, as they would appear normally in the browser.

If the contents of the <DIV> tag exceed the space provided by the `Width` and `Height` attributes, the section's height will be increased accordingly by default. To change this behavior, you can specify yet another attribute, the `Overflow` attribute, whose valid values are:

Scroll The section's dimensions remain unchanged, and scroll bars are attached automatically.

Hidden The section's dimensions remain unchanged, and part of the document is invisible.

The following HTML document (it's the `PLACMNT.HTM` document) is rendered as shown in Figure 23.3:

```
<HTML>
<CENTER>
<FONT FACE="Comic Sans MS" SIZE=4>
<DIV STYLE="width:400; height:60; background-color:yellow">
This text will be rendered in a box that's 400 pixels wide and 60 pixels
tall
</DIV>
<BR>
<DIV STYLE="width:120; height:60; background-color:cyan">
This text will be rendered in a square box that's 120 pixels wide and 60
pixels tall
</DIV>
</FONT>
</CENTER>
</HTML>
```

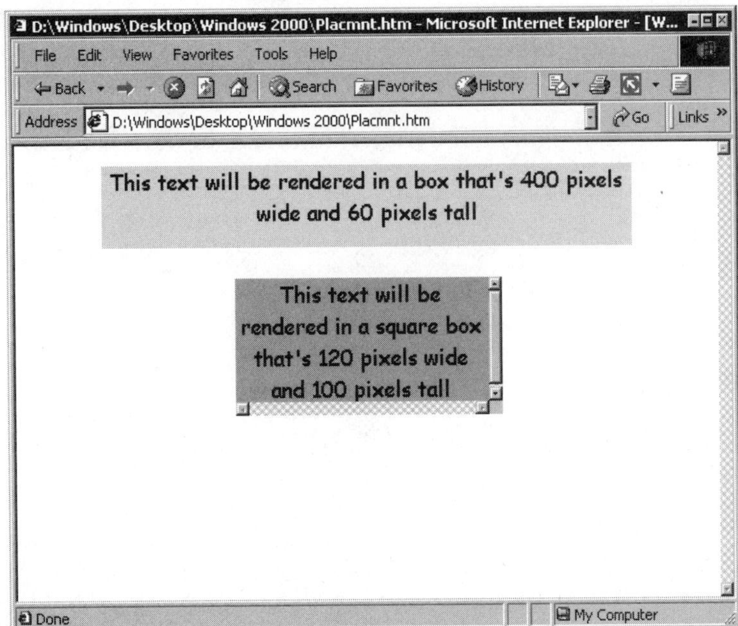

FIGURE 23.3
The PLACEMNT.HTM document demonstrates the Width and Height attributes of the <DIV> tag's style.

Another attribute that's commonly used in DHTML is the Display attribute, which determines whether the <DIV> tag is visible. If you set the visible attribute to "none," the section will be invisible. You can make it visible again by manipulating the visible attribute through VBScript code, following a user action. To make a hidden element visible again, set its visibility attribute to an empty string (""). The example in the following section demonstrates how to manipulate the attributes of the <DIV> and create dynamic documents.

Manipulating the Styles

Being able to define your own styles gives you freedom in placing HTML elements on a Web page, but it doesn't make the page dynamic. To make the page dynamic, you should be able to program the elements through VBScript. Dynamic pages contain scripts that manipulate the tag's styles.

Figure 23.4 shows a simple page with information about some Sybex titles. The titles are grouped together under the name of the series to which they belong, as nested lists. The series names are the outer list, and the titles in each series are the nested lists. The document shown in Figure 23.4 is static: it displays all the information available at once in a lengthy document and doesn't react to user actions.

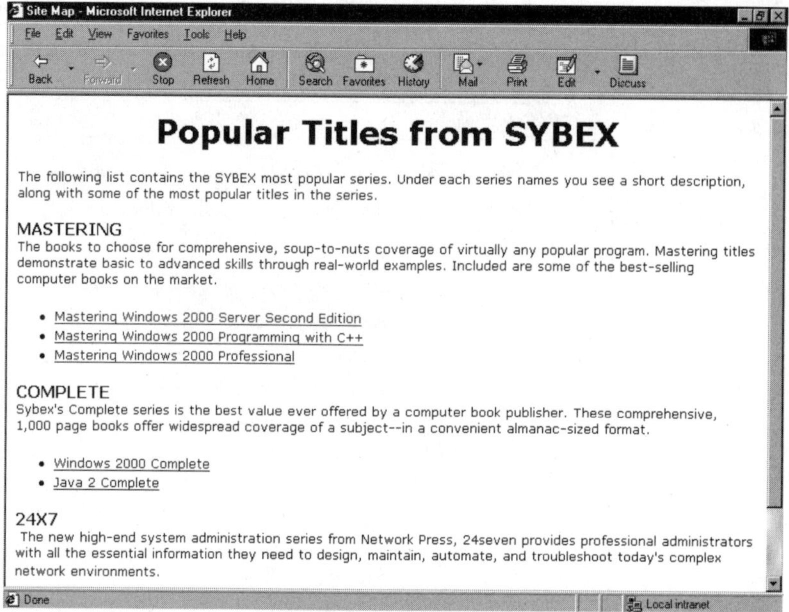

FIGURE 23.4 *The SBXHTML.HTM document is a static page that contains nested lists.*

NOTE For more information on displaying nested lists, see Chapter 22.

If you were seeing this page in any other application, such as your word processor, you might expect to be able to expand and collapse this list at will. A user who's interested in the titles of the Mastering series, for example, should not have to wade through all the other titles. You can do something similar with HTML, namely use the names of the series as hyperlinks to separate documents with the titles in each series. This is how titles are currently organized at the Sybex Web site.

With DHTML, it is possible to organize the series and their titles in an expandable list without having to make additional trips to the server and retrieve new documents. Each series title is a hotspot, and, when clicked, it expands the following list. The first time you open this document, you will see the title "Popular Titles from SYBEX" and the following text. If you hover the pointer over the document's title, the title will turn red. Click the title, and it will be expanded to display the names of the series, as shown in Figure 23.5. If you click it again, the list will collapse.

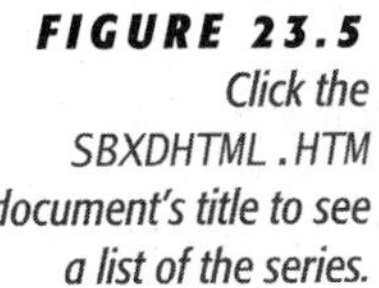

FIGURE 23.5 *Click the* SBXDHTML.HTM *document's title to see a list of the series.*

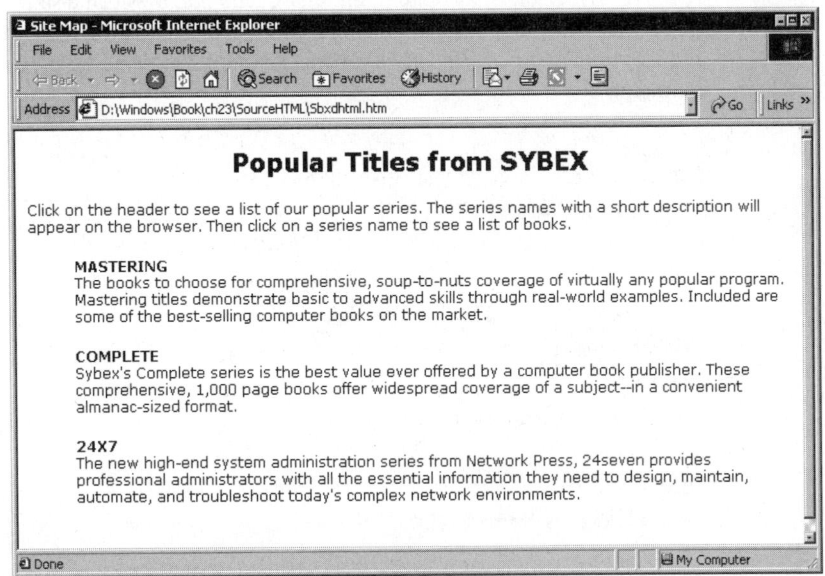

If you click the name of a series, you will see a list of titles that belong to the series. The titles are hyperlinks, which take you to the corresponding book's page on the Sybex Web site. Each series name turns red as you hover the pointer over it.

As you might guess, this dynamic page reacts to two mouse events: the `onMouseOver` event (by turning the corresponding element to red) and the `onClick` event (by expanding or shrinking the selected list). We'll look at the code of the document, but let's start by examining the code of the `SBXHTML.HTM` document, which is simpler. Then, we'll modify this document to create the dynamic lists.

HTML Lists

Next you'll see the HTML code that produced the list in Figure 23.4. In the interest of conserving space and demonstrating the topic of lists, I've omitted the descriptions and the hyperlinks. If you want to know how the list items are displayed as hyperlinks, here's the tag that corresponds to the item *Mastering Windows 2000 Server Second Edition* (the first title in the Mastering series):

```
<LI TYPE=DISC>
<A HREF="http://www.sybex.com/cgi-bin/bookpg.pl?1911back.html">Mastering
Windows 2000 Server Second Edition</A>
```

The title is surrounded by <A> tags, which mark a hyperlink. The hyperlink's destination is a Perl script that returns the description of the book. (Don't worry—you don't have to know anything about Perl. This is the URL that will be displayed in the browser's Address Box when you select the specific title.)

NOTE Hyperlinks may point to another document; they can also point to programs on a Web server. When the destination points to a program, this program is invoked on the server, and the result of the processing (an HTML file that's generated on the fly) is sent to the client computer.

Here is the HTML code that produces the nested lists with the series names and the corresponding titles:

```
<HTML>
<HEAD>
                <TITLE>Site Map</TITLE>
</HEAD>
<BODY>
<FONT FACE="Verdana" SIZE=2>
<CENTER>
<H1>
Popular Titles from SYBEX
</H1>
</CENTER>
The following list contains the SYBEX most popular series.
Under each series names you see a short description, along with some
of the most popular titles in the series.
<FONT SIZE=3>
<P>
<B>MASTERING</B><BR>
<FONT SIZE=2>
The books to choose for comprehensive, soup-to-nuts coverage
of virtually any popular program. Mastering titles demonstrate
basic to advanced skills through real-world examples.
Included are some of the best-selling computer books on the market.
<UL>
</font></font>
<LI TYPE=DISC><a href="http://www.sybex.com/cgi-bin/
rd_bookpg.pl?2774back.html">Mastering
  Windows 2000 Server Second Edition</a>
<LI TYPE=DISC><a href="http://www.sybex.com/cgi-bin/
rd_bookpg.pl?2642back.html">Mastering
  Windows 2000 Programming with C++</a>
<LI TYPE=DISC><a href="http://www.sybex.com/cgi-bin/
rd_bookpg.pl?2448back.html">Mastering
  Windows 2000 Professional</a>
```

```
</UL>
</font>
<p><font size="3" face="Verdana"><b>COMPLETE<br>
</b>
</font>
<font face="Verdana" size="2">Sybex's Complete series is the best value ever
offered by a computer book publisher. These comprehensive, 1,000 page books
offer widespread coverage of a subject--in a convenient almanac-sized
format.</font></p>
<ul>
  <li><a href="http://www.sybex.com/cgi-bin/
rd_bookpg.pl?2721back.html"><font face="Verdana" size="2">Windows
    2000 Complete</font></a></li>
  <li><a href="http://www.sybex.com/cgi-bin/
rd_bookpg.pl?2468back.html"><font face="Verdana" size="2">Java
    2 Complete</font></a></li>
</ul>
<P><font size="3" face="Verdana"><b>24X7</b><br>
<font size="-1"> The new high-end system administration series from
Network Press, 24seven provides professional administrators with all the
essential information they need to design, maintain, automate, and
troubleshoot today's complex network environments.</font></font>
<ul>
  <li><font size="3" face="Verdana"><a href="http://www.sybex.com/cgi-bin/
rd_bookpg.pl?2593back.html">Netware
    5 24X7</a></font></li>
  <li><font size="3" face="Verdana"><a href="http://www.sybex.com/cgi-bin/
rd_bookpg.pl?2532back.html">Windows
    Client Administration 24X7</a></font></li>
</ul>
<FONT FACE="Verdana" SIZE=2>
<FONT SIZE=3>
<UL>
</font>
</UL>
<UL>
<FONT SIZE=2>
</UL>
</FONT>
</BODY>
</HTML>
```

As you can see, each series contains a list of titles. To display a list with HTML, you must enclose the entire list in a pair of <UL> tags (UL stands for Unordered List), and each new item in the list must be prefixed with an <LI> tag. The TYPE=DISC attribute simply displays a little bullet in front of each item, and you can omit it if you don't like it.

DHTML Lists

The dynamic version of this page is a bit more complicated, but it uses the same structure. Each item that acts like a hotspot must be named so that we can reference it through the code. To name a section of the document, we must enclose it in a pair of <DIV> tags and use the <DIV> tag's ID attribute. Here is the definition of the Mastering series:

```
<DIV ID="Head1">
<FONT SIZE=3>
<B>MASTERING</B><BR>
<FONT SIZE=2>
</DIV>
```

The <DIV> tags mark the beginning and the end of an object. The header "Mastering" is a distinct object, and the ID attribute is the object's name.

Following the Mastering hotspot is the list of Mastering titles. The entire list is another object, because we must be able to expand and collapse it. The definition of the Mastering list is based on the straight HTML code I presented earlier, but it's enclosed in a pair of <DIV> tags, which is named TOC1. Here's the code that produces the Mastering list:

```
<DIV ID="Head1">
      <FONT SIZE=2>
      <FONT SIZE=3>
      <B>MASTERING</B><BR> <FONT SIZE=2>
      The books to choose for comprehensive, soup-to-nuts coverage
      of virtually any popular program. Mastering titles demonstrate
      basic to advanced skills through real-world examples.
      Included are some of the best-selling computer books on the market.</
font></font>
      </DIV><DIV ID="TOC1" STYLE="display:none">
        <ul>
          <li type="DISC"><a href="http://www.sybex.com/cgi-bin/
rd_bookpg.pl?2774back.html">Mastering Windows 2000 Server Second Edition</a>
          <li type="DISC"><a href="http://www.sybex.com/cgi-bin/
rd_bookpg.pl?2642back.html">Mastering Windows 2000 Programming with C++</a>
```

```
        <li type="DISC"><a href="http://www.sybex.com/cgi-bin/
rd_bookpg.pl?2448back.html">Mastering Windows 2000 Professional</a></li>
      </ul>
  </DIV>
```

Again, I omitted the definitions of the hyperlinks to make the code easier to read. Notice that this object is named TOC1 and it has a style, too. The attribute

```
<STYLE="display:none">
```

tells Internet Explorer not to display the object initially. The list is still loaded, but it remains invisible.

As you've probably guessed, we must also supply the code to hide and display the list each time the user clicks the Mastering hotspot. The Mastering hotspot is called Head1. Therefore, we must supply an event handler (a subroutine) that will react when the user clicks the Head1 object. This subroutine is the Head1_onClick(), and its definition is

```
Sub Head1_onclick()
    If TOC1.style.display = "" then
        TOC1.style.display = "none"
    Else
        TOC1.style.display = ""
    End If
End Sub
```

This event handler is invoked when the user clicks the Mastering hotspot. It examines the value of the Display attribute of the TOC1 object. If the TOC1 object is visible (its Display attribute is empty), the script hides it by setting its display property to "none." If not, the script displays the object by setting its display attribute to nothing.

In addition to reacting to the mouse click, the various hotspots react to mouse movements. Every time you move the mouse over another series name, the previously highlighted one is reset to black. Each series title is a separate object, so all you have to do is change its Color attribute.

The two subroutines that detect when the pointer moves in or out the area of the Head1object are the Head1_onMouseOver() and Head1_onMouseOut() subroutines. You must use these subroutines to change the color of the Head1 object so that when the mouse enters the area of the object, the text color is set to red, and when it leaves the same area, the text color is reset to black. Here are the corresponding event handlers:

```
Sub Head1_onmouseover()
    Head1.style.color= "#FF3300"
End Sub

Sub Head1_onmouseout()
    Head1.style.color= "#000000"
End Sub
```

Dynamic HTML is nothing more than programmable HTML. When building a Web page with DHTML, you are basically building an HTML document, and you must make sure that each section of the document that should react to user actions is delimited with a pair of `<DIV>` tags. Everything that appears between `<DIV>` and `</DIV>` tags is a separate object and can be manipulated through VBScript commands.

To write the commands that manipulate the document's objects, you supply an event handler for each external action to which your document must react. The name of the event handler is made up of the name of the object that will react (this name is usually the `ID` of a `<DIV>` tag) and the name of the event to which it must react. The subroutine `Head1_onMouseOver()` is activated every time the user moves the pointer over the object `Head1`.

ActiveX Controls

In addition to introducing objects to HTML and programming them with VBScript, you can also add tremendous functionality to your Web pages by means of ActiveX controls. ActiveX controls are in essence small programs that you can embed in a Web page and activate from within the page. With ActiveX controls, you can give your Web pages functionality that simply can't be achieved with HTML—not even with VBScript.

Unlike scripts, which are downloaded along with the page, an ActiveX control is a *system component*, an object that must be installed on your system before an application can use it. Once an ActiveX control is installed, many pages can use it, but the first time you run into a given control, it must be downloaded and installed. Internet Explorer can automatically download and install ActiveX controls, but some intervention on your part is required.

ActiveX Controls and Security Issues

Because ActiveX controls are system components, they aren't as safe as HTML or VBScript. HTML is a document-formatting language that can't harm your computer. HTML can't access your local disk, and it can't create any executable files or in any other way distort your files. The same is true for VBScript. VBScript was designed to be safe for your computer. It can't access your local disk, and it can't interact with any of the processes running at the same time. Both HTML and VBScript are quite safe (and consequently quite limited).

Continued

ActiveX controls, on the other hand, have access to your system's resources, and it is possible for a Web page to harm your computer through an ActiveX control. This is not a problem of the ActiveX technology. *Any* application you install on your computer without thinking twice about it has the potential of ruining your system. The same is true of ActiveX controls. You may wonder, "How do I protect my system from ill-designed controls?" Microsoft has built some safety mechanisms into its ActiveX technology. To help ensure that the ActiveX controls you download are from reputable sources, Microsoft introduced the *Authenticode Security* technology. When Internet Explorer downloads a control, you'll be presented with an Authenticode certificate on the screen that describes the control and its source. You either accept the certificate to download the control or reject it to cancel the download.

In the following sections we are going to look at a few ActiveX controls and how to use them from within your code. We will explore the multimedia controls that are installed along with Internet Explorer and are totally safe.

The Multimedia Controls

The *multimedia controls* were introduced to simplify the development of DHTML pages. To understand what these controls do and how to use them on a Web page, you must first understand why they were introduced. The constant struggle of Web authors is to add as much graphic content as possible to their pages (in the form of backgrounds, images, animated GIFs, and so on), without increasing the size of the page—a difficult balancing act. The multimedia controls allow Web authors to create visually rich and animated content without including lengthy images or video files. The multimedia controls included with Internet Explorer are as follows:

Structured Graphics Control This control lets you create graphics by inserting commands in your code. The commands are rendered on the computer to produce interesting graphics. For example, you can turn a simple element, such as text, into a graphic design element by changing its direction or by printing it along an arbitrary path.

Filter Control You can use this control to apply various effects to the elements of a page, such as illuminating them with spotlights of different colors and shapes.

Multimedia Sequencer This control allows you to sequence the various effects and time them, effectively adding animation features to static elements.

You'll see examples of all three controls in the following sections.

The Structured Graphics Control

The Structured Graphics control can produce an image on your computer based on a few commands. Not all images are bitmaps. Some of them can be constructed with simple geometric shapes, such as boxes, circles, ovals, polygons, and text. These images need not be coded in GIF or JPG files, and they can be easily reproduced on the browser from a textual description. Once the browser receives the descriptions of the objects, it can reproduce the images. It can also scale an image to fill the available space without distortion. Such graphics are called *vector graphics*. They are described in terms of basic shapes, color, and text, instead of pixels.

Figure 23.6 shows a very simple page that was produced with the Structured Graphics control. This page contains text elements, but it's not the type of text you'd see on a typical HTML page. The title at the top has an outline (this is not an HTML option), and the two words at the bottom of the page are printed at an angle. This is typical of what the Structured Graphics control can do for your page. It can take the simplest element of all—plain text—and turn it into a graphic element.

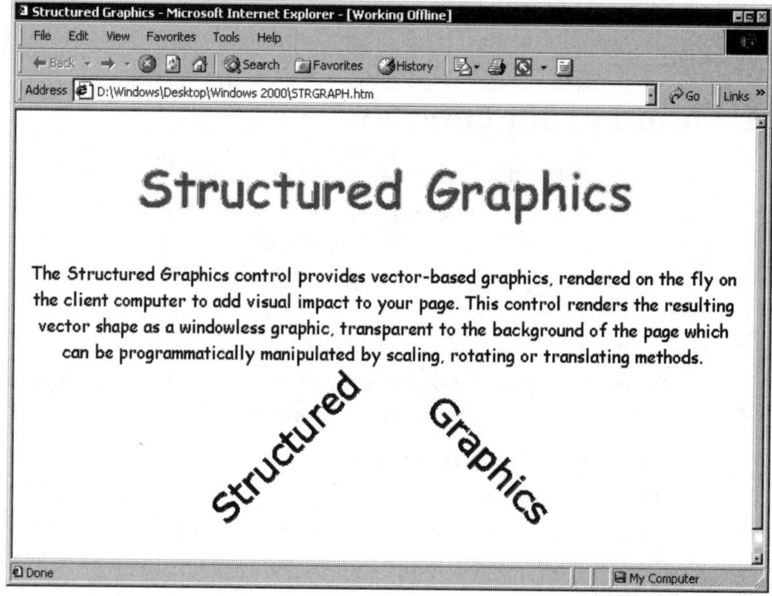

FIGURE 23.6 *The STRGRAPH.HTM page uses the Structured Graphics control to turn text into a graphic element.*

To use the Structured Graphics control on a Web page, you must first embed it in the page with the following statement:

```
<OBJECT ID=string1
STYLE="HEIGHT:98;WIDTH:480;TOP:0;LEFT:0;ZINDEX: 0"
CLASSID="CLSID:369303C2-D7AC-11d0-89D5-00A0C90833E6">
<PARAM NAME="Line0001" VALUE="SetFont('Comic Sans MS',65,1200,0,0,0)">
<PARAM NAME="Line0002" VALUE="SetLineColor(255,255,0)">
<PARAM NAME="Line0003" VALUE="SetFillColor(255,0,255,0,0,255)">
<PARAM NAME="Line0004" VALUE="SetFillSTYLE(1)">
<PARAM NAME="Line0005" VALUE="SetLineSTYLE(1)">
```

```
<PARAM NAME="Line0006" VALUE="Text('Structured Graphics',-225,20,0)">
</OBJECT>
```

`String1` is a name you assign to the control (you can have multiple Structured Graphics controls on the same page). The entry `STYLE` specifies the basic properties of the control: its dimensions on the page, its position, and its Z-Index (objects with larger Z-Index values appear in front of other object with smaller values, should they overlap). The last line is the control's Class `ID`: a unique string by which the control is registered on the system. This string can be found in the Registry, but it's always easier to copy it from an example.

The following lines specify various parameters of the control. In essence, they define the graphic element to be produced by the control. The first parameter is the control's `SetFont` method, which lets you define the font properties of the text. The `SetLineColor` on the following line determines the color of the pen used to draw the elements on the screen. The `SetFillColor` and `SetFillStyle` methods specify the color and style used for filling the element (in our case, it's text). The last parameter, `Text`, specifies the string to be displayed, the coordinates of the text, and the angle at which the text will printed.

The two words at the bottom of the page are placed with the following `<OBJECT>` tags. Notice that they differ in the text and the angle at which the text is displayed (45 and –45 degrees respectively).

```
<OBJECT ID=String2 CLASSID="CLSID:369303C2-D7AC-11d0-89D5-00A0C90833E6"
STYLE="WIDTH:180;HEIGHT:180">
<PARAM NAME="Line0001" VALUE="SetFillColor(0,0,255)">
<PARAM NAME="Line0002" VALUE="SetFont('Verdana', 40, 400, 0, 0, 0)">
<PARAM NAME="Line0003" VALUE="Text('Structured', -50, 50, -45)">
</OBJECT>

<OBJECT ID=String3 CLASSID="CLSID:369303C2-D7AC-11d0-89D5-00A0C90833E6"
STYLE="WIDTH:180;HEIGHT:180">
<PARAM NAME="Line0001" VALUE="SetFillColor(0,0,255)">
<PARAM NAME="Line0002" VALUE="SetFont('Verdana', 40, 400, 0, 0, 0)">
<PARAM NAME="Line0003" VALUE="Text('Graphics', -50, -50, 45)">
</OBJECT>
```

The Filter Control

The `Filter` control lets you apply multimedia-style effects to the elements of the page. To apply a filter to an HTML element, you insert the filter's description into the corresponding tag through the `filter` attribute, whose syntax is

```
filter:filtername(parameters)
```

The *filtername* entry is the name of the filter (one of the values that appear in Table 23.1), and *parameters* are the filter's parameters.

TABLE 23.1: THE VARIOUS EFFECTS OF THE FILTER CONTROL

Filter	Description
Alpha	Sets a transparency level
Blur	Creates the impression of moving at high speed
Chroma	Makes a specific color transparent
Drop Shadow	Creates an offset solid silhouette
FlipH	Creates a horizontal mirror image
FlipV	Creates a vertical mirror image
Glow	Adds radiance around the outside edges of the object
Grayscale	Drops color information from the image
Invert	Reverses the hue, saturation, and brightness values
Light	Projects light sources onto an object
Mask	Creates a transparent mask from an object
Shadow	Creates a solid silhouette of the object
Wave	Creates a sine wave distortion along the x-axis and y-axis
Xray	Shows just the edges of the object

To apply the blur effect to an image, use the following tag:

```
<IMG ID=sample SRC="NYSKY.GIF" style="filter:blur(strength=50)">
```

The `blur()` filter accepts a single parameter, which is the strength of the filter (the maximum value is 100). Other filters require more arguments. The `Glow()` filter, shown in Figure 23.7, requires two arguments: the color of the glow and the strength of the filter (the larger the value, the greater the glow effect). Some filters, such as `FlipV()` and `FlipH()`, which mirror an image vertically and horizontally, have no parameters. All filters and transitions have an `Enabled` property, and all transitions have a `Duration` property. You can also apply multiple filters to the same object as two style attributes (just separate their names with a semicolon).

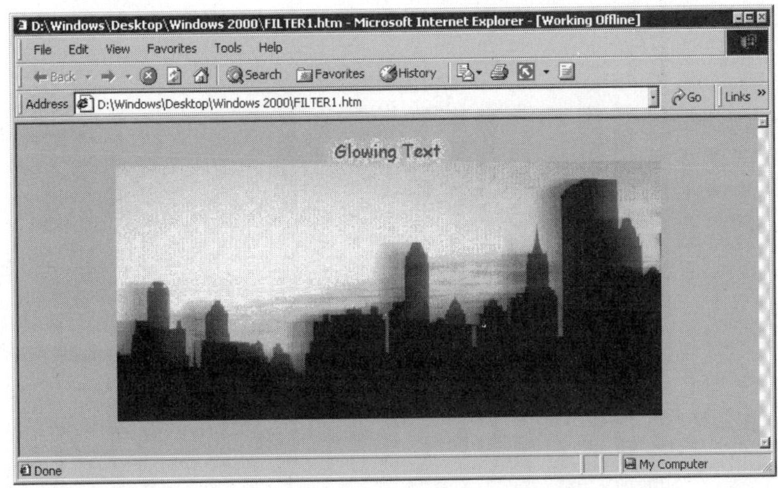

FIGURE 23.7 *The `FILTER1.HTM` document demonstrates the `Glow` and `Blur` special effects.*

The following HTML code produced the page in Figure 23.7. The title is a string to which the `Glow` effect was applied, and the image was distorted with the `blur()` filter. Here's the code:

```
<HTML>
<BODY BGCOLOR=silver>
<CENTER>
<FONT FACE="Comic Sans MS" SIZE=60 COLOR=red>
<DIV id=bob style="width:100%; filter:glow(Color=#F0F000,Strength=10);">
Glowing Text
</DIV>
<IMG ID=sample SRC="NYSKY.GIF" style="filter:blur(strength=30)">
</CENTER>
</BODY>
</HTML>
```

The Lights Effect

There's another interesting `Filter` effect. Consider a level-1 header. The `<H1>` tag will create the same header on every page. But if you apply some special lighting to the same header, it will stand out and look more like an image. You can illuminate normal text with a colored spotlight. The spotlight affects all the elements on the page. Moreover, each time you click the header, a new light is added. Its color is chosen randomly, giving a different look to the image.

The following code creates this effect:

```
<HTML>
<HEAD>
<TITLE>Filter Effects</TITLE>
<SCRIPT language="VBScript">
Dim Light

Sub window_onLoad()
    divText.style.filter = "Light"
    Set Light = divText.filters(0)
    Light.addPoint 350,75,125,255,125,55,120
    Call Light.changecolor(1, 50+rnd*80,50+rnd*220,50+rnd*120,1)
    divText.style.filter = "Light"
End sub

Sub divText_onclick()
    Light.addPoint 350,75,125,255,125,55,120
    Call Light.changecolor(1, 50+rnd*80,50+rnd*220,50+rnd*120,1)
    divText.style.filter = "Light"
End sub
</SCRIPT>

</HEAD>
<BODY BGCOLOR=darkgray>

<CENTER>
<DIV id=divText style="POSITION:RELATIVE; WIDTH:100%"><FONT SIZE=5
FACE='Comic Sans MS' color="WHITE">
<OBJECT ID=sgText1
STYLE="HEIGHT:98;WIDTH:480;TOP:0;LEFT:0;ZINDEX: 0"
CLASSID="CLSID:369303C2-D7AC-11d0-89D5-00A0C90833E6">
<PARAM NAME="Line0001" VALUE="SetFont('Verdana',80,1200,0,0,0)">
<PARAM NAME="Line0002" VALUE="SetLineColor(255,255,0)">
<PARAM NAME="Line0003" VALUE="SetFillColor(255,0,255,0,0,255)">
<PARAM NAME="Line0004" VALUE="SetFillSTYLE(1)">
<PARAM NAME="Line0005" VALUE="SetLineSTYLE(1)">
<PARAM NAME="Line0006" VALUE="Text('Light Filters',-225,20,0)">
</OBJECT>
<P>
<B>Filters can affect any HTML element,
including text, Active X controls and images.
```

```
Click on the text to change the color of the spotlights
illuminating it.</B>
</FONT>
</DIV>

</CENTER>
</FONT>
</DIV>
</BODY>
</HTML>
```

When the page is loaded, and the `Window_onLoad` event occurs, the script applies the Light filter to the `divText` element (the graphic and the following text). Then a new spot is added (`Light.AddPoint` method), and its color is set to the value (255, 255, 55, which is a shade of magenta). The `AddPoint` method's first three arguments are the coordinates of the spot, and the following three values are the color of the spotlight (its red, green, and blue components). The last argument is the spot's cone, expressed in degrees.

Each time the user clicks the `divText` element, the `divText_onClick()` event occurs. In this event's handler, we add a new spotlight (at the same place, pointing at the same direction) and set its color to a random value. If you click the text repeatedly, the effects accumulate.

The Multimedia Sequencer Control

The Multimedia Sequencer control lets you control how the various effects are applied on your page, effectively animating it. For example, you can program the various parameters of the special effects, change the values of certain attributes over time, or even reposition the various elements.

To use the Sequencer control, you first set up an *action set*, which is a logical grouping of named procedures that are used to control the timing and behavior of the elements you want to animate on the page. The Sequencer control calls scripts, which can be executed once, or they can be repeated by the Sequencer.

Like all other controls, you must place an instance of it on the page before you can call its methods. The `<OBJECT>` tag for inserting the Sequencer control is

```
<OBJECT id=SeqName
    STYLE=""
    CLASSID=clsid:B0A6BAE2-AAF0-11d0-A152-00A0C908DB96>
</OBJECT>
```

To create an action set, you call the `At` method of the object, passing the desired animation parameters. The statement

```
call SeqName("Action").At(0.000, "Play(1)", -1, 15.0, 1)
```

defines an action set named `Action` and specifies it with the `At` method. The `At` method's syntax is

```
At(startTime, scriptName, loop, interval, tiebreak, threshold)
```

The *startTime* argument is a value in the format `seconds.milliseconds` (`ss.mmm`), which sets the start time for the specified action. This is not an absolute time; instead, it's the time that must elapse after the page has been loaded. *ScriptName* is the name of the script to be called at the specified time. If the script expects any arguments, you can specify this as follows:

```
scriptName(arg1, arg2,...)
```

The remaining arguments are all optional. The *loop* argument determines how many times the action will be repeated. The default is 1, and it can be set to –1 to repeat the loop forever. The value 0 will prevent the execution of the script. The argument *interval* is another optional argument in the form `seconds.milliseconds` (`ss.mmm`), which specifies the delay between consecutive iterations of the action. The argument *tiebreak* is an integer, which sets the priority of the action. If two or more actions occur simultaneously, the action with the lower tiebreak value will be performed first (the value 0 is the highest priority). The *threshold* argument specifies for how long the action will be executed, or repeated, before it's dropped from the queue. Its default value is –1 (never).

Here's a simple example:

```
Seq("Action").At(0.000, "Play(1)", -1, 15.0, 1)
```

The `Action` action set will start its execution as soon as the page is loaded (the *startTime* argument is 0). To execute this action, the Sequencer control will call the procedure `Play()`, passing the value `1` as an argument. The `-1` argument tells the control to repeat the action forever, and the argument `15.0` is the execution interval: the action will be repeated every 15 seconds (provided it completes within that time frame). The action's threshold is `1` (a high priority, but not the highest).

You can use the same Sequencer control to control multiple actions in the same action set, and you must call the control's `At` method for each action. For optimal performance, use only one sequencer on a page with a single action set that calls a lot of actions. Then, you can start the execution of an action sequence by calling the `Play` method:

```
Seq("Action").Play()
```

Other Sequencer methods are `Start` (which starts or resumes the execution of an action set) and `Pause` (which pauses the execution).

In addition to its methods, the Sequencer control supports a number of events, through which you can better control the Sequencer's actions. The `onPlay` event is triggered when an action set's execution begins and the `onStop` event when the execution is paused (with the `Pause` method). The `onInit` event occurs when the Sequencer is completely loaded into memory, and this is where the action sets are defined. The onInit event occurs before the Window_onLoad event, which is where we start the actions (with the Play method).

The best way to understand how the Sequencer control is used on a Web page is to look at an example. The COUNTER.HTM page, shown in Figure 23.8, contains five hyperlinks to sites such as Microsoft, Sybex, and so on. In front of the hyperlinks is a counter that counts down from 5 to 1 and then starts over again. When the counter's value is 5, the CNET hotspot is active (it's displayed in yellow, and all other destinations are displayed in white). In addition, the URL of the active hyperlink is displayed, along with a short description of the site in the upper-right corner of the page. Three seconds later, the counter's value will become 4, the CNET hotspot will be reset to white, and the Microsoft Network hotspot will be activated. The process is repeated for all hotspots, and then it starts over again. This page combines the Structured Graphics and Sequencer controls to animate text and uses DHTML to display the descriptions in the same area on the page.

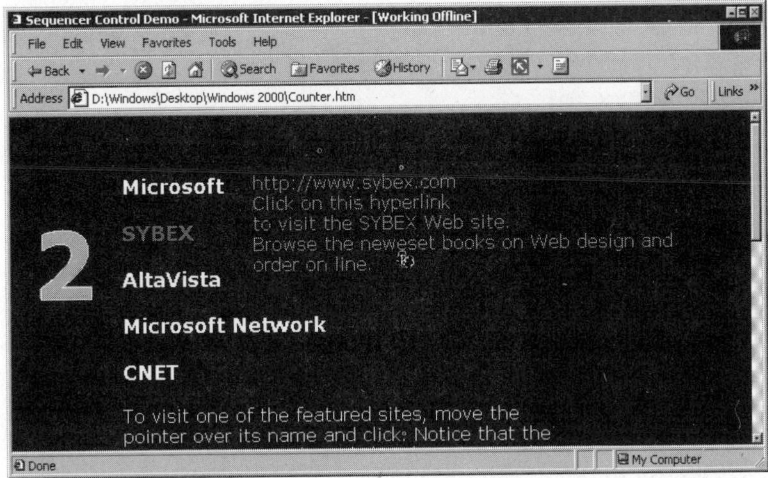

FIGURE 23.8 *The COUNTER.HTM page demonstrates how to use the Sequencer control to animate various elements on a page.*

The number in front of the hyperlink is displayed with the help of the Structured Graphics control. The page contains five graphic elements and the digits 1–5. All elements are generated with similar <OBJECT> tags. Here's the tag for the digit 1:

```
<OBJECT ID="Num1"
    CLASSID="CLSID:369303C2-D7AC-11D0-89D5-00A0C90833E6"
    STYLE="position:absolute; VISIBILITY:VISIBLE; WIDTH:800; HEIGHT:800;
TOP:-40; LEFT:-575;">
    <PARAM NAME="Line0001" VALUE="SetFont('Verdana', 100, 650, 0, 0, 0)">
    <PARAM NAME="Line0002" VALUE="SetLineColor(255,255,255)">
    <PARAM NAME="Line0003" VALUE="SetFillColor(255,255,0)">
```

```
    <PARAM NAME="Line0004" VALUE="SetFillStyle(1)">
    <PARAM NAME="Line0005" VALUE="Text('1', 200, -200, 0)">
</OBJECT>
</DIV>
```

The other digits are created with similar Structured Graphics objects.

NOTE Although you can animate many types of objects, the Structured Graphics control provides the most appropriate objects for animation on a Web page.

Then the Seq Sequencer control is placed on the page with the following tag:

```
<OBJECT ID="Seq"
    CLASSID="CLSID:B0A6BAE2-AAF0-11d0-A152-00A0C908DB96">
</OBJECT>
```

The Seq control's `At` method is then used to create the action set. The actions are quite simple. Every three seconds a new digit is displayed (all others are made invisible) and a new description appears on the page. The action set is defined in the control's `onInit` event, with the following statements:

```
Sub Seq_OnInit
    call Seq("Action").At(0.000, "Play(1)", -1, 15.0, 1)
    call Seq("Action").At(3.000, "Play(2)", -1, 15.0, 2)
    call Seq("Action").At(6.000, "Play(3)", -1, 15.0, 3)
    call Seq("Action").At(9.000, "Play(4)", -1, 15.0, 4)
    call Seq("Action").At(12.000, "Play(5)", -1, 15.0, 5)
End Sub
```

The script `Play(1)` displays the digit "1" and makes all others invisible. This script is called as soon as the page is loaded and is repeated every 15 seconds. The script `Play(2)` displays the digit "2" and starts three seconds after the page is loaded (which is also three seconds after the digit "1" was initially displayed). The last digit is displayed 12 seconds after the page is loaded. It will remain on the screen for three seconds, since the digit "1" will be displayed again 15 seconds after the page's `Load` event. The `Play()` subroutine is shown next:

```
Sub Play(Element)
    Select Case Element
    Case 1
        HideAll
        Num1.style.visibility = "Visible"
        URL1.style.color="#FF3000"
        URL5.style.color="white"
        caption1.style.visibility="Visible"
```

```
    Case 2
        HideAll
        Num2.style.visibility = "Visible"
        URL1.style.color="white"
        URL2.style.color="#FF6000"
        caption2.style.visibility="Visible"
    Case 3
        HideAll
        Num3.style.visibility = "Visible"
        URL2.style.color="white"
        URL3.style.color="#FF9000"
        caption3.style.visibility="Visible"
    Case 4
        HideAll
        Num4.style.visibility = "Visible"
        URL3.style.color="white"
        URL4.style.color="#FFC000"
        caption4.style.visibility="Visible"
    Case 5
        HideAll
        Num5.style.visibility = "Visible"
        URL4.style.color="white"
        URL5.style.color="#FFFF00"
        caption5.style.visibility="Visible"
    End Select
End Sub
```

The `Play()` subroutine handles all the animation on the page by turning on and off the visibility of the various elements. The elements *`URLX`* and *`captionX`* are the address of the current Web site and its caption. They are described with statements similar to the following:

```
<H3 ID=URL1 onclick="Window.Navigate 'http://www.microsoft.com'">Microsoft</
H3>
```

and

```
<DIV ID=caption1 STYLE="position:absolute; font-size: 10 pt;
color:lightblue; font-family: Verdana, Arial, Helvetica; TOP: 50; LEFT:220;
visibility:hidden">
http://www.microsoft.com<BR>
Click on this hyperlink<BR>
to visit the Microsoft Web site.<BR>
Learn about the new browser and Dynamic HTML,<BR>
see demos and download new tools.
</DIV>
```

NOTE The Sequencer and Structured Graphics controls are complicated, and programming them is quite a task. These controls aren't meant to be programmed manually. You should expect to see applications that will allow you to build animation with point-and-click operations, and they'll generate the required code for these controls. Unfortunately, at the time of this writing no such tools exist.

If you've come this far in this chapter, you probably have a good idea how to combine DHTML, VBScript, and ActiveX controls to write interactive, dynamic pages. You may be wondering what Web pages have to do with administering and scripting Windows 2000 Professional. So far, I've covered the prerequisites for the "real thing"—how to use VBScript and ActiveX controls to write scripts that manipulate the Windows environment. In the next two chapters, you'll see how to apply this knowledge to scripting the operating system itself. Before we leave this chapter, however, there's another interesting ActiveX control I'd like to discuss, a control that lets you integrate voice into your Web pages and scripts.

Voice-Enabled Pages

Have you ever felt like yelling at your computer? Most of us probably have. With the Agent control, a new ActiveX control from Microsoft, the computer might actually hear you—and do something about it.

The Agent control understands spoken commands and responds in a synthesized voice. Although the control itself is substantially more involved than most ActiveX controls you'll run into, adding the Agent control to a Web page and programming it to react to voice commands is a simple task. This section also provides an interesting example of using VBScript to control a page and make it highly interactive.

To use the Agent control, you'll need a sound card and a microphone. The control adds multimedia capabilities to a Web page and allows the user to interact with the page by speaking. Instead of clicking buttons or hyperlinks, you can actually say the commands out loud. The computer responds in a synthesized voice—a glimpse into the future of human-computer interaction.

To install the Agent control, you must first download a number of files from Microsoft's Web site at `http://msdn.microsoft.com/workshop/c-frame.htm#/workshop/imedia/agent/default.asp`. Figure 23.9 shows this page.

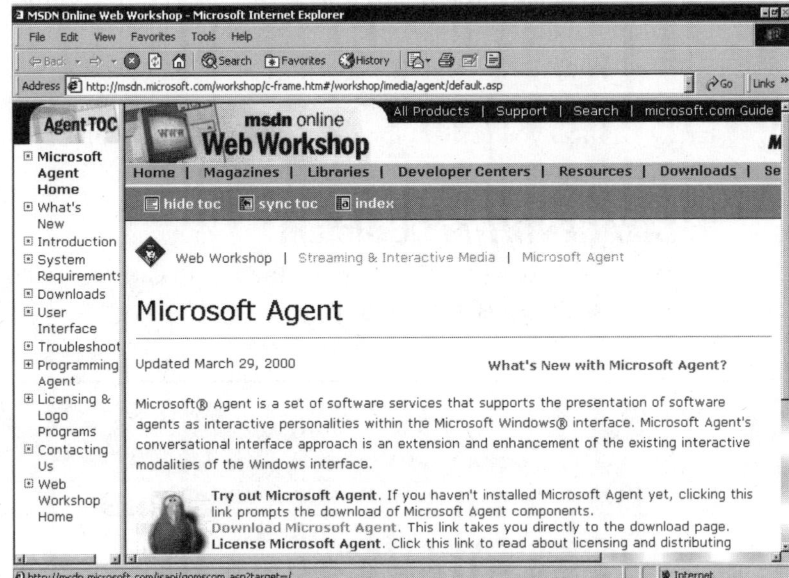

FIGURE 23.9
The Agent ActiveX control's home page

In the left pane, click Downloads to read about and download the following components:

Agent Essentials The basic functionality of the control

Speech Engines The speech synthesis and speech recognition engines

Characters The data needed for each of the available characters

The ActiveX Agent control supports three animated characters who help the user interact with the page: Genie, Merlin, and Robby. These characters appear on the screen while you're interacting with the Agent. The required support files are quite lengthy, so you might want to download them at an idle time.

After you download all the required files, click the hyperlink. Hear Genie, Merlin, and Robby tell you about Microsoft Agent for an introduction to this exciting technology. The three characters will appear on an empty page and tell you all about the Agent control. This page uses the Agent control's speech synthesis capabilities only. The three characters engage in a conversation and discuss the features of the Agent control.

TIP To display this page, Internet Explorer may download additional components as needed, so please be patient. The Agent ActiveX control will take up a few megabytes on your hard disk. At any point, you can remove all or some of its components using the Add/Remove Programs applet in Control Panel.

To display this page, Internet Explorer 5 will need to install some additional ActiveX components. You will be prompted to accept the control, it will be installed, and then a minute or two later the Web page will activate.

Beyond understanding voice commands and responding in voice, the characters perform gestures that make the interface even more intuitive. For example, Merlin starts yawning if you're silent for a spell or shrugs his shoulders if he doesn't understand a command.

The *AXAGENT.HTM* Document

The page shown in Figure 23.10 deploys the Merlin character, who welcomes the user to the page with a spoken message.

FIGURE 23.10 *The AXAGENT.HTM page demonstrates the use of the Agent control.*

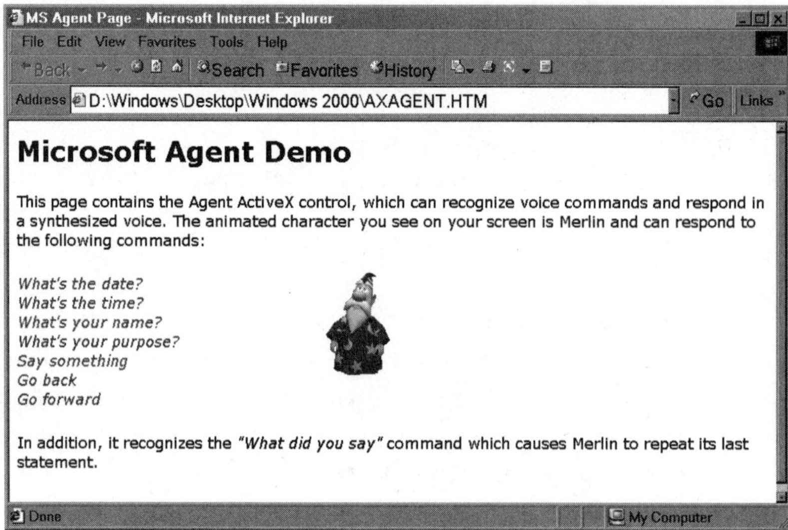

This page understands the following commands:

- What's the date?
- What's the time?
- What's your name?
- What's your purpose?
- Say something.
- Go back.
- Go forward.
- What did you say?

Programming the Agent Control

To use the ActiveX Agent control on an HTML document, you must insert all three components I mentioned earlier (the Agent control, the speech synthesis engine, and the speech recognition engine) with the following code:

```
<OBJECT ID="AgentControl" width=0 height=0
CLASSID="CLSID:F5BE8BD2-7DE6-11D0-91FE-00C04FD701A5"

CODEBASE="http://activex.microsoft.com/controls/agent/
msagent.exe#VERSION=1,3,0,0">
</OBJECT>

<OBJECT ID="TruVoice" width=0 height=0
CLASSID="CLSID:B8F2846E-CE36-11D0-AC83-00C04FD97575"

CODEBASE="http://activex.microsoft.com/controls/agent/
cgram.exe#VERSION=1,3,0,0">
</OBJECT>

<OBJECT ID="CnC" width=0 height=0
CLASSID="CLSID:161FA781-A52C-11D0-8D7C-00A0C9034A7E"
CODEBASE="http://www.research.microsoft.com/research/srg/
actcnc.exe#VERSION=3,0,0,1827">
</OBJECT>
```

The CODEBASE attribute tells Internet Explorer where to find the corresponding components, should they not be already installed on the host computer.

The Agent control can't recognize and react to just anything and everything you say. It must be told which commands to look for and how to respond to each one. This is done with the help of a script. The script of the AXAGENT.HTM page is concentrated in two subroutines:

- The first subroutine initializes the control and tells the control which commands to look for and how to respond to them.
- The second subroutine processes the commands spoken by the user.

The first subroutine, which initializes the control, is executed when the window is loaded. It's the Window_onLoad() subroutine, shown here:

```
Sub Window_onLoad()
AgentControl.Connected = True      '
AgentControl.Characters.Load "Merlin", "c:\msdownloads\merlin.acs"
Set Merlin = AgentControl.Characters("Merlin")
Merlin.Commands.Add "GetTime", "Current Time", "what's the [current] time"
Merlin.Commands.Add "GetDate", "Current Date", "what's the [current] date"
```

```
Merlin.Commands.Add "GetName", "Current Name", "what's your name"
Merlin.Commands.Add "GetPurpose", "Agent's purpose", "what's your purpose?"
Merlin.Commands.Add "Say", "Say Something", "say [something]"
Merlin.Commands.Add "GoBack", "Go Back", "go back"
Merlin.Commands.Add "GoForward", "Go Forward", "go forward"
Merlin.Show
Merlin.Speak "Hello, O great one!"
End Sub
```

The subroutine starts by loading Merlin's character and animation data. Notice that the code expects to find the `Merlin.asc` file in a specific folder (you must change it accordingly for your system). Then it enables the control's command interface so that the control can recognize voice commands and display them in a list of commands.

The subroutine then tells the control which commands to look for and how to respond to them. Each new command you add to the control's repertoire has the following:

- An ID (a name that distinguishes it from all other commands)
- A name (which appears in the list of commands when the user right-clicks the control)
- The phrase to be recognized

The statement

```
Merlin.Commands.Add "GetTime", "Current Time", "what's the [current] time"
```

tells the control to recognize the `GetTime` command (this is the command's ID). When the user says, "What's the time?" the control should register the question as the `GetTime` command. The string `Current Time` appears in the list of commands so that the user can select it with the mouse, too.

You can also specify that the control ignore certain words. The word *current* in the date and time commands is optional, so it's included in square brackets. The control will understand both questions: "What's the time?" and "What's the current time?"

The second subroutine in the page's script is `Agent1_Command(UserInput)`, which is invoked every time the user issues a command with the microphone. To issue a voice command to the Agent, hold down the Scroll Lock key and speak into the mike. `Command` is an event that signifies that the user has issued a command (by voice or by choosing a command from the list of arguments). The command, as recognized by the control, is passed to the subroutine as an argument (the `UserInput` argument specifies the ID of the command issued by the user). If the user has asked, "What's the time?" the `Agent1_Command("GetTime")` subroutine is invoked. The `Agent1_Command` event handler is shown next:

```
Sub AgentControl_Command(UserInput)
Dim cmdName

cmdName = UserInput.Name
```

```
Select Case cmdName
    Case "GetTime"
        Merlin.Speak "the time is "  & FormatDateTime(Now, vbLongTime)
    Case "GetDate"
        Merlin.Speak "the date is "  & FormatDateTime(Now, vbLongDate)
    Case "GetName"
        Merlin.Speak "my name is Merlin"
    Case "GetPurpose"
        Merlin.Speak "my purpose is to demonstrate how to use voice on a Web
        page"
    Case "Say"
        Merlin.speak "I'm old and tired. What can I say?"
    Case "GoBack"
on error resume next
        call window.history.back(0)
    Case "GoForward"
on error resume next
        call window.history.forward(0)
    End Select

End Sub
```

The event handler extracts the name of the command and assigns it to the variable cmdName. It then examines the value of the cmdName variable. If the command's name is GetTime, the Agent tells you what time it is. Speak is a method of the Agent control, which causes the Agent to say something (to convert text to synthesized voice). The statement

```
FormatDateTime(Now, vbLongDate)
```

formats the current date as "September 20, 2000." The Speak method of the control pronounces this string. By default, the date is returned in the format "9/20/2000," which isn't the most appropriate format for the purposes of this page.

The GoBack and GoForward commands call a VBScript statement that causes the browser to move to the previous or next page in the history list, as though the user had clicked the Back or the Forward button. The Agent control can be integrated with the browser but cannot simply respond to spoken commands. In the future, you'll see Desktop applications that use the Agent control to interact with the user. For example, you'll be able to start an application by saying its name, start a new file by saying "New," close the file by saying "Close," and so on.

An ActiveX control is an object: a piece of code that implements some functionality and makes it available to other applications. You can contact the control from within an HTML page and manipulate it through its methods and properties with VBScript. By now, you should have a good idea of how ActiveX controls are inserted into HTML pages and how they are programmed. To find out the control's properties and methods, you must look up their documentation and use the samples as your starting point, to simplify the process.

Summary

In this chapter, we looked at how to extend HTML with styles and classes, how to use ActiveX controls, and how to create voice-enabled pages.

In the next two chapters, you'll see more objects, which let you access parts of the operating system, such as its file system, the networked drives and printers, and so on. You'll also learn how to use VBScript outside HTML pages—and how to use VBScript to script not an HTML page but the operating system itself.

CHAPTER 24

VBScript and Windows 2000 Professional

FEATURING:

In the last two chapters, you saw how to use VBScript within HTML pages. VBScript was introduced to "activate" Web pages. As such, it is a safe language. In other words, a script can't access your file system and affect your computer in any way. It's limited within the scope of the HTML document that contains it and has no access to your system. If every page you view on the Web had the option to delete a few files on your system, the Web would be a *very* unpopular place.

Making VBScript safe also made it seriously limited (not to say crippled). It's a simple language indeed, and every user could think of a few useful new features. If you think about it, though, you'll realize that most of these new features would end up making the language unsafe.

VBScript, however, is also the scripting language of the Windows 2000 Professional operating system, similar to the batch language of DOS. It should be able to move files around, process entire folders, and so on. In addition, it should be possible for scripts to be executed outside the context of HTML pages. To write a script that moves a few files around, you wouldn't have to develop a Web page. Traditionally, scripts don't have user interfaces. They contain commands that are executed silently, one after the other. They are not programs with a user interface, and they don't interact with the user. Scripts are meant to carry out simple, repetitive tasks without user interaction.

This chapter discusses the features of VBScript that are unique to Windows 2000 Professional and can be executed on the local computer only. You'll see how you can access the computer's file system and write useful scripts to automate simple, repetitive tasks. Notice that the scripts discussed in this chapter can be executed on their own and not in the context of Web pages. In other words, you can't use the objects of VBScript discussed in this chapter to enhance your Web pages.

NOTE Let me say this one more time: You can't execute these scripts over a network, only on your local computer. And you must be logged on as an administrator to do so.

Writing and Executing Scripts

Scripts are text files with the extension VBS that contain VBScript statements. The following VBScript statements display the number of days to the turn of the century:

```
DAYS2000 = #01/01/2100# - Date()
MsgBox DAYS2000 & " days left in this century"
```

The first line of the script calculates the difference between two dates: the current date and the first date of the year 2100. In VBScript, the symbol # is used to delimit dates (just as double quotes are used to delimit strings).

NOTE I know, I know—technically this century ends on the last day of 2100. I'm just using the popular concept.

Start Notepad, enter the two lines of code, and save them in the file `2100.VBS`.

NOTE Don't forget to select All Files in the Save As Type drop-down list in the File Save dialog box. If you don't, the file will be saved as `2100.VBS.TXT`.

Execute the file `2100.VBS` by double-clicking its icon. You will see a message box like the one in Figure 24.1.

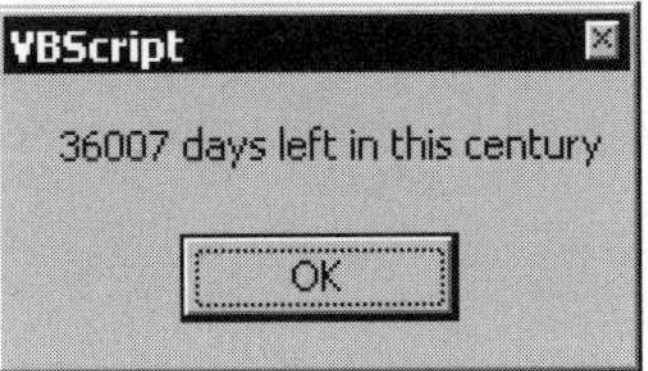

FIGURE 24.1
The output of the 2100.VBS script

NOTE In the unlikely event that you double-click the icon of a VBS file and nothing happens, the operating system will prompt you to select the application that can open the file. In the dialog box, select the application WSCRIPT. After that, all VBS files will be associated with the WSCRIPT application.

This is a simple, almost useless script. You would probably prefer a program that displays the number of years, days, minutes, even seconds to the turn of the century on your Desktop. This example simply shows you how you can write and execute a script with VBScript.

You're probably wondering what kind of useful scripts you can write. As I mentioned, VBScript is a safe—and thus seriously limited—language. Scripting languages are best at manipulating files, starting applications, performing repetitive tasks (such as printing a bunch of files at midnight), and so on. And, so far, you haven't seen any VBScript commands to manipulate files.

VBScript has been enhanced with file manipulation commands, but you can't use these extensions with HTML pages. The VBScript objects we are going to examine in this chapter can only be used in stand-alone scripts. You can't include them in HTML documents. (Actually, you *can* include them in your Web pages, but when these pages are opened with Internet Explorer 5, a warning will be displayed that the page contains an unsafe script that may harm the local computer. And most people won't view the page.)

Because of space limitations, I can't elaborate on all the objects provided to give you access to the various components of the Windows 2000 Professional operating system. This chapter is more a reference than a tutorial. I have tried, however, to include as many practical examples as possible. My goal is to help you get acquainted with the objects of VBScript for manipulating the Windows 2000 Professional file system. Once you familiarize yourself with objects, their properties, and their methods, you'll be able to develop really useful scripts for your daily needs. You will find more scripts in the next chapter.

A unique feature of VBScript is its ability to contact other applications and automate them. You will see later in this chapter how you can use VBScript to start Excel and instruct it to perform a sequence of operations. Applications that can be automated are called *servers,* and you probably have many servers installed on your system already. If you want, you can develop your own server applications (but that is a topic beyond the scope of this book).

Objects, Properties, and Methods

I'm assuming that many of you are not familiar with the principles of object-oriented programming, so here's a quick introduction to the latest buzzwords in programming. An *object* is a program that floats around in the operating system. It actually lives in a file on the disk, but it's also registered with the system. You don't need to know the name of the executable file, just the name it's registered with. Because objects are registered with the operating system, they are parts of the operating system, or extensions to the operating system, if you prefer.

An object knows how to perform certain actions, and its role is to provide its services and capabilities to other applications. An object provides information and allows itself to be configured by *properties*. An object performs some action by calling its *methods*. Let's say, for example, that you have an object that knows about the file system on the computer. As a programmer, you really don't want to be writing the low-level code that communicates directly with the hard disk controller, reads sectors, and figures out where folders and files are on the disk. This is the job of the `FileSystemObject` object (an object I will talk a lot about in this chapter).

Let's say that you want to use `FileSystemObject` to create a text file. The code would look like this:

```
Dim fso, file1
Set fso = CreateObject("Scripting.FileSystemObject")
Set file1 = fso.CreateTextFile("tempfile.txt", True)
```

Here's the sequence of steps. Two variables are declared—*fso*, which will keep track of a *reference* to a `FileSystemObject`, and *file1*, which will keep a *reference* to a file created by the `CreateTextFile` method of the `FileSystemObject`. A *reference* is a variable that allows you to act on, or interact with, your own copy of a `FileSystemObject`. Fear not—I will be discussing these terms in more depth later on.

Another important point needs to be made here. Every time you want to use a `FileSystemObject`, you need to create a reference to one by using the `CreateObject()` function (more later). What is important now is that `CreateObject()` takes an argument that is a Class name—here, the Scripting class. A Class is the code that implements the functionality of the "object," with the name of the object describing what the object is intended to do. (It would not make sense for Ford to write automotive software and use a `FileSystemObject` to start the windshield wipers, for example. A `Wipers` object would make much more sense.) Classes are cookie cutters. The object's properties and methods are accessed through the variable that refers to the object that has just been created—with the properties and methods being the object interface.

Windows 2000 Professional is a complicated operating system, and there's no reason its internal code shouldn't be used by applications, as well. As you have undoubtedly noticed, all Windows 2000 Professional applications use the same dialog box to allow the user to select a file (the Open dialog box) or specify a color (the Color dialog box). Obviously, this is no coincidence. A Class somewhere in the system displays these dialog boxes. The dialog box you see on the screen is an instance of the Class, which is an object. Some Open dialog boxes display the names of text files, others display the names of image files, and so on. The Class is implemented so that it can display all filenames. The individual objects derived from this Class have different characteristics, but they share a common design philosophy.

As a programmer, you need only contact this Class and ask it to display the Open or Color dialog box. The Class displays the dialog box, handles the interaction with the user, and returns the name of the selected file to the program. Using the objects built into the operating system, you can access a lot of functionality with a few simple commands. In addition, all the applications maintain a consistent look, which significantly reduces the learning curve of any application.

The same is true for applications. Excel uses many math functions internally, and Word provides many text-processing functions. Two typical examples are Excel's `Evaluate` method, which evaluates math expressions, and Word's `CheckSpelling` method, which spell-checks a word. Using VBScript's `CreateObject()` function, you can contact both applications and use their functionality from within your scripts. As you will see, the application's window doesn't appear on the screen, and, for all practical purposes, users think the operations are all performed by the script (provided they have the corresponding application installed on their system).

You probably have many questions regarding objects—I'll get to those in the examples of this chapter. So, instead of discussing objects at large, let's get down to the objects exposed by VBScript for accessing the components of the Windows 2000 Professional file system.

Collections and Dictionaries

In this section, I'll discuss briefly a data structure that is new to many programmers, but it's a real prerequisite for working with objects: the *collection*. A collection is a data structure for storing information, similar to an array. Collections, however, can store all types of information. Many of the objects you'll encounter in this (and the following) chapter are collections. The `Files` collection, for example, stores references to the files of a given folder. Not the names of the files, nor the entire files—just references to files, which you can access with an index value. If you are familiar with another popular scripting language, Perl, you can think of a collection as an associative array or a hash.

In order for you to get a handle on collections, you need to make sure that you understand what an array is. An *array* is a sequential list of identical items. To make it a little more concrete, think of an array as lined paper, with each line having a number, starting with 1 and ending with the highest line where you have written information. If the lined paper had names on it, you could say "names(2)" refers to the second line on the paper, or the second element in the array. Arrays can also have more than one dimension. A spreadsheet program is a great example of a two-dimensional array. You have lines (or rows) going down and fields (or cells, or columns) separating out the rows into smaller chunks of information.

The `Dictionary` object is like a one-dimensional array that stores data values. The difference between an array and a `Dictionary` object is that in the array you use an index value to access the array's elements, and in a `Dictionary` object you use a key.

Let's say you have an array in which you store temperatures for various cities. To read the temperature in a given city, you must know the city's index to the array and request the corresponding element. If your city's index to the array is 6, the temperature in your city is `Temperature(6)`. If `Temperature` was a `Dictionary` object, you would access the desired temperature by the name of the corresponding city, as `Temperature("Greensboro")`.

This illustrates a powerful difference between an array and a `Dictionary`. An array takes a number as an index; `Dictionary` takes a text string. This means that you can add items to an array and access them by a number, say 4, for the fourth element in the array. With a `Dictionary` object, you need to know only the key value, not its position in the array (this is a thinker...).

To use a Dictionary object in your code, you must first create an object variable with the CreateObject() function:

```
Set Temperatures = CreateObject("Scripting.Dictionary")
```

Temperatures is an object variable, not an array. The Temperatures *variable* holds items, which can be any type (numeric or strings). Each item is associated with a unique key, which is used to retrieve an individual item and is usually an integer or a string.

After creating a Dictionary variable, you must populate it with items. To add a key and data pair to a Dictionary object, use the Add method, whose syntax is

```
object.Add key, item
```

Here, *object* is a Dictionary variable (like Temperatures), *key* is the value you'll use later to retrieve the data value, and *item* is the actual data you want to store in the Dictionary. The following lines add city temperature values to the Temperatures variable:

```
Temperatures.Add "Greensboro", 82
Temperatures.Add "Charlotte", 79
Temperatures.Add "Durham", 73
```

If you attempt to add a pair with a key that already exists, an error will occur. You can either insert the appropriate error-trapping code or use the Exists method. The Exists method accepts as argument a key and returns True if the key exists in the Dictionary and False otherwise. Call the Exists method every time you want to add a new pair to the Dictionary:

```
If Not Temperatures.Exists("Greensboro") Then
    Temperatures.Add "Greensboro", 82
End If
```

You can also remove items from the Dictionary with the Remove method, which accepts a key as argument and removes the corresponding pair from the Dictionary. To remove the entry that corresponds to the temperature in Greensboro, use statements such as the following:

```
If Temperatures.Exists("Greensboro") Then
    Temperatures.Remove "Greensboro"
End If
```

Once again, the real power in these data structures is that the program does not need to keep track of the order of how data was put into the data storage mechanism. The program just needs to make sure that the data is in there by key value (still got your thinking cap on?).

You can also clear the entire Dictionary by removing all the pairs with the RemoveAll method, whose syntax is

```
Temperatures.RemoveAll
```

These are the methods that let you set up Dictionaries and assign data to them. To retrieve a value stored in a Dictionary object, use the name of the Dictionary variable, and pass to it the key as argument. To display the temperature in Greensboro, use the statement:

```
Temperatures("Greensboro")
```

By default, keys are case-sensitive, and the keys "GREENSBORO" or "greensboro" won't locate the desired item in the Dictionary. To change this behavior, use the CompareMode property, which sets (or returns) the comparison mode for comparing string keys in a Dictionary object. Its syntax is

```
object.CompareMode = compare
```

The *compare* value can be 0 (for binary or case-sensitive comparisons) or 1 (for text or case-insensitive comparisons). These are the same values as for the compare arguments of VBScript's StrComp() function.

To access the items and their keys in the Dictionary object, you must use the Items and Keys methods. The Items method returns an array containing all the items in a Dictionary object. Likewise, the Keys method returns an array containing all the keys in a Dictionary object. To access the elements of these two arrays, declare a new variable, and then assign the result of the corresponding method to the variable. The following lines demonstrate how to access the keys and their items:

```
{statements to assign values to the collection Temperatures}
DItems = Temperatures.Items
DKeys = Temperatures.Keys
For i = 0 To Temperatures.Count - 1
    txt = txt & DKeys(i) & " " & DItems(i) & vbCrLf
Next
MsgBox txt
```

This code segment displays the list of cities and their temperatures in a message box. In addition to the Items and Keys methods, which let you examine the items in a Dictionary object, you can use the Item and Key properties to manipulate the Dictionary's items. The Item property sets (or returns) an item for a specified key in a Dictionary object. To change the temperature of a city in the Dictionary object of the example, use a statement such as the following:

```
Dictionary.Item("Greensboro") = 84
```

You can also change the key of a given item with the Key property, although this isn't common practice. If users are looking up the temperature in Los Angeles using the key "LA", you can change the key of this item with a statement such as the following:

```
Dictionary.Key("Los Angeles") = "LA"
```

Finally, the Count property of the Dictionary object returns the number of items stored in it. To scan all the items in a Dictionary object, set up a For…Next loop that goes from 0 to the value of the Count property minus 1.

```
For i = 0 To Temperatures.Count - 1
    {process the current item, Temperatures.Item(i)
Next
```

There's a better structure for iterating through the items of a collection, namely the loop For Each...Next, as shown here:

```
For Each city In Temperatures
    {process current item, city}
Next
```

This loop automatically scans all the items in the Temperatures collection. At each iteration, the city variable represents the current item.

There is also something quite subtle in the code snippets above. These collections are "zeros based," which means that when you want to iterate over the collection by using a For loop, you need to start at 0 and end at one less than the Count of items in the collection. *Some collections are ones based.*

The *Files* Collection

One of the objects exposed by VBScript is the Files collection, which represents all the files in a folder. As you might have guessed, you don't have to populate this collection. It's created automatically by VBScript, and it contains the files of a specific folder. Obviously, you can't remove any items from this collection, either. You can only access the items of the collection and their properties (such as the size of a file, its attributes, and so on).

To create a Files collection, use the following statements (which I'll discuss later in this chapter):

```
set FileSys = CreateObject ( "Scripting.FileSystemObject" )
set List = FileSys.GetFolder ( "d:\windows\desktop\windows 2000" )
msgbox "count " & List.files.Count
for each aFile in List.files
        msgbox "file: " & aFile.name
    {process the current file, aFile}
    {aFile.Name is the name of the file}
    {aFile.Size is the size of the file}
Next
```

The variable *aFile* represents a file in the collection. It's a File type variable, and you use it to access the properties of the specific file. I'll discuss the various properties of the File object, as well as the methods for copying, moving, or deleting files, later in this chapter.

Similar to the Files collection is the Folders collection, which contains the subfolders of a given folder. It is accessed in the same way, only the loop's variable represents the current subfolder, and through its properties and methods you can manipulate folders (request their size, move them to a new location, and so on).

As you can see, collections are simple but flexible structures. They can be used for storing all types of information, yet they can be accessed quite simply, and the script doesn't have to know anything about the objects stored in the collection. Then, you can use a single variable to access the properties of the current object and manipulate the object through the same variable's methods. You will see many examples of collections in the following sections, but for now you should keep in mind the structure of a collection and the few properties it provides (`Item` and `Count`), as well as the `For Each...Next` structure for iterating through its items.

The *FileSystemObject* Object

The first objects of VBScript I'll discuss are the `TextStream` and `FileSystemObject` objects. The `FileSystemObject` lets you open an existing text file or create a new one and read from and write to it. The `TextStream` object provides the methods for reading and writing data from and to the file.

The `FileSystemObject` gives your script access to the computer's file system and is only available with stand-alone scripts (VBS files). To gain access to your computer's file system, you must create a `FileSystemObject` variable with the `CreateObject` method (as I explained earlier):

```
Set FSys = CreateObject("Scripting.FileSystemObject")
```

The variable *FSys* represents the file system. To access text files on the computer's disk, you must use the `FileSystemObject` object's methods, which I'll describe next.

The *CreateTextFile* Method

This method creates a new text file and returns a `TextStream` object that can be used to read from or write to the file. The syntax of the `CreateTextFile` method is

```
Set TStream = FSys.CreateTextFile(filename, overwrite, unicode)
```

The *`filename`* argument specifies the name of the file to be created and is the only required argument. The `overwrite` argument is a Boolean value that indicates whether you can overwrite an existing file (if `True`) or not (if `False`). If you omit the `overwrite` argument, existing files are not overwritten. The last argument, `unicode`, indicates whether the file is created as a Unicode or an ASCII file. If the `unicode` argument is `True`, the new file is created as a Unicode file; otherwise, it is created as an ASCII file. If you omit the `unicode` argument, an ASCII file is assumed.

To create a new text file, create a `FileSystemObject` object variable, and then call its `CreateTextFile` method as follows:

```
Set FSys = CreateObject("Scripting.FileSystemObject")
Set TStream = FSys.CreateTextFile("c:\testfile.txt", True)
```

The *`TStream`* variable represents a `TextStream` object, whose methods allow you to write to or read from the specified file (I'll discuss these methods later in this chapter).

The *OpenTextFile* Method

In addition to creating new text files, you can open existing files with the `OpenTextFile` method, whose syntax is

```
FSys.OpenTextFile(filename, iomode, create, format)
```

The `OpenTextFile` method opens the specified file and returns a `TextStream` object that can be used to read from or write to the file.

The *`filename`* argument is the only required one. The value of the `iomode` argument is one of the constants, as you can see in Table 24.1.

TABLE 24.1: THE VALUES OF THE OPENTEXTFILE METHOD'S IOMODE ARGUMENT

Constant	Description
`ForReading`	The file is opened for reading existing data.
`ForAppending`	The file is opened for appending new data.

The *`create`* optional argument is a Boolean value that indicates whether a new file can be created if the specified filename doesn't exist. If it's `True`, a new file is created. The last argument, *`format`*, is also optional and can be `True` (the file is opened in Unicode mode) or `False` (the file is opened in ASCII mode). If omitted, the file is opened using the system default (ASCII).

To open a `TextStream` object for reading, use the following statements:

```
Set FSys = CreateObject("Scripting.FileSystemObject")
Set TStream = FSys.OpenTextFile("c:\testfile.txt", ForReading)
```

Like the `CreateTextFile` method, the `OpenTextFile` method returns a `TextStream` object, whose methods allow you to write to or read from the specified file.

Now that you have seen how the `FileSystemObject` is used to open and create files, you are ready to look at the `TextStream` object, which lets you read from and write to files. The `FileSystemObject` has more methods, which allow you to access the various drives, copy and delete files or entire folders, and more. I'll come back to the methods of the `FileSystemObject`, but first let's see how you can manipulate text files through the `TextStream` object.

The *TextStream* Object's Methods

After you create a `TextStream` object with the `CreateTextFile` or the `OpenTextFile` method of the `FileSystemObject`, you can use the following methods to read from and write to the file.

Read

The `Read` method reads a specified number of characters from a `TextStream` object. Its syntax is

```
TStream.Read(characters)
```

Here, *`characters`* is the number of characters to be read from, and *`TStream`* is a `TextStream` variable.

ReadAll

The `ReadAll` method reads the entire `TextStream` (text file) and returns the text in a string. Its syntax is

```
fileText = TStream.ReadAll
```

ReadLine

The `ReadLine` method reads one line of text at a time (up to, but not including, the newline character) from a text file and returns the resulting string. Its syntax is

```
fileText = TStream.ReadLine
```

Skip

This method skips a specified number of characters when reading a text file. Its syntax is

```
TStream.Skip(characters)
```

Here, *`characters`* is the number of characters to be skipped.

SkipLine

The `SkipLine` method skips the next line of the text file, and its syntax is

```
TStream.SkipLine
```

The characters of the skipped lines are discarded, up to and including the next newline character.

Write

The `Write` method writes the specified string to a `TextStream` file. Its syntax is

```
TStream.Write(string)
```

Here, *`string`* is the string (literal or variable) to be written to the file. Strings are written to the file with no intervening spaces or characters between each string. Use the `WriteLine` method to write a newline character or a string that ends with a newline character.

WriteLine

The `WriteLine` method writes the specified string followed by a newline character to the file. Its syntax is

```
TStream.WriteLine(string)
```

Here, *string* is the text you want to write to the file. If you call the `WriteLine` method without an argument, a newline character is written to the file.

WriteBlankLines

The `WriteBlankLines` method writes a specified number of blank lines (newline characters) to the file. Its syntax is

```
TStream.WriteBlankLines(lines)
```

Here, *lines* is the number of blank lines to be inserted in the file.

The *TextStream* Object's Properties

Besides its methods, the `TextStream` object provides a number of properties that allow your code to know where the pointer is in the current `TextStream`.

AtEndOfLine

This is a read-only property that returns `True` if the file pointer is at the end of a line in the `TextStream` object, and `False` otherwise. The `AtEndOfLine` property applies to files that are open for reading. You can use this property to read a line of characters, one at a time, with a loop similar to the following one:

```
Do While TSream.AtEndOfLine = False
    newChar = TStream.Read(1)
    {process character newChar}
Loop
```

This loop scans the file represented by the `TStream` object, and while it hasn't reached the end of the current line, it reads and processes another character.

AtEndOfStream

This is another read-only property that returns `True` if the file pointer is at the end of the `TextStream` object. The `AtEndOfStream` property applies only to `TextStream` files that are open for reading. You can use this property to read an entire file, one line at a time, with a loop such as the following:

```
Do While TStream.AtEndOfStream = False
    newLine = TStream.ReadLine
    {process line}
Loop
```

Column

This is another read-only property that returns the column number of the current character in a `TextStream` line. The first character in a line is in column 1. Use this property to read data arranged in columns, without tabs or other delimiters between them.

Line

The Line property is another read-only property that returns the current line number in the TextStream. The Line property of the first line in a TextStream object is 1.

Using the *TextStream* Object

The TSTREAM.VBS script demonstrates several of the TextStream object's methods. When this script is executed, it creates a text file and writes a few lines in it. Then it opens the file, reads its lines, and displays them in a message box. Let's start with the script's code:

```
Set FileObj = CreateObject("Scripting.FileSystemObject")
TestFile = "c:\textfile.txt"
Set OutStream = FileObj.CreateTextFile (TestFile, True, False)
str1 = "This file was created on " & Now()
OutStream.WriteLine Str1
OutStream.WriteLine "This is the second line in the file"
OutStream.WriteBlankLines(1)
OutStream.WriteLine "This is the fourth line in the file"
Set OutStream = Nothing
Set InStream = FileObj.OpenTextFile (TestFile, 1, False, False)
While InStream.AtEndOfStream = False
   TLine = Instream.ReadLine
   txt = txt & TLine & vbCrLf
Wend
MsgBox "The following text was read from the file" & vbcrlf & txt
Set Instream=Nothing
```

The CreateObject method creates a FileSystemObject variable (the variable *FileObj*), through which the script can access the computer's hard disk and create the file c:\textfile.txt. OutStream is a TextStream object, whose Write method you use to write to the file. After the desired lines have been written to the file, you set the TextStream object variable to Nothing to release the resources allocated to it. See Figure 24.2 for the output of the TSTREAM.VBS script.

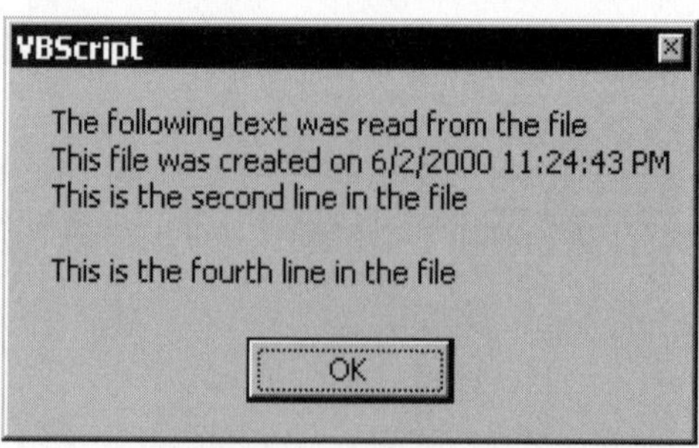

FIGURE 24.2 *The output of the TSTREAM.VBS script, which reads the lines of a text file on the local disk and displays them in a message box*

In the second half of the script, you create another `TextStream` object (the `InStream` object variable) to read the lines of the same file. The file's lines are read with a `While...Wend` loop, which examines the value of the `TextStream` object's `AtEndOfStream` property to find out how many lines to read from the file:

```
While InStream.AtEndOfStream = False
    TLine = Instream.ReadLine
    {process Tline variable}
Wend
```

The script doesn't do any real processing; it simply appends the current line to the *txt* variable, which is then displayed in the message box. In the next chapter, you will see how to use external files to store arguments for the script (such as a list of files to move to another folder or to print late at night).

More *FileSystemObject* Methods

In the previous sections, I discussed the methods of the `FileSystemObject` object, which allow you to access files on the local disk(s). The `FileSystemObject` supports many more methods, which apply to files and folders—methods that allow you to copy and delete files or folders, which are the bread and butter of scripting.

CopyFile

The `CopyFile` method copies one or more files from one folder to another, and its syntax is

```
FSys.CopyFile source, destination, overwrite
```

The *source* argument is the path of the file to be moved and may contain wildcard characters (for copying multiple files). The *destination* argument is the path of the destination folder that the files will be copied to. The *destination* argument may not contain wildcard characters. The last argument, `overwrite`, is optional and it's a Boolean value (`True`/`False`) that indicates whether existing files are to be overwritten. The `CopyFile` method will produce a run-time error if the destination file has its read-only attribute set, regardless of the value of the overwrite argument. See the discussion of the `Attributes` property for an example of how to overwrite read-only files.

CopyFolder

This method copies a folder from one location to another, including the subfolders (this is called *recursive* copying). The syntax of the `CopyFolder` method is

```
FSys.CopyFolder source, destination, overwrite
```

where *source* is the path of the source folder (where files will be copied from) and may include wildcard characters, in case you want to copy multiple files. The *destination* argument is the path of the destination folder (where the files will be copied to), and it may not contain wildcard characters. The last argument, `overwrite`, is optional, and it's a Boolean value that indicates whether existing folders can be overwritten. If it's True, the destination files can be overwritten, if they exist. To protect existing files in the destination folder, set it to False.

To copy all the DOC files from the folder MyDocuments to the folder WorkDocs\February, use the following statement:

```
Set FSys = CreateObject("Scripting.FileSystemObject")
FSys.CopyFolder "c:\MyDocuments\*.DOC", "c:\WorkDocs\February"
```

NOTE If you are going to use these statements in a script, you must also delete the original files (or move them, instead of copying them).

The CopyFolder method stops on the first error it encounters. This means that some files have been copied, some have not. The method isn't going to move the copied files back to their source folder; neither will it continue with the remaining files.

DeleteFile

The DeleteFile method deletes one or more files, and its syntax is

```
FSys.DeleteFile filespec, force
```

where *filespec* is the name of the file(s) to delete and may contain wildcard characters. The force argument is optional, and it's a Boolean value that indicates whether read-only files will be deleted (if True) or not (if False). Like the CopyFile method, the DeleteFile method stops on the first error it encounters.

DeleteFolder

This method deletes a specific folder and its contents, including its subfolders and their files. Its syntax is identical to the syntax of the DeleteFile method:

```
FSys.DeleteFolder folderspec, force
```

Here, *folderspec* is the name of the folder to delete. The specified folder is deleted, regardless of whether it contains files or not (unlike the RMDIR command of DOS).

MoveFile

The MoveFile method moves one or more files from one folder to another, and its syntax is

```
FSys.MoveFile source, destination
```

where *source* is the path of the file(s) to be moved and *destination* is the path where the file(s) will be moved to. The MoveFile method works identically to the Copy method, but the original files are deleted after they have been copied. The *source* argument string can contain wildcard characters to move multiple files, but the *destination* argument can't contain wildcard characters.

NOTE If the destination is an existing file's name or an existing folder's name, an error occurs.

MoveFolder

The `MoveFolder` method moves a folder to another location. Its syntax is

```
FSys.MoveFolder source, destination
```

where *`source`* and *`destination`* are the specifications of the source and destination folders.

FileExists, FolderExists

These two methods return `True` if the specified file or folder exists. Use them to make sure a file or folder exists before attempting to use it from within your script. Their syntax is

```
FSys.FileExists(fileSpec)
```

and

```
FSys.FolderExists(folderSpec)
```

GetFile, GetFolder

The `GetFile` method of the `FileSystemObject` returns a `File` object, which represents a specific file.

NOTE The `GetFile` method doesn't return the entire file; neither does it return the name of the file. It's a reference to a file, through which you can access the file's properties.

To create a `File` object variable with the `GetFile` method, you must first create a `FileSystemObject` variable and then call its `GetFile` method:

```
Set FSys = CreateObject("Scripting.FileSystemObject")
Set thisFile = Fsys.GetFile ( "c:\somefile.txt")
```

NOTE If you do not have a file named c:\somefile.txt, this might produce an error.

The `GetFolder` method is quite similar to the `GetFile` method, but it returns a `Folder` object. The argument of the `GetFolder` method must be an absolute or relative path name:

```
Set FSys = CreateObject("Scripting.FileSystemObject")
Set AdminsDocs = Fsys.GetFolder ( "C:\Documents and
Settings\Administrator\My Documents")
```

Here, you would get a list of the administrator's files in their My Documents folder (assuming that you had at least read access to the files).

GetFileName

This method returns the last component of specified path, which is a filename with its extension. The `GetFileName` method is usually called with a `File` object as argument to retrieve the filename without having to provide your own routine for parsing the path name. Notice that the `GetFileName` method works on its argument, whether such a path exists or not.

The *COPYFILES* Script

The `COPYFILES.VBS` script demonstrates how to manipulate multiple files using the `FileSystemObject` object's methods. The script reads a list of files from a text file (filenames are stored in the file one per line) and copies them to another folder.

The script expects to find the list of files to be copied in the C:\Documents and Settings\Administrator\My Documents text file. This file contains a full filename per line (it may contain blank lines but no comments). Here's a typical text file populated with file specifications:

```
c:\personal\Resume.doc
c:\personal\contracts\Pub.doc
c:\personal\contacts.xls
c:\Documents and Settings\Administrator\My Documents\Resume.doc
c:\Documents and Settings\Administrator\My Documents\SalaryHistory.xls
c:\Documents and Settings\Administrator\My Documents\DreamJob.ppt
```

The script creates a `TextStream` object (variable *`InStream`*), whose methods are used to read lines from the text file. Each line is the full name of a file to be copied. The script creates a `File` object for each filename in the text file with the `GetFile` method and assigns it to the variable *`thisFile`*. Then it calls the variable's `Copy` method to copy the file to its destination folder, which is the `c:\backup` folder. Here's the script's listing:

```
Set FileObj = CreateObject("Scripting.FileSystemObject")
InputFile = "C:\Documents and Settings\Administrator\My
Documents\filelist.txt"
Set InStream = FileObj.OpenTextFile (InputFile)
While InStream.AtEndOfStream = False
   currFileName = Instream.ReadLine
   If currFileName <> "" Then
      msgbox "copying " & currFileName
       Set thisFile = FileObj.GetFile(currFileName)
' NOTICE: THE FOLDER c:\backup MUST EXIST!
       thisFile.Copy "c:\backup\"  & thisFile.Name
```

```
    End If
Wend
Set Instream = Nothing
```

TIP Notice that the C:\backup folder must exist, and its name is hard-coded in the script. You can revise the script so that it reads the name of the destination folder from the text file (it could be the first line in the text file). Also, the `filelist.txt` file must exist. Create a text file with the names of the files you want to copy, and adjust the script's code accordingly. And one last important detail: the script needs to be run from the folder specified by the *`InputFile`* variable, or the `filelist.txt` file needs to include fully qualified path names (as shown above).

The *FTYPES* Script

This script renames and moves one or more files. Let's say you want to rename a bunch of files according to the date and time they were created, and then move them to another folder. Renaming files is a very common operation in scripting, and you can easily adjust this script's code to accommodate other practical situations.

The FTYPES.VBS script renames all the TIF files in the folder Images on the system to *YYMMDDHHNNSS*.TIF, where *YY* is the year, *MM* is the month, *DD* is the day, *HH* is the hour, *NN* is the minute, and *SS* the second of the file's creation stamp. If two files were created within less than a second of each other, a letter is appended to this name. This script produces names like 20000411150343.TIF or 20000411150343A.TIF.

NOTE In testing this script, you might have to copy a number of files to a new folder. In this case, all files will have the same creation date and they will be renamed to the same name (such as 2000041150343) and a different suffix (A, B, C, and so on).

This script starts by making sure that the destination folder exists. If not, it creates the folder with the following statements:

```
Set FSys = CreateObject("Scripting.FileSystemObject")
If Not FSys.FolderExists(DestFolder) Then
    FSys.CreateFolder DestFolder
End If
```

The `GetFolder` method is used to create a reference to the source folder, and then this variable's `Files` property is ready to retrieve the collection of all files in the folder:

```
Set FolderFiles = FSys.GetFolder(SourceFolder)
Set FileCollection = FolderFiles.Files
```

Then the script scans all the files in the *`FileCollection`* variable with a For Each…`Next` loop and renames them according to their creation time and date. Most of the script's code builds the new filename according to the parts of the property `DateCreated`.

Notice also the nested loops that use the `FileExists` property to make sure that each new filename is unique. As long as a file by that name exists, the code appends a different character to the end of the name. There's a statement in this loop that may confuse you:

```
ext = Chr(Asc(ext)+1)
```

`Ext` is the character that will be appended to the end of the filename to make it unique (for example, A, B, and so on). Since you can't increase a character value (in other words, you can't add 1 to A to get B), you must convert the character to a numeric value:

```
Asc(ext)
```

then add 1 to this value:

```
Asc(ext) + 1
```

and finally convert the new numeric value back to a character

```
Chr(Asc(ext)+1)
```

Here's the complete listing of the `FTYPES.VBS` script. As with all the examples of this chapter, the arguments (the names of the source and destination folders) are hard-coded.

NOTE The topic of passing arguments to your scripts is covered in Chapter 25.

```
 Copies All TIF files in the SourceFolder to the DestFolder
' and renames them according to the date/time of their creation
' You will need to modify the SourceFolder and DestFolder variables for
' your particular system!
   SourceFolder="c:\Images"
   DestFolder="c:\Backup"
   Set FSys = CreateObject("Scripting.FileSystemObject")
   If Not FSys.FolderExists(DestFolder) Then
       FSys.CreateFolder DestFolder
   End If
   Set FolderFiles = FSys.GetFolder(SourceFolder)
   Set FileCollection = FolderFiles.Files
   For Each thisFile in FileCollection
       If UCase(Right(thisFile.Name,4))=".TIF" Then
           newName = Year(thisFile.DateCreated)
           MN = Month(thisFile.DateCreated)
           If MN < 10 Then MN = "0" & MN
```

```
            DY = Day(thisFile.DateCreated)
            HR = Hour(thisFile.DateCreated)
            MT = Minute(thisFile.DateCreated)
            newName = newName & MN & DY & HR & MT
            If FSys.FileExists(DestFolder & "\" & newName & ".TIF") Then
                ext = "A"
                While FSys.FileExists(DestFolder & "\" & newName & ext &
                    ".TIF")
                     ext = Chr(Asc(ext)+1)
                Wend
            End If
       newName = DestFolder & "\" & newName & ext & ".TIF"
            ThisFile.Copy newName
       'msgbox "copying " & thisFile.Name & " to " & newName
            ThisFile.Delete
        End If
    Next
```

Renaming a large number of files is a common operation in scripting, and you can use this script as your starting point for similar scripts. You need to change only the statements that build the new filename according to different criteria.

TIP If you have problems running the `FTYPES.VBS` script, make sure the folders Images and Backup exist on the system and that you have set the *`SourceFolder`* and *`DestFolder`* variables correctly.

FileSystemObject Properties

The `FileSystemObject` object provides a significant number of properties, which you can use from within your script to access the drives and files of the computer's file system. These properties are discussed in the following sections, along with example scripts.

The *Drives* Collection

The `Drives` collection contains all the available drives. To access the `Drives` collection, you must first create a `FileSystemObject` variable and then access the `Drives` property of this variable:

```
Set FSys = CreateObject("Scripting.FileSystemObject")
Set AllDrives = FSys.Drives
```

The `AllDrives` variable is a collection of `Drive` objects (described in the next section). To list all the available drives, use a `For Each...Next` loop like the following:

```
For Each drive in AllDrives
    {process current drive, which is
     represented by the drive variable}
    MsgBox "Drive " & drive.Letter & " processed"
Next
```

The DriveLetter property returns the letter assigned to the specific drive. The Drives collection has the two properties of every collection: Count and Item. To access individual drives, you can also use an index value, as shown here:

```
AllDrives.Item(i)
```

or

```
AllDrives(i)
```

Each Drive object provides a number of properties, which are described next.

The *Drive* Object

The Drive object provides access to the properties of a particular local drive or shared network drive.

AvailableSpace

This property returns the amount of space available on the specified drive. The value returned by the AvailableSpace property is usually the same as that returned by the FreeSpace property, described later in this section (the two properties return different values for file systems that support quotas).

DriveLetter

The DriveLetter property returns the drive letter of a physical local drive or a shared network drive. Local drives always have a letter associated with them, but network drives may not be mapped to a letter. In this case, the DriveLetter property returns an empty string ("").

The DRIVES.VBS script displays the properties of all drives on the computer:

```
' This script scans the drives on your computer
' and displays their characteristics on a message box
' Notice the use of the statement ON ERROR RESUME NEXT
' Without it, the script will stop if a drive can't be
' accessed (drive A: is usually unavailable)
Set FSys = CreateObject("Scripting.FileSystemObject")
Set AllDrives = FSys.Drives
On Error Resume Next
For Each iDrive In AllDrives
    s = s & "Drive " & iDrive.DriveLetter & ": - "
    s = s & iDrive.VolumeName  & vbCrLf
```

```
    s = s & "Free Space: " & FormatNumber(iDrive.FreeSpace/1024, 0)
    s = s & " Kbytes"
    s = s & vbCrLf
Next
MsgBox s
```

The script's output is shown in Figure 24.3.

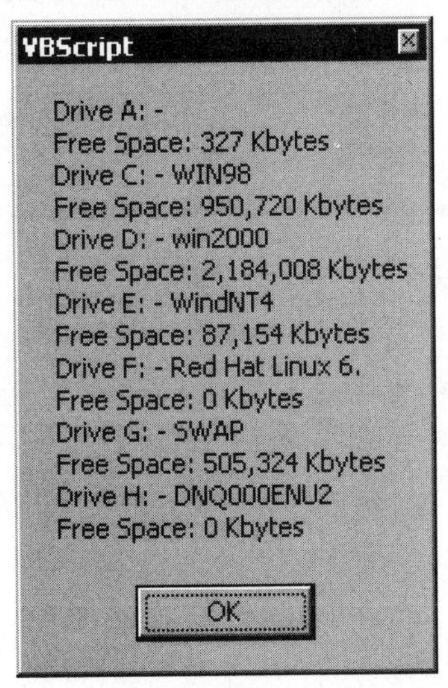

FIGURE 24.3 *The output of the DRIVES.VBS script*

The script's code is straightforward, but there is a statement I need to explain further. When you execute this script, the A drive (and possibly the B drive, if you have one) will grind for a few seconds. If, like most people, you don't have a diskette inserted in the drive, the drive isn't ready, and the script can't read its properties. The script would stop at this point with an error message, if it weren't for the statement

```
On Error Resume Next
```

This statement tells VBScript to continue the execution of the script with the next statement, should an error occur. The only thing that can go wrong in this script is that a drive isn't ready. In this case, the script will display the drive's letter, but not its volume name and size (see the entry for drive A in Figure 24.3).

DriveType

The `DriveType` property returns a value indicating the type of the specified drive. The values that correspond to each drive type are shown in Table 24.2.

TABLE 24.2: THE DRIVE TYPES

Value	Description
0	Unknown
1	Removable
2	Fixed
3	Network
4	CD-ROM
5	RAM Disk

FileSystem

This property returns the type of file system in use on the specified drive. DOS and Windows 95/98 use the FAT file system, Windows NT uses the NTFS system, and Windows 2000 Professional uses NTFS, FAT, or FAT32. Since the main drive is usually the C drive, the following statements read the file system type:

```
Set FSys = CreateObject("Scripting.FileSystemObject")
Set Drive = FSys.GetDrive("C:")
MsgBox Drive.FileSystem
```

FreeSpace

The `FreeSpace` property returns the amount of free space available on the specified drive; it has the same value as the `AvailableSpace` property. See the earlier entry `AvailableSpace` for more information.

IsReady

This property returns `True` if the specified drive is ready, `False` otherwise. Use this property before attempting to access removable-media drives and CD-ROM drives. `IsReady` will return `True` if the appropriate media is inserted into the drive and is ready to be accessed. If you want to access the CD-ROM drive from within your script, use the following statements:

```
Set FSys = CreateObject("Scripting.FileSystemObject")
Set Drive = FSys.GetDrive("D: ")
If Drive.IsReady Then
    {access drive}
Else
    MsgBox "Drive not ready. Please insert CD-ROM and try again"
End If
```

Path

The Path property returns the current path on a Drive object. Path is also a property of the File object (in which case it returns the path of the specified file) and the Folder object (in which case it returns the path of the specified folder).

RootFolder

This property returns an object that represents the root folder of a drive. You must use this property to create a variable, which will give you access to the files and folders contained on a specific drive's root folder.

SerialNumber

This property returns the decimal serial number used to uniquely identify a disk volume. You can use the SerialNumber property to ensure that the correct disk is inserted in a drive with removable media.

ShareName

The ShareName property returns the shared name for a network drive, and its syntax is

```
DriveObject.ShareName
```

If the DriveObject is not a network drive, the ShareName property returns a zero-length string ("").

TotalSize

The TotalSize property returns the total space, in bytes, of a drive (local or shared). The following statements use a drive's TotalSize and AvailableSpace properties to calculate the percentage of the free space:

```
Set FSys = CreateObject("Scripting.FileSystemObject")
Set drv = FSys.GetDrive("C:\")
s = "Drive " & drv.DriveLetter & ": is "
s = s & FormatNumber(drv.AvailableSpace/drv.TotalSize, 2)*100 & "% free"
MsgBox s
```

VolumeName

This property sets or returns the volume name of the specified drive. To request a drive's volume name, use the statement:

```
DriveObject.VolumeName
```

To change the drive's volume, use the statement:

```
DriveObject.VolumeName = newname
```

The *Files* Collection

The Files collection contains a File object for each file in a folder. The following script iterates through the files of a specific folder using the For Each...Next statement:

```
Set FSys = CreateObject("Scripting.FileSystemObject")
Set ThisFolder = FSys.GetFolder(folderName)
Set AllFiles = ThisFolder.Files
For Each file in AllFiles
    {process current file}
Next
```

In the loop's body you can access the various properties of the current file. Its name is file.Name, its creation date is file.DateCreated, and so on.

We'll look at the various properties and methods of the File object next.

The *File* Object

The File object represents a file and provides properties, which represent the various properties of the actual file, and methods, which let you copy, move, and delete files.

To obtain a File object and examine its properties, use the following sequence of statements:

1. Create a FileSystemObject variable:

   ```
   Set FSys = CreateObject("Scripting.FileSystemObject")
   ```

2. Use the *FSys* variable to obtain an object that represents a specific file:

   ```
   Set file = FSys.GetFile(fileName)
   ```

   where *fileName* is the desired file's path name (c:\backup\F001.jpg, for example).

3. Access the file's properties through the File object variable:

   ```
   Fname = file.Name
   FDate = file.DateCreated
   FSize = file.Size
   ```

   and so on.

Next we'll take a look at the properties of the File object.

The *File* Object's Properties

The File object provides the following properties. Most of these properties apply to the Folder object as well, which you'll read about later in this chapter.

Attributes

The Attributes property is used to read or set a file's attributes. To read the attributes of a file, use the syntax

```
aFile.Attributes
```

You can also set selected attributes (as long as they are not read-only attributes), using the syntax

```
AFile.Attributes = new_attribute_value
```

The *new_attribute_value* can have any of the values shown in Table 24.3. To change multiple attributes, combine the corresponding values with the logical OR operator. (The attributes are read-write except for volume, directory, alias, and compressed, which are read-only.)

TABLE 24.3: THE VALUES OF NEW_ATTRIBUTE_VALUE

Constant	Value	Description
Normal	0	Normal file
ReadOnly	1	Read-only file
Hidden	2	Hidden file
System	4	System file
Volume	8	Disk drive volume label
Directory	16	Folder or directory (read-only)
Archive	32	File has changed since last backup
Alias	1024	Link or shortcut (read-only)
Compressed	2048	Compressed file (read-only)

To determine if the archive attribute is cleared for a file, use this code:

```
If f.attributes and 32 Then
  ' archive bit is cleared
Else
  ' Archive bit is set
   End If
```

You can also use the MsgBox() function to prompt the user to change the read-only attribute:

```
If aFile.Attributes And 1 Then
   reply = MsgBox("This is a read-only file. Delete it anyway?", vbYesNo)
   If reply = vbYes Then
      aFile.Attributes = aFile.Attributes + 32
      aFile.Delete
   End If
Else
   aFile.Delete
End If
```

Delete is a method of the File object, which deletes the specific file. I'll discuss that in the next section.

Normally, when you set a file's attributes, you don't reset the existing ones. For example, you may choose to add the Hidden attribute from a file that has its ReadOnly attribute set. To turn on the Hidden attribute without affecting the other ones, use a statement like

```
aFile.Attributes = aFile.Attributes + 2
```

or

```
aFile.Attributes = aFile.Attributes Or 2
```

To remove a specific attribute, first find out whether this attribute is already set, then subtract its value from the Attributes property's value. To remove the Hidden attribute, use a structure like the following:

```
If aFile.Attributes And 2 Then
    aFile.Attributes = aFile.Attributes - 2
End If
```

DateCreated

The DateCreated property returns the date and time that the specified file or folder was created, and it's read-only. To retrieve the date a specific file was created, use the syntax

```
aFile.DateCreated
```

The following code segment calculates the age of a file in days. You can calculate the file's age in any other time interval by replacing the function Day() with Month() for months, Minute() for minutes, and so on.

```
Set FSys = CreateObject("Scripting.FileSystemObject")
Set thisFile = FSys.GetFile("c:\Documents and Settings\Administrator\My
Documents\PTLink.htm")
DateCreated = FSys.DateCreated
MsgBox Day(now() - DateCreated)
```

DateLastAccessed

This property returns the date and time that the specified file or folder was last accessed. The DateLastAccessed property is identical in its use to the DateCreated property.

DateLastModified

This property returns the date and time that the specified file or folder was last modified. The DateLastModified property is identical in its use to the DateCreated property.

TIP The `DateCreated`, `DateLastAccessed`, and `DateLastModified` properties are read-only. Sometimes, it's useful to be able to *touch* the files in a folder (change the `DateLastAccessed` property). If you are using scripts or another automated mechanism for deleting or moving old files, touching them will enable you to exclude certain files from an automatic deletion operation. It would be convenient to touch a file by changing the value of its `DateLastAccessed` property, but this is impossible. To change the `DateLastAccessed` property, you should copy the file, delete the original, and then rename the copied file back to the name of the original file.

Drive

The `Drive` property returns the drive letter of the drive on which the specified file or folder resides. It's read-only and its syntax is

```
object.Drive
```

where *`object`* is always a `File` or `Folder` object.

Name

The `Name` property returns or sets the name of a file or folder (the last part of the path). To find out the name of a file, use the statement

```
FileObject.Name
```

To rename an existing file (or folder), use the following syntax:

```
FileObject.Name = new_name
```

where *`new_name`* is the new name of the file represented by the `FileObject` variable (or the corresponding `Folder` object variable).

ParentFolder

The `ParentFolder` property returns a `Folder` object, which represents the parent folder of the specified file or folder. This property is read-only.

Path

The `Path` property returns the path for a specified file or folder. If the file resides in the root folder, the backslash character (\)is not included. In other words, the path for the file C:\\SomeFile.cmd is "C:" and not "C:\".

If the `FileObject` object variable represents the file C:\Documents and Settings\Administrator\My Documents\TOC.doc, then the expressions

```
FileObject.Path
```

and

```
FileObject.Name
```

return the following values:

```
c:\Documents and Settings\Administrator\My Documents
```

and

```
TOC.doc
```

ShortName

This property is similar to the Name property, but it returns the short name (eight-dot-three convention) of the specified file or folder.

Size

When applied to File objects, this property returns the size, in bytes, of the specified file. For folders, it returns the size, in bytes, of all files and subfolders contained in the folder.

Type

This property returns information about the type of a file or folder. For example, for files ending in .TXT, the string Text Document is returned.

The *File* Object's Methods

The File object provides a number of methods for moving files around that are similar to the methods of the FileSystemObject, and they are described in the following sections. The difference between the methods of the FileSystemObject and those of the File object is that with the File object's methods you can't move multiple files at once. Each method is applied to a specific file only.

Copy

This method copies a file (or folder) from one location to another. The syntax of the Copy method is

```
FileObject.Copy destination, overwrite
```

where *destination* is the new name or folder of the file and may not contain wildcard characters. The second argument, overwrite, is optional, and it's a Boolean value that indicates whether existing files or folders are to be overwritten (if True) or not (if False).

Delete

This method deletes a file (or folder). The syntax of the Delete method is

```
FileObject.Delete force
```

The force argument is optional and indicates whether files with their read-only attributes should be deleted anyway (if True) or not (if False). Unlike the DOS RMDIR command, the Delete method removes a folder regardless of whether it contains files or subfolders.

Move

The Move method moves a file to a new location (it's equivalent to copying the file to a new location, then deleting the original file). The syntax of the Move method is

```
FileObject.Move destination
```

where *destination* is the path where the file is moved to. If the *destination* argument is a folder name, the file is moved to the specified folder with the same name. If the destination argument contains a filename, too, the file is moved and renamed. You can call the `Move` method with a different filename to simply rename the original file.

OpenAsTextStream

This method opens a specified file and returns a `TextStream` object that can be used to read from or write to the file. The syntax of the `OpenAsTextStream` method is

```
FileObject.OpenAsTextStream(iomode, format)
```

Both arguments are optional. The `iomode` argument specifies whether the file will be opened for input, output, or appending, and it can have one of the values shown in Table 24.4.

TABLE 24.4: TABLE 24.4: THE SETTINGS OF THE IOMODE ARGUMENT OF THE OPENASTEXTSTREAM

Constant	Value	Description
ForReading	1	Opens a file for reading only. You can't write to this file.
ForWriting	2	Opens a file for writing. If a file with the same name exists, its previous contents are overwritten.
ForAppending	8	Opens a file and writes to the end of the file.

The second argument, *format*, indicates whether the file should be opened as Unicode or ASCII, and it can have one of the values shown in Table 24.5.

TABLE 24.5: TABLE 24.5: THE SETTINGS OF THE FORMAT ARGUMENT OF THE OPENASTEXTSTREAM

Constant	Value	Description
TristateUseDefault	–2	Opens the file using the system default.
TristateTrue	–1	Opens the file as Unicode.
TristateFalse	0	Opens the file as ASCII.

The `OpenAsTextStream` method does the same thing as the `OpenTextFile` method of the `FileSystemObject`. They both prepare a file for input or output. Use the `OpenAsTextStream` method when you have an object variable that represents the file you want to open. If you know the name of the file, use the `OpenTextFile` method of the `FileSystemObject`.

The *Folders* Collection

The Folders collection contains a Folder object for each subfolder in a folder. The following script iterates through the subfolders of a specific folder using the For Each...Next statement:

```
Set FSys = CreateObject("Scripting.FileSystemObject")
Set ThisFolder = FSys.GetFolder(folderName)
Set AllFolders = ThisFolder.SubFolders
For Each folder in AllFolders
    {process current folder}
Next
```

In the loop's body you can access the various properties of the current folder. Its name is folder.Name, its creation date is folder.DateCreated, and so on.

The various properties of the Folder object are described next. But first, let's look at the AddFolder method, the Folder object's single method.

AddFolder

The AddFolder method adds a new Folder object to a Folders collection, and its syntax is

```
FolderObject.AddFolders folderName
```

where *folderName* is the name of the new Folder object to be added.

The *Folder* Object

The Folder object represents a folder on a disk; it allows you to manipulate the actual folders on your disk through its properties and methods. To create a Folder object, you must first create a FileSystemObject variable and then call its GetFolder method, using the folder's path as argument:

```
Set FSys = CreateObject("Scripting.FileSystemObject")
Set thisFolder = FSys.GetFolder("C:\Documents and Settings\Administrator\My
Documents")
```

After these lines are executed, the variable *thisFolder* represents the folder D:\Documents and Settings\Administrator\My Documents, and you can manipulate the folder through the variable's properties and objects.

I'll discuss the Folder object's properties next. Since many of these properties are quite similar to corresponding properties of the File object, I'll just mention them briefly and focus on the unique properties of the Folder object.

Attributes

The Attributes property returns, or sets, the attributes of files or folders. To read a folder's attributes, use the statement

```
FolderObject.Attributes
```

To change an attribute, use the statement

```
FolderObject.Attributes = FolderObject.Attributes or newAttributes
```

See the discussion of the Attributes property of the File object for more information on using this property.

DateCreated

The DateCreated property returns the date and time that the specified file or folder was created, and it's read-only.

DateLastAccessed

This property returns the date and time that the specified file or folder was last accessed, and it's read-only.

DateLastModified

This property returns the date and time that the specified file or folder was last modified, and it's read-only.

Drive

The Drive property returns the letter of the drive on which the specified file or folder resides, and it's read-only.

IsRootFolder

This property returns True if the specified folder is the root folder, False otherwise. There is no equivalent property for the File object. You can use the IsRootFolder property to calculate the depth of a folder, with a subroutine like the following:

```
Sub GetDepth(FolderObject)
If FolderObject.IsRootFolder Then
        MsgBox "The specified folder is the root folder."
Else
    Do Until FolderObject.IsRootFolder
        Set FolderObject = FolderObject.ParentFolder
        fdepth = fdepth + 1
    Loop
    MsgBox "The specified folder is " & fdepth & " levels deep."
End If
End Sub
```

Name

The Name property returns the name of a specified file or folder (the last part of the folder's path name). See the Name property of the File object for details on using this property.

ParentFolder

This property returns the parent folder of a `Folder` object. See the discussion of the property `IsRootFolder` for an example.

Path

The `Path` property returns the path of a specified file or folder (the folder's path name without the last part). See the `Path` property of the `File` object for details on using this property.

ShortName

This property returns the short folder name (eight-dot-three convention) of a `Folder` or `File` object.

ShortPath

This property returns the short path name of a `Folder` or `File` object.

Size

`Size` is a property of both files and folders, and it returns the size (in bytes) of a file, or the total size of all the files in a folder and its subfolders. To find out the size of a file or folder, you must first create the appropriate `File` or `Folder` object variable and then read the variable's `Size` property:

```
Set FSys = CreateObject("Scripting.FileSystemObject")
Set thisFile = FSys.GetFolder(" D:\Documents and Settings\Administrator\My
Documents\messages.doc")
MsgBox "The MESSAGE.DOC file is " & thisFile.Size & " bytes long."
Set thisFolder = FSys.GetFolder("C:\Documents and Settings\Administrator\My
Documents")
MsgBox "The  My Documents folder's size is " & thisFolder.Size/(1024*1024) &
" Mbytes."
```

Subfolders

The `Subfolders` property returns a `Folders` collection, which contains all the subfolders of a specific folder. To obtain the collection of subfolders under the folder C:\Winnt, create a `FileSystemObject` variable, use its `GetFolder` method to obtain a reference to the specific folder, and then read the value of the `SubFolders` property, as shown in the following statements:

```
Set FSys = CreateObject("Scripting.FileSystemObject")
Set thisFolder = FSys.GetFolder("c:\winnt")
Set allFolders = aFolder.SubFolders
For Each f in allFolders
    {process folder f}
Next
```

The current folder's name in the loop's body is `f.Name`. The processing of the current folder could be to examine its files, and this is exactly what you are going to do next.

Scanning a Folder Recursively

The `SCAN.VBS` script will come in handy for processing files in multiple folders. This script scans a folder recursively: first it scans the folder's files, and then it visits its subfolders, one at a time, where it does the same—scans its files and then visits each one of its subfolders. This script doesn't do much. It simply prints the names of the folders it visits and their files to a text file. You can use it as a starting point for a number of scripts that must perform some operations on many files scattered through multiple folders.

This script is more complicated than the other ones presented in this chapter, but you should try to understand how it works, so that you can modify its code according to your needs. It is also the first script in this chapter that uses a subroutine. Here's the main script:

```
Dim FSys, DFile
Set FSys = CreateObject("Scripting.FileSystemObject")
Set DFile = FSys.CreateTextFile("c:\allfiles.txt", True)
' Specify the folder you wish to map in the following line
ScanFolder("C:\winnt")
DFile.Close
MsgBox "File List created"
```

The *`DFile`* variable represents the file where the output is printed. The file is created with the `CreateTextFile` method of the `FileSystemObject` object, and it overwrites an existing file with the same name. The name of the file and the name of the folder to be scanned are hard-coded in the script, but you'll see in Chapter 25 how to call scripts with arguments. Then, the program calls the `ScanFolder()` subroutine with the name of the folder to be scanned (C:\Winnt).

The `ScanFolder()` subroutine first scans the files in the folder specified as argument and then its subfolders. When the program control returns, the main script closes the file and displays a message on the screen. The implementation of the `ScanFolder()` subroutine, shown next, is quite interesting:

```
Sub ScanFolder(folderSpec)

    Set thisFolder = FSys.GetFolder(folderSpec)
    Set fc = thisFolder.SubFolders
    Set AllFiles=thisFolder.Files
    For Each iFile in AllFiles
        DFile.WriteLine iFile.path
    Next
```

```
    For Each iFolder in FoldersCollection
        DFile.WriteLine
        DFile.WriteLine "*** FOLDER  " & iFolder.path & "***"
        ScanFolder(iFolder.path)
    Next
End Sub
```

The `ScanFolder()` subroutine starts by creating a reference to the subfolder specified by its argument. It creates a collection with all the files in the folder and scans the collection to print the names of the files to the file represented by the object variable *DFile*.

After printing the names of the files in the current record, the subroutine must scan all the subfolders and print their contents. At this point, I want to repeat the same process that the `ScanFolder()` performs. That's why I call the `ScanFolder()` again, from within `ScanFolder()`.

TIP You might find this type of coding strange, but it's a very powerful programming technique. A procedure can call itself recursively. Each new copy of the procedure is executed afresh; it has its own copy of local variables and runs independently of the previous copies of the procedures.

When a recursive procedure calls itself, the current instance of the procedure is suspended and waits for the copy it just called to terminate. Then it resumes its execution. Even if you are not familiar with recursive programming, you can use the `SCAN.VBS` script as your starting point to develop all kinds of scripts that must perform the same operations on multiple folders and their subfolders.

The `ALLFILES.TXT` file generated by the `SCAN.VBS` script contains a list of files, grouped by the folder they belong to. Here's a typical file generated by the script:

```
C:\WINNT\ade.dll
C:\WINNT\Ade001.bin
C:\WINNT\Blue Lace 16.bmp
C:\WINNT\certocm.log
C:\WINNT\clock.avi

...

C:\WINNT\Zapotec.bmp
C:\WINNT\_default.pif

*** FOLDER  D:\WINNT\addins***
C:\WINNT\addins\faxext.ecf
```

```
*** FOLDER  D:\WINNT\Application Compatibility Scripts***
C:\WINNT\Application Compatibility Scripts\aciniupd.exe
C:\WINNT\Application Compatibility Scripts\acregl.exe
```


Automating Other Applications

The most important functions of VBScript are the CreateObject and GetObject functions, which allow your script to contact other applications and automate them. In other words, the script will start an application, send commands to it, and close the application. For example, if you need to calculate a complicated math expression from within a script, you can contact Excel, pass the expression to be evaluated to it, and read the result.

Another example is a script that starts Word, opens one or more documents and prints them without any user interaction. Such a script is even more useful if coupled with the Task Scheduler, so that you can do massive printouts at midnight, when your computer and the printer are both available.

The applications you can contact with the CreateObject and GetObject functions must be ActiveX servers (formerly known as OLE servers). As I mentioned earlier, a server is an application that exposes its objects, so that other applications can use them. Again, if you are not familiar with object programming, the topic of server applications is easier to understand through an example. The following two lines contact Excel and request the calculation of an expression:

```
Set EXL = CreateObject("Excel.Application")
MsgBox EXL.Evaluate(log(3.45/abs(cos(0.34))))
```

Figure 24.4. shows the output.

FIGURE 24.4
The output of an Excel calculation

The first line creates an object variable, EXL, which represents the Excel application. The next line calls Excel's Evaluate method, which accepts a math expression as an argument and returns its value. The result is displayed on a message box.

Now, VBScript is quite capable of calculating an expression like log(3.45/abs(cos (0.34))), so why bother with Excel? The reason is that the expression must be hard-coded into the script, as I've done in this example. But what if you want to calculate a user-supplied expression? Writing a function that calculates arbitrary expressions (a so-called *math parser*) is quite a task. Using Excel's `Evaluate` method, you can calculate any math expression from within your script.

The `MATH.VBS` script prompts the user to enter a math expression, calculates, and displays the result. The script's code is surprisingly simple:

```
Set EXL = CreateObject("Excel.Application")
Expression = InputBox("Enter an expression")
MsgBox Expression & " = " & EXL.Evaluate(Expression)
Set EXL = Nothing
```

This script works nicely, provided you have Excel installed on your computer and you enter a valid math expression. Expressions like 14/0, or Sqr(–9) are invalid—they can't be calculated. To prevent run-time errors, you must add some error-trapping code (run-time errors are discussed later in this chapter).

Excel is a server application because it exposes its properties and methods so that other applications can use them. The idea is that programmers need not duplicate the functionality already built into existing applications. Excel is the proper program for doing math, so why shouldn't it make its functionality available to other applications? Notice that the server application (Excel, in this case) isn't displayed while the script is running. Let's look at the syntax of these two methods and then at some more examples.

The *CreateObject()* Function

The `CreateObject()` function returns a reference to an ActiveX component. The function returns an object, which can be assigned to an object variable:

```
Set objVar = CreateObject(ClassName)
```

The `ClassName` argument has the form `servername.typename`, where ***`servername`*** is the name of the application providing the object and ***`typename`*** is the type or class of the object to be created. An ActiveX server provides at least one type of object. For example, Excel provides the `Application` object (which provides methods and properties that expose the application's basic functionality) or a `WorkSheet` (which provides methods and properties for manipulating the cells of a worksheet).

In the previous section, you saw an example of the `Excel.Application` object. Let's see another script that starts Excel and enters a few values in selected cells. The `XLAUTO.VBS` script starts Excel and instructs it to create a new worksheet, populate it, and then save it. See Figure 24.5.

```
Dim EXLSheet
Set EXLSheet = CreateObject("Excel.Application")
If ( Err.number <> 0 ) then
      Msgbox "Error opening excel " & Err.Description
End If

exlsheet.workbooks.add
exlsheet.worksheets.add
```

```
EXLSheet.WorkSheets(1).Cells(1,1).Value = "1997 Q1"
EXLSheet.WorkSheets(1).Cells(2,1).Value = "1997 Q2"
EXLSheet.WorkSheets(1).Cells(3,1).Value = "1997 Q3"
EXLSheet.WorkSheets(1).Cells(4,1).Value = "1997 Q4"
EXLSheet.WorkSheets(1).Cells(5,1).Value = "TOTAL"
EXLSheet.WorkSheets(1).Cells(1,2).Value = "3342.00"
EXLSheet.WorkSheets(1).Cells(2,2).Value = "5324.00"
EXLSheet.WorkSheets(1).Cells(3,2).Value = "5227.00"
EXLSheet.WorkSheets(1).Cells(4,2).Value = "3673.00"
EXLSheet.WorkSheets(1).Cells(5,2).Value = "=SUM(B2:B4)"
EXLSheet.Save "c:\test.xls"
set EXLSheet = Nothing
```

FIGURE 24.5 *The XLAUTO.VBS script starts Excel and creates this worksheet automatically.*

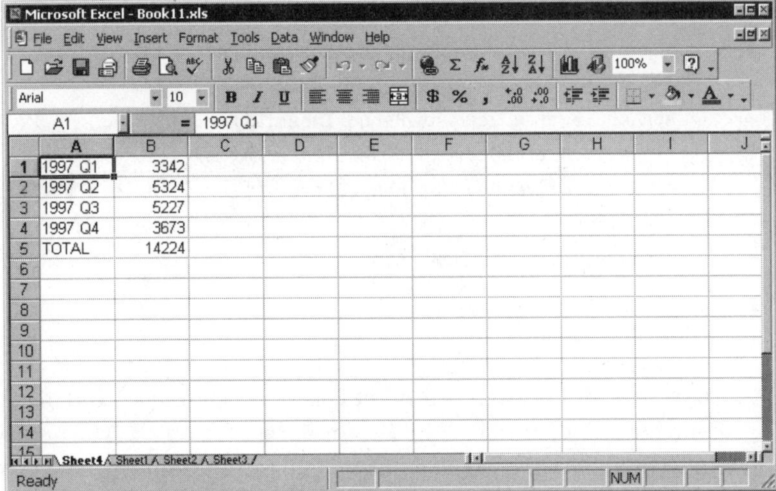

You will notice that this script has an `If...Then` statement right below the `CreateObject()` function call. It is good programming practice to always check for errors, and I will discuss error trapping in a few pages.

The `WRDAUTO.VBS` script does something similar with Word. It starts Word, inserts a few paragraphs in the document, and then leaves the application open. The user can edit the text and then save it (or discard the changes).

You should not start any instances of the `WRDAUTO.VBS` script without closing the current instance of Word first. Each new instance of the script will start another instance of Word—and this will deplete your system's resources quickly. Here is the script's source code:

```
' The WRDAUTO.VBS script starts Word, creates a new document
' and then makes the application visible. The user can edit
```

```
' the document and then close it.

' Don't run multiple instances of this script without
' terminating the active instance of the script.

Set AppWord = CreateObject("Word.Application")
AppWord.Documents.Add
AppWord.ActiveDocument.Range.InsertAfter "Document Title" & vbCr
AppWord.ActiveDocument.Range.Font.Bold = True
AppWord.ActiveDocument.Range.Font.Size = 16
AppWord.ActiveDocument.Range.Font.Name = "Comic Sans MS"
AppWord.ActiveDocument.Range.InsertAfter "This is the document's first
paragraph, aligned to the left." & vbCrLf
AppWord.ActiveDocument.Range.InsertAfter "This is the document's second
paragraph. "
AppWord.ActiveDocument.Range.InsertAfter "It was inserted with the statement
"
AppWord.ActiveDocument.Range.InsertAfter
"AppWord.ActiveDocument.Range.InsertAfter "
AppWord.ActiveDocument.Range.InsertAfter "and is also left aligned." &
vbCrLf
AppWord.ActiveDocument.Range.InsertAfter "The last line in the document." &
vbCrLf
AppWord.Visible = True
```

The variable AppWord represents the running instance of Word. The documents open in Word are members of the Documents collection, and to create a new document you must call the Add method of the Documents object. The newly added document is the currently active document, and you can access it with the expression AppWord.ActiveDocument. See Figure 24.6.

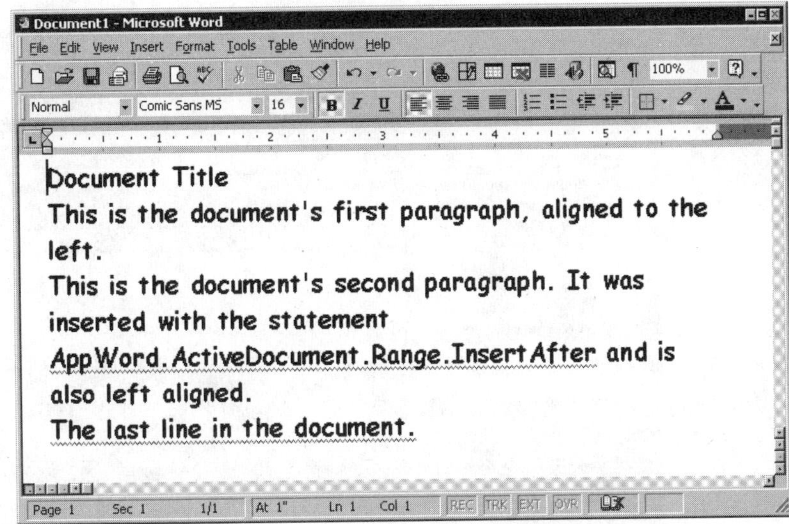

FIGURE 24.6 *The* WRDAUTO.VBS *scripts starts Word, inserts a few lines in a new document, and leaves the application open for editing.*

The text in a document is accessed via the Range object, which may represent a few characters, words, sentences, or the entire document. The Range object, in turn, supports numerous properties and methods, which correspond to nearly every editing and formatting command in the application's menus. The `InsertAfter` method inserts some text after the current paragraph in the document (there's also an `InsertBefore` method, which inserts text before the current paragraph in the text). The Range object's Font property lets you set the font for the text that follows it. To change the appearance of existing text, you can use the `Selection` object.

In order to see the object model—the capabilities of Excel (or other Office applications)—you need to invoke the scripting editor. In Excel 2000, follow these steps:

1. Choose Tools ➢ Macro ➢ Visual Basic Editor to open the editor.
2. Press F2.

By browsing through the display (see Figure 24.7), you will see the various objects, methods, and properties that Excel provides. Look in the lowest pane to see a description of the particular method or property you are looking at.

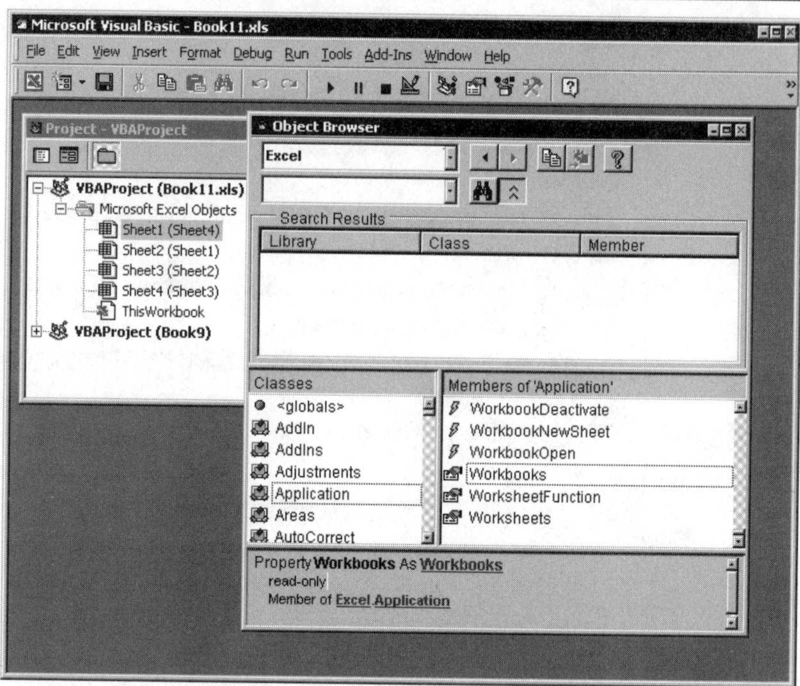

FIGURE 24.7
Objects, methods, and properties in Excel

TIP For further information on scripting with Microsoft Office 97 and 2000, see `http://msdn.microsoft.com/library/default.asp?URL=/library/techart/sampauto.htm`.

The *GetObject()* Function

If you want to start an application and open an existing file, use the `GetObject()` function, whose syntax is

```
GetObject(pathname, class)
```

Both arguments are optional, but you must specify at least one. The *`pathname`* argument is the path name of the file you want to open. If it's omitted, then you must supply the second argument. The *`class`* argument has the form `servername.typename`, where *`servername`* is the name of the application providing the object and *`typename`* is the type or class of the object to be created.

If you specify the `class` argument only, then `GetObject` returns a new instance of the specified type (a new DOC or XLS file, for example).

You should also use the `GetObject()` function when there is a running instance of the application that can edit the type of file you want to open. If Word is running, for example, you need not start another instance of Word with the `CreateObject()` function. Instead, use the `GetObject()` function to open the file with the current instance of the application.

Handling Run-Time Errors

A script is a program that runs without user intervention. As such, it should be carefully designed so that it won't stop when it encounters an error. I'm assuming that you will test your scripts and make sure they don't contain any syntax errors. There are some errors, however, that can't be caught at design time. For example, an extremely simple script that calculates the square root of a user-supplied value is very vulnerable to user input. If the user supplies a negative number, the function `SQR()`, which returns the square root of a number, will abort the execution of the script with an error message, as you can see in Figure 24.8.

FIGURE 24.8 *Errors within scripts display this dialog box and terminate the execution of the script.*

Similarly, a script that calls Excel and works perfectly on your system will not work on another system without Excel. These are typical examples of what can go wrong with a script, no matter how well you design and test it. And, of course, you can't expect the user to deal with such situations.

Trapping Errors

Every major language provides a number of mechanisms for catching errors before they cause a run-time error. These mechanisms are known as *error traps*, and the corresponding code is called *error-trapping* code. VBScript's error-trapping capability leaves a lot to be desired, but it provides a mechanism that will help you write more robust applications. This mechanism is implemented with the statement

```
On Error Resume Next
```

and the `Err` object. The `On Error Resume Next` statement tells VBScript not to interrupt the execution of the current script but to continue with the following statement. Just by inserting this statement at the beginning of the script, you make sure that the script won't terminate abruptly should an error occur. But the results will be unpredictable. For example, if you attempt to execute the `MATH.VBS` script described in this section on a system without Excel, you won't see the error message, but the result displayed will be incorrect (no matter what the expression is, the result will be 0).

To take advantage of the `On Error Resume Next` statement, you must examine the `Err` object. The `Err` object holds the last error that occurred during the execution of the script. Its `Number` property returns the error's number, and its `Description` property returns the error's description. To find whether an error occurred, examine the `Err.Number` property:

```
If Err.Number <> 0 Then
    {process error}
End If
```

Let's revise the `MATH.VBS` script to make it more robust. The first place an error may occur is in the statement that creates an instance of Excel. Insert the `On Error Resume Next` statement at the beginning of the script. After the execution of the statement that creates the Excel object, examine the `Err.Number` property. If it's not zero, then an error occurred, because Excel couldn't start.

```
On Error Resume Next
Set EXL = CreateObject("MSExcel.Application")
If Err.Number <> 0 Then
    MsgBox "Could not start Excel. Please make sure Excel is
      installed on your system before running this script."
    Wscript.Quit
End If
```

If an error occurred during the creation of the `EXL` variable, there is no point in continuing the execution of the script. You simply display a message (which is more descriptive and certainly friendlier than the default error message) and quit. To quit the script, call the `Wscript.Quit` method (the `Wscript` object is discussed in detail in Chapter 25). To test the behavior of this script on a system with Excel installed, use the name MSExcel, instead of Excel (as I've done in the listing shown above). Since there's no MSExcel application, the `CreateObject()` function will fail. Figure 24.9 shows the error message from VBScript.

FIGURE 24.9
An error message from VBScript

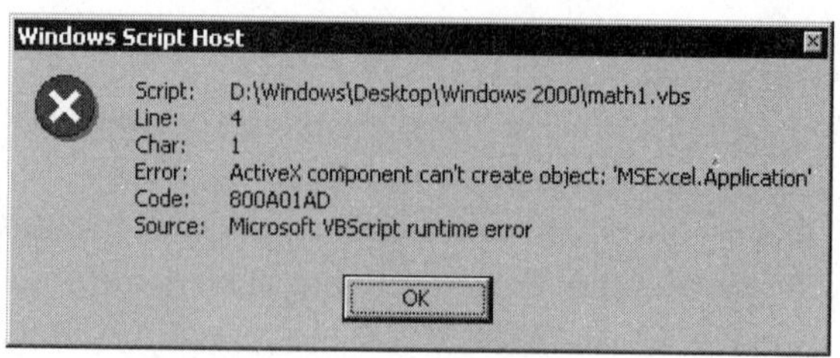

Another potential error is that the user-supplied expression can't be evaluated (for example, if the user requests the square root of a negative number). This is handled by the following statements:

```
Expression = InputBox("Enter a expression")
MsgBox Expression & " = " & EXL.Evaluate(Expression)
If Err.Number <> 0 Then
    MsgBox "Excel returned the following error: " & vbCrLf & Err.Description
End If
```

If the expression can be calculated, the `MsgBox` statement will be executed and the `Err.Number` property will be zero (which means that the error-trapping code won't be executed). If Excel raises an error, the `MsgBox` statement *won't* be executed, and the error-trapping code will be executed instead. To test for this type of error, change the name of the class from `MSExcel.Application` to `Excel.Application`, run the script and enter an expression like SQR(–16), or LOG(–45), which are invalid expressions. The script will display the message returned by Excel (which is `Type Mismatch`). You can find out the error's number and display a friendlier message, such as "You supplied an invalid expression, which Excel can't calculate."

Summary

In this chapter, we looked at how to write and execute scripts on a Windows 2000 Professional local computer. I gave you some examples that show how to write scripts that access the file system and in other ways manipulate files and folders. Obviously, my intention is that you now have enough information that you can extrapolate and write scripts that can take care of repetitive tasks on your system.

CHAPTER 25

The Windows Scripting Host

FEATURING:

The Windows Scripting Host is an engine for executing scripts. It comes with Windows 98, Windows NT, and Windows 2000 (Professional and the three editions of Server). The Scripting Host is an executable file, `WSCRIPT.EXE`, that can execute scripts written in VBScript and JScript. This means that a company that wants to provide a new scripting language for the Windows operating system can provide its own scripting engine.

NOTE You may also see scripting languages such as Perl or IBM's REXX on Windows. Currently, however, there are only two scripting languages for Windows 2000 Professional: VBScript and JScript. In this book, we'll explore VBScript exclusively, which is the simplest one yet.

A *scripting host* is an environment in which scripts can be executed. The same host is also used by Internet Explorer (in fact, it started out as a component of Internet Explorer), which executes scripts embedded in Web pages, so the scripting engine is used by multiple components of the operating system. As you'll recall from previous chapters, VBScript is a language that allows you to manipulate the elements of a Web page. Its role in the operating system is the same: it allows you to manipulate the elements of the operating system (access its file system, connect to shared resources on the network, and so on).

In this chapter we'll develop even more scripts with VBScript, but this time with the objects exposed by Wscript. Specifically, you'll learn how to:

- Run scripts with `WSCRIPT.EXE` and pass arguments to them
- Process the arguments from within your scripts
- Access the Windows environment and the Registry from within your scripts
- Access the network resources from within your scripts and automate setup tasks

NOTE The current Microsoft Web site for VBScripting is `http://msdn.microsoft.com/scripting/default.htm?/scripting/vbscript/samples/vbssamp.htm`.

Running a Script

To run a script, you have two options:

- Double-click a file or an icon that has a VBS extension.
- Use the `WSCRIPT.EXE` application.

To use the first option, locate the script on your computer and double-click its icon. This is the method we used in Chapter 24. The disadvantage to this method is that you can't supply arguments to a script. As you'll recall from the last chapter, the only way to modify the script's behavior was to store the "arguments" in a text file and have the script open the text file and read its arguments. Scripts that can be called with arguments are very flexible and can be called repeatedly to act on different data.

Alternatively, you can start `WSCRIPT.EXE` by opening the Run dialog box and supplying the name of the script as an argument. You can append any number of arguments to the name of the script. Since calling scripts with arguments is quite important, I'll start the discussion of the Windows Scripting Host with this topic.

The *Wscript* Object

Besides providing an environment for executing the scripts, `WSCRIPT.EXE` provides a few objects that let you access special features of the Windows shell, which you can't access through VBScript. Practically speaking, you can think of the objects of Wscript as an extension of VBScript (as long as you don't use the objects discussed in this chapter in scripts included in HTML pages).

The `Wscript` object provides several properties for obtaining information about the scripting engine itself, the script being executed, and the arguments passed to the script.

The *Arguments* Property

So far, you've seen how to build and execute scripts but not how to pass arguments to them. VBScript on its own can't handle command-line arguments. The `Arguments` property of the `Wscript` object lets your script read the arguments passed to it. To access the actual arguments, you must create an object variable with the statement

```
Set Args = Wscript.Arguments
```

The *`Args`* variable is a collection, which provides the `Item` and `Count` properties. `Arguments` is a property of the `Wscript` object, which happens to be a collection. To iterate through the collection's items, you can use a `For...Next` loop like the following:

```
For i = 0 to Args.Count - 1
    {process each argument}
Next
```

Or you can use a `For Each...Next` loop like this one:

```
For Each arg In Args
    {process each argument}
Next
```

In the case of the `For...Next` loop, you can access each argument with the expression *`Args(i)`*; in the case of the `For Each...Next` loop, you can access them through the variable *arg*. The ARGS1.VBS and ARGS2.VBS scripts demonstrate how to access the script's argument with both methods.

Here's the ARGS1.VBS script:

```
Set Args = Wscript.Arguments
For i=0 to Args.Count - 1
    txt = txt & Args(i) & vbCrLf
Next
MsgBox txt
```

Each argument is a member of the collection Args, and the elements appear in the order in which they were passed to the script. The ARGS2.VBS script is shown next:

```
Set Args = Wscript.Arguments
For Each arg In Args
    txt = txt & arg & vbCrLf
Next
MsgBox txt
```

To pass one or more arguments to a script, choose Start ➢ Run to open the Run dialog box. In the Open box, enter the following string:

```
C:scripts\args1.vbs One Two Three
```

You must modify the path to the script ARGS1.VBS according to your hard disk's structure. After the script's name, supply the arguments using a space as a separator. If you call the script with these arguments, their values will appear in a message box, as shown in Figure 25.1.

FIGURE 25.1 *The Args1.vbs displays its arguments in a message box.*

Do not use a comma to separate the arguments of your script. The comma will be attached to the argument that proceeds it. If you supply the arguments

```
C:\scripts\args1.vbs One, Two, Three
```

the script will display its arguments as shown in Figure 25.2. The comma is treated like any other character; only the space character is treated differently.

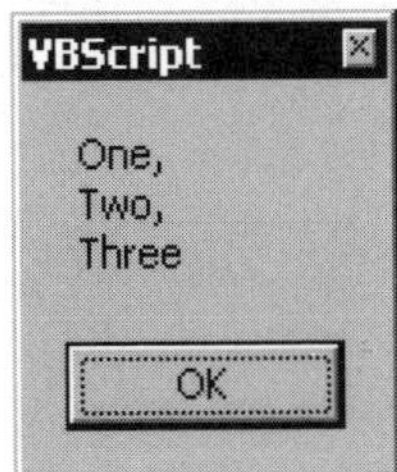

FIGURE 25.2 *Script arguments should not be delimited with the comma character.*

If any of the arguments include spaces, you must enclose the entire argument in double quotes. For example, if the last argument in our example were a string with a space in it, like the one shown here:

```
c:\scripts\args1.vbs one two "three four"
```

without the double quotes, the `Arguments` collection would contain four arguments: `one`, `two`, `three`, and `four` (the double quotes themselves are not included in the argument). Instead, it contains three arguments: `one`, `two`, and `three four`.

In Chapter 24, we developed the `MATH.VBS` script, which contacts Excel to evaluate a user-supplied expression. Here, we are going to modify this script, so that it can accept the expression to be evaluated as an argument. The modified `MATH.VBS` script is shown here:

```
' This script contacts Excel to calculate
' a math expression and displays the result

Set EXL = CreateObject("Excel.Application")
Set Args = Wscript.Arguments
On Error Resume Next
MsgBox Args(0) & " = " & EXL.Evaluate(Args(0))
If Err.Number > 0 Then
    MsgBox Err.Description
End If
```

`Args(0)` is the expression to be evaluated. To execute this script, call it with a command like the following:

```
c:\scripts\math.vbs "LOG(ABS(3+SIN(3.34)/0.033))"
```

Notice that this expression does not require double quotes around it because the expression doesn't contain spaces. On the other hand, the path of the script *does* require double quotes because this string contains a space.

TIP Don't forget to modify the path name of the script so that it points to the folder where you have copied the script.

This script is not very robust. If it's called without an argument, it will display the message "Subscript out of range" (not the most descriptive message for your users). This error message refers to the expression `Args(0)`. The `Args` collection is empty, and there's no such element.

You can trap this error from within your code by examining the value of the `Args.Count` property. If this value is zero, you can prompt the user from within your script to enter a math expression. If the script was called with an argument (possibly more, which are ignored), the script can go on and evaluate it. Here's the revised `MATH.VBS` script:

```
Set EXL = CreateObject("Excel.Application")
Set Args = Wscript.Arguments
If Args.Count = 0 Then
    Expression = InputBox("Please enter a math expression")
Else
    Expression = Args(0)
End If
On Error Resume Next
MsgBox Expression & " = " & EXL.Evaluate(Expression)
If Err.Number > 0 Then
    MsgBox Err.Description
End If
EXL.Disconnect
```

As you can see, the `Wscript` object's `CreateObject` method is identical to VBScript's `CreateObject()` function, and the `Disconnect` method is equivalent to releasing an object variable in VBScript by setting it to `Nothing`.

More *Wscript* Properties

The `Wscript` object provides other properties in addition to the Arguments property. They relate to the Scripting Host (the `WSCRIPT.EXE` executable) and the script being executed.

Application

The `Application` property returns the friendly name of the `Wscript` object, which is the string "Windows Scripting Host" (the same value is returned by the property `Name`).

FullName

The `FullName` property returns the path and filename of the executable file of the Windows Scripting Host (`WSCRIPT.EXE`).

Name

The Name property returns the friendly name of the Wscript object, which is the string "Windows Scripting Host."

Path

The Path property returns the name of the folder where the WSCRIPT.EXE or CSCRIPT.EXE resides (usually C:\Winnt).

ScriptFullName

The ScriptFullName property returns the path and filename of the script being executed by the Windows Scripting Host.

Version

The Version property returns the version of the Windows Scripting Host (WSCRIPT.EXE). The version of the Scripting Host that ships with Windows 2000 Professional is 5.1.

ScriptName

The ScriptName property provides the filename of the script being executed by the Windows Scripting Host.

The script SCRIPT.VBS demonstrates several of the properties of the Wscript object. The script's code is

```
msg ="Script File Name      " & Wscript.ScriptName & vbCrLf
msg = msg & "Script Path Name     " & Wscript.ScriptFullName & vbCrLf
msg = msg & "Executed by            " & Wscript.Application & "Â
  (version " & Wscript.Version & ")" & vbCrLf
MsgBox msg
```

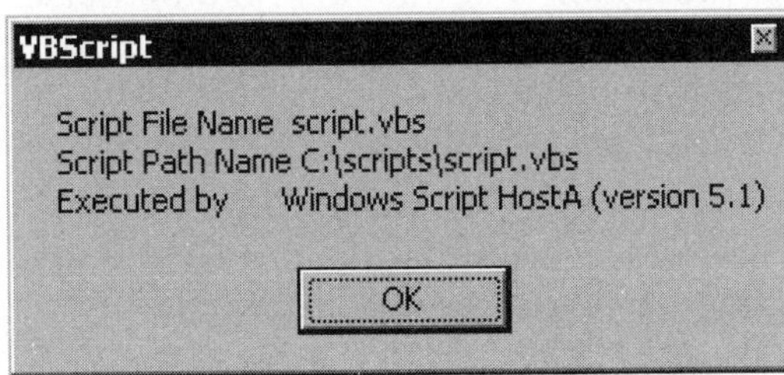

Wscript Methods

The Wscript object provides a number of methods, most of which have an equivalent VBScript function. The most important methods are the CreateObject and GetObject methods, which are identical to the VBScript functions of the same name. Let's start with the simpler methods of the Wscript object.

Echo

The Echo method displays one or more values in a message box. You can display the friendly name of the Windows Scripting Host with the Echo method in a message box that is identical to the box displayed by the MsgBox() function:

```
Wscript.Echo Wscript.Name
```

You can display multiple values, as long as they are delimited by a comma character. Multiple values are displayed next to each other with a space between them. The following statement will display the message box shown in Figure 25.3:

```
Wscript.Echo "string argument", Wscript.Name, 98.9+1
```

Notice that the Name property is replaced by its value and the expression 98.9+1 is calculated and replaced by its result.

FIGURE 25.3 *The Echo method can display multiple values next to each other.*

NOTE Echo is a very simple method and is provided as a primitive debugging tool. The MsgBox() function and the Popup method (described later) provide many more options, and you will probably prefer these.

Quit

The Quit method quits the execution of the script and, optionally, returns an error code. Its syntax is

```
Wscript.Quit errorCode
```

The optional argument *errorCode* is the error code to be returned. If *errorCode* is omitted, the Quit method returns the error code 0. You can use the error code to show whether the script ended its execution normally or to specify the error that prevented the script from completing its execution.

The *WshShell* Object

The WshShell object provides a number of properties for accessing the environment variables and the special folders, as well as a number of methods for manipulating the Registry. Let's start with the object's properties.

Environment

The `Environment` property returns a collection with all environment variables. To iterate through the environment variables, create a `WshShell` object and then request its `Environment` collection:

```
Set WshShell = Wscript.CreateObject("Wscript.Shell")
Set AllVars = WshShell.Environment
For Each evar In AllVars
    txt = txt & evar & vbcrlf
Next
Msgbox txt
```

The *`evar`* variable represents an environment variable in the form

```
Variable = setting
```

The output of the `ENVVARS.VBS` script is shown in Figure 25.4. To access the values of specific environment variables, you can use the `WshEnvironment` object, which is described later in this chapter. Table 25.1 lists the name of the available environment variables.

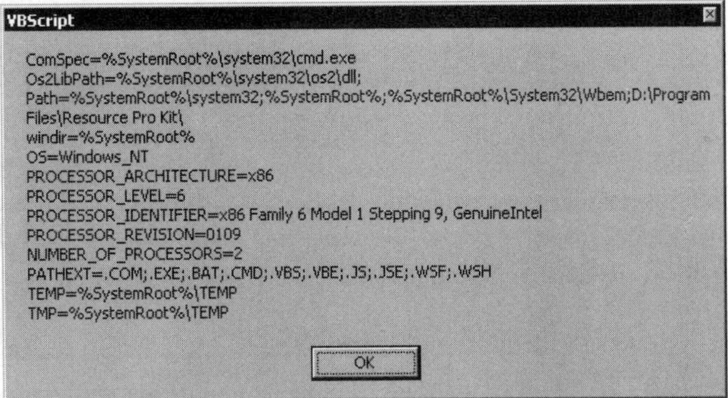

FIGURE 25.4 *The `ENVVARS.VBS` script displays the names and values of the environment variables.*

TABLE 25.1: THE `ENVIRONMENT` VARIABLES' NAMES

Name	Description
`NUMBER_OF_PROCESSORS`	Number of processors running on the machine
`PROCESSOR_ARCHITECTURE`	Processor type of the user's workstation
`PROCESSOR_IDENTIFIER`	Processor ID of the user's workstation
`PROCESSOR_LEVEL`	Processor level of the user's workstation

TABLE 25.1: THE ENVIRONMENT VARIABLES' NAMES (CONTINUED)

Name	Description
PROCESSOR_REVISION	Processor version of the user's workstation
OS	Operating system on the user's workstation
COMSPEC	Executable for command Command Prompt (typically CMD.EXE)
HOMEDRIVE	Primary local drive (typically the C drive)
PATH	PATH environment variable
PATHEXT	Extensions for executable files (typically COM, EXE, BAT, or CMD)
PROMPT	Command prompt (typically PG) when defined. This environment variable is not normally defined.
SYSTEMDRIVE	Local drive on which system folder resides
SYSTEMROOT	System folder (e.g., C:\Winnt); this is the same as WINDIR
WINDIR	System folder (e.g., C:\Winnt); this is the same as SYSTEMROOT
TEMP	Folder for storing temporary files (e.g., C:\temp)
TMP	Folder for storing temporary files (e.g., C:\temp)

SpecialFolders

The SpecialFolders property gives your script access to the special folders on your system. The special folders provide the Desktop folder, the Start Menu folder, and the personal documents folder.

NOTE The SpecialFolders property returns the path name of the Desktop folder (for example, "C:\Documents and Settings\Administrator\Desktop") and not a Folder object. To access the files and subfolders of the Desktop folder, you must first create a Folder object variable with the GetFolder method of the FileSystemObject object, as shown in the example that follows.

Use this property to create new shortcuts on the Desktop or to place new applications in the Start Menu folder. The following script displays the names of the files on the Desktop, along with their type. This script uses the FileSystemObject to iterate through the files of the Desktop folder, as explained in the previous chapter.

```
' This script displays all files on the Desktop,
' along with their types
Set WShell = Wscript.CreateObject("Wscript.Shell")
```

```
DTOPfolder = WShell.SpecialFolders("Desktop")

Set FSys = CreateObject("Scripting.FileSystemObject")
Set ThisFolder = FSys.GetFolder(DTOPfolder)
Set AllFiles = ThisFolder.Files
For Each file in AllFiles
    txt = txt & file.Name & "  (" & file.Type & ")" & vbCrLf
Next
MsgBox txt
```

You can also access all the special folders on the computer using the `SpecialFolders` collection. The following script iterates through the computer's special folders and prints their names:

```
' List all special folders on the host computer
  Set WShell = Wscript.CreateObject("Wscript.Shell")
  For Each Folder In WShell.SpecialFolders
     msg = msg & Folder & vbCrLf
  Next
  MsgBox msg
```

If you execute this script, it will print the path names of the folders as follows:

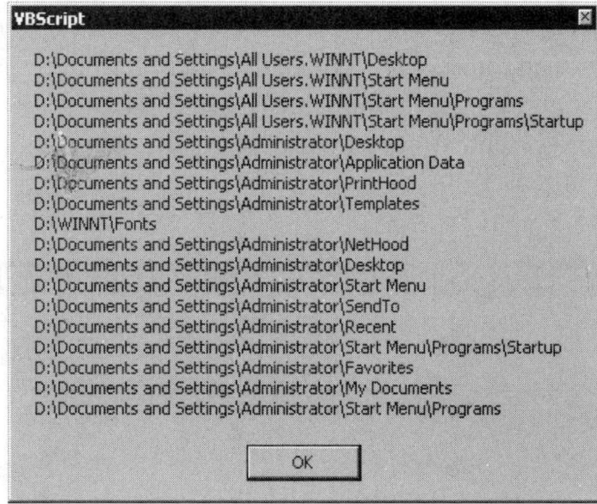

CreateShortcut

The `CreateShortcut` method creates a `Shortcut` or a `URLShortcut` object. (A `URLShortcut` object is a link to a URL, instead of a file on the local disk. When you click `URLShortcut`, the corresponding page is opened with Internet Explorer.)

Creating an actual shortcut on the Desktop is a bit more complicated than using the `CreateShortCut` method, since you must specify the properties of the shortcut (its name, icon, target, and so on) and then save it. The first step in creating a shortcut, however, is to create a Shortcut object and then use it to set its properties. The process of creating shortcuts is described later in this chapter, but here is a short script that creates a shortcut:

```
Set WShell = Wscript.CreateObject("Wscript.Shell")
Set ShellLink = WShell.CreateShortcut("Run Any Script.lnk")
ShellLink.TargetPath = "WSCRIPT.EXE"
ShellLink.Save
```

If you place these lines into a VBS file and execute it, it will create a shortcut on the Desktop. The shortcut's icon will be the icon of the WSCRIPT application, and the shortcut starts the WSCRIPT.EXE application. It is not a very useful shortcut unless you drop a script on it, in which case it will execute the script as though you'd double-clicked the script's icon.

Popup

The Popup method displays a message box, similar to VBScript's MsgBox() function. It has the same syntax, and the only advantage to using this method is that it allows you to specify how many seconds it will remain active on the screen before it will shut itself down. The syntax of the method is

```
Popup(msg, seconds, title, type)
```

where *msg* is the message to be displayed; this is the only mandatory argument. If the second argument, *seconds*, is supplied, the message box will automatically close after the specified number of seconds. The argument *title* is the message box's title, and the last argument, *type*, is the same as in the MsgBox() function. It determines which buttons and which icon will appear in the message box. Its possible values are shown in Table 25.2.

TABLE 25.2: BUTTON COMBINATIONS YOU CAN DISPLAY IN A POP-UP WINDOW

Value	Button
0	OK
1	OK and Cancel
2	Abort, Retry, and Ignore
3	Yes, No, and Cancel
4	Yes and No
5	Retry and Cancel

The icon is specified by one of the values shown in Table 25.3, which must be added to the value specifying the button to appear in the message box.

TABLE 25.3: THE ICONS YOU CAN DISPLAY IN A POP-UP WINDOW

Value	Icon
16	Stop
32	Question Mark
48	Exclamation Mark
64	Information

Depending on which button in the message box was clicked, the Popup method returns a value, which is one of those shown in Table 25.4.

TABLE 25.4: THE VALUES RETURNED BY THE POPUP METHOD

Value	Description
1	OK button
2	Cancel button
3	Abort button
4	Retry button
5	Ignore button
6	Yes button
7	No button

The following script, POPUP.VBS, displays a pop-up dialog box and waits for 10 seconds. If the user doesn't click a button during this interval, the dialog box will close automatically and the program will resume.

```
Set WShell = Wscript.CreateObject("Wscript.Shell")
Reply = WShell.Popup("Display long file names?", 10, "Timed Dialog Box",
4+64)
If Reply = 6 Then
    Wscript.Echo "OK, here are a few long file names..."
Else
    If Reply = 7 Then
        Wscript.Echo "OK, here are a few short file names..."
    Else
```

```
        Wscript.Echo "I selected long file names for you"
    End If
End If
```

As I said, the dialog box expires after 10 seconds. In this case, the Popup method returns the value –1, and the script makes the default selection (as though the Yes button were clicked).

Manipulating the Registry

The WshShell object of Wscript provides methods for manipulating the Registry entries too. They are the RegWrite (to write information into the Registry), RegRead (to read information from the Registry), and RegDelete (to delete information from the Registry).

The Registry is an enormous database that contains all the information needed for the proper operation of Windows itself. It contains initialization information for the applications, uninstall information, settings for networked computers, the file types and the associated applications, and much more. It consists of several files located in *systemroot*\System32\Config.

WARNING It's very easy to mess up the Registry, and the degree to which an error can affect your system depends on the error. You can make mistakes that you'll never notice—but you can also make your operating system unusable. So it's always a good idea to back up the Registry before fiddling with it. Make sure you know what you are doing before you make *any* changes to the Registry!

Registry Manipulation Methods

The Wscript object provides three methods for reading or deleting existing keys or values and adding new ones.

RegRead

The RegRead method returns a specific registry key or value. Its syntax is

```
RegRead(name)
```

where *name* is the Registry key, or value, to be read from the Registry. If the argument ends with the backslash character (\), the RegRead method returns the key. Otherwise, it returns the key's value.

Some of the main branch names are abbreviated as shown in Table 24.5.

TABLE 25.5: THE ABBREVIATIONS OF THE MAIN REGISTRY KEYS

Short Name	Long Name
HKCU	HKEY_CURRENT_USER
HKLM	HKEY_LOCAL_MACHINE
HKCR	HKEY_CLASSES_ROOT
	HKEY_USERS
	HKEY_CURRENT_CONFIG

NOTE The branches HKEY_USERS and HKEY_CURRENT_CONFIG don't have an abbreviation; check the Wscript documentation on the Microsoft Web site for up-to-date information on the abbreviations of these branches.

To read a key or a value from the Registry, you first create a WShell object variable and then call the RegRead method to read a key:

```
Set WShell = WScript.CreateObject("Wscript.Shell")
TileMode = WShell.RegRead(name)
```

The *name* argument is the name of a key or a value. If it's a key, it must end with the backslash character (\). The name of the image that's displayed on the Desktop's background is the value "HKCU\Control Panel\Desktop\TileWallpaper". The expression

```
WShell.RegRead("HKCU\Control Panel\Desktop\Wallpaper")
```

will return the name of the image, which the operating system displays on the Desktop.

The other option you can set is the mode in which the image will be displayed (whether it will be centered, tiled, or stretched to cover the entire Desktop). This setting is stored in the value WShell.RegRead("HKCU\Control Panel\Desktop\TileWallpaper"). This value can be 0 (centered), 1 (tiled), or 2 (stretched).

The following script reads the settings of the two values in the Registry. Notice that the program sets up an array with the possible values of the TileMode setting so that we can translate a numeric value to textual description.

```
Dim Tiles(2)
Tiles(0) = "Centered"
Tiles(1) = "Tiled"
Tiles(2) = "Stretched"
Set WShell = Wscript.CreateObject("Wscript.Shell")
TileMode = WShell.RegRead("HKCU\Control Panel\Desktop\TileWallpaper")
WallPaper = WShell.RegRead("HKCU\Control Panel\Desktop\Wallpaper")
```

```
If WallPaper = "" Then WallPaper = "None"
msg ="The current wallpaper is " & WallPaper
msg = msg & vbCrLf & "and it's " & Tiles(TileMode)
MsgBox msg
```

If you execute the REGREAD.VBS script, you'll see a message box like the one shown in Figure 25.5, with the name of the background image and its tiling mode.

FIGURE 25.5
The output of the REGREAD.VBS script

RegWrite

The RegWrite method sets the Registry key or value specified by its argument. The syntax of the RegWrite method is

```
RegWrite name, value
```

The first argument, *name*, is the name of a key if it ends with a backslash character (\), or it's the name of a value. The same abbreviations discussed in the section RegRead apply to the name argument of the RegWrite method. The second argument, *value*, is the value to be written to the Registry.

Let's revise the REGREAD.VBS script so that it changes the background image on the Desktop. The revised script is called REGWRITE.VBS:

```
Set WShell = Wscript.CreateObject("Wscript.Shell")
WShell.RegWrite "HKCU\Control Panel\Desktop\Wallpaper", "C:\WINNT\Blue Lace
16.bmp"
WShell.RegWrite "HKCU\Control Panel\Desktop\TileWallpaper", "1"
```

Running this script will update the Registry but not the Desktop. This change will take effect the next time you restart the computer. Also, depending on the background you select, you may need to enable the Active Desktop.

Example: Manipulating the Shortcut Menu

Our next example manipulates the Registry and does something more practical: it manipulates the shortcut menu of the text files. When you right-click a text file's icon, you'll see a shortcut menu. This menu contains commands that can be executed directly on the file. For example, you can print the file on the current printer without having to open the document in Notepad first. You can add more entries to the shortcut menu by manipulating the Registry.

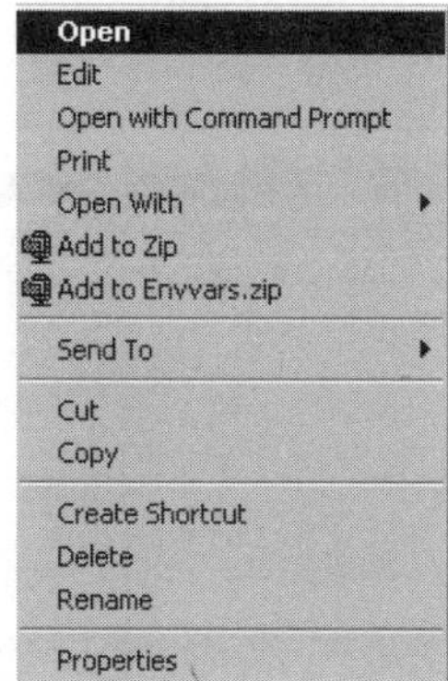

Let's find out where the commands of the shortcut menu for text files are stored in the Registry. Start `REGEDIT`, and locate the key `txtfile` (the complete path to this key is HKEY_CLASSES_RROT\txtfile). Expand the key `txtfile` and you'll see the following keys:

DefaultIcon The location of the icon that's displayed for text files

Shell The information about the commands of the shortcut menu

Expand the `Shell` key and you'll see two more keys:

Open The `Open` command

Print The `Print` command

Expand these two keys to see the commands that are executed when the corresponding command is selected on the shortcut menu. To add a new command to the shortcut menu, all you have to do is add the corresponding key and its command under the `txtfile\Shell` key in the Registry.

Let's say you have a program that encrypts text files. If you encrypt files frequently, you could add the `Encrypt` command to the shortcut menu. To automate this process, create a script that consists of the following two lines:

```
Set WShell = Wscript.CreateObject("Wscript.Shell")
WShell.RegWrite "HKCR\txtfile\Shell\Encrypt\command\",
 "C:\UTILS\ENCRYPT.EXE %1"
```

The entry `"HKCR\txtfile\Shell\Encrypt\command\"` is a key, because it ends with a backslash. Since there is no `Encrypt` key under `Shell`, a new key will be added. The command key will be added under the `Encrypt` key. The string following the key in the `RegWrite` method is the name of the command that implements the Encrypt option. (`ENCRYPT.EXE` is an imaginary program name used as an example; there's no such tool in Windows 2000 Professional.)

If you execute this script and then run REGEDIT (or, if you have the REGEDIT application open, press F5 to refresh it), you'll see that a new key was added under the `txtfile` key, as shown in Figure 25.6.

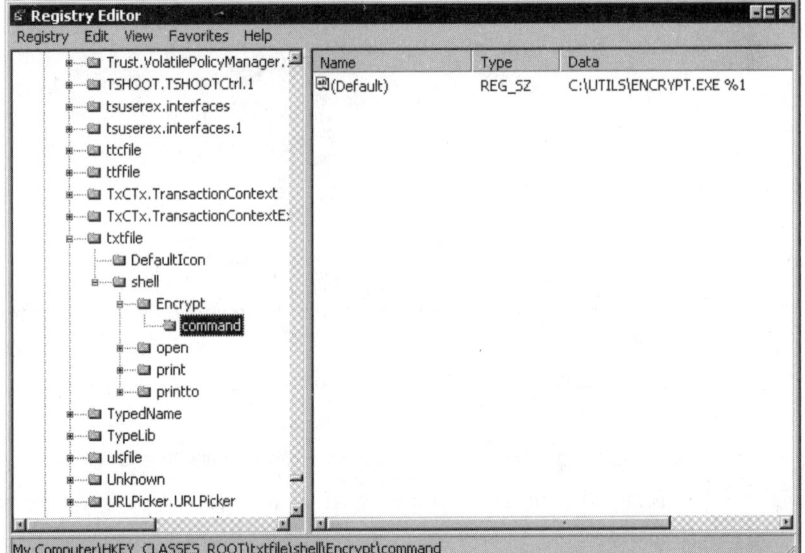

FIGURE 25.6 *Use the Registry manipulation methods to add new keys to the Registry.*

RegDelete

The `RegDelete` method deletes a key or value from the Registry. Its syntax is

```
WShell.RegDelete name
```

where *name* is a key if it ends with a backslash character (\), or it's a value. The same abbreviations discussed in the section RegRead apply to the name argument of the `RegDelete` method.

The script REGDEL.VBS demonstrates this method. This script removes the `txtfile\Shell\Encrypt` key from the Registry and, consequently, from the text files' shortcut menu. The REGDEL.VBS script calls the `RegDelete` method using the same key as the REGADD.VBS script:

```
Set WShell = Wscript.CreateObject("Wscript.Shell")
WShell.RegDelete "HKCR\txtfile\shell\Encrypt\"
```

Execute this script and then examine the Registry and the shortcut menu of a text file.

Run

The Run method starts another application, whose name is specified as the method's argument. The script that invokes the application may continue its execution or wait for the application to terminate. The method's syntax is

```
Run cmd, windowStyle, wait
```

The first argument, *cmd*, contains the command that will start the application. It is the path name of an executable file, like NOTEPAD.EXE. The cmd string may also contain environment variables, which are automatically expanded. The string

```
%windir%\notepad.exe
```

will be expanded to something like

```
c:\Windows\notepad.exe
```

depending on your Windows installation.

The last argument, *windowStyle*, determines the style of the window in which the application will run. It can be 0 (normal window), 1 (minimized window), or 2 (maximized window).

The last argument, wait, determines whether the script will suspend its execution until the application has terminated. If it's False (or omitted), the script continues its execution. If it's True, the script waits for the application to terminate. In the second case, the Run method will return the error code returned by the application.

To start the Notepad application from within your script, you must first create a WShell object and then call the Run method, passing the name of the application to be invoked:

```
Set WShell = Wscript.CreateObject("Wscript.Shell")
WShell.Run ("%windir%\notepad")
```

Starting *Wscript* from within a Script

You can use the Run method to start Wscript and execute another script from within your script. Here's a simple script that calls the MATH1.VBS script presented earlier in this chapter. The CALLSCR.VBS script starts Wscript and passes as argument the path name of the MATH1.VBS script along with the expression to be evaluated.

```
Set WShell = Wscript.CreateObject("Wscript.Shell")
cmd = "WSCRIPT " & chr(34) & "c:scripts\math1.vbs" &
  chr(34) & " sin(3.33)/log(13.5)"
WShell.Run (cmd)
```

Here, cmd is the argument passed to the Run method. The expression chr(34) corresponds to the double-quote character ("). We use this expression because we want to embed a pair of double quotes *within* the double quotes that delimit the entire string. The actual value of the cmd argument is

```
WSCRIPT "c:\\scripts\math1.vbs" "sin(3.33)/log(13.5)"
```

The entire line, including the double quotes, must be stored in another string variable. The outer quotes would ruin the order of the existing ones, so we must use the expression chr(34). This is a simple trick for embedding double quotes within a string already delimited by double quotes.

The *WshNetwork* Object

The WshNetwork object provides the properties and methods you need to manipulate the various objects on the network (shared drives and printers), as well as the properties of the local computer on the network (its name, domain name, and so on).

ComputerName

The ComputerName property returns a string, which is the name of the computer.

UserDomain

The UserDomain property returns a string, which is the user domain name.

UserName

The UserName property returns a string, which is the username. The following script (NAMES.VBS) displays the computer, domain, and usernames in a message box:

```
Set WNet = Wscript.CreateObject("Wscript.Network")
On Error Resume Next
Txt = "Domain Name " & WNet.UserDomain & vbCrLf
Txt = Txt & "Computer Name " & WNet.ComputerName & vbCrLf
Txt = Txt & "User Name " & WNet.UserName & vbCrLf
MsgBox Txt
```

Notice the statement On Error Resume Next. If this script is executed on a non-networked computer, it will display the computer's name only. The other two properties do not exist outside a network, and the corresponding lines will generate a runtime error. The NAMES.VBS script resumes execution with the following line.

Connecting to Network Printers

The following methods let you connect to and disconnect from network printers. They are the EnumPrinterConnections method, which returns the network printer mapping; the AddWindowsPrinterConnection method, which connects to a network printer; and the RemovePrinterConnection method, which removes a currently connected printer. You can also set the default printer with the SetDefaultPrinter method.

EnumPrinterConnections

The `EnumPrinterConnections` method returns the current network printer mappings as a `Collection` object. The items in the collection are the names of the local and remote printers. To access the currently connected printers, you must first create a variable with the statements

```
Set WNet = Wscript.CreateObject("Wscript.Network")
Set AllPrinters = WNet.EnumPrinterConnections
```

You can then access each printer's local port and the remote name of each connected printer. The local port of the first connected printer is `AllPrinters(0)`, and its remote name is `AllPrinters(1)`. The corresponding entries for the second connected printer are `AllPrinters(2)`, `AllPrinters(3)`, and so on. The number of connected printers is given by the property `AllPrinters.Count/2`.

AddWindowsPrinterConnection

The `AddWindowsPrinterConnection` method maps a remote printer to a local resource. This method accepts several arguments, which are shown in its syntax:

```
WNetwork.AddWindowsPrinterConnection localName, remoteName, updateProfile,
user, password
```

where *`localName`* is the name of a local resource that the remote printer will be mapped to (such as LPT1) and *`remoteName`* is the name of the shared printer. The remaining arguments are optional. The `updateProfile` argument is a Boolean value that specifies whether the mapping will be stored in the user profile (so that it can be restored every time the user logs in). The last two arguments, *`user`* and *`password`*, let you connect to a shared network printer from another user's computer. If you want to temporarily connect a user to a printer that requires special privileges, specify the name and password of a user who has the appropriate privileges.

TIP In general, this is not a great idea, since VBS files are simple text files and you shouldn't store passwords in text files (everyone can read them). If you do, you should make this file hidden from most users.

To connect to a shared printer, create a `WshNetwork` variable and call its `AddWindowsPrinterConnection` method, as shown here:

```
Set WNet = Wscript.CreateObject("Wscript.Network")
WNet.AddWindowsPrinterConnection "LPT1", "\\PServer\Laser500"
```

RemovePrinterConnection

The `RemovePrinterConnection` method removes the connection to a network printer, and its syntax is

```
WNet.RemovePrinterConnection name, force, updateProfile
```

The *name* argument is either a local name or a remote name, depending on how the printer is connected. If the printer is mapped to a local resource, *name* must be set to the local name. If the shared network printer isn't mapped to a local name, *name* must be set to the remote name. The `updateProfile` argument is the same as in the `AddPrinterConnection` method.

SetDefaultPrinter

This method sets a remote printer as the default printer. The syntax of the method is

```
WNet.SetDefaultPrinter printerName
```

where *printerName* is the name of the remote printer that will become the default printer. When a shared printer is being used and you attempt to disconnect it, you'll see a warning displayed. To skip this warning and disconnect the drive anyway, set the `Force` argument to `True`. If this argument is `False` or omitted, you'll get a warning when the script attempts to disconnect the printer while it's in use by an application. This argument must be the remote printer's name (such as `\\PServer\Laser500`).

Connecting to Network Drives

The `Wscript.Network` object provides a similar set of properties and methods for connecting to and disconnecting from network drives. The method `EnumNetworkDrives` returns all the connected drives, and the `MapNetworkDrive` and `RemoveNetworkDrive` methods let you connect to and disconnect from network drives.

EnumNetworkDrives

The `EnumNetworkDrives` method returns the current network drive mappings as a collection. The items in the collection are the names of the local and remote drives. To access the currently connected drives, you must first create a variable with the statements

```
Set WNet = Wscript.CreateObject("Wscript.Network")
Set AllDrives = WNet.EnumNetworkDrives
```

Just like the `Printers` collection, the local names and the remote drive names are stored in sequential items. The local name of the first connected drive is `AllDrives(0)`, and its remote name is `AllDrives(1)`. The corresponding entries for the second connected drive are `AllDrives(2)`, `AllDrives(3)`, and so on. The number of connected drives is given by the property `AllDrives.Count/2`.

MapNetworkDrive

The `MapNetworkDrive` method maps a shared network drive to a local resource. The syntax of the method is

```
WNet.MapNetworkDrive localName, remoteName, updateProfile, user, password
```

The first argument, *localName*, is the local resource name the drive will be mapped to (a drive letter such as S). The *remoteName* argument is the name of the shared network drive. If you want to connect to the drive Backup on the PServer computer, use the statements

```
Set WNet = Wscript.CreateObject("Wscript.Network")
WNet.MapNetworkDrive "S:", "\\PServer\Backup"
```

NOTE The name of the network drive must be prefixed by the name of the computer it belongs to.

The following arguments are all optional. The `updateProfile` argument is a Boolean value; if it's `True`, the mapping is stored in the user profile and is restored every time the user logs on to the specific workstation. The last two arguments, *`user`* and *`password`*, let you connect to a shared network drive from another user's computer. If you want to connect a user temporarily to a drive that requires special privileges, specify the name and password of a user who has the appropriate privileges. (Remember, this file should be hidden from most users.)

RemoveNetworkDrive

To disconnect from a network drive, use the `RemoveNetworkDrive` method. This method removes the connection specified by its argument. The syntax of the method is

```
WNet.RemoveNetworkDrive driveName, force, updateProfile
```

The *`driveName`* argument, which is the only required argument, can be either a local or a remote name, depending on how the drive is mapped. If the mapped drive has a local name, this is the name you must specify. If the drive doesn't have a local name (that is, drive letter), *`driveName`* must be set to the drive's remote name.

TIP If you connected to the drive with the `MapNetworkDrive` method, the shared drive has a local name, which must be specified in the `RemoveNetworkDrive` method. If you used the `NET USE` command (from within a command file) to connect to the drive, you must use the drive's remote name.

When a shared drive is being used and you attempt to disconnect it, you'll see a warning displayed. To skip this warning and disconnect the drive anyway, set the `Force` argument to `True`. If this argument is `False` or omitted, you'll get a warning when the script attempts to disconnect the drive while it's in use by an application.

The last argument, `updateProfile`, is described in the `MapNetworkDrive` entry.

To disconnect the drive I presented in the last example, use the statements

```
Set WNet = Wscript.CreateObject("Wscript.Network")
WNet.RemoveNetworkDrive "S:"
```

The *WshShortcut* Object

The WshShortcut object represents a shortcut and lets you manipulate the properties of an existing shortcut or create a new shortcut. To create a WshShortcut, use the statements

```
Set WShell = Wscript.CreateObject("Wscript.Shell")
strDesktop = WShell.SpecialFolders("Desktop")
Set aShortcut = WShell.CreateShortcut(strDesktop & "\Encrypt.lnk")
```

If the Encrypt.lnk file exists, the *aShortcut* variable represents the shortcut on the Desktop. If no such shortcut exists, a new one is created.

NOTE The new shortcut will not appear on the Desktop until you save it with the Save method.

The properties of the WshShortcut object and its Save method are explained in the following sections.

Arguments

The Arguments property specifies the arguments to be passed to the shortcut represented by the variable.

Description

The Description property specifies the description of a shortcut.

FullName

The FullName property specifies the full path name of the shortcut.

Hotkey

The HotKey property provides the *hotkey* of a shortcut, which is a keyboard shortcut to start or switch to a program. The hotkey consists of a modifier and a key and has the form Alt+E, or Ctrl+Shift+A. The available modifiers are

- ALT+
- CTRL+
- SHIFT+
- EXT+

The keys you can use in hotkey combinations are the characters A–Z and the digits 0–9. To assign a hotkey combination to the shortcut represented by the variable myShortCut, use the statement

```
myShortCut.Hotkey = "ALT+SHIFT+F"
```

IconLocation

The IconLocation property specifies the location of the icon to be used for a shortcut. Usually, multiple icons are stored in the same file and the format of the IconLocation property is Path.index. If you look up the key for Icon in the Registry, you will find values such as the following:

```
C:\Program Files\NetMeeting\conf.exe,1
```

Here, the icon to be used with NetMeeting is the first one in the CONF.EXE file.

TargetPath

The TargetPath property specifies the target path of a shortcut object (the object it refers to).

WindowStyle

This property specifies the window style of a shortcut object. This is the style of the window when the referenced application starts, and it can have one of the values shown in Table 25.6.

TABLE 25.6: POSSIBLE VALUES FOR THE WINDOWSTYLE PROPERTY

Value	Description
0	Normal
1	Minimized
2	Maximized

WorkingDirectory

The WorkingDirectory property specifies the working directory of a shortcut object.

Save

The Save method saves the shortcut object to the location specified by the TargetPath property. To save a shortcut object, call the method:

```
WShortcut.Save
```

Example: Creating a New Shortcut

The following script creates a new shortcut on the Desktop:

```
Set WShell = Wscript.CreateObject("Wscript.Shell")
strDesktop = WShell.SpecialFolders("Desktop")
Set aShortcut = WShell.CreateShortcut(strDesktop & "\Encrypt.lnk")
aShortcut.TargetPath = "C:\UTILS\ENCRYPT.EXE"
```

```
aShortCut.Hotkey = "ALT+CTRL+E"
aShortCut.Save
```

The variable *strDesktop* is the path to the Desktop (which is a special folder), and the variable *aShortcut* represents the new shortcut. The new shortcut is created when the Save method is called.

Summary

This concludes our discussion of the Windows Scripting Host. With VBScript and the objects exposed by Wscript, you can write useful scripts to automate file operations, set up a workstation's environment, connect to shared resources on a network, and even manipulate the Registry.

CHAPTER 26

Supporting New Hardware and Installing Drivers

FEATURING:

The process of installing new hardware in Windows 2000 Professional has changed radically from the procedure used in NT 4. For one thing, you now have Plug and Play to assist you in locating and configuring new hardware. The other important thing is that you can locate all your hardware configuration information in Device Manager. To display your current hardware settings, follow these steps:

1. On the Desktop, right-click My Computer and choose Properties from the shortcut menu to open the System Properties dialog box.
2. Click the Hardware tab, and then click the Device Manager button to open the Device Manager window:

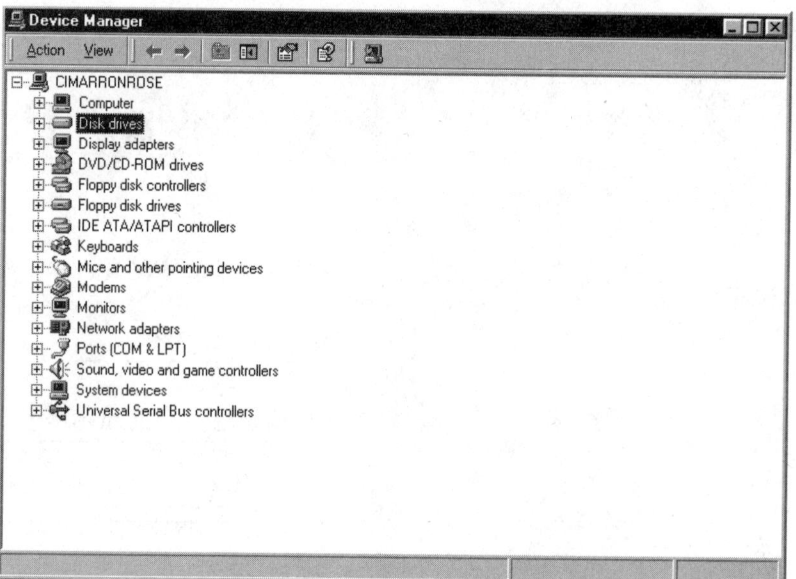

3. Expand an item to display the specific devices installed on your system.
4. Right-click a device, and choose Properties from the shortcut menu to display the Properties dialog box for that device, which contains all the current settings.

TIP Only users with Administrator permissions are allowed to add or change hardware on a workstation.

Display Adapters

Generally, the only time you'll need to install a new display adapter is when you muck up your video driver—that is, if you can still see what you're doing. If you still have the VGA mode option available to you when loading Windows 2000 Professional, you'll be able to boot the machine and detect the new display adapter.

Installing the driver is easy. Follow these steps:

1. Shut down your computer and turn off the power. Install the new display adapter according to the manufacturer's instructions.
2. Reboot the computer, and when you see the menu options to start Windows 2000 Professional, press the F8 key. From the F8 menu, select Safe Mode VGA to start the computer with a standard VGA driver.
3. Once Windows 2000 Professional has started, log on to the system, and then choose Start ➢ Settings ➢ Control Panel.
4. Click Add/Remove Hardware to start the Add/Remove Hardware Wizard:

5. At the Welcome screen, click Next to open the Choose A Hardware Task screen.
6. Click the Add/Troubleshoot A Device option, and then click Next to open the New Hardware Detection screen.
7. After Windows 2000 Professional searches for a device, you'll see the Choose A Hardware Device screen. In the Devices list, select Add A New Device, and then

click Next to open the Find New Hardware screen:

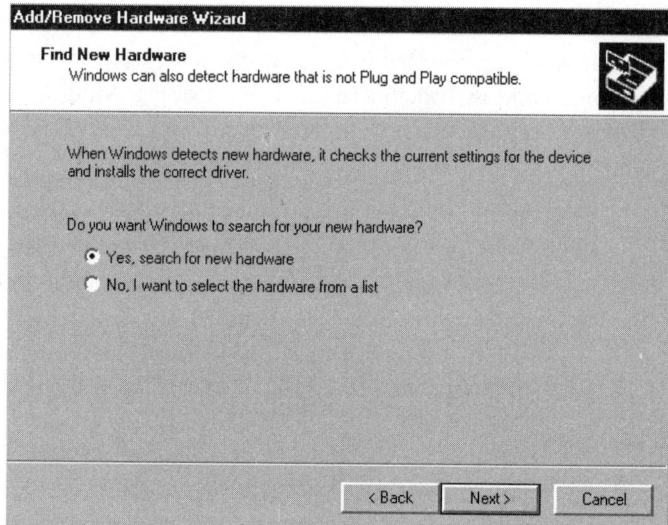

8. Select the Yes, Search For New Hardware option, and then click Next. If things go well at this point, Windows 2000 Professional will correctly identify your new display adapter and remove the settings for your old adapter.
9. Click Finish to allow Windows 2000 Professional to complete the installation.

Here are some additional points concerning display adapters:

- When troubleshooting your video platform, remember that VGA is a standard. If your video card is behaving poorly, first move your resolution back to 640 by 480. If this setting does not resolve your problem, reinstall your video driver in VGA mode.
- When choosing to use a Super VGA card, try to find one that supports the S3 standard—it seems to be a de facto standard in the industry.
- Visit the manufacturer's Web site to determine if they have Windows 2000 Professional drivers for your card. This might actually become a part of your hardware selection process.

SCSI Cards and Devices

In this section I'll focus on how to install three SCSI (Small Computer System Interface) devices: SCSI hard drives, CD-ROMs, and tape drives. Keep in mind that purchasing a device that simply has the SCSI designation is no guarantee that it will work with other SCSI devices. Always look for the SCSI-2 or SCSI-3 designation, which ensures that your SCSI host adapter and SCSI devices will interact. Also check to make sure that the SCSI devices you are installing are on the Hardware Compatibility List (HCL) for Windows 2000 Professional. You can find the HCL either in the package with Windows 2000 Professional or on Microsoft's Web site at `www.microsoft.com/isapi/hwtest/hcl.idc`.

NOTE SCSI, pronounced "scuzzy," is a high-speed parallel interface that is used to connect a computer to peripheral devices using only one port.

Hard Drives and CD-ROMs

Although hard drives and CD-ROMs are usually part of the initial installation of Windows 2000 Professional, you might add a hard drive or a CD-ROM drive after Windows 2000 Professional has been installed. If so, the basic approach is the same as adding a display adapter. In fact, this approach is the same no matter what type of new hardware you are installing.

Tape Drives

Even though tape drives can also be SCSI drives, you configure them differently from SCSI hard drives and CD-ROMs. However, thanks to SCSI, this particular driver is probably the easiest driver to install. To add a tape drive to your system, follow these steps:

1. Make sure that the SCSI address for the tape drive is set to a number that is not being used by another SCSI device. SCSI addresses range from 0 to 7 for SCSI-2 and from 0 to 15 for SCSI-3. For example, say you are adding an APS DAT drive to your workstation. On the back of the drive is a switch clearly labeled "SCSI address" that lets you change the address easily. When the drive was purchased, the switch was set to 6. That address is already being used by a SCSI hard drive, however. So, you simply flip the switch to 5. If you don't change the setting, the two SCSI drives will conflict at startup, and the computer won't operate at all. The only remedy is to remove the tape drive or change the SCSI address so that the computer can start properly.
2. After you set the address, connect the drive into the SCSI port on your computer.
3. Start the computer. If Windows 2000 Professional doesn't automatically find your tape drive during the startup, open Control Panel, and run the Add/Remove Hardware Wizard to detect the drive.
4. After the tape drive is detected, you need to install the driver. Click OK, and Windows 2000 Professional loads the driver for you. Device Manager lists the tape drive that has been detected and confirms that its driver has been loaded.

Mouse Drivers

Changing mouse drivers is easy in Windows 2000 Professional. Let's say that instead of the usual Microsoft serial mouse driver, you want to install a Logitech mouse. Follow these steps:

1. Shut down your computer, and connect the new mouse.

NOTE Windows 2000 Professional should automatically recognize your new mouse without rebooting. If Windows 2000 Professional doesn't recognize your new mouse immediately, shut down and restart the computer.

2. If the mouse wasn't detected correctly during startup, open Control Panel, and run the Add/Remove Hardware Wizard to detect it.
3. You may be prompted to provide drivers for the mouse if Windows 2000 Professional does not support it. Click the Have Disk button if you need to select the driver from a manufacturer's disk.
4. Specify the path where the driver files are located, and click OK. Your new mouse driver is now successfully installed.

Click the Close button and restart your computer in order for the settings to take effect.

Keyboard Drivers

Changing keyboard drivers is similar to changing mouse drivers, and you can do it using the Add/Remove Hardware Wizard. You can also use Device Manager to change the drivers. To change a keyboard driver using Device Manager, follow these steps:

1. Shut down your computer, and connect the new keyboard. Restart your system.
2. On the Desktop, right-click My Computer, and choose Properties from the shortcut menu to open the System Properties dialog box.
3. Click the Hardware tab, and then click the Device Manager button to open the Device Manager window.
4. Expand the Keyboards item, and then double-click the name of your keyboard to open its Properties dialog box.
5. Click the Driver tab, and then click the Update Driver button to start the Upgrade Device Driver Wizard:

6. Click Next to open the Install Hardware Device Drivers screen.
7. Click the option to display a list of drivers, and then click Next to open the Select A Device Driver screen.
8. Select the manufacturer and model of the new keyboard. Click the radio button to Show All Hardware Of This Device Class to display a list of all the keyboard drivers. Or, if you have drivers on disk, you can click the Have Disk button.
9. Click Next and then click Next again, and the Wizard will install the driver.
10. When the process is complete, click Finish, and then restart the computer in order for the settings to take effect.

Sound Cards

If you have a multimedia system or are thinking about upgrading to one, you may want to install a new sound card to enhance your presentations or games. Adding a sound card in Windows NT 4 involved several tricky steps. But in Windows 2000 Professional it's as easy as running the Add/Remove Hardware Wizard to detect the card and its settings.

Depending on the type of sound card you're installing, you may have to make some settings on the card itself before inserting it in the slot. If the card is fully Plug and Play, Windows 2000 Professional will be able to detect and configure the card if there are enough available resources in your computer.

TIP Make sure that the addresses you specify aren't already being used by another device, or you'll have problems with both devices. You might want to keep a written record of the settings for all your devices. That way, if something does happen, the first thing you can do is look at the list to make sure that the new device doesn't conflict with any existing ones.

Table 26.1 lists some of the most common settings for a sound card.

TABLE 26.1: SOUND CARD DEVICE SETTINGS

Parameter	Definition
Interrupt	Range is from 0 to 15. Just as with I/O addresses, make sure that no other device uses the same interrupt number.
DMA channel (8-bit)	Sets the DMA channel your card will use for 8-bit digitized sound.
DMA channel (16-bit)	Sets the DMA channel your card will use for 16-bit digitized sound.
MPU401 I/O address	Different from the normal I/O address. Tells the system the port address at which the MPU401 feature of the sound card is located.

To display a list of the current settings for any device, in Device Manager, double-click the name of the device to open the Properties dialog box for the device, and click the Resources tab. You'll see something similar to the following:

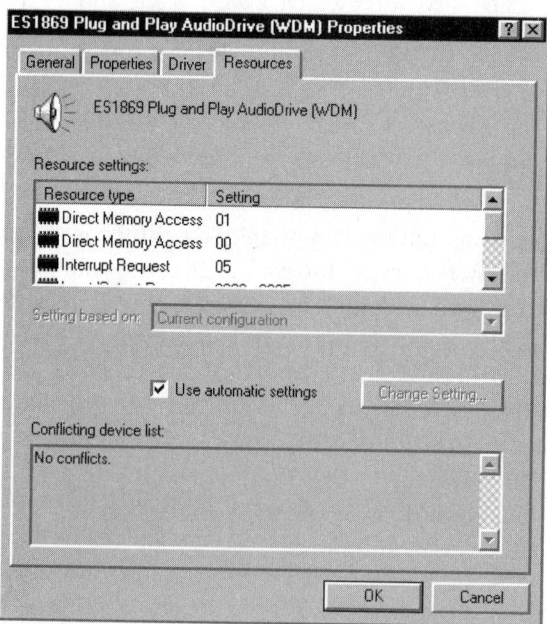

Doing this before installing a new piece of hardware can save you a lot of grief if there aren't any free resources.

Many newer sound cards are coming with software packages designed to help install them in Windows NT. They will probably be updated with install routines for Windows 2000 Professional also. Consult the documentation for the card, or visit the manufacturer's Web site for details. If your sound card supports this, the documentation will direct you to run a setup program on a disk provided with the sound card.

NOTE For information on installing modems, see Chapter 10. For information on installing network interface cards, see Chapter 17.

EIDE and IDE Adapters

Generally, if you have an IDE (Integrated Drive Electronics) or EIDE (Enhanced IDE) hard drive, you'll have Plug-and-Play support. After you configure your drives and install them on your system, Windows 2000 Professional will automatically detect Plug-and-Play compatible devices.

The IDE driver, `atapi.sys`, controls all IDE and EIDE devices on a PCI (Peripheral Component Interconnect) machine. AT Attachment Protocol Interface (ATAPI) is the specification that defines the IDE drive interface. AT refers to the IBM/PC personal computer and its bus architecture.

If you have a hard drive that Windows 2000 Professional can't detect, Windows 2000 Professional may think that it's a SCSI drive and use a SCSI driver for it. If you don't have a SCSI adapter driver installed, install the SCSI adapter following the instructions given earlier in this chapter. Reboot, and Windows 2000 Professional should be able to detect your hard drive.

The ATAPI driver in Windows 2000 Professional will also work with UltraDMA hard drives, though you will probably want to install the driver specific to your disk controller for maximum performance. Be sure that the driver was designed for Windows 2000 Professional, however, or you may be troubleshooting a blue screen later.

PCMCIA Adapters

Just like the tape driver, this driver is automatically detected when Windows 2000 Professional is loaded. If you're not sure if a PCMCIA (Personal Computer Memory Card International Association) adapter card exists on your system, check Device Manager to see if there is an entry beneath PCMCIA Adapters.

In general, the PC Card entry in Device Manager is for monitoring the status of PCMCIA devices and changing the driver for the PCMCIA *socket*. If you want to change the PCMCIA socket settings, double-click the entry in Device Manager, and click the Driver or Resource tab.

NOTE The terms PCMCIA and PC Card refer to the same type of devices and are used interchangeably today.

Troubleshooting Drivers

If your system doesn't work after the initial install, it is best to delete everything, format the drive, and reinstall from scratch. Microsoft found that some DLL files or system files could become corrupt, so they recommend reinstalling from scratch to correct the bugs.

If some drivers—such as those for video adapters, NICs, and modems—don't work after the initial install, they may be incompatible. In addition, certain multimedia systems may not be compatible. Check with the manufacturer, and be sure that you have drivers that support Windows 2000 Professional. You can often find these drivers at the manufacturer's Web site.

Also, sometimes you'll lose a communications port or a printer port after the initial install. If you know what you are doing, you can get these ports back by disabling Plug and Play in the BIOS.

Summary

This is a short and, in some ways, unnecessary chapter because Windows 2000 Professional is Plug and Play. The problem arises if some of your devices are not Plug and Play. In that case, you can follow the steps in this chapter to try to make them work.

CHAPTER 27

Fixing Windows 2000 Professional When It Breaks

FEATURING:

Despite Windows 2000 Professional's resilient nature, it still sometimes crashes. Some crashes are caused by random events: It really *is* possible for a cosmic ray to hit a critical part of a chip and freeze up a PC (and in that case there's not much to do other than to turn the machine off and then back on). But if you find Windows 2000 Professional crashing *regularly*, you have to do something about it, 'cause it's not supposed to. Of course, to do something effective about system crashes, you'll need a method, and that's what this chapter offers.

I'll avoid trotting out all the old an-ounce-of-prevention bromides (though there *is* a lot of truth to those old saws). I start off with a discussion of preventing trouble in the first place and then look at techniques you can use to gather the information needed to ascertain, attack, and fix problems that may sooner or later arise.

Avoiding Windows 2000 Professional Crashes

You can keep Windows 2000 Professional trouble at bay in a few basic ways:

- Buy reliable hardware, preferably hardware that is on the Windows 2000 Hardware Compatibility List.
- Protect the machine from environmental hazards, most notably substandard electric power.
- Install Windows 2000 Professional properly, or, in some cases, *re*install Windows 2000 Professional properly.
- Obtain the latest tested drivers for your hardware.
- Always shut down Windows 2000 Professional properly.
- Back up your hard disk.
- Be sure you have the proper security level for whatever function you're performing.

Let's look quickly at each of these.

Buy Reliable Hardware

One of the things that causes instability for *any* PC operating system is the hardware that the operating system must sit atop. PCs made by IBM were once the standard and, right or wrong, "PC-compatible" meant that they "did the same thing that the IBM machines did, including the bugs." Nowadays, there *is* no standard, and so no two brands of computers work exactly the same way.

A major point of difference between makes and models of computers is the expansion bus, the slots on a PC motherboard into which you plug expansion cards such as video boards, sound cards, network boards, and sound boards. Because these slots must accommodate the connectors on the bottom of the expansion cards, the person who designs the motherboard and the person who designs the expansion card must agree on how that interface should work; the interface must be *standard*.

That's where the problem arises. The most common PC interface standard is called the Industry Standard Architecture, or ISA, board. The *problem* with the ISA standard is that it's not really a standard; there is no carved-in-stone specification for it, just an informal industry consensus. The result is that if you take a "standard" ISA board and plug it into a "standard" ISA slot, it may not work perfectly 100 percent of the time. It'll probably work most of the time, but some small percentage of the time, data may get lost passing between the expansion card and the motherboard. If that data is crucial, the PC may lock up.

What can Windows 2000 Professional do about that? In other words, how can an operating system that wants to be stable work around an inherently unstable hardware platform? To a certain extent, there's nothing that the operating system can do, and some crashes are unavoidable. But some ISA boards are designed better than others, and only experimentation will separate the good from the bad. Further, the operating system can incorporate drivers for the hardware that are a bit more "forgiving." By forgiving, I mean that the driver is built to *anticipate* a certain number of hardware errors and to simply step around them.

"Aha!" you cry. "If they can make drivers 'forgiving,' why don't they *always* do that?" Well, for one thing, it's harder to write such drivers. For another, most driver authors resent writing drivers to support hardware that isn't really standard. Talk to them for a bit, and they start muttering about hitting moving targets and the like. Finally, and most important, adding forgiveness to a driver *slows it down*, and as all PC speed freaks know, slow is bad.

Again, what can you do about it? For one thing, stay as far away from ISA boards as you can. Yes, they're the most common and the cheapest boards, but there's usually a reason that cheap things are cheap.

TIP Buy systems that have PCI slots (at least three slots), and use only PCI boards. Most of these systems also have ISA, but don't use them. Multiprocessor systems usually have a combination of PCI and EISA slots; both of those are fine to use because both are truly standard interfaces.

The Peripheral Component Interconnect (PCI), Extended Industry Standard Architecture (EISA), and MicroChannel Architecture (MCA) buses were all designed by a central authority that published specifications, which, if followed, yield an expansion board that works predictably. That's why I strongly recommend staying with those three expansion slot types. In reality, however, you won't find many of today's systems with the MCA bus; it's about dead. Again, you'll find EISA slots on many multiprocessor systems, but not many EISA expansion boards are on the market. PCI is becoming more and more widespread and almost unavoidable in new hardware; in my opinion, it's the way to go.

Guard against Environmental Hazards

A decent number of PCs die each year because they get bad power. It's not something you can easily detect; it just happens. But you can prevent it.

PC power problems fall into three categories:

- Incorrect voltage—usually too low. Low voltage is called a voltage sag or brownout.
- Loss of power altogether.
- Extremely brief (under one 1/100 of a second) increases in voltage and power, called surges or spikes.

Low voltage causes your PC's power supply to try to compensate by drawing more current, which heats up the PC components and shortens their lives. You change voltage on an electrical circuit with a device called a transformer. A transformer that's smart enough to know whether to move the voltage up or down is called a *voltage regulator,* and for most PC applications, the name of the device that contains a voltage regulator is a *power conditioner*. A power conditioner costs $50 and up.

Loss of power altogether requires a battery of some kind. The two kinds of battery backup are *standby power supply* (*SPS*) and *uninterruptible power supply* (*UPS*). An SPS has a battery that "wakes up," so to speak, when power to the PC is interrupted. Because an SPS doesn't always wake up fast enough, you need an SPS with a switching time (wake-up time) of 4 milliseconds or less. A UPS, in contrast, is always supplying power from the battery (while refilling it, of course) and so has no switching time. Clever marketers call their SPSs "UPSs." If in doubt, ask about the switching time.

Surges and spikes can be brushed aside by a power conditioner. Do *not* buy a surge protector, a cheap device that does little to protect you from power problems. A surge protector is based on a device called a Metal Oxide Varistor (MOV), which is a "kamikaze" device: After you get a little surge, the MOV stops the surge but dies in the process. The *next* surge goes through without trouble.

I recommend devices created by American Power Conversion called the Smart-UPS line. Despite their name, these devices are not UPSs but rather a combination of an SPS and a power conditioner. They start at about $200 discounted. (To read more about PC power problems and solutions, pick up the latest edition of my book *The Complete PC Upgrade and Maintenance Guide* [Sybex Inc., 2000].)

Install Windows 2000 Professional Properly

A look back at Chapter 2 will remind you that you've got a lot of choices to make when you install Windows 2000 Professional. If you end up with a bad installation, reinstall Windows 2000 Professional or your Windows 2000 Professional applications. If you reinstall a piece of software, however, don't install it on top of an existing installation; that often doesn't wipe the old installation clean. Before reinstalling any software, remove it completely and check the Registry for any leftover pieces.

In Chapter 2, I tell you how to upgrade from an earlier version of Windows or NT, but the truth is, the most stable and reliable installations are built from the ground up. This usually means installing on a freshly formatted hard drive and then installing applications. If you simply must perform an upgrade, be sure to disable all third-party services. Heck, disable all the services you can easily live without for a while. The less that Setup has to worry about, the fewer things that can go wrong.

Obtain the Latest Tested Drivers for Your Hardware

Although Windows 2000 Professional is a solidly built system, it does have one fairly large Achilles' heel (or maybe a whole Achilles' foot): drivers. Third-party drivers don't often get tested thoroughly. All drivers are suspect; so try the simplest drivers available.

For example, when updating a driver, keep the old one around just in case the update isn't so "up." If you're experiencing video problems, you can always rely on the VGA driver.

Always Shut Down Windows 2000 Professional Properly

Most people seem to know this by now, but it's worth repeating that you should *shut down Windows 2000 Professional properly*. Don't just turn off the computer; choose Start and then Shut Down.

If you don't do that, you stand not only to lose data from your applications, but you may damage the operating system. If you are using only NTFS-formatted disks, the damage will be less than it would be with a FAT disk (NTFS incorporates fault-tolerant features), but you could lose data nevertheless.

Back Up Your Disk Regularly

I shouldn't have to say this, but…

The hard disks in most people's PCs aren't backed up. And there are as many excuses for this as there are PCs. But there's no reason for it, at least not any more. Iomega's Zip drives are a terrific way to quickly and easily save 100MB of data onto a thing that *looks* like a floppy but that stores much more data. Tape drives get cheaper all the time. And I just can't say enough about the value of CD-ROM burners for backups.

And Windows 2000 Professional even comes with a backup program, Backup, that I'll discuss later in this chapter.

Be Sure You're Authorized to Do Something before Doing It

As you've read elsewhere in this book, living with Windows 2000 Professional means thinking differently because you're now living in a more secure world. That means that you may run into a kind of trouble fairly new to PC users—the inability to do a particular function on your system.

For example, imagine that when someone logs on to your network, they run a logon batch script that synchronizes their PC's clock with the time on the server; the command is `net time\\`*`servername`*` /set/yes`. When you log on to a Windows 2000 Professional workstation as a simple domain user, you get an error indicating that you don't have the right to set the PC's clock.

Now, if you are a network techie, you would likely understand this error message and where it comes from—again, the account you used to log on is too low on the network's totem pole, so to speak. But for a regular, less-technical user, it could be somewhat disconcerting.

In general, remember that a Windows 2000 Professional computer runs different kinds of user accounts—administrators, users, power users, and so on. You'll make your life easiest if you remember to log on as an administrator for that particular workstation before trying to change permissions on files or do anything with the Administrative Tools.

An Ounce of Prevention…

Before I get into what you can do to fix Windows 2000 Professional before it breaks, I want to point you toward some tools you can use from time to time that might well prevent some common, everyday problems: Disk Defragmenter, Disk Cleanup, and Check Disk.

Defragmenting Files

As files on your computer grow, they will not fit back into their original locations on your hard disk, so Windows 2000 Professional divides the files into pieces and spreads the files over several different disk locations. This is how Windows is designed to work and how the system juggles constantly changing file sizes. An unfortunate side-effect as a file is divided into more and more pieces is that it takes longer and longer for your system to find and retrieve the whole file when you open it. A disk defragmenter keeps your hard disk performance at its peak by finding fragmented files on your system and rewriting them into contiguous continuous areas of your hard disk.

Disk Defragmenter works behind the scenes; although the files on your hard disk have actually been moved, you will still find them in the same folders. Follow these steps to use the Disk Defragmenter:

1. Choose Start ➢ Programs ➢ Accessories ➢ System Tools ➢ Disk Defragmenter. Alternatively, right-click the drive, choose Properties, click the Tools tab to bring it to the front, and click Defragment Now.
2. Choose the disk you want to defragment, and click the Analyze button. Disk Defragmenter looks at the drive and prepares a display and reports on the condition of the files on that drive; the Analysis Display box shows fragmented files, contiguous files, system files, and hard disk free space as stripes of different colors, as seen in Figure 27.1. Once the analysis is complete, click the View Report button to open the Analysis Report dialog box. At the top of the Analysis Report dialog box, you will see volume information, including the amount of fragmentation, free space, and file and directory fragmentation. In the lower part of this dialog box, you will see detailed information on specific files. Click the heading at the top of the columns to sort the data in that column. On the basis of the data collected, Disk Defragmenter also recommends whether or not you should continue with the defragmentation.
3. Click Defragment to continue, or click Close to return to the main window.

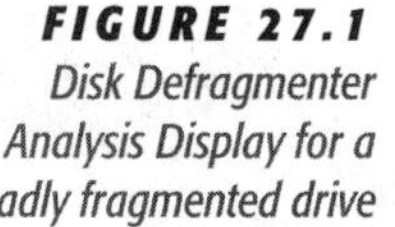

FIGURE 27.1
Disk Defragmenter Analysis Display for a badly fragmented drive

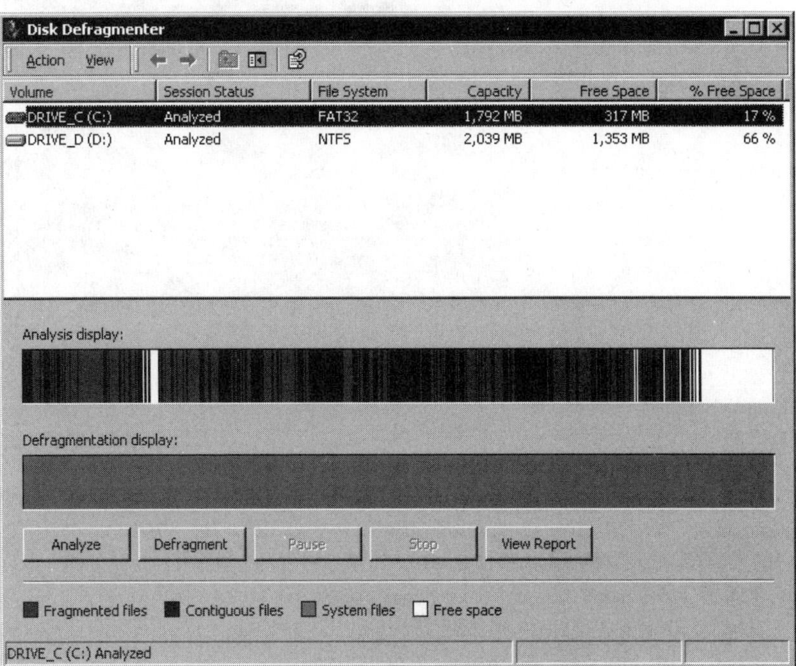

4. If you click the Defragment button, the Disk Defragmenter starts working. Buttons are available so that you can stop or pause Disk Defragmenter.

You can certainly perform other work on the computer while Disk Defragmenter is running, but the response time will be much slower, and Disk Defragmenter will start over each time you write a file to your hard disk. The best time to run Disk Defragmenter is while you are out for lunch or after you've finished your work for the day.

Cleaning Up Disks

Have you ever wished there was some way you could just wave a magic wand and get rid of all the unused or temporary files that take up space on your hard disk? Well, now there is such a tool, and it is called Disk Cleanup. Choose Start ➢ Programs ➢ Accessories ➢ System Tools ➢ Disk Cleanup to open the Select Drive dialog box. Choose the drive you want to work with, and click OK to open the Disk Cleanup dialog box shown in Figure 27.2.

FIGURE 27.2 *The Disk Cleanup dialog box*

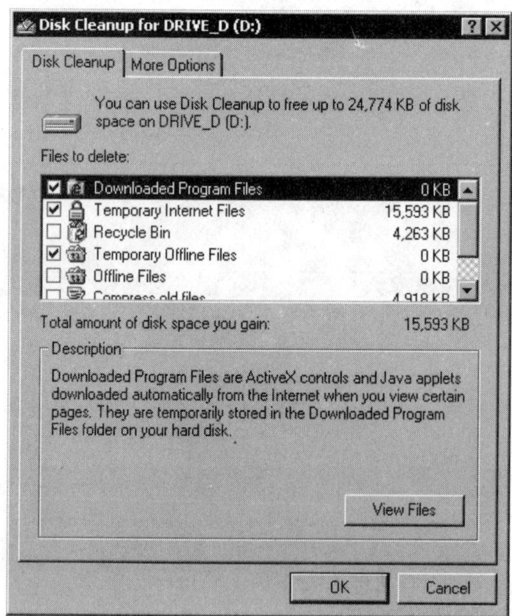

Alternatively, you can open Explorer or My Computer, right-click the disk you want to work with, and then choose Properties from the shortcut menu. On the General tab, click the Disk Cleanup button.

The Disk Cleanup dialog box has these tabs:

Disk Cleanup Displays the amount of free space that could be recovered by deleting temporary files in certain categories, including Internet files and downloaded program files, or by emptying the Recycle Bin on your Desktop. As you check the boxes to delete files, a running counter tells you how much disk space will be recovered. Click View Files to open an Explorer window so you can check the files a little more closely before you delete them from your hard disk.

More Options Lets you remove applications or Windows components that you don't use. Click either of the Clean Up buttons to open the Add/Remove Programs applet, and then select the Windows Setup tab to remove Windows components you don't use, or select the Install/Uninstall tab to remove application programs you don't use.

Checking Disks for Errors

Another disk-management task you might have to perform from time to time is to check a hard disk for errors, and Windows 2000 Professional includes a tool for checking FAT32 volumes. All NTFS volumes log file transactions and replace bad clusters automatically. To check out a hard disk, open Explorer or My Computer, right-click the disk you want to work with, and then choose Properties from the shortcut menu. On the Tools tab, click the Check Now button to open the Check Disk dialog box, which contains these two options:

- Automatically Fix File System Errors
- Scan For And Attempt Recovery Of Bad Sectors

Check the appropriate boxes, and then click Start to begin scanning the disk. A status bar across the bottom of the Check Disk dialog box indicates the progress of the tests, and you will see a message when the disk check is complete.

Restoring a Configuration

Sometimes, no matter how vigilant you've been, mistakes happen or something just goes wrong, and you need to fix your system. These fixes range from easy to horrific.

I'll start with a relatively easy one. What happens if you successfully install Windows 2000 Professional, try to adjust your system configuration, and render your PC unusable or even unbootable? Something as simple as changing the video driver to something that your system can't handle will do that, and it's hard to restore the original driver if you can't read what's on your screen. If you've messed up your system's configuration, what do you do?

One thing that you *could* do is reinstall Windows 2000 Professional. But not only do you have to do the installation process itself, you have to set up all services and user accounts again, and this gets very boring and/or frustrating very quickly. Fortunately, there are other ways to fix your setup when something's gone wrong.

Using the "Last Known Good" Menu

If you've changed your system so that it can't boot Windows 2000 Professional, one of these better solutions can be seen while you're rebooting. If you watch while your machine's booting up, you'll see a message on a black screen that says "For troubleshooting and advanced startup options for Windows 2000 Professional, press F8." If you press the F8 key, you'll see a menu asking you whether you want to:

- Boot Into Safe Mode
- Boot Into Safe Mode With Networking Enabled
- Boot To Safe Mode With A Command Prompt
- Enable Boot Logging
- Enable VGA Mode
- Use The *Last Known Good Configuration*—the configuration that was used the last time the machine booted successfully
- Enable Debugging Mode

These options cover most of the possible troubleshooting scenarios involving the boot process. If your machine won't boot, you probably don't want to use the current configuration; so choose the Last Known Good configuration. This should make your machine bootable.

When Does (and Doesn't) It Work?

What are the criteria for a configuration being the Last Known Good one? To qualify, a configuration must not have produced any critical errors involving a driver or a system file, and a user must have been able to log on to the system at least once.

The Last Known Good configuration can't always help you. If any of the following are true, you'll have to use another solution:

- You made a change more than one successful boot ago and want to restore things as they were before the change.
- The information that you want to change is not related to control-set information—user profiles and file permissions fall into the category of information that can't be changed with the Last Known Good menu.
- The system boots, a user logs on, and then the system hangs.
- You change your video driver to an incompatible driver, restart the system, and then log on with the bad driver (you can still type, even if you can't see).

NOTE The key to getting Last Known Good to work is knowing what constitutes a successful logon. A *successful logon* is when you have entered your username and password and *have been authenticated*. Ever seen the message that a domain controller could not be found but you have been logged on with cached credentials? Windows 2000 Professional considers that a successful logon. If you suspect even for a moment that the change you made might not work, don't log on. Let the computer sit at the Ctrl+Alt+Del prompt for a couple of minutes. If you do not receive any messages about failed services, then log on.

Recovering from Bad Video Drivers

You may recall from the earlier discussion of the Last Known Good configuration that if you change the video drivers to something that your system can't handle and then reboot and log on with the bad drivers (you can still type a password even if the screen is messed up), the Last Known Good solution can no longer help you. You have, after all, successfully rebooted and logged on to the system; the fact that you can't *see* anything is immaterial.

Under NT 3.1, this was something of a rigmarole. But NT 4 built into `boot.ini` the option NT Workstation 4.0 (VGA Drivers). All you had to do was shut down the PC, restart it, and choose the setup with VGA drivers. Then, after you got the system back up, you simply selected Display from Control Panel, and then you could take a second shot at choosing a video driver. Even better, the Display applet included a Test button that NT forced you to use *before* you committed yourself to whether the video drivers work.

Windows 2000 Professional takes this safety net a bit further. When you change a video driver in Windows 2000 Professional, you are forced to test the new driver before the change becomes permanent. The system will apply the change and try the new configuration for 15 seconds. During this time, you are prompted to decide whether you want to keep this new setting. If you click Cancel, the system reverts to its previous setting with no harm done. If you select OK, the setting is made permanent. The really nice part is that you won't even have to reboot the computer to make the change!

The Recovery Console

Recovery Console is a command-line tool that you can use to start and stop services, format drives, and repair your system. To use Recovery Console, you really should be a power user, and you must be logged on as an administrator. This tool is not installed by default when you install Windows 2000 Professional, so the first order of business in this section is telling you how to install it.

Installing the Recovery Console

You install the Recovery Console from the Windows 2000 Professional installation CD. Insert your CD in the drive, and then follow these steps:

1. Choose Start ➢ Run, and in the Open box type **d:\i386\winnt32/cmdcons** where d: is the drive letter of your installation CD. The first time you do this, Windows 2000 Professional displays the following message box:

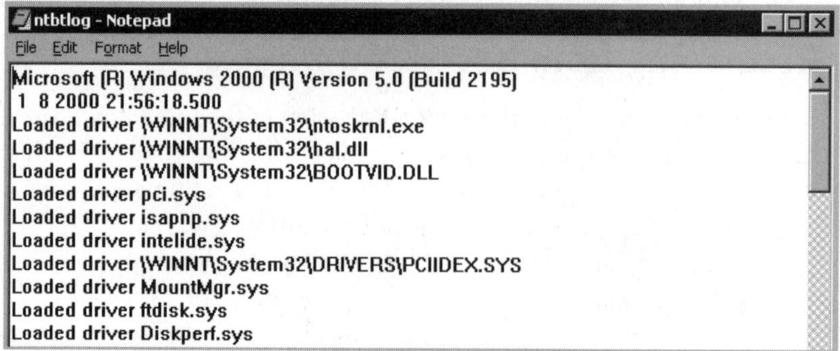

2. Windows 2000 Professional Setup will copy some files from the installation CD and then prompt you to restart the computer.
3. After you restart, the Recovery Console will be in the Startup menu (the text menu you see when you start up the computer), listed as Microsoft Windows 2000 Professional Command Console. To start it, just choose that option before the 30-second timeout to whatever your default start-up option is.

Creating the Emergency Repair Disk

Every time you successfully edit your system's configuration, you should back the configuration up against the time when you unsuccessfully edit the settings. This backup disk is called the Emergency Repair Disk.

TIP Re-create the Emergency Repair Disk after you have successfully booted with the new configuration information. This way, you'll know that the configuration you're backing up works.

Previous versions of NT had a utility called RDISK that you could use to create a repair disk after installation. If you're looking for RDISK in Windows 2000 Professional, you won't find it. Yes, Windows 2000 Professional still offers the same Emergency Repair Disk (ERD) functionality, but you now use a utility in the Backup program to make it, and it is not the same disk. Strictly speaking, the ERD is no longer a repair disk, but a boot disk to run the repair tools on the CD.

To create the ERD, follow these steps:

1. Choose Start ➢ Programs ➢ Accessories ➢ System Tool ➢ Backup.
2. On the initial screen of the utility, you'll find buttons for three Wizards: Backup Wizard, Restore Wizard, and Emergency Repair Disk. Click the Emergency Repair Disk button
3. When prompted, put a blank, formatted disk in the A drive, and click OK. You'll have the option of copying the Registry files to the Repair folder. I strongly recommend that you do so.
4. Click OK to begin the process.

NOTE The updated files will be in `%systemroot%\Repair\RegBack`.

Windows 2000 Professional copies `AUTOEXEC.NT`, `CONFIG.NT`, and `SETUP.LOG` to the disk. The two NT files are not bootable—this isn't a boot disk. Rather, they're the files that Windows 2000 Professional needs to boot the files necessary for running 16-bit applications such as the Repair utility. `AUTOEXEC.NT` installs support for the CD-ROM (which you'll need to repair Windows 2000 Professional), the network redirector, and DPMI Memory. `CONFIG.NT` loads DOS into the Upper Memory Block (UMB), out of conventional memory, and loads `HIMEM.SYS`, needed to read memory above 640KB.

Know Thy ERD

It's important that you realize that the ERD you get with Windows 2000 Professional is different from the NT 4 ERD. The Windows 2000 Professional ERD does not include Registry data—probably a reflection of the fact that people with complex systems could easily have a `Security` key file too big to fit on a disk. You can see the contents of the two ERD types below (the Windows 2000 Professional ERD is on top):

Continued

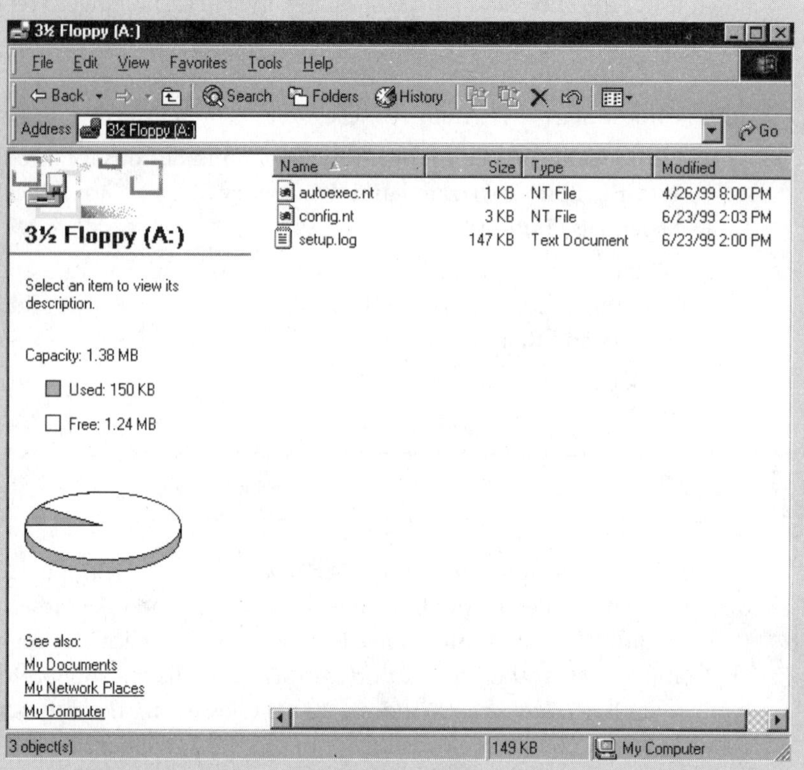
3½ Floppy (A:)
File Edit View Favorites Tools Help
Back Search Folders History
Address 3½ Floppy (A:)
Go
3½ Floppy (A:)
Select an item to view its description.
Capacity: 1.38 MB
Used: 150 KB
Free: 1.24 MB
See also:
My Documents
My Network Places
My Computer
Name Size Type Modified
autoexec.nt 1 KB NT File 4/26/99 8:00 PM
config.nt 3 KB NT File 6/23/99 2:03 PM
setup.log 147 KB Text Document 6/23/99 2:00 PM
3 object(s)
149 KB
My Computer

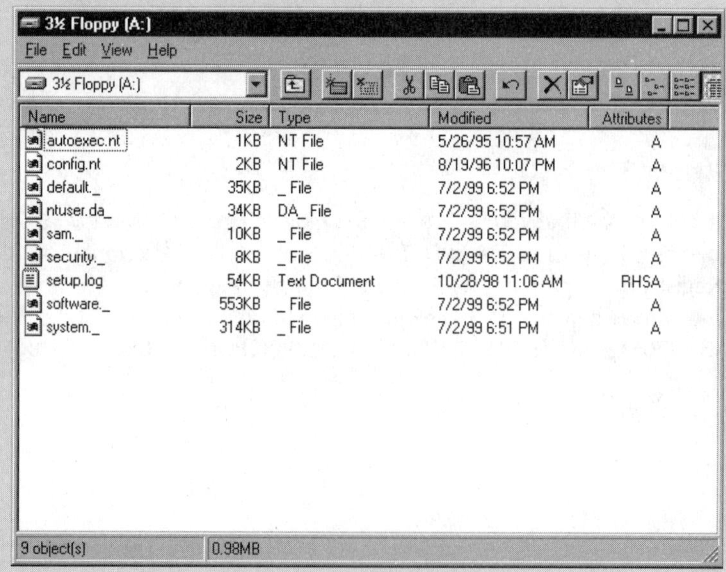
3½ Floppy (A:)
File Edit View Help
3½ Floppy (A:)
Name Size Type Modified Attributes
autoexec.nt 1KB NT File 5/26/95 10:57 AM A
config.nt 2KB NT File 8/19/96 10:07 PM A
default._ 35KB _ File 7/2/99 6:52 PM A
ntuser.da_ 34KB DA_ File 7/2/99 6:52 PM A
sam._ 10KB _ File 7/2/99 6:52 PM A
security._ 8KB _ File 7/2/99 6:52 PM A
setup.log 54KB Text Document 10/28/98 11:06 AM RHSA
software._ 553KB _ File 7/2/99 6:52 PM A
system._ 314KB _ File 7/2/99 6:51 PM A
9 object(s)
0.98MB

Continued

You can replace parts of the system Registry from the Recovery Console, if you update the information in the RegBack folder on a regular basis. (The original files are in the \Config folder; the backups in \Repair\RegBack.) Just don't expect to have that information anywhere if you don't back it up when creating the ERD.

Curious about what you *do* with the ERD? Read the next section.

Repairing—or Recovering—a Damaged Installation

The Last Known Good menu and the Safe Mode boot options aren't always enough to get a wounded installation back on its feet again. You've still got some options before reinstalling, though. As I discussed in the previous section, Windows 2000 Professional offers two repair tools: the Recovery Console and the Emergency Repair Disk. Both work on volumes formatted with either FAT or NTFS—one of the cool things about Windows 2000 Professional, since this means that you can now format a system partition with NTFS but still have access to troubleshooting tools.

NOTE For a refresher on Safe Mode, look back in Chapter 2.

Understanding Repair Options

The two repair options aren't identical. The Emergency Repair Disk is a simple procedure for those times when you don't know precisely what the problem is, but you want to fix it and get on with your life. There's little finesse involved: you start installing Windows 2000 Professional; when asked whether you're doing a real installation or a repair, you choose to repair, and then you plug in the ERD and let Setup repair files that are different from the ones originally installed. (There's a little more to it than that, but that's the basic story. I'll go through the procedure a bit later in this chapter.) As long as you haven't replaced any drivers or DLLs in your system folders with new ones, you can safely choose to restore all system files to their originals, and you'll still get your Windows 2000 Professional installation back as you left it—just fixed.

The Recovery Console is a little more complicated. Rather than a means of restoring damaged files, it's a command-line utility from which you can perform a variety of tasks:

- Copy system files from a floppy disk or CD to a hard disk (although not from a hard disk to a floppy disk)
- Start and stop services
- Read and write data in the system directory on the local hard disk
- Format disks
- Repartition disks

Use the Recovery Console when you know precisely what's wrong and what you want to accomplish. If you don't know what's wrong, this is not an easy way of finding out.

In short, if your Windows 2000 Professional installation is dead and you're not sure why, use the Emergency Repair Disk to see whether restoring the original installation files will fix the problem. If you know what the problem is—like, for example, a bad or missing SYS file or a runaway service—you can use the Recovery Console to copy the missing file to its new location without changing any other files.

If you didn't set up the Recovery Console before Windows 2000 Professional became unbootable (or you want to run the ERD repair utility), you'll need to run Setup from the installation CD. After Setup has copied all the files it needs to access the hardware it needs to run Setup, it will ask you whether you want to install Windows 2000 Professional, repair it, or exit Setup. Press R to open the Windows 2000 Professional Repair Options menu, from which you can either repair an installation with the Recovery Console (press C) or with the Emergency Repair Disk (press R).

Using the Recovery Console

When you choose to run the Recovery Console, it will scan the disk and find any installations of Windows NT/2000 on the disk. Select the one you want to repair. Type the number of the option you want, and supply the password for the admin account. You're in.

If the term "console" led you to expect some kind of GUI, you'll be surprised to see a simple command-line interface. Although it looks like an ordinary command prompt, the Recovery Console is not the command prompt that you can open from the Accessories menu. First, it supports only a few commands and only locally—this is not a network tool. Second, those commands are specialized for this interface and only perform a limited set of functions. The wildcard options in the copy command don't work in the console, you can only copy files from removable media to the system partition (but not the other way around—you can't use the console to back up files to other media), and although you can move to other logical drives on the hard disk, you can't read files on any partition other than the system partition—or even perform a `dir` function on them. If you try, you'll get an Access Denied error. The Recovery Console is not a command-line version of Windows 2000 Professional, cool as that would be.

NOTE I'd expected that the Recovery Console would include a command-line version of RegEdit, as Windows 95/98 does. Sadly, it does not.

You can't back up files. You can't read the contents of any folder not in the system root. You can't use wildcards. You can't edit security information. What can you do with the Recovery Console?

Mostly, you can fix your system partition to make it usable again. As you can see in Table 27.1, the Recovery Console is a set of commands that you can use to manipulate the files and structure of the system partition. There are a lot of functions with duplicate commands that use the same syntax; unless I specify otherwise, there's no difference between the two commands.

TABLE 27.1: SUPPORTED RECOVERY CONSOLE COMMANDS

Command Name	Function
`attrib`	Changes the attributes of a selected file or folder.
`batch`	Runs the commands specified in a text file so that you can complete many tasks in a single step.
`cd` or `chdir`	Displays the name of the current directory, or changes directories. Typing **cd..** closes the current directory and moves you up one in the tree.
`chkdsk`	Runs CheckDisk.
`cls`	Wipes the screen of any previous output, so you can see better.
`copy` or `extract`	Copies files from removable media to the system folders on the hard disk. Does not accept wildcards.
`del` or `delete`	Deletes one or more files (does not accept wildcards).
`dir`	Lists the contents of the current or selected directory.
`disable`	Disables the named service or driver.
`enable`	Enables the named service or driver.
`diskpart`	Replaces the FDISK tool you're probably familiar with. Creates or deletes disk partitions.
`fixboot`	Writes a new partition boot sector on the system partition.
`fixmbr`	Writes a new Master Boot Record (MBR) for the partition boot sector.
`format`	Formats the selected disk.
`listsvc`	Lists all the services running on the Windows 2000 Professional installation.
`logon`	If you have multiple Windows 2000 Professional (or NT) installations on the local hard disk, you can use this command to select the installation you want to repair.
`map`	Displays the drive letter mappings currently in place. Handy for getting the information you need to use DISKPART.
`md` or `mkdir`	Creates a directory.

Continued

TABLE 27.1: SUPPORTED RECOVERY CONSOLE COMMANDS (CONTINUED)

Command Name	Function
`more, type`	Displays the contents of the chosen text file.
`rd` or `rmdir`	Deletes a directory.
`rename` or `ren`	Renames a single file.
`Systemroot`	Makes the current directory the system root of the drive you're logged into.
`Extract`	Extracts a compressed installation file (one with a CAB extension) to the local fixed disk. Only works if you're running the Recovery Console from the installation disk.

WARNING If you thought the Registry Editor was potentially dangerous, the Recovery Console is just as bad or worse. You can really screw up your system here, to the point that the only thing to do is reinstall and reload your backups. There's no Undo feature, not all the commands ask for confirmation, and there's no Read-Only setting like the one in `regedt32`. If you're not used to working from the command line, review what you want to do and the tools you need to do it before you open the console.

Some of the commands shown in Table 27.1 will look familiar to old DOS hands, but many of them work a little differently from the way they did under DOS, using a slightly different syntax or only working under specific circumstances. Let's take a look at how you can use these commands to get things back up and running.

Enabling and Disabling Services

Why would you need to enable or disable services from the command line? Therein lies a tale...

Earlier this year, I bought a new PC. Installed everything, ran the installation program for the 3Com network card in the server. Life was good.

Until I rebooted the computer.

You see, a diagnostic program was part of the setup for the NIC—an unavoidable part that you could not choose to not install. (Trust me: I tried, on several computers with the same set of hardware.) Whenever I started up NT, this diagnostic program would scan the system and display a message that a newer version of my NIC's driver was available—did I want to use the new driver? Click OK or Cancel, and the message box would close for a second and then reopen, with the same message. Add to this that the searching and displaying was using up 100 percent of CPU time for a 350MHz Pentium II doing *nothing else but running the diagnostic.* Running the Task Manager (when I could get a spare cycle here or there to open it) didn't help, because the program wouldn't shut down even when I killed the process.

NOTE Worried about this happening to you? Although I've run into several people who've had the same problem with one version of the driver for the 3Com 3C905X Ethernet 10Base-T card, this issue seems to be fixed in the driver published in April 1999. Other than this glitch, I've been very happy with these NICs.

OK, I figured—the problem is a runaway service, so if I can shut down the service I will resolve the problem. But shutting down the service is hard when you're clicking OK in a repeatedly reappearing dialog box and then frantically grabbing CPU cycles to open Control Panel and then Services before the dialog box opens and the CPU usage starts running at 100 percent again.

In this case, I was finally able to get to the Services applet, find the service (named 3Com Diagnostics, or some such, so identifying the problem child wasn't hard), and then stop and disable it. Problem solved. But it took a lot of time and mouse-clicking to get to that point. A tool that would enable me to boot to the command prompt and disable that service without having to work around the CPU-eating message box would have been nice. And that's where the services-related tools in the Recovery Console come in.

The first step to fixing a problem like this is running the `listsvc` utility from the Recovery Console. There are no arguments to this—just type **`listsvc`** at the command prompt, and Windows 2000 Professional will display a list of all the services and drivers currently installed for that installation of Windows 2000 Professional, a short description of what they are, and their start type (boot, automatic, manual, system, or disabled). Seeing all the services will probably take a few pages of screen, but the services are listed alphabetically, so you can find the one you want fairly easily. Write down its name.

TIP The names of services and drivers are not case-sensitive.

Once you've found the suspected problem child, it's time for the disable command. The syntax is simple: `disable` *`servicename`*. Windows 2000 Professional will then notify you that it found the Registry entry for this service (or tell you that it can't find an entry for this service, in which case you need to check your spelling and try again). It will also display the current start type and new start type for the service. Write down the current start type for the service in case you want to start it again.

To make the change take effect, type **exit** to leave the Recovery Console and restart the computer. See if disabling that service fixed the problem. If it did, you're home free. (Not sure how you'd know? Depends on what the problem was. In the case of the runaway 3Com diagnostics, the fix was pretty immediate. As soon as I turned off the service, the problem disappeared.) If it didn't, you can return to the console, enable that service, and try something else.

You don't have to disable a service to keep it from running when Windows 2000 Professional starts, however. Instead, you could change its start type from automatic to manual. To do so, or to reenable a service you disabled, you'll need to use the enable command. Like disable, enable's syntax is simple: `enable` *`servicename`*. If run on a disabled service, this syntax will enable the service and restore it to whatever its start type was when it was disabled.

To change a service's start type without disabling it, add the new start type to the end of the enable command, like this:

enable *servicename start_type*

where *start_type* is one of the options in Table 27.2.

TABLE 27.2: START TYPES

Start Type	Meaning
Service_boot_start	Boot
Service_system_start	System
Service_demand_start	Manual
Service_auto_start	Automatic

So, for example, instead of disabling the 3Com diagnostic service, I could have changed its start type from automatic to manual. That way, I could have started it at any time during the Windows 2000 Professional session, but it wouldn't start automatically.

Replacing Damaged Files

Perhaps the problem isn't a runaway driver or service, but a corrupted part of the operating system, as in error messages that say `Bad or Missing NTOSKRNL.EXE`. In such a case, you may need to replace all or part of your operating system (although, if we're talking about more than a few files here or you aren't sure what's broken, you might consider hauling out the Emergency Repair Disk). The tools most likely to apply to this scenario are the ones to create and delete folders, rename files, change attributes, and copy or extract files from other media.

Creating folders is simple. The command syntax is as follows:

```
md [drive:]path
mkdir [drive:]path
```

where *drive:* is the drive letter of the drive on which you want to create the folder, if it's not the current one, and *path* is the name of the folder you want to create. Just make sure that, if you don't spell out the location of the new folder, you're currently in the place where the new folder should be created.

The syntax for the `rmdir` and `rd` commands (for deleting folders) is the same as that for `md`. The only part of folder deletion that you have to watch is that you can't delete folders unless they're empty, with no subfolders. If you try, you'll get an error message telling you that the folder is not empty, and there's no switch to make `rd` act like `deltree` (an old DOS command that would delete subdirectories).

Before you delete a folder, run the `dir` command to check out its contents and make sure that you really do want to remove it. Conveniently, `dir` displays all files, hidden or not, and shows their attributes.

Rather than deleting entire folders, however, you're more likely to need to replace individual files. That's where `copy` and `extract` come in. The `copy` command is what it sounds like: a method for copying a file from one location to another, with the caveat I've mentioned before that you can only copy files *to* the system folder, not copy files *from* the system folder to removable media such as a Jaz drive. The syntax for copying files is simple:

```
copy source [destination]
```

where *source* is the name of the original file and *destination* is the folder where you're pasting the original (along with a new name, if you need it). If you don't specify a folder, the file will be copied to the folder from which you're running the command. The `extract` utility works the same way as `copy` and uses the same syntax, with one exception: you can only use `extract` if you started the Recovery Console from the Repair option in Setup. Neither copying utility supports wildcards (so you can't copy the entire contents of a folder very easily), but `copy` automatically decompresses compressed installation files for you. Both utilities will alert you if a file with the name of the one you're pasting already exists in that location.

If you're not sure that you want to replace an existing file, try renaming it and then copying the new file to the relevant location. The syntax for `rename` is as follows:

```
rename [drive:][path] filename1 filename2
```

This command works only on single files, and the renamed file must be in the same place as the original. That is, you can't use `rename` to move files. To do that, you'd need to use `copy`.

Fixing Boot Sectors and Boot Records

Your computer uses a couple of pieces of information to navigate your hard disk. Those two pieces are the boot sector and the Master Boot Record (MBR). Most of the time, these pieces are pretty safe, but some things (such as some viruses) can target and infect them, or they can be lost. In such a case, you'll need a way to restore them.

First, a little background. The partition boot sector contains the information that the file system uses to access the volume. The Master Boot Record (discussed below) examines the information in the boot sector to load the boot loader.

The Windows 2000 Professional boot sector contains the following information:

- A jump instruction
- The name and version of the operating system files (such as Windows 2000 Professional)
- A data structure called the BIOS Parameter Block, which describes the physical characteristics of the partition
- A data structure called the BIOS Extended Parameter Block, which describes the location of the Master File Table for NTFS volumes
- The bootstrap code

Most of the information in the boot sector describes the physical characteristics of the disk (for example, the number of sectors per track and clusters per sector), in addition to the location of the File Allocation Table (for FAT volumes) or the Master File Table (for NTFS volumes). The layout and exact information included in the boot sector depends on the disk format used.

Given that a disk may have more than one partition, how does the hard disk know where to find the different partitions? The first sector on every hard disk (whether the hard disk has an operating system on it or not) contains that disk's Master Boot Record (MBR). The MBR contains the partition table for that disk and a small amount of code used to read the partition table and find the system partition for that hard disk. Once it finds that partition, the MBR loads a copy of that partition's boot sector into memory. If the disk is not bootable (has no system partition), the code never gets used, and the boot sector is not loaded.

In short, a hard disk needs a functioning MBR to boot. The MBR is in the same place on every hard disk, so it's potentially an easy virus target.

OK—all that said, to write a new boot sector to a drive, type **`fixboot`**. This will write a new boot sector to the current boot drive. To create a new MBR, type **`fixmbr`**.

Deleting, Creating, and Formatting Partitions

The Recovery Console includes tools not only for fixing Windows 2000 Professional, but also for completely wiping things out and starting over. With these tools you can repartition and reformat your hard disk. Partitioning is setting up logical drives on the disk; formatting is placing a file system on those drives so you can store data on them.

WARNING You probably already know this, but just in case you've forgotten, repartitioning and formatting are *destructive*. Any data on the hard disk you've reformatted or repartitioned is history. Keep your backups.

Before you start formatting or repartitioning, you might want to take a look at what you've already got in place. The Recovery Console's map command can help you do that. Type **map** at the command prompt, and you'll see output like the following:

```
?              0MB          Device\HardDisk0\Partition0
C:   FAT16  1028MB          Device\HardDisk0\Partition1
?           3310MB          Device\HardDisk0\Partition0
E:   NTFS   1028MB          Device\HardDisk0\Partition2
H:   NTFS   1028MB          Device\HardDisk0\Partition3
G:          1028MB          Device\HardDisk0\Partition4
?            227MB          Device\HardDisk0\Partition0
A:                          Device\Floppy0
D:                          Device\CDROM0
```

You can see from this that logical drive G on the hard disk hasn't been formatted, because it's not showing any file system. To format it, you would use the following syntax:

```
format g: [/q] [/fs:filesystem]
```

Here, `/q` tells `format` to do a quick format (not checking for bad sectors), and the `/fs` switch is for specifying the file system to use. You don't have to specify a file system (your options are NTFS, FAT32, and FAT), but if you don't, Windows 2000 Professional will format it to NTFS. When you run this command, Windows 2000 Professional will tell you that all data on that drive will be lost and ask you to confirm that the format should proceed. Do so, and a few seconds later you will have a newly formatted drive.

TIP You can convert a FAT partition to NTFS, but you cannot convert an NTFS partition to FAT.

You can format the G drive safely, or at least without affecting any other logical drives. What you can't do, even before formatting, is repartition to make the G drive bigger, perhaps giving it some of that space that isn't used on the disk.

When you're done with the Recovery Console, type **exit** and press Enter. The computer will reboot.

Using the Emergency Repair Disk

You have two options for the Emergency Repair Disk: Manual Repair, in which you can choose from a list of repair options (not another one!) or Fast Repair, which repairs your installation for you. I'm not a trusting type, so I recommend that you choose M for Manual to be sure that you get the options you want.

NOTE If you choose Fast Repair, the repair utility will perform all the tasks proffered by the Manual Repair utility.

By default, the repair utility will inspect the start-up environment, verify the Windows 2000 Professional system files to make sure none are missing, and inspect the boot sector. Choose the options you want, and press Enter to continue.

Now, you'll need that ERD. Make sure it's in the floppy drive and press Enter. If you don't have an ERD, you may still be able to repair the installation by pressing L to let Setup try to find the Windows 2000 Professional installation for you. Setup will look around to find a Windows 2000 Professional installation and then ask you whether the installation found at such and such a location is the one you want to repair. If it is, press Enter.

Setup will read from `Setup.log` on the ERD and then start doing the operations you selected. If it comes across any files in your existing installation that don't match the ones logged in `Setup.log`, which is a record of all files installed originally, it will tell you and then offer you a choice of skipping the file, repairing it (that is, replacing it with the one that Windows 2000 Professional would install), or choosing to repair all files that differ from the original. There is no "skip all" function, so you'll have to make a decision for each file if you're pretty sure that you want to keep some of the files logged in `Setup.log`. It's inspecting the entire Windows 2000 Professional folder, so this may take a while.

There's really no way to know which file represents the problem, unfortunately. All this process does is note which files are different from what Setup would have installed. If you've run Windows 2000 Professional for any length of time and made any modifications, quite a number of files may be different. However, replacing these files won't restore Windows 2000 Professional to a just-installed condition because your Registry files are not replaced.

When it's done, the computer will reboot and (hopefully) run Windows 2000 Professional.

NOTE Your security information—policies, accounts, passwords—will be as you left it. The ERD does not record or replace security information.

The Driver Verifier—a Condom for Your Drivers

It goes without saying that reliable hardware is the number one most important consideration when building reliable Windows 2000 Professional systems. However, equally as important is making sure that reliable drivers are used.

A hardware device—as far as Windows 2000 Professional is concerned—is only as good as its associated driver. The driver is the software that resides in the "kernel" of Windows 2000 Professional and actually talks to the hardware. The kernel is more or less the brains of your Windows 2000 Professional operating system; therefore, it is one of the areas that should be protected the most. However, Microsoft's own Web site states that "most third-party code that causes blue screens runs in the operating system kernel."

So what is the solution to this problem? A new program released in Windows 2000 Professional called the Driver Verifier. So, what exactly does the Driver Verifier do and why would you want to use it? I'm glad you asked, because in the course of writing this chapter, I had to ask myself the same question.

If you've been lucky, all the hardware on your system has well-behaved drivers that don't cause any problems. But what if you wanted to add an old, slightly outdated card to your system? How would that impact your system's stability? Or what if you found a new driver on the Internet for some existing hardware you have? Will the new driver be as stable on your system as your current driver? How can you be sure that updating to a new driver won't compromise your system stability in some way?

The Driver Verifier is the answer to all these questions and more. In reality, what the Driver Verifier does is quite simple. During normal Windows operations, all the drivers on your system reside in the kernel of the Windows 2000 Professional operating system and are supposed to play nicely together and with the operating system. Windows 2000 Professional doesn't really look at what they are doing. It more or less assumes that the drivers will be on their best behavior as long as they respond appropriately when called on. As an analogy, imagine a bunch of children playing around unsupervised in a back yard. Now, as long as they respond when you call to them, would you assume that they aren't doing anything they shouldn't be doing? I should hope not!

As anyone who has children knows, just because you don't find out that your kids are misbehaving doesn't mean that they're not causing trouble. Kids need supervision. Well, sometimes the drivers in your system need supervision. That's basically what the Driver Verifier does—it acts as a babysitter for your drivers. It puts them under a microscope and scrutinizes every single thing they do. Using our children analogy, imagine taking one of the children, putting him or her in their own private sandbox, and standing over them watching every single thing they do.

In effect, this is what the Driver Verifier does. By keeping an eye on how the drivers on your system utilize and access memory, your system will display a blue screen if a driver misbehaves. So, what does Windows 2000 Professional consider misbehaving? Well, the list is rather long—and *extremely* technical—to the point where addressing those issues would take up far more pages than are allocated to this book. Therefore, let's just take a look at the common circumstances in which you would want to use the Driver Verifier and how to use it.

Running the Driver Verifier

As I mentioned before, you will probably want to use the Driver Verifier if you want to add a new piece of hardware to your system or if you want to update an existing driver. In any case, if you are concerned about system stability, run the Driver Verifier in order to place the new (or updated) driver in its own private sandbox for the first few weeks.

WARNING During the course of writing this chapter, I placed the driver for my network adapter in the Driver Verifier to make sure it was behaving appropriately. For whatever reason, when I took the driver back out, my system would no longer access the Internet without causing a blue screen. Eventually, I figured out that this was due to a conflict with some personal firewall software that I was using. The personal firewall software worked fine before I started testing the Driver Verifier, but after I took my network adapter in and out of the Driver Verifier, my personal firewall would no longer work consistently. I'm sure that this was an atypical symptom of using the Driver Verifier program—and more likely a problem with my personal firewall software—but it does warrant a bit of caution. Even though this is a great diagnostic utility, unless you have something specific that you want to troubleshoot, it may not be wise to play around with it. And just in case you do want to use it, you might want to back up your system first.

You can start the Driver Verifier in two ways:

- At the command prompt, type **VERIFIER**.
- Choose Start ➢ Run to open the Run dialog box, and in the Open box, type **Verifier**.

In either case, the Driver Verifier Manager dialog box opens at the Driver Status tab, as shown in Figure 27.3.

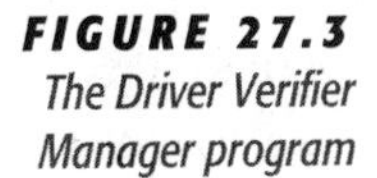

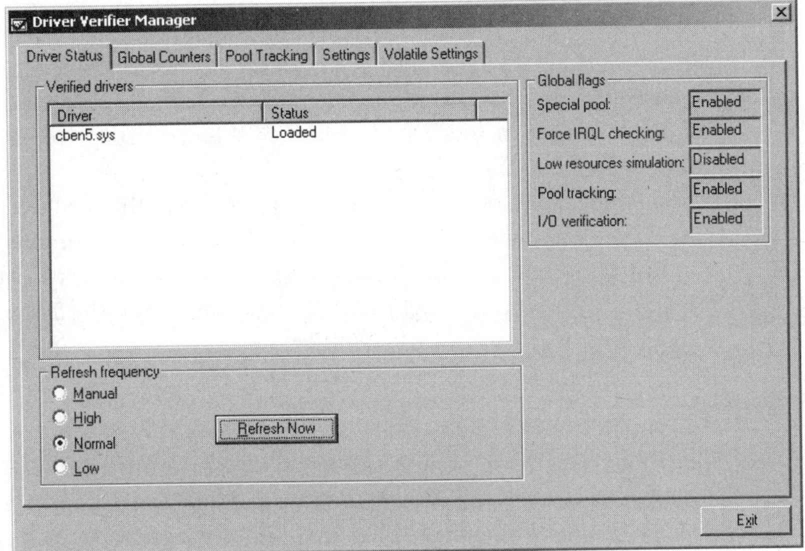

FIGURE 27.3
The Driver Verifier Manager program

The Driver Status tab shows you which drivers are currently being scrutinized. To add a driver into the Driver Verifier (to put the driver "in its sandbox"), select the Settings tab, and find the driver. All the drivers for your system will probably be listed in that tab with a status of Not Verified. Although you could tell your system to verify all drivers by selecting the Verify All Drivers radio button at the top of the Settings tab, I advise against this. As you will see in the list of drivers on your system, quite a lot of them are running. Instead, test them individually, if you suspect a problem, by selecting a driver and then clicking the Verify button at the bottom of the tab.

More often than not, staging a driver to be verified will require rebooting your system. And when you reboot , you might notice that it takes significantly longer to start up. This is normal behavior and not any cause for concern. After you restart your system, start the Driver Verifier again to make sure that your driver is now listed in the Verified Drivers window of the Driver Status tab. If your driver is correctly listed in there, all its activities are now being monitored by the Driver Verifier.

So, what's next? Other than working with some of the specific settings for what to test and how, you should go about using your system normally. If you are able to run for a few weeks without any sort of blue screen bug-check error messages, it is reasonably safe to assume that your driver is behaving correctly within your system, and you can move it out of the verifier and back into normal operation.

So what are some of the specific settings for what to test and how? Well, many options are available, and again they are extremely technical in nature and far beyond the scope of this chapter. You can read more about them—in painstaking detail—at Microsoft's online DDK (driver development kit) documentation for the Driver Verifier program at `www.microsoft.com/ddk/ddkdocs/win2k/drverif_5nqf.htm`.

System File Checker

One of the things that Microsoft has learned over the years is that more often than not unreliable behavior in Windows can often be directly attributed to missing, corrupted, or conflicting versions of critical system components. In an effort to resolve this problem, Microsoft has included a new utility in Windows 2000 Professional called the System File Checker (SFC).

The System File Checker is a command-line utility that will scan the critical system files on your computer and replace any suspicious files with original copies either from your installation media or a special folder on your system. If you suspect that a Windows file on your system might have been damaged, run the System File Checker to find out for sure.

Running the SFC

The SFC will check approximately 2700 files on your system—namely most of the SYS, DLL, EXE, TTF, FON, and OCX files that were originally installed. When you run the SFC, you are in effect telling the utility to compare all the files on your system against the original installation media. Therefore, the SFC will need a copy of the original files to work from. Make sure that you have your original Windows 2000 Professional CD-ROM handy when you need to run this utility.

The SFC is a command-line utility, so you won't find it on any of the menus in your system. To launch the SFC, type **SFC** at a command prompt. If everything is working correctly, you should see a help screen giving you the available command options. The options are listed in Table 27.3:

TABLE 27.3: SFC COMMAND LINE OPTIONS

Command Line Options	Description
`/scannow`	Forces an immediate scan of your system
`/scanonce`	Tells your system to scan all files on your system at the next boot up
`/scanboot`	Tells your system to scan all files on your system at every boot up
`/cancel`	Cancels any and all pending scans of your system
`/enable`	Enables Windows File Protection during normal system operation
/purgecache	Purges the Dllcache folder and begins scanning all protected system files immediately
/quiet	Used in conjunction with other switches, tells the system to automatically replace incorrect files without prompting the user
/?	Displays commands

Since you're reading this chapter, you're most likely looking for troubleshooting information, either to repair a system that is currently experiencing problems or for future reference. For most troubleshooting purposes, a simple SFC /SCANNOW will suffice. This will begin checking each of the critical system files on your computer, comparing them against the original copies, and determining if any of the file have been corrupted.

As the tool is running, a status monitor will keep you informed as to how far the system has proceeded with its checking. If the SFC finds any files that are missing or corrupted (when compared with the Windows 2000 Professional source media), it will replace the file with the original version either from its cache on your hard drive or from the original media.

Just for giggles, I tested this capability on my system by overwriting one of the TrueType Font (TTF) files. Sure enough, once I ran the SFC, it saw that one of my files was corrupted and replaced it with an original copy of the file. I can definitely see where the SFC is useful in the case of corrupted files, virus infections, or just plain ol' human error. The SFC is a life-saver!

The Registry Entry That Lets You Force a Blue Screen (Core Dump)

OK, so far in this chapter, I've been talking about ways to avoid blue screens or at least to minimize their impact. But what if you actually *want* to cause a blue screen?

Although unusual, on occasions you might want to force your system to crash via a blue screen. For example, you might want to test that Windows 2000 Professional will reboot itself properly and that all the necessary services on your system will start again. Or, you might want to see how well an application that is running on your system will perform in the event of a critical failure. For whatever the reasons, if you want to force your system to blue screen, you can do it.

All you need is one simple Registry modification. To modify the Registry in Windows 2000 Professional, you use RegEdit. As always, before making *any* modifications to your Registry, back it up.

After you back up your Registry, you will need to navigate to the HKEY_LOCAL_MACHINE\SYSTEM\CurrentControlSet\Services\i8042prt\Parameters. In there, you will create a create a key called CrashOnCtrlScroll as a DWORD type. Enter a value of 1 for the Registry key, and then reboot your system.

So what does this do? Well, the i8042prt service is responsible for handling your keyboard input. So this Registry entry allows you to force the system to crash through the use of a special keystroke. Useful for both diagnostic testing purposes and practical joking! Once you have this Registry key in your system, a simple Ctrl+ScrollLock+ScrollLock will cause your system to immediately blue screen (you must use the Ctrl key on the right side of the keyboard).

Backing Up and Restoring

A lot of what I've talked about in this chapter won't do you any good unless you've backed up your system. So, as I promised, early on in this chapter, here are the steps for backing up and for restoring.

Making a Backup

The next thing you can do to make life easier for yourself is to back up important files. Yes, we know you have heard all this before; everybody's heard about making backups, but why should *you* make a backup?

To protect against hard disk failure A hard disk can fail at almost any time, but when it does, it is always at the most inconvenient moment.

To protect against accidental deletion of a file If you work on many projects, your chances of accidentally deleting a file are far higher than if you work on only one at a time.

To create an archive at the end of a project You can make a backup that contains all the files relating to a single project when the work is done; then if you need to refer to the files again, you know where to find them.

These are the main reasons to make a backup, but there are others. You might back up the files of a terminating employee in case the computer is reassigned within your department or is transferred to another department. In either case, the new user will likely clean up the hard disk—in other words, delete all the most important files. In addition, making a backup is one way to transfer a large number of files from one computer system to another. Finally, you should always back up before making a substantial change to your system such as installing new hardware, upgrading the operating system, or making a major configuration change to your application software.

Once you decide to make a backup, you need to plan your backup strategy and, most important, stick to it. With no plan, you will simply accumulate floppy disks or tapes haphazardly, you will waste tapes, and you will waste time looking for a file when you need to restore a file deleted by accident.

So how often should you make a backup? For an answer that fits the way you work, answer these questions:

- How often do your data files change? Every day? Every week? Every month?
- How important to your day-to-day operations are these files? Can you work without them? How long would it take you to recreate them?
- How much will it cost to replace lost files in terms of time spent and business lost?

In our computerized world, it takes hours to create an HTML page with just the right look or a budget spreadsheet that everyone agrees to, but either can be lost or destroyed in milliseconds. A hard-disk failure, a mistaken delete command, overwriting the file with an earlier version with the same name—these can destroy a file just as surely as fire, flood, or earthquake. You just have to lose one important file to become an instant convert for life to a program of regular, planned backups.

To start the Windows 2000 Professional backup program, choose Start ➢ Programs ➢ Accessories ➢ System Tools ➢ Backup. The first time you start the program, a dialog box welcomes you to Microsoft Backup and leads directly into the Backup Wizard.

Using the Backup Wizard

Using the Backup Wizard is a quick and easy way to learn about backups; it gets you going quickly with the minimum of technical knowledge. If you would rather not use the Wizard, click Backup; you can always restart it from the Tools menu inside the Backup program if you change your mind.

The Wizard walks you through the following sequence:

What to Back Up You can back up all files and folders on your computer or selected files and folders; you can also back up only those files that have changed since the last time you made a backup.

Where to Store the Backup Select a destination drive for the backup. You can back up to a network drive, but check with your system administrator before you do so for the first time.

Type of Backup You can compare the backup against the original copies of your files to ensure that the files are backed up properly, and you can specify whether Backup should compress your files as they are backed up to save space on the destination drive.

Once you have made your selections, click the Start button to begin the backup; a small progress indicator tracks the backup as it proceeds.

A time will come when you want a little more control over your backups, and that is when you stop using the Wizard and take charge of the process yourself. At the Welcome dialog box, rather than invoking the Wizard, click the Backup tab. Using the Backup program involves essentially the same tasks that the Backup Wizard does for you—selecting the files, deciding where to put them, and specifying how the backup should actually be made. Let's take a look.

TIP You must have the right permissions to make a backup or a restore. Make sure you are logged on as an administrator or as a backup operator if you are backing up files on a local computer. If you are not logged on as an administrator or backup operator, you must be the owner of the file or folders you want to back up, or you must have one or more of the following permissions: Read, Read and Execute, Modify, or Full Control.

Making a Manual Backup

If you have previously specified and saved a backup job, you can select it for use again using Job ➢ Load Selections. That done, all you have to do is click the Start Backup button to begin the backup.

If you don't have a previously saved backup job or if you want to do things a little differently this time, the first task is to decide which files to back up. You can back up all the files and folders selected in the Backup window, shown in Figure 27.4, or you can back up only files that have changed, along with any new files never before backed up.

FIGURE 27.4
The main Backup window

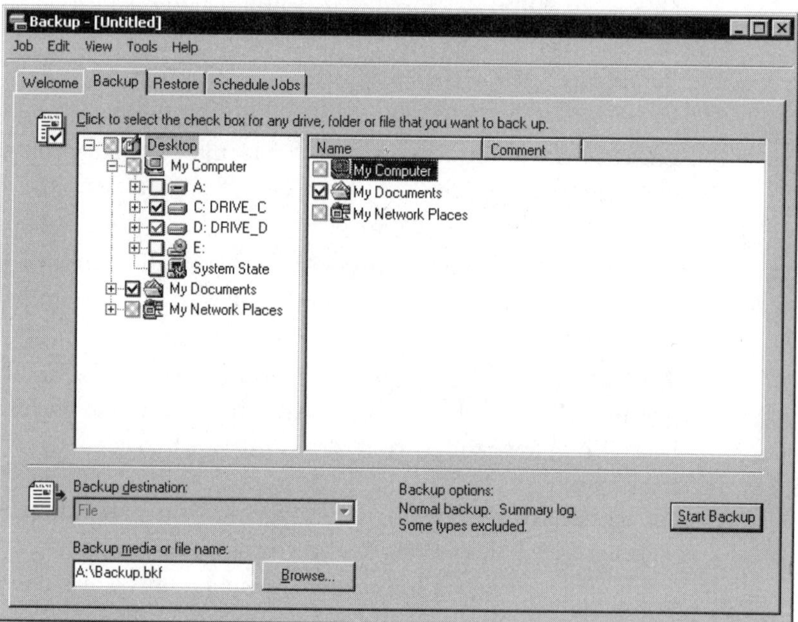

In the Backup window, check the box next to the files and folders you want to back up. A blue checkmark indicates that the folder or file is selected for backup; a gray checkmark indicates that some of the files in the folder or on the drive have been selected for backup.

The next task is to select the destination device or drive for the backup and to name the backup file itself. Use the Backup Destination list below the main window to select the destination, and the Backup Media Or File Name box to specify a name for this backup.

The last part of the process is to review the backup configuration settings. Choose Tools ➢ Options to open the Options dialog box shown in Figure 27.5.

FIGURE 27.5
The Options dialog box

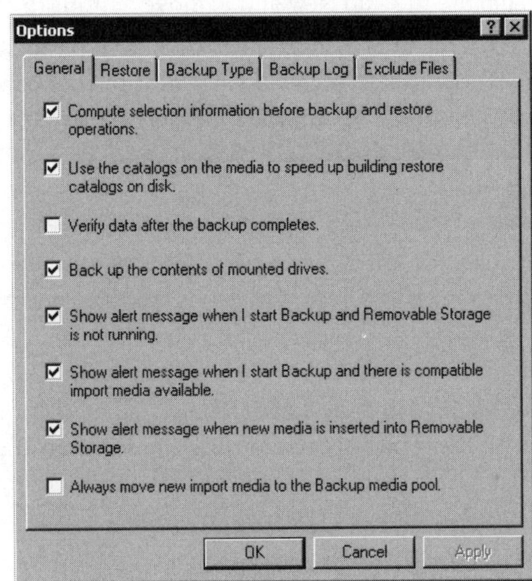

Across the top of the Options dialog box you will see the following tabs:

General Lets you specify that the backed-up data are compared against the original files to ensure the data were properly backed up. You can also specify how data compression is performed and how you want the Backup program to respond if it finds that the medium (tape, disk, or CD) you are using already contains a backup.

Restore Lets you specify what happens when duplicate files are found during a restore operation.

Backup Type Lets you choose how the backup is made:

> **Normal** Backs up all the selected files and clears the archive bit.
>
> **Copy** Backs up all the selected files but does not clear the archive bit.
>
> **Differential** Backs up all the selected files that changed since the last Normal or Incremental backup. When the backup is complete, the archive bit for each file is left on.
>
> **Incremental** Backs up all the selected files that have changed since the last Incremental or Normal backup. When the backup is complete, the archive bit for each file is turned off.
>
> **Daily** Backs up all the files that have been modified today.

Backup Log Lets you specify the elements you want to include in the backup log file.

Exclude Files Lets you specify file types that you want to exclude from this backup; use the Add New and Remove buttons to select files for exclusion.

All that remains is to click the Start Backup button to begin the backup. Keep the backup in a safe place, preferably not next to your computer; if your computer is damaged by the sprinklers going off by accident, there is a very good chance that the backup will be destroyed at the same time.

TIP Click the Schedule Jobs tab to specify the date for a backup.

Restoring a Backup

Most of the time, making a backup is a simple precaution, and you put it on the shelf along with the other tapes or Zip disks. But there will come a time, after a hard-disk controller failure perhaps, when you will need to restore a backup. Again, as when making the backup, you can use a Wizard, or you can do it manually.

Using the Restore Wizard

Using the Restore Wizard is a quick and easy way to learn about restoring backups; it gets you going quickly with the minimum of technical knowledge. To access this feature, click Restore Wizard. If you would rather not use the Wizard, click the Restore tab, which is described in the next section.

The Wizard walks you through a sequence of dialog boxes that specify the following:

What to Restore You can restore all files and folders in the backup set, or you can restore selected files and folders.

Restore From Specify the type and location of the backup you want to restore.

Select Backup Sets Select a backup set for the restore.

Where to Restore Specify the target of the restore; most of the time, selecting Original Location to put the file back where it came from makes the most sense.

How to Restore Specify whether existing files on your hard disk should be overwritten during the restore.

Click the Start Restore button to begin the restore; a small progress indicator tracks the restore as it proceeds.

Using the Restore Tab

Using the Restore tab in the Backup program involves essentially the same tasks that the Restore Wizard does for you—selecting the files, deciding where to put them, and specifying how the restore should actually be made. A checkmark in a gray check box means that only some of the files in a folder have been selected. A checkmark in a white box means that all files in a folder have been selected.

Summary

This chapter introduced you to some of the vital skills needed for troubleshooting Windows 2000 Professional when things go wrong. I discussed how to avoid Windows 2000 Professional crashes, which is the best troubleshooting technique of all, and how to restore a configuration. I then introduced you to Recovery Console, a tool that is new in Windows 2000 Professional. Following that, we took a look at the Driver Verifier, the System File Checker, and the Registry entry that lets you force a core dump. Fixing Windows is no fun, but at least now you have an idea of how to go about it. You also know why it's important to back up your files, you know how to back up, and you know how to restore.

CHAPTER 28

Administrative and Diagnostic Tools

FEATURING:

Windows 2000 Professional comes with new administrative tools for you to use when you add new disk volumes and check on existing ones, track system events, watch system performance, and run general diagnostics. Let's take a look at these tools and how they can help you keep your system running smoothly.

Running Disk Management

In Windows NT, you use the Disk Administrator tool to manage disk partitions and handle all your formatting chores. In Windows 2000 Professional, the corresponding tool is Disk Management, which is part of the Computer Management console in Administrative Tools. To open Disk Management, follow these steps:

1. Choose Start ➢ Settings ➢ Control Panel to open Control Panel.
2. Click Administrative Tools, and then click Computer Management to open the Computer Management window.
3. In the Tree pane, expand Storage, and then click the Disk Management folder. You'll see something similar to the following:

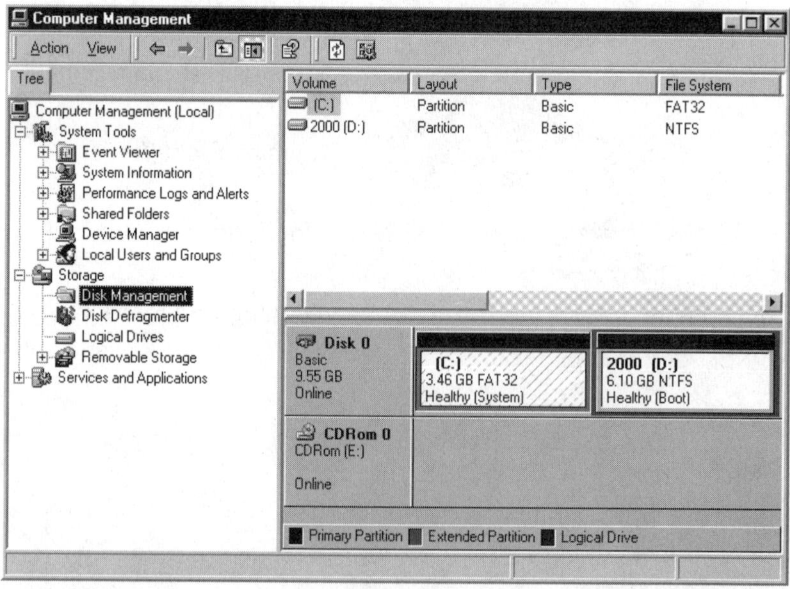

The Disk Management tool, which is displayed in the right pane of the Computer Management window, gives you a graphical representation of the hard disks and CD-ROM devices in your computer. You can, however, customize the way information is presented in a variety of ways.

TIP If you will be using the Administrative Tools frequently, place this group on the Programs menu. To do so, choose Start ➢ Settings ➢ Taskbar & Start Menu to open the Taskbar And Start Menu Properties dialog box. Click the Advanced tab, and in the Start Menu Settings list, click the Display Administrative Tools check box, and then click OK.

The Disk Management window is in three parts. On the left is the Tree pane of the Computer Management console. The lower-right pane contains the information for all the physical disks installed in the computer, excluding floppy drives. The upper-right pane contains descriptions of those disks, including data on the amount of space used and free, the type of file system, and the health of that system.

To use Disk Management to create or delete partitions, format drives, and create stripe or volume sets, simply click the disk that you want to modify, and select the change that you want to make from the Action menu. Or, you can right-click the drive that you want to modify, and then select the appropriate action from the shortcut menu.

Deciding Which File System Is Best

Windows 2000 Professional can use the File Allocation Table (FAT) file system supported by DOS and Windows 95/98, the File Allocation Table 32 (FAT32) file system supported by Windows 95/98, and the New Technology File System (NTFS) supported by Windows NT. Each has its respective upsides and downsides. Here's a quick rundown.

FAT's main advantage is its backward compatibility with DOS and with Windows 95/98 systems using FAT. FAT's main disadvantage is that it's a 16-bit file system with a minimum cluster size of 32KB. The result is that FAT can address partitions only up to 2GB. If your drive is larger than this, you'll have to create two partitions to use FAT. Also, FAT has no security features. As a positive note, under Windows NT, the FAT file system has a maximum file and partition size of 4GB.

The FAT32 file system evolved from the traditional FAT file system used by DOS and Windows. This file system also allows for much larger volumes—it supports volumes of as much as 16GB in size—with smaller cluster sizes than FAT, yet it doesn't support as large a volume size as NTFS. Another downside to FAT32 is that, like FAT, it does not provide any local security.

In contrast, NTFS is a robust, 32-bit file system with many security features, including password protection for specific files, the capability to limit access to specific files, file compression, file recovery, and the capability to address very large partitions. Although a system using NTFS will run a bit slower than one using FAT in some cases, NTFS is your best bet if you want the additional features of Windows 2000 Professional.

To add another twist, Windows 2000 Professional provides support for usage quotas on NTFS partitions. To use the quota systems, you must have upgraded your NTFS from the version supported in Windows NT 4 to the version of NTFS that is provided by Windows 2000 Professional.

NOTE If you dual-boot Windows 2000 Professional formatted with NTFS and another operating system formatted with FAT or FAT32, Windows 2000 Professional can read the FAT and FAT32 files, but the other system will not be able to read NTFS files. The same is true of a network. If one machine uses NTFS and another uses FAT or FAT32, the NTFS machine will be able to read FAT and FAT32 files, but the FAT and FAT32 machine will not be able to read files on the NTFS machine.

Using File Compression in NTFS

One cool feature of the NTFS file system is its compression capability. Windows 2000 Professional can compress entire volumes, individual subfolders (also called subdirectories), and files. The compression ratio usually winds up being about 1.5:1, or 33 percent. For example, Windows 2000 Professional would compress a 100MB file to about 67MB. Generally, it's better not to compress files that contain multimedia data because more often than not, they're already using their own compression algorithm. Also, because multimedia files are played back in real time (at a specified data rate rather than as fast as possible), the added overhead of NTFS decompression may adversely affect audio or video quality, causing breaks in the audio or frames to be skipped in the video.

Database files are probably also best left uncompressed because decompressing the database each time you run a query on it will slow performance.

NTFS compression is great for files that you need to keep around but don't access often. It's also good for files you access regularly if you don't mind a slight performance hit because of the extra hard-disk real estate you gain.

To compress an NTFS file or folder, follow these steps:

1. In Explorer, right-click the file or folder you want to compress, and choose Properties from the shortcut menu to open the Properties dialog box for that file or folder.
2. On the General tab, click the Advanced button to open the Advanced Attributes dialog box:

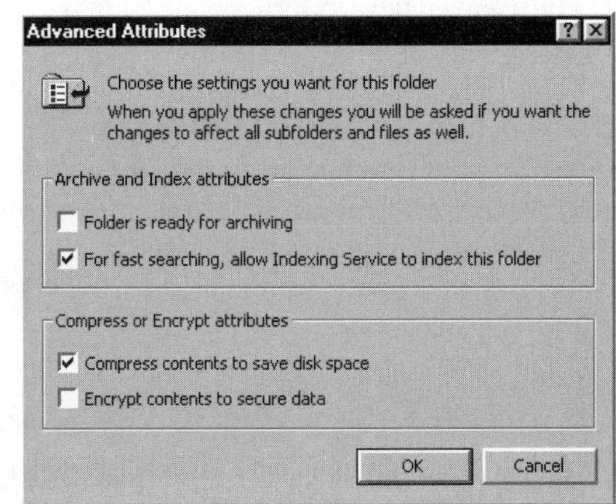

3. Click the Compress Contents To Save Disk Space check box, and then click OK.

The next time you use the file or folder, it will automatically be uncompressed.

To compress an NTFS hard-disk volume, follow these steps:

1. On the Desktop, open My Computer.
2. Right-click the volume you want to compress, and choose Properties from the shortcut menu to open the Properties dialog box for that drive:

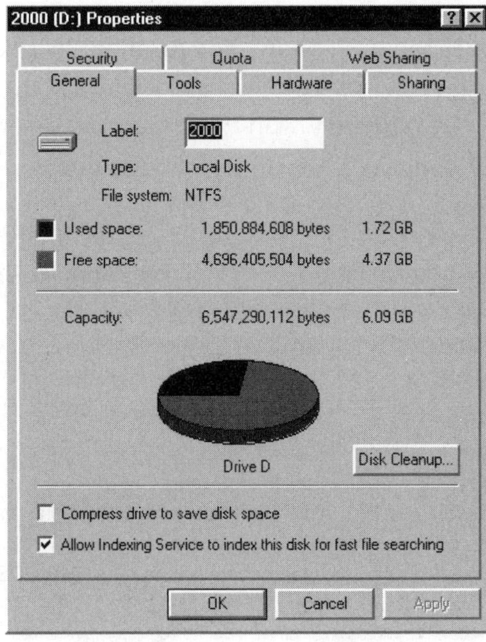

3. On the General tab, click the Compress Drive To Save Disk Space check box, and then click OK.

Using NTFS File Security Features

NTFS file security lets you change settings for disk drives, folders, and even files. These features can be useful if your machine stores many files that you share with other users on your network as well as your private files.

For information on how to set permissions for NTFS drives, folders, and files, see Chapter 18.

Setting Up a New Disk Drive in Windows 2000 Professional

If you've added a new disk drive to your system, Disk Management will be able to see it, but you'll need to create a partition and a volume on it before Windows 2000 Professional can use it.

NOTE After you create a partition on a new disk and format it, you can use it in Windows 2000 Professional without rebooting. The new dynamic volumes in Windows 2000 Professional will even let you change the size of a partition or extend it across several hard drives without rebooting.

Let's step through adding a new partition and creating a volume on a new disk:

1. In the Disk Management window, select the new disk, and choose Action ➢ Create Partition to start the Create Partition Wizard.
2. Select the type of partition you want to create, either primary or extended. By default, Windows 2000 Professional assigns all available space on a disk to its primary partition. To create other extended partitions on the disk, set the size of the primary partition smaller. For example, you've added a 1GB hard drive, and you want to create two 500MB partitions. Select 500MB as the size for your primary partition. This leaves the other 500MB of space free for an extended partition that you'd create later.

NOTE Windows 2000 Professional supports a maximum of four "basic" partitions per hard drive. Windows 2000 Professional supports only one extended partition per drive, but it allows as many as four primary partitions. Basic partitions are the same as traditional partition types found under earlier versions of NT or MS-DOS. The new dynamic volumes allow as many logical volumes per disk as you want.

3. After setting the partition size, click OK. The primary partition has now been created.
4. To format the new partition, click the drive and select Format from the Action menu.
5. Select the type of file system you want to use—FAT, FAT32, or NTFS. Remember, FAT will give you somewhat better speed performance but with limited volume size; NTFS enables you to use Windows 2000 Professional file compression, security features, and file recovery.
6. After selecting the file system, you can enable/disable the QuickFormat feature. Disabling QuickFormat tells Windows 2000 Professional to first scan the partition for bad sectors. If you know the disk is free of bad sectors, go ahead and QuickFormat it. If you're not sure, it's better to have Windows 2000 Professional scan for bad sectors. It will take considerably longer than a QuickFormat but could save you trouble up the road.
7. Click OK. When Windows 2000 Professional asks you to confirm your choice, click OK again. Windows 2000 Professional begins the formatting process. The time depends on the type of format and the partition size.
8. When formatting is complete, Windows 2000 Professional assigns a drive letter to the new volume, and you can begin using it.

WARNING You can apply the `Set Active` command to a newly created partition. Use this command *only* if you want your machine to boot from this new partition.

Creating Extended Partitions and Logical Drives

The main difference between a primary partition and an extended partition is that you can create multiple logical drives only on an extended partition. So what's a logical drive? Simply put, a logical drive is a designated portion of a physical drive. Windows 2000 Professional is aware of two kinds of drives, physical and logical. A physical drive is the actual drive itself, and Windows 2000 Professional can create partitions on it and format it. You can create a logical drive on an extended partition that may be only part of a physical disk, but Windows 2000 Professional will see that logical drive as a separate unit, and you can map a drive letter to it.

Let's say you've added a 2GB hard disk to a dual-boot system, and you have created a 1GB primary partition and formatted it using FAT (so that Windows 98 can see it). You've decided to make an extended partition, using the remainder of the hard drive (1GB). You've also decided to create two logical drives that will use the NTFS file system. The steps that follow take you through creating an extended partition and logical drives.

NOTE Only extended partitions can contain logical disk volumes.

1. Right-click the portion of the new hard drive labeled Free Space or select the region labeled Free Space, and from the Action menu, choose Create Partition. In the Create Partition Wizard, select Extended as the partition type. If DOS clients aren't going to be able to access the newly created partition, Windows 2000 Professional will warn you of this fact and verify that you want to continue. Click OK. Windows 2000 Professional now creates your new extended partition.
2. Next, right-click the newly created extended partition—or select the region labeled Free Space—and from the Partition menu, choose Create Partition again.
3. Windows 2000 Professional now prompts you for the size of the logical drive, defaulting to using all available space—1024MB. For our example, we'll create two 512MB logical drives, one at a time; so specify the size of the logical drive as 512MB and click OK. Windows 2000 Professional now creates the logical drive and assigns it the next sequentially available drive letter.
4. Right-click the new logical drive (or click the Partition menu) and select Commit Changes Now. This step is necessary before you can format the drive. Windows 2000 Professional saves your disk information to the hard drive on which the operating system is installed and then advises you to update the Emergency Repair Disk you created during initial installation. More on that later.
5. To format the newly created logical drive, right-click it (or click the Action menu) and select Format. Windows 2000 Professional prompts for which file system you'd like to use. Select NTFS and leave the QuickFormat box unchecked.
6. Windows 2000 Professional now scans for bad sectors and then begins formatting. When the format is complete, Windows 2000 Professional displays a window with disk and volume space information.
7. To create the second logical drive, repeat steps 2 through 6.

TIP If you want to create an Emergency Repair Disk (ERD) outside of Disk Management, open Administrative Tools and run Backup. Windows 2000 Backup includes a Wizard that will enable you to create a new ERD.

Creating Striped and Spanned Volumes

Windows 2000 Professional can create large volumes that span several hard drives, which can be useful if you work with large amounts of data. Windows 2000 Professional can also create a *striped volume,* which consists of two or more disks "striped" together; stripe sets let you access large data files faster. In other words, when you tell an application to write to disk, data is written to all disks in the stripe set simultaneously, with each one receiving part of the file. The result is faster throughput for both reads and writes.

NOTE You may have heard the term RAID, which stands for Redundant Array of Inexpensive Disks. RAID technology is usually used only on servers that process a great deal of data or that get many data requests from many users. There are different RAID levels, and each has its benefits and liabilities. The Windows 2000 Professional striped volume is considered RAID 0—data is striped across at least two drives. The benefit is increased performance. The liability is added risk: If one of the drives fails, the *entire* volume will be lost if it hasn't been backed up. Also, most file servers have hardware RAID disk controllers, but Windows 2000 Professional's implementation of RAID 0 is done in "software." Your CPU, therefore, has to do the work of splitting and reassembling files that are read from or written to the striped volume.

TIP Disk striping is the fastest partitioning scheme available in Windows 2000 Professional. It can use either FAT or NTFS but cannot contain the system or boot partition. In addition, in Windows 2000 Professional, striped volumes can only be created on dynamic disks.

Windows 2000 Professional can also create a *spanned volume*, which groups several formatted disks to create a single, larger volume that Windows 2000 Professional sees as one unit. This technique is more commonly known as *spanning* of disks or parts of disks. For example, it offers the advantage of letting you create a single, very large data drive for general storage rather than having to use each drive individually. The drives or drive parts you're including should contain no partition information and should read Free Space. Here's how to create a volume set:

1. In Control Panel, click Administrative Tools, and then click Computer Management to open the Computer Management window.
2. Expand Storage, and then click the Disk Management folder.
3. Hold down the Ctrl key, and select the drives or parts of drives you want to include in the new volume set.
4. Next, choose Action ➢ Create Volume Set.
5. Windows 2000 Professional asks for the volume set size. If you decide you want the size to be less than the sum total of the included drives, Windows 2000 Professional will try to distribute the volume set evenly across its member drives.
6. To format the new volume set partition, choose Partition ➢ Commit Changes Now.

7. Next, right-click the volume set (or click the Action menu) and select Format. Windows 2000 Professional prompts for which file system you'd like to use. Select NTFS and leave the QuickFormat box unchecked. Windows 2000 Professional now formats the new volume set. Depending on the volume set size, this process may take some time.
8. To save these new changes to your configuration, run the Windows Backup utility to create a new ERD.

Creating a striped volume is similar to creating a spanned volume, but there is a consideration: if you dual-boot your system, you won't be able to see this striped volume when running Windows 3.1 or Windows 95/98. Here's how to create a striped volume:

1. The drives or drive parts you're including should contain no partition information. They should read Free Space.
2. Hold down the Ctrl key and select the drives or parts of drives you want to include in the new striped volume.
3. Next, from the Action menu, choose Create Striped Volume.
4. Windows 2000 Professional asks for the striped volume size. If you decide you want the striped volume size to be less than the sum total of the included drives, Windows 2000 Professional will try to distribute the striped volume evenly across its member drives.
5. To format the new volume set partition, from the Partition menu, select Commit Changes Now.
6. Next, select the striped volume and right-click it (or click the Action menu) and select Format. Windows 2000 Professional asks which file system you'd like to use. Select NTFS and leave the QuickFormat box unchecked. Windows 2000 Professional will now format the new striped volume. Depending on the striped volume size, this process may take some time.
7. To save these new changes to your configuration, run the Windows Backup utility and create a new ERD.

TIP A Windows 2000 Professional striped volume is non-fault-tolerant: if one drive goes south, the whole stripe set is history. Be sure to back up stripe sets regularly.

Using Dynamic Volumes

Dynamic volumes are a new concept in Windows 2000 Professional. Traditional partition types stored their information in a *partition table* that was located in the first physical sector of the hard disk. It was this location and its limited storage space for partition information that limited us to four partitions per physical disk. The partition table stores information for the size and location of each partition and is used to find the bootable partition during the startup procedure.

Dynamic volumes store their partition information in the data portion of the drive, and thus they are not limited in the amount of information they can store. To convert a basic disk to a dynamic disk, right-click the disk in the Disk Management tool, and select Dynamic from the shortcut menu. You will have to reboot to perform the conversion. After the restart, you will be able to create or modify dynamic volumes on the disk, including expanding the volume across multiple disks.

Dynamic volumes come in various flavors:

Simple A simple dynamic volume is similar to a traditional partition in that it exists on a single drive. It can be resized by extending the volume if it is on a dynamic disk that was created as a dynamic disk and not upgraded from a basic disk.

Spanned This dynamic volume spans two or more disks to create one logical volume, as its name implies, but it can be extended. Spanned volumes are the same as volume sets in NT 4, but in Windows 2000 Professional they are only available on dynamic disks.

Mirrored This volume type is only available on Windows 2000 Server. Mirrored volumes provide fault tolerance by keeping an exact mirror image of all data in the volume. If you lose one disk, you still have an exact copy of all the data.

Striped Striped volumes are the fastest type of dynamic volume and yield great benefits in performance. They are not fault tolerant, however. If you lose one disk, you lose all the data in the volume. They are the same as the traditional stripe sets available in NT, but stripe volumes are only available in Windows 2000 Professional on dynamic disks.

RAID 5 This type of dynamic volume is only available in Windows 2000 Server. RAID 5 is also known as striping with parity. RAID 5 allows the volume to lose one hard disk without failing. It does this by combining the remaining data with the parity information to recreate the data on the fly.

Running Event Viewer

One of Windows 2000 Professional's more handy tools is the Event Viewer, which can be helpful for troubleshooting a misbehaving PC, or for getting a better handle on what Windows 2000 Professional is doing behind the scenes. To open Event Viewer, follow these steps:

1. Choose Start ➢ Settings ➢ Control Panel to open Control Panel.
2. Click Administrative Tools, and then click Event Viewer.

3. In the Tree pane, select Application Log, Security Log, or System Log. If you select System Log, you'll see something similar to the following:

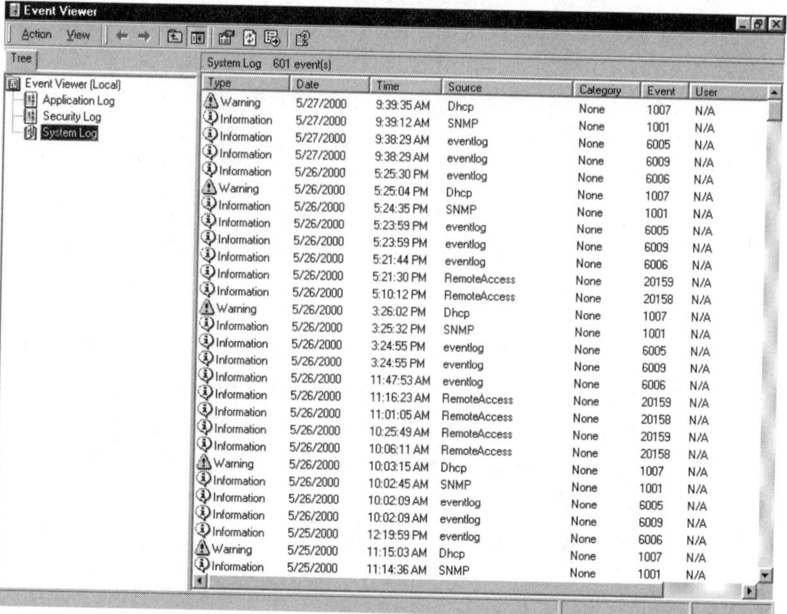

Type	Date	Time	Source	Category	Event	User
Warning	5/27/2000	9:39:35 AM	Dhcp	None	1007	N/A
Information	5/27/2000	9:39:12 AM	SNMP	None	1001	N/A
Information	5/27/2000	9:38:29 AM	eventlog	None	6005	N/A
Information	5/27/2000	9:38:29 AM	eventlog	None	6009	N/A
Information	5/26/2000	5:25:30 PM	eventlog	None	6006	N/A
Warning	5/26/2000	5:25:04 PM	Dhcp	None	1007	N/A
Information	5/26/2000	5:24:35 PM	SNMP	None	1001	N/A
Information	5/26/2000	5:23:59 PM	eventlog	None	6005	N/A
Information	5/26/2000	5:23:59 PM	eventlog	None	6009	N/A
Information	5/26/2000	5:21:44 PM	eventlog	None	6006	N/A
Information	5/26/2000	5:21:30 PM	RemoteAccess	None	20159	N/A
Information	5/26/2000	5:10:12 PM	RemoteAccess	None	20158	N/A
Warning	5/26/2000	3:26:02 PM	Dhcp	None	1007	N/A
Information	5/26/2000	3:25:32 PM	SNMP	None	1001	N/A
Information	5/26/2000	3:24:55 PM	eventlog	None	6005	N/A
Information	5/26/2000	3:24:55 PM	eventlog	None	6009	N/A
Information	5/26/2000	11:47:53 AM	eventlog	None	6006	N/A
Information	5/26/2000	11:16:23 AM	RemoteAccess	None	20159	N/A
Information	5/26/2000	11:01:05 AM	RemoteAccess	None	20158	N/A
Information	5/26/2000	10:25:49 AM	RemoteAccess	None	20159	N/A
Information	5/26/2000	10:06:11 AM	RemoteAccess	None	20158	N/A
Warning	5/26/2000	10:03:15 AM	Dhcp	None	1007	N/A
Information	5/26/2000	10:02:45 AM	SNMP	None	1001	N/A
Information	5/26/2000	10:02:09 AM	eventlog	None	6005	N/A
Information	5/26/2000	10:02:09 AM	eventlog	None	6009	N/A
Information	5/25/2000	12:19:59 PM	eventlog	None	6006	N/A
Warning	5/25/2000	11:15:03 AM	Dhcp	None	1007	N/A
Information	5/25/2000	11:14:36 AM	SNMP	None	1001	N/A

System events are logged by Windows 2000 Professional's system components, including hardware drivers. For example, if a driver fails to load, it will write a system event to the System Log. Or if a Windows 2000 Professional service fails to initialize, the service reports its failure in the System Log. There are three types of System Log events:

Information Logged when a driver or service starts successfully and indicated by the blue letter *i*. For example, each time you boot up Windows 2000 Professional, a system event is logged, indicating that the Event Log service was started.

Warning Logged when a condition occurs that could mean future trouble, for example, a nearly full hard drive. Indicated by an exclamation point in a yellow triangle.

Error Logged when a service or a driver fails to start or load and indicated by an X in a red circle. For example, if your network card driver fails, that error is logged, as is an error indicating that any network protocols communicating with that network card have failed.

Security events occur if you've enabled auditing on a shared disk, subfolder, or file. Audited events are written to the Security Log when someone accesses your shared area and logs in. An administrator can specify which events are logged into the Security Log. There are two types of Security Log events:

Success Logged when a user successfully logs on to one of your shared areas: a disk, a subfolder, or a file.

Failure Logged when a user fails to log on to one of your shared areas.

Windows 2000 Professional applications write status and error messages in the Application Log. If an application is crashing or behaving oddly, it's usually a good idea to check the Application Log for error messages. The Application Log uses the same three event types as the System Log: Information, Warning, and Error. Application developers specify which events to log.

Each time you boot Windows 2000 Professional, it runs CHKDSK (CheckDisk) on the volume containing the system files and logs the report to the Application Log. The event is called Autochk.

With Event Viewer, you can look at only one event log at a time. To change views, select the log you want to see.

TIP When opening old log files, be careful not to confuse them with your system's actual logs. The system log files live in the C:\Winnt\System32\Config subfolder. If you open a log other than one of your system's three primary logs, its name will be displayed in the title bar of the Event Viewer window. Each time you open Event Viewer, it loads the system's three event logs.

For any of your three logs, Event Viewer supports two viewing modes: All Records and Filter. The default view is the All Records view. In this view, you see all the events currently stored in a log. To view only specific events, follow these steps:

1. Choose View ➢ Filter to open the Properties dialog box for the log you are viewing.
2. Click the Filter tab:

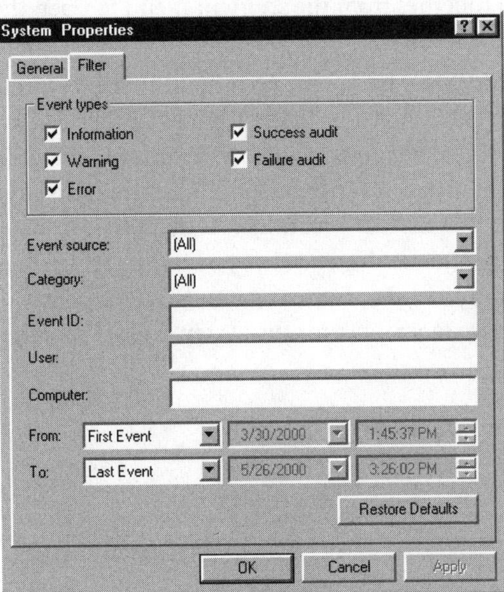

3. Select the types of events, their source, category, and so on, and then click OK.

If a hardware device isn't loading or is behaving oddly, one of the first places to look for the cause is the Event Viewer because a misbehaving device will likely document its problems in the System Log. And even though Warning and Error events are sometimes short on specifics, they can often be good indicators of where to begin looking. Here's what a troubleshooting session might look like.

On start-up, the driver for a Sound Blaster card fails to initialize; the result is a lack of wave audio in Windows 2000 Professional. The first indicator you get is a message like the one below informing you that at least one Windows 2000 Professional service failed to start.

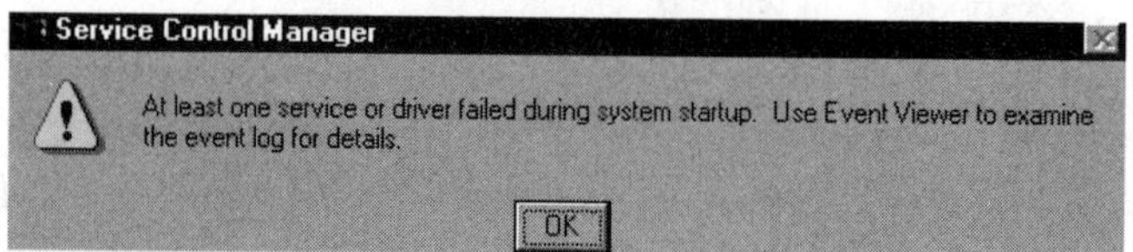

Upon opening Event Viewer, you'd see an Error event in the System Log reported by Windows 2000 Professional's Service Control Manager. After clicking it, you'd see the message "The following boot-start or system-start driver(s) failed to load: sndblst." Although this somewhat terse message doesn't provide any specifics from Event Viewer, you could then check your Sound Blaster driver's status by following these steps:

1. Right-click My Computer, and choose Properties from the shortcut menu to open the System Properties dialog box.
2. Click the Hardware tab, and then click the Device Manager button to open Device Manager.
3. Expand Sound, Video And Game Controllers, right-click Sound Blaster, choose Properties from the shortcut menu to open the Properties dialog box, and check the settings.

Event Viewer has a few other handy features to check out. From the Action menu, you can clear all events from all three logs. Be careful here, however. Although Windows 2000 Professional will issue a warning, there's no Undo for clearing the logs. If you think you want to access event information contained in the logs, save them as backups in a different subfolder so that you can access them later if need be.

To change the size of a log or overwrite its settings, right-click the log, and choose Properties from the shortcut menu to open the log's Properties dialog box. Figure 28.1 shows the General tab for the System Log's Properties dialog box.

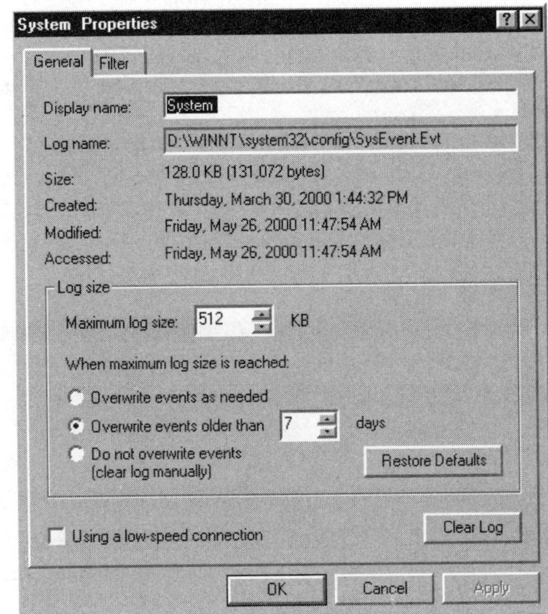

FIGURE 28.1
You can change log settings in the log's Properties dialog box.

Log size can be anywhere from 64KB on up (the default is 512KB). Windows 2000 Professional defaults to overwriting events more than seven days old; so if your network administrator wants to back up your event logs weekly, all events will be catalogued. This can pose a problem only if your system is generating an unusually large amount of log events—for example, an application or device isn't working properly or a network protocol stack is continuously issuing warning events.

If you're getting Event Log information about other computers (or they're getting Event Log information about your computer) on your network and if you are connected to that network via a modem, click the Using A Low-Speed Connection check box.

NOTE If you've set event overwriting to be cleared manually or have specified to overwrite events of a certain age, the Windows 2000 Professional System Log can fill up and can no longer be updated until you make more room in the log. If your system is having problems and can't update the System Log, diagnosing a problem may be more difficult. If your log file has filled, you can't re-enable event logging by increasing the logs' file sizes. You'll have to back up your logs, clear all events from them, and then increase the files' sizes.

WARNING Be careful to watch the size of logs as they grow. If you have set the logs to never overwrite and they fill up, Windows 2000 Professional may hang. If you are auditing for security events, the recommended setting is to never overwrite because security events should be documented over long periods of time. Clearing and archiving the log should be a part of routine maintenance.

Using the View menu in Event Viewer, you can sort events chronologically, listing either the oldest or the newest events first. To find a specific event, choose View ➢ Find to open the Find In Local System dialog box:

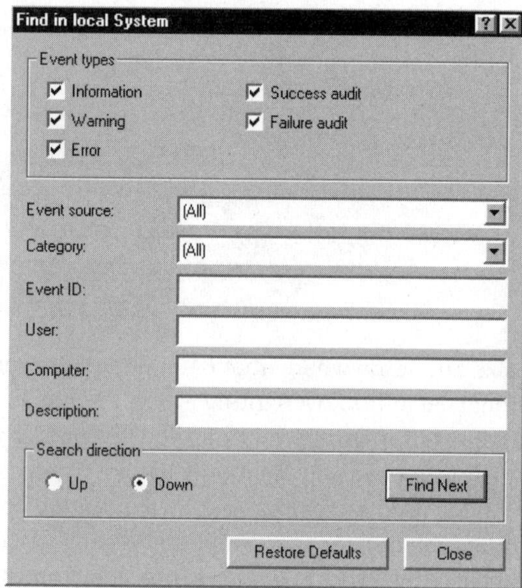

This feature essentially duplicates the Filter function, except that Event Viewer's Find displays, one by one, events that fit a certain description rather than listing them all at once.

To modify the display in Event Viewer, choose View ➢ Customize to open the Customize View dialog box:

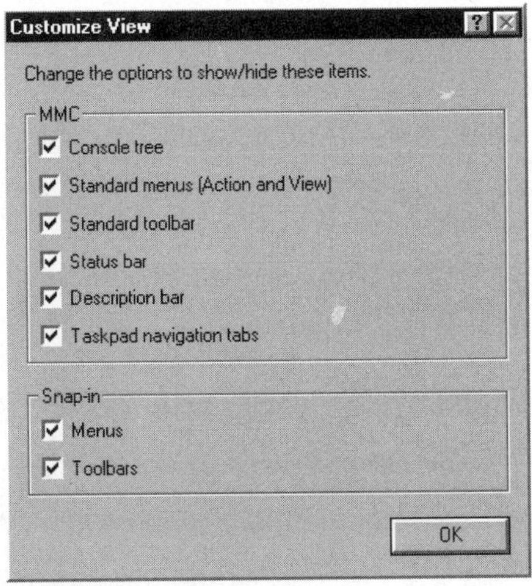

Click or clear a check box to show or hide an item.

Monitoring Performance

Windows 2000 Professional is designed to "self-tune" for optimal performance but also provides several tools for detecting possible performance bottlenecks. You can use the Windows 2000 Professional Performance console to monitor and log the performance of hundreds of variables, including some very esoteric ones intended to be used by developers and network administrators when tracking application and system behavior. In addition to tracking performance on your system, you can track performance counters on other Windows 2000 Professional machines on your network. We'll take a look at the Performance console and some of its components. Rather than cover every variable counter you can assign in Performance, we'll look at about a dozen or so key counters that deliver the most relevant system information.

NOTE If you want only a quick read on Windows 2000 Professional "vitals," right-click the Taskbar and select Task Manager from the shortcut menu. Though not new to Windows 2000 Professional, Task Manager has many added features, including a Performance tab that reports CPU usage and memory statistics. Task Manager also lists applications you have open, as well as processes that are running (those created by programs and Windows 2000 Professional services). Task Manager is discussed in detail at the end of this chapter.

To open the Performance console, in Control Panel click Administrative tools, and then click Performance. Figure 28.2 shows the Performance console.

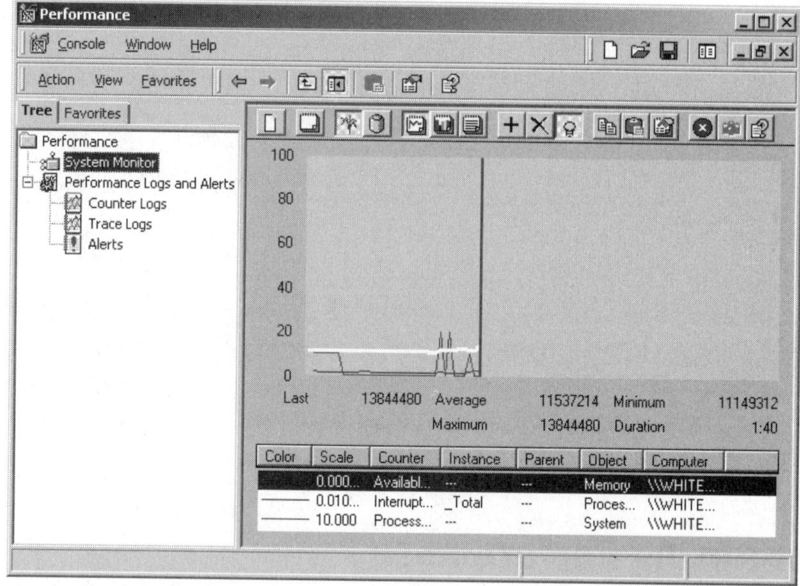

FIGURE 28.2
The System Monitor in the Performance console delivers constantly updated information about the performance of subsystems, and it can update its display dozens of times a second.

Performance provides three views of real-time data in System Monitor. To access one of these views, click the corresponding button on the toolbar. (To display a button's label, simply place the cursor over it.) The three views are simply different displays of the data that Performance can report. Here's a quick rundown:

View Chart Displays counters graphically. You can add as many counters as you like, although more than about a half-dozen makes for a rather cluttered graph.

View Histogram Displays bar graphs that dynamically update as the data changes.

View Report Displays counters in real time (as Chart view does). Selected counters are listed and their values are updated at a specified rate.

Before getting into detail about each of these views, let's look at some counters you're most likely to monitor.

Windows 2000 Professional classifies its subsystem components into objects, and each object has anywhere from two to more than a dozen counters that you can monitor. In addition, certain objects—such as processors, physical disks, and logical disks—also have instances because your Windows 2000 Professional system may have more than one of these types of hardware.

To display an explanation of what any counter monitors, follow these steps:

1. Click the Add button on the toolbar (it has a plus sign) to open the Add Counters dialog box:

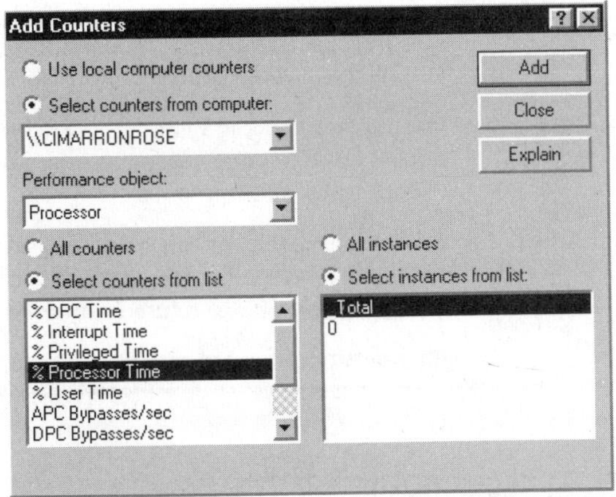

2. Select an object from the Performance Object drop-down list.
3. Select a counter from the Select Counters From List drop-down list.
4. Click the Explain button.

Obviously, you also use the Add Counters dialog box to specify which counters you want to monitor, and we'll look at how to do that shortly.

So without further ado, let's take a look at several objects and some of their counters. Tables 28.1, 28.2, 28.3, and 28.4 show you the counters, their functions, and their importance for four objects: the Paging File object, the Processor object, the Physical-Disk object, and the Server object. Before you can monitor disk performance, you need to enable the Disk Performance option. To do so, at the command prompt, type **DISKPERF -Y**. To turn off this feature, type **DISKPERF -N** at the command prompt.

TABLE 28.1: THE PAGING FILE (SWAP FILE) OBJECT

Counter	Importance
% Usage	A value that stays persistently high is one indicator that additional RAM would noticeably improve system performance, given the type of work you're doing.

TABLE 28.2: THE PROCESSOR OBJECT

Counter	Importance
% Processor Time	May indicate that an application or a service is using the CPU excessively, cutting into overall system performance.
% Interrupt Time	Interrupts execute in Windows 2000 Professional's kernel mode; applications execute in user mode. Excessive hardware interrupts can hamper overall system performance.
% Privileged Time	Similar to % Interrupt Time; if your system is spending excessive amounts of time in Privileged mode, applications, which all run in user mode, have to wait for the CPU to return to user mode to access the CPU.
% User Time	An indicator of how much CPU time applications have available to them.

TABLE 28.3: THE PHYSICALDISK OBJECT

Counter	Importance
Disk Read Bytes/sec	Gives a general indication of a disk's read performance.
Disk Write Bytes/sec	Gives a general indication of a disk's write performance.

TABLE 28.4: THE SERVER OBJECT

Counter	Importance
Bytes Total/sec	Excessive network access of your system by other users can drag down your overall performance.
Errors Logon	Repeated failed logon attempts may mean a password-guessing program is trying to crack into your system.
Sessions Timed Out	Useful for setting idle time-out values. Each active peer connection to your system slightly diminishes overall system performance.

Adding a Counter in Chart View

Performance defaults to Chart view, which graphically displays any selected counters. Let's go through the steps to add the Processor object and % Processor Time counter and the Paging File object and % Usage counter:

1. In the Performance console, select System Monitor, and click the Add button to open the Add Counters dialog box.
2. In the Performance Object drop-down list, select Processor.
3. In the Select Counter From List drop-down list, select %Processor Time, and then click Add.
4. In the Performance Object drop-down list, select Paging File.
5. In the Select Counter From List drop-down list, select %Usage, and then click Add.
6. Click Close.

Back in the Performance console, you'll see something similar to the following:

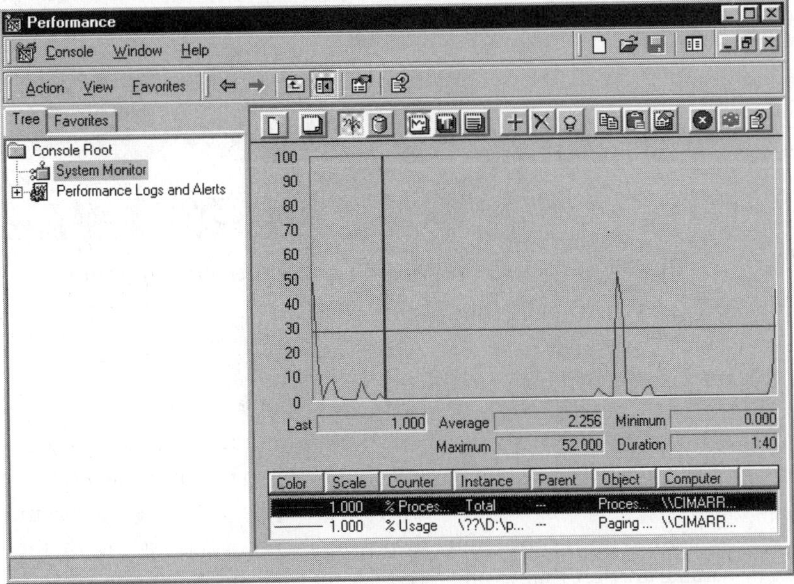

To save this view at any point in time, right-click the chart, choose Save As from the shortcut menu to open the Save As dialog box, give the file a name, and click Save. You can save the view as a Web page or as a report.

TIP To highlight a counter, select it at the bottom of the window, and press Ctrl+H.

To customize the chart's colors, fonts, and other graphical elements, follow these steps:

1. Right-click the chart, and choose Properties from the shortcut menu to open the System Monitor Properties dialog box:

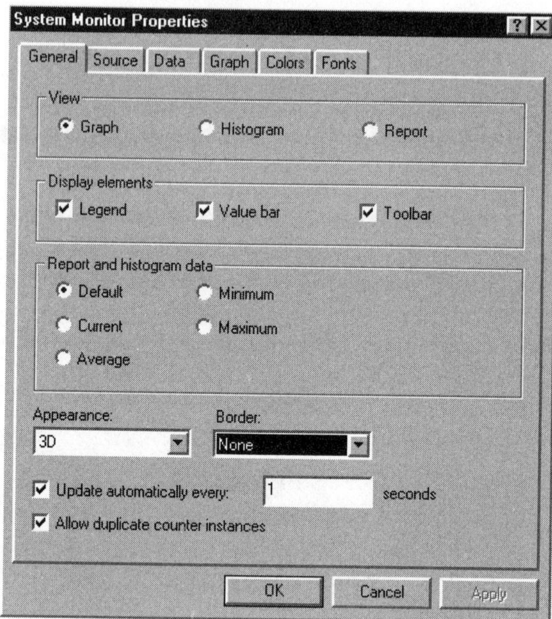

2. Click one of the six tabs, and then specify your options.
3. When you're finished, click OK.

Using Alerts

Alerts can be very useful when monitoring the computer system over a long period of time or when you have several computers to monitor. An alert is triggered when a condition you have selected occurs. For example, if you wanted to find out how often your CPU was being stressed by the normal level of activity throughout the day, you could make an alert that would trigger whenever the System object Processor Queue Length counter exceeded a count of two.

To set Alert counters, follow these steps:

1. In the Performance window, expand the Performance Logs And Alerts entry in the Tree pane, and then click Alerts.

2. Right-click in the right pane, and choose New Alert Settings from the shortcut menu to open the New Alert Settings dialog box:

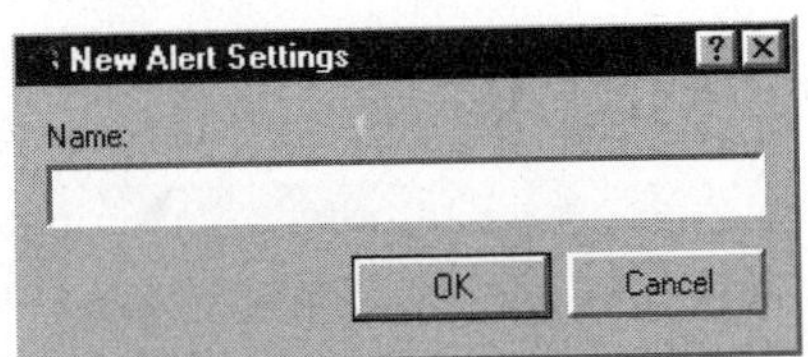

3. In the Name box, enter a name for this group of Alert settings, and then click OK to open the Properties dialog box for the new Alert group.
4. Enter a comment that describes the settings, and then click the Add button to open the Select Counters dialog box:

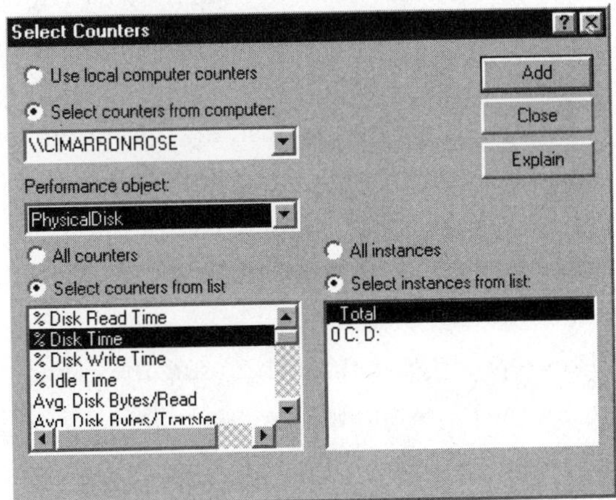

5. Select Use Local Computer Counters.
6. In the Performance Object drop-down list box, select an object.
7. In the Select Counters From List drop-down list box, select a counter, and then click Add.
8. When you're finished, click Close.
9. Back in the Properties dialog box, you can set a trigger using the Alert When The Value Is drop-down list box. Set a limit by entering a percentage in the Limit box.
10. Specify the frequency at which data is sampled using the Interval spin box and the Units drop-down list box.
11. Click OK.

To save this view of the Alert log, choose Action ➢ Save As.

NOTE You cannot set an alert for both over and under conditions on the same counter.

Using Counter Log View

Performance lets you track hundreds of counters in real time (as they happen), but often you may want to review system events one by one. To do this, you set Counter Logs to capture objects' counters to a file for later review. Let's step through logging Processor and Memory counters.

1. In the Tree pane of the Performance console, expand Performance Logs And Alerts.
2. Select Counter Logs, right-click in the right pane, and choose New Log Settings from the shortcut menu to open the New Log Settings dialog box.
3. Enter a name that will describe this log, and click OK to open the Properties dialog box for this log.
4. Click the Add button to open the Select Counters dialog box.
5. Click Use Local Computer Counters, and then select the Processor Performance Object.
6. Click the All Counters button to add all the counters for this object.
7. Click the Add button.
8. Now repeat steps 5 through 7 using the Memory object.
9. Click the Close button.
10. Click OK to close the Properties dialog and return to Performance.
11. Right-click the icon for the log settings you just created, and select Start from the shortcut menu to start the log. When you want to stop the log, right-click the icon again and select Stop from the shortcut menu.

WARNING Carefully watch the size of the log file as it grows. It is easy to gather enough data to fill a hard drive if left unattended for too long. When monitoring performance over a long period of time, it is more common to set the time interval to several minutes to avoid gathering too much data.

Viewing specific data points is a little tricky here because the timeframe "slider" controller works differently in each of the three views. Let's take a look at it. Follow these steps:

1. In the Performance console, select System Monitor, right-click in the right pane, and choose Properties from the shortcut menu to open the System Monitor Properties dialog box.
2. Click the Source tab:

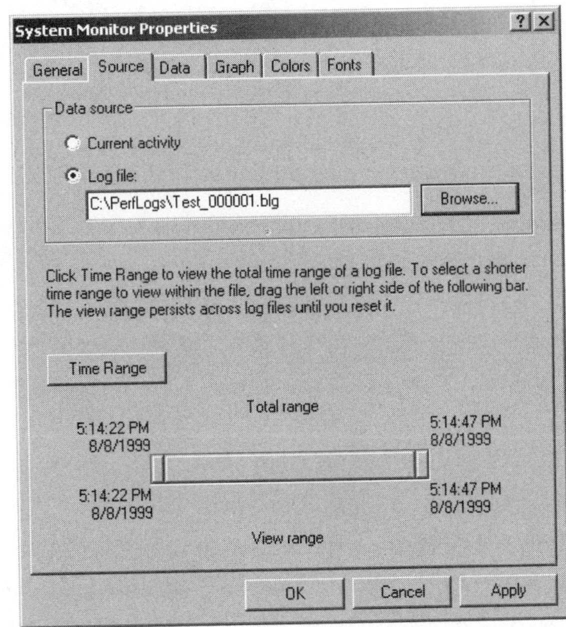

3. Click the Time Range button, and then set the beginning and ending time to view using the end handles on the slider bar.
4. Click OK.

Because Log view shows only one data point at a time, you can change the data point by using the Time Range slider to change the start point. After you click OK, you'll see a data point for that time value. This view is useful for zeroing in on data at an exact time, but it isn't very useful for looking at multiple data points.

Using Report View

Similar to Chart view, Report view shows up-to-the minute statistics on object counters but displays them numerically rather than graphically. If you want to watch many counters simultaneously, Report view is your best bet because Chart view gets to be a cluttered mess when you try to display too many counters simultaneously. To display counters in Report view, click the View Report button. You'll see something similar to the following:

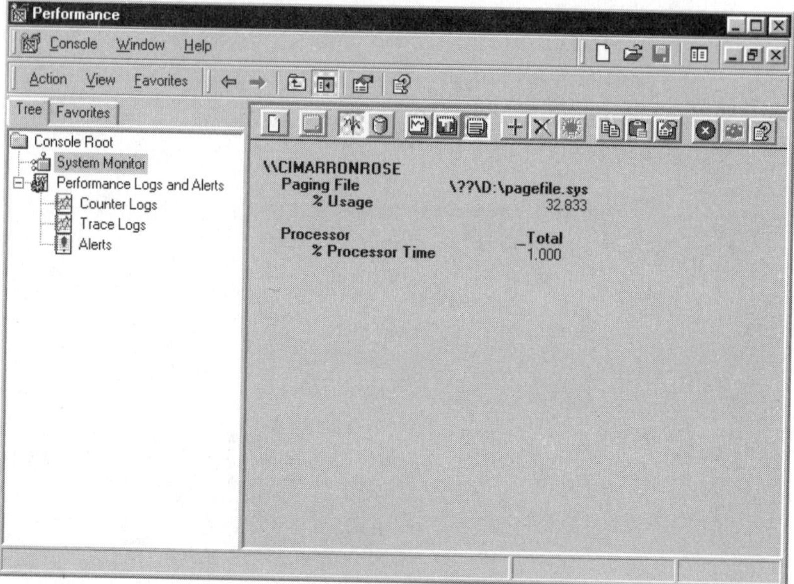

Running System Information

When everything on your system works, new devices install painlessly, and services work right the first time, life is good. If only it were always so. Alas, the general headaches of new hardware installation follow—cracking the box open, finding an available I/O slot, dealing with the mysterious force that makes your system's box much easier to rip open than it is to put back together... Then, after you restart the system, there may be I/O resource conflicts or services may fail for whatever reason. The fun never ends...

Fortunately, Windows 2000 Professional provides some tools to ease system troubleshooting. Chief among them is System Information, which you can use to display system information ranging from detailed display driver data to the services that are installed and the other services or devices on which they depend. To open System Information, follow these steps:

1. In Control Panel, click Administrative Tools, and then click Computer Management to open the Computer Management window.
2. In the Tree pane, expand System Information.

To display a lot of information about your system, click the System Summary folder. The pane on the right displays the version and build of Windows 2000 Professional you're running, your CPU type, a serial number, and registration information, as well as information ranging from the manufacturer on your system and its model number to the amount of memory free or the amount of page file in use. Figure 28.3 shows information about my system.

FIGURE 28.3
The System Summary folder displays local configuration details.

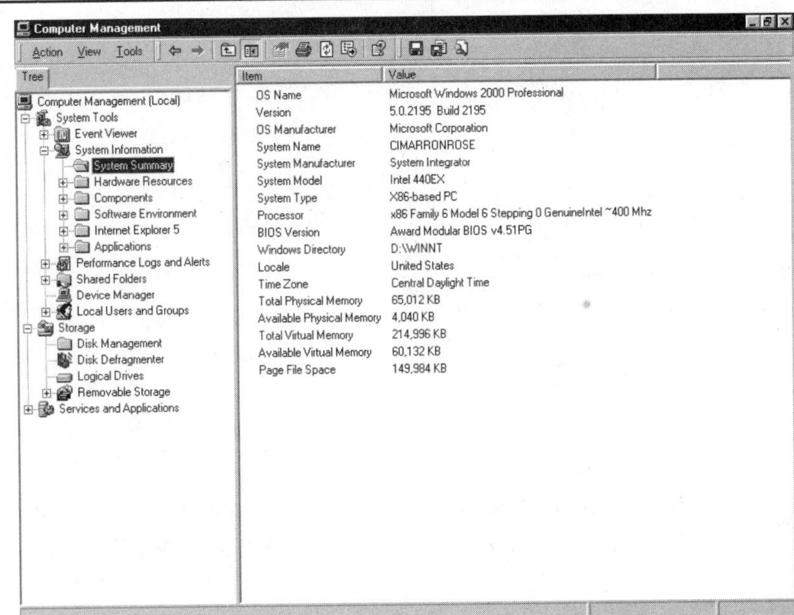

To view information on the hardware installed in your computer, expand the Components folder. For information about display hardware and drivers, click the Display folder. You'll see something similar to the following:

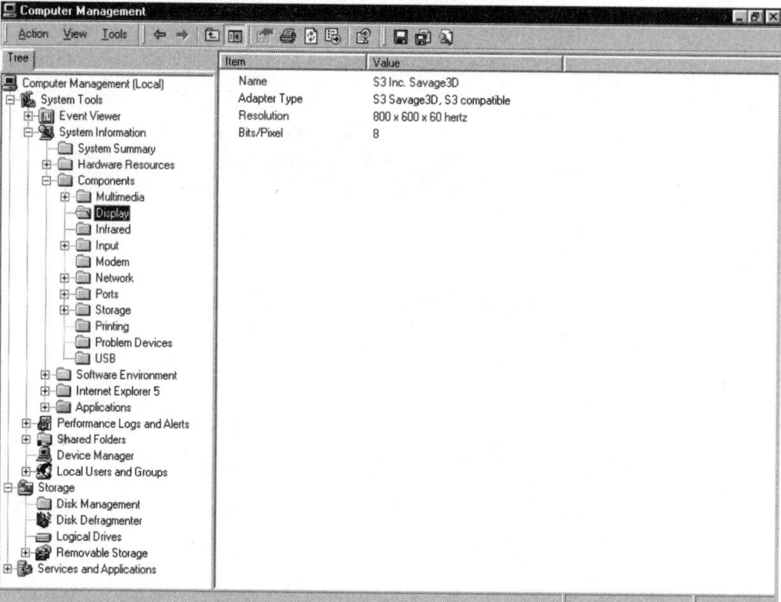

For information about the drives on your system, expand the Storage folder under System Information, and then click the Drives folder. You'll see something similar to the following:

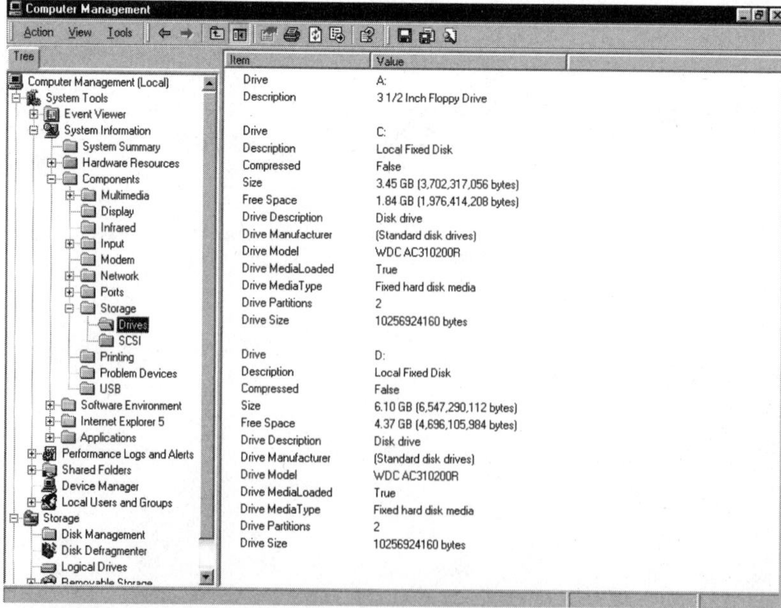

The Drives folder gives detailed information about local floppy, hard, and CD-ROM drives. Although there isn't really any diagnostic information available here per se, the Drives folder can indicate trouble with a drive simply by showing you that Windows 2000 Professional cannot see the drive. For example, say you have a second hard drive that is *not* displayed on this list. The drive's absence may indicate either a faulty data or power cable connection to the unit. If the drive is a SCSI device, the SCSI chain may be incorrectly terminated. If it's a second EIDE hard drive, there may be an incorrect master-slave configuration on the second drive. Before looking at more complicated problems, always check your physical connections. Often, the solution is simpler than you think.

TIP You cannot get information about floppy, removable disk, or CD-ROM drives unless a disk is in the drive. With a disk present, you'll get information about that specific disk.

For information about services, expand the Software Environment folder, and click the Services folder. You'll see something similar to the following:

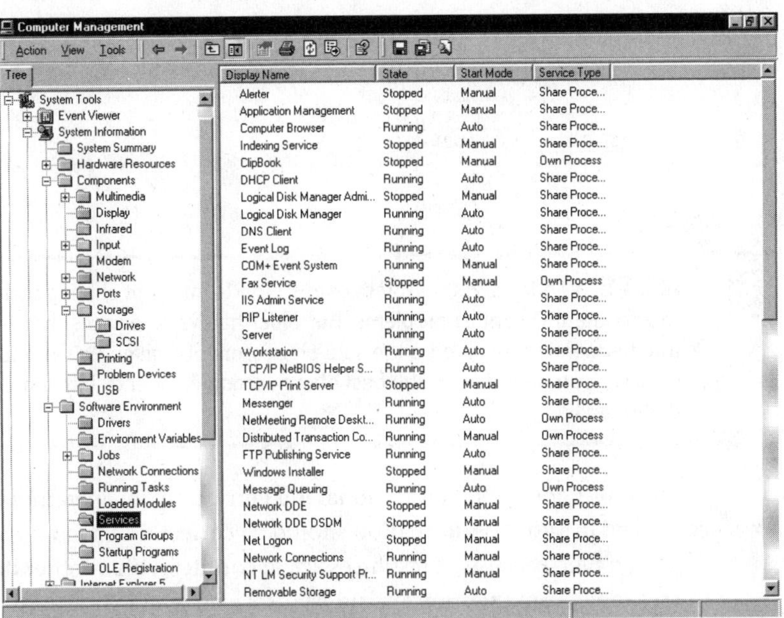

NOTE You can't use the Services folder to start and stop services. For that, you use the Services node under Services And Applications.

For information about system resources, expand the Hardware Resources folder, and select one of the subfolders. Figure 28.4 shows the IRQs in use on my system, which I displayed by selecting the IRQs folder.

FIGURE 28.4
The contents of the IRQs folder on my system

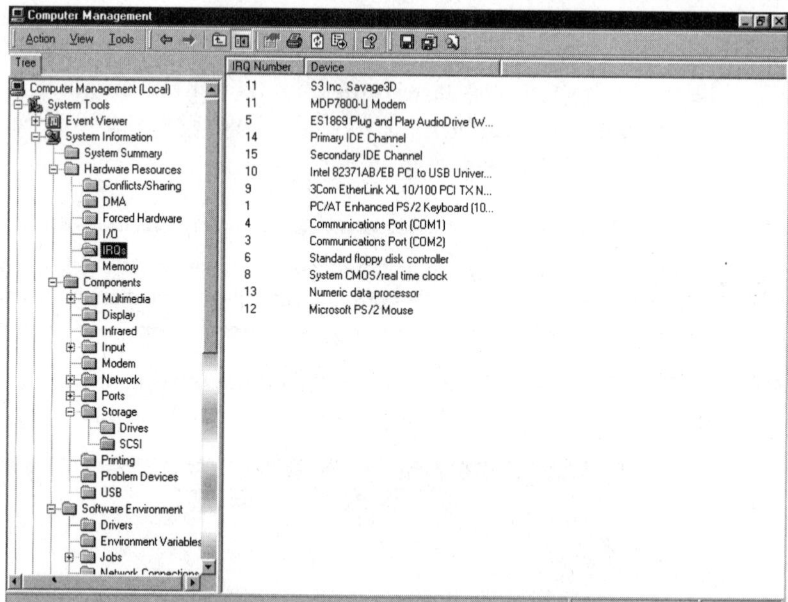

NOTE Windows 2000 Professional supports interrupt sharing by hardware devices to try to alleviate IRQ conflict problems. But older hardware devices that aren't aware of this feature frequently expect to be the sole possessors of a given IRQ and won't do very well sharing it with another device. The best plan of action is for each hardware device to have its own dedicated IRQ(s).

Since Windows 2000 Professional is a Plug-and-Play operating system, the values contained in System Information should be correct. But sometimes, a device won't be displayed here because its resources are in conflict with another device. In this case, the two devices in question should be displayed when you click the Conflicts/Sharing folder. It's a good idea to check here before you install a new device so that you can figure out which resources are allocated and which are available. Be sure to check all three resource types: IRQ, DMA, and base I/O.

For Registry information, expand the Software Environment folder, and click the Environment Variables folder. You'll see something similar to the following:

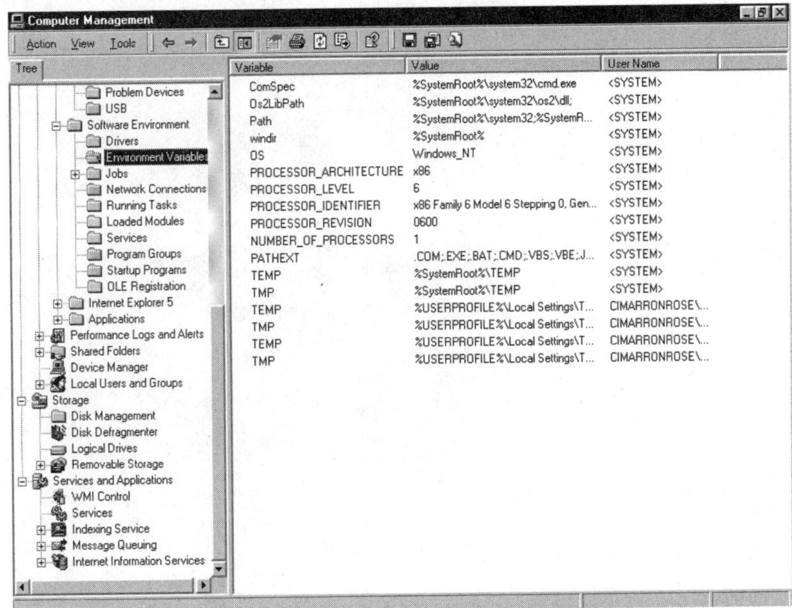

The Environment Variables folder is another view-only portion of System Information; it displays Registry information about CPUs and system paths. You can't edit this information, but it may be valuable for a technical support engineer trying to troubleshoot your system. Windows applications, in addition to using the system's pagefile, will often write temporary files for storing less frequently used data rather than using system memory. It's a method of "cheating" on the amount of memory the application allocates or using allocated memory for more immediate or more frequently used tasks.

To create and print a report from any of the System Information folders, right-click the folder and select Print. Because System Information generates so much information, you might want to save the information in a file rather than printing it. You can save the file as a text file or as a System Info File. Choose either from the Action menu.

Running Task Manager

Task Manager (see Figure 28.5) is a tool that lets you quickly monitor and troubleshoot Windows 2000 Professional, particularly in terms of the programs you are running. Task Manager in Windows 2000 Professional is significantly improved over previous versions of Task Manager, most notably in its capability to gauge system performance.

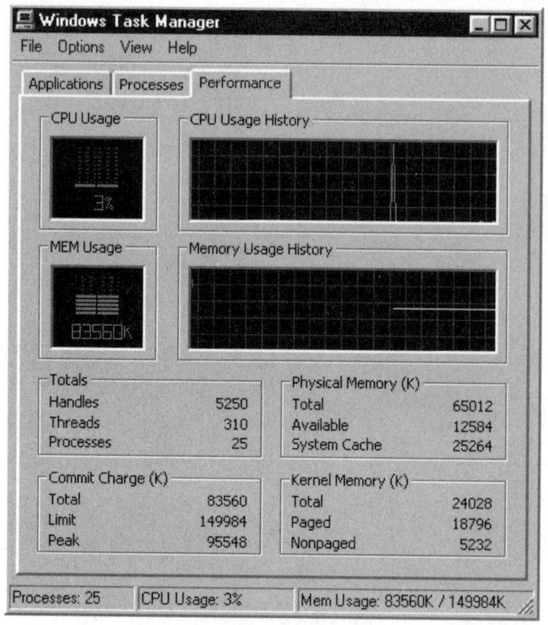

FIGURE 28.5
Use Task Manager to easily monitor programs you are running.

To run Task Manager, do one of the following:

- Right-click your Taskbar, and choose Task Manager from the shortcut menu.
- Choose Start ➢ Run, type **`taskmgr`** in the Open box, and click OK.

TIP If your system is causing some difficulty that makes the above methods unavailable, press Ctrl+Alt+Delete to open a Windows Security dialog box, and click the Task Manager button to open Task Manager. Go ahead—try it.

By default, Task Manager opens at the Performance tab. Regardless of which tab you are looking at, though, the bottom of Task Manager displays the number of processes being run, the percentage of CPU usage, and the amount of memory being used, including any virtual memory you may be using. This quick reference tells you everything you need to know in order to immediately understand the operating condition of your system.

Task Manager Applications

Task Manager's Applications tab lists all running applications and their current status (see Figure 28.6). An application's status will either be Running, if the program is behaving properly, or Not Responding, if the program is having problems.

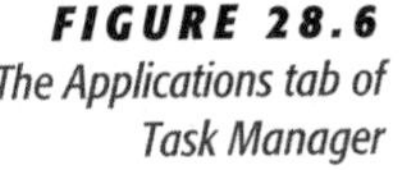

FIGURE 28.6
The Applications tab of Task Manager

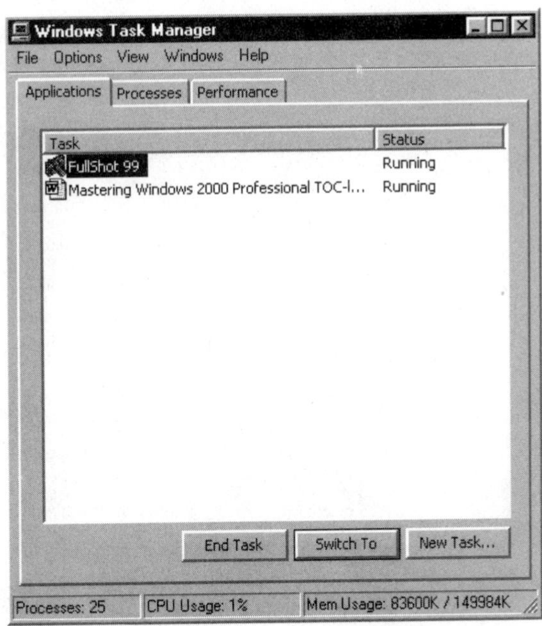

To close a running application, select it, and click End Task. To switch to a running application, select it, and click Switch To. To start a new application, follow these steps:

1. Click the New Task button to open the Create New Task dialog box:

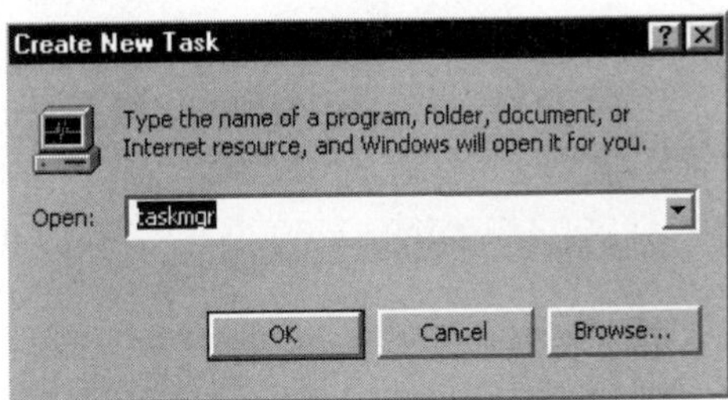

2. Type the name of the application in the Open box, and click OK.

Task Manager Processes

You can use the list on the Processes tab (see Figure 28.7) to monitor and halt any processes that are running on your computer. Processes are measured in all the separate executables that Windows 2000 Professional runs concurrently. This includes any applications you are running and all the background executables that Windows 2000 Professional runs automatically, including services. To terminate a running process, select it, and click the End Process button.

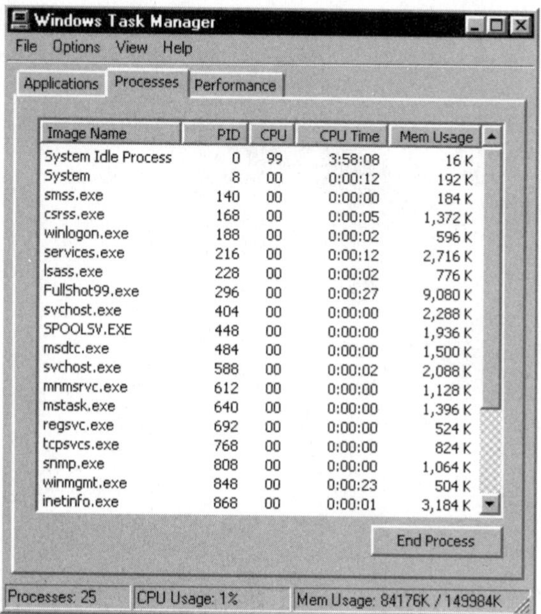

FIGURE 28.7
Task Manager lets you monitor running processes.

WARNING Don't end a process unless it is marked as being errant. Ending a process that is running may crash other programs that are running correctly if they depend on that process.

Task Manager Performance

You use the Performance tab to monitor your computer's usage of memory, processor time, and other resources. The two central graphs on the page measure the amount of memory used and the amount of processor time used. For multiple processors, you can choose to show one graph for each CPU or one graph for combined CPUs. The Performance tab also contains information on how much physical memory is being used and how much memory the Windows 2000 Professional kernel is using.

TIP When you run Task Manager, a small green square appears on your Taskbar next to your clock. This is a CPU usage meter. Point to the usage meter to display the percentage of CPU usage at the current moment.

Summary

Windows 2000 Professional's suite of administrative tools cover the gamut of system functions, ranging from providing networking settings to detailed information about the operating system's main "plumbing."

Most of the tools are intended to help troubleshoot system problems; using them in concert, you can gather sufficient information to remedy most system hiccups and even avert larger ones by catching them early. Although no set of tools is a panacea for all problems, those in Windows 2000 Professional will do a good job of helping you keep your system up and running.

CHAPTER 29

Additional Customization Options

FEATURING:

The best-laid plans of mice and men oft gang a-gley, as the saying goes. And so, despite the tens of thousands of work hours invested in designing and coding Windows 2000 Professional to make intelligent use of your system's hardware, not every scenario could possibly be foreseen. Now that Windows 2000 Professional includes the simplicity of Plug and Play, configuring and troubleshooting the system is much easier than before. Clearly, much thought has gone into reducing the perceived complexity of the operating system. Still, as we all know, human intervention can be highly advantageous at times. If you're a system administrator, computer jock, or power user and you haven't found the options you need discussed elsewhere in this book, check out this chapter—I've gathered all the rest of the customization and optimization options here.

Keyboard Options

Without modifying anything via the Control Panel's Keyboard applet, your keyboard will likely work just fine. But you might want to see what you're missing. Check out this applet's settings (see Figure 29.1) for changing several behavioral characteristics of your keyboard—you might never go back to the defaults.

FIGURE 29.1
The Keyboard Properties dialog box

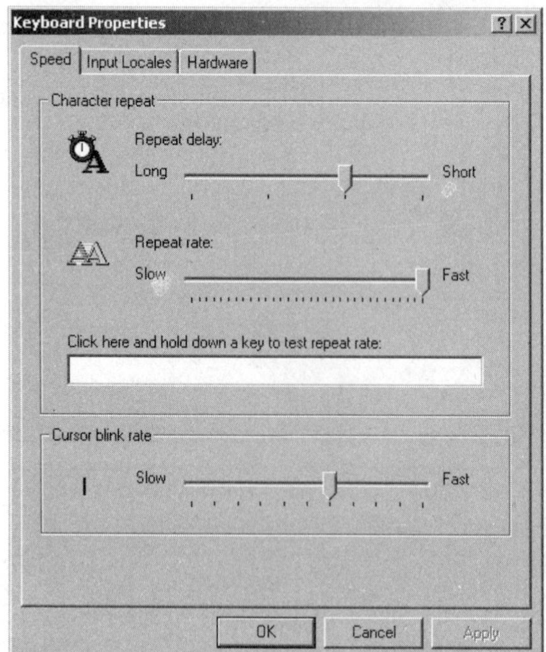

On the Speed tab, the first thing you'll want to fiddle with is the Repeat Delay setting. This setting determines how long you have to hold down a key before it starts repeating. If you tend to hesitate more than the average typist and you find your screen responding with *tthhee* instead of *the*, lengthen the repeat delay.

The Repeat Rate setting controls the rate at which characters appear on your screen after you press the keys on your keyboard. Most keys repeat on-screen when you hold them down for a while, but this setting also controls the rate at which the spacebar, arrow keys, PgUp, and PgDn keys work as well. To alter the default setting, simply drag the slider to a faster or slower setting. You can test the effect of a setting by clicking in the test box and holding down a letter key. If the setting is too slow or fast, adjust and try again.

At the bottom of the Speed tab, you can change the cursor blink rate. This setting determines how fast the insertion point (or *I-beam*) blinks when you're editing text. If this setting is too slow, the cursor can vanish for too long. Too fast, on the other hand, can be annoying. Drag the speed slider, and then check out the blinking cursor to observe the effect.

Multiple Keyboard-Layout and Keyboard-Language Support

Because of differences in language and alphabet, computers marketed abroad have different key assignments from the standard U.S. business computer. Key assignments in Windows 2000 Professional for special characters such as accented letters, umlauts, and the like are determined by choices you can make on the Input Locales tab. During installation of Windows 2000 Professional, you're asked to confirm the language that Setup has assumed is correct for your location, so typically this will already be correct. If your line of work calls for text in several languages, you can install any number of language drivers on your system and switch between them as you need them. Clicking the Taskbar or pressing a key is all you need to do to switch from one driver (and thus keyboard layout) to another.

Typically you'll have only one language showing when you select the Input Locales tab. To add a new language, follow these steps:

1. Click Add to open the Add Input Locale dialog box.
2. In the Input Locale drop-down list box, select the new language, and click OK. You may be prompted to insert a disk or CD-ROM so that the applet can locate the proper driver.
3. Back in the Input Locales tab of the Keyboard Properties dialog box, you'll see the language added to the Input Language list. If you want the new language to be the default, click Set As Default.

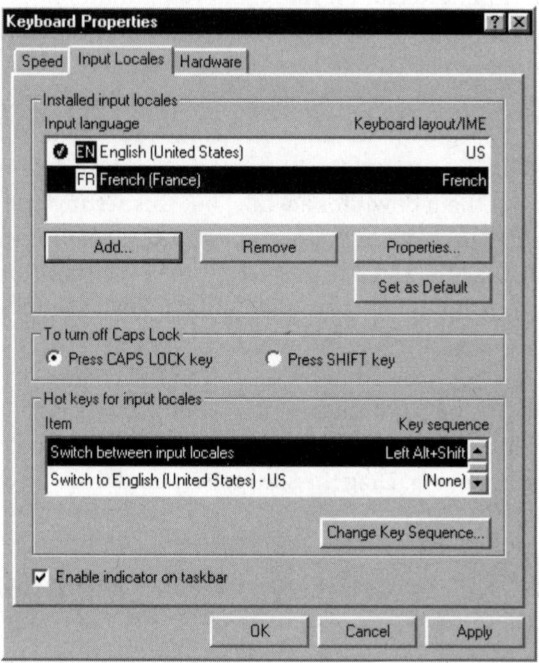

4. In the Hot Keys For Input Locales section, you'll notice that a shortcut key is selected. You can use this to switch between languages. To change the shortcut key, click Change Key Sequence to open the Change Key Sequence dialog box.
5. If you check Enable Indicator On Taskbar, your Taskbar will indicate which language driver is active at any one time. Clicking the indicator in the status area displays a menu that lets you easily switch between languages.
6. Click OK.

Once set to another language, some keys (shifted and unshifted) will type letters that are different from those printed on your keyboard. Unfortunately, you'll have to experiment a bit to determine where your new keys are—Windows 2000 Professional doesn't include a utility that will display a keyboard map for each language driver.

If you want to remove a language/locale driver, select it in the Input Language list, and click Remove. To change a locale's keyboard layout without changing the corresponding Input Locale, click the Properties button to open the Input Locale Properties dialog box, select a keyboard layout, and click OK. In most cases, however, you will want to keep the keyboard layout the same as the Language/Locale setting.

TIP Are you tired of the plain-old QWERTY layout? Think it could be holding you back? If you're willing to learn a new keyboard layout, try one of the *Dvorak* layouts, which are scientifically designed to increase the efficiency of your keystrokes. In the Input Locales Properties dialog box, select normal, left-handed, or right-handed Dvorak layouts from the Keyboard Layout/IME drop-down list.

Hardware Settings

The Hardware tab in the Keyboard Properties dialog box displays the name and some of the properties of the keyboard installed on your system. In most cases, Plug and Play detected the correct driver for your keyboard and installed it when you installed Windows 2000 Professional.

However, if you're having trouble with your keyboard, for example, sounds repeat continually after you press a key, click Troubleshoot to start the Keyboard Troubleshooter. Click Properties to open the Properties dialog box for your keyboard. On the General tab, you'll see some of the same information you saw in the Hardware tab. On the Driver tab, you can get details about the specific keyboard driver installed on your system, and you can click Update Driver to start the Upgrade Device Driver Wizard, which helps you find and install an updated driver. The Resource tab displays the resource settings for your keyboard and lets you change them if necessary.

Regional Options

You use the Regional Options applet in Control Panel to customize Windows 2000 Professional for use in a specific country. If you're using Windows 2000 Professional in English in the United States, don't bother making any changes in the Regional Options dialog box (unless someone has already gotten to your settings and changed them before you began working). The settings in the Regional Options dialog box pertain exclusively to Windows and Windows applications; other programs won't take advantage of them. Actually, even some Windows applications won't take advantage of them. Experiment with the settings to see if they make any difference in your applications, or check out the application's manual for information about how to set the formats for it.

In Control Panel, click Regional Options to open the Regional Options dialog box you see in Figure 29.2.

TIP Windows 2000 Professional may ask you to insert one of the application's disks when making changes, so have them on hand.

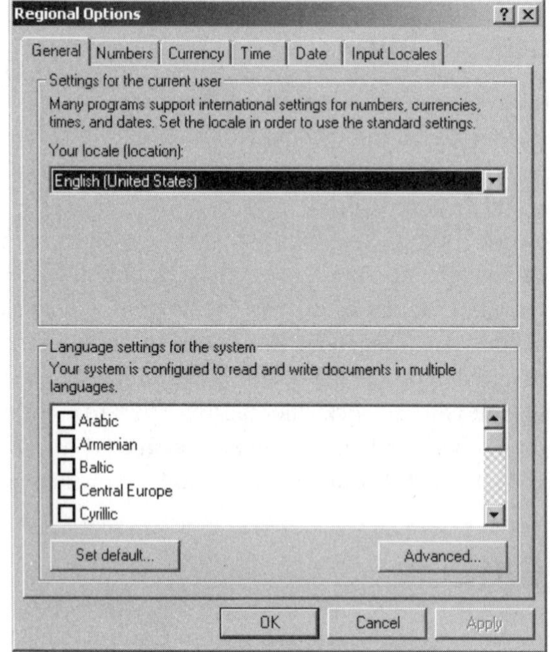

FIGURE 29.2 *Changes you make in the Regional Options dialog box affect only the applications that use the internal Windows settings for such functions.*

The Regional Options dialog box has the following tabs:

General Tells Windows 2000 Professional which country you're in. All other settings change in accordance with Windows 2000 Professional's understanding of the accepted practices in that country. Only bother changing the other options if you deem them necessary.

Numbers Specifies the appearance of numbers and symbols to use for the country you indicated on the General tab.

Currency Sets the currency symbol and the location and number of decimal digits.

Time Allows for 12- or 24-hour time indication, AM or PM indicators, choice of separators, and leading zeros.

Date Sets dates from myriad formats such as 3/6/00; 03/06/00; 3/6/2000; 06–03–2000; March 6, 2000; and others. This is useful for programs that pop the date into text at the touch of a key or translate dates from one format to another.

Input Locales Is identical to the Input Locales tab of the Keyboard Properties dialog box. This tab lets you install additional keyboard input languages and layouts, which you can then easily switch between via a special keystroke (also configurable).

To change any of the Regional Options settings, simply click the appropriate tab, and then click the drop-down list box for the setting in question. Examples of the current settings are shown in each section, so you don't need to change them unless they look wrong.

System Settings

At times in your experience with Windows 2000 Professional you will need to adjust settings that enhance the performance of your computer. This section introduces you to the primary applets in Control Panel for this purpose.

System Applet

The System applet provides a number of system settings. Be forewarned, however, that many of these settings are intended only for advanced users. If you happen to be familiar with the System applet in Windows 95/98, you will notice that the Windows 2000 Professional System applet is quite different—it lacks the Device Manager tab, for instance. Chances are, if you're a power user who digs around in the computer and goofs around with boards and various upgrades, you'll probably be using this applet from time to time. It displays information about your system's internals—amount of RAM, type of processor, environment settings, user profiles, hardware profiles, and start-up configuration. It also lets you adjust the foreground/background multitasking performance and the size and location of your paging file(s).

Clicking System in Control Panel opens the System Properties dialog box, as shown in Figure 29.3.

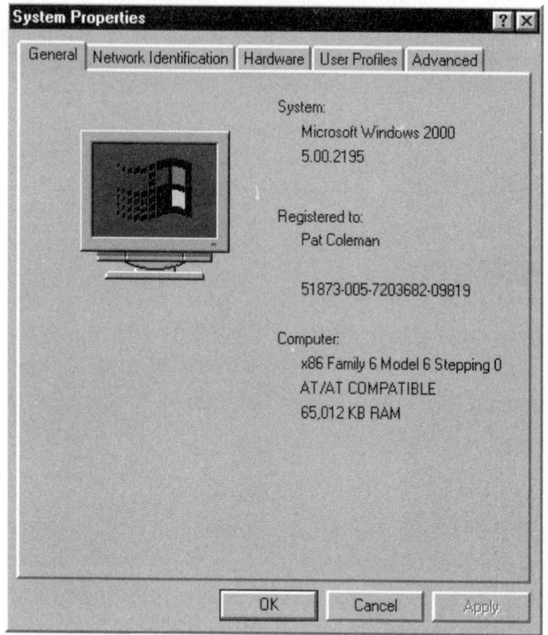

FIGURE 29.3
The System Properties dialog box provides advanced system settings.

The General Tab

The General tab simply displays useful information about your system, such as the version of Windows 2000 Professional installed, the system processor type, and how much RAM is installed.

The Network Identification Tab

On this tab, which is shown in Figure 29.4, you can change your workgroup or domain membership or the name of your computer.

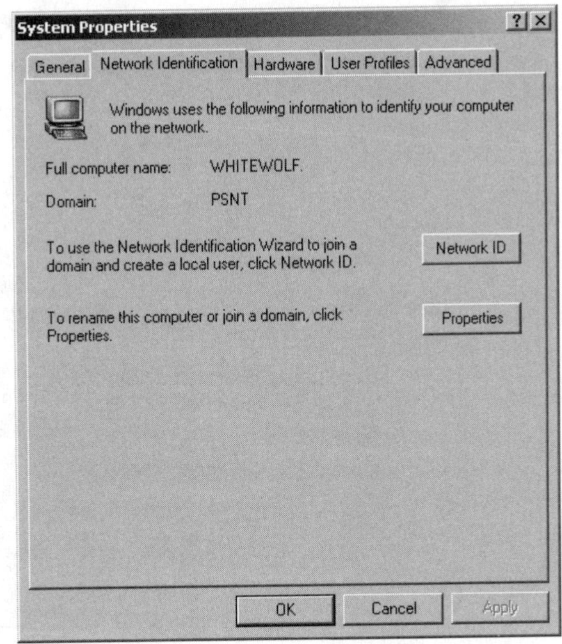

FIGURE 29.4
The Network Identification tab lets you change your computer name or domain membership.

The Hardware Tab

The Hardware tab, shown in Figure 29.5, gives you access to many of the hardware-specific settings in Windows 2000 Professional, including the Hardware Wizard, the Device Manager, and Hardware Profiles. Let's take a closer look at these options.

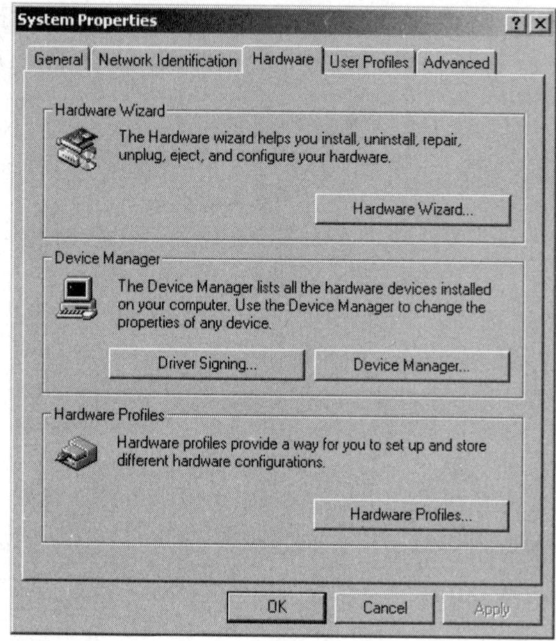

FIGURE 29.5
The Hardware tab gives you access to most of your computer's hardware settings.

Hardware Wizard

Click the Hardware Wizard button to start the Add/Remove Hardware Wizard, which is useful if you are trying to add or troubleshoot hardware devices in your computer. (You can also start this Wizard by clicking Add/Remove Hardware in Control Panel.) You can use this Wizard to unplug or eject hot swappable devices such as PC cards, to install new hardware, to remove hardware, and to troubleshoot devices that aren't working correctly. Figure 29.6 shows the Welcome screen of the Add/Remove Hardware Wizard.

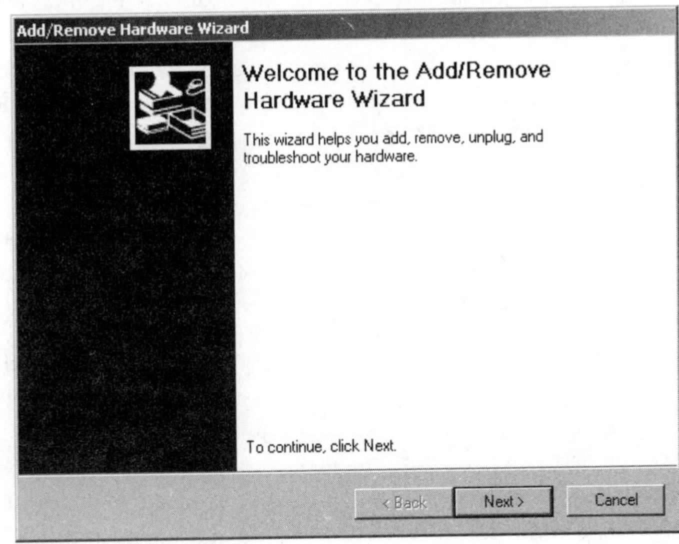

FIGURE 29.6 *The Add/Remove Hardware Wizard is useful for adding or removing hardware.*

Device Manager

Click the Device Manager button to open the Device Manager window, which is shown in Figure 29.7.

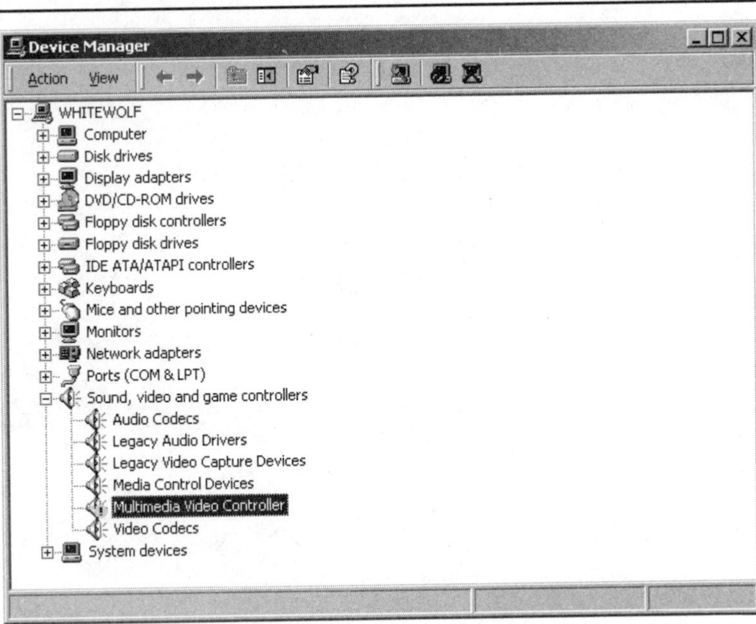

FIGURE 29.7 *The Device Manager lets you troubleshoot and adjust devices in your computer.*

To use Device Manager to view or modify a device, expand the console tree for the type of device you want to view, and double-click the individual device. For example, to display the properties for your video card, expand Display Adapters (click its plus sign), and double-click your video card's entry to open the Properties dialog box for your video card. In the Properties dialog box for a typical device you can enable or disable a device, change the driver, or modify the resources used by that device.

Remember that Windows 2000 Professional is a Plug-and-Play operating system, so the settings you make in Device Manager will be applied to any Plug-and-Play devices in your computer. Use this power carefully; if you make a mistake, you could potentially make your computer non-bootable.

Hardware Profiles

Click the Hardware Profiles button to open the Hardware Profiles dialog box, as shown in Figure 29.8. This applet is handy when you're adding or removing hardware or system drivers and want to create a backup trail. You can also use a hardware profile to switch between two or more sets of connected/installed hardware devices on a regular basis. For example, they can come in handy when you need to use a laptop on the road and then connect it to a docking station at home or at the office.

FIGURE 29.8
The Hardware Profiles dialog box

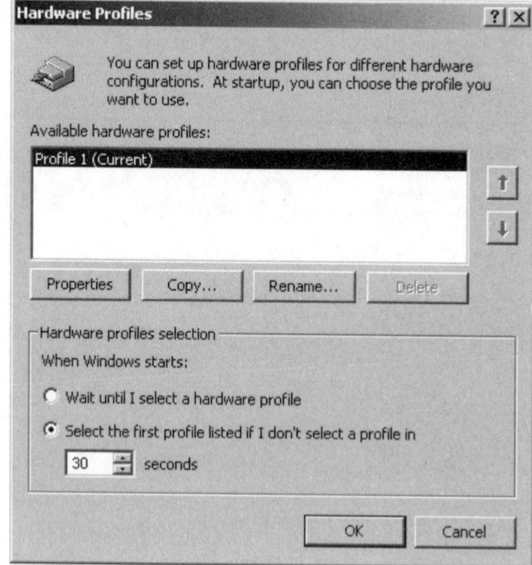

Select a configuration in the Available Hardware Profiles list, and click Properties to open the Properties dialog box (see Figure 29.9) for that profile.

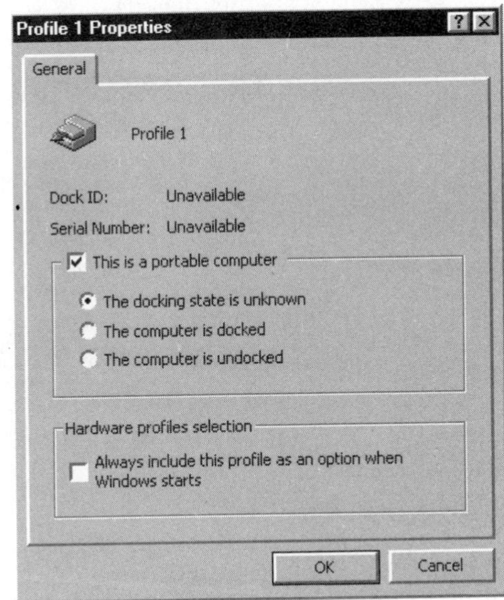

FIGURE 29.9
The Properties dialog box for a hardware profile

You can specify the current docking status, which means you can create one hardware configuration for docked mode and another one for undocked modes. Windows 2000 Professional then tries to automatically determine at bootup whether you're docked or undocked and uses the appropriate hardware configuration. If Windows 2000 Professional cannot determine the docking status while booting, you will have to select which mode to use (or else settle for Windows 2000 Professional choosing the unknown docking state mode, which might not load all the drivers you need).

The User Profiles Tab

If more than one user has logged in to your system, you will find multiple profiles displayed in the profiles list on the User Profiles tab (see Figure 29.10). You can delete unused, no-longer-needed profiles by simply highlighting them and clicking the Delete button. To change a *local profile* into a *roaming profile*, and vice versa, click the Change Type button to open the Change Profile Type dialog box. Local profiles apply only to the one PC; roaming profiles can give you the same Desktop no matter where on the network you log in.

NOTE For slow-link network connections, you can use a cached profile, which avoids the overhead of downloading this information from a remote server.

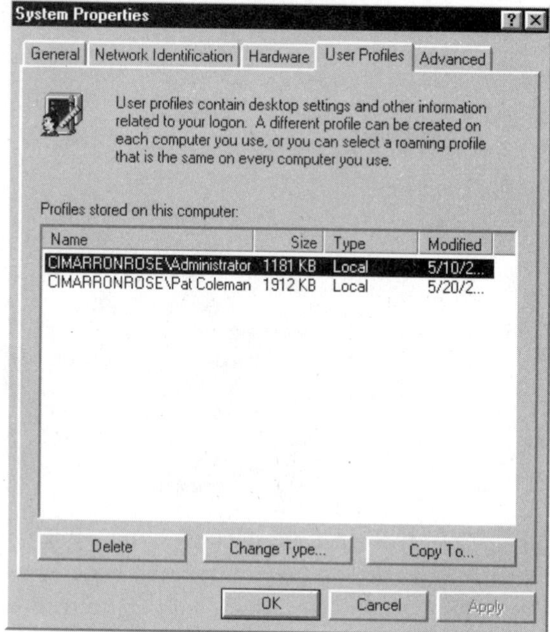

FIGURE 29.10
The User Profiles tab

Clicking the Copy To button opens the Copy To dialog box, which you can use to copy a selected profile to a floppy or to some other location on the network. This gives you the ability to carry your favorite Desktop configuration with you to another system.

The Advanced Tab

You use the options on the Advanced tab to access some of the more, well, *advanced* options. If you're familiar with Windows NT 4, you're probably thinking that there are some tabs missing in the System applet. The good news is that they aren't missing. They've just been moved to the Advanced tab, which is shown in Figure 29.11. In this section, we'll take a look at some of things you can do from this tab.

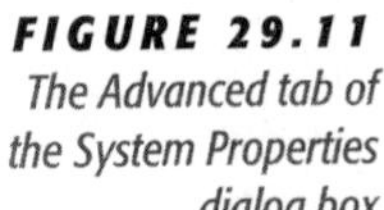

FIGURE 29.11
The Advanced tab of the System Properties dialog box

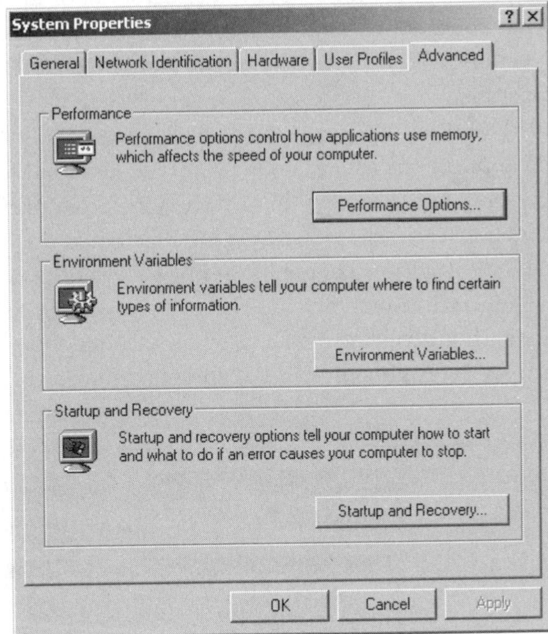

Performance Options

Clicking the Performance Options button opens the Performance Options dialog box, as shown in Figure 29.12. As the name implies, the two settings on this page affect system performance—in most cases, changing these will have an adverse impact on performance, so do so with care.

FIGURE 29.12
The Performance Options dialog box

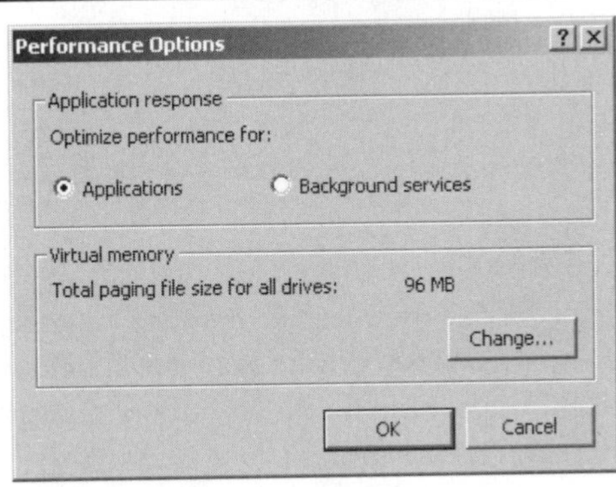

In the Optimize Performance For section are radio buttons that adjust how much extra processing time is given to the foreground, or focused application, as opposed to any other applications running in the background. The default setting of Applications gives the foreground application maximum priority, which is good if the primary use of your system is as a workstation. If your system will be used primarily as a server, however, it makes sense to click the Background Services radio button so that background applications get the same priority as any foreground application.

Click the Change button to open the Virtual Memory dialog box, which shows you how much disk space is being used for all paging files. In Windows 2000 Professional, you can have multiple paging files—one for each drive, in fact. This scheme lets Windows 2000 Professional increase disk performance by using a paging file located on one drive while accessing data located on another drive. As you can see in Figure 29.13, you can set the paging file's initial and maximum sizes for each drive.

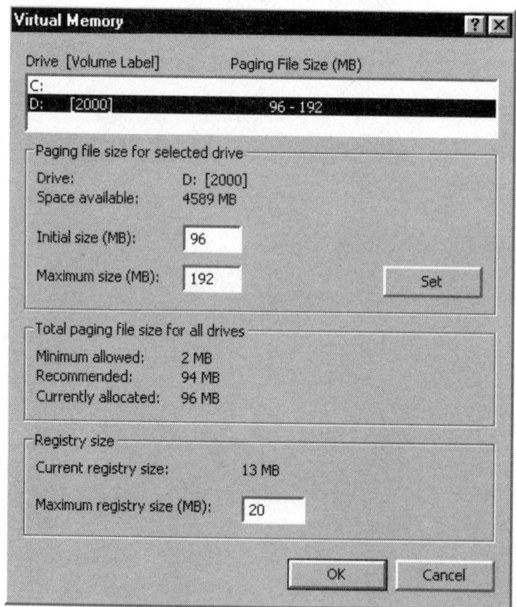

FIGURE 29.13 *To improve performance, Windows 2000 Professional can have separate paging files on each physical drive.*

In the Virtual Memory dialog box, you can also adjust the maximum Registry size. This does not *allocate* the specified amount of space, and therefore it does not guarantee that the space will actually be available should the Registry ever need it. Instead, it simply sets the upper limit on the amount of disk space the system Registry files will be permitted to use. This is another good reason (besides affecting general system performance) to prevent your drives from filling up completely.

Environment Variables

If you've used NT, Windows, DOS, or for that matter, even Unix, you are probably familiar with the idea of environment settings. An *environment setting*, also known as an environment variable or system variable, comprises a setting name and its value. Certain applications or the operating system itself occasionally needs to look at these settings. One of the most common of these variables is Path, which holds a concatenated list of all folders the system should search when looking for an application or dynamically loaded library file. In the Advanced tab, click the Environment Variables button to open the Environment Variables dialog box:

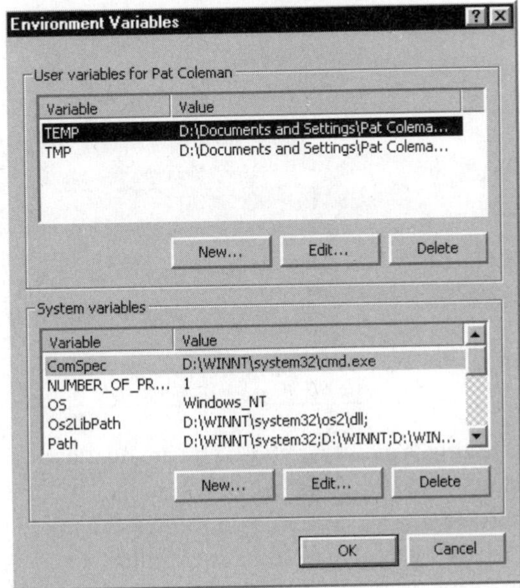

To change an existing setting, select it in either the User Variables section or the System Variables section, and then click the Edit button. In the Edit User Variable (or Edit System Variable) dialog box, enter the new value in the Variable Value field, and click OK. Similarly, to add a new setting click the New button, type the name of the new variable, enter the value in the Value field, and click OK. To delete a variable, highlight it, and click the Delete button.

I believe that eventually environment variables are going to be phased out completely in favor of using the Registry, and in fact these settings are currently stored in the Registry.

Startup and Recovery

Click the Startup And Recovery button to open the Startup And Recovery dialog box, as shown in Figure 29.14. In the System Startup section, you select the operating system that will boot next time. You can specify how long at bootup the operating system menu should wait for a user to change this setting before proceeding to boot the operating system selected in this dialog box.

FIGURE 29.14
The Startup And Recovery dialog box lets you select which operating system will boot when the system is rebooted.

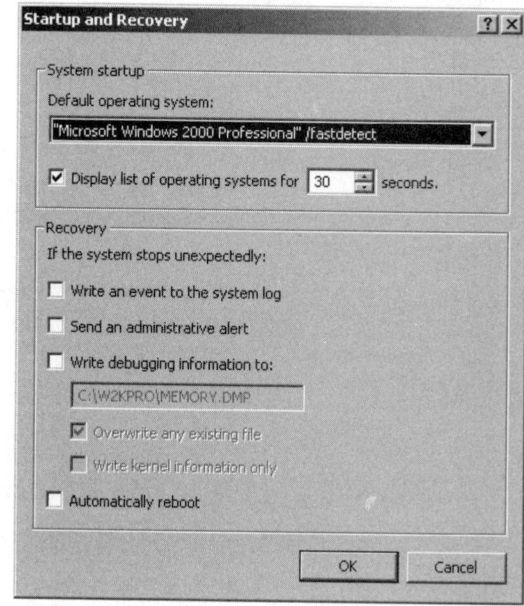

This setting is mainly useful if you are dual-booting, for example, Windows 2000 Professional and Windows 95/98. If you need to select from among other (non-Microsoft) operating systems, you will need a more extensive third-party boot manager, such as the System Commander utility. If you clear the Display List Of Operating Systems check box, the boot menu won't be displayed. This has the same effect as setting the timeout value in the `boot.ini` file to zero.

The lower portion of this dialog box has to do with how the system behaves when encountering a serious system error. Although these errors are quite rare, if a system process or thread is forced to terminate unexpectedly, Windows 2000 Professional may become unstable; when this happens, usually the safest action is to restart the system (the last choice, Automatically Reboot). In addition you can choose whether to log an event, send an alert, or perform a memory dump when an error occurs.

Device Manager

To open Device Manager, follow these steps:

1. In Control Panel, click System to open the System Properties dialog box.
2. Click the Hardware tab, and then click the Device Manager button. You'll see the window shown in Figure 29.15.

FIGURE 29.15
The Device Manager window

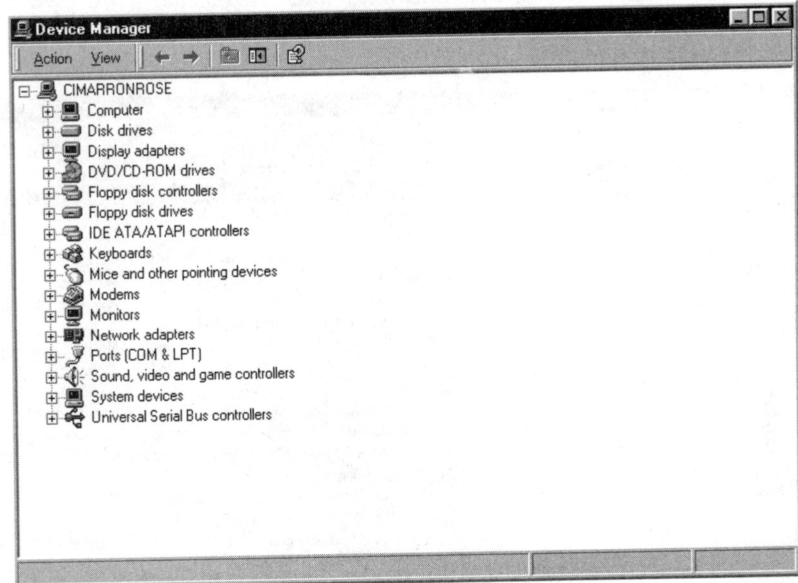

You use Device Manager to manage the many device drivers that Windows 2000 Professional uses to communicate with the hardware installed in your system. A quick look at the Device list can tell you whether a particular device driver is loaded and running.

If a device is malfunctioning, its console tree will be expanded and the icon will have either a *red splat* or *yellow bang* on it. The red splat is a common slang term for a device displaying the red X through the icon, and the yellow bang means a device with the yellow symbol containing an exclamation point. If you see one of these, you'll know there is a problem with either the device or its driver. Right-click the device, and from the shortcut menu, choose Disable or Uninstall.

If you happen to be using multiple hardware profiles, each profile will be listed by name in the Properties dialog box for a device. Simply check the box beside each profile name where the device should be used.

Services Console

The main difference between a service and an application is that a service loads whenever the system is booted, regardless of whether any user logs into the system. Examples of services include tape backup services, Web server services, and mail services. You can get involved, however, and start, stop, pause, or resume specific services by means of the Start Service, Stop Service, Pause Service, and Restart Service buttons in the

Services console, which is shown in Figure 29.16). As with devices, you can enable and disable services automatically for a hardware profile.

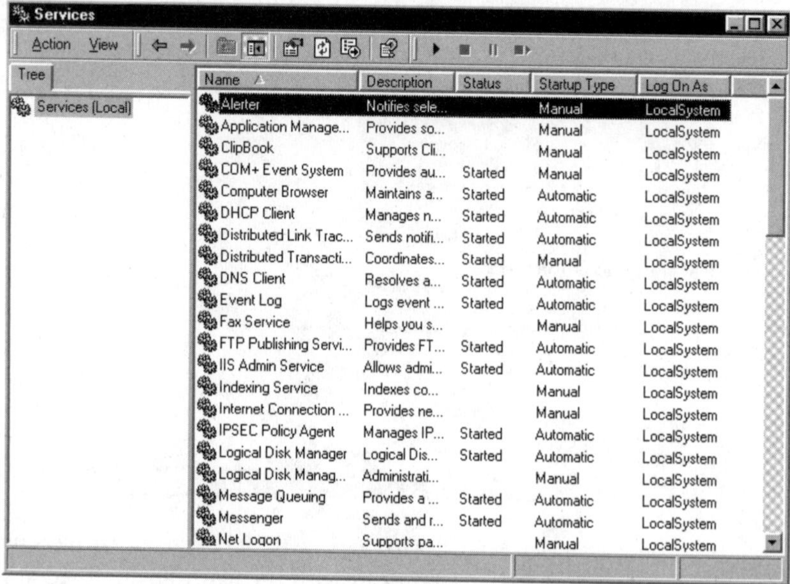

FIGURE 29.16 *The Services console lets you specify when various services should be started and which logon account they will use.*

Because services can start prior to or irrespective of who logs in, there needs to be some way to specify which user account a service should log in with. Normally, services default to use the System account, but in some cases this creates a security risk. For example, if a Web server starts up using administrator privileges and allows server-side includes, it is entirely possible for someone out on the Internet to gain complete access to the system, because any program started via the Web server gains the same security rights as the Web server itself.

So how do you change the login account for a service? Follow these steps:

1. In the Services console, double-click the service to open the Properties dialog box for that service, and select the Log On tab:

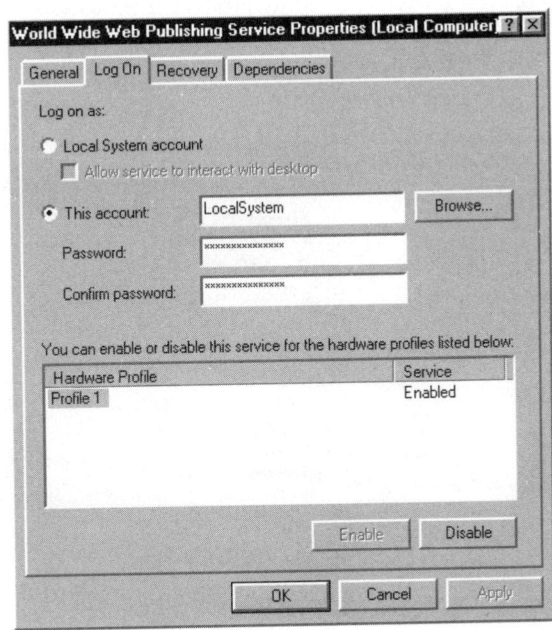

2. Click the This Account radio button, and then click the Browse button to open the Select User dialog box.
3. Select the account the service should use when it logs in, and then click OK.
4. Click OK again to close the service's Properties dialog box, and then close the Services console.

The Recycle Bin's Properties

Recall that when you delete files, they aren't actually erased (unless you remembered to press the Shift key at the same time as the Delete key when you deleted them). They get moved to the Recycle Bin, which is a folder on your hard disk. If your hard disk is modest in size or is getting crammed, decreasing the size of the Recycle Bin might be in order. If you decrease its size, though, remember that you'll be cutting down on the number (and/or the size) of the files that can be recovered. In some cases, you might even want to increase the size of the Recycle Bin to keep yourself from worrying about whether you're making the right decision when clearing off certain projects (for instance, if you've ever worked for clients who change their mind after giving their "final" instructions). The options in the Recycle Bin Properties dialog box are therefore worth a look.

To open the Recycle Bin Properties dialog box (see Figure 29.17), right-click the Recycle Bin icon, either on the Desktop or in Explorer, and then choose Properties from the shortcut menu.

FIGURE 29.17
You can set specifics of the Recycle Bin's behavior from its Properties dialog box.

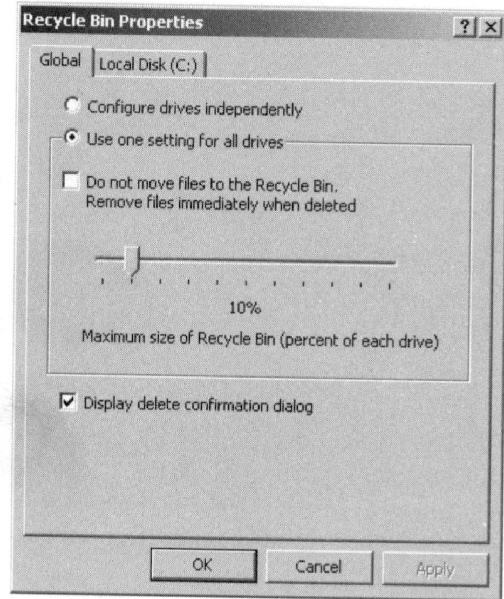

In addition to a Global tab, there is also a tab for each of your local hard disks. If you choose Configure Drives Independently on the Global tab, you'll have to go to each tab as needed to make individual drive settings. Otherwise you can just use the Global tab.

If you don't want to be able to reclaim deleted files, check the Do Not Move Files To The Recycle Bin check box. Why would you do this? For one thing, it speeds up the deletion process. For another, it frees up disk space immediately on deletion. Finally, if you're paranoid that someone else is going to access your system and expose your old mistakes, it destroys the evidence.

As a default, 10 percent of each drive is used for the Recycle Bin. When you delete a file on drive C, it goes to drive C's Recycle Bin until you empty the Bin. When you delete from drive D (if you have a second hard drive), it goes into drive D's Recycle Bin. As a Recycle Bin reaches capacity, newly deleted files will push older files off the bottom of the list, deleting them permanently. In practical terms, the Recycle Bin's size determines how long a file will be recoverable before it's pushed off the list.

WARNING The size of a drive's Recycle Bin unfortunately limits the size of the largest file that can be recovered after an accidental deletion. If a file is larger than the maximum size of the Recycle Bin, it won't be recyclable. As of this writing, you won't be warned of this either; it will just be erased.

If you want to alter the size of your Recycle Bins, use the percentage slider. Usually, the default of 10 percent works just fine, but if you work with very large files, you may want to increase this percentage to accommodate them. If you're short on disk space and don't tend to make deletion mistakes, decrease it.

The Display Delete Confirmation Dialog check box is normally checked so that you can confirm before Windows 2000 Professional will empty the bin. If you find the confirmation boxes annoying, clear this check box.

Here are a few other points you might want to keep in mind concerning the Recycle Bin in Windows 2000 Professional:

- If you delete a folder, only the files within that folder appear in the Recycle Bin—the folder itself will not appear. However, if you restore a file that was originally located in a deleted folder, Windows 2000 Professional re-creates the folder and then restores the file to it.
- If you delete files via the command prompt (typing **del** or **erase**), these files *are* immediately erased. If you ever need to restore these files (or files deleted from the Recycle Bin), you'll need a third-party tool that will work with Windows 2000 Professional, but Windows 2000 Professional itself provides no such means of "undeleting" files that were deleted via a DOS command.

A Microsoft Management Console Primer

Let's face it, NT 4 admins. Our old familiar administrative tools—such as the User Manager and User Manager for Domains, Server Manager, Event Viewer, and even Disk Administrator—have been assimilated into these things called Microsoft Management Console (MMC) tools.

To master the Windows 2000 Professional graphical changes, you must fully understand the MMC. In this section, I'll explain how MMC is not evil, discuss key MMC terms you should know, and then look briefly at the Computer Management console.

What Is This MMC Thing?

In NT 4, administrators had to master multiple administration tools. A whole set of built-in tools, plus independent third-party tools, made administration sort of a mess. Although many admin tools functioned remotely, you had to install some of them separately (unless your desktop happened to be an NT server), and with third-party tools, you often had to jump through hoops to get them to work remotely, if at all. Even worse, with menus, buttons, toolbars, Wizards, tabs, HTML, Java (you get the picture), just learning how to navigate new software was a chore. Also, there was no simplified version of User Manager for Domains that could be given to account operators and no way to hide menu items in administrative tools for those without full administrator rights.

So we complained. "As administrators, we need to be able to administer our networks from the comfort and luxury of our cubicles. And we don't want to waste time exploring all the windows, Wizards, and tabs in every new tool. And we need more flexible tools," we said. Behold, Microsoft has heard our cries, and their response was the MMC.

MMC is a framework for management applications, providing a unified interface for Microsoft and third-party management tools. MMC doesn't replace management applications; it integrates them into one single interface. There are no inherent management functions in MMC at all. It uses component tools called snap-ins, which do all the work. MMC provides a user interface; it doesn't change how the snap-ins function.

Why Is MMC Good and Not Evil?

The following benefits are associated with MMC:

- You only have to learn one interface to drive a whole mess of tools.
- Third-party (ISV) tools will probably use MMC snap-ins. At least, Microsoft is encouraging software vendors to do so.
- You can build your own consoles, which is practical and fun. Admins can even create shortcuts on the console to non-MMC tools such as executables, URLs, Wizards, and scripts.
- By customizing MMC consoles, admins can delegate tasks to underlings without giving them access to all functions and without confusing them with a big scary tool.
- Help in MMC is context sensitive; it displays subjects for only the appropriate components. Okay, that's not really new, but it's still cool (the Action menu is also context sensitive, but nobody uses menus anymore; everybody just right-clicks instead).

MMC Terms to Know

This section defines important terms you'll need to know when working with MMC.

A *console*, in MMC-speak, is one or more administrative tools in an MMC framework. The prebuilt admin tools, such as Active Directory Users and Computers, are console files. You can also make your own consoles without any programming tools—you needn't be a C or Visual Basic programmer, as I'll discuss a bit later. The saved console file is a *Microsoft saved console (MSC)* file and it carries the MSC extension.

NOTE It's important to distinguish between Microsoft Management Console and console tools. MMC provides a framework to create customized console-based tools. `MMC.EXE` is a program that presents administrators (and others creating console tools) with a blank console to work with. It might help to think of a new instance of `MMC.EXE` as providing the raw material for a tool. In that case, Microsoft Management Console provides the rules and guidelines for building the tool, and the new console you create is the finished product.

Snap-ins are what we call administrative tools that can be added to the console. For example, the DHCP admin tool is a snap-in, and so is the Disk Defragmenter. Snap-ins can be made by Microsoft or by other software vendors. (You *do* need programming skills to make these, in other words.) A snap-in can contain components called nodes, or containers, or even leaves, in some cases. Although you can load multiple snap-ins in a single console, most of the prebuilt administrative tools contain only a single snap-in (including the Computer Management tool).

An *extension* is basically a snap-in that can't live by itself on the console but depends on a stand-alone snap-in. It adds some functionality to a snap-in. Some snap-ins work both ways. For example, the Event Viewer is a stand-alone snap-in, but it's implemented as an extension to the Computer Management snap-in. The key point is that extensions are optional. You can choose not to load them. For example, Local Users and Groups is an extension to the Computer Management snap-in. If you remove the extension from the `COMPMGMT.MSC` file used by your support folk, or simply don't include it in a custom console that uses the snap-in, those who use the tool won't have the option to create or manage users and groups with the tool. They won't even see it. (Please note that this will not prevent them from creating users and groups by other means, if they have the correct administrative privileges.)

Admins can create new MSC files by customizing an existing MSC file or by creating one from a blank console. The `MMC.EXE` plus the defined snap-ins create the tool interface. Also, it's possible to open multiple tools simultaneously, but each console runs one instance of MMC. Open an MSC file and look in Task Manager while it's running—you only see the `MMC.EXE` process running, not the MSC file, just as you see `WINWORD.EXE` running in Task Manager, but not the Word document's name.

By default, prebuilt console tools open in *User mode*. Changes cannot be made to the console design. You can't add or remove snap-ins, for example. To create or customize a console, use *Author mode*. When a user is running a tool and not configuring it, it should be running in one of the User modes. The tool will actually look different in User mode than it does in Author mode.

Figure 29.18 shows a sample console tool, with the parts of the interface labeled. This console is running in Author mode to show all the parts of the MMC interface. This is a custom console, but to open any existing tool in Author mode, choose Start ➢ Run to open the Run dialog box and invoke it with the /a switch.

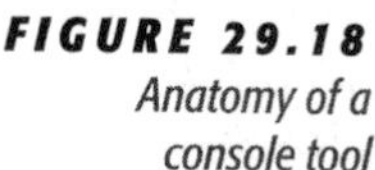

FIGURE 29.18
Anatomy of a console tool

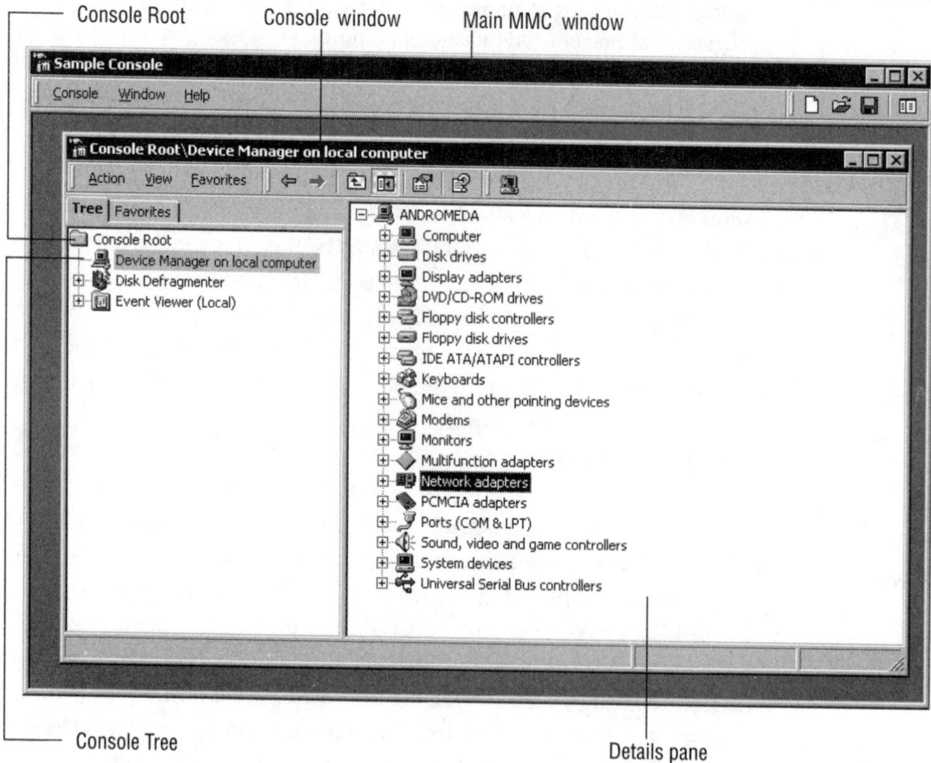

In Figure 29.18, the Main MMC window is present because the tool is open in Author mode. In User mode, the Main MMC window, with menus and buttons, is hidden, and you only see the Console window. The Console menu in the Main window is basically a File menu, but it's also used to add and remove snap-ins and set console options. The Console window Action menu is context sensitive and will reflect the options of the selected snap-in tool or component. The hierarchical list of items shown by default in the left pane is called the *console tree* (hence the "tree" label on the tab), and at the top is the *console root*. The Favorites tab displays any created links to places in the console tool. The right pane is called the *details pane*. Snap-ins appear as nodes on the console tree. The contents of the details pane depend on the item selected on the console tree.

The Computer Management Console

The Computer Management console is *the* main tool for administering a single server, local or remote. If you only have one server on your network and you only want to use one admin tool, Computer Management fits the bill. To open the Computer Management console, right-click My Computer and choose Manage from the shortcut menu.

There are three nodes in the Computer Management console tree: System Tools, Storage, and Services and Applications (see Figure 29.19). Notice that the focus is on the local machine by default; to connect to other computers on the network, right-click the Computer Management icon at the root of the tree and choose Connect To Another Computer from the shortcut menu.

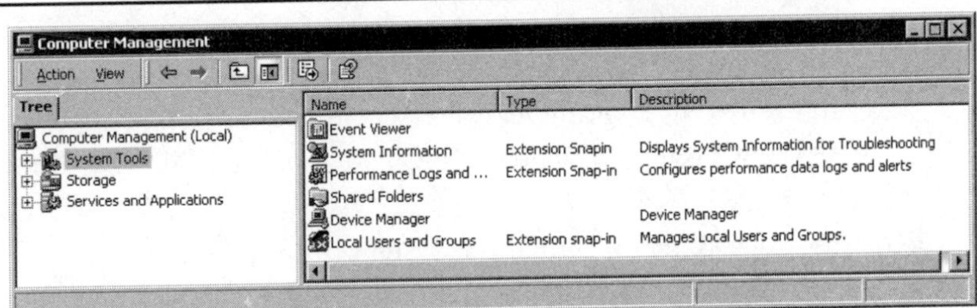

FIGURE 29.19 *The Computer Management console tree*

Expand the nodes in the Computer Management console tree to reveal the configuration tools and objects, as shown in Figure 29.20. Most of the core functions are under System Tools. Some functions even work remotely on NT 4 machines (you can view a remote machine's Event Logs, for example), but new features require the remote machine to be a Windows 2000 Professional box.

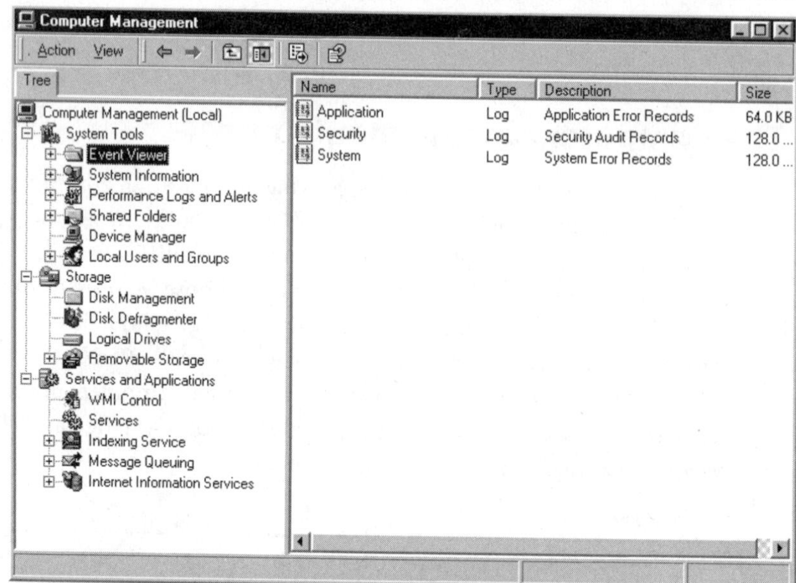

FIGURE 29.20 *The expanded Computer Management console tree*

In the System Tools node, you can complete the following tasks:

- View events and manage the Event Logs. Basically the Event Viewer tool turned into an MMC snap-in.
- View system information. System Information provides details about hardware resources, system components configuration information, and software components (see Figure 29.21).

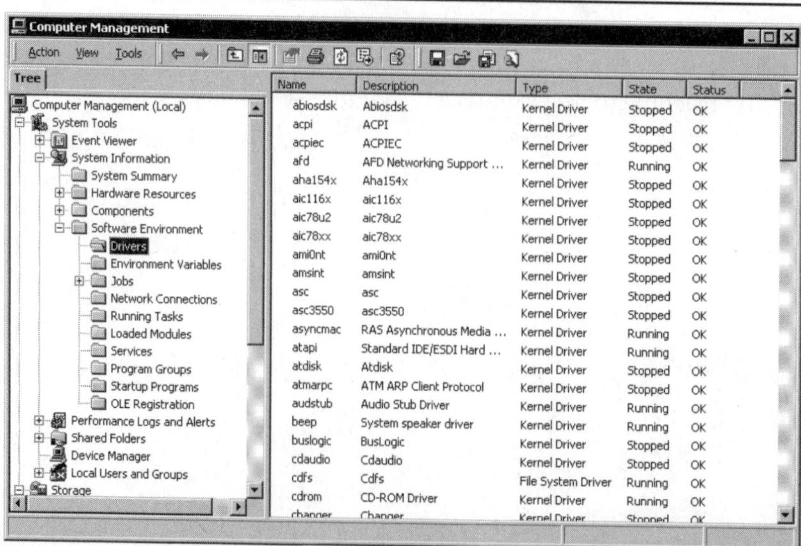

FIGURE 29.21 *Viewing system information*

- Manage shared folders. View, create, and manage shares; view sessions and open files; and disconnect sessions.
- Manage devices. The long-awaited Device Manager is fully remotable and a great place to track down information about your hardware, update drivers, and troubleshoot resource conflicts.
- Create and manage local users and groups.

The Storage node includes options for managing removable storage (a new feature), along with the new Disk Defragmenter tool and the Disk Management tool, which is the equivalent of the Disk Administrator in NT 4. There is also a component to view logical drives, including network drive mappings, and their properties. This is useful if you want to quickly view free space or set NTFS security at the root of a partition, for example. Too bad you can't browse folders as you can in Explorer. Oh well, I guess we don't need *another* desktop shell program, do we?

The Services and Applications node includes telephony settings, services configuration, Windows Management Instrumentation (WMI), indexing, and IIS management stuff, the last of which is also available in the Administrative Tools group by itself (the tool is called Internet Services Manager, while the extension in Computer Management is called Internet Information Services). The components available in the Services and Applications node depend on what services are installed on your system. For instance, if Internet Information Services is not installed (and it isn't by default), you won't see that component.

Summary

In this chapter, we talked about some of Windows 2000 Professional's other configuration settings, the ones that don't seem to fit elsewhere in our discussions. We explored setting keyboard options and regional settings. We looked at system settings such as performance, startup and shutdown, hardware profiles, and user profiles. We then went on to discuss the Recycle Bin's configuration and use and finished by taking a look at the Microsoft Management Console.

CHAPTER 30

Advanced Troubleshooting Methodology

FEATURING:

Ever have one of *those* days? A day when nothing seems to go right with your computer? Unfortunately, an operating system such as Windows 2000 Professional is extremely complex, and any complex system will inevitably have those days. Just remember this quote from a favorite Scottish engineer: "The more they over-tink the plumbing, the easier it is to stop up the drains." With a system such as Windows 2000 Professional, things can go wrong in so many places that it's often difficult to find a place to start.

In this chapter, we take a look at the "how" of troubleshooting Windows 2000 Professional. Much of what I cover here will be equally useful on Windows 2000 Server, but the main focus is, of course, Professional. I want to give you a workable method for finding your way through the maze.

The Tao of Troubleshooting

At first it seems that troubleshooting mostly involves memorizing a lot of details about everything. When working with an experienced troubleshooter, you've probably even found yourself thinking, "How do they know that?" Truth is, most people never do well by simply trying to memorize everything. Human beings succeed best when working from their strengths; we all have problems when working from our weaknesses. To make troubleshooting a strength, you need to find the pattern in the chaos.

NOTE The process of troubleshooting is the process of moving from "Big Picture" to small detail. Asking questions is the tool for breaking the big picture into small details.

Consider this scenario: A friend tells you that he is having trouble getting a vending machine to accept a dollar bill. If you happen to be a vending machine expert, you might know everything about how the dollar bill is drawn into the machine, every detail of the mechanisms that control the entire process. Probably not. Instead, being a good troubleshooter, you consider the directions on the machine. Then you start asking questions:

"Has it ever worked before?"

"Did you put the dollar in facing the right direction?"

"Is the dollar bill folded?"

With this last question, your friend admits that the corners of the bill are a bit folded. So you try straightening them out. Then you test your solution by reinserting the bill. It works, and you are a hero. Of course, solving a problem like this has a low glory quotient, but it serves to illustrate the basics.

Define the Problem: "It's Broken."

The first step to successful troubleshooting is to define the problem accurately. Many times people will define a problem in very simple terms and expect you to know what they are talking about. Your job as a troubleshooter is to define the details of the problem: "So what *exactly* is broken?" This is a good question to start the conversation. (Incidentally, this may be a conversation with yourself if you are trying to solve your own problem.) Start by getting a clear description of what the customer—the person who is reporting the problem—feels is the issue. It is often a good technique to take the time to write these points out on paper.

Try to get all the details that describe the problem as the customer sees it. Ask questions like "Has it ever worked before?" or "When did you notice that it stopped working?"

Explore the Boundaries

This can be a painful lesson to learn. Often the person you are working with to solve a problem (yes, this can even be yourself) leaves out important details. This is almost never because they want you to fail, but rather because they don't think that a particular detail is relevant. This is a painful lesson because you may spend a great deal of time pursuing irrelevant issues when the real problem is very simple. Consider the following illustration.

You are talking with a customer about their computer problem. The issue, as reported, is that the new internal modem isn't working. So right away you dig in to the settings and configuration for the modem. You try initialization strings, but the operating system cannot even detect the modem. About 30 minutes go by and you're no closer to a solution. You ask the customer to double-click something in Control Panel and he replies, "I can't do that." When you ask why, you are told that the mouse doesn't work either. Slapping your forehead, you know the answer: The modem is installed on IRQ4, and so is the mouse.

Exploring the boundaries means finding out everything that may be wrong with the system. The proper question here is, "Is there anything else that doesn't appear to be working?" If you had asked this question in the preceding scenario, you could have solved the problem in about 10 minutes instead of 40 minutes. The extra information you get here *may* be unrelated to the problem, but it may be exactly the piece you need to solve the puzzle.

Brainstorm and Document

Now that you have a clue about where the problem lies, it's time to come up with some ideas to help focus in on the real issue. While you are gathering your thoughts, write them down. Try to have at least three things to try before proceeding.

Writing down your ideas is important. You will be trying each possible approach, and this may take time. It may be difficult to remember each idea when you're in the heat of battle (figuratively speaking). Don't be afraid to add to this list as you go. Often you will discover the best approach while trying one of your initial ideas.

Test Your Ideas

This is a critical point: Test each approach—one at a time.

It is impossible to overemphasize this point. Many troubleshooters will try the "shotgun" approach, meaning that they test every idea they can muster all at once. Most likely one of the ideas will work, but which one?

During the course of troubleshooting an operating system, you will frequently be disabling certain functionalities. If you try every idea at the same time, you may fix the problem, but you'll be left with an operating system that has been crippled by your actions. Worse yet, you won't know which areas to re-enable and which one to repair.

Testing each idea one at a time enables you to discover clearly what's broken and to easily find your way back through the maze of settings that have been changed.

Repair the Problem

This is the easy part—usually. Finding the problem can often be a time-consuming process, but repairing the broken portion of the system can be as simple as replacing a corrupt file. Perhaps the issue arises from bad hardware. This is easy to fix; just replace the hardware. (The hard part here is to find the money for the replacement.)

Clean Up after Yourself

Remember how I said earlier to test each possible solution individually? This is the phase where you undo some of the ideas that were unsuccessful. Never leave the system worse than you found it. There are few support issues worse than a customer who is upset that the previous support person made their problems worse or caused new ones.

Again, it's helpful to have documented the approaches you tried—especially if you kept notes about what you did during the troubleshooting phase. If you did, it is simple to backtrack and turn features back on. When troubleshooting Windows 95, I often renamed the `config.sys` and `autoexec.bat` files to get them out of the way. Ever notice that your CD-ROM won't work if the driver doesn't load in the `config.sys`? Most customers will view this as a serious problem.

Provide Closure

If you are dealing with other people in your troubleshooting process, providing closure means informing them of what the problem was and what you did to resolve it. If you are going through this process to solve your own problem, it means reviewing what you did and understanding how to avoid this problem in the future.

Nearly every person you work with when supporting an operating system will want to know what the problem was and how to fix it. We all like to feel that we have been included in finding a solution, that we are part of a team effort. A word of advice here: If you are supporting people on Windows 2000 Professional as part of your job, always try to include the customer in the troubleshooting process. It helps them to feel better about the incident and about your presence. That, in turn, helps them to participate by giving you good information. And that makes everyone's day go better.

Now a moment for the darker side of support. If the problem was caused by the user's ignorance, getting closure is your opportunity to educate. If you do this with some sensitivity, you can turn this into a positive experience. If you give in to the temptation to tell the person that they're an idiot, you will be burning bridges that will be difficult to rebuild later. Your choice. If *you* are the customer, this is where you can ask advice or discover an opportunity for education.

Troubleshooting Printing

Printing is one of those areas that is most important to users of computer systems. Remember the promise of the "paperless office"? Anyone ever seen one? Printing is one of the highest causes of support calls, and one of the hardest areas to get good support in. This area in particular is one in which you need to think simple. Don't forget to ask yourself the easy questions, such as, "Is it plugged in?" and, "Is it turned on?" If they are answered up front, these two questions can save you a lot of time troubleshooting printing issues. Just remember to ask diplomatically when troubleshooting someone else's printing problem. No one likes to feel dumb.

Let's work through a scenario to get a feel for how to apply the methodology to printing issues in Windows 2000 Professional. Here is your trouble ticket:

User:	Bob
Telephone:	12345
Problem:	Can't print
Description:	Nothing comes out when I try to print.
Priority:	URGENT!

As you can see, your user Bob is having trouble trying to print a document and feels that it is urgent that this be resolved quickly. The first step is to define the problem, so you contact Bob at his cubicle. Bob informs you that the job he is trying to print is a monthly profit-and-loss report for The Boss. Sounds pretty important, so you get right to work on the problem.

Scenario 1: Printer Is Unplugged

Simple questions first. Has it ever worked? Bob tells you that the printer worked fine the last time he tried to print, which was yesterday. What happened when he tried to print this time? He clicked Print in Word 97 and got a message that the printer was offline or out of paper.

Test the approach. You look at the print device, an HP LaserJet 5MP that is on Bob's desk, and see that the lights are on. This indicates that the printer is plugged in to electricity. Next, you try toggling the online/offline switch and find that the print device is online. Still thinking simple, you next check the back of Bob's print device to make sure the parallel cable is firmly attached. It is. Bob's computer is a tower and is located under his desk. You crawl under the desk to check the parallel cable and find that it has fallen off the back of the computer. You reconnect the cable and try to print a test page. It works!

Provide closure. The closure comes with the determination that Bob may have accidentally kicked loose the cable when he stretched his feet out under his desk. One possible solution to avoid this is to be sure that the retaining clips of the parallel cable are correctly fastened on the computer's parallel port. Providing an explanation of the cause along with a solution gives the customer some closure on the issue.

This sounds ridiculously easy, right? You might be surprised to find out that this ticket, or a slight variation thereof, is a very common answer for help desks.

Scenario 2: Nothing in the Print Queue Will Print

Explore the boundaries. When you contact Bob regarding his printing issue, he tells you that he has been trying to print for the last two hours but nothing is coming out of the printer. Bob tells you that there were no messages when he tried to print other than the pop-up message that the job was successfully printed. Windows 2000 Professional is accepting the print jobs when he submits them, but nothing is coming out.

Ask the simple questions. You investigate the simple issues first. The print device is connected and plugged in. It does display indicator lights, so you know that it is turned on and getting power. The cables are connected. Bob tells you that it printed fine yesterday, but it hasn't printed at all this morning. He insists that nothing has been changed on his computer, no software added, no hardware changed.

Track the possible approaches. You decide that some of the possibilities are that he might be printing to a different printer and doesn't realize it, or that something is wrong with the print queue.

Test the approaches. You check the Printers folder on Bob's computer and verify the setting for his locally attached HP LaserJet. Next, you verify that this printer is set as the default and that he has not redirected the output to another network printer. Opening the printer icon, you discover a long list of jobs that Bob submitted earlier today. Every job he has tried to print is listed, and the job on top of the list is a report from Excel.

You try checking to make sure that the printer has not been Paused. Everything looks fine, but no print jobs will process. You determine that the queue itself has become either corrupted or jammed.

Repair the problem. After closing the Printers folder, you open the Administrative Tools folder and double-click the Services icon. You scroll down the list to find the Print Spooler service and highlight it. You stop the service, wait a few seconds, then start it again.

TIP When the Print Spooler service becomes corrupt, or a job gets jammed in the queue, stopping and restarting the service may be enough to resolve the issue with no further effort.

After restarting the Print Spooler service, you examine the queue and find that the jobs are unchanged. At this point, the most likely cause is a corrupted document stuck at the top of the queue. Make a note as to the document size and timestamp. Stop the Print Spooler again, and then open Explorer.

Using Explorer, open the %SystemRoot%\System32\Spool\Printers folder. Find the files with the approximate timestamp of the print job that was stuck at the top of the queue. There will be two files, one with the extension SPL, the other with the extension SHD. If you have trouble deleting the SPL file, you may still be able to fix the problem by renaming the SHD file and restarting the Print Spooler service.

NOTE Windows 2000 Professional uses two files for each print job submitted. The first is the actual spool file (`*.spl`), which contains the formatted data to be printed. The second is the shadow file (`*.shd`), which is basically a transaction file for the print job.

After successfully deleting the two files, you restart the Print Spooler and immediately the print jobs begin to print.

Provide closure. Talking with Bob, you describe the issue as a corrupted print job that acted like a cork in a bottle, plugging up the queue. This could have been caused by a problem with the printer settings, the queue itself being corrupt, or most likely the document being corrupt. In the last case, Bob could open the document in the original program and select Save As from the File menu to save a new copy of the document without the corruption.

Other Print Troubleshooting Steps

There are several standard troubleshooting steps that you can add to your support toolbox. We have already discussed one of the most important—asking simple questions. Believe it or not, verifying that the print device is plugged in and turned on can solve many problems. This is no reflection on either the intelligence of the user or their knowledge of computing. Some *very* experienced people have called support with printing issues that were solved by either plugging in the print device or turning it on. We've all done it at some time.

Assuming that the print device is plugged in and turned on, and that you have verified the parallel cable as well, you need to test the print subsystem directly. To do so, follow these steps:

1. Choose Start ➢ Settings ➢ Printers to open the Printers folder.
2. Right-click the icon for your printer, and choose Properties from the shortcut menu to open the Properties dialog box for your printer.
3. On the General tab, click Print Test Page.

If you are troubleshooting a non-PostScript print device, you can try the following command at a command prompt:

```
Type dir > lptl:
```

This copies the output of a `dir` command directly to the print device and bypasses the spooling provided by Windows 2000 Professional. If this fails or if the output is garbled, the issue may be a bad cable, faulty parallel port, or other hardware problem. If it works, then you know the problem exists in Windows 2000 Professional or the program.

NOTE Redirecting the output of a command to the port will not work if you are testing a PostScript device.

If any devices are connected to the computer's parallel port between the computer and the print device, you should remove them and try printing again. Windows 2000 Professional is often not very forgiving about sharing ports with multiple devices.

Try a generic driver for the print device. If you are using a PostScript device, try installing the Apple LaserWriter driver. This is a very basic PostScript driver. If it works, then you have identified the problem as a bad `*.ppd` driver for the PostScript print device. If it is a non-PostScript device, try the Generic-Text Only driver.

NOTE PostScript printers don't really have a printer driver. Instead they use a PostScript Printer Description file (*.ppd), which is essentially a text file that describes how to send print jobs to the print device.

An issue that is often overlooked is the amount of space available for the spool file. Check to make sure that plenty of free space remains on the partition where Windows 2000 Professional is installed. Try printing from another operating system on the same computer if there is a dual-boot configuration. Or you could even try printing from the same application on a different computer.

One last possibility is that there is a problem with your document. It is possible that you will be able to print a less complex document from the same application. If this is the case, the problem is probably within the application.

Troubleshooting Windows 2000 Professional Setup

Many people encounter problems during the installation of Windows 2000 Professional, though most of the problems are minor and can be easily avoided. This section helps with troubleshooting the more difficult Setup issues.

In this section, we talk about troubleshooting Setup on the Intel and compatible platforms. The techniques work well for machines that are on the Hardware Compatibility List (HCL) and also for most machines that aren't on the list. Why would you want to install Windows 2000 Professional on a "noncompatible" system? Ever build your own computer? It wouldn't likely be on the HCL unless you want to pay Microsoft to test your computer and certify it for Windows 2000 Professional.

We've broken this section into parts that address problems you might encounter when planning for or during the text mode portion of Setup, during the transition to GUI mode, and during the final phase of rebooting.

Planning and Text Mode Setup

If you can restrain yourself from simply tearing the shrink-wrap from the box and whipping the CD-ROM out to start Setup, you should think about some things before you begin. Does your computer meet or exceed all the requirements? You may want to take the time to consult Chapter 2 again for setup guidance and hardware requirements. Assuming that you have done this and your computer meets all the requirements, there are some additional points you will want to document before starting.

What cards are installed in your computer? Do you have a network card? A sound card? What about a 3D accelerator card? Do you have the settings for all these devices written down? Remember that Windows 2000 Professional is a Plug-and-Play operating system; it can find the settings for most of your hardware on its own, but you should still know what those settings are in case it can't find them. Do you have the latest drivers for Windows 2000 Professional? Are the drivers on floppy disk or CD-ROM where you can get to them easily? Or are they on a network share? By the way, it won't do you any good to have your network card drivers out on a network server somewhere if you don't already have a functioning network card. Keep these handy on a floppy disk. Use Table 30.1 as a guide for the information you should have on hand prior to running Setup.

TABLE 30.1: USEFUL INFORMATION FOR SETUP

Device	Information to Gather
Video display	Adapter brand and model, chipset
Network adapter	IRQ, I/O address, DMA, transceiver type
SCSI adapter	Manufacturer and model, chipset, IRQ, bus type
Mouse (pointing device)	Manufacturer and model, bus type, port
I/O ports	Serial, parallel, IRQ, and I/O addresses
Internal modem	Port, IRQ, I/O address
Sound card	Manufacturer and model (or compatible model), IRQ, I/O address, DMA
Other devices	Hardware resources, device type, drivers

Now let's look at another troubleshooting scenario involving setup issues. In this situation, imagine you are the person responsible for installing Windows 2000 Professional and for providing general technical support to a group of users.

Scenario 3: Drives Not Found

You are responsible for installing Windows 2000 Professional on a computer for one of the users in your department. You build and use the four Setup floppies to boot the computer and begin Setup. When Setup reaches the point where it displays your current disk and partition information, Setup displays the following error message:

```
Setup did not find any hard drives on your computer.
```

You know that there are two hard drives in this computer and you can hear them spinning, so you know that they are receiving power. The first step in your troubleshooting methodology is to explore the boundaries of the problem.

You open the case of the computer to find out exactly what kind of hard drives are installed (after turning off the power, of course). You find that the drives are SCSI-2 2.1GB, and that they are attached to an Adaptec 2940 controller. No other SCSI devices are installed in this computer. When you investigate, you find that the computer had IDE drives and has recently been updated with a new SCSI controller and SCSI disks.

What you know and don't know at this point:

1. The computer has never worked before in this configuration.
2. The drives are SCSI, which require electronic termination and unique ID numbers on each bus.
3. You do not know the state of the termination.
4. You do not know the SCSI ID numbers for each drive.

Based on this information, you should already be suspecting that something is wrong with the hardware configuration. You reach into the case to ensure that the cables are tightly attached and find that they are. On these hard drives the SCSI IDs are set by jumpers on the rear of the drive (you will probably have to remove the drives to get at them).

Your plan of attack:

1. Verify the SCSI ID numbers of the drives and controller.
2. Verify the termination of the drive chain.
3. Check the BIOS settings of the controller.

Before you go through the work to remove the hard drives to check their ID numbers, you boot the computer to run the SCSI BIOS program. This program enables you to view and modify the configuration of the devices, as well as run diagnostics and other utilities. This utility tells you that it sees both hard drives, one as SCSI ID #0, the other as SCSI ID #1. This means the ID numbers are not the issue.

NOTE SCSI ID numbers are important. Having a conflict between two or more devices on the same SCSI bus can cause Setup to fail to recognize installed hard drives. It can also cause the system to fail when booting or to hang after booting.

The BIOS utility on the Adaptec controller also provides the capability to enable or disable termination on the controller card itself. You check and find that it is enabled correctly. Now you have verified the SCSI ID numbers, the controller settings, and half of the termination. The only thing left on your list is termination. To do this on older hardware, you have to pull out the last hard drive on the ribbon cable and check its termination.

Checking the last drive on the chain, you find that its terminator packs (resistors) are not set. This means that the SCSI bus is not terminated at one end. This may or may not be the problem, but it certainly needs to be fixed. You correct the termination and are ready to test the setup again. You start Setup, and this time everything runs fine.

Today, many SCSI drives are self-terminating, and you can also terminate on the ribbon cable instead of the drive. Today's SCSI is usually terminated on the SCSI controller and on the ribbon cable if building internal (to the PC) SCSI chains.

When you are troubleshooting problems on a SCSI-based system, always remember to check the termination. With SCSI, both ends of each drive chain must be terminated. Windows 2000 Professional is so sensitive about the stability of the hardware components that improper termination can be fatal to Setup. Even if you succeed with Setup, termination issues can result in hanging or even a blue-screen error. Even mismatched termination levels can cause this situation. If your controller has active termination and your hard drive has passive termination, you may have problems. Upgrading your SCSI chain to active termination or even forced-perfect termination at both ends can relieve the problem.

SCSI Troubleshooting

In the previous scenario, we looked at the possible importance of SCSI termination. In my experience, nearly 90 percent of the troubleshooting issues of Windows 2000 Professional Setup on SCSI-based computers involve termination problems. But there are other issues to be aware of as well. For instance, is the BIOS of the SCSI controller activated? This is another problem that would cause the preceding scenario.

A low-level format that is incorrect for the current drive geometry could cause file corruption, drives not being recognized by Setup, and system crashes. If you are installing a new SCSI drive or changing to a new make or model of SCSI controller, you should perform a low-level format of the drive to assure that the drive geometry will line up correctly.

In simpler terms, the drive controller performs a format of the disks within the drive so that the operating system will be able to write data to the individual sectors on the drive. In a way, sectors are like tiny boxes that are meant to contain information. Imagine trying to drop golf balls into small boxes. If you are lining them up correctly, it's easy. The balls simply drop right into place every time. But imagine now that you're slightly off your aim. The balls usually go in the boxes, but sometimes they bounce off the edges and roll away. That's what's happening when your drive isn't low-level formatted correctly for the specific controller. Each SCSI controller has its own geometry—its way of laying out those little boxes.

If multiple SCSI controllers are in the computer, does more than one of them have an active BIOS? If so, they may be competing for Int13 calls. This means that the "wrong" controller may be trying to boot the computer and therefore prevents the "right" controller from doing its job.

It's common today for people to try to mix SCSI device types—that is, to add 50-pin SCSI-2 devices to the same chain as SCSI-3 devices with 68 pins. That means that the cable has to change sizes from 68 wires to 50 wires. If you mix these devices, be certain that you buy the proper cable to make the conversion. If you don't, or if you try to convert from 68 to 50 wires and then back to 68, you will have wires that are not being terminated correctly. It is better by far to have only "wide" devices with 68 pins on one chain and "narrow" devices with 50 pins on a separate chain.

Troubleshooting Text Mode to GUI Mode

The transition from the character-based portion of Setup to the graphical portion is the number one point for problems to occur. This is a delicate time when Windows 2000 Professional (albeit a limited version of Windows 2000 Professional) is being booted for the first time. During this phase, Windows 2000 Professional is loading the kernel for the first time and initializing hardware and drivers. Some of the Setup specialists at Microsoft say that this is the toughest test of your computer hardware configuration that Windows 2000 Professional will ever make.

During this transition, Windows 2000 Professional is switching your CPU to a flat memory model and initiating multithreading. Windows 2000 Professional is also loading the Hardware Abstraction Layer (HAL) at this time. If your computer requires a customized HAL, you may have severe problems here. Normally, it's only the top-of-the-line computer brands that require custom HALs. If you don't know, consult the manual for your system or contact the manufacturer.

This is the most likely point for blue screens, also called *STOP screens* because of the text at the top of the screen. Some people insist on calling these the "Blue Screen of Death," though you should be aware that there may be hundreds of possible blue-screen errors in Windows 2000 Professional. None of us will likely ever see them all. We've included some of the most common below.

Blue Screens During Setup

There are two blue screens that are most commonly seen during Setup. The first is

```
STOP: 0x0000001E
KMODE_EXCEPTION_NOT_HANDLED
```

And the second is:

```
STOP: 0x0000000A
IRQL_NOT_LESS_OR_EQUAL
```

Both of these blue screens can be indications of faulty hardware, especially memory. A misbehaving driver most commonly generates these, though a hardware issue can cause them. One of the first things to rule out is any third-party driver you may be installing. Try to use only drivers supplied with Windows 2000 Professional, if possible. If you can't avoid using a driver supplied by someone else, then be certain the driver was written specifically for Windows 2000 Professional and not for an earlier version of NT. Try contacting the vendor for an updated driver file, possibly through their Web site.

Another common blue-screen error involves Windows 2000 Professional's inability to access the hard drive to boot the computer. The STOP code is

```
STOP 0x0000007B
INACCESSIBLE_BOOT_DEVICE
```

This one is usually not nearly as bad as it seems at first. What Windows 2000 Professional is telling you is that it can't use the driver you chose during the text mode portion of Setup. This blue screen can be worked through by using standard hard-disk troubleshooting. That means asking questions such as, "Is it plugged in?" Check the cables, and if it's a SCSI drive, check the termination. Be sure the drive is getting power and is spinning normally.

One of the most interesting causes of the STOP 0x7B is adding an IDE drive to a SCSI-based system. IDE controllers are enumerated before the SCSI controllers, meaning that the BIOS of the computer looks for them first. If you add an IDE drive to a computer that is already working fine with SCSI hard drives, you may very well see this blue screen. That situation can be fixed in the computer's BIOS. If your BIOS supports the option, set the boot order to go to the SCSI drives first, then the IDE.

One last thing to mention about blue screens applies more to upgrading Windows 2000 Professional from an earlier version than to a fresh installation. During an upgrade, Setup will notify you that you must remove an application before you can continue. As soon as the application is removed, Setup continues with the installation.

One last critical error to talk about here:

```
Setup has encountered a fatal error that prevents it from continuing.
Contact your software representative for help. Status code (0x4, 0, 0, 0)
```

This error message is displayed on a blue screen but is not actually considered a "blue screen" because it does not display the typical STOP message. This indicates a problem with the Master Boot Record (MBR). Either the MBR has become corrupted or it's infected with a boot-sector virus. Yes, even NTFS can become infected with a virus. This usually happens only on dual-boot systems that use FAT as their primary boot partition, but it can also happen if you boot the computer with an infected floppy disk. NTFS is resistant to viruses in that Windows 2000 Professional doesn't allow any program to access the hardware directly. In theory, this should prevent any boot-sector virus.

It is possible to repair the MBR if you have a bootable floppy that you know is clean of any virus infection. (That's the hard part in getting rid of a virus). An emergency boot disk from Windows 95/98 is especially helpful for this because you need `fdisk.exe`. After booting the infected computer with the boot floppy (you did write-protect the floppy, didn't you?), run `mem.exe` at the command prompt. The total bytes of memory (before anything is subtracted) should equal 640K. Next, run `chkdsk.exe` and look at the line for Total Bytes Memory (it's near the bottom), which should read 655,360. If either amount of memory is off, and especially if only *one* of them is off, you probably have a boot-sector virus loaded in memory. If both of these programs correctly report the amount of conventional memory, you can be reasonably certain that the virus is not in memory. If that's the case, you can type **FDISK/MBR** at the command prompt to rebuild the MBR. This command won't do anything else, provided the virus is not in memory. If the virus is in memory, this command may be fatal to your data.

WARNING The FDISK/MBR command is dangerous and should never be used without being absolutely positive that the boot-sector virus is not loaded in memory. *The result could be total data loss.* Most boot-sector viruses work by moving the MBR elsewhere on the disk, then replacing it with their own code. Anything that tries to scan the MBR is first infected by the virus, then redirected out to the real MBR in its new location.

NOTE It's interesting to note that the Master Boot Record is operating system–independent. It's quite possible to rebuild the MBR for a Windows 2000 Professional computer using an emergency boot disk from Windows 98.

Miscellaneous Setup Issues

If your computer hangs during the final reboot of Windows 2000 Setup, try removing the CD-ROM from the drive. Windows 2000 Professional supports the "El Torito" standard of bootable CD-ROMs using the No Emulation mode. If the BIOS of your computer supports bootable CD-ROMs but not the No Emulation mode, your system may hang. It may also give the error message below:

```
BOOT: Couldn't find NTLDR
Please insert another disk.
```

This is fixed the same way—just remove the CD-ROM from the drive and reboot the computer. Setup should continue normally after booting.

NOTE El Torito is the official name for a bootable CD-ROM name and is derived from the place of its creation—a restaurant where the engineers were having a few drinks.

Addressing GUI Mode and Initial Boot Issues

During this phase of Setup, Windows 2000 Professional installs drivers and configures the system. Problems in this portion of Setup are typically fewer and generally related to configuration rather than failing hardware or drivers. This is also where Windows 2000 Professional will try to load the network for the first time in a full configuration.

It is possible to encounter video problems at this phase of Setup. On some computers the display will not reset correctly during a warm boot under Windows 2000 Professional. If this occurs, your display will be black or very distorted. Try turning off the power to the computer (yes, this is one of those rare cases where you power down without shutting down first), then restarting it. If this resolves the issue, you will have to power down the computer every time you reboot. This is a hardware issue related to the video and system BIOS and not a Windows 2000 Professional problem. If you've tried this and the display is still distorted, then you will need to boot Windows 2000 Professional with the VGA option and change your display properties (and possibly the driver) to one that does work with your hardware.

Now let's apply this information to a common troubleshooting issue for Setup. In this scenario, you are again the support person installing Windows 2000 Professional, but this time the CD-ROM drive is not supported by Windows 2000 Professional.

Scenario 4: Unsupported CD-ROM

You are installing Windows 2000 Professional on your computer. Your machine is running NT 3.51 and has a SCSI CD-ROM attached to a MediaVision Pro Audio Spectrum-16 sound card with built-in SCSI controller. This configuration was supported under your old version of NT Workstation so you begin Setup by running `Winnt32/makelocalsource` from the I386 folder on the CD-ROM. Setup copies all the files from the I386 folder to the hard drive and then reboots your computer.

Setup proceeds normally until you reach the GUI mode and need to install a network adapter driver ROM provided by the NIC's manufacturer from the CD. When you attempt to load the driver, you receive the following error message:

```
NONCRITICAL ERROR
The external library procedure, CopySingleFile, reported the following
error: Unable to do the specified file copy operation.
```

If you choose to continue, the driver will not be installed correctly.

You load the Windows 2000 Professional CD-ROM on another computer to look for the file that is missing and notice that it is located in the `Drvlib` folder, which contains third-party drivers. You also happen to notice that the driver for your Trantor MediaVision sound card is not supported in the Windows 2000 Professional Setup program but has instead been "retired." Microsoft occasionally retires drivers for devices that are not very common, although they were once supported on NT.

NOTE In this particular case, the driver is not provided for Windows 2000 Professional. You will have to either acquire a new driver or replace the sound card with a newer, supported card.

Returning to the first computer, you complete the installation, ignoring the errors. When Setup has completed and the system has rebooted, you find that your CD-ROM is no longer available even though the sound card is installed. Why not?

When you chose to perform the upgrade using the `Winnt32 /makelocalsource` command, all the files from the I386 folder were copied to your hard drive, but no files from Valueadd were copied. In addition, although you could find the options to install the drivers from Valueadd, you could no longer access that folder because the driver for the controller was never installed. This error occurs when you try to install optional drivers from the CD-ROM that are no longer accessible in Setup. It can be caused by either an unsupported CD-ROM drive (as in this scenario) or by a network install.

Troubleshooting Windows 2000 Professional Networking

Because Windows 2000 Professional is a network operating system, it makes sense that you will probably encounter issues with your network from time to time. In most documentation you find today, the troubleshooting text tells you to perform "standard network troubleshooting" without ever telling you what that is. This section lets you in on that secret. Troubleshooting networking is one area in particular where my basic methodology will help you.

First, you start with any error message that Windows 2000 Professional gives you. This is always the first step in troubleshooting Windows 2000 Professional: Use whatever information it provides. Write the error message exactly as it appears because you can later use that to query the Knowledge Base. Next, you want to see what the Event Viewer can tell you. Event Viewer is probably the best friend you have in troubleshooting Windows 2000 Professional. It's not always clear and concise, but it will often tell you exactly what the problem is. It's always worth checking.

These things are true for any type of troubleshooting in Windows 2000 Professional. But basic network troubleshooting goes beyond Windows 2000 Professional's systems to encompass any network operating system. That's what we need to focus on in this section.

Is It Plugged In?

What do you need in order to have a conversation? You must have some kind of medium to carry the information from one person to another. You must also have some rules to determine how that conversation will take place. Imagine what happens when you meet someone on the street and strike up a conversation. You probably start by making eye contact, then smiling and speaking. If you both happen to speak at least one language in common, you can communicate easily. There may be a few failed attempts before you both find a language you can use, but eventually you will succeed.

A network is just like that. In its simplest form, a network can be two computers connected by a wire. When one wants to talk to the other, the first computer needs some kind of attention signal; then they both need to negotiate a common language and follow the rules of that language to communicate.

Networks can be simple systems or they can be complex. But however complicated they get, they all have certain things in common. They all have something connecting the nodes, and they all have at least one language. On most networks, the nodes are individual computers as well as intermediary systems such as routers, bridges, switches, and gateways. The language of a network is the protocol.

When troubleshooting any network system, keep these fundamental concepts in mind. Start with the communications medium. Is a proper cable plugged into the computer? Is the other end of the cable plugged into a hub or wall drop? If you are using coax cable, do you have a T-connector and possibly a terminator? Are the drivers for the network card installed and working? Do you have at least one protocol in common with the other computer?

These sound like simple questions, and they are, really. You might be surprised how often these simple questions will resolve your networking issues.

Is Anybody Out There?

Most of the troubleshooting I've talked about so far has dealt with working on one computer at a time. Network troubleshooting often involves the connecting systems between the computers as much or more than the computers themselves. I've shown you many ways to work with problems on computers, but how do you see what's wrong with a whole network? That's what this section is about. Here I introduce you to some of the tools included in Windows 2000 Professional to troubleshoot the network.

Troubleshooting TCP/IP

The single most common network protocol today is TCP/IP. Its popularity is most likely due to the Internet, but also because TCP/IP is an industry standard suite of protocols. It is not just one protocol, but rather a group of them designed to perform specific tasks. The part that most people like is the industry standard part. That means that if you have Macs and NetWare and Unix computers on your network, your Windows 2000 Professional computer can communicate with all of them using TCP/IP. TCP/IP is also popular with support people because it has so many troubleshooting tools built into it.

Ping

The Packet Inter-Network Groper (Ping) is the most basic test of network communication over TCP/IP. What Ping does for you is bounce a series of packets off of a remote host. You're essentially just saying "Hello?" over and over and (hopefully) getting a response each time. The basic syntax is `ping www.host.com` or `ping 10.1.0.44`.

So what does this tell you? Getting a response when pinging by IP address means that your network card is installed correctly, the driver is working, the TCP/IP protocol is working, Windows Sockets is working, the other computer is working, and everything in between is working. That's quite a lot of information for just one small command! When you ping by host name, you get all the previous information, plus you know that your hostname resolution is working.

You can also ping the address 127.0.0.1. This address is reserved for the local host (the local computer) and is a loop-back diagnostic test of your installed TCP/IP software. Successfully pinging the local host verifies that TCP/IP is successfully installed on the local computer.

Hostname

The hostname utility returns the hostname of the local computer. This can be helpful when you aren't exactly sure what it is.

IPConfig

IPConfig is right up there with ping when it comes to valuable TCP/IP utilities. This tool enables you to view some or all of your TCP/IP configuration (as the name might imply). To use it, type **`ipconfig`** at the command prompt to receive your IP address, subnet mask, and default gateway. If you type **`ipconfig /all`**, you will see a listing of every TCP/IP configuration for every interface on your computer. To give you some idea of the scope of information, Figure 30.1 shows the output of the `ipconfig /all` command.

IPConfig can also be used to release and renew IP addresses acquired through DHCP. The process for this is `ipconfig/release` then `ipconfig /renew`.

NOTE Windows 95/98 has a utility called `winipcfg.exe` that provides the same functionality as `ipconfig` in a GUI interface. `Winipcfg.exe` is available for Windows 2000 Professional in the Windows 2000 Professional Resource Kit.

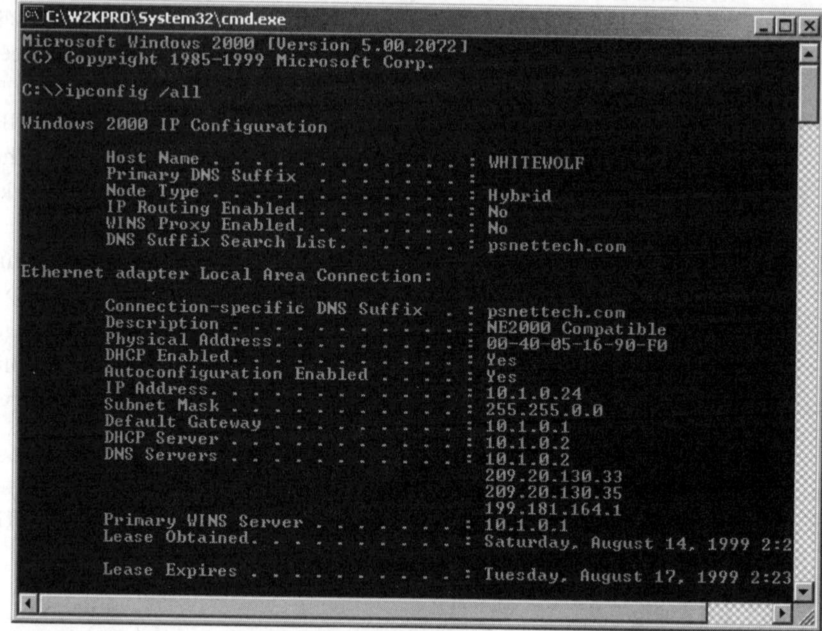

FIGURE 30.1 *Output of the* `ipconfig /all` *command*

ARP

The ARP command views and modifies the Address Resolution Protocol (ARP) cache. ARP is used by TCP/IP to resolve an IP address such as 10.1.0.1 to a unique hardware address or MAC address.

The process that TCP/IP uses to communicate between two computers is shown in Figure 30.2. At the Application layer, the user types in a Universal Resource Locator (URL) to browse a favorite Web site. The user's computer is configured to use a certain Domain Name System (DNS) server that is responsible for resolving the name in the URL to an IP address. Then TCP/IP uses ARP to resolve that IP address to a unique physical address. Every network card has a unique hexadecimal number assigned to it when it is manufactured. That's the physical address or MAC address of the card.

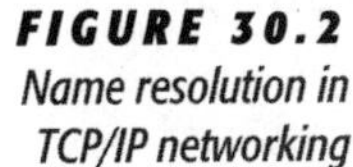

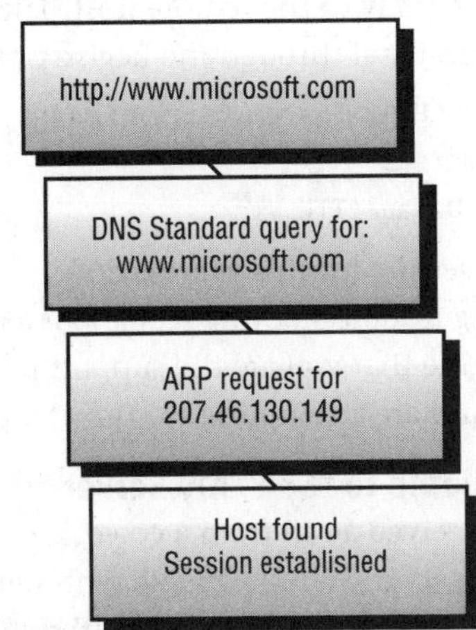

FIGURE 30.2
Name resolution in TCP/IP networking

When ARP resolves an IP address to a unique hardware address, it stores the resolution in its cache. One thing you can do to improve the connection speed to a server that you use frequently is to make a static entry in the ARP cache. The command string below will add a static entry for a computer:

```
ARP -s 10.1.0.1 00-40-05-16-DA-8A
```

The –s switch tells the ARP command to make the entry permanent. You should be aware that *permanent* in this case means only until the computer is rebooted. If you want this entry to really be permanent, you must use the ARP command in a logon script or batch file in your Startup group.

TraceRT

The Trace Route (TraceRT) command is very much like Ping in that it bounces several packets of information off of a remote computer. But TraceRT does more than that. It also shows a response from every router that the packets go through on their way to the remote computer.

This can be especially useful when dealing with communications issues with a remote host that is very far away (as in many routers away). TCP/IP uses a mechanism called a Time To Live (TTL) to determine how long a packet of data should be allowed on the network. If it didn't drop packets after a set period of time, packets would still be roaming the Internet from 20 years ago or more. The TTL is decremented automatically by at least one at each and every router it passes through (also called a *hop*). If a packet is forced to wait in a router due to network congestion, its TTL may be decremented by more than one.

TraceRT can reveal when the default TTL isn't high enough to allow for network congestion on the way to the remote host. The TTL setting can be adjusted in Windows 2000 Professional through the Registry at this location:

```
HKEY_LOCAL_MACHINE\System\CurrentControlSet\Services
\Tcpip\Parameters
Value name: DefaultTTL
```

The maximum setting for this value is 255.

The following troubleshooting scenario is a common support call in most networks. This time, imagine that you are the support person for a group of users on your company network and are attempting to correct a problem with network connectivity.

Scenario 5: Unable to "See" My Server

You have just received a call from a coworker, Mary, who is having trouble retrieving e-mail from her server. When you talk with her at her office, you learn that she is unable to open her e-mail application without receiving an error that the server could not be found. She is using TCP/IP as the only network protocol.

Has it ever worked before? Mary tells you that she was able to get e-mail until yesterday when someone installed the latest version of the e-mail client. Ever since then, no luck.

Track possible approaches. The problem could be the e-mail client but is more likely a simple configuration problem. You decide to do the following:

1. Verify IP address and configuration.
2. Test communication with server.
3. Test communication with another computer other than the server.

The first thing to do is run `ipconfig /all` to verify the computer's current settings. You do this and find that the computer's IP address, subnet mask, and default gateway are all correct.

Next you try pinging the server and get no response. You now try using Ping in a methodical process to determine where the failure is. You try pinging the default gateway (router) and you do receive a response. You don't know if there is another router between your default gateway and the e-mail server, but you can find out by using TraceRT. TraceRT returns success messages from three routers but fails to find the e-mail server.

You now know that the local computer's configuration is fine and that the default gateway is up and running. You know that at least three routers between the local computer and the e-mail server are functional. What you need to know is whether the last router is passing the information directly to the e-mail server and the e-mail server is down, or if there is another router beyond the third router that may be down.

When you pinged the e-mail server earlier, you did it by IP address. Now you try pinging by host name. The attempt fails, but it does resolve the name to an IP address, so you can tell that name resolution is happening correctly. Looking at the address of the e-mail server, you try another address that should be another server on that same section of the network. The Ping attempt to that address does respond.

NOTE Many network designers assign IP addresses in a set, predictable pattern. One common pattern is to assign all routers to the first 5 addresses on a subnet and servers to the last 20 addresses.

What you know now is that the network is working correctly all the way to the remote subnet where the server is located, but the server itself is still not responding. This would be a great time to call the administrator of that server to see if the server is running. Another possible solution is that the server may have an incorrect TCP/IP configuration. If the server *is* running, you should verify the configuration on the server to see if it can communicate with any other computer.

Troubleshooting IPX/SPX

IPX/SPX used to be the protocol of choice on Novell networks, and it still is in many. It's a fine, routable protocol, relatively fast and easy to configure. So why is it being mentioned in a troubleshooting section? Because there are settings that are frequently misconfigured. The problems with the IPX/SPX protocol stem from those options for configuration that must be set correctly for two computers to hold a conversation. Most notable is the setting for frame type.

Frame type refers to the manner in which data is packaged when placed on the physical wire. It describes the header and addressing fields, the error correction, and the overall size of the data that can be sent at one time. IPX/SPX supports five frame types: 802.2, 802.3, Ethernet II, Ethernet SNAP, and Token Ring. The most common are 802.2 and 802.3. Windows 2000 Professional (like most operating systems) uses only one frame type at a time. Windows 2000 Server, on the other hand, can use up to all five at once. Frame types are important because you must have the same frame type as the computer you are trying to communicate with. Mismatched frame types are probably the most common reason for failed communication over IPX/SPX.

In Microsoft networking, NWLink is called the IPX/SPX–compatible protocol even though it is fully compliant with all IPX/SPX standards. It is different only in that it provides a NetBIOS layer to facilitate name services on Microsoft network operating systems. For troubleshooting, that may or may not be important to know. What is important to know is that it is fully compliant with everyone else's IPX/SPX protocol.

Unlike TCP/IP in Windows 2000 Professional, NWLink doesn't ship with a bunch of troubleshooting utilities. That's usually not a problem because most issues will be resolved in the configuration. The primary tool for checking your NWLink configuration will be either the Network applet in Control Panel or `ipxroute.exe`. Using `ipxroute.exe` enables you to view the current configuration of NWLink for each network adapter in the computer and to modify the IPX/SPX routing table if the computer has more than one network interface. Entering the command `ipxroute config` at the command prompt will display the current configuration of NWLink.

Figure 30.3 shows the properties sheet for NWLink on Windows 2000 Professional. The properties on Windows 2000 Server are a bit different, so you may find this a little confusing if you are more familiar with Windows 2000 Server. The essentials are covered here—the adapter, the frame type, and the network number. The default setting for the frame type is Auto Detect. Microsoft tells us that this setting enables Windows 2000 Professional to scan the frame types being transmitted across the wire and then pick the most prevalent type. In fact, what appears to happen is that Windows 2000 Professional uses the very first frame type it comes across. Usually this will be correct. But on a network that utilizes multiple frame types, your Windows 2000 Professional computer may choose the wrong frame type when it starts up, causing you to be cut off from the servers you need.

FIGURE 30.3
The Properties dialog box for NWLink on Windows 2000 Professional

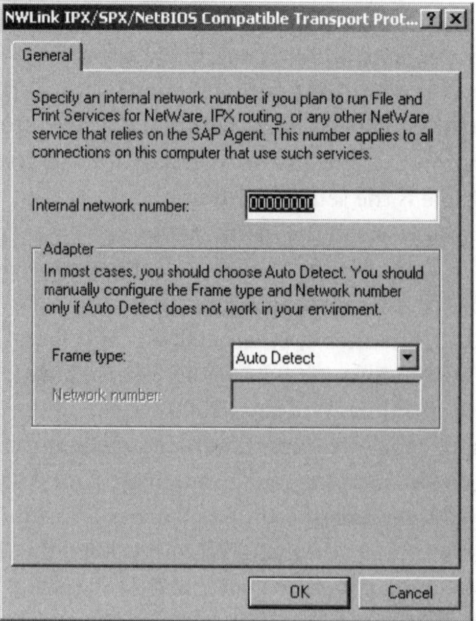

The other important setting on this page is the network number. IPX/SPX handles routing of information by using these network numbers to identify each unique section of a network. Every segment (the section of network between two routers) must be assigned a unique network number. The default setting in Windows 2000 Professional takes care of that for you. When you are using Auto Detect for the frame type, it will also detect the local network number. If you change from Auto Detect to a specific frame type, you will need to enter a valid network number. Contact your network administrator if necessary.

If you need more information than these tools provide, you will need to resort to a network analyzer such as Microsoft's Network Monitor, which is included with their Systems Management Server (SMS) package.

Troubleshooting NetBEUI

Network issues regarding the NetBEUI protocol usually involve name resolution and NetBIOS. NetBEUI is a great protocol for the right environment—typically a small network consisting of 50 or fewer computers. It's a good choice if you will never need to route data from one network to another and if you will not be connecting directly to the Internet.

NetBEUI is self-tuning and self-optimizing. It's truly a protocol that you can install and it "just works." The biggest troubleshooting issue you are likely to see is when browsing. Browsing through My Network Places is something that nearly all users do, and it's almost always what they mean when they say, "I can't see the server."

If you need to resolve something deeper than browsing issues, you will need a network analyzer because NetBEUI doesn't provide any built-in tools for troubleshooting.

How Do You Troubleshoot Windows 2000 Professional Network Architecture?

Although it's true that a good troubleshooting method can work you through almost any problem, at times you need to know more. In fact, I believe that the more you know about how something's put together, the easier it is to find what's wrong. That's certainly true of a complex system such as Windows 2000 Professional.

At the beginning of this chapter, I noted that troubleshooting is the process of going from a big picture view of things to a small detail view. Asking questions is the primary tool for accomplishing this, but knowledge is also a valuable tool. Figure 30.4 shows the overall network architecture of Windows 2000 Professional.

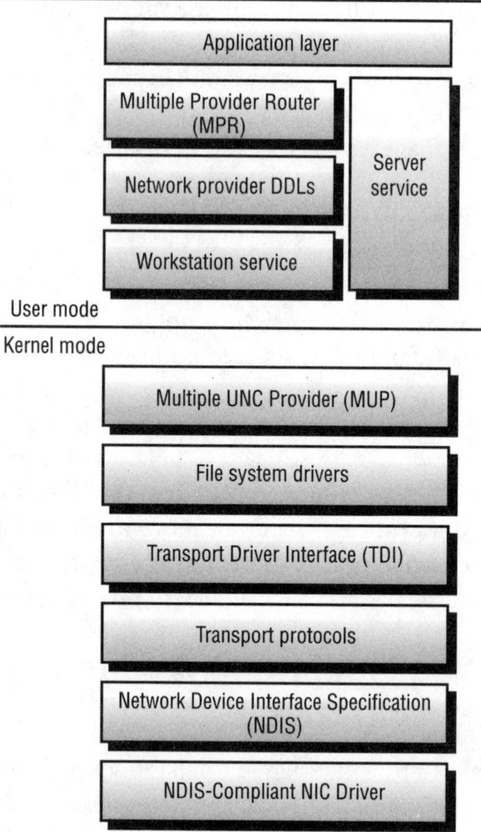

FIGURE 30.4 *The network architecture of Windows 2000 Professional*

User Mode Components

The following are components of the user mode.

Application Layer

The Application layer is where your program is accepting your network requests. For example, when you type in the URL of your favorite Web site, you are interacting with the Application layer.

Multiple Provider Router

The Multiple Provider Router (MPR) is kind of like a traffic cop in that its job is to direct the flow of communication. Windows 2000 Professional uses the MPR only when you are mapping a network drive. Its task is to decide which of the installed network clients will do the best job in making the drive mapping.

The MPR is contained in the file `mpr.dll`.

Network Provider DLL

A DLL is a dynamic link library, which is basically a file that contains support functions for a program. In this case, the library of functions is part of a network client that is installed in Windows 2000 Professional.

There will be one provider DLL for each installed network client. The file for the native Windows 2000 Professional client, LanmanWorkstation, for example, is `ntlanman.dll`.

Workstation Service and Server Service

These are the user mode components of the Workstation and Server services. Essentially, these are "stubs" that provide user mode applications with access to the kernel mode Workstation and Server services of Windows 2000 Professional.

Kernel Mode Components

The following are components of the kernel mode.

Multiple UNC Provider

The Multiple UNC Provider (MUP) is a traffic cop like the MPR, except that instead of directing traffic when mapping drives, the MUP directs traffic when you are using a Universal Naming Convention (UNC) path.

You will be using the MUP's services whenever you click Start ➢ Run and type a path such as `\\Server5\Public`, or when your application connects to a server resource without mapping a drive letter first. An example is your e-mail program, which is configured to talk with one particular server to retrieve mail but doesn't require that you first map a drive to the share on the server.

When the MUP receives a request for service, its job is to decide which file system driver (which network client) can best answer the request, and then send the request to that driver.

The MUP is contained in the file `mup.sys`.

File System Drivers

File system drivers are the network redirectors and servers. When you install network support in Windows 2000 Professional, you always get two of these drivers by default. The first, `rdr.sys`, is the kernel mode component of the Workstation service, your native Windows 2000 Professional client. The second, `srv.sys`, is the kernel mode portion of the Server service.

There may be other file system drivers installed for other network clients. One common example is the `nwrdr.sys` driver for the Client Services for NetWare in Windows 2000 Professional.

Transport Driver Interface

Transport Driver Interface (TDI) doesn't actually exist as a file. It is what its name implies, an interface between the file system drivers and the transport protocols. The

TDI is *exposed* by the two layers—that is to say that any file system driver for Windows 2000 Professional networking must support the functions used by TDI, and the same for the transport protocols.

This layered approach allows for portability and extensibility. Because of the TDI boundary layer, you can (in theory) install as many network clients and servers or as many protocols as you want on Windows 2000 Professional.

Transport Protocols

These are the protocols used to communicate on your network. The files for each should be easy to identify because they are usually just the name of the protocol with a SYS extension.

In theory, you can install an unlimited number of protocols in Windows 2000 Professional so long as they conform to the two boundaries in the network stack. Transport protocols must expose the TDI boundary on top and the NDIS layer on the bottom.

Network Device Interface Specification

Network Device Interface Specification (NDIS) is a boundary layer between the protocols and the adapter driver. But it has a more important job than that.

Years ago, when you wanted to develop a new driver for a network adapter card, you needed to think about details and settings like the media access scheme, error detection and correction, frame types, and so on, before you ever got to the part of the driver that just ran the card. NDIS was an effort by Microsoft, Intel, 3Com, and other companies to solve this problem. By conforming to a known standard, they could remove the common functions from the driver and load them into a library of functions that every network needs. Essentially, they wanted to stop reinventing the wheel every time they brought out another card.

NDIS, as it is implemented in Windows 2000 Professional, is an interesting component. It is both a file and a boundary layer. As a file, `ndis.sys` is a driver file that acts like a DLL in that it loads into memory and anybody who knows how to talk to it can ask NDIS for support. As a boundary, it defines a standard form of communication between the transport protocols and the network adapter card.

NDIS-Compliant Network Adapter Driver

At the bottom of the stack but certainly very important, the Network Interface Card (NIC) driver is responsible for error-free transmission and reception of data on the physical network medium.

Using the NDIS standard enables you to install as many NICs as you want in a computer (of course, you only have so many slots in your computer). As long as the drivers comply with the NDIS standard, you can bind multiple cards to one protocol or multiple protocols to one NIC.

The file containing the driver is named according to the naming convention of the manufacturer, but they all end with a SYS extension.

Finding More Information

This chapter provided you with a general method for troubleshooting and some specifics about applying the method to Windows 2000 Professional. It also made the point that sometimes you need more than a good method; you need good information. This final section introduces you to some of the premier sources of Windows 2000 Professional troubleshooting information.

The Microsoft Knowledge Base

This is the number one source of up-to-date information used to fix problems with Windows 2000 Professional (or any Microsoft product, for that matter). The Knowledge Base (KB) is a SQL database containing articles that describe known problems in Microsoft products, how to diagnose them, and most importantly, how to resolve them. The articles are typically written by the engineers in Microsoft Technical Support—the people who have the hands-on knowledge of dealing with the problems.

The typical life of a KB article begins when an engineer hangs up the phone after fixing a new problem. "Wow," he exclaims, "that was the weirdest thing I've seen yet." The engineer mentions the issue to his neighbor, who starts taking notes because *she's* never seen it either. Then the local KB editor hears about it and starts pestering the engineer to write it up in an article. Now, not every engineer can or will write articles, but there is always someone looking to expand their writing career who will tackle the article if the engineer can explain it well enough. So one way or another the article gets written. Then it is edited for style and reviewed for technical accuracy. If it passes all the reviews, it is added to the Knowledge Base.

The support engineers at Microsoft use these articles to resolve issues for customers, and once in a while the engineers find an article that isn't quite accurate. They can then submit a comment to the editors describing the problem with the article so it can be fixed. On occasion the comments are helpful; sometimes they're just very emotional. The point is, these articles are constantly being reviewed and updated for accuracy.

Accessing the Knowledge Base

The Knowledge Base can be accessed in a few ways. The first is to call Microsoft Technical Support and let them do the browsing through the KB. This might be a better answer than you realize because they have access to articles that aren't released to the public. This isn't some dark Microsoft conspiracy; it's mostly out of consideration for other companies' reputations (and their own). If a problem is serious but hasn't been fully documented by all parties involved, Microsoft isn't going to expose itself to possible litigation over a KB article. The information will be marked as MSONLY or PARTNER so that only support engineers can see the information. After all parties have confirmed the issues, the article can be released to the public.

The easiest way for us mere mortals to use the Knowledge Base is to access it through the Support Online pages at Microsoft's Web site (`www.microsoft.com`). This location is updated approximately twice a week to contain the latest information. If there is a hot issue that needs to be dealt with immediately (such as a bug in Internet Explorer's security), the fix is released overnight and an article is sent into the KB right away.

The third way is to use TechNet, which is a subscription-based product from Microsoft for Information Systems and support professionals. TechNet is sent out once a month on several CD-ROMs. The first CD-ROM contains the entire public Knowledge Base, additional white papers, Resource Kits, and training materials. The remaining CD-ROMs contain the entire Microsoft driver library; all the current Service Packs, patches, and device drivers that Microsoft provides for their operating systems; and other products.

Understanding the Art of Query

Finding information in the Knowledge Base can be difficult. Face it, this thing is *huge.* Microsoft support engineers spend time in training after they're hired just learning to use the KB effectively. Don't feel bad if you have trouble at first finding the information you want. I've listed some helpful hints here that should make the task easier.

Start specific, and move outward. Try querying on a specific error message (if you have one). If that doesn't work, try a few words from the error and the names of the files or devices involved in the problem. For example, if you wanted to find an article about a blue-screen error and your Adaptec 2940 controller, you might submit this query:

```
Winnt and adaptec and 2940 and STOP and 0x1E
```

If there were any issues related to a blue screen with the STOP code 0x1E dealing with an Adaptec 2940 controller, the list of articles would be displayed (there aren't any, in case you're wondering). Notice the *and* between each of the query words. When querying the KB using this structure, the results will be articles that contain *all* the words. You are literally asking for all articles containing the words *Winnt, Adaptec, 2940, STOP,* and *0x1E.* Any article that has only some of the words will not be returned. The default action when you type a string of query words is to find any article that contains *at least one* of those words.

There is a way to increase the likelihood of success in querying the KB. If you include certain *keywords* in your search, you will find specific articles more easily. In Table 30.2 I have included some keywords that can help improve your KB query skills.

TABLE 30.2: KNOWLEDGE BASE KEYWORDS FOR WINDOWS 2000 PROFESSIONAL

KB Keyword	Description
Kberrmsg	Returns articles dealing with error messages. Can be used with all products.
Kbsetup	Articles dealing with setup issues. Can be used with all products.
Kbtool	Concerns articles about commands or utilities. Can be used in all products.
Ntboot	Articles dealing with the NT boot process. NT specific.
Ntdirlist	Directory listing of distribution disks. NT specific.
Ntdomain	Deals with NT domain administration. NT specific.
Ntras	Articles concerning Remote Access Service. NT specific.
Ntsetup	Returns articles pertaining to NT Setup issues. NT specific.
Ntsp	Lists articles with information about NT Service Packs. NT specific.
NtSrv	Articles that apply only to NT Server. NT specific.
NtSrvWkst	Articles that apply to *both* NT Server and NT Workstation. NT specific.
Ntstart	Boot process and start-up of NT. NT specific.
Ntstop	Articles concerning STOP screen messages or blue screens. NT specific.
NtWkst	Articles that apply to NT Workstation *only*. NT specific.

The Windows 2000 Professional Resource Kits

With the release of NT 4, Microsoft separated the NT Resource Kit into two parts: a Resource Kit for NT Workstation and one for NT Server. They both covered different material and were targeted at the specific type of environment that the operating systems will be used in. This philosophy continues with Windows 2000 Professional due to the sheer size of the information being provided.

The Windows 2000 Professional Resource Kit covers the basics of installation, configuration, and administration of Windows 2000 Professional, though much of the material will work on Server as well. The Server Resource Kit focuses mostly on domain and Enterprise networking issues and how Windows 2000 Server fits into that picture. Both kits come with a CD-ROM full of helpful utilities. I've heard some people joke that Windows 2000 is the add-on companion product for the Resource Kit. What they're trying to say is that anyone who is serious about supporting Windows 2000 Professional will want access to the information in both kits.

Summary

No matter what your interest is in Windows 2000 Professional, there will be times when understanding the process of troubleshooting will be helpful to you. Even if troubleshooting is never going to be part of your responsibility, things may go wrong. If you have even a basic understanding of the process, you will convey much more meaningful information to the person who *is* responsible for the troubleshooting.

Use the methods listed in this chapter when troubleshooting your own computer. Follow the guidelines for documenting the steps taken and the possible approaches to use. Always remember to think simple at first, and then move on to the more exotic as you eliminate basic possibilities.

Take the time to become familiar with the Microsoft Knowledge Base. It can help you to find solutions to your own computer problems without spending additional money or time on support. If you are a support professional, the KB provides the raw information needed to excel in your job.

INDEX

Note to the Reader: Throughout this index **boldfaced** page numbers indicate primary discussions of a topic. *Italicized* page numbers indicate illustrations.

A

D

F

G

H

I

J

M

N

O

P

Q

R

S

U

V

W

Z